NATIONAL AND INTERNATIONAL
ANTI-MONEY LAUNDERING LAW

NATIONAL AND INTERNATIONAL ANTI-MONEY LAUNDERING LAW

Developing the Architecture of Criminal Justice, Regulation and Data Protection

Edited by
Benjamin VOGEL
Jean-Baptiste MAILLART

INTERSENTIA
Cambridge – Antwerp – Chicago

Intersentia Ltd
8 Wellington Mews
Wellington Street | Cambridge
CB1 1HW | United Kingdom
Tel: +44 1223 736 170
Email: mail@intersentia.co.uk
www.intersentia.com | www.intersentia.co.uk

Distribution for the UK and
Rest of the World (incl. Eastern Europe)
NBN International
1 Deltic Avenue, Rooksley
Milton Keynes MK13 8LD
United Kingdom
Tel: +44 1752 202 301 | Fax: +44 1752 202 331
Email: orders@nbninternational.com

Distribution for Europe
Lefebvre Sarrut Belgium NV
Hoogstraat 139/6
1000 Brussels
Belgium
Tel: +32 (0)800 39 067
Email: mail@intersentia.be

Distribution for the USA and Canada
Independent Publishers Group
Order Department
814 North Franklin Street
Chicago, IL 60610
USA
Tel: +1 800 888 4741 (toll free) | Fax: +1 312 337 5985
Email: orders@ipgbook.com

National and International Anti-Money Laundering Law. Developing the Architecture of Criminal Justice, Regulation and Data Protection

Artwork on cover: Seb Antoniou / sebantoniou.com

ISBN 978-1-78068-954-8
D/2020/7849/109
NUR 824

British Library Cataloguing in Publication Data. A catalogue record for this book is available from the British Library.

PREFACE

The present volume contains the fruits of a collaborative research project at the Max Planck Institute for Foreign and International Criminal Law. Led by Benjamin Vogel, the research group comprised three postdoctoral researchers at the Institute, Giovanna Amato, Ana Carolina Carlos de Oliveira and Jean-Baptiste Maillart. For the analysis of the United Kingdom's legal framework, the group was furthermore supported by Michael Levi at Cardiff University and by Liliya Gelemerova at the University of Manchester. The editors were fortunate to benefit from the rich insights of their colleagues who, through countless hours of discussion, built a highly stimulating collaborative research environment.

The project owes a particular debt of gratitude to Ulrich Sieber, director emeritus at the Max Planck Institute. All project collaborators greatly benefited from his generous advice and continuous guidance throughout the project. With his pioneering approach towards legal research into security law against the background of digitalisation, globalisation and the rising policy paradigm of risk prevention, Professor Sieber prepared the groundwork for this study both in terms of substance and methodology. Over the course of several decades of research, he was one of the first to highlight the profound changes which legal orders would increasingly undergo as a result of the rapid development of information technology, the rise of transnational crime and new associated risks. Resulting from those profound changes, he recognised the need, which also forged the design of the present study, to expand research on criminal policy beyond the confines of traditional criminal law and towards States' wider security architecture based on normative, empirical and comparative research.

The project furthermore owes an immense debt to numerous experts, including policymakers and competent authorities at supranational and national levels as well as the private sector, who – in the course of more than one-hundred hours of interviews – shared their experiences and allowed the authors to grasp the practical realities of today's efforts in the fight against money laundering. Without their commitment and generosity, and in light of the many uncodified and unreported practices of AML, it would have been simply impossible to attempt the following study. The collaborators are indeed profoundly thankful for the open and engaging atmosphere that marked the interviews. In fact, this experience demonstrates both the need for and the feasibility of greater mutual engagement between academic research institutions and competent authorities when inquiring into future challenges of criminal and wider security policy.

Particular thanks is due to Jürgen Storbeck, former director of Europol, who was not only of invaluable help in organising interviews but who also, through numerous discussions, challenged the collaborators and thereby allowed them to further refine their understanding of the many pitfalls as well as the opportunities brought about by transnational cooperation in criminal matters. A special debt is also owed to Alexandra Schenk, who provided crucial methodological assistance in the conduct and evaluation of interviews. Obviously, this book would not have been possible without the diligent work of the outstanding team of Intersentia, in particular Ann-Christin Maak, Rebecca Moffat and Ahmed Hegazi.

Last but not least, thanks is also due to the material support that allowed the project's scope and depth to adapt to the size of the challenges encountered in today's AML frameworks. The collaborators are grateful to Philip Morris Germany for supporting the research on anti-money laundering at the Max Planck Institute. To the extent that the study inquires into public-private partnerships for the sharing of information by competent authorities with the private sector, the collaborators furthermore extend their gratitude to the European Commission. In this regard, this research was funded by the European Union's Internal Security Fund – Police.* Statements about the law in this book aspire to reflect the state of affairs on 31 January 2020, though some subsequent developments of particular relevance have also been included.

Benjamin Vogel and Jean-Baptiste Maillart
Freiburg, July 2020

* The content of this study represents the views of the authors only and is their sole responsibility. The European Commission does not accept any responsibility for use that may be made of the information it contains.

CONTENTS

LIST OF CASES

EUROPEAN COURT OF HUMAN RIGHTS

COURT OF JUSTICE OF THE EUROPEAN UNION

GERMANY

ITALY

SPAIN

SWITZERLAND

UNITED KINGDOM

LIST OF ABBREVIATIONS

4AMLD	Directive 2015/849/EU
5AMLD	Directive 2018/843/EU
AEOI	Automatic Exchange of Information
AktG	Aktiengesetz
AML	Anti-money laundering
AMLA	Anti-Money Laundering Act (RS 955.0)
AMLD	Anti-Money Laundering Directive
AMLO	Anti-Money Laundering Ordinance (RS 955.01)
AMLO-CFMJ	Federal Gaming Board Anti-Money Laundering Ordinance (RS 955.021)
AMLO-DFJP	Federal Department of Justice and Police Anti-Money Laundering Ordinance (RS 955.022)
AMLO-FINMA	Swiss Financial Market Supervisory Authority Anti-Money Laundering Ordinance (RS 955.033.0)
AO	Abgabenordnung
Art.	Article
ASA	Association suisse des assurances
ASSL	Association suisse des sociétés de leasing
AsylG	Asylgesetz
AT	Austria
ATF	Arrêt du Tribunal fédéral
AufenthG	Gesetz über den Aufenthalt, die Erwerbstätigkeit und die Integration von Ausländern im Bundesgebiet
AUPER	Automated Registration System of Persons
AWG	Außenwirtschaftsgesetz
AZRG	Gesetz über das Ausländerzentralregister
Bafin	Bundesanstalt für Finanzdienstleistungsaufsicht
BayZustV	Bayerische Zuständigkeitsverordnung
BE	Belgium
BFH	Bundesfinanzhof
BFHE	Entscheidungen des Bundesfinanzhofs
BG	Bulgaria
BGB	Bürgerliches Gesetzbuch
BGBl.	Bundesgesetzblatt
BGH	Bundesgerichtshof

BGHSt	Entscheidungen des Bundesgerichtshofes in Strafsachen
BI	Banca d'Italia
BKAG	Bundeskriminalamtgesetz
BMG	Bundesmeldegesetz
BNDG	Gesetz über den Bundesnachrichtendienst
BR	Bundesrat
BT	Bundestag
BtMG	Gesetz über den Verkehr mit Betäubungsmitteln
BVerfG	Bundesverfassungsgericht
BVerfGE	Entscheidungen des Bundesverfassungsgerichts
BVerfGK	Kammerentscheidungen des Bundesverfassungsgerichts
BVerfSchG	Bundesverfassungsschutzgesetz
BVerwG	Bundesverwaltungsgericht
BZRG	Bundeszentralregistergesetz
C. Cass.	Corte di Cassazione
CAP	Codice delle Assicurazioni Private
CC	Criminal Code
CDB	Agreement on the Swiss Banks' code of conduct with regard to the exercise of due diligence
CDD	Customer due diligence
CEO	Chief Executive Officer
CFMJ	Federal Gaming Board
CFT	Countering the financing of terrorism
CITCO	Intelligence Center against Terrorism and Organized Crime
CNCA	Centre for Counter Terrorism Coordination
CNI	Centro Nacional de Inteligencia
CNMV	Comisión Nacional del Mercados de Valores
CO	Code of Obligations (Switzerland)
CO	Compliance Officer (Spain)
Confidi	Consorzio di garanzia collettiva dei fidi
Consob	Commissione Nazionale per le Società e la Borsa
CPS	Crown Prosecution Service
CRAB	Centro Registral Anti-blanqueo de Capitales del Colegio de registradores de la Propiedad, mercantiles y bienes Inmuebles
CRR	Capital Requirements Regulation (EU) No. 575/2013
CTF	Counter-terrorist financing
CY	Cyprus
CZ	Czech Republic
D.L.	Decreto legge

D.P.R.	Decreto del Presidente della Repubblica
DAML	Defence Against Money Laundering
DB-AMLA	Draft bill amending the Anti-Money Laundering Act
DB-Terr	Draft bill on the fight against terrorism
DE	Germany
Decree	Real Decreto 304/2014
DK	Denmark
DNFBP(s)	Designated Non-Financial Businesses and Profession(s)
DStR	Das deutsche Steuerrecht
EBA	European Banking Authority
EC	European Community
ECHR	European Convention on Human Rights
ECtHR	European Court of Human Rights
EDD	Enhanced Due Diligence
EE	Estonia
EEA	European Economic Area
EEAS	European External Action Service
EGMLTF	Expert Group on Anti-Money Laundering and Countering Terrorist Financing
EIOPA	European Insurance and Occupational Pensions Authority
EL	Greece
ES	Spain
ESAs	European Supervisory Authorities
ESMA	European Securities and Markets Authority
EU	European Union
FATF	Financial Action Task Force
FCA	Financial Conduct Authority
FDF	Federal Department of Finance
FedPol	Federal Office of Police
FF	Feuille fédérale
FFA	Forensic Financial Analysis
FI	Finland
FINMA	Swiss Financial Market Supervisory Authority
FIU	Financial Intelligence Unit
FKAustG	Finanzkonten-Informationsaustauschgesetz
FR	France
FSMA	Financial Services and Markets Act
FSRBs	FATF-style regional body
G 10	Gesetz zur Beschränkung des Brief-, Post- und Fernmeldegeheimnisses

G20	Group of Twenty
G7	Group of Seven
GCMF	Interdepartmental Coordinating Group on Combating Money Laundering and the Financing of Terrorism
GDPR	General Data Protection Regulation
GenG	Gesetz betreffend die Erwerbs- und Wirtschaftsgenossenschaften
GEWA	MROS' data processing system
GewO	Gewerbeordnung
GmbHG	Gesetz betreffend die Gesellschaften mit beschränkter Haftung
GWG	Geldwäschegesetz
HGB	Handelsgesetzbuch
HMRC	HM Revenue & Customs
HR	Croatia
HU	Hungary
IBAN	International Bank Account Number
ICO	Initial coin offering
ICRG	International Co-operation Review Group
IE	Ireland
INDEX SRC	Federal Intelligence Service's indexing system
ISIL	Islamic State in Iraq and the Levant
IT	Italy
IVASS	Istituto per la vigilanza sulle assicurazioni
JMLIT	Joint Money Laundering Intelligence Taskforce
JMLSG	Joint Money Laundering Steering Group
KAGB	Kapitalanlagegesetzbuch
KWG	Kreditwesengesetz
KYC	Know Your Customer
L.	Legge
L.D.	Decreto legislativo
LEA	Law enforcement agencies
LPP	Legal Professional Privilege
LT	Lithuania
LU	Luxembourg
LV	Latvia
MADG	Gesetz über den militärischen Abschirmdienst
MER	Mutual Evaluation Report
ML	Money laundering
ML/TF	Money laundering/Terrorism financing
MLCP	Money laundering compliance principal

MLRO	Money Laundering Reporting Officer
MoU(s)	Memorandum(s) of understanding
MPC	Ministère public de la Confédération
MROS	Money Laundering Reporting Office Switzerland
MT	Malta
NCA	National Crime Agency
NCIS	National Criminal Intelligence Unit
NDIU	National Drugs Intelligence Unit
NGO(s)	Non-governmental organisation(s)
NJW	Neue Juristische Wochenschrift
NL	Netherlands
NRA	National risk assessment
N-SIS	Schengen Information System's National Part
NStZ	Neue Zeitschrift für Strafrecht
NStZ-RR	NStZ Rechtsprechungsreport
NVwZ	Neue Zeitschrift für Verwaltungsrecht
OAG	Office of the Attorney General
OAR-G	Organisme d'Autorégulation des Gérants de Patrimoine
OCP- Notars	Organo Centralizado de Prevención de blanqueo de capitales del Colegio Notarial
OECD	Organisation for Economic Cooperation and Development
OLG	Oberlandesgericht
O-MROS	Ordinance on MROS (RS 955.23)
OPBAS	Office for Professional Body Anti-Money Laundering Supervision
OWiG	Gesetz über Ordnungswidrigkeiten
P.D.	Decreto Presidenziale
PEP(s)	Politically exposed person(s)
PL	Poland
PNC	Police National Computer
POCA	Proceeds of Crime Act 2002
PrüfbV	Verordnung über die Prüfung der Jahresabschlüsse der Kreditinstitute und Finanzdienstleistungsinstitute sowie über die darüber zu erstellenden Berichte
PrüfV	Verordnung über den Inhalt der Prüfungsberichte zu den Jahresabschlüssen und den Solvabilitätsübersichten von Versicherungsunternehmen
PSC	Persons with Significant Control
PT	Portugal
RCE	Central Register of Foreigners

RIPOL	Police Computerised Research System
RO	Romania
RPS	Revue pénale suisse
RS	Recueil systématique
RUMACA	Customs' database
SAAM	Swiss Association of Asset Managers
SächsGwGZustVO	Sächsische Geldwäschegesetz-Zuständigkeitsverordnung
SAR(s)	Suspicious activity report(s)
SARAs	Segnalazioni antiriciclaggio aggregate
SAV/SNV	Selbstregulierungsorganisation des Schweizerischen Anwaltsverbandes und des Schweizerischen Notarenverbandes
SBA	Swiss Bankers Association
SchwarzArbG	Gesetz zur Bekämpfung der Schwarzarbeit und illegalen Beschäftigung
SE	Sweden
SEPBLAC	Servicio Ejecutivo de la Comisión de Prevención del Blanqueo de Capitales e Infracciones Monetarias
SFO	Serious Fraud Office
SI	Slovenia
SK	Slovakia
SPC	Spanish Penal Code
SRA	Solicitors Regulation Authority
SRO(s)	Self-regulatory organisation(s)
SRO-SVV	Selbstregulierungsorganisation des Schweizerischen Versicherungsverbandes
StGB	Strafgesetzbuch
StPO	Strafprozessordnung
STR(s)	Suspicious transaction report(s)
STS	Sentencia del Tribunal Supremo
StVG	Straßenverkehrsgesetz
SYMIC	Central Migration Information System
SYSC	The Senior Management Arrangements, Systems and Controls sourcebook
TF	Terrorist financing
TUB	Testo Unico Bancario
TUF	Testo Unico della Finanza
UCITS	Undertakings for Collective Investments in Transferable Securities
UIF	Unità di Informazione Finanziaria
UK	United Kingdom

UN	United Nations
UNODC	United Nations Office on Drugs and Crime
UNSC	United Nations Security Council
UTR(s)	Unusual transaction report(s)
VAG	Gesetz über die Beaufsichtigung der Versicherungsunternehmen
VAT	Value added tax
VOSTRA	Computerised Criminal Records Database
VQF	Verein zur Qualitätssicherung von Finanzdienstleistungen
WpHG	Gesetz über den Wertpapierhandel
ZAG	Zentrale Aufbereitung Geldwäschereiverdachtsmeldung (Switzerland)
ZAG	Gesetz über die Beaufsichtigung von Zahlungsdiensten (Germany)
ZFdG	Gesetz über das Zollkriminalamt und die Zollfahndungsämter
ZollVG	Zollverwaltungsgesetz

LIST OF CONTRIBUTORS

Giovanna Amato
Research fellow at the Max Planck Institute. She graduated and obtained her PhD from the University of Bologna, where she received numerous scholarships and was an assistant professor. She is currently working towards qualifying as an associate professor and her work focuses on organised crime, corporate criminal liability, AML and, more generally, crime prevention. She is also a practicing lawyer and has acted as compliance officer for various companies.

Ana Carolina Carlos de Oliveira
Research fellow at the Max Planck Institute. She is also an assistant professor, member of the research group on corporate and economic crime and PhD candidate at the Pompeu Fabra University, Barcelona. She graduated and received a first PhD from the University of Sao Paulo, where, among other awards, she was distinguished by the Instituto Brasileiro de Ciencias Criminais. She also acts as a consultant specialised in the prevention of financial crimes.

Liliya Gelemerova
Holds a PhD from Tilburg University and is honorary senior lecturer at the University of Manchester. Her specialism is anti-financial crime which she has developed working in various roles across the public and private sectors, starting with the Bulgarian FIU in the late 1990s. She currently works in financial crime compliance in the banking industry in London.

Michael Levi
Professor of Criminology at the School of Social Sciences, Cardiff University. He has been researching economic crime since 1972 and money laundering since 1988. In 2019, he received lifetime achievement awards from the American Society of Criminology, the British Society of Criminology, and for Tackling Economic Crime.

Jean-Baptiste Maillart
Research fellow at the Max Planck Institute. He holds law degrees from the University of Paris I Pantheon-Sorbonne, the Geneva Academy of International Humanitarian Law and Human Rights, and the University of Geneva. His PhD thesis analysed the challenges of the territoriality principle in the context of cybercrime. He is a former fellow of the Swiss National Science Foundation.

Benjamin Vogel
Head of the research group on illicit financial flows at the Max Planck Institute and, since 2013, in charge of the Institute's desk on English criminal law. He holds law degrees from the Universities of Potsdam, Paris X and Cambridge. He is currently working on his habilitation; his research focuses on comparative law, criminal law theory, financial crime, and supranational security law.

QUESTIONNAIRE

I. INTRODUCTION

A. HISTORY OF ANTI-MONEY LAUNDERING

Please provide a brief overview of the history of AML efforts in your country.

B. CURRENT CONCERNS AND REFORM AGENDA

Which specific concerns currently arise in your jurisdiction regarding AML (e.g. regarding its effectiveness, constitutional law concerns, implementation of international instruments)? Which proposals/demands currently surface in the AML reform debate?

II. AIMS AND SCOPE OF AML SYSTEM

A. AIMS OF AML REGIME

The precise objectives of AML are sometimes somewhat unclear, in particular when political statements at the international and national levels and actual enforcement practice differ. How then would you describe the purpose of AML instruments in your country? Please refer both to legislation and political statements as well as the known practice of competent authorities.

B. SCOPE OF MONEY LAUNDERING

1. *Definition of Money Laundering in Criminal Law*

a. *Actus Reus*

i. Predicate Offences

Please specify the predicate offences under your money laundering offence. Please also indicate whether/to what extent these offences must fulfil a certain threshold of seriousness in order to be considered predicate offences (e.g. depending on the potential or actual length of the custodial sentence of the predicate offence).

ii. Definition of Money Laundering Acts

How is the act of money laundering described in your criminal law (e.g. concealment, possession)? Is the laundering of the proceeds of one's own criminal activity ("self-laundering") covered, and how is this defined? What objective link must there be between the property that was generated by the predicate offence and the act of money laundering (e.g. only direct link, or also laundering of substitutes for illicit gains)? How does your law treat property that partially originates from illicit gains and partially from legitimate income (e.g. when only 10% of the purchase price of real estate originates from illicit sources)? How does the law treat the gains originating from tax evasion?

b. *Mens Rea*

Which *mens rea* is required by your general money laundering offence (intent, negligence, wilful blindness, recklessness)? Please briefly explain how your law defines these mental states. To what extent must the respective *mens rea* cover the predicate offence (e.g. knowledge of the exact details of the predicate offence or only awareness of any illicit origin)?

2. *Money Laundering by Omission*

Does your law provide for criminal liability for money laundering by omission? Where appropriate, how is this defined, in particular, what circumstances give rise to such responsibility (e.g. being a compliance officer)? If your law provides for negligent money laundering, to what extent does this produce delimitation problems between negligence and omission?

3. *Aggravated Forms of Money Laundering*

Does your law provide for aggravated forms of money laundering, and how are these defined?

4. *Statutes of Limitation*

What statute of limitation applies to money laundering? Please also indicate how this issue is addressed with regard to continued forms of money laundering (in particular, laundering through possession or tax evasion).

Are there temporary limits regarding the predicate offence that precludes criminal liability for money laundering? Do the statutes of limitation of the predicate offences impact on the criminal liability for money laundering?

5. *Jurisdictional Rules*

To what extent can acts of money laundering committed abroad, in whole or in part, be punished in your jurisdiction? To what extent does your money laundering offence apply to predicate offences committed abroad?

C. NON-CRIMINAL DEFINITION OF MONEY LAUNDERING

Does your legal system have a separate money laundering definition outside criminal law? If so, please specify the difference to the criminal law definition and to what extent this definition is relevant.

D. SCOPE OF OBLIGED ENTITIES

1. *Financial and Banking Institutions*

Which financial institutions are designated as obliged entities under your law?

2. *Virtual Currency System Participants*

To what extent are virtual currency system participants (e.g. virtual currency exchange platforms, custodial wallet providers) considered to be obliged entities?

3. *Legal Profession and Tax Advisors*

To what extent are members of the legal profession and tax advisors designated as obliged entities?

4. *Informal Value Transfer Systems*

To what extent are informal value transfer system (e.g. *hawala* providers) considered as obliged entities?

5. *Non-Profit Sector*

To what extent are non-profit entities (in particular NGOs) considered as obliged entities?

6. *Overview of Other Obliged Entities*

Please provide a brief overview of the other professions that are designated as obliged entities under your law.

E. RELATIONSHIP BETWEEN AML AND ANTI-TERRORISM FINANCING FRAMEWORK(S)

AML and counter-terrorism financing (CTF) are often addressed with the same instruments. Are there any particularities/differences in the treatment of AML and CTF in your country? Is there any debate on whether these two issues should be more clearly separated, due to differences between the two phenomena (CTF often involving legally acquired property) or to differences in the applicable constitutional law standards (particularly with regard to proportionality) or to differences in their objectives (e.g. CTF might be more focused on financial intelligence than on the suppression of cash flows)?

III. THE SYSTEM OF MONEY LAUNDERING PREVENTION

A. CUSTOMER DUE DILIGENCE

1. *Standard CDD Rules*

a. Triggers and Timing

When do obliged entities have to apply CDD measures? Where necessary, please differentiate between different types of obliged entities.

b. CDD Measures

What CDD measures does your law require? Where necessary, please differentiate between different types of obliged entities (especially financial industry institutions, real estate agents, dealers in goods).

c. Individual Responsibility

Is there any executive position at the obliged entities' senior/most senior level (e.g. board members, directors) who, according to the law, bear overall responsibility for the company's AML, even if this person is not operationally involved in day-to-day AML compliance?

d. Further CDD Guidance

Please provide a brief overview of the most relevant binding guidance issued by supervisory authorities (e.g. the financial market authority, the bar association) or other public authorities (e.g. FIUs) to specify the law's standard CDD requirements, in particular guidance for risk assessment.

2. Simplified CDD

a. Scope

In which cases does your law allow for simplified CDD measures, i.e. for a simplification of standard CDD requirements? Where necessary, please differentiate between different types of obliged entities.

b. Requirements

How are the applicable requirements for simplified CDD under your law simplified compared to standard CDD? Where necessary, please differentiate between different types of obliged entities.

c. Further Simplified CDD Guidance

Please provide a brief overview of the most relevant binding guidance issued by supervisory authorities (e.g. the financial market authority, the bar association) or other public authorities (e.g. FIUs) to specify the law's simplified CDD requirements, in particular guidance for risk assessment. Are these authorities under a legal duty to provide such guidance?

3. *Enhanced CDD*

a. Scope

In which cases does your law require enhanced CDD measures, i.e. measures that are more ambitious than the standard requirements? Where necessary, please differentiate between different types of obliged entities.

b. Requirements

How are the applicable enhanced requirements under your law more demanding than standard CDD? Where necessary, please differentiate between different types of obliged entities.

c. Further Enhanced CDD Guidance

Please provide a brief overview of the most relevant binding guidance issued by supervisory authorities (e.g. the financial market authority, the bar association) or other public authorities (e.g. FIUs) to specify the law's enhanced CDD requirements, in particular guidance for risk assessment.

4. Rules on Politically Exposed Persons

a. Definition

How does your law define "politically exposed persons"? Where applicable, please specify differences in the definition between domestic/foreign PEP and other categories (e.g. "international" PEPs).

b. Requirements

How do CDD rules for PEPs differ from the aforementioned enhanced CDD?

c. Further Enhanced CDD Guidance on PEPs

Please provide a brief overview of the most relevant binding guidance issued by supervisory authorities (e.g. the financial market authority, the bar association) or other public authorities (e.g. FIUs) to specify the law's enhanced CDD requirements applicable to business relationships and occasional transactions involving PEPs.

5. Rules on High-Risk Third Countries

a. Scope

Certain countries pose a particularly high money laundering risk, leading the international community to call for precautions when dealing with such countries. How does your law define "high-risk third countries"? Does this definition refer to relevant international, regional or national "blacklists" or other authoritative designation mechanisms?

b. Requirements

How do CDD rules for high-risk third countries differ from the aforementioned enhanced CDD?

c. Further Enhanced CDD Guidance on High-Risk Third Countries

Please provide a brief overview of the most relevant binding guidance issued by supervisory authorities (e.g. the financial market authority, the bar association) or other public authorities (e.g. FIUs) to specify the law's enhanced CDD requirements applicable to business relationships and occasional transactions involving high-risk third countries.

6. Private Sector CDD Guidance

Are there any private sector standards/rules that provide further guidance for the exercise of CDD, in particular risk assessment? Please provide a brief overview of such instruments.

B. PRELIMINARY RISK ANALYSIS

To what extent does your law impose an obligation on obliged entities to carry out a risk analysis of their business operations prior to the conduct of any client-specific or transaction-specific CDD measures in order to identify/assess its risk exposure and adapt its CDD practice accordingly?

C. REPORTING AND ASSET FREEZING

1. First-Time Reporting

a. Trigger for/Degree of Suspicion

When do obliged entities have to file a suspicious activity report (SAR)? What degree of suspicion is required? Please specify when such reporting is mandatory and when it is at the discretion of the obliged entity. If necessary, please differentiate between the types of obliged entities.

b. Content and Direct Addressee(s) of SARs

Who is the direct addressee of the SAR (e.g. FIU, police, prosecutor, bar association)? What information must it contain?

c. Duty not to Disclose

To what extent is the obliged entity under an obligation not to disclose to its customer the fact that it filed a SAR?

d. Power or Duty to Freeze

To what extent is the obliged entity under an obligation, or at least authorised, to temporarily suspend its business relationship with the customer concerned, to stop transactions, or to freeze property? For how long can such measures be imposed?

e. Instant Collateral Duties

Is the obliged entity under any collateral obligations when filing a SAR (e.g. further monitoring of the client's business activities)?

2. Follow-Up

a. Duty to Provide FIU with Additional Data

To what extent is the obliged entity under an obligation to provide the FIU or other addressees of the SAR with further information?

b. Continued Duty not to Disclose SAR to Client

To what extent is there a continued duty on the part of the reporting obliged entity not to disclose to the client the filing of the SAR, even if it has not led to a discovery of illegal conduct?

c. Continued Collateral Duties

After having filed a SAR, is the obliged entity under any collateral obligations, even if the initial suspicion has not been confirmed (e.g. further monitoring of the client's business activities)?

3. *Special Rules for Privileged Professions*

a. Trigger for/Degree of Suspicion

Do special rules on the degree of suspicion or other triggering factors required for a SAR apply to privileged professions (e.g. lawyers, tax advisors)? Where relevant, please differentiate between types of professions.

b. Content and Addressee(s) of SARs

Are there special rules regarding the addressees, procedure and content of SARs filed by privileged professions? Where applicable, please differentiate between professions.

c. Duty not to Disclose to Client

Are there special rules for privileged professions on the disclosure of a SAR filing?

4. Protection of SAR's Source

Does your law provide special rules for the protection of a SAR's source (e.g. anonymity of the obliged entity that filed the SAR, anonymity of the individual employee that filed the SAR)? If so, please specify.

D. RECORD KEEPING

To what extent does your law provide for record keeping obligations of CDD information, records of transactions and/or SAR-related information?

E. COMPLIANCE OFFICERS

To what extent are obliged entities under a legal obligation to appoint compliance officers or create a similar position to ensure respect for AML regulations? What competences and powers must such a compliance officer have? Which rules ensure the independence of the compliance officer vis-à-vis the obliged entity?

F. INTERNAL COMPLAINT MECHANISM

Is an obliged entity under an obligation to put in place an internal complaint mechanism that allows employees or third persons to inform senior management about AML CDD violations committed within the obliged entity? If so, please specify the scope of such an obligation, the design of such a mechanism, and possible safeguards that serve to protect the complainant (e.g. by insuring his anonymity).

G. ADDITIONAL PREVENTIVE MEASURES

Are any further obligations applicable to obliged entities in order to ensure effective CDD (especially training of staff, background screening of employees)? In this respect, are there any obligations on the part of the FIU to support the obliged entities?

H. RULES ON OBLIGED ENTITIES' CIVIL LIABILITY TOWARDS CLIENT

If a client suffers economic damage from CDD measures (e.g. by the sudden disruption of banking services) or the freezing of assets after the filing of an unjustified SAR, under what conditions can an obliged entity be held responsible and forced to compensate the client?

I. SUPERVISORY AUTHORITIES' ROLE

1. *Supervisory Measures to Ensure Application of CDD and Other AML-Related Obligations*

Briefly describe the preventive functions of supervisory authorities, or other competent authorities, to ensure the application of AML CDD and related AML obligations by obliged entities.

2. *Complaint Mechanism*

Does your law provide for a mechanism (at the level of supervisory authorities or other competent authorities) that allows individuals (in particular employees of obliged entities) to report violations of CDD and related obligations by an obliged entity? If so, please specify. To what extent does special protection exist for the person who made such a complaint (e.g. the right to remain anonymous)?

J. STATISTICS ON SARs BY OBLIGED ENTITIES

Are any statistics available on the number of SARs and the value of transactions associated with them, as well as on the number of follow-up reports filed by obliged entities and the outcome of such reports?

IV. THE SYSTEM OF FINANCIAL INTELLIGENCE UNITS

A. INSTITUTIONAL AND FUNCTIONAL CHARACTERISTICS

1. *Organisational Position*

Is the FIU situated within or connected to the organisational structure of another authority (e.g. supervisory authority, other administrative authority, criminal justice, police, customs)?

2. *Purpose and Tasks*

How are the FIU's purpose and its tasks defined?

3. *Independence*

To what extent is the FIU independent from political actors and other authorities? Can other authorities give instructions to the FIU (e.g. prosecutor, police, supervisory authorities, ministers)? If so, in which cases?

4. Powers

Which investigative and which coercive powers are given to the FIU (e.g. freezing of assets, giving instructions to and requesting information from other authorities, telecommunications interceptions, search and seizure of documents, interrogations)?

B. TREATMENT OF SARs

1. Data Processing

How does the FIU proceed with SARs filed by obliged entities and other authorities? How and to what end are the SARs analysed by the FIU? When and how are SARs forwarded to other authorities (e.g. to the prosecution)?

2. *Special Procedures for Privileged Professions*

Do special procedures for the processing of SARs exist for privileged professions (e.g. lawyers, tax advisors)? If so, please specify (e.g. SAR screening by a profession's self-governing body).

3. *Feedback Obligations*

a. Obligation of the FIU

Is the FIU under an obligation to inform the reporting entity about the outcome of the SAR? If so, what information will be provided to the reporting entity?

b. Obligation of Investigative Authorities

In the event that the FIU or a reporting entity communicates a SAR to a law enforcement authority (e.g. police, prosecutor, tax authorities), is this law enforcement authority under an obligation to inform the FIU about the outcome of the SAR? If so, what information will be provided to the FIU?

4. *Disclosure Obligations Towards "Suspect"*

To what extent is the FIU entitled or obliged to inform the "suspect" about the investigation conducted by the FIU following a SAR?

C. PROACTIVE INVESTIGATIONS

Does the FIU have the power to initiate an investigation even in the absence of a SAR? If so, please specify the conditions of initiation of such investigations, as well as the powers the FIU has to this end. Is such an investigation necessarily directed against a particular suspect? To what extent is an obliged entity under an obligation not to disclose to its client that the FIU has requested information with regard to this client?

D. ACCESS TO DATA

1. *Design and Content of FIU's Own Data Banks*

To what extent does the FIU collect SARs? What other data can be collected and/or stored by the FIU?

2. *Access to Other Public Data Banks*

Which other data banks of public authorities does the FIU have access to, and under what conditions (e.g. criminal justice, tax office)?

3. *Access to Private Data Banks*

Which data banks of private entities does the FIU have access to, and under what conditions?

4. *Data Analytics*

To what extent is the FIU authorised to conduct data analytics (data mining, data matching) in or between the aforementioned data banks, in particular to automatically process the content of such data banks in order to identify possible suspects?

5. *International Cooperation*

Does your FIU have any special cooperation agreements with foreign authorities? If so, please briefly summarise their main content.

E. PARTICIPATION OF "SUSPECTS"

1. *Defence Rights*

To what extent are "suspects" involved in the FIU process? Which defence rights apply (e.g. legal privilege, right against self-incrimination, access to file, right to be heard)?

2. *Judicial Review or Other Remedies*

Are there ways for the "suspect" to apply for judicial review of the FIU's action? Are there review mechanisms other than judicial ones?

F. SIMILAR POWERS OF SUPERVISORY BODIES

1. Financial Supervision

Do supervisory bodies of financial markets (e.g. the financial market authority) have the right to investigate a suspicion of money laundering on their own? If so, please specify the competent supervisory body, and when and how such investigations are conducted.

2. Non-Financial Sector Supervision

Do other supervisory bodies (e.g. the bar association) have the right to investigate a suspicion of money laundering on their own? If so, please specify the competent supervisory authority, when, and how such investigations are conducted as well as which coercive measures can be applied by the supervisory body to prevent money laundering.

G. REPORTING OBLIGATIONS OF SUPERVISORY AUTHORITIES

Which supervisory authorities (e.g. the financial market authority, the bar association) have to file reports about suspicious activities to the FIU? Please specify whether and to what extent reporting requirements differ from those applicable to obliged entities.

H. REPORTING BY OTHER AUTHORITIES

Do other authorities have to file reports about suspicious activities to the FIU (e.g. tax authorities, customs, prosecutors)? If not, are they allowed to do so? If yes, please specify. Do they report to the FIU or to other bodies?

I. STATISTICS

1. Number of Reports by Supervisory Authorities and Other Authorities

Are there statistics on the number of reports about suspicious activities filed by supervisory authorities and other authorities?

2. FIU Analysis

Are there statistics on the number of FIU investigations and the value of transactions associated with these investigations? If available, please differentiate between investigations following a SAR and investigations on the FIU's own initiative.

3. Communications to Law Enforcement Authorities

Are there statistics on the number of communications by the FIU to other authorities, in particular regarding the forwarding of SARs (e.g. to the prosecution, police)?

V. DATA FLOW AND DATA PROTECTION

A. DATA EXCHANGE BETWEEN FIU AND PRIVATE SECTOR

1. From FIU to Private Sector

Which data protection restrictions exist for the transfer of personal data from the FIU to obliged entities?

2. From Private Sector to FIU

Which data protection restrictions exist for the transfer of personal data from obliged entities to the FIU?

B. DATA EXCHANGE BETWEEN FIU AND CRIMINAL JUSTICE SYSTEM

1. From FIU to Criminal Justice System

Which data protection restrictions exist for the transfer of personal data from the FIU to the criminal justice system?

2. From Criminal Justice System to FIU

Which data protection restrictions exist for the transfer of personal data from the criminal justice sector to the FIU?

C. DATA EXCHANGE BETWEEN FIU AND INTELLIGENCE AGENCIES

1. From FIU to Intelligence Agencies

Which data protection restrictions exist for the transfer of personal data from the FIU to intelligence agencies?

2. From Intelligence Agencies to FIU

Which data protection restrictions exist for the transfer of personal data from intelligence agencies to the FIU?

D. DATA EXCHANGE BETWEEN FIU AND TAX AUTHORITIES

1. From FIU to Tax Authorities

Which data protection restrictions exist for the transfer of personal data from the FIU to tax authorities?

2. From Tax Authorities to FIU

Which data protection restrictions exist for the transfer of personal data from tax authorities to the FIU?

E. DATA EXCHANGE BETWEEN FIU AND CUSTOMS AUTHORITIES

1. *From FIU to Customs Authorities*

Which data protection restrictions exist for the transfer of personal data from the FIU to customs authorities?

2. *From Customs Authorities to FIU*

Which data protection restrictions exist for the transfer of personal data from customs authorities to the FIU?

F. INFORMATION FLOW BETWEEN FIU AND FOREIGN COUNTERPARTS

1. *Restrictions on Data Transfer from FIU to Foreign FIUs*

Which data protection restrictions exist for the transfer of personal data from the FIU to a foreign FIU?

2. Restrictions on Use of Data Obtained from Foreign FIUs

Which data protection restrictions exist for the use of personal data the FIU received from a foreign FIU?

G. INFORMATION FLOW BETWEEN FIU AND FOREIGN NON-COUNTERPARTS

1. Restrictions on Data Transfer from FIU to Other Foreign Authorities

Which data protection restrictions exist for the transfer of personal data from the FIU to other foreign authorities?

2. Restrictions on Use of Data Obtained from Other Foreign Authorities

Which data protection restrictions exist for the use of personal data the FIU received from other foreign authorities?

H. EVIDENTIAL VALUE OF FIU-GENERATED DATA IN COURT PROCEEDINGS

Are there special rules on the admissibility of FIU-generated information as evidence in court proceedings?

I. USE OF CDD DATA FOR PROFIT MAKING

To what extent can personal data gathered by obliged entities for the purpose of CDD, or received by them from the FIU, be used for profit-oriented purposes, i.e. for purposes not directly related to the prevention of financial crime? In particular, to what extent are obliged entities authorised to use data mining systems?

J. DATA SHARING BETWEEN OBLIGED ENTITIES REGARDING SARs AND FIU REQUESTS

1. Data Sharing Inside a Group

To what extent are obliged entities authorised to share information regarding the filing of SARs or regarding requests by the FIU with other obliged entities within the same group of companies?

2. *Data Sharing with Similar Professions*

To what extent are obliged entities authorised to share information regarding the filing of SARs or regarding requests by the FIU with other obliged entities outside the group, but within a similar profession?

3. *Data Sharing with Obliged Entities Outside the EU*

To what extent are obliged entities authorised to share information regarding the filing of SARs or regarding requests by the FIU with other obliged entities in third countries?

K. DATA SHARING BETWEEN OBLIGED ENTITIES REGARDING POSSIBLE CASES OF MONEY LAUNDERING

1. *Data Sharing Inside a Group*

To what extent are obliged entities authorised to share information regarding suspicious transactions or similarly unusual events with other obliged entities within the same group of companies?

FATF 58
European Union 137
Germany 269
Italy 383
Spain 501
Switzerland 622
Comparative Analysis 860

2. *Data Sharing with Similar Professions*

To what extent are obliged entities authorised to share information regarding suspicious transactions or similarly unusual events with other obliged entities outside the group, but within a similar profession?

FATF 58
European Union 138
Germany 270
Italy 383
Spain 502
Switzerland 622
Comparative Analysis 861

3. *Data Sharing with Obliged Entities Outside the EU*

To what extent are obliged entities authorised to share information regarding suspicious transactions or similarly unusual events with other obliged entities in third countries?

FATF 59
European Union 138
Germany 271
Italy 383
Spain 502
Switzerland 622
Comparative Analysis 862

L. DATA MINING BY OBLIGED ENTITIES

To what extent are obliged entities authorised to conduct data mining (instead of mere data matching) within their data banks in order to identify possible cases of money laundering?

VI. BENEFICIAL OWNERSHIP TRANSPARENCY

A. BENEFICIAL OWNERSHIP INFORMATION

1. *General Framework*

Does your country impose obligations on legal entities and trusts to disclose their beneficial ownership situation? If so, please specify who is subject to such obligations (e.g. citizens, residents, domestic entities, foreign entities operating in the country)? How are these categories defined?

2. *Definition of "Beneficiary" and "Effective Control"*

How does your country define the terms "beneficiary" and "effective control" or any other equivalent criteria for beneficial ownership?

3. *Definition of "Information"*

In the present context, how does your country define the term "information"?

4. *Special Rules for Entities with a Cross-Border Dimension*

Does the law provide for special requirements and mechanisms for the disclosure of foreign nationals, foreign entities or foreign trusts? If so, please specify who is covered and what information must be disclosed.

B. BENEFICIAL OWNERSHIP REGISTRIES

1. *Scope and General Procedure*

Does your country have centralised or decentralised mechanisms to disclose beneficial ownership information (e.g. a national registry)? If so, please specify who is covered by such mechanisms and which information they contain.

2. *Ex Ante Verification of Accuracy*

Are there procedures to verify the accuracy of the beneficial ownership information before it is fed into the aforementioned mechanism(s)? If so, please specify.

3. *Ex Post Review of Accuracy*

Are there procedures to verify the accuracy of beneficial ownership information after it has been fed into the aforementioned mechanism(s)? If so, please specify, in particular, the reasons that trigger such *ex post* verification.

C. ACCESS TO BENEFICIAL OWNERSHIP INFORMATION

1. *Access by FIU and Other Authorities*

To what extent do the FIU and other authorities have access to beneficial ownership information and under which conditions?

2. Access by Obliged Entities

To what extent do obliged entities have access to beneficial ownership information and under which conditions?

3. Access by Interested Third Parties

To what extent do interested third parties or the public at large have access to beneficial ownership information and under which conditions?

VII. SANCTIONS

A. SANCTIONS FOR MONEY LAUNDERING

1. Requirement of a Conviction for a Predicate Offence

To what extent does the commission of a predicate offence have to be proven? Is a criminal conviction for the predicate offence a necessary prerequisite for a criminal conviction of money laundering?

2. Forms of Sanctions

Which types of sanctions can be applied following a criminal conviction for money laundering?

3. Confiscation

In addition to the aforementioned sanctions, what kinds of confiscation can be imposed in the context of money laundering (e.g. conviction-based confiscation, non-conviction-based confiscation)? Please specify the respective conditions.

4. Statistics

a. Number of Criminal Proceedings

Are statistics available on the number of criminal proceedings for money laundering and the value of transactions associated with these proceedings? If possible, please specify whether these proceedings are the result of a SAR or another origin.

b. Number of Convictions

Are statistics available on the number of criminal convictions for money laundering and the value of transactions associated with these convictions? If possible, please specify whether they are the result of a SAR or another origin.

B. SANCTIONS FOR VIOLATIONS OF PREVENTIVE MEASURES

1. Money Laundering by Violating Preventive Obligations

Does your law allow for criminal convictions of money laundering for violations of omission in the course of preventive duties (e.g. due diligence, reporting obligations)?

2. CDD, Reporting and Other AML-Related Obligations

a. Special Criminal Laws against Individuals

Does your law provide for criminal sanctions against individuals for a violation of CDD, reporting and/or other AML-related obligations? If so, please specify, in particular, the type of obligations and the range of sanctions available.

b. Administrative Sanctions against Individuals

Does your law provide for administrative sanctions against individuals for a violation of CDD, reporting and/or other AML-related obligations? If so, please specify, in particular, the type of and the range of sanctions available? Who imposes these sanctions, and upon whose initiative are they imposed?

c. Sanctions against Legal Entities

Does your law provide for sanctions against legal entities for a violation of CDD, reporting and/or other AML-related obligations? If so, please specify, in particular, the type of obligations and the range of sanctions available? Who imposes these sanctions, and upon whose initiative are they imposed?

3. *Statistics*

a. Number of Investigations and Sanctions

Are statistics available on the number of criminal and administrative investigations launched against individuals and legal entities for the aforementioned offences? If so, please specify.

b. Number of Convictions

Are statistics available on the number of criminal or administrative convictions/ sanctions imposed on individuals and legal entities for the aforementioned offences? If so, please specify.

C. CUMULATION OF MONEY LAUNDERING AND OTHER AML-RELATED SANCTIONS

To what extent can sanctions for money laundering be combined with sanctions for the violation of preventive obligations? For example, can one be held criminally responsible for money laundering and subjected to criminal or administrative sanctions for the same criminal conduct for violating reporting obligations?

VIII. THE USE OF CASH AS A MEANS OF PAYMENT

A. LIMITS

Are there legal limits on the use of cash as a means of payment, in particular any maximum amounts?

B. STATISTICS

Are there statistics on the use of cash in relation to the overall volume of (cash and non-cash) transactions conducted in the country?

IX. SUMMARY, EVALUATION AND FUTURE PERSPECTIVES

INTRODUCTION

Benjamin VOGEL

I. RESEARCH OBJECT AND CONTEXT

Money laundering has over recent years become a pivotal security concern in the European Union and beyond. Originating initially from efforts against drug trafficking, anti money laundering (AML) today is driven by broader considerations that reflect the diversity of criminal activity resulting in illicit financial flows. Several factors had a particularly strong impact on policymakers. With rising political concern about terrorism, the resulting focus on related financial flows and close alignment of AML and counter-terrorism financing (CTF) measures, counterterrorism has ultimately also served as a catalyst for a growth of AML.[1] The dividing line between money laundering and terrorist financing has in fact been blurred, both because terrorists can have recourse to organised crime as a means of financing their political agenda and because the aims and methods of profit-seeking organised crime can oftentimes closely resemble or equate to terrorism. AML policies have also been stimulated by types of criminality that, while not necessarily corresponding to the initial focus on organised criminal groups, are equally profit-driven and therefore in need of ensuring that assets are concealed from competent authorities, notably corruption and tax-related offences. Extensive data leaks, such as the "Panama Papers",[2] involving professional enablers (such as criminal attorneys

---

1 See e.g. European Commission, Communication from the Commission to the European Parliament and the Council on an Action Plan for strengthening the fight against terrorist financing of 2 February 2016, COM(2016) 50 final.

2 European Parliament, Report on the inquiry into money laundering, tax avoidance and tax evasion of 16 November 2017, A8-0357/2017.

and bankers) and anonymity-friendly jurisdictions have furthermore provided important insights into the complexity and magnitude of transnational schemas to hide assets, and into the implication therein of organised crime, corrupt officials and tax offenders. Resulting from the scale of hidden and potentially criminal assets and the involvement of financial institutions and other professional enablers, policymaking has more recently been devoting greater attention to the role of obliged entities.[3] Increasing awareness in this regard can be explained in particular by the threat that the involvement of financial institutions and other obliged entities in criminal activity poses to themselves, notably due to sometimes heavy sanctions being imposed by third states, and to the wider economy, not least the potential of criminal assets to distort competition in lawful markets.

In reaction to the aforementioned concerns, norm-setters at both the supranational and domestic levels have responded by successively expanding the scope of AML in many crucial respects. The definition of money laundering has been expanding to cover an increasing variety of profit-generating predicate offences. The circle of obliged entities is continuously widening to encompass additional types of businesses. Customer due diligence (CDD) obligations have been tightened in order to ensure greater scrutiny of higher-risk situations. Financial intelligence units (FIUs) are in many cases transforming from mere data depositories into intelligence bodies with an increasing operational mandate. Supervisory authorities are being entrusted with growing responsibility for enforcing the private sector's CDD and reporting obligations and to this end are being equipped with enhanced sanctioning powers. Gateways for competent authorities to share relevant information with one another are being expanded. Beneficial ownership transparency is being strengthened through instruments like publicly accessible registers. And increasing emphasis is being put on the monitoring of crypto assets, that is assets traded outside the conventional financial system.

Unsurprisingly, the introduction of a multitude of new concepts and instruments into pre-established AML frameworks is in many cases proving difficult. Reforms are often adopted without scrutinising the effectiveness of pre-existing concepts and the validity of underlying assumptions.[4] As importantly, new instruments frequently pose a compatibility challenge with regard to other elements of AML. The consistency of particular national legal frameworks can be complicated by demands under national constitutional law. Sometimes profound differences between national legal orders and their social

---

3 See European Commission, Report on the assessment of recent alleged money laundering cases involving EU credit institutions of 24 July 2019, COM(2019) 373 final.

4 M Levi/P Reuter/T Halliday, Can the AML system be evaluated without better data?, 69 *Crime, Law and Social Change* (2018), pp. 307–328.

and institutional realities complicate the search for consistency in global and regional AML policies. Torn between supranational demands and difficulties with integrating these demands into a national legal order, policymakers will frequently prioritise formal compliance with those demands over the actual effectiveness of the respective measures.

II. OVERALL OBJECTIVE OF THE STUDY

In light of the aforementioned difficulties, the present study aims to develop remedies to the primary inconsistencies and challenges of today's AML frameworks. It seeks to improve existing instruments by proposing the essential components of a comprehensive AML architecture that is both effective as to the objectives pursued and respectful of fundamental rights. While the study is primarily concerned with the development of recommendations for the European Union, large parts of the insights and conclusions are expected to be relevant or oftentimes even equally valid for jurisdictions outside the EU. In that sense, and while this is not its main objective, the following study also hopes to make a contribution to discussion about the future shape of global AML standards.

III. STARTING HYPOTHESES AND KEY QUESTIONS

The research design of the study is guided by four primary starting hypotheses that constitute evident points of contention observable within national AML frameworks in the EU.

First, the application of today's AML instruments are frequently characterised by a sense of uncertainty about the specific objectives of the overall framework.[5] While originally focused on organised crime, the expanding scope of supranational and national frameworks and with it the purposes pursued by the various public and private actors have now moved in various additional directions,[6] not least towards the detection of tax offences. At the same time, to the extent that AML is also meant to serve the protection of the integrity of financial institutions, there appears to be little consensus about the actual meaning of this objective. This raises the question to what extent supranational and national frameworks do in essence agree on the purposes they pursue, and

5 PC van Duyne/JH Harvey/LY Gelemerova, The Critical Handbook of Money Laundering: Policy, Analysis and Myths, 2018, pp. 321–324.

6 G Stessens, Money Laundering: A New International Enforcement Model, 2000, pp. 11–14.

whether any particular purpose reflects a consistent understanding of how a framework should actually function.[7]

Second, even where objectives are clearly defined, the role of the private sector's preventive obligations are often not well understood. While obliged entities are obviously expected to detect money laundering and report any suspicion to this effect to the authorities, the ambiguity inherent in a risk-based approach to CDD and the lack of a precise definition of relevant suspicion can lead to great uncertainty about what is expected by the law. Despite vast resources being spent on private compliance efforts, this may call into question the actual suitability of the regulatory framework to effectively contribute to the detection and prevention of money laundering.[8] Furthermore, expectations of supervisory and other authorities towards the private sector alternate between a desire to have obliged entities serve as gatekeepers of the financial system or instead primarily as sources of financial intelligence. Differences of opinion in this respect can reflect rather antagonistic visions of the purpose of private sector involvement and so, in order to not produce contradictory practices, require clarification.

Third, the place of FIUs within the national security architecture is often not clearly understood. FIUs are indeed a rather new actor within states' institutional settings, and there still does not seem to be much consensus at the supranational level as to how exactly they should operate.[9] Such uncertainty is unhelpful not only because national legislators can, as a consequence, find it difficult to define the competences and powers of the FIU in a way that makes effective use of the operational benefits offered by financial intelligence. FIUs are of course a central component of the AML framework, as they are intermediaries between the private sector and the competent authorities. The less effective the performance of their role, the more limited the usefulness of obliged entities' reporting of suspicious activity thus is. In addition, ambiguity about the exact purpose and the powers of FIUs can also complicate their relationship with other authorities, especially criminal justice authorities. It is therefore necessary to gain a better understanding of the role that FIUs can and should play while at the same time recognising that diversity between national legal orders might be partially explained by differences in the design of national criminal justice systems.

---

7 See MF Cuéllar, The tenuous relationship between the fight against money laundering and the disruption of criminal finance, 93(2/3) *The Journal of Criminal Law and Criminology* (2003), pp. 394–402.

8 Europol, From Suspicion to Action: Converting financial intelligence into greater operational impact, 2017; see WS Laufer, The Missing Account of Progressive Corporate Criminal Law, 14 *New York University Journal of Law & Business* (2017), pp. 110–116.

9 See K Stroligo et al., Financial Intelligence Units Working With Law Enforcement Authorities and Prosecutors, International Bank for Reconstruction and Development/The World Bank 2018.

Fourth, supranational as well as national frameworks have so far only tentatively addressed the interaction between AML and data protection law.[10] AML is to a very large extent about the processing of personal data by public and private players. With the ever-growing role of electronic transactions as a payment method and the decline of cash, the amount of financial data is constantly expanding. The establishment of beneficial ownership registries and the increasing data sharing between competent authorities, as well as between obliged entities, are accentuating concerns in this regard. To the extent that data protection considerations today occupy a central place in the constitutional order of many jurisdictions, uncertainty about data protection limits in the gathering and further processing of financial data is a major flaw. For insofar as the constraints imposed by data protection law are not sufficiently reflected in the shape of AML instruments, the competent authorities and obliged entities lack legislative guidance on how to resolve conflicting normative expectations, thereby creating the potential for abuse and at the same time exposing competent authorities and obliged entities to judicial challenges.

IV. METHODOLOGY

In order to examine the starting hypotheses, thereby identify the flaws in current laws and subsequently develop potential remedies, the analysis of AML frameworks is confronted with four key challenges that need to be addressed by the methodology of this study. At the same time, these challenges already point to some important limits on the knowledge production that can be expected from the analysis.

Constituting a first challenge, AML laws at the national level are heavily predefined by supranational demands, in particular the FATF standards and, as far as obliged entities in the Member States and their subsidiaries in third states are concerned, EU legislation. Frameworks at the national level can therefore not be understood, and consequently must not be analysed, without taking into consideration the applicable supranational requirements. Otherwise, recommendations for national policymakers are at risk of falling short of internationally accepted standards and thus would potentially provoke tensions and contradictions that would very likely not be politically or legally acceptable and would ultimately contribute to more distortions rather than to more coherence of a given national framework. Starting with an analysis of

---

10 Opinion of the European Data Protection Supervisor (EDPS) on a proposal for a Directive of the European Parliament and of the Council on the prevention of the use of the financial system for the purpose of money laundering and terrorist financing, and a proposal for a Regulation of the European Parliament and of the Council on information on the payer accompanying transfers of funds of 4 July 2013.

supranational frameworks of the FATF and EU before moving to the individual national frameworks of Germany, Italy, Spain, Switzerland and the United Kingdom does not of course mean that reflections about the shape and potential reform of national frameworks should blindly follow supranational demands. In fact, the analysis of national frameworks in the light of supranational standards can also help to explain whether deficiencies at the national level might have their origin in the supranational sphere, notably in that particular supranational demands might at times clash with national constitutional requirements and thereby present national policymakers with great and sometimes unsurmountable problems. In such cases, a multilevel analysis of both supranational and national legal frameworks will then also provide insights into the possible need to amend or even fundamentally rethink some supranational standards. Nevertheless, given the very internationalised nature of AML and the highly transnational nature of modern financial services, solutions at the national level, and therefore by implication any methodological design aimed at developing legal reform, will as far as possible need to accommodate supranational standards.

As a second challenge, any analysis of AML is confronted with the need to include a plurality of areas of law, notably criminal law, the law of business regulation and data protection provisions. It is impossible to understand the obligations of private businesses and professionals under regulatory law without having a clear understanding of the applicable criminal law. Similarly, the scope as well as the deficiencies of criminal offences pertaining to money laundering will usually not be fully appreciated if one misses the regulatory context in which money laundering is occurring. The applicable regulatory law as well as relevant powers of competent authorities will in turn usually not been fully understood if the applicable limitations stemming from data protection law are left out of the picture. In light of the overreaching purpose of AML to provide leads for criminal investigations, the obligations and powers of competent authorities and of obliged entities cannot be assessed in complete isolation from the principles and safeguards of criminal procedure law. Lastly, the actual impact of obligations under regulatory law will not least also depend on the shape of the respective system of regulatory supervision, including the availability of administrative sanctions and administrative preventive measures. In short, only by approaching the AML framework as a legal architecture that consists of various independent but interrelated elements can one fully appreciate the functioning of its individual components and on this basis make sense of its deficiencies. AML is thus a paradigmatic example of a phenomenon visible in many areas of modern criminal policy of legislators going well beyond the traditional contours of criminal justice and criminal sanctions and instead developing broader and more diverse approaches towards an encompassing "security law".[11]

---

11 U Sieber, The New Architecture of Security Law: Crime Control in the Global Risk Society, in U Sieber et al. (eds.), Alternative Systems of Crime Control, 2018.

In addition to criminal justice authorities, this includes extensive crime prevention and detection duties of private businesses, a greater role for non-criminal sanctions and the gathering of criminal intelligence outside the confines of criminal investigations. Only by combining these different elements can an analysis of today's AML frameworks succeed in producing meaningful findings.

As a third challenge, AML is at the national level usually characterised by considerable variations as regards both policy concepts and underlying objectives. Such variations demonstrate that supranational standards in many respects still allow for extensive flexibility. In fact, due to the above-described nature of AML as constituting a complex architecture of various areas of law, supranational harmonisation of national frameworks is effectively limited by the often-important differences in how individual national legal orders define the function and scope of the relevant areas of law. This may for example concern the question whether a national legal order requires criminal investigations to be closely supervised by judicial authorities or to what extent it emphasises data protection as a constraint on public and private data processing. It then becomes clear that AML cannot be adequately understood by merely looking at supranational frameworks because those will in many respects be too unspecific. In turn, the framework of one particular national jurisdiction might merely reflect a singular interpretation of supranational standards and therefore potentially reveal little about common features of AML. Given the necessary limitation of the number of national frameworks compared, one can of course not realistically hope to gain a conclusive understanding of all the different options through which supranational standards can be transposed at the national level.[12] Nevertheless, the comparative analysis of five national jurisdictions will, as a minimum outcome, ensure that the shape of the AML framework of individual jurisdictions is put into perspective. Such perspective is essential not only to get inspiration for how one and the same supranational standard might be implemented at the national level in more or less effective ways, but in particular to understand whether deficiencies at the national level are primarily the result of national policy choices or rather of supranational demands.

Fourthly, inquiries into AML are confronted with the problem that large parts of a legal framework's actual functioning is neither publicised through case law nor otherwise made transparent. While some statistics and available research[13] shed light on some elements of AML practice, key aspects are still marked by very limited public availability of relevant data, not least as regards the manner in which obliged entities perform their CDD obligations and as

---

12 See already M Pieth/G Aiolfi, A Comparative Guide to Anti-Money Laundering, 2004.

13 See e.g. B Unger et al. (eds.), The Economic and Legal Effectiveness of the European Union's Anti-Money Laundering Policy, 2014.

regards the work of FIUs. Such empirical findings are however a necessary precondition for understanding to what extent current law leads to deficiencies in practice as well as for identifying further considerations that a holistic AML framework should address. Consequently, the study also requires extensive empirical research to understand how the various elements of a framework are applied. Obviously, within a primarily normative study, such empirical inquiry does not aspire to produce statistically representative findings, but merely to provide starting points for identifying focus areas and substantiating reform proposals. The resulting normative theory of AML then obviously invites further empirical research to test the underlying assumptions, a task that must be reserved to future research.

Following from the above, the methodology of the study can be sketched in three steps. First, the study analyses national legal orders with a view to identifying whether they address questions that are relevant for remedying the starting hypotheses, and to what extent the responses currently given by national law are insufficient or incoherent in this regard. Second, through an analysis of the FATF and EU frameworks and a comparison of these framework with national legal orders, the study inquires whether the deficiencies identified at the national level are already predefined by supranational demands or have their causes in the respective national arrangements. In a third step, and on the basis of the insights developed through the prior steps, the study explains the key deficiencies of the current EU framework and develops remedies for them. In order to gain the necessary understanding of AML practice and underlying policymaking, the study included about 100 hours of semi-structured qualitative interviews with practitioners from criminal justice authorities, FIUs, supervisory authorities and obliged entities, as well as with policymakers from relevant supranational bodies.

Due to its necessarily comparative nature, the study is based on a comparative legal analysis of supranational and national frameworks. This required a uniform and detailed comparative meta-structure that extends to all relevant elements of the AML architecture. Adopting the functional method of comparative law as a starting point, the meta-structure inquires into how the various legal orders find solutions to the same factual problems, irrespective of the label or categorisation (for example whether something is called "punishment" or "measure") that an individual legal order attaches to those solutions. The functionalist starting point is enriched by structuralist considerations,[14] in that the analysis contextualises factual problems against the backdrop of the wider AML architecture, thereby aiming to avoid misunderstanding as regard an instrument's role and relevance within a particular national legal order.

[14] J Bomhoff, Comparing Legal Argument, in M Adams/J Bomhoff (eds.), Practice and Theory in Comparative Law, 2012.

Recognising the limits inherent in designing any comparative structure,[15] the latter has been continuously evaluated, and where necessary refined, throughout the analysis, notably in view of the findings of the empirical research. This allowed individual country rapporteurs to uncover instances where national concepts that at first glance seemed to be similar turned out to be significantly different in nature and therefore unapt for comparative purposes. Finally, and thus taking into account that the perspectives adopted in the process of legal research, and the resulting findings, are heavily dependent on the legal and political culture in which the respective researcher was educated,[16] the analyses of the various legal orders covered by the study was guided and enriched by continuous dialogue between the different rapporteurs. This communication aimed at ensuring that the various authors followed a consistent vision of the questions addressed in the meta-structure, both when inquiring into the state of their respective laws and when questioning practitioners.

Finally, it is worth pointing out that the present study's research interest focuses on money laundering and not also on terrorism financing. While both phenomena as well as their applicable legal frameworks do extensively overlap, CTF is in many ways characterised by additional features, in particular special investigative powers of competent authorities, which will usually modify the perspective from which one must assess the practical relevance and effectiveness of the AML/CTF framework. CTF is furthermore heavily reliant on targeted sanctions at the supranational level.[17] Including those particularities would however have required a further significant extension of the scope of the study and was therefore rejected from the start. Consequently, references to terrorism financing in this study are merely supposed to adequately present the content of laws where these laws do not further differentiate between money laundering and terrorism financing. In many cases, however, it did appear more appropriate to omit references to terrorism financing altogether, not least in order to avoid confusion. Such references are thus not meant to express views on the current design of CTF, in particular on whether differences in the (largely backward-looking, thus concerned with the origin of assets) nature of the concept of money laundering and the (essentially forward-looking, thus primarily concerned with the intended future use of assets) concept of terrorism financing would suggest that both frameworks should follow largely identical rules or, instead, that the applicable rules should differentiate more than they currently do.

---

15 R Michaels, The Functionalist Method of Comparative Law, in M Reimann/R Zimmermann (eds.), The Oxford Handbook of Comparative Law, 2006.

16 See H-H Jescheck, Entwicklung, Aufgaben und Methoden der Strafrechtsvergleichung, 1955; R Cotterell, Comparatists and sociology, in P Legrand/R Munday (eds.), Comparative Legal Studies: Traditions and Transitions, 2003.

17 See U Sieber/B Vogel, Terrorismusfinanzierung: Prävention im Spannungsfeld von internationalen Vorgaben und nationalem Tatstrafrecht, 2015.

THE ANTI-MONEY LAUNDERING ARCHITECTURE OF THE FATF

Jean-Baptiste MAILLART

I. INTRODUCTION

A. HISTORY OF ANTI-MONEY LAUNDERING AND THE FATF

The Financial Action Task Force (FATF) is an inter-governmental policy-making body[1] that was established during the 1989 G7 Summit held in Paris, in response to the increasing concern over the laundering of drug crime proceeds.[2] The FATF was commissioned with the mandate "to assess the results of cooperation already undertaken in order to prevent the utilisation of the banking system and financial institutions for the purpose of money laundering, and to consider additional preventive efforts in this field, including the adaptation of the legal and regulatory systems so as to enhance multilateral judicial assistance".[3] As a result, in 1990, the FATF issued a report containing the original 40 Recommendations which were intended to provide a comprehensive plan of action to fight against the misuse of financial systems by persons laundering drug money.

Since then, the FATF Recommendations have been thoroughly and comprehensively revised three times, in 1996, 2003 and, most recently, 2012,

1 The membership of the FATF has grown over the years. At the time of its creation, the FATF had 16 members. In 1991 and 1992, the FATF expanded its membership to 28. In 2000, the FATF expanded to 31 members and has since increased to its current 39 members, which include two regional organisations, the European Commission and the Gulf Co-operation Council. It should also be noted that there are numerous sub-organisations that supplement the work of the FATF and have specific AML and CTF functions. These sub-organisations can be split into three groups: Observers, Associate Members and Observer Organisations.

2 In this regard, see FATF (2014), *25 Years and Beyond: The Financial Action Task Force setting the standards to combat money laundering and the financing of terrorism and proliferation*, p. 4. On the history of anti-money laundering prior to 1989, in particular the influence of the United States on the development of the regime, see P. van Duyne, J. Harvey and L. Gelemerova, *The Critical Handbook of Money Laundering: Policy, Analysis and Myths*, Palgrave Macmillan, London, 2018, pp. 41–89.

3 G7 Group of Nations, *Economic Declaration*, Paris Summit, 1989, para. 53.

in order to broaden their scope beyond drug money laundering,[4] and to close loopholes and further address the evolving nature and associated risks of money laundering. Furthermore, it is worth noting that, after the terrorist attacks of 9/11, the FATF saw its mandate expand to include the financing of terrorism[5] so that today the FATF functions as the universally recognised standard-setting and assessment body, not only in the fight against money laundering in relation to all "serious offences",[6] but also in the fight against terrorist financing. Though not being legally binding (soft law),[7] the FATF Recommendations have been endorsed at the highest level by 205 jurisdictions worldwide (as at June 2019),[8] which, in so doing, agreed to being assessed by other jurisdictions using the FATF mutual evaluation methodology. The FATF Standards set out the essential measures that countries should have in place to:

> identify the risks, and develop policies and domestic coordination; pursue money laundering, terrorist financing and the financing proliferation; apply preventive measures for the financial sector and other designated sectors; establish powers and responsibilities for the competent authorities (e.g. investigative, law enforcement and supervisory authorities) and other institutional measures; enhance the transparency and availability of beneficial ownership information of legal persons and arrangements; and facilitate international cooperation.[9]

B. CURRENT CONCERNS AND REFORM AGENDA

Countering terrorist financing has undoubtedly been the "top priority" for the FATF in recent years.[10] Terrorist financing has been an ongoing item on the

---

4 The scope of the FATF Recommendations was broadened beyond drug-money laundering in 1996 when the Recommendations were revised for the first time. See FATF Recommendation 4 (1996): "[e]ach country should extend the offence of drug money laundering to one based on serious offences".

5 On the expansion of the FATF's mandate to include the financing of terrorism, see *infra* section II.E.

6 FATF Recommendation 3 (2012).

7 Although the influence of soft law on the development of international law is indisputable, soft law rules are not a source of international law (art. 38 Statute of the International Court of Justice *a contrario*).

8 Remarks by FATF President Marshall Billingslea, FATF Ministerial meeting, Washington DC, 12 April 2019.

9 FATF (2012), *International Standards on Combating Money Laundering and the Financing of Terrorism and proliferation*, updated June 2019, p. 6.

10 See e.g. Objectives for FATF – XXXI (2019–2020), Paper by the Incoming President, Chinese Presidency Priorities for the FATF, p. 1; Objectives for FATF XXIX (2017–2018), Paper by the Incoming President, Priorities for the Argentine Presidency, Executive Summary, para. 5; FATF (2018), *Annual Report 2017–2018*, p. 11; FATF President Juan Manuel

agenda of the FATF since the attacks of September 11, 2001, but the terrorist attacks in 2015 in Paris, Brussels and other parts of the world called for further action by the FATF to enhance efforts in counter-terrorist financing (CTF) at the global level. As part of its *Consolidated Strategy on Combating Terrorist Financing* agreed in February 2016, the FATF reviewed nearly 200 jurisdictions to determine whether they had established adequate legal frameworks and mechanisms to criminalise terrorist financing and implement targeted financial sanctions. At the Busan Plenary in June 2016, Recommendation 8 on non-profit organisations and its Interpretative Note were also revised with the same objective to improve the fight against terrorism financing, in particular as regards foreign terrorist fighters and tackle the resources used by the Islamic State in Iraq and the Levant (ISIL).[11] More recently, the FATF Plenary adopted a new report entitled *The Financing of Recruitment for Terrorist Purposes*,[12] and agreed on a new Counter-Terrorist Financing Operational Plan.[13] Though these measures were primarily targeting terrorism financing, it should be noted that they also automatically impact the anti-money laundering (AML) legal framework.

Despite the strong current focus of the FATF on CTF, AML remains high on its agenda. In particular, effective implementation of the FATF Standards on beneficial ownership appears to be to be one of the FATF's most important preoccupations at the moment.[14] The information leaked in the Panama Papers in April 2016 revealed that many countries are still not effectively implementing the measures to prevent the misuse of companies, trusts and other corporate vehicles. In addition, a recent review by the FATF of the first nine assessments in the fourth round of mutual evaluations identified multiple implementation challenges on beneficial ownership.[15] In this context, the FATF

Vega-Serrano's remarks at Joint Special Meeting of UN Security Council Committees and the FATF, 12 December 2016.

11 The revisions take into account the findings of the following reports: FATF Report (2014), *Risk of Terrorist Abuse in Non-Profit Organisations*, and FATF Best Practices (2015), *Combating the Abuse of Non-Profit Organisations*. On the financing of ISIL, see also FATF Report (2015), *Financing of the Terrorist Organisation Islamic State in Iraq and the Levant (ISIL)*.

12 FATF Report (2018), *The Financing of Recruitment for Terrorist Purposes*. This report sets out how terrorist organisations fund the recruitment of new members.

13 The new Counter-Terrorist Financing Operational Plan was adopted by the Plenary in February 2018 and focuses on improving and updating the understanding of terrorism financing risks, promoting more effective coordination, including improving information sharing domestically and internationally, ensuring the FATF Standards provide up-to-date and effective tools to combat terrorism financing, and ensuring effective implementation and application of tools, including targeted financial sections to combat terrorism financing. See Outcomes of the Plenary meeting of the FATF, Paris, 21–23 February 2018.

14 See e.g. Objectives for FATF – XXXI (2019–2020), Paper by the Incoming President, Chinese Presidency Priorities for the FATF, p. 1; Outcomes of the Plenary meeting of the FATF, Orlando, 16–21 June 2019; FATF (2018), *Annual Report 2017–2018*, p. 11.

15 See FATF (2017), *Annual Report 2015–2016*, p. 27.

Plenary adopted in June 2018 a joint FATF–Egmont Group study that looks at the mechanisms and techniques, in particular those involving professional intermediaries, that can be used to obscure the ownership and control of illicitly obtained assets, drawing on over 100 case studies, the experiences of law enforcement experts, the outcomes of FATF mutual evaluation reports, and the insights provided by academic reports and other studies.[16] Furthermore, upon the 18 April 2016 request of the G20 Finance Ministers and Central Bank Governors, the FATF is now working with the Global Forum on Transparency and Exchange of Information for Tax Purposes "to reinforce each other's work to improve the effective implementation of international standards in this area".[17]

Information sharing between public authorities and between private entities is also currently on the radar of the FATF. In June 2016, the FATF issued the *Consolidated FATF Standards on Information Sharing* containing the relevant excerpts from the FATF Recommendations and Interpretative Notes with respect to information sharing.[18] The consolidation of existing Standards was done in order to add value and to help clarify the requirements with respect to the sharing of information. The Consolidated Standards help to define the types of information that should be shared, including the types of information that competent authorities are required to make publicly available, the circumstances in which such information should be shared, and the safeguards and protections that should apply to information sharing. The FATF has also recently issued a report on inter-agency information sharing,[19] not publicly available,[20] and *Guidance on Private Sector Information Sharing*.[21] This Guidance identifies the key challenges that inhibit the sharing of information between financial institutions of the same group and financial institutions not belonging to the same group. It also articulates how the FATF Standards on information sharing should be applied by national authorities and private sector for sharing of customer, account and transaction information, including information on unusual or suspicious transactions, sets out practical

---

16 FATF/Egmont Group of Financial Intelligence Units (2018), *Concealment of Beneficial Ownership*. On professional money laundering, see also FATF Report (2018), *Professional Money Laundering*.

17 G20 Finance Ministers and Central Bank Governors' Meeting, Washington, 15 April 2016.

18 FATF (2016), *Consolidated FATF Standards on Information Sharing*, updated November 2017.

19 The report "outlines challenges to effective information sharing between key operational authorities, as well as good practices and practical tools to improve inter-agency cooperation for counter financing terrorist purposes" (FATF Report to the G20 Leaders' Summit, July 2017, para. 8).

20 "The report will be made available to key agencies involved in tackling terrorism and its financing, as well as agencies not traditionally involved in counter-terrorist financing activities" (Outcomes of the Plenary meeting of the FATF, Valencia, 21–23 June 2017).

21 FATF Guidance (2017), *Private Sector Information Sharing*. On the content of this guidance, see notably *infra* sections V.J.1 and V.K.1.

examples of how authorities can facilitate such sharing of information, and highlights recent initiatives in information sharing, including public–private partnerships in a number of countries for wider mutual benefits.

Lastly, two further recent initiatives by the FATF should be mentioned here. First, the Plenary adopted at the end of 2017 a supplement to the 2013 FATF Guidance on AML/CTF measures and financial inclusion that provides country examples of customer due diligence (CDD) measures adopted in the context of financial inclusion.[22] Those examples illustrate how a simplified set of CDD measures or alternative forms of identity verification (e.g. the use of digital identity tools) can support financial inclusion, while appropriately mitigating money laundering and terrorism financing risks. Second, the Argentine Presidency of the FATF (2017–2018) made outreach to the prosecutorial services and criminal justice system a key priority of the FATF's work. Through a series of regional workshops, the FATF brought together 450 judges and prosecutors from over 150 jurisdictions to share experience, challenges and best practices in investigating and prosecuting money laundering and terrorism financing, and in confiscating the proceeds of crime. The final report, published in June 2018, provides good practices in the investigation, prosecution and conviction of both money laundering and terrorism financing.[23] Given the transnational nature of many criminal networks, the report also highlights the need for international cooperation.[24]

II. AIMS AND SCOPE OF AML SYSTEM

A. AIMS OF AML REGIME

Although the original 40 Recommendations of the FATF were specifically designed to track down organised criminal groups involved in drug trafficking and to disrupt their activities by seizing their criminal proceeds,[25] the ultimate aim of the FATF's mandate has, since then, shifted towards the protection of "the integrity of the international financial system", as stated in the introduction to the 2012 Recommendations.[26] The FATF indeed considers today that the

22 FATF Guidance (2017), *Anti-Money Laundering and Terrorist Financing Measures and Financial Inclusion With a Supplement on Customer Due Diligence.*

23 FATF President's Paper (2018), *Anti-money laundering and counter terrorist financing for judges & prosecutors*, pp. 20–57.

24 *Ibid.*, pp. 58–61.

25 See *supra* section I.A.

26 FATF (2012), *International Standards on Combating Money Laundering and the Financing of Terrorism and proliferation*, updated June 2019, p. 8. See also Declaration of the Ministers of the Financial Action Task Force, Washington, DC, 12 April 2019, para. 3.

high-level objective in implementing AML measures is that "[f]inancial systems and the broader economy are protected from the threats of money laundering".[27] In view of the breath of this definition, the actual purpose of the FATF's framework remains ambiguous. It appears that the framework moved away from primarily addressing drug trafficking, but it now seems unclear whether the threat from money laundering is understood as being the threat from organised crime or even more broadly from crime or serious crime. The ambiguity of the objective(s) is highlighted by a statement of the former President of the FATF, Santiago Otamendi, who said: "[b]y effectively enforcing [AML] laws, at the end of the day these measures protect our economies, ensure their transparency, predictability and increase their competitiveness, attracting direct foreign investment".[28]

B. SCOPE OF MONEY LAUNDERING

1. *Definition of Money Laundering in Criminal Law*

a. *Actus Reus*

i. Predicate Offences

Pursuant to Recommendation 3, "[c]ountries should apply the crime of money laundering to all serious offences, with a view to including the widest range of predicate offences".

According to the Interpretative Note to Recommendation 3, States may determine the scope of predicate offences by reference to all offences, to a list of offences, to a threshold linked either to a category of serious offences or to the penalty of imprisonment applicable to the predicate offence, or a combination of these approaches.[29] Where the threshold approach is followed, predicate offences should at least comprise offences that fall within the category of serious offences under national law, or that are punishable by a maximum penalty of more than one year's imprisonment, or that are punished by a minimum penalty of more than six months' imprisonment (for countries that have a minimum threshold for offences in their legal system).[30]

Whichever approach is adopted, paragraph 4 of the Interpretative Note to Recommendation 3 requires countries to include, at least, a range of offences

---

27 FATF (2016), *Methodology for Assessing Compliance with the FATF Recommendations and the Effectiveness of AML/CFT Systems*, updated February 2019, p. 15.

28 Speech at the GALIFAT Plenary, Buenos Aires, 27 July 2017.

29 Interpretative Note to FATF Recommendation 3 (2012), para. 2.

30 *Ibid.*, para. 3.

within each of the "designated categories of offences", identified in the FATF Glossary as follows:

- participation in an organised criminal group and racketeering;
- terrorism, including terrorist financing;
- trafficking in human beings and migrant smuggling;
- sexual exploitation, including sexual exploitation of children;
- illicit trafficking in narcotic drugs and psychotropic substances;
- illicit arms trafficking;
- illicit trafficking in stolen and other goods;
- corruption and bribery;
- fraud;
- counterfeiting currency;
- counterfeiting and piracy of products;
- environmental crime;
- murder, grievous bodily injury;
- kidnapping, illegal restraint, and hostage-taking;
- robbery or theft;
- smuggling (including in relation to customs and excise duties and taxes);
- tax crimes (related to direct taxes and indirect taxes);
- extortion;
- forgery;
- piracy;
- and insider trading and market manipulation.[31]

ii. Definition of Money Laundering Acts

Although the FATF specifies the scope of predicate offences to which countries should apply money laundering, the intergovernmental body does not define itself the offence of money laundering. Instead, Recommendation 3 urges countries to "criminalise money laundering on the basis of the Vienna Convention and the Palermo Convention". It should be noted, however, that the Interpretative Note to Recommendation 3 provides guidance on how States could or should criminalise money laundering.

Art. 3(1)(b) and (c) of the 1988 United Nations Convention against Illicit Traffic in Narcotic Drugs and Psychotropic Substances (Vienna Convention)[32]

---

31 FATF Glossary (2012), "Designated categories of offences". With respect to the very first category (participation in an organised criminal group and racketeering), the FATF explains that "[i]t is sufficient if a country meets either of the two options set out in the Palermo Convention, i.e. either a separate offence or an offence based on conspiracy" (FATF MER Technical Compliance (2012), Criterion 3.2, footnote 10).

32 United Nations, Convention against Illicit Traffic in Narcotic Drugs and Psychotropic Substances, Vienna, 19 December 1988.

and art. 6(1) of the 2000 United Nations Convention against Transnational Organized Crime (Palermo Convention)[33] require States parties to take all the necessary measures to establish as money laundering offences, when committed intentionally, three distinct sets of criminal conducts. The first set of criminal conducts involves the "conversion or transfer of property".[34] According to United Nations Office on Drugs and Crime's (UNODC) commentary on the Palermo Convention, "conversion" includes "instances in which financial assets are converted from one former type to another, for example, by using illicitly generated cash to purchase real estate or the sale of illicitly acquired real estate", while "transfer" may be carried out for instance when "the same assets are moved from one place or jurisdiction to another or from one bank account to another".[35] The "concealment or disguise of the true nature, source, location, disposition, movement, rights with respect to, or ownership of property" constitutes the second sets of criminal conducts.[36] The third set includes the "acquisition, possession or use of property".[37] As provided for by art. 3(1)(c) of the Vienna Convention, the obligation on States to criminalise the third set of conducts is subject to their constitutional principles and the basic concepts of their legal system. Similarly, this obligation to criminalise is, in the Palermo Convention, a legislative option subject to the basic concepts of the legal system of each country.[38]

Pursuant to Recommendation 3, "[c]ountries may provide that the offence of money laundering does not apply to persons who committed the predicate offence, where this is required by fundamental principles of their domestic law".[39] This mirrors art. 6(2)(e) of the Palermo Convention.[40] It should be noted that the Vienna Convention is silent on this issue.

In the Vienna Convention as well as in the Palermo Convention, the term "property" means "assets of every kind, whether corporeal or incorporeal, movable or immovable, tangible or intangible, and legal documents or instruments evidencing title to, or interests in, such assets".[41]

---

33 United Nations, Convention against Transnational Organised Crime, New York, 15 November 2000.

34 Vienna Convention, art. 3(1)(b)(i); Palermo Convention, art. 6(1)(a)(i).

35 UNODC (2004), *Legislative Guides: United Nations Convention against Transnational Organized Crime*, para. 100.

36 Vienna Convention, art. 3(1)(b)(ii); Palermo Convention, art. 6(1)(a)(ii).

37 Vienna Convention, art. 3(1)(c)(i); Palermo Convention, art. 6(1)(b)(i). Such offences require the actual "receipt" of the property.

38 Palermo Convention, art. 6(1)(b). Moreover, the criminalisation of the first and second sets of acts should be, pursuant to art. 6(1) of the Palermo Convention, in accordance with the fundamental principles of the domestic law of each country.

39 Interpretative Note to FATF Recommendation 3 (2012), para. 6.

40 Palermo Convention, art. 6(2)(e): "If required by fundamental principles of the domestic law of a State Party, it may be provided that the offences set forth in paragraph 1 of this article do not apply to the persons who committed the predicate offence".

41 Vienna Convention, art. 1(q); Palermo Convention, art. 2(d).

Under the Vienna Convention, property shall be "derived from" any predicate offence or offences, as defined in art. 3(1)(a),[42] or from an act of participation in such offence or offences.[43] As pointed out by UNODC, "the reference to property being 'derived from' certain offences [raises the question whether it] can be taken to cover property 'obtained directly or indirectly' from those offences".[44] UNODC does not provide a clear-cut answer to this question but explains that "[o]n a broad understanding of 'derivation' it would seem possible to include also certain cases of 'indirect derivation'".[45] The situation is much clearer in the context of the Palermo Convention, as art. 6(1) requires the property to be the "proceeds of crime", defined as "any property derived from or obtained, directly or indirectly, through the commission of an offence".[46] Similarly, the Interpretative Note to Recommendation 3 provides that "[t]he offence of money laundering should extend to any type of property, regardless of its value, that directly or indirectly represents the proceeds of crime".[47]

b. *Mens Rea*

Neither the Vienna Convention nor the Palermo Convention require the criminalisation of unintentional conducts, such as acts of negligence.[48] These two legal instruments only aim to criminalise money laundering "when committed intentionally".[49] Moreover, acts of conversion or transfer of property must not only be committed intentionally but also for the purpose of either concealing or disguising the criminal origin of the property or helping a person evade criminal liability for the crime that generated the property.[50] The other acts of money laundering do not require such a *dolus specialis* to amount to money laundering.

Money laundering acts must also be committed with knowledge, at the time of commission, that the property is the "proceeds of crime"

42 Art. 3(1)(a) refers to various offences, namely activities related to drug trafficking, cultivation of certain narcotic plants, possession or purchase of narcotic drugs, manufacturing and distribution of drug-related equipment, organisation management or financing of drug-related offences.

43 Vienna Convention, art. 3(1)(b)(i), (ii) and (c)(i).

44 UNODC (1998), *Commentary on the United Nations Convention against Illicit Traffic in Narcotic Drugs and Psychotropic Substances*, para. 3.46.

45 *Ibid.*

46 Palermo Convention, art. 2(e).

47 Interpretative Note to FATF Recommendation 3 (2012), para. 4.

48 Yet it is worth mentioning that negligence as an optional basis for criminal liability was considered during the negotiations of the Palermo Convention. It was however dropped during the seventh session of the ad hoc committee (17–18 January 2000; A/AC.254/4/Rev.7).

49 Vienna Convention, art. 3(1); Palermo Convention, art. 6(1).

50 Vienna Convention, art. 3(1)(b)(i); Palermo Convention, art. 6(1)(a)(i).

(Palermo Convention)[51] or is "derived from an offence or offences established in accordance with [art. 3(1)] subparagraph a) … or from an act of participation in such an offence or offences" (Vienna Convention).[52]

2. *Money Laundering by Omission*

Neither the FATF nor the Vienna Convention or the Palermo Convention require the criminalisation of money laundering by omission. As was already mentioned above, even the criminalisation of the possession of proceeds of crime is subject to the constitutional principles of national jurisdictions.

3. *Aggravated Forms of Money Laundering*

The FATF Standards do not provide for aggravated forms of money laundering or particular sentencing level applicable to money laundering.

However, it should be noted that art. 3(5) of the Vienna Convention provides a non-exhaustive list of factual circumstances which could render the commission of money laundering "particularly serious".[53] According to this provision, the obligation on States parties is merely to ensure that their courts and other competent authorities having jurisdiction are able to take into account those factual circumstances in sentencing. Therefore, "[a] party is not required to ensure that the courts or other authorities do in practice avail themselves of this power, nor is there any attempt to state the effect that those circumstances have on the sanction imposed".[54]

---

51 Palermo Convention, art. 6(1)(a)(i), (ii) and (b)(i).

52 Vienna Convention, art. 3(1)(b)(i), (ii) and (c)(i). See UNODC (1998), *Commentary on the United Nations Convention against Illicit Traffic in Narcotic Drugs and Psychotropic Substances*, para. 3.68.

53 These factual circumstances referred to in this article are: the involvement in the offence of an organised criminal group to which the offender belongs; the involvement of the offender in other international organised criminal activities; the involvement of the offender in other illegal activities facilitated by commission of the offence; the use of violence or arms by the offender; the fact that the offender holds a public office and that the offence is connected with the office in question; the victimisation or use of minors; the fact that the offence is committed in a penal institution or in an educational institution or social service facility or in their immediate vicinity or in other places to which school children and students resort for educational, sports and social activities; and prior convictions, particularly for similar offences, whether foreign or domestic, to the extent permitted under the domestic law of a State party. For a brief commentary of each of these factual circumstances, see UNODC (1998), *Commentary on the United Nations Convention against Illicit Traffic in Narcotic Drugs and Psychotropic Substances*, paras. 3.116–3.126.

54 UNODC (1998), *Commentary on the United Nations Convention against Illicit Traffic in Narcotic Drugs and Psychotropic Substances*, para. 3.115.

4. *Statutes of Limitation*

The FATF Recommendations do not specify what statute of limitation should or could apply to money laundering. They also do not specify whether there should or could be temporary limits regarding the predicate offence that would preclude criminal liability for money laundering.

5. *Jurisdictional Rules*

The FATF is silent regarding the principles on the basis of which States could or should exercise their jurisdiction over money laundering offences.

With respect to predicate offences, the FATF considers that those offences "should extend to conduct that occurred in another country, which constitutes an offence in that country, and which would have constituted a predicate offence had it occurred domestically".[55] However, dual incrimination is not an absolute requirement as States "may provide that the only prerequisite is that the conduct would have constituted a predicate offence, had it occurred domestically".[56]

C. NON-CRIMINAL DEFINITION OF MONEY LAUNDERING

The FATF does not provide a non-criminal definition of money laundering.

D. SCOPE OF OBLIGED ENTITIES

1. *Financial and Banking Institutions*

The FATF designates "financial institutions" as obliged entities. Under the FATF framework, "financial institutions" are defined as follows:

> any natural or legal person who conducts as a business one or more of the following activities or operations for or on behalf of a customer:
>
> 1. Acceptance of deposits and other repayable funds from the public [this also captures private banking].
> 2. Lending [this includes *inter alia* consumer credit; mortgage credit; factoring, with or without recourse; and finance of commercial transactions (including forfeiting)].

55 Interpretative Note to FATF Recommendation 3 (2012), para. 5.
56 *Ibid.*

3. Financial leasing [this does not extend to financial leasing arrangements in relation to consumer products].
4. Money or value transfer services [this does not apply to any natural or legal person that provides financial institutions solely with message or other support systems for transmitting funds].
5. Issuing and managing means of payment (e.g. credit and debit cards, cheques, traveller's cheques, money orders and bankers' drafts, electronic money).
6. Financial guarantees and commitments.
7. Trading in:
   (a) money market instruments (cheques, bills, certificates of deposit, derivatives etc.);
   (b) foreign exchange;
   (c) exchange, interest rate and index instruments;
   (d) transferable securities;
   (e) commodity futures trading.
8. Participation in securities issues and the provision of financial services related to such issues.
9. Individual and collective portfolio management.
10. Safekeeping and administration of cash or liquid securities on behalf of other persons.
11. Otherwise investing, administering or managing funds or money on behalf of other persons.
12. Underwriting and placement of life insurance and other investment related insurance [this applies both to insurance undertakings and to insurance intermediaries (agents and brokers)].
13. Money and currency changing.[57]

2. *Virtual Currency System Participants*

In 2012, when the FATF Recommendations were last comprehensively revised, virtual currency system participants were not designated as obliged entities by the FATF, virtual currencies (which are also often referred to as virtual assets) and related financial services being still at an early stage of development.

However, in light of the rapid emergence of virtual currency payment products and services and associated risks of money laundering and terrorist financing, the FATF considered that virtual currency system participants (or at least some of them) had to be included in the scope of obliged entities and thus apply AML/CTF preventive measures.[58] As a result, the FATF first issued in 2015 a Guidance on a risk-based approach to virtual currencies where

---

[57] FATF Glossary (2012), "Financial institutions". The content in brackets comes from the Glossary.

[58] See e.g. FATF Report (2014), *Virtual Currencies Key Definitions and Potential AML/CFT Risks*. In addition to proposing a common definitional vocabulary that clarifies what virtual currency is, classifying the various types of virtual currencies and identifying the

it stated that "virtual currency exchangers, and any other types of institution that act as nodes where convertible virtual activities intersect with the regulated fiat currency system" fall within the scope of the FATF Recommendations and their Interpretative Notes.[59] More recently, in October 2018, the FATF Plenary amended Recommendation 15 and the Glossary[60] to clarify how the FATF Standards apply to financial activities and operations involving virtual assets. Accordingly, countries should now ensure that virtual asset service providers, notably wallet providers, providers engaged in exchange services between virtual currencies or between virtual currencies and fiat currencies, and providers of financial services for initial coin offerings (ICOs), are subject to AML/CTF regulations. Furthermore, virtual asset service providers should be licensed or registered and subject to monitoring to ensure compliance. In June 2019, the FATF formally adopted and issued the text of the Interpretive Note to Recommendation 15. At the same time, the FATF also updated its Guidance on the application of the risk-based approach to virtual assets and virtual assets service providers.[61]

3. *Legal Profession and Tax Advisors*

In addition to financial institutions, the FATF defines as obliged entities the so-called "Designated Non-Financial Businesses and Professions" (DNFBPs). DNFBPs include notably "lawyers, notaries [and] independent legal professionals". According to the FATF Glossary, "[t]his refers to sole practitioners, partners or employed professionals within professional firms".[62] In other words, "[i]t is not meant to refer to 'internal' professionals that are employees of other types of businesses, nor to professionals working for government agencies, who may already be subject to AML/CFT measures".[63]

4. *Informal Value Transfer Systems*

Informal value transfer systems, in particular *hawala*, are the subject of typology studies by the FATF,[64] but are not designated as obliged entities under the FATF

participants in typical virtual currency systems, the FATF report also aims at identifying potential uses of virtual currencies for money laundering or terrorism financing purposes.

59 FATF Guidance for a Risk-based Approach (2015), *Virtual Currencies*, para. 14.

60 The definitions of "virtual asset" and "virtual asset service providers" were added to the Glossary.

61 FATF Guidance for a Risk-Based Approach (2019), *Virtual Assets and Virtual Asset Service Providers.*

62 FATF Glossary (2012), "Designated Non-Financial Businesses and Professions".

63 *Ibid.*

64 See e.g. FATF Report (2013), *The Role of Hawala and Other Similar Service Providers in Money Laundering and Terrorist Financing.*

Recommendations. The FATF does not provide for any special rules on the treatment of informal value transfer systems.

5. *Non-Profit Sector*

While Recommendation 8 provides rules on the treatment of the non-profit sector in the area of CTF,[65] the FATF does not extend these rules to the area of AML. However, one should point out that, when NGOs serve the function of transferring assets to particular beneficiaries, they qualify as "financial institutions" in the sense of the FATF Recommendations, in that they provide money transfer services.

6. *Overview of Other Obliged Entities*

In addition to "lawyers, notaries [and] independent legal professionals", the scope of DNFBPs includes "accountants", "casinos" (including internet- and ship-based casinos), "real estate agents", "dealers in precious metals" and "dealers in precious stones". It also extends to "trust and company service providers" defined as follows:

> all persons or businesses that are not covered elsewhere under these Recommendations, and which as a business, provide any of the following services to third parties: acting as a formation agent of legal persons; acting as (or arranging for another person to act as) a director or secretary of a company, a partner of a partnership, or a similar position in relation to other legal persons; providing a registered office; business address or accommodation, correspondence or administrative address for a company, a partnership or any other legal person or arrangement; acting as (or arranging for another person to act as) a trustee of an express trust or performing the equivalent function for another form of legal arrangement; acting as (or arranging for another person to act as) a nominee shareholder for another person.[66]

E. RELATIONSHIP BETWEEN AML AND ANTI-TERRORISM FINANCING FRAMEWORK(S)

As mentioned *supra*,[67] the FATF's original purpose was to tackle money laundering by organised criminal groups involved in drug trafficking.

---

65 See *infra* section II.E.

66 FATF Glossary (2012), "Trust and company service providers".

67 See *supra* section I.A.

Nevertheless, following the September 11 attacks in the United States, the FATF expanded its mandate to deal with the issue of terrorism financing and issued the Eight Special Recommendations on Terrorist Financing in October 2001.[68] In 2004, the FATF published a Ninth Special Recommendation, which sets out requirements relating to the cross-border movement of cash and negotiable instruments. The 40+9 Recommendations were merged during the 2012 Revision into the current 40 Recommendations, which are now universally recognised as the international standard in the fight against both money laundering and terrorism financing. Three Recommendations are, however, unique to terrorist financing, namely Recommendation 5 (terrorist financing offence), Recommendation 6 (targeted financial sanctions related to terrorism and terrorist financing), and Recommendation 8 (non-profit organisations).

III. THE SYSTEM OF MONEY LAUNDERING PREVENTION

A. CUSTOMER DUE DILIGENCE

1. *Standard CDD Rules*

a. Triggers and Timing

Pursuant to Recommendation 10, financial institutions should be required by law to apply CDD measures in five situations: (i) when establishing a business relationship; (ii) when carrying out an occasional transaction above US$/€15,000;[69] (iii) when carrying out an occasional transaction that is a wire transfer falling within the scope of the Interpretative Note to Recommendation 16; (iv) when there is a suspicion of money laundering

---

[68] These Eight Recommendations set out the basic framework for combating terrorist financing. They required implementation of a range of measures, including taking immediate steps to ratify the 1999 United Nations Convention for the Suppressing of the Financing of Terrorism and the relevant United Nations Resolutions; criminalising the financing of terrorism, terrorist acts and terrorist organisations; freezing and confiscating their assets; and providing the widest possible range of assistance to other countries' law enforcement and regulatory authorities for terrorist investigations.

[69] "Financial transactions above the designated threshold include situations where the transaction is carried out in a single operation or in several operations that appear to be linked" (Interpretative Note to FATF Recommendation 10 (2012), para. 22).

or terrorism financing;[70] or (v) when the financial institution has doubts about the veracity or adequacy of previously obtained customer identification data.[71]

Different triggers apply to DNFBPs. Those should be required to undertake CDD measures in the following situations:

(a) Casinos – when customers engage in financial transactions equal to or above the applicable designated threshold [US$/€3,000].
(b) Real estate agents – when they are involved in transactions for their client concerning the buying and selling of real estate.
(c) Dealers in precious metals and dealers in precious stones – when they engage in any cash transaction with a customer equal to or above the applicable threshold [US$/€15,000].
(d) Lawyers, notaries, other independent legal professionals and accountants – when they prepare for or carry out transactions for their client concerning the following activities:
   - buying and selling of real estate;
   - managing of client money, securities or other assets;
   - management of bank, savings or securities accounts;
   - organisation of contributions for the creation, operation or management of companies;
   - creation, operation or management of legal persons or arrangements, and buying and selling of business entities.
(e) Trust and company service providers – when they prepare for or carry out transactions for a client concerning the following activities:
   - acting as a formation agent of legal persons;
   - acting as (or arranging for another person to act as) a director or secretary of a company, a partner of a partnership, or a similar position in relation to other legal persons;
   - providing a registered office, business address or accommodation, correspondence or administrative address for a company, a partnership or any other legal person or arrangement;
   - acting as (or arranging for another person to act as) as trustee of an express trust or performing the equivalent function for another form of legal arrangement;

70 A suspicion of money laundering or terrorism financing may arise "during the establishment or course of the customer relationship, or when conducting occasional transactions" (Interpretative Note to FATF Recommendation 10 (2012), para. 1).

71 "Examples of situations that might lead an institution to have such doubts could be where there is a suspicion of money laundering in relation to that customer, or where there is a material change in the way that the customer's account is operated, which is not consistent with the customer's business profile" (Interpretative Note to FATF Recommendation 10 (2012), para. 10).

- acting as (or arranging for another person to act as) a nominee shareholder for another person.[72]

With respect to the timing of verification of the identity of the customer and beneficial owner,[73] the FATF requires this to take place "before or during the course of establishing a business relationship or conducting transactions for occasional customers".[74] However, if permitted by law, financial institutions and DNFBPs may proceed to the verification after the business relationship is established or the transaction is performed, provided that this takes place as soon as reasonably practicable, this is essential not to interrupt the normal conduct of business and the money laundering/terrorism financing risks are effectively managed.[75] According to the FATF, obliged entities should be required to adopt risk management procedures concerning the conditions under which a customer may utilise the business relationship or perform the transaction prior to verification.[76]

b. CDD Measures

The FATF requires the following CDD measures to be taken for all customers. First, obliged entities should "identify the customer and verify that customer's identity using reliable, independent source documents, data or information".[77] Second, obliged entities should "verify that any person purporting to act on behalf of the customer is so authorised, and should identify and verify the identity of that person".[78] Third, obliged entities should "identify the beneficial

72 FATF Recommendation 22 (2012). The designated thresholds for transactions performed by casinos, dealers in precious metals and dealers in precious stones are set out in paragraph 1 of the Interpretative Note to FATF Recommendations 22 and 23 (2012), which also provides that transactions above these thresholds "include situations where the transaction is carried out in a single operation or in several operations that appear to be linked".

73 On these CDD measures, see *infra* section III.A.1.b.

74 FATF Recommendation 10 (2012). For DNFBPs, see FATF Recommendation 22 (2012). For life or other investment-related insurance business, "the verification of the identity of the beneficiary(ies) should occur at the time of the payout" (Interpretative Note to FATF Recommendation 10 (2012), para. 7). On CDD measures for life or other investment-related insurance business, see *infra* section III.A.1.b.

75 FATF Recommendations 10 and 22 (2012). "Examples of the types of circumstances ... where it would be permissible for verification to be completed after the establishment of the business relationship, because it would be essential not to interrupt the normal conduct of business, include: Non face-to-face business [and] securities transactions" (Interpretative Note to FATF Recommendation 10 (2012), para. 11).

76 Interpretative Note to FATF Recommendation 10 (2012), para. 12; Interpretative Note to FATF Recommendations 22 and 23 (2012), para. 2.

77 FATF Recommendation 10 (2012).

78 Interpretative Note to FATF Recommendation 10 (2012), para. 4.

owner and take reasonable measures to verify the identity of the beneficial owner, such that the financial institution is satisfied that it knows who the beneficial owner is".[79] Fourth, "the purpose and intended nature of the business relationship" should be understood and, as appropriate, information should be obtained in this regard.[80] Fifth, obliged entities should be required to "conduct ongoing due diligence on the business relationship".[81] This includes scrutinising "transactions undertaken throughout the course of that relationship to ensure that the transactions being conducted are consistent with the institution's knowledge of the customer, their business and risk profile, including, where necessary, the source of funds",[82] and ensuring "that documents, data or information collected under the CDD process is kept up-to-date and relevant, by undertaking reviews of existing records, particularly for higher-risk categories of customers".[83]

Regarding customers that are legal persons or legal arrangements,[84] the FATF requires obliged entities, in addition to the aforementioned CDD measures, to understand "the ownership and control structure of the customer".[85] Moreover, it should be noted that, for the same type of customers, the FATF provides a list of elements on the basis of which obliged entities should conduct the identification and the verification of the identity of the beneficial owners.[86]

With respect to life or other investment-related insurance business, the FATF requires financial institutions, in addition to the aforementioned CDD measures required for the customer and the beneficial owner, to conduct the following specific CDD measures with respect to the beneficiary(ies) of life insurance and other investment-related insurance policies: "(a) For beneficiary(ies) that are identified as specifically named natural or legal persons or legal arrangements – taking the name of the person; (b) For beneficiary(ies) that are designated by characteristics or by class (e.g. spouse or children at the time that the insured event occurs) or by other means (e.g. under a will) – obtaining sufficient information concerning the beneficiary to satisfy the financial institution that it will be able to establish the identity of the beneficiary at the time of the payout".[87]

---

79 FATF Recommendation 10 (2012). The verification of the identity of the beneficial owner should be done on the basis of "the relevant information or data obtained from a reliable source" (FATF MER Technical Compliance (2012), Criterion 10.5).

80 FATF Recommendation 10 (2012).

81 *Ibid.*

82 *Ibid.*

83 Interpretative Note to FATF Recommendation 10 (2012), para. 23.

84 See FATF definitions of legal persons and legal arrangements *infra* section VI.A.1.a.

85 FATF Recommendation 10 (2012).

86 Interpretative Note to FATF Recommendation 10 (2012), para. 5.

87 Interpretative Note to FATF Recommendation 10 (2012), para. 6.

c. Individual Responsibility

The FATF requires financial institutions and DNFBPs to appoint a compliance officer at the management level.[88]

d. Further CDD Guidance

The FATF Recommendations do not provide further standard CDD guidance.

2. Simplified CDD

a. Scope

Under the FATF framework, a country may allow its obliged entities to undertake simplified CDD measures in circumstances where the risks of money laundering are lower and provided that there has been an adequate analysis of the risk by the country or by the obliged entity.[89] Simplified CDD measures should therefore never be permitted whenever there is a suspicion of money laundering or terrorism financing.[90]

b. Requirements

With respect to the nature of simplified CDD measures, the FATF merely indicates that these measures "should be commensurate with the lower risk factors".[91]

c. Further Simplified CDD Guidance

The Interpretative Note to Recommendation 10 provides examples of potentially lower-risk situations and examples of possible simplified CDD measures to be taken in such situations. As underlined in paragraph 14 of the Interpretative Note, these examples "are not mandatory elements of the FATF Standards, and are included for guidance only". Furthermore, it is pointed out that "[t]he examples are not intended to be comprehensive, and although they are considered to be helpful indicators, they may not be relevant in all circumstances".

---

88 Interpretative Note to FATF Recommendation 18 (2012), para. 3; Interpretative Note to FATF Recommendations 22 and 23 (2012), para. 2.

89 Interpretative Note to FATF Recommendation 1 (2012), paras. 2 and 11; Interpretative Note to FATF Recommendation 10 (2012), para. 16; Interpretative Note to FATF Recommendations 22 and 23 (2012), para. 2.

90 Interpretative Note to FATF Recommendation 1 (2012), para. 2; Interpretative Note to FATF Recommendation 10 (2012), para. 21; Interpretative Note to FATF Recommendations 22 and 23 (2012), para. 2.

91 Interpretative Note to FATF Recommendation 10 (2012), para. 21.

The examples of potentially lower-risk situations are:

(a) Customer risk factors:
  - Financial institutions and DNFBPs – where they are subject to requirements to combat money laundering and terrorist financing consistent with the FATF Recommendations, have effectively implemented those requirements, and are effectively supervised or monitored in accordance with the Recommendations to ensure compliance with those requirements;
  - Public companies listed on a stock exchange and subject to disclosure requirements (either by stock exchange rules or through law or enforceable means), which impose requirements to ensure adequate transparency of beneficial ownership;
  - Public administrations or enterprises.

(b) Product, service, transaction or delivery channel risk factors:
  - Life insurance policies where the premium is low (e.g. an annual premium of less than USD/EUR 1,000 or a single premium of less than USD/EUR 2,500);
  - Insurance policies for pension schemes if there is no early surrender option and the policy cannot be used as collateral;
  - A pension, superannuation or similar scheme that provides retirement benefits to employees, where contributions are made by way of deduction from wages, and the scheme rules do not permit the assignment of a member's interest under the scheme;
  - Financial products or services that provide appropriately defined and limited services to certain types of customers, so as to increase access for financial inclusion purposes.

(c) Country risk factors:
  - Countries identified by credible sources, such as mutual evaluation or detailed assessment reports, as having effective AML/CFT systems;
  - Countries identified by credible sources as having a low level of corruption or other criminal activity.[92]

The examples of possible simplified CDD measures are:

- Verifying the identity of the customer and the beneficial owner after the establishment of the business relationship (e.g. if account transactions rise above a defined monetary threshold).
- Reducing the frequency of customer identification updates.
- Reducing the degree of on-going monitoring and scrutinising transactions, based on a reasonable monetary threshold.
- Not collecting specific information or carrying out specific measures to understand the purpose and intended nature of the business relationship,

---

92 *Ibid.*, para. 17.

but inferring the purpose and nature from the type of transactions or business relationship established.[93]

3. *Enhanced CDD*

a. Scope

Under the FATF framework, obliged entities should, in addition to performing standard CDD measures, apply enhanced CDD measures in circumstances where the risks of money laundering or terrorism financing are higher.[94]

Pursuant to Recommendations 12, 13 and 19, business relationships and occasional transactions involving foreign politically exposed persons (PEPs),[95] cross-border correspondent banking and other similar relationships,[96] and natural persons or legal entities established in high-risk third countries identified as such by the FATF[97] should always be considered by financial institutions as high-risk situations. According to the Interpretative Note to Recommendation 10, all "unusual large transactions, and all unusual patterns of transactions, which have no apparent economic or lawful purpose" should also always be treated as high risk. The same triggers for enhanced CDD measures apply to DNFBPs.[98]

b. Requirements

The FATF Recommendations do not include a list of minimum enhanced CDD measures applicable in all high-risk situations. The FATF sets out specific enhanced CDD measures only with respect to foreign PEPs,[99] cross-border correspondent banking and other similar relationships,[100] and unusual large transactions/unusual patterns of transactions, which have no apparent economic or lawful purpose.[101]

---

93 *Ibid.*, para. 21.

94 Interpretative Note to FATF Recommendation 1 (2012), paras. 2 and 10; Interpretative Note to FATF Recommendation 10 (2012), para. 15; Interpretative Note to FATF Recommendations 22 and 23 (2012), para. 2.

95 On the definition of foreign PEPs, see *infra* section III.A.4.a.

96 "The similar relationships to which financial institutions should apply criteria (a) to (e) include, for example those established for securities transactions or funds transfers, whether for the cross-border financial institution as principal or for its customers" (Interpretative Note to FATF Recommendation 13 (2012)).

97 On the FATF lists of high-risk third countries, see *infra* section III.A.5.a.

98 FATF Recommendations 22 and 23 (2012); Interpretative Note to FATF Recommendations 22 and 23 (2012), para. 2.

99 See *infra* section III.A.4.b.

100 See FATF Recommendation 13 (2012) and its interpretative Note.

101 See Interpretative Note to FATF Recommendation 10 (2012), para. 20.

c. Further Enhanced CDD Guidance

The Interpretative Note to Recommendation 10 provides examples of potentially higher-risk situations and examples of possible enhanced CDD measures to be taken in such situations. As underlined in paragraph 14 of the Interpretative Note, these examples "are not mandatory elements of the FATF Standards, and are included for guidance only". Furthermore, it is underlined that "[t]he examples are not intended to be comprehensive, and although they are considered to be helpful indicators, they may not be relevant in all circumstances".

The examples of potentially higher-risk situations are:

(a) Customer risk factors
  - The business relationship is conducted in unusual circumstances (e.g. significant unexplained geographic distance between the financial institution and the customer);
  - Non-resident customers;
  - Legal persons or arrangements that are personal asset-holding vehicles;
  - Companies that have nominee shareholders or shares in bearer form;
  - Business that are cash-intensive;
  - The ownership structure of the company appears unusual or excessively complex given the nature of the company's business.

(b) Country or geographic factors:
  - Countries identified by credible sources, such as mutual evaluation or detailed assessment reports or published follow-up reports, as not having adequate AML/CFT systems;
  - Countries subject to sanctions, embargos or similar measures issued by, for example, the United Nations;
  - Countries identified by credible sources as having significant levels of corruption or other criminal activity;
  - Countries or geographic areas identified by credible sources as providing funding or support for terrorist activities, or that have designated terrorist organisations operating within their country.

(c) Product, service, transaction or delivery channel risk factors:
  - Private banking; anonymous transactions (which may include cash);
  - Non-face-to-face business relationships or transactions;
  - Payment received from unknown or un-associated third parties.[102]

The examples of possible enhanced CDD measures are:

- Obtaining additional information on the customer (e.g. occupation, volume of assets, information available through public databases, internet, etc.), and updating more regularly the identification data of customer and beneficial owner.

---

102 *Ibid.*, para. 15.

- Obtaining additional information on the intended nature of the business relationship.
- Obtaining information on the source of funds or source of wealth of the customer.
- Obtaining information on the reasons for intended or performed transactions.
- Obtaining the approval of senior management to commence or continue the business relationship.
- Conducting enhanced monitoring of the business relationship, by increasing the number and timing of controls applied, and selecting patterns of transactions that need further examination.
- Requiring the first payment to be carried out through an account in the customer's name with a bank subject to similar CDD standards.[103]

4. *Rules on Politically Exposed Persons*

a. Definition

A PEP is defined by the FATF as an individual who is or has been entrusted with a prominent public function. The FATF distinguishes between foreign PEPs, domestic PEPs and international organisation PEPs. The Glossary provides the following definitions, which do not cover "middle ranking or more junior individuals":[104]

> *Foreign PEPs* are individuals who are or have been entrusted with prominent public functions by a foreign country, for example Heads of State or of government, senior politicians, senior government, judicial or military officials, senior executives of state owned corporations, important political party officials.
>
> *Domestic PEPs* are individuals who are or have been entrusted domestically with prominent public functions, for example Heads of State or of government, senior politicians, senior government, judicial or military officials, senior executives of state owned corporations, important political party officials.
>
> *Persons who are or have been entrusted with a prominent function by an international organisation* refers to members of senior management, i.e. directors, deputy directors and members of the board or equivalent functions.[105]

---

103 *Ibid.*, para. 20.

104 FATF Glossary (2012), "Politically Exposed Persons". With respect to "middle ranking and more junior officials", the FATF explains, however, that "there should be awareness that middle ranking and more junior officials could act on behalf of a PEP to circumvent AML/CFT controls. These less prominent public functions could be appropriately taken into account as customer risk factors in the framework of the overall assessment of risks associated with the business relationship in accordance with Recommendation 10 when they are acting on behalf of a PEP" (FATF Guidance (2013), *Politically Exposed Persons (Recommendations 12 and 22)*, para. 37).

105 FATF Glossary (2012), "Politically Exposed Persons".

b. Requirements

With respect to foreign PEPs, Recommendations 12 and 22 require countries to ensure that financial institutions and DNFBPs have "appropriate risk management systems" in place to determine whether the customer or beneficial owner is a foreign PEP.[106] Since foreign PEPs are always considered a high risk, obliged entities are required, in addition to performing the standard CDD measures required under Recommendation 10, to take the three following enhanced CDD measures set out in Recommendation 12: "obtain senior management approval for establishing (or continuing, for existing customers) such business relationships",[107] "take reasonable measures to establish the source of wealth and source of funds",[108] and "conduct enhanced ongoing monitoring of the business relationship".[109]

Contrary to foreign PEPs, obliged entities must, for domestic PEPs and international organisation PEPs, only take "reasonable measures", based on the assessment of the level of risk, to determine whether the customer or beneficial owner is a domestic/international organisation PEP.[110] According to the 2013 FATF Guidance on PEPs, "[t]he different sets of requirements to detect PEPs (one for foreign PEPs, and one for domestic/international organisation PEPs) reflect that the level of risks are different".[111] If a customer or beneficial owner is determined to be a domestic PEP or an international organisation PEP, enhanced CDD measures do not always have to be applied. It is only in cases of a "higher risk business relationship" that financial institutions and DNFBPs should take enhanced CDD measures consistent with those applicable to foreign PEPs,[112] in addition to the aforementioned standard CDD measures. If the risk assessment establishes that the business relationship with the

106 FATF Guidance (2013), *Politically Exposed Persons (Recommendations 12 and 22)*, para. 16: "This means that proactive steps must be taken, such as assessing customers on the basis of risk criteria, risk profiles, the business model, verification of CDD information, and the institution's own research, to determine whether a customer or a beneficial owner is a foreign PEP". See paras. 54–78 for further guidance on the use of sources of information for the determination of foreign PEPs.

107 For further guidance on the implementation of this measure, see FATF Guidance (2013), *Politically Exposed Persons (Recommendations 12 and 22)*, paras. 81–85.

108 For further guidance on the implementation of this measure, see *ibid.*, paras. 86–94.

109 For further guidance on the implementation of this measure, see *ibid.*, paras. 95–98.

110 FATF Recommendations 12 and 22 (2012). FATF Guidance (2013), *Politically Exposed Persons (Recommendations 12 and 22)*, para. 17: "This means reviewing, according to relevant risk factors, CDD data collected pursuant to Recommendation 10 in order to determine whether a customer or beneficial owner is a domestic PEP".

111 FATF Guidance (2013), *Politically Exposed Persons (Recommendations 12 and 22)*, para. 17. See paras. 54–78 for further guidance on the use of sources of information for the determination of domestic PEPs and international organisation PEPs.

112 FATF Recommendations 12 and 22 (2012). Specific enhanced CDD measures for foreign PEPs, see *supra* section III.A.4.b.

domestic/international organisation PEP presents a normal or low risk, the financial institution or DNFBP is not required to apply enhanced due diligence measures.

All the aforementioned measures should also be applied to family members and close associates of PEPs.[113]

c. Further Enhanced CDD Guidance on PEPs

The FATF Recommendations does not provide further enhanced CDD guidance on PEPs.

5. *Rules on High-Risk Third Countries*

a. Scope

At FATF level, the geographical/country risk is defined through two public statements issued three times a year at the end of each Plenary meeting on the basis of the results of the International Co-operation Review Group's (ICRG) reviews.[114] Each statement provides a short summary of the specific risks emanating from each listed country, as well as any measures that countries should take.

The "Public Statement" identifies two groups of countries. The first group is composed of jurisdictions with such serious strategic deficiencies that they are subject to a FATF call on its members and other jurisdictions to apply counter-measures on the basis on Recommendation 19 paragraph 2.[115] The second group is composed of jurisdictions which are subject to a FATF call on its members and other jurisdictions to ensure, on the basis of Recommendation 19 paragraph 1 and Recommendation 23, that financial institutions and DNFBPs are required to apply enhanced due diligence measures proportionate to the risks arising from the jurisdiction.[116]

The "Improving Global AML/CFT Compliance: On-going Process" Statement identifies countries or jurisdictions with strategic weaknesses in their AML/CFT

113 FATF Recommendations 12 and 22 (2012). The FATF does not define these terms "as this depends to some extent on the social-economic and cultural structure of the country of the PEP" (FATF Guidance (2013), *Politically Exposed Persons (Recommendations 12 and 22)*, para. 46).

114 For further information about the review process of high risk and non-cooperative jurisdictions by the ICRG, see http://www.fatf-gafi.org/publications/high-riskandnon-cooperativejurisdictions/more/more-on-high-risk-and-non-cooperative-jurisdictions.html?hf=10&b=0&s=desc(fatf_releasedate).

115 In January 2020, the Democratic People's Republic of Korea was the only country in the first group (Public Statement, 18 October 2019).

116 In January 2020, Iran was the only country in the second group (Public Statement, 18 October 2019).

measures but that have provided a high-level commitment to an action plan developed with the FATF.[117]

b. Requirements

The FATF does not provide for specific enhanced CDD measures applicable to business relationships and transactions involving high-risk third countries. The FATF merely indicates that the enhanced CDD measures that could be applied by financial institutions to business relationships and transactions with natural and legal persons from countries for which this is called for by the FATF "include those measures set out in paragraph 20 of the Interpretative Note to Recommendation 10 [see *supra* section III.A.3.c], and any other measures that have a similar effect in mitigating risks".[118] The same applies to DNFBPs.[119]

c. Further Enhanced CDD Guidance on High-Risk Third Countries

The FATF Recommendations does not provide further enhanced CDD guidance on high-risk third countries.

6. Private Sector CDD Guidance

The FATF Recommendations do not refer to any private sector standards that would provide further guidance for the exercise of CDD.

B. PRELIMINARY RISK ANALYSIS

Pursuant to Recommendation 1, countries should ensure that financial institutions and DNFBPs "identify, assess and take effective action to mitigate their money laundering and terrorist financing risks." In implementing a risk-based approach, obliged entities should take into account several factors, including countries or geographic areas (for customers), and services, transactions or delivery channels (for products).[120]

---

117 In January 2020, the following countries were considered by the FATF as having strategic weaknesses in their AML/CFT measures but having provided a high-level commitment to an action plan developed with the FATF: the Bahamas, Botswana, Cambodia, Ghana, Iceland, Mongolia, Pakistan, Panama, Syria, Trinidad and Tobago, Yemen and Zimbabwe ("Improving Global AML/CFT Compliance: On-going Process" Statement, 18 October 2019).

118 Interpretative Note to FATF Recommendation 19 (2012), para. 1. See *supra* section III.A.3.c.

119 Interpretative Note to FATF Recommendations 22 and 23 (2012), para. 2.

120 Interpretative Note to FATF Recommendation 1 (2012), para. 8.

C. REPORTING AND ASSET FREEZING

1. *First-Time Reporting*

a. Trigger for/Degree of Suspicion

Under the FATF framework, a financial institution is required to submit a suspicious activity report (SAR; or STR in the FATF terminology) whenever it "suspects or has reasonable grounds to suspect that funds are the proceeds of a criminal activity or are related to terrorist financing".[121]

While the same requirement applies to casinos and real estate agents,[122] the reporting requirement imposed by the FATF upon trust and company service providers, and dealers in precious stones or metals is narrower. Trust and company service providers should indeed report only "when, on behalf of or for a client, they engage in a transaction in relation to the activities referred to in paragraph (e) or Recommendation 22".[123] With respect to dealers in precious stones or metals, those should only report suspicious transactions "when they engage in any cash transaction with a customer equal to or above the applicable designated threshold [US$/€15,000]."[124]

b. Content and Direct Addressee(s) of SARs

According to the FATF, obliged entities are required to report their suspicions to the FIU.[125] All suspicious transactions should be reported, regardless of the amount of the transaction and whether it actually went through.[126] Moreover, the reporting requirement should be a free-standing obligation and not be subject to further conditions. Therefore, "any indirect or implicit obligation to report suspicious transactions, whether by reason of possible prosecution for a money laundering or terrorist financing offence or otherwise (so called 'indirect reporting'), is not acceptable".[127]

c. Duty not to Disclose

Pursuant to Recommendation 21, "financial institutions, their directors, officers and employees should be … prohibited by law from disclosing ('tipping-off')

---

121 FATF Recommendation 20 (2012).

122 FATF Recommendation 23 (2012).

123 FATF Recommendation 23(c) (2012).

124 FATF Recommendation 23(b) (2012). The designated threshold is provided by Interpretative Note to FATF Recommendations 22 and 23 (2012), para. 1.

125 FATF Recommendations 20 and 23 (2012).

126 Interpretative Note to FATF Recommendation 20 (2012), para. 3.

127 *Ibid.*, para. 4.

the fact that a STR or related information is being filed with the FIU". The same requirement applies to DNFBPs.[128] As underlined in the *Guidance on Private Sector Information Sharing*:

> [e]nsuring the confidentiality of STRs is critical to an effective functioning of the reporting regime. Confidentiality of STRs is needed so that the subject of STR and third parties are not tipped-off, as this can adversely affect intelligence gathering and investigation, and can enable persons to abscond or dispose of assets. Confidentiality also protects the reputation of the person who is the subject of an STR. Finally, confidentiality protects the safety and security of the person filing the report, and breaches of confidentiality have the potential to undermine the entire suspicious transaction reporting regime.[129]

d. Power or Duty to Freeze

The FATF Recommendations do not address whether reporting obliged entities, as a result of their suspicion, should be under an obligation to freeze assets, or at least be entitled to this effect.

e. Instant Collateral Duties

The FATF Standards do not indicate whether obliged entities should be under any further obligations after having filed a SAR.

2. Follow-Up

a. Duty to Provide FIU with Additional Data

Pursuant to Recommendation 29, obliged entities which have filed a SAR shall, if requested to do so, provide additional information to the FIU.[130] However, the FATF does not further define the ambit of this obligation.

b. Continued Duty not to Disclose SAR to Client

According to the FATF, financial institutions and DNFBPs should be prohibited from disclosing the fact that a SAR *is being* filed with the FIU.[131] The FATF does not however explicitly say to what extent there should also be a continued

---

128 FATF Recommendation 23 (2012).

129 FATF Guidance (2017), *Private Sector Information Sharing*. See also Interpretative Note to FATF Recommendation 10 (2012), para. 2.

130 Interpretative Note to FATF Recommendation 29 (2012), para. 5.

131 FATF Recommendations 21 and 23 (2012).

duty on the part of the reporting obliged entity not to disclose to the client the filing of a SAR, even if it has not led to a discovery of illegal conduct.

c. Continued Collateral Duties

The FATF Recommendations do not specify to what extent there is a continued duty on the part of the reporting obliged entity not to disclose to the client the filing of the SAR, even if it has not led to a discovery of illegal conduct.

3. *Special Rules for Privileged Professions*

a. Trigger for/Degree of Suspicion

Pursuant to Recommendation 23(a), lawyers, notaries, other independent legal professionals and accountants should be bound by the reporting obligation when, on behalf of or for a client, they engage in a financial transaction in relation to any of following activities: buying and selling of real estate; management of client money, securities or other assets; management of bank, savings or securities accounts; organisation of contributions for the creation, operation or management of companies; creation, operation or management of legal persons or arrangements; and buying and selling of business entities.

The requirement to file a SAR should however not be mandatory "if the relevant information was obtained in circumstances where they are subject to professional secrecy or legal professional privilege".[132] The material scope of professional secrecy is left to the discretion of States. However, according to the Interpretative Note to Recommendation 23, this "would normally cover information lawyers, notaries or other independent legal professionals receive from or obtain through one of their clients: (a) in the course of ascertaining the legal position of their client, or (b) in performing their task of defending or representing that client in, or concerning judicial, administrative, arbitration or mediation proceedings."[133]

b. Content and Addressee(s) of SARs

In principle, lawyers, notaries, other independent legal professionals and accountants are required to submit their SARs directly to the FIU.[134] However, according to the Interpretative Note to Recommendation 23, "[c]ountries may allow lawyers, notaries, other independent legal professionals and accountants to send their SAR to their appropriate self-regulatory organisations, provided

132 Interpretative Note to FATF Recommendation 23 (2012), para. 1.
133 *Ibid.*, para. 2.
134 FATF Recommendation 23 (2012).

that there are appropriate forms of cooperation between these organisations and the FIU".[135]

c. Duty not to Disclose to Client

In principle, the FATF does not exempt lawyers, notaries, other independent legal professionals and accountants from the non-disclosure requirement.[136] However, according to the Interpretative Note to Recommendation 23, where they "seek to dissuade a client from engaging in illegal activity, this does not amount to tipping-off".[137] This exception thus goes beyond dissuasion from money laundering, its predicate offences and terrorism financing, and extends to cases where privileged professionals try to dissuade their clients from other illegal acts, including acts that are merely unlawful and not criminal.

4. Protection of SAR's Source

The FATF considers the protection of SAR sources as a relevant element of reporting, which notably also highlights the tip-off requirement described above. However, the FATF does not require further measures to protect the employees of obliged entities that file a SAR.

D. RECORD KEEPING

Pursuant to Recommendation 11, financial institutions should be required to maintain "all necessary records on transactions, both domestic and international". It is provided that such records must contain sufficient detail to enable the reconstruction of individual transactions and should be kept for at least five years.[138] Financial institutions should also be required to maintain "records obtained through CDD measures ..., account files and business correspondence, including the results of any analysis undertaken".[139] Such records should be kept for at least five years following the end of a business relationship or the date of the occasional transaction.[140] The same

135 Interpretative Note to FATF Recommendation 23 (2012), para. 3.
136 FATF Recommendation 23 (2012).
137 Interpretative Note to FATF Recommendation 23 (2012), para. 4.
138 FATF Recommendation 11 (2012).
139 *Ibid.* The principle that financial institutions should maintain records on transactions and information obtained through CDD measures should be set out in law.
140 *Ibid.*

record-keeping requirements should be applied to DNFBPs in the situations set out in Recommendation 22.

E. COMPLIANCE OFFICERS

The FATF requires the establishment of compliance management arrangements, which should include the appointment of a compliance officer at management level.[141] However, the FATF does not provide further requirements with respect to, for instance, the competences and powers that compliance officers should have.

F. INTERNAL COMPLAINT MECHANISM

The FATF does not require obliged entities to have in place an internal complaint mechanism that would allow employees or third persons to inform senior management about violations of AML-related obligations committed within the obliged entity.

G. ADDITIONAL PREVENTIVE MEASURES

In order to mitigate and manage effectively the risks of money laundering, financial institutions and DNFBPs should be required to implement programmes against money laundering.[142] These programmes should include: "(a) the development of internal policies, procedures and controls, including appropriate compliance management arrangements, and adequate screening procedures to ensure high standards when hiring employees; (b) an ongoing employee training programme; and (c) an independent audit function to test the system".[143]

To the same end, countries may only permit obliged entities to rely on third parties to perform CDD obligations under very strict conditions set out in Recommendation 17, such as the fact that the third party must be regulated, supervised or monitored for, and has measures in place for compliance with, CDD and record-keeping requirements. Where such reliance is permitted, the ultimate responsibility for CDD measures should remain with the financial institution relying on the third party.[144]

---

141 FATF Recommendation 18 (2012); Interpretative Note to FATF Recommendation 18 (2012), paras. 1 and 3.

142 FATF Recommendations 18 and 23 (2012).

143 Interpretative Note to FATF Recommendation 18 (2012), para. 1.

144 FATF Recommendation 17 (2012).

H. RULES ON OBLIGED ENTITIES' CIVIL LIABILITY TOWARDS CLIENT

Pursuant to Recommendation 21(a), financial institutions as well as their directors, officers and employees should be "protected by law from criminal and civil liability for breach of any restriction on disclosure of information imposed by contract or by any legislative, regulatory or administrative provision, if they report their suspicions in good faith to the FIU, even if they did not know precisely what the underlying criminal activity was, and regardless of whether illegal activity actually occurred". The same applies to DNFBPs.[145]

I. SUPERVISORY AUTHORITIES' ROLE

1. *Supervisory Measures to Ensure Application of CDD and Other AML-Related Obligations*

In order to ensure the effective application of AML-related obligations by obliged entities, countries are required to designate one or more supervisors that have the responsibility for regulating and monitoring, on the basis of a risk-based approach,[146] obliged entities' compliance with AML requirements.[147] With respect to DNFBPs other than casinos, supervisory responsibilities may be conferred to "an appropriate self-regulatory body, provided that such a body can ensure that its members comply with their obligations to combat money laundering".[148]

- Regulation of Obliged Entities

First, Core Principles financial institutions[149] and casinos should be required to be licensed, and other financial institutions, including those providing a money or value transfer service or a money or currency changing service, should be

145 FATF Recommendation 23 (2012).

146 See Interpretative Note to FATF Recommendation 26 (2012) and Interpretative Note to FATF Recommendation 28 (2012), paras. 1–3.

147 See FATF Recommendations 26–28 (2012) and their Interpretative Notes.

148 FATF Recommendation 28 (2012).

149 According to the FATF Glossary, "Core Principles refers to the Core Principles for Effective Banking Supervision issued by the Basel Committee on Banking Supervision, the Objectives and Principles for Securities Regulation issued by the International Organization of Securities Commissions, and the Insurance Supervisory Principles issued by the International Association of Insurance Supervisors."

licensed or registered.[150] Second, supervisors should take the necessary measures to prevent criminals or their associates from holding, or being the beneficial owner of, a significant or controlling interest, or holding a management function in financial institutions and DNFBPs.[151]

– Monitoring of Obliged Entities

According to Recommendation 26, financial supervisors should have "adequate powers to supervise or monitor, and ensure compliance by, financial institutions with requirements to combat money laundering". These powers should include "the authority to conduct inspections" and the possibility to "compel production of any information from financial institutions that is relevant to monitoring such compliance".[152]

The FATF does not indicate which powers supervisors of DNFBPs should be provided with. The intergovernmental body only indicates that DNFBPs should be subject to effective systems for monitoring and ensuring compliance with AML/CFT requirements.[153]

2. Complaint Mechanism

The FATF Recommendations do not provide for a mechanism (at the level of supervisory authorities or other competent authorities) that allows individuals (in particular employees of obliged entities) to report violations of CDD and related obligations by an obliged entity.

J. STATISTICS ON SARs BY OBLIGED ENTITIES

According to Recommendation 35, the FATF requires countries to maintain "comprehensive statistics ... on the STRs received".

---

150 FATF Recommendations 26 and 28 (2012).

151 *Ibid.* With respect to casinos, supervisory authorities should also take the necessary measures to prevent criminals or their associates from being an operator of a casino. With respect to DNFBPs, supervisory authorities should also take the necessary measures to prevent criminals or their associates from being professionally accredited, and as regards casinos from being an operator.

152 FATF Recommendation 27 (2012). "The supervisor's power to compel production of or to obtain access for supervisory purposes should not be predicated on the need to require a court order" (FATF MER Technical Compliance (2012), Criterion 27.3, footnote 60).

153 FATF Recommendation 28 (2012).

IV. THE SYSTEM OF FINANCIAL INTELLIGENCE UNITS

A. INSTITUTIONAL AND FUNCTIONAL CHARACTERISTICS

1. *Organisational Position*

The FATF does not require FIUs to be of any particular type.[154] That means that countries are free to establish their FIU in the institutional context of their choice, notably within administrative authorities (such as supervisory authorities), police authorities, or even within the intelligence community.

2. *Purpose and Tasks*

Pursuant to the Interpretative Note to Recommendation 29, "[t]he FIU plays a central role, in a country's AML/CFT operational network, and provides support to the work of other competent authorities".[155] The FATF requires FIUs to carry out three core functions. First, the FIU should serve as "a national centre for the receipt … of: (a) suspicious transaction reports; and (b) other information relevant to money laundering, associated predicate offences and terrorist financing".[156] Second, the FIU should analyse the information received.[157] Third, the FIU should disseminate information and the results of its analysis to the relevant competent authorities.[158]

3. *Independence*

According to the FATF, "[t]he FIU should be operationally independent and autonomous".[159] To this end, "the FIU should have the authority and capacity to carry out its functions freely, including the autonomous decision to analyse, request and/or disseminate specific information".[160] Furthermore, the FIU is required "to obtain and deploy the resources needed to carry out its functions, on an individual or routine basis, free from any undue political, government or industry influence or interference, which might compromise its operational independence".[161] Under the FATF framework, operational independence and autonomy of the FIU also means that if it is established within

---

154 Interpretative Note to FATF Recommendation 29 (2012), para. 1.
155 *Ibid.*
156 FATF Recommendation 29 (2012).
157 *Ibid.*
158 *Ibid.*
159 Interpretative Note to FATF Recommendation 29 (2012), para. 8.
160 *Ibid.*
161 *Ibid.*, para. 12.

the existing structure of another authority, its core functions should remain distinct from those of the other authority, and that it should always be able "to make arrangements or engage independently with other domestic competent authorities or foreign counterparts on the exchange of information".[162]

4. *Powers*

– Power to Obtain Additional Information from Obliged Entities

According to Recommendation 29, "[t]he FIU should be able to obtain additional information from reporting entities" in order to conduct proper analysis. The FATF specifies that the FIU should be able to obtain additional data from any obliged entity, and not only from entities that have previously filed a SAR.[163]

– Power to Access Beneficial Ownership Information

Additionally, pursuant to Recommendations 24 and 25, countries should ensure that the FIU can obtain or access in a timely manner adequate, accurate and timely information on the beneficial ownership of legal persons and legal arrangements (including trusts).[164]

B. TREATMENT OF SARs

1. *Data Processing*

Pursuant to Recommendation 29, SARs as well as any other information relevant to money laundering, associate predicate offences and terrorist financing received by the FIU should be analysed by the FIU. According to the FATF, "FIU analysis should add value to the information received"[165] but should not necessarily focus on each disclosure. FIUs can indeed decide on "appropriate selected information, depending on the type and volume of the disclosures received, and on the expected use after dissemination".[166] FIUs should use SARs and other information received to perform both operational and strategic analysis.[167] Operational analysis aims "to identify specific targets

---

162 *Ibid.*, paras. 9 and 11.
163 FATF MER Technical Compliance, Criterion 29.3, footnote 62. On the limits of this request power, see *infra* section V.A.1.b.
164 See *infra* section VI.C.1.
165 Interpretative Note to FATF Recommendation 29 (2012), para. 3.
166 *Ibid.*
167 *Ibid.*

(e.g. persons, assets, criminal networks and associations), to follow the trail of particular activities or transactions, and to determine links between those targets and possible proceeds of crime, money laundering, predicate offences or terrorist financing."[168] Strategic analysis aims to decipher the underlying patterns and trends related to money laundering, which will enable the FIU or other State entities to draw conclusions for the strategic prevention of money laundering, and to provide input for policy formulation and for setting operational priorities.[169]

2. *Special Procedures for Privileged Professions*

As already seen above, the FATF allows national legislators to provide that privileged professions report their suspicions to their self-regulated bodies.[170] However, the FATF does not specify whether these self-regulatory bodies are required to forward the SARs to the FIU, or whether they can analyse the SARs by themselves.

3. *Feedback Obligations*

a. Obligation of the FIU

Pursuant to Recommendation 34, "the competent authorities … should … provide feedback, which will assist financial institutions and designated non-financial businesses and professions in applying national measures to combat money laundering and terrorist financing, and, in particular, in detecting and reporting suspicious transactions". The FIU falls within the FATF definition of "competent authorities".[171] However, the FATF does not provide any information regarding the content, the type (general or individual case-by-case feedback), the form and/or the frequency of the feedback that the FIU should provide to obliged entities.

b. Obligation of Investigative Authorities

The FATF does not explicitly require investigative authorities to provide feedback to the FIU. That said, it is worth mentioning that, in the context of mutual evaluations, the incorporation of feedback from competent authorities into the FIU's function is considered by the FATF as a Specific Factor that

168 *Ibid.*
169 *Ibid.*
170 See *supra* section III.C.3.b.
171 See FATF Glossary (2012), "Competent authorities".

could support the conclusions on the Core Issues examined in determining whether Immediate Outcome 6 ("Financial intelligence and all other relevant information are appropriately used by competent authorities for money laundering and terrorist financing investigations") is being achieved.[172]

4. *Disclosure Obligations Towards "Suspect"*

The FATF does not provide for any interaction between the FIU and individuals or entities that appear as possible suspects in SARs. In particular, the FATF Recommendations do not state that the FIU, following the analysis of SAR, may provide information to persons concerned.

C. PROACTIVE INVESTIGATIONS

Considering that, under the FATF framework, the FIU should serve as the central agency for the receipt of SARs filed by obliged entities, but also of any other information as required by national legislation, one can assume that the FATF implicitly allows FIUs to initiate an analysis even in the absence of a SAR. Suspicion of money laundering and terrorism financing may be triggered by the FIU's own analysis, information reported by the press or a third party or even information spontaneously shared by a foreign FIU.[173]

D. ACCESS TO DATA

1. *Design and Content of FIU's Own Data Banks*

Under the FATF framework, the FIU should serve as the central agency for receiving SARs filed by obliged entities, as well other information relevant to money laundering, associate predicate offences and terrorist financing, as required by national legislation.[174] The FATF mentions cash transaction reports, wire transfer reports and other threshold-based reports as examples of such information that could be disclosed to the FIU.[175] Moreover, it is important to stress that, pursuant to Recommendation 40 and its Interpretative Note, FIUs can also receive information spontaneously shared by foreign FIUs and non-counterparts.

---

172 FATF MER Effectiveness Assessment, Immediate Outcome 6 (2012), 8: "To what extent does the FIU incorporate feedback from competent authorities ... into its functions?"

173 See *infra* section V.F.

174 FATF Recommendation 29 (2012).

175 Interpretative Note to FATF Recommendation 29 (2012), para. 2.

2. *Access to Other Public Data Banks*

The FATF requires countries to ensure that FIUs have access to "the widest possible range of … administrative and law enforcement information", which includes "information from open or public sources, as well as relevant information collected and/or maintained by, or on behalf of, other authorities".[176]

3. *Access to Private Data Banks*

The FATF requires countries to ensure that FIUs have access "to the widest possible range of financial … information", as well as, "where appropriate, commercially held data".[177] However, as seen below[178] regarding the limits provided by the FATF on the powers of FIUs to request additional information, it seems clear that the access to commercially held financial data does not mean indiscriminate access to private data banks.

4. *Data Analytics*

Whilst acknowledging the fact that data analytics tools "cannot fully replace the human judgment element of analysis",[179] the FATF recommends the use of data analytics systems by FIUs to perform their operational and strategic analysis functions. The Interpretative Note to Recommendation 29 indeed states that "FIUs should be encouraged to use analytical software to process information more efficiently and assist in establishing relevant links".[180] Moreover, in the context of mutual evaluations, the use of "IT tools for data mining and analysis of financial intelligence" is considered by the FATF as a Specific Factor that could support the conclusions on the Core Issues examined in determining if Immediate Outcome 6 (that is whether the FIU has adequate resources) is being achieved.[181]

---

176 *Ibid.*, para. 6.

177 *Ibid.*

178 See *infra* section V.A.2.

179 Interpretative Note to FATF Recommendation 29 (2012), para. 3.

180 *Ibid.*

181 FATF MER Effectiveness Assessment, Immediate Outcome 6, 12: "Do the relevant authorities have adequate resources (including IT tools for data mining and analysis of financial intelligence …) to perform its functions?" In the 2016 Mutual Evaluation Report of Austria, the Austrian FIU's IT system was criticised by the FATF assessors because it "only permits the FIU to perform very basic search queries such as on the number of the file, name of the suspect, and name of the victim … [and offers] no possibility to perform search on accounts numbers or other financial details, cross-match STRs, or conduct data-mining to find trends and patterns across STRs" (FATF (2016), *Anti-money laundering and counter-terrorist*

5. *International Cooperation*

Pursuant to Recommendation 40 and its Interpretative Note, countries should ensure that FIUs can request from foreign FIUs and non-counterparts any information that may be relevant for the processing or analysis of information related to money laundering, associate predicate offences or terrorist financing.

E. PARTICIPATION OF "SUSPECTS"

Under the FATF framework, individuals or entities that form the object of operational analysis do not yet, as a result of the analysis, reach the level of the suspect of a criminal investigation. Rather, the FIU's operational analysis is meant to be a precursor to possible subsequent criminal or other investigations. As a result, the Recommendations do not foresee that a suspect must enjoy procedural rights in relation to the FIU.

F. SIMILAR POWERS OF SUPERVISORY BODIES

The FATF does not specify whether supervisory bodies should or could have the right to investigate a suspicion of money laundering on their own.

G. REPORTING OBLIGATIONS OF SUPERVISORY AUTHORITIES

The FATF only requires financial institutions and DNFBPs to report suspicious transactions.[182] It does not indicate whether the supervisory authorities should also be required to report their suspicions to the FIU.

H. REPORTING BY OTHER AUTHORITIES

The FATF also does not indicate whether other competent authorities, such as law enforcement or customs, should be required to report their relevant suspicions to the FIU.

---

financing measures – Austria, Fourth Round Mutual Evaluation Report, para. 127). See also FATF (2016), *Anti-money laundering and counter-terrorist financing measures – Switzerland, Fourth Round Mutual Evaluation Report*, para. 129.

182 On the reporting obligation of obliged entities, see *supra* section III.C.

I. STATISTICS

1. Number of Reports by Supervisory Authorities and Other Authorities

Pursuant to Recommendation 33, the FATF requires countries to maintain "comprehensive statistics ... on the STRs received". It is not clear, however, whether this also covers reports from supervisory authorities to the extent that they are subject to a reporting obligation under national law.

2. FIU Analysis

The FATF does not provide global statistics on the number of FIU investigations carried out throughout the world and the value of transactions associated with these investigations.

3. Communications to Law Enforcement Authorities

Pursuant to Recommendation 33, the FATF requires countries to maintain "comprehensive statistics ... on the STRs ... disseminated" to competent authorities, which include "authorities that have the function of investigating and/or prosecuting money laundering and predicate offences".[183]

V. DATA FLOW AND DATA PROTECTION

A. DATA EXCHANGE BETWEEN FIU AND PRIVATE SECTOR

1. From FIU to Private Sector

The FATF does not make any statement on the transfer of data, in particular personal data, from the FIU to the private sector. On the other hand, the Recommendations also do not provide rules that would oblige countries to allow data transfer from the FIU to obliged entities. In particular, the FIU's power to request additional information from obliged entities does not necessarily entail that it also has the power to provide data to the obliged entities, at least data that is not strictly necessary to answer the request.

---

183 FATF Glossary (2012), "Competent authorities".

2. *From Private Sector to FIU*

The FATF specifies that the FIU should be able to obtain additional data from any obliged entity, and not only from entities that have previously filed a SAR.[184] However, requests for information must relate to a suspicion of money laundering or terrorism financing.[185] Therefore, "[t]his does not include indiscriminate requests for information to reporting entities in the context of the FIU's analysis (e.g. 'fishing expeditions')".[186] The information that the FIU should be permitted to obtain from obliged entities could include all the information gathered in the CDD process, consistent with the risk circumstances and the type of CDD measures applied.[187]

Under the FATF framework, FIUs should also have access to "financial data" and, "where appropriate, commercially held data".[188] However, it does not further specify the term "appropriate", thus presumably referring to national law standards.

B. DATA EXCHANGE BETWEEN FIU AND CRIMINAL JUSTICE SYSTEM

1. *From FIU to Criminal Justice System*

When there are grounds to suspect money laundering, predicate offences or terrorist financing, FIUs are required, under the FATF framework,[189] to disseminate information and the results of their analysis to competent authorities, including "authorities that have the function of investigating and/or prosecuting money laundering and predicate offences".[190] The FATF does not further specify to what extent the FIU is required to disseminate information, or whether it is only meant to be authorised to transmit all the information it deems relevant.

The FIU should also be able to respond to information requests from criminal justice authorities pursuant to Recommendation 31.[191] However, dissemination

184 FATF MER Technical Compliance, Criterion 29.3, footnote 65.

185 *Ibid.*

186 *Ibid.*

187 Interpretative Note to FATF Recommendation 29 (2012), para. 5.

188 FATF Recommendation 29 (2012).

189 Interpretative Note to FATF Recommendation 29 (2012), para. 4.

190 FATF Glossary (2012), "Competent authorities".

191 FATF Recommendation 31 (2012): "When conducting investigations of money laundering, associated predicate offences and terrorist financing, competent authorities should be able to ask for all relevant information held by the FIU".

upon request is not compulsory for the FIU and the decision to disclose the information should thus remain with the FIU.[192]

2. *From Criminal Justice System to FIU*

The FATF requires countries to ensure that the FIU has access on a timely basis to law enforcement information.[193] However, access should only be permitted for the purpose of performing its analysis function properly.[194] The FATF Recommendations do not further elaborate on possible transfer limits under national law.

C. DATA EXCHANGE BETWEEN FIU AND INTELLIGENCE AGENCIES

The FATF Recommendations do not explicitly address the relationship between the FIU and intelligence agencies. It might be argued however that intelligence services can fall under the category of "competent authorities", with whom the FIU, under Recommendation 31, is required to share relevant data, without a clear statement to this effect. It does however seem unlikely that States would accept implicit interference in core institutional questions of national security, notably as regards data sharing by and with intelligence services.

D. DATA EXCHANGE BETWEEN FIU AND TAX AUTHORITIES

1. *From FIU to Tax Authorities*

Where tax authorities qualify as competent authorities in the sense of the FATF definition, that is when they investigate tax offences,[195] the transfer of data from the FIU to the tax authorities is regulated by the same rules as those referred to above applying to the transfer of data from the FIU to the criminal justice authorities.[196]

However, where tax authorities carry out purely administrative functions (e.g. processing of tax declarations), the FATF Recommendations do not explicitly address this issue.

192 Interpretative Note to FATF Recommendation 29 (2012), para. 4.
193 FATF Recommendation 29 (2012).
194 *Ibid.*
195 See FATF Glossary (2012), "Competent authorities".
196 See *supra* section V.B.1.

2. *From Tax Authorities to FIU*

The FATF requires countries to ensure that the FIU, in order to conduct proper analysis, has access to the widest possible range of administrative information.[197] It does not however further specify to what extent this might necessitate access by the FIU to tax data, though the term "possible" seems to allow for adequate limits under national law, in particular the secrecy of tax proceedings.

E. DATA EXCHANGE BETWEEN FIU AND CUSTOMS AUTHORITIES

1. *From FIU to Customs Authorities*

Where custom authorities qualify as competent authorities in the sense of the FATF definition, that is when they investigate customs-related offences,[198] the transfer of data from the FIU to the tax authorities is regulated by the same rules as those referred to above applying to the transfer of data from the FIU to the criminal justice authorities.[199]

However, where custom authorities carry out purely administrative functions, the FATF Recommendations do not explicitly address this issue.

2. *From Customs Authorities to FIU*

The FATF requires countries to ensure that the FIU, in order to conduct proper analysis, has access to the widest possible range of administrative information.[200] As already said, the FATF requires the widest access to administrative information to perform its analysis function properly, but without providing how that might be limited under national law.

F. INFORMATION FLOW BETWEEN FIU AND FOREIGN COUNTERPARTS

1. *Restrictions on Data Transfer from FIU to Foreign FIUs*

Under the FATF framework, FIUs should exchange information with their foreign counterparts.[201] In particular, FIUs should have the power to exchange

197 FATF Recommendation 29 (2012).
198 See FATF Glossary (2012), "Competent authorities".
199 See *supra* section V.B.1.
200 FATF Recommendation 29 (2012).
201 Interpretative Note to FATF Recommendation 40 (2012), para. 7.

with foreign FIUs all information required to be accessible or obtainable directly or indirectly by the FIU under the FATF Recommendations, and under domestic law, provided, however, that the principle of reciprocity is met.[202] The same requirements are set out in the *Egmont Group Principles for Information Exchange Between Financial Intelligence Units for Money Laundering and Terrorism Financing Cases*,[203] to which FIUs should have regard pursuant to paragraph 13 of the Interpretative Note to Recommendation 29.

According to the FATF, FIUs "should not prohibit or place unreasonable or unduly restrictive conditions on exchanging information or providing assistance".[204] In particular, FIUs should not refuse a request for assistance on the grounds that:

(a) the request is also considered to involve fiscal matters; and/or
(b) laws require financial institutions or designated non-financial businesses and professions (except where the relevant information that is sought is held under circumstances where legal privilege or legal professional secrecy applies) to maintain secrecy and confidentiality; and/or
(c) there is an inquiry, investigation or proceeding underway in the country receiving the request, unless the assistance would impede that inquiry, investigation or proceeding; and/or
(d) the nature or status (civil, administrative, law enforcement etc.) of the requesting counterpart authority is different to its foreign FIU.[205]

However, FIUs may refuse to provide information to a foreign counterpart "if the requesting FIU cannot protect the information effectively".[206]

2. *Restrictions on Use of Data Obtained from Foreign FIUs*

According to the FATF, the overarching principle with respect to the use of information obtained by FIUs from counterparts is that information "should be used only for the purpose for which the information was sought or provided".[207] In this context, "[a]ny dissemination of the information to other authorities or third parties, or any use of this information for administrative, investigative,

202 *Ibid.*, para. 9.
203 Egmont Group (2013), *Principles for Information Exchange Between Financial Intelligence Units for Money Laundering and Terrorism Financing Cases*, Principle 22.
204 Interpretative Note to FATF Recommendation 40 (2012), para. 2. See also Egmont Group (2013), *Principles for Information Exchange Between Financial Intelligence Units for Money Laundering and Terrorism Financing Cases*, Principle 24.
205 *Ibid.*
206 Interpretative Note to FATF Recommendation 40 (2012), para. 4; Egmont Group (2013), *Principles for Information Exchange Between Financial Intelligence Units for Money Laundering and Terrorism Financing Cases*, Principle 25.
207 Interpretative Note to FATF Recommendation 40 (2012), para. 3.

prosecutorial or judicial purposes, beyond those originally approved, should be subject to prior authorisation by the requested [FIU]".[208] It is important to stress, however, that "[t]he FIU receiving the request should not refuse consent to such dissemination unless this would fall beyond the scope of application of its AML/CFT provisions, could impair a criminal investigation, would be clearly disproportionate to the legitimate interests of a natural or legal person or the State of the providing FIU, or would otherwise not be in accordance with fundamental principles of its national law".[209] Moreover, "[a]ny such refusal to grant consent should be appropriately explained".[210]

G. INFORMATION FLOW BETWEEN FIU AND FOREIGN NON-COUNTERPARTS

1. *Restrictions on Data Transfer from FIU to Other Foreign Authorities*

Under the 2012 FATF Recommendations, direct exchange of information between the FIU and foreign non-counterparts is only "encouraged",[211] reflecting the risk that direct exchange between non-counterparts may circumvent international cooperation rules, such as mutual legal assistance rules. In contrast, indirect exchange of information between the FIU and foreign non-counterparts through one or more domestic or foreign authorities (for example from a FIU through a domestic criminal justice authority to a foreign criminal justice authority) should be allowed by countries.[212] It is important to stress, however, that this does not entail an obligation for FIUs to share information with foreign non-counterparts. In other words, FIUs, based on domestic law, should be empowered but not compelled to cooperate diagonally.

According to the Interpretative Note to FATF Recommendation 40, FIUs should not refuse a request of assistance on a number of specified grounds, notably the ground that national law require obliged entities (except where legal privilege or legal professional secrecy applies) to maintain secrecy and confidentiality.[213] It should however be noted that the FATF does not refer to the shape of rules on mutual legal assistance between criminal justice authorities, resulting from the fact that the role of FIUs and thus also the purpose of any cooperation between FIUs and foreign criminal justice authorities consist in the collection of intelligence and not evidence. Accordingly, the Interpretative

208 *Ibid.*
209 Egmont Group (2013), *Principles for Information Exchange Between Financial Intelligence Units for Money Laundering and Terrorism Financing Cases*, Principle 26.
210 *Ibid.*
211 Interpretative Note to FATF Recommendation 40 (2012), para. 18.
212 *Ibid.*, para. 17.
213 Interpretative Note to FATF Recommendation 40 (2012), para. 4.

Note to FATF Recommendation 40 should seemingly not be understood as applying to national mutual legal assistance rules.

2. *Restrictions on Use of Data Obtained from Other Foreign Authorities*

As for the exchange of information between FIUs, the Interpretative Note to FATF Recommendation 40 provides that information received by FIUs from foreign non-counterparts should be used only for the purpose for which the information was sought or provided.[214] In this context, any use beyond that originally approved should be authorised by the authority that provided the information.[215]

H. EVIDENTIAL VALUE OF FIU-GENERATED DATA IN COURT PROCEEDINGS

The FATF Recommendations do not treat FIU-generated data as evidence, but as intelligence that can then serve as the basis for further investigations by other authorities. Whilst this does not exclude under national law using FIU data as evidence, the FATF does not make any further statement on such use.

I. USE OF CDD DATA FOR PROFIT MAKING

The FATF does not address possible limits on the use of data collected through CDD, in particular regarding the possible use of such data for purely commercial purposes.

J. DATA SHARING BETWEEN OBLIGED ENTITIES REGARDING SARs AND FIU REQUESTS

1. *Data Sharing Inside a Group*

According to Recommendation 18, financial institutions are required to implement group-wide policies and procedures for sharing information within the same financial group[216] for the purpose of CDD and money laundering and terrorist financing risk management. In this framework, group-level compliance,

---

214 Interpretative Note to FATF Recommendation 40 (2012), para. 3.

215 *Ibid.*

216 As per the FATF Glossary, "Financial group means a group that consists of a parent company or of any other type of legal person exercising control and coordinating functions over the

audit and AML/CFT functions should be provided with information from branches and subsidiaries when necessary for AML/CFT purposes.[217] Such information "could include an STR, its underlying information, or the fact that an STR has been submitted".[218] Similarly, "branches and subsidiaries should receive such information from these group-level functions when relevant and appropriate to risk management".[219]

According to the FATF *Guidance on Private Sector Information Sharing*, group-wide sharing of SARs "allows financial institutions to identify higher risk customers across the group's business and deploy specific monitoring mechanisms or enhanced measures".[220] Additionally, it "enables emergence of a global picture of the risk exposure of the financial institution to such customers, thereby promoting implementation of an effective risk-based approach".[221] Moreover, "[s]uch sharing, which may occur before or after filing of an actual STR by the financial institutions, where required will enable the group compliance to look at the suspect customer's activities or transactions across different verticals, lines of business and jurisdictions. This will also allow them to conduct sophisticated analyses of suspicious activities, assess these analyses against the client database and build the scenario across its global operations".[222]

2. *Data Sharing with Similar Professions*

The FATF Recommendations only address the issue of data sharing between financial institutions that are not part of the same group in the context of correspondent banking relationships (Recommendation 13), money or value transfer services (Recommendation 14), wire transfer (Recommendation 16), and third party reliance (Recommendation 17). The FATF does not specify to what extent obliged entities are authorised to share information regarding SARs with other obliged entities outside the group, but within a similar profession.

3. *Data Sharing with Obliged Entities Outside the EU*

The FATF Recommendations do not provide for special rules regarding data sharing regarding SARs and FIUs requests between obliged entities within the EU and obliged entities outside the EU.

---

rest of the group for the application of group supervision under the Core Principles, together with branches and/or subsidiaries that are subject to AML/CFT policies and procedures at the group level".

217 Interpretative Note to FATF Recommendation 18 (2012), para. 4.

218 *Ibid.*

219 *Ibid.*

220 FATF Guidance (2017), *Private Sector Information Sharing*, para. 43.

221 *Ibid.*

222 *Ibid.*

K. DATA SHARING BETWEEN OBLIGED ENTITIES REGARDING POSSIBLE CASES OF MONEY LAUNDERING

1. *Data Sharing Inside a Group*

According to the Interpretative Note to Recommendation 18, group-level compliance, audit and AML/CFT functions should be provided with "information and analysis of transactions or activities which appear unusual (if such analysis was done)" from branches and subsidiaries when necessary for AML/CFT purposes.[223] Similarly, "branches and subsidiaries should receive such information from these group-level functions when relevant and appropriate to risk management".[224]

Considering that sharing a SAR itself is prohibited in certain jurisdictions, the FATF allows countries to share only information and analysis of transactions or activities which appear unusual, if such analysis was carried out (e.g. facts, transactions, circumstances and documents, including personal information) without disclosing the fact that a SAR was filed.[225] It also allows disclosure of the fact that a SAR has been filed or that a SAR has been filed and sharing underlying information (e.g. information on suspicions and the results of any internal analysis or examination, but not the STR itself).[226] What matters is that shared information is only used for AML/CFT purposes and that it adds value to improving compliance with risk management and reporting obligations in all the locations where a multinational group may be operating.[227] Information should then only be shared if there is a cross-jurisdictional element to it, "such as a customer that has exposure to operations of the group in more than one location or aspects of the flow of transactions or funds that affect operations in the relevant jurisdictions".[228]

2. *Data Sharing with Similar Professions*

As noted above, the FATF Recommendations only address the issue of data sharing between financial institutions that are not part of the same group in the context of correspondent banking relationships (Recommendation 13), money or value transfer services (Recommendation 14), wire transfer (Recommendation 16), and third party reliance (Recommendation 17). The

223 Interpretative Note to FATF Recommendation 18 (2012), para. 4.
224 *Ibid.*
225 FATF Guidance (2017), *Private Sector Information Sharing*, para. 50.
226 *Ibid.*
227 *Ibid.*, para. 51.
228 *Ibid.*

FATF does not specify to what extent obliged entities are authorised to share information regarding suspicions beyond SARs and FIU requests with other obliged entities outside the group, but within a similar profession.

3. *Data Sharing with Obliged Entities Outside the EU*

The FATF Recommendations do not provide for special rules regarding data sharing regarding suspicious transactions or similarly unusual events between obliged entities within the EU and obliged entities outside the EU.

L. DATA MINING BY OBLIGED ENTITIES

The FATF Recommendations do not specify to what extent obliged entities should or could conduct data mining (instead of mere data matching) within their data banks in order to identify possible cases of money laundering.

VI. BENEFICIAL OWNERSHIP TRANSPARENCY

A. BENEFICIAL OWNERSHIP INFORMATION

1. *General Framework*

Pursuant to Recommendations 24 and 25, countries are required to ensure that there is adequate, accurate and timely information on the beneficial ownership situation that can be obtained or accessed in a timely fashion by competent authorities. Countries should apply this requirement with respect to legal persons incorporated or created by any other mechanism in their territory[229] and to legal arrangements governed under their law.[230]

Under the FATF framework, legal persons refers to "any entities other than natural persons that can establish a permanent customer relationship with a financial institution or otherwise own property [such as] companies, bodies corporate, foundations, Anstalt, partnerships, or associations".[231] Legal arrangements refers to "express trusts or other similar legal arrangements [such as *fiducie*, *Treuhand* and *fideicomiso*]".[232]

---

229 Interpretative Note to FATF Recommendation 24 (2012), para. 1, footnote 41.
230 Interpretative Note to FATF Recommendation 25 (2012), para. 1.
231 FATF Glossary (2012), "Legal persons".
232 FATF Glossary (2012), "Legal arrangements".

2. *Definition of "Beneficiary" and "Effective Control"*

The FATF definition of beneficial owners in the context of legal persons refers, first of all, to the "[t]he natural persons who ultimately have a controlling ownership of the structure in a legal person".[233] Where, however, there is a doubt "as to whether the person(s) with the controlling ownership interest are the beneficial owner(s) or where no natural person exerts control through ownership interests",[234] the beneficial owners are "the natural persons (if any) exercising control of the legal person or arrangement through other means".[235] In the event that no natural person can be identified on the basis of this criterion, "the relevant natural person who holds the position of senior managing official"[236] should be designated as a last resort as the beneficial owner of the legal person. As underlined in the FATF *Guidance on Transparency and Beneficial Ownership*, an essential element of the FATF definition of beneficial owners in the context of legal persons is therefore that it "focuses that on the natural person (not legal) persons who actually own and take advantage of capital or assets of the legal person; as well as on those who really exert effective control over it (whether or not they occupy formal positions within that legal person), rather than just the (natural or legal) persons who are legally (on paper) entitled to do so".[237]

With respect to trusts, the FATF defines beneficial owners as "the settlor, the trustee(s), the protector (if any), the beneficiaries or class of beneficiaries, and any other natural person exercising ultimate effective control over the trust (including through a chain of control/ownership)".[238] Regarding other types of legal arrangements, the FATF refers to "persons in equivalent or similar positions".[239]

3. *Definition of "Information"*

Under the FATF framework, beneficial ownership information refers to "the identity"[240] of the beneficial owner(s). The FATF does not specify what information is necessary to verify the identity.

---

233 Interpretative Note to FATF Recommendation 10 (2012), para. 5(b)(i.i). According to the FATF, "[a] controlling ownership interest depends on the ownership structure of the company. It may be based on a threshold, e.g. any person owning more than a certain percentage of the company (e.g. 25%)" (*ibid.*, footnote 32).

234 *Ibid.*, para. 5(b)(i.ii).

235 *Ibid.*

236 *Ibid.*, para. 5(b)(i.iii).

237 FATF Guidance (2014), *Transparency and Beneficial Ownership*, p. 8.

238 Interpretative Note to FATF Recommendation 10 (2012), para. 5(b)(ii.i).

239 *Ibid.*, para. 5(b)(ii.ii).

240 *Ibid.*, para. 5(b).

4. *Special Rules for Entities with a Cross-Border Dimension*

The FATF Recommendations do not provide for special requirements and mechanisms for the disclosure of foreign nationals, foreign entities or foreign trusts.

B. BENEFICIAL OWNERSHIP REGISTRIES

1. *Scope and General Procedure*

The fundamental requirement underlying Recommendations 24 and 25 is that countries should ensure that competent authorities can obtain or access in a timely manner adequate, accurate and timely information on the beneficial ownership of legal persons and legal arrangements.

The FATF Standards maintain a certain level of flexibility as to the means through which information on the beneficial ownership of legal persons should be made available to competent authorities. The FATF indeed recognises "the need to provide flexibility for countries to implement the requirements in a manner that corresponds with their legal, regulatory, economic and cultural characteristics".[241] Countries should use or more of the following mechanisms:

(a) Requiring companies or company registries to obtain and hold up-to-date information on the companies' beneficial ownership;
(b) Requiring companies to take reasonable measures to obtain and hold up-to-date information on the companies' beneficial ownership;
(c) Using existing information, including: (i) information obtained by financial institutions and/or DNFBPs, in accordance with Recommendations 10 and 22 [CDD]; (ii) information held by other competent authorities on the legal and beneficial ownership of companies (e.g. company registries, tax authorities or financial or other regulators); (iii) [basic information such as information about the status and powers of the company, its shareholders and its directors]; and (iv) available information on companies listed on a stock exchange, where disclosure requirements (either by stock exchange rules or through law or enforceable means) impose requirements to ensure adequate transparency of beneficial ownership.[242]

241 FATF Guidance (2014), *Transparency and Beneficial Ownership*, p. 18.
242 Interpretative Note to FATF Recommendation 24 (2012), para. 8. See FATF Guidance (2014), *Transparency and Beneficial Ownership*, pp. 19–27 for further guidance on the implementation each of these mechanisms.

The FATF is less flexible as regards trusts and other similar legal arrangements, since it requires countries to ensure that trustees and persons in equivalent or similar positions obtain and hold beneficial ownership information.[243]

2. Ex Ante *Verification of Accuracy*

The FATF requires countries to ensure that information on beneficial ownership of legal persons and legal arrangements is "accurate and … as current and as up-to-date as possible".[244] However, the FATF Standards do not specify any procedure that countries should put in place in order to ensure that beneficial ownership information meets these requirements.

3. Ex Post *Review of Accuracy*

The FATF requires countries to ensure that information on beneficial ownership of legal persons and legal arrangements is "updated within a reasonable period following any change".[245] However, FATF Standards do not specify any procedure that countries should put in place in order to ensure that beneficial ownership information is kept updated after it has been disclosed.

C. ACCESS TO BENEFICIAL OWNERSHIP INFORMATION

1. *Access by FIU and Other Authorities*

Under the FATF framework, countries should ensure that competent authorities – including FIUs[246] – can obtain and access in a timely fashion beneficial ownership information.[247]

2. *Access by Obliged Entities*

Financial institutions and DNFBPs should have access to beneficial ownership information on legal persons and legal arrangements within the framework of CDD.

243 Interpretative Note to FATF Recommendation 25 (2012), paras. 1 and 9.
244 Interpretative Note to FATF Recommendation 24 (2012), para. 11; Interpretative Note to FATF Recommendation 25 (2012), para. 6.
245 *Ibid.*
246 See FATF Glossary (2012), "Competent authorities".
247 Interpretative Note to FATF Recommendation 24 (2012), para. 12; Interpretative Note to FATF Recommendation 25 (2012), para. 4.

3. *Access by Interested Third Parties*

The FATF does not specify to what extent interested third parties or the public at large should or could have access to beneficial ownership information and under what conditions.

VII. SANCTIONS

A. SANCTIONS FOR MONEY LAUNDERING

1. *Requirement of a Conviction for a Predicate Offence*

The FATF makes it clear that a prior conviction for the predicate offence is irrelevant for the punishment of subsequent money laundering, stating that "[w]hen proving that property is the proceeds of crime, it should not be necessary that a person be convicted of a predicate offence".[248] However, the FATF does not further indicate to what extent the commission of a predicate offence has to be proven.

2. *Forms of Sanctions*

The FATF requires countries to apply criminal sanctions to natural persons convicted of money laundering.[249]

If permitted by national law, criminal sanctions should also be applied to legal persons in relation to money laundering.[250] If that is not possible due to the fundamental principles of domestic law, "civil or administrative liability and sanctions should apply".[251] The FATF underlines that "[t]his should not preclude parallel criminal, civil or administrative proceedings with respect to legal persons in countries in which more than one form of liability is available".[252] Moreover, it provides that "[s]uch measures should be without prejudice to the criminal liability of natural persons".[253]

All sanctions for money laundering should be "effective, proportionate and dissuasive".[254]

---

248 Interpretative Note to FATF Recommendation 3 (2012), para. 4.
249 *Ibid.*, para. 7(b).
250 *Ibid.*, para. 7(c).
251 *Ibid.*
252 *Ibid.*
253 *Ibid.*
254 *Ibid.*, paras. 7(b) and (c).

3. *Confiscation*

Pursuant to Recommendation 4, competent authorities should be able, following a criminal conviction for money laundering, to confiscate, without prejudicing the rights of *bona fide* third parties "property laundered, ... proceeds from, or instrumentalities used in or intended for use in money laundering or predicate offences ... or property of corresponding value". Furthermore, "[c]ountries should consider adopting measures that allow such proceeds or instrumentalities to be confiscated without requiring a criminal conviction (non-conviction based confiscation), or which require an offender to demonstrate the lawful origin of the property alleged to be liable to confiscation, to the extent that such a requirement is consistent with the principles of their domestic law."[255]

4. *Statistics*

a. Number of Criminal Proceedings

Pursuant to Recommendation 33, the FATF requires countries to maintain "comprehensive statistics on ... money laundering ... investigations [and] prosecutions".

b. Number of Convictions

Pursuant to Recommendation 33, the FATF requires countries to maintain "comprehensive statistics on ... money laundering ... convictions".

B. SANCTIONS FOR VIOLATIONS OF PREVENTIVE MEASURES

1. *Money Laundering by Violating Preventive Obligations*

The FATF clearly distinguishes between criminal proceedings for money laundering (Recommendation 3 and its Interpretative Note)[256] and criminal proceedings for violations of preventive measures (Recommendation 35). It also does not address the question whether a violation of AML preventive obligations can give rise to criminal responsibility for money laundering by omission.

---

255 FATF Recommendation 4 (2012).

256 See *supra* section VII.A.

2. *CDD, Reporting and Other AML-Related Obligations*

a. Special Criminal Laws against Individuals

Recommendation 35 requires countries to apply effective, proportionate and dissuasive sanctions to natural persons who fail to comply with the CDD, record keeping, reporting and other AML-related preventive requirements set out in Recommendations 10–23. In addition, Recommendation 35 incorporates a requirement that, where obligations apply to financial institutions and DNFBPs that are legal persons, sanctions should be available not only in relation to the legal persons but also to their directors and senior management.

However, the FATF does not require that sanctions necessarily be of a criminal nature.[257]

b. Administrative Sanctions against Individuals

According to the FATF, sanctions described in the previous section can also be of an administrative nature.[258] Pursuant to Recommendations 27 and 28, supervisory authorities should be authorised to impose such sanctions. As regards specifically financial institutions' supervisors, the FATF indicates that they "should have powers to impose a range of disciplinary and financial sanctions, including the power to withdraw, restrict or suspend the financial institution's license, where applicable".[259]

c. Sanctions against Legal Entities

Recommendation 35 requires countries to apply effective, proportionate and dissuasive sanctions, whether criminal, administrative or civil, to legal persons who fail to comply with the CDD, record keeping, reporting and other AML-related preventive requirements set out in Recommendations 10–23.

Pursuant to Recommendations 27 and 28, supervisory authorities should be authorised to impose administrative sanctions on legal entities. Again, the FATF requires that financial institutions' supervisors "should have powers to impose a range of disciplinary and financial sanctions, including the power to withdraw, restrict or suspend the financial institution's license, where applicable".[260]

---

257 FATF Recommendation 35 (2012).
258 *Ibid.*
259 FATF Recommendation 27 (2012).
260 *Ibid.*

3. *Statistics*

a. Number of Investigations and Sanctions

The FATF does not provide global statistics on the number of criminal and administrative investigations launched throughout the world against individuals and legal entities for the aforementioned offences.

b. Number of Convictions

The FATF does not provide global statistics on the number of criminal and administrative convictions/sanctions imposed throughout the world on individuals and legal entities for the aforementioned offences.

C. CUMULATION OF MONEY LAUNDERING AND OTHER AML-RELATED SANCTIONS

The FATF Recommendations do not specify to what extent sanctions for money laundering can be combined with sanctions for the violation of preventive obligations.

VIII. THE USE OF CASH AS A MEANS OF PAYMENT

A. LIMITS

The FATF Recommendations do not require countries to impose legal limits on the use of cash as a means of payment.

B. STATISTICS

The FATF does not provide global statistics on the use of cash in relation to the overall volume of (cash and non-cash) transactions conducted throughout the world.

IX. SUMMARY, EVALUATION AND FUTURE PERSPECTIVES

June 2019 marked the 30-year anniversary of the FATF, and April 2020 will mark the same anniversary of the First 40 Recommendations. Over the past three decades, the FATF undoubtedly functioned as the universal standard setter and global watchdog in the fight against money laundering and terrorist financing. As at October 2019, the FATF Recommendations have been endorsed by over 200 jurisdictions worldwide (although not being legally binding),[261] and very often serve as a point of reference in other international instruments addressing AML/CTF, such as EU directives[262] and United Nations Security Council (UNSC) Resolutions.[263] The FATF Recommendations and mutual evaluations have led to positive awareness and driven forwards numerous legislative reforms around the world over the years, so that the inter-governmental body could nearly be labelled as a quasi-legislator in the field of AML/CTF. The ongoing reform of the AML law in Switzerland, following the 2016 mutual evaluation, reflects this very well.[264] Moreover, one should also note that the one of the strengths of the FATF has always been carrying out an ongoing assessment of money laundering and terrorist financing risks in order to rapidly identify new threats and risks to the financial system and propose measures needed to reduce these risks. Recently, for instance, the FATF amended Recommendation 15 and the Glossary to clarify how the FATF Standards apply to financial activities and operations involving virtual assets,[265] and it now considers the opportunity to work on money laundering associated with the illegal wildlife trade.[266]

During its 30-year leadership of the global fight against financial crime, the FATF has certainly enhanced the integrity of the international financial

---

261 See *supra* section I.A.

262 Recital (4) 4AMLD: "Union action should continue to take particular account of the FATF Recommendations and instruments of other international bodies active in the fight against money laundering and terrorist financing. With a view to reinforcing the efficacy of the fight against money laundering and terrorist financing, the relevant Union legal acts should, where appropriate, be aligned with the International Standards on Combating Money Laundering and the Financing of Terrorism and Proliferation adopted by the FATF in February 2012"; Recital (3) Directive 2018/1673/EU: "Union action should continue to take particular account of the Financial Action Task force (FATF) Recommendations … The relevant Union legal acts should, where appropriate, be further aligned with the International Standards on Combating Money Laundering and the Financing of Terrorism and Proliferation by the FATF in February 2012".

263 See e.g. UNSC Resolution 1617 (2005), Resolution 2161 (2014) and Resolution 2462 (2019). Resolution 2462 (2019) urges all countries to implement the FATF Recommendations, including the standards to assess the specific terrorist financing risks they face. In addition, the resolution requires countries to criminalise terrorist financing in line with FATF Recommendation 5, recognising that countries must criminalise the financing of a terrorist act but also the financing of support to terrorist organisations and individual terrorists for any purpose, even in the absence of a link to a specific terrorist act. The new resolution, which also welcomes FATF's ongoing work to mitigate the risks from virtual assets and virtual assets service providers, reaffirms the close collaboration between the FATF and the United Nations in the fight against terrorist fighting.

264 See Switzerland report in this volume, section I.B.

265 See *supra* section II.D.2.

266 Objectives for FATF XXXI (2019–2020), Paper by the Incoming President, Chinese Presidency Priorities for the Financial Action Task Force (FATF), p. 2.

system and contributed to the establishment of a robust and wide-reaching AML/CTF architecture. However, in spite of the major successes achieved so far,[267] four main concerns about the FATF's work must be raised today. First of all, the risk-based approach, according to which countries should ensure that measures to prevent or mitigate money laundering and terrorist financing are commensurate with the risks identified, and which is at the core of the 2012 Recommendations,[268] is not reflected in the FATF's own assessment method. The FATF indeed uses the same evaluation framework for all countries, regardless of their weight on the international financial stage and their vulnerability to money laundering and terrorist financing. Second, the FATF approach to reporting is still very much quantity-oriented,[269] which has proved highly ineffective,[270] and has not yet started reflecting (at least publicly) on how to increase the quality of private sector reporting to the public sector by improving the former's ability to identify illicit financial flows and thus render due diligence more efficient. In contrast, various initiatives along these lines have been launched at national level in the past few years, notably through the development of public–private partnerships.[271] Third, as highlighted several times in this study, the FATF Recommendations include a few terminological contradictions, thereby weakening the entire AML/CTF architecture and preventing a harmonised application of the FATF Standards. An example is Recommendation 12, which requires financial institutions to obtain *senior* management approval for establishing (or continuing, for existing customers) business relationships with PEPs, whereas, according to para. 3 of the Interpretative Note to Recommendation 18, the head compliance officer should simply be appointed at the management level.[272] Last but not least, the FATF's decision-making process and assessment procedure severely lack transparency and remain too politicised. From the appointment of the assessment teams in charge of mutual evaluations to the strong participation of the national authorities in the drafting of such reports and the updating of the black and grey lists of high-risk third countries after each plenary,[273] the FATF does not provide enough assurance of independence and oversight.

---

267 For a comprehensive review of the what the FATF has achieved in the past 30 years, see FATF (2019), *Financial Action Task Force – 30 years.*

268 See e.g. FATF Recommendations 1 and 10 (2012).

269 See e.g. FATF (2016), *Anti-money laundering and counter-terrorist financing measures – Switzerland, Fourth Round Mutual Evaluation Report*, para. 315; FATF (2014), *Anti-money laundering and counter-terrorist financing measures – Spain, Fourth Round Mutual Evaluation Report*, pp. 96–97.

270 See e.g. Europol, *From suspicion to action: Converting financial intelligence into greater operation impact*, 2017.

271 See e.g. JMLIT in the UK. See UK report in this volume, section I.B.

272 See *supra* sections III.E and III.A.4.b.

273 See *supra* section III.A.5.a.

China took over the presidency of the FATF in June 2019. For the first time, the FATF President was appointed for a term of two years with the aim to "establish a higher profile for the FATF and increase its capacity in dealing with stakeholders at the international level".[274] As agreed by FATF members in February 2019, and following the adoption of an open-ended mandate by ministers in April,[275] under the Chinese Presidency the FATF will conduct a strategic review of its core work. The review will focus on the mutual evaluation and follow-up processes. It will consider experience from the evaluations done to date, and it will inform agreement by the FATF Plenary on the future of this work after the current round. As the determining factor for the majority of the costs for members, in terms of being assessed, providing assessors and funding the Secretariat, the review should "strengthen the efficiency and the effectiveness of FATF and make the FATF's country assessments and monitoring processes more timely, effective and risk-based."[276] In addition to the strategic review, other priorities of the Chinese Presidency include mitigating the risks and exploiting the opportunities of new technologies, promoting and enabling more effective supervision by national authorities, strengthening coordination and capacity for training on the FATF standards throughout the FATF Global Network, and developing best practices on beneficial ownership.[277]

---

274 Outcomes of the Plenary meeting of the FATF, Buenos Aires, 1–3 November 2017.

275 Declaration of the Ministers of the Financial Action Task Force, Washington, DC, 12 April 2019.

276 Objectives for FATF XXXI (2019–2020), Paper by the Incoming President, Chinese Presidency Priorities for the Financial Action Task Force (FATF), p. 2.

277 *Ibid.*, pp. 2–4.

THE ANTI-MONEY LAUNDERING ARCHITECTURE OF THE EUROPEAN UNION

Jean-Baptiste MAILLART

I. INTRODUCTION

A. HISTORY OF ANTI-MONEY LAUNDERING WITHIN THE EU

The very first legal instrument to address the threat of money laundering within the European Union (EU) was Council Directive 91/308/EEC.[1] Adopted in 1991, it defined money laundering in terms of drugs offences only and imposed obligations solely on the financial sector. Ten years later, the second Anti-Money Laundering (AML) Directive (Directive 2001/97/EC)[2] extended the scope of Council Directive 91/308/EEC both in terms of the predicate offences covered and in terms of the range of obliged entities covered. In 2005, the third AML Directive (Directive 2005/60/EC)[3] was introduced with the aim of bringing the EU legal framework in line with the revised Financial Action Task Force (FATF) Recommendations, which provided more detailed requirements in relation to customer identification and verification, the situations where a higher risk of money laundering or terrorist financing may justify enhanced measures and also the situations where a reduced risk may justify less rigorous controls.

More recently, on 20 May 2015, the fourth AML Directive (Directive 2015/849/EU, 4AMLD)[4] was adopted. Following to a large extent the 2012 FATF

1 Council Directive 91/308/EEC of 10 June 1991 on prevention of the use of the financial system for the purpose of money laundering (OJ L 166, 28.06.1991, p. 77).

2 Directive 2001/97/EC of the European Parliament and of the Council of 4 December 2001 amending Council Directive 91/308/EEC on prevention of the use of the financial system for the purpose of money laundering (OJ L 344, 28.12.2001, p. 76).

3 Directive 2005/60/EC of the European Parliament and of the Council of 26 October 2005 on the prevention of the use of the financial system for the purpose of money laundering and terrorist financing (OJ L 309, 25.11.2005, p. 15).

4 Directive 2015/849/EU of the European Parliament and of the Council of 20 May 2015 on the prevention of the use of the financial system for the purposes of money laundering or terrorist financing, amending Regulation (EU) No 648/2012 of the European Parliament and

Recommendations,[5] the 4AMLD, which had to be transposed by 26 June 2017,[6] aimed at strengthening the EU legal framework for the prevention of money laundering and terrorist financing, notably by:

(i) requiring the European Commission to publish an EU-level risk assessment report and each Member State to produce a national risk assessment every two years to ensure effective management and identification of money laundering and terrorist financing risks;
(ii) requiring obliged entities to conduct a documented AML/ counter-terrorist financing (CTF) risk assessment in respect of their business and take risk mitigation measures that are commensurate with this assessment;
(iii) lowering the threshold for the application of customer due diligence (CDD) measures by dealers in goods to €10,000;
(iv) designating offline gambling services as obliged entities;
(v) removing the automatic entitlement to apply simplified CDD measures for specific customers and products;
(vi) broadening the definition of politically exposed persons (PEPs) to encompass people entrusted with a prominent public position domestically, as well as domestic PEPs who work for international organisations;
(vii) making tax crimes a predicate offence for money laundering;
(viii) requiring Member States to ensure that beneficial ownership information related to corporate and other legal entities, as well trusts which generate tax consequences, is held, at national level, in a central register; and
(ix) defining minimum administrative penalties to be applied in the event of violation of preventive measures.

Despite its recent adoption, it soon became clear, in light of emerging threats (namely the terrorist attacks in Europe in 2015, which also impacted the AML legal framework due to the close connection between AML and CTF, and the offshore leaks investigated in the Panama Papers), that the 4AMLD was

---

of the Council, and repealing Directive 2005/60/EC of the European Parliament and of the Council and Commission Directive 2006/70/EC (OJ L 141, 20.05.2015, p. 73).

5 On some issues, however, the 4AMLD goes beyond the FATF requirements and provides for additional safeguards (e.g. scope of obliged entities, beneficial ownership information, sanctions).

6 At the time of writing, all Member States have transposed the 4AMLD. It should be noted, however, that some Member States were late in transposing the 4AMLD. By 26 June 2017, only 11 Member States (the United Kingdom, France, Germany, Italy, Spain, Slovenia, Sweden, Austria, Belgium, the Czech Republic and Croatia) had brought into force the laws, regulations and administrative provisions necessary to comply with the Directive.

insufficient to fully address the challenges facing the EU's preventive AML framework. As a result, the European Commission presented in February 2016 an Action Plan for how the Commission would seek to upgrade the 4AMLD in order to ensure that Member States have the necessary tools to tackle new threats and challenges related to terrorist financing and money laundering in the Union.[7] The Action Plan, which builds on the 2015 European Security Agenda,[8] set out a series of measures that led to the publication on 5 July 2016 of a Proposal for a Directive amending the 4AMLD.[9] After nearly two years of negotiations and counterproposals, Directive 2018/843/EU (5AMLD)[10] was finally adopted by the European Parliament and the Council and entered into force on 10 July 2018. Member States had until 10 January 2020 to transpose it.[11] The 5AMLD, which is not a comprehensive overhaul of the existing legislative framework but rather a series of amendments to the 4AMLD, made the following key changes to the 4AMLD:

(i) definition of the specific enhanced CDD measures that obliged entities shall take when dealing with economical operators coming from high-risk third countries identified as such by the European Commission;
(ii) expansion of the definition of obliged entities to include other professional businesses, notably auction houses, art dealers, digital wallet providers and virtual currency exchange services, and specification of the scope of application of the 4AMLD with respect to tax advisors and estate agents;
(iii) reduction in the threshold for identifying the holders of general purpose anonymous prepaid cards from €250 to €150 and suppression of the CDD exemption in the case of remote payment transactions where the amount paid exceeds €50;

---

7 European Commission, Action Plan for strengthening the fight against terrorist financing, 2 February 2016, COM(2016) 50 final.

8 European Commission, The European Agenda on Security, 28 April 2015, COM(2015) 185 final.

9 European Commission, Proposal for a Directive amending Directive (EU) 2015/849 on the prevention of the use of the financial system for the purposes of money laundering or terrorist financing and amending Directive 2009/101/EC, 5 July 2016, COM(2016) 450 final.

10 Directive 2018/843/EU of the European Parliament and of the Council of 30 May 2018 amending Directive 2015/849/EU on the prevention of the use of the financial system for the purposes of money laundering or terrorist financing, and amending Directives 2009/138/EC and 2013/36/EU (OJ L 156, 19.06.2018, p. 43).

11 Art. 4(1) 5AMLD. One should note, however, that different deadlines exist for: (i) the establishment of beneficial ownership registers for trusts and similar legal arrangements (10 March 2020); (ii) the interconnection of beneficial ownership registries via the European Central Platform (10 March 2021); and (iii) the setting up of the centralised automated mechanisms allowing the identification of holders of bank and payment accounts and safe deposit boxes (10 September 2020).

(iv) broadening of the criteria for the assessment of high-risk third countries and improving the safeguards for financial transactions to and from such countries;
(v) granting financial intelligence units (FIUs) new powers, in particular the power to request information from any obliged entity even without there having been a suspicious transaction report;
(vi) enhanced protection for whistleblowers who report money laundering;
(vii) requirement that a limited set of information on beneficial ownership of corporate and other legal entities held in national beneficial ownership registries is accessible by the general public (but not the register of beneficial owners of trusts, which will still require demonstration of a legitimate interest);
(viii) requirement that each Member State put verification mechanisms in place to enhance the accuracy of the information and reliability of beneficial ownership registries; and
(ix) interconnection of beneficial ownership registries within the EU to facilitate cooperation and exchange of information between Member States.

Besides a preventive-regulatory AML regime, the EU has also developed a "complementary"[12] criminal law approach to money laundering. On 21 December 2016, the European Commission presented a proposal to establish minimum rules concerning the definition of offences and sanctions in the area of money laundering[13] with the aim of bringing national laws across the EU in line with international obligations, in particular those arising from the Council of Europe Convention on Laundering, Search, Seizure and Confiscation of the Proceeds from Crime and on the Financing of Terrorism (Warsaw Convention),[14] signed by the EU in 2009, and the relevant FATF Recommendations. The European Commission proposed these measures as it believed that arts. 1(b) and 2 of Council Framework Decision 2001/500/JHA,[15] which lay down requirements for the criminalisation of money laundering and also establish the minimum level of the maximum sanctions in respect of certain acts of money laundering, are neither comprehensive nor coherent

12 Recital (1) 4AMLD.
13 European Commission, Proposal for a Directive on countering money laundering by criminal law, 21 December 2016, COM(2016) 826 final.
14 Council of Europe Convention on Laundering, Search, Seizure and Confiscation of the Proceeds from Crime and on the Financing of Terrorism, CETS No 198, Warsaw, 16 May 2005.
15 Council Framework Decision 2001/500/JHA of 26 June 2001 on money laundering, the identification, tracing, freezing, seizing and confiscation of instrumentalities and the proceeds of crime (OJ L 182, 05.07.2001).

enough to effectively combat money laundering across the EU.[16] In particular, the Commission suggested that national differences in the definition, scope and sanctioning of money laundering offences create a risk of forum shopping in the Union and hinder cross-border judicial and police cooperation as well the exchange of information between competent authorities.[17] Directive 2018/1673/EU on combating money laundering by criminal law,[18] which will replace the aforementioned provisions of Council Framework Decision 2001/500/JHA with regard to the Member States bound by this Directive,[19] was adopted by the Union co-legislators on 23 October 2018 and entered into force on 2 December 2018. Member States are expected to bring into force laws and administrative provisions necessary to comply with it by 3 December 2020.[20]

B. CURRENT CONCERNS AND REFORM AGENDA

As observed above, the EU has recently been bolstering its legal framework to fight against money laundering and terrorist financing. Between May 2015 and October 2018, three Directives were adopted to strengthen the EU regulatory and criminal law framework in this regard, which is merely one fewer than for the period 1991–2015. In addition to these legislative reforms, five recent developments pertaining to the EU AML/CTF legal framework are worth mentioning.

First, Directive 2019/1153 facilitating the use of financial and other information was adopted on 20 June 2019[21] following a European Commission's proposal of 17 June 2018,[22] which was then significantly revised by the Council

16 European Commission, Proposal a Directive on countering money laundering by criminal law, Explanatory memorandum, p. 1.

17 *Ibid.*

18 Directive 2018/1673/EU of the European Parliament and of the Council of 23 October 2018 on combating money laundering by criminal law (OJ L 284, 12.11.2018, p. 22).

19 Recital (20) and art. 12 Directive 2018/1673/EU. All Member States are bound by Directive 2018/1673/EU, except for Denmark, the United Kingdom and Ireland, which declined "opt-in" as permitted by arts. 1 and 2 of Protocols Nos. 21 and 22, annexed to the Treaty on European Union and to the Treaty on the Functioning of the European Union (see recitals (23) and (24) Directive 2018/1673/EU).

20 Art. 13(1) Directive 2018/1673/EU.

21 Directive 2019/1153/EU of the European Parliament and of the Council of 20 June 2019 laying down rules facilitating the use of financial and other information for the prevention, detection, investigation or prosecution of certain criminal offences, and repealing Council Decision 2000/642/JHA (OJ L 186, 11.7.2019, p. 122).

22 European Commission, Proposal for a Directive laying down rules facilitating the use of financial and other information for the prevention, detection, investigation or prosecution of certain criminal offences and repealing Council Decision 2000/642/JHA, 17 April 2018, SWD(2018) 114 final – SWD(2018) 115 final, https://ec.europa.eu/home-affairs/sites/homeaffairs/files/what-we-do/policies/european-agenda-security/20180417_directive-

and the European Parliament.[23] The Directive further strengthens the criminal law legal framework by speeding up the access to financial information for law enforcement authorities and by enhancing the exchange of financial information between law enforcement authorities and Financial Intelligence Units. Member States will have until August 2021 to transpose it. The relevant provisions will be addressed in this report.[24]

Second, the EU Parliament criticised in 2017 the fact that the European Commission's methodology for identifying high-risk third countries was not sufficiently autonomous and called on the Commission to adopt a roadmap describing the milestones for developing and implementing a new methodology.[25] This methodology was issued on 22 June 2018.[26]

In accordance with the new methodology, the Commission carried out a pre-assessment to determine the relevant countries to be assessed, in addition to those already listed by the FATF,[27] and the level of priority for the assessment of those countries. Countries were selected for further analysis if they met any of the following non-cumulative criteria: countries identified by the European External Action Service (EEAS) or by Europol as having a systemic impact on the integrity of the EU financial system; jurisdictions reviewed by the International Monetary Fund as international offshore financial centres; or countries considered economically relevant based on the strength of their economic ties with the EU and the size of their financial sector.

The Commission thus identified 132 jurisdictions as falling within the scope of the EU assessment. Out of these 132 jurisdictions, the Commission identified 54 so-called "Priority 1 countries" (countries of the highest priority),[28] to be

proposal-facilitating-use-information-prevention-detection-investigation-prosecution-criminal-offences_en.pdf.

23 See e.g. European Parliament legislative resolution of 17 April 2019 on the proposal for a Directive laying down rules facilitating the use of financial and other information for the prevention, detection, investigation or prosecution of certain criminal offences and repealing Council Decision 2000/642/JHA (COM(2018)0213 – C8-0152/2018 – 2018/0105(COD)).

24 See notably *infra* section V.B.1.

25 European Parliament resolution of 17 May 2017 on the Commission delegated resolution of 24 March 2017 amending Delegated Regulation (EU) 2016/1675 supplementing Directive (EU) 2015/849, as regards deleting Guyana from the table in point I of the Annex and adding Ethiopia to that table (C(2017)01951 – 2017/2634(DEA)).

26 European Commission, Methodology for identifying high risk third countries under Directive (EU) 2015/849, 22 June 2018, SWD(2018) 362 final.

27 According to the new methodology, the Commission indeed considered as a starting point that any third country presenting a risk for the international financial system, as identified by the FATF, are presumed to represent a risk for the EU internal market.

28 Afghanistan, Albania, Algeria, American Samoa, Armenia, Australia, Bahamas, Bangladesh, Bosnia and Herzegovina, Botswana, China, China Hong Kong SAR, Colombia, Costa Rica, Democratic People's Republic of Korea, Ethiopia, former Yugoslav Republic of Macedonia, Ghana, Guam, Guatemala, Guyana, Iran, Iraq, Isle of Man, Laos, Libya, Malaysia, Mauritius, Mexico, Morocco, Nigeria, Northern Mariana Islands, Pakistan, Panama, Puerto Rico, Russian Federation, Samoa, Saudi Arabia, Serbia, Singapore, Sri Lanka, Switzerland, Syrian

assessed by the end of 2018, and 78 so-called "Priority 2 countries",[29] to be assessed progressively from 2019 onwards as soon as new information sources become available. "Priority 1 countries" were identified on the basis of the following set of non-cumulative criteria: countries identified by Europol/ EEAS as being exposed to money laundering or terrorist financing threats considering money laundering and terrorist financing risk factors; countries listed in the EU list of non-cooperative jurisdictions for tax purposes adopted by the Council of the EU; countries listed in Regulation (EU) 2016/1675 but de-listed by the FATF between 14 July 2016 and 15 November 2018; or countries which have been subject to a mutual evaluation process against the 2012 FATF Recommendations carried out by the FATF or a FATF-style regional body (FSRB) – where the evaluation report was finalised by June 2018 and the country has been identified by Europol as having a systemic impact on the integrity of the EU financial system.

On the basis of its assessment of the 54 "Priority 1 countries", the Commission identified, by way of a delegated act published on 13 February 2019, 23 jurisdictions with strategic deficiencies in their AML/CTF regimes.[30] This included 12 countries listed by the FATF at the time (Bahamas, Botswana, the Democratic People's Republic of Korea, Ethiopia, Ghana, Iran, Pakistan, Sri Lanka, the Syrian Arab Republic, Trinidad and Tobago, Tunisia and Yemen) and 11 additional jurisdictions (Afghanistan, American Samoa, Guam, Iraq, Libya, Nigeria, Panama, Puerto Rico, Samoa, Saudi Arabia and the US Virgin Islands). The following eight criteria, set out in art. 9(2) 4AMLD as modified by 5AMLD,[31] were the basis for the assessment: criminalisation of money laundering and terrorist financing; measures relating to CDD, record keeping

Arab Republic, Thailand, Trinidad and Tobago, Tunisia, Turkey, Uganda, Ukraine, United Arab Emirates, United States, US Virgin Islands, Vanuatu and Yemen.

29 Andorra, Anguilla, Antigua and Barbuda, Argentina, Aruba, Azerbaijan, Bahrain, Barbados, Belarus, Belize, Bermuda, Bolivia, Brazil, British Virgin Islands, Cabo Verde, Cameroon, Canada, Cayman Islands, China Macao SAR, Congo, Cook Islands, Côte d'Ivoire, Curaçao, Dominica, Dominican Republic, Ecuador, Egypt, Faroe Islands, Fiji, Gambia, Georgia, Greenland, Grenada, Guernsey, Honduras, India, Indonesia, Israel, Jamaica, Japan, Jersey, Jordan, Kazakhstan, Kenya, Republic of Korea, Kosovo, Kyrgyzstan, Lebanon, Maldives, Marshall Islands, Mauritania, Moldova, Monaco, Mongolia, Montenegro, Montserrat, Namibia, Nauru, New Caledonia, Nicaragua, Niue, Oman, Palau, Papua New Guinea, Peru, Philippines, Qatar, Saint Kitts and Nevis, Saint Lucia, Saint Vincent and the Grenadines, San Marino, Senegal, Seychelles, Somalia, South Africa, Suriname, Swaziland, Taiwan, Tajikistan, Thailand, Turkmenistan, Turks and Caicos Islands, Uruguay, Venezuela and Vietnam.

30 Commission Delegated Regulation (EU) … / … of 13.2.2019 supplementing Directive (EU) 2015/849 by identifying high-risk third countries with strategic deficiencies, http://www.ipsoa.it/~/media/Quotidiano/2019/02/15/antiriciclaggio-23-paesi-a-rischio-nella-black-list-ue/regolamento_delegatoENG%20pdf.ashx.

31 The 5AMLD has significantly broadened the criteria set out in art. 9(2) 4AMLD, including notably the availability of information on the beneficial ownership of companies and legal arrangements.

and reporting of suspicious transactions by financial institutions; measures relating to CDD, record keeping and reporting of suspicious transactions by Designated Non-Financial Business and Professions (DNFBPs); powers and procedures of the third country's competent authorities for the purposes of combating money laundering and terrorist financing; existence of dissuasive, proportionate and effective sanctions; third country's practice in cooperation and exchange of information with Member States' competent authorities; availability of accurate and timely information of the beneficial ownership of legal persons arrangements to competent authorities; and implementation of targeted financial sanctions related to terrorism and terrorist financing.

The list of high-risk third countries, which had to be endorsed by the Council and the European Parliament within one month after notification of the delegated act to both institutions,[32] was, however, unanimously rejected by the Justice and Home Affairs Ministers of the EU (Council).[33] In a statement, the Council justified its decision on the grounds that it "cannot support the current proposal that was not established in a transparent and resilient process that actively incentivizes affected countries to take decisive action while also respecting their right to be heard".[34] The European Parliament has been disapproving of the Council's rejection of the new list, recognising that many listed countries applied diplomatic pressure on members of the Council to influence their position. Questions have also been raised about the Commission's attitude towards countries that have not been listed but are well known for weaknesses in their AML/CTF frameworks, like Russia for example. In any case, the Commission will now have to propose a new draft list of high-risk third countries that will address Member States' concerns.

The third development worth mentioning is the adoption of the 5th Capital Requirements Directive (CRD 5).[35] In relation to AML/CTF, amendments introduced an explicit cooperation obligation between prudential authorities and AML/CTF competent authorities and FIUs and removed confidentiality barriers to effective information sharing between those authorities.[36]

---

32 Art. 64(5) 4AMLD.

33 https://data.consilium.europa.eu/doc/document/ST-6964-2019-REV-1/en/pdf.

34 *Ibid.* It should be noted that the US Department of the Treasury also expressed its "significant concerns about the substance of the list and the flawed process by which it was developed" and rejected the inclusion of American Samoa, Guam, Puerto Rico and the US Virgin Islands on the list (see Treasury Statement on European Commission List of Jurisdictions with Strategic AML/CFT Deficiencies, https://home.treasury.gov/news/press-releases/sm610).

35 Directive (EU) 2019/878 of the European Parliament and of the Council of 20 May 2019 amending Directive 2013/36/EU as regards exempted entities, financial holding companies, mixed financial holding companies, remuneration, supervisory measures and powers and capital conservation measures (OJ L 150, 07.06.2019, p. 253).

36 See art. 117(5) Directive 2013/36/EU as modified by CRD 5.

Moreover, the Directive clarifies the possibility for prudential supervisors to use available prudential tools to address AML/CTF concerns from a prudential perspective and mentions explicitly the AML/CTF dimension in the context of the supervisory review and evaluation process, requiring competent authorities to take necessary measures using the tools and powers at their disposal should money laundering/terrorist financing concerns be significant from a prudential perspective.[37]

The fourth development pertaining to the EU AML/CTF legal framework that is worth mentioning is the publication on 16 December 2019 by the three European Supervisory Authorities (ESAs) – the European Banking Authority (EBA), the European Securities and Markets Authority (ESMA) and the European Insurance and Occupational Pensions Authority (EIOPA) – of Joint guidelines on cooperation and information exchange, thereby establishing colleges of AML/CTF supervisors for the first time in the EU.[38] These Guidelines require that in situations where a firm operates in more than three Member States, supervisors establish an AML/CTF college. To this end, the Guidelines have laid down rules that govern the establishment and operation of the AML/CTF colleges. These colleges will bring together AML/CTF supervisors of the same firm, as well as other relevant parties, such as prudential supervisors and AML/CTF supervisors from third countries for example. This is to ensure that all supervisors have access to comprehensive information about the firm and use it to inform their risk assessment and supervisory approach. The colleges will also allow the supervisors to agree on a common approach, including coordinated actions. The Guidelines also include provisions to structure supervisory cooperation in situations where the conditions for setting up an AML/CFT college are not met.

Last but not least, one should mention the new powers given to the EBA by the European legislature in late 2019 to lead, coordinate and monitor EU supervisors' fight against money laundering and terrorist financing, thereby consolidating the AML/CTF mandates of all three ESAs within the EBA.[39]

---

37 See *infra* III/I/1.

38 ESAs, Joint guidelines on cooperation and information exchange for the purpose of Directive (EU) 2015/849 between competent authorities supervising credit and financial institution, JC 2019 81, 16 December 2019.

39 Regulation (EU) 2019/2175 of the European Parliament and of the Council of 18 December 2019 amending Regulation (EU) No 1093/2010 establishing a European Supervisory Authority (European Banking Authority), Regulation (EU) No 1094/2010 establishing a European Supervisory Authority (European Insurance and Occupational Pensions Authority), Regulation (EU) No 1095/2010 establishing a European Supervisory Authority (European Securities and Markets Authority), Regulation (EU) No 600/2014 on markets in financial instruments, Regulation (EU) 2016/1011 on indices used as benchmarks in financial instruments and financial contracts or to measure the performance of investment

The Regulation implementing these powers and this mandate, which follows a proposal made on 12 September 2018 by the European Commission,[40] came into effect on 1 January 2020.[41] The ultimate aim of such reform is to ensure that financial institutions and competent authorities apply effective and robust AML/CTF controls wherever they operate in the single market. The EBA's new mandate includes notably:[42]

(i) developing EU-wide AML/CFT policy and setting clear regulatory expectations of the components of an effective and risk-based approach to AML/CFT that financial institutions and competent authorities have to implement;
(ii) fostering comparable approaches and the consistent and effective implementation of EU AML/CFT legislation by assisting competent authorities through training and bilateral support where necessary;
(iii) identifying, assessing and disseminating information on EU-wide ML/TF risks and developing a common approach to mitigating these risks strategically;
(iv) conducting thematic peer reviews where necessary to test compliance by a cross-section of national competent authorities with a particular legal AML/CTF requirement;
(v) investigating possible breaches of EU AML/CTF law where there is clear evidence to suggest that an AML/CFT authority may be in breach of such law;
(vi) establishing a permanent internal AML/CTF standing committee (the AMLSC) to provide subject matter expertise to inform the EBA's work;
(vii) creating a new AML/CTF database containing both quantitative and qualitative data that will be analysed and used notably to share information and inform competent authorities across the EU of emerging and priority risks, and inform the EBA's AML/CFT policy and strategy;
(viii) cooperating with FIUs; and
(ix) facilitating cooperation with third country authorities to ensure that AML/CFT breaches by financial institutions that operate on a cross-border basis are addressed comprehensively and in a timely manner.

---

funds, and Regulation (EU) 2015/847 on information accompanying transfers of funds (OJ L 334, 27.12.2019, p. 1).

40 Communication from the Commission, *Strengthening the Union framework for prudential and anti-money laundering supervision for financial institutions*, 12 September 2018, https://ec.europa.eu/commission/sites/beta-political/files/soteu2018-anti-money-laundering-communication-645_en.pdf.

41 See art. 7 Regulation (EU) 2019/2175.

42 See in particular art. 9a Regulation (EU) No 1093/2010 as modified by Regulation (EU) 2019/2175.

II. AIMS AND SCOPE OF AML SYSTEM

A. AIMS OF AML REGIME

Since the very first AML Directive, the EU's discourse on AML has mainly focused on the protection of the financial system.[43] For instance, recital (2) 4AMLD stresses the absolute urgency of preserving "[t]he soundness, integrity and stability of credit institutions and financial institutions, and confidence in the financial system as a whole [which] could be seriously jeopardised by the efforts of criminals and their associates to disguise the origin of criminal proceeds or to channel lawful or illicit money for terrorist purposes". Another recent example is that of recital (50) 5AMLD, which expressly states that the objective of the 4AMLD is "the protection of the financial system by means of prevention, detection and investigation of money laundering and terrorist financing".

At the same time, however, the objective of protecting society from crime and the internal security of the Union seems to also play an important role in the development of AML instruments at EU level. In line with the 2015 European Agenda on Security,[44] the preamble of the 4AMLD[45] and the preamble of Directive 2018/1673/EU[46] expressly refer to this objective. One should also mention the Commission Staff Working Document of 26 June 2017 on improving cooperation between EU FIUs, according to which "[t]he fight against money laundering is ... essential to combating criminal activities ... not only to deprive criminals from their incentive to commit crimes when profit is their ultimate objective, but also to detect criminals and their associates and bring them to justice".[47]

B. SCOPE OF MONEY LAUNDERING

1. *Definition of Money Laundering in Criminal Law*

a. *Actus Reus*

i. Predicate Offences

Pursuant to art. 2(1) Directive 2018/1673/EU, the definition of criminal activities which shall constitute predicate offences for money laundering in all Member

43 See e.g. recital (1) Council Directive 91/308/EEC.

44 See European Commission, The European Agenda on Security, 28 April 2015, COM(2015) 185 final, p. 17.

45 See recital (2).

States refers to "any kind of criminal involvement in the commission of any offence punishable, in accordance with national law, by deprivation of liberty or a detention order for a maximum of more than one year or, as regards Member States that have a minimum threshold for offences in their legal systems, any offence punishable by deprivation of liberty or a detention order for a minimum of more than six months". Moreover, to the extent that the application of those penalty thresholds does not already do so, art. 2(1) Directive 2018/1673/EU requires Member States to include a range of predicate offences within each of the following 22 categories of offences:

(a) participation in an organised criminal group and racketeering, including any offence set out in Council Framework Decision 2008/841/JHA;
(b) terrorism, including any offence set out in Directive (EU) 2017/541 ...;
(c) trafficking in human beings and migrant smuggling, including any offence set out in Directive 2011/36/EU of the European Parliament and the Council and Council Framework Decision 2002/946/JHA;
(d) sexual exploitation, including any offence set out in Directive 2011/93/EU ...;
(e) illicit trafficking in narcotic drugs and psychotropic substances, including any offence set out in Council Framework Decision 2004/757/JHA;
(f) illicit arms trafficking;
(g) illicit trafficking in stolen goods and other goods;
(h) corruption, including any offence set out in the Convention on the fight against corruption involving officials of the European Communities or officials of Member States of the European Union and in Council Framework Decision 2003/568/JHA;
(i) fraud, including any offence set out in Council Framework Decision 2001/413/JHA;
(j) counterfeiting of currency, including any offence set out in Directive 2014/62/EU ...;
(k) counterfeiting and piracy of products;
(l) environmental crime, including any offence set out in Directive 2008/99/EC ... or in Directive 2009/123/EC ...;
(m) murder, grievous bodily injury;
(n) kidnapping, illegal restraint and hostage-taking;
(o) robbery or theft;
(p) smuggling (including in relation to customs and excise duties and taxes);
(q) tax crimes relating to direct and indirect taxes, as laid down in national law;
(r) extortion;
(s) forgery;
(t) piracy;

---

46 See recital (1).

47 European Commission, Commission Staff Working Document, 26 June 2017, SWD(2017) 275 final, p. 2.

(u) insider trading and market manipulation, including any offence set out in Directive 2014/57/EU ...;
(v) cybercrime, including any offence set out in Directive 2013/40/EU ... [footnotes omitted]

With the only exception of cybercrime,[48] the scope of predicate offences provided in art. 2(1) Directive 2018/1673/EU mirrors the FATF list of "designated categories of offences", as well as the range of criminal activities listed in the appendix of the Warsaw Convention, to which the offence of money laundering should be applied according to paragraph 4 of the Interpretative Note to FATF Recommendation 3 and art. 9(4) of the Warsaw Convention.

ii. Definition of Money Laundering Acts

Art. 3(1) Directive 2018/1673/EU requires Member States to take all the necessary measures to establish as punishable money laundering offences three distinct sets of criminal conducts. The first set involves the "conversion or transfer of property".[49] The "concealment or disguise of the true nature, source, location, disposition, movement, rights with respect to, or ownership of, property" constitutes the second set of money laundering offences.[50] The third set includes the "acquisition, possession or use of property".[51]

Art. 3(5) Directive 2018/1673/EU requires Member States to criminalise self-laundering. However, this obligation is limited to the first and second sets of money laundering acts.[52] In other words, the obligation to criminalise self-laundering does not apply to the mere possession or use of property. According to the European Commission, "[t]his approach takes into account that prosecuting a person for the mere 'personal enjoyment' of the proceeds of the own crime for which he has already been judged, in some Member States, is considered to infringe the principle of *ne bis in idem*".[53]

The term "property" is defined in Directive 2018/1673/EU as follows: "assets of any kind, whether corporeal or incorporeal, movable or immovable, tangible

48 The committing of a cybercrime is not envisaged by the FATF as a predicate offence. The rationale set out by the European Commission to include cybercrime within the scope of predicate offences is that "cases show that proceeds from cybercrime are laundered through sophisticated schemes, involving both traditional and new payment methods" (European Commission, Proposal a Directive on countering money laundering by criminal law, Explanatory memorandum, p. 13).

49 Art. 3(1)(a) Directive 2018/1673/EU.

50 Art. 3(1)(b) Directive 2018/1673/EU.

51 Art. 3(1)(c) Directive 2018/1673/EU.

52 Art. 3(5) Directive 2018/1673/EU.

53 European Commission, Proposal for a Directive on countering money laundering by criminal law, Explanatory memorandum, pp. 14–15.

or intangible, and legal documents or instruments in any form including electronic or digital, evidencing title to or an interest in such assets".[54]

Pursuant to art. 3(1) Directive 2018/1673/EU, property must be "derived from criminal activity", as defined in art. 2(1) Directive 2018/1673/EU.[55] This includes property derived both directly and indirectly from criminal activity.[56]

b. *Mens Rea*

Directive 2018/1673/EU does not require the criminalisation of unintentional conduct, such as negligent money laundering. Art. 3(1) requires Member States to criminalise money laundering when it is committed intentionally and with the knowledge that the property is derived from criminal activity. Intention and knowledge can be inferred from objective, factual circumstances.[57] Directive 2018/1673/EU further states that Member States "may" criminalise money laundering where the offender "suspected or ought to have known that the property was derived from criminal activity".[58]

As regards to acts of conversion and transfer of property, such acts must be committed intentionally and also "for the purpose of concealing or disguising the illicit origin of the property or of assisting any person who is involved in the commission of such an activity to evade the legal consequences of that person's action".[59] The other acts of money laundering do not require such a *dolus specialis* to amount to money laundering.

2. *Money Laundering by Omission*

Directive 2018/1673/EU does not require the criminalisation of money laundering by omission.

3. *Aggravated Forms of Money Laundering*

Art. 6(1) Directive 2018/1673/EU requires Member States to ensure that aggravated penalties apply where one of the aforementioned money laundering offences[60] is committed within the framework of a criminal organisation in the

---

54 Art. 2(2) Directive 2018/1673/EU.
55 On the definition of criminal activity, see *supra* section II.B.1.a.i.
56 Recital (19) Directive 2018/1673/EU.
57 Recital (13) Directive 2018/1673/EU.
58 Art. 3(2) Directive 2018/1673/EU.
59 Art. 3(1)(a) Directive 2018/1673/EU.
60 See *supra* section II.B.1.a.ii.

sense of art. 1(1) Council Framework Decision 2008/841/JHA[61] or where the perpetrator is an obliged entity within the meaning of art. 2 4AMLD[62] and has committed the offence in the exercise of his/her professional activities.

According to art. 6(2) Directive 2018/1673/EU, further aggravating circumstances "may" include the fact that the laundered property is of considerable value or that it derives from one of the six predicate offences referred to in points (a)–(e) and (h) of art. 2(1) (participation in an organised criminal group and racketeering, terrorism, trafficking in human beings and migrant smuggling, sexual exploitation, illicit trafficking in narcotic drugs and psychotropic substances, and corruption).[63]

4. *Statutes of Limitation*

Directive 2018/1673/EU does not specify what statute of limitation shall or could apply to money laundering within the Union. It also does not specify whether there shall or could be temporary limits on the predicate offence that would preclude criminal liability for money laundering.

5. *Jurisdictional Rules*

Art. 10(1) Directive 2018/1673/EU requires Member States to establish their criminal jurisdiction over the money laundering offences described above[64] where the offence is committed in whole or in part on their territory (territoriality principle) or when the perpetrator is one of their nationals (active personality principle). Moreover, art. 10(2) Directive 2018/1673/EU authorises Member States to establish their jurisdiction over such offences committed outside their territory where the perpetrator is a habitual resident on their territory or when the offence is committed for the benefit of a legal person established on their territory. In the event of a conflict of jurisdiction, Member States are expected to cooperate in order to decide which of them will prosecute the offender.[65] The following factors shall be taken into account: the territory of the Member State on which the offence was committed, the nationality or residency of the offender, the country of origin of the victim or victims, and the territory on which the offender was found.[66] Where appropriate, and in accordance with art. 12 of

61 Council Framework Decision 2008/841/JHA of 24 October 2008 on the fight against organised crime (OJ L 300, 24.10.2008, p. 42).
62 On art. 2 4AMLD (scope of obliged entities), see *infra* section II.D.
63 See *supra* section II.B.1.a.i.
64 See *supra* section II.B.1.a.ii.
65 Art. 10(3) Directive 2018/1673/EU.
66 *Ibid.*

Framework Decision 2009/948/JHA,[67] Directive 2018/1673/EU requires the matter to be referred to Eurojust.[68]

With respect to property derived from conduct that occurred on the territory of another Member State or of a third country, Member States are required to ensure that the money laundering offences extend to such property where that conduct would have constituted a predicate offence had it occurred domestically.[69] However, with the exception of six specific predicate offences, Member States are allowed to further require that the relevant conduct also constitutes a criminal offence under the national law of the other Member State or of the third country where it was committed.[70] The six specific predicate offences with respect to which the dual incrimination requirement cannot be applied are those listed in points (a)–(e) and (h) of art. 2(1) Directive 2018/1673/EU (participation in an organised criminal group and racketeering, terrorism, human trafficking, sexual exploitation, illicit trafficking in narcotic drugs and psychotropic substances, and corruption).[71]

C. NON-CRIMINAL DEFINITION OF MONEY LAUNDERING

Art. 1(3) 4AMLD provides the definition of money laundering for the purposes of this Directive. In terms of *actus reus* and *mens rea*, this definition is strictly identical to the criminal law definition enshrined in art. 3(1) Directive 2018/1673/EU.[72]

It should be noted, however, that, with respect to property derived from conduct that occurred on the territory of another Member State or of a third country, the money laundering definition provided in the 4AMLD is broader than its criminal law counterpart (art. 3(3)(c) and (4) Directive 2018/1673/EU) in that it extends to such property regardless of whether the dual incrimination requirement is met.[73] In contrast, the 4AMLD in much less extensive than Directive 2018/1673/EU regarding the scope of predicate offences for money laundering. Art. 2(1) Directive 2018/1673/EU indeed refers to 22 categories of offences, within which Member States are required to include a range of

[67] Council Framework Decision 2009/948/JHA of 30 November 2009 on prevention and settlement of conflicts of exercise of jurisdiction in criminal proceedings (OJ L 328, 15.12.2009, p. 42).

[68] Art. 10(3) Directive 2018/1673/EU. See also recital (18) Directive 2018/1673/EU.

[69] Art. 3(3)(c) Directive 2018/1673/EU.

[70] Art. 3(4) Directive 2018/1673/EU.

[71] See *supra* section II.B.1.a.i.

[72] On art. 3(1) Directive 2018/1673/EU, see *supra* section II.B.1.a.ii. In comparison, see art. 3(3)(c) and (4) Directive 2018/1673/EU (*supra* section II.B.5).

[73] Art. 1(4) 4AMLD.

predicate offences,[74] whereas art. 3(4) 4AMLD only refers to six categories, namely terrorism, illicit trafficking in narcotic drugs and psychotropic substances, organised crime, fraud, corruption, and tax offences. It now remains to be seen whether the 4AMLD will be revised with a view to aligning the definition of predicate offences as reflected in this Directive with the wider definition provided in Directive 2018/1673/EU.

D. SCOPE OF OBLIGED ENTITIES

1. *Financial and Banking Institutions*

Pursuant to art. 2(1) and (2) 4AMLD, the Directive is applicable to "credit institutions" and "financial institutions" as defined under EU law.[75]

2. *Virtual Currency System Participants*

Virtual currency system participants did not originally fall within the scope of the 4AMLD. However, it soon became clear that the anonymity of virtual currencies may allow their potential misuse for criminal purposes, in particular terrorist financing.[76] The 5AMLD has thus amended art. 2 4AMLD to add providers engaged in exchange services between virtual currencies[77] and fiat currencies

---

74 See *supra* section II.B.1.a.i.

75 Pursuant to art. 3(1) 4AMLD, "'credit institution' means a credit institution as defined in point (1) of Article 4(1) of Regulation (EU) No 575/201, including branches thereof, as defined in point (17) of Article 4(1) of that Regulation, located in the Union, whether its head office is situated within the Union or in a third country." According to art. 3(2) 4AMLD, "'financial institution' means: (a) an undertaking other than a credit institution, which carries out one or more of the activities listed in points (2) to (12), (14) and (15) of Annex I to Directive 2013/36/EU … including the activities of currency exchange offices (bureaux de change); (b) an insurance undertaking as defined in point (1) of Article 13 of Directive 2009/138/EC … insofar as it carries out life assurance activities covered by that Directive; (c) an investment firm as defined in point (1) of Article 4(1) of Directive 2004/39/EC …; (d) a collective investment undertaking marketing its units or shares; (e) an insurance intermediary as defined in point (5) of Article 2 of Directive 2002/92/EC … where it acts with respect to life insurance and other investment-related services, with the exception of a tied insurance intermediary as defined in point (7) of that Article; (f) branches, when located in the Union, of financial institutions as referred to in points (a) to (e), whether their head office is situated in a Member State or in a third country."

76 European Commission, Proposal for a 5AMLD, Explanatory memorandum, p. 12: "Transactions with virtual currencies benefit from a higher degree of anonymity than classical financial fund transfers and therefore entails a risk that virtual currency may be used by terrorist organisations to conceal financial transfers". See also recital (8) 5AMLD.

77 Pursuant to art. 3(18) 4AMLD as modified by 5AMLD, "'virtual currencies' means a digital representation of value that is not issued or guaranteed by a central bank or a public authority,

(that is to say legal tender that is designated as such, and electronic money, of a particular country, accepted as a medium of exchange in the issuing country) as well as custodial wallet providers[78] to the list of obliged entities, thereby requiring them to apply CDD measures and to report suspicious transactions that may involve money laundering or terrorist financing to FIUs.[79] According to the European Commission, this amendment should strengthen the effectiveness of the EU AML/CTF framework but also reinforce the credibility of virtual currencies, as anonymity will become more an obstacle than an advantage for virtual currencies in further developing their economic potential.[80] It should be noted that the exchange from one virtual currency to another remains outside the scope of the 5AMLD and can therefore still be carried out without any monitoring.[81]

3. *Legal Profession and Tax Advisors*

Pursuant to art. 2(1)(3)(b) 4AMLD, the Directive applies to:

> notaries and other independent legal professionals, where they participate, whether by acting on behalf of and for their client in any financial or real estate transaction, or by assisting in the planning or carrying out of transactions for their client concerning the:
>
> (i) buying and selling of real property or business entities;
> (ii) managing of client money, securities or other assets;
> (iii) opening or management of bank, savings or securities accounts;
> (iv) organisation of contributions necessary for the creation, operation or management of companies;
> (v) creation, operation or management of trusts, companies, foundations, or similar structures.

---

is not necessarily attached to a legally established currency and does not possess a legal status of currency or money, but is accepted by natural or legal persons as a means of exchange and which can be transferred, stored and traded electronically".

78 Pursuant to art. 3(19) 4AMLD as modified by 5AMLD, "'custodian wallet provider' means an entity that provides services to safeguard private cryptographic keys on behalf of its customers, to hold, store and transfer virtual currencies."

79 Art. 2(1)(3)(g) and (h) 4AMLD as modified by 5AMLD.

80 European Commission, Proposal for a 5AMLD, Explanatory memorandum, p. 11.

81 Recital (9) 5AMLD. See also Opinion of the European Central Bank of 12 October 2016 on the proposal for a 5AMLD, para. 1.1.1: "[T]he ECB also mentions that digital currencies do not necessarily have to be exchanged into legally established currencies. They could also be used to purchase goods and services, without requiring an exchange into a legally established currency or the use of a custodial wallet provider. Such transactions would not be covered by any of the control measures provided for in the proposal and could provide a means of financing illegal activities".

The 4AMLD is also applicable to "tax advisors".[82] The 5AMLD specifies that this includes "any other person that undertakes to provide, directly or by means of other persons to which that other person is related, material aid, assistance or advice on tax matters as a principal business or professional activity."[83]

4. *Informal Value Transfer Systems*

All providers of payment services as defined in art. 4(3) *cum* Annex I of Directive 2015/2366/EU[84] should be appropriately registered and regulated. Those providers should seek the status of authorised payment institutions or, under certain conditions, registered payment institutions. *Hawala* and other such informal value transfer services, however, usually qualify as illegal since they are normally not registered and do not comply with the requirements of Directive 2015/2366/EU.

5. *Non-Profit Sector*

The 4AMLD does not explicitly mention non-profit entities in the list of obliged entities. However, non-profit entities can be payment institutions, and thus obliged entities, where they transfer money from the donor to the ultimate beneficiary if the selection of the ultimate beneficiary is done by the donor him- or herself and not left to the transferring non-profit entity. Non-profit entities may furthermore fall under other categories of obliged entities if they fulfil the respective statutory criteria, for example in the case of a credit institution that provides loans and thus banking services to beneficiaries.

6. *Overview of Other Obliged Entities*

In addition to the obliged entities described above, the scope of the 4AMLD extends to "auditors",[85] "external accountants",[86] "trust or company service providers not already covered under [art. 2(1)(3)] point (a) or (b)",[87] "providers

---

82 Art. 2(1)(3)(a) 4AMLD.

83 Art. 2(1)(3)(a) 4AMLD as modified by 5AMLD.

84 Directive 2015/2366/EU of the European Parliament and of the Council of 25 November 2015 on payment services in the internal market, amending Directives 2002/65/EC, 2009/110/EC and 2013/36/EU and Regulation (EU) No 1093/2010, and repealing Directive 2007/64/EC (OJ L 337, 23.12.2015, p. 35).

85 Art. 2(1)(3)(a) 4AMLD.

86 Art. 2(1)(3)(a) 4AMLD.

87 Art. 2(1)(3)(c) 4AMLD. According to art. 3(7) 4AMLD, "'trust or company service provider' means any person that, by way of its business, provides any of the following services to third parties: (a) the formation of companies or other legal persons; (b) acting as, or arranging for

of gambling services"[88] and "persons trading in goods to the extent that payments are made or received in cash in an amount of EUR 10 000 or more, whether the transaction is carried out in a single operation or in several operations which appear to be linked".[89]

The 5AMLD has further broadened the scope of obliged entities to cover "persons trading or acting as intermediaries in the works of art, including when this is carried out by art galleries and auction houses" and "persons storing, trading or acting as intermediaries in the trade of works of art when this is carried out by free ports" where the transaction amounts to €10,000 or more, including where this amount is exceeded upon aggregated several partial payments.[90] The 5AMLD also specifies that the 4AMLD is applicable to estate agents "including when acting as intermediaries in the letting of immovable property, but only in relation to transactions for which the monthly rent amounts to EUR 10 000 or more".[91]

E. RELATIONSHIP BETWEEN AML AND ANTI-TERRORISM FINANCING FRAMEWORK(S)

All the preventive measures laid down in the 4AMLD address money laundering as well terrorist financing. In other words, with respect to the prevention and regulation of money laundering and terrorist financing, the applicable legal regime is the same at EU level. The criminal law approach is, however, provided for by different legal instruments, namely Directive 2017/541/EU on combating terrorism (CTF)[92] and Directive 2018/1673/EU (AML).

---

another person to act as, a director or secretary of a company, a partner of a partnership, or a similar position in relation to other legal persons; (c) providing a registered office, business address, correspondence or administrative address and other related services for a company, a partnership or any other legal person or arrangement; (d) acting as, or arranging for another person to act as, a trustee of an express trust or a similar legal arrangement; (e) acting as, or arranging for another person to act as, a nominee shareholder for another person other than a company listed on a regulated market that is subject to disclosure requirements in accordance with Union law or subject to equivalent international standards".

88 Art. 2(3)(3)(f) 4AMLD. With the exception of casinos, Member States are allowed, however, to remove these providers partially or completely from the list of obliged entities if a low money laundering risk is evidenced (art. 2(2) 4AMLD).

89 Art. 2(1)(3)(e) 4AMLD.

90 Art. 2(1)(3)(i) and (j) 4AMLD as modified by 5AMLD.

91 Art. 2(1)(3)(d) 4AMLD as modified by 5AMLD.

92 Directive 2017/541/EU of the European Parliament and of the Council of 15 March 2017 on combating terrorism and replacing Council Framework Decision 2002/475/JHA and amending Council Decision 2005/671/JHA (OJ L 8, 15.03.1988, p. 6).

III. THE SYSTEM OF MONEY LAUNDERING PREVENTION

A. CUSTOMER DUE DILIGENCE

1. *Standard CDD Rules*

a. Triggers and Timing

Pursuant to art. 11 4AMLD, obliged entities are required to perform CDD measures in the following circumstances:

> (a) when establishing a business relationship;
> (b) when carrying out an occasional transaction that:
>   (i) amounts to EUR 15 000 or more, whether that transaction is carried out in a single operation or in several operations which appear to be linked; or
>   (ii) constitutes a transfer of funds, as defined in point (9) of Article 3 of Regulation (EU) 2015/847 ..., exceeding EUR 1 000;
> (c) in the case of persons trading in goods, when carrying out occasional transactions in cash amounting to EUR 10 000 or more, whether the transaction is carried out in a single operation or in several operations which appear to be linked;
> (d) for providers of gambling services, upon the collection of winnings, the wagering of a stake, or both, when carrying out transactions amounting to EUR 2 000 or more, whether the transaction is carried out in a single operation or in several operations which appear to be linked;
> (e) when there is a suspicion of money laundering or terrorist financing, regardless of any derogation, exemption or threshold;
> (f) when there are doubts about the veracity or adequacy of previously obtained customer identification data.

According to art. 14(5) 4AMLD as modified by 5AMLD, CDD measures shall be applied to: (i) "new customers"; (ii) "existing customers on a risk-sensitive basis [and at appropriate times]"; (iii) "when the relevant circumstances of a customer change"; and (iv) "when the obliged entity has any legal duty [in particular under national law] in the course of the relevant calendar year to contact the customer for the purpose of reviewing any relevant information relating to the beneficial owner(s), or if the obliged entity has had this duty under Council Directive 2011/16/EU [on administrative cooperation in the field of taxation]".

With respect to the timing of verification of the identity of the customer and beneficial owner,[93] the 4AMLD requires this to take place "before the

---

[93] On these CDD measures, see *infra* section III.A.1.b.

establishment of a business relationship or the carrying out of the transaction".[94] However, obliged entities may be allowed to proceed to the verification during the establishment of a business relationship, provided that this takes place as soon as reasonably practicable after initial contact, this is essential not to interrupt the normal conduct of business and the money laundering risk is deemed low.[95] Moreover, it should be noted that Member States may allow the opening of an account with a credit institution or financial institution, including accounts that permit transactions in transferable securities, provided that there are adequate safeguards in place to ensure that transactions are not carried out by the customer or on its behalf until the identity of the customer and the beneficial owner was verified.[96]

b. CDD Measures

According to art. 13(1) 4AMLD as modified by 5AMLD, obliged entities are required to take the following CDD measures for all customers:

> (a) identifying the customer and verifying the customer's identity on the basis of documents, data or information obtained from a reliable and independent source, including, where available, electronic identification means, relevant trust services as set out in Regulation (EU) No 910/2014 [on electronic identification and trust services for electronic transactions in the internal market] or any other secure, remote or electronic identification process regulated, recognised, approved or accepted by the relevant national authorities;
>
> (b) identifying the beneficial owner and taking reasonable measures to verify that person's identity so that the obliged entity is satisfied that it knows who the beneficial owner is, including, as regards legal persons, trusts, companies, foundations and similar legal arrangements, taking reasonable measures to understand the ownership and control structure of the customer. Where the beneficial owner identified is the senior managing official as referred to in Article 3(6)(a)(ii), obliged entities shall take the necessary reasonable measures to verify the identity of the natural person who holds the position of senior managing official and shall keep records of the actions taken as well as any difficulties encountered during the verification process;

---

94 Art. 14(1) 4AMLD. For life or other investment-related insurance business, "the verification of the identity of the beneficiaries shall take place at the time of the payout. In the case of assignment, in whole or in part, of the life or other investment-related insurance to a third party, credit institutions and financial institutions aware of the assignment shall identify the beneficial owner at the time of the assignment to the natural or legal person or legal arrangement receiving for its own benefit the value of the policy assigned" (art. 13(5) 4AMLD). On CDD measures for life or other investment-related insurance business, see *infra* section III.A.1.b.

95 Art. 14(2) 4AMLD.

96 Art. 14(3) 4AMLD.

(c) assessing and, as appropriate, obtaining information on the purpose and intended nature of the business relationship;
(d) conducting ongoing monitoring of the business relationship including scrutiny of transactions undertaken throughout the course of that relationship to ensure that the transactions being conducted are consistent with the obliged entity's knowledge of the customer, the business and risk profile, including where necessary the source of funds and ensuring that the documents, data or information held are kept up-to-date.

For life insurance or other investment-related insurance business, which includes contract-based pension insurance,[97] the 4AMLD requires financial and credit institutions, in addition to the aforementioned CDD measures required for the customer and the beneficial owner, to conduct the following specific CDD measures with respect to the beneficiaries of life insurance and other investment-related insurance policies:

(a) in the case of beneficiaries that are identified as specifically named persons or legal arrangements, taking the name of the person;
(b) in the case of beneficiaries that are designated by characteristics or by class or by other means, obtaining sufficient information concerning those beneficiaries to satisfy the credit institutions or financial institution that it will be able to establish the identity of the beneficiary at the time of the payout.[98]

c. Individual Responsibility

According to art. 46(4) 4AMLD, obliged entities are required, where applicable, to " identify the member of the management board who is responsible for the implementation of the laws, regulations and administrative provisions necessary to comply with this Directive".

d. Further CDD Guidance

The EU AML legal framework does not provide further standard CDD guidance.

2. Simplified CDD

a. Scope

The 4AMLD authorises Member States to allow obliged entities to apply simplified CDD measures in areas of lower risk that are identified by Member

[97] See art. 3(2)(b) 4AMLD *cum* art. 2(3)(a)(ii) Directive 2009/138/EC of the European Parliament and of the Council of 25 November 2009 on the taking-up and pursuit of the business of Insurance and Reinsurance (Solvency II) (OJ L 335, 17.12.2009, p. 1).

States or by the obliged entities' own preliminary risk analysis as long as obliged entities, before applying such simplified measures, always ascertain that the particular business relationship or the transaction does indeed present a lower degree of risk, and that they carry out sufficient monitoring of the transactions and business relationships to enable the detection of unusual or suspicious transactions.[99] However, the 4AMLD does not set out in detail how obliged entities should assess the risk associated with a business relationship or transaction. Annex II of the Directive, in accordance with art. 16(4), nonetheless provides the following non-exhaustive list of factors of potentially lower-risk situations that Member States and obliged entities shall consider when assessing the money laundering risks:

(1) Customer risk factors:
  (a) public companies listed on a stock exchange and subject to disclosure requirements (either by stock exchange rules or through law or enforceable means), which impose requirements to ensure adequate transparency of beneficial ownership;
  (b) public administrations or enterprises;
  (c) customers that are resident in geographical areas of lower risk as set out in point (3);
(2) Product, service, transaction or delivery channel risk factors:
  (a) life insurance policies for which the premium is low;
  (b) insurance policies for pension schemes if there is no early surrender option and the policy cannot be used as collateral;
  (c) a pension, superannuation or similar scheme that provides retirement benefits to employees, where contributions are made by way of deduction from wages, and the scheme rules do not permit the assignment of a member's interest under the scheme;
  (d) financial products or services that provide appropriately defined and limited services to certain types of customers, so as to increase access for financial inclusion purposes;
  (e) products where the risks of money laundering and terrorist financing are managed by other factors such as purse limits or transparency of ownership (e.g. certain types of electronic money);
(3) Geographical risk factors:
  (a) Member States;
  (b) third countries having effective AML/CFT systems;
  (c) third countries identified by credible sources as having a low level of corruption or other criminal activity;
  (d) third countries which, on the basis of credible sources such as mutual evaluations, detailed assessment reports or published follow-up reports, have requirements to combat money laundering and terrorist financing

98 Art. 13(5) 4AMLD.
99 Art. 15 4AMLD.

consistent with the revised FATF Recommendations and effectively implement those requirements.

Pursuant to art. 12(1) 4AMLD as modified by 5AMLD, Member States are also granted the possibility to exempt electronic money products from certain CDD measures[100] under the following cumulative conditions:

(a) the payment instrument is not reloadable, or has a maximum monthly payment transactions limit of EUR 150 which can be used only in that Member State;
(b) the maximum amount stored electronically does not exceed EUR 150;
(c) the payment instrument is used exclusively to purchase goods or services;
(d) the payment instrument cannot be funded with anonymous electronic money;
(e) the issuer carries out sufficient monitoring of the transactions or business relationship to enable the detection of unusual or suspicious transactions.

Member States shall ensure, however, that the aforementioned exemption "is not applicable in the case of redemption in cash or cash withdrawal of the monetary value of the electronic money where the amount redeemed exceeds EUR 50, or in the case of remote payment transactions as defined in point (6) of Article 4 of the Directive (EU) 2015/2366 ... where the amount paid exceeds EUR 50 per transaction".[101] Further, the 5AMLD requires that transactions with anonymous prepaid cards that have been issued outside the EU be restricted to only those issued by countries deemed to be sufficiently compliant with requirements set out in the current EU AML framework.[102]

b. Requirements

According to art. 12(1) 4AMLD as modified by 5AMLD, the CDD measures that obliged entities may be allowed not to apply with respect to electronic money are those set out in points (a), (b) and (c) of art. 13(1) and art. 14.[103]

The 4AMLD does not, however, specify the content of the simplified CDD measures which could be taken by obliged entities in other situations presenting a lower risk of money laundering or terrorist financing.

c. Further Simplified CDD Guidance

As prescribed in arts. 17 and 18(4) 4AMLD, the European Supervisory Authorities (ESAs), namely the European Banking Authority (EBA), the European Securities and Markets Authority (ESMA) and the European Insurance

[100] On these CDD measures, see *infra* section III.A.2.b.
[101] Art. 12(2) 4AMLD as modified by 5AMLD.
[102] Art. 12(3) 4AMLD as modified by 5AMLD.
[103] On the content of these CDD measures, see *supra* section III.A.1.a and b.

and Occupational Pensions Authority (EIOPA), issued guidelines on 26 June 2017 with the aim of promoting the development of a common understanding, by credit and financial institutions across the EU, of what the risk-based approach to AML/CTF entails and how it should be applied.[104] These guidelines set out risk factors credit and financial institutions, as defined in art. 3(1) and (2) 4AMLD,[105] should consider when assessing the risk of money laundering and terrorist financing associated with individual business relationships and occasional transactions.[106] Moreover, these guidelines set out how firms can adjust the extent of their CDD measures in a way that is commensurate to the risk of money laundering and terrorist financing they have identified. In other words, the ESAs' guidelines also provide guidance on simplified CDD measures that credit and financial institutions within the Union could take in low-risk situations, as well as guidance on enhanced CDD measures that such obliged entities should take in high-risk situations.

It would fall outside the ambit of this study to analyse in detail the content of the ESAs' guidelines, in particular the sectoral guidelines on the risk-sensitive application of CDD measures by credit and financial institutions operating in certain specific sectors, namely correspondent banking, retail banking, electronic money issuance, money remittance, wealth management, trade finance business, life insurance business, and investment funds.[107] However, it is deemed appropriate hereafter to provide examples of simplified CDD measures that, according to the ESAs, could potentially be applied in *all* situations where the risk of money laundering and terrorist financing has been assessed as low.

– Adjusting the Timing of CDD

Adjusting the timing of CDD means verifying the customer's or beneficial owner's identity after the establishment of the business relationship or the carrying out of the transaction. In low-risk situations, the ESAs indeed consider that this can be done either "during the establishment of the business relationship" or only "once transactions exceed a defined threshold or once a reasonable time

---

104 ESAs, Joint Guidelines under Articles 17 and 18(4) of Directive (EU) 2015/849 on simplified and enhanced due diligence and the factors credit and financial institutions should consider when assessing the money laundering and terrorist financing risk associated with individual business relationships and occasional transactions, JC 2017 37, 26 June 2017.

105 On the content of art. 3(1) and (2) 4AMLD, see *supra* section II.D.1.

106 See ESAs, Joint Guidelines under Articles 17 and 18(4) of Directive (EU) 2015/849 on simplified and enhanced due diligence and the factors credit and financial institutions should consider when assessing the money laundering and terrorist financing risk associated with individual business relationships and occasional transactions, JC 2017 37, 26 June 2017, paras. 17–33.

107 *Ibid.*, paras. 72–226.

limit has elapsed".[108] Credit and financial institutions must ensure, however, that: (i) "this does not result in a de facto exemption from CDD"; (ii) "the threshold or time limit is set at reasonably low level"; (iii) "they have systems in place to detect when the threshold or time limit has been reached"; and (iv) "they do not defer CDD or delay obtaining relevant information about the customer where applicable legislation ... require[s] that this information be obtained at the outset".[109]

- Adjusting the Quantity of Information Obtained for Identification, Verification or Monitoring Purposes

According to the ESAs' guidelines, credit and financial institutions are also allowed, in low-risk situations, to adjust the quantity of information obtained for identification, verification or monitoring purpose.[110] For example, this can be done by "verifying the identity on the basis of information obtained from [only] one reliable, credible and independent document or data source", or by "assuming the nature and purpose of the business relationship because the product is designed for one particular use only, such as a company pension scheme or a shopping centre gift card".[111]

- Adjusting the Quality or Source of Information Obtained for Identification, Verification or Monitoring Purposes

On the basis of the ESAs' guidelines, credit and financial institutions are allowed, in low-risk situations, not only to adjust the quantity of information obtained for identification, verification or monitoring purposes, but also to adjust the quality or source of this information.[112] For example, "where the funds are state benefit payments or where the funds have been transferred from an account in the customer's name at an [European Economic Area] firm", credit and financial institutions are allowed to only rely upon the source of funds.[113]

- Adjusting the Frequency of CDD Updates and Reviews of the Business Relationship

Adjusting the frequency of CDD updates and reviews of the business relationship is another example of simplified CDD measure which, according to the ESAs, can be taken in low-risk situations. This can entail, for instance,

108 *Ibid.*, para. 45.
109 *Ibid.*
110 *Ibid.*
111 *Ibid.*
112 *Ibid.*
113 *Ibid.*

"carrying [such updates and reviews] out only when trigger events occur such as the customer looking to take out a new product or service or when a certain transaction threshold is reached".[114]

– Adjusting the Frequency and Intensity of Transaction Monitoring

On the basis of the ESAs' guidelines, credit and financial institutions are allowed, in low-risk situations, not only to adjust the frequency of CDD updates and reviews of the business relationship, but also to adjust the frequency and intensity of transaction monitoring, for example "by monitoring transactions above a certain threshold only".[115] However, "[w]here firms choose to do this, they must ensure that the threshold is set at a reasonable level and that they have systems in place to identify linked transactions that, together, would exceed that threshold".[116]

3. *Enhanced CDD*

a. Scope

The 4AMLD requires obliged entities to apply, in addition to standard CDD measures, enhanced CDD measures in cases of higher risks that are identified by Member States or by the obliged entities' own preliminary risk analysis.[117] However, the 4AMLD does not set out in detail how obliged entities should assess the risk associated with a business relationship or transaction. Annex III of the Directive, in accordance with art. 18(3), nonetheless provides the following non-exhaustive list of factors of potentially higher-risk situations that Member States and obliged entities shall consider when assessing the money laundering risks:

(1) Customer risk factors:
   (a) the business relationship is conducted in unusual circumstance;
   (b) customers that are resident in geographical areas of higher risk as set out in point (3);
   (c) legal persons or arrangements that are personal asset-holding vehicles;
   (d) companies that have nominee shareholders or shares in bearer form;
   (e) businesses that are cash-intensive;
   (f) the ownership structure of the company appears unusual or excessively complex given the nature of the company's business;
   (g) customer is a third country national who applies for residence rights or citizenship in the Member State in exchange of capital transfers, purchase of property or government bonds, or investment in corporate entities in that Member State;

---

114 *Ibid.*
115 *Ibid.*
116 *Ibid.*
117 Art. 18(1) 4AMLD.

(2) Product, service, transaction or delivery channel risk factors:
  (a) private banking;
  (b) products or transactions that might favour anonymity;
  (c) non-face-to-face business relationships or transactions, without certain safeguards, such as electronic identification means, relevant trust services as defined in Regulation (EU) No 910/2014 or any other secure, remote or electronic, identification process regulated, recognised, approved or accepted by the relevant national authorities;
  (d) payment received from unknown or unassociated third parties;
  (e) new products and new business practices, including new delivery mechanism, and the use of new or developing technologies for both new and pre-existing products;
  (f) transactions related to oil, arms, precious metals, tobacco products, cultural artefacts and other items of archaeological, historical, cultural and religious importance, or of rare scientific value, as well as ivory and protected species;
(3) Geographical risk factors:
  (a) without prejudice to Article 9, countries identified by credible sources, such as mutual evaluations, detailed assessment reports or published follow-up reports, as not having effective AML/CFT systems;
  (b) countries identified by credible sources as having significant levels of corruption or other criminal activity;
  (c) countries subject to sanctions, embargos or similar measures issued by, for example, the Union or the United Nations;
  (d) countries providing funding or support for terrorist activities, or that have designated terrorist organisations operating within their country.

Pursuant to arts. 18(1) and 18*a*–24 4AMLD as modified by 5AMLD, business relationships and occasional transactions involving high-risk third countries identified as such by the European Commission,[118] business relationships and occasional transactions where the customer or the customer's beneficial owner is a PEP,[119] and cross-border correspondent relationships with a third-country respondent institution, shall always be considered by obliged entities as high-risk situations requiring the application of enhanced CDD measures. According to art. 18(2) 4AMLD as modified by 5AMLD, all complex and unusually large transactions, and all unusual patterns of transactions, which have no apparent economic or lawful purpose, shall also always be treated as high risk.

b. Requirements

The 4AMLD does not include a list of minimum enhanced CDD measures applicable in all high-risk situations in addition to standard CDD measures.

---

118 On the EU list of high-risk third countries, see *infra* section III.A.5.a.

119 On the EU definition of "politically exposed persons", see *infra* section III.A.4.a.

However, the 4AMLD sets out specific enhanced CDD measures with respect to certain high-risk situations, namely: (i) transactions which are either complex or unusually large, as well unusual patterns of transactions, which do not have an apparent economic or lawful purpose; (ii) cross-border correspondent banking with third-country respondent institutions; (iii) business relationships and occasional transactions where the customer and/or the customer's beneficial owner is a PEP; and (iv) business relationships and occasional transactions involving high-risk third-countries identified as such by the European Commission.

With respect to high-risk transactions and patterns of transactions referred to under (i), art. 18(2) 4AMLD as modified by 5AMLD requires obliged entities "to examine, as far as reasonably possible, the background and purpose of [such transactions and patterns of transactions]." Further, obliged entities "shall increase the degree and nature of monitoring of the business relationship, in order to determine whether those transactions or activities appear suspicious."

As regards cross-border correspondent relationships involving the execution of payments with a third-country respondent institution (high-risk situations referred to under (ii)), art. 19 4AMLD as modified by 5AMLD requires obliged entities to apply, in addition to standard CDD measures, the following enhanced CDD measures:

(a) gather sufficient information about the respondent institution to understand fully the nature of the respondent's business and to determine from publicly available information the reputation of the institution and the quality of supervision;
(b) assess the respondent institution's AML/CFT controls;
(c) obtain approval from senior management before establishing new correspondent relationships;
(d) document the respective responsibilities of each institution;
(e) with respect to payable-through accounts, be satisfied that the respondent institution has verified the identity of, and performed ongoing due diligence on, the customers having direct access to accounts of the correspondent institution, and that it is able to provide relevant customer due diligence data to the correspondent institution, upon request.

The specific enhanced CDD measures required by the 4AMLD with respect to high-risk situations referred to under (iii) and (iv) will be presented at a later stage.[120]

c. Further Enhanced CDD Guidance

As seen earlier, the ESAs issued in 2017, in accordance with arts. 17 and 18(4) 4AMLD, joint guidelines on simplified and enhanced CDD measures and

---

120 See *infra* sections III.A.4.b (business relationships and occasional transactions involving PEPs) and III.A.5.b (business relationships and occasional transactions involving high-risk third countries identified as such by the European Commission).

the factors credit and financial institutions should consider when assessing the money laundering and terrorist financing risk associated with individual business relationships and occasional transactions.[121]

In particular, these guidelines provide guidance on how enhanced CDD measures set out in art. 18(2) 4AMLD (enhanced CDD measures applicable to all complex and unusually large transactions, and all unusual patterns of transactions, which have no apparent economic or lawful purpose) and art. 19 4AMLD (enhanced CDD measures applicable to cross-border correspondent relationships with third-country respondent institutions) could be applied. For example, paragraph 57 provides that credit and financial institutions could understand the background and purpose of complex and unusually large transactions, and all unusual patterns of transactions, which have no apparent economic or lawful purpose by "establishing the source and destination of the funds or finding out more about the customer's business to ascertain the likelihood of the customer making such transactions". Another example is that of paragraph 92, according to which, in the context of a cross-border correspondent relationship with a third-country respondent institution, the determination of the reputation of the institution and the quality of supervision could be based upon publicly available information, such as FATF and Financial Sector Assessment Programme assessments.

As will be seen later, the ESAs' guidelines also provide guidance on the enhanced CDD measures credit and financial institutions should take where the customer, or the customer's beneficial owner, is a PEP, or where they deal with high-risk third countries.[122]

4. *Rules on Politically Exposed Persons*

a. Definition

Art. 3(9) 4AMLD defines "politically exposed persons" as follows:

> [A] natural person who is or has been entrusted with prominent public functions and includes the following:
>
> (a) heads of State, heads of government, ministers and deputy or assistant ministers;
> (b) members of parliament or of similar legislative bodies;

---

[121] ESAs, Joint Guidelines under Articles 17 and 18(4) of Directive (EU) 2015/849 on simplified and enhanced due diligence and the factors credit and financial institutions should consider when assessing the money laundering and terrorist financing risk associated with individual business relationships and occasional transactions, JC 2017 37, 26 June 2017. See *supra* section III.A.2.c.

[122] See *infra* sections III.A.4.c (business relationships and occasional transactions involving PEPs) and III.A.5.c (business relationships and occasional transactions involving high-risk third countries identified as such by the European Commission).

(c) members of the governing bodies of political parties;
(d) members of supreme courts, of constitutional courts or of other high-level judicial bodies, the decisions of which are not subject to further appeal, except in exceptional circumstances;
(e) members of courts of auditors or of the boards of central banks;
(f) ambassadors, chargés d'affaires and high-ranking officers in the armed forces;
(g) members of the administrative, management or supervisory bodies of State-owned enterprises;
(h) directors, deputy directors and members of the board or equivalent function of an international organisation.

This definition, which does not cover middle-ranking or more junior individuals,[123] shall be specified by Member States. According to art. 20a(1) 4AMLD as modified by 5AMLD, each Member State shall indeed "issue and keep up to date a list indicating the exact functions which, according to national laws, regulations and administrative provisions, qualify as prominent public functions". Moreover, "Member States shall request each international organisation accredited on their territories to issue and keep up to date a list of prominent public functions at that international organisation".[124]

b. Requirements

The 4AMLD sets out specific enhanced CDD measures that obliged entities shall take vis-à-vis PEPs.[125] Art. 20 requires obliged entities to:

(a) have in place appropriate risk management systems, including risk-based procedures, to determine whether the customer or the beneficial owner of the customer is a politically exposed person;
(b) apply the following measures in case of business relationships with PEPs:
    (i) obtain senior management approval for establishing or continuing business relationships with such persons;[126]
    (ii) take adequate measures to establish the source of wealth and source of funds that are involved in business relationships or transactions with such persons;
    (iii) conduct enhanced, ongoing monitoring of those business relationship.

---

123 Art. 3(9) 4AMLD.

124 Art. 20a(1) 4AMLD as modified by 5AMLD.

125 According to Recital (33) 4AMLD, enhanced CDD measures relating to PEPs "should not be interpreted as stigmatising politically exposed persons as being involved in criminal activity. Refusing a business relationship with a person simply on the basis of the determination that he or she is a politically exposed person is contrary to the letter and spirit of this Directive and of the revised FATF Recommendations".

126 According to recital (34), "[o]btaining approval from senior management for establishing business relationships does not need to imply, in all cases, obtaining approval from the board of directors. It should be possible for such approval to be granted by someone with sufficient knowledge of the institution's money laundering and terrorist financing risk exposure and of sufficient seniority to take decisions affecting its risk exposure".

The aforementioned enhanced CDD measures shall also be applied to "family members"[127] and "persons known to be close associates"[128] of PEPs. Obliged entities shall also monitor the risk posed when a person ceases to hold the position yielding PEP status for a period of at least 12 months.[129]

c. Further Enhanced CDD Guidance on PEPs

The ESAs' joint guidelines of 26 June 2017 provide details on how to apply some of the specific enhanced CDD measures set out in art. 20 4AMLD that obliged entities shall take where the customer, or the customer's beneficial owner, is a PEP.

First, credit and financial institutions should verify the source of wealth and source of funds that are involved in business relationships or transactions with PEPs "on the basis of reliable and independent data, documents or information where the risk associated with the PEP relationship is particularly high".[130] Second, with respect to the requirement that senior management approval must be obtained for entering into, or continuing, a business relationship with a PEP, the ESAs consider that "[t]he appropriate level of seniority for sign-off should be determined by the level of increased risk associated with the business relationship, and [that] the senior manager approving a PEP business relationship should have sufficient seniority and oversight to take informed decisions on issues that directly impact the firm's risk profile."[131]

5. *Rules on High-Risk Third Countries*

a. Scope

Following the mandate given by art. 9 4AMLD, the European Commission is empowered to identify, through the adoption of delegated acts subject to the conditions laid down in art. 64 of that Directive, third-country jurisdictions with strategic deficiencies in their national AML/CFT regimes that pose significant

---

127 The 4AMLD defines "family members" as follows: "(a) the spouse, or a person considered to be equivalent to a spouse, of a politically exposed person; (b) the children and their spouses, or persons considered to be equivalent to a spouse, of a politically exposed person; (c) the parents of a politically exposed person" (art. 3(10)).

128 The 4AMLD defines "persons known to be close associates" as follows: "(a) natural persons who are known to have joint beneficial ownership of legal entities or legal arrangements, or any other close business relations, with a politically exposed person; (b) natural persons who have sole beneficial ownership of a legal entity or legal arrangement which is known to have been set up for the de facto benefit of a politically exposed person" (art. 3(11)).

129 Art. 22 4AMLD.

130 ESAs, Joint Guidelines under Articles 17 and 18(4) of Directive (EU) 2015/849 on simplified and enhanced due diligence and the factors credit and financial institutions should consider when assessing the money laundering and terrorist financing risk associated with individual business relationships and occasional transactions, JC 2017 37, 26 June 2017, para. 52.

131 *Ibid.*

threats to the financial system of the Union ("high-risk third countries"). The Commission is assisted in the preparation of delegated acts by the Expert Group on Anti-Money Laundering and Countering Terrorist Financing (EGMLTF).[132]

The European Commission adopted the first such act on 14 July 2016 (Delegated Regulation (EU) 2016/1675)[133] and has regularly updated it since then to put the EU list of high-risk third countries in line with the FATF list.[134] According to recital (6) of Delegated Regulation (EU) 2016/1675, the Commission indeed deems it "of the highest importance that the list of third countries laid down at Union level is closely aligned, as appropriate, with those lists agreed internationally". At the time of writing, the EU list of high-risk third countries is aligned with the FATF list as updated in June 2018,[135] and consists of the following categories and countries:

- *high-risk third countries which have provided a written high-level political commitment to address the identified deficiencies and have developed an action plan with the FATF:* Ethiopia, Pakistan, Serbia, Sri Lanka, Syria, Trinidad and Tobago, Tunisia and Yemen;
- *high-risk third countries which have provided a written high-level political commitment to address the identified deficiencies and have decided to seek technical assistance in the implementation of the FATF Action Plan, which are identified by FATF Public Statement:* Iran; and
- *high-risk third countries which present ongoing and substantial money-laundering and terrorist-financing risks, having repeatedly failed to address the identified deficiencies and which are identified by FATF Public Statement:* Democratic People's Republic of Korea.

---

132 EGMLTF is a Commission expert group composed of representatives of high administrative level responsible for anti-money laundering in national administrations of the EU Member States and the European Economic Area. More information is available at: http://ec.europa.eu/transparency/regexpert/index.cfm?do=groupDetail.groupDetail&groupID=2914.

133 Commission Delegated Regulation (EU) 2016/1675 of 14 July 2016 supplementing Directive (EU) 2015/849 of the European Parliament and of the Council by identifying high-risk third countries with strategic deficiencies (OJ L 254, 20.09.2016, pp. 1–4).

134 Commission Delegated Regulation (EU) 2018/105 of 27 October 2017 amending Delegated Regulation (EU) 2016/1675, as regards adding Ethiopia to the list of high-risk third countries in the table in point I of the Annex (OJ L 19, 24.01.2018, pp. 1–2); Commission Delegated Regulation (EU) 2018/212 of 13 December 2017 amending Delegated Regulation (EU) 2016/1675 supplementing Directive (EU) 2015/849 of the European Parliament and of the Council, as regards adding Sri Lanka, Trinidad and Tobago, and Tunisia to the table in point I of the Annex (OJ L 41, 14.02.2018, pp. 4–5); Commission Delegated Regulation (EU) 2018/1467 of 27 July 2018 amending Delegated Regulation (EU) 2016/1675 supplementing Directive (EU) 2015/849 of the European Parliament and of the Council, as regards adding Pakistan to the table in point I of the Annex (OJ L 246, 02.10.2018, p. 1).

135 See the "Public Statement" (http://www.fatf-gafi.org/publications/high-risk-and-other-monitored-jurisdictions/documents/public-statement-june-2018.html) and the "Improving Global AML/CFT Compliance: On-going Process" Statement (http://www.fatf-gafi.org/

b. Requirements

Before being modified by the 5AMLD, the 4AMLD did not specify the nature of enhanced CDD measures that obliged entities shall take with respect to business relationships and financial transactions involving high-risk third countries identified as such by the European Commission.[136] Each Member State could therefore determine at national level the type of enhanced CDD measures to be taken with regard to high-risk third countries. However, this has caused several disparities in the application of enhanced CDD measures across the EU and created weak spots where terrorists or criminal groups could potentially transfer or retrieve illicit funds more easily.[137] The 5AMLD thus aimed to provide a solution to these regulatory discrepancies by requiring obliged entities to apply a minimum set of predefined enhanced CDD requirements when dealing with high-risk third countries as identified by the Commission.[138] This formalised approach aims to lessen differences in the application of regulatory requirements between obliged entities, harmonising these measures at EU level.

Pursuant to art. 18a(1) 4AMLD as modified by 5AMLD, obliged entities shall apply all of the following enhanced CDD measures with respect to business relationships and transactions involving high-risk third countries identified as such by the Commission:

(a) obtaining additional information on the customer and on the beneficial owner(s);
(b) obtaining additional information on the intended nature of the business relationship;
(c) obtaining information on the source of funds and source of wealth of the customer and of the beneficial owner(s);
(d) obtaining information on the reasons for the intended or performed transactions;

---

publications/high-risk-and-other-monitored-jurisdictions/documents/fatf-compliance-june-2018.html) issued after the FATF Plenary meeting which took place on 24–29 June 2018.

136 See *supra* section III.A.5.a.

137 See recital (12) 5AMLD and Proposal for a 5AMLD, Impact Assessment, para. 2.1.3.

138 It should be noted that the 5AMLD also provides an illustrative list of counter-measures that Member States shall apply, where applicable, with regard to listed high-risk third countries. According to art. 18a 4AMLD as modified by 5AMLD, those measures shall consist of one or more of the following: "(a) refusing the establishment of subsidiaries or branches or representative offices of obliged entities from the country concerned, or otherwise taking into account the fact that the relevant obliged entity is from a country that does not have adequate AML/CFT regimes; (b) prohibiting obliged entities from establishing branches or representative offices in the country concerned, or otherwise taking into account the fact that the relevant branch or representative office would be in a country that does not have adequate AML/CFT regimes; (c) requiring increased supervisory examination or increased external audit requirements for branches and subsidiaries of obliged entities located in the country concerned; (d) requiring increased external audit requirements for financial groups with respect to any of their branches and subsidiaries located in the country concerned; (e) requiring credit and financial institutions to review and amend, or if necessary terminate, correspondent relationships with respondent institutions in the country concerned."

(e) obtaining the approval of senior management for establishing or continuing the business relationship; [and]
(f) conducting enhanced monitoring of the business relationship by increasing the number and timing of controls applied, and selecting patterns of transactions that need further examination.

In addition to these measures, obliged entities are required to apply one or several of the following additional risk mitigating measures to persons and legal entities carrying out transactions involving high-risk third countries as identified by the Commission:

(a) the application of additional elements of enhanced due diligence;
(b) the introduction of enhanced relevant reporting mechanisms or systematic reporting of financial transactions;
(c) the limitation of business relationships or transactions with natural persons or legal entities from the third countries identified as high risk countries [by the European Commission].[139]

c. Further Enhanced CDD Guidance on High-Risk Third Countries

The ESAs' joint guidelines of 26 June 2017 provide guidance on what could entail some the specific enhanced CDD measures set out in art. 18a 4AMLD as modified by 5AMLD that obliged entities shall take with respect to all business relationships and transactions involving high-risk third countries identified as such by the European Commission.

– Increasing the Quantity of Information about the Customer or Beneficial Owner's Identity, or the Customer's Ownership and Control Structure

According to the ESAs, increasing the quantity of information about the customer or beneficial owner's identity, or the customer's ownership and control structure, "may include obtaining and assessing information about the customer's or beneficial owner's reputation and assessing any negative allegations against the customer or beneficial owner".[140] The following examples are provided: "a. information about family members and close business partners; b. information about the customer's or beneficial owner's past and present business activities; and c. adverse media searches".[141]

---

139 Art. 18a(2) 4AMLD as modified by 5AMLD.

140 ESAs, Joint Guidelines under Arts. 17 and 18(4) of Directive 2015/849/EU on simplified and enhanced due diligence and the factors credit and financial institutions should consider when assessing the money laundering and terrorist financing risk associated with individual business relationships and occasional transactions, JC 2017 37, 26 June 2017, para. 60.

141 *Ibid.*

- Increasing the Quantity of Information about the Intended Nature of the Business Relationship

According to the ESAs, increasing the quantity of information about the intended nature of the business relationship may include obtaining information on "a. the number, size and frequency of transactions that are likely to pass through the account, to enable the firm to spot deviations that might give rise to suspicion (in some cases, requesting evidence may be appropriate); b. why the customer is looking for a specific product or service, in particular where it is unclear why the customer's needs cannot be met better in another way, or in a different jurisdiction; c. the destination of funds; d. the nature of the customer's or beneficial owner's business, to enable the firm to better understand the likely nature of the business relationship".[142]

- Obtaining Additional Information on the Source of Funds and Source of Wealth of the Customer and the Beneficial Owner

The ESAs' guidelines also provide guidance on how to further verify the source of funds and source of wealth of the customer and the beneficial owner. According to the three ESAs, this can be done, *inter alia*, "by reference to VAT and income tax returns, copies of audited accounts, pay slips, public deeds or independent media reports".[143]

6. *Private Sector CDD Guidance*

The 4AMLD does not refer to any private sector standards that would provide further guidance for the exercise of CDD within the whole European Union.

B. PRELIMINARY RISK ANALYSIS

According to art. 8(1) 4AMLD, obliged entities shall "take appropriate steps to identify and assess the risks of money laundering and terrorist financing, taking into account risk factors including those relating to their customers, countries or geographic areas, products, services, transactions or delivery channels."[144] This preliminary risk analysis, which "shall be proportionate to the nature and

---

142 *Ibid.*

143 *Ibid.*

144 According to art. 8(2) 4AMLD, "[t]he risk assessments referred to in paragraph 1 shall be documented, kept up-to-date and made available to the relevant competent authorities and self-regulatory bodies concerned. Competent authorities may decide that individual documented risk assessments are not required where the specific risks inherent in the sector are clear and understood."

size" of the obliged entity,[145] is meant to tailor the particular entity's subsequent CDD to its individual risk exposure. The risk analysis can notably define triggers for the performance of simplified and enhanced CDD measures.[146]

C. REPORTING AND ASSET FREEZING

1. *First-Time Reporting*

a. Trigger for/Degree of Suspicion

Pursuant to art. 33(1)(a) 4AMLD, an obliged entity is required to file a suspicious activity report (SAR) whenever it "knows, suspects or has reasonable grounds to suspect that funds are the proceeds of criminal activity or are related to terrorist financing".[147] All suspicious transactions, including attempted transactions, shall be reported.[148]

b. Content and Direct Addressee(s) of SARs

Obliged entities are required to report their suspicions to the FIU.[149] However, in the case of estate agents, Member States have the possibility to designate an appropriate self-regulatory body as the authority to receive the SARs.[150]

c. Duty not to Disclose

Pursuant to art. 39(1) 4AMLD, "obliged entities and their directors and employees shall not disclose to the customer concerned or to other third persons

---

145 Art. 8(1) 4AMLD.

146 See *supra* section III.A.2.a and III.A.3.a.

147 The term "criminal activity" means "any kind of criminal involvement in the commission of the following serious crimes: (a) terrorist offences, offences related to a terrorist group and offences related to terrorist activities as set out in Titles II and III of Directive (EU) 2017/541; (b) any of the offences referred in Article 3(1)(a) of the 1988 United Nations Convention against Illicit Traffic in Narcotic Drugs and Psychotropic Substances; (c) the activities of criminal organisations as defined in Article 1(1) of Council Framework Decision 2008/841/JHA; (d) fraud affecting the Union's financial interests, where it is at least serious, as defined in Article 1(1) and Article 2(1) of the Convention on the protection of the European Communities' financial interests; (e) corruption; (f) all offences, including tax crimes relating to direct taxes and indirect taxes and as defined in the national law of the Member States, which are punishable by deprivation of liberty or a detention order for a maximum of more than one year or, as regards Member States that have a minimum threshold for offences in their legal system, all offences punishable by deprivation of liberty or a detention order for a minimum of more than six months" (art. 3(4) 4AMLD as modified by 5AMLD).

148 Art. 33(1) *in fine* 4AMLD.

149 Art. 33(1)(a) 4AMLD.

150 Art. 34(1) 4AMLD.

the fact that information is being [or] will be ... transmitted [to the FIU] ... or that a money laundering or terrorist financing analysis is being, or may be, carried out".

d. Power or Duty to Freeze

Pursuant to art. 35(1) 4AMLD, obliged entities are required "to refrain from carrying out transactions which they know or suspect to be related to proceeds of criminal activity or to terrorist financing until they have [reported these transactions to the FIU] ... and have complied with any further specific instructions from the FIU or the competent authorities in accordance with the law of the relevant Member State". Obliged entities are therefore required, before carrying out reported transactions, to at least briefly wait in order to give the FIU the opportunity to give instructions.[151] However, "[w]here refraining from carrying out transactions ... is impossible or is likely to frustrate efforts to pursue the beneficiaries of a suspected operation, the obliged entities concerned shall inform the FIU immediately afterwards".[152]

e. Instant Collateral Duties

The 4AMLD does not further specify whether obliged entities are under any collateral obligations when filing a SAR (e.g. further monitoring of the client's business activities).

2. Follow-Up

a. Duty to Provide FIU with Additional Data

According to art. 33(1)(a) 4AMLD, obliged entities which have transmitted a SAR to the FIU shall "promptly respond to requests by the FIU for additional information".

b. Continued Duty not to Disclose SAR to Client

Under the 4AMLD, obliged entities shall not disclose to the customer concerned the fact that a SAR "has been" made to the FIU.[153] Considering that there is nothing in the Directive implying that this obligation would be subject to a temporal limit, one can therefore conclude that there is a continued duty on the

---

151 See also art. 32(7) 4AMLD.
152 Art. 35(2) 4AMLD.
153 Art. 39(1) 4AMLD.

part of the reporting obliged entity not to disclose to the client the filing of a SAR, even if it has not led to a discovery of illegal conduct.

c. Continued Collateral Duties

The 4AMLD does not specify to what extent there is a continued duty on the part of the reporting obliged entity not to disclose to the client the filing of the SAR, even if it has not led to a discovery of illegal conduct.

3. Special Rules for Privileged Professions

a. Trigger for/Degree of Suspicion

As seen earlier,[154] notaries and other independent legal professionals are deemed obliged entities under the 4AMLD "where they participate, whether by acting on behalf of and for their client in any financial or real estate transaction, or by assisting in the planning or carrying out of transactions for their client concerning the: (i) buying and selling of real property or business entities; (ii) managing of client money, securities or other assets; (iii) opening or management of bank, savings or securities accounts; (iv) organisation of contributions necessary for the creation, operation or management of companies; (v) creation, operation or management of trusts, companies, foundations, or similar structures".[155]

Art. 34(2) 4AMLD provides, however, an exception with respect to the reporting requirement enshrined in art. 33(1)(a) 4AMLD. According to this provision, notaries and other independent legal professionals, such as lawyers, are not subject to the obligation to report in so far as they are bound in their activities by professional secrecy, that is when the matter "relates to information that they receive from, or obtain on, one of their clients, in the course of ascertaining the legal position of their client, or performing their task of defending or representing that client in, or concerning, judicial proceedings, including providing advice on instituting or avoiding such proceedings, whether such information is received or obtained before, during or after such proceedings."[156] This exemption from the reporting obligation also applies to tax advisors, external accountants and auditors.[157]

---

154 See *supra* section II.D.3.

155 Art. 2(1)(3)(b) 4AMLD.

156 In its report on the assessment of the risks of money laundering and terrorist financing affecting the internal market and relating to cross-border activities published in June 2017, the European Commission noted that this exemption from the reporting obligation is often abused by legal professionals (European Commission, *Report on the assessment of the risks of money laundering and terrorist financing affecting the internal market and relating to cross-border activities*, 26 June 2017, COM(2017) 340 final, para. 2.1.5.).

157 Art. 34(2) 4AMLD.

b. Content and Addressee(s) of SARs

In principle, notaries and other independent legal professionals, as well as auditors, external accountants and tax advisors, are required to submit their SARs directly to the FIU.[158] However, according to art. 34(1) 4AMLD, Member States may allow them to send their SARs to their appropriate self-regulatory bodies, which will then have to forward the information to the FIU promptly and unfiltered.[159]

c. Duty not to Disclose to Client

In principle, the 4AMLD does not exempt notaries and other independent legal professionals, as well as auditors, external accountants and tax advisors, from the non-disclosure obligation.[160] However, according to art. 39(6) of that Directive, where they "seek to dissuade a client from engaging in illegal activity, that shall not constitute disclosure". This exception thereby goes beyond dissuasion from money laundering, its predicate offences and terrorist financing, and extends to cases where privileged professionals try to dissuade their clients from other illegal acts, including acts that are merely unlawful and not criminal.

4. *Protection of SAR's Source*

According to recital (41) 4AMLD, "[t]here have been a number of cases where employees who have reported their suspicions of money laundering have been subjected to threats or hostile action". As a result, Member States are required to "ensure that individuals, including employees and representatives of the obliged entity who report suspicions of money laundering or terrorist financing internally or to the FIU, are legally protected from being exposed to threats, retaliatory or hostile action, and in particular from adverse or discriminatory employment actions".[161] Moreover, Member States "shall ensure that individuals who are exposed to threats, retaliatory or hostile actions, or adverse or discriminatory employment actions for reporting suspicions of money laundering or terrorist financing internally or to the FIU are entitled to present a complaint in a safe manner to the respective competent authorities".[162]

---

158 Art. 33(1)(a) 4AMLD.

159 Art. 34(1) 4AMLD.

160 Art. 39(1) 4AMLD.

161 Art. 38(1) 4AMLD as modified by 5AMLD. See also art. 61(3) 4AMLD as modified by 5AMLD.

162 Art. 38(2) 4AMLD as modified by 5AMLD. See also art. 61(3) 4AMLD as modified by 5AMLD.

D. RECORD KEEPING

Obliged entities are required to keep records of transactions and information obtained through the performance of CDD measures for a period of five years after the end of a business relationship or occasional transaction.[163] Upon expiry of the retention period, obliged entities shall delete personal data, unless otherwise provided for by national law, which shall determine under which circumstances obliged entities may or shall further retain data.[164]

E. COMPLIANCE OFFICERS

According to art. 8(4)(a) 4AMLD, obliged entities are required to appoint a compliance officer at management level, when deemed appropriate with regard to the size and nature of the business.[165] The compliance officer shall be responsible for transmitting SARs to the FIU and answer requests for additional information from the latter.[166]

F. INTERNAL COMPLAINT MECHANISM

Art. 61(3) 4AMLD as modified by 5AMLD requires obliged entities "to have in place appropriate procedures for their employees, or persons in a comparable position, to report breaches internally through a specific, independent and anonymous channel, proportionate to the nature and size of the obliged entity concerned".

G. ADDITIONAL PREVENTIVE MEASURES

In order to mitigate and manage effectively the risks of money laundering, obliged entities are required to have in place programmes against money laundering.[167]

---

163 Art. 40(1) 4AMLD. One should note, however, that art. 40(1)(a) 4AMLD allows Member States to extend the retention period for up to an additional five years if deemed necessary for the purposes of prevention, detection or investigation of money laundering and terrorist financing, and after carrying out an assessment of the necessity and proportionality.

164 Art. 40(1) 4AMLD.

165 See also art. 46(4) 4AMLD: "Member States shall require that, where applicable, obliged entities identify the member of the management board who is responsible for the implementation of the laws, regulations and administrative provisions necessary to comply with this Directive".

166 Art. 33(2) 4AMLD.

167 The 4AMLD provides specific requirements regarding financial groups' programmes against money laundering (see art. 45).

These programmes shall include: (i) "the development of internal policies, controls and procedures, including model risk management practices";[168] (ii) "employee screening";[169] (iii) "an independent audit function to test" the system;[170] and (iv) "special ongoing training programmes to help [employees] recognize operations which may be related to money laundering or terrorist financing and to instruct them as to how to proceed in such cases".[171]

H. RULES ON OBLIGED ENTITIES' CIVIL LIABILITY TOWARDS CLIENT

According to art. 37 4AMLD:

> [d]isclosure of information in good faith by an obliged entity or by an employee or director of such an obliged entity in accordance with Articles 33 and 34 [filing of SARs and provision of additional data to the FIU] shall not constitute a breach of any restriction on disclosure of information imposed by contract or by any legislative, regulatory or administrative provision, and shall not involve the obliged entity or its directors or employees in liability of any kind even in circumstances where they were not precisely aware of the underlying criminal activity and regardless of whether illegal activity actually occurred.

I. SUPERVISORY AUTHORITIES' ROLE

1. *Supervisory Measures to Ensure Application of CDD and Other AML-Related Obligations*

In order to ensure the effective application of AML-related obligations by obliged entities, the 4AMLD requires Member States to ensure that competent authorities have the responsibility for regulating and monitoring, on the basis of a risk-based approach,[172] obliged entities' compliance with AML requirements.[173] With respect to notaries and other independent legal professionals, as well as auditors, external accountants and tax advisors, Member States may, under certain conditions, confer the supervisory responsibilities to self-regulated bodies.[174]

---

168 Art. 8(4) 4AMLD.
169 *Ibid.*
170 *Ibid.*
171 Art. 46(1) 4AMLD.
172 See art. 48(6), (7) and (8) 4AMLD.
173 See arts. 47 et 48 4AMLD as modified by 5AMLD.
174 See art. 48(9) 4AMLD.

According to art. 48(2) 4AMLD as modified by 5AMLD:

> Member States shall ensure that the competent authorities have adequate powers, including the power to compel the production of any information that is relevant to monitoring compliance and perform checks, and have adequate financial, human and technical resources to perform their functions. Member States shall ensure that staff of those authorities are of high integrity and appropriately skilled, and maintain high professional standards, including standards of confidentiality, data protection and standards addressing conflicts of interest.

According to art. 47(1) 4AMLD as modified by 5AMLD, "Member States shall ensure that providers of exchange services between virtual currencies and fiat currencies, and custodian wallet providers, are registered, that currency exchange and cheque cashing offices, and trust or company service providers are licensed or registered, and that providers of gambling services are regulated." Additionally, "Member States shall require competent authorities to ensure that the persons who hold a management function in [these entities] ... or are the beneficial owners of such entities, are fit and proper persons".[175] Finally, with respect to auditors, external accountants, tax advisors, notaries, other independent legal professionals and estate agents, "Member States shall ensure that competent authorities take the necessary measures to prevent criminals convicted in relevant areas or their associates from holding a management function in or being the beneficial owners of those obliged entities".[176]

In addition to the aforementioned rules laid down in the 4AMLD, it is also worth addressing supervisory measures to ensure application of AML-related obligations from the perspective of recent prudential regulatory developments, in particular the adoption of the CRD 5. This Directive provides more details on the assessment of the internal controls and risk management systems during the authorisation process. It also introduces an explicit power to remove members of the management board in case of concerns related to their suitability, including from an AML/CTF perspective. Moreover, the Directive mentions explicitly the AML/CTF dimension in the context of the supervisory review and evaluation process, requiring competent authorities to take necessary measures using the tools and powers at their disposal should money laundering/terrorist financing concerns be significant from a prudential perspective. There is also an obligation for competent authorities to notify the European Banking Authority and the authority responsible for anti-money laundering supervision where they identify weaknesses in the governance model, business activities or business model, which give reasonable grounds to suspect money laundering or terrorist financing. Complaint Mechanism.

175 Art. 47(2) 4AMLD.
176 Art. 47(3) 4AMLD.

2. *Complaint Mechanism*

Pursuant to art. 61(1) 4AMLD as modified by 5AMLD, Member States shall ensure that competent authorities, as well as, where applicable, self-regulatory bodies, have in place effective and reliable mechanisms to encourage the reporting of AML-related violations within obliged entities. These mechanisms shall include secure communication channels to ensure that the identity of the reporting person is known only to the competent authorities, as well as, where applicable, self-regulatory bodies.[177] These mechanisms shall also include:

(a) specific procedures for the receipt of reports on breaches and their follow-up;
(b) appropriate protection for employees or persons in a comparable position, of obliged entities who report breaches committed within the obliged entity;
(c) appropriate protection for the accused person;
(d) protection of personal data concerning both the person who reports the breaches and the natural person who is allegedly responsible for a breach, in compliance with the principles laid down in [Regulation (EU) 2016/679 and Directive 2016/680/EU];
(e) clear rules that ensure that confidentiality is guaranteed in all cases in relation to the person who reports the breaches committed within the obliged entity, unless disclosure is required by national law in the context of further investigations or subsequent judicial proceedings.[178]

J. STATISTICS ON SARs BY OBLIGED ENTITIES

The only statistics on SARs available at EU level at the moment are those provided by Europol in its report "From suspicion to action: Converting financial intelligence into greater operation impact", published in September 2017.[179] In this report, Europol provides detailed figures on various aspects of SAR reporting across the 28 Member States for the period 2006–2014, thereby offering a recent and unique pan-European perspective of the reporting regime. The most relevant SAR-related statistics contained in this report are mentioned in what follows.

The number of SARs filed across the EU has steadily increased since 2006. In 2014, EU FIUs received a total of 960,463 SARs, representing an increase of almost 70% compared to 2006 (see Figure 1 below). However, it should be pointed out that 67% of all reporting in the EU between 2006 and 2014 is accounted for by just two Member States, the United Kingdom and the Netherlands (see Table 1 below). According to Europol, the high number of

---

177 Art. 61(1) 4AMLD as modified by 5AMLD.
178 Art. 61(2) 4AMLD.
179 https://www.europol.europa.eu/publications-documents/suspicion-to-action-converting-financial-intelligence-greater-operational-impact.

SARs received by the Dutch FIU can be explained by the fact that the Dutch FIU does not receive SARs, but rather unusual transaction reports (UTRs), which are based on objective indicators with little analysis conducted by obliged entities, hence the high number.[180] As regards the high reporting volume in the UK, Europol considers that it is due to the fact that the UK is home to one of the largest financial markets in Europe and that it operates a suspicious activity regime which broadens the types of reports the FIU can receive.[181]

Figure 1. Total annual SARs across all Member States 2006–2014

Source: Europol, "From suspicion to action: Converting financial intelligence into greater operation impact", 2017, p. 9.

Table 1. Total SARs across all Member States 2006–2014

Member State	SAR reporting volume (2006–2014)	Percentage of total
UK	2,329,609	36
NL	2,026,299	31
IT	310,228	5
LV	269,871	4
PL	228,868	4
FI	197,980	3
FR	188,570	3
BE	165,899	3
IE	120,971	2
DE	117,217	2
EE	100,509	2
SE	88,060	1

(continued)

180 Report, pp. 9–10.
181 Report, p. 10.

Table 1 *continued*

Member State	SAR reporting volume (2006–2014)	Percentage of total
HU	80,744	1
LU	40,382	< 1
RO	30,833	< 1
ES	28,046	< 1
DK	28,141	< 1
EL	27,442	< 1
SK	25,290	< 1
PT	23,741	< 1
CZ	22,033	< 1
AT	13,827	< 1
BG	11,505	< 1
HR	11,332	< 1
CY	4,197	< 1
SI	3,003	< 1
LT	2,127	< 1
MT	940	< 1

Source: Europol, "From suspicion to action: Converting financial intelligence into greater operation impact", 2017, p. 10.

As shown in Figure 2 below,[182] banks and credit institutions were overwhelmingly the most frequent reporting entities within the financial sector in the EU for the period 2013–2014. Money transfer services, such as money remitters and money service businesses, also account for a significant proportion of SARs filed with EU FIUs. As regards the non-financial sector, three categories of obliged entities report most frequently to the FIUs: the gambling industry, public notaries and accountants (see Figure 3 below).[183] In contrast, certain sectors are noted for their low levels of reporting, in particular gold dealers, trustees and fiduciaries, real estate agents, and insurance brokers.

Another interesting outcome of the Europol study is that the use of cash (deposits, withdrawals and cash transactions) remains the primary reason prompting obliged entities to report suspicions (see Figure 4 below).[184] By comparison, 20% of FIUs cited suspicious transaction patterns as the main reason behind reporting. Furthermore, two categories, namely "economic background of the account user" and "unusual behavior", were cited by 15% of FIUs as the main reason triggering reporting.

---

182 Figure 2 represents the proportion of FIUs citing the obliged entities within the financial sector as the most frequent reporting entities in 2013/2014.

183 Figure 3 represents the proportion of FIUs citing the obliged entities within the non-financial sector as the most frequent reporting entities in 2013/2014.

184 Figure 4 is based on total weighed results of FIUs' responses for the years 2013–2014.

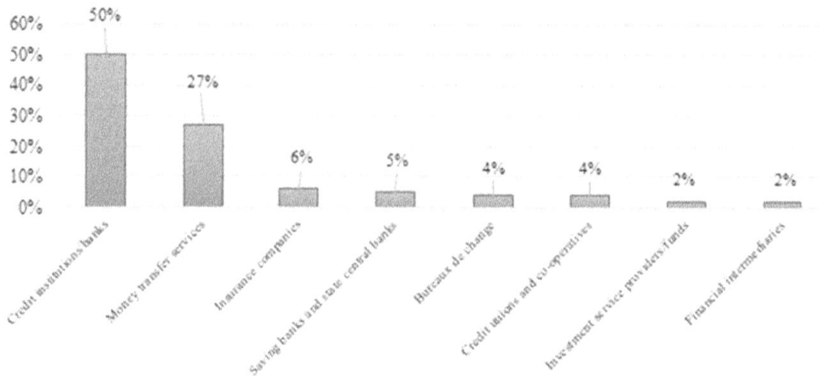

Figure 2. Most frequent reporting entities 2013/2014 (financial sector)

Source: Europol, "From suspicion to action: Converting financial intelligence into greater operation impact", 2017, p. 15.

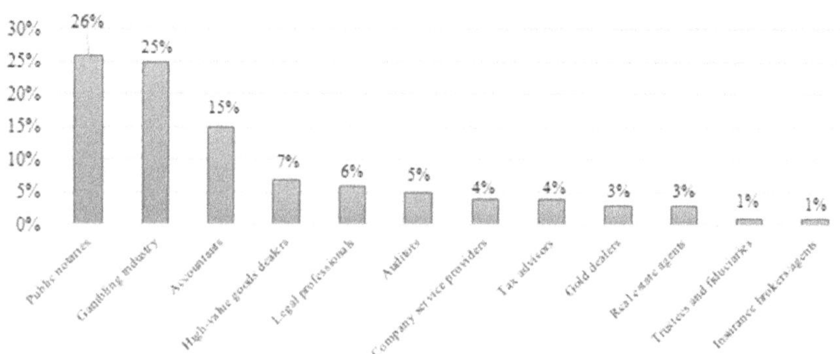

Figure 3. Most frequent reporting entities 2013/2014 (designated non-financial sector)

Source: Europol, "From suspicion to action: Converting financial intelligence into greater operation impact", 2017, p. 15.

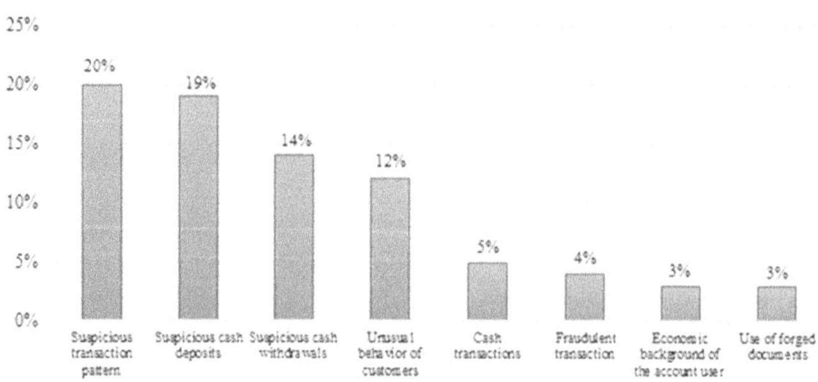

Figure 4. Main reasons behind reporting 2013/2014

Source: Europol, "From suspicion to action: Converting financial intelligence into greater operation impact", 2017, p. 22.

IV. THE SYSTEM OF FINANCIAL INTELLIGENCE UNITS

A. INSTITUTIONAL AND FUNCTIONAL CHARACTERISTICS

1. *Organisational Position*

The EU AML framework does not require FIUs to be of any particular type. That means that Member States are free to establish their FIU in the institutional context of their choice, notably within police authorities, administrative authorities (such as supervisory authorities), or even within the intelligence community.

2. *Purpose and Tasks*

According to art. 32(1) 4AMLD, "[e]ach Member State shall establish an FIU in order to prevent, detect and effectively combat money laundering and terrorist financing". Under the Directive, the FIU shall carry out the three following core functions:

(i) serve as "the central unit … responsible for *receiving* … suspicious transaction reports and other information relevant to money laundering, associated predicate offences or terrorist financing";[185]
(ii) *analyse* the information received and, if necessary, obtain additional information from obliged entities and other sources in order to perform its analysis properly, namely to establish links between suspicious transactions and underlying criminal activity;[186] and
(iii) *disseminate* the results of its analysis and any additional relevant information to the relevant competent authorities, notably investigative and prosecuting authorities,[187] where there are grounds to suspect money laundering, associated predicate offences or financing of terrorism.[188]

3. *Independence*

Pursuant to art. 32(3) 4AMLD, FIUs shall be "operationally independent and autonomous, which means that the FIU shall have the authority and capacity

185 Art. 32(3) 4AMLD.
186 Art. 32(3) and (4) 4AMLD.
187 Recital (44) 5AMLD.
188 Art. 32(3) 4AMLD.

to carry out its functions freely, including the ability to take autonomous decisions to analyze, request and disseminate specific information".

4. *Powers*

- Power to Suspend or Withhold Consent to a Suspicious Transaction that is Proceeding

According to art. 32(7) 4AMLD, FIUs shall be "empowered to take urgent action, directly or indirectly, where there is a suspicion that a transaction is related to money laundering or terrorist financing, to suspend or withhold consent to a transaction that is proceeding, in order to analyse the transaction, confirm the suspicion and disseminate the results of the analysis to the competent authorities". Additionally, FIUs shall be "empowered to take such action, directly or indirectly, at the request of an FIU from another Member State for the periods and under the conditions specified in the national law of the FIU receiving the request".[189]

- Power to Obtain Additional Information from Obliged Entities

According to art. 32(3) 4AMLD, FIUs shall be able "to obtain additional information from obliged entities" in the context of their analysis function provided, however, that information requests are based on sufficiently defined conditions and thereby do not amount to fishing expeditions.[190] The 5AMLD has clarified the fact that FIUs "shall be able to request, obtain and use additional information from *any* obliged entity ... even if no prior [SAR] is filed".[191] This clarification was deemed necessary as certain Member States have chosen to limit the power of their FIU to request and obtain additional information from obliged entities by the requirement that a prior SAR has first been made by an obliged entity.[192] Yet, as underlined in recital (17) 5AMLD, "the need for FIUs to obtain additional information from obliged entities based on a suspicion of money laundering or financing of terrorism might be triggered by a prior SAR reported to the FIU, but might also be triggered through other means such as the FIU's own analysis, intelligence provided by competent authorities or information held by another FIU." Granting FIUs the power to request and obtain additional information regardless of whether a SAR has previously been filed by a reporting entity therefore seems necessary for them to perform their analysis function properly.

---

189 Art. 32(7) 4AMLD.
190 Recital (17) 5AMLD.
191 Art 32(9) 4AMLD as modified by 5AMLD.
192 See European Commission, Proposal for a 5AMLD, Explanatory memorandum, p. 14.

The 5AMLD also suppressed the word "indirectly" from art. 33(1)(b) 4AMLD[193] to ensure that FIUs always have direct access to information held by obliged entities and cannot therefore be required to rely upon a third party (e.g. the prosecutor or judicial authority) to obtain this information.[194] According to the Commission, such indirect access would indeed increase the delay for the FIU in accessing information from obliged entities, which is "particularly problematic where an FIU needs to rapidly access information in view of taking a decision for suspending/withholding consent for processing a transaction".[195]

– Power to Access Beneficial Ownership Information

According to art. 30(6) 4AMLD as modified by 5AMLD, FIUs shall be able to access in a timely manner beneficial ownership information held by legal entities incorporated within their territory, on the one hand, and by legal arrangements administered in their territory, on the other hand.[196] Moreover, Member States shall ensure that the information held in the central beneficial ownership register[197] is accessible in all cases to FIUs, without any restriction.[198]

– Power to Access Information from Other Domestic Sources

According to art. 32(4) 4AMLD, FIUs shall have access, "directly or indirectly [and] in a timely manner, to the financial, administrative and law enforcement information that they require to fulfil their tasks properly".[199]

B. TREATMENT OF SARs

1. *Data Processing*

Pursuant to art. 32(8) 4AMLD, SARs and other information relevant to money laundering, associate predicate offences and terrorist financing – such as information shared by foreign counterparts[200] or by supervisory authorities referred to in art. 48 of that Directive and entities in charge of overseeing the

193 According to art. 33(1)(b) 4AMLD, obliged entities are required to provide the FIU "directly or indirectly, at its request, with all necessary information, in accordance with the procedures established by the applicable law".

194 See European Commission, Proposal for a 5AMLD, Impact assessment, para. 2.4.2.

195 *Ibid.*

196 Art. 30(2) and 31(3) 4AMLD.

197 See *infra* section VI.B.1.

198 Art. 30(5)(a) and 31(4)(a) 4AMLD as modified by 5AMLD.

199 For further details on the information held by public authorities that FIUs shall have access to, see *infra* section IV.D.2.

200 See art. 53(1) 4AMLD.

stock, foreign exchange and financial derivatives markets[201] – shall be used by the FIU to perform both operational and strategic analysis. "focuses on individual cases and specific targets or on appropriate selected information, depending on the type and volume of the disclosures received and the expected use of the information after dissemination".[202] As this wording shows, the Directive does not provide a very specific definition of operational analysis, leaving it to Member States to define the shape of this function under national law. The purpose of the strategic analysis is to address money laundering trends and patterns.[203] According to art. 32(4) 4AMLD, the decision on conducting an analysis, whether strategic and/or operational, shall remain within the FIU. Accordingly, the decision on whether a report of suspected money laundering or terrorist financing is analysed in the first place is taken autonomously by the FIU.

Under the 4AMLD, "[t]he FIU shall be responsible for disseminating the results of its analyses and any additional relevant information to the competent authorities where there are grounds to suspect money laundering, associated predicate offences or terrorist financing".[204] In these specific circumstances, FIUs are therefore authorised to disseminate information to competent authorities, notably investigative and prosecuting authorities.[205] The 4AMLD does not, however, indicate whether FIUs are also obliged to do so.

2. *Special Procedures for Privileged Professions*

In principle, notaries and other independent legal professionals, as well as auditors, external accountants and tax advisors, are required to submit their SARs directly to the FIU.[206] However, according to art. 34(1) 4AMLD, Member States may allow them to send their SARs to their appropriate self-regulatory bodies, which will then have to forward the information to the FIU promptly and unfiltered.[207]

3. *Feedback Obligations*

a. Obligation of the FIU

The 4AMLD does not provide for an explicit feedback obligation on the part of the FIU. During the 2017 European Commission's assessment of the risks

201 See art. 36 4AMLD.
202 Art. 32(8)(a) 4AMLD.
203 Art. 32(8) 4AMLD.
204 Art. 32(3) 4AMLD.
205 Recital (44) 5AMLD.
206 Art. 33(1)(a) 4AMLD.
207 Art. 34(1) 4AMLD.

of money laundering and terrorist financing affecting the internal market and relating to cross-border activities, "all obliged entities have stressed the need for proper feedback mechanisms from FIUs".[208] According to art. 46(3) 4AMLD, "Member States shall ensure that, where practicable, timely feedback on the effectiveness of and follow-up to reports of suspected money laundering or terrorist financing is provided to obliged entities". The 4AMLD does not specify, however, the authority or authorities which shall provide this feedback.

b. Obligation of Investigative Authorities

Under the 4AMLD, "competent authorities" are required to "provide feedback to the FIU about the use made of the information provided … and about the outcome of the investigations or inspections performed on the basis of that information".[209] Pursuant to recital (44) 5AMLD, "authorities that have the function of investigating or prosecuting money laundering, associated predicate offences and terrorist financing" fall within the definition of "competent authorities".

4. Disclosure Obligations Towards "Suspect"

EU law does not foresee direct contact between the FIU and obliged entities' clients even though it provides for the FIU's power to suspend or withhold consent to a transaction.[210]

C. PROACTIVE INVESTIGATIONS

As seen earlier, EU FIUs shall now be able to request and obtain additional information from any obliged entity, regardless of whether a SAR has previously been filed.[211] In other words, since the adoption of the 5AMLD, Member States are no longer authorised to limit the power of their FIU to request additional information from obliged entities by the requirement that a SAR has previously been made.[212] As a result, FIUs within the Union can no longer be understood as State agencies whose sole duty would be the analysis of SARs. EU FIUs can also initiate an investigation in the absence of a SAR on the basis, for example, of information received from a foreign counterpart, or information reported

208 European Commission, *Report on the assessment of the risks of money laundering and terrorist financing affecting the internal market and relating to cross-border activities*, 26 June 2017, COM(2017) 340 final, para. 2.2.5.

209 Art. 32(6) 4AMLD.

210 Art. 32(7) 4AMLD. See *supra* section IV.A.4.

211 See *supra* section IV.A.4.

212 *Ibid.*

by the media, and, in the context of this investigation, request and obtain additional information from obliged entities.

D. ACCESS TO DATA

1. *Design and Content of FIU's Own Data Banks*

The 4AMLD only requires FIUs to record SARs.[213] The 4AMLD does not, however, specify what kind of other information FIUs shall or could register in their own databases, and in particular to what extent information received from other public authorities or private entities should or could be permanently registered and thereby made available to the FIU. Equally, the 4AMLD does not specify that the FIUs' databases should contain particular content or use a particular method.

2. *Access to Other Public Data Banks*

According to art. 32(4) 4AMLD, FIUs shall "have access, directly or indirectly, in a timely manner, to the financial, administrative and law enforcement information that they require to fulfil their tasks properly". However, no indication is provided as to what specific sources of information qualify, respectively, as "financial", "administrative" and "law enforcement".[214]

Before being modified by the 5AMLD, the 4AMLD did not require Member States to set up an automated central mechanism at national level to provide competent authorities, including FIUs, with direct access to information on the identity of holders of bank and payment accounts as well as beneficial owners. The 4AMLD only encouraged the creation of such mechanisms but did not make it mandatory for Member States.[215] However, since the adoption of the 5AMLD and the introduction of new art. 32a into the 4AMLD, Member States are now required to put in place, by 10 September 2020, "centralised automated mechanisms, such as central registries or central electronic data retrieval systems, which allow the identification, in a timely manner, of any natural

---

213 Art. 33(1)(a) 4AMLD.

214 In this context, one should, however, point out a particular type of disclosure foreseen as mandatory for Member States by Regulation (EC) 1889/2005 on controls of cash entering or leaving the Union. Under art. 3 of this Regulation, "any natural person entering or leaving the Community and carrying cash of a value of EUR 10 000 or more shall declare that sum to the competent authorities of the Member State through which he is entering or leaving the Community". According to art. 5(1), such declarations shall be "made available" to the FIU of that Member State.

215 See recital (57) 4AMLD.

or legal persons holding or controlling payment accounts and bank accounts identified by IBAN … and safe deposit boxes held by a credit institution within their territory".[216] The information held in the centralised mechanisms shall be "directly accessible in an immediate and unfiltered manner to national FIUs"[217] and shall include at least the following:

- for the customer-account holder and any person purporting to act on behalf of the customer: the name, complemented by either the other identification data required under the national provisions transposing point (a) of Article 13(1) [identification and verification of the customer's identity] or a unique identification number;
- for the beneficial owner of the customer-account holder: the name, complemented by either the other identification data required under the national provisions transposing point (b) of Article 13(1) [identification and verification of the beneficial owner's identity] or a unique identification number;
- for the bank or payment account: the IBAN number and the date of account opening and closing;
- for the safe-deposit box: name of the lessee complemented by either the other identification data required under the national provisions transposing Article 13(1) [CDD measures] or a unique identification number and the duration of the lease period.[218]

According to the European Commission, central automated mechanisms are necessary for the timely identification by FIUs of all the bank and payment accounts held by a person suspected of money laundering in view of a rapid and efficient detection of criminal financial flows at both national and international level.[219] Without such mechanisms, FIUs wanting to obtain a list of the bank and payment accounts belonging to one person would indeed need to "formulate a

216 Art. 32a(1) 4AMLD as modified by 5AMLD.

217 Art. 32a(2) 4AMLD as modified by 5AMLD. In contrast, pursuant to the same provision, the information held in the centralised bank account registries shall only be "accessible" to other national authorities competent for the prevention of money laundering, terrorist financing and associated predicate offences. One should note, however, that, according to art. 4(1) Directive 2019/1153/EU, the information held in the centralised bank account registries shall now be rendered "directly and immediately" accessible to all Member States' designated competent authorities "when necessary for the performance of their tasks for the purpose of preventing, detecting, investigating or prosecuting a serious criminal offence or supporting a criminal investigation concerning a serious criminal offence, including the identification, tracing and freezing of the assets related to such investigation".

218 Art. 32a(3) 4AMLD as modified by 5AMLD. Member States may include other information they deem necessary for preventing money laundering and terrorist financing (art. 32a(4) 4AMLD as modified by 5AMLD).

219 See recital (20) 5AMLD. See also EU FIU's Platform, *Mapping exercise and gap analysis on FIUs powers and obstacles for obtaining and exchanging information*, 15 December 2016, pp. 88–91, http://ec.europa.eu/transparency/regexpert/index.cfm?do=groupDetail.groupDetailDoc&id=33583&no=2.

'blanket request' to all credit and payment institutions in their country [which is] time consuming".[220]

3. *Access to Private Data Banks*

According to art. 32(4) 4AMLD, "Member States shall ensure that their FIUs have access, directly or indirectly, in a timely manner, to the financial … information that they require to fulfil their tasks properly". However, the Directive does not specify which private data banks exactly the FIU shall have access to and under what conditions.

4. *Data Analytics*

Neither the 4AMLD nor the 5AMLD indicate whether FIUs are required or authorised to conduct data mining in or between their own data banks, in particular to automatically process the content of these data banks in order to identify possible suspects.

However, Directive 2016/680/EU,[221] which applies to the processing of data by FIUs by virtue of art. 1(1) *cum* art. 3(7)(a),[222] provides that FIUs' decisions "based solely on automated processing, including profiling, which produce an adverse legal effect concerning the data subject or significantly affects him or her, [shall] be prohibited unless authorised by Union or Member State law to which the [FIU] is subject and which provides appropriate safeguards for the rights and freedoms of the data subject, at least the right to obtain human intervention on the part of the controller."[223] The Directive also provides that, where authorised, such FIU decisions "shall not be based on special categories of personal data referred to in Article 10 [personal data revealing racial or ethnic origin, political

---

220 European Commission, Proposal for a 5AMLD, Impact Assessment, para. 2.5.2. According to the European Commission, sending blanket requests also "creates unnecessary cost" and may be "from a cost and administrative perspective – simply not a feasible option". Furthermore, it may result "in the dissemination of personal data in a non-targeted way to financial institutions, which can create problems from a data protection and fundamental rights perspective" (European Commission, Proposal for a 5AMLD, Impact Assessment, para. 2.5.2).

221 Directive 2016/680/EU of the European Parliament and of the Council of 27 April 2016 on the protection of natural persons with regard to the processing of personal data by competent authorities for the purposes of the prevention, investigation, detection or prosecution of criminal offences or the execution of criminal penalties, and on the free movement of such data, and repealing Council Framework Decision 2008/977/JHA (OJ L 119, 04.05.2016, p. 89).

222 FIUs indeed qualify as public authorities competent for the prevention, detection and, to a certain extent, investigation, of criminal offences. Yet, considering that FIUs are not criminal justice authorities per se and are not placed, in most cases, under judicial supervision, one may argue that the processing of data by FIUs is not subject to Directive 2016/680/EU but rather to Regulation (EU) 2016/679 (so-called "General Data Protection Regulation").

223 Art. 11(1) Directive 2016/680/EU.

opinions, religious or philosophical beliefs, or trade union membership, … genetic data, biometric data for the purpose of uniquely identifying a natural person, data concerning health or data concerning a natural person's sex life or sexual orientation], unless suitable measures to safeguard the data subject's rights and freedoms and legitimate interests are in place",[224] and that profiling resulting in discrimination against natural persons on the basis of these special categories of personal data shall be prohibited in any case.[225]

5. *International Cooperation*

Pursuant to art. 53(1) 4AMLD as modified by 5AMLD, FIUs shall be able to request from their EU counterparts "any information that may be relevant for the processing or analysis of information … related to money laundering or terrorist financing and the natural or legal person involved, regardless of the type of associated predicate offences and even if the type of predicate offences is not identified at the time of exchange". The use of the decentralised computer network FIU.net[226] for the exchange of information between EU FIUs is encouraged but not mandatory.[227]

E. PARTICIPATION OF "SUSPECTS"

Neither the 4AMLD nor the 5AMLD provide for administrative or judicial remedies against the FIU's action, but they do not exclude it neither.

F. SIMILAR POWERS OF SUPERVISORY BODIES

The 4AMLD does not indicate whether the supervisory bodies referred to in art. 48 of the Directive are required, or at least entitled, to investigate a suspicion of money laundering on their own. Moreover, the 4AMLD does not address parallel proceedings whereby the FIU's operational analysis and supervisory authorities' investigations in possible breaches of AML-related obligations by obliged entities might potentially overlap.

---

224 Art. 11(2) Directive 2016/680/EU.

225 Art. 11(3) Directive 2016/680/EU.

226 FIU.net is a decentralised platform that connects all the EU FIUs and allows them to exchange information between themselves in a secure way. FIU.net, which was established in 2007 and embedded in EUROPOL in 2016 is quite a sophisticated and technologically advanced computer network. It is not just a channel of communication as financial information can be retrieved on the platform and integrated directly in FIUs' national databases. FIU.net also permits multilateral operational cooperation. The exchanges can vary from a minimal approach (such as 'known/unknown requests' to check whether individual's names are found in another EU Member State's database) to a 'case file' giving further details and justification to obtain information from the other FIUs.

227 Recital (56) and art. 56(1) 4AMLD.

G. REPORTING OBLIGATIONS OF SUPERVISORY AUTHORITIES

Under the 4AMLD, supervisory authorities referred to in art. 48 of that Directive shall promptly inform the FIU of any fact that could be related to money laundering or to terrorist financing they discover when performing checks on the obliged entities.[228]

H. REPORTING BY OTHER AUTHORITIES

In addition to obliged entities as defined in art. 2(1) 4AMLD and supervisory authorities referred to in art. 48 4AMLD, "supervisory bodies empowered by law or regulation to oversee the stock, foreign exchange and financial derivative markets [shall] inform the FIU if they discover facts that could be related to money laundering or terrorist financing".[229]

I. STATISTICS

1. *Number of Reports by Supervisory Authorities and Other Authorities*

The EU does not provide statistics on the number of reports about suspicious activities filed by supervisory authorities and other authorities.

2. *FIU Analysis*

The EU does not provide statistics on either the number of FIU investigations in the Union or the value of transactions associated with these investigations.

3. *Communications to Law Enforcement Authorities*

In its report "From suspicion to action: Converting financial intelligence into greater operational impact",[230] Europol provides the best available picture of the conversion rate at EU level (see Figure 5 below). On average, just over 10% of the SARs submitted to EU FIUs were forwarded to law enforcement authorities between 2006 and 2014. According to Europol, the fact that the conversion rate is higher in 2013 and 2014 "is entirely the result of outlier figures reported by the Italian FIU, which reports a conversion rate for these years in excess of 100%".[231]

---

228 Art. 36(1) 4AMLD.

229 Art. 36(2) 4AMLD.

230 https://www.europol.europa.eu/sites/default/files/documents/ql-01-17-932-en-c_pf_final.pdf.

231 *Ibid.*, pp. 29–30.

Without the figures reported by the Italian FIU, the conversion rate for the other Member States remains at 10%.

Figure 5. Conversion rate across all Member States 2006–2014[232]

Source: Europol, "From suspicion to action: Converting financial intelligence into greater operation impact", 2017, p. 30.

V. DATA FLOW AND DATA PROTECTION

A. DATA EXCHANGE BETWEEN FIU AND PRIVATE SECTOR

1. *From FIU to Private Sector*

Neither the 4AMLD nor the 5AMLD give the FIU the power to share its data with the private sector. Art. 33(1)(b) 4AMLD as modified by 5AMLD does give the FIU the power to directly request all the necessary information from obliged entities in accordance with the procedures established by the applicable law. Nothing in the Directive, however, indicates that this request should allow the FIU to communicate more information than is strictly necessary for specifying the scope of its request.

2. *From Private Sector to FIU*

According to art. 32(4) 4AMLD, FIUs shall "have access, directly or indirectly, in a timely manner, to the financial … information that they require to fulfil their tasks properly". FIUs' requests to obliged entities for additional information shall comply with the requirements set out in Directive 2016/680/EU.[233] As regards the decision of obliged entities to share information with the FIU,

232 *Ibid.*, p. 30.

233 See art. 1(1) *cum* art. 3(7)(a) Directive 2016/680/EU.

notably following a request for additional information, or in the context of a SAR,[234] obliged entities have to respect the additional requirements set out in Regulation (EU) 2016/679.[235]

B. DATA EXCHANGE BETWEEN FIU AND CRIMINAL JUSTICE SYSTEM

1. *From FIU to Criminal Justice System*

Where there are grounds to suspect money laundering, associated predicate offences or terrorist financing, FIUs are responsible, under the 4AMLD, for disseminating the results of their analyses and any additional relevant information to the competent authorities,[236] including "authorities that have the function of investigating or prosecuting money laundering, associated predicate offences and terrorist financing".[237] The information that shall be disseminated does not include all the information that has been received by the FIU through the initial disclosures or obtained in the course of its analysis, but only the "results of its analysis" and "specific information".[238] The 4AMLD, however, does not further specify what information is covered by the aforementioned power. It should therefore be recalled that the additional limits provided by Directive 2016/680/EU apply, in particular the principles relating to the processing of personal data set out in art. 4(1).[239]

---

234 One could argue, however, that the reporting obligation is a delegation of public power and would therefore fall within the scope of Directive 2016/680/EU. This would notably mean that different proportionality requirements would apply. In particular, art. 5(1)(c) Regulation (EU) 2016/679 provides that personal data shall be "adequate, relevant and limited to what is necessary in relation to the purposes for which they are processed ('data minimisation')", while art. 4(1)(c) Directive 2016/680/EU provides that personal data shall be "adequate, relevant and not excessive in relation to the purposes for which they are processed".

235 Regulation (EU) 2016/679 of the European Parliament and of the Council of 27 April 2016 on the protection of natural persons with regard to the processing of personal data and on the free movement of such data, and repealing Directive 95/46/EC (OJ L 119, 04.05.2016, p. 1).

236 Art. 32(3) 4AMLD. See *supra* section IV.B.1.

237 Recital (44) 5AMLD.

238 Art. 32(3) 4AMLD.

239 Art. 4(1) Directive 2016/680/EU: "1. Member States shall provide for personal data to be: (a) processed lawfully and fairly; (b) collected for specified, explicit and legitimate purposes and not processed in a manner that is incompatible with those purposes; (c) adequate, relevant and not excessive in relation to the purposes for which they are processed; (d) accurate and, where necessary, kept up to date; every reasonable step must be taken to ensure that personal data that are inaccurate, having regard to the purposes for which they are processed, are erased or rectified without delay; (e) kept in a form which permits identification of data subjects for no longer than is necessary for the purposes for which they are processed; (f) processed in a manner that ensures appropriate security of the personal data, including protection against unauthorised or unlawful processing and against accidental loss, destruction or damage, using appropriate technical or organisational measures."

Pursuant to art. 32(4) 4AMLD *cum* recital (44) 5AMLD, the FIU shall also be able to respond to information requests from criminal justice authorities provided that such requests are "motivated by concerns relating to money laundering, associated predicate offences or terrorist financing". One should note, however, that, according to art. 7(1) Directive 2019/1153/EU, law enforcement authorities shall now be given the possibility to request information from the FIU for the wider purpose of fighting serious crime, rather than being limited to money laundering and terrorist financing. More precisely, FIUs shall "be able to reply, in a timely manner, to reasoned requests for financial information or financial analysis by those designated competent authorities in their respective Member State, where that financial information or financial analysis is necessary on a case-by-case basis and where the request is motivated by concerns relating to the prevention, detection, investigation or prosecution of serious criminal offences".

Dissemination upon request shall never be mandatory for the FIU. In particular, "[w]here there are objective grounds for assuming that the provision of such information would have a negative impact on ongoing investigations or analyses, or, in exceptional circumstances, where disclosure of the information would be clearly disproportionate to the legitimate interest of a natural or legal person or irrelevant with regard to the purposes for which it has been requested, the FIU shall be under no obligation to comply with the request for information".[240] Finally, to the extent that the data was initially collected by the FIU for a different purpose than the one for which the data will be processed by the criminal justice authorities, such transfer of data shall be permitted in so far as the "processing is necessary and proportionate to that other purpose in accordance with Union or Member State law."[241]

2. *From Criminal Justice System to FIU*

The 4AMLD requires Member States to ensure that the FIU has access on a timely basis to law enforcement information.[242] However, access shall only be permitted for the purpose of performing the analysis function properly.[243] In addition, to the extent that the data was initially collected for a different purpose, such transfer of data shall be permitted in so far as the processing by the FIU is necessary and proportionate to the purpose it pursues.[244]

240 Art. 32(5) 4AMLD.
241 Art. 4(2)(b) Directive 2016/680/EU.
242 Art. 32(4) 4AMLD.
243 *Ibid.*
244 Art. 4(2)(b) Directive 2016/680/EU.

C. DATA EXCHANGE BETWEEN FIU AND INTELLIGENCE AGENCIES

The EU has no jurisdiction in matters of national security, which includes legislation on information sharing involving intelligence agencies.[245] In any case, the 4AMLD does not exclude the possibility of national legislators regulating the sharing of information between intelligence agencies and FIUs. In fact, in light of FIUs' function to gather information about events prior to the establishment of a suspicion within the meaning of criminal procedural law, it is clear that FIU operational and strategic analyses are likely to frequently overlap with inquiries by intelligence services, thereby potentially triggering an interest in cooperation between the two sides.

D. DATA EXCHANGE BETWEEN FIU AND TAX AUTHORITIES

1. *From FIU to Tax Authorities*

Where tax authorities qualify as competent authorities in the sense of recital (44) 5AMLD, that is when they investigate tax offences, the transfer of data from the FIU to the tax authorities is regulated by the same rules as those referred to above applying to the transfer of data from the FIU to the criminal justice authorities.[246]

However, where tax authorities carry out purely administrative functions (e.g. processing of tax declarations), neither the 4AMLD nor Directive 2016/680/EU explicitly address this issue. This does not mean that information sharing is not permitted. However, in light of the purpose of Directive 2016/680/EU of harmonising a common level of data protection standards for criminal justice data throughout all the Member States, it seems at least plausible that the purpose limitation principle enshrined in art. 4(2) of this Directive explicitly excludes the sharing of information with authorities acting outside art. 1(1). Indeed, otherwise cross-border information sharing between criminal justice authorities could be hampered if data they provided to counterparts with other Member States could further be shared with purely administrative authorities.

2. *From Tax Authorities to FIU*

The EU legal framework does not explicitly set out data protection restrictions regarding the transfer of personal data from the tax authorities to the FIU.

---

245 Art. 4(2) *in fine* Treaty on European Union.

246 See *supra* section V.B.1.

The regulation of this question is therefore left to the discretion of Member States. However, it should be noted that, when the FIU processes the information received from the tax authorities, the requirements set out in art. 4(1) Directive 2016/680/EU, referred to above,[247] apply.

E. DATA EXCHANGE BETWEEN FIU AND CUSTOMS AUTHORITIES

1. *From FIU to Customs Authorities*

Where custom authorities qualify as competent authorities in the sense of recital (44) 5AMLD, that is when they investigate custom-related offences, the transfer of data from the FIU to the custom authorities is regulated by the same rules as those referred to above applying to the transfer of data from the FIU to the criminal justice authorities.[248]

However, where custom authorities carry out purely administrative functions (e.g. processing of tax declarations), neither the 4AMLD nor Directive 2016/680/EU explicitly address this issue. This does not mean that information sharing is not permitted. However, in light of the purpose of Directive 2016/680/EU of harmonising a common level of data protection standards regarding criminal justice data throughout all Member States, it seems at least plausible that the purpose limitation principle enshrined in art. 4(2) of this Directive explicitly excludes the sharing of information with authorities acting outside art. 1(1). Indeed, otherwise cross-border information sharing between criminal justice authorities could be hampered if data they provided to counterparts with other Member States could further be shared with purely administrative authorities.

2. *From Customs Authorities to FIU*

The EU legal framework does not explicitly set out data protection restrictions regarding the transfer of personal data from the custom authorities to the FIU. The regulation of this question is therefore left to the discretion of Member States. However, it should be noted that, when the FIU processes the information received from the custom authorities, the requirements set out in art. 4(1) Directive 2016/680/EU, referred to above,[249] apply.

---

247 *Ibid.*
248 See *supra* section V.B.1.
249 *Ibid.*

F. INFORMATION FLOW BETWEEN FIU AND FOREIGN COUNTERPARTS[250]

1. *Restrictions on Data Transfer from FIU to Foreign FIUs*

Under the 4AMLD, Member States shall ensure that FIUs exchange information with EU counterparts.[251] To this end, "the FIU to whom the request is made is required to use the whole range of its available powers which it would normally use domestically for receiving and analysing information when it replies to a request for information …] from another FIU".[252] Information exchange can be done upon request from a foreign FIU seeking information, or spontaneously whenever the providing FIU believes that information available to it can be of use to a counterpart.[253]

The fact that the type of predicate offences that may be involved is not identified at the time of the exchange shall be without prejudice to the exchange of information.[254] However, this provision seems to mean that, at a later stage of the analysis, a predicate offence may well be identified by the FIU and that this may become relevant as a condition for providing cooperation, notably through consent for further use or dissemination of the information transmitted.

Pursuant to art. 53(1) 4AMLD, information shall only be shared by FIUs "for the processing or analysis of information by the FIU related to money laundering or terrorist financing and the natural or legal person involved". In other words, information shall only be exchanged for analytical or strategic purposes in relation to money laundering or terrorist financing. Moreover, an FIU may refuse to exchange information.[255] It is important to stress, however, that the exchange of information may only be denied "in exceptional circumstances where the exchange could be contrary to fundamental principles of its national law".[256] In addition, the exceptions shall be specified *ex ante* in a way which prevents misuse and does not unduly limit the general rule of free exchange of information for analytical purposes.[257]

---

250 For an assessment of the framework for FIUs' cooperation with third countries and obstacles and opportunities to enhance cooperation between FIUs in the European Union, including the possibility of establishing a coordination and support mechanism, see Report from the Commission to the European Parliament and the Council assessing the framework for cooperation between Financial Intelligence Units, 24 July 2019, COM(2019) 371.

251 Art. 53(1) 4AMLD as modified by 5AMLD.

252 Art. 53(2) 4AMLD as modified by 5AMLD.

253 Art. 53(1) 4AMLD as modified by 5AMLD.

254 *Ibid.*

255 Art. 53(3) 4AMLD.

256 *Ibid.*

257 *Ibid.*

2. *Restrictions on Use of Data Obtained from Foreign FIUs*

Under the 4AMLD, information that FIUs receive from foreign counterparts shall only be used "for the accomplishment of the FIU's tasks as laid down in this Directive".[258] In addition, the transmitting FIU "may impose restrictions and conditions for the use of that information".[259]

In particular, the information exchanged shall be used only "for the purpose for which it was sought or provided".[260] In this context, any further use of that information, as well as its dissemination to other authorities is strictly dependent on the "prior consent" of the providing FIU.[261] It is however important to stress that art. 55(2) 4AMLD as modified by 5AMLD establishes that "[t]he requested FIU shall not refuse its consent to such dissemination unless this would fall beyond the scope of application of its AML/CFT provisions or could lead to impairment of a criminal investigation, or would otherwise not be in accordance with fundamental principles of national law of that Member State". Moreover, "[a]ny such refusal to grant consent shall be appropriately explained".[262]

G. INFORMATION FLOW BETWEEN FIU AND FOREIGN NON-COUNTERPARTS

The EU legal framework does not explicitly set out data protection restrictions regarding the transfer of personal data from FIUs to other foreign authorities. Such information sharing does, however, seem to be possible when the information exchanged is not ultimately used as evidence in court proceedings, and provided that the principles set out in art. 4(1) Directive 2016/680/EU referred to above are respected.[263]

H. EVIDENTIAL VALUE OF FIU-GENERATED DATA IN COURT PROCEEDINGS

The EU legal framework does not provide special rules on the admissibility of FIU-generated information as evidence in court proceedings.

---

258 Art. 54 4AMLD.

259 *Ibid.*

260 Art. 55(1) 4AMLD.

261 *Ibid.*

262 Art. 55(2) 4AMLD as modified by 5AMLD.

263 See *supra* section V.B.1.

I. USE OF CDD DATA FOR PROFIT MAKING

The 4AMLD makes clear that processing of personal data by obliged entities for commercial purposes shall be strictly prohibited.[264] Obliged entities shall process personal data on the basis of this Directive only for the purposes of the prevention of money laundering and terrorist financing.[265]

J. DATA SHARING BETWEEN OBLIGED ENTITIES REGARDING SARs AND FIU REQUESTS

1. *Data Sharing Inside a Group*

Art. 39(3) 4AMLD as modified by 5AMLD permits credit institutions and financial institutions from the EU and belonging to the same group to share between them information about the filing of SARs and FIUs' requests for additional information.

2. *Data Sharing with Similar Professions*

Art. 39(5) 4AMLD permits credit institutions, financial institutions, auditors, external accountants, tax advisors, notaries and other independent legal professionals, in cases relating to the same customer and the same transaction involving two or more obliged entities, to share information about the filing of SARs and FIUs' requests for additional information with obliged entities from the same professional category, provided that they are subject to obligations as regards professional secrecy and personal data protection.

3. *Data Sharing with Obliged Entities Outside the EU*

According to art. 39(3) 4AMLD as modified by 5AMLD, credit and financial institutions from the EU are allowed to share information regarding the filing of SARs and FIUs' requests for additional information with their branches and majority-owned subsidiaries established in third countries, provided, however, "that those branches and majority-owned subsidiaries fully comply with the group-wide policies and procedures, including procedures for sharing information within the group, in accordance with Article 45, and that the group-wide policies and procedures comply with the requirements set out in

---

264 See recital (43) and art. 41(2) 4AMLD.

265 *Ibid.*

the Directive."[266] Data sharing regarding SARs and FIUs' requests with credit and financial institutions established in a third country, but which are not part of the same group, is also allowed if the third country "imposes requirements equivalent to those laid down in this Directive, and that they are from the same professional category and are subject to obligations as regards professional secrecy and personal data protection".[267]

As regards auditors, external accountants, tax advisors, notaries and other independent legal professionals, such entities are allowed, in cases relating to the same customer and the same transaction involving two or more obliged entities, to share information about the filing of SARs and FIUs' requests for additional information with obliged entities from the same category who are established outside the EU, provided, here again, that the relevant third country imposes requirements equivalent to those laid down in the 4AMLD.[268]

K. DATA SHARING BETWEEN OBLIGED ENTITIES REGARDING POSSIBLE CASES OF MONEY LAUNDERING

1. *Data Sharing Inside a Group*

Pursuant to art. 45(8) 4AMLD, "[i]nformation on suspicion that funds are the proceeds of criminal activity or are related to terrorist financing reported to the FIU shall be shared within the group, unless otherwise instructed by the FIU".

---

266 In this regard, one should note that "where obliged entities have branches or majority-owned subsidiaries located in third countries where the minimum AML/CFT requirements are less strict than those of the Member State, their branches and majority-owned subsidiaries located in the third country [shall] implement the requirements of the Member State, including data protection, to the extent that the third country's law so allows" (art. 45(3) 4AMLD). In case a third country's law does not permit the implementation of the requirements of the Member State, and thereby the implementation of group-wide anti-money laundering and countering the financing of terrorism policies and procedures, obliged entities are required to "ensure that branches and majority-owned subsidiaries in that third country apply additional measures to effectively handle the risk of money laundering or terrorist financing, and inform the competent authorities of their home Member State" (art. 45(5) 4AMLD). These additional measures, including minimum action, are laid down in art. 8 Commission Delegated Regulation (EU) 2019/758 of 31 January 2019 supplementing Directive (EU) 2015/849 of the European Parliament and of the Council with regard to regulatory technical standards for the minimum action and the type of additional measures credit and financial institutions must take to mitigate money laundering and terrorist financing risk in certain third countries (OJ L 125, 14.05.2019, p. 4). If the additional measures are not sufficient, the competent authorities of the home Member State "shall exercise additional supervisory actions, including requiring that the group does not establish or that it terminates business relationships, and does not undertake transactions and, where necessary, requesting the group to close down its operations in the third country" (art. 45(5) 4AMLD).

267 Art. 39(5) 4AMLD.

268 *Ibid.*

2. *Data Sharing with Similar Professions*

The 4AMLD does not specify to what extent obliged entities are authorised to share information regarding suspicious transactions or similarly unusual events with other obliged entities outside the group, but within a similar profession.

3. *Data Sharing with Obliged Entities Outside the EU*

Unless otherwise instructed by the FIU, obliged entities from the EU are allowed to share information regarding suspicious transactions or similarly unusual events with their branches and majority-owned subsidiaries established in third countries, provided, however, that those branches and majority-owned subsidiaries fully comply with the group-wide policies and procedures, including procedures for sharing information within the group, in accordance with art. 45, and that the group-wide policies and procedures comply with the requirements set out in the Directive.[269]

L. DATA MINING BY OBLIGED ENTITIES

Neither the 4AMLD nor the 5AMLD indicate to what extent obliged entities are authorised to conduct data mining within their data banks in order to identify possible cases of money laundering. Art. 22(1) Regulation (EU) 2016/679[270] provides, however, that each data subject "shall have the right not to be subject to a decision based solely on automated processing, including profiling, which produces legal effects concerning him or her or similarly significantly affects him or her."

VI. BENEFICIAL OWNERSHIP TRANSPARENCY

A. BENEFICIAL OWNERSHIP INFORMATION

1. *General Framework*

Pursuant to art. 30(1) 4AMLD, "Member States shall ensure that corporate and other legal entities incorporated within their territory are required to

---

269 Art. 45(8) 4AMLD. On branches and majority-owned subsidiaries established in third countries where the law does not permit the implementation of the requirements of the Member State, see *supra* footnote 263.

270 Regulation (EU) 2016/679 of the European Parliament and of the Council of 27 April 2016 on the protection of natural persons with regard to the processing of personal data and on the free movement of such data, and repealing Directive 95/46/EC (OJ L 119, 04.05.2016, p. 1).

obtain and hold adequate, accurate and current information on their beneficial ownership". Member States shall also ensure that the same requirement applies to trustees of express trusts and other similar legal arrangements administered in their territory.[271] In the event of non-compliance, the Directive provides that proportionate, effective and dissuasive sanctions shall be applied.[272]

2. *Definition of "Beneficiary" and "Effective Control"*

The 4AMLD sets out a differentiated approach with respect to the definition of "beneficial owner", distinguishing between corporate entities, on the one hand, and trusts, similar legal arrangements and legal entities such as foundations, on the other hand.

a. Corporate Entities

In the case of corporate entities, other than a company listed on a regulated market that is subject to disclosure requirements consistent with Union law or subject to equivalent international standards which ensure adequate transparency of ownership information, the 4AMLD provides that the term "beneficial owner" includes at least the following: "natural person(s) who ultimately owns or controls a legal entity through direct or indirect ownership of a sufficient percentage of the shares or voting rights or ownership interest in that entity, including through bearer shareholdings, or through control via other means".[273] If, however, "after having exhausted all possible means and provided there are no grounds for suspicion, no [natural] person ... is identified [on the basis of these criteria], or if there is any doubt that the person(s) identified are the beneficial owner(s)", the 4AMLD provides that "the natural person(s) who hold the position of senior managing official(s)" shall be designated as a last resort as the beneficial owner(s).[274]

Art. 3(6)(a)(i) 4AMLD further specifies the meaning of "direct or indirect ownership", and thereby specifies the meaning of beneficial ownership. First, it states that "[a] shareholding of 25% plus one share or an ownership interest of more than 25% in the customer held by a natural person shall be an indication of direct ownership". Second, it provides that "[a] shareholding of 25% plus one share or an ownership interest of more than 25% in the customer held by a corporate entity, which is under the control of a natural person(s), or by multiple corporate entities, which are under the control of the same natural person(s), shall be an indication of indirect ownership." In its

271 Art. 31(1) 4AMLD as modified by 5AMLD.
272 Arts. 201(1) and 31(1) 4AMLD as modified by 5AMLD.
273 Art. 3(6)(a)(i) 4AMLD.
274 Art. 3(6)(a)(ii) 4AMLD.

proposal for a 5AMLD, the Commission proposed to lower this threshold to 10% in respect of corporate entities that have no active business and which are mostly used as an intermediary structure between the assets or income and the ultimate beneficial owner (defined as "Passive Non-Financial Entities" under Directive 2011/16/EU).[275] The European Commission indeed noted that for such entities, which present "a specific risk of being used for money laundering and tax evasion",[276] "the set threshold is easily circumvented, leading to no identification of the natural persons who ultimately own or control the legal entity".[277] However, this proposal was not retained by the EU co-legislators in the final version of the 5AMLD.

b. Trusts, Similar Legal Arrangements, and Legal Entities such as Foundations

In the case of trusts, the 4AMLD provides that the term "beneficial owner" includes at least the following: "(i) the settlor(s); (ii) the trustee(s); (iii) the protector(s), if any; (iv) the beneficiaries or where the individuals benefiting from the legal arrangement or entity have yet to be determined, the class of persons in whose main interest the legal arrangement or entity is set up or operates; (v) any other natural person exercising ultimate control over the trust by means of direct or indirect ownership or by other means".[278]

As regards legal entities such as foundations, and legal arrangements similar to trusts, "beneficial owner" means any "natural person(s) holding equivalent or similar positions to those referred to [with respect to trusts]".[279]

3. *Definition of "Information"*

As regards corporate and other legal entities, the 4AMLD only provides that beneficial ownership information shall include "the details of the beneficial interests held",[280] without providing further details on that. With respect to trusts and similar legal arrangements, the Directive only refers to "the identity" of the beneficial owner(s).[281]

4. *Special Rules for Entities with a Cross-Border Dimension*

EU law does not provide for special requirements and mechanisms for the disclosure of foreign nationals, foreign entities or foreign trusts.

---

275 See European Commission, Proposal for a 5AMLD, art. 1(2)(a).
276 European Commission, Proposal for a 5AMLD, Explanatory memorandum, p. 17.
277 European Commission, Proposal for a 5AMLD, recital (18).
278 Art. 3(6)(b) 4AMLD as modified by 5AMLD.
279 Art. 6(c) 4AMLD.
280 Art. 30(1) 4AMLD.
281 Art. 31(1) 4AMLD.

B. BENEFICIAL OWNERSHIP REGISTRIES

1. *Scope and General Procedure*

As mentioned above, Member States are required to ensure that corporate and other legal entities incorporated within their territory, as well as trustees of express trusts and similar legal arrangements administered in their territory, obtain and hold adequate, accurate and current information on their beneficial ownership.[282]

At the same time, the 4AMLD also requires Member States to ensure that beneficial ownership information is held, at national level, in a central register. This requirement applies to all corporate and other legal entities incorporated in their territory,[283] as well as, since the adoption of the 5AMLD, to all express trusts and similar legal arrangements (and no longer only to trusts generating tax consequences, as initially provided by the 4AMLD).[284] In the case of trusts and similar legal arrangements, beneficial ownership information "shall be held in a central beneficial ownership register set up by the Member State where the trustee of the trust or person holding an equivalent position in a similar legal arrangements is established or resides".[285] Where, however, "the place of establishment or residence of the trustee of the trust or person holding an equivalent position in similar legal arrangement is outside the Union, [the beneficial ownership information] shall be held in a central register set up by the Member State where the trustee of the trust or person holding an equivalent position in a similar legal arrangement enters into a business relationship or acquires real estate in the name of the trust or similar legal arrangement".[286]

Beneficial ownership information shall be kept for at least five years and no more than 10 years after the legal entity has been struck off the register, or after the grounds for registering the beneficial ownership information of the trust or similar legal arrangement have ceased to exist.[287]

By 10 March 2021, the national beneficial ownership registers of the different Member States are expected to be interconnected via the European Central Platform established by art. 22(1) of Directive 2017/1132/EU relating to certain aspects of company law.[288] The connection of the Member States' central registers to the platform shall be set up in accordance with the technical specifications and procedures established by implementing acts adopted by

282 Arts. 30(1) and 31(1) 4AMLD as modified by 5AMLD. See *supra* section VI.A.1.a.
283 Art. 30(3) 4AMLD.
284 Art. 31(3a) 4AMLD as modified by 5AMLD.
285 *Ibid.*
286 *Ibid.*
287 Arts. 30(10) and 31(9) 4AMLD as modified by 5AMLD.
288 *Ibid.*

the Commission in accordance with art. 24 of Directive 2017/1132/EU and with art. 31a of the 5AMLD.[289]

2. Ex Ante *Verification of Accuracy*

The 4AMLD requires Member States to ensure that the information held in the beneficial ownership register is adequate, accurate and current.[290] However, the Directive does not specify any procedure that Member States shall put in place in order to ensure that the information actually meets these requirements when it is fed into the register.

3. Ex Post *Review of Accuracy*

Before being modified by the 5AMLD, the 4AMLD did not specify neither any procedure that Member States shall put in place in order to ensure that information held in the beneficial ownership register is kept up to date. Since the adoption of the 5AMLD, however, Member States are required to establish specific mechanisms to this effect. According to arts. 30(4) and 31(5) 4AMLD as modified by 5AMLD, "[s]uch mechanisms shall include requiring obliged entities and, if appropriate and to the extent that this requirement does not interfere unnecessarily with their functions, competent authorities to report any discrepancies they find between the beneficial ownership information available in the central registers and the beneficial ownership information available to them". In the case of reported discrepancies, "Member States shall ensure that appropriate actions be taken to resolve the discrepancies in a timely manner and, if appropriate, a specific mention be included in the central register in the meantime."[291]

C. ACCESS TO BENEFICIAL OWNERSHIP INFORMATION

1. *Access by FIU and Other Authorities*

EU FIUs and competent authorities, which, according to art. 30(6) 4AMLD as modified by 5AMLD, includes notably investigative authorities, tax authorities and supervisors of obliged entities, shall be able to obtain in a timely manner from legal entities incorporated within their territory, and legal arrangements administered in their territory, their beneficial ownership information.[292]

---

289 *Ibid.*

290 Arts. 30(4) and 31(5) 4AMLD.

291 Arts. 30(4) and 31(5) 4AMLD as modified by 5AMLD.

292 Arts. 30(2) and 31(3) 4AMLD.

Moreover, Member States shall ensure that the information held in the beneficial ownership register referred to above[293] is accessible in all cases to competent authorities and FIU, without any restriction.[294]

2. *Access by Obliged Entities*

The 4AMLD requires Member States to ensure that obliged entities are able to obtain in a timely manner from the aforementioned entities and arrangements their beneficial ownership information when performing CDD measures.[295]

Moreover, Member States shall ensure that the information held in the beneficial ownership register referred to above[296] is also accessible in a timely manner by obliged entities within the framework of CDD.[297] Where, however, such access "would expose the beneficial owner to disproportionate risk, risk of fraud, kidnapping, blackmail, extortion, harassment, violence or intimidation, or where the beneficial owner is a minor or otherwise legally incapable, Member States may provide for an exemption from such access to all or part of the information on the beneficial ownership on a case-by-case basis."[298] These exemptions, which may be applied to all obliged entities, except for credit institutions, financial institutions, and notaries and other legal professionals that are public officials,[299] shall be "granted upon a detailed evaluation of the exceptional nature of the circumstances".[300] Moreover, "[r]ights to an administrative review of the exemption decision and to an effective judicial remedy shall be guaranteed".[301]

3. *Access by Interested Third Parties*

a. Corporate and Other Legal Entities

Before being modified by the 5AMLD, the 4AMLD granted access to the information on the beneficial ownership of corporate and other legal entities

---

293 See *supra* section VI.B.1.

294 Arts. 30(5)(a) and 31(4)(a) 4AMLD as modified by 5AMLD.

295 Arts. 30(1) and 31(2) 4AMLD.

296 See *supra* section VI.B.1.

297 Arts. 30(5)(b) and 31(4)(b) 4AMLD as modified by 5AMLD. Before being modified by the 5AMLD, the 4AMLD only required Member States to ensure that obliged entities could, in the framework of CDD, have access to information on the beneficial ownership of legal entities held in the central beneficial ownership register. In contrast, art. 31(4) 4AMLD only allowed Member States to apply the same requirement with respect to trusts and similar legal arrangements.

298 Arts. 30(9) and 31(7a) 4AMLD as modified by 5AMLD.

299 *Ibid.*

300 *Ibid.*

301 *Ibid.*

held in the central beneficial ownership register referred to above[302] to FIUs and competent authorities (without any restriction), obliged entities (within the framework of CDD), as well as "any other organization who [could] demonstrate a legitimate interest".[303] The 5AMLD has replaced this third category with "any member of the general public", thereby abolishing the need to establish a legal interest.[304] According to the Preamble of the 5AMLD, "[p]ublic access to beneficial ownership information allows greater scrutiny of information of information by civil society, including by the press or civil society organisations, and [therefore] contributes to preserving trust in the integrity of business transactions and of the financial system".[305] Making corporate ownership information public is also notably expected to reduce the use of shell companies for money laundering or terrorist financing purposes, "both by helping investigations and through reputational effects, given that anyone who could enter into transactions is aware of the identity of the beneficial owners".[306]

At a minimum, members of the general public shall have access to "the name, the month and year of birth and the country of residence and nationality of the beneficial owner as well as the nature and extent of the beneficial interest held".[307] Where, however, such access "would expose the beneficial owner to disproportionate risk, risk of fraud, kidnapping, blackmail, extortion, harassment, violence or intimidation, or where the beneficial owner is a minor or otherwise legally incapable, Member States may provide for an exemption from such access to all or part of the information on the beneficial ownership on a case-by-case basis."[308]

b. Trusts and Similar Legal Arrangements

Originally, the 4AMLD only required Member States to grant access to the information on the beneficial ownership of trusts and similar legal arrangements held in the central beneficial ownership register referred to above[309] to FIUs and competent authorities.[310] Since the adoption of the 5AMLD, however, such information shall also be accessible to obliged entities (in the framework of CDD),[311] as well as to any person that can demonstrate a "legitimate interest".[312]

---

302 See *supra* section VI.B.1.
303 Art. 30(5)(c) 4AMLD.
304 Art. 30(5)(c) 4AMLD as modified by 5AMLD.
305 Recital (30) 5AMLD.
306 *Ibid.*
307 Art. 30(5)(c) 4AMLD as modified by 5AMLD.
308 Art. 30(9) as modified by 5AMLD.
309 See *supra* section VI.B.1.
310 Art. 31(4) 4AMLD.
311 Art. 31(4)(b) 4AMLD as modified by 5AMLD. See *supra* section VI.C.2.
312 Art. 31(4)(c) 4AMLD as modified by 5AMLD. According to recital (41) 5AMLD, "the definition of legitimate interest should be governed by the law of the Member State where the trustee of a

Additionally, access shall also now be granted to any person that files a written request in relation to a trust or similar legal arrangement which holds or owns a controlling interest in any corporate or other legal entity incorporated outside the EU, through direct or indirect ownership, including through bearer shareholdings, or through control via other means.[313]

The new aforementioned categories of persons shall have access to "the name, the month and year of birth and the country of residence and nationality of the beneficial owner as well as the nature and extent of the beneficial interest held".[314] Where, however, such access "would expose the beneficial owner to disproportionate risk, risk of fraud, kidnapping, blackmail, extortion, harassment, violence or intimidation, or where the beneficial owner is a minor or otherwise legally incapable, Member States may provide for an exemption from such access to all or part of the information on the beneficial ownership on a case-by-case basis."[315]

VII. SANCTIONS

A. SANCTIONS FOR MONEY LAUNDERING

1. Requirement of a Conviction for a Predicate Offence

Under Directive 2018/1673/EU, Member States shall provide for a margin of leeway when proving money laundering offences. More specifically, in order to secure a conviction for money laundering, according to Directive 2018/1673/EU, it is irrelevant whether there is a prior or simultaneous conviction for the predicate offence.[316] Moreover, it does not require "that all the factual elements or all circumstances relating to that criminal activity, including the identity of the perpetrator" are established.[317]

trust or person holding an equivalent position in a similar legal arrangement is established or resides". Alternatively, "[w]here the trustee of the trust or person holding equivalent position in similar legal arrangement is not established or does not reside in any Member State, access to information and the definition of legitimate interest should be governed by the law of the Member State where the beneficial ownership information of the trust or similar legal arrangement is registered in accordance with the provisions of this Directive." The Preamble of the 5AMLD also states that the definition of "legitimate interest" "should not restrict the concept of legitimate interest to cases of pending administrative or legal proceedings, and should enable to take into account the preventive work in the field of anti-money laundering, counter terrorist financing and associate predicate offences undertaken by non-governmental organisations and investigative journalists, where appropriate" (recital (42) 5AMLD).

313 Art. 31(4)(d) 4AMLD as modified by 5AMLD.

314 Art. 31(4)(d) 4AMLD as modified by 5AMLD.

315 Art. 31(7a) 4AMLD as modified by 5AMLD.

316 Art. 3(3)(a) Directive 2018/1673/EU.

317 Art. 3(3)(b) Directive 2018/1673/EU.

2. *Forms of Sanctions*

Directive 2018/1673/EU requires Member States to apply effective, proportionate and dissuasive criminal penalties to natural persons convicted of money laundering[318] and establishes the minimum maximum penalty at four years of imprisonment.[319] Member States shall also ensure that natural persons who have committed money laundering are, where necessary, subject to additional sanctions or measures.[320] Recital (14) Directive 2018/1673/EU indicates what could constitute such sanctions or measures, stating that they may include "fines, temporary or permanent exclusion from access to public funding, including tender procedures, grants and concessions, temporary disqualifications from the practice of commercial activities or temporary bans on running for elected or public office".

Pursuant to art. 7(1) Directive 2018/1673/EU, Member States shall also take the necessary measures to establish the liability of legal persons[321] for money laundering committed "for their benefit". The underlying conduct can be committed "by any person, acting either individually or as part of an organ of the legal person and having a legal position within the legal person, based on any of the following: (a) a power of representation of the legal person; (b) an authority to take decisions on behalf of the legal person; or (c) the authority to exercise control within the legal person".[322] In addition, art. 7(2) Directive 2018/1673/EU includes a "failure to prevent" basis for corporate liability, where a "lack of supervision or control" by a person referred to in art. 7(1) has made possible the commission of a money laundering offence for the benefit of that legal person by a person under its authority.

With respect to sanctions for legal persons, art. 8 Directive 2018/1673/EU requires Member States to apply effective, proportionate and dissuasive sanctions. These sanctions shall include:

> criminal or non-criminal fines and may include other sanctions, such as:
>
> (a) exclusion from entitlement to public benefits or aid;
> (b) temporary or permanent exclusion from access to public funding, including tender procedures, grants and concessions;
> (c) temporary or permanent disqualification from the practice of commercial activities;
> (d) placing under judicial supervision;

---

318 Art. 5(1) Directive 2018/1673/EU.

319 Art. 5(2) Directive 2018/1673/EU.

320 Art. 5(3) Directive 2018/1673/EU.

321 Under Directive 2018/1673/EU, "'legal persons' means entity having legal personality under the applicable law, except for states or public bodies in the exercise of state authority and for public international organisations" (art. 2(3)).

322 Art. 7(1) Directive 2018/1673/EU.

(e) a judicial winding-up order;
(f) temporary or permanent closure of establishments which have been used for committing the offence.[323]

3. *Confiscation*

Pursuant to art. 9 Directive 2018/1673/EU, Member States shall ensure that their competent authorities freeze or confiscate, in accordance with Directive 2014/42/EU, the proceeds derived from and instrumentalities used or intended to be used in the commission or contribution to the commission of money laundering. Directive 2014/42/EU of 3 April 2014 on the freezing and confiscation of instrumentalities and proceeds of crime in the European Union,[324] which replaced arts. 1(a), 3 and 4 of Council Framework Decision 2001/500/JHA,[325] lays down minimum rules approximating the Member States' freezing and confiscation regimes.[326] Art. 4 requires Member States to confiscate the "instrumentalities and proceeds [of crime] or property the value of which corresponds to such instrumentalities or proceeds, subject to a final conviction for a criminal offence, which may also result from proceedings in absentia". The term "criminal offence" refers to a set of criminal offences defined in art. 3, which includes money laundering. Art. 5 sets out rules on extended confiscation where a court is satisfied that the property in question has been obtained through other criminal activities by the convicted person. Art. 6 requires Member States to enable confiscation where property was transferred from the suspect to a third party, or directly acquired by a third party, who "knew or ought to have known that the purpose of the transfer or acquisition was to avoid confiscation". Art. 7 requires Member States to enable the freezing of property with a view to possible subsequent confiscation.

4. *Statistics*

a. Number of Criminal Proceedings

The EU does not provide statistics on either the number of criminal proceedings for money laundering within the Union or the value of transactions associated with these proceedings. However, pursuant to art. 44(2)(b) 4AMLD, Member States are required, on an annual basis, to maintain comprehensive statistics on "the number of cases investigated [and] the number of persons prosecuted … for

323 Art. 8 Directive 2018/1673/EU.
324 Directive 2014/42/EU of the European Parliament and of the Council of 3 April 2014 on the freezing and confiscation of instrumentalities and proceeds of crime in the European Union (OJ L 127, 29.04.2014, p. 39).
325 Art. 14(1) Directive 2014/42/EU.
326 See recital (5) Directive 2014/42/EU.

money laundering". The statistics shall include, "if available, data identifying the number and percentage of reports resulting in further investigation".[327]

b. Number of Convictions

The EU does not provide statistics on either on the number of convictions for money laundering within the Union or the value of transactions associated with these convictions. However, pursuant to art. 44(2)(b) 4AMLD, Member States are required, on an annual basis, to maintain comprehensive statistics on "the number of persons convicted for money laundering".

B. SANCTIONS FOR VIOLATIONS OF PREVENTIVE MEASURES

1. *Money Laundering by Violating Preventive Obligations*

The EU AML framework does not explicitly address the issue of money laundering by omission. However, as was already noted,[328] art. 7(2) Directive 2018/1673/EU provides for corporate liability for a "failure to prevent" where a "lack of supervision or control" by a person referred to in art. 7(1) Directive 2018/1673/EU has made possible the commission of a money laundering offence for the benefit of that legal person by a person under its authority.

2. *CDD, Reporting and Other AML-related Obligations*

a. Special Criminal Laws against Individuals

Neither the 4AMLD nor Directive 2018/1673/EU require Member States to provide for and apply criminal sanctions to natural persons who fail to comply with the CDD, reporting and other AML-related requirements set out in the 4AMLD. The 4AMLD only requires Member States to impose administrative sanctions and measures. However, as provided for by art. 58(2), "[M]ember States may decide not to lay down rules for administrative sanctions or measures for breaches which are subject to criminal sanctions in their national law".

b. Administrative Sanctions against Individuals

The 4AMLD requires Member States to provide for and apply effective, proportionate and dissuasive sanctions and measures of an administrative

[327] Art. 44(2)(c) 4AMLD.
[328] See *supra* section VII.A.2.

nature to natural persons who are liable for breaches that are serious, repeated, systematic, or a combination thereof, of the CDD, reporting, record keeping and internal controls requirements set out in the Directive.[329] In addition, the 4AMLD provides that, "where obligations apply to [obliged entities that are] legal persons ..., sanctions and measures can be applied to the members of the management body and to other natural persons who under national law are responsible for the breach".[330]

Pursuant to art. 59(2) 4AMLD, Member States shall ensure that the range of administrative sanctions and measures that can be applied include at least the following:

> (a) a public statement which identifies the natural ... person and the nature of the breach;
> (b) an order requiring the natural ... person to cease the conduct and to desist from repetition of that conduct;
> (c) where an obliged entity is subject to an authorisation, withdrawal or suspension of the authorisation;
> (d) a temporary ban against any person discharging managerial responsibilities in an obliged entity, or any other natural person, held responsible for the breach, from exercising managerial functions in obliged entities;
> (e) maximum administrative pecuniary sanctions of at least twice the amount of the benefit derived from the breach where that benefit can be determined, or at least EUR 1 000 000.

Derogating from art. 58(2)(e) 4AMLD, for breaches involving financial institutions, to the extent that they are natural persons, art. 59(3)(b) 4AMLD provides specific sanctions in that it specifies the maximum administrative fine to be no less than €5,000,000.

Member States shall also ensure that all decisions imposing an administrative sanction or measure for breach of the national provisions transposing the Directive against which there is no appeal are published by the competent authorities on their website after the person sanctioned is informed of that decision.[331] Unless overriding reasons require otherwise, the identity of the person responsible for the breach as well as the nature of the breach shall be mentioned in the publication.[332]

---

329 Art. 59(1) 4AMLD.

330 Art. 58(3) 4AMLD.

331 Art. 60(1) 4AMLD. According to art. 60(3), "[c]ompetent authorities shall ensure that any publication in accordance with this Article shall remain on their official website for a period of five years after its publication. However, personal data contained in the publication shall only be kept on the official website of the competent authority for the period which is necessary in accordance with the applicable data protection rules".

332 Art. 60(1) 4AMLD.

Finally, the ESAs shall be informed by the competent authorities of all administrative sanctions and measures imposed on financial institutions.[333] According to art. 62(3) 4AMLD, "[t]he ESAs shall maintain a website with links to each competent authority's publication of administrative sanctions and measures imposed [on] financial institutions, and shall show the time period for which each Member State publishes administrative sanctions and measures".

c. Sanctions against Legal Entities

The 4AMLD requires Member States to provide for and apply effective, proportionate and dissuasive sanctions and measures of an administrative nature to legal persons who are liable for breaches that are serious, repeated, systematic, or a combination thereof, of the CDD, reporting, record keeping and internal controls requirements set out in the Directive.[334] In addition, the 4AMLD requires Member States to ensure "that legal persons can be held liable for the breaches ... committed for their benefit by any person, acting individually or as part of an organ of that legal person, and having a leading position within the legal person based on any of the following: (a) power to represent the legal person; (b) authority to take decisions on behalf of the legal person; or (c) authority to exercise control within the legal person".[335]

Art. 59(2) 4AMLD specifies that the aforementioned range of administrative sanctions and measures (points (a)–(e)) also applies to legal entities.[336]

With respect to breaches involving credit or financial institutions, specific sanctions are provided for by art. 59(3)(a) 4AMLD, by way of derogation from art. 58(2)(e) of this Directive. In this case indeed, the maximum administrative fine shall be no less than €5,000,000 or 10% of the total annual turnover according to the latest available accounts approved by the management body.

In the same way as for natural persons above, the Directive provides that Member States shall ensure that decisions imposing an administrative sanction or measure for breach of the national provisions transposing the Directive against which there is no appeal are published by the competent authorities on their website.[337] Unless overriding reasons require otherwise, the identity of the person responsible as well as the nature of the violation shall be mentioned in the publication.[338]

The ESAs shall be informed by the competent authorities of all administrative sanctions and measures imposed on credit and financial institutions, to be

---

333 Art. 62(1) 4AMLD.
334 Art. 59(1) 4AMLD.
335 Art. 60(5) 4AMLD.
336 See *supra* section VII.B.2.b.
337 Art. 60(1) 4AMLD. See *supra* section VII.B.2.b.
338 Art. 60(1) 4AMLD.

published on their website in line with the above-mentioned requirements of art. 62(3) 4AMLD.[339]

3. *Statistics*

a. Number of Investigations

There are no statistics available on the number of investigations launched in the EU by supervisory authorities against individuals and legal entities for the aforementioned offences. One should note, however, that, according to art. 44(2)(f) 4AMLD as modified by 5AMLD, Member States are required to maintain comprehensive statistics on "the number of on-site and off-site supervisory actions [and] the number of breaches identified on the basis of supervisory actions".

b. Number of sanctions

There are no statistics available on the number sanctions imposed on individuals and legal entities by supervisory authorities for the aforementioned offences. One should note, however, that, according to art. 44(2)(f) 4AMLD as modified by 5AMLD, Member States are required to maintain comprehensive statistics on the number of "sanctions/administrative measures applied by supervisory authorities".

C. CUMULATION OF MONEY LAUNDERING AND OTHER AML-RELATED SANCTIONS

The EU legal framework does not specify to what extent sanctions for money laundering can be combined with sanctions for the violation of preventive obligations.

VIII. THE USE OF CASH AS A MEANS OF PAYMENT

A. LIMITS

Legislative attempts at EU level to introduce limits on the use of cash as means of payment have failed. While a number of Member States have in place

339 Art. 62(1) 4AMLD. See *supra* section VII.B.2.b.

restrictions for cash payments above a specific threshold,[340] there is no limit on the use of cash as a means of payment imposed at EU level. It should be noted, however, that the European Commission explored the relevance of potential upper limits to cash payments across the EU. Following the 2016 Action Plan to further step up the fight against the financing of terrorism, the European Commission launched in January 2017, via the publication of an Inception Impact Assessment,[341] an initiative to examine the impacts of restrictions on payments in cash. According to an impact study commissioned by the Commission in this context,[342] it was observed in particular that restrictions on cash payments are a sensitive issue for European citizens, many of whom view the possibility of paying in cash to be a fundamental freedom, which should not be disproportionally restricted. On the basis of these findings, the European Commission decided in June 2018 not to consider any legislative initiative to restrict cash use across the EU.[343]

B. STATISTICS

The European Central Bank does not provide statistics on the use of cash in relation to the overall volume of (cash and non-cash) transactions conducted in the Union.

IX. SUMMARY, EVALUATION AND FUTURE PERSPECTIVES

Cases of money laundering have hit headlines all around Europe in the past few years.[344] An investigation found for instance that up to $30 billion of

---

340 Restrictions on cash payments at national level are generally considered compatible with Union law. For the Euro area, recital (19) of Council Regulation (EC) No 974/98 states that "limitations on payments in notes and coins, established by Member States for public reasons, are not incompatible with the status of legal tender of euro banknotes and coins, provided that other lawful means for the settlement of monetary debts are available".

341 Inception Impact Assessment, http://ec.europa.eu/smart-regulation/roadmaps/docs/plan_2016_028_cash_restrictions_en.pdf.

342 ECORY/CEPS, Study on an EU initiative for a restriction on payments in cash, 15 December 2017, https://ec.europa.eu/info/sites/info/files/economy-finance/final_report_study_on_an_eu_initative_ecorys_180206.pdf.

343 See Report from the Commission to the European Parliament and the Council on restrictions on payments in cash, 12 June 2018, COM(2018) 483 final.

344 On some of these cases, see notably Report from the Commission to the European Parliament and the Council on the assessment of recent alleged money laundering cases involving EU

ex-Soviet and Russian money had potentially passed through the Estonian branch of Denmark's largest bank, Danske Bank.[345] Another one led to the conviction of Dutch bank ING to pay €775m in fines after it allowed 'structural infringement' of the Netherlands' Money Laundering and Terrorist Financing Act.[346]

Against this backdrop, combined with the emergence of new threats, namely the terrorist attacks in Europe in 2015 and the offshore leaks investigated in the Panama Papers,[347] the Juncker Commission made the strengthening of the EU AML/CTF legal framework a top priority of its mandate.[348] As a result, three directives were adopted in just over three years, which is merely one fewer than for the period 1991–2015.[349] From the lowering of the threshold for the application of CDD measures to the inclusion of tax offences within the scope of predicate offences to money laundering, the mandatory creation of a beneficial ownership register in each Member State, the definition of minimum administrative penalties to be applied in the event of violation of preventive measures, the establishment of minimum rules concerning the definition of criminal offences and sanctions in the area of money laundering and the new powers granted to FIUs, the three directives adopted between May 2015 and October 2018 have comprehensively amended and bolstered the EU AML/CTF regime.

In addition to the normative acceleration described above, what is striking about the EU AML/CTF framework today is that most recent developments have occurred on an independent basis, whereas, previously, EU directives were always adopted following a revision of the FATF Recommendations, the latter forming a blueprint for the EU's AML/CTF framework. In fact, the 4AMLD, the 5AMLD and Directive 2018/673/EU are the first directives to provide rules which do not all arise from the FATF Recommendations. Beneficial ownership registries are a good example in this regard. Indeed, the FATF Recommendations maintain a certain level of flexibility as to the means through

---

credit institutions, 27 July 2019, COM(2019) 373. The analysis of the selected cases revealed substantial incidents of failures by credit institutions to comply with core requirements of the 4AMLD, such as risk assessment, customer due diligence, and reporting of suspicious transactions and activities to Financial Intelligence Units.

345 See e.g. "Scandal-hit Danske branch handled $30bn of Russian money", *Financial Times*, 3 September 2018, available at: https://www.ft.com/content/d1efae70-af80-11e8-8d14-6f049d06439c.

346 See e.g. "ING to pay €775m in money laundering case", *Financial Times*, 4 September 2018, available at: https://www.ft.com/content/f3e64e3e-b02b-11e8-99ca-68cf89602132.

347 See *supra* section I.A.

348 European Commission, The European Agenda on Security, 28 April 2015, COM(2015) 185 final.

349 See *supra* section I.A.

which information on the beneficial ownership of legal persons[350] should be made available to the competent authorities and obliged entities.[351] Countries may choose to rely upon a national beneficial ownership registry which would hold the beneficial ownership information of all legal persons incorporated or created by any other mechanism in their territory, but they do not have to.[352] They may also, for instance, merely require companies themselves to obtain and hold information on the companies' beneficial ownership without also imposing on them an obligation to disclose the information to a beneficial ownership registry.[353] In contrast, the 4AMLD requires Member States to ensure that legal persons obtain and hold information on their beneficial ownership, and communicate it to a central beneficial ownership register at national level.[354] According to the 5AMLD, this register shall be publicly available,[355] whereas the FATF Recommendations do not even address the question of access to beneficial ownership registries.

Another strong signal of the EU's emancipation in the fight against money laundering and terrorist financing, which one could even qualify as a leadership shift, is that, since it was amended by the 5AMLD, the 4AMLD now requires obliged entities to apply a minimum set of predefined enhanced CDD requirements when dealing with high-risk third countries,[356] whereas the FATF Recommendations do not specify the type of enhanced CDD measures to be taken with regard to high-risk third countries.[357] One could also mention the attempt to establish an autonomous EU list of high-risk third countries.[358] Previously, before the EU Parliament criticised in 2017 the fact that the European Commission's methodology for identifying high-risk third countries was not sufficiently autonomous and called on the Commission to develop and implement a new methodology, the European Commission confined itself to copying and pasting the FATF list of high-risk third countries.[359]

Now that a new European Commission is in place, it remains unclear whether AML/CTF will remain high on the EU's political agenda. However, in view of the recently adopted Communication *Towards a better implementation*

---

350 The FATF is less flexible as regards express trusts since it requires countries to ensure that trustees and persons in equivalent or similar positions obtain and hold beneficial ownership information. See *supra* section VI.A.1.

351 See FATF report in this volume, section VI.B.1.

352 *Ibid.*

353 *Ibid.*

354 See *supra* section VI.B1.

355 See *supra* section VI.C.3.

356 See *supra* section III.A.5.b.

357 See FATF report in this volume, section III.A.5.b.

358 See *supra* section I.B.

359 *Ibid.*

of the EU's anti-money laundering and countering the financing of terrorism framework,[360] in which the European Commission stresses the need for the full implementation of the AML Directives while underlining that a number of structural shortcomings in the implementation of the Union's anti-money laundering and counter-terrorist financing rules still need to be addressed, it is something to wish for.

[360] Communication from the European Commission to the European Parliament and the Council, Towards better implementation of the EU's anti-money laundering and countering the financing of terrorism framework, 24 July 2019, COM(2019) 360 final.

THE ANTI-MONEY LAUNDERING ARCHITECTURE OF GERMANY

Benjamin VOGEL

I. INTRODUCTION[1]

A. HISTORY OF ANTI-MONEY LAUNDERING IN THE COUNTRY

Anti-money laundering (AML) in German law is a rather recent phenomenon. The criminal offence of money laundering was first introduced in 1992 in transposition of Article 3 of the 1988 UN Convention Against Illicit Traffic in Narcotic Drugs and Psychotropic Substances.[2] The list of predicate offences was then limited to felonies (that is, crimes punishable by a minimum of one year imprisonment), drug trafficking and any offences committed as a member of a criminal organisation.[3] As results from legislative materials of the time, AML was initially taken to be a tool to fight organised crime, and therein not limited to drug trafficking.[4] Subsequent reforms have continuously expanded the catalogue of predicate offences, notably in 1994[5] and 1998 through the inclusion, independently of whether or not committed as part of a criminal

1 Unless otherwise provided, statutory provisions cited in this chapter refer to the Money Laundering Law (Geldwäschegesetz) of 23 June 2017, BGBl. I p. 1822, as modified by Article 1 of the Act of 12 December 2019, BGBl. I, p. 2602. Citations of the GWG refer to the Federal Financial Supervisory Authority's translation; https://www.bafin.de/SharedDocs/Veroeffentlichungen/EN/Aufsichtsrecht/Gesetz/GwG_en.html. Citations of the StGB refer to the translation by Michael Bohlander as revised by Ute Reusch, citations of the StPO to the translation by Brian Duffett and Monika Ebinger (updated by Kathleen Müller-Rostin and Iyamide Mahdi) as revised by Ute Reusch, both available on the webpage of the Federal Ministry of Justice and Consumer Protection; https://www.gesetze-im-internet.de/englisch_stgb/index.html and https://www.gesetze-im-internet.de/englisch_stpo/index.html.

2 BT-Drucksache 12/3533, p. 10.

3 Gesetz zur Bekämpfung des illegalen Rauschgifthandels und anderer Erscheinungsformen der organisierten Kriminalität of 15 July 1992, BGBl I 1992, p. 1304.

4 BT-Drucksache 12/989, p. 26; BT-Drucksache 12/3533, p. 12.

5 Gesetz zur Änderung des Strafgesetzbuches, der Strafprozeßordnung und anderer Gesetze (Verbrechensbekämpfungsgesetz) of 28 October 1994, BGBl I 1994, p. 3186.

organisation, of the taking of bribes, certain serious forms of smuggling and a variety of particularly serious forms of property offences.[6] In transposition of European Directive 91/308/EEC,[7] customer identification, documentation and suspicious activities reporting obligations for credit institutions and financial institutions were first introduced in 1993.[8] In line with Directive 2001/97/EC, the scope of obliged entities was, in 2002, extended to numerous other professions, including auditors, tax advisors, real estate agents, notaries, some independent legal professionals, dealers in high-value goods and casinos; furthermore, the reform notably introduced beneficial ownership verification obligations and a Financial Intelligence Unit as central analysis body to support criminal justice authorities in the processing of obliged entities' reports.[9] Following Directive 2005/60/EC,[10] this preventive framework was comprehensively reformed in 2008, in particular through the introduction of a risk-based approach to customer due diligence (CDD) and the obligation to continuously monitor business relationships,[11] and, to remedy deficits established in the 2010 FATF mutual evaluation, supplemented in 2011.[12] In transposition of Directive 2015/849/EU,[13] the preventive framework was again comprehensively reformed in 2017, especially by reshaping the FIU as an administrative body and introducing a beneficial ownership registry.[14]

B. CURRENT CONCERNS AND REFORM AGENDA

Ongoing debates about AML in Germany continue to reflect concerns that the framework is still lacking sufficient effectiveness. Such charges do partially result from what is in some cases framed as a discrepancy between a *de facto* involvement of financial institutions in money laundering on the one hand and

---

6 Gesetz zur Verbesserung der Bekämpfung der Organisierten Kriminalität of 4 May 1998, BGBl I 1998, p. 845.

7 Council Directive of 10 June 1991 on prevention of the use of the financial system for the purpose of money laundering.

8 Gesetz über das Aufspüren von Gewinnen aus schweren Straftaten of 25 October 1993, BGBl I 1993, p. 1771.

9 Gesetz zur Verbesserung der Bekämpfung der Geldwäsche und der Bekämpfung der Finanzierung des Terrorismus of 8 August 2002, BGBl I 2002, p. 3105; BT-Drucksache 14/8739, pp. 1, 14.

10 Directive of 26 October 2005 on the prevention of the use of the financial system for the purpose of money laundering and terrorist financing.

11 Gesetz zur Ergänzung der Bekämpfung der Geldwäsche und der Terrorismusfinanzierung of 13 August 2008, BGBl I 2008, p. 1690; BT-Drucksache 16/9038, p. 33.

12 Gesetz zur Optimierung der Geldwäscheprävention of 22 December 2011, BGBl I 2011, p. 2959; BT-Drucksache 17/6804.

13 Directive of 20 May 2015 on the prevention of the use of the financial system for the purposes of money laundering or terrorist financing.

14 Geldwäschegesetz of 23 June 2017, BGBl. I, p. 1822.

an absence of legal liability for such involvement on the other hand, in the sense that even full compliance with their AML obligations does not prevent obliged entities from contributing to money laundering.[15] While the recently concluded National Risk Analysis has confirmed the widely held view that Germany, due to its stability and the size of its economy, is an attractive destination for the investment of proceeds of crime, the extent of money laundering in the country is unsurprisingly subject to much speculation.[16] Irrespective of the actual volume of laundered proceeds in Germany, political and wider public discourse is mostly about perceived lacunas in the design and practical implementation of the national framework. This concerns in particular the consequences of the creation, in 2017, of an administrative FIU and the resulting readjustment of the relationship between criminal justice authorities and the FIU. In this respect, questions continue to arise notably as regards the FIU's (largely lacking) access to operational data of police authorities, which is relevant because policing in Germany falls predominantly under the competence of the 16 *Länder* (federal states) and not the federal government. Ostensibly partially also resulting from the mounting number of suspicious activity reports (SARs) received by the FIU as well as from recruitment difficulties following the 2017 reform, questions are still being asked about the quality of the FIU's operational analysis, though those concerns might first and foremost constitute a transitory phenomenon.[17] Another area of the national AML framework frequently criticised as being insufficient or even largely ineffective regards the supervision of obliged entities' preventive measures in the financial,[18] but especially in the non-financial sector. Supervision over non-financial obliged entities falls largely under the competence of the federal states and is marked by a multitude of distinct supervisory authorities, potentially leading to a fragmentation of relevant findings, and by an oftentimes insufficient commitment of local governments as regards the staffing level of those authorities[19] and, arguably as a result, a low number of supervisory inspections and sanctions.[20] Political concern seems accentuated in respect of the property market, which is regularly judged to entail a heightened money laundering risk, as both notaries and estate agents fall under the responsibility of diverse *Länder* authorities and are subjected to only relatively few inspections.[21] Prior to the

---

15 See BT-Drucksache 19/7840, pp. 8–9; Bafin, Jahresbericht 2017, p. 79.

16 See BT-Drucksache 19/2449; K-D Bussmann, Geldwäscheprävention im Markt, Springer 2018, p. 102.

17 See BT-Drucksache 18/12405, pp. 156–157; BT-Drucksache 19/9326, pp. 13–15; BT-Drucksache 19/10218, p. 12.

18 See BT-Drucksache 19/3818, pp. 9–12; BT-Drucksache 19/7840, pp. 6–7.

19 See BT-Drucksache 19/3818, pp. 15–17.

20 See BT-Drucksache 19/2449, pp. 24–26.

21 See BT-Drucksache 19/10218, p. 5; BT-Drucksache 19/2449, p. 24; BT-Drucksache 19/10218, pp. 9–10.

transposition of Directive (EU) 2018/843, controversy was also created by the design of the beneficial ownership register, in particular the prior lack of a verification mechanism for the register's content and the non-existence of an obligation of foreign entities to notify the German registry of their beneficial owner even in cases where this entity acquires real estate in Germany.[22] These concerns were now somewhat addressed by the legislator, in particular by the introduction of an obligation of obliged entities (and to a more limited degree also of supervisory authorities and the FIU) to notify the register if they detect inconsistencies, by strengthening the role of administrative sanctions proceedings into violations of beneficial ownership transparency obligations, and by requiring third-country entities to register their beneficial ownership information when they acquire real estate property in Germany.[23] At the same time, the recent reform raises renewed concerns about the compatibility of beneficial ownership transparency with data protection requirements, especially as regards the now foreseen public access to large parts of the registry.[24] Finally, it should be noted that a decision of the Federal Constitutional Court declared that the meaning of numerous core terms of the preventive AML framework – such as "appropriate, risk-oriented procedures", "enhanced risk" or "particularly complex and large" transactions – was in need of clarification by the lower courts, though the Constitutional Court did not yet express itself on the constitutionality of the respective provisions;[25] in any case, this decision can be understood as an indication that – absent further clarification by the legislator, supervisory authorities and the competent courts – constitutional jurisprudence might, in future cases of doubt, favour a rather narrow reading of obliged entities' obligations.

II. AIMS AND SCOPE OF AML SYSTEM

A. AIMS OF AML REGIME

The purpose of AML is debated primarily around the criminal offence of money laundering. Adopting the viewpoint of the legislator, jurisprudence and commentators predominantly assume that the criminalisation of money laundering protects the administration of justice.[26] In addition, insofar as the

---

22 See BT-Drucksache 19/11098, p. 2; BT-Drucksache 19/10218, pp. 5–6.

23 See section 18 para. 3a, section 20 para. 1 s. 2 and section 23a GWG.

24 See BT-Drucksache 19/10716, pp. 2–4; BT-Drucksache 19/13827, p. 21.

25 BVerfG, NJW 2019, 659, 660.

26 BT-Drucksache 12/989, p. 27; OLG Karlsruhe 2006, 767, 768; S Neuheuser, in W Joecks/ K Miebach (eds.), Münchener Kommentar zum Strafgesetzbuch, volume 4, §§185–262, 3rd ed., C.H. Beck 2017, §261 para. 7.

offence covers the procurement, keeping and use of proceeds of crime, it is also taken to protect those interests that were, in the particular case, protected by the respective predicate offence;[27] this for example means that property is considered to be a protected interest if the predicate offence was a property crime. As results from the legislative materials, money laundering is deemed to serve the administration of justice for two reasons: first, because the criminalisation of money laundering is taken to offer investigative authorities an opportunity to penetrate criminal organisations and, by following back the money and paper trail, reach the centre of such organisations;[28] second – as regards the concealment, hiding or endangerment of the detection of the proceeds – because these acts frustrate or endanger the authorities' ability to remedy the consequences of crime.[29] As regards the procurement, keeping and use of proceeds of crime, the additional purpose of strengthening the purpose of the predicate offence seemingly results from the idea that these three variations of money laundering aim to economically isolate the proceeds of crime and thereby render the commission of the predicate offence less attractive in the first place.[30] In contrast, as regards the Anti-Money Laundering Act and thus the preventive obligations of obliged entities, there is little debate about a particular protected interest, implying that, by transposing subsequent EU directives, Germany has implicitly adopted the rationale of the Union legislature, including both the integrity and stability of financial institutions and – as becomes clear especially with regard to the Financial Intelligence Unit – a strengthening of the goals pursued through the criminalisation of money laundering.[31]

B. SCOPE OF MONEY LAUNDERING

1. *Definition of Money Laundering in Criminal Law*

a. *Actus Reus*

i. Predicate Offences

Section 261 of the StGB defines the offence of money laundering and provides a list of predicate offences. Accordingly, conduct can constitute money laundering

---

27 BT-Drucksache 12/989, p. 27; BGH NJW 2018, 2742, 2743; BGH NStZ-RR 2013, 253.

28 BT-Drucksache 12/989, p. 26; BT-Drucksache 12/3533, p. 11.

29 BT-Drucksache 12/3533, p. 12.

30 BT-Drucksache 12/3533, p. 11; BT-Drucksache 12/4795; BGH NJW 2010, 3730, 3733.

31 See Directive 2015/849/EU at recital 2; BT-Drucksache 18/11555, p. 87; section 30 para. 2 GWG.

only if the assets originate from one of the enumerated offences, which are as follows:

(i) felonies, that is criminal acts that are punishable by a minimum sentence of one year's imprisonment;[32]
(ii) taking or giving bribes for the exercise of the function of an elected representative, including of foreign legislative organs, according to section 108e StGB; taking or giving bribes meant as an incentive to violate duties of a domestic or foreign official function, according to sections 332 paras. 1 and 3, 334 and 335a StGB; the illegal production, trading, transport or procurement of narcotics, according to section 29 para. 1 s. 1 no. 1 Drugs Act; the illegal possession, production, trading, transport or procurement of precursors of narcotics, according to section 19 para. 1 no. 1 Drug Precursors Control Act;
(iii) the commercial or armed smuggling and the smuggling as a member of a gang, as well as the procurement and trading, commercially or as member of a gang, of smuggled goods, according to sections 373 and 374 para. 2 Tax Code;[33]
(iv) to the extent that the perpetrator (not merely a person aiding and abetting him)[34] acted on a commercial basis or as a member of a gang whose purpose was the continued commission of such offences, thus in the form of organised criminality,[35] each of the following offences: the counterfeiting, procurement or use of, or trading in, payment cards, cheques or promissory notes, according to section 152a StGB; the exploitation or profit-oriented supervision of prostitution, according to section 181a StGB; human trafficking for the purpose of sexual or for other forms of exploitation, according to section 232 StGB; forced prostitution, according to section 232a StGB; forced labour, according to section 232b StGB; work exploitation, according to section 233 StGB; exploitation under unlawful imprisonment, according to section 233a StGB; theft, according to section 242 StGB; embezzlement, according to section 246 StGB; blackmail, according to section 253 StGB; handling stolen goods, according to section 259 StGB; fraud, computer fraud and subsidy fraud, according to sections 263, 263a and 264 StGB; sports betting fraud, according to section 265c StGB; abuse of trust, according to section 266 StGB; forgery, according to section 267 StGB; forgery of electronic data, according to section 269 StGB; causing wrong

---

32 Section 12 StGB.
33 According to section 261 para. 1 s. 1 no. 3 StGB, this also applies to evasion of duties imposed as part of the EU's common agricultural market according to section 12 para. 1 of the Common Market Organisation Implementation and Direct Payments Act (Gesetz zur Durchführung der gemeinsamen Marktorganisationen und der Direktzahlungen).
34 BGH NJW 2009, 326.
35 See BT-Drucksache 13/8651, p. 12; BT-Drucksache 18/4350, p. 20.

entries in public records, according to section 271 StGB; organising unlawful gambling, according to section 284 StGB; taking or giving bribes in commercial dealings, according to section 299 StGB; the intentional unlawful disposal of waste, according to section 326 StGB; the intentional unlawful handling of radioactive or similarly dangerous substances, according to section 328 paras. 1, 3 and 4 StGB; the making of false entries in public records, according to section 348 StGB; the smuggling of foreigners into the federal territory, according to section 96 Residence Act; the incitement to submit fraudulent asylum applications, according to section 84 Asylum Act; tax evasion according to section 370 Tax Code; market manipulation, insider dealing in greenhouse gas emission allowances and insider trading, according to section 119 Securities Trading Act; infringements of trade mark rights or the unlawful use of indications of geographical origin, according to sections 143, 143a and 144 Trade Mark Act; copyright infringements, according to sections 106–108b Copyright Act; infringements of utility model rights, according to section 25 Utility Model Act; infringements of design rights according to sections 51 and 65 Protection of Designs Act; patent infringements, according to section 142 Patent Act; infringements of semiconductor-related property rights, according to section 10 Semiconductor Protection Act; infringements of plant variety property rights, according to section 39 Plant Variety Protection Act;

(v) the preparation of serious violent offences endangering the state, according to section 89a StGB; terrorism financing, according to section 89c StGB; participation in, or support of, a domestic or foreign criminal or terrorist organisation, according to sections 129, 129a and 129b StGB; any[36] crime committed by a member of a domestic or foreign criminal or terrorist organisation.

Beyond the preceding specifications, in particular that the offences enumerated under (iv) above must have been committed on a commercial basis or by a member of a gang,[37] the law does not require that the predicate offence crosses a particular seriousness threshold.

ii. Definition of Money Laundering Acts

– Definition

According to section 261 para. 1 StGB, whosoever (i) hides an object which constitutes proceeds of one of the above-mentioned predicate crimes,

---

36 T Fischer, Strafgesetzbuch, 67th ed., C.H. Beck 2020, §261 para. 22.

37 BGH NStZ 2009, 326.

(ii) conceals its origin, or (iii) obstructs or endangers the establishment of its origin, its discovery, its confiscation or its seizure is guilty of money laundering. Variant (iii) does not require that the perpetrator is him- or herself directly dealing with criminal proceeds, but is in particular meant to cover cases where somebody is helping another to hide or conceal such proceeds. Unlike variants (i) and (ii), variant (iii) requires that the conduct does have an actual impact on the authorities' ability to recover the criminal proceeds; the conduct must at least endanger such recovery. Endangerment means that the conduct does in fact complicate the authorities' access to the proceeds, in that the conduct brings about a real (and not merely abstract) possibility that recovery of the property will fail.[38]

According to section 261 para. 2 StGB, whosoever (iv) procures such an object for himself or a third person, or (v) keeps it in his custody or (vi) uses it for himself or a third person is also guilty of money laundering. These three variants of money laundering aim to economically isolate criminal proceeds.[39] They do not require that the conduct in any way affects the likelihood of a recovery of the criminal proceeds by the authorities.[40] Procurement in variant (iv) requires that the perpetrator or a third person obtains effective control of the object from another;[41] procurement does not require collusion between the transferring and the receiving person.[42] Custody in variant (v) refers to the conscious exercise of custody over an object and includes the case that the perpetrator keeps the object for the predicate offender. For being in the custody of someone, it is however not enough that the object is under his or her control; rather it must be shown that the person deliberately decided to take the object under his or her control.[43]

Section 261 para. 6 StGB does provide that a person is not liable under section 261 para. 2 StGB if a third person previously acquired the object without having thereby committed a criminal offence. This exception does not however cover cases where criminal proceeds are kept by a *bona fide* third person (for example in the trust account of an attorney) if this third party is bound to follow instructions of a *mala fide* person; if such assets are, on the *male fide* person's instructions, then transferred by the *bona fide* person to a another, the receiver of the assets can still be liable under section 261 para. 2 StGB.[44] Furthermore, it must be noted that the exception of section 261 para. 6 StGB does not apply to the money laundering variants of section 261 para. 1 StGB;

38 BGH NJW 1999, 436, 437; BGH NStZ 2017, 28, 29–30; OLG Karlsruhe NStZ 2009, 269, 270.
39 BT-Drucksache 12/989, p. 27; BGH NJW 2001, 2891, 2892.
40 BGH NStZ-RR 2013, 253.
41 BGH NStZ 2010, 222, 223.
42 BGHSt 55, 36 = BGH NStZ 2010, 517.
43 OLG Frankfurt NJW 2005, 1727, 1733.
44 BGHSt 55, 36 = BGH NStZ 2010, 517, 518–519.

somebody who receives criminal proceeds from a *bona fide* person can thus still be liable for money laundering if the receiver thereby obstructs or endangers the recovery of the proceeds by the authorities, or at least accepts this to be the possible consequence of him or her receiving the proceeds.[45] Similarly, section 261 para. 6 StGB does not negate the criminal liability of a person who received the criminal proceeds in good faith, but after becoming aware of their criminal origin intentionally obstructs or endangers their recovery, for example by transferring immovable property to a spouse.[46]

Reflecting the principle that the same wrongful conduct must not be punished repeatedly,[47] section 261 para. 9 s. 2 StGB provides that whosoever is liable because of his or her participation in the antecedent act cannot be punished for money laundering. This includes the case that a person is liable for aiding the commission of the antecedent crime, which notably covers acts aimed at helping the perpetrator to secure the spoils in the immediate aftermath of a property crime.[48] If a person's participation in the antecedent act cannot be established beyond reasonable doubt, she can however still be punished for money laundering.[49] Furthermore, if a person cannot be punished for the antecedent crime in Germany, the fact that her involvement in the antecedent crime could be punished in a foreign jurisdiction does not exclude her punishment for money laundering in Germany.[50] Importantly, as a derogation from section 261 para. 9 s. 2 StGB, section 261 para. 9 s. 3 StGB provides a form of self-laundering by the predicate offender, stating that the exemption from liability does not apply if the perpetrator of a predicate offence, or a person aiding and abetting it, put the acquired object on the market by concealing its unlawful origin. Such concealment has been found notably where the convicted predicate offender made payments into an account that nominally belonged to another person but effectively served to cover the predicate offender's personal expenses, as he thereby concealed himself as the true beneficial owner of the payments.[51] Such criminalisation of self-laundering is based on the assumption that the concealment constitutes an additional wrong that goes beyond the wrong inherent in the predicate offence and does not therefore infringe the constitutional prohibition on punishing the same act repeatedly.[52]

45 T Fischer, Strafgesetzbuch, 67th ed.,C.H. Beck 2020, §261 para. 44.

46 BGH NJW 2001, 2891, 2894; BGH NStZ 2017, 28, 29.

47 See C Schröder/M Bergmann, Warum die Selbstgeldwäsche straffrei bleiben muss, 2013, pp. 55–58.

48 See BGH NStZ-RR 1999, 208.

49 BT-Drucksache 13/8651, pp. 10–11; BGH NStZ 2000, 653, 654; BGHST 50, 224 = BGH NStZ 2006, 237, 238 f.

50 BGHSt 53, 205 = BGH NStZ 2009, 328, 329.

51 BGH NJW 2019, 533, 535.

52 See BR-Drucksache 116/1/17, p. 2; BGH NStZ 2019, 533, 534.

As regards the object of money laundering, section 261 para. 1 primarily focuses on the origin of an object as being criminal. Such object comprises any tangible and intangible assets, including rights, shares and real estate, cash and book money.[53] The object must originate from a predicate offence, though it must not be the same object as the one directly obtained through the respective offence. Section 261 StGB does not provide much detail on the required link between the property generated by the predicate offence and the money laundering act, and the precise contours of this link still remain undefined by the courts.[54] It is however accepted that section 261 StGB also covers objects that, possibly even through a chain of multiple consecutive transactions, were obtained through conversion of, or in exchange for, the initial object of the predicate offence. It suffices that, from an economic perspective, the predicate offence and the object are causally linked.[55] An object is however not deemed to originate from the predicate offence if, as a result of subsequent processing, the economic value of the object is primarily the result of independent efforts of a third person.[56] Furthermore, as section 261 para. 1 StGB contains numerous predicate offences that are not characterised by the obtaining of assets, it is clear that rewards obtained by the predicate offender as well as substitutes for such rewards can also be objects within the meaning of section 261 StGB.[57]

The integration of tainted assets into a larger amount of untainted assets can affect the status of the newly constituted whole, depending on the share of the tainted assets.[58] The Federal Court of Justice has accepted that book money on a bank account is, in its entirety, an object for the purpose of section 261 StGB if the share originating from predicate offences is not entirely insignificant.[59] This was taken to be the case where, within a time span of three years, the share of criminal inflows to the bank account amounted to between 6% and 35% annually. In this case, all the money in the account is deemed to be an object derived from criminal activity.[60] Similarly, where 10% of the money used for the purchase of an item originated from a predicate offence, the purchased item in its entirety is deemed an object within the meaning of section 261 StGB.[61]

---

53 BT-Drucksache 12/989, p. 27.

54 T Fischer, Strafgesetzbuch, 67th ed., C.H. Beck 2020, §261 para. 7.

55 BGHSt 5, 205, 209 = BGH NStZ 2009, 328 f.; BGH NStZ-RR 2010, 109, 110; BGH NStZ 2017, 28, 29.

56 BT-Drucksache 12/989, p. 27.

57 BGHSt 53, 205 = BGH NStZ 2009, 328, 329; see T Fischer, Strafgesetzbuch, 67th ed., C.H. Beck 2020, §261 para. 7.

58 S Barton, NStZ 1993, 159, 163; S Neuheuser, in W Joecks/K Miebach, Münchener Kommentar zum StGB 3rd ed., C.H. Beck 2017, §261 para. 58.

59 BGH, judgment of 15 August 2018 – 5 StR 100/18, at para. 30.

60 BGH NJW 2015, 3254; see also OLG Karlsruhe NJW 2005, 767, 769.

61 BT-Drucksache 12/3533, p. 12.

Where money is transferred from a bank account that contained criminal assets to several other bank accounts, the credit balance of each of those other accounts will be deemed tainted in proportion to the overall amount of the tainted assets and the distribution of those assets between the different accounts.[62]

Arguably departing from the concept of a causal link between predicate offence and the object,[63] section 261 para. 1 StGB specifies that in cases of tax evasion, money laundering can also be committed in respect of expenditure saved by virtue of the tax evasion, in respect of unlawfully acquired tax repayments and allowances, and, in cases of smuggling or the procurement of smuggled goods, in respect of an object in relation to which fiscal charges have been evaded.[64] The precise scope of this extension to section 261 StGB is however not clear yet, in particular to what extent the evasion of taxes might contaminate the overall fortune of the taxable person.[65]

– Exclusion of Liability

Section 261 para. 9 StGB provides for a special exclusion of criminal liability (usually called "active repentance"), stipulating that a person who committed an act of grossly negligent money laundering will not be criminally liable if he or she voluntarily reports the offence to the competent public authority or voluntarily causes such a report to be made, unless the act had already been discovered in whole or in part at the time and the offender knew this or could reasonably have known. Where a person committed an act of intentional money laundering, he or she must, in order to gain immunity from prosecution, in addition cause the criminal proceeds to be officially secured. The competent authorities in the aforementioned sense are state prosecution offices, the police and local courts.[66] Section 261 para. 9 StGB is notably of relevance for the employees of obliged entities in that they can protect themselves from liability for grossly negligent money laundering. The liability exception covers not only the person who directly reported to the authorities (notably a company's head of AML compliance), but also those employees that reported the case internally to the competent (compliance) officers.[67] Given that SARs by obliged entities under section 43 GWG have to be reported exclusively to the FIU and not to the criminal justice authorities, section 43 para. 4 GWG clarifies that the filing

62 OLG Frankfurt NJW 2005, 1727, 1732.

63 T Fischer, Strafgesetzbuch, 67th ed., C.H. Beck 2020, §261 para. 5; S Neuheuser, NStZ 2009, 327.

64 BT-Drucksache 14/7471, p. 9.

65 See T Fischer, Strafgesetzbuch, 67th ed., C.H. Beck 2020, §261 para. 12.

66 See section 158 para. 1 Criminal Procedure Code. (Strafprozessordnung, StPO)

67 BT-Drucksache 12/989, p. 28.

of an SAR will, under the aforementioned conditions, equally negate criminal liability for money laundering.

b. *Mens Rea*

– Intentional Money Laundering

Section 261 paras. 1 and 2 StGB require that the perpetrator acted with intent as regards each of the elements of the money laundering conduct and the origin of the object as resulting from one of the predicate offences enumerated by the law. In order to be intentional, *dolus eventualis* suffices. Accordingly, the perpetrator is deemed to act intentionally already if he or she was aware of the risk that all the elements of the crime of money laundering were present and accepted that this risk might materialise, in the sense that the perpetrator accepted that his or her own objectives were more important than respect for the law.[68] For being intentional, it is thus not necessary that the perpetrator acted with the clear objective to handle proceeds of crime or that he realised that a criminal origin was virtually certain. For the conduct to be intentional, it suffices that the perpetrator was aware of the risk that the object was of criminal origin and accepted this possibility as constituting no reason for abandoning his or her plans. Furthermore, the perpetrator does not have to be aware of the precise circumstances of the predicate offence; rather it suffices that he or she was aware of facts that, from a legal standpoint, provide a rough idea of the predicate offence.[69] It is also even immaterial whether the perpetrator erred about the type of the actual predicate offence, as long as what he or she imagined corresponds to any other of the predicate offences enumerated by the law.[70]

– Grossly Negligent Money Laundering

Partially departing from money laundering as being an intent-based crime, section 261 para. 5 StGB also provides for criminal liability if, in any of the above-mentioned objective forms of money laundering defined under section 261 paras. 1 or 2 StGB, the perpetrator is, through gross negligence, unaware of the fact that the object stems from one of the enumerated predicate offences. Gross negligence thereby refers to cases where, in light of the circumstances, the criminal origin of the object was blatant and the

---

68 Section 15 StGB; BGHSt 7, 363; BGH NStZ-RR 2009, 13, 14, BGH NStZ 2008, 453, 454; B Vogel, in M Dyson/B Vogel, The Limits of Criminal Law, Intersentia 2018, p. 50.

69 BGHSt 43, 158 = BGH NStZ 1998, 42, 43; KG, NStZ-RR 2013, 13.

70 BGH, Decision of 26 July 2018 – 3 StR 626/17, para. 14.

perpetrator demonstrated particular indifference or gross carelessness towards its origin.[71]

– Special Standards for Criminal Defence Attorneys

As regards the receipt of their professional fee by criminal defence attorneys and in order to address the heightened risk that such attorneys, due to the nature of their professional activity, might be suspected of money laundering and thereby the attorney–client relationship severely impaired, the jurisprudence of the Federal Constitutional Court has in this respect stipulated a more demanding intent requirement. For such receipt to constitute money laundering (usually in the form of procurement of criminal proceeds according to section 261 para. 2 StGB) the attorney must positively know that the fees were the proceeds of a predicate offence.[72] Thus in such cases, *dolus eventualis* regarding the criminal origin of the fees does not suffice to found liability for intentional money laundering. In the same vein, the receipt of fees that originate form a predicate offence does not give rise to liability for grossly negligent money laundering according to section 261 para. 5 StGB.[73]

2. *Money Laundering by Omission*

German law does in principle accept liability for money laundering by omission according to section 13 StGB regarding persons who are under a duty to avert the respective act provided that they become aware that another person is about to commit an act of money laundering and fail to take appropriate measures against it. Such duty will normally apply to state agents who are under law tasked with the aversion of crimes, especially police officers within the range of their area of competence,[74] and also officers of the FIU. In contrast, it is controversial and has not yet been decided by the courts to what extent private individuals can be liable for money laundering by omission when they are subject to AML obligations, in particular AML compliance officers of an obliged entities.[75] In any case, one should point out that obliged entities' CDD obligations require them and their employees to establish the risk entailed in particular business relationships and transactions, and for this purpose to

---

[71] BGHSt 43, 158 = BGH NStZ 1998, 42, 44; BGHSt 50, 347 = BGH NJW 2006, 1297, 1298–1299; BGH NJW 2008, 2516, 2517; BGH NStZ-RR 2019, 145, 146.

[72] BVerfGE 110, 226 = BVerfG NJW 2004, 1304, 1311.

[73] BVerfGE 110, 226 = BVerfG NJW 2004, 1304, 1312.

[74] T Fischer, Strafgesetzbuch, 67th ed., C.H. Beck 2020, §13 para. 30.

[75] C Nestler/M El-Ghazi, in F Herzog/O Achtelik (eds.), Geldwäschegesetz, §261, paras. 117–118.

perform measures to be able to detect cases of money laundering. This does not necessarily equal a responsibility to prevent money laundering, but primarily an obligation to gather sufficient relevant information.[76] One should also note that responsibility to decide upon the permissibility of a transaction is, through the reporting of suspicious activities and the obligation of obliged entities to then wait for three working days before carrying out the reported transaction, ultimately left to the FIU.[77] In light of the differentiated system of internal information flows and the allocation of corresponding individual responsibilities resulting from the GWG (not least the obligation, in many cases of high risk, to obtain senior management approval),[78] one must doubt whether the law in addition contains an implicit duty of senior management officials to intervene even in situations where they are not actively involved in the processing of a particular business relationship or transaction.

3. *Aggravated Forms of Money Laundering*

Section 261 para. 4 StGB provides for an aggravated form of intentional money laundering in especially serious cases. The provision specifies that such a case typically occurs if the money laundering is done on a commercial basis or as a member of a gang whose purpose is the continued commission of money laundering. An act of money laundering is deemed to be committed on a commercial basis if the perpetrator had the plan to commit several offences of money laundering to produce a regular income for more than merely a short time and of more than merely negligent volume.[79] Money laundering is committed as a member of a gang if at least three persons agree to join forces to commit several offences of money laundering, even if the details of those further offences have not yet been determined.[80] Beyond these two examples in which aggravated money laundering will usually be established, the law does not provide an exhaustive definition of aggravating circumstances. Aggravated cases are those that, as regards the objective seriousness and the degree of culpability, clearly distinguish themselves from average cases of the same offence and therefore require the use of a more severe sentencing range.[81] Such particular seriousness can notably result from a particularly high volume of the criminal proceeds.[82]

---

[76] See section 10 para. 9 and section 15 para. 9 GWG.
[77] Section 43 para. 1 and section 46 para. 1 s. 1 no. 2 GWG.
[78] Section 15 para. 4 s. 1 no. 1, para. 5 no. 2, para. 7 no. 2 GWG.
[79] BGH NStZ 2009, 326; see BGH NStZ-RR 2011, 373.
[80] See BGHSt 46, 321 = BGH NStZ 2001, 421–422.
[81] BVerfGK 14, 177 = BVerfG NJW 2008, 3627, 3628; BGH NStZ 1992, 229.
[82] See BGH 1981, 692, 693; T Fischer, Strafgesetzbuch, 67th ed., C.H. Beck 2020, §46 para. 89.

4. *Statutes of Limitation*

According to section 78 para. 3 in conjunction with section 261 paras. 1 and 2 StGB, punishment for intentional and for grossly negligent money laundering is in principle precluded five years after its commission. Certain procedural measures will however interrupt or stay the limitation period. According to section 78c paras. 1 and 3 StGB the limitation period restarts again after certain investigative measures (such as the interrogation of the suspect or a search warrant), though the limitation period will in any case run out at the latest 10 years after the commission of the offence. In addition, according to section 78b para. 4 StGB, in aggravated cases of intentional money laundering the limitation period is stayed for a maximum of five years once proceeding have been commenced before a district court. According to section 78b para. 3 StGB, the limitation period is also stayed by a first-instance judgment in the matter until the time of the judgment of the court of last resort. As regards the determination of the applicable time of the commission of the offence where the perpetrator keeps criminal proceeds in his or her custody, the limitation period runs only from the moment when the unlawful state of affairs is terminated, that is at the time when the perpetrator stops to consciously exercise custody over the proceeds;[83] this rule seems however inapplicable as regards expenditure saved by virtue of the tax evasion, where for the purpose of the limitation period one will need to refer to the moment when the tax payment would normally have been due.[84] The time of the commission of the predicate offence is of no legal relevance for the liability for money laundering; in particular the expiry of the limitation period of the predicate offence does not preclude punishment for money laundering.[85]

5. *Jurisdictional Rules*

As regards acts of money laundering, the general rules on jurisdiction of the StGB apply. According to section 3 StGB, German law is in principle only applicable to acts committed on German territory.[86] Section 9 para. 1 StGB defines the place of the offence in particular as the place where the offender acted or, in the case of an omission, should have acted. The law thereby primarily refers to the physical presence of the perpetrator on the national territory at the

---

83 See BGHSt 20, 227 = BGH NJW 1965, 1817; N Bosch, in A Eser et al., Strafgesetzbuch, 30th ed., C.H. Beck 2019, §78a para. 11.

84 See T Fischer, Strafgesetzbuch, 67th ed., C.H. Beck 2020, §78a para. 15.

85 B Hecker, in A Eser et al., Strafgesetzbuch, 30th ed., C.H. Beck 2019, §261 para. 11; S Neuheuser, in W Joecks/K Miebach, Münchener Kommentar zum StGB, volume 4, 3rd ed., C.H. Beck 2017, §261 para. 136.

86 For offences committed on German ships and aircraft, see section 4 StGB.

time of the offence. The presence of one joint perpetrator (not merely a person aiding and abetting the money laundering) on the national territory gives rise to the applicability of German law to other joint perpetrators that acted outside the national territory, even if the one who acted on the national territory was him- or herself performing merely preparatory acts.[87] In contrast, as a definitive loss of the proceeds by the victim of the predicate offence does not constitute an element of the offence of money laundering, the place of such loss is immaterial for establishing the place of the offence of money laundering.[88] In respect of offences committed abroad, section 7 para. 1 StGB provides that German criminal law applies to offences committed against a German, if the act is also a criminal offence at the locality of its commission. In this regard, the Federal Court of Justice has accepted German jurisdiction over money laundering acts committed abroad if the criminal proceeds originated from a predicate offence committed against a national person of German nationality, though not if the immediate victim was merely a legal person established in Germany.[89] According to section 7 para. 2, German criminal law furthermore applies to offences committed abroad if the act is also a criminal offence at the locality of its commission, provided that the offender was German at the time of the offence or became German after the commission or was a foreigner and, despite him being discovered in Germany and despite his prosecution by another state being possible, is not extradited.[90]

As regards objects that are the proceeds of a predicate offence committed abroad, section 261 para. 8 StGB provides that such objects are equivalent to the objects of predicate offences committed in Germany if such offence is also punishable at the place of its commission. For the proceeds of an offence committed abroad to be covered by section 261 StGB, it is thus necessary that such offence fulfils the elements of a predicate offence under German law.[91] In this respect, one must note that some predicate offences do in principle only cover conduct directed against domestic institutions and extend to foreign interests only where the law explicitly provides for it. For example, as already stated above, the catalogue of predicate offences in section 261 para. 1 StGB covers the taking or giving of bribes meant as an incentive to violate duties of an official function both as regards domestic and foreign official functions, since section 335a StGB, to which section 261 StGB explicitly refers, provides for such extension. Similarly, section 129b StGB, to which section 261 StGB

[87] BGHSt 39, 88 = BGH NStZ 1993, 180; BGH NStZ-RR 2009, 197.

[88] BGH NStZ-RR 2013, 253; BGH NJW 2018, 2742, 2743.

[89] BGH NJW 2018, 2743, 2743.

[90] See T Fischer, Strafgesetzbuch, 67th ed., C.H. Beck 2020, §7 para. 10.

[91] BT-Drucksache 13/8651, p. 12; BGHSt 53, 205 = BGH NStZ 2009, 328; K Kühl, in K Kühl/M Heger, Strafgesetzbuch, 29th ed. 2018, §261, para. 4.

again explicitly refers, extends the scope of criminal liability for the involvement in a criminal or terrorist organisation to organisations operating outside of the European Union, provided that the particular case is in some important way related to Germany. In contrast, as regards tax evasion, the law does not provide an extension to the evasion of foreign taxes, thus tax-evading conduct committed abroad (which is anyway covered by section 261 StGB only if done on a commercial basis or as a member of a gang) is not a predicate offence where it aims exclusively at the evasion of foreign tax duties.[92]

C. NON-CRIMINAL DEFINITION OF MONEY LAUNDERING

Section 1 subsection 1 of the GWG refers to the StGB's definition of money laundering without adding any modifications. Accordingly, the criminal law definition underpins obliged entities' preventive obligations as well as the responsibilities of the FIU.

D. SCOPE OF OBLIGED ENTITIES

1. *Financial and Banking Institutions*

According to section 2 para. 1, the following financial services providers are obliged entities:[93] (i) credit institutions[94] within the meaning of section 1 para. 1 of the Banking Act (Kreditwesengesetz, KWG), that is undertakings that provide banking services, and domestic branches of foreign-domiciled credit institutions;[95] (ii) financial services institutions, that is undertakings that, commercially or in a business-like manner, provide financial services for others without being a credit institution,[96] and domestic branches of foreign-domiciled

---

92 See section 370 para. 7 AO; T Fischer, Strafgesetzbuch, 67th ed., C.H. Beck 2020, §261 para. 27.

93 According to section 50 no. 1 GWG, the enumerated obliged financial businesses, including branches of foreign businesses as well payment institutions and electronic money institutions domiciled in another EEA contracting state, are mostly supervised by the Federal Financial Supervisory Authority (Bundesanstalt für Finanzdienstleistungsaufsicht); exceptions notably apply to financial undertakings (vi), whose supervision will depend on the particular services they perform; see e.g. section 34f Trade Regulations Act (Gewerbeordnung, GewO).

94 According to section 25l KWG, this also covers financial holding companies and mixed financial holding companies that are subordinated companies within the meaning of section 10a KWG or have been designated as such; see Article 4(1)(20) and (21) of Regulation (EU) 575/2013.

95 For exceptions see section 2 para. 1 nos. 3–8 KWG, notably businesses that provide banking services exclusively to other businesses within the same group of companies.

96 Section 1 para. 1a KWG.

financial services institutions;[97] (iii) payment institutions and electronic money institutions, that is in particular providers of payment services or electronic money services that are not credit institutions within the meaning of Regulation 575/2013,[98] and domestic branches of foreign-domiciled similar institutions; (iv) agents of payment institutions and agents of electronic money institutions as well as payment institutions and electronic money institutions domiciled in another EEA contracting state insofar as they established domestic agents;[99] (v) independent traders that sell or re-exchange electronic money of a credit institution; (vi) financial undertakings that primarily perform certain statutorily defined finance-related services[100] and domestic branches of such foreign-domiciled undertakings, provided that they do not already fall under one of the preceding categories and are also not insurance undertakings, investment management companies,[101] independent lawyers, patent attorneys, notaries, accountants, tax advisors or company or trust service providers; (vii) investment management companies[102] and domestic branches of foreign investment companies, notably[103] those that are domiciled in another Member State of the EU or the European Economic Area and fulfil the requirements of a management company or of an internally managed investment company

---

97 For exceptions see section 2 para. 6 s. 1 nos. 3–10 and 12, notably businesses whose financial service consists exclusively in the management of a system of employees' ownership in their own or affiliated companies.

98 See section 1 para. 1 no. 1 and para. 2 no. 1 Payment Services Supervision Act (Zahlungsdiensteaufsichtsgesetz, ZAG).

99 Section 1 paras. 9 and 10 ZAG.

100 According to section 1 para. 24 s. 1 GWG, financial undertakings are those whose main activity consists of the purchasing, holding or selling of shares, purchasing money claims with a financing function, trading in financial instruments for one's own account (which usually excludes mere debt collection activities; BT-Drucksache 19/13827, p. 65), advising others on investments in financial instruments, advising undertakings on the capital structure, industrial strategy and related questions, advising other undertakings on mergers and acquisitions, or brokering loans between credit institutions. For exceptions regarding holding companies whose activity is confined to the management of their shareholding outside the sector of credit and financial institutions and insurance undertakings, see section 1 para. 24 s. 2 GWG and BT-Drucksache 19/13827, pp. 64–65.

101 Section 1 para. 3 KWG.

102 See in particular section 17 para. 1 of the Investment Act (Kapitalanlagegesetzbuch, KAGB).

103 For the further scope of domestic branches of foreign-domiciled investment companies, see section 1 para. 1 no. 9 GWG in conjunction with section 1 para. 17 KAGB, which includes domestic branches of those foreign companies that are alternative investment fund managers within the meaning of Directive 2011/61/EU (that is, companies which are not undertakings for collective investment in transferable securities (UCITS) within the meaning of Directive 2009/65/EC), and with section 1 para. 18 KAGB, which covers management companies that meet the requirements of Directive 2011/61/EU. According to section 1 para. 1 no. 9 GWG, alternative investment fund management companies domiciled in a third state that, according to section 57 para. 1 KAGB, are subject to the supervision of the Federal Financial Supervisory Authority are also covered.

within the meaning of Directive 2009/65/EC, and those domiciled in a third state that are alternative investment fund managers within the meaning of Directive 2011/61/EU.

Insurance undertakings[104] within the meaning of Directive 2009/138/EC as well as domestic branches of such undertakings are obliged entities to the extent that they offer life insurance (including contractual pension insurances) activities that fall under the Directive,[105] accident insurances with return of premiums, loans or capitalisation products. To the extent that they provide the preceding products and services, insurance agents and insurance brokers,[106] and domestic branches of foreign insurance intermediaries, are obliged entities as well.[107]

2. *Virtual Currency System Participants*

With the transposition of Directive 2018/843/EU, the German legislator has extended the definition of financial services, and thereby the scope of financial service institutions, to the keeping, management and safeguarding, for others, of virtual assets or of private cryptographic keys that serve to hold, store or transfer virtual assets.[108] The definition of financial instruments was expanded to virtual assets. The law defines such assets as digital representations of value that is not issued or guaranteed by a central bank or a public authority and does not possess a legal status of currency or money, but due to an agreement or actual practice, is accepted by natural or legal persons as a means of exchange or payment or serves investment purposes, and which can be transferred, stored and traded electronically.[109] Given that virtual currencies constitute financial instruments,[110] those who purchase and sell or exchange them in

---

104 According to section 50 no. 2 GWG in conjunction with sections 320 and 321 Insurance Supervision Act (Versicherungsaufsichtsgesetz, VAG), the supervision of private insurance undertakings usually falls under the responsibility of the Federal Financial Supervisory Authority, if this task has not been attributed to the competent authorities of the federal states (*Länder*) in particular due to the comparatively limited economic significance of the undertaking.

105 Article 2(3)(a) of Directive 2009/138/EC.

106 Section 59 Insurance Contract Act (Versicherungsvertragsgesetz). According to section 34d GewO, the licensing of insurance agents and the revocations of licences, and therefore the supervision, is performed by the local Chamber of Industry and Commerce.

107 For narrow exceptions in this regard see section 34d paras. 6 and 7 no. 1 GewO.

108 Section 1 para. 1a s. 2 no. 6 KWG.

109 Section 1 para. 11 s. 2 no. 10 and s. 3 KWG.

110 To this effect, see already Bundesanstalt für Finanzdienstleistungsaufsicht, Merkblatt – Hinweise zum Zahlungsdiensteaufsichtsgesetz of 22.12.2011 as modified on 29.11.2017, at (4)(a)(aa); Bundesanstalt für Finanzdienstleistungsaufsicht, Bafin Journal, January 2014, pp. 27–29.

their own name on behalf of another are providing a banking service within the meaning of the law and are therefore a credit institution, provided that they do so in a commercial way. Those who are acting as intermediaries, in particular by operating a multilateral trading platform, are providing a financial service and are therefore a financial service institution.[111] Accordingly, traders in virtual currency and providers of virtual currency exchange platforms (including virtual currency to virtual currency exchange platforms),[112] and domestic branches of such foreign businesses, are obliged entities.

3. *Legal Profession and Tax Advisors*

According to section 2 para. 1, attorneys at law, legal advisers that are member of a bar associations,[113] patent attorneys[114] and notaries[115] are obliged entities to the extent that they assist a client in the planning or carrying out of one of the following businesses: (i) buying and selling of real property or business entities; (ii) managing of money, securities or other assets; (iii) opening or management of bank, savings or securities accounts; (iv) organisation of contributions necessary for the creation, operation or management of companies; (v) creation, operation or management of trusts, companies or similar structures. Furthermore, these legal professionals are also obliged entities to the extent that they execute, on behalf of and for their client, financial or real estate transactions, advise the client on the capital structure, industrial strategy or related questions, provide advice or services in relation to mergers and acquisitions, or assist on tax matters in a business-like manner. To the extent that they perform the aforementioned activities, independent legal advisors who are not members of a bar association, and natural persons and entities that, due to their special knowledge, have been authorised to provide certain legal services, such as the provision of advice on foreign law, are also covered.[116] In contrast, tax advisors

---

111 See section 1 para. 1 no. 6 and para. 1a s. 2 no. 1 KWG.

112 Bundesanstalt für Finanzdienstleistungsaufsicht, Virtuelle Währungen/Virtual Currency (VC) of 28.04.2016; Bundesanstalt für Finanzdienstleistungsaufsicht, Konsultation 17/2018, Entwurf Rundschreiben Sorgfaltspflichten im Zusammenhang mit virtuellen Währungen – Hinweise für ein angemessenes risikoorientiertes Vorgehen of 18.10.2018, para. II.

113 According to section 50 no. 3 GWG, the local bar association performs the function of the supervisory authority.

114 According to section 50 no. 4 GWG, the Chamber of Patent Attorneys performs the function of the supervisory authority.

115 According to section 50 no. 5 GWG, the president of the local Regional Court (Landgericht) performs the function of the supervisory authority.

116 See section 10 para. 1 of the Legal Services Act (Rechtsdienstleistungsgesetz). This does not cover the provision of debt collection services; section 2 para. 1 no. 11 GWG.

(including income tax self-help organisations) and tax agents[117] are obliged entities irrespective of any particular type of professional activity.

4. *Informal Value Transfer Systems*

Value transfer systems will usually constitute a provision of payment services and, if conducted commercially or otherwise at a scale that requires business-like organisational arrangements, constitute payment institutions, and as such require a permission by the Federal Financial Supervisory Authority.[118] If, despite fulfilling the aforementioned conditions, they operate informally without permission, such systems are illegal and their operation constitutes a criminal offence.[119] In contrast, if informal value transfer services are not provided commercially and only at a scale that, due to its limited scope, does not require being organised in a business-like manner, they do not constitute payment institutions and are then also not obliged entities.

5. *Non-Profit Sector*

The law does not explicitly say to what extent non-profit entities might constitute an obliged entity. Section 2 para. 1 no. 15 ZAG clarifies that the receiving and delivery of cash, if done in the context of a non-profit activity, does not constitute a payment service, and the acting entity is thus not a payment institution and so also not an obliged entity. Beyond this particular and narrow exception,[120] no special rules apply. In particular, non-profit entities can be payment institutions and thus obliged entities where they transfer money from the donor to the ultimate beneficiary if the selection of the ultimate beneficiary is done by the donor him- or herself and not left to the transferring non-profit entity.[121] Non-profit entities will furthermore fall under other categories of obliged entities if they fulfil the respective statutory criteria, for example if

---

117 According to section 50 no. 7 GWG, the local Chamber of Tax Advisors performs the function of the supervisory authority.

118 Section 1 para. 1 s. 2 no. 6 and section 10 para. 1 ZAG; Bundesanstalt für Finanzdienstleistungsaufsicht, Merkblatt – Hinweise zum Zahlungsdiensteaufsichtsgesetz of 22.12.2011 as modified on 22.11.2017, at (2)(e).

119 Section 63 para. 1 no. 4 ZAG; see BGH NStZ-RR 2016, pp. 15–16; S Warius, Das Hawala-Finanzsystem in Deutschland – ein Fall für die Bekämpfung von Geldwäsche und Terrorismusfinanzierung?, Duncker & Humblot 2009, pp. 119–123.

120 See Bundesanstalt für Finanzdienstleistungsaufsicht, Merkblatt – Hinweise zum Zahlungsdiensteaufsichtsgesetz of 22.12.2011 as modified on 22.11.2017.

121 See section 1 para. 1 s. 2 no. 6 ZAG; Bundesanstalt für Finanzdienstleistungsaufsicht, Merkblatt – Hinweise zum Zahlungsdiensteaufsichtsgesetz of 22.12.2011 as modified on 22.11.2017, at (2)(e).

they are a credit institution that provides loans and thus banking services to beneficiaries.[122]

6. *Overview of Other Obliged Entities*

Beyond the aforementioned, section 2 para. 1 extends the scope of obliged entities to several other commercial or professional activities. The law notably covers auditors[123] in all their commercial or professional activities.

Furthermore, trust or company service providers and trustees are designated as obliged entities if they provide one of the following services to another: (i) establishing a legal person or partnership; (ii) performing a directorship or management function of a legal person or a partnership, performing the function of a partner of a partnership or performing a similar function; (iii) providing a domicile or an address, and related services, for a legal person, a partnership or trust; (iv) performing the function of a trustee for an entity that serves to manage or allocate fiduciary assets; (v) performing the function of a nominal shareholder for another person, provided that this person is not a company listed on an organised market that, as regards the distribution of voting rights, is subject to transparency requirements of EU law or to equivalent international standards; (vi) creating the opportunity for another person to perform the functions described under (ii), (iv) and (vi).

Section 2 para. 1 also designates estate agents, who are defined as persons who commercially broker the purchase, sale or lease of real estate and equivalent rights, commercial premises or accommodation.[124] Gambling organisers and gambling agents[125] are equally obliged entities.[126] The law also includes persons trading in goods, that is persons who commercially sell goods, irrespective of in whose name and on whose account the person acts.[127] Also covered are art

122 See S Winheller/L Auffenberg, Benötigen Stiftungen eine Bafin-Genehmigung?, BW-Bank Stiftungsmanagement, 1/2017, pp. 11–12.

123 According to section 50 no. 6 GWG, the Chamber of Public Accountants performs the function of the supervisory authority.

124 Section 1 para. 11 GWG.

125 According to section 50 no. 8 GWG, the function of the AML supervisory authority is performed by the authority that is competent for the general supervision of such entities. This can vary between federal states and between the particular types of gambling.

126 For exceptions, see section 2 para. 1 no. 15 GWG, excluding notably game machine operators and lotteries that are organised outside the internet, provided, in both cases, that they are licensed by the competent authority.

127 See section 1 para. 9 GWG. The supervisory authorities competent for estate agents and traders in goods are designated by state (*Länder*) regulations; see section 50 no. 9 GWG. See for example section 8a s. 1 Bavarian Ordinance on Jurisdiction (BayZustV); Article 1 nos. 4 and 6 Saxon Ordinance on Jurisdiction in Matters of the Money Laundering Act (SächsGwGZustVO); section 1 Baden-Wuerttemberg Ordinance on Jurisdiction (Zuständigkeitenverordnung BW).

brokers, that is persons who, on a commercial basis, act as intermediaries in the trade of works of art[128] (including art galleries auction houses), and art warehouse keepers, that is persons who on a commercial basis, store works of art in free-trade zones, in both cases irrespective of in whose name and on whose account.[129] Finally, section 2 para. 3 provides that, while they are not considered to be obliged entities, customer identification and reporting obligations as well as obligations to cooperate with the FIU also apply to courts that perform public auctions for the purpose of a foreclosure sale of real estate, registered vessels and aircraft, but only insofar as the auction involves cash transactions of at least €10,000. According to section 2 para. 4, the same obligations apply to authorities and corporations under public law that perform public auctions, though again only insofar as this involves cash transactions of at least €10,000; these obligations do not however apply to the auction sale of items that were seized through foreclosure.

E. RELATIONSHIP BETWEEN AML AND ANTI-TERRORISM FINANCING FRAMEWORK(S)

The GWG does not provide for substantial differences in the treatment of money laundering and terrorism financing, thus obliged entities' obligations as well as the competences and powers of the FIU are, in principle, the same for both types of crime. The law does, however, somewhat differentiate as regards preventive and investigative powers of competent authorities. If facts indicate that assets would serve the financing of terrorism, the Federal Financial Supervisory Authority may prohibit transactions and issue instructions to the management of credit institutions, financial service institutions, payment service institutions, electronic money institutions and investment management companies.[130] Furthermore, the Criminal Procedure Code provides criminal justice authorities with some investigative powers in cases of a suspicion of terrorism financing that may not be available against money laundering.[131]

---

128 See Annex II no. 53 UStG; BT-Drucksache 19/13827, p. 68.

129 Section 1 para. 23 and section 2 para. 1 no. 16 GWG.

130 Section 6a KWG; section 27 subsection 2 s. 1 ZAG; section 6 KAGB.

131 Compare in particular section 100a subsection 2 no. 1 (a) and (m), allowing telecommunications interception in cases of self-laundering only where the assets originate from a number of particularly serious predicate offences, section 100b subsection 2 no. 1 (a) and (l) StPO, allowing remote online searches of digital devices only in aggravated cases of money laundering, section 112a subsection 1 s. 1 no. 1 StPO, lowering the requirements for the ordering of pretrial detention, and section 443 subsection 1 s. 1 no. 1 StPO, facilitating the freezing of assets of individuals that are indicted or arrested for a suspicion of terrorism financing.

III. THE SYSTEM OF MONEY LAUNDERING PREVENTION

A. CUSTOMER DUE DILIGENCE

1. *Standard CDD Rules*

a. Triggers and Timing

– General Triggers

According to section 10 para. 3, obliged entities must apply general CDD measures in the following cases:

- when establishing a business relationship,[132] that is, according to section 1 para. 4, a relationship that is directly related to the commercial or professional activities of obliged entities and that, at the moment of its establishment, is meant to have an element of duration;[133]
- in the case of transactions that are carried out outside a business relationship if they are (i) a money transfer within the meaning of Article 3(9) Regulation 2015/847 and this transfer amounts to €1,000 or more,[134] or (ii) the performance of any other transaction worth €15,000 or more; according to section 1 para. 5, a transaction means any act, or where there seems to be a link between them,[135] multiple acts, that aim at, or result in, a movement of money or movement of other assets;

---

132 Supervisory guidance for the financial sector specifies that this usually does not include the establishment of new contracts with the same client within an existing contractual relationship; Bafin, Auslegungs- und Anwendungshinweise zum Geldwäschegesetz of December 2018, at III.4.1.

133 Guidance by the Federal Ministry of Finance in Bundesministerium der Finanzen, Auslegungshinweise des Bundesministeriums der Finanzen zur Handhabung des Verdachtsmeldewesens of 6 November 2014, p. 2, clarifies that this already covers the initiation of the relationship.

134 According to financial sector supervisory guidance, this also coves cash payments to another person's account; Bafin, Auslegungs- und Anwendungshinweise zum Geldwäschegesetz of December 2018, at III.4.2.2.

135 As specified by financial sector supervisory guidance Bafin, Auslegungs- und Anwendungshinweise zum Geldwäschegesetz of December 2018, at III.4.1.2, a link is usually established if a significant number of transactions within a limited time span are similar with regard to the underlying business deal, purpose or business processing, even if the contract partners are not identical. For credit institutions, financial services institutions, financial holding companies and investment management companies, this will usually require the use of IT systems to detect relevant links; see section 25h para. 2 KWG and section 28 para. 1 s. 4 KAGB.

- irrespective of any derogation, exemption or threshold amount according to the GWG or other laws, if there are facts that indicate that (i) assets that are related to a transaction or business relationship are an object of money laundering, or (ii) assets a related to terrorism financing;
- when there are doubts whether information that was obtained on the basis of the GWG regarding the identity of the contract partner, the person representing the contract partner or the beneficial owner is accurate.

According to section 10 para. 3a, obliged entities must fulfil general CDD duties with respect all new customers; as regards existing business relationships, these duties must be fulfilled at an appropriate time on a risk-sensitive basis, in particular when (i) significant circumstances of a customer change, or (ii) the obliged entity is legally obliged to contact the customer in the course of the respective year in order to verify beneficial ownership information, or (iii) the obliged entity is required to verify the account holder's place of residence under Directive 2011/16/EU to identify accounts belonging to a person that, for taxation purposes, is a resident in another Member State.[136]

- Special Triggers for Particular Obliged Entities

The GWG provides a number of further CDD triggers for particular types of obliged entities that, in some cases, go beyond the aforementioned standard triggers and, in other cases, are less demanding.

Section 10 para. 4 lowers the threshold amount for transactions outside a business relationship for payment institutions and electronic money institutions within the meaning of section 1 para. 3 ZAG, agents of payment institutions and agents of electronic money institutions within the meaning of section 1 paras. 9 and 10 ZAG, and independent businesses that sell or re-exchange electronic money of a credit institution within the meaning of section 1 para. 2 no. 2 ZAG. Every time these obliged entities receive cash in the performance of payment services, independently of the amount or the establishment of a business relationship, they have to identity the contract partner and, where relevant, the person representing him or her, to verify whether the person representing the contract partner is entitled to this effect, and to identify the beneficial owner.

136 Sections 9–17 Act on the Automatic Exchange of Information on Financial Accounts in Tax Matters (Gesetz zum automatischen Austausch von Informationen über Finanzkonten in Steuersachen, FKAustG); see also Article 8 para. 3a and Annex 1 section II–VII of Council Directive 2011/16/EU of 15 February 2011 on administrative cooperation in the field of taxation and repealing Directive 77/799/EEC as amended by Council Directive (EU) 2016/2258 of 6 December 2016.

Section 25i para. 1 KWG and section 27 para. 2 s. 1 ZAG provide that credit institutions, payment service institutions and electronic money institutions,[137] when they issue electronic money, must apply general CDD to all transactions outside a business relationship, irrespective of any threshold amount. However, according to section 25i para. 2 KWG, they are exempted from this obligation under certain cumulative conditions, in particular where the instruments of payment are non-rechargeable or where monthly payments with a rechargeable instrument are limited to €150, the electronically stored value does not exceed €150, the instrument cannot be bought or recharged with anonymous electronic money, and a re-exchange of the electronic money through a cash pay-out or through distance payment cannot exceed €50.

Similarly, when they are involved in the issuing of electronic money, agents of electronic money institutions and independent businesses that sell or re-exchange electronic money of a credit institution must, according to section 10 para. 7, apply CDD to all transactions outside a business relationship, irrespective of any threshold amount. However, in this case they only need to identify the contract partner, where relevant identify the person representing him or her and verify whether this person is entitled to represent the contract partner, and determine if the contract partner is a politically exposed person, a close relative of such a person or somebody who is known to be closely related to such a person. Furthermore, according to section 25i para. 2 of the KWG and section 10 para. 7 GWG, the aforementioned obliged entities are exempted from those due diligence obligations under the same cumulative conditions as those that, as mentioned above, apply to the issuing of electronic money by credit institutions.

For transactions in foreign notes and coins of a value of €2,500 or more that are not processed through an account set up for the client at this institution, section 25k para. 1 KWG provides that credit institutions and financial services institutions[138] must identify the contract partner, where relevant identify the person representing him or her and verify whether this person is entitled to represent the contract partner, clarify whether the contract partner is acting for a beneficial owner and where this is the case identify the beneficial owner, and determine if the contract partner or the beneficial owner is a politically exposed person, a close relative of such a person or somebody who is known to be closely related to such a person.

Gambling provides and gambling brokers, to the extent that they are obliged entities, have to apply CDD, according to section 10 para. 5, already

[137] Where relevant, the same obligation also applies to investment management companies; see section 28 para. 1 s. 4 KAGB.

[138] Where relevant, the same obligation also applies to investment management companies; section 28 para. 1 s. 4 KAGB.

where a player's winnings or stakes amount to €2,000 or more, except where the gambling is provided or brokered online. For online gambling, additional CDD obligations apply.

Estate agents must, according to section 10 para. 6, perform standard CDD only (i) when they broker sales contracts, or (ii) when they broker rental contracts that involve a monthly rent of €10,000 or more.

According to section 10 para. 6a, traders in goods have to perform standard CDD in the case of (i) transactions of works of art worth €10,000 or more; (ii) transactions of precious metals,[139] if the trader, him- or herself or through a third person, makes or received cash payments of €2,000 or more; and (iii) transactions of other goods, if the trader, him- or herself or through a third person, makes or received cash payments of €10,000 or more. Art brokers and art warehouse keepers must perform standard CDD in the case of transactions worth €10,000 or more.

Section 11 para. 1 specifies that the identification of contract partners, of persons representing them and of beneficial owners must, in principle, be carried out before the establishment of a business relationship or before the performance of a transaction. However, the identification can also be carried out, without undue delay, during the establishment of the business relationship if this is necessary in order not to interrupt the normal course of business, provided that the risk of money laundering and terrorism financing is low.[140]

Providing an exception to the aforementioned rule, section 11 para. 2 specifies that estate agents have to identify the contract partners of the purchase, persons representing them and the beneficial owner as soon as the contract partner of the estate agent expresses a genuine interest in the performance of the purchase agreement, provided that the parties to the purchase agreement are sufficiently determined.

Furthermore, as regards credit institutions, financial service institutions and investment management companies, section 25j KWG and section 28 para. 1 s. 4 provide that the verification of the identity of the contract partner,

---

139 According to section 1 para. 10, high-value goods are those which, due to their nature, value or intended use, stand out from commodities of daily use, or which, due to their price, do not constitute an everyday purchase. This notably includes precious metals, such as gold, silver and platinum, gemstones, jewellery and watches, works of arts, antiquities, cars, vessels, motorboats and aircraft.

140 For the criteria of a low risk, see below section III.2.a. Section 54 para. 2 s. 2 VAG specifies that, where claims from an insurance policy are ceded to a third person, the identity of the new beneficiary and, where applicable, its beneficial owner must be established when the insurance undertaking is informed of the cession. According to section 54 para. 2 s. 3 VAG, the identification of an insurance beneficiary who is not the policyholder, and where relevant the beneficiary's beneficial owner, can be completed after the establishment of the business relationship, but at the latest at the moment of the payout or when the beneficiary intends to avail herself of her rights.

of a person representing him and of the beneficial owner can also be done immediately after the opening of an account or securities account (and thus after the establishment of the business relationship). In this case, it must however be ensured that no funds can be transferred from the account before the verification has been completed. A repayment of deposited funds shall only be disbursed to the depositor.

Identification of the contract partner is, according to section 11 para. 3, not required if the obliged entity has already identified the respective person on a previous occasion as part of the entity's due diligence obligations and recorded the information that was thereby obtained. If the objective circumstances give rise to doubt as to whether the information is still accurate, the obliged entity must perform a new identification.

b. CDD Measures

– General CDD Measures

General CDD measures are specified by section 10 para. 1. They include:

(i) identification of the contract partner and, where relevant, the person representing him, as well as verification of whether the person representing the contract partner is entitled to do so.[141] Section 11 para. 4 provides further details on the scope of the identification, including notably the address of the natural or legal person, and, as regards a legal person, the name of the members of its representative body.[142] Section 12 paras. 1 and 2 provide an exhaustive catalogue of documents or methods that are deemed sufficiently reliable for the purpose of identification,[143] including for natural persons notably the person's ID card or a qualified electronic

141 According to Regulation 2015/847, payment service providers are furthermore under an obligation to provide information on the payer's identity to the payee's payment service provider or, where relevant, to any intermediary payment service provider. The payee's payment service provider as well as any intermediary payment service providers are under an obligation to implement effective procedures to detect whether such information on the payer is missing and, following a risk-sensitive approach, either reject the transfer or request further information. Section 14 para. 5 GWG provides an exception to Regulation 2015/847, which is not applicable to some purely domestic transfers if they serve the payment of goods or services and do not exceed the amount of €1,000.

142 Section 11 para. 6 GWG provides a corresponding duty of the contract partner to provide and update the relevant information and documentation.

143 According to supervisory guidance, this does not exclude remote identification via video link with the client; see Bafin, Rundschreiben 3/2017 (GW) – Videoidentifizierungsverfahren of 10 April 2017.

signature within the meaning of Regulation 910/2014,[144] and, as regards legal persons or commercial partnerships, in particular an extract from commercial or similar registries;

(ii) clarification whether the contract partner is acting for a beneficial owner,[145] and where this is the case, identification of the beneficial owner, which according to section 11 para. 5 includes at least the name and, insofar as this is appropriate in light of a particular money laundering or terrorism financing risk, further identification criteria.[146] Through risk-adequate means,[147] the obliged entity has to verify that the collected information is accurate;[148] to this end it must not exclusively rely on the content of the beneficial ownership registry.[149] Where the contract partner is not

---

144 For the additional requirements applicable to identification by electronic signature, see section 12 para. 1 s. 2–3 GWG.

145 Bafin, Auslegungs- und Anwendungshinweise zum Geldwäschegesetz of December 2018, at III.5.2.1 provides that the establishment of a beneficial owner will usually not be feasible if the contracting party is an entity established under public law or if 100% of a private company's shares are held by public entities. The same guidance states that (in light of section 3 para. 2 GWG) this obligation is not only inapplicable to publicly listed companies that are subject to EU or equivalent transparency rules regarding voting rights, but also does not apply to other companies that, despite not themselves being publicly listed, are controlled by a publicly listed company.

146 As regards insurance undertakings, section 54 para. 1 VAG specifies that this duty also applies to the identification of any insurance beneficiary who is not identical to the policyholder, and where the beneficiary is not a natural person, to its beneficial owner.

147 According to supervisory guidance, the obliged entity can in principle rely on the information provided by the client without further inquiries on its own, unless it becomes aware of obvious suspicious facts; Bafin, Auslegungs- und Anwendungshinweise zum Geldwäschegesetz of December 2018, at III.5.2.3.2.

148 Section 11 para. 6 GWG provides for a corresponding duty of the contract partner to disclose whether the business relationship or transaction is meant to be established, continued or performed for a beneficial owner, and, if so, provide proof of his or her identity. According to section 11 para. 6 GWG, in the case of estate agents, the same obligation applies to the contract partners of the brokered sales contract that are not themselves contract partners of the estate agent. Bafin, Auslegungs- und Anwendungshinweise zum Geldwäschegesetz of December 2018, at III.5.2.2.2, does however specify that if the obliged entity is unable to identify the actual beneficial owner and therefore has to establish merely the fictional beneficial owner according to section 3 para. 2 s. 6 GWG (see below section VI.A.1.b), it will normally suffice to identify only one single individual (for example one board member), even if several individuals meet the statutory criteria of a fictional beneficial owner.

149 See below section VI.B. In any case, according to section 11 para. 5 s. 2 GWG, when establishing a new business relationship with a legal person, commercial partnership, foundation or similar structure, the obliged entity must request proof of registration with the beneficial ownership register or directly obtain relevant information from this register. Furthermore, according to section 11 para. 5 s. 5 GWG, in the case that a particular person could not be established as the actual beneficial owner, and thus the legal representative, managing shareholder or partner of the contract partner is deemed to be the beneficial owner, the obliged entity has to perform adequate measures to verify the identity of this person.

a natural person,[150] this includes the obligation to adopt appropriate measures to understand the ownership and control structure of the contract partner;[151]

(iii) to the extent that this does not already follow unequivocally from the business relationship, obtaining and assessing of information on the purpose and the intended nature of the business relationship;

(iv) determination, through appropriate, risk-oriented procedures, if the contract partner or the beneficial owner[152] is a politically exposed person[153] or a close relative of such a person or somebody who is known to be closely related to such a person;[154]

(v) ongoing monitoring of the business relationship, including of transactions that are carried out in its course, in order to ensure that those transactions correspond (a) to the documents and information in possession of the obliged entity about the contract partner and beneficial owner, and about their business activity and customer profile, and (b) to the extent that this is required, to the information in possession of the obliged entity on the sources of funds.

In a similar vein, if the identity of the beneficial owner of trusts and similar structures is determined according to special characteristics or categories, the obliged entity must gather adequate data so that it can, at the moment of the performance of the transaction or of the exercise of his or her rights, identify the beneficial owner. According to section 11 para. 7 GWG, when trustees, in this capacity, enter a business relationship or perform a transaction above the applicable thresholds of standard CDD, they have to disclose their status and, without undue delay, provide the relevant beneficial ownership information.

150 As specified by supervisory guidance, identification of the beneficial owner will usually not be necessary if the contract partner is a public body; Bafin, Auslegungs- und Anwendungshinweise zum Geldwäschegesetz of December 2018, at III.5.2.

151 Supervisory guidance specifies that such measures go beyond the need to check whether individual shareholders control more than 25% of shares; in addition, the analysis of the control structure requires at least "rudimentary verification" of whether there are indications that natural persons have control over the contract partner irrespective of the nominal allocation of shares. Instead of analysing the client's control structure, it is also permissible to treat as the beneficial owners all natural persons who hold a substantial share (meaning more than 25%) in an interposed company; Bafin, Auslegungs- und Anwendungshinweise zum Geldwäschegesetz of December 2018, at III.5.2.3.3.

152 As regards insurance undertakings, according to section 54 para. 2 s. 1 VAG this duty extends to any insurance beneficiary who is not the policyholder and, where relevant, to the beneficial owner of this beneficiary.

153 Supervisory guidance specifies that, while there is in principle no obligation to use commercially available databases for the identification of PEPs, the use of such databases will usually indicate an adequate performance of obliged entities' duty to this effect; Bafin, Auslegungs- und Anwendungshinweise zum Geldwäschegesetz of December 2018, at III.5.4.2.

154 For details of these categories see below section III.A.4. Supervisory guidance states that the obligation to clarify whether the contract partner is closely related to a PEP only applies if such relationship is publicly known or the obliged entity has reasons to believe in such relationship; Bafin, Auslegungs- und Anwendungshinweise zum Geldwäschegesetz of December 2018, at III.5.4.

As part of their ongoing monitoring, obliged entities have furthermore to ensure that documents, data and information are updated, in line with the particular risk, within adequate time periods.[155]

According to section 10 para. 2, the particular scope of the aforementioned general CDD measures (ii)–(v) must correspond to the individual money laundering or terrorism financing risk, in particular in view of the contract partner, business relationship or transaction. To this end, obliged entities shall take into account in particular a catalogue of criteria provided for in Annex 1 and 2 of the GWG.[156] Furthermore, their risk assessment shall take into account (i) the purpose of the account or the transaction, (ii) the value of assets deposited by the client or the volume of transactions, and (iii) the regularity and duration of the business relationship.

According to section 10 para. 9, if an obliged entity is not able to fulfil the above-mentioned general CDD obligations (i)–(iv),[157] it must not establish or continue the business relationship, and must not perform any transaction. If

---

155 Supervisory guidance specifies that updates can be triggered in particular by anomalies discovered through the ongoing monitoring of the business relationship, by correspondence with the contract partner or by doubts about the accuracy of client data. As regards the regular verification of client data, the length of adequate time intervals will depend on the risk category of the respective client or product, in line with the obliged entity's own risk analysis. In the case of an average risk, verification measures must be taken at least every 10 years; in the case of a high risk, at least every two years; Bafin, Auslegungs- und Anwendungshinweise zum Geldwäschegesetz of December 2018, at III.5.5.2.

156 According to the non-exhaustive list in Annex 1, possible indications of a potentially lower risk include the following: in view of the nature of the customer, notably listed companies that are subject to adequate transparency obligations as regards their beneficial owners; public entities and customers domiciled in a country with effective AML/CTF frameworks; in view of the nature of the business relationship, notably life insurances with low premiums and employees' pension systems that do not allow beneficiaries to transfer their entitlements. According to the non-exhaustive list in Annex 2, possible indications of a potentially high risk include the following: in view of the nature of the customer, notably exceptional circumstances of the business relationship; customers that are domiciled in countries with inadequate AML/CTF frameworks; legal persons that serve the purpose of private asset management; businesses with nominal shareholders or that emit bearer shares; cash-intensive businesses; businesses with an ownership structure that, in light of the nature of their activity, is unusually or overly complex; customers that are third-country nationals who received a residency title or citizenship of an EU Member State in exchange for the transfer of capital, for the purchase of real estate or government bonds or for investments in companies in this Member State; in view of the nature of the business relationship, notably private wealth management; products and transactions that favour anonymity; business relationships or transactions without personal contact and without particular security measures (such as electronic signatures).

157 As specified by supervisory guidance, if the obliged entity, following an extensive inquiry to this effect, is unable to identify the beneficial owner, the prohibition of section 10 para. 9 GWG does not apply. Rather, section 3 para. 2 s. 5 GWG points out that in this case the legal representative, managing associate or partner of the contract partner is deemed to be beneficial owner; Bafin, Auslegungs- und Anwendungshinweise zum Geldwäschegesetz of December 2018, at III.5.8.1.

the business relationship was already established, it must be terminated by the obliged entity,[158] irrespective of any other legal or contractual obligations.[159] This duty does not apply to independent lawyers, patent attorneys, notaries, auditors, tax advisors and tax agents, if their client seeks legal advice or legal representation, except where the obliged entity knows that the client is consciously using the legal advice or representation for the purpose of money laundering or terrorism financing.

- Special CDD Measures for Particular Obliged Entities

As regards gambling providers and brokers, according to section 10 paras. 5 and to the extent that they are obliged entities and are not provided online, identification requirements can be satisfied by identifying the player the moment he or she enters the casino or other venue, if it is ensured that that transactions amounting to €2,000 or more, including the purchase or re-exchange of tokens, can be attributed to the respective player.

For the providers of online gambling, additional CDD requirements apply. Notably, according to section 16 paras. 2 and 3, before allowing an individual player to participate in a game, the gambling provider must first set up a player account in the name of this individual; the player account must not contain deposits or other refundable money of the player other than the money deposited for the purpose of participating in the game,[160] and interest must not be paid on the account balance. Each player shall have only one player account.[161] According to section 16 para. 4, the gambling provider must furthermore ensure that the player's transactions into the account are carried out via direct debit, a bank transfer or a payment card from a payment account

---

158 As the statutorily provided termination of a business relationship and the non-performance of transactions constitute a restriction on the client, obliged entities must always have due regard to the proportionality principle. Supervisory guidance therefore states that the duty according to section 10 para. 9 GWG does not apply where, in view on the one hand of the interest of the obliged entity and of the contract partner, and on the other hand the money laundering or terrorism financing risk in the specific case, termination or non-performance would be inappropriate. Such exceptions must however be substantiated in each individual case and must be approved by the obliged entity's management; Bafin, Auslegungs- und Anwendungshinweise zum Geldwäschegesetz of December 2018, at III.5.8.2.

159 Supervisory guidance states that an obliged entity cannot rely on section 10 para. 9 GWG if the inability to comply with its obligations is due to a reason that falls with its sphere of responsibility; Bafin, Auslegungs- und Anwendungshinweise zum Geldwäschegesetz of December 2018, at III.5.8.1.

160 See section 16 para. 3 s. 3 GWG and section 3 para. 3 s. 3 ZAG; O Achtelik, in F Herzog/ O Achtelik (eds.), Geldwäschegesetz, 2018, §16 para. 7.

161 BT-Drucksache 18/11555, p. 122; Gemeinsame Hinweise der Obersten Glücksspielaufsichtsbehörden der Länder gemäß §51 Absatz 8 GWG, Auslegungs- und Anwendungshinweise zum Geldwäschegesetz für Veranstalter und Vermittler von Glücksspielen of 1 February 2019, p. 48.

that has been set up in the name of the player at a credit institution, payment institution or electronic money institution. If the transaction into the player's account is done by means of a payment card, the obligation to identify the name of the holder of the payment account does not apply where the payment by a single transaction does not exceed €25 and the overall value of payments per month does not exceed €100.[162] According to section 16 para. 7, transactions from the gambling provider to the player shall only be made into a payment account that has been set up in the player's name at a credit institution, payment institution or electronic money institution.

Insurance intermediaries, according to section 10 para. 8, where they collect premiums for insurance undertakings that are obliged entities, have to inform the insurance undertaking when premium payments are performed in cash and thereby exceed €15,000 within one calendar year.

The GWG does not impose a general obligation on obliged entities to apply particular technologies in the performance of their CDD. Section 25h para. 2 KWG and section 28 para. 1 s. 4 KAGB do however provide that, irrespective of their obligation to conduct ongoing monitoring of business relationships, credit institutions and capital management companies have to use and update data processing systems. These systems must enable them to identify business relationships and individual transactions which, in light of empirical knowledge about the methods of money laundering, terrorism financing and other crimes that can endanger assets of the institution, and compared to similar cases, are particularly complex or large, follow an unusual transaction pattern, or have no apparent economic or lawful purpose.[163]

– Performance of CDD by Third Parties

For the performance of some exhaustively[164] listed standard CDD obligations (the identification of the contracting party and of persons representing her, verification whether persons representing the contracting party are authorised to do so, clarification of the beneficial owner, obtaining and assessing information about the purpose and nature of the business relationship, and verification whether the contracting party or the beneficial owner are politically exposed persons or family member or close associates of such persons), section 17

---

162 BT-Drucksache 18/12405, p. 167.

163 Supervisory guidance suggests that such systems will in particular allow for the creation of client profiles and the filtering of transactions on the basis of relevant risk parameters. Resulting hits have subsequently to be manually assessed as to their actual relevance; Bafin, Auslegungs- und Anwendungshinweise zum Geldwäschegesetz of December 2018, at III.5.5.1.

164 Bafin, Auslegungs- und Anwendungshinweise zum Geldwäschegesetz of December 2018, at III.8, clarifies that consequently neither the continuous monitoring of business relationships nor enhanced CDD measures can be delegated to third parties.

para. 1 allows obliged entities to rely on certain third parties (in particular on other obliged entities) even in the absence of a contractual basis between the two sides to this effect and without the need to verify the reliability of the third party.[165] Third parties for this purpose can be (i) other obliged entities in Germany, (ii) obliged entities from other EU Member States, (ii) member organisations or federations of obliged entities from EU Member States, or (iv) obliged entities from third states which are subject to due diligence and data retention obligations equivalent to the obligation applicable to obliged entities within the EU and which are supervised in a way that also ensures respect for tip-off prohibitions regarding communication between obliged entities and the FIU. Section 17 para. 2 specifies that obliged entities must not rely on third parties located in a high-risk third country, except for (i) branches of obliged entities that are domiciled within the EU and (ii) subsidiaries which are under the majority ownership of an obliged entity domiciled within the EU, provided that the branches or subsidiaries fully participate in group-wide AML and CTF strategies and procedures.[166] If the obliged entity relies on third party, it must, according to section 17 para. 3, ensure that this third party (i) when identifying persons domiciled in Germany, complies with German law, (ii) gathers all the necessary information for the performance of the above-listed standard CDD obligations, (iii) transmits this information directly and without undue delay to the obliged entity, and (iv) upon request produces copies of all documentation relevant for identification purposes and other relevant documentation.[167] According to section 17 para. 4, these conditions are presumed to be met if the third party is part of the same group as the obliged entity, provided that the group effectively complies with EU or equivalent AML and CTF standards. Section 17 paras. 5 and 6 furthermore authorises obliged entities to also delegate the performance of the above-mentioned standard CDD measures to other persons or businesses than those already mentioned, provided that such transfer is done on a contractual basis, the obliged entity ensures that the other person or business complies with the above requirements, and the delegation does not adversely affect the obliged entity's compliance, the management and monitoring capacity of its executive management, or its supervision by the competent supervisory authority. Section 17 para. 7 specifies that a transfer to such other third party requires prior verification of this party's reliability and subsequently ongoing random checks of measures adopted by it.

---

165 Bafin, Auslegungs- und Anwendungshinweise zum Geldwäschegesetz of December 2018, at III.8.1.

166 On group-wide compliance programmes see below section III.G.

167 Section 17 para. 4 GWG and Bafin, Auslegungs- und Anwendungshinweise zum Geldwäschegesetz of December 2018, at III.8.1 clarify that this covers in particular assistance between obliged entities that are part of the same group.

c. Individual Responsibility

Section 4 para. 3 determines that responsibility for obliged entities' risk management and for compliance with AML obligations rests with a member of the executive management. The entity's risk analysis and its internal safeguards, as well as major updates thereof,[168] require the approval of this person. It results from section 7 para. 11[69] that, unlike the compliance officer, the designated member of the executive management is not supposed to be operationally involved in the day-to-day implementation of AML obligations,[170] but rather to ensure that AML and CTF are duly taken into account at the board or directorate level.[171] Accordingly, this member of the executive management bears overall responsibility for compliance with the respective obligations,[172] not least in view of possible measures to be adopted by the supervisory authority in the event of a breach of those obligations.[173]

d. Further CDD Guidance

The competent supervisory authority must, according to section 51 para. 8, provide obliged entities with regularly updated guidance for the interpretation and implementation of CDD obligations. The guidance of the Federal Financial Supervisory Authority provides some important clarifications on the performance of standard CCD obligations, in particular as regards the determination of the beneficial owner.[174] Guidance is also issued by supervisory authorities in the

---

168 See Bafin, Auslegungs- und Anwendungshinweise zum Geldwäschegesetz of December 2018, at II.2.2.

169 See also BT-Drucksache 18/11555, p. 112.

170 According to Bafin, Auslegungs- und Anwendungshinweise zum Geldwäschegesetz of December 2018, at II.3.2, if, after having been informed about deficiencies in the entity's preventive framework, the responsible member of the executive management does not follow the recommendations of the AML compliance officer, this has to be recorded.

171 According to Bafin, Auslegungs- und Anwendungshinweise zum Geldwäschegesetz of December 2018, at II.2.2, this does however require that he or she has detailed knowledge of the obliged entity's money laundering and terrorism financing risks and their evaluation, which requires that he or she is regularly (and if necessary promptly) provided with all the key relevant information. In a similar vein see section 53 para. 2 VAG.

172 Bafin, Auslegungs- und Anwendungshinweise zum Geldwäschegesetz of December 2018, at II.2.2, clarifies that this does not exclude the possible collective responsibility of the executive management.

173 See below section VII.B.2.b.

174 Bafin, Auslegungs- und Anwendungshinweise zum Geldwäschegesetz of December 2018, pp. 38–49. For details see *supra* and *infra* in the notes referring to the respective CDD obligations. See also Bafin, Auslegungs- und Anwendungshinweise zum Geldwäschegesetz – Besonderer Teil für Versicherungsunternehmen (January 2020), providing some special guidance for insurance undertakings, and specifying *inter alia* conditions under which, for reasons of proportionality, insurance undertaking may be allowed to continue a business relationship even when some information about the customer's identity is lacking (see p. 12).

non-financial sector and focuses especially on the formal requirements of customer and beneficial owner identification.[175] In some sectors guidance will substantially not go beyond a concise summary of the GWG's content.[176]

2. *Simplified CDD*

a. Scope

According to section 14 para. 1, obliged entities need to perform only simplified CDD measures where they determine, having regard to the risk factors contained in Annexes 1 and 2 to the GWG,[177] that in certain areas, notably as regards the type of customers, transactions and services or products, there exists only a low risk of money laundering or of terrorism financing.[178] Before applying simplified measures, obliged entities must ascertain that the business relationship or transaction in the particular case does in fact present a lower degree of risk. The application of simplified CDD measures thus presupposes two steps, first a preliminary risk assessment by the obliged entity that categorises a particular area of its business as usually being of low risk, and second a determination in the particular case whether a specific business relationship or transaction, which belongs to a category that was assessed as usually being of low risk, does in fact present a lower risk. Cases that, by law or the obliged entity's own risk analysis or by an order of a supervisory authority, were categorised as being of higher risk are from the outset not eligible for simplified CDD.[179]

---

[175] See for example for auditors Wirtschaftsprüferkammer, Auslegungs- und Anwendungshinweise der Wirtschaftsprüferkammer zum Gesetz über das Aufspüren von Gewinnen aus schweren Straftaten (Geldwäschegesetz -GwG) of 26 June 2019, pp. 19–38; for notaries Bundesnotarkammer, Anwendungsempfehlungen zum Geldwäschegesetz of March 2018, pp. 14–18; for example for lawyers Bundesrechtsanwaltskammer, Auslegungs- und Anwendungshinweise zum Gesetz über das Aufspüren von Gewinnen aus schweren Straftaten (Geldwäschegesetz -GwG) of October 2019, pp. 9–20.

[176] See for example Senatsverwaltung für Wirtschaft, Energie und Betriebe, Basisinformation Geldwäschegesetz (GwG) für Güterhändler, Immobilienmakler und andere Nicht-Finanzunternehmen of February 2018.

[177] See above section III.A.1.b. For obliged entities supervised by the Federal Financial Supervisory Authority, guidance furthermore points to the Risk Factors Guidelines of the European Supervisory Authorities according to Articles 17 and 18(4) of Directive 2015/849/EU; Bafin, Auslegungs- und Anwendungshinweise zum Geldwäschegesetz of December 2018, at III.6.1.

[178] Supervisory guidance specifies that this usually applies in particular in the case of transactions and business relationships with credit institutions or financial services institutions established in the EU or in an equivalent third State, and with listed companies from the EU or an equivalent third State; Bafin, Auslegungs- und Anwendungshinweise zum Geldwäschegesetz of December 2018, at III.6.2.

[179] See sections 15 paras. 2, 3 and 8 GWG; Bafin, Auslegungs- und Anwendungshinweise zum Geldwäschegesetz of December 2018, at III.8.6.2.

b. Requirements

According to section 14 para. 2, when they are entitled to apply simplified CDD, obliged entities are allowed to adequately reduce the scope of CDD measures and in particular verify the identity of the contracting party, of the person representing him or her, and of the beneficial owner not on the basis of the documents and methods provided by section 12 paras. 1 and 2,[180] but merely on the basis of suitable documents, data or information which originate from a credible and independent source. In any case, obliged entities must ensure a screening of transactions and a monitoring of business relationships to an extent that enables identifying and reporting unusual or suspicious transactions. Thus, recourse to simplified CDD does in principle not exempt obliged entities from their standard CCD obligations,[181] but only affects the intensity of measures to this effect.

3. *Enhanced CDD*

a. Scope

In addition to standard CDD measures, section 15 para. 2 provides that obliged entities must apply enhanced CDD measures if they determine, within the obliged entity's general risk analysis or in an individual case, and having regard to the risk factors contained in Annexes 1 and 2 to the GWG,[182] that a higher risk of money laundering or terrorism financing might be present.[183] Accordingly, if the obliged entity's risk analysis has categorised a particular type of business or transaction as being of higher risk, enhanced CDD measures must be applied to all businesses and transactions falling within this category. Furthermore, if a business or transaction had not previously been categorised as being of high risk, obliged entities must still assess whether the individual case might constitute a higher risk.

Section 15 para. 3 no. 3 specifies, without being exhaustive in this regard,[184] that a higher risk is present in particular if a transaction, compared to similar

---

180 See above section III.A.1.b.

181 J Figura, in F Herzog/O Achtelik (eds.), Geldwäschegesetz, §14, para. 8.

182 See above section III.A.1.b.

183 For obliged entities supervised by the Federal Financial Supervisory Authority, guidance furthermore points to the Risk Factors Guidelines of the European Supervisory Authorities according to Articles 17 and 18(4) of Directive 2015/849/EU; Bafin, Auslegungs- und Anwendungshinweise zum Geldwäschegesetz of December 2018, at III.7.1.

184 Section 15 para. 10 s. 1 no. 1 GWG authorises the Federal Ministry of Finance to decree additional circumstances, in which a higher risk of money laundering or terrorism financing is deemed to be present, and also decree particular enhanced CDD measures that obliged entities then have to apply. Section 15 para. 10 s. 1 no. 2 GWG furthermore authorises

cases, is particularly complex or unusually large, follows an unusual transaction pattern, or has no apparent economic or lawful purpose.[185]

Section 15 para. 3 no. 4 furthermore provides that a higher risk is also present in the case of a cross-border correspondent relationship[186] of a credit or financial services institution, of a payment or electronic money institution, of another financial undertaking, or of an insurance undertaking or insurance agent, provided that the respondent institution is domiciled in a state outside the EU and the European Economic Area, or, if the obliged entity has previously assessed this state to be a higher risk, in a Member State of the European Economic Area.

According to section 15 para. 3 no. 1 and no. 2, a high risk is also deemed to be present if the contracting party or a beneficial owner is a politically exposed person or a close relative of such a person or somebody who is known to be closely related to such a person, or if the contracting partner or beneficial owner is a natural or legal person domiciled in a high-risk third state designated as such by the European Commission, or if the business relationship or transaction in other ways involves such a state.[187]

b. Requirements

Section 15 para. 2 specifies that, if obliged entities establish that a higher risk of money laundering or terrorism financing might be present, they determine

the Ministry of Finance, with regard to cases involving a high-risk third country, to order particular CDD measures and countermeasures; in this respect, the Ministry can also specify details as regards the ordering of enhanced CDD measures by competent supervisory authorities.

185 Supervisory guidance specifies that the unusual character of a transaction is already established where, in view of the obliged entity's or its employee's general understanding of the respective business activity, and without further clarification of the case, one notices deviations from the usual behaviour of a client or of a third person. Criteria for the unusual character of a transaction can for example be the volume of the obliged entity's overall business activity or the scope of the particular business relationship; Bafin, Auslegungs- und Anwendungshinweise zum Geldwäschegesetz of December 2018, at III.7.4.

186 According to section 1 para. 21 GWG, correspondent relationships are business relationships within which one of the following services are performed: (i) banking services by credit institutions within the meaning of section 2 para. 1 no. 1 GWG (correspondent) for CRR credit institutions within the meaning of the Capital Requirements Regulation (EU) No. 575/2013 or for businesses in a third state that perform activities equivalent to CRR credit institutions (respondent); or(ii) services other than banking services, if they can be legally performed by a credit institution, a financial services institution, a payment or electronic money institution, another financial undertaking, an insurance undertaking, an insurance agent or an investment management company within the meaning of section 2 para. 1 GWG (correspondent) for other CRR credit institutions or financial institutions within the meaning of Directive 2015/849/EU or for businesses or persons in a third state that perform services equivalent to those of such credit institutions or financial institutions (respondent).

187 See below section III.A.4 and 5.

the particular scope of CDD measures in accordance with this higher risk. Section 15 para. 4 s. 1 provides a cumulative list of minimum enhanced CDD requirements in cases where obliged entities determine that there might be a higher risk, specifying that in such a case (i) the establishment or continuation of the business relationship requires senior management approval, (ii) adequate measures must be applied that allow to establish the source of assets that are involved in the business relationship or transaction, and (iii) the business relationship must be submitted to enhanced, continuous monitoring. According to section 1 para. 15, senior management refers to an officer or senior employee of the obliged entity who has sufficient knowledge of the institution's money laundering and terrorist financing risk exposure and sufficient seniority to take decisions in this regard, without necessarily being a member of the executive management.

For cases of higher risk as set forth by section 15 para. 3 no. 3 (that is, in the case of unusually complex or large transactions, unusual transaction patterns or where a transaction has no apparent economic or lawful purpose), section 15 para. 6 specifies that enhanced CDD entails at least the duty (i) to analyse, through adequate means, the transaction and its background and purpose in order to monitor and assess the risk of the business relationship or transaction risk to examine, where appropriate, whether it should be reported to the FIU, and (ii) to submit the business relationship, if one underlies the transaction, to enhanced continuous monitoring in order to assess the relationship's and individual transactions' money laundering or terrorism financing risk, and, in case of higher risk, to continue enhanced monitoring of the relationship.[188]

For cases of higher risk according to section 15 para. 3 no. 4 (that is, in the case of a cross-border correspondent relationship), section 15 para. 7 provides that enhanced CDD entails a cumulative list of duties. When entering a business relationship, obliged entities must then at least: (i) gather sufficient information about the respondent institution to fully understand the nature of the respondent's business and to assess the respondent's reputation and money laundering and terrorism financing controls and the quality of supervision; (ii) obtain approval from senior management before establishing a business relationship with the respondent; (iii) before establishing such a business relationship determine and document the respective responsibilities of each institution with regard to the performance of CDD duties; (iv) adopt measures to ensure that no business relationships are established or continue with a respondent institution that is known to allow its accounts to be used by a shell bank, that is a credit institution within the meaning of Regulation 575/2013[189] or financial institution within the meaning of

188 See BT-Drucksache 18/11555, p. 122.

189 Section 1 para. 3d s. 1 KWG; see BT-Drucksache 18/11555, p. 104. Section 25m no. 1 KWG, section 27 para. 2 s. 1 ZAG and section 28 para. 1 s. 4 KAGB furthermore prohibit the

Directive 2015/849/EU or an undertaking that carries out activities equivalent to those of such credit or financial institutions and that is registered in the companies' register or a comparable register in a country in which the actual direction and management does not take place and that is not affiliated with a regulated group of credit or financial institutions;[190] and (v) adopt measures to ensure that the respondent institution does not allow payable-through accounts.[191]

If an obliged entity is not in a position to fulfil the above-mentioned enhanced CDD obligations, it must, according to section 10 para. 9 and section 15 para. 9, not establish or continue the business relationship and must not perform any transaction. This prohibition does not apply to independent lawyers, patent attorneys, notaries, auditors, tax advisors and tax agents, if they are asked to provide legal advice or legal representation, except if they know that the legal advice or representation has been consciously used or will be used for the purpose of money laundering or terrorism financing.

Finally, section 10 para. 9 s. 4 provides that notaries must not perform a notarisation if the client is a legal entity, partnership, trust or similar structure which has not yet provided him or her with documentation about its ownership and control structure; notaries must furthermore not perform a notarisation if a legal entity or partnership that is domiciled abroad wants to acquire real estate in Germany as long as this entity or partnership has provided its beneficial ownership information neither to the German beneficial ownership registry nor to an equivalent registry in another Member State.[192]

c. Further Enhanced CDD Guidance

As already stated, the supervisory authorities must provide obliged entities with regularly updated guidance on the interpretation and application of CDD duties. Guidance of the Federal Financial Supervisory Authority provides some basic clarification on the triggers of enhanced CDD and furthermore refers to the European Supervisory Authorities' Guidelines on risk factors and simplified and enhanced customer due diligence.[193] In contrast, guidance in the non-financial

---

establishment or continuation by credit institutions, financial services institutions, payment institutions, electronic money institutions and investment management companies of any business relationship with a shell bank.

190 Section 1 para. 22 GWG.

191 Section 25m no. 2 Banking Act furthermore prohibits any establishment or management of such accounts, described by the law as accounts established in the name of the respective credit or financial institution or of another credit or financial institution through which customers of this institution or of the other institution can autonomously carry out their own transactions.

192 Section 11 para. 5a and section 20 para. 1 s. 2 and 3 GWG.

193 European Banking Authority et al., Joint Guidelines under Articles 17 and 18(4) of Directive (EU)2015/849 on simplified and enhanced customer due diligence and the factors credit and

sector usually provides little detail about enhanced CDD triggers and the measures that obliged entities shall adopt in cases of higher risk.[194]

Furthermore, according to section 15 para. 8, in addition to the criteria provided by the law, if findings, evaluations, reports or assessments by national or international bodies that are tasked with AML or CTF (such as criminal justice authorities or the FATF)[195] justify the assumption of a higher risk, the competent supervisory authority can order obliged entities to perform enhanced monitoring, adopt necessary countermeasures, and apply additional risk-adequate CDD measures to the relevant business relationships or transactions.

4. *Rules on Politically Exposed Persons*

a. Definition

Section 15 para. 3 no. 1 provides that a higher risk is present where the contracting party or a beneficial owner is a politically exposed person (PEP). Section 1 para. 12 s. 2 no. 1 specifies that a PEP is any person who exercises or has exercised a high-ranking prominent public function at the international, European or national level or a public function of comparable political importance below the national level. The law does not differentiate between domestic and foreign PEPs, and it provides non-exhaustive examples to this effect, in particular heads of government and ministers, secretaries of state, members of parliament, members of governing bodies of political parties, members of governing bodies of courts of auditors, members of executive or supervisory bodies of state owned undertakings and members of governing bodies of international or European intergovernmental organisations. According to section 1 para. 12 s. 2 no. 2, those holding an office contained in the single list of prominent public functions published by the European Commission are also PEPs.[196]

---

financial institutions should consider when assessing the money laundering and terrorist financing risk associated with individual business relationships and occasional transactions of 4 January 2018; JC 2017 37.

194 See Wirtschaftsprüferkammer, Auslegungs- und Anwendungshinweise der Wirtschaftsprüferkammer zum Gesetz über das Aufspüren von Gewinnen aus schweren Straftaten (Geldwäschegesetz –GwG) of 26 June 2019, pp. 44–45; Bundesrechtsanwaltskammer, Auslegungs- und Anwendungshinweise zum Gesetz über das Aufspüren von Gewinnen aus schweren Straftaten (Geldwäschegesetz –GwG) of October 2019, p. 22. For an insofar notable detail, see Bundesnotarkammer, Anwendungsempfehlungen zum Geldwäschegesetz of March 2018, p. 20, which specifies that notaries' duty of confidentiality prevents them, when inquiring into the origin of assets, from gathering information from third parties.

195 BT-Drucksache 18/11555, p. 122.

196 See Article 20a(3) of Directive 2015/849/EU of 20 May 2015 on the prevention of the use of the financial system for the purposes of money laundering or terrorist financing as amended by Directive (EU) 2018/843.

According to section 15 para. 3 no. 1, a high risk is also present where the contracting party or a beneficial owner is a close relative of a PEP (that is, spouses, children and their spouses, parents)[197] or somebody who is known to be closely related to such a person within the meaning of section 1 para. 14, that is somebody whom the obliged entity has reasons to believe that he or she (i) together with the PEP is the beneficial owner of a private legal person, a registered partnership, a trust or a self-serving endowment, (ii) entertains other close business relationships with a PEP, or (iii) is the exclusive beneficial owner of a private legal entity, a registered partnership, a trust or a self-serving endowment in relation to which the obliged entity has reasons to believe that it was in fact established for the benefit of a PEP.

b. Requirements

The aforementioned[198] minimum enhanced CDD requirements of section 15 para. 4 also apply where a contracting partner or beneficial owner is a PEP, is a close relative of, or closely related to, such a person. They thus require the business relationship's approval by senior management, adequate measures to determine the source of the assets[199] and enhanced continuous monitoring of the relationship. Section 15 para. 4 s. 2 furthermore specifies that, if the contracting party or beneficial owner becomes a PEP only after the commencement of the business relationship or if the obliged entity only then learns of it, the obliged entity must ensure that the continuation of the relationship takes place with the approval of senior management. Section 15 para. 4 s. 3 furthermore provides that the risk specific to PEPs must be taken into account by obliged entities for a period of at least 12 months after the person left the respective public function, and that appropriate and risk-sensitive measures must be applied until such time as it is deemed that such risk is no longer present.[200]

197 Section 1 para. 13 GWG.

198 See above section III.A.3.b.

199 Supervisory guidance clarifies that, in the eyes of the obliged entity, the source of assets must be plausible; Bafin, Auslegungs- und Anwendungshinweise zum Geldwäschegesetz of December 2018, at III.7.2.

200 As regards insurance undertakings, according to section 55 VAG (Insurance Supervision Act), if the insurance beneficiary who is not the policyholder, or the beneficial owner of such beneficiary, is a PEP, a close relative of, or closely linked to, such a person, and provided that the obliged entities establish a higher risk of money laundering or terrorism financing, they must then, in addition to its duties under section 15 para. 4 GWG, inform senior management prior to any payout, submit the entire business relationship to the policyholder to an enhanced review, and assess whether the conditions of a report to the FIU are present.

5. *Rules on High-Risk Third Countries*

a. Scope

Section 15 para. 3 no. 2 specifies that a higher risk is present if the contracting partner or beneficial owner is a natural or legal person domiciled in a high-risk third state designated by the European Commission under Article 9 of Directive 2015/849/EU, or if such third state is otherwise involved in a business relationship or transaction; however this does not apply to branches or majority-owned subsidiaries of EU-domiciled obliged entities that are located in a high-risk third state, provided that those branches or subsidiaries unreservedly comply with the group-wide policies and procedures within the meaning of Article 45(1) of Directive 2015/849/EU, that is group-wide data protection and AML/CTF information sharing policies and procedures.

b. Requirements

Section 15 para. 5 contains a cumulative list of minimum enhanced CDD obligations that obliged entities are required to perform when a high-risk third state is involved. In such cases, they must obtain additional information on the customer and on the beneficial owner; additional information on the intended nature of the business relationship; information on the source of funds and source of wealth of the customer and of the beneficial owner;[201] and information on the reasons for the intended or performed transactions.[202] Obliged entities must furthermore ensure the approval of senior management for establishing or continuing the business relationship. In the case of a business relationship, they must also conduct enhanced monitoring of it by increasing the number and timing of controls applied, and selecting patterns of transactions that need further examination.

c. Further Guidance on High-Risk Third Countries

Under section 15 para. 5a, competent supervisory authorities can require obliged entities, insofar as this is risk-adequate and in compliance with the EU's international obligations, to apply additional enhanced CDD measures. Such measures can in particular include the following: (i) reporting of

---

201 According to section 15 para. 5 no. 1(d), this excludes fictional beneficial owners within the meaning of section 3 para. 2 s. 5 GWG.

202 According to section 15 para. 5 no. 1(f) GWG, and insofar as this is necessary to assess the risk of terrorism financing, obliged entities must, in view of the involvement of a high-risk third state, furthermore obtain information about the intended use of funds.

financial transactions to the FIU; (ii) the limitation of business relationships or transactions with natural persons or legal entities from high-risk third countries; (iii) prohibiting obliged entities domiciled in a high-risk third country from establishing subsidiaries, branches or representative offices in Germany; (iv) prohibiting obliged entities from establishing branches or representative offices in the high-risk third country; (v) requiring domestic branches and subsidiaries of obliged entities domiciled in a high-risk third country to undergo increased supervisory examination by the competent supervisory authority or by an external audit; (vi) applying increased requirements for an external audit of branches and subsidiaries of obliged entities domiciled in a high-risk third country; and (vii) requiring credit institutions, financial services institutions, payment institutions, electronic money institutions, other financial businesses, insurance undertakings and agents, and capital management businesses, to review and amend, or if necessary terminate, correspondent relationships with respondent institutions in the high-risk third country.

B. PRELIMINARY RISK ANALYSIS

In order to comprehensively identify, categorise and weight their individual money laundering and terrorism financing risks and on this basis adopt adequate preventive measures,[203] section 5 para. 1 requires obliged entities[204] to identify and assess the risks of money laundering and terrorist financing that come along with the business activities they engage in, having regard in particular to the risk factors contained in Annexes 1 and 2 to the GWG[205] as well as the results of the national risk assessment.[206] The scope of the preliminary risk analysis depends on the nature and size of the obliged entity's business. According

203 BT-Drucksache 18/11555, p. 109.

204 Estate agents must, according to section 4 paras. 2 and 4 GWG, perform a preliminary risk analysis only (i) when they broker sales contracts, or (ii) when they broker rental contracts that involve a monthly rent of €10,000 or more. According to section 4 paras. 2 and 5, traders in goods must perform a preliminary risk analysis only in the case of (i) transactions of works of art worth €10,000 or more; (ii) transactions of precious metals, if the trader, him- or herself or through a third person, makes or received cash payments of €2,000 or more; or (iii) transactions of other goods, if the trader, him- or herself or through a third person, makes or received cash payments of €10,000 or more. Art brokers and art warehouse keepers must have an effective risk management in the case of transactions worth €10,000 or more.

205 See above section III.A.1.b. For credit institutions, financial services institutions, payment institutions, electronic money institutions, insurance undertakings and agents and investment management companies, Bafin, Auslegungs- und Anwendungshinweise zum Geldwäschegesetz of December 2018, at II.3, specifies they must also observe the Joint Guidelines of the European supervisory authorities according to Articles 17 and 18 of Directive 2015/849/EU.

206 On Member States' obligation to conduct such an assessment, see Article 7 of Directive 2015/849/EU.

to section 5 para. 2, the obliged entity must regularly (that is, at least once per year)[207] review and, if necessary, update the risk analysis, and must, upon request, make the most recent version available to the competent supervisory authority. Section 5 para. 3 specifies that insofar as the obliged entity is the parent company of a group of companies, the preliminary risk analysis must cover the entire group.

C. REPORTING AND ASSET FREEZING

1. *First-Time Reporting*

a. Trigger for/Degree of Suspicion

According to section 43 para. 1, if facts exist which indicate that (i) assets related to a business relationship, brokerage or transaction are derived from a criminal offence which could constitute a predicate offence of money laundering, (ii) a business occurrence, a transaction or property is related to terrorism financing, or (iii) the contracting party has not fulfilled its obligation to disclose to the obliged entity whether it intends to establish, continue or perform the business relationship or transaction on behalf of a beneficial owner, the obliged entity must report this matter without delay, irrespective of the amount involved. As regards a breach of the obligation to disclose the beneficial owner, the purpose of the reporting duty suggests that an SAR is not required in circumstances in which such disclosure would normally be considered unusual and materially irrelevant; in contrast, an SAR will always have to be filed if it appears that the client intended to deceive the obliged entity and also if (in particular due to an unequivocal instruction) the client must have been in no doubt that he or she was required to disclose any beneficial owner.[208]

In line with the purpose of section 43, it must be assumed that the reporting duty also covers cases where a transaction is not carried out or a business relationship is not established as a result of obliged entities' CDD measures.[209] Section 43 para. 5 furthermore provides that the FIU in consultation with the competent supervisory authority may define types of transactions which must always be reported to the FIU.

Beyond the aforementioned requirements, the law does not explicitly elaborate on the degree of suspicion that triggers a duty to file a report. The legislative drafting history makes it clear that section 43 is meant to remain below

---

207 BT-Drucksache 18/11555, p. 109.

208 See Bafin, Auslegungs- und Anwendungshinweise zum Geldwäschegesetz of December 2018, at IV.10.

209 Bafin, Rundschreiben 3/2012 of 6 July 2012.

the standard of suspicion of a criminal complaint, and that obliged entities and their employees enjoy a margin of judgment, which will however be sharply reduced if the circumstances[210] of the particular case correspond to indications that have been defined and communicated as such to obliged entities by the FIU.[211] Obliged entities are not required to perform a detailed legal analysis of whether a case satisfies the definition of money laundering or terrorism financing; rather it suffices that, in view notably of the circumstances of the case and professional experience, a money laundering or terrorism financing background cannot be excluded.[212] In essence, the reporting duty does thus not depend on a subjective suspicion of the obliged entity's employee, but on the presence of known facts that, in light of objective assessment standards, typically indicate a link with money laundering or terrorism financing.[213] Given the necessarily remaining ambiguity, in cases where it is doubtful whether the facts at hand indicate money laundering or terrorism financing, the reporting duty will thus not be reducible to a clear-cut definition of suspicion; rather, if the facts at hand give rise to an enhanced risk, a violation of a reporting duty will then depend on whether, in view of the facts known to the obliged entity, a decision not to file an SAR was influenced by irrelevant considerations or false assumptions or was based on manifestly unreasonable valuation standards.[214]

As regards the territorial scope of the reporting obligation, section 43 para. 3 specifies that it applies if the obliged entity operates an establishment in Germany and the reportable matter in question is related to an activity of the German establishment. This in particular means that a reporting duty in Germany does not arise where the situation relates exclusively to the activities of an obliged entity's branch abroad. Legislative drafting materials explain that a relevant relationship to Germany is deemed to exist where the situation (such as a transaction) concerns legal relations in Germany.[215]

It results from section 7 para. 5 that the filing of SARs is incumbent upon the obliged entity's AML compliance officer or one of his or her deputies, and

---

210 Bafin, Auslegungs- und Anwendungshinweise zum Geldwäschegesetz of December 2018, at IV.10, requests increased vigilance with regard to transactions that are particularly complex or large, are carried out in an unusual way, or have no apparent economic or lawful purpose.

211 Bafin, Auslegungs- und Anwendungshinweise zum Geldwäschegesetz of December 2018, at IV.10.

212 See BT-Drucksache 18/11555, p. 156; Bundesministerium der Finanzen, Auslegungshinweise des Bundesministeriums der Finanzen zur Handhabung des Verdachtsmeldewesens of 6 November 2014, pp. 2–4; S Barreto da Rosa, in F Herzog/O Achtelik (eds.), Geldwäschegesetz, 2018, §43, para. 6.

213 BT-Drucksache 17/6804, p. 21; Bafin, Auslegungs- und Anwendungshinweise zum Geldwäschegesetz of December 2018, at IV.10.

214 In this vein Bafin, Auslegungs- und Anwendungshinweise zum Geldwäschegesetz of December 2018, at IV.10.

215 BT-Drucksache 18/11555, p. 157.

that this decision is not subject to interference by the obliged entity's executive management.[216]

b. Content and Direct Addressee(s) of SARs

The report is directly addressed to the FIU, and must, according to section 45, be filed electronically. Transmission by post (which would seem to include transmission by telefax)[217] is allowed only if electronic data transmission is temporarily disrupted. To avoid undue hardship, the FIU can, upon request by an obliged entity, dispense with the electronic transmission of a report by an obliged entity and authorise transmission by post. In any case, obliged entities have to electronically sign up with the FIU irrespective of the filing of an SAR.[218] According to section 45 para. 4, obliged entities are allowed to delegate the reporting to an external body if the latter can guarantee confidentiality and an effective performance of the duty.[219] Section 45 para. 5 authorises the Federal Ministry of Finance to define, by means of an ordinance, formal details for the submission of a report; however, even in the absence of such an ordinance, section 45 is meant to imply that the FIU has the power to define the format of the electronic submission, notably by providing an electronic user interface[220] that obliged entities are required to use to this effect.[221]

In line with the relatively low standard of suspicion that triggers a reporting duty and the requirement that the report be filed without delay,[222] obliged entities are not required to provide the FIU with an extensive analysis of the reported case, in particular not to extensively investigate the transaction on

216 See below section III.E. Accordingly, Bafin, Auslegungs- und Anwendungshinweise zum Geldwäschegesetz of December 2018, at IV.10 states that it would be incompatible with the reporting duty for an obliged entity to require the internal communication of suspicious activity by the employee who detected it to be first submitted to a person other than the AML compliance officer and to allow this other person to stop the communication to the compliance officer where this other person disagrees with the initial assessment.

217 See BVerwG NVwZ 2017, 967, 969.

218 According to section 59 para. 6 GWG, this duty enters into force once a new FIU information network has been established, at the latest on 1 January 2024.

219 See above section III.F.

220 See Financial Intelligence Unit, Merkblatt zum Vordruck 033573 – Verdachtsmeldung ohne Transaktion of 9 June 2017; Financial Intelligence Unit, Merkblatt zum Vordruck 033572 – Verdachtsmeldung mit Transaktion of 10 June 2017.

221 See BT-Drucksache 18/11555, p. 157. According to the FIU's webpage, obliged entities are, as of 1 February 2018, in principle required to submit their reports via the goAML Web Portal or, in the event of disruption of this interface for a period of at least 12 hours, via telefax; see Financial Intelligence Unit, Ende der Übergangsphase der parallelen Abgabemöglichkeit von Verdachtsmeldungen zum 1. February 2018, 9 January 2018.

222 According to guidance by the Federal Ministry of Finance in Bundesministerium der Finanzen, Auslegungshinweise des Bundesministeriums der Finanzen zur Handhabung des Verdachtsmeldewesens of 6 November 2014, p. 3, the internal assessment of the case must be completed as quickly as possible.

their own.[223] Nevertheless, in order for a report to be meaningful, obliged entities will be required to provide all the facts (which might in particular include details on multiple transactions and information on account turnover)[224] that allow the FIU to comprehend why, in the eyes of the obliged entity, the situation gave rise to a suspicion.[225] When weighting their obligation to report without delay on the one hand and a possible further analysis of the case on the other hand, obliged entities will however usually need to prioritise the former.[226]

c. Duty not to Disclose

According to section 47 para. 1, an obliged entity must not disclose to the contracting party, the instructing party of the transaction or other third parties the intended or past filing of a report, a criminal investigation launched on the basis of an SAR or a request for information by the FIU addressed to the obliged entity. In light of the clear legislative objective of preventing the tipping-off of clients that might endanger the success of any subsequent criminal investigation or of any preventive measures[227] (in particular the confiscation of the assets), the prohibition of section 47 para. 1 also applies to the disclosure of any intended or past filing of a criminal complaint. The prohibition does however not apply to disclosure to state authorities, including to self-regulatory bodies, and to certain other obliged entities.[228]

As regards the prohibition to disclose the intended filing of an SAR, given that frequently multiple employees of the obliged entity will be involved in the decision to file an SAR (notably account managers and compliance officers), the specific intention of the individual employee is irrelevant once he or she is aware that all the preconditions of a reporting duty are present.[229] As disclosure can also be done implicitly, an obliged entity has to ensure that its communication with the client does not reveal that it assumes itself to be under an obligation to report or that it suspects a case of money laundering

---

223 In this vein, Bafin, Auslegungs- und Anwendungshinweise zum Geldwäschegesetz of December 2018, at IV.10, specifies that the obliged entity's judgement must only take into account and inquire into facts that have been generated in direct connection with the respective business relationship and that are therefore available to the AML compliance officer and can be consulted at short notice. In particular, it is not required (and in view of the duty to report without delay even not allowed) to interview the client about the origin and purpose of assets before filing the SAR; in this sense see also OLG Frankfurt, Order of 10 April 2018 – 2 Ss-OWi 1059/17, at para. 36.

224 S Barreto da Rosa, in F Herzog/O Achtelik (eds.), Geldwäschegesetz, 2018, §45, paras. 6–7.

225 BR-Drucksache 317/11, p. 48.

226 S Barreto da Rosa, in F Herzog/O Achtelik (eds.), Geldwäschegesetz, 2018, §43, para. 56.

227 See already BT-Drucksache 16/9038, p. 46.

228 See Article 39(2) of Directive 2015/849/EU and below section V.J.

229 See BT-Drucksache 17/6804, p. 36; S Barreto da Rosa, in F Herzog/O Achtelik (eds.), Geldwäschegesetz, 2018, §47, para. 1.

or terrorism financing; this does not exclude the possibilities of merely asking the client questions in the performance of CDD and of explaining to the client that, due to its legal obligations, the obliged entity will not carry out a transaction or establish a business relationship. Furthermore, an obliged entity is exceptionally entitled to disclose the filing of an SAR or of a criminal complaint to a client where, due to a very serious criminal suspicion against one client and a resulting duty of care towards other clients, the disclosure is necessary to avert property damage to an unsuspected client.[230]

d. Power or Duty to Freeze

In order to enable the ordering of provisional measures by the FIU or asset freezing measures by the criminal justice authorities, obliged entities must, according to section 46 para. 1, not execute a transaction about which an SAR has been filed (i) before being informed by the FIU or a public prosecution office that it consents to the execution, or (ii) before the third working day (which does not include Saturdays) after the day on which the SAR was filed has elapsed without the execution of the transaction having been prohibited by the FIU or the competent public prosecution office.[231] Section 46 para. 2 adds that execution is also permitted if a postponement is not possible or could frustrate possible criminal proceedings; the obliged entity must then however subsequently file an SAR without delay. A postponement will usually be impossible if the client had explicitly insisted on the instant execution of a transaction or if, in view of the circumstances of the transaction (for example in the case of usual cash transactions, including cash withdrawals) a postponement is not feasible.[232] In view of the objective of this exception to avoid excessive constraints on business operations, which could have the undesirable effect of inducing obliged entities to adopt excessively demanding reporting standards, section 46 para. 2 does however seem inapplicable if the criminal nature of a transaction is blatant; otherwise, section 46 could have the unintended effect of inciting conduct for which the obliged entity's employee (were it not for the subsequent filing of an SAR)[233] would normally be criminally liable for grossly negligent money laundering even if the postponement was not motivated by concerns that a postponement and a resulting implicit tip-off would frustrate criminal proceedings.

---

230 BGH NJW 2008, 2245, 2246; S Barreto da Rosa, in F Herzog/O Achtelik (eds.), Geldwäschegesetz, 2018, §47, para. 6.

231 BT-Drucksache 18/11555, p. 158.

232 See BT-Drucksache 12/2704, p. 18; S Barreto da Rosa, in F Herzog/O Achtelik (eds.), Geldwäschegesetz, 2018, §47, para. 15.

233 See section 261 paras. 5 and 9 s. 1 StGB; Bafin, Auslegungs- und Anwendungshinweise zum Geldwäschegesetz of December 2018, at IV.10.

If, despite not having been vetoed by the FIU or a prosecutor, the obliged entity continues to doubt the lawfulness of the transaction, it may refuse to execute it or may terminate the relationship with the particular client altogether. This is so even if the obliged entity would otherwise be under a contractual obligation to the contrary insofar as, in light of objective reasons that indicate a criminal origin, the entity and its employees cannot be expected to carry out the transaction and thereby assume the risk of sanctions. However, the law does not explicitly provide for a power of obliged entities to withhold a client's assets beyond the three-day period following the filing of an SAR solely on the basis of a suspicion. In particular, as long as the obliged entity's employees did not establish a criminal origin of assets but consider this to be merely a possibility, a transfer of the respective assets back to the client or to any related third person following the filing of an SAR will not give rise to criminal liability for grossly negligent money laundering; accordingly in this case the obliged entity cannot rely on the prohibition of grossly negligent money laundering as a justification for withholding and thereby effectively freezing the assets.[234]

e. Instant Collateral Duties

Besides the duty not to execute a transaction for a period of at least[235] three days, the law does not specify particular collateral measures that obliged entities would be expected to perform after the filing of an SAR. Insofar as an SAR refers to a particular transaction, the obliged entity remains in principle free to carry out other transactions for the same client or from the same account.[236] Subject to the circumstances of the particular case, the filing of an SAR will however constitute a crucial factor in guiding the obliged entity's CDD towards the same client or business relationship and will thus usually give rise to enhanced CDD measures according to section 15 para. 6,[237] namely trigger at least an obligation to perform enhanced continuous monitoring of the underlying business relationship and analyse any other transactions that are closely related to the reported transaction. Similar considerations apply insofar as an SAR does not refer to a particular transaction, but rather (triggered for example by the behaviour of the client) to an entire business relationship. For this case, the

234 See section 261 paras. 1 and 9 s. 1 no. 1 StGB and above section II.B.1.a.ii.

235 On possible provisional measures by the FIU see below section IV.A.4.

236 Bafin, Auslegungs- und Anwendungshinweise zum Geldwäschegesetz of December 2018, at IV.10, recommends that, insofar as the obliged entity considers a termination of the relationship, it should first approach the FIU and possible the competent criminal justice authorities in order not to compromise an ongoing investigation.

237 Bafin, Auslegungs- und Anwendungshinweise zum Geldwäschegesetz of December 2018, at IV.10.

law does not provide for an obligation to suspend the relationship,[238] yet its suspicious nature will at least trigger enhanced CDD obligations for all incoming and outgoing transactions within the affected business relationship.

2. *Follow-Up*

a. Duty to Provide FIU with Additional Data

According to section 30 para. 3 s. 1, the FIU can request information from obliged entities irrespective of the filing of an SAR by the requested entity. The FIU can thus ask the reporting obliged entity to provide it with additional information about the reported transaction that it requires to assess the possible criminal nature of the assets in question.[239] Such requests may not least aim to uncover developments following the execution of a transaction in order to establish whether subsequent observations by the obliged entity might help to substantiate an initially inconclusive SAR. Due to the broad scope of section 30 para. 3 s. 1, the FIU can however also request information that is not related to any prior SAR, as well as information that is only indirectly related to a prior SAR in that the request may for example aim to find out whether other unreported transactions of the same client might share similarities to the previously reported transaction. If an SAR is passed on by the FIU to the criminal justice authorities, information requests of those authorities to the obliged entity are then based on the Criminal Procedure Code, namely on the power of criminal courts and public prosecutors and, on the instruction of a prosecutor, of the police to request witness testimony.[240] The criminal justice authorities notably have the power to request the surrender of documents and, in the event of a refusal, seize them. In this respect, it should be noted that constitutional jurisprudence allows for an extensive seizure of banking data in criminal proceedings, including files that are not directly related to the suspect in order to counter the risk that relevant evidence is concealed in inconspicuous places.[241]

b. Continued Duty not to Disclose SAR to Client

The law does not provide for temporal limits on the above-mentioned disclosure prohibitions. It must therefore be assumed that these prohibitions apply permanently and in particular even if, after the FIU's analysis or after an investigation by judicial authorities, an initial suspicion is not substantiated.

---

238 S Barreto da Rosa, in F Herzog/O Achtelik (eds.), Geldwäschegesetz, 2018, §46, para. 6.

239 Bafin, Auslegungs- und Anwendungshinweise zum Geldwäschegesetz of December 2018, at IV.10.

240 Section 48 para. 1, section 161a para. 1 and section 163 para. 3 StPO.

241 BVerfG, NStZ 1994, 349; sections 94, 95 and 98 para. 1 s. 1 StPO.

The continued non-disclosure obligation might effectively be curtailed by disclosure within subsequent administrative or judicial proceedings. As already stated, section 47 para. 2 provides that the non-disclosure obligation does not apply to disclosure to state authorities, which could be understood as including disclosure within court proceedings. However, section 47 para. 3 also provides that, unless otherwise stated by the law, state authorities other than the FIU which have gained knowledge of an SAR are prohibited from disclosing this information to the contracting party of the obliged entity, the instructing party of the transaction, the beneficial owner, a person who acted as their representative or to their legal advisor. Disclosure to these persons is only allowed with the prior consent of the FIU and only if the disclosure would not alter the initial purpose of the SAR.[242]

This raises the question how information contained in SARs should be treated within criminal proceedings. The reference to "unless otherwise stated by the law" in section 47 para. 3 can be understood as giving preference to the criminal court's duty to comprehensively investigate the case and, to this end, make use of all available legally obtained information. Section 47, as well as section 49, which sets limits on the disclosure of personal data by the FIU to a person concerned, however show that it is the intention of the legislator to ensure that at least some parts of an SAR and of the FIU's further communication with obliged entities remain, in principle, inaccessible to the persons directly affected by the report and thus to the public at large. On the one hand, it is inconceivable that information having found its way into a criminal court file (be it provide by the FIU or by an obliged entity) would not be disclosed to the defendant and his or her legal counsel.[243] On the other hand, it results from section 32 para. 4 s. 1 and section 49 para. 2 s. 2 that some information, including SAR-related information, is not disclosed by the FIU, not even to the criminal justice authorities. As a result, while the FIU cannot be entitled to prevent the disclosure of information that has otherwise be obtained by the criminal justice authorities, these authorities must in principle respect the FIU's decision not to communicate information about an SAR or about other communication between the FIU and obliged entities, including as regards any information held in this regard by obliged entities themselves.[244] Exceptions to this obligation can however result from a criminal court's constitutional obligation to establish the truth[245] if the disclosure of information is relevant for this purpose and

---

242 The explanatory notes to the GWG specify that this non-disclosure duty of authorities applies equally to reports to the FIU by supervisory authorities according to section 44 GWG and reports to the FIU by the tax authorities according to section 31b AO; BT-Drucksache 18/11555, p. 158.

243 BVerfGE 57, 250; BVerfG NJW 2006, 1048, 1049; BVerfG NStZ-RR 2013, 379.

244 See sections 54 and 96 StPO.

245 Section 244 para. 2 StPO.

the FIU's interest in non-disclosure is not preponderant.[246] In such cases, defendants in a criminal trial can seek disclosure by the FIU despite the FIU's unwillingness to give its consent. To decide upon such application for disclosure, the administrative courts are entitled to request the surrender of relevant confidential files from the FIU, and can thereby review the relevant material in private in order to decide whether it should be disclosed to the applicant due to his or her preponderant interest.[247]

To assess whether the FIU's interest in the non-disclosure of information is preponderant, it has to be noted that, according to section 47 para. 2, information about SARs and about information requests by the FIU can widely be disclosed within groups of obliged entities, and to a lesser extent even beyond groups. One must therefore assume that such communications do not enjoy a comprehensive claim to confidentiality. Accordingly, the FIU's right to deny disclosure to a defendant and to a criminal court only extends to particular elements of its communication with obliged entities. This in particular covers those elements of an SAR the disclosure of which could endanger the individual that filed it.[248] Depending on the circumstances of the particular case, the FIU's right to refuse disclosure might also extend to such content of an SAR or of an information request of the FIU the disclosure of which could endanger the effectiveness of AML/CTF measures, in particular details about the obliged entity's CDD practice or about the communication between the obliged entity and the FIU publication of which could negatively affect the effectiveness of the FIU's operational capabilities.[249]

c. Continued Collateral Duties

As already stated, the GWG does not provide details regarding the further treatment of a reported transaction or business relationship beyond the duty not to execute a reported transaction for a period of at least three days. Insofar as the reporting entity subsequently learns that the suspicion was perfectly legal, this will of course be relevant for the extent of CDD measures. However, and despite a general duty of the FIU to provide feedback,[250] reporting entities will usually not learn whether their suspicion was well-founded or not. The further treatment of a reported business relationship therefore depends mainly on obliged entities' risk appetite and, insofar as they are willing to keep the customer, on the outcome of their enhanced CDD.

---

246 See BVerfGE 57, 250, 284 = BVerfG NJW 1981, 1719, 1724; BGH NJW 2007, 3010, 3012; BVerwG NVwZ 2010, 905, 909.

247 Section 99 Code of Administrative Court Procedure (Verwaltungsgerichtsordnung).

248 See section 49 para. 2 s. 3 GWG.

249 See section 49 para. 2 s. 2 no. 2 GWG.

250 See *infra* IV.B.3.

3. *Special Rules for Privileged Professions*

a. Trigger for/Degree of Suspicion

According to section 43 para. 2, members of a bar association, patent attorneys, notaries, auditors, tax advisors and tax agents are exempted from the reporting obligation if the matter relates to information they obtained in the context of the provision of legal advice or of legal representation.[251] This is meant to ensure that all activities that are subject to professional secrecy[252] are comprehensively covered,[253] thereby avoiding potential uncertainty about the limits of professional secrecy that could arise if only selected elements of the professional activity (for example the provision of legal advice or the legal representation of the client) were covered. However, the reporting obligation remains in force if the obliged entity knows that the contracting party has used or is using the legal advice or legal representation for the purpose of money laundering or terrorism financing or another criminal offence. Insofar as a member of a privileged profession is acting in the exercise of such profession, the conditions triggering a reporting duty are thus much more demanding. A mere suspicion is not enough; the respective professional must, from his or her subjective perspective, be sure that the client relationship has been used or is used for criminal purpose. However, according to section 43 para. 6, the Federal Ministry of Finance can, in agreement with the Ministry of Justice, through legislative degree, determine certain types of real estate transactions in which the aforementioned privilege does not apply.

To determine the actual scope of the reporting duty of privileged professions, it must be noted that for members of a bar association, patent attorneys and notaries, the question of a reporting duty only arises where they are obliged entities, which, as seen earlier, is only the case when they participate in a number of defined commercial activities.[254] This notably means that, to the extent that a member of those professions is not participating in such activities

---

[251] See BT-Drucksache 19/13827, p. 94, which clarifies in particular that mere business audit activities do not enjoy privilege.

[252] See section 43a para. 2 Federal Lawyers' Act (Bundesrechtsanwaltsordnung); section 39a para. 2 Patent Attorneys' Act (Patentanwaltsordnung); section 18 para. 1 Federal Notaries' Act (Bundesnotarordnung); section 43 para. 1 and section 130 para. 1 Auditors' Act (Wirtschaftsprüferordnung); section 57 para. 1 Tax Advisors' Act (Steuerberatungsgesetz).

[253] See BT-Drucksache 18/12405, p. 166.

[254] See above sections II.D.3. From a constitutional law perspective, this reporting duty of the legal profession as regards commercial activities is arguably rather unproblematic: the Federal Constitutional Court has (in the case of the seizure of client-related documents in the possession of the attorney) explicitly accepted that outside the sphere of criminal defence, the legislature was entitled to give priority to the interests of criminal justice over the secrecy interest of the client even if the attorney herself was not suspected of a crime; BVerfG NJW 2018, 2385, 2389.

and is merely providing legal advice to the client or representing the client in court proceedings, a reporting duty does not arise even if the legal professional has knowledge that the client has used or is using the client relationship for the purpose of a criminal offence. However, where legal professionals are sure that, through their participation in the defined commercial activities, they are used for the purpose of money laundering or terrorism financing, they have to report; furthermore, they might through such participation themselves become criminally liable for aiding and abetting those offences.[255]

b. Content and Addressee(s) of SAR

Unlike in the pre-2017 law, there are no longer special rules as regards the addressees of reports from privileged professions. Under the old law, privileged professions were required to file their reports to their federal-level chamber, which then had to forward the report without delay to the old FIU and the state prosecution office.[256] This approach has been abandoned as of 2017, meaning that reports are now always directly addressed to the FIU.

c. Duty not to Disclose to Client

In principle, the law does not exempt privileged professions from the above-mentioned non-disclosure obligations. However, according to section 47 para. 4, where members of the bar association, patent attorneys, notaries, independent legal advisors who are not members of a bar association, tax advisors and auditors seek to dissuade a client from engaging in illegal activity, this does not constitute a disclosure. The provision thereby goes beyond dissuasion from money laundering, its predicate offences and terrorism financing, and extends to cases where privileged professionals try to dissuade their clients from other illegal acts, including acts that are merely unlawful and not criminal.[257]

4. Protection of SAR's Source

According to section 49 para. 1 s. 2 and para. 2 s. 3, in the event that the FIU provides information to a person affected by an SAR,[258] it must redact the

---

255 As for the constitutionality of such limits on the exercise of the legal profession, see BVerfG NJW 2004, 1305, 1312; BVerfG NJW 2015, 2949, 2953, affirming that criminal defence attorneys can themselves be criminally liable for money laundering by accepting payment of fees from illegal sources if they are sure of this origin; see S Barreto da Rosa, in F Herzog/O Achtelik (eds.), Geldwäschegesetz, 2018, §43, para. 75.

256 Section 11 para. 4 of the old GWG, which remained in force until 26 June 2017.

257 S Barreto da Rosa, in F Herzog/O Achtelik (eds.), Geldwäschegesetz, 2018, §47, para. 31.

258 See below section IV.B.4.

personal data of the individual who filed the SAR, except if legitimate interests of the requesting person are preponderant. Although the disclosure prohibition does in principle also extend to subsequent proceedings conducted by other authorities, disclosure of the reporting individual's identity may in particular be required within a criminal trial in which the respective SAR is relevant; disclosure might then depend on the concrete interests at stake, in particular on the one hand on the relevance of the reporting individual's identity for the establishment of truth and on the other hand on the probability and intensity of any endangerment of the reporting individual.[259] In a similar vein, section 49 para. 4 adds that, if the person who filed an SAR or reported a matter internally is an employee of the obliged entity, this person must not suffer any disadvantages in his or her employment as a consequence of the report.[260] As regards a possible protection of the obliged entity itself (and provided that, as may be the case with independent individual professionals, it is not already covered by the above-mentioned section 49), the law does not provide special provisions to hide its identity. In exceptional cases,[261] it is however conceivable that the FIU may refrain from disclosing the identity of a legal entity to the person affected by an SAR if such disclosure would allow for the identification of the reporting individual and thereby endanger this individual. Similarly, the FIU might then, in line with section 47 para. 3, refuse a disclosure of such information in criminal or other proceedings.

D. RECORD KEEPING

According to section 5 para. 2 no. 1, obliged entities must document their preliminary risk analysis,[262] and do so in a way that enables the supervisory authority to comprehend how the assessment results, and in particular the differentiation between different risk categories, were reached.[263] According to section 8 para. 1, they must furthermore record and retain (i) information

---

259 See above section III.C.2.b.

260 Section 49 para. 5 now provides that otherwise such a person can, irrespective of any judicial remedy (in particular before a labour court), lodge a complaint with the competent supervisory authority; BT-Drucksache 19/13827, p. 96.

261 See section 49 para. 2 s. 2 GWG and below section IV.B.4.

262 See above section III.B. For possible exemptions by the supervisory authority from this duty in cases where the money laundering or terrorism financing risks are clearly discernible, see section 5 para. 4 GWG. According to Bafin, Auslegungs- und Anwendungshinweise zum Geldwäschegesetz of December 2018, at II.2.3, exceptions will in principle only apply to non-financial obliged entities.

263 See Bafin, Auslegungs- und Anwendungshinweise zum Geldwäschegesetz of December 2018, at II.2.3.

gathered as part of their CDD on contracting parties, persons representing the contracting parties, beneficial owners;[264] information about the steps taken to identify the beneficial owner;[265] and information about business relationships and transactions insofar as it may be necessary for the analysis of transactions; (ii) sufficient information on the performance and the results of CDD risk grading, as well as about the adequacy of the measures adopted as a result of it; (iii) the results of the analysis of transactions that are particularly complex or large, follow an unusual transaction pattern, or have no apparent economic or lawful purpose;[266] and (iv) the motives and a plausible justification of the evaluation result regarding any case where the filing of an SAR was considered.[267] Obliged entities must also record measures they performed to identify the beneficial owner of legal entities and commercial partnerships. According to section 8 para. 4, information that was gathered in the performance of CDD about contract partners, persons representing contract partners, and beneficial owners, as well as information about business relationships and transactions, insofar as they can be relevant for the analysis of transactions, must be retained for five years counting from the end of the year in which the business relationship is terminated, provided that no other legal duties stipulate a longer period.[268] Other information must be retained for five years counting from the end of the year in which the information was gathered, subject again to a possible longer period specifically provided by law. Insofar as no other retention duties require otherwise,[269] records must be destroyed after ten years at the latest.[270]

264 According to section 8 para. 1 s. 1 no. 1(a) GWG, in the case of estate agents this includes information about the parties of a sales contract. If, in the absence of other information to this effect, the contract partner's legal representative, managing shareholder or partner is deemed to be the beneficial owner, obliged entities must, according to section 8 para. 1 s. 3 GWG, furthermore document the steps undertaken to verify the identity of such person as well as any difficulties they encountered in this respect.

265 According to section 8 para. 1 s. 2 and section 11 para. 5a s. 1 GWG, in the case of a transaction pertaining to the transfer of real estate property, notaries must furthermore retain documentation of the client's ownership and control structure if the client is a legal entity, partnership, foundation, trust or similar structure.

266 For credit institutions, financial service institutions and capital management companies, section 25h para. 3 s. 2 KWG and section 28 para. 1 s. 4 KAGB clarify that the documentation must demonstrate that the particular transaction did not lead to the conclusion that a criminal offence was committed or attempted.

267 See Bafin, Auslegungs- und Anwendungshinweise zum Geldwäschegesetz of December 2018, at IV.10.

268 To this effect, see for example section 147 para. 3 AO and section 257 para. 4 HGB; BT-Drucksache 19/13827, p. 72.

269 BT-Drucksache 19/13827, p. 72.

270 For requirements as to the form of the documentation, see section 8 paras. 2 and 3 GWG.

E. COMPLIANCE OFFICERS

Section 7 para. 1 requires credit institutions, financial services institutions, payment institutions, electronic money institutions, other financial businesses,[271] insurance undertakings, capital management businesses, and gambling providers and brokers to have a money laundering compliance officer at their management level as well as a deputy. The compliance officer shall be responsible for compliance with money laundering-related obligations. He or she must be directly subordinated to the executive management. The supervisory authority can exempt an obliged entity from the duty to have a compliance officer where it is ensured that (i) a risk of a loss of information or of information deficits as a consequence of the businesses organisational structure does not arise;[272] and, (ii) following a risk-oriented approach, steps are taken to avoid business relationships or transactions that are related to money laundering or terrorism financing. The competent supervisory authority can also order obliged entities other than the aforementioned to appoint a compliance officer if the supervisory authority deems this appropriate. As regards dealers in goods, such appointment must normally be ordered where the main activity of the dealer concerns the trade in high-value goods. Section 7 para. 5 specifies that the compliance officer must exercise his or her function on the national territory.[273] He is notably the contact person for criminal justice authorities, the FIU and the supervisory authority. Compliance officers must be equipped with sufficient powers and means;[274] in particular they have to be provided with unhindered access to all information, data, records and systems that could be relevant for the exercise of their function.[275] The compliance officer reports directly to the member of the executive management responsible for AML and

---

271 Within the meaning of section 2 para. 1 no. 6 GWG; see above section II.D.1.

272 According to Bafin, Auslegungs- und Anwendungshinweise zum Geldwäschegesetz of December 2018, at II.3.2, such a risk will normally be presumed in obliged entities with a staff of 15 or more and in the case of cross-border business structures.

273 On the particular requirements for a group-wide compliance officer according to section 6 para. 2 no. 2 GWG, see Bafin, Auslegungs- und Anwendungshinweise zum Geldwäschegesetz of December 2018, at IV.11.3.

274 Bafin, Auslegungs- und Anwendungshinweise zum Geldwäschegesetz of December 2018, at II.3.2, specifies that the obliged entity's internal supervisory body must be informed about any significant cuts of means.

275 Bafin, Auslegungs- und Anwendungshinweise zum Geldwäschegesetz of December 2018, at II.3.2, specifies these functions as advising and supporting preventive efforts, notably by developing the entity's risk analysis and of internal principles and procedures, being involved in the assessment of new products, business areas and client categories, and in the development of internal work instructions, and in a timely manner monitoring (including where appropriate through random samples) of compliance with internal procedures and instructions and processing any cases of suspicion. The same guidance furthermore provides that the compliance officer has to examine any transaction that is particularly complex or large, is carried out in an unusual way, or has no apparent economic or lawful purpose.

CTF compliance.[276] As regards the filing of SARs or requests by the FIU, the compliance officer is not subject to instructions by the executive management.[277]

F. INTERNAL COMPLAINT MECHANISM

Section 6 para. 5 provides that obliged entities must adopt measures appropriate to the entity's nature and size that enable employees and individuals in a similar position to notify violations of AML provisions to suitable bodies while ensuring the confidentiality of the identity of the notifying person. Such violations notably include the case that an employee notified a case of money laundering to the obliged entity's competent compliance officer who then did not to file an SAR.[278] The particular design of this mechanism is left to the obliged entities.[279] In line with section 6 para. 7, the obliged entity can also designate an external body to be responsible for receiving and processing internal notifications if this external body can guarantee confidentiality and an effective follow-up treatment of the notifications. Analogous to section 53 para. 5, one must furthermore assume that notifying employees must not as a result of the notification be held liable, including under criminal or labour law, except if the notification was intentionally false or false due to gross negligence.[280]

G. ADDITIONAL PREVENTIVE MEASURES

– Internal Safeguards

To manage and mitigate the risk of money laundering and terrorism financing, section 6 para. 1 requires obliged entities[281] to implement adequate internal

---

276 See above section III.A.1.c. According to Bafin, Auslegungs- und Anwendungshinweise zum Geldwäschegesetz of December 2018, at II.3.2, the appointment of a member of the executive management as the compliance officer or deputy is admissible only where the obliged entity has a staff of less than 15. To avoid conflicts of interest, the AML compliance officer should furthermore in principle not simultaneously occupy the position of data protection compliance officer. He or she is furthermore excluded from exercising internal audit functions.

277 Bafin, Auslegungs- und Anwendungshinweise zum Geldwäschegesetz of December 2018, at II.3.2, requires the compliance officer, insofar as relevant for the function, to have the power of representation for the obliged entity, and, in the matter of the prevention of money laundering and terrorism financing, the power to issue internal instructions.

278 Bafin, Auslegungs- und Anwendungshinweise zum Geldwäschegesetz of December 2018, at IV.10.

279 BT-Drucksache 18/11555, p. 111.

280 See below section III.I.2.

281 Real estate agents must, according to section 4 paras. 2 and 4 GWG, implement internal safeguards only (i) when they broker sales contracts, or (ii) when they broker rental contracts

safeguards through principles, procedures and controls that correspond to and sufficiently cover the risk of the particular obliged entity. The adequacy of safeguards[282] depends notably on the obliged entity's size, organisational structure and risk exposure, including its client structure.[283] Obliged entities must monitor the functioning of the safeguards and update them when necessary.[284] Section 6 para. 2 specifies that internal safeguards are in particular the following: (i) the development of internal principles, procedures and controls with regard to money laundering and terrorism financing risks, CDD obligations, reporting duties, documentation and compliance with other AML-related obligations; (ii) the appointment of a money laundering compliance officer and a deputy;[285] (iii) as regards parent companies of a group of companies, the establishment of group-wide procedures; (iv) the development and updating of adequate measures in order to prevent the abuse of new products and new technologies for money laundering and terrorism financing ends or for the purpose of facilitating the anonymity of business relationships or transactions; (v) the screening of employees in regards to their reliability;[286] (vi) initial and ongoing training of employees regarding typologies and current methods of money laundering and terrorism financing, as well as the relevant obligations, including data protection obligations; and (vii) a review of the aforementioned principles and procedures by an independent[287] audit insofar as such review is appropriate to the nature and size of the business activity.[288] Section 6 para. 3 specifies that if, insofar

---

that involve a monthly rent of €10,000 or more. According to section 4 paras. 2 sand 5, traders in goods must implement internal safeguards only in the case of (i) transactions of works of art worth €10,000 or more; (ii) transactions of precious metals, if the trader, him- or herself or through a third person, makes or received cash payments of €2,000 or more; or (iii) transactions of other goods, if the trader, him- or herself or through a third person, makes or received cash payments of €10,000 or more. Art brokers and art warehouse keepers must implement internal safeguards in case of transactions worth 10,000 Euro or more.

282 Bafin, Auslegungs- und Anwendungshinweise zum Geldwäschegesetz of December 2018, at II.3, specifies that the adequacy of safeguards is determined on the basis of the obliged entities' own risk analysis.

283 BT-Drucksache 18/11555, p. 110.

284 According to Bafin, Auslegungs- und Anwendungshinweise zum Geldwäschegesetz of December 2018, at II.3, an obligation to update may notably be triggered by a significant change of the risk exposure or in light of new money laundering or terrorism financing methods.

285 See above section III.E. Bafin, Auslegungs- und Anwendungshinweise zum Geldwäschegesetz of December 2018, at II.3.5, specifies that this includes both a risk-oriented screening at the moment of recruitment and subsequent screening if the behaviour of the employee gives rise to doubts about his or her reliability.

286 See section 1 para. 20 GWG.

287 Bafin, Auslegungs- und Anwendungshinweise zum Geldwäschegesetz of December 2018, at II.3.7, provides that this can also be done through an internal audit, but must cover the work of the AML compliance officer; the audit may be performed by random samples the number of which is adequate to the total number of relevant transactions.

288 According to section 29 para. 2 s. 1 KWG, the annual audit of credit institutions and financial services institutions has to include a verification of the institution's AML

as they are an obliged entity, attorneys at law, patent attorneys, notaries, other legal advisors, auditors, tax advisors, tax agents, trust service providers, trustees, estate agents and traders in goods exercise their profession as the employee of a company, the obligation to implement internal safeguards lies with the company.

Credit institutions, financial services institutions, financial holding companies, mixed financial holding companies and capital management companies must, according to section 25h para. 1 KWG and section 28 para. 1 s. 4, additionally implement internal safeguards to prevent money laundering, terrorism financing and other crimes that may endanger the institution's assets. This requires an adequate and regularly updated system of safeguards and controls, including strategies and safeguards to prevent the abuse of new financial products and technologies for purposes of money laundering, terrorism financing or for the facilitation of the anonymity of business relationships and transactions. Section 25h para. 2 KWG and section 28 para. 1 s. 4 KAGB add that credit institutions and capital management companies have to operate and update data processing systems that enable them to identify business relationships or transactions that, in light of the publicly and internally available knowledge about the methods of money laundering and terrorism financing and about other crimes that may endanger the institution's assets, are particularly complex or large, are carried out in an unusual way, or have no apparent economic or lawful purpose. Similarly, section 27 para. 1 s. 2 no. 5 ZAG requires payment service institutions and electronic money institutions to operate data processing systems to ensure compliance with the GWG. In a similar vein, section 6 para. 4 GWG adds that gambling providers and brokers must, in addition to the above-mentioned internal safeguards, operate and update data processing systems which enable them to identify business relationships and individual transactions that in light of the publicly or internally available knowledge about the methods of money laundering and terrorism financing appear dubious or unusual. The supervisory authority is entitled to define conditions under which payment service institutions, electronic money institutions and gambling providers are allowed to refrain from operating data processing systems.[289]

compliance; see similarly section 35 para. 5 VAG for insurance undertakings, section 24 para. 1 s. 3 no. 1 ZAG for payment institutions and electronic money institutions, and section 38 para. 4 s. 1, section 121 para. 3 s. 2 and section 136 para. 3 s. 2 KAGB for capital management companies. On the substantive and formal requirements of the audit, see section 27 Ordinance on the Annual Audit of Credit Institutions and Financial Service Institutions (Prüfungsberichtsverordnung, PrüfbV) and section 43b Ordinance on the Annual Audit of Insurance Undertakings (Prüfungsberichteverordnung, PrüfV).

289 Section 27 para. 3 s. 2 ZAG; section 6 para. 4 s. 3 GWG.

Section 6 para. 6 requires obliged entities to ensure that that they can expeditiously[290] answer requests by the FIU or other competent authorities as to whether, within a period of five years prior to the request, they maintained a business relationship with a particular person and what the nature of this business relationship was; obliged entities must ensure that this information is transmitted securely and confidentially. Attorneys at law, patent attorneys, notaries, auditors, tax advisors and tax agents may refuse to answer the request if it relates to information they obtained in the context of the provision of legal advice or of legal representation, except if they positively know that the legal advice or representation was or is used for money laundering or terrorism financing.

According to section 6 para. 7, obliged entities may, on a contractual basis, task third parties with implementing internal safeguards,[291] provided that they notify the competent supervisory authority in advance. This authority may prohibit the transfer if (i) the third party cannot guarantee an orderly performance of safeguards, (ii) the control capabilities of the obliged entity would be adversely affected, or (iii) supervision would be adversely affected.[292]

– Group-wide Compliance

According to section 9 para. 1, obliged entities that are parent companies of a group of companies must conduct a risk analysis for all branches, branch offices and group companies that are subject to AML obligations. Based on this analysis, they have to adopt the following measures throughout the group and, insofar as the branches, branch offices and group companies are subject to AML obligations and are under the controlling influence of the parent company, ensure their effective implementation: (i) the implementation of uniform[293] internal safeguards in line with those mentioned above; (ii) the appointment of an AML compliance officer tasked with the development of a group-wide prevention strategy and with its coordination and monitoring; (iii) the implementation of procedures to ensure group-wide information exchange; and (iv) the implementation of arrangements for the protection of

290 See BT-Drucksache 18/11555, p. 111, which does however explain that, depending on the obliged entity's nature and size, this does not necessarily require an electronic mechanism.

291 Bafin, Auslegungs- und Anwendungshinweise zum Geldwäschegesetz of December 2018, at II.3.10, specifies that this might in principle include any type of safeguard, including the AML compliance officer.

292 See also section 25h KWG.

293 Bafin, Auslegungs- und Anwendungshinweise zum Geldwäschegesetz of December 2018, at IV.11.3, specifies that such uniformity does not mean that the standards must be the same for all group companies independently of the nature of their business activity, but merely that, within one category of activities, there must be group-wide standards irrespective of a company's or branch's location.

personal data. Insofar as branch offices and majority-owned group companies are situated in another EU Member State, the parent company of the group must, according to section 9 para. 2, furthermore ensure that they comply with the local AML and CTF obligations. According to section 9 para. 3, insofar as branches and majority-owned group companies are situated in a third state where less stringent preventive obligations than those applicable in Germany apply, and to the extent that this is compatible with local laws, parent companies must ensure compliance with the standards of German law. Insofar as, due to the law of the third state, the implementation of the above measures (i), (iii) and (iv) is not allowed, parent companies must ensure that the branches and group companies concerned apply additional measures to effectively counter money laundering and terrorism financing risks;[294] parent companies must furthermore inform the competent supervisory authority in Germany of those measures. If these measures do not suffice, the supervisory authority must order parent companies to ensure that the branches and subsidiaries in the third state neither establish or continue business relationships nor perform transactions. According to section 9 para. 4, if the group's parent company is not subject to the obligation to implement group-wide measures, the preceding obligations also apply to group companies that are obliged entities and have a controlling influence over at least one other group company.

H. RULES ON OBLIGED ENTITIES' CIVIL LIABILITY TOWARDS CLIENT

CDD measures (notably a sudden termination of contractual services) and the filing of SARs (which might lead to provisional measures by the FIU) can in principle give rise to civil liability of the obliged entity towards its clients if the measure or reporting, despite being motivated by obligations under the GWG, were performed on the basis of unsubstantiated factual elements and were causal for the prejudice that the client suffered. Section 48 does however comprehensively[295] exclude liability for (i) the filing of an SAR or a criminal complaint, (ii) the internal reporting of suspicious transactions by employees to their superior or another in-house body, and (iii) the obliged entity's or an employee's compliance with an information request from the FIU, unless the report, complaint or the information provided to the FIU was intentionally false or false due to gross negligence. The law does not explicitly provide for an exemption from liability in the case of other deficient measures, in particular

294 For examples of such measures, see Bafin, Auslegungs- und Anwendungshinweise zum Geldwäschegesetz of December 2018, at IV.11.3.

295 BT-Drucksache 12/2704, p. 19; BT-Drucksache 18/11555, p. 158.

the termination of a business relationship due to CDD obligations. However, insofar as such measures are less prejudicial to the client than the obliged entity's communication with the FIU, which may ultimately even trigger a criminal investigation and thus entails significant reputational and economic risks for the client, it would not seem appropriate to apply less demanding liability standards to factually unsubstantiated CDD measures than to SARs and FIU information requests. Obliged entities are then also exempted from liability for the erroneous performance of CDD, unless they acted intentionally or due to gross negligence.

I. SUPERVISORY AUTHORITIES' ROLE

1. *Supervisory Measures to Ensure Application of CDD and Other AML-Related Obligations*

Section 6 para. 8 provides that the supervisory authority may, in a particular case, issue adequate and necessary orders to an obliged entity to ensure implementation of the necessary internal safeguards.[296] This allows the supervisory authority to address both a complete lack as well as mere insufficiencies of internal safeguards.[297] Going further, according to section 6 para. 9, the competent supervisory authority may order that individual obliged entities or groups of obliged entities, due to the nature and size of their business and in light of the present money laundering or terrorism financing risks, have to implement internal safeguards in a particular risk-adequate manner. According to section 7 para. 4, the supervisory authority may furthermore order the dismissal of the AML compliance officer or of his or her deputy if this person lacks the required qualification or is unreliable.

Furthermore, according to section 51 para. 2, the competent supervisory authority can "take the appropriate and necessary measures and issue orders to ensure compliance" with the GWG and with regulations adopted on its basis,

[296] For the obligation of supervisory authorities to comprehensively cooperate with each other as well as with other authorities, including the FIU and criminal justice authorities, see section 55 para. 1 GWG. For the duty to cooperate with supervisory authorities of another EU Member State in cases in which the parent company of a domestic branch or branch office is domiciled in this Member State, see section 55 para. 5 GWG. As for the sharing of data with supervisory authorities of other EU Member States, section 55 para. 7 GWG provides a number of grounds on the basis of which such sharing must not be refused, in particular not because the information is deemed confidential, except where the information is protected by the right to refuse to give evidence or is covered by a professional secrecy privilege of legal professionals.

[297] Bafin, Auslegungs- und Anwendungshinweise zum Geldwäschegesetz of December 2018, at II.3.11.

and the supervisor can to this end also make use of the powers granted to it for supervisory functions outside AML law. Within these limits, supervisors can in particular adopt appropriate measures and issue orders to ensure that obliged entities in the particular case comply with these requirements and do not, in violation thereof, enter or continue business relationships or perform transactions.

Section 51 para. 3[298] specifies that supervisory powers notably include inspections, which may be conducted on-site or elsewhere, without the need to give specific reasons, and whose "frequency and intensity" depends on the obliged entity's risk profile. The supervisory authority must re-evaluate an obliged entity's risk profile at regular intervals and also "when important events or developments occur in relation to the obliged entity's senior management and business activity." According to section 52 para. 1, to ensure respect for the GWG, obliged entities, their organs and employees must, upon request and free of charge, provide the supervisory authority and any person or entity used by the supervisory authority in the performance of its functions with information about all relevant business matters and transactions, as well as relevant documentation. If facts indicate that particular persons are obliged entities, they have, according to section 52 para. 6, upon request and free of charge, provide the competent supervisory authority information about all business matters as well as related documents insofar as this is necessary to determine whether they are in fact obliged entities. According to section 52 para. 4,[299] individuals may refuse to respond to questions if they would otherwise expose themselves or a close relative to the risk of criminal prosecution or administrative sanctions. According to section 52 para. 5, attorneys at law, patent attorneys, notaries, auditors, tax advisors and tax agents can furthermore refuse to respond to questions regarding information they obtained in the context of providing legal advice or legal representation, except if they positively know that the client used or is using the legal advice for the purpose of money laundering or terrorism financing. The aforementioned exemptions however only apply to the obligation to answer questions, and do not affect the supervisory authority's right to access relevant documents.

---

298 For equivalent powers regarding those obliged entities that are not directly covered by section 51 para. 3 GWG, see section 44 para. 1 KWG for credit institutions and financial service institutions, section 305 para. 1 VAG for insurance undertakings, section 19 para. 1 ZAG for payment service institutions and electronic money institutions, and section 14 KAGB in conjunction with section 44 para. 1 KWG for investment management companies.

299 For equivalent exceptions regarding those obliged entities that are not directly covered by section 51 para. 4 GWG, see section 44 para. 6 KWG for credit institutions and financial service institutions, section 305 para. 5 VAG for insurance undertakings, section 19 para. 4 ZAG for payment service institutions and electronic money institutions, and section 14 KAGB in conjunction with section 44 para. 6 KWG for investment management companies.

For some financial institutions, the competent supervisory authority can appoint an external special representative to fully or partially replace an organ of the institution,[300] in particular if conditions for a dismissal of members of the organ are met.[301] In the case of credit institutions and financial services institutions, the special representative may also be tasked with implementing adequate organisational measures to prevent further sustained legal infringements by the institution or supervise compliance with supervisory orders.[302] The special representative is authorised to attend all meetings of the institutions' organs and other internal bodies, request information from members of the organs and from employees as well as access all documentation.[303]

2. *Complaint Mechanism*

Supervisory authorities must, according to section 53 para. 1, provide a mechanism for receiving notices about potential and actual contraventions of AML and CTF obligations that fall under the remit of the respective supervisory authority; it must ensure that those notices can also be filed anonymously through protected communication channels. Notifiable violations notably include the case where an obliged entity's employee internally reported a case of money laundering to the compliance officer, who then did not file an SAR.[304] Section 53 para. 3 adds that the supervisory authority must not disclose the identity of a notifying person without this person's explicit consent, and must furthermore not disclose the identity of the person who forms the object of the notification. These disclosure prohibitions do not however apply if the transfer of the information, due to a legal requirement, is necessary in the context of further investigations or in subsequent administrative or court proceedings, or if the disclosure is ordered by a court. In line with this limited protection of anonymity, section 53 para. 7 confirms that the supervisory authority's notification mechanism does not restrict the procedural rights of persons that form the object of a notification, in particular not the right to be informed about the subject matter of administrative or administrative or criminal proceedings against him or her and the right to inspect the file of the proceedings.[305]

---

300 See section 45c para. 2 no. 3 KWG for credit institutions and financial services institutions, section 307 para. 1 VAG for insurance undertakings, and section 20 paras. 1 and 2 ZAG for payment service institutions and electronic money institutions.

301 On such conditions, see below section VII.B.2.b.

302 Section 45c paras. 1 and 2 nos. 5 and 6 KWG; in a similar vein section 293 para. 3 VAG.

303 Section 45c para. 1 KWG; section 307 para. 2 VAG.

304 Bafin, Auslegungs- und Anwendungshinweise zum Geldwäschegesetz of December 2018, at IV.10.

305 See BT-Drucksache 18/11555, p. 162.

Section 53 para. 5 furthermore specifies that notifying employees of companies and persons falling under the supervision of the respective supervisory authority, as well as notifying employees of companies and persons to whom the functions of a supervised company or person have been outsourced, must not, as a result of the notification, be held liable under criminal or labour law or for any compensation of damages or otherwise disadvantaged, except if the notification was intentionally false or false due to gross negligence.[306] Section 53 para. 8 adds that the right of employees to make a notification to the competent supervisory authority cannot be restricted by contract.

J. STATISTICS ON SARs BY OBLIGED ENTITIES

Statistics for 2018 provide that obliged entities filed 77,252 SARs, though without specifying the value of the related assets. This compares to 59,845 in 2018, 45,597 in 2016, and 32,008 in 2015.[307] This increase can largely be attributed to a greater willingness of obliged entities to file SARs and to a change in how obliged entities perceive the nature of SARs. Not least because, since 2017, SARs no longer have to also be reported to the criminal justice authorities but now exclusively to the FIU, it seems that obliged entities less and less equate SARs with a criminal complaint and more and more perceive SARs only as a quasi-supervisory instrument, thereby meaning they have fewer inhibitions about reporting their clients. In 2018, 58% of SARs were forwarded to competent authorities as being possibly related to money laundering, terrorism financing or other criminal offences. However, in the same year the FIU received only 14,065 feedback communications from state prosecution offices; only 275 of those communications mentioned that the SAR subject matter led to a criminal conviction, to an out-of-trial criminal fine or to an indictment. The remainder of the feedback communications stated that proceedings by the criminal justice authorities were discontinued; according to the FIU, this does not however exclude the possibility that the criminal justice authorities used the SAR as a lead for an investigation for offences other than money laundering and terrorism financing, though this assertion is not further specified through statistics.[308]

306 Section 53 para. 5a GWG provides that such persons can, irrespective of any judicial remedy (in particular before a labour court), lodge a complaint with the competent supervisory authority; BT-Drucksache 19/13827, p. 100.

307 Financial Intelligence Unit, Jahresbericht 2018, Cologne 2019, pp. 13–14. The number for 2018 also includes 54 reports filed by supervisory authorities and 414 filed by tax authorities.

308 Financial Intelligence Unit, Jahresbericht 2018, Cologne 2019, pp. 17–19.

IV. THE SYSTEM OF FINANCIAL INTELLIGENCE UNITS

A. INSTITUTIONAL AND FUNCTIONAL CHARACTERISTICS

1. *Organisational Position*

The *Zentralstelle für Finanztransaktionsuntersuchungen* (Focal Point for the Analysis of Financial Transactions, hereafter: FIU) is integrated into the General Directorate of Customs (*Generalzolldirektion*) and therein attached to the Customs Criminal Office (*Zollkriminalamt*).[309] The FIU is thereby subordinated to the Federal Ministry of Finance.

2. *Purpose and Tasks*

According to section 28 para. 1 GWG, the FIU is tasked with collecting and analysing information related to money laundering or terrorist financing and disseminating this information to the competent domestic authorities for the purpose of the investigation, prevention or prosecution of such offences. For this purpose, the FIU is responsible for the following: receiving and collecting SARs; conducting operational analyses; exchanging information and coordinating with supervisory authorities; cooperating and exchanging information with foreign FIUs; prohibiting transactions and ordering other urgent measures; transmitting the results of operational analyses and other relevant information to the competent domestic authorities; providing feedback following the filing of an SAR; conducting strategic analyses and producing reports on this basis; engaging in dialogue with the relevant domestic authorities, in particular about typologies and methods; keeping statistics in accordance with Article 44(2) of Directive 2015/849/EU; publishing an annual report on operational analyses; and attending meetings of national and international working groups.

The GWG extends the utilisation of the FIU's data well beyond the investigation, prevention or prosecution of money laundering and terrorist financing. According to section 28 para. 3 GWG, the FIU and other domestic public authorities competent in the investigation, prevention and prosecution of money laundering and terrorist financing as well as other criminal offences, authorities competent in the prevention of threats, and domestic supervisory authorities shall work together to implement the GWG and provide mutual support. This might imply that, within the limits of the applicable data protection rules, the FIU shall lend support to other domestic authorities even with regard to events that have no money laundering or terrorism financing component. Furthermore, according to section 28 para. 4 GWG, the FIU shall,

[309] Section 5a para. 2 s. 3 Tax Administration Law (Finanzverwaltungsgesetz, FVG).

where necessary, inform the competent tax authorities or the authorities charged with the protection of the social security systems of matters which come to its knowledge in the performance of its tasks and which it has not transmitted to another competent government agency.

3. *Independence*

The FIU is organisationally autonomous and operates with professional independence in the framework of its tasks and powers, as provided for by section 27 para. 2 GWG. It is subject to the supervision of the Federal Ministry of Finance. However, according to section 28 para. 2 GWG, insofar as it receives and collects SARs, conducts operational analyses, prohibits transactions and orders other urgent measures, and transmits to the competent domestic authorities the results of the operational analyses and additional relevant information, the supervision by the Federal Ministry of Finance is limited to "legal supervision", meaning that insofar the Ministry can only interfere where it deems the FIU's action to be illegal, but it is not allowed to interfere into the FIU's policy considerations.

4. *Powers*

- Requests for Information

According to section 30 para. 3 s. 1, the FIU may, irrespective of whether it received an SAR, obtain information from obliged entities insofar as this is necessary for the performance of its tasks. Furthermore, according to section 31 para. 1, the FIU may, insofar as it is necessary for the performance of its tasks, collect data from domestic public authorities. The latter shall provide information to the FIU at its request for the performance of its tasks insofar as no transmission restrictions preclude the provision of information.[310]

- Coercive Powers

If the FIU has indications that a transaction is related to money laundering, terrorist financing or particular cases of proliferation financing,[311] it may adopt urgent measures, notably, according to section 40 para. 1, prohibiting the execution of the transaction in order to verify the indications and analyse the transaction. The FIU can also (i) prohibit credit institutions, financial services

---

310 On such limits see below section V.

311 See Article 23(2) of Council Regulation (EU) 2017/1509 of 30 August 2017 concerning restrictive measures against the Democratic People's Republic of Korea and repealing Regulation (EC) 329/2007.

institutions and payment services[312] from executing dispositions in relation to an account or securities account it holds, and from executing other financial transactions; (ii) instruct a credit institution to deny access to a safe deposit box; or (iii) issue other orders to an obliged entity in relation to a transaction. The aforementioned measures may, according to section 40 para. 2, also be taken on the basis of a request from a foreign FIU. According to section 40 paras. 3 and 4, measures shall be rescinded by the FIU as soon as or insofar as the conditions for the measure are no longer met. Measures end at the latest one month after their ordering, or when the fifth working day has elapsed since the matter was passed on to the competent law enforcement agency.

B. TREATMENT OF SARs

1. *Data Processing*

According to section 30 para. 2, the FIU shall analyse SARs filed by obliged entities, reports filed by supervisory authorities[313] and notifications from the tax authorities in order to verify whether the reported matter is related to money laundering, terrorist financing or another criminal offence.

2. *Special Procedures for Privileged Professions*

The GWG does not provide for special procedures regarding the treatment of SARs filed by privileged professions. Reports must always be submitted directly to the FIU, whose data processing does not, in principle, differentiate between the types of obliged entity that reported a transaction.

3. *Feedback Obligations*

a. Obligation of the FIU

According to section 41 para. 2, the FIU must provide a reporting obliged entity with "feedback on the relevance of its report within an appropriate period". The law does not however further specify the content of such communication and in particular does not further specify whether or to what extent the feedback must contain specific information on the particular reported activity or whether it might perhaps suffice for the reporting entity to only be informed about the nature of the FIU's follow-up measures without providing specific

312 See section 2 para. 1 nos. 1–3 GWG.
313 See section 44 GWG.

results of an operational analysis. By providing that the obliged entity "may only use personal data obtained in this way to improve its risk management, its fulfilment of its due diligence requirements and its reporting behaviour", section 41 para. 2 does however indicate that the feedback may contain personal data and thereby potentially also details about the FIU's analysis.

b. Obligation of Investigative Authorities

According to section 42 para. 1, if the FIU has provided information to the criminal justice authorities, the public prosecution office must notify the FIU of the filing of an indictment and of the outcome of the proceedings. The law specifies that the public prosecution office must perform this notification "by sending a copy of the indictment, the reasoned decision to terminate proceedings, or the verdict". Furthermore, according to section 42 para. 2, if the FIU has provided information to another domestic authority, the latter must notify the FIU of the use made of the information and of the outcome of the measures taken on the basis of the information, subject to the condition that other legal provisions do not preclude such notification.

4. Disclosure Obligations Towards "Suspect"

The law allows the FIU to disclose details about an operational analysis to the person concerned, but does not clarify whether or when there might be a duty to this effect. According to section 49 para. 1 s. 1, if the analysis of an SAR has not been concluded yet, the FIU "may, upon request, provide the person concerned with details of the available information concerning him if this will not interfere with the purpose of the analysis." In light of the operational analysis' function to serve as a precursor for criminal investigations, the purpose of the analysis includes possible follow-up measures (such as an asset freeze) by criminal justice authorities.[314] Despite the law's wording, the clear legislative intent to protect the FIU's data leads one to conclude that section 49 applies to any operational analysis, including analyses based not on an SAR but on information provided by other authorities.[315] A person concerned is anybody who is directly involved in the reported matter, in particular any contract partner or beneficiary of a transaction or business relationship.[316] Similarly, at the request of the person concerned, the FIU may, according to section 49 para. 2 s. 1, provide such information if the analysis of an SAR has been concluded but its results were not forwarded to the criminal justice authorities. In contrast, according

314 S Barreto da Rosa, in F Herzog/O Achtelik (eds.), Geldwäschegesetz, 2018, §49, para. 12.
315 S Barreto da Rosa, in F Herzog/O Achtelik (eds.), Geldwäschegesetz, 2018, §49, para. 5.
316 BT-Drucksache 18/11555, p. 159.

to section 49 para. 3, the FIU is no longer allowed to provide information to the person concerned once it has transmitted the matter to the criminal justice authorities; the FIU regains the right to provide information to the person concerned once proceedings by the public prosecution office or the court have been concluded.

Imposing limits on any disclosure by the FIU to the person concerned, section 49 para. 2 s. 2 provides that the FIU must refuse to provide information if such disclosure "would have negative effects" on (i) "international relations", (ii) "matters concerning the internal or external security of Germany", (iii) "the conduct of another criminal investigation", or (iv) "the conduct of ongoing judicial proceedings".[317] Effects on international relations seem particularly relevant where the FIU processed personal data that it obtained, on the basis of confidentiality, from domestic or foreign intelligence agencies or a foreign FIU. Matters concerning the internal security of Germany may justify non-disclosure in particular where information relates to investigative techniques (such as the design of investigative software) the publication of which might hamper the effectiveness of the technique.[318] Furthermore, according to section 49 para. 1 s. 2 and para. 2 s. 3, the FIU must in principle redact the personal data of the individual who filed an SAR, except if legitimate interests of the requesting person are preponderant. According to section 49 para. 2 s. 3, the same applies to the personal data of the individual who complied with a demand for information from the FIU. In view of the purpose of these rules to protect individuals from threats or reprisals, the FIU must not disclose the identity not only of the obliged entity's representative who filed the SAR, but in particular also of the employee who triggered the SAR inside the obliged entity in the first place.[319]

C. PROACTIVE INVESTIGATIONS

Section 28 para. 1 s. 2 no. 2 clarifies that the FIU's operational analysis does not consist merely of an assessment of reports by obliged entities and supervisory or tax authorities, but also of other information. In view of the various sources of data that the FIU is tasked with analysing, including information from public sources as well as non-public sources,[320] its operational analysis thus does not require an SAR as a starting point. Though section 30 para. 2 seems to impose a general duty on the FIU to analyse each SAR as well as each report submitted to the FIU by supervisory and by tax authorities,[321] this must be understood as

317 For similar, albeit narrower powers of supervisory authorities to deny disclosure of personal data to the data subject, see section 51a para. 2 GWG.

318 See VG Wiesbaden, judgment of 4 September 2015 – 6 K 687/15.WI.

319 See BT-Drucksache 18/11555, p. 159.

320 See section 30 para. 1 no. 4 GWG.

321 BT-Drucksache 18/11555, p. 140.

allowing for a margin of appreciation as to when and how the FIU processes reports. For unlike criminal justice authorities with regard to a criminal suspicion,[322] the FIU is not subject to a duty to comprehensively investigate each SAR. The fact that the GWG, unlike the Criminal Procedure Code,[323] does not provide for a formal decision to discontinue the analysis of an SAR confirms that the FIU's operational action is not meant to follow a highly formalised procedure. Section 30 para. 2 therefore does not exclude the possibility that the FIU, after a preliminary assessment of an SAR and in light of the degree of suspicion and the volume and nature of the respective transaction, decides not to continue its analysis of the report. In turn, and analogous to the suspicion threshold of an SAR according to section 43 para. 1, one must assume that the FIU is allowed to start an operational analysis on the basis of any information other than an SAR and other than reports by supervisory or tax authorities if this information contains facts that indicate that property is derived from a criminal offence which could constitute a predicate offence of money laundering, or facts that indicate that a transaction or property is related to terrorism financing. As already explained,[324] this standard merely requires that in view notably of the circumstances of the case and professional experience, a money laundering or terrorism financing background cannot be excluded. Following from its margin of appreciation, the FIU is empowered to prioritise certain operational analyses over others, provided that the resulting case selection is, from a criminal policy point of view, in line with the significance of the available cases and is not based on illegitimate discriminatory considerations. Operational analyses can therefore also be triggered not least by information provided by other domestic or foreign authorities. While the operational analysis does primarily consist of data matching with data found in a variety of public and, to a lesser extent, private data banks,[325] it notably also includes the power, according to section 30 para. 3, to obtain information from obliged entities irrespective of whether the FIU has received a prior SAR. Inevitably, while a suspicion is not necessarily directed against a particular suspect, an operational analysis will regularly correlate with a suspicion against one or more particular individuals. As a result, and in order to avoid an interference in the competence of the criminal justice authorities and prevent a circumvention of defence rights under the Criminal Procedure Code, the FIU will, despite the ambiguous wording to this effect of section 32 para. 2 s. 1, have to refer the case to the criminal justice authorities at the latest when the FIU must assume that, on the basis of the available information, the criminal justice authorities will necessarily initiate a criminal investigation.

322 See section 160 para. 1 and section 244 para. 2 StPO.
323 See section 170 para. 2 StPO.
324 See above section III.C.1.a.
325 See below sections IV.D.2 and IV.D.3.

D. ACCESS TO DATA

1. *Design and Content of FIU's Own Data Banks*

The GWG does not explicitly specify the form and content of the FIU's databases, but delegates this decision. According to section 39 GWG, the FIU shall issue, for every automated file containing personal data it operates for the performance of its tasks, an order opening the file. This order requires the consent of the Federal Ministry of Finance; prior to the opening order being issued, the Federal Commissioner for Data Protection and Freedom of Information shall be heard. The opening orders must include in particular the purpose of processing the data, the type of personal data to be stored, the group of persons about whom the data are stored, the conditions under which stored data may be transmitted, the possible recipients of such transmission, the time of review of the stored data and the period for which they are stored. According to section 29 para. 1 GWG, the FIU may process personal data insofar as this is necessary for the performance of its tasks.

The FIU's data stock consists of the following reports and information that, according to section 30 para. 1 GWG, it shall process for the performance of its tasks: SARs from obliged entities and from supervisory authorities,[326] suspicious activities notifications and other relevant information obtained from revenue authorities,[327] the content of declarations required for the cross-border transport of cash and related information resulting from border controls,[328] further information from the customs authorities regarding the cross-border transport of cash and equivalent means of payment,[329] and other information from public and non-public sources within the framework of the FIU's tasks, which may notably include information that was spontaneously shared by a foreign FIU.

2. *Access to Other Public Data Banks*

Insofar as this is necessary for conducting operational analyses (i.e. in order to verify whether a reported activity or other information is related to money laundering, terrorist financing or another criminal offence),[330] the FIU, according to section 31 para. 4 GWG, is entitled to compare, by automated means, the personal data stored in its information system with the personal data contained in the police information network. The latter constitutes the central gateway for

326 Sections 43 f. GWG.
327 Section 31b AO.
328 As required by Article 5(1) of Regulation (EC) 1889/2005 of the European Parliament and the Council of 26 October 2005 on controls of cash entering or leaving the Community.
329 Section 12a Customs Administration Act (Zollverwaltungsgesetz, ZollVG).
330 Section 28 para. 1 s. 2 no. 2 and section 30 para. 2 GWG.

the exchange of data between the Federal Criminal Police, the Federal Police, state police authorities, the Customs Criminal Office, regional customs investigation offices, and (insofar as they exercise border policing functions) the authorities of the customs administration;[331] the network contains information on crimes (including on suspects, suspects' contact persons, victims and witnesses, and data enabling their identification; under narrower conditions also data of individuals who are expected to commit a serious offence and other personal data that is needed to avert a substantial danger)[332] that are of relevance for more than one federal state, or that are of international or otherwise significant relevance.[333] If this results in a match between the transmitted data and data stored in the police information network, the FIU is allowed to retrieve, by automated means, the relevant data from the police information network. However, if other agencies participating in the police information system have categorised data as being especially sensitive and have for this reason prevented data retrieval by the FIU, the agency holding the data receives, by automated means, the information that a match exists. At the same time, the FIU is also automatically informed about the match and about which agency holds the data.[334] The agency holding the data is required to contact the FIU without delay and transmit the data to it, insofar as no transmission restrictions preclude this. The FIU is, according to section 31 para. 4a, furthermore entitled to automatically retrieve information from the Central Register of Prosecution Offices (which covers in particular the name of the defendant, and the type, time and place of the suspected offences) about all ongoing criminal proceedings in Germany; this notably also includes information about criminal proceedings by *Länder* authorities that, in particular due to a merely local or regional relevance, are not contained in the above-mentioned police information network.[335]

For the purpose of fulfilling its tasks, the FIU can, according to the Act on the Customs Investigations Service, also retrieve personal data from the customs investigation information system. It contains information on customs-related crimes and administrative offences, suspects, suspects' contact persons, witnesses, and, under narrow circumstances, data on individuals who are expected to commit a relevant serious offence,[336] as well as data on persons

[331] Section 29 para. 3 s. 1 Act on the Federal Criminal Police Office (Bundeskriminalamtgesetz, BKAG).

[332] Section 16 para. 5 s. 1 no. 2b and section 19 paras. 1 and 2 BKAG.

[333] See section 30 para. 1 no. 1 BKAG.

[334] On the rationale for this parallel notification see BT-Drucksache 19/13827, p. 90.

[335] Section 492 para. 2, para. 3 s. 3 and section 494 para. 2 StPO; BT-Drucksache 19/13827, p. 110. From 1 January 2021, the FIU will furthermore be able to automatically retrieve information from the beneficial ownership register; Article 1 no. 25 and Article 20 para. 2 of the law transposing Directive (EU) 2018/843, BGBl. 2019 I p. 2602.

[336] Section 11 para. 2 s. 1 and3, section 8 Customs Investigations Act (Zollfahndungsdienstgesetz, ZFdG).

who participate in the domestic and cross-border movement of goods, capital and services.[337] This system includes the Customs Criminal Office, customs investigation offices, other investigating bodies of the Customs Administration and the Federal Criminal Police.[338]

As preparation to request data from tax offices, the FIU is, according to section 31 para. 5 s. 2 GWG, entitled to retrieve, by transmitting the name and address or date of birth and by automated means, a person's tax number and the address of the competent tax office. According to section 31 para. 5 s. 3 f. GWG, automated retrieval by the FIU of other data which are stored by the revenue authorities and subject to the tax secrecy requirement[339] are only possible insofar as this is permitted by the Tax Code or the tax laws.[340] In contrast, regarding data which are stored by the revenue authorities of the Customs Administration and which the FIU is legally entitled to receive,[341] the FIU is mandated to establish an automated process to retrieve such data, insofar as this is appropriate because of the large number of transmissions or because of the transmission's particular urgency.[342]

Insofar as is necessary to verify the particulars of the person concerned, the FIU can, according to section 31 para. 7 GWG, retrieve, through an automated process, the personal details (namely name, date and place of birth, and address), nationalities, previous addresses and details of identity documents.[343]

For the purpose of the operational analyses of reports and other information, the FIU can be authorised, insofar as this is appropriate because of the large number of transmissions or because of the transmission's particular urgency,[344] to automatically retrieve data from the Central Register of Foreign Nationals on foreigners who are not entitled to freedom of movement under EU law, notably the following: the particulars, possible alias, and details on identity documents;[345] if relevant, details of the asylum seeker registration certificate;[346] details of asylum requests, illegal entry, illegal residence, asylum applications, decisions regarding residency status, applications regarding residency status or passport-related measures,[347] grounds for suspecting that the person belongs, belonged or plans to belong to an organisation or group in the federal territory

---

337 Section 3 para. 1 s. 1 no. 1, section 9 and section 11 para. 2 s. 3 ZFdG.
338 Section 11 para. 2 s. 1 ZFdG.
339 See section 30 AO.
340 On this see below section V.D.2.
341 See below section V.E.
342 See section 31 para. 3 GWG.
343 Section 38 Federal Act on Registrations (Bundesmeldegesetz, BMG).
344 Section 22 para. 1 s. 1 no. 7, para. 2 s. 1 Act on the Central Register of Foreign Nationals (Ausländerzentralregistergesetz, AZRG).
345 Section 17a in conjunction with section 14 AZRG.
346 Section 17a no. 6 AZRG in conjunction with section 63a Asylum Act (Asylgesetz, AsylG).
347 Section 17a no. 7 in conjunction with section 3 para. 1 no. 7, section 2 paras. 1a, 2 nos. 1, 3 AZRG.

whose existence, aims or activities are concealed from the authorities in order to avert the prohibition of said organisation or group;[348] grounds for suspecting that the person, on the federal territory, is planning, is committing or has committed aggravated drug offences;[349] grounds for suspecting that the person, on the federal territory, is planning, is committing or has committed offences related to a terrorist organisation or other terrorism-related offences;[350] grounds for suspecting that the person is endangered by terrorism-related offences;[351] grounds for suspecting that the person is preparing or has prepared a serious violent offence endangering the state, or is establishing or has established contacts with a terrorist organisation for the purpose of committing such an act;[352] and information regarding any interview of the person by immigration authorities which served to clarify reservations against entry or continued residence.[353]

The FIU can also retrieve data from the Federal Central Criminal Register, which contains relevant information on judgments of criminal courts, certain preventive decisions of administrative bodies and courts (notably the revocation of passports, prohibitions on possessing weapons or explosives, decisions barring the person from exercising a profession due to unreliability or ineptitude, decisions imposing a prohibition on taking care of or supervising children and young people), decisions of criminal courts and state prosecutors regarding a person's lack of criminal responsibility, and certain follow-up decisions, especially details of the execution of a criminal sentence.[354]

Furthermore, the FIU can retrieve data from the Customs Administration's central information system for financial controls against illegal work and illegal employment.[355] This database contains data on companies and individuals that have been subjected to an investigation aimed at identifying illegal work and illegal employment, i.e. work or employment relations that illegally circumvent the application of social security or tax regulations.[356] It notably contains a person's particulars, tax identification and social security numbers, bank

---

348 Section 17a no. 7 in conjunction with section 3 para. 1 no. 7, section 2 para. 2 no. 7 AZRG in conjunction with section 95 para. 1 no. 8 Residence Act (Aufenthaltsgesetz, AufenthG).

349 Section 17a no. 7 in conjunction with section 3 para. 1 no. 7, section 2 para. 2 no. AZRG in conjunction with sections 30 f. Act on Narcotics (Betäubungsmittelgesetz, BtMG).

350 Section 17a no. 7 in conjunction with section 3 para. 1 no. 7, section 2 para. 2 no. 7 AZRG in conjunction with sections 129a f. StGB.

351 Section 17a no. 7 in conjunction with section 3 para. 1 no. 7, section 2 para. 2 no. 7 AZRG.

352 Section 17a no. 7 in conjunction with section 3 para. 1 no. 7, section 2 para. 2 no. 7a AZRG in conjunction with sections 89a f. StGB.

353 Section 17a no. 7 in conjunction with section 3 para. 1 no. 7, section 2 para. 2 no. 12 AZRG in conjunction with section 54 para. 2 no. 7 AufenthG.

354 Section 3 Act on the Federal Central Criminal Register (Bundeszentralregistergesetz, BZRG).

355 Section 17 para. 1 s. 1 no. 5, para. 2 s. 2 Act on Illegal Work and Illegal Employment (Schwarzarbeitsgesetz, SchwarzArbG).

356 See section 1 para. 2 SchwarzArbG.

account number, the number of personal documents, details of the company, and the status of the investigation, including information on any final decision by a court or state prosecutor.[357]

According to section 36 para. 2 s. 1 no. 4 of the Road Traffic Code, the FIU can also automatically retrieve data from the Vehicle Registry, which specifies the identity of vehicle owners as well as vehicle data.[358]

According to section 150a para. 2 no. 5 of the Trade Code, the FIU can request data from the Central Trade Registry, which in particular contains all decisions by administrative authorities on cases in which such authorities have rejected or withdrawn the granting of a trade licence or have prohibited someone from exercising a particular trade due to a person's unreliability or ineptitude, as well as all decisions on the imposition of trade-related fines.[359]

Finally, section 31 para. 1 provides a general power of the FIU to collect data from domestic public authorities, "insofar as no transmission restrictions preclude the provision of information". While this provision does not by itself grant the power to automatically retrieve data from other authorities, it potentially allows for indirect access to many other data stocks than those already mentioned above,[360] including access to land registries.[361]

3. *Access to Private Data Banks*

All credit institutions, and also, as far as relevant, payment service institutions and electronic money institutions, must establish a database which contains the number of accounts, securities accounts, deposit boxes, the date of their opening and dissolution, the name and date of birth of the account holder as well as of the person authorised to dispose, and the name and the address of the beneficial owner.[362] According to section 31 para. 6 GWG, the FIU can retrieve this data through an automated search without the institution being made aware of the retrieval, and is thereby enabled to swiftly find out whether and where an individual or entity is holding accounts.[363]

4. *Data Analytics*

The difference between mere data matching and more powerful data analytics technologies is of great significance for assessing the intrusiveness and thus

357 Section 16 para. 2 SchwarzArbG.
358 Sections 32 para. 2 and 33 StVG.
359 Section 149 para. 2 no. 1(a)(b) and no. 3 GewO.
360 See on this in more detail below section V.
361 See section 12 Land Register Regulation (Grundbuchordnung, GBO).
362 Section 24c para. 1 KWG; section 27 para. 2 ZAG.
363 See section 24c para. 1 s. 6.

proportionality of the processing of personal data. While the exact content of these two categories of data processing are not defined by law, existing legislation and in particular the jurisprudence of the Federal Constitutional Court provide insights into the need for differentiation. Broadly speaking, by relying on partial correlation of two or more data sets, data matching leads to an amalgamation of multiple findings that are scattered within one or more database, and through the compilation of those data sets provides authorities with a more meaningful picture of the situation.[364] To understand data matching and how it is distinct from more potent data analytics technologies, one must point out that data processing in essence builds on a correlation between distinct data sets. Such correlation is first formulated as a hypothesis that is then tested by comparing the potentially correlating data sets (in particular by automatically matching different data banks). Only by formulating a hypothesis of a possible correlation of certain parameters (for example by assuming that a particular suspect's name, address or bank account number might reappear in other files) can the agent determine what to look for, that is which particular correlation parameters (for example a particular name or and address) and which data stocks (for example which particular police files) to include in the data processing. In contrast to the mere matching of data from different data pools, data analytics techniques may work without the agent having a clear idea of specific correlation parameters. Instead, data analytics techniques can use statistical methods to identify correlation parameters (for example an analytical software may within one database be able to detect a suspect's behavioural pattern, this pattern however being invisible to the agent, and then detect a similar but anonymous behavioural pattern within another database, thereby generating the assumption that the behaviour recorded in the second database is also attributable to the same suspect).[365] Even more importantly, data analytics techniques may operate without starting with an already individualised suspect, but rather may use statistical methods to identify suspects in the first place (for example by scanning data for behaviour patterns that are typically characteristic of a particular type of criminal).

---

364 See BVerfGE 133, 277, 333.

365 For an example of where such enhanced data processing is authorised under German law, see the definition in section 6a para. 5 Act on the Central Counter-Terrorism Database (Antiterrordateigesetz, ATDG): "An extended use [of data] covers the establishment of correlations between persons, groups, institutions, objects and items, the exclusion of irrelevant information and findings, the attribution of incoming information to known situations and the statistical analysis of stored data. To this end, the participating authorities of the federal government might also retrieve data from the database by relying on (1) phonetic or incomplete data, (2) the search through a plurality of data fields, (3) the linking of persons, institutions, organizations, objects or (4) the temporal narrowing of search criteria, depict spatial or other ties between person as well as connections between persons, groups, institutions, objects and items, and weight search criteria."

Germany constitutional jurisprudence has repeatedly stated that statistical methods of data processing as a criminal policy tool raise grave data protection concerns and therefore require narrow legislative limitations. In its 2006 decision on automated dragnet techniques,[366] the Federal Constitutional Court set stringent limits against any data processing that extensively includes personal data of individuals against whom there is no suspicion, even where the processed data are by themselves of rather limited relevance for affected individuals' personality. The Court stressed that even the linking of innocuous data allows insights into someone's personality. The interference into the fundamental right to informational self-determination would be particularly intensive where such data processing extends to a large number of public and private data banks, not least data banks of private businesses that contain detailed information about a customer's shopping behaviour or whereabouts.[367] The Court underlined the danger that the use of such data processing would expose a high number of innocent persons to the risk of being treated as suspect, thereby potentially leading to further and more intrusive rights infringements without having behaved in any way that would give rise to suspicion. The Court furthermore pointed to the risk that dragnet data processing could reproduce prejudices in social perception; entire groups, in particular social minorities, could be stigmatised and as a consequence unjustly discriminated against through the use of broad correlation parameters (for example ethnic background or religious beliefs).[368] The interference into the right to informational self-determination was particularly strong where bulk data processing included data of persons who were in no way related to a specific wrongdoing and had also not given cause to be subjected to investigative measures. Such measures could also have an intimidating effect on the wider population and thereby constrain citizens' self-determination; their broad scope could threaten the

---

366 For a definition of dragnet techniques in criminal procedure, see section 98a para. 1 StPO: "where there are sufficient factual indications to show that a criminal offence of substantial significance has been committed (1) relating to the illegal trade in narcotics or weapons or the counterfeiting of money or official stamps, (2) relating to national security (sections 74a, 120 of the Courts Constitution Act), (3) relating to offences which pose a danger to the general public, (4) relating to endangerment of life and limb, sexual self-determination or personal liberty, (5) on a commercial or habitual basis, or (6) by a member of a gang or in some other organized way, personal data relating to individuals who manifest certain significant features which may be presumed to apply to the perpetrator may be automatically matched against other data in order to exclude individuals who are not under suspicion or to identify individuals who manifest other significant characteristics relevant to the investigations. This measure may be ordered only where other means of establishing the facts or determining the perpetrator's whereabouts would offer much less prospect of success or be much more difficult."

367 See BVerfGE 115, 320 = BVerfG NJW 2006, 1939, 1942–1943.

368 BVerfGE 115, 320 = BVerfG NJW 2006, 1939, 1943.

naturalness of behaviour in that they contribute to a risk of abuse and a feeling of being under surveillance.[369]

Modern data analytics technologies only amplify the concerns raised by constitutional jurisprudence. In particular with the advent of self-learning automated systems, it might often not be possible to retrace how the system came to a particular conclusion, in particular what statistical assumptions were underlying the processing. This is because a self-learning system does not just apply algorithms that were conceptualised and fed into it by human agents, but it can analyse data on the basis of hitherto unknown patterns and establish correlations on the basis of correlation parameters and patterns that it discovered autonomously.[370] Such technology seems to offer vast new opportunities to better understand data and improve human decision-making. Yet self-learning systems also pose a serious challenge in assessing the proportionality of data processing and thus the latter's legality. Not only can it be difficult or even impossible to identify the data that the system included in its analysis. Given that the proportionality of data processing depends in particular on the level of sensitivity of the processed data, uncertainty about the nature and scope of the processed data might potentially negate the proportionality of the processing. Furthermore, to the extent that the underlying correlation parameters and patterns remain opaque,[371] citizens are at risk of being subjected to discriminatory or otherwise arbitrary selection criteria and thereby to further rights infringements. Reflecting such concerns, the Federal Constitutional Court has, in a judgment of 2013, clarified that it was one thing to authorise criminal justice or intelligence agencies to retrieve data from the data banks of another security agency for the purpose of an individual data query, but that it is, from the viewpoint of constitutional law, a very different thing to allow such authorities to access another agency's data bank for the purpose of including this data bank in a dragnet investigation, to perform a bulk data retrieval or to establish a correlation between persons through as-yet unknown correlation parameters.[372]

The GWG does not explicitly mention enhanced data processing powers. In fact, section 29 para. 2 GWG explicitly addresses the FIU's data processing methods only by specifying that it may compare personal data that it has stored for the performance of its tasks with other data. In light of constitutional jurisprudence, one must therefore assume that at least for the purpose of an operational analysis the FIU must not use data analysis technologies that

369 BVerfGE 115, 320 = BVerfG NJW 2006, 1939, 1944.
370 B Körffer, Datenschutz Nachrichten 4/2014, p. 149.
371 B Körffer, Datenschutz Nachrichten 4/2014, p. 150.
372 BVerfGE 133, 277, 361.

extensively rely on the processing of personal data of unsuspected individuals or that otherwise lead to an automated compilation of personal data from multiple public and private databases without such compilation being guided by a specific pre-existing suspicion. As a minimum requirement, these limits have at least two consequences for both the design of the FIU's databases and of its data processing methods. First, the FIU must not record and process large amounts of data transmitted by obliged entities or by other authorities insofar as such data does not directly refer to suspected individuals or transactions. Accordingly, the FIU must in particular not request obliged entities to provide financial bulk data that to a great extent covers transactions not directly related to a suspected client. Second, the FIU must not use its access to various public databases for the purpose of an operational analysis that is not yet directed at a particular suspicious business relationship or transaction, but merely applies statistical figures in order to identify individual suspects.

E. PARTICIPATION OF "SUSPECTS"

1. *Defence Rights*

Individuals targeted by an operational analysis of the FIU have, in this respect, only limited procedural rights. As already explained above,[373] affected persons may request relevant information, but the law, in section 49, provides extensive grounds to the FIU to deny such requests. In any case, given that the FIU's operational analysis is meant to be merely a precursor to subsequent criminal investigations and is expected to protect the confidentiality of its communication with the FIU's sources, in particular as regards communication with obliged entities,[374] a person targeted by an operational analysis is not meant to be heard by the FIU. Insofar as the FIU is collecting information about a particular person by requesting CDD information from an obliged entity, the law furthermore does not provide for a privilege against self-incrimination of a client vis-à-vis the obliged entity. This reflects the fact that a client, in the context of CDD, finds him- or herself not directly confronted with a state body and in principle remains free not to provide the obliged entity with requested information,[375] though the client must in this case usually expect the obliged entity to refrain from providing the service sought. For the ultimate benefit of the client, section 30 para. 3 s. 3 does however provide for a legal privilege of lawyers, patent attorneys, notaries, auditors, tax advisors and tax agents as

[373] See above section IV.B.4.
[374] Section 32 para. 2 s. 1 and section 47 paras. 1 and 2 s. 2 GWG.
[375] See BGH, NJW 1996, 2940, 2941.

regards information requests from the FIU. These obliged entities may refuse to provide the FIU with information insofar as the request relates to information they obtained in the context of providing legal advice or the legal representation of the contracting party.[376] However, according to section 30 para. 3 s. 4, the obligation to provide information continues to exist if the obliged entity knows that the contracting party has used or is using its legal advice for the purpose of money laundering or terrorist financing.

After having ordered an urgent measure,[377] the FIU may, according to section 40 para. 5, release property at the request of the person concerned, insofar as this property serves to cover the basic needs of the person or the person's family members, to pay pensions or maintenance, or comparable purposes. Furthermore, the obliged entity or another adversely affected party (which can be the obliged entity's contracting party or another affected person) may, according to section 40 para. 6, lodge an objection to urgent measures imposed by the FIU, leading to an administrative review of the measures.

2. *Judicial Review or Other Remedies*

Following an unsuccessful objection to the imposition of urgent measures by the FIU, the interested parties can apply for judicial review before the administrative court. The law specifies that the objection does not have suspensory effect. Interested parties can however lodge an emergency appeal with the administrative court to apply for interim measures.[378] Furthermore, to the extent that a person was affected by an SAR and information requested from the FIU in that regard, he or she can, insofar as the request is denied, seek judicial review of the lawfulness of the denial before the administrative court.[379]

F. SIMILAR POWERS OF SUPERVISORY BODIES

Suspected criminal offences, including money laundering, are investigated by the public prosecution office and, under its direction, by the police.[380] If a supervisory authority, in investigating an administrative offence, is becoming aware of indications that the offence is actually a criminal one, it must transfer the case to the public prosecution office.[381]

376 See section 2 para. 1 nos. 10 and 12 GWG.
377 See above section IV.A.4.
378 Section 80 para. 5 of the Code of Administrative Court Procedure. (Verwaltungsgerichtsordnung)
379 See BVerwG, NJW 2018, 590; OVG Bautzen, Decision of 11 April 2017 – 5 B 262/16.
380 Section 152 para. 1, section 160 and section 163 para. 1 StPO; section 152 para. 1 GVG.
381 Section 41 para. 1 Act on Regulatory Offences (Ordnungswidrigkeitensgesetz, OWiG).

G. REPORTING OBLIGATIONS OF SUPERVISORY AUTHORITIES

If the facts indicate that assets are related to money laundering or terrorist financing, the supervisory authorities tasked with the supervision of obliged entities must, according to section 44 para. 1 GWG, report these facts to the FIU without delay. According to section 44 para. 2 GWG, the aforementioned reporting obligation "applies mutatis mutandis to authorities responsible for supervision of the stock, foreign exchange and financial derivatives markets".

H. REPORTING BY OTHER AUTHORITIES

Under the preceding conditions, section 31b para. 2 of the Tax Code imposes an obligation on the revenue authorities to report to the FIU without undue delay. The law specifies that this applies irrespective of the value involved.

I. STATISTICS

1. *Number of Reports by Supervisory Authorities and Other Authorities*

According to statistics for 2018, 54 reports were filed by supervisory authorities and 414 by tax authorities, though the value of the associated assets is not specified.[382]

2. *FIU Analysis*

The statistics for 2018 do not provide the number of SARs effectively processed by the FIU or the number of operational analyses commenced on the basis of information other than an SAR. Some, albeit only tentative, conclusions can however be drawn from the statistics, according to which in 2018 the FIU received 10,674 instances of feedback from the criminal justice authorities regarding the outcome of cases communicated by the FIU to these authorities between mid-2017 and the end of 2018, as well as from the percentage of operational analyses that, in 2018, led to a communication from the FIU to the criminal justice authorities, namely 58%.[383]

---

382 Financial Intelligence Unit, Jahresbericht 2018, Cologne 2019, p. 14.

383 Financial Intelligence Unit, Jahresbericht 2018, Cologne 2019, pp. 17–18. See section 42 para. 1 GWG on the obligation of criminal justice authorities to report to the FIU the outcome of any criminal investigation for which the FIU had provided information.

V. DATA FLOW AND DATA PROTECTION

A. DATA EXCHANGE BETWEEN FIU AND PRIVATE SECTOR

1. *From FIU to Private Sector*

Every transfer of personal data constitutes an interference in the fundamental right to informational self-determination and thus requires legislative authorisation.[384] The GWG authorises a transfer of personal data to private entities only to a very limited extent. Insofar as it is empowered to request information from obliged entities according to section 30 para. 3 s. 1, one must assume that the FIU is authorised to pass on to the requested obliged entity such information as is needed to enable a meaningful response to the request. To be proportionate, such transfer of personal data must however be limited to what is strictly necessary in order to protect the obliged entity's client, who might, as a result of the mere request, become suspicious in the eyes of the obliged entity, from unjustified adverse repercussions.[385] Similar considerations apply to the FIU's power according to section 41 para. 2 to provide reporting obliged entities with feedback to their SARs; such feedback must not include personal data that is unrelated to the reported suspicion. Furthermore, in light of the FIU's power under section 40 to order urgent preventive measures to prevent money laundering and terrorism financing, the law implies that the FIU has authority to transfer to any obliged entity such personal data as is necessary to effectively implement these measures, in particular the identity and personal details of a suspect and other personal data enabling the obliged entity to identify accounts or transactions covered by the urgent measure.

Beyond this, given the lack of any explicit authorisation, the FIU is not allowed to transfer personal data to obliged entities. In particular, the FIU is not entitled to forward unstructured volumes of data (for example data sets that contain personal data of both suspects and unsuspected person) with the aim of comprehensively matching such data with the data banks of an obliged entity in order to thereby identify particular persons. To the extent that the

---

384 BVerfGE 65, 1, 43–44.

385 Unlike the GWG, the law on the federal domestic intelligence agency provides rules that aim at avoiding such adverse effects and might thereby offer some guidance on how to ensure the proportionality of such transfer of personal data. Section 8b para. 5 Act on the Federal Office for the Protection of the Constitution (Bundesverfassungsschutzgesetz, BVerfSchG) states that, as regards information requests by the intelligence agency notably to credit institutions or financial services institutions, the obliged private entity is prohibited from unilaterally taking actions that would negatively affect the customers solely because of the information request, in particular by limiting services to the customer or by increasing fees. Furthermore, the agency must explicitly point out this prohibition and must also declare that the information request does not entail a claim that the person concerned is suspected of an illegal act.

FIU is, according to section 42 para. 5, authorised, together with the supervisory authorities, to "define types of transactions" which obliged entities shall always report as an SAR, this clearly refers to merely typological information and is not meant to allow the transfer of data that can be attributed to particular persons.[386] Thus, while typologies will often be the product of a processing of personal data originating from relevant investigations, section 42 para. 5 does not authorise the transfer of data by the FIU that would enable obliged entities to reconstruct the transferred data as referring to a particular person.[387]

2. *From Private Sector to FIU*

Section 30 para. 3 s. 1 authorises the FIU to request information from obliged entities "insofar as this is necessary for the performance of its tasks",[388] but does not further specify conditions for the exercise of this power, such as any particular degree of suspicion or the nature and scope of relevant information. Given the law's silence on these issues, one might, as a standard of comparison, refer to the requirements that are applicable under German tax law to information requests from the revenue authorities to private entities in non-criminal tax investigations. This analogy would reflect the fact that both the FIU's and the tax authorities' information requests are to some extent similar. Both will regularly (though not necessarily) be addressed to financial institutions; both requests are situated outside criminal proceedings and aim to uncover a third party's wrongdoing before a criminal suspicion in the sense of the Criminal Procedure Code has been established.[389] The revenue authorities are authorised to request information from any person insofar as the information is needed to ascertain facts which are of significance for taxation.[390] According to the jurisprudence of the Federal Fiscal Court, it suffices that the revenue authorities can demonstrate an elevated probability that the information requested will lead to the detection of unidentified tax situations. This prognosis can be based on case-specific clues or general experience which indicate that the detection of unidentified tax situations is particularly likely. In contrast, an information request by the tax authorities must

---

[386] ECJ, judgment of 20 December 2017, C 434/16 (Nowak/Data Protection Commissioner), at para. 28.

[387] Similar considerations apply to the power of supervisory authorities according to section 15 para. 8 GWG to order, on the basis of findings of national or international bodies responsible for preventing or combating money laundering or terrorist financing (thus, where appropriate, on the basis of information provided by the FIU), to implement enhanced CDD measures.

[388] Section 30 para. 3 s. 1 GWG.

[389] See section 208 para. 1 s. 1 no. 3 AO; BFHE 91, 351; BFH, judgment of 29 October 1986 – VII R 82/85; BFH, judgment of 29 June 2005 – II R 3/04.

[390] Section 93 para. 1 AO: "The participants [in tax proceedings] and other persons shall provide the revenue authority with the information needed to ascertain facts which are of significance for taxation".

not be based solely on pure speculation. Equally, the information request must not be part of a dragnet investigation,[391] that is an investigation that, as a precursor to the subsequent singling out of particular suspects, solely aims to identify a group of individuals who share characteristics with the suspect. In a similar vein, the tax authorities are not allowed to request information with the aim of comprehensively screening bank clients' data in order to obtain a complete picture of unidentified tax situations without there being prior specific clues indicating the existence of such situations.[392]

However, it is questionable whether an information request by the FIU according to section 30 para. 3 can be compared to the tax authorities' power to request information from third parties in non-criminal tax investigations. Both powers do cover the procurement of personal data from a third party (that is, not the potential suspect) prior to a criminal suspicion, and both may include similarly sensitive data, as they enable the authorities to get to know the account holder's financial situation and, as far as they have a financial component, often also his or her social contacts.[393] The more even routine daily cash transactions are replaced by digital transactions, and the more the provision of goods and services online leads to an increase in low-value digital transactions, the greater the amount of personal data that the authorities can access via an information request to credit and financial services institutions and payment service providers. Yet, as regards the scope of accessible data, FIU requests according to section 30 para. 3 might even go much further than that. In light of the FIU's function to detect cases of money laundering and terrorism financing, such requests will also extend to the requested obliged entity's CDD documentation, which the obliged entity must keep for five years,[394] and which will in many cases include vast amounts of data provided by customers, not least about their personal or business background and the purpose of transactions. Depending on the circumstances of the particular case, information requests by the FIU can therefore be highly intrusive.

Beyond the nature of the data sought, the intrusiveness of a public authority's data gathering is, according to constitutional jurisprudence, also determined by how the data is obtained, to what extent the data collection may have detrimental effects for the person concerned, notably as regards the risk of being subjected to investigative measures due to an unfounded suspicion, and what remedies are available to fend off such effects.[395]

---

391 BVerfG NJW 2007, 2464, 2468; BFH, judgment of 29 October 1986 – VII R 82/85; BFH DStR 2002, 993, 995; BFH, DStRE 2009, 625, 627 f.; BFH DStRE 2013, 1068, 1072 f.; BFH DStR 2015, 2846, 2848; BFH DStR 2016, 1862, 1865; B Rätke, in F Klein, Abgabenordnung, 14th ed., C.H. Beck 2018, §93 Rn. 6 f.

392 See BFH DStR 2000, 1511, 1514 f.; BFH, DStR 2002, 993, 996.

393 See BVerfG NJW 2007, 2464, 2466.

394 Section 8 para. 4 GWG.

395 BVerfG NJW 2007, 2464, 2469.

In light of these constitutional standards, it is then particularly relevant that the FIU's operational analysis is meant to detect criminal offences and thus usually to prepare criminal investigations against individuals involved in suspicious activities. The FIU's information requests within its operational analysis are thus not unlikely to have severe detrimental effects on the person concerned, in that they can subsequently form the basis of highly intrusive investigative measures. In this context, it is also important to note that the requested obliged entity's answer to the FIU might at times be influenced by interests of its own that might negatively affect the answer's veracity, not least because the obliged entity will often have an interest in deflecting doubts about the quality of its CDD and reporting practice. Besides the risk of a criminal investigation as the result of an unfounded suspicion, information requests by the FIU are frequently also likely to stigmatise the client in the eyes of the requested obliged entity and other obliged entities,[396] and thereby notably lead to termination of banking services and even difficulties in opening accounts with other financial institutions. In this respect, it is particularly relevant that the FIU's data request must, according to section 47 para. 1 no. 3, not be disclosed by the requested obliged entity to its client, and thus in principle remain secret. Furthermore, section 49 provides multiple grounds that prevent the FIU from subsequently disclosing its information request to the person concerned even after the conclusion of the FIU's operational analysis and after a possible transfer of the case to the criminal justice authorities. As a result of this essentially covert nature of the FIU's request, the availability of judicial remedies for the requested obliged entity's client before an administrative court is regularly practically excluded or at least significantly delayed.

Finally, it must be recalled that obliged entities are under an obligation to continuously monitor their business relationships as part of their standard CDD duties, and to subject an individual client to increased monitoring in cases where the obliged entity must assume that the client poses an enhanced risk.[397] It seems likely that information requests by the FIU will often lead the requested obliged entity to treat the client concerned as a risk and therefore apply extra CDD measures to him or her, for example by asking the client questions[398] or by collecting information from other obliged entities or third parties. In such cases, the FIU's request can amount to much more than a request for information

396 Note that the obliged entities' disclosure prohibition regarding the FIU's requests in many cases does not apply to a disclosure towards other obliged entities; section 47 para. 2 s. 1 nos. 2–5 GWG.

397 Section 10 para. 1 s. 1 no. 5 and section 15 para. 4 s. 1 no. 3 GWG.

398 Importantly, as the requested obliged entity is, according to section 47 para. 1 no. 3 GWG, under an obligation not to disclose the FIU's request to the client, it will usually not be allowed to warn its client that by providing additional information to the obliged entity he or she might effectively incriminate him- or herself.

that the requested obliged entity had already obtained before the information request and might rather also include elements of proactive monitoring triggered by the information request.

In view of the potentially highly personal nature of the requested data, the possible serious repercussions of the FIU's request, the limited availability of judicial remedies for obliged entities' clients, and possible enhanced monitoring by the requested obliged entity, the power to request information under section 30 para. 3 must be considered significantly more intrusive than information requests by tax authorities outside criminal proceedings.[399] The data gathering powers in the Criminal Procedure Code of course demonstrate that even very sensitive data (such as the content of telecommunications) can in principle be gathered covertly to build a criminal case. The lack of judicial oversight over the FIU's information requests and the possible collateral effects of such requests on the conduct of obliged entities towards the persons concerned does however suggest that FIU requests are subject to considerable substantive requirements, at least where the FIU is seeking access to large quantities of customer data, including CDD documentation. Having regard to constitutional jurisprudence and the proportionality standards of the legal order, notably in view of the respective standards of the Criminal Procedure Code and in light of the comparatively more limited availability of procedural safeguards under the GWG, it would appear that the FIU's power to request information (beyond terrorism financing) is limited to cases of money laundering and its predicate offences that are of particular gravity in the individual case.[400] Depending on the scope of the information requested in a given case, this might in particular bar the FIU from requesting information regarding cases of money laundering and predicate offences where the suspected offences' seriousness would not allow for similarly intrusive covert investigative measures under the Criminal Procedure Code.[401]

As the FIU's power to request information can thus be subject to stringent proportionality limits, it must be asked whether similar limiting considerations also apply to obliged entities' duty to file SARs. The GWG indeed specifies neither the precise suspicion threshold[402] nor the nature and scope of data that obliged entities must provide to the FIU as part of an SAR, merely stating that the "matter" has to be reported "correctly" and "completely".[403] Due to the potentially highly personal nature of the client information, the possible serious

399 See BVerfG NJW 2007, 2464, 2469 f.; BFH, judgment of 29 October 1986 – VII R 82/85; BFH, DStRE 2009, 625, 629; BFH DStRE 2013, 1068, 1073 f.; BFH DStR 2015, 2846, 2849; BFH DStR 2016, 1862, 1866 f.

400 See section 100a para. 1 no. 2 and para. 2 StPO.

401 See section 100a para. 2, section 100e para. 1, section 100g para. 2 s. 2 and section 101a StPO.

402 See above section III.C.1.a.

403 Section 43 para. 1 and section 56 para. 1 no. 59 GWG.

repercussions of an SAR as a trigger for investigative measures against the client, and the limited remedies available to him or her, the client's fundamental right to informational self-determination requires that the duty to file an SAR be limited by adequate proportionality considerations. As a minimum requirement, SARs must then not be filed on the basis of an overly low suspicion threshold that would, from an objective point of view, appear arbitrary. Furthermore, the content of an SAR must not go beyond what is necessary for the SAR to serve its function, that is to enable the FIU to understand the reporting obliged entity's suspicion and to assess whether to conduct an analysis of the matter. As regards the serious threshold of the suspected offence, the reporting obliged entity can itself hardly be expected to legally assess the reported matter, not least because the reporting entity will usually not have sufficient contextual information to this end. It would therefore seem unfeasible to limit the reporting duty based on the nature of the predicate offence. The amount of assets that form part of the reported activity can however provide some limiting guidance, at least in that the volume and sensitivity of personal data included in an SAR should usually not be out of proportion to the quantitative importance of the suspicious activity.[404]

B. DATA EXCHANGE BETWEEN FIU AND CRIMINAL JUSTICE SYSTEM

1. *From FIU to Criminal Justice System*

According to section 32 para. 2 s. 1, if the FIU "finds in the operational analysis that property is related to money laundering, terrorist financing or another criminal offence, it shall transmit the result of its analysis and all relevant information to the competent criminal justice agencies without delay." Unlike what this wording might indicate,[405] the government's explanatory notes to the provision state that the relevant suspicion threshold is already reached if, in light of all the information considered in the analysis, sufficient factual indications of the commission of a criminal offence may be present.[406] In any case, the wording

---

404 Beyond these considerations, one should note that negative follow-up repercussions of the filing of an SAR on the respective client relationship (notably the cancellation of the contractual relationship) are not so much consequences of the reporting duty, but rather follow from obliged entities' risk management. Consequently, the adoption of such measures by obliged entities concern the proportionality not of the reporting duty, but rather of the CDD duty, in particular the duty not to establish or not to continue a business relationship where the risk is deemed inappropriate; see section 10 para. 9 and section 15 para. 9 GWG.

405 BT-Drucksache 18/11928, p. 12.

406 BT-Drucksache 18/11555, p. 144.

of section 32 para. 2 s. 1 makes it clear that if the presence of a criminal offence is conclusively established, the FIU has no discretion and, absent particular transmission restrictions, must communicate the relevant data to the criminal justice authorities. In line with the operational analysis' primary function to provide a starting point for criminal investigations rather than to be itself an investigation to collect criminal evidence, the wording of section 32 para. 2 s. 1 furthermore indicates that the FIU's communication to the criminal justice authorities will not necessarily include all the information taken into account in the operational analysis, but needs to include at least as much information as is necessary for the criminal justice authorities to commence a criminal investigation.

According to section 32 para. 3 s. 1, the FIU shall furthermore transmit personal data, upon request, to the law enforcement agencies insofar as this is necessary for (i) the investigation of money laundering and terrorist financing or the conduct of criminal proceedings related to these, or (ii) the conduct of other criminal proceedings not covered by (i).

According to section 32 para. 5 s. 1 no. 2, personal data shall not be transmitted insofar as the dissemination of the data would be disproportionate to the legitimate interests of a natural or legal person, or if it could negatively affect ongoing investigations of other domestic competent authorities.[407] Further restrictions apply with regard to information that, according to section 32 para. 4 s. 1, is subject to transmission restrictions. Such restrictions notably cover data that the FIU obtained from a foreign FIU, as a transfer of such information is subject to the approval of this foreign FIU,[408] information that was provided by other foreign authorities on a confidential basis,[409] and information whose disclosure within criminal proceedings could negatively affect the analytical capabilities of the FIU.[410]

The Federal Constitutional Court has clarified that, even where transferred data is subsequently not used as evidence but only as an investigative lead in criminal investigations, the principle of proportionality imposes restrictions on the data transfer from one public authority to another. Irrespective of whether the data is used as evidence or merely as an investigative lead, it must always be ensured that any use of the data by another authority takes account of the level of severity of the interference with fundamental rights caused by the initial data gathering. Information that was obtained through particularly intrusive measures can subsequently be used only for particularly important purposes.[411]

407 BT-Drucksache 18/11555, p. 145.
408 Section 34 para. 3 s. 2 and 3 GWG.
409 See section 49 para. 2 s. 2 no. 1 GWG.
410 See section 49 para. 2 s. 2 no. 2 GWG and above section III.C.2.b.
411 BVerfG NJW 2016, 1781, 1801, 1804.

In this respect, it must be recalled that the FIU's operational analyses, unlike the commencement of investigations by criminal justice authorities, do not require a pre-established suspicion within the meaning of the Criminal Procedure Code,[412] despite the fact that the FIU's analyses are in essence geared towards the identification of crimes and their subsequent prosecution. The FIU can then already analyse SARs and process information obtained from other sources when, in view of the circumstances of the case and professional experience, a money laundering or terrorism financing background cannot be excluded.[413] This power to effectively investigate the possible commission of a criminal offence well before a criminal suspicion has been established means that such investigation is of a particular gravity. For such power allows individuals to be targeted with a view to establishing a criminal suspicion against them, not on the basis of objective facts that give rise to a clear suspicion, but rather on the basis of considerations that will regularly rely more on subjective judgments of the acting agents[414] and thereby significantly increase the risk of objectively unjustified investigative measures.

Furthermore, the FIU's analysis will in many cases be based on information from sources whose identity will at no point during subsequent criminal proceedings be disclosed to the defendant, and information from analytical methods (in particular data analytics) whose precise functioning will equally be shielded from the public.[415] In this context, one must also underline that the FIU's analytical function will in many cases rely on information provided by a foreign FIU, and that information communicated between FIUs is usually only for intelligence purposes, meaning that such information cannot be provided by the receiving FIU to another public authority without the foreign FIU's consent.[416] In order to protect the FIU's functioning, in particular to ensure that private sources as well as foreign FIUs are willing to communicate relevant information, the law thus appears to emphasise a need for the FIU's sources to be shielded from the person concerned and the wider public. This means that suspects and the criminal courts will often not be able to access all the details of the circumstances under which an SAR was filed,[417] in particular information about related communication between the obliged entity and the FIU and, to the extent that this would lead to the disclosure of the identity of the person who filed it, sometimes even not precise information about why exactly the obliged entity decided to file the SAR. To the extent that the primary sources of the operational analysis are as a result not disclosed by the FIU and thereby

412 See section 160 para. 1 StPO.
413 See above sections III.C.1.a and IV.C.
414 See above section IV.C.
415 See above section IV.B.4.
416 See section 34 para. 3 s. 3 GWG.
417 See above section III.C.2.b.

shielded from judicial scrutiny, the gravity of the FIU's data processing does increase further.

Finally, in order to assess the gravity of the FIU's processing of personal data, and hence to determine to what extent such data can be transferred to the criminal justice authorities, it is important to take into account the scope of the FIU's data processing powers. In this respect, it must be noted that the FIU receives SARs from all obliged entities and thus from a great number of businesses and independent professionals whose activities directly or indirectly cover almost the entirety of economic activity in Germany. It must furthermore be noted that with the decline of the use of cash, and the nowadays primary role played by electronic transactions, the FIU, through the reporting obligations imposed on obliged entities as well as through its power to request information from obliged entities independently of an SAR, has access to an ever-growing amount of financial data, thereby enabling it to monitor the financial transactions of virtually all individuals and businesses in Germany. Beyond goods and services acquired over the internet, the transactions records will in many cases allow deep insights into the private and not infrequently even intimate life of individuals, without access to the records being limited by the requirement of a criminal suspicion. Accordingly, the nature and potential scope of the processed data confirm that the FIU's operational analysis is of particular gravity.

In view of the above observations and the constitutional jurisprudence on information sharing between criminal justice authorities and intelligence services, one must note that the FIU shares many characteristics of an intelligence service, which in turn has repercussions for its ability under constitutional law to provide information to other state authorities, not least criminal justice authorities. In this regard, it is particularly relevant that the FIU, in light of the legislative intention apparent from the GWG, is collecting information largely without disclosing details about its sources, and that obliged entities that file SARs or respond to the FIU's request for information are themselves not allowed to disclose their communication with the FIU to the suspect or third parties. Furthermore, the FIU's access to SARs and its power to request information from obliged entities cannot be assessed in isolation from obliged entities' obligation, as part of the standard CDD duties, to continuously monitor their client relationships. Given their reporting duty to the FIU, obliged entities' obligation to monitor their clients' business conduct must ultimately be attributed to the FIU as a key part of the FIU's data collection and data analysis capacity. Through the culmination of obliged entities' CDD and reporting obligations and the FIU's power to request information from obliged entities independently of an SAR, the FIU does in essence command a network of private informers that, in view of the number of employees of obliged entities as well as the sensitivity of the financial data collected, may well reach the data collection powers of an intelligence service or – at least as regards data collection powers other than telecommunications surveillance[418] – even go beyond it. Finally, and in this regard equally characteristic of an intelligence service, the FIU is authorised to collect and analyse information about threats before a criminal suspicion arises. It is here that the FIU's mandate goes particularly far, as it is tasked not only with the monitoring of systemic threats through its strategic analysis power,[419] but first and foremost with the identification of criminal suspects in view of preparing a criminal investigation against particular individuals. In going beyond the monitoring of strategic threats as the traditional role of German intelligence services,[420] and also – even primarily – focusing on the establishment of criminal responsibility of individuals, and doing so before a criminal suspicion arises, the FIU does in fact partially dissolve German constitutional law's basic separation between intelligence gathering and criminal investigations.[421]

Accordingly, the FIU's processing of personal data does in principle constitute a substantial interference with the fundamental right to informational self-determination. As regards a possible transfer of personal data to the criminal justice authorities, the intensity of this interference is further increased by the fact that the FIU, according to section 30 para. 2, is tasked with analysing SARs not only with regard to money laundering and terrorism financing, but also as regards "another criminal offence", which includes, but is not limited to, the predicate offences of money laundering. In view of the considerations that shape the Constitutional Court's jurisprudence on the transfer of data from intelligence services to police authorities, any transfer of personal data by the FIU to criminal justice authorities must thus necessarily be limited and require a narrow reading of the data transfer powers conferred by section 32 para. 2 s. 1 and para. 3. The FIU's data transfer powers might arguably include information on all crimes that reach the seriousness threshold of money laundering. However, the above-described extensive scope of the FIU's data processing powers and the broad scope of section 261 StGB (which includes self-laundering by the predicate offender of only small amounts of ill-gotten gains)[422] indicate that not all cases of money laundering and not all predicate offences reach an adequate seriousness threshold.

The exact scope of the FIU's power to transfer data to criminal justice authorities thus currently remains not entirely clear. A determination to this

---

418 Note that, in light of the legislation on the federal domestic intelligence service, the covert nature of data collection other than telecommunications surveillance (in particular informants) is in itself already a sufficient reason to limit the data sharing between the intelligence service and other state authorities; see section 8 para. 2 and section 19 para. 1 BVerfSchG; see section 4 para. 4 Act on Restrictions on the Secrecy of Mail, Post and Telecommunications (G 10).

419 Section 28 para. 1 s. 2 no. 8 GWG.

420 See section 28 para. 1 s. 2 no. 8; BVerfG NJW 2013, 1499, 1505.

421 See BVerfG NJW 2013, 1499, 1504–1505.

422 See section 261 para. 1 s. 2 and para. 9 s. 3 StGB.

effect will depend not least on the actual overall volume of the FIU's data collection activities (notably on the question of to what extent it receives SARs, on the level of detail of these reports, and to what extent the FIU uses its power to request information from obliged entities), the extent of its willingness to disclose its sources and data processing methods within criminal proceedings, and the extent to which it collaborates with intelligence services.[423] In any case, and in light of the legislative thresholds accepted in the law applicable to intelligence services, the FIU is allowed to share personal data on more serious criminality,[424] that is criminal offences that, according to the seriousness standards of the law, generally constitute offences of a particular weight, and that also in view of the circumstances of the specific case (in particular in view of the damage caused or the extent of the threat caused to the public) are of particular significance.[425]

2. *From Criminal Justice System to FIU*

According to section 31 para. 1 s. 1, the FIU "may, insofar as this is necessary for the performance of its functions, collect data from domestic public authorities". This includes personal data from the criminal justice authorities the transfer of which is necessary for the prosecution or prevention of a criminal offence.[426] Section 31 para. 1 s. 1 specifies that the requested authority shall transfer requested data "insofar as no transmission restrictions preclude the provision of information".[427]

The law does not explicitly specify further transmission limitations as regards information flows from the criminal justice authorities to the FIU. However, in order to ensure proportionality between the collection and the use of personal data within criminal justice, section 477 para. 2 s. 2 of the

423 On the latter point see section 1 no. 6 Security Clearance Ordinance (Sicherheitsüberprüfungsfeststellungsverordnung, SÜFV).

424 See for example section 19 para. 1 no. 4 BVerfSchG, allowing for the transfer of personal data from the domestic intelligence service to the criminal justice authorities only in the case of criminality of significant importance.

425 BVerfGE 107, 299, 322; this includes, but is not necessarily limited to, offences the seriousness of which would permit the ordering of telecommunications surveillance according to section 100a StPO.

426 See section 17 nos. 1 and 3 Introductory Act to the Courts Constitution Act (Einführungsgesetz zum Gerichtsverfassungsgesetz, EGGVG); section 474 para. 2 s. 1 no. 2 StPO.

427 See also section 474 para. 2 StPO. Transmission restrictions result notably from section 100d para. 5 StPO (use of personal data from covert recordings of private speech on private premises in another proceeding only if such covert recording could also be ordered in the other proceeding or to avert particularly serious threats; according to BVerfGE 109, 279, 347 this excludes proceedings for offences that carry a maximum sentence of not more than five years' imprisonment) and section 101a paras. 4 and 5 StPO (telecommunications connection data for another proceeding only if the production of such data could be ordered in the other proceeding or to avert particularly serious threats).

Criminal Procedure Code provides restrictions on the transfer between different criminal proceedings of personal data that has been obtained by the criminal justice authorities through particularly intrusive investigative measures. It states that "[i]f a [investigative] measure pursuant to this statute is only admissible where specified [more serious] criminal offences are suspected, then any personal data obtained on the basis of such a measure may only be used … for evidential purposes in [criminal proceedings for] other criminal offences, in respect of which the [same investigative measure] could have been ordered". It would however appear that this limitation is not applicable to the transfer of personal data to the FIU for two reasons, despite the FIU's functional nature as a precursor to criminal proceedings. First, section 477 para. 2 s. 2 of the Criminal Procedure Code is according to its wording only concerned with the use of personal data as evidence; in contrast, the provision does not bar the use of personal data as mere intelligence.[428] An evidentiary use of personal data by the FIU will however usually not occur as the FIU's function is primarily analytical and not itself concerned with the imposition of coercive measures.[429]

Second, it was already observed above[430] that the FIU shares many of the characteristics of an intelligence service, as it aims to detect criminality but does so primarily by analysing suspicious transactions without disclosing its intelligence collection to suspected individuals and largely outside judicial supervision. The Federal Constitutional Court has stressed that the fundamental differences in tasks and procedural safeguards between the police authorities on the one hand and the intelligence services on the other hand require "a principle of separation of information" and that the transfer of personal data between police authorities and intelligence services is subject to "heightened constitutional requirements". The Court added that "if exceptions are granted for operational tasks, they constitute a particularly serious interference".[431] This jurisprudence primarily follows from the concern that the transfer of information by intelligence services to the criminal justice authorities might exploit the much less demanding procedural requirements applicable to the intelligence services to circumvent the requirements of criminal procedure law. While similar concerns are raised by the transfer of personal data from the FIU to

---

428 B Schmitt, in L Meyer-Goßner/B Schmitt, Strafprozessordnung, 62nd ed., C.H. Beck 2019, §477, para. 5a; P Wittig, in J-P Graf (ed.), BeckOK StPO, 33rd ed., 2019, §477, para. 5; cf. G Gieg, in R Hannich (ed.), Karlsruher Kommentar zur Strafprozessordnung, 8th ed., C.H. Beck 2019, §477, para. 3; T Singelnstein, in C Knauer/H Kudlich/H Schneider (eds), Münchener Kommentar zur StPO, 1st ed., C.H. Beck 2019, §477, para. 34.

429 Personal data used within an operational analysis might however need to be used as evidence if the FIU, according to section 40 GWG, orders temporary urgent measures, such as the prohibition of a transaction, as such measures might subsequently be subject to review before an administrative court.

430 Above section V.B.1.

431 BVerfGE 133, 277, 329.

the criminal justice authorities,[432] transfers from the criminal justice authorities to the FIU highlight another dimension of the separation of information between both sides of the state security architecture. This extra dimension results from the fact that, at the core of its mission, the FIU's operational analysis targets individual transactions and thus particular individuals, and thus unlike traditional intelligence services under German law[433] is not primarily concerned with the strategic monitoring of threats.[434] The resulting functional proximity of the FIU to the criminal justice authorities can lead to an overlap between operational analyses and criminal investigations that, in targeting particular individuals suspected of having committed a criminal offence, might circumvent the transparency and formality of the law of criminal procedure.[435]

In this respect, it has first to be noted that, due to the largely covert nature of the FIU's operational analysis, the transfer of sensitive personal data from the criminal justice authorities to the FIU exposes this data to a heightened risk of being used in a way that is not compliant with the purpose for which the data was originally collected or transferred. Due to the extensive powers of the FIU not to disclose data in its possession to persons concerned, the availability of judicial remedies against the potential misuse of such data is effectively very limited. The secrecy of the data processing and the resulting limited availability of a remedy increases the intensity of an interference with the fundamental right to informational self-determination.[436]

Furthermore, any assessment of the proportionality of a transfer of personal data from the criminal justice authorities to the FIU has to take into account that the FIU extensively interacts with obliged entities and thus with the private sector. Data that the FIU has received from criminal justice authorities is then highly likely to have an indirect but nevertheless often detrimental effect on obliged entities' clients, in particular if, on the basis of criminal justice data, the FIU learns that an individual is being targeted for, or associated with, a suspected criminal offence. While the FIU is not allowed to transfer personal data that it has received from the criminal justice authorities to obliged entities, the mere fact that the FIU suddenly shows itself to be interested in a particular client will regularly lead the respective obliged entity, once it receives a request for information from the FIU, to reassess its relationship with the client and often even terminate the client relationship. Such indirect consequences of a data transfer by criminal justice authorities appears problematic not least because the FIU, not being the authority in charge of the criminal investigation at the source of the data transfer, will usually not be well placed to assess the

432 See above section V.B.1.

433 BVerfGE 133, 277, 326.

434 For the FIU's strategic analysis, see section 28 para. 1 s. 2 no. 8 GWG.

435 See BVerfGE 133, 277, 327–328.

436 BVerfGE 115, 320, 353–354.

significance and reliability of the transferred data. As the FIU cannot normally know the precise investigative context of the data received from the criminal justice authorities and therefore in particular cannot assess the strength of the resulting suspicion,[437] there is a significant risk of obliged entities' clients being subjected to detrimental CDD measures that ultimately have their origin in de-contextualised information from a criminal investigation.

A factual overlap between the FIU's operational analysis and criminal investigations also poses the risk that obliged entities' clients, while already being investigated by the criminal justice authorities, might as a result of an operational analysis by the FIU be induced to incriminate themselves as a consequence of questions being asked of the client by an obliged entity after this obliged entity has received a request for information from the FIU. As, according to section 47 para. 1 no. 3, the requested obliged entity is not allowed to disclose the FIU's information request to its client, the client will then usually be unaware that the obliged entity's question is effectively meant to contribute to an already ongoing criminal investigation against him or her. Given that the FIU's request according to section 30 para. 3 is not subject to judicial authorisation, and furthermore given that the obliged entity is not allowed to disclose the FIU's request to its client,[438] the GWG does not currently provide for a procedural mechanism that would effectively prevent the FIU's auxiliary involvement in criminal investigations from leading to self-incrimination by suspects. This risk can appear particularly significant to the extent that an obliged entity, having received a request from the FIU, might sometimes have strong reasons to emphasise its client's wrongdoing in order to deflect criticism regarding the quality of its own CDD practice – for example by portraying the client as particularly deceptive and thus as hard to detect through CDD measures; the obliged entity might then have reason to frame communication with this client in a way that deliberately seeks to confirm the underlying suspicion.

Finally and crucially, the GWG raises the question of to what extent the FIU as an intelligence-gathering agency can play a *de facto* investigative role prior to an initial suspicion in the sense of the Criminal Procedure Code and thus prior to, or outside of, a criminal investigation by the criminal justice authorities. Section 30 para. 2 authorises the collection of intelligence on particular crimes before the suspicion threshold for a criminal investigation has been reached. Constitutional jurisprudence accepts that intelligence agencies, beside their primary function of providing strategic information to policy makers, may also be authorised to monitor individual wrongdoing with a view to subsequently providing their observations to the criminal justice authorities.[439] If, however, the

---

437 In that sense BVerfGE 133, 277, 332.

438 Section 47 para. 1 nos. 1 and 3 GWG.

439 See section 3 para. 1 s. 1, para. 2 G10, section 18 para. 6 BVerfSchG; BVerfG NJW 2004, 279, 280.

FIU had extensive access to personal data from the criminal justice authorities, it would be enabled to act as a quasi-subsidiary of the criminal justice authorities, though without acting under the control of the criminal courts and, unlike the criminal justice authorities, without being constrained by the requirement of an initial suspicion as the precondition of an investigation. This would allow the FIU in particular to subject individuals to an operational analysis on the basis of personal data obtained from criminal justice authorities where this data had been insufficient to open or to continue a criminal investigation. For example, where a criminal justice authority discontinued a money laundering investigation because it was unable to establish the predicate offence, the FIU, not being constrained by the requirement of an initial suspicion, might still use the information available from the criminal justice authority as the basis for an operational analysis in the hope of establishing a degree of suspicion that would allow the criminal justice authorities to take back control of the case. The decision to launch or continue a criminal investigation will in such cases depend on the FIU's autonomous[440] decision to analyse a particular case, as well as on the depth of this analysis. As a consequence, the launch or the continuation of criminal investigations by the criminal justice authorities is then effectively not based on whether the information in the hands of the criminal justice authorities gives rise to a reasonably substantiated suspicion against a particular individual, but on the FIU's autonomous selection of suspicious transactions or targets.

In German criminal procedure law, the initial suspicion plays a fundamental role in ensuring that criminal investigations are not triggered by unreasonable or otherwise arbitrary considerations.[441] If the decision to trigger criminal investigations, even if to a significant degree taken on the basis of data from the criminal justice authorities, is effectively exempted from this requirement, this constitutes a severe interference with a fundamental rule of law guarantee. The Federal Constitutional Court has nevertheless admitted the possibility of a rather extensive operational sharing of personal data between the police and intelligence services if this serves a "particularly important public interest",[442] which it recognised notably in the fight against terrorism.[443] In this case, the Court even accepted a joint database of police and intelligence agencies, although this did not (except in urgent cases) provide the requesting authority with direct access to the gist of the sought data, but only allowed the requesting agency to identify data matches in order to then request the matching data through personal communication between officer. Following

440 On the FIU's operational autonomy see above sections IV.A.3. and IV.C.
441 See BVerfGE 112, 284, 297; BVerfGE 115, 320, 361.
442 BVerfGE 133, 277, 329.
443 BVerfGE 133, 277, 333–334.

from this constitutional reluctance to allow a broad sharing of personal data between the police and intelligence services, and furthermore given the FIU's function as a precursor to criminal investigations acting as a trigger for criminal proceedings without being confined by the requirement of an initial suspicion, and lastly in light of the above-mentioned section 477 para. 2 s. 2 of the Criminal Procedure Code that presupposes a heightened sensitivity of personal data collected through qualified investigative measures, it would seem that the FIU is allowed to extensively access such data only in exceptional cases.[444] Access to such sensitive personal data (notably information obtained through telecommunications surveillance and undercover investigators)[445] is then only proportionate if the FIU's respective operational analysis focuses on terrorism[446] or on criminal conduct the potential threat of which is comparable to terrorism. This will often be the case for organised crime,[447] but usually not for cases of serious criminality outside organised crime.

C. DATA EXCHANGE BETWEEN FIU AND INTELLIGENCE AGENCIES

1. *From FIU to Intelligence Agencies*

According to section 32 para. 1, the FIU must transmit "without delay" SARs and equivalent reports from supervisory authorities to the Federal Office for the

---

444 See also the narrow purpose limitation rules of the StPO for a transfer of personal data from the criminal justice authorities to the federal internal intelligence service in section 18 paras. 1b and 3 BVerfSchG.

445 See sections 101 para. 4, 100a and 110a StPO. Note that telecommunications surveillance in a criminal investigation into money laundering by the predicate offender is only admissible if the predicate offence constituted a serious crime; section 100a para. 2 no. 1(m). Note also that covert recordings on private premises and the use of particularly sensitive telecommunications connection data is only allowed in criminal proceedings for cases of particularly serious crimes and in preventive proceedings to avert concrete or imminent major threats, which might exclude a transfer to intelligence services; see section 100d para. 5 and section 101a para. 4 s. 1 StPO.

446 Possible investigative methods at the origin of the accessible criminal justice data then include notably sections 98a para. 1 s. 1 no. 2 (dragnet investigations), 100a para. 2 no. 2(a) and (d) (telecommunications surveillance), 100f para. 1 (covert recording outside private premises), 100h para. 1 s. 2 (other surveillance measures outside private premises), and 110a para. 1 s. 1 no. 2 (undercover investigators) StPO.

447 For a definition of organised crime, see for example section 4 para. 2 of the State Intelligence Law of the state of Bavaria (*Bayerisches Verfassungsschutzgesetz*): "Organized crime … is the systematic commission of criminal offenses … which are of major importance to the legal order by more than two parties acting on a long-term or indefinite basis for the purpose of seeking profit or power (1) by using commercial or business-like structures, (2) by using force or equivalent threats, or (3) by exerting influence on politics, the administration, the judiciary, the media or businesses" (translated by the author).

Protection of the Constitution (that is, the federal internal intelligence service) "insofar as there are factual indications that the transmission of this information is necessary for the [Federal Office] to perform its functions." These functions notably include the monitoring of endeavours directed against the democratic order, the security of the state or the functioning of constitutional bodies, of counter-espionage, of domestic violence-oriented endeavours against Germany's foreign policy interests, and of domestic endeavours against the peaceful coexistence of peoples.[448] Furthermore, according to section 32 para. 2, the FIU must transmit the results of its operational analysis "and all relevant information" on this matter to the Federal Office for the Protection of the Constitution and to the Federal Intelligence Service (that is, the foreign intelligence service) "insofar as there are factual indications that this transmission is necessary" for the performance of their functions. As regards the Federal Intelligence Service, it should be noted that its task, defined as the production of knowledge about activities abroad that are of relevance for Germany's foreign and security policy,[449] explicitly also extends to the monitoring of large-scale organised money laundering.[450]

Beyond the aforementioned transmission of information *ex officio*, section 32 para. 3 provides that the FIU must provide personal information to the Federal Office for the Protection of the Constitution, the Federal Intelligence Service and the Military Intelligence Service[451] insofar as this is necessary for the clearing up of money laundering or terrorism financing or the clearing up of other threats. Section 32 para. 5 s. 1 no. 2 clarifies that personal data shall not be transmitted insofar as the dissemination of the data would be disproportionate to the legitimate interests of a natural or legal person. Furthermore, the FIU has to respect data transmission restrictions. Such restrictions notably apply to data that the FIU obtained from a foreign FIU, as a transfer of such information is subject to the approval of this foreign FIU,[452] and to personal data originally obtained by the FIU from criminal justice authorities that, according to the Criminal Procedure Code and thereby specifying proportionality limits, preclude a use for the particular purpose pursued by the requesting intelligence service.[453]

448 Section 3 para. 1 BVerfSchG.

449 Section 1 para. 2 Act on the Federal Intelligence Service (Bundesnachrichtendienstgesetz, BNDG).

450 Section 5 para. 1 s. 1 no. 6 G10.

451 See section 1 para. 1 Act on the Military Counterintelligence Service (Gesetz über den militärischen Abschirmdienst, MADG).

452 Section 34 para. 3 s. 2 and 3 GWG.

453 For data obtained through telecommunications surveillance, see section 18 para. 6 BVerfSchG.

2. *From Intelligence Agencies to FIU*

As already mentioned,[454] according to section 31 para. 1 s. 1, the FIU can, for the performance of its functions, collect data from domestic public authorities, which in principle also covers the intelligence services. Limits on this power are set by the data transfer provisions of the laws regulating the respective intelligence services. The intelligence services can provide personal data to other domestic public authorities if this is necessary to respond to past or imminent crimes of more than minor seriousness.[455] The intelligence services are thereby however not entitled to provide personal data that they have obtained through certain covert methods,[456] though this does not exclude the provision of non-personal data (in particular strategic data) that the services have assembled on the basis of personal data obtained by such methods. As regards personal data obtained by the intelligence services through the surveillance of telecommunication or postal services, the law allows for the transfer of such data to other public authorities for the prevention or clearing up of a number of listed criminal offences, which would seem to include data transfer to the FIU; such personal data can then be transferred in particular if there are indications that suggest that a person is planning or committing terrorism financing or another listed offence directed against the state or the democratic order, or if particular facts give rise to the suspicion that a person is planning or committing other (mostly serious) crimes, amongst them notably also money laundering and many of its predicate offences.[457]

D. DATA EXCHANGE BETWEEN FIU AND TAX AUTHORITIES

1. *From FIU to Tax Authorities*

According to section 32 para. 3 s. 2 no. 2, the FIU shall transmit personal data, *ex officio* or upon request, to the competent domestic authorities insofar as this is necessary for taxation procedures. The broad wording of this provision seems to indicate that the FIU shall transfer personal data even if it does not point towards the commission of a criminal offence. Such a broad reading

454 See above section V.B.2.

455 Section 19 para. 1 s. 3 BVerfSchG; section 24 para. 1 s. 1 BNDG; W Bock, in W-R Schenke/K Graulich/J Ruthig (eds.), Sicherheitsrecht des Bundes, 2nd ed., C.H. Beck 2019, BVerfSchG §19, para. 18.

456 See section 19 para. 1 in conjunction with section 8 para. 2 BVerfSchG; section 24 para. 1 s. 2 in conjunction with section 5 BNDG; note that the FIU (despite its integration into the Customs Criminal Office) is not a customs investigation authority within the meaning of section 19 para. 1 BVerfSchG; see section 5a para. 3 s. 2 FVG.

457 Section 4 para. 4 s. 1 no. 1, section 3 paras. 1 and 1a, and section 7 para. 4 s. 1 G10.

would however be difficult to reconcile with the Federal Constitutional Court's jurisprudence on covert intelligence gathering, which, as pointed out above, suggests that the FIU's processing of personal data is highly intrusive and akin to an intelligence service.[458] As a result, and in light of the proportionality standards of the legal order, it would seem that a transfer of personal data by the FIU to the tax authorities is admissible only where the information is meant to prevent or investigate serious tax crimes that, compared to other tax crimes, are of particular significance,[459] and possibly also independently of a criminal suspicion where the FIU detects a particularly large tax loss.[460]

2. *From Tax Authorities to FIU*

Section 31 para. 5 s. 1 GWG in conjunction with section 31b para. 1 no. 5 of the Tax Code stipulates that, as an exception to the tax secrecy governing the treatment of personal data in tax proceedings, the revenue authorities, *ex officio* or upon request, shall transfer personal data insofar as such disclosure serves the performance of the FIU's tasks.[461] According to section 31b para. 2 s. 1 of the Tax Code, the revenue authorities are even under an obligation to report to the FIU any facts indicating that property is the object of money laundering or related to terrorism financing.[462]

Reflecting the fundamental right not to incriminate oneself,[463] section 393 para. 2 of the Tax Code provides that "[w]here during criminal proceedings the public prosecutor's office or the court learns from the tax records of facts or evidence which the taxpayer, in compliance with his obligations under tax law, revealed to the revenue authority before the initiation of criminal proceedings or in ignorance of the initiation of criminal proceedings, this knowledge may not be used against him for the prosecution of an act that is not a tax crime." This exclusionary rule follows from the fact that the privilege against self-incrimination does not exempt a taxable person from the obligation to provide the revenue authorities with all necessary information to establish her tax liability.[464] However, the exclusion of such material from criminal proceedings does "not apply to crimes for the prosecution of which there is a compelling

---

458 See above section V.B.1.

459 See section 19 para. 1 s. 1 nos. 3 and 4 BVerfSchG; BVerfG NJW 2003, 1787, 1791.

460 See section 19 para. 1 s. 1 no. 2 BVerfSchG; BVerfGE 133, 277, 365.

461 As regards the rather broad powers of the revenue authorities to share personal data with other authorities, see BVerfG, NJW 2008, 3489, 3490; BFH, DStRE 2003, 1287, 1289.

462 On the proportionality of section 31a AO (reporting of illegal employment by the revenue authorities) see BFH, DStR 2007, 2009, 2011.

463 See ECtHR, judgment of 3 May 2001, app. no. 31827/96 (J.B./Switzerland), at para. 64; BVerfGK 17, 253.

464 See BVerfGE 56, 37, 47; BVerfG NJW 2005, 352; BGH NStZ-RR 2004, 242, 243; BGH NJW 2005, 763, 764.

public interest",[465] at least in cases where the incriminating information was not directly contained in a compelled statement of the taxable person him- or herself but contained in documents produced by him or her as a result of any prior record-keeping obligations.[466] According to section 30 paras. 4 and 5 of the Tax Code, a compelling public interest is deemed to exist in particular if the disclosure is necessary "to prevent or prosecute crimes punishable by a minimum of one year's imprisonment or other intentional serious offences that aim to cause human injury or loss of life or that aim to cause damage to the state and its institutions"; furthermore a compelling public interest is also deemed to exist if "economic crimes are being or are to be prosecuted, and which in view of the method of their perpetration or the extent of the damage caused by them are likely to substantially disrupt the economic order or to substantially undermine general confidence in the integrity of business dealings or the orderly functioning of authorities and public institutions".[467] While section 393 para. 2 of the Tax Code does directly apply only to the criminal justice authorities, the provision explicitly refers not only to evidence, but also to "facts" that are not evidence, and thus apparently also refers to mere intelligence.[468] In view of the FIU's function as a precursor to criminal proceedings, the limitation on the use of material contained in section 393 para. 2 of the Tax Code then also applies to any operational analysis that targets the taxpayer who provided the relevant information, and in this respect restricts its transfer by the revenue authorities to the FIU.

E. DATA EXCHANGE BETWEEN FIU AND CUSTOMS AUTHORITIES

1. *From FIU to Customs Authorities*

The FIU is allowed to transmit personal data on customs-related suspicious activity and customs-related crimes to the customs authorities via the customs

465 Section 393 para. 2 s. 2 AO; see BGHSt 49, 136, 147; BGHSt 50, 299, 317.

466 On whether or how to accommodate section 393 para. 2 s. 2 AO with the privilege against self-incrimination, see BVerfGK 17, 253; BGH NJW 2006, 925, 926; M Jäger, in F Klein/G Orlopp (eds), Abgabenordnung, 14th ed., C.H. Beck 2018, §393, para. 59; M Lindemann, in S Hüls/T Reichling (eds.), Steuerstrafrecht, C.F. Müller 2016, §393, paras. 41, 74; J Sprenger, in W Leitner/H Rosenau (eds.), Wirtschafts- und Steuerstrafrecht, Nomos 2017, §393, paras. 10–11.

467 For doubts regarding the constitutionality of this provision, see W Joecks, in Steuerstrafrecht, Kommentar, 8th ed., C.H. Beck 2015, §393 AO, para. 97.

468 See BVerfGE 56, 37, 51; W Joecks, in Steuerstrafrecht, Kommentar, 8th ed., C.H. Beck 2015, §393 AO, para. 92; M Lindemann, in S Hüls/T Reichling (eds.), Steuerstrafrecht, C.F. Müller 2016, §393, para. 71.

investigation information system.[469] Insofar as the customs authorities investigate customs-related crimes and in this case serve as criminal justice authorities,[470] they are also covered by the FIU's obligation according to section 32 para. 2 s. 1 to inform the competent criminal justice authorities about cases of money laundering or other criminal offences, that is as regards the customs authorities' customs-related money laundering or other customs-related criminal offences. Either way, the transmission of personal data by the FIU to the customs authorities in view of suspected criminal offences is subject to the above-mentioned proportionality limits, which exclude less serious forms of criminality.[471]

2. *From Customs Authorities to FIU*

The customs authorities are, *ex officio* or on request, entitled to transfer to the FIU personal data for the performance of its tasks, in particular for operational analyses but also, in view of the possible money laundering implications of cross-border commerce, for strategic analyses. However, for the reasons explained above, personal data originating from qualified investigative measures of the customs authorities (such as telecommunications surveillance and informants) can be transferred to the FIU only in exceptional cases.[472] The FIU is furthermore allowed to retrieve data from the customs investigation information system. The FIU can thereby notably access information on customs-related crimes, but also on non-crime-related personal information regarding the domestic and cross-border movement in goods, capital and services, and personal data for the monitoring of individuals suspected of the future commission of serious violations of customs-related obligations.[473]

F. INFORMATION FLOW BETWEEN FIU AND FOREIGN COUNTERPARTS

1. *Restrictions on Data Transfer from FIU to Foreign FIUs*

According to section 35 para. 2 s. 1, the German FIU may, upon request, transmit personal data to a foreign FIU (i) for an operational analysis by a foreign FIU,

---

469 Section 11 para. 2 s. 1 and section 13 para. 1 in conjunction with section 3 para. 1 s. 1 no. 2 ZFdG; see above section IV.D.2.

470 Section 26 para. 1 s. 1 ZFdG.

471 See above section V.B.1.

472 See above section V.B.2. As regards powers of the customs authorities in criminal investigations, see section 26 para. 1 ZFdG; as regards their preventive investigative powers, see notably sections 20, 22a and 23a ZFdG.

473 See section 11 para. 2 s. 3 in conjunction with sections 8–10 ZFdG.

(ii) for the purpose of a planned urgent measure (in particular the temporary prohibition of transactions)[474] by the German FIU, insofar as facts indicate that the property in question is located in Germany and is connected with a matter which is before the foreign FIU, or (iii) "for the performance of the functions of another foreign public authority acting against money laundering, its predicate offences or terrorist financing."[475]

To respond to the request by a foreign FIU, the German FIU may, according to section 35 para. 2 s. 2, use information already held by it. According to section 35 para. 2 s. 3, "[i]f this information also includes data collected or transmitted by other domestic or foreign authorities, the disclosure of these data is only permissible with the consent of these authorities, unless the information comes from publicly accessible sources." Furthermore, section 35 para. 2 s. 3 specifies that the FIU "may request information from other domestic public authorities or demand information from obliged entities."[476] If the request stems from the FIU of another EU Member State, the German FIU is, according to section 33 para. 2 s. 2, obliged to use its data gathering and transmission powers, thus in this respect enjoys no discretion.

According to section 35 para. 4, the FIU may, even without a request from a foreign FIU, also transmit personal data to a foreign FIU "if facts indicate that natural or legal persons in the territory of that country have committed money laundering or terrorist financing offences", notwithstanding the nature of the predicate offence or whether or not the predicate offence has already been established.[477] Irrespective of such indications, according to section 33 para. 1 s. 3, if the FIU receives an SAR that concerns another EU Member State, it must promptly forward this SAR to the competent FIU. According to section 35 para. 1, the FIU can also forward an SAR that concerns a third state to the respective foreign FIU, though in that regard it is not under an obligation to do so. For both the transfer of data upon request and on its own initiative, section 35 para. 5 provides that the German FIU can (and in many cases indeed must)[478] impose restrictions and conditions on the use of the data by the foreign FIU; this may be relevant in particular if the use of the data is limited by national

---

474 Section 40 GWG; see above section IV.A.4.

475 According to BT-Drucksache 18/11555, p. 148, this is meant to include foreign supervisory authorities as the ultimate recipients of the requested information.

476 For the limits applicable to such requests, see above sections V.A.2, B.2, C.2, D.2 and E.2.

477 Under EU law, transmission must not be preconditioned by a particular suspected predicate offence, but only as regards cooperation between FIUs of Member States, and not, as the explanatory notes of the German law imply, also for cooperation with FIUs from third states; see Article 53(1)(1) of Directive 2015/849/EU of 20 May 2015 on the prevention of the use of the financial system for the purposes of money laundering or terrorist financing, as amended by Directive (EU) 2018/843 of 30 May 2018 and BT-Drucksache 19/13827, p. 93.

478 S Barreto da Rosa, in F Herzog/O Achtelik (eds.), Geldwäschegesetz, 2018, §35, para. 19.

proportionality considerations[479] or limitations stipulated by another authority from whom the data was originally obtained.[480]

For limits on the transfer of data by the FIU, the GWG differentiates between the FIUs of EU Member States and those of third states. According to section 33 para. 1, the exchange of data with the FIUs of other EU Member States "is to be ensured irrespective of the type of predicate offence for money laundering and also if the type of predicate offence has not been established. In particular, a differing definition in an individual case of the tax crimes which, under national law, can qualify as a predicate offence for money laundering does not preclude an exchange of information with Financial Intelligence Units of other member states of the European Union."

According to section 33 para. 4, the FIU may reject an information request from another EU FIU only if: (i) "the transmission of information could jeopardise the internal or external security or other essential interests of the Federal Republic of Germany", which means that the discretion of the German FIU to deny a request out of policy considerations is confined to cases of particular importance, such as a substantiated risk that the data transfer could compromise covert intelligence operations and their methods, or exceptional national economic interests;[481] (ii) in the individual case, the transmission can, even with due regard for the public interest in it, not be reconciled with fundamental principles of German law; this would seem to include respect for the fundamental right to informational self-determination[482] and resulting from it the requirement that the purpose of the foreign FIU's data processing is proportionate to the data gathering method through which the requested data was originally obtained;[483] (iii) "the transmission of information could hinder or jeopardise criminal investigations or the conduct of judicial proceedings", notably if the transfer to a foreign FIU could lead to a premature disclosure of the data to the suspect of an ongoing domestic investigation;[484] or (iv) if the German FIU previously received the requested data from another foreign

479 On such limits see notably above section V.B.1.

480 BT-Drucksache 18/11555, p. 146.

481 See BT-Drucksache 18/11555, p. 147; BGH NJW 1979, 1556, 1557; OLG Köln, Beschluss vom 20.10.2010 – 6 AuslS 101/09, 95; S Barreto da Rosa, in F Herzog/O Achtelik (eds.), Geldwäschegesetz, 2018, §33, para. 18; W Bock, in W-R Schenke/K Graulich/J Ruthig (eds.), Sicherheitsrecht des Bundes, 2nd ed., C.H. Beck 2019, BVerfSchG §23, para. 6.

482 See BT-Drucksache 19/13827, p. 92; J Ruthig, in W-R Schenke/K Graulich/J Ruthig (eds.), Sicherheitsrecht des Bundes, 2nd ed., C.H. Beck 2019, BKAG §28, para. 7.

483 On the constitutional requirement to safeguard the proportionality between the original gathering of data and its subsequent use also in cases of transfer of data to foreign authorities, see BVerfGE 141, 220, 330–331. This is relevant in particular where the foreign FIU requests personal data that the German FIU obtained from another domestic authority who had acquired this data by qualified investigative methods; see above section V.B.2.

484 S Barreto da Rosa, in F Herzog/O Achtelik (eds.), Geldwäschegesetz, 2018, §33, para. 20.

authority and the transmission to the foreign FIU is precluded by conditions imposed by this authority.

As regards information requests from FIUs of third states, the law does not impose an obligation to cooperate. Section 35 para. 7 merely provides that personal data must not be transmitted if: (i) the transmission could harm the security or other essential interests of Germany; (ii) special federal provisions preclude transmission, which includes cases that fall outside the scope of particular data transfer provisions;[485] or (iii) the legitimate interests of the data subject are overriding, which notably covers the constitutional requirement of adequate human rights standards in the requesting state.[486] The same provision clarifies that "legitimate interests of the data subject" include an appropriate level of data protection in the receiving country. Furthermore, according to section 35 para. 8, personal data should usually not be transmitted if the transmission could hinder or jeopardise criminal investigations or judicial proceedings, or if it is not clear that the requesting FIU would respond to a German request of the same kind.

2. *Restrictions on Use of Data Obtained from Foreign FIUs*

Section 34 para. 3 states that the German FIU may use the data transmitted by a foreign FIU only "for the purposes for which the data were requested", and "in compliance with the conditions under which the data were made available". The provisions adds that "[i]f the data transmitted are subsequently to be disclosed to another public authority or used for a purpose beyond the original purposes", this requires the prior consent of the transmitting foreign FIU.

G. INFORMATION FLOW BETWEEN FIU AND FOREIGN NON-COUNTERPARTS

Section 35 para. 6 s. 3 states that if information transferred by the FIU to a foreign FIU "is to be used as evidence in criminal proceedings, the rules of cross-border cooperation in criminal matters apply." This underlines that the exchange of data by the FIU is meant to serve intelligence purposes only and is not meant to directly produce evidence. The law does not authorise the direct transfer of personal data from the German FIU to non-counterpart

---

485 See J Ruthig, in W-R Schenke/K Graulich/J Ruthig (eds.), Sicherheitsrecht des Bundes, 2nd ed., C.H. Beck 2019, BKAG §28, para. 11; for such transmission limits see above sections V.A.2, B.2, C.2, D.2 and E.2.

486 See BVerfGE 141, 220, 334–335; J Ruthig, in W-R Schenke/K Graulich/J Ruthig (eds.), Sicherheitsrecht des Bundes, 2nd ed., C.H. Beck 2019, BKAG §28, para. 7.

foreign authorities,[487] but envisages the forwarding of data by the requesting foreign FIU to other national authorities of the same country. Section 35 para. 2 s. 1 no. 3 explicitly clarifies for information requests by FIUs both from EU Member States and from third states that information can also be transferred in particular "for the performance of the functions of another foreign public authority which serves to prevent, detect and combat money laundering or predicate offences for money laundering or terrorist financing." Section 35 para. 6 provides that, if personal data is to be disclosed by the foreign FIU to another authority in that country, this requires the prior consent of the German FIU, which must have "due regard for the purpose and the legitimate interests of the data subject regarding the data."

To simplify the transfer of data to non-counterpart authorities within the EU, section 33 para. 5 s. 1 states that the German FIU, if it transmits information to the FIU of another EU Member State, "should normally express its consent promptly for this information to be disclosed to other authorities of that member state". According to section 33 para. 5 s. 2, the German FIU can however refuse to give its consent for the same reasons for which it may reject a request in the first place, notably because the forwarding of the information would constitute a disproportionate infringement of a person's right to informational self-determination or would expose the information to a risk of disclosure that could compromise essential national interests.[488] As results from the recent change introduced in the course of the transposition Directive 2018/843/EU, as regards money laundering, the law now requires the German FIU to give its consent irrespective of the nature of the predicate offence, meaning that the forwarding of information by the receiving EU FIU to another national authority (in particular to a foreign criminal justice authority) should, as regards transmission to another EU Member State, in principle not be subject to a dual incrimination requirement. This seems to go beyond what is required by the Directive;[489] in any case, consent may, at least if a departure from the dual incrimination requirement is in the particular case not stipulated by EU law,[490] still be refused as being irreconcilable with a fundamental principle of German law.[491]

---

487 See also BT-Drucksache 18/11555, p. 147.

488 BT-Drucksache 18/11555, p. 147.

489 See Article 55(2) of Directive 2015/849/EU of 20 May 2015 on the prevention of the use of the financial system for the purposes of money laundering or terrorist financing, as amended by Directive (EU) 2018/843 of 30 May 2018: "The requested FIU shall not refuse its consent to such dissemination unless this would fall beyond the scope of application of *its* AML/CFT provisions" (emphasis added).

490 Relating thereto, see in particular Article 3(4) of Directive 2018/1673/EU of 23 October 2018 on combating money laundering by criminal law.

491 See BT-Drucksache 19/13827, p. 92.

H. EVIDENTIAL VALUE OF FIU-GENERATED DATA IN COURT PROCEEDINGS

The law does not explicitly address the admissibility of FIU-generated information as evidence in court proceedings, and notably does not provide for a prohibition of such use. The admissibility of FIU-generated information as evidence thus depends on whether its transfer to judicial proceedings is allowed in the first place,[492] which might in some cases in particular also depend on whether a foreign FIU whose information was fed into the domestic FIU's analysis agrees to the further transfer of its information to the domestic judicial authorities.[493] Furthermore, as explained above,[494] while the law does effectively restrict the use of SARs in court proceedings, it does not categorically exclude such disclosure. Yet one must remember that, in view of the FIU's function to detect criminal conduct and thus to serve as a precursor for criminal investigations, the results of the FIU's analysis are not primarily meant to establish criminal guilt, but to provide a basis for investigative measures to be carried out by the criminal justice authorities. This does not exclude findings that played a role in the FIU's analysis also being subsequently used in a criminal court's final decision. However, the jurisprudence of the Federal Constitutional Court and of the criminal courts regarding the probative value of the testimony of hearsay evidence is then highly relevant.[495] Where evidence is based on information that, for reasons of public interest and in particular to protect sources or honour confidentiality commitments towards foreign authorities, is withheld from the court and the defendant, the reliability of this evidence is considerably reduced, and accordingly the courts are required to subject it to a particularly critical examination.[496] Accordingly, to the extent that the FIU's conclusions are based on information that during the subsequent criminal proceedings is not disclosed to the court and the defendant, the results of the FIU's analysis are of limited evidential value.

Further limits on the evidential use of FIU-generated information are imposed in the Criminal Procedure Code (StPO). Section 161 para. 2 s. 1 StPO provides that "[w]here measures pursuant to this statute are only admissible where the commission of particular criminal offences is suspected, personal data that has been obtained as a result of a corresponding measure taken pursuant to another statute may be used as evidence in criminal proceedings without the consent of the person affected by the measure only to clear up one of the criminal offences in respect of which such a measure could have been ordered to clear up the offence pursuant to this statute." As a consequence,

---

492 On this see above section V.B.1.

493 See section 34 para. 3 s. 2 and 3 GWG.

494 See above section III.C.2.b.

495 See BVerfG NJW 2010, 925, 926; BGH NJW 2007, 237, 239; BGH NStZ-RR 2014, 246, 249.

496 BVerfG NJW 1981, 1719, 1725; NJW 2010, 925, 926; BGH NJW 2004, 1259, 1261.

criminal justice authorities in particular may not use as evidence data that they received from the FIU where this data had initially been produced by secret investigative measures of another authority (such as covert surveillance by an intelligence service) and such measures would, according to the StPO, not have been admissible in the particular case. However, the limitation contained in section 161 para. 2 StPO only concerns the use of the respective data as evidence and does not extend to its use by investigative authorities for the purpose of commencing a criminal investigation or providing new investigative leads. Consequently, investigative measures by criminal justice authorities can also be triggered by information obtained through an investigative measure of another authority that would not have been allowed in the criminal investigation, though such information then cannot be used as evidence in court.[497]

I. USE OF CDD DATA FOR PROFIT MAKING

Section 11a para. 1 provides a narrow purpose limitation for personal data collected by obliged entities under the GWG,[498] stating that they are allowed to process such data only insofar as this is necessary for the purpose of preventing money laundering and terrorism financing. This does not however exclude that the same data is at the same time collected and further processed for other lawful reasons, notably for a legitimate interest of the obliged entity, provided that the scope of the data gathering is adequate and necessary in relation to such purpose.[499] Depending on the actual scope and nature of the processed data, such a legitimate interest may notably lie in an obliged entity's interest in evaluating the risk profile of the customer, as well as for determining whether, in view of economic and other risks and the resulting intensity and thus costs of the performance of CDD, the entering into, continuation or performance of a particular business relationship or transaction is economically reasonable.

J. DATA SHARING BETWEEN OBLIGED ENTITIES REGARDING SARs AND FIU REQUESTS

1. *Data Sharing Inside a Group*

According to section 47 para. 2 s. 1 no. 2, the prohibition on disclosing the filing of an SAR, the launch of a criminal investigation or a request for information by

497 BVerfG NJW 2005, 2766.

498 BT-Drucksache 19/13827, p. 75.

499 See Article 5(1)(c) and Article 6(1)(f) of Regulation (EU) 2016/679 of 27 April 2016 on the protection of natural persons with regard to the processing of personal data and on the free movement of such data, and repealing Directive 95/46/EC.

the FIU does not apply to disclosure between credit institutions, financial services institutions, payment institutions and electronic money institutions, other financial undertakings, insurance undertakings and insurance agents belonging to the same group.[500] However, for disclosure to subordinate obliged entities of the same group established outside the EU and the European Economic Area, the law provides special requirements.[501]

Section 47 para. 2 s. 2 specifies that information disclosed between obliged entities may be used solely for the purpose of preventing money laundering or terrorism financing; this notably excludes the commercial use of the disclosed information.[502]

2. *Data Sharing with Similar Professions*

According to section 47 para. 2 s. 1 no. 5, the prohibition on disclosing the filing of an SAR, the launch of a criminal investigation or a request for information by the FIU does also not apply to disclosure between certain types of obliged entities (namely credit institutions, financial services institutions, payment institutions and electronic money institutions, other financial undertakings, insurance undertakings, investment management companies, attorneys at law, patent attorneys, notaries, tax advisors and auditors) in cases which relate to the same contracting party and the same transaction involving two or more obliged entities, if the obliged entities are from the same professional category, and are subject to comparable obligations as regards professional secrecy and personal data protection.

Furthermore, and independently of the identity of the particular transaction and contracting party, section 47 para. 2 s. 1 no. 4 allows disclosure between some obliged entities (notably attorneys at law, patent attorneys, notaries, independent legal advisors who are not members of a bar association, tax advisors, and auditors), provided that the persons concerned perform their professional activities by means of self-employment, as employees within the same legal person, or as employees within a structure that shares common ownership, management or compliance control in relation to AML/CTF requirements.

Again, according to section 47 para. 2 s. 2, information disclosed between obliged entities can be used solely for the purpose of preventing money laundering or terrorism financing.

---

500 See section 1 para. 16 GWG; Article 22(1) of Directive 2013/34/EU.
501 See below section V.J.3.
502 BT-Drucksache 18/11555, p. 158.

3. *Data Sharing with Obliged Entities Outside the EU*

The law sets out special requirements for the disclosure of the filing of an SAR, the launch of a criminal investigation or a request for information by the FIU to entities located in third countries, that is countries that are neither EU Member States nor members of the European Economic Area.

As regards disclosure between financial entities (that is credit institutions, financial services institutions, payment institutions and electronic money institutions, other financial undertakings, insurance undertakings and insurance agents) and their branches and majority-owned subsidiaries in third countries,[503] section 47 para. 2 s. 1 no. 3 requires that the group is subject to a group-wide AML/CTF compliance programme that satisfies the requirements set forth by the law and that these requirements are effectively implemented.[504]

As regards disclosure between certain types of obliged entities belonging to the same profession (namely credit institutions, financial services institutions, payment institutions and electronic money institutions, other financial undertakings, insurance undertakings, investment management companies, attorneys at law, patent attorneys, notaries, tax advisors, and auditors) in cases which relate to the same contracting party and the same transaction involving two or more obliged entities, if the obliged entities are domiciled in a third country, section 47 para. 2 s. 2 no. 5 requires, in addition to the above-mentioned conditions,[505] that this third country imposes AML/CTF requirements equivalent to Directive 2015/849/EU.

Finally, as regards disclosure between certain other obliged entities (notably attorneys at law, patent attorneys, notaries, independent legal who that are not members of a bar association, tax advisors, and auditors) and such entities from third countries, section 47 para. 2 s. 1 no. 4 requires, in addition to the above-mentioned requirements,[506] that the third country imposes AML/CTF requirements equivalent to those laid down in Directive 2015/849/EU.

K. DATA SHARING BETWEEN OBLIGED ENTITIES REGARDING POSSIBLE CASES OF MONEY LAUNDERING

1. *Data Sharing Inside a Group*

Section 47 para. 5 s. 1 provides that some obliged entities (namely credit institutions, financial services institutions, payment institutions and

503 See BT-Drucksache 18/11555, p. 158.
504 Section 9 GWG.
505 See above section III.J.2.
506 See above section III.J.2.

electronic money institutions, agents of payment institutions and agents of electronic money institutions, independent traders that sell or re-exchange electronic money of a credit institution, other financial undertakings, insurance undertakings, insurance agents and investment management companies) can also provide each other with information beyond the above-mentioned cases (SARs, follow-up criminal investigations and information requests by the FIU) about specific matters which involve abnormalities or unusual circumstances indicating money laundering, one of its predicate offences or terrorism financing,[507] if they can assume that other obliged entities require this information for their risk assessment of a corresponding or similar transaction or business relationship or the assessment of whether an SAR or a criminal complaint should be filed.[508] The law does not add further details about the type and scope of the data that can thus be shared, but it is clear from the reference to "specific matters" as well as from the provision's objective that the obliged entity is also authorised to share personal data about particular clients and transactions. This notably covers cases where an obliged entity itself does not have sufficient information to file an SAR but seeks additional information about a transaction or business relationship from other obliged entities in order to enrich its risk assessment.[509] Section 47 para. 5 s. 2 states that this information may also be provided using databases, irrespective whether these databases are operated by obliged entities themselves or third parties; potentially relevant data may thus be made available to unspecified other obliged entities who will then, by querying the database, be able to access it on their own initiative. The information provided may be used solely for the purpose of preventing money laundering, its predicate offences or terrorist financing and only subject to any conditions imposed by the obliged entity that provided the information.

2. *Data Sharing with Similar Professions*

The aforementioned section 47 para. 5 does not differentiate between obliged entities inside and outside a group of companies. It is therefore clear that the

---

507 According to section 25h para. 3 s. 4 KWG and section 28 para. 1 s. 4 KAGB, credit institutions, financial services institutions and investment management companies can also share information regarding any other criminal offence.

508 For insurance undertakings, see also section 53 para. 1 VAG. Unlike section 47 para. 5 GWG, this provision is seemingly more limited as regards when insurance undertakings might provide others with information: unlike section 47 para. 5 GWG, section 53 para. 1 VAG envisages the use of the information provided only for the receiving entity's case-specific assessment of whether an SAR or a criminal complaint should be filed, not also for a receiving entity's broader risk assessment.

509 BT-Drucksache 16/9038, p. 46–47; S Barreto da Rosa, in F Herzog/O Achtelik (eds.), Geldwäschegesetz, 2018, §47, para. 33.

obliged entities listed in this provision can also share relevant information with other obliged entities outside the group.[510]

3. *Data Sharing with Obliged Entities Outside the EU*

Section 47 para. 5, which provides for the sharing of information about specific matters which involve abnormalities or unusual circumstances indicating money laundering, one of its predicate offences or terrorism financing, does not mention entities in third states and therefore does not authorise disclosure to such entities.

L. DATA MINING BY OBLIGED ENTITIES

The GWG does not specify the limits of the use of big data analytics techniques by obliged entities. In this respect, one must then note Article 22(1) of Regulation (EU) 2016/679, which provides that "[t]he data subject shall have the right not to be subject to a decision based solely on automated processing, including profiling, which produces legal effects concerning him or her or similarly significantly affects him or her." Therefore, and unless the contract partner explicitly consents to such processing, obliged entities must, in the performance of CDD, not rely on automated processing of personal data in a way that effectively delegates decisions about customers to automated processing. While this does not exclude the possibility of using such techniques to assist human decision-making (not least for the identification of red flags through the automated monitoring of business relationships), a human agent must still verify the automated findings. Consequently, the obliged entity, in taking significant decisions about an actual or potential contract partner, is not allowed to substantially rely on inferences that the competent employee was unable to comprehend.

VI. BENEFICIAL OWNERSHIP TRANSPARENCY

A. BENEFICIAL OWNERSHIP INFORMATION

1. *General Framework*

According to section 20 para. 1 s. 1, legal persons under private law and registered partnerships have to obtain and hold information on their beneficial ownership,

510 For information sharing between insurance undertakings, see also section 53 para. 1 VAG.

keep this information updated, and communicate it in electronic form and without undue delay to the agency in charge of the beneficial ownership register. Section 20 para. 1a adds that entities also have to inform the register about their renaming, merger, dissolution or change of legal status.

The disclosure obligation according to section 20 para. 1 is imposed on the legal persons and registered partnerships themselves. To enable them to comply with this duty, the law provides for corresponding duties of beneficial owners and, to some extent also of shareholders. According to section 20 para. 3 s. 1, beneficial owners have to provide the legal person or partnership with the necessary information to comply with its disclosure obligation and update this information without undue delay. According to section 20 para. 3 s. 2, the same obligation applies to shareholders that are not themselves the beneficial owner, but only if they are directly controlled by a beneficial owner.[511] In the case of associations or cooperatives – thus legal persons that do not have a share-based ownership structure – the duty to provide the necessary information rests on any member that controls more than 25% of the voting rights.[512] In the case of foundations, to the extent that they have legal personality, the necessary information must be provided by: (i) any natural person who acts as trustor, trustee or protector; (ii) any natural person who is a member of the foundation's board; (iii) any natural person who has been designated as a beneficiary; (iv) if the natural person who will be the beneficiary has not been designated yet, the group of natural persons for the benefit of whom the estate shall be managed or distributed,; or (v) any natural person who, in any other way, directly or indirectly, exerts a controlling influence on the estate's management or the distribution of returns, and (vi) any natural person who can directly or indirectly exert a controlling influence over a legal person or partnership that is a member of the board of the foundation or that has been designated as beneficiary of the foundation.[513]

According to section 20 para. 3a, if a legal person or partnership did not receive beneficial ownership information in line with the preceding obligations, it must, to the extent that it is known, request adequate information from its shareholders. Shareholders must respond to such request in due course. The obligation to request information does not however apply if the beneficial ownership information is already in other ways known to the legal person or partnership. Both a request and the information received must be documented.

According to section 20 para. 3b, if the shareholder realises that the beneficial ownership of the legal person or partnership has changed, it must notify it in due course, except if the information about the new beneficial owner

511 Such direct control will notably exist where the shareholder is itself a legal entity that is directly controlled by the beneficial owner; see section 3 para. 2 s. 3 GWG.
512 Section 20 para. 3 s. 2 and 4 GWG.
513 Sections 20 para. 3 s. 3 and 4 and section 3 para. 3 GWG.

is already accessible via the central registry or if it is otherwise known to the shareholder that the legal person or partnership is already aware of the change. The shareholder has to document the notification.

According to section 20 para. 4, the duty of shareholders, members and beneficial owners to provide the legal person or partnership with the necessary information on beneficial ownership is cancelled if the information can already be retrieved from the commercial register, the register of partnerships, the register of cooperatives, the association register or the business register, or because the entity is listed on an organised market or otherwise operates under adequate voting shares transparency obligations. The said duty is furthermore also cancelled if other shareholders, members and beneficial owners have already provided the legal person or partnership with the necessary information.

Beyond legal persons under private law and registered partnerships, the GWG also imposes beneficial ownership transparency obligations on trusts, foundations that have no legal personality and serve the founders' self-interest, and other legal structures that are similar to the structure or function of such foundations,[514] on the condition that the trustee or fiduciary has a place of residence in Germany or, if the trustee or fiduciary is a legal entity, is domiciled in Germany. According to section 21 paras. 1 and 2, trustees and fiduciaries must obtain and hold information on the ownership of the trust, foundation or similar structure that they administer, keep this information updated, and communicate it in electronic form and without undue delay to the agency in charge of the beneficial ownership register. According to section 21 paras. 1 b and 2, they must also inform the register if the trust, foundation or similar structure is renamed, dissolved or no longer required to register.

2. *Definition of "Beneficiary" and "Effective Control"*

Section 3 para. 1 defines the beneficial owner as the natural person who ultimately owns or controls the contract partner, or the natural person on whose initiative a transaction is ultimately carried out or a business relationship is ultimately established. Without being exhaustive, the law provides examples of natural persons that constitute beneficial owners in this sense.

Section 3 para. 2 s. 1 specifies the meaning of beneficial ownership in the case of legal persons (except for foundations) and other companies that are not listed on an organised market in the EU or the European Economic Area and that are not subject to transparency requirements under EU law as regards voting shares or to equivalent international standards. In this case, a beneficial owner is at least every person that, directly or indirectly, (i) holds more than 25% of

---

514 Section 21 para. 4 GWG authorises the Federal Ministry of Finance to specify, in agreement with the Ministry of Justice, the scope of trusts and similar legal structures covered by these obligations.

capital shares, (ii) controls more than 25% of voting rights, or (iii) in a similar way exercises control. According to section 3 para. 2 s. 2, indirect control in particular covers situations where such shares or voting rights are held by one or more legal persons or partnerships that are controlled by a natural person. According to section 3 para. 2 s. 3, control in particular means that the natural person can, directly or indirectly, exercise a controlling influence over the legal person or partnership.[515]

Section 3 para. 2 s. 5 provides that if after a comprehensive examination and provided that no facts exist that would trigger an SAR, no beneficial owner pursuant to the preceding criteria can be identified, then the contract partner's legal representative, managing shareholder or partner is deemed to be the beneficial owner.

Section 3 para. 3 specifies the beneficial owner of foundations with legal personality, fiduciary structures through which assets are administered or distributed and similar legal structures. In these cases, a beneficial owner is: (i) any natural person who acts as trustor (settlor), trustee or protector; (ii) any natural person who is a member of the foundation's board; (iii) any natural person who has been designated as a beneficiary; (iv) if the natural person who will be the beneficiary has not been designated yet, the group of natural persons for the benefit of whom the estate shall be managed or distributed; (v) any natural person who, in any other way, directly or indirectly, exerts a controlling influence on the estate's management or the distribution of returns; and (vi) any natural person who can directly or indirectly exert a controlling influence over a legal person or partnership that is a member of the board of the foundation or that has been designated as beneficiary of the foundation.

3. *Definition of "Information"*

According to section 19 para. 1, legal persons, registered partnerships and trustees are required to obtain, hold and register the following information on the beneficial owner: (i) first and last name, (ii) date of birth, (iii) place of residence, (iv) the nature and extent of the economic interest; and (v) nationality. According to section 19 para. 3, information on the nature and extent of the economic interest must show why the person is a beneficial owner,

---

515 For the meaning of a controlling influence, see section 3 para. 2 s. 4 GWG and section 290 paras. 2–4 HGB. It is established notably where a person (i) holds the majority of the company's voting rights, (ii) has the right to appoint or dismiss the majority of members of the management or supervisory body that determines the company's financial or business policy, (iii) due to an agreement with the company or according to the company's statute has the right to determine the company's financial or business policy, or (iv) from an economic point of view bears most of the company's risks and chances, if the company serves a tightly limited and clearly defined goal of that person.

in the case of legal persons (with the exception of foundations)[516] and registered partnerships requiring information about: (i) the person's share in the entity, in particular the extent of capital or voting shares; (ii) the exercise of control in any other way, in particular due to an agreement between the person and a shareholder or between multiple shareholders or due to the person's entitlement to appoint legal representatives or members of executive bodies of the company; or (iii) the person's function as the company's legal representative or managing partner.

4. *Special Rules for Entities with a Cross-Border Dimension*

According to section 20 para. 1 s. 2, the obligation to obtain beneficial ownership information and communicate it to the beneficial ownership registry also applies to entities which are established abroad once they agreed to acquire ownership of real estate in Germany, provided that they did not yet communicate the required information to an equivalent register of another Member State.

According to section 21 para. 1 s. 2, the above obligations of trustees and fiduciaries also apply to those who are domiciled or established abroad if, for the trust, foundation or similar legal structure, they enter into a business relationship with a contract partner that is domiciled in Germany or agree to acquire ownership of real estate in Germany; according to section 21 para. 1 s. 3; the above obligations do not, however, apply if the trustee or fiduciary has already communicated the required information to an equivalent register of another Member State where the trustee or fiduciary is domiciled or established or where the trusts, foundation or similar legal structure entertains a business relationship with a contract partner that is established in this Member State.

B. BENEFICIAL OWNERSHIP REGISTRIES

1. *Scope and General Procedure*

The obligation to communicate the entirety of the above-described information on the beneficial owner to the national beneficial ownership registry in principle applies to all legal persons, registered partnerships and, to the extent that they are domiciled in Germany, to trustees of trusts and similar legal structures. Section 20 para. 2 s. 2 does however provide exceptions to this obligation. It is deemed to have been met if the beneficial ownership

---

516 As regards the communication of the economic interest of beneficial owners of trusts, foundations and similar structures, the trustee must designate the natural persons specified in section 3 para. 3 GWG; see above section VI.A.1.b.

information can, via the beneficial ownership register,[517] already be retrieved electronically from the commercial register,[518] the register of partnerships,[519] the register of cooperatives,[520] the association register[521] or the business register.[522] The obligation to communicate to the beneficial ownership register is also deemed to have been met for companies that are listed on an organised market that allows supervised trading in financial instruments in a Member State of the EU or the European Economic Area,[523] and for companies subject

---

517 Electronic access to these registers via the beneficial ownership register is enabled by section 22 para. 1 GWG.

518 For commercial partnerships (*Offene Handelsgesellschaften*) and partly limited commercial partnerships (*Kommanditgesellschaften*), see sections 8, 106 and 162 para. 1 HGB, providing the name, date of birth and place of residence of each partner. For stock corporations (*Aktiengesellschaften*), see sections 81 and 106 Stock Corporation Act (Aktiengesetz, AktG), providing notably the identity of members of the board and the name and place of residence of the members of the supervisory board. For limited liability companies (*Gesellschaften mit beschränkter Haftung*), see sections 7, 8 and 40 para. 1 s. 1 Limited Liability Companies Act (Gesetz betreffend die Gesellschaften mit beschränkter Haftung, GmbHG), providing notably the shareholders' name, date of birth and place of residence, and the relevant percentage interest in the share capital. According to section 40 para. 1 s. 2 GmbHG, "[i]f a shareholder is himself a company, then in the case of registered companies the list shall include the business name, registered office, the relevant register and number of the entry in the register, in the case of non-registered companies their shareholders including family name, given name, date of birth and place of residence under a summarising designation."

519 Section 3 para. 2 and section 5 para. 1 of the Partnerschaftsgesellschaftsgesetz (Partnership Companies Code) for partnerships of members of independent professions.

520 Sections 10 and 11 Cooperatives Act (Genossenschaftsgesetz, GenG) for cooperatives (*Genossenschaften*).

521 Section 55 BGB for associations (*Vereine*).

522 Section 8b HGB and section 22 para. 1 s. 1 GWG. See in particular section 40 para. 1 Wertpapierhandelsgesetz (WpHG, Securities Trading Act) for disclosures of significant voting rights in domestic issuers of securities. For securities that have been issued by an issuer whose country of origin is Germany, section 33 para. 1 WpHG provides that whosoever, through acquisition, sale or by any other means, reaches, exceeds or falls below 3%, 5%, 10%, 15%, 20%, 25%, 30%, 50% or 75% of voting rights from shares in the issuer belonging to him must without undue delay communicate this to the issuer and the Federal Financial Supervisory Authority. According to section 34 para. 1 WpHG, for the purpose of calculating the aforementioned threshold the following are also in particular taken into account: voting rights in the issuer that are held by a subsidiary of the registrant, voting rights held by a third party for the account of the registrant, and voting rights that can otherwise be exercised by the registrant. According to section 38 paras. 1 and 2 WpHG, the duty to communicate also applies to persons who directly or indirectly hold instruments that entitle them to acquire shares and resulting voting rights (in particular options, futures contracts and swaps). Similarly see section 20 paras. 1, 2 and 4 AktG for the disclosure of significant shareholding in stock corporations. When more than one quarter or the majority of the shares, or the majority of voting rights, in a stock corporation having its seat in Germany belongs to another enterprise, this enterprise must notify the company, which must then publicly disclose this ownership interest.

523 See section 2 para. 11 WpHG; section 12 of the Decree on the ascertainment of notification, communication and publication duties according to the Securities Trading Act (Verordnung zur Konkretisierung von Anzeige-, Mitteilungs- und Veröffentlichungspflichten nach dem Wertpapierhandelsgesetz).

to transparency requirements under EU law as regards voting shares or to equivalent international standards.[524]

2. *Ex Ante Verification of Accuracy*

According to section 18 para. 3, if a communication by a legal person, registered partnership, trust or similar structure is incomplete or unclear, the agency in charge of the beneficial ownership register can request the communicating entity to provide the necessary information within a reasonable time. The law does not provide for an ex ante verification of the accuracy of the information provided before it is entered into the register. However, according to section 18 para. 3a, the register can, on a case-by-case basis, communicate information and documents to the authority competent for investigating and sanctioning violations of beneficial ownership transparency obligations, in particular if the register suspects that the information provided is incorrect or incomplete, thereby potentially triggering an administrative investigation into the case.[525]

3. *Ex Post Review of Accuracy*

The law envisages that entries in the beneficial ownership register can be verified by inquiring into the veracity of the information held by the disclosing entity. To this end, section 20 para. 5 and section 21 para. 3 provide that the FIU as well as the competent supervisory authority are, within the framework of their duties and powers, entitled to look into, or request, the beneficial ownership information held by the respective entities. The requested information must be provided without undue delay.

Furthermore, according to section 23a para. 1, obliged entities that, for the performance of CDD, accessed information from the beneficial ownership register have to report, without undue delay, to the agency in charge of the register discrepancies which they discover between the beneficial ownership information in the register and their own findings. This includes findings to the effect that the register appears to be incomplete. The same obligation applies to supervisory authorities, to the administrative authority tasked with investigating and sanctioning violations pertaining to the beneficial ownership registry, and to the FIU,[526] provided that such duty does not adversely affect their functioning. According to section 23a para. 3, the register agency then has to review the discrepancy report without undue delay, and can, for this purpose, request necessary information and documentation from the reporting

524 See Directive 2004/109/EC on the harmonisation of transparency requirements in relation to information about issuers whose securities are admitted to trading on a regulated market.
525 Section 56 para. 1 nos. 55 and 61 and para. 5 s. 2 GWG; section 47 para. 1 OWiG.
526 Section 23a para. 1 s. 3 and section 23 para. 1 s. 1 no. 1(a) and (b) GWG.

person as well as from the respective registered entity. According to section 23a para. 4, it must forward the discrepancy report together with all relevant documentation to the authority competent for investigating and sanctioning violations of beneficial ownership transparency obligations if it reaches the conclusion that information contained in the register is not accurate or if, due to factual uncertainty, it is unable to conclude the review. The fact that information is subject to review must, according to section 23a para. 6, be shown in the register.

C. ACCESS TO BENEFICIAL OWNERSHIP INFORMATION

1. *Access by FIU and Other Authorities*

According to section 23 para. 1 s. 1 no. 1, the following authorities are allowed to access the beneficial ownership register: (i) the supervisory authorities and the authority competent for investigating and sanctioning violations of beneficial ownership transparency obligations; (ii) the FIU; (iii) the Federal Office for Economic Affairs and Export Control and other agencies tasked with responsibilities of foreign trade law;[527] (iv) the criminal justice authorities; (v) the Federal Central Tax Office and the local tax authorities,[528] (vi) the authorities tasked with the investigation, prevention and removal of dangers;[529] (vii) courts; and (viii) authorities and corporations under public law that perform public auctions.

2. *Access by Obliged Entities*

According to section 23 para. 1 s. 1 no. 2, access to the beneficial ownership register is also authorised for obliged entities to the extent that they demonstrate that such access is necessary for the fulfilment of their CDD obligations.

According to section 23 para. 2 s. 1, upon request by the beneficial owner, the agency in charge of the beneficial ownership register shall partially or completely restrict access to the register if the beneficial owner demonstrates that, after a balancing of interests and in view of all circumstances of the particular case, the interests of the beneficial owner that are worthy of protection oppose the provision of access. According to section 23 para. 2 s. 2, an interest in this sense is established if facts justify the assumption that the provision of access would expose the beneficial owner to the risk of becoming a victim of a fraud,

527 See section 13 Foreign Trade and Payments Act (Außenwirtschaftsgesetz, AWG).

528 See section 6 para. 2 no. 5 AO.

529 This, *inter alia*, includes police authorities when acting outside the context of a criminal investigation.

abduction, hostage-taking, extortion, homicide or intentional causing of bodily harm, or criminal threats, or if the beneficial owner is a minor or incapable.[530] According to section 23 para. 2 s. 4, access by obliged entities to the register cannot however be restricted in respect of credit institutions, financial service institutions, payment institutions and electronic money institutions, insurance undertakings and notaries.

3. *Access by Interested Third Parties*

According to section 23 para. 1 s. 1 no. 3, access to the beneficial ownership register is finally also authorised for all members of the public. However, according to section 23 para. 1 s. 2, in this case access shall only be granted to the name and the nature and scope of the beneficial owner's economic interest, the month and year of his or her birth, the country of residence and nationality, unless the complete date of birth or the complete place of residence is already accessible through other public registers. Furthermore, access to the register on the basis of section 23 para. 1 s. 1 no. 1 can be partially or completely restricted if the beneficial owner demonstrates preponderant interests as described above. In order to access information, section 23 para. 3 requires that users must first sign up with the register; this condition is meant to ensure an adequate balance between transparency needs and privacy and data protection rights of affected persons, not least by averting abusive access to the register.[531]

VII. SANCTIONS

A. SANCTIONS FOR MONEY LAUNDERING

1. *Requirement of a Conviction for a Predicate Offence*

According to section 261 StGB, conduct can constitute money laundering only if the assets originate from one of the listed predicate offences.[532] The court must establish the presence of the main factual elements of the predicate offence. For this purpose, a conviction of the predicate offender is neither necessary nor sufficient.[533] Rather the court must establish at least in broad outline the presence of a predicate offence, in order to exclude beyond reasonable doubt that the assets were acquired legally or that they originate from a crime that is not a predicate offence. In this case, it is not necessary for the court to establish

530 See sections 263, 239a, 239b, 253, 255, 211, 212, 223, 224, 226, 227, 240 and 241 StGB.
531 BT-Drucksache 19/13827, p. 86.
532 See above section II.B.1.a.i.
533 KG, NStZ-RR 2013, 13.

the identity of the victims of the predicate offence or specify to what extent individual victims suffered economic damage.[534] Insofar as it is established beyond reasonable doubt that the assets originate from a predicate offence, it is also not necessary for the court to establish which of several possible types of predicate offences were at the source, or to establish the identity of the predicate offender, the place of commission of the predicate offence or the exact modality of its commission.[535]

2. *Forms of Sanctions*

Section 261 paras. 1 and 4 StGB provides that intentional money laundering can be sanctioned by three months' to five years' imprisonment, and in aggravated cases[536] by six months' to 10 years'. According to section 261 para. 5 StGB, grossly negligent money laundering is punished by imprisonment of up to two years or a fine. While section 261 para. 1 StGB does not explicitly mention the possibility of a fine, it results from section 46 and section 47 para. 2 StGB that intentional money laundering will, in principle, be sanctioned by a fine and not by imprisonment if, in light of the seriousness of the offence and the level of culpability of the offender, a punishment of six months' imprisonment or more would not be appropriate. Furthermore, according to section 41 StGB, if the offence led to the actual or attempted enrichment of the offender, a fine can be imposed in addition to a custodial sentence, provided that, in view of the offender's personal and financial circumstances, this seems appropriate. Section 40 para. 2 StGB specifies that the amount of a fine is calculated *per diem* and in this respect on the basis of the offender's average daily net income. In addition, according to section 70 para. 1 StGB, if the offence was committed in abuse of the offender's profession or business, or in gross breach of his or her attendant duties, the court can issue an order disqualifying the offender from exercising that profession or business for a period of one to five years, and in exceptional cases indefinitely, if there is a specific danger that he or she will commit further serious crimes of such type. According to section 262 and section 68 StGB, the court may in addition order supervision of the offender's conduct if it imposes a custodial punishment of at least six months and there is a danger that the person will commit further crimes. Such supervision will, in principle last for a minimum of two and a maximum of five years; it can in particular include court directions not to engage in specific activities which may be misused for criminal purposes.[537]

534 BGH, judgment of 15 August 2018 – 5 StR 100/18, at paras. 25–26.

535 BGH NStZ 2016, 538.

536 See above under II.B.3.

537 Section 68b para. 1 s. 1 no. 4 and section 68c para. 1 StGB; OLG Hamm, NStZ-RR 2010, 90; T Fischer, Strafgesetzbuch, 67th ed., C.H. Beck 2020, §68b para. 7.

3. *Confiscation*

– Confiscation of the Instruments and Products of Money Laundering

Section 74 paras. 1 and 2 and section 261 para. 7 StGB provide for the confiscation of means and objects of money laundering. Means are notably the assets that the perpetrator used to hide the proceeds of crime,[538] while objects are the assets produced by the laundering.[539] According to section 74a StGB, if the instrument or object belongs to a person other than the perpetrator or an accessory, its confiscation is permitted if this person (i) by being at least grossly negligent contributed to the object's involvement in a criminal offence or (ii) in knowledge of the circumstances that would have allowed its confiscation acquired it in a reprehensible way. If the confiscation of an instrument or object of the offence is not possible because the perpetrator or accessory disposed of it, consumed it or in any other way frustrated its confiscation, the court can, according to section 73c StGB, order the confiscation of a corresponding amount of money.

– Confiscation of Proceeds of Crime

Section 73 StGB provides for the confiscation of anything that the perpetrator or an accessory obtained through or for a criminal offence, including the fruits of such proceeds and any surrogates that the perpetrator or accessory acquired through the sale of what he or she had initially obtained, as a compensation for its destruction, damaging or loss, or by virtue of an obtained right. Section 73 thereby covers any benefit that the perpetrator received from the commission of a crime, which includes both the proceeds directly resulting from a crime as well as rewards for a crime received from a third person.[540] In the case of money laundering, section 73 thereby covers any proceeds that the money launderer received for the laundering, but not the product of money laundering (such as a bank account balance produced by the laundering of cash), which, as stated above, is instead confiscated under sections 74 and 74a StGB as an object of the crime.[541]

In addition to confiscation for the criminal offence that formed the primary object of a criminal process, section 73a StGB provides for the extended

538 K Altenhein, in U Kindhäuser/U Neumann/H-U Paeffgen (eds.), Strafgesetzbuch, 5th ed, Nomos 2017, §261, para. 146.

539 BGH NJW 2019, 533, 535–536; BGH, judgment of 23 January 2019 – 5 StR 143/18, at para. 56; BGH NJW 2019, 2182, 2183; see also BT-Drucksache 18/9525, p. 66.

540 BGH NStZ-RR 2019, 22; BGH NJW 2019, 2182, 2183; M Köhler, Die Reform der strafrechtlichen Vermögensabschöpfung, NStZ 2017, pp. 503–504.

541 BGH NJW 2019, 2182, 2183–2184.

confiscation of other objects of the perpetrator or accessory if it is established that they were obtained through or for other criminal offences. As a consequence, if a person is convicted of money laundering, the court will also confiscate property that is not the proceeds of the respective money laundering if it is established that this property originated from other crimes of the convicted person. As a determination to this effect does not require that a particular crime is identified as the source of the respective assets, section 73a essentially lowers, for the purpose of confiscation, the evidential standard, though the court must still be fully convinced of the other assets' criminal origin.[542]

Section 73b StGB specifies that confiscation shall be ordered against another person (that is, somebody who was neither the perpetrator nor the accessory, which could also be a legal entity or commercial partnership)[543] if this other person (i) obtained anything through the criminal offence and the perpetrator or accessory had acted for this other person; (ii) obtained it at no cost or without legal cause, or if the other person knew or should have known that the object originated from a criminal offence; or (iii) inherited or otherwise obtained it by virtue of inheritance law. The preceding causes (ii) and (iii) are however not applicable if the object, before having been obtained by the other person, had been acquired by a third person against payment and with legal cause and this third person did not know and should not have known that the object originated from a criminal offence. If the other person, under the preceding conditions (ii) and (iii), instead of the object that was initially obtained through the criminal offence (directly from the perpetrator or accessory, or through several intermediate transactions that may involve *bona fide* intermediaries)[544] obtained another object the value of which corresponds to that of the initial object, or if the other person obtains fruits of this object, these shall equally be confiscated. Confiscation under the preceding conditions (ii) and (iii) can also be ordered of any surrogates that the other person acquired through the sale of what he or she had initially obtained, as a compensation for its destruction, damaging or loss, or by virtue of an obtained right.

According to section 73c StGB, if the confiscation of what was obtained is not possible, or, as regards surrogates, not feasible, the court shall order the confiscation of a corresponding amount of money. Confiscation of an amount of money shall also be ordered to the extent that the current value of a confiscated object falls short of what was initially obtained. As regards the determination of

---

542 BGH NStZ 2019, 271; BR-Drucksache 418/16, p. 71; G Trüg, Die Reform der strafrechtlichen Vermögensabschöpfung, NJW 2017, p. 1915.

543 BGH NJW 2000, 297, 299–300; M Köhler/C Burkhard, Die Reform der strafrechtlichen Vermögensabschöpfung, NStZ 2017, p. 666.

544 BGH NJW 2000, 297, 300; OLG Hamburg, NStZ 2005, 584–585; M Köhler/C Burkhard, Die Reform der strafrechtlichen Vermögensabschöpfung, NStZ 2017, pp. 667–668.

what was obtained, section 73d StGB clarifies that expenses of the perpetrator, accessory or of the third person must be deducted. This shall however in general not apply for expenses spent for the commission or preparation of the criminal offence (for example bribes paid for the conclusion of a contract or investments for illegal sales of goods). Section 73e StGB specifies that the confiscation of what was obtained for or through the offence, or of surrogates, or of a corresponding amount of money is precluded insofar as compensation claims of the victim have been fulfilled or are otherwise barred. As regards a person other than the perpetrator or accessory,[545] confiscation is also precluded insofar as the value of what this person initially obtained no longer exists within his or her assets, except if the person, at the moment of losing this value, knew or due to gross negligence ignored the circumstances that would have justified a confiscation.

– Confiscation from Legal Entities

Under German law, criminal responsibility only extends to natural persons. Section 74e StGB therefore provides special rules for the confiscation of objects that are used for or are the result of a criminal offence and belong to a legal entity or partnership. It specifies that if the director or another person who represents or manages a legal entity or commercial partnership, or supervises or controls the management, commits an act that would justify the confiscation of an object of crime, his or her act is attributed to the legal entity or partnership. As a result, an object of money laundering that belongs to a legal entity or commercial partnership can be confiscated not only if members of the senior management committed the offence, but also if they acquired the object for the entity or partnership and in doing so were at least grossly negligent regarding the criminal origin of the object. In contrast, as regards proceeds of a crime committed by an employee (wholly or at least in part) for the benefit of a legal entity or partnership, their confiscation does not depend on the internal status of the perpetrator.[546] Resulting from section 73c para. 1 s. 1 no. 1 StGB, if anybody, in committing the crime, acted for a legal entity or partnership (for example as a sales agent) and the entity or partnership received a benefit from the crime, this benefit must be confiscated.[547]

---

545 Regarding a loss of enrichment of the perpetrator or accessory, see section 459g para. 5 s.1 StPO.

546 M Köhler/C Burkhard, Die Reform der strafrechtlichen Vermögensabschöpfung, NStZ 2017, p. 666.

547 See A Eser/F Schuster, in A Eser et al. (eds), Schönke/Schröder, Strafgesetzbuch, 30th ed., 2019, §74e, para. 1; M Köhler, Die Reform der strafrechtlichen Vermögensabschöpfung, NStZ 2017, p. 501.

– Non-conviction-based Confiscation

Section 76a para. 1 StGB provides for the confiscation of the proceeds of a proven criminal offence, or that were the object of a proven criminal offence, if no particular person has been prosecuted or convicted for the offence, for example because the perpetrator is on the run.[548] According to section 76a para. 2, the confiscation of the proceeds of a criminal offence is allowed even if the prosecution of the offence is time-barred. Going further, section 76a para. 4 StGB allows for the confiscation of an object even if it cannot be attributed to a particular criminal offence, provided that it can be established that the object originated from one of the listed types of offences, which include terrorism financing, intentional money laundering and some other serious offences that are typically linked to organised crime. For this purpose, section 437 of the Code of Criminal Procedure specifies that the criminal origin of the object can be established in particular based on a gross disparity between the object's value and the legal income and also having regard to the circumstances under which the object was detected. If the claim of a criminal origin of assets is accordingly substantiated, confiscation will only be averted if the interested person explains the assets' legal origin.[549]

4. *Statistics*

According to federal statistics for the year 2018, 240 persons were convicted for intentional money laundering in the form of concealment of criminal assets, and 35 persons in the form of having acquired, kept or used such assets. In the same year, 49 persons were convicted for an aggravated case of money laundering, and 403 for grossly negligent money laundering.[550] While the statistics do not specify the value associated with these convictions, they do provide the type and level of sanctions imposed on convicted persons. 92 adults were convicted to a prison sentence for concealment (of which 77 were suspended sentences) and 134 to a fine, 14 for acquiring, keeping or using criminal assets (of which 12 were suspended) and 21 to a fine, 35 for aggravated cases (of which 25 were suspended) and 11 to a fine, and 35 for grossly negligent money laundering (of which 33 were suspended) and 354 to a fine. As for those adults convicted to a prison sentence of more than two years, seven pertained

548 M Köhler, Die Reform der strafrechtlichen Vermögensabschöpfung, NStZ 2017, p. 499.

549 BR-Drucksache 418/16, p. 104; G Trüg, Die Reform der strafrechtlichen Vermögensabschöpfung, NJW 2017, p. 1916.

550 Statistisches Bundesamt, Rechtspflege Strafverfolgung, Fachserie 10 Reihe 3, 2019, p. 36–39.

to concealment, one to the acquisition, keeping or use, and eight to aggravated cases.[551]

B. SANCTIONS FOR VIOLATIONS OF PREVENTIVE MEASURES

1. *Money Laundering by Violating Preventive Obligations*

Insofar as an employee of the company is directly involved in the respective transaction and is aware of the illicit origin of the assets, and by processing the transaction deliberately violates preventive obligations in order to enable the transaction, this employee is him- or herself liable for money laundering, either as a principle offender or, depending on the scope of his or her involvement, for aiding and abetting the client. In contrast, the question of possible liability for omission by failing to conform with preventive obligations is relevant primarily as regards employees who are not personally involved in the processing of illicit transactions, but due their role within the obliged entity (in particular as a member of the board who is responsible for AML or as a compliance officer)[552] are under a general obligation to prevent money laundering within the company. As already explained above, it is currently not clear whether the law recognises the criminal liability of obliged entities' employees for money laundering by omission.[553] Thus it cannot be said with certainty to which extent the deliberate omission to perform adequate preventive measures would, even if it enables the transfer of illicit assets, constitute intentional money laundering.

As regards the potential liability of employees involved in the processing of the transaction, one must also have regard to section 261 para. 5 StGB, which, as already explained, stipulates criminal liability for grossly negligent money laundering.[554] An employee can thus be criminally liable if, in light of the circumstances, the origin of the assets as being the proceeds of a predicate offence is blatant and the employee demonstrates particular indifference or gross carelessness towards the origin.[555] Violations of preventive duties, notably CDD measures that are clearly inconsistent with the money laundering risk of the particular case, will often go hand in hand with cross carelessness as to the origin of assets. However, for a finding of grossly negligent money laundering it is not enough that the criminal origin of the assets was objectively blatant; the

---

551 Statistisches Bundesamt, Rechtspflege Strafverfolgung, Fachserie 10 Reihe 3, 2019, p. 176–177 and 226–227.

552 See section 4 para. 3 and section 7 para. 1 GWG.

553 See above section II.B.2.

554 See above section II.B.1.b.

555 BGH NJW 2008, 2516, 2517; BGH NStZ-RR 2019, 145, 146; OLG Hamburg NStZ 2011, 523–524.

individual employee must have been personally able to readily understand, at least in broad outline,[556] that the crimes at the source of the assets were indeed predicate offences.[557] Furthermore, the scope of section 261 para. 5 StGB with regard to obliged entities' employees is further limited by the fact that the standard of gross negligence only applies to the assets' illicit origin, whereas the offender's conduct must still be intentional. As a consequence, in cases where the employee does not personally obtain the criminal assets or provide them to a third party[558] (but merely helps the client to dispose of the assets, for example by providing advice) this employee, even if particularly indifferent or grossly careless towards the origin of the assets, will be liable for grossly negligent money laundering only if he or she is aware of the possibility that the client wants to conceal the assets from the authorities and deliberately accepts this possibility.[559] In light of this overall narrow scope of section 261 para. 5 StGB, its practical relevance as regards violations of preventive obligations by obliged entities' employees is thus limited.

2. *CDD, Reporting and Other AML-Related Obligations*

a. Special Criminal Laws against Individuals

Violations of preventive AML obligations are not explicitly criminalised under German law. The offence of "assisting in avoiding prosecution or punishment" according to section 258 StGB[560] can however be fulfilled with regard to a violation of an obliged entity's AML obligations, provided that the employee acted with the purpose or in the knowledge to impede a criminal investigation against a customer. This covers in particular the situation where an employee is actively preventing the obliged entity from filing an SAR, for example by providing false information to the competent compliance officer, or is disclosing the filing of an SAR or of an FIU information request to the suspected client. As concerns employees that are personally responsible for filing SARs to the FIU (in particular as a compliance officer or any other member of the senior management tasked with the duty of filing SARs),[561] one must furthermore assume that a violation of a reporting obligation, thus an omission, can equally give rise to criminal liability. By providing the FIU with information about

556 See above section II.B.1.b.

557 BGH NStZ-RR 2015, 13, 14.

558 See section 261 para. 2 StGB; C Nestler/M El-Ghazi, in: F Herzog/O Achtelik (eds.), Geldwäschegesetz, §261, para. 128.

559 See OLG Karlsruhe NStZ 2009, 269, 270.

560 Section 258 para. 1 StGB provides that "[w]hosoever intentionally or knowingly obstructs in whole or in part the punishment of another in accordance with the criminal law because … shall be liable to imprisonment not exceeding five years or a fine."

561 See section 7 para. 5 s. 2 and section 43 para. 3 GWG.

suspicious activities that, if confirmed, is then forwarded to the criminal justice authorities,[562] the individual in charge of an obliged entity's reporting obligation is required to actively contribute to the prosecution of offenders. Therefore, both section 258 StGB and the obligation to file SARs are meant to serve the same purpose, namely the administration of justice.[563] By withholding relevant information, the competent employee can thus be liable for assisting in avoiding prosecution, provided he or she acts with the purpose or in the knowledge to at least significantly delay prosecution or to ensure that the offender will only be punished for a lesser crime.[564]

b. Administrative Sanctions against Individuals

– Fines

For a large number of listed AML-related obligations,[565] the GWG and related legislation[566] make the intentional or grossly negligent violation of these obligations an administrative offence, and in some cases already a violation

---

562 Section 32 para. 2 s. 1 GWG.

563 See BGH NStZ 1992, 540; BGH NStZ 1997, 597–598; K Altenhein, in U Kindhäuser/U Neumann/H-U Paeffgen (eds.), Strafgesetzbuch, 5th ed., Nomos 2017, §258 para. 44, S Cramer, in W Joecks/K Miebach (eds), Münchener Kommentar zum StGB, 3rd. ed., C.H. Beck 2017, volume 4, §258 para. 17.

564 BGH NStZ-RR 2011, 43, 43; S Cramer, in W Joecks/K Miebach (eds), Münchener Kommentar zum StGB, 3rd. ed., C.H. Beck 2017, volume 4, §258 paras. 23–24.

565 Section 56 para. 2 GWG defines the following as administrative offences: (1) failing to conduct a preliminary risk analysis as part of the obliged entity's risk management, (2) failing to document, regularly review and update the entity's risk analysis; (3) failing to implement appropriate internal safeguards or failing to monitor the functioning of these safeguards or failing to update them regularly or as necessary; (4) as a gambling provider failing to operate adequate data processing systems or failing to update them; (5) failing to comply with an supervisory order requesting the implementation of particular safeguards; (6) failing to adequately record or retain CDD data (including the results of an examination, the reasons considered and a plausible explanation of the assessment result) or failing to do so correctly or completely; (7) failing to retain CDD documentation or other evidence for a period of five years; (8) as a parent company, failing to devise uniform group-wide precautions, procedures and measures; (9) as a parent company, failing to ensure that the uniform group-wide obligations and measures are effectively implemented; (10) as a parent company, failing to ensure that group companies situated in another EU Member State comply with the local AML legal requirements; (11) as a parent company, failing to ensure that group companies domiciled in a third country with lower AML/CTF standards adopt adequate measures to effectively counter the risk of money laundering and terrorist financing, or failing to inform the supervisory authority about the measures taken; (12) contravening a supervisory order requesting a parent company to ensure that group companies do not establish business relationships or perform transactions in a particular third state; (13) as a group company failing to implement group-wide measures; (14) in violation of standard CDD obligations failing to adequately identify the contracting party or a person acting on her behalf, or failing to verify whether the person acting for the contracting party is authorised to this effect; (16) in violation of standard CDD obligations failing to verify whether the contracting party

is acting on behalf of a beneficial owner; (17) in violation of standard CDD obligations failing to identify the beneficial owner; (18) in violation of standard CDD obligations failing to obtain information on the purpose and nature of the business relationship or failing to evaluate this information; (19) in violation standard CDD obligations failing to correctly establish whether the contracting party or the beneficial owner is a PEP, a family member or a close associate; (20) in violation of standard CDD obligations failing to continuously and correctly monitor a business relationship; (21) in violation of standard CDD obligations failing to adequately determine the extent of CDD measures in accordance with the respective risk of money laundering or terrorist financing; (22) failing to demonstrate that they have applied risk-adequate standard or simplified CDD measures; (23) as an estate agent failing to comply with applicable standard CDD requirements; (24) as an insurance agent failing to notify the insurance undertaking about cash premium payments of more than €15,000 per year; (25) in violation of standard, simplified or enhanced CDD obligations establishing, continuing or failing to terminate a business relationship or performing a transaction; (26) in violation of standard CDD obligations failing to identify the contracting party, person acting on her behalf or beneficial owners in due time; (27) as an estate agent failing to identify the contract parties in due time; (28) despite reasons for doubt about the continuing accuracy of previously obtained identification data failing to carry out a new identification; (29) in violation of standard CDD obligations failing to properly collect the required identification information about a natural person, legal entity or partnership; (30) in violation of standard CDD obligations failing to establish the name of the beneficial owner; (31) in violation of simplified CDD obligations failing to ensure the monitoring of transactions and business relationships to an extent that enables the detection of unusual or suspicious transactions; (32) failing to perform required enhanced CDD measures in cases where a higher risk of money laundering or terrorism financing might be present; (33) in violation of enhanced CDD obligations failing to obtain approval of senior management before establishing or continuing a business relationship in cases where a higher risk of money laundering or terrorism financing might be present or when the contacting partners are politically exposed persons, their family members or close associates; (34.) in violation of enhanced CDD obligations failing to take measures to identify the origin of assets in cases where a higher risk of money laundering or terrorism financing might be present or when the contacting partners are politically exposed persons, their family members or close associates; (35) in violation of enhanced CDD obligations failing to conduct enhanced ongoing monitoring of a business relationship in cases where a higher risk of money laundering or terrorism financing might be present or when the contracting partners are PEPs, their family members or close associates; (36) in violation of enhanced CDD obligations, in the case of a business relationships or transactions involving high-risk third countries failing to obtain required information, including on the origin of assets, and their intended use; (37) in violation of enhanced CDD obligations, in the case of business relationships or transactions involving high-risk third countries failing to obtain senior management approval; (38) in violation of enhanced CDD obligations, in the case of business relationships or transactions involving high-risk third countries failing to conduct enhanced monitoring; (39) in violation of enhanced CDD obligations, in the case of particularly complex, large or unusual transactions failing to adequately examine the transaction and its background; (40) in violation of enhanced CDD obligations, in the case of a particularly complex, large or unusual transactions failing to conduct enhanced ongoing monitoring of the underlying business relationship; (41) in violation of enhanced CDD obligations failing to gather sufficient information about the respondent of a cross-border correspondent relationship; (42) in violation of enhanced CDD obligations failing to obtain the approval of senior management for establishing a cross-border correspondent relationship; (43) in violation of enhanced CDD obligations, in the case of cross-border correspondent relationships failing to determine and document responsibilities pertaining to compliance with CDD requirements; (44) in violation of enhanced CDD obligations failing to take measures within a correspondent relationship against shell banking or payable-through accounts; (45) contravening a supervisory order requesting enhanced CDD measures regarding particular business relationships or transactions; (46) in the case of an online gambling provider, admitting a player without first setting up a player account in his or her name; (47) in the case of an online gambling provider, accepting deposits or other refundable monies; (48) in the case of an online gambling provider, allowing transactions of the player to the obliged entity through channels other than those authorised by the law; (49) in the case of an online gambling provider, failing to notify the supervisory authority about payment accounts that receive monies from players; (50) in the case of an online gambling provider, carrying out transactions to the player through channels other than those authorised by the law; (51) in the case of an online gambling provider, failing to sufficiently specify the reason of payment to a player despite a request by the supervisory authority; (52) in the case of an online gambling provider, failing to fully identify the player in due time; (53) delegating the performance of CDD measures to a third party domiciled in a high-risk third country; (54) failing to provide additional information in due time to the beneficial ownership registry after having been requested to do so by the register; (55) failing to obtain, correctly and completely retain and update beneficial ownership information of a private legal entity or commercial partnership and correctly and completely notify it to the register; (56) failing to notify the beneficial ownership register correctly and completely about changes to the registered entity's or partnership's name, merger, dissolution or change of legal status; (57) without having been authorised to this effect by the notifiable entity, electronically communicating beneficial ownership information to the register; (58) as beneficial owner of a notifiable legal entity or commercial partnership or as its shareholder, provided this shareholder is directly controlled by the beneficial owner, failing to correctly, completely and in due time provide this legal entity or commercial partnership with the required beneficial ownership information; (59) as a shareholder of notifiable legal entities or partnerships failing to respond correctly, completely and in due time to their requests by the notifiable entity or partnership for beneficial ownership information, or failing to inform them completely, correctly and in due time about changes of the beneficial owner; (60) as a notifiable entity or partnership failing to document beneficial ownership information requests made to its shareholders or failing to document the information thereby obtained; (61)) as administrator of a trust or trustees of a foundation or similar legal structure failing to obtain, correctly or completely retain, update beneficial ownership information and correctly and completely notify it to the register; (62) as administrator of a trust or trustee of similar structures failing to inform the register correctly, completely, and in due time, about the trust's or structure's change of name, dissolution or about the fact that it no longer qualifies as a notifiable entity; (63) as a notifiable entity failing to rectify incorrect notifications to the register; (64) under false pretence gaining permission to access the beneficial ownership register or otherwise gaining unlawful access to it; (65) as an obliged entity failing to report to the beneficial ownership register discrepancies between the register's content and the obliged entity's own finding; (66) as an obliged entity which reported possible discrepancies to the beneficial ownership register or as an entity affected by such report failing to provide the agency in charge of the register upon request with information and documentation, or failing to do so in due time; (67) as an obliged entity failing to completely, correctly and in due time respond to an information request by the FIU; (68) as an obliged entity failing to completely and in due time respond to an order of provisional measures by the FIU; (69) as an obliged entity failing to correctly, completely and in due time submit an SAR to the FIU; (70) failing to file an SAR without undue delay after having lawfully performed a suspicious transaction; (71) disregarding a prohibition by the supervisory authority on exercising a particular business or profession or on performing executive management functions; (72) in the case of a credit institution, payment institution or electronic money institution, failing to correctly, completely and in due time respond to a request of a supervisory authority about the payment account of a gambling provider or player; (73) failing to completely, correctly and in due time respond to information requests by the competent supervisory authority, or failing to completely, correctly and in due time provide requested documentation; and (74) failing to tolerate a supervisory inspection.

by simple negligence.[567] Offences are usually sanctioned by the competent supervisory authority within its discretion.[568]

According to section 56 para. 1 s. 2 and para. 2 s. 2, an offence, when committed intentionally, may be punished by a fine of up to €150,000,[569] when committed through gross negligence by a fine of €100,000, and by a fine of

566 See section 332 para. 4f VAG, which notably covers violations of the obligation to identify the allottee, to verify whether he or she is a PEP, and to obtain senior management approval before any payout to such a person.

567 This concerns notably the following cases: (i) failing to appoint a member of the senior management responsible for AML; where applicable, failing to appoint a money laundering compliance officer or a deputy; failing to comply with a supervisory order requesting the appointment of a money laundering compliance officer or failing to do so in due time; where applicable, failing to appoint a group compliance officer; entering, continuing or performing a business relationship or transaction that involves a high-risk third country despite being unable to comply with enhanced CDD obligations; performing a reported transaction within a delay of three working days after its submission without being authorised to this effect by the FIU or a prosecutor; unlawfully disclosing the filing of an SAR, a criminal investigation or an FIU information request to a third party (section 56 para. 2 GWG); (ii) violations by credit institutions and financial service institutions as well as by financial holding companies of their obligation to apply and keep up to date adequate data processing systems to identify business relationships and individual transactions that are particularly complex, large or unusual or that do not have an obvious economic or lawful purpose (section 56 para. 11b in conjunction with section 25h para. 2 KWG), (iii) violations by credit institutions to perform adequate measures for examining such transactions in order to monitor and assess the risk of money laundering, terrorism financing or other crimes endangering the institution's assets (section 56 para. 2 no. 11c in conjunction with section 25h para. 3 KWG), (iv) violations by credit institutions, payment institutions and electronic money institutions of their obligation to apply required standard CDD measures when issuing electronic money irrespective of a threshold amount and to keep records about issued rechargeable electronic money carriers (section 56 para. 2 no. 11d in conjunction with section 25i paras. 1 and 3 KWG, section 64 para. 3 nos. 9 and 10 ZAG), and violation of payment institutions and electronic money institutions to have adequate safeguards, including data processing systems, to comply with their AML obligations (section 64 para. 3 no. 5a in conjunction with section 27 para. 1 ZAG). See also section 56 para. 4 KWG, which defines as administrative offences intentional and negligent violations of Regulation (EU) 2015/847 on information accompanying transfers of funds. This covers notably violations by payment service providers to transmit the required information about the payer and payee; adequately and in due time verify the information; implement procedures to detect missing information; implement effective risk-based procedures for determining whether or not to execute a transfer of funds lacking the required payer and payee information; take adequate measures where another payment service provider repeatedly fails to provide the required information and report the failure to the competent supervisory authority; or record the required information for up to five years (section 56 para. 4 KWG in conjunction with As 4(1), (2) and (4), 7, 8 and 16(1)(2) of Regulation 2015/847).

568 Section 36 para. 1 no. 1 and section 47 para. 1 OWiG; section 56 para. 5 s. 1 GWG. See also section 73b para. 1 BRAO for attorneys at law, section 76 para. 8 StBerG for tax advisors, and section 69a para. 1 PAO for patent attorneys.

569 For violations of Regulation (EU) 2015/847 see section 56 para. 6 no. 3 KWG (€200,000) for violations by individuals and section 56 paras. 6a and 6c KWG for sustained violations by legal entities and partnerships (€5 million, 10% of annual turnover or up to twice the economic benefit derived from the contravention).

€50,000 when committed through simple negligence; these thresholds may be exceeded if the perpetrator's economic benefit from the offence exceeds that maximum.[570] Section 56 para. 3 adds that a fine can be up to €1 million or "up to twice the economic benefit derived from the contravention" if the contravention was "serious, repeated or systematic", provided that it was also committed intentionally or through gross negligence. Under these qualifying conditions, if the individual is him- or herself an obliged entity providing certain financial services (that is, falling under the categories of credit institution, financial services institution, payment institution or electronic money institution, another financial undertaking, insurance undertaking, insurance agent or investment management company),[571] the fine can be up to €5 million, which again may be exceeded if the perpetrator's economic benefit exceeds that maximum.[572]

- Other Supervisory Measures

Besides being fined, violations of AML duties can also result in further supervisory measures. As regards individuals who are themselves obliged entities and whose activity requires a licence, section 51 para. 5 s. 1 GWG authorises the competent supervisory authority to prohibit their business or profession or withdraw the licence if they intentionally or negligently and in a sustained manner violated obligations under the GWG or regulations or supervisory orders adopted or issued on its basis,[573] and continued this conduct despite having been cautioned by the supervisory authority.[574]

According to section 36 para. 1 of the Banking Act, instead of revoking the licence of a credit institution or financial service institution, the Financial Services Supervisory Authority can demand the dismissal of executive management officials responsible for a sustained violation by the institution of obligations under the GWG or of related regulations or orders; it can furthermore prohibit such officials from exercising their activity for another legal person and,

---

570 Section 17 para. 4 OWiG.

571 Section 2 para. 1 nos. 1–3 and 6–9 GWG.

572 See section 17 para. 4 OWiG.

573 As regards trust or company service providers and trustees, section 51 para. 5b s. 3 GWG furthermore adds that the competent supervisory authority can prohibit the provision of such services if facts indicate that the beneficial owner does not have the necessary suitability or reliability.

574 For agents of payment institutions and agents of electronic money institutions, payment institutions and electronic money institutions domiciled in another EEA contracting state, and independent traders that sell or re-exchange electronic money of a credit institution, insofar as these businesses are subject to supervision by authorities in another EU Member State or EEA contracting state, section 51 para. 5a GWG provides that the Financial Supervisory Authority can adopt temporary and adequate measures to remedy serious violations if the foreign authority does not adopt the necessary measures or if its measures are insufficient.

in the case of some violations, for any obliged entity.[575] Responsibility in this sense does not require that the executive management official personally committed the contravention, but rather that a contravention which was committed by another employee could have been prevented, for example through adequate internal controls or other organisational measures.[576] According to section 36 para. 2 of the Banking Act, the Federal Financial Supervisory Authority can furthermore demand the dismissal of executive management officials and prohibit such officials from exercising their activity for another legal person if they personally, intentionally or through gross negligence violated obligations under the GWG or regulations or supervisory orders adopted or issued on its basis, and continued with this conduct despite having being cautioned by the supervisory authority. According to section 36a para. 1 s. 4 of the Banking Act, in the case of particular contraventions by an obliged entity (notably as regards the prohibition in certain dealings with shell banks),[577] the Financial Services Supervisory Authority can prohibit a company official who was responsible for the violation from assuming an executive management position with any obliged entity for up to two years, even if this official had not been acting in an executive management position.

Similarly, the Financial Services Supervisory Authority can, instead of revoking the licence of a capital management company, demand the dismissal of executive management officials responsible for serious, repeated or systematic violations by the company of obligations under the GWG or of related regulations or orders; it can also prohibit any other individual who was acting within the company and was responsible for such violations from exercising their activity.[578] The Financial Services Supervisory Authority can furthermore order the dismissal of members of the executive management of investment management companies, and prohibit these individuals from carrying out their activity in the future, if the executive management or any of its members violated obligations under the GWG in a sustained manner.[579]

The competent supervisory authority can also order the dismissal of executive management officials or other key officials of an insurance undertaking and prohibit them from carrying out their activity if, intentionally or negligently,

---

575 See section 36 para. 1 s. 3 in conjunction in particular with sections 25i (violations of standard CDD obligations concerning electronic money), 25k (violation of enhanced CDD obligations concerning foreign exchange and factoring) or 25m (violations of certain prohibitions regarding shell banking) KWG. See also BR-Drucksache 963/96, p. 91.

576 R Fischer/C Müller, in K-H Boos/R Fischer/H Schulte-Mattler (eds.), Kreditwesengesetz, volume 1, 5th ed., C.H. Beck 2016, §36, at para. 10.

577 Section 25m KWG; see also sections 25i and 25k KWG and Regulation (EU) 2015/847.

578 Section 40 para. 1 in conjunction with section 39 para. 3 no. 7 KAGB.

579 Section 119 para. 5 no. 2, section 128 para. 4 no. 2, section 147 para. 5 no. 2, and section 153 para. 5 no. 2 KAGB.

they committed serious, systematic or repeated violations of the GWG or of regulations or orders adopted or issued on its basis.[580]

The Financial Services Supervisory Authority can furthermore demand the permanent or temporary dismissal of executive management officials of payment institutions and electronic money institutions, and prohibit them from carrying out their activity in other such institutions or obliged entities if they are responsible for a serious, repeated or systematic violation of AML obligations by the institution. Against any other individuals who are responsible for the violation, such an order can only be temporary. Executive management officials can also be ordered to be dismissed and prohibited from carrying out their activity with other institutions if they personally committed intentional or grossly negligent violations of AML obligations and continued with this conduct after having been cautioned by the supervisory authority.[581]

For other obliged entities than those mentioned above, section 51 para. 5 s. 2 GWG specifies that the competent supervisory authority can impose on a member of the executive management or on another employee of the obliged entity a temporary prohibition on occupying an executive management position with obliged entities if this individual intentionally or negligently and in a sustained manner violated obligations under the GWG or regulations or supervisory orders adopted or issued on its basis and continued this conduct despite having been cautioned by the supervisory authority.[582]

- Publication

According to section 57, the competent authority must for the duration of five years publish fines and measures that were imposed as a result of a contravention of the GWG or of provisions adopted on the basis of it on this authority's website or on a joint website, and must therein state the type and nature of the contravention and the individuals, entities or partnerships who were responsible. The publication must be suspended or alternatively can be anonymised if it (i) would infringe the personality rights of individuals or would for other reasons constitute a disproportionate disclosure of personal data, (ii) would endanger the stability of the financial markets of Germany or of another EEA contracting state, or (iii) would endanger an ongoing investigation; the publication must not happen if suspension or anonymisation would not prevent the endangerment of financial markets or ensure proportionality.[583]

---

580 Section 303 para. 2 no. 4 VAG.

581 Section 20 para. 1 in conjunction with section 13 para. 2 no. 5 and section 20 para. 3 ZAG.

582 As regards trust or company service providers and trustees, section 51 para. 5b s. 2 GWG adds that the competent supervisor can dismiss members of the senior or executive management if facts indicate that they do not have the necessary suitability or reliability.

583 See also section 319 para. 2 s. 3 VAG.

c. Sanctions against Legal Entities

– Fines

Fines for legal entities and partnerships can, according to section 56 para. 1 s. 2 and para. 2 s. 2, be up to €150,000 when committed intentionally, €100,000 when committed through gross negligence, and €50,000 Euro when committed through simple negligence. According to para. 3 s. 1, the fine can amount up to €1 million or up to twice the benefit derived from the contravention if the contravention was serious, repeated or systematic, provided that is was also committed intentionally or through gross negligence. Under those qualifying conditions, according to section 56 para. 3 s. 3 and 4, fines for providers of financial services that are legal entities or partnerships can be up to €5 million or up to 10% of the entity's or partnership's total turnover in the previous fiscal year (whichever is higher).[584]

– Other Supervisory Measures

Section 35 para. 2 no. 6 of the Banking Act gives the Financial Services Supervisory Authority the power to revoke the licence of a banking institution or financial services institution if this institution violated its obligations under the GWG or the Banking Act or regulations or orders adopted or issued on the basis of these Acts in a sustained manner. Similarly, the licence of an insurance undertaking, payment institution, electronic money institution or investment management company can be revoked if it violated its obligations under the GWG in a serious, repeated or systematic manner.[585] For all other obliged entities, the aforementioned 51 para. 5 GWG provides corresponding powers.

3. *Statistics*

As required by law, supervisory authorities keep statistics *inter alia* on the number of cases in which, through supervisory audit measures or otherwise, they detected a violation of AML-related administrative obligations, and the number

584 For the calculation of the total turnover, see section 56 para. 3 GWG: if the fined obliged entity is a parent company or subsidiary, the total turnover is not calculated on the basis of turnover of the sole obliged entity, but on the basis of the total turnover according to the consolidated financial statements of the parent company covering the largest number of group-affiliated companies.

585 Section 304 para. 3 no. 4 VAG; section 13 para. 2 no. 5 ZAG; section 39 para. 3 no. 7 and section 44 para. 5 no. 4 KAGB.

of sanctions and other measures imposed for these violations.[586] For 2018, the Federal Financial Supervisory Authority (with regard to its competence for credit and financial service institutions, payment service institutions, electronic money institutions, agents of payment institutions, agents of electronic money institutions, insurance undertakings and capital management companies) became aware of violations in 1,711 cases, of which 297 appeared in the performance of supervisory audit measures. They resulted in 25 fines in the range of €1,750 to €3.5 million.[587] As regards supervisory action undertaken by *Länder* authorities, that is regarding most of those obliged entities not covered by the Federal Financial Supervisory Authority, supervisory authorities identified violations in 994 cases, all of which except 29 were appearing within the performance of supervisory audit measures. They resulted of 162 fines,[588] and in 13 cases in in a licence withdrawal.

C. CUMULATION OF MONEY LAUNDERING AND OTHER AML-RELATED SANCTIONS

If an act constitutes at the same time an administrative offence and a criminal offence, only the latter is applied.[589] This does not, however, cover cases where an administrative and a criminal offence, while resulting from distinct acts, are merely closely linked in time and space. One situation (such as a grossly negligent money laundering that is accompanied by a violation of documentation duties) can thus give rise to both criminal and administrative sanctions. If a court has imposed a sanction for an administrative offence and this decision has become final, the same situation cannot be prosecuted any longer for a criminal offence; a prosecution for the criminal offence, however, remains possible if the administrative sanction was imposed only by a supervisory authority.[590]

---

586 The following numbers are provided online by the Federal Ministry of Finance at https://www.bundesfinanzministerium.de/Content/DE/Standardartikel/Themen/Internationales_Finanzmarkt/Finanzmarktpolitik/2019-07-03-aufsichtstaetigkeit-geldwaeschegesetz.html.

587 The level of fines was distributed as follows: 5 x €1,750, 6 x €3,850, 1 x €6,500, 1 x €12,500, 9 x €19,450, 1 x €25,000, 1 x €150,000, and 1 x €3,500,000. The statistics also specify that the Federal Financial Supervisory Authority carried out altogether 2,762 audit measures, 90 of which were on-site checks.

588 The level of fines was distributed as follows: 28 fines of up to €500, 12 fines of €500–1,000, 31 fines of €1,000–5,000, 9 fines from €5,000–10,000, and 82 fines of more than €10,000 (adding up to €152,987 in total). The statistics specify the following number of supervisory audit measures by *Länder* authorities: 283 (of which 2 on-site) for insurance agents; 815 (of which 2 on-site) for external accountants, tax advisors and tax agents; 887 (of which 185 on-site) for estate agents; 1,302 (of which 313 on-site) for gambling service providers; 2,710 (of which 503 on-site) for traders in goods.

589 Section 21 para. 1 s. 1 OWiG.

590 See section 84 para. 2 s. 1 OWiG.

VIII. THE USE OF CASH AS A MEANS OF PAYMENT

National law does not provide for an upper limit on cash transactions. The latest available statistics cover the year 2017 and specify that 74% of transactions were carried out in cash. The share of cash with regard to absolute transaction turnover was, however, more limited and amounted to only 45%.[591]

IX. SUMMARY, EVALUATION AND FUTURE PERSPECTIVES

The German AML framework is extensively aligned to the EU rules and FATF recommendations. It therefore also shares many structural weaknesses of these frameworks.[592] At the same time, some deficiencies of national law are rooted in difficulties with coherently accommodating supranational demands within Germany's legal culture and institutional structure.

To begin with, and crucially, German law still suffers from considerable uncertainty in its understanding of the objectives of AML. Current jurisprudence sees the criminal offence of money laundering as primarily serving the investigation and prosecution of predicate offences and the recovery of ill-gotten gains. In contrast, while the protection of the integrity of financial institutions is in principle recognised as relevant, this further aim has so far not significantly impacted on the shape of criminal policy. Very much in line with this understanding of AML, criminal investigations for money laundering in Germany are regularly marked by a strong focus on identifiable predicate offences.[593] A recent decision of the Federal Constitutional Court has further reinforced German law's focus on the predicate offence, deciding that when ordering house searches within criminal proceedings for money laundering, authorities must at least in broad outline already specify a possible predicate offence. Such investigative measures, and by implication similarly intrusive measures, are therefore not admissible as long as the investigative authorities lack any information about the source of the suspect assets.[594] The offence of money laundering and thus AML are in this way essentially relegated to tools for addressing predicate offences. Though more recently there seems to be a change of awareness in this respect,[595] policymakers and criminal justice authorities

591 Deutsche Bundesbank, Zahlungsverhalten in Deutschland 2017, p. 8.

592 On these see *infra* Conclusions.

593 See also V Zoppei, Anti-Money Laundering Law: Socio-Legal Perspectives on the Effectiveness of German Practices, Springer 2017, p. 189 f.

594 BVerfG NJW 2020, 1351, 1353.

595 See Bundesministerium der Finanzen, Erste Nationale Risikoanalyse 2018/2019, 2019, p. 25; Bundesministerium der Finanzen, Strategie gegen Geldwäsche und Terrorismusfinanzierung, 2020, p. 5.

may often still find it difficult to fully appreciate the wrongfulness of money laundering as a danger that is substantially different from the predicate crime. As long as legislation and criminal justice authorities emphasise the predicate crime as key to the offence of money laundering, German law will continue to see money laundering as being merely ancillary to the predicate offence. In doing so, it fails to appreciate the dangers that result from the inflow of criminal proceeds into financial institutions and, through them, into wider society. So far, law and practice remain rather unconcerned by the possibility that criminal actors and especially organised crime can penetrate the national economy by increasingly engaging in business activities. Money laundering is therefore rarely, if at all, understood as a tool of criminals to expand their power in society. While the actual scope of this danger is an empirical question that, for Germany, undoubtedly requires more research, it is in any case hardly satisfactory that current law as well as policy debates have so far not usually addressed this danger.

In light of the aforementioned focus of German law on the detection and investigation of predicate offences, two weaknesses of the current national framework are rather logical consequences. First, directly following from the strongly predicate-offence-oriented shape of the German (and indeed supranational) definition of money laundering, criminal proceedings against complex and professional types of laundering are difficult to conduct and thus apparently rare. Instead judicial practice focuses rather often on subordinate agents within a chain of transaction, not least on individuals that, against remuneration, allow their personal account to be used by criminal groups.[596] The more recent criminalisation of self-laundering under German law is likely to enhance a trend towards the punishment of low-complexity laundering activities, indicating that, as with the above-described uncertainty about the aims of AML, weaknesses of the national framework can in many cases partially also result from misunderstandings in the dialogue between supranational standard-setters and national policymakers. If not complemented by future legislative guidance to the contrary, both the law's continuing strong emphasis on the predicate offences and a far-reaching criminalisation of self-laundering will provide little incentive to competent authorities to put time and resources into the investigation of complex and professional laundering schemes. For the latter to happen, the law would need to considerably reduce the relevance of the predicate offence in the definition of the offence of money laundering. At the same time, crucially, the law should make it clear that the seriousness of money laundering, and thus the setting of investigative priorities, should depend not so much on the seriousness of the predicate offence, but primarily on the scope and complexity of the dissimulation efforts.

---

596 See also K Bussmann, Abschlussbericht zur 'Geldwäschestudie' der 'Nationalen Risikoanalyse Bekämpfung von Geldwäsche u. Terrorismusfinanzierung- Ermittlungs- u. Strafverfahren' of 31 October 2019.

Second, German law's limited appreciation of the integrity of financial institutions as a primary aim of AML can also explain why national law has, at least in the past, arguably paid insufficient attention to the supervision of obliged entities. For if AML is primarily taken to serve the prosecution of predicate offences, respect for AML obligations by obliged entities and thus the quality of AML supervision is effectively only of indirect usefulness, namely insofar as the level of AML compliance is then ultimately meant to strengthen the ability of criminal justice authorities to investigate predicate crime. From this standpoint, it could then be argued that AML supervision is in this respect either not very necessary (as the effectiveness of investigations in predicate crime will in most cases ultimately not depend on the effectiveness of AML, but rather on the overall strength of the criminal justice system) or at least not the best way to spend limited resources (as it might then seem more rational to allocate sparse resources to criminal justice authorities rather than to AML supervisory authorities). If, in contrast, the integrity of financial institutions is recognised as an objective of AML the relevance of which is at least equal to the investigation of predicate offences, it would seem much more plausible to emphasise the importance of an effective supervision and allocate resources accordingly. In a similar vein, German law puts rather little emphasis on AML violations by obliged entities' employees, as most administrative offences to this effect require at least the comparatively high subjective standard of gross negligence and furthermore as there are no special criminal offences that focus on deliberate AML violations. This confirms the impression that the defence of obliged entities against the influence of criminal actors is, in German law, still not so much seen as a goal in itself, but foremost merely as an instrument to impede the commission of predicate offences and to facilitate their investigation.

Besides those deficiencies, which ultimately result from uncertainties about the objectives pursued, German law also encounters problems pertaining to the alignment between supranational demands and the structure of its national legal architecture. In this respect, the creation of an administrative FIU outside the confines of the criminal justice system was an important step in the right direction which responded to the limits that exist in the German criminal procedure law as regards the collection of criminal intelligence. Being located outside the criminal procedure allows the FIU to become a key institution for the confidential and expeditious gathering of financial intelligence while at the same time limiting secrecy in criminal proceedings. The creation of a dedicated body for the collection of financial intelligence appears to be important not least because of the openness and global integration of the German economy,[597] which makes it vulnerable to foreign criminal investments and, for AML

[597] See Bundesministerium der Finanzen, Erste Nationale Risikoanalyse 2018/2019, pp. 31–33.

purposes, requires the extensive and swift cross-border sharing of information. Such sharing will usually be much slower and, in light of the transparency of criminal proceedings, also much less effective if performed within the confines of criminal procedure law. German AML law does not however yet fully accept the consequences which, from the standpoint of its national constitutional law, result from the intelligence nature of the FIU. In order to ensure the constitutionality and thus sustainability of the FIU, the legislator will therefore need to provide appropriate limits to the FIU's operational competence and powers. In light of the above considerations, the FIU's operational competence needs to be limited to the analysis of organised crime, terrorism financing and equivalently serious criminality only. Furthermore, its powers will need to be specified and appropriately limited especially with regard to the scope of the FIU's authority to secretly request personal data from obliged entities and its power to share information with other authorities. In a similar vein, German AML law does not yet sufficiently accommodate the comparatively high constitutional data protection standards in other areas of AML, especially as regards the powers of obliged entities to automatically process large stocks of personal data and to secretly share personal data with other obliged entities. The lack of sufficient safeguards both as regards the FIU and as regards obliged entities not only gives rise to the risk of fundamental rights violations, but also, by making AML law vulnerable to legal challenges, threatens the ultimate viability of the national framework.

Very similar to many other jurisdictions, German law is also confronted with doubts about the effectiveness of its SAR reporting regime and the underlying ability of obliged entities to detect money laundering. The recently created Anti-Financial Crime Alliance public-private partnership aims to address this deficit by providing better strategic information to obliged entities in order to improve the performance of their CDD. While this initiative potentially constitutes an important step, one must not overlook the fact that, for obliged entities' CDD to become effective, competent authorities, not least supervisors and the FIU, will need to show considerable commitment to assisting obliged entities.[598] Cooperation between competent authorities and only a small number of obliged entities on a limited number of financial crime risks will not suffice to broadly improve the risk-detection capacity of obliged entities. Instead, this requires cooperation mechanisms that go well beyond the sporadic provision of strategic information and instead provide obliged entities with operational guidance, where appropriate on a case-by-case basis, in the managing of concrete risks. At any rate, obliged entities' AML obligations should not serve as an excuse for insufficient resourcing of competent authorities, but

[598] In this vein also Bundesministerium der Finanzen, Strategie gegen Geldwäsche und Terrorismusfinanzierung, 2020, p. 9.

should instead be designed in a more collaborative way. Currently, German law however provides little detail in this respect. While the law authorises supervisory authorities to determine particular types of business relationships or transactions as constituting enhanced risks, it so far provides no specific mechanisms that would ensure adequate operational collaboration between supervisors and obliged entities. As importantly, while supervisors, the FIU and criminal justice authorities are required to collaborate for the purpose of AML, the law provides little detail in this respect, not least as regards the operational cooperation between supervisors and the FIU. As long as the law does not specify permanent and effective information gateways and assign clear responsibilities to particular authorities, it is unlikely that supervisors will have the necessary crime-related information to regularly provide obliged entities with adequate guidance or, alternatively, that the FIU will play this role.

Beyond the lack of appropriate information gateways to assist obliged entities in the performance of their CDD, the contribution of the private sector to AML is furthermore hampered by continuing uncertainty about the actual rationale of SAR reporting. Both the German legislator and supervisors now seem to emphasise a more quantitative approach to reporting, as they require obliged entities to report indications of money laundering and terrorism financing before the performance of extensive CDD inquiries. This approach can lead to greater transparency as regards the risk exposure of obliged entities and is in this respect potentially helpful. Due to the resulting numbers of SARs received by the FIU, it however also makes it likely that reporting obliged entities will, in most cases, not receive feedback from the FIU as regards the merits of a specific reported business relationship or transaction. Obliged entities are then usually left in the dark about the quality of their findings, which ultimately weakens rather than strengthens CDD and reporting.

Finally, the German AML framework is heavily influenced by the country's federal structure, a fact that becomes particularly obvious with regard to obliged entities in the non-financial sector when looking at the multitude of different supervisory authorities at *Länder* level that are competent in this regard. The same applies to criminal justice authorities, which, for the most part, are organised at *Länder* level. On the one hand, a decentralised institutional structure is not a weakness in itself. In fact, and as just observed with regard to the FIU's treatment of vast amounts of SARs, a high level of centralisation can be an obstacle in particular for cooperation between competent authorities and obliged entities, but also for cooperation between competent authorities. On the other hand, decentralised competences carry the risk that related information is scattered around numerous authorities who therefore fail to understand the bigger picture of a particular business relationship or transaction. German law requires AML supervisory authorities to extensively collaborate with each other and with the FIU. However, little detail is again provided on how this should work in practice, which makes it unlikely that collaboration will, in most cases, go beyond more or less frequent strategic exchanges between those authorities. Similarly, a significant part of the information held by *Länder* police authorities will not be accessible to the FIU within one central information gateway. Accumulating information in central structures is of course not a remedy that would by itself ensure greater collaboration. The added operational value of such structures will indeed often be outweighed by the resulting drawbacks. In particular, wide-ranging access to sensitive data can weaken accountability and thus render the mistaken and even abusive use of the data more likely, thereby threatening the interests of affected individuals and potentially also compromising investigations. Instead of overly centralising supervisory functions or providing more far-reaching direct access of the FIU to *Länder* police data, the legislator could provide for more specific collaborative mechanisms that assign clear responsibilities to different authorities. These could include in particular a framework for case-by-case cooperation between the FIU and supervisory authorities that would, where useful, give the FIU the responsibility to bring together and disseminate information of relevance for multiple supervisors. FIU secondments to *Länder* police authorities, and vice versa, could further help to bridge the gap between state and federal level while respecting *Länder*'s interest in protecting the integrity of their data and at the same time, as a basis for trust-based collaboration, assigning individual accountability for the handling of shared data to the seconded agent.

THE ANTI-MONEY LAUNDERING ARCHITECTURE OF ITALY

Giovanna Amato

I. INTRODUCTION

A. HISTORY OF ANTI-MONEY LAUNDERING IN THE COUNTRY

The history of anti-money laundering (AML) efforts in Italy involves different instruments, both repressive and preventive.

In the international context, Italy is the first country to have adopted repressive legal tools against money laundering. Law (L.) 18 May 1978, no. 191 first introduced the offence of money laundering into the Italian Criminal Code (CC).[1] In creating this offence, the Italian legislator wanted to confront the serious phenomenon of terrorism in Italy in the 1970s. According to the original provision, art. 648-*bis* criminalised – in cases of complicity in the predicate offence – acts and facts aimed at the *replacement* of money and things of value coming from aggravated forms of robbery, extortion or kidnapping with the intent of extortion with other money or things of value, in order to obtain a profit for oneself or others or to help the perpetrator of the predicate offence to assure him/herself that profit. The real criminological target in criminalising these acts and facts was not properly and only the replacement of money itself, but rather offences like robbery, extortion or kidnapping, which represent typical forms of economical provision for terrorism. The aim of this "emergency reform" was to extend the scope of certain offences, with the result that the Italian doctrine has spoken of money laundering as "a special form of fencing and/or of abetment".[2]

---

1 The provision was introduced after art. 648, concerning the offence of fencing. Art. 648 criminalises anyone who, in order to procure profit for himself/herself or for others, purchases, receives or conceals money, assets or property derived from any crime, or is involved in acquiring, receiving or concealing such money, assets or property.

2 Angelini, *Il reato di Riciclaggio. Aspetti dogmatici e problemi applicativi*, Giappichelli, Turin, 2008, 3; Castaldo/Naddeo, *Il denaro sporco. Prevenzione e repressione del riciclaggio*, Cedam, Padua, 2010, 69; Palombi (a cura di), *Il riciclaggio dei proventi illeciti. Tra politica criminale e diritto vigente*, ESI, Naples, 1996, 38.

It was not until L. 19 March 1990, no. 55 that the offence of money laundering became autonomous and the repressive AML system further developed in the Italian Criminal Code,[3] with the introduction of a new offence at art. 648-*ter*, which criminalises the *use* of money, goods and other benefits of criminal provenance. Art. 648-*ter* defines the use of money, goods and other benefits of criminal provenance as the act of anyone who uses money, assets or other benefits derived from crime in their economic or financial activities.

The current expression of the offence of money laundering is the result of L. 9 August 1993, no. 328 which ratifies and gives effect to the Council of Europe's 1990 Convention on Laundering, Search, Seizure and Confiscation of the Proceeds of Crime.

L. 15 December 2014, no. 186 finally introduced art. 648-*ter.*1, which contains the provision of self-money laundering, into the Italian Criminal Code.

Legislative Decree (L.D.) 231/2007 added art. 25-*octies* to L.D. 8 June 2001, no. 231, which provides for corporate criminal liability in relation to "[f]encing, money laundering and use of money, goods and benefits of illicit origin".[4] It also added to the Criminal Code art. 648–*quater*, which provides for the confiscation of assets that are the product or profit of the money laundering offences established by arts. 648-*bis* and 648-*ter*.[5]

L.D. 15 January 2016, no. 8 decriminalised some offences, with the declared intention of reducing the size of the penal system by introducing administrative sanctions, rendering the AML system more effective. In particular, any offence previously punished with solely a fine or penalty was decriminalised.

---

3 According to the Italian doctrine, this restyling concerned not only the existing provision of art. 648-*bis*, but also the whole AML system, which was rethought in a "two-stage development" sense: on the one hand, the money laundering itself, as a form of replacement, and on the other hand, recycling. See Castaldo/Naddeo, *Il denaro sporco. Prevenzione e repressione del riciclaggio*, Cedam, Padua, 2010, 71; Palombi (a cura di), *Il riciclaggio dei proventi illeciti. Tra politica criminale e diritto vigente*, ESI, Naples, 30.

4 The possibility to punish companies for the commission of a money laundering offence was first introduced by L. 16 March 2006, no. 146, later substituted by the general provision of art. 63.3 of L.D. 231/2007, which ratified and implemented the UN Convention against Transnational Organized Crime adopted by the General Assembly in 2001. The provision originally only punished companies for the commission of *transnational* money laundering. On the topic see Castaldo/Naddeo, *Il denaro sporco. Prevenzione e repressione del riciclaggio*, Cedam, Padua, 2010, 403 ff.; Mezzetti/Piva (a cura di), *Punire l'autoriciclaggio. Come, quando, perché*, Giappichelli, Turin, 2016, 41 ff.; Cappa/Cerqua, *Il riciclaggio del denaro. Il fenomeno, il reato, le norme di contrasto*, Giuffrè, Milan, 2012, 101 ff.; Angelini, *Il reato di Riciclaggio. Aspetti dogmatici e problemi applicativi*, Giappichelli, Turin, 2008, 17.

5 Art. 648-*quater* also provides for the confiscation of equivalent sums of money, assets or other property, which the offender has available, including through intermediaries, for a value equivalent to the product, reward or profit of the offence. Goods may be confiscated in application of art. 240 CC. To this end, the provision gives the public prosecutor the power to take any investigative measures necessary to trace the assets, money or other property to be confiscated.

The first preventive legal tool against money laundering in Italy was L. 5 July 1991, no. 197, which contained "[u]rgent measures to limit the use of cash and bearer securities in transactions and to prevent the use of the financial system for the purpose of money laundering". It implemented Decree Law (D.L.) 3 May 1991, no. 143 and the first AML Directive. The law has been defined as "the official birth certificate of the anti-money laundering legislation in Italy",[6] setting out the new preventive framework for the fight against money laundering. Its innovative approach can be seen in the attribution to the Italian Foreign Exchange Office – which became the FIU in 2008 – of the task of identifying, through appropriate statistical analyses, irregularities that may be used as indicators of activities related to money laundering.[7]

With the entrance into force of L.D. 26 May 1997, no. 153,[8] the Italian Foreign Exchange Office became the key player in the financial efforts against money laundering. The reporting of suspicious transactions was centralised,[9] and the Foreign Exchange Office became the buffer between obliged entities and investigative authorities, like the Bureau of Anti-Mafia Investigation and the Special Foreign Exchange Unit of the Finance Police. The main purpose of the legislative intervention was the institutionalisation of the AML strategy, through the separation of the financial analysis from the investigative activity.[10]

L.D. 20 February 2004, no. 56 implemented the second AML Directive, extending the scope of the first Directive to the "non-financial" sector. It was not until L.D. 21 November 2007, no. 231 that a structured preventive AML system and the introduction of criminal sanctions for the violations of AML duties in Italy came into effect. This L.D. implemented the third AML Directive.[11]

Art. 15 of L. 12 August 2016, no. 170 contains the guiding principles and criteria for the implementation of that law and for the implementation of the

6 Bruni/Masciandaro (a cura di), *Mercati finanziari e riciclaggio. L'Italia nello scenario internazionale*, Egea, Milan, 1998, 101 ff.

7 *Ibid.*, 102, also refer to the duty to collaborate of bank intermediaries and to the obligation to register, in a standardised form, all transactions exceeding 20 million lire on IT archives to be compulsorily established among the authorised intermediaries. See also Palombi (a cura di), *Il riciclaggio dei proventi illeciti. Tra politica criminale e diritto vigente*, ESI, Naples, 28. With particular reference to the duty to collaborate, see Manna (a cura di), *Riciclaggio e reati connessi all'intermediazione mobiliare*, Utet, Turin, 2000, 367 ff.

8 It definitively implemented in Italy the first Directive on prevention of the use of the financial system for the purpose of money laundering.

9 According to art. 3.2 of Law 197/1991, the SARs shall be transmitted by financial intermediaries to the local Office of the Chief of Police responsible for the area.

10 Bruni/Masciandaro (a cura di), *Mercati finanziari e riciclaggio. L'Italia nello scenario internazionale*, Egea, Milan, 1998, 122 and 143.

11 On the topic Castaldo/Naddeo, *Il denaro sporco. Prevenzione e repressione del riciclaggio*, Cedam, Padua, 2010, 253 ff.; Cappa/Cerqua, *Il riciclaggio del denaro. Il fenomeno, il reato, le norme di contrasto*, Giuffrè, Milan, 2012, 121 ff.; Palmieri, *La tutela penale della libertà di iniziativa economica. Riciclaggio e impiego di capitali illeciti tra normativa vigente e prospettive di riforma*, ESI, Naples, 2013, 134; Gambogi, *Riciclaggio e antiriciclaggio*, in *Officina del diritto*, Giuffrè, Milan, 2015.

provisions of the EU Regulation 2015/847 on information accompanying the transfers of funds. L.D. 25 May 2017, no. 90 essentially rewrites L.D. 231/2007, introducing several innovations concerning the obligations receivers, record keeping, communications to the competent authorities, the notion of the beneficial owner, customer due diligence (CDD) measures, controls, and the sanctioning system.[12] L.D. 231/2007, as replaced (but not repealed) by the recent L.D. 25 May 2017, no. 90, establishes the normative framework of the system of prevention of money laundering in Italy.

On 3 October 2019, the Council of Ministers approved Legislative Decree no. 125, which transposes into Italian law Directive no. 2018/843 of the European Parliament and of the Council on the prevention of the use of the financial system for the purpose of money laundering and terrorist financing, better known as the fifth anti-money laundering directive. The decree, which bears the date of 4 October 2019, was published in the Official Gazette on the following 26 October 2019 and entered into force on 11 November 2019. The text introduces amendments and additions to the previous Legislative Decree no. 231/2007 as amended by Legislative Decree 90/2017.

B. CURRENT CONCERNS AND REFORM AGENDA

Defining the main issues relating to AML in Italy currently requires distinguishing between repression and prevention of money laundering. In general, the debate on both aspects of the fight against money laundering is affected by the discussion on organised crime and the legal tools to prevent and fight it.

On the repression side, the debate does not focus on the offence of money laundering itself, but rather on the measures of patrimonial prevention, such as confiscation, and on the crime of external participation in the Mafia association. The Italian jurisprudence[13] and doctrine[14] deal in particular with constitutional law concerns, such as legality, proportionality and predictability, highlighted in some important decisions of the ECtHR.[15]

---

12 See the Government Act no. 389/2017 and the illustrative Report on the Decree, at www.documenti.camera.it.

13 C. Cass., Sez. Un., sentence, no. 40076, 27 April 2017, at www.penalecontemporaneo.it; C. Cass., Sez. Un., sentence, no. 111, of 30 November 2017, at www.penalecontemporaneo.it; C. Cass., Sec. I, sentence of 6 July 2017, Contrada, at www.penalecontemporaneo.it.

14 Viganò, *La Corte di Strasburgo assesta un duro colpo alla disciplina italiana delle misure di prevenzione personali*, at www.penalecontemporaneo.it; id., *Strasburgo ha deciso, la causa è finita: la Cassazione chiude il caso Contrada*, at www.penalecontemporaneo.it; Manes, *Dalla "fattispecie" al "precedente": appunti di "deontologia ermeneutica"*, at www.penalecontemporaneo.it.

15 With regard to preventive measures, see ECtHR, Grand Chamber, sentence of 23 February 2017, *De Tommaso v. Italy*, at https://hudoc.echr.coe.int, with regard to Mafia association; see ECtHR, Sec. IV, sentence of 14 April 2015, *Contrada v. Italy*, at https://hudoc.echr.coe.int.

On the prevention side, the debate that followed the recent implementation of the fourth AML Directive (4AMLD) has been superficial and mainly focused on such aspects as the reduction of the area of criminal relevance, the application of *ne bis in idem*, and the change to the normative technique. All these aspects concern the changes to the AML sanctioning system.[16] The main criticisms concern the Italian AML provision on cryptocurrency, which is considered inadequate to fully address the problem. This has led some authors to consider the possibility of criminalising virtual currency exchange under arts. 648-*bis* or 648-*ter*.1 CC.[17]

II. AIMS AND SCOPE OF AML SYSTEM

A. AIMS OF AML REGIME

Defining the precise objectives of AML requires making a distinction between the repressive and the preventive system.

The Italian Criminal Code distinguishes two kind of offences against property, based specifically on how the act is carried out: either committed with violence or committed through fraud. Even though money laundering is among the crimes against property committed through fraud, it escapes a univocal systematisation. From this perspective, money laundering is more like a multi-offence crime, and its position in the Criminal Code is merely the consequence of its origin as a special form of fencing.[18] Nowadays, property represents a secondary and eventual protection objective. The extension of the catalogue of predicate offences reveals that money laundering covers a wide range of objectives, which have as a common denominator the administration of justice.[19] Money laundering only indirectly harms the economic order, the public order and property, which has to be interpreted not just as property, but also in the dynamic sense of savings and investment. Italian doctrine and jurisprudence agree that money laundering is an offence against the administration of justice, because of its nature as a "concrete danger offence", in which the different acts must pose an obstacle to the identification of the predicate offences and of the money, goods and benefits coming from them.[20]

---

16 Giacometti/Formenti, *La nuova disciplina in materia di prevenzione del riciclaggio e di finanziamento del terrorismo*, at www.penalecontemporaneo.it.

17 Sturzo, *Bitcoin e riciclaggio 2.0*, at www.penalecontemporaneo.it; see also among the practitioners Di Vizio, *Le cinte daziarie del diritto penale alla prova delle valute virtuali degli internauti*, at www.uif.bancaditalia.it.

18 See above, section I.A.

19 See above, section II.B.1.a.i.

20 Castaldo/Naddeo, *Il denaro sporco. Prevenzione e repressione del riciclaggio*, Cedam, Padua, 2010, 76 ff.; Angelini, *Il reato di Riciclaggio. Aspetti dogmatici e problemi applicativi*,

With regard to the preventive tools against money laundering, their purposes have been much clearer from outset, given the fact that the EU Directives set out the framework for achieving their objectives. Nevertheless, the Italian system maintains a strong specificity with regard to AML objectives. In addition to the protection of the integrity of the financial system, the Italian AML law that implements the 4AMLD, through the coordinating role assigned to the National Anti-Mafia and Counter-Terrorism Bureau, shows that the fight against organised crime is one of its main purposes. This purpose does not expressly arise from the text of the law (art. 2 of L.D. 90/2017 on "Purposes and principles"), but emerges from the statements of the Italian authorities involved in the fight against money laundering.[21] This statement is reinforced by the adaptation of the Italian system to the 5AMLD Directive.

B. SCOPE OF MONEY LAUNDERING

1. *Definition of Money Laundering in Criminal Law*

a. *Actus Reus*

i. Predicate Offences

Art. 648-*bis* of the Italian Criminal Code punishes, apart from cases of participation in the predicate offence, anyone who replaces or transfers money, goods or other benefits resulting from an intentional felony, or carries out other transactions in relation to them, in order to hinder the identification of their unlawful provenance.

Money, goods and benefits must originate from an intentional felony; in other words, the predicate offence cannot consist in a negligent felony or in a misdemeanour. The Italian Criminal Code distinguishes, without defining them, between felonies and misdemeanours on the basis of how they are punished. In particular, art. 39 establishes that the offence is considered either a felony or a misdemeanour depending on the type of penalty provided for that offence. In the context of crimes against property, a typical example of a misdemeanour is the purchase of things of suspicious provenance.[22] Apart from these excluded cases, there is no other limit on what may count as a possible predicate offence.

Giappichelli, Turin, 2008, 19 ff.; Cappa/Cerqua, *Il riciclaggio del denaro. Il fenomeno, il reato, le norme di contrasto*, Giuffrè, Milan, 2012, 54 ff. Among the jurisprudence, see C. Cass., sentence no. 43295, 24 November 2010, in *Ced Cass.*, RV 248949.

21 See Clemente, *Presentazione del Rapporto Annuale dell'Unità di Informazione Finanziaria per l'Italia*, 13 July 2018, 4, at www.uif.bancaditalia.it, according to whom organised crime is one of the most significant threats that the AML system is called to prevent and intercept in Italy.

22 See Fiandaca/Musco, *Diritto penale. Parte generale*, Zanichelli, Bologna, 2014, 168 ff.

ii. Definition of Money Laundering Acts

The current provision refers to three kinds of act:[23] *substitution*, *transfer* or in general any *other transaction* intended to impede the identification of the criminal origin of money, goods and other benefits.[24] *Substitution* refers to all those acts aimed at exchanging or transforming criminal proceeds with or into other goods, making difficult to trace their illicit provenance. The jurisprudence clarifies that the act is not complete when the proceeds to recycle are received, but when the substitution has been carried out and the recycled goods have been passed on.[25] *Transfer* refers to all situations – material (for example, bulk smuggling) and juridical (for example, legal negotiation) – where the criminal proceeds are made part of another person's assets.[26] Unlike substitution, in *transfer* the qualitative and quantitative composition of the criminal proceeds remains the same. The act of carrying out *any other transaction*, apart from substitution and transfer, involves attempting to impede the identification of the criminal origin of money, goods or other benefits. By including this type of act, the Italian legislator outlines money laundering as an "openly structured" offence.[27] According to the Italian jurisprudence, the obstacle does not necessarily need to be final, but it is sufficient that it makes the ascertainment of predicate offences more difficult.[28] To prove the danger that these acts might be realised, as a common requirement of the different acts, the judge should use a subsequent *prognosis in concreto* and on a partial or total *basis*, which takes into consideration some or all of the circumstances existing at the time of the action.[29] The material objects of recycling are *money*, *goods* and any other *assets* that come from an "intentional crime". In particular, the concept of *goods* coincides with that of art. 810 of the Italian Civil Code, namely with "things that can form the object of rights". The definition includes both material and intangible properties,

---

23 The offence of money laundering is a conduct offence.

24 Castaldo/Naddeo, *Il denaro sporco. Prevenzione e repressione del riciclaggio*, Cedam, Padua, 2010, 109 ff.; Gambogi, *Riciclaggio e antiriciclaggio*, in *Officina del diritto*, Giuffrè, Milan, 2015, 16; Lanzi/Insolera, *Codice penale d'impresa. Commento articolo per articolo alle norme penali per l'Impresa*, Dike Giuridica Editrice, Rome, 2015, 976.

25 Castaldo/Naddeo, *Il denaro sporco. Prevenzione e repressione del riciclaggio*, Cedam, Padua, 2010, 119 ff.; Gambogi, *Riciclaggio e antiriciclaggio*, in *Officina del diritto*, Giuffrè, Milan, 2015, 17; recently, see C. Cass., sentence no. 1857, 16 November 2016, in *Ced Cass.*, RV 269316.

26 Castaldo/Naddeo, *Il denaro sporco. Prevenzione e repressione del riciclaggio*, Cedam, Padua, 2010, 123 ff.; Gambogi, *Riciclaggio e antiriciclaggio*, in *Officina del diritto*, Giuffrè, Milan, 2015, 17.

27 Castaldo/Naddeo, *Il denaro sporco. Prevenzione e repressione del riciclaggio*, Cedam, Padua, 2010, 128 ff.; Gambogi, *Riciclaggio e antiriciclaggio*, in *Officina del diritto*, Giuffrè, Milan, 2015, 18.

28 C. Cass., 14 December 2012, no. 1422, in *Cassazione Penale*, 2013, 3530.

29 Gambogi, *Riciclaggio e antiriciclaggio*, in *Officina del diritto*, Giuffrè, Milan, 2015, 19.

like financial instruments or shares. The concept of *assets* represents any object with an economic value. The Italian doctrine underlines that the diversity and scope of the material object of money laundering – the properties mentioned above – is not devoid of problematic questions. One such question concerns the risk of overlap between money laundering and fencing, which punishes the acts of acquiring, receiving and hiding money or things resulting from a crime, and consequently the risk of losing its own objectives in protecting the same interests.[30]

The concept of things of *criminal provenance* has been interpreted in the Italian jurisprudence and doctrine in a wide sense, as covering money, goods and benefits *directly* or *indirectly* resulting from the predicate offence.[31] Consequently, the expression "things of criminal provenance" refers to the *profit*, the *product* and the *reward* of a crime. The *profit* is the economic income deriving from the commission of a crime, the *product* represents the result of the illicit activity and the *reward* is the payment received for committing the crime. Traditionally, Italian doctrine and jurisprudence have interpreted the concept of *gain* in a physical-material sense, as an effective enrichment, immediately identifiable, consequent upon the commission of the predicate offence. Recently, this has developed towards an economical meaning, including the patrimonial "non-decrease" (non-reduction of one's assets – that is, an enrichment deriving from the failure to pay taxes).[32] From this perspective, gains originating from tax evasion are usually related to licit activities and they merely represent a *lack of deprivation*, even if this property forms part of a much larger property of the perpetrator of the predicate offence, and even where its exact value cannot be identified. The evolution of the concept of *provenance*, together with an undefined catalogue of predicate offences, results in the extension of money laundering to tax crimes.[33]

---

30 This is testified, for example, by the jurisprudence, which applies the offence of money laundering in the case of licence-plates forgery. See C. Cass., sentence no. 56391, 23 November 2017, in *Ced Cass.*, RV 271553. From this point of view, in order to contain the application of money laundering, Italian doctrine takes advantage of the expression "originated from crime". See Castaldo/Naddeo, *Il denaro sporco. Prevenzione e repressione del riciclaggio*, Cedam, Padua, 2010, 142.

31 See C. Cass., sentence no. 6061, 17 January 2012, in *Ced Cass.*, RV 252701.

32 Lanzi/Insolera, *Codice penale d'impresa. Commento articolo per articolo alle norme penali per l'Impresa*, Dike Giuridica Editrice, Rome, 2015, 979; Cadoppi/Canestrari/Manna/Papa, *Diritto penale dell'economia*, vol. I, Utet, Milan, 2017, 965. Among the jurisprudence, see C. Cass., sentence no. 49427, 17 November 2009, in *Ced Cass.*, RV 246469; C. Cass., sentence no. 6061, 17 January 2012, in *Ced Cass.*, RV 252701; C. Cass., sentence no. 42120, 9 October 2012, in *Ced Cass.*, RV 253830; C. Cass., sentence no. 29452, 17 May 2013, *in Ced Cass.*, RV 256468.

33 The tax crimes contained in L.D. no. 74 of 10 March 2000 – such as fraudulent financial statements, false financial statements, omitted financial statements, issue of fake invoices, concealment or destruction of accounting documents – constitute predicate offences.

Under the Italian Criminal Code, the case of assets that originates partially from illicit gains and partially from legitimate income is irrelevant. Art. 648-*bis* is fulfilled in both cases.[34]

In accordance with its reserve clause ("apart from cases of participation in the predicate offence"), the perpetrator of the predicate offence or his/her accomplice are not punishable under art. 648-*bis*. Italian doctrine and jurisprudence use two different criteria in order to define what it means to participate in the predicate offence. On the one hand, an older interpretation, supported by minority doctrine, uses a *temporal* criterion.[35] If the offender and his/her accomplice come to an agreement on committing the offence before or during the execution of the predicate offence, they cannot be punished under art. 648-*bis*. On the other hand, the majority of doctrine and the United Sections of the Italian Court of Cassation[36] use a *causal* criterion.[37] The offender and accomplice may reach an agreement to recycle the profits resulting the offence before or during the commission of the predicate offence, but it is necessary to verify, on a case-by-case basis, whether that agreement made an effective contribution to the predicate offence, in terms of influencing or strengthening the decision to commit a crime (i.e. the predicate offence).[38]

However, the so-called "self-money laundering privilege" mentioned in art. 648-*bis* coexists with the provision of art. 648-*ter.*1, which contains the offence of self-money laundering, recently introduced by L. 15 December 2014, no. 186. Art. 648-*ter.*1, paragraph 1 CC punishes any person who, having committed or participated in committing an intentional crime, employs, replaces or transfers within economic, financial, business or speculative activities, the money, assets, property or other benefits resulting from the commission of this crime, so as to concretely hinder the identification of their criminal origin. The reference of the provision to the sentence "within economic, financial, business or speculative activities" refers to the "re-introduction" or "re-entry" into legitimate economic activities, which is the key element that distinguishes the punishable activities from those that constitute *post factum* activities, which are not punishable in light of the fundamental principle of *ne bis in idem*. Art. 648-*ter.*1, paragraph 4 CC provides that, in cases other than those described above, acts are not punishable if money, assets or other benefits are intended merely for personal use or enjoyment.[39]

---

34 The question arises rather in terms of limits on the seizing and confiscation.

35 Gambogi, *Riciclaggio e antiriciclaggio*, in *Officina del diritto*, Giuffrè, Milan, 2015, 14.

36 C. Cass., Sez. Un., 27 February 2014, no. 25191, in *Ced Cass*, RV 259587.

37 Gambogi, *Riciclaggio e antiriciclaggio*, in *Officina del diritto*, Giuffrè, Milan, 2015, 15.

38 Castaldo/Naddeo, *Il denaro sporco. Prevenzione e repressione del riciclaggio*, Cedam, Padua, 2010, 146 ff.; Gambogi, *Riciclaggio e antiriciclaggio*, in *Officina del diritto*, Giuffrè, Milan, 2015, 14; Amore, *Il punto e l'accapo sull'autoriciclaggio dei proventi delle consorterie criminali di stampo mafioso dopo le SS.UU. n. 25191 del 2014*, 13, at www.penalecontemporaneo.it.

39 See Mezzetti/Piva (a cura di), *Punire l'autoriciclaggio. Come, quando, perché*, Giappichelli, Turin, 2016; with reference to the criminal liability of enterprises, see

b. *Mens Rea*

Currently, art. 648-*bis* requires a general intent, namely knowledge and willingness, to replace or transfer money, goods or assets, or to carry out other operations that are capable of impeding objectively and *in concreto* the identification of the criminal origin of the money, goods or assets.[40] Furthermore, knowledge of the criminal provenance of the material objects is required. This means awareness that the benefits generally come from another, even unspecified, crime; thus, it is not required that the perpetrator knows precisely the legal nature and/or the definition of the predicate offence.[41] Italian doctrine highlights that the lack of specified predicate offences in the statutory definition facilitates proof of the perpetrator's awareness of the criminal origin of the money, goods or assets, especially in relation to a perpetrator who is just not part to the predicate offence and thus is not punishable under art. 648-*bis*. However, the doctrine also underlines the tension with the constitutional principle of culpability by admitting forms of *dolus in re ipsa* (inferring guilt from purely objective events) and the risk of ineffectiveness of the offence of money laundering.[42]

In the recent Italian jurisprudence,[43] there is a tendency to admit *dolus eventualis* with regard to the illicit origin of money, goods and benefits as a form of mental state of money laundering. In consideration of the fact that the different acts involve hiding that illicit origin, the mental state should at least require awareness of the possibility and acceptance of the risk of that illicit provenance, but not simply suspicion, negligence, disregard or lack of interest about it.[44]

The Italian provision on money laundering (art. 648-*bis* CC) does not refer to any form of criminal liability by omission or by negligence.

Cadoppi/Canestrari/Manna/Papa, *Diritto penale dell'economia*, vol. II, Utet, Milan, 2017, 3024; Parodi (diretto da), *Diritto penale dell'impresa*, Giuffrè, Milan, 2017, 477 ff. For a recent application, see C. Cass., sentence no. 33074, 14 July 2016, in *Ced Cass.*, RV 267459.

40 Gambogi, *Riciclaggio e antiriciclaggio*, in *Officina del diritto*, Giuffrè, Milan, 2015, 21; Castaldo/Naddeo, *Il denaro sporco. Prevenzione e repressione del riciclaggio*, Cedam, Padua, 2010, 171 ff.

41 The knowledge of the exact nature of the predicate offence can be relevant for the level of culpability of the offender, according to different provisions of the Criminal Code, such as art. 5 CC; for the relationship between intent and normative elements, according to art. 47.3 CC; and for the relationship between intent and awareness of the offence. See Fiandaca/Musco, *Diritto penale. Parte generale*, Zanichelli, Bologna, 2014, 366 ff.

42 Gambogi, *Riciclaggio e antiriciclaggio*, in *Officina del diritto*, Giuffrè, Milan, 2015, 21; Castaldo/Naddeo, *Il denaro sporco. Prevenzione e repressione del riciclaggio*, Cedam, Padua, 2010, 171 ff.

43 See C. Cass., sentence no. 8330, 26 November 2013, in *Ced Cass.*, RV 259010.

44 Gambogi, *Riciclaggio e antiriciclaggio*, in *Officina del diritto*, Giuffrè, Milan, 2015, 22; Castaldo/Naddeo, *Il denaro sporco. Prevenzione e repressione del riciclaggio*, Cedam, Padua, 2010, 178.

2. *Money Laundering by Omission*

According to a minority of the doctrine,[45] which is however followed by the courts, money laundering by omission could be abstractly possible in the form of participation by omission in the other's act of money laundering. From this perspective, bank managers and potentially others can be punished under art. 648-*bis* for participation by omission if they do not impede money laundering operations committed by their subordinates. This concept entails, on the one hand, the acknowledgment that the superior holds a guarantee position on to the superior and, on the other hand, the acceptance of an "improper omission", which is one of the two types of omission recognised in the Italian criminal law system.[46] The most recent Italian jurisprudence has stated a bank director is liable for omission in money laundering offences, because of – among other acts – the violation of the duty to report suspicious transactions.[47] In particular, anomalous transactions, the hierarchical position of the bank director, his competence in bank matters and the precision of the AML legislation would all oblige him not to authorise the transactions and to observe the duty to report, and they are all indicators of acceptance of the risk of the commission of money laundering. According to the jurisprudence,[48] *dolus eventualis* would have supported the conviction for money laundering.

3. *Aggravated Forms of Money Laundering*

Art. 648-*bis*, paragraph 2, introduces one aggravated form of the offence when the perpetrator of money laundering is a professional. There are two different problematic issues concerning this aggravated form of money laundering that have affected the Italian doctrinal debate. On the one hand, there is not definition

45 Zanchetti, *Il riciclaggio di denaro proveniente da reato*, Giuffrè, Milan, 1997, 374 ff.

46 The Italian Criminal Code distinguishes between two different forms of omission: *proper* omission and *improper* omission. The distinction is based on two criteria, namely the structure of the offence and how it is categorised. *Proper omission* is a conduct offence and is expressly included in the special part of the Criminal Code or in any other complementary legislation. *Improper omission* is an offence of result and is not expressly included in the Criminal Code. It represents the result of the combined provisions of art. 40.2 CC on the causal link, and an offence of result by commission contained in the special part of the Criminal Code. Furthermore, the possibility of carrying out an *improper omission* depends on the type of offence by commission, which has to be a free-form one, and on the possibility of recognising that the perpetrator holds a guarantee position. See Fiandaca/Musco, *Diritto penale. Parte generale*, Zanichelli, Bologna, 2014, 615 ff.

47 See C. Cass., sentence no. 9472, 14 January 2016, and C. Cass., sentence no. 29452, 17 May 2013. Both of the decisions are unpublished. For references to less recent decisions, see Manna (a cura di), *Riciclaggio e reati connessi all'intermediazione mobiliare*, Utet, Turin, 2000, 388 ff.

48 C. Cass., sentence no. 9472, 14 January 2016, and C. Cass., sentence no. 29452, 17 May 2013.

of what "professional activity" means; on the other hand, the legislation is not clear as to whether there is a causal relationship between the professional activity and money laundering.[49] The jurisprudence has not yet addressed either question.

Another form of aggravated money laundering is found in art. 71.1 of L. 6 September 2011, no. 159, the Code of Anti-Mafia Law and Prevention Measures. According to the provision, the penalty increases if a person who is subject to a personal preventive order commits the offence of money laundering during the application period of the order and for three years after.

4. *Statutes of Limitation*

In principle, money laundering is perpetrated when the offender carries out the act of substituting, transferring or performing another action intended to impede the identification of the criminal origin of money, goods and other assets.[50] The statute of limitation begins to run at the moment the offence is completed. It is 12 years (eight years in case of self-money laundering), but increases to 15 years (10 years in case of self-money laundering) if there are causes of interruption of the limitation period pursuant to art. 160 CC Examples of events that would interrupt the limitation period are judgment, an order that applies the personal precautionary measures, an order of validation of arrest, or questioning before the public prosecutor.[51]

Furthermore, it is necessary to consider that money laundering is usually made up of numerous operations, for example depositing money in a bank account followed by many withdrawals and/or transferring money to other bank accounts in order to conceal the paper trail. From a phenomenological point

---

49 For references, see Castaldo/Naddeo, *Il denaro sporco. Prevenzione e repressione del riciclaggio*, Cedam, Padua, 2010, 198. Among the Italian jurisprudence, the issues have not been subject to discussion. See C. Cass., sentence no. 43534, 24 April 2012, in *Ced Cass.*, RV 253796.

50 As already clarified, the consummation of the *replacement* does not occur when the proceeds to recycle are received, but when the substitution has been done and the recycled goods have been given back. See above, section II.B.1.a.ii.

51 Apart from felonies punishable by life imprisonment, art. 157.1 CC limits the time for the prosecution of all crimes to a period equal to the maximum penalty provided for by law, which cannot, however, be less than six years for felonies and four years for misdemeanours. It is not enough that the criminal proceedings be started before the statute of limitations ran out: it is the definitive sentence that must be handed down before the term expires. According to art. 157.2 CC, to determine the time necessary to extinguish the offence, reference shall be made only to the penalty established for the committed or attempted offence, without taking into account its reduction in the case of attenuating circumstances, or its increase in the case of aggravating circumstances. Time shall start to run from the day on which the offence was committed or, in the case of attempted or continuing offences, from the date on which the offender's activity or continuing activity ceased (art. 158 CC). See also Lanzi/Insolera, *Codice penale d'impresa. Commento articolo per articolo alle norme penali per l'Impresa*, Dike Giuridica Editrice, Rome, 2015, 982.

of view, the Italian doctrine recognises in these acts a form of "indirect money laundering".[52] The admissibility of indirect money laundering requires money laundering itself to have taken place between the predicate offences, which is feasible in view of the wide meaning of *criminal provenance*.[53] According to the majority of the Italian doctrine and the jurisprudence, when in the same factual context there are different and subsequent perpetration acts with reference to the same material object, there is a form of "crime with a progressive development"[54] or "a crime with a prolonged consummation",[55] in which the different operations follow on from each other. These interpretative solutions have an impact on the limitation period for the crime, which starts to run from each single identifiable and documentable operation or transfer. According to a minority view, admitting money laundering as a predicate offence has as its consequence the application of the self-money laundering privilege.[56] In order to settle the debate, the doctrine suggests that the Italian lawmaker should intervene.

The statute of limitation for the predicate offences does not affect the criminal liability for money laundering, according to art. 170 CC.[57] However, if the laundering act occurs after the limitation period of the predicate offence has run out, there is no liability for money laundering.[58]

5. *Jurisdictional Rules*

Art. 6 CC states that anyone – therefore citizen of any nationality – may be punished under Italian law if he/she commits a crime in the territory of Italy. The offence shall be considered to have been committed in the territory of Italy when the action or the omission has occurred there in whole or in part, or the event that is the consequence of the action or the omission occurred there. It follows that also acts of money laundering *partially* committed abroad can be punished according to the Italian Criminal Code. The jurisprudence clarifies

52 For more references see Castaldo/Naddeo, *Il denaro sporco. Prevenzione e repressione del riciclaggio*, Cedam, Padua, 2010, 164; Mantovani, *Diritto penale. Delitti contro il patrimonio*, Cedam, Padua, 2002, 254.

53 See above, section II.B.1.a.i. With regard to this specific aspect, see Zanchetti, *Art. 648* bis *c.p.*, in Crespi/Stella/Zuccalà (a cura di), *Commentario breve al codice penale*, Cedam, Padua, 2008, 1944.

54 C. Cass., sentence no. 52645, 20 November 2014, in *Ced Cass.*, RV 261624; C. Cass., sentence no. 34511, 29 April 2009, in *Ced Cass.*, RV 246561.

55 C. Cass., sentence no. 43881, 9 October 2014, in *Ced Cass.*, RV 260694; C. Cass., sentence no. 546, 7 January 2011, in *Ced Cass.*, RV 249446. For a comment on the decision, see Razzante, *Riciclaggio, operazioni bancarie e prescrizione*, in *Giurisprudenza Italiana*, 2011, 2374 ff.

56 Castaldo/Naddeo, *Il denaro sporco. Prevenzione e repressione del riciclaggio*, Cedam, Padua, 2010, 168.

57 According to this disposition, when a crime is a predicate offence of another crime, the cause that determines its extinction does not extend to the main offence.

58 See Gambogi, *Riciclaggio e antiriciclaggio*, in *Officina del diritto*, Giuffrè, Milan, 2015, 24.

that in these cases Italian jurisdiction can be affirmed when even just a *fragment* of the act has occurred in the territory of Italy, even if the events that occur in there fall far below the substantive requirements of an attempt.[59]

According to art. 9 CC, an Italian citizen who commits a crime abroad for which Italian law establishes imprisonment of not less than three years – thus covering money laundering – may be punished under Italian law provided that he/she is in the territory of Italy. According to art. 10, the foreigner who commits a crime abroad to the detriment of the Italian State or an Italian citizen for which the Italian law establishes imprisonment of not less than one year – thus also covering money laundering – may be punished under Italian law provided that he/she is in the territory of Italy and the Minister of Justice or the injured person so requests.

The Italian Criminal Code does not specify whether the predicate offences for money laundering extend to acts that occur exclusively in another country. However, the jurisprudence has clarified that the offence of money laundering is applicable when the predicate offence has been committed exclusively abroad and is an offence under Italian law.[60]

C. NON-CRIMINAL DEFINITION OF MONEY LAUNDERING

Art. 2.4 of L.D. 90/2017 contains a separate definition of money laundering, outside the criminal law, which is the reference for the AML preventive regime. In line with art. 1 4AMLD, the provision distinguishes four groups of acts that make the preventive offence of money laundering wider than the one in the Criminal Code.

There are many differences with the crime established by art. 648-*bis* CC.

In particular, according to art. 2.4(a), the following shall be regarded as money laundering: "the conversion or transfer of property, knowing that such property is derived from criminal activity or from an act of participation in such activity, for the purpose of concealing or disguising the illicit origin of the property or of assisting any person who is involved in the commission of such an activity to evade the legal consequences of that person's action". The reference to the purpose of helping whoever is involved in the criminal activity to avoid the legal consequences of his/her own actions cannot be punished under

---

59 What is necessary is that these fragments of conduct have an objective relevance, namely a material tangibility, which can be appreciable in such a way as to connect the part of the conduct carried out in Italy to that realised in the foreign country. See C. Cass., sentence no. 13085, 3 October 2013, in *Ced Cass.*, RV 259486; C. Cass., sentence no. 6151, 5 February 2014, in *Ced Cass.*, RV 258634; C. Cass., sentence no. 6001, 4 February 2014, in *Ced Cass.*, RV 258633; C. Cass., sentence no. 44837, 11 October 2012, in *Ced Cass.*, RV 254968.

60 C. Cass., sentence no. 42120, 9 October 2012, in *Ced Cass.*, RV 253830.

art. 648-*bis* CC but is potentially punishable under art. 379 CC, which covers aiding and abetting property crimes.

According to art. 2.4(b), the following shall be regarded as money laundering: "the concealment or disguise of the true nature, source, location, disposition, movement, rights with respect to, or ownership of, property, knowing that such property is derived from criminal activity or from an act of participation in such an activity". Unlike art. 648-*bis* CC, disguising relates not only to the illegal origin of goods or rights on them, but also to their "location, disposition, movement and property". The provision also refers to awareness that such property comes from criminal activity or "participation in it", although participation in the predicate offence is not punishable under art. 648-*bis* CC, because of the "self-money laundering privilege".[61]

According to art. 2.4(c), the following shall be regarded as money laundering: "the acquisition, possession or use of property, knowing, at the time of receipt, that such property was derived from criminal activity or from an act of participation in such an activity". The conduct described here covers acts that are already potentially punishable under art. 648 CC, which deals with "fencing". The provision also refers to awareness that such property comes from criminal activity or "participation in it", although the participation in the predicate offence is not punishable under art. 648-*bis* CC, because of the "self-money laundering privilege".[62]

According to art. 2.4(d), the following shall be regarded as money laundering: "the participation in, association to commit, attempts to commit and aiding, abetting, facilitating and counselling the commission of any of the actions referred to in points (a), (b) and (c)". The "association with the purpose of money laundering" is not punishable under art. 648-*bis* CC and is generally punished under art. 416 CC, which provides for "association to commit offences".[63]

According to art. 2.5, the predicate offence can also count as money laundering if it is committed abroad.

D. SCOPE OF OBLIGED ENTITIES

1. *Financial and Banking Institutions*

According to art. 3.2 of L.D. 90/2017, a wide range of natural persons and legal entities with their registered office in Italy fall under the category of "financial and banking institutions". In particular, the definition includes banks, Poste

61 See above, section II.B.1.a.i.

62 See above, section II.B.1.a.i.

63 With reference to L.D. 231/2007, see Gambogi, *Riciclaggio e antiriciclaggio*, in *Officina del diritto*, Giuffrè, Milan, 2015, 11.

Italiane SpA, providers of electronic money services,[64] payment providers,[65] movable brokerage companies,[66] savings management companies,[67] variable capital investment companies,[68] fixed capital investment (movable or real estate) companies,[69] exchange rate agents as defined by art. 201 of the Consolidated Law on Financial Intermediation (TUF, L.D. 24 May 1998, no. 58), intermediaries as defined by art. 106 of the Consolidated Banking Act (TUB, L.D. 1 September 1993, no. 385), Cassa Depositi e Prestiti SpA (a State-controlled company that sells e.g. State loans), micro-credit providers,[70] *consorzio di garanzia collettiva dei fidi* (Confidi),[71] and subjects covered by art. 2.6 L. 130/1999,[72] with reference to credit securitisation operations,[73] fiduciary companies as defined by art. 106 TUB,[74] financial consultants and financial consultant companies.[75] The definition also includes insurance companies that operate in the areas provided for by art. 2.1 of the Private Insurance Code, (CAP),[76] and insurance intermediaries, who operate in the branches provided for by art. 2.1 CAP.[77]

---

64 Art. 1.2(h-*bis*) TUB defines them as companies, other than banks, which issue electronic money.

65 Art. 1.2(h-*sexies*) TUB defines them as companies, other than banks and electronic money providers, authorised to provide payment services.

66 Art. 1.1(e) TUF defines them as investment companies having the form of a legal entity with registered office and general management in Italy, different from the banks and financial intermediaries registered in the register provided for by art. 106 TUB, authorised to carry out investment services or activities.

67 Art. 1.1(o) TUF defines them as joint-stock companies with registered office and general management in Italy authorised to provide the collective asset management service.

68 Art. 1.1(i) TUF defines them as joint-stock companies with share capital with a registered office and general management in Italy, having as sole object the collective investment of assets collected through the offer of own shares.

69 Art. 1.1(i-*bis*) TUF defines them as limited liability companies with a registered office and head office in Italy, having as exclusive object the collective investment of assets raised through the offer of own shares and other financial instruments.

70 According to art. 111 TUB, these subjects, registered in a special list held by Bank of Italy, can grant loans to natural persons or companies of persons or companies with limited liability or associations or cooperative societies, for the start-up or exercise of self-employment or micro-enterprise activities.

71 These are bodies with a cooperative or *consortium* structure, which carry out collective guarantee activities to facilitate member or partner companies in accessing bank credit. Art. 112 TUB covers their activity.

72 The provision refers to subjects in charge of the collection of transferred receivables and of cash and payment services.

73 Letter (r) was deleted by L.D. no. 125 2019.

74 According to this provision, the exercise – in relation to the public – of the concession activity of loans in any form are reserved to authorised financial intermediaries, registered in a special register held by Bank of Italy.

75 These two are regulated by art. 18-*bis* TUF and art. 18-*ter* TUF.

76 Art. 2.1 CAP defines the branches of life insurance.

77 In particular, those included in art. 109.2(a), (b) and (d) CAP: (a) refers to insurance agents, as intermediaries acting in the name or on behalf of one or more insurance or reinsurance companies; (b) refers to insurance or reinsurance mediators, also called brokers, as intermediaries acting on behalf of the client and without powers of representation of

According to art. 3.2, the category of "financial and banking institutions" also covers: (i) the branch offices of financial and banking institutions and insurance companies set up in Italy that have their legal head office and central administration in another EU State or in a third State; (ii) financial and banking institutions and insurance companies that have their legal head office and central administration in another EU State but are established in Italy, although without branch offices in Italy.

Art. 3 of L.D. 90/2017 also defines the category of "other financial operators" (art. 3.3), which includes trust companies,[78] financial intermediaries,[79] agents engaged in financial activities,[80] and subjects professionally practicing currency exchange, consisting of spot trading of cash payments.

Banks, Poste Italiane SpA, electronic money providers, payment providers, intermediaries, Cassa Depositi e Prestiti SpA, micro-credit providers, Confidi, fiduciary companies, professional traders in gold and obliged entities governed by the TUB are subject to the supervision, i.e. regulatory and sanctioning power, of the Bank of Italy. The following provisions of the Bank of Italy, which have the normative value of secondary legislation and implement the AML legal provisions, are applicable to the above-mentioned obliged entities:

- "Implementing provisions concerning the organisation, procedures and internal controls aimed at preventing the use of intermediaries and other entities engaged in financial activities for the purpose of money laundering and terrorism financing, according to the (former) Article 7.2, of L.D. 21 November 2007, no. 231", adopted on 10 March 2011;
- "Implementing provisions for the maintenance of the Unified Database and for the simplified record keeping methods, according to the (former) Article 37.7 and 8, of L.D. 21 November 2007, no. 231", adopted on 3 April 2013;[81]

insurance or reinsurance companies; and (d) refers to banks authorised pursuant to art. 14 TUB, financial intermediaries included in the special list referred to in art. 107 TUB, securities companies authorised pursuant to art. 19 TUF, and the company Poste Italiane (Bancoposta services division) authorised pursuant to art. 2 of D.P.R. 14. March 2001, no. 144.

78 According to L. 23 November 1939, no. 1966, containing "provisions on fiduciary or auditing companies".

79 According to art. 128-*sexies* TUB, financial intermediaries are those who connect, including through consulting activity, banks or financial intermediaries envisaged by the Consolidated Banking Act, with potential clients for the granting of finance in any form.

80 According to art. 128-*quater*.2 TUB, agents engaged in financial activities are those who promote and conclude contracts relating to the granting of finance in any form or to the provision of payment services, on the basis of a direct mandate from financial intermediaries envisaged by the TUB, payment institutions, electronic currency providers, banks or the Poste Italiane.

81 According to Bank of Italy, *Comunicazione della Banca d'Italia in materia di obblighi antiriciclaggio per gli intermediari bancari e finanziari*, published on 9 February 2018 at www.bancaditalia.it, due to the entry into force of L.D. 90/2017 and the repeal of the

- "Implementing provisions concerning customer due diligence for combating money laundering and terrorist financing", adopted on 30 July 2019; and
- "Provisions concerning irregularity indicators for intermediaries", adopted on 24 August 2010.

Movable brokerage companies, savings management companies, variable capital investment companies, fixed capital investment (movable or real estate) companies, exchange rate agents, financial consultants and financial consultant companies, financial intermediaries, agents engaged in financial activities, and those governed by the TUF are subject to the supervision of Consob (the National Commission for Companies and Stock Exchange). However, the above-mentioned implementing provisions of the Bank of Italy are also applicable to these obliged entities.

Insurance companies and intermediaries are subject to the supervision of IVASS (the Institute for the Supervision of Private Insurances). IVASS's "Implementing provisions concerning the organisation, procedures, internal controls and CDD, aimed at preventing the use of insurance companies and intermediaries for the purpose of money laundering and terrorism financing, according to the (former) Article 7.1, let. a), of L.D. 21 November 2007, no. 231", adopted by IVASS on 22 May 2018, which have the normative value of secondary legislation and implement the AML legal provisions, are applicable to these obliged entities.

The "Implementing provisions for the maintenance of the Unified Database and for the simplified record keeping methods, according to the (former) Article 37.7 and 8, of L.D. 21 November 2007, no. 231", and the "Provisions concerning irregularity indicators for intermediaries", adopted by Bank of Italy are also applicable to insurance companies operating in the area of life insurance.

The FIU's provisions implementing the AML legislation are also applicable to all financial institutions, in particular the "Implementing provisions for sending aggregate AML reports", adopted on 23 December 2013, and its annexes. The FIU's "Instructions on data and information to be included in suspicious transactions reports", adopted on 4 May 2011, and its annexes have to be taken into account.

2. *Virtual Currency System Participants*

Art. 1.1(qq) of L.D. 90/2017 defines "virtual currency" as the digital representation of value, not issued *or guaranteed* by a central bank or by a public authority,

---

Unique Database, these provisions are no longer in force. However, arts. 31 and 32 of L.D. 90/2017 provide for record-keeping duties and assigns the Bank of Italy the power to issue implementing rules that can allow supervised obliged entities to use the existing databases for the purpose of record keeping. In the absence of new regulations, Bank of Italy suggests the use, on a voluntary basis, of the Unique Database in order to fulfil the record-keeping duty.

not necessarily linked to legal tender, which is used as a means of exchange for the purchase of goods and services *or for investment purposes* and which is electronically transferred, archived and negotiated.[82]

An innovative aspect of L.D. 90/2017 is that it takes into consideration participants in virtual currency systems, defining them and making them subject to the AML preventive regime. Indeed, according to art. 3.5 L.D. 90/2017, "service providers related to the use of virtual currency" and, following the entry into force of L.D. 125/2019, the "providers of digital portfolio services" are considered to be obliged entities. They fall under the category of "other non-financial operators". With reference to the definition, art. 1.1(ff) of L.D. 90/2017, as modified by L.D. no. 125/2019, defines the "service providers related to the use of virtual currency", as any natural or legal person that provides to third parties, on a professional basis, *including online*, services for the use, exchange, storage and conversion of virtual currency from or into currencies having legal tender *or digital representations of value, including those convertible into other virtual currencies as well as services of issue, offer, transfer and clearing and any other service related to the acquisition, negotiation or intermediation in the exchange of the same currencies.*[83] According to art. 1.1(ff-bis) of L.D. 90/2017, as introduced by L.D. 125/2019, "providers of digital portfolio services" are defined as any natural or legal person that provides, to third parties, on a professional basis, including online, services for safeguarding private cryptographic keys on behalf of its customers, in order to hold, store and transfer virtual currencies.

3. *Legal Profession and Tax Advisors*

According to art. 3.4 of L.D. 90/2017, the legal profession and tax advisors are considered to be obliged entities, falling under the category of professionals, during the exercise of their profession, in an individual or in an associate form or in companies.[84]

With reference to legal professions, art. 3.4(c) includes notaries and lawyers in that category where they participate, whether by acting on behalf of and for their client in a financial or real estate transaction, or by assisting in the planning or carrying out of transactions for their client, in the following activities: buying and selling real estate or business entities (subpara. (1)); managing their client's money, securities or other assets (subpara. (2)); opening or managing banks, savings or securities accounts (subpara. (3)); organising contributions necessary

---

82 The words in italics have been included in the definition of virtual currency by L.D. 125/2019.

83 The words in italics have been included in the definition of service providers related to the use of virtual currency by L.D. 125/2019.

84 The provision does not present particular changes compared to arts. 12 and 13 of L.D. 231/2007. For an analysis of the previous legislation with reference to professionals, see Gambogi, *Riciclaggio e antiriciclaggio*, in *Officina del diritto*, Giuffrè, Milan, 2015, 9 ff.

for the creation, operation or management of companies (subpara. (4)); and creating, operating or managing trusts, companies, foundations or similar structures (subpara. (5)).

According to art. 3.7 L.D. 90/2017, branches established in Italy of the above-mentioned entities, which have their head office and central administration in a foreign country, are also considered obliged entities.

Notaries are subject to the supervision, i.e. regulatory and sanctioning power, of the National Council of Notaries. The National Council of Notaries' "Technical Rules on AML", adopted on 27 July 2017 and 27 October 2017, following the favourable opinion of the Financial Security Committee on 18 September 2017, are applicable to this category of professional. These Rules implement the new AML provisions with regard to the following matters: the scope of the AML provisions in relation to notaries, CDD measures and record keeping.

Lawyers are subject to the supervision, i.e. regulatory and sanctioning power, of the National Council of the Bar. The National Council of the Bar's "Technical Rules on AML", adopted on 15 December 2017, are applicable to this category of professionals. These Rules implement the new AML provisions with regard to the following matters: CDD measures, record keeping, duty to report and politically exposed persons (PEPs).

Tax advisors are under the supervision of the Board of Professional Accountants and Auditors. The Board of Professional Accountants and Auditors is going to adopt the "Technical Rules on AML" to implement the new AML provisions with regard to the following matters: risk assessment, CDD measures and record keeping.

The provisions of the Ministry of Justice concerning the "Determination of irregularity indicators in order to facilitate the identification of money laundering suspicious transactions by certain categories of professionals and auditors", adopted on 16 April 2010, are applicable to all of the above-mentioned professionals.

The FIU's "Instructions on data and information to be included in suspicious transactions reports", adopted on 4 May 2011, are also applicable to the above-mentioned professionals.

4. *Informal Value Transfer Systems*

The Italian law on AML does not consider informal value transfer systems (e.g. *hawala* providers) to be obliged entities.

The activity of value transfer becomes formal as soon as it is carried out in line with L.D. 27 January 2010, no. 11, which regulates payment services.[85] Under the

[85] The Legislative Decree implemented in Italy the First Payment Services Directive of 2007. The law contains the rules under which payment services can be provided (art. 2) and payment providers can be established (arts. 114-*sexies* and ff. TUB).

conditions set by the law, value transfer systems can be considered to be *payment services* provided by *payment providers*, subject to the AML regulation and considered as obliged entities.[86] Regardless of the distinction between informal and formal value transfer systems, the limit set by art. 49 of L.D. 90/2017 on the use of cash as a mean of payment has to be taken into account.[87]

5. *Non-Profit Sector*

The Italian law on AML does not consider non-profit entities (in particular NGOs) to be obliged entities.[88]

6. *Overview of Other Obliged Entities*

Art. 3 of L.D. 90/2017 identifies other two categories as obliged entities: other non-financial operators (art. 3.5), and game service providers (art. 3.6).

The first category includes other companies and trust service providers that do not fall under the other categories of obliged entities, *subjects who trade in antique goods, subjects who trade in works of art or who act as intermediaries in these trades, if the value of the transaction is equal to or greater than €10,000;*[89] *subjects who store or trade works of art or who act as intermediaries in these trades, if this activity is carried out within free ports and the value of the transaction is equal to or greater than €10,000;*[90] traders in gold,[91] estate agents[92] *even when they act as intermediaries in the letting of real estate and, in this case, limited to transactions for which the monthly fee is equal to or greater than €10,000,*[93] guarded custody and guarded transport service providers for cash, titles and values,[94] civil mediators,[95] and extrajudicial debt collectors on behalf of third parties.[96]

---

86 See above, section II.D.1.

87 See below, section VIII.A.

88 Their nature of non-profit-making business prevents considering them as companies, such as those listed in art. 3 of L.D. 90/2017, regardless of the legal form adopted for their establishment, for example that of a foundation.

89 The provision has been modified by L.D. 125/2019.

90 The provision has been modified by L.D. 125/2019.

91 L. 17 January 2000, no. 7, containing the "New regulation of the gold market", provides for these activities.

92 L. 3 February 1989, no. 39, concerning the regulation of the profession of mediator, provides for these activities.

93 The words in italics have been included in the definition by L.D. 125/2019.

94 For carrying out these activities, art. 134 T.U.L.P.S. requires the possession of a licence from the local Public Safety Authority.

95 Art. 60 of L. 18 June 2009, no. 60, on mediation in civil and commercial matters, provides for these activities.

96 For carrying out these activities, art. 115 TULPS requires the possession of a licence from the local Public Safety Authority.

The second category includes casinos, registered online-gambling operators,[97] and registered gambling operators that operate through a physical distribution network.[98]

Both of the above-mentioned categories of obliged entities, according to art. 9.14 of L.D. 90/2017, are under the supervision of the Special Foreign Exchange Unit of the Finance Police. It has the duty to verify that the obliged entities comply with CDD and related obligations, and the power to carry out inspections and monitoring. The AML implementing provisions on "Determination of irregularity indicators in order to facilitate the identification of money laundering suspicious transactions by certain categories of non-financial operators", adopted by the Ministry of the Interior on 17 February 2011, are applicable.

The category of professionals during the exercise of their profession, in an individual or in an associate form or in companies (art. 3.4), should also be considered to be obliged entities. This category includes, for example: chartered accountants, expert accountants and labour consultants (subpara. (a)); anyone who works professionally as an expert or consultant in the field of accounting and taxes, for associations of entrepreneurs and traders, for CAF (the Italy-wide tax assistance centre) and for Istituti di patronato (subpara. (b)); and legal auditors and legal auditor companies, including when they carry out legal auditing of public-interest entities or entities subject to the intermediate regime (subpara. (d) and (e)).

According to art. 3.7 L.D. 90/2017, branches established in Italy of the above-mentioned entities, which have their head office and central administration in a foreign country, are also considered to be obliged entities.

The above-mentioned professionals are under the supervision of different authorities: accountants and tax consultants are under the supervision of the Board of Professional Accountants and Auditors, CAF is under the supervision of the Revenue Agency, and legal auditors are under the supervision of the Ministry of Finance and Economy. The provisions of the Ministry of Justice, adopted on 16 April 2010, concerning the "Determination of irregularity indicators in order to facilitate the identification of money laundering suspicious transactions by certain categories of professionals and auditors", are applicable to the above-mentioned professionals. The Board of Professional Accountants and Auditors is going to adopt the "Technical Rules on AML", to implement the new AML provisions with regard to the following matters: risk assessment, CDD measures and record keeping.

---

97 They offer, through the Internet or other telecommunications networks, games with cash prizes, on the basis of the concession of the Italian Customs and Monopoly Agency.

98 They offer games with cash prizes, on the basis of the concession of the Italian Customs and Monopoly Agency.

The following provisions are also applicable to auditors who have auditing arrangements with all the above-mentioned financial entities:

- "Implementing provisions of L.D. 21 November, no. 231 and subsequent amendments and additions for statutory auditors and auditing firms with auditing engagements on public-interest entities or entities subject to intermediate regime", adopted by Consob on 4 September 2018;
- "Provisions concerning irregularity indicators for statutory auditors and auditing firms with auditing engagements on public-interest entities or entities subject to intermediate regime", adopted by the Bank of Italy on 30 January 2013.

The FIU's "Instructions on data and information to be included in suspicious transactions reports", adopted on 4 May 2011, are also applicable to professionals.

E. RELATIONSHIP BETWEEN AML AND ANTI-TERRORISM FINANCING FRAMEWORK(S)

L. 15 December 2001, no. 438, containing "Urgent measures for the fight against international terrorism", represents the first Italian response to terrorism as a global phenomenon. The law, amending art. 270-*bis* CC, extended the scope of the offence of criminal association to cover terrorism and added terrorism financing to the list of offences. L. 14 December 2001, no. 431, containing "Urgent measures to counter international terrorism financing", first established within the Ministry of Economy and Finance the Financial Security Committee, which is in charge of the coordination of authorities and activities in the fight against terrorism. Since then, various regulatory additions have followed, adding new offences to the Criminal Code – such as the organisation of transfers for the purposes of terrorism, training activities for the purposes of international terrorism, financing of acts for the purposes of terrorism – and also modifying L.D. 231/2007 on the prevention of money laundering, introducing counter-terrorism financing (CTF) as one of its purposes. In addition, L.D. 22 June 2007, no. 109, implementing the third AML Directive and CTF Directive, represents the organic legal framework for the prevention of the use of the financial system and for the freezing of assets for terrorism financing purposes. L.D. 109/2007 provides for different duties: on the one hand, a duty to report suspicious transactions to the FIU that is regulated by L.D. 231/2007, and on the other hand, a duty to communicate to the FIU all the information relating to the relevant persons and transactions and the measures adopted by obliged entities in order to be able freeze the assets of listed persons.

L.D. 90/2017, modifying both L.D. 231/2007 and L.D. 109/2007,[99] does not change this normative setting. It follows that AML and CTF are only partially addressed through the same instrument. Despite the differences between the two phenomena, and the applicable constitutional law standards or objectives, there is no debate on whether these issues should be more clearly separated.

III. THE SYSTEM OF MONEY LAUNDERING PREVENTION

A. CUSTOMER DUE DILIGENCE

1. *Standard CDD Rules*

a. Triggers and Timing

Art. 17 of L.D. 90/2017 defines the cases in which obliged entities shall apply CDD measures.[100]

Obliged entities shall apply CDD measures when establishing a business relationship, namely a continuous relationship or a professional assignment. They shall also apply CDD measures when carrying out an occasional transaction that amounts to €15,000 or more, whether that transaction is carried out in a single operation or in several operations that appear to be linked, or constitutes a transfer of funds exceeding €1,000.[101]

Obliged entities shall also apply CDD measures: (i) when there is a suspicion of money laundering or terrorism financing, regardless of any derogation, exemption or threshold[102] (however, the law does not define when "there is a suspicion of money laundering"); and (ii) when there are doubts about the veracity or adequacy of previously obtained customer identification data.

---

99 The reference goes, for example, to art. 4-*bis* of L.D. 109/2007, and to the new measure of assets freezing. See Carfeda, *Le "nuove" misure di congelamento nazionale e il traffic di capitali volti al finanziamento del terrorismo*, at www.penalecontemporaneo.it. The author criticises the lack of juridicalisation and the low standard of proof required for its application.

100 See also the Illustrative Report on the L.D. 90/2017, p. 7, at www.documenti.camera.it.

101 As defined in art. 3(9) Regulation (EU) 2015/847 of the European Parliament and of the Council.

102 According to art. 4.2 of the FIU's Instruction on the data and information to include in suspicious transaction reports, issued 2011, in implementation of L.D. 231/2007, "the suspicion must be based on a complete evaluation of the objective and subjective elements of the transaction … also in the light of FIU's anomaly indicators and abnormal behaviour schemes".

Providers of gambling services shall apply CDD measures because they carry out gaming operations. According to art. 53.1, online providers of gambling services shall apply CDD measures when they open or modify an individual user's account. According to art. 53.6, providers of offline gambling services shall apply CDD measures when a wager is placed and when carrying out transactions with a value of €2,000 or more. According to art. 53.7, with reference to the games offered by video lottery devices, providers of gambling services shall apply CDD measures when the nominal value of the ticket is €500 or more.

According to art. 53.9, casinos shall apply CDD measures when the value of the transactions made for the purchase or the exchange of tokens or other means of gaming or for the collection of winnings is €2,000 or more.

Art. 17.5 specifies that banks, electronic currency providers, payment providers and Poste Italiane SpA shall apply CDD measures when they act as a means of transferring cash or they take part in any way in the transfer of cash or bearer bonds, whether in euros or in foreign currency, between different parties for an amount €15,000 or more.

In the provision of payment services and in the issuance and distribution of electronic money effected by financial agents,[103] banks, electronic currency providers, payment providers and Poste Italiane SpA, including such entities with head offices in another EU Member State, as well as their branches, shall also apply CDD measures for occasional transactions of less than €15,000.[104] According to art. 17.7, obliged entities are not required to apply CDD measures in relation to the carrying out of the mere preparation and transmission of tax declarations or obligations related to employees' salaries.

Art. 18.2–4 defines the timing of CDD measures, stating that obliged entities shall identify the customer and the beneficial owner and verify his/her identity before the establishment of the business relationship or the occasional transaction.

If there is a low risk of money laundering or terrorism financing, obliged entities shall immediately acquire the person's identifying data and the data concerning the nature and amount of the transaction. They can verify the customer's identity later, but in any case within 30 days.

Furthermore, professionals can verify the identity of the customer or beneficial owner at a later time. They are required to identify the customer and beneficial owner at least when the professional is assigned, or when they perform their legal analysis or defend or represent the customer in judicial proceedings, including giving advice to start proceedings. They have the obligation only to identify the customer or the beneficial owner.

---

103 As defined at arts. 3.3(c) and 1.2(nn) of L.D. 90/2017.

104 As defined in art. 3(9) of Regulation (EU) 2015/847 of the European Parliament and of the Council.

b. CDD Measures

Art. 17.3, which takes the risk-based approach,[105] provides a general rule for all CDD measures. The provision requires obliged entities to adopt CDD measures that shall be proportionate and adequate to the size of the risk of money laundering and terrorism financing. In order to graduate the measures, obliged entities shall use criteria concerning the client and the transaction.[106]

Art. 18 defines the content of CDD measures, which shall comprise, first, identifying the customer and verifying the customer's identity, through the presentation of an identity card or other equivalent identity document, or on the basis of documents, data or information obtained from a reliable and independent source. The same measures are applicable to the person purporting to act on behalf of the customer; the law also requires verifying the existence and extent of the power to act on behalf of the customer (art. 18.1(a)).[107] According to art. 19.1(b), the verification of the customer's identity requires checking the accuracy of the identification data contained in the documents and information acquired at the time of identification, where there are doubts, uncertainties and inconsistencies relating to them.

Secondly, CDD measures shall also comprise identifying the beneficial owner and verifying the beneficial owner's identity, through the adoption of risk-proportional measures including, with regard to the beneficial ownership of trusts and other legal entities, measures that allow retracing – with reasonable reliability – the ownership and the control structure of the customer (art. 18.1(b));

---

105 According to art. 15.2 of L.D. 90/2017, obliged entities shall adopt objective procedures for the analysis and evaluation of the risk of money laundering and terrorism financing. For the risk assessment, they shall take into account risk factors associated with the type of customer, the geographical area of transactions, the channel of distribution and the products or services offered.

106 The criteria concerning the client include his/her/its juridical nature, his/her/its prevalent activity, behaviour at the moment of the transaction or the establishment of the business relationship, and the geographical location of his/her/its residence or legal head office. The criteria concerning the transaction include its type and form, the amount and frequency of transactions, whether the transaction makes sense in relation to the client's activity and the amount of his/her economic resources, its object and the geographical location of the its destination.

107 According to art. 19.1(a) of L.D. 90/2017, providing for the mode of fulfilment of CDD measures, the identification of the customer is carried out in the presence of the customer or the agent. The provision considers several cases in which the identification duty is fulfilled even without the physical presence of the customer, for example that of customers whose identification data comes from public registries, authenticated private contracts or certificates used to generate a digital signature; or of customers who have been already identified by the obliged entity in relation to another existing business relationship or service. The check can be made by consulting the public system for the prevention of the identity theft according to L.D. 11 April 2011, no. 64, or using other reliable and independent sources, both public and private.

and obtaining and assessing information on the purpose and intended nature of the business relationship, in particular information on the conditions of the establishment, on the relationship between customer and agent, and between customer and beneficial owner, and on the business activity (art. 18.1(c)).[108] According to art. 19.1(c), this is done by verifying the compatibility of the data and information provided by the customer with the information autonomously acquired by the obliged entity, as well as having regard to all the transactions performed during the existing business relationship or to the establishment of further professional relationships.

Lastly, CDD measures shall comprise conducting ongoing monitoring of the business relationship with the customer, through the examination of his overall activity, the verification and updating of data and information already acquired according to art. 18.1(a), (b) and (c), and also of the source of the funds in the customer's possession (subpara. (d)). According to art. 19.1(d), the ongoing monitoring is carried out by analysing the transactions and activities performed, to verify that they are consistent with the obliged entity's knowledge of the customer and the risk profile, including where necessary the source of funds.

According to art. 42, where an obliged entity is unable to comply with the CDD requirements listed in art. 19.1(a), (b) and (c), it shall refrain from establishing, performing or continuing the business relationship or the transaction and consider making a suspicious activity report (SAR) to the FIU about the customer, in accordance with art. 35.

Art. 19.3 specifies that in the case of life or other investment-related insurance business, obliged entities shall also apply specific CDD measures to the beneficiary of the insurance contract, as soon as he/she is identified or designated, and to the actual recipient of the awarded benefit and the respective beneficial owners.[109]

c. Individual Responsibility

The AML law does not create an executive position at the obliged entities' senior/most senior level with overall responsibility for the company's AML, even if this person is not operationally involved in day-to-day AML compliance.

---

108 According to this provision, further information, including concerning the customer's economic and patrimonial situation, may be acquired at a later stage, depending on the risk of money laundering and terrorism financing. Where there is a high risk of money laundering or terrorism financing, obliged entities acquire and evaluate the information even in the case of occasional transactions or services.

109 The measures consists in taking the name of the person specifically identified or designated as the beneficiary and, in the case of beneficiaries that are designated by characteristics or by class, obtaining sufficient information to satisfy that it will be able to establish the identity of the beneficiary at the time of the payout.

The criminal and administrative sanctions provided for in the AML law are applied in accordance with the principles of personal responsibility and culpability.

Art. 16.2(b) of L.D. 90/2017 only provides that supervisory authorities shall define the requirements in terms of size and structure that mean obliged entities must set up an AML unit and appoint an AML officer responsible for AML compliance.[110]

Arts. 2380 ff. of the Civil Code assign overall responsibility to the board of directors, which is considered to be responsible to the shareholders for the management of the company, i.e. including for the consequences of the application of criminal and administrative penalties to the legal entity.

d. Further CDD Guidance

Art. 7.1(c) and art. 15.1 of L.D. 90/2017 assign supervisory authorities the task of specifying the law's standard CDD requirements, in particular giving guidance on risk assessment.[111] The main binding provisions giving guidance for financial and banking institutions are the Bank of Italy's "Implementing provisions concerning customer due diligence for combating money laundering and terrorist financing",[112] and IVASS's "Implementing provisions concerning the organisation, procedures, internal controls and CDD, aimed at preventing the use of insurance companies and intermediaries for the purpose of money laundering and terrorism financing, according to the (former) Article 7.1, let. a), of L.D. 21 November 2007, no. 231". The Bank of Italy's guidance lists several risk assessment criteria, covering the characteristics of the customer, the activities performed and the economic interests, the behaviour at the time of carrying out the transaction or establishing the business relationship, the geographical location of the customer or of the counterpart, the type of transaction or business relationship, its amount and frequency, its reasonableness, and the business relationship or the occasional transaction. Art. 30 of the guidance adopted by IVASS lists risk assessment criteria only cover to the characteristics of the customer, the activities performed and the economic interests, and the behaviour at the time of carrying out the transaction or establishing the business relationship.[113]

---

110 For more references, see Bank of Italy, *Regulatory framework providing rules on the organization, procedures and internal controls aimed at preventing the use of intermediaries and other entities engaged in financial activities for the purpose of money laundering and terrorist financing*, 10 March 2011, 15 ff., at www.bancaditalia.it.

111 Both articles provide that supervisory authorities shall establish criteria and methodologies commensurate with the nature of the activity carried out and the size of the obliged entities, for the analysis and assessment of the risk of money laundering and terrorism financing to which obliged entities are exposed in the exercise of their activity.

112 See, in particular, p. 11 ff. For more references see above, section II.D.1.

113 For more references see above, section II.D.1.

According to art. 10.3 of L.D. 90/2017, the Italian Financial Security Committee shall draw up guidelines for the assessment of the risk of money laundering and terrorism financing to which the offices of public administrations are exposed in the exercise of their institutional activities. On the basis of the aforementioned guidelines, public administrations shall adopt internal procedures suitable to assessing the level of exposure of their offices to the risk and shall set out the measures necessary to mitigate it. Neither the guidelines nor the internal procedures have been adopted yet by the public administration.

With regard to professionals, art. 11.2 of L.D. 90/2017 assigns the self-regulatory bodies the responsibility for developing and updating technical rules on CDD measures and the procedures and methodologies for analysing and assessing the risk of money laundering and terrorism financing to which professionals are exposed in the exercise of their activities. The "Technical Rules on AML" adopted by the National Council of Notaries refers to the same risk assessment criteria mentioned in the Bank of Italy's guidance. The "Technical Rules on AML" adopted by the National Council of the Bar solely provide that the risk assessment can be carried out with the help of a consulting firm.

2. *Simplified CDD*

a. Scope

According to art. 23.1 of L.D. 90/2017, if there is a low risk of money laundering or terrorism financing, obliged entities may apply simplified CDD measures, in terms of the scope and frequency of CDD measures generally required by art. 18.[114] However, the law does not define what a "low risk of money laundering" means. It only provides, at art. 23.2, different criteria for a low risk, related to the type of customers,[115] the type of goods, services, transactions and channel of distribution,[116]

---

114 See above, section III.A.1.b.

115 The criteria relating to the customers include companies admitted to the listing on a regulated market and subject to disclosure obligations which require them to ensure adequate transparency about their beneficial ownership; public administrations or institutions or bodies performing public functions, in accordance with EU law; and customers who are residents in low-risk geographical areas.

116 The criteria relating to the types of goods, services and transactions include life insurance contracts whose annual premium does not exceed €1,000 or whose single premium does not exceed €2,500; supplementary pension schemes, according to L.D. 5 December 2005, no. 252, on the condition that they do not include redemption clauses other than those referred to in art. 14 and that they cannot serve as a guarantee for a loan outside the cases provided for by law; pension schemes or similar schemes which provide pension benefits to employees, in which the contributions are paid by deduction from remuneration and which do not allow beneficiaries to transfer their rights; financial products or services that offer services appropriately defined and circumscribed to certain types of customers, aimed at encouraging financial inclusion; and products in which the risks of money laundering or terrorism financing are mitigated by factors such as spending limits or transparency about beneficial ownership.

and the geographical location.[117] According to art. 23.3, supervisory authorities and self-regulatory bodies may identify additional risk factors in order to complete or modify this list.

The Italian AML legislation does not define in general the cases in which obliged entities are allowed to apply simplified CDD measures.[118] It is only in relation to electronic money products that art. 23.3 of L.D. 90/2017 identifies the conditions under which supervisory authorities have to define simplified CDD measures that banks and electronic money providers are authorised to apply.[119]

Art. 23.4 clarifies that where there is a *suspicion* of money laundering or terrorism financing, simplified measures cannot be applied.

b. Requirements

L.D. 90/2017 does not define the content of simplified CDD measures.

c. Further Simplified CDD Guidance

Art. 23.3 of L.D. 90/2017 assigns supervisory authorities and self-regulatory bodies the task of defining simplified CDD measures. Supervisory authorities also have to define simplified CDD measures that banks and electronic money providers may apply in relation to the offer of electronic money products in low-risk conditions.[120]

The Bank of Italy's guidance just offers some examples of the regulatory provisions on simplified CDD measures, the exact definition of which is delegated to obligated entities.[121] Obliged entities verify that the conditions

117 The criteria relating to the geographical area include Member States; third countries with effective systems to prevent money laundering and terrorism financing; third countries that authoritative and independent sources consider to be characterised by a low level of corruption or permeability to other criminal activities; and third countries that, on the basis of reliable and independent sources, such as mutual evaluations or published detailed evaluation reports, provide for and effectively implement AML and terrorism financing safeguards, consistent with the FATF's recommendations.

118 See also the Illustrative Report on the L.D. 90/2017, p. 10, at www.documenti.camera.it.

119 The risk-mitigating conditions have to be present cumulatively. In particular, following the entrance into force of L.D. 125/2019, the payment instrument must not be reloadable or must have a maximum monthly payment transaction of €*150*, which can be used only in the territory of Italy; the maximum amount stored on the device cannot exceed €*150*; the payment instrument must be used exclusively to purchase goods or services; the payment instrument must not be funded by anonymous electronic money; and the issuer must carry out sufficient monitoring of the transactions to enable the detection of unusual or suspicious transactions in the case of redemption in cash or cash withdrawal of the monetary value of the electronic money where the amount redeemed exceeds €*50*; *the payment instrument must not be used for remote payment transactions where the amount of the transaction exceeds €50.*

120 See also the Illustrative Report on the L.D. 90/2017, p. 10, at www.documenti.camera.it.

121 Bank of Italy, *Implementing provisions concerning customer due diligence for combating money laundering and terrorist financing*, 30 July 2019, 18, at www.bancaditalia.it.

allowing simplified CDD measures to be applied are permanent, following the risk-based approach. Therefore, obliged entities are not exempted from the obligation to carry out a risk analysis, identify the customer or beneficial owner, acquire their data, and assess the purpose and nature of the professional service being provided.[122] Art. 43 of IVASS's guidance refers to simplified CDD requirements provided for by the law.[123]

According to the Technical Rules of the National Council of the Bar, a low-risk situation is one where there is a repeated and continuous assignment of professional duties to the lawyer by the same customer, in a context of consistency of the services required with the customer's risk profile (Technical Rule no. 7). In a low-risk situation, lawyers can fulfil their CDD obligations by using structured collection and processing of data and information, even predefined IT procedures, that are able to automatically assign a risk class to the customer. Lawyers can also fulfil their CDD obligations by acquiring a statement confirming the data and information provided by the customer, in particular relating to the ownership structure and beneficial ownership (Technical Rule no. 8). In any case, if there is a low risk, lawyers are exempted from gathering detailed information on the economic-patrimonial situation of the client, and from carrying out specific verification of the origin of funds and resources available to the client (Technical Rule no. 9).[124] The Technical Rules of the National Council of Notaries refer to the law's simplified CDD requirements. They only specify that legal persons, such as supervised companies, and public administrations or institutions that carry out public functions represent customers with a low risk profile.

3. *Enhanced CDD*

a. Scope

Art. 24 of L.D. 90/2017 defines the cases in which obliged entities shall apply enhanced CDD measures.[125] Art. 24.2 identifies three factors indicating high risk: the type of customer;[126] the type of product, service, transaction or delivery

[122] Bank of Italy, *Implementing provisions concerning customer due diligence for combating money laundering and terrorist financing*, 30 July 2019, 19, at www.bancaditalia.it.

[123] See above, section II.D.1.

[124] For more details, see above, section II.D.3.

[125] See also the Illustrative Report on the L.D. 90/2017, p. 11, at www.documenti.camera.it.

[126] The customer risk factors include the following cases: business relationships conducted in unusual circumstances; customers that are resident or based in geographical areas of higher risk; legal persons or arrangements that are personal asset-holding vehicles; companies that have shares in bearer form or are held by trustees; business that are cash-intensive; and where the ownership structure of the company appears unusual or excessively complex given the nature of the company's business.

channel;[127] and to the geographical location.[128] Art. 24.3 requires obliged entities to examine the context and the purposes of particularly high-value transactions or of transactions where there are doubts as to its concrete purposes. In these cases, obliged entities shall apply enhanced CDD measures. According to art. 24.4, supervisory authorities and self-regulatory bodies may identify additional risk factors in order to complete or modify this list.

According to art. 24.5, obliged entities shall always apply enhanced CDD measures in the following cases: *ongoing business relationships and transactions involving high-risk third countries;*[129] *cross-border correspondent relationships involving the execution of payments with a credit institution or correspondent financial institution in a third country;*[130] ongoing business relationships or transactions with clients and their beneficial owners who are PEPs, except where such PEPs act in their capacity as public administration bodies.[131]

b. Requirements

Art. 25 of L.D. 90/2017 defines the content of enhanced CDD measures.[132] According to art. 25.1, applying enhanced CDD measures where there is a high risk of money laundering or terrorism financing means that obliged entities are required to acquire additional information about the customer and beneficial owner, examine the elements forming the basis of the assessment of the purpose and nature of the relationship in depth, and intensify the frequency of monitoring of the permanent business relationship.

---

[127] Following the entrance into force of L.D. 125/2019, the product, service, transaction or delivery channel risk factors include: services with a high degree of customisation, offered to customers with a significant amount of assets; products or transactions that might favour anonymity; non-face-to-face business relationships or transactions, without certain safeguards, such as electronic signatures; payments received from third parties that do not have a clear connection with the customer or his/her business; new products and new business practices, including new delivery mechanisms, and the use of new or developing technologies for both new and pre-existing products; and *transactions involving oil, arms, precious metals, tobacco products, cultural goods and other movable property of archaeological, historical, cultural and religious importance or of rare scientific value, as well as ivory and protected species.*

[128] Geographical risk factors include: countries identified by credible sources, such as mutual evaluations, as not having effective AML/CTF systems; countries identified by credible sources as having significant levels of corruptions or other criminal activity; countries subject to sanctions, embargos or similar measures, issued by the competent national or international bodies; and countries providing funding or support for terrorist activities, or that have designated terrorist organisations operating within their country.

[129] The provision has been modified by L.D. 125/2019.

[130] The provision has been modified by L.D. 125/2019.

[131] The exception has been introduced by L.D. 125/2019. For more details, see below, section III.A.4.a.

[132] See also the Illustrative Report on the L.D. 90/2017, p. 11, at www.documenti.camera.it.

In the case of *cross-border correspondent relationships involving the execution of payments with a credit institution or correspondent financial institution in a third country*, obliged entities apply the enhanced CDD measures listed at art. 25.2. In particular, they shall gather additional information about the respondent institution to understand fully the respondent's ownership structure, the nature of its business and the quality of supervision. Obliged entities shall also assess the quality of the respondent institution's AML/CTF controls; obtain approval from senior management before establishing new bank correspondent accounts; document the respective responsibilities of each institution; and make sure of the application of CDD measures to customers who directly access respondent bank accounts, of the ongoing monitoring of their customers' business relationships and of the possibility to receive CDD data. Lastly, obliged entities ensure the constant monitoring of their business relationships with third-country institutions.

In any case, art. 25.3 prohibits opening or maintaining, even indirectly, respondent bank accounts between shell banks.

c. Further Enhanced CDD Guidance

According to art. 24.4, in a high-risk situation, supervisory authorities and self-regulatory bodies may establish additional enhanced CDD measures beyond those listed at art. 25.

The Bank of Italy's guidance does not go into more detail than the law on enhanced CDD measures.[133] The Bank of Italy clarifies that enhanced CDD measures consist in adopting measures characterised by greater depth, extent and frequency.[134] More specific and detailed provisions cover the following cases: occasional business relationships and transactions involving high-risk third countries; cross-border correspondent business relationships with a responding bank or financial intermediary in a third country; PEPs; transactions characterised by unusually large amounts of money or for which there are doubts about the purposes.[135] Art. 46 of the IVASS's guidance adds further detail on the law's enhanced CDD requirements, taking into consideration factors related to the customer, such as indicators of a negative reputation; to public offices not included in the definition of PEPs; to the transaction, such as some types

133 Bank of Italy, *Implementing provisions concerning customer due diligence for combating money laundering and terrorist financing*, 30 July 2019, 20–21, at www.bancaditalia.it.

134 Bank of Italy, *Implementing provisions concerning customer due diligence for combating money laundering and terrorist financing*, 30 July 2019, 20, at www.bancaditalia.it.

135 Bank of Italy, *Implementing provisions concerning customer due diligence for combating money laundering and terrorist financing*, 30 July 2019, 20–25, at www.bancaditalia.it.

of insurance contracts; or to the beneficiaries, such as not being related to the customer by some kind of affective relationship.[136]

The binding guidance adopted by self-regulatory bodies does not add to or provide further detail on the enhanced CDD measures provided by the law.

4. *Rules on Politically Exposed Persons*

a. Definition

Art. 1.2(dd) of L.D. 90/2017 defines "politically exposed persons" as natural persons who hold or have been assigned within the last year prominent public functions, as well as their relatives and people who are known to have a close relationship to them. The definition refers to domestic, foreign and international PEPs.[137]

b. Requirements

According to art. 24.5 of L.D. 90/2017, obliged entities shall always apply enhanced CDD measures in the case of a business relationship or transactions with customers and the beneficial owner who are PEPs, *unless the aforementioned PEPs act as bodies of public administrations. In such cases, obligated entities shall adopt CDD measures commensurate with the risk actually detected.*[138]

According to art. 25.4, in the case of PEPs, enhanced CDD measures consist of: obtaining senior management approval for establishing or continuing business

---

136 For more details, see IVASS, *Implementing provisions concerning the organization, procedures, internal controls and CDD, aimed at preventing the use of insurance companies and intermediaries for the purpose of money laundering and terrorism financing, according to the (formerly) Article 7.1, let. a), of L.D. 21 November 2007, no. 231*, at www.ivass.it.

137 In more detail, the following figures belong to the category: heads of State, heads of government, ministers and undersecretaries; presidents of regions, region assessors, mayors and equivalent offices in other States; members of parliament, senators, members of the European Parliament, regional council members and equivalent offices in other States; members of the governing bodies of political parties; judges of the Constitutional Court, judges of the Supreme Court or the Court of Auditors, accountant State councillors, other members of the council of administrative justice for Sicily and equivalent offices in other States; members of the boards of central banks or supervisory authorities; ambassadors, chargés d'affaires and equivalent offices in other States; high-ranking officers in the armed forces and equivalent offices in other States; members of the administrative, management or supervisory bodies of Italian or foreign State-owned enterprises or region-, district-, province- or metropolis-owned enterprises; management of legal entities belonging to the national health service; and directors, deputy directors and members of the board of or equivalent functions in international organisations.

138 Indeed, Article 23, paragraph 2, letter a), no. 2, referring to simplified CDD measures applied in case of "public administrations or institutions or bodies performing public functions, in accordance with European Union law", has to be taken into account. The provision has been modified by L.D. 125/2019.

relationships or carrying out occasional transactions with such persons; taking adequate measures to establish the source of assets that are involved in business relationships or transactions with such persons; and ensuring enhanced, ongoing monitoring of those business relationships. Art. 25.5 also specifies that, in the event that the insurance beneficiary or the beneficial owner is a PEP, obliged entities shall inform the senior management before paying out insurance policy proceeds and shall conduct enhanced scrutiny of the business relationship with the policyholder.

According to art. 24.6, where there is a high risk of money laundering or terrorism financing, obliged entities shall apply enhanced CDD measures when the customer, originally a PEP, has no longer held a prominent public function for more than a year. The provision is applicable even if the beneficiary of the insurance or the beneficial owner are still PEPs. These measures also apply to family members and persons known to be close associates of PEPs.[139]

c. Further Enhanced CDD Guidance on PEPs

According to the Bank of Italy's guidance, the following enhanced CDD measures shall be applied to business relationships and occasional transactions involving PEPs.[140] In particular, in order to identify whether a customer is a PEP, obliged entities, in addition to obtaining the relevant information from the customer, shall use other sources, such as official open sources. If the customer or the beneficial owner falls within the definition of PEP, the senior management or their delegate shall authorise the establishment or the carrying out of the ongoing business relationship. In the case of ongoing transactions or business relationships with PEPs, obliged entities shall act appropriately to establish the origin of the funds used in the transactions or business relationships. To this end, they shall acquire a specific statement from the customer and verify the information therein using publicly available documents. The constant monitoring of the business relationship shall be carried out more intensively and frequently.

---

139 The category of family members of PEPs includes: the parents, spouse, cohabitant, and children and their spouses and cohabitants. Following the entrance into force of L.D. 125/2019, the category of persons known to be close associates of PEPs includes: *natural persons who, in accordance with the AML legislation, together with the PEP, hold the effective ownership of legal entities, trusts and similar legal entities or who have close business relations with the PEP* and natural persons who have sole beneficial ownership of a legal entity or legal arrangements which is known to have been set up for the *de facto* benefit of a PEP.

140 Bank of Italy, *Implementing provisions concerning customer due diligence for combating money laundering and terrorist financing*, 30 July 2019, 23–24, at www.bancaditalia.it.

Art. 49 of the IVASS's guidance lists the same enhanced CDD measures, which shall be applied to business relationships and occasional transactions involving PEPs.[141]

The binding guidance adopted by self-regulatory bodies does not add to or provide further detail on the enhanced CDD measures provided by the law.

5. *Rules on High-Risk Third Countries*

a. Scope

Art. 1.2(bb) of L.D. 90/2017 defines "high-risk third countries" as those non-EU countries whose systems have strategic deficiencies in the prevention of money laundering and terrorism financing, in accordance with arts. 9 and 64 4AMLD.

b. Requirements

According to art. 24.5 of L.D. 90/2017, obliged entities shall always apply enhanced CDD measures *in case of ongoing business relationships and transactions involving high-risk third countries.*[142] An exception is represented by paragraph 6-*bis*, introduced by L.D. 125/2019, according to which obliged entities assess, on a risk-based approach, whether to apply enhanced CDD measures to branches located in high-risk third countries, which are however controlled by obliged entities located in the Italian State or in another Member State, if such branches comply with the policies and procedures of the group, in accordance with Article 45 of the 5AML Directive.

L.D. 125/2019 has significantly modified the current text of law, adding further paragraphs to the provision for regulating enhanced CDD measures in case of business relationships involving high-risk countries. In particular, according to paragraph 4-*bis*, obliged entities shall acquire additional information about the purpose and nature of the business relationship, on the origin of the funds and the economic and financial situation of the customer and beneficial owner, on the reasons of the planned or executed transactions. Obliged entities shall also acquire the authorisation of management before starting or maintaining a business relationship or carrying out a transaction involving high-risk third countries, and ensure a constant and strengthened control of the ongoing business relationship, increasing the frequency and intensity of the controls carried out and identifying operational schemes to be subject to further investigation.

---

141 For more details, see IVASS, *Implementing provisions concerning the organization, procedures, internal controls and CDD, aimed at preventing the use of insurance companies and intermediaries for the purpose of money laundering and terrorism financing, according to the (formerly) Article 7.1, let. a), of L.D. 21 November 2007, no. 231*, at www.ivass.it.

142 The provision has been modified by L.D. 125/2019.

c. Further Enhanced CDD Guidance on High-Risk Third Countries

Article 25.4-*ter* of L.D. 125/2019 has strengthened the role of the supervisory authorities and self-regulating bodies, providing that in the cases referred to in paragraph 4-*bis*, they may provide for additional enhanced CDD measures, for periodic reporting obligations concerning transactions involving high-risk third countries, and for limitations on the opening or continuation of ongoing relationships or the prohibition to carry out transactions with persons resident in these countries.

According to Article 25.4-*quater*, in order to limit the risk of money laundering and terrorist financing associated with high-risk third countries, supervisory authorities may also adopt, where deemed necessary, one or more of the following measures. They may deny authorisation to carry on banking or financial activities in the territory of the Italian State to companies controlled by intermediaries established in high-risk third countries or deny them authorisation to establish branches in the territory of the Italian State. They may deny banking and financial intermediaries established in the territory of the Italian State authorisation to establish branches in the territory of high-risk third countries. They may require banking and financial intermediaries established in the territory of the Italian State to strengthen controls on correspondent current accounts and similar relationships with correspondent intermediaries established in the aforementioned third countries and, if they cease to exist, to close them. Finally, they may require banking and financial intermediaries established in the territory of the Italian State to intensify controls, including inspections, on branches established in high-risk third countries.

The Bank of Italy's guidance does not go into more detail than the law on enhanced CDD measures applicable to business relationships and occasional transactions involving high-risk third countries.

Art. 48 of the IVASS's guidance provides for further enhanced CDD measures, stating that obliged entities shall exercise a constant monitoring to identify the moment when a third country in which the customer, the beneficiary or the beneficial owners are resident or have their registered office becomes a high risk one. This is in order to comply with the duty to abstain from business relationships or occasional transactions involving, directly or indirectly, trust companies, trusts, anonymous companies and companies controlled by means of bearer shares that have their registered office in a high-risk third country.[143]

The binding guidance adopted by self-regulatory bodies does not add to or provide further detail on the enhanced CDD measures provided by the law.

---

[143] For more details, see IVASS, *Implementing provisions concerning the organization, procedures, internal controls and CDD, aimed at preventing the use of insurance companies and intermediaries for the purpose of money laundering and terrorism financing, according to the (formerly) Article 7.1, let. a), of L.D. 21 November 2007, no. 231*, at www.ivass.it.

6. *Private Sector CDD Guidance*

There are no private sector rules that provide further guidance on the carrying out of CDD.

B. PRELIMINARY RISK ANALYSIS

According to art. 15.2 of L.D. 90/2017, obliged entities shall carry out the analysis and assessment of the risk of money laundering and terrorism financing. For the risk assessment, obliged entities shall take into account risk factors associated with the type of customer, the geographical area of activity, the distribution channels and the products and services offered.

The risk analysis and assessment procedures shall comply with the criteria and methodologies defined by supervisory authorities and self-governing bodies.[144]

According to art. 15.4 of L.D. 90/2017, the risk assessment procedure shall be documented, periodically updated and made available to the authorities and to self-regulatory bodies for the exercise of their functions and powers with regard to the prevention of money laundering and terrorism financing.

C. REPORTING AND ASSET FREEZING

1. *First-Time Reporting*

a. Trigger for/Degree of Suspicion

According to art. 35.1 of L.D. 90/2017, before carrying out the transaction, obliged entities shall send, without delay, a SAR when they know, suspect or have reasonable grounds to suspect that money laundering or terrorism financing transactions are in progress or have been carried out or attempted or that the funds, regardless of their amount, derive from criminal activity.[145]

According to art. 35.1, the suspicion can arise from the type, amount and nature of the transactions, from their structure or from any other relevant element, including the economic background and activity of the customer. The

---

[144] According to art. 15.1 of L.D. 90/2017, supervisory authorities and self-regulatory bodies shall define criteria and methodologies commensurate with the nature of the activity carried out and the size of obligated entities, for the analysis and assessment of the risk of money laundering and terrorism financing to which they are exposed in the exercise of their activity.

[145] art. 1.2(b) defines "criminal activity", such as the achievement or involvement in the achievement of a felony committed with criminal intent.

provision specifies that frequent and unjustified recourse to cash transactions (even below the statutory limit of cash transactions of €3,000) can give rise to suspicion, and, in particular, cash withdrawals or deposits that do not align with the customer's risk profile. In addition to these indicators of suspicion, it is up to the FIU to establish and update the indicators of anomalies.[146]

b. Content and Direct Addressee(s) of SARs

According to art. 35 of L.D. 90/2017, the FIU is the addressee of SARs. Art. 36 specifies how art. 35 applies in relation to particular financial sector institutions.[147]

With regard to the content of the SAR, art. 35.3 only states that obliged entities shall transmit a report containing data, a description of the transaction, and the reasons for the suspicion.

More information on how to compile SARs and the content thereof is provided in the FIU's "Instructions on the data and information to include in suspicious transaction reports", and its technical annexes, posted on the FIU's website.[148] SARs are composed of four main sections. The first section contains data on the report itself, i.e. the information that identifies and describes the report and the reporting institution. The second section contains structured lists of information on the transactions, persons and accounts involved and their interrelations. The third section is a free-form description of the transactions reported and the grounds for suspicion. The fourth section is for annexes.

As a non-exhaustive example of the information on the transactions, persons and accounts involved and their interrelations that needs to be included in an SAR, Annex 2 of the FIU's Instructions lists the following: identification data, tax code, legal status, PEPs, appearance on CTF lists, contractual position and credit situation in relation to the reporting entity, employment status if a natural person, knowledge of prejudicial procedures, risk profile, identification

146 See the combined provisions of arts. 35.1 and 6.4(e) of L.D. 90/2017. See also Unità di Informazione Finanziaria, *Instructions on the data and information to include in suspicious transaction reports issued in implementation of Legislative Decree 231/2007, Article 6.6, let.* e-bis, 4 May 2011, at www.uif.bancaditalia.it.

147 In particular, bank and financial intermediaries, other financial operators, financial instruments management companies, subjects under convention and agents according to art. 1.2(nn).

148 Unità di Informazione Finanziaria, *Instructions on the data and information to include in suspicious transaction reports issued in implementation of Legislative Decree 231/2007, Article 6.6, let.* e-bis, 4 May 2011, at www.uif.bancaditalia.it. The reports are compiled and transmitted using the data entry function on the INFOSTAT-UIF portal or by uploading from the portal files containing proprietary applications that comply with the standards mandated in Annexes 3a and 3b of the *Instructions*. The reports are subjected to two sets of automatic controls – one by the reporting institution itself, through diagnostic tools available on the portal and one by the FIU's information system (in the report acquisition phase) – to ensure data integrity and compatibility.

number assigned to the transaction, its date and place of execution, number of transactions, the type of transaction depending on the type of obliged entity that carries it out, its status, if it is a suspicious transaction, if CDD measures have been carried out, currency, and amount. Other specific attributes of the transaction and the business relationship between the customer and the obliged entity, relating to the specific situation of the reporting entity, also have to be taken into account.[149]

c. Duty not to Disclose

Art. 39 of L.D. 90/2017 contains a general prohibition on disclosing SARs. Art. 39.1 prohibits obliged entities and anybody who knows about a SAR from giving notice to the "suspected" customer or third parties of the submission of the SAR, or of the probable existence of an investigation on money laundering or terrorism financing.

From another perspective, art. 41.3 of L.D. 90/2017, regulating the "return flow" of the report's outcome from the FIU to the reporting entity, includes the same prohibition on communication provided in art. 39.

d. Power or Duty to Freeze

Obliged entities shall refrain from carrying out the transaction when they report to the FIU. According to art. 35.2 of L.D. 90/2017, in the presence of elements of suspicion, obliged entities shall not carry out the transaction until they send the FIU the SAR. According to the same provision, this duty to postpone is subject to three exceptions. Obliged entities shall not freeze if there is a legal obligation to perform the act in question, if it cannot be delayed due to the normal flow of transactions, or if it would prejudice a judicial investigation – in particular considering that these are often complex investigations into organised crime. In these cases, obliged entities shall inform the FIU immediately after the transaction has been carried out.

The law does not define the duration of the temporary suspension: art. 35.1 only specifies that obliged entities, before carrying out the transaction, shall send a SAR to the FIU without delay. The question can be better answered by looking at art. 6.4(c), which confers on the FIU the power to suspend suspicious transactions for a maximum of five working days, including at the request of investigative or judicial authorities or of another FIU, if it does not frustrate judicial investigations.[150]

---

149 For more details, see Unità di Informazione Finanziaria, *Instructions on the data and information to include in suspicious transaction reports issued in implementation of Legislative Decree 231/2007, Article 6.6, let.* e-bis, 4 May 2011, Annex 2, 9 ff.

150 Postponements are usually already ordered in response to unsolicited communications from banks that provide advance information on the contents of the SARs. This is an incisive

e. Instant Collateral Duties

The law does not mention any collateral obligations when filing a SAR, other than those listed in art. 18 concerning standard CDD measures[151] and in art. 31 concerning the duty to store information about the customer. However, it should be noted that the filing of a SAR generally needs to be taken into account when deciding on CDD measures, in particular standard measures under art. 18, as those measures have to be conducted on a risk-oriented basis.

2. Follow-Up

a. Duty to Provide FIU with Additional Data

According to art. 35.3 of L.D. 90/2017, obliged entities shall collaborate with the FIU, responding promptly to requests for further information. Neither L.D. 90/2017 nor the FIU's Instructions define the content of this further information.

b. Continued Duty not to Disclose SAR to Client

The AML system does not contain an explicit provision setting out an eventual continuing duty on the part of the reporting obliged entities not to disclose the filing of a SAR to the client, even when the SAR has not led to the discovery of illegal conduct.

However, art. 39 of L.D. 90/2017 contains a general prohibition regarding disclosure of additional information requested by the FIU. In addition, art. 41.3 of L.D. 90/2017, regulating the "return flow" of the report's outcome from the FIU to the reporting entity, – includes the same prohibition provided for in art. 39.

c. Continued Collateral Duties

The law does not mention any collateral obligations after a SAR has been filed, even when the initial suspicion has not been confirmed. Art. 18.1(d) of L.D. 90/2017, concerning CDD measures and, in particular, the duty to continue monitoring the customer relationship, remains unaffected.[152]

power, particularly effective in delaying the execution of suspicious transactions for a limited period, until precautionary measures can be taken by the judiciary. See Unità di Informazione Finanziaria, *Annual Report for 2016*, May 2017, 54, at www.uif.bancaditalia.it.

151 See above, section III.B.1.b.

152 See above, section III.A.1.b.

3. *Special Rules for Privileged Professions*

a. Trigger for/Degree of Suspicion

L.D. 90/2017 does not provide for special rules on the degree of suspicion or other triggering factors for forwarding SARs to members of privileged professions.[153] The only exception is art. 35.5 of L.D. 90/2017, which specifies that the duty to report does not apply to legal professionals, who receive information from their clients or otherwise obtain information on their clients in, or concerning, judicial proceedings, including providing advice on instituting or avoiding such proceedings, whether such information is received or obtained before, during or after such proceedings.

The binding "Resolution on anomaly indexes in order to support the identification of money laundering or terrorism financing suspicious operations for professionals and tax advisors" and its two annexes, implemented by the Minister of Justice, provides for other triggering factors required for a SAR.[154] Arts. 3 and 4 are particularly relevant. According to art. 3.4, the impossibility of attributing transactions or customer behaviour to the anomaly indicators set out in Annex 1 to the Resolution is not sufficient to prevent the transaction from giving rise to a suspicion of money laundering or terrorism financing. Therefore, professionals must consider further behaviour and further characteristics of the transaction that *in concreto* reveal factors giving cause for suspicion. According to art. 4.1 of the Resolution, in order to properly fulfil the duty to report suspicious transactions, professionals shall also have regard to the principles and general instructions contained in Annex 2 to the Resolution. It requires professionals to send a SAR even if they refuse to provide the professional service or carry out the transaction, or if they do not do so because they have reasons for suspicion.[155]

b. Content and Addressee(s) of SARs

There are special rules about the addressees of SARs filed by privileged professionals. Art. 37 of L.D. 90/2017, at paragraphs 1 and 2, provides that professionals can choose whether to report directly to the FIU or, in accordance with art. 11.4 of L.D. 90/2017, to their self-governing bodies. The latter, upon reception of the SAR, shall immediately transmit the entire report to the FIU, but without the name of the reporter.

---

153 See above, section III.A.1.a.

154 See Minister of Justice, *Resolution on anomaly indexes in order to support the identification of money laundering or terrorism financing suspicious operations for professionals and tax advisors*, 16 April 2010, in *Gazzetta Ufficiale della Repubblica Italiana*, Serie generale no. 101, 3 May 2010. The document is available at www.giustizia.it.

155 Ibid., 14.

The procedures that lead to the forwarding of SARs filed by privileged professionals and the content of a SAR are not defined by L.D. 90/2017, but by the above-mentioned Resolution of the Minister of Justice and its annexes. With regard to procedures, Annex 2 gives professionals the responsibility for defining internal procedures. They shall record the evaluative process followed, in order to *a posteriori* retrace the reasons for suspicion and share the responsibilities of the different people taking part in the process, in case of a request from the competent authorities. The measures shall be adopted taking into account the specific nature of each profession, including its organisational and operational dimensions. With regard to the content of a SAR, art. 4.2 of the Resolution specifies that the report shall contain data, a description of the transactions, and the reasons for suspicion determined by the FIU.[156]

c. Duty not to Disclose to Client

Art. 39 of L.D. 90/2017 contains a general prohibition on disclosing SARs, making no distinction between whether the SAR is filed by privileged professionals or by other obliged entities.[157] Art. 39.6 clarifies that the case of privileged professionals who dissuade clients from committing an illegal act does not constitute a violation of the duty not to disclose.

Further rules for privileged professions on disclosure of a SAR are contained in the above-mentioned Resolution, at Annex 2. It provides for a prohibition on disclosure for professionals who file a SAR and for anyone who knows about it. It also provides that the "return flow" from the FIU to professionals is subject to a strict confidentiality regime and to the prohibition of disclosure.[158]

4. Protection of SAR's Source

Arts. 36 and 37 of L.D. 90/2017 offer protection to the SAR's source in relation the FIU: in general, obliged entities and professionals transmit SARs to the FIU without disclosing the reporter's identity.[159]

Art. 38 of L.D. 90/2017 contains a general provision on protecting the SAR's source, opting for the anonymity of the individual employee or the professional

---

156 The FIU's *Instructions on data and information to include in suspicious transaction reports* represent therefore the reference provision, both for obliged entities both for professionals. See Minister of Justice, *Resolution on anomaly indexes in order to support the identification of money laundering or terrorism financing suspicious operations for professionals and tax advisors*, 16 April 2010, in *Gazzetta Ufficiale della Repubblica Italiana*, Serie generale no. 101, 3 May 2010, 8 and 15.

157 See above, section III.A.1.b.

158 Minister of Justice, *Resolution on anomaly indexes in order to support the identification of money laundering or terrorism financing suspicious operations for professionals and tax advisors*, 16 April 2010, in *Gazzetta Ufficiale della Repubblica Italiana*, Serie generale no. 101, 3 May 2010, 16.

159 See above, sections III.B.1.b and III.B.3.b.

that filled the report.[160] In detail, according to art. 38.1, obliged entities and self-governing bodies shall adopt all "appropriate measures" to ensure the confidentiality of the reporter's identity. Art. 38.2, which applies to obliged entities that have a complex organisation, provides that the function holder, the legal representative or his/her delegate has the responsibility to keep safe acts and documents containing the reporter's personal data. Art. 38.3 specifies that in any phase of the criminal proceeding, from the inquiry to the process, the judicial authorities adopt "appropriate measures" to ensure the confidentiality of the reporter's identity. In any case, the name of the reporter cannot appear in either the public prosecutor's folder or the case file. His/her identity cannot be revealed, unless the judicial authority provides otherwise, with a motivated decree ensuring the adoption of "appropriate measures"[161] to guarantee his/her protection and only if it is necessary for the detection of the offence.

With reference to banks and financial institutions, the protection is provided both in the obliged entities and externally: arts. 52-*bis* and 52-*ter* of TUB on internal reporting systems and reporting systems to the Bank of Italy, in addition to providing for the "adequate protection" of the reporter against retaliatory, discriminatory or otherwise unfair conduct resulting from the reporting, specifies that the submission of a report does not in itself constitute a breach of the obligations arising from the employment relationship.[162]

D. RECORD KEEPING

Art. 31 of L.D. 90/2017 provides for the general duty to store information about the customer. In particular, art. 31 provides that obliged entities shall store documents, data and information useful in preventing, identifying or verifying any money laundering or terrorism financing activities and allowing the FIU or other competent authority to carry out its analysis. For this purpose, obliged entities store a copy of the customer's documents and the originals of the records of the transactions. Documents, data and information acquired are stored for a period of 10 years from the end of the business relationship or the occasional

160 With regard to professionals, see also Minister of Justice, *Resolution on anomaly indexes in order to support the identification of money laundering or terrorism financing suspicious operations for professionals and tax advisors*, 16 April 2010, in *Gazzetta Ufficiale della Repubblica Italiana*, Serie generale no. 101, 3 May 2010, 16.

161 These measures also comprehend, in the case of organised crime and terrorism criminal proceedings, those concerning covert operations, like preventing the informer's face from being visible during the process, under art. 9 of L. 16 March 2006, no. 146, on the "Ratification of UN Convention on transnational organized crime", modified by L. 13 August 2010, no. 136.

162 For more details, see also Bank of Italy, *Circular no. 285 containing supervisory provisions for the banks*, 17 December 2013, at www.bancaditalia.it. On the topic, Amato, *Obbligo di segnalazione (c.d. Whistleblowing)*, at www.treccani.it.

transaction. These documents must at least make it possible to univocally reconstruct the establishment of the business relationship with the customer; the data identifying the customer, the beneficial owner and the executor; information about the purpose and nature of the business relationship; the date, the amount and the purpose of the transaction; and the means of payment used.[163]

E. COMPLIANCE OFFICERS

According to art. 16.2(b) of L.D. 90/2017, supervisory authorities and self-governing bodies have the task of defining dimensional and organisational requirements, according to which obliged entities shall introduce an AML unit, appoint an AML officer and establish an independent review body to check policies, monitoring and procedures. However, it should be taken into consideration that this provision can only apply to corporate structures. Therefore, of the obliged entities, professionals are not under a legal obligation to appoint a compliance officer.

The law does not define the competences and powers of such compliance officers, nor the rules for ensuring their independence vis-à-vis the obliged entity.

More information about compliance officers or similar positions intended to ensure respect for AML regulations is provided in the measures adopted by the Bank of Italy 2011, in accordance with L.D. 231/2007.[164] The measures adopted by the Bank of Italy provide guidance on the implementation of compliance functions, but without explicitly attributing them to a particular officer or body. This regulatory framework, in defining the organisational arrangements necessary to prevent and mitigate the risk of money laundering and terrorism financing, does not refer to corporate bodies properly identified, but rather to different functions like the "strategic supervision function", the "management function" or the "control function" assigned to corporate bodies or their members in accordance with civil law or supervisory regulations.

According to the measures adopted by the Bank of Italy, the AML unit has the task of continuously verifying the coherence of internal procedures, with the

---

[163] Art. 32 specifies that obliged entities shall adopt systems for the record keeping of documents, data and information that are in line with the provisions on data protection and, in particular, the processing of personal data exclusively for the purposes of prevention of money laundering and terrorism financing.

[164] See Bank of Italy, *Regulatory framework carrying rules on organization, procedures and internal controls aimed at preventing the use of intermediaries and other entities engaged in financial activities for the purpose of money laundering and terrorism financing*, 11 March 2011, 12 ff., at www.bancaditalia.it.

aim of preventing and curbing the violation of external and internal AML and terrorism financing regulations.[165]

The AML officer, who is at the head of the AML unit, is responsible for complex tasks, to be carried out across all the various organisational levels. The tasks involve both verifying the functioning of procedures and structures, and supporting and advising on management choices. The AML officer has to be in possession of adequate independence, authority and professionalism. In order to achieve this, the person appointed to the AML unit shall not be directly responsible for operative areas or be hierarchically dependent on those who are responsible for these areas.[166]

F. INTERNAL COMPLAINT MECHANISM

The AML law does not provide for an obligation to put in place an internal compliant mechanism that allows employees or third persons to inform the senior management about AML CDD violations being committed within the obliged entity. Nonetheless, according to art. 46 of L.D. 90/2017, the members of the board of statutory auditors, the supervisory board and the management control committee of the obliged entities shall communicate, without delay, to the legal representative or his/her delegate any potentially suspicious transactions of which they become aware in the exercise of their functions, and

165 See Bank of Italy, *Regulatory framework carrying rules on organization, procedures and internal controls aimed at preventing the use of intermediaries and other entities engaged in financial activities for the purpose of money laundering and terrorism financing*, 11 March 2011, 16–17, at www.bancaditalia.it. Specifically, the AML unit has to identify the applicable rules and to evaluate their impact on internal processes and procedures; to collaborate in identifying the internal control and procedures system aimed at preventing and fighting the risk of money laundering and terrorism financing; to verify the suitability of the internal control and procedures systems; and to propose organisational and procedural changes that are necessary or worthwhile to ensure adequate risk management. For these purposes, it has the power to control and inspect. It also has to give advice and assistance to the enterprise bodies and the upper management; to evaluate in advance the offer of new products or services; to verify the reliability of the flow of information that feeds the unique informatics archive (*archivio unico informatico*); to transmit to the FIU, on a monthly basis, the aggregate data registered in the unique informatics archive; to arrange the training of employees; and to provide the flow of information to the enterprise bodies and the upper management. The AML unit can also be requested to carry out enhanced CDD measures if the risk of money laundering is particularly high. The AML unit also has to draw up a document defining the responsibilities, tasks and operational measures for managing the risk of money laundering and terrorism financing. These provisions have to be read having regard to the new AML legislation and coordinated with it, for example taking into account the abolition of the unique informatics archive.

166 See Bank of Italy, *Regulatory framework carrying rules on organization, procedures and internal controls aimed at preventing the use of intermediaries and other entities engaged in financial activities for the purpose of money laundering and terrorism financing*, 11 March 2011, 15, at www.bancaditalia.it.

to the supervisory authorities, public administrations and interested bodies facts that may represent serious or repeated, systematic or multiple violations of the AML provisions of which they become aware in the exercise of their functions.

With regard only to the banking and credit sector, L.D. 1 September 1993, no. 385, as modified by L.D. 12 May 2015, no. 72, includes an obligation to set up internal reporting systems. In particular, art. 52-*bis* defines the specific reporting procedures that banks are required to adopt, such as the provision of specific, independent and autonomous channels for this purpose (art. 52-*bis*.2(c)), so as to ensure that the person responsible for receiving, examining and evaluating the report is not hierarchically or functionally subordinate to any reported subject, is not him/herself the alleged perpetrator of the violation, and has no potential interest related to the report, thereby compromising its impartiality and independence.[167]

With regard to private corporate criminal liability, such an obligation can be found in art. 6.2(d) of L.D. 231/2001. According to this provision, in order to prevent crimes and to avoid corporate criminal liability, compliance programmes have to provide for the *duty to inform* the internal body that is in charge of operating and overseeing such programmes. In particular, art. 6.2-*bis*, concerning the content of compliance programmes, requires IT channels to guarantee *confidential reporting* of conduct involving the commission of a crime or the violation of compliance programmes and disciplinary sanctions against those who violate such programmes. The provision means anonymous reports are not possible.[168]

G. ADDITIONAL PREVENTIVE MEASURES

The AML statute provides for further obligations applicable to obliged entities in order to ensure effective CDD.

According to art. 16.3 of L.D. 90/2017, obliged entities shall adopt measures proportionate to their risks, nature and size, that ensure their staff are aware of their obligations, including those regarding data protection. To this end, obliged entities shall guarantee the execution of permanent training programmes aimed at ensuring the correct application of the AML provisions, the recognition of

---

167 The author of the report may be any employee of the bank and anyone who in any way operates on the basis of relationships that mean they are involved in the corporate organisation, even in a form other than a subordinate employment relationship (art. 1.2(h-*novies*). The subject of the report is those acts or events that may constitute a violation of the provisions on banking activity (art. 52-*bis*.1).

168 Art. 6 has recently been modified by the entrance into force of L. 30 November 2017, no. 179, containing "Provisions for the protection of the reporter of crimes or irregularities in the context of a public or private employment", in *Gazzetta Ufficiale*, Serie generale no. 291, 14 December 2017.

operations related to money laundering or terrorism financing, and the adoption of the behaviours and procedures that have to be implemented by law.

With reference to such further obligations, the FIU does not have a duty to support obliged entities.

H. RULES ON OBLIGED ENTITIES' CIVIL LIABILITY TOWARDS CLIENT

Art. 35.4 of L.D. 90/2017 provides that any communication of information, carried out in good faith by obliged entities, their employees or managers, for the purpose of a SAR, does not constitute a violation of contractual, legislative, administrative or regulatory duties. The provision also specifies that these exemptions apply even if the reporter has no actual knowledge of any possible criminal activity and regardless of whether the illegal activity has been carried out.[169]

Therefore, if a client suffers economic damage from the freezing of assets after the filing of an unjustified SAR, the obliged entity can be held responsible and forced to compensate the client.

I. SUPERVISORY AUTHORITIES' ROLE

1. *Supervisory Measures to Ensure Application of CDD and Other AML-Related Obligations*

According to art. 7.1 of L.D. 90/2017, supervisory authorities have a general duty to verify that the obliged entities they supervise comply with CDD and related AML obligations.

For this purpose, supervisory authorities have, among others, the following powers.[170] They carry out inspections and monitoring, including the request of documents, acts and any other information useful to the fulfilment of the supervisory and monitoring functions. In the exercise of such competences, supervisory authorities have the power to summon the management and the employees of the obliged entities to appear before them, and to demand the submission of periodic reports concerning prevention of money laundering and

---

169 In the same way, see art. 3 of L. 30 November 2017, no. 179, containing "Provisions for the protection of the reporter of crimes or irregularities in the context of a public or private employment", in *Gazzetta Ufficiale*, Serie generale no. 291, 14 December 2017.

170 Art. 7.1 of L.D. 90/2017 refers to the adoption, with regard to the supervised obliged entities, of provisions implementing L.D. 90/2017 on organisation, procedures, internal controls and CDD measures (subpara. (a)). It also refers to the control of the adequacy of the organisational and procedural structures (subpara. (b)) and the definition of procedures and methodologies for the risk assessment (subpara. (c)).

terrorism financing[171] (art. 7.2(b)). The frequency and intensity of monitoring and inspections is based on the risk profile, size and nature of the obliged entity (art. 7.2(a)).

The preventive powers of supervisory authorities also include summoning administrative or monitoring bodies for the adoption of specific decisions (art. 7.2(c)), and the adoption of measures concerning the prohibition of new transactions, in the event of serious defects or violations (art. 7.2(d)). In the context of their preventive powers, supervisory authorities have access to information about the beneficial ownership of companies and trusts (art. 7.3). Supervisory authorities shall also promptly inform the FIU and the Bureau of Anti-Mafia Investigation of situations they consider to be linked to the crimes of money laundering and terrorism financing of which they become aware in the exercise of their institutional activities, and provide other European supervisory authorities with any information useful for the effective carrying out of their own tasks (art. 7.4).

With regard to groups of companies L.D. 125/2019 amended art. 7, providing for further powers. In particular, supervisory authorities may issue to the holding company, by means of general or specific measures, instructions concerning the group as a whole or its companies, in relation to the fulfilment of AML duties (art. 7.4-*bis*(a)), and they may carry out inspections and require the production of documents that they deem necessary (art. 7.4-*bis*(b)). According to art. 7.4-*quater*, in case of banking or financial intermediaries controlled by an Italian holding or group branches, established in the territory of a Member State, supervisory authorities may request to the supervisory authorities of that Member State to carry out such inspections. According to art. 7.4-*quinques*, the same power may be exercised by Italian supervisory authorities at request of foreign supervisory authorities with regard to banking and financial intermediaries having their registered office in Italy but falling under the supervision of foreign supervisory authorities. Italian supervisory authorities may also allow the inspection to be carried out by foreign supervisory authorities, auditors or experts or to be participated in by the requesting supervisory authority.

According to art. 9.1 of L.D. 90/2017, the Special Foreign Exchange Unit of the Finance Police has the duty to verify that obliged entities that are not supervised comply with CDD and related AML obligations.[172] According to art. 9.3, the frequency and intensity of monitoring and inspections is based on the risk profile, size and nature of the obliged entity. According to art. 9.4, the Special Foreign Exchange Unit of the Finance Police has the power to carry out inspections and monitoring.

171 L.D. 125/2019 has modified art. 7.2(b), providing that inspection and control powers may also be exercised over persons to whom obliged entities have outsourced business functions that are essential or important for the fulfilment of anti-money laundering duties.

172 See above, section II.D.6.

According to art. 11.1 of L.D. 90/2017, self-regulatory bodies have the duty to verify that professionals listed in their registries comply with CDD and related AML obligations.

2. *Complaint Mechanism*

The AML legislation does not provide for any other complaint mechanisms, at the level of supervisory authorities, for reporting violations of CDD and related obligations by employees of supervised obliged entities, beyond those listed above.[173]

As already clarified,[174] with reference to the banking and credit sector, L.D. 385/1993 contains a specific provision, at art. 52-*ter*, on the system of reporting to the Bank of Italy.

J. STATISTICS ON SARs BY OBLIGED ENTITIES

Statistics regarding SARs by the private sector can be found in the Annual Report of the Italian FIU, in the sections on "Reporting flow" and "Operational analysis".[175]

The data show a steady increase in the number of SARs, with the sole exception of 2017: from 64,601 in 2013 to 101,065 in 2016. The number of SARs then decreased to 93,820 in 2017. As the Annual Report for 2017 explains, the decrease in 2017 was not the result of less reporting by obliged entities, as that continues to rise. Rather, it is the result of overstated growth of SARs in 2016 because of voluntary disclosure and the return of funds held abroad.[176]

The number of SARs progressively increases again in 2018 and 2019: during 2018, the FIU received 98,030 SARs, approximately 4,200 more than the previous year, and 105,789 SARs in 2019, about 7,759 units more than the previous year.[177]

---

173 See above, section III.F.

174 See above, sections III.C and III.F.

175 The first contains data on the "reports received", the "suspicious transactions", the "quality of active cooperation", and the "communications of cases where due diligence is not possible". The first subsection on "reports received" contains data divided into the following categories: "STRs by type of reporting entity", "STRs by category of banking and financial intermediary" and "STRs received from professionals and non-financial operators". The second subsection on "suspicious transactions" contains data divided into the following categories: "distribution of STRs by category of crime", "STRs received in numbers", "distribution of STRs received by region where transaction occurred", "main types of transaction reported in the year (per cent of total transactions reported)" and "distribution by transmission time of STRs". See, as the most recent example, available only in Italian, Unità di Informazione Finanziaria, *Annual Report for 2019*, May 2020, no. 12, 9 ff., at www.uif.bancaditalia.it.

176 Unità di Informazione Finanziaria, *Annual Report for 2017*, May 2018, no. 10, 23, at www.uif.bancaditalia.it.

177 Unità di Informazione Finanziaria, *Annual Report for 2018*, May 2019, no. 11, 11, and Unità di Informazione Finanziaria, *Annual Report for 2019*, May 2020, no. 12, 11, both at www.uif.bancadiitalia.it.

With regard to the reporters, the Annual Report for 2019 shows that the largest number of SARs (64.5% of the total) came from banks and Poste Italiane SpA; this, however, represents a reduction of 4% compared to 2018. The number of SARs from intermediaries and other financial operators continued to grow, confirming its position as the second-largest macro-category of obligated entities in terms of the number of reports submitted, with an increase of around 52%. SARs from non-financial operators and gaming service providers also increased compared to 2018 (on average +27%). There was a minimal increase in percentage terms of reports sent by public administrations, although the absolute values were extremely low: 47 SARs compared to 43 in 2018.[178]

The sector of privileged professionals showed an increase (+5.3%) in the number of SARs for 2019, primarily driven by notaries' reports (+6.6%). The contributions from other professional categories remained numerically ancillary, although the previously declining trends regarding accountants (from 319 to 327) and lawyers (from 38 to 48) were reversed. Relatively more significant was the increase of reporting by auditing firms and statutory auditors (from 13 to 30). The contribution of associated, interprofessional and inter-lawyer firms continued to decrease (from 81 to 18). As such, the National Council of Notaries is now almost the only source of reports (98.2%). Although, to a much lesser extent, reports by accountants are transmitted mainly by the National Council of Chartered Accountants and Accounting Experts (73.4% compared to 72.3% in 2018).[179]

With regard to the value of transactions associated with SARs, the Annual Report for 2019 shows that the total value of suspicious transactions actually executed came to over €91 billion, compared to €71 billion in 2018. The distribution of SARs by value range remained substantially unchanged: most of them were suspicious transactions of between €50,000 and €500,000. The increase in the number of SARs continued in 2020. In the first four months of the year the FIU received 35,927 SARs, an increase of 6.3% compared to the same period in 2019. The increase in SARs sent to investigative authorities was 9%.[180]

Statistics on the outcome of the reports are contained in the section on "Operational analysis".[181]

---

178 Ibid., 13.

179 Unità di Informazione Finanziaria, *Annual Report for 2019*, May 2020, 13, at www.uif.bancaditalia.it.

180 Ibid., 15.

181 This section is divided into subsections on "the numbers", "the process of analysis", "risk assessment", "the methodology", "issues of major concern", "no further action", and "postponements of transactions". See Unità di Informazione Finanziaria, *Annual Report for 2016*, May 2017, 41 ff., at www.uif.bancaditalia.it.

The Annual Report for 2019 shows that, having acquired and processed the SARs, the FIU considered 20.5% of the total reports analysed to be high risk, 29.9% medium risk, and 13.5% lower risk.[182]

A total of 106,318 SARs were analysed and forwarded to the investigative authorities. This represents an increase compared to 2018: the data show a steady increase in the number of reports analysed and forwarded, amounting to 98,117 in 2018 and 106,318 in 2019.[183]

In addition to the Annual Reports, the Italian FIU used to published, up to the first half of 2012, a "Half-Yearly Bulletin" and a yearly "Notebook of Anti-Money Laundering", both available on the FIU's website. They simply offer statistics on SARs and the outcome of such reports.

IV. THE SYSTEM OF FINANCIAL INTELLIGENCE UNITS

A. INSTITUTIONAL AND FUNCTIONAL CHARACTERISTICS

1. *Organisational Position*

Pursuant to art. 6.1 of L.D. 90/2017 (art. 6 of L.D. 231/2007), Italy's FIU is set up within the Bank of Italy, which is a "public law institution".

The Italian legislator chose an administrative model for the FIU, in order to keep the task of financial analysis separate from that of investigative analysis and to emphasise the independent role of prevention, the purpose of which is to preserve the economic and financial system.[184]

The legal status assigned to the Italian FIU within the Bank of Italy is peculiar: the FIU has no legal personality; its organisation and operation are governed by a regulation of the Bank of Italy; and the Bank of Italy is also obliged to provide the FIU with the financial, material, human and technical resources necessary for the effective pursuit of its institutional goals.[185]

---

182 Unità di Informazione Finanziaria, *Annual Report for 2019*, May 2020, no. 12, 31, at www.uif.bancaditalia.it.

183 Unità di Informazione Finanziara, *Annual Report for 2018*, May 2019, no. 11, 25, and Unità di Informazione Finanziara, *Annual Report for 2019*, May 2020, no. 12, 29, both at www.uif.bancaditalia.it.

184 Castaldo/Naddeo, *Il denaro sporco. Prevenzione e repressione del riciclaggio*, Cedam, Padua, 2010, 333 ff.; Castaldi, *L'Unità di Informazione finanziaria per l'Italia (UIF) a un anno dalla sua istituzione*, 3 February 2009, 4, at www.bancaditalia.it, according to whom Italy "has opted for an administrative FIU model, focused on the functional independence of the authority responsible for receiving and deepening the financial reporting of suspicious transactions. This activity is distinguished both by the investigative analysis and by the subsequent repression of the crime, enhancing the function of connection and of filter, assigned to the FIU to protect the integrity of the financial and economic system".

185 Banca d'Italia, *Regolamento per l'organizzazione e il funzionamento della Unità di Informazione Finanziaria per l'Italia (UIF), ai sensi dell'art. 6, comma 2, del d.lgs. 21 novembre 2007, n. 231*, 18 July 2014, at www.bancaditalia.it.

2. *Purpose and Tasks*

Art. 6 of L.D. 90/2017 sets out the functions of the Italian FIU.

In particular, the FIU receives SARs and performs the financial analysis of them (operational analysis), and analyses financial flows in order to identify and prevent money laundering and terrorism financing (strategic analysis), receiving regularly updated statistical data from obliged entities (aggregate data, or SARA (*segnalazioni anti-riciclaggio aggregate*)).[186] The difference between operational and strategic analysis can be explained as follows. Operational analysis is a process aimed at confirming the existence of a suspicion of money laundering or terrorism financing. It is a process of transformation in which the data obtained from SARs are processed through automated systems, enriched by cross-checking the data against databases and open sources. SARs are classified according to risk and transaction type in order to identify those that are most significant and warrant being passed on for further investigation.[187] Strategic analysis, on the other hand, draws on the information and the indications obtained through the analysis of SARs and aggregate data, and any other relevant information available to the FIU, both open and confidential. The data are processed and combined to help guide the FIU's actions, the planning of its activities and the selection of the priorities it chooses to pursue. Strategic analysis rests on two pillars: the identification of the types and patterns of anomalous financial conduct, and the monitoring and study of financial flows and money laundering phenomena. An additional purpose of strategic analysis is to assess the risk of money laundering or financing of terrorism activities for the system as a whole or for selected geographical areas, means of payment and economic sectors. Defining risk levels enables the FIU to develop its own vision of the threats to and the vulnerabilities of Italy's anti-money-laundering system.[188]

---

186 With reference to the aggregate AML reports, art. 33 of L.D. 90/2017 states that banking and financial intermediaries and trust companies shall transmit aggregate data relating to their transactions to the FIU, in order to allow the carrying out of analysis aimed at identifying any phenomena of money laundering or terrorism financing in certain territorial areas. According to the second paragraph, the FIU shall identify the types of data to be transmitted, the methods and frequency of their transmission, verifying the compliance with this obligation through direct access to data and information held by them.

187 Unità di Informazione Finanziaria, *Annual Report for 2017*, May 2018, no. 10, 41, at www.uif.bancaditalia.it, which clarifies that the process follows the risk-based approach defined in the international standards and allows intelligence efforts to be adapted, taking into account the risks and vulnerabilities identified in the course of risk assessments and the results of strategic analyses. The wealth of knowledge that comes from the selection and financial analysis of SARs also allows the FIU to classify suspicious transactions and to identify and define types and patterns of abnormal behaviour to be shared with the obliged entities.

188 Unità di Informazione Finanziaria, *Annual Report for 2016*, May 2017, 75, at www.uif.bancaditalia.it, which clarifies that the data used by the FIU come from the aggregate AML reports, information derived from operational analysis, cooperation with national and international authorities, and inspections. The main aggregation criteria are determined by

The Italian FIU also gives instructions on data and information that must be contained in SARs, when the SAR should be drawn up, and how the reporter's identity should be kept confidential.

In order to facilitate the detection of suspicious transactions, the FIU periodically issues and updates anomaly indicators, so-called "typologies".[189] These are recurring elements that are important for assessing the threats posed by money laundering and terrorism financing, such as the improper use of certain financial instruments and payment methods, the geographic location of transactions, the economic sectors at greatest risk, the precise subjective profiles of persons and entities reported on, and the complex and opaque company structures designed to disguise beneficial ownership. According to art. 6 of L.D. 90/2017, the Italian FIU – using the information gathered in carrying out its functions – has the task of developing and disseminating typologies, and indicating the risk of money laundering and terrorism financing in specific sectors of the Italian economy, in specific categories of payment instruments and in specific parts of the Italian territory.

The Italian FIU shares information with several Italian authorities. In particular:

(i) it transmits any data, information on reported transactions or on suspects, or analyses of financial flows or the results of its analyses, related to investigations on organised crime or on terrorism financing to the National Anti-Mafia and Counter-Terrorism Bureau;
(ii) it transmits SARs indicating a risk of money laundering or terrorism financing, the analysis of the SARs and the pertinent information related to the predicate offences to the Bureau of Anti-Mafia Investigation and the Special Foreign Exchange Unit of the Finance Police;
(iii) it provides the judicial authority with the general results of the analysis carried out and any other information that the judicial authority, in the context of investigations concerning the crimes of money laundering, self-money laundering, and their predicate offences, or of terrorism financing, considers necessary for beginning criminal proceedings;
(iv) in cases of specific interest, it communicates the results of the analysis carried out, including the pertinent information related to the predicate offences, to the intelligence agencies; and

---

the FIU and include the type of payment instrument, the location of the reporting branch, the customer's economic sector and residence, and the location of the counterparty and the latter's financial intermediary. Both inward and outward transactions are reported; the value of cash transactions is indicated separately. The FIU draws on the results of the strategic analysis while taking part in the preparation of the national risk assessment.

189 In the spirit of active collaboration, the FIU publishes its results as case studies. See Unità di Informazione Finanziaria, *Annual Report for 2017*, May 2018, no. 10, 58 ff., at www.uif.bancaditalia.it.

(v) it provides police forces, supervisory authorities, the Ministry of Economy and Finance, the Customs and Monopoly Agency, the Ministry of Justice and the National Anti-Mafia and Counter-Terrorism Prosecutor with the general results of its studies.

Art. 6 does not erase the FIU's duty to denounce, provided at art. 331 of the Italian CCP. According to this provision, public officers and persons in charge of a public service who, in the exercise or because of their functions or their service, become aware of a crime that can be prosecuted *ex officio* must report it in writing, even when the person to whom the crime is attributed has not yet been identified. The complaint shall be immediately transmitted to the public prosecutor or to a police officer.

The FIU also exchanges information and collaborates with foreign FIUs, respecting the condition of reciprocity, including regarding the confidentiality of information.

In relation to its duties, the FIU verifies reports of violations under the AML/CTF legislation and transmits that information to the relevant authorities. In particular, it notifies supervisory authorities of violations of CDD measures and reporting obligations. If the relevant obliged entities are not supervised, it addresses the violations itself.[190]

The Italian FIU is also involved in the fight against the sexual exploitation of children and paedophilic pornography on the Internet in compliance with L. 6 February 2006, no. 38.

The Italian FIU draws up a yearly report on its activity, which the Director transmits to the Ministry of the Economy and Finance by 30 May to be forwarded to Parliament, together with a report by the Bank of Italy on the funds and resources allocated to the FIU.

3. *Independence*

According to art. 6.1 of L.D. 90/2017, the Italian FIU is "autonomous and operationally independent" from all authorities, including vis-à-vis Bank of Italy. According to this principle, the structure and operation of the Italian FIU are governed by a regulation of the Governor of Bank of Italy, first issued on 21 December 2007 and renewed after the Unit was reorganised on 18 July 2014.[191]

The FIU's Director is appointed by the Directorate of the Bank of Italy, on the proposal of its Governor, from among those persons meeting suitable standards of integrity, experience and knowledge of the financial system. The Director

---

190 See below, section VII.B.2.

191 Banca d'Italia, *Regolamento per l'organizzazione e il funzionamento della Unità di Informazione Finanziaria per l'Italia (UIF), ai sensi dell'art. 6, comma 2, del d.lgs. 21 novembre 2007, n. 231*, 18 July 2014, at www.bancaditalia.it.

has full authority over and responsibility for the Unit, while the Bank of Italy provides financial, material, human and technical resources.[192] According to art. 6.4, the Director has autonomy over the management of the FIU, for which he defines guidelines and directs and controls its activity.

A Committee of Experts, composed of the Director of the FIU and four members nominated by the Ministry of the Economy and Finance after consultation with the Governor of the Bank of Italy, acts in an advisory capacity, without having any executive capacity.[193]

4. *Powers*

Art. 6 of L.D. 90/2017 establishes the powers of the Italian FIU. The FIU's coercive powers can be described as follows: (a) suspending suspicious transactions; (b) requesting information from the private and public sector; and (c) a quasi-supervision power to inspect obliged entities.

In particular, the FIU can suspend suspicious transactions for a maximum of five working days, including at the request of the investigative or judicial authorities or of another FIU, so long as it does not impede the investigation or prosecution of crimes.[194] As clarified by the FIU, suspensions are usually ordered in response to communications from banks that provide advance information on the contents of SARs.[195] This is an incisive power, particularly effective in delaying the execution of suspicious transactions for a limited period, until precautionary measures can be taken by the judiciary pursuant to the Code of Criminal Procedure.[196]

---

192 Art. 6.1–2 of L.D. 90/2017, and arts. 2 and 4 of the Bank of Italy's Regulation on the Organisation and Functioning of the FIU. See Banca d'Italia, *Regolamento per l'organizzazione e il funzionamento della Unità di Informazione Finanziaria per l'Italia (UIF), ai sensi dell'art. 6, comma 2, del d.lgs. 21 novembre 2007, n. 231*, 18 July 2014, 2, at www.bancaditalia.it.

193 Art. 6.3 of L.D. 90/2017, and art. 3 of the Bank of Italy's Regulation on the Organisation and Functioning of the FIU. See Banca d'Italia, *Regolamento per l'organizzazione e il funzionamento della Unità di Informazione Finanziaria per l'Italia (UIF), ai sensi dell'art. 6, comma 2, del d.lgs. 21 novembre 2007, n. 231*, 18 July 2014, 3, at www.bancaditalia.it.

194 The Italian legislator does not clarify if the FIU is *obliged* to suspend suspicious transactions upon request of the judicial authorities. The operational autonomy and independence of the FIU, according to art. 6.1 of L.D. 90/2018, as well as the wording "can", seem to come out on the side of a negative response.

195 In this way, Unità di Informazione Finanziaria, *Annual Report for 2017*, May 2018, no. 10, 56, at www.uif.bancaditalia.it.

196 The above-mentioned precautionary measure is that of art. 321 CCP, namely preventive seizure. According to art. 321.1–2, when there is a danger that the free availability of goods pertaining to the crime may aggravate or prolong its consequences or facilitate the commission of other crimes, at the request of the public prosecutor, the judge may order its seizure with a reasoned decree. The judge may also order the seizure of goods for which confiscation is permitted. Among the Italian jurisprudence, with particular reference to money laundering, see C. Cass., sentence no. 24785, 12 May 2015, in *Ced Cass.*, RV 264282; C. Cass., sentence no. 15804, 25 March 2015, in *Ced Cass.*, RV 263391; C. Cass., sentence no. 9392, 18 February 2015, in *Ced Cass.*, RV 263301.

The FIU carries out targeted requests from obliged entities to supplement the specific information acquired as a consequence of the filing of a SAR, but also – according to the Annual Report for 2019[197] – regardless of a SAR, as a consequence of foreign FIUs' analyses, or else to meet the requirements regarding cooperation with judicial authorities, investigative bodies and supervisory authorities in the sector. Investigative bodies also provide the FIU with the investigative information necessary to enable the authority to carry out its analysis.

Lastly, the FIU contributes through inspection and auditing to the observance of the duty to report and to the uncovering of violations of SARs and SARA obligations, also collaborating with investigative authorities. As regards the enforcement of the duty to report, the FIU carries out inspections on a selective basis. It also conducts general inspections to look more closely at sectors and transactions that are judged as being at risk, in order to verify that obliged entities' cooperation duties are being fulfilled and that their internal procedures for drawing up SARs are adequate.

B. TREATMENT OF SARs

1. *Data Processing*

Art. 40 of L.D. 90/2017 focuses on the analysis and development of SARs. The FIU, using the results of its analysis and studies, carries out the financial analysis of SARs filed by obliged entities (art. 40.1(a)), in particular operational analysis. The financial analysis process begins with a first-level analysis to assess the actual level of risk of each SAR and to determine the most appropriate treatment. Based on the information received through automatic data enrichment and from other sources, the FIU determines whether the suspicion of money laundering appears to be founded and whether further investigation is needed. If further investigation is needed to retrace the movement of the suspicious funds, the SAR undergoes a second-level analysis, which produces a detailed report on the findings of the additional investigation. In this phase, a multitude of options and tools for in-depth analysis are available. In addition to contacting the reporting institution and other obliged entities to obtain additional information, the analyst may for example consult the national database of financial account holders in order to identify the banks with which the reported persons maintain accounts, access the national tax database and involve foreign FIUs if the transaction

197 In this sense, Unità di Informazione Finanziaria, *Annual Report for 2019*, May 2020, no. 12, 63 ff., at www.uif.bancaditalia.it.

involves cross-border connections or if notable recurrences emerge from the periodic multilateral matching function ("Ma3tch") of FIU.NET, the network shared by all the European FIUs.[198] According to the AML law, the FIU has direct access to the data and information contained in the account and deposit register, the tax register (art. 6.6(a)) and the real estate register (art. 6.6(b)), and to information concerning the beneficial owner of legal entities and trusts found in a special section of the companies register (art. 6.6(c)).

Operational analysis is a *process of transformation* in which the data obtained from the SARs are processed through automated systems, enriched by cross checking databases and open sources; SARs are classified according to risk and transaction type in order to identify those that are most significant and warrant being disseminated for subsequent investigative developments.[199] The analysis of SARs is therefore central to the Unit's financial intelligence activities and is instrumental in extracting from the reports the investigative elements to be forwarded – according to arts. 6, 8 and 40 of L.D. 90/2017[200] – to the authorities responsible for investigating cases of money laundering, its predicate offences and terrorism financing.

It should be noted that the filter function of the FIU does not seem to be clarified by the AML law. On the one hand, according to art. 40.1(d), the FIU shall transmit to the Bureau of Anti-Mafia Investigation and the Special Foreign Exchange Unit of the Finance Police those SARs "presenting a risk of money laundering" or terrorism financing and the results of the analysis it has carried out. On the other hand, according to art. 40.1(c), the FIU shall transmit to the National Anti-Mafia and Counter-Terrorism Bureau "data relating to the received SARs", so that the Bureau can verify whether such data are relevant to ongoing judicial proceedings.

The law does not define how SARs are forwarded to the other authorities, especially to judicial authorities. The FIU's Annual Report underlines that for the information exchanges with obliged entities and judicial authorities the FIU mainly use electronic channels: for the former, the FIU has developed the pre-existing SAR transmission platform,[201] while for the latter, it has developed

198 Ibid., 47 ff.

199 Ibid., 41, which clarifies that the process follows the risk-based approach defined in the international standards and allows intelligence efforts to be adapted, taking into account the risks and vulnerabilities identified in the course of risk assessments and the results of strategic analyses.

200 See above, on the tasks of FIU, section IV.A.2.

201 See Unità di Informazione Finanziaria, *Annual Report for 2016*, May 2017, 115, at www.uif.bancaditalia.it. According to the FIU, the project for the exchange of information with the reporters is of great importance. The FIU explains that communications usually take place via channels external to the SAR sending platform, through the acquisition of documents mostly in free format. To overcome the current situation, the project "Exchange and management of confidential documentation" was planned for 2017.

new platforms on the basis of protocol agreements.[202] The Annual Report also clarifies that the FIU may uncover evidence of criminal activity, which is then reported to the competent judicial authorities pursuant to art. 331 CCP, either directly by means of a report or via the technical reports sent to the investigative bodies together with the relevant SARs. If the FIU is aware of an ongoing investigation, it provides information to the judiciary, mainly acquired during on-site inspections.

The wealth of knowledge that comes from the selection and financial analysis of SARs also allows the FIU to classify suspicious transactions and to identify and define general categories of suspicious transactions and patterns of abnormal behaviour to be shared with the obliged entities.[203] Thanks to the exchange of information with the judicial authorities, the FIU can work more effectively and expand its knowledge of criminal typologies and practices, which also serves to produce indicators of irregularities and representative models of anomalous conduct. In turn, the judicial authorities can take advantage of the Unit's vast stock of information resources and analyses in order to prosecute criminal offences.[204]

2. *Special Procedures for Privileged Professions*

According to art. 37.1–2 of L.D. 90/2017, privileged professionals report directly to the FIU or, according to art. 11.4, to their self-governing bodies. These, upon receiving an SAR from one of their members, shall immediately transmit the full SAR to the FIU, without the name of the reporter.

3. *Feedback Obligations*

a. Obligation of the FIU

According to art. 41.2 of L.D. 90/2017, the FIU is under an obligation to inform the reporting entity about the outcome of a SAR. The law provides that the FIU – ensuring the protection of confidentiality – shall communicate, directly or through the self-governing bodies, the outcome of the reports to the reporting entity, taking into account the information received from the investigative

202 See Unità di Informazione Finanziaria, *Annual Report for 2016*, May 2017, 115, at www.uif.bancaditalia.it, which refers to the "SAFE project" for the management of information exchanges with the judicial authorities and foreign FIUs. The project involves the use of telecommunications channels for the acquisition of information and the digitalisation of the entire procedure for processing requests.

203 Unità di Informazione Finanziaria, *Annual Report for 2017*, May 2018, no. 10, 41, at www.uif.bancaditalia.it.

204 Ibid., 93, confirms that the data can also come from the inspection.

authorities, in particular the Bureau of Anti-Mafia Investigation and the Special Foreign Exchange Unit of the Finance Police.

The law does not specify what the *protection of confidentiality* consists of. The concept cannot be confused with that of *investigative secret*, since the AML regulation calls for the retention of two different concepts.

The "return flow" of information shall be subject to the same prohibition of communication to customers or third parties provided for by art. 39.[205]

b. Obligation of Investigative Authorities

According to arts. 8.1(c), and 41.1 of L.D. 90/2017, the National Anti-Mafia and Counter-Terrorism Bureau, the Bureau of Anti-Mafia Investigation and the Special Foreign Exchange Unit of the Finance Police are under an obligation to inform the FIU of the investigative results that follow from the analysis of SARs previously forwarded by the FIU to these authorities.[206]

The provisions do not clarify what information shall be provided. The provisions only specify that the forwarding of information to the FIU does not compel the authorities to keep the investigation secret.[207]

4. Disclosure Obligations Towards "Suspect"

The AML law does not provide for an obligation of disclosure to the "suspect" on the part of the FIU.

C. PROACTIVE INVESTIGATIONS

The AML regulation does not describe the FIU's activities as *investigations*, instead always using the term *analysis*. Nevertheless, the way the FIU processes data shows that the treatment of financial data goes well beyond the mere analysis of SARs. In fact, the close collaboration between the FIU and other authorities, in particular judicial authorities, indicates that the FIU's action frequently gives rise to suspicion of a particular suspect.

L.D. 90/2017 does not require there to be an pre-existing SAR for the FIU to carry out its analysis, and also allows the FIU to analyse transactions not reported

---

205 See above, section III.B.2.c.

206 See above, sections IV.A.2 and IV.B.1.

207 According to art. 329.1 CCP, the investigative measures carried out by the public prosecutor and the judicial police, the requests from the public prosecutor for the authorisation to carry out investigative measures and the judge's orders that provide for such requests are subject to secrecy until the defendant can have access to the investigative file and, in any case, not later than the closure of the preliminary investigations.

by obliged entities and identified on the basis of third-party information, in particular from foreign FIUs or judicial authorities. In particular, art. 6.4(f) provides that the FIU shall perform audits, including through inspections, in order to ensure the observance of the duty to report and to discover cases where SARs have omitted information or not been sent at all, also in collaboration with the investigative authorities.[208] The provision recognises the power to conduct proactive investigations ("performs, also through inspections, audits"), with the purpose of "ensuring the observance of the duty to report" and "discovering cases of omission of suspicious transaction reports". These two purposes therefore seem to mean that a SAR does not have to already exist. The law does not provide for any special power related to this form of proactive investigation. Art. 39 only prohibits obliged entities and anybody who knows about a SAR from giving notice to the "suspected" client or third parties – among others – of "additional information requested by the FIU".

The power to initiate an investigation even in the absence of a SAR also appears in the FIU's Annual Report for 2017. It clarifies that the Unit conducts general inspections to look more closely at sectors and transactions at risk, and to check that the active cooperation obligations are being fulfilled and that the procedures for making SARs are adequate.[209]

D. ACCESS TO DATA

1. *Design and Content of FIU's Own Data Banks*

SARs and SARAs are kept by the FIU, in order to conduct its financial analysis in accordance with art. 6.4(a) and (b) of L.D. 90/2017. The limits on which data can be stored by the FIU are not defined by the AML law, but can be inferred from arts. 6–10 of the FIU's "Instructions on data and information to include in suspicious transaction reports" and its technical annexes.[210] According to art. 6, the content of the report is divided into: identification data, namely the information that identifies and qualifies the report and the reporter;[211]

[208] Furthermore, art. 6.4(g) provides that the Italian FIU, in relation to its duties, ascertain the violations under the AML legislation.

[209] See Unità di Informazione Finanziaria, *Annual Report for 2017*, May 2018, no. 10, 93 ff., at www.uif.bancaditalia.it.

[210] See Unità di Informazione Finanziaria, *Istruzioni sui dati e le informazioni da inserire nelle segnalazioni di operazioni sospette*, 4 May 2011, at www.uif.bancaditalia.it.

[211] With reference to identification data, art. 7 states that the report shall indicate the event that gave rise to it being forwarded; it may also indicate the phenomenon to which the suspicious transaction is attributable, if it corresponds to one of the patterns representing abnormal behaviour. The obliged entity shall indicate the level of risk attributed to the reported activity, according to its prudent assessment. The report shall also contain the reference (identification number or protocol number) to any reports deemed to be connected and the reason for that connection.

structured lists of information on transactions, subjects, relationships and the links between them;[212] a free-form description of the transactions reported and on the reasons for suspicion;[213] and any annexes.[214] Art. 6.1 clarifies that the reporting format is the same for all categories of obliged entities, with a different level of informational detail in relation to the particularities of the obliged entity itself and the reported transactions.

The other data collected and stored by the FIU are those obtained through the FIU's inspections (art. 6.4(f) or requests for further information (art. 35.3), or through its access to public data banks (art. 6.6), or following the exchange of data and information with other national or international authorities, on the basis of protocol agreements (art. 12). In none of these cases does the AML law precisely define which data can be requested and stored, nor the limits on how long it can be kept.

With particular regard to art. 6.6 of L.D. 90/2017, the framework of accessible data can be inferred from a wide range of provisions and refers to the following data:

(i) data contained in the register of accounts and deposits referred to in art. 20.4, L. 30 December 1991, no. 413, in particular: tax code, bank accounts, account balances and total value of the transfers carried out over the year;
(ii) data contained in the tax register referred to in art. 37 of D.L. 4 July 2006, no. 223, converted by L. 4 August 2006, no. 248, in particular: tax code or VAT number, income received or paid, value of and counterparties to the VAT transactions, insurance contracts, cancellations from the business register, contracts for the supply of electricity, gas and telephone services, any application aimed at obtaining a licence, concession or other authorisation and at exercising professional activities, and declaration of start of activities;
(iii) data contained in the real estate register referred to in art. 19 of D.L. 31 May 2010, no. 78, converted by L. 30 July 2010, no. 122, in particular: cadastral

212 The informative elements, according to art. 8, shall include structured data concerning transactions, relationships and subjects to which/whom the transactions or reports are related, and the links between them. The report shall contain a reference to at least one subject and to one transaction, even if not carried out, regardless of its value. The report may contain references to transactions deemed not to be suspicious if necessary for understanding the transactions described or the reason for suspicion.

213 The free-form description shall include, according to art. 9, the description of the transactions reported and reference to the economic and financial context, illustrating in a comprehensive and detailed way the reasons for suspicion, i.e. the reasons that have led the report to believe the transaction related to money laundering or terrorism financing and to report it. In particular, it shall include the logical process followed by the reporter in the assessment of the anomalies.

214 The documents that the reporter deems to be necessary for describing the suspicious transaction are attached to the report in electronic format, according to art. 10.

data such as location, consistency, graphic representation and tax value, and data from real estate registers, such as ownership of real rights or mortgages;
(iv) data contained in the beneficial ownership register, established pursuant to art. 21 of L.D. 90/2017.[215]

Limits on the FIU's collection and conservation of data derive from the data protection legislation, in particular from L.D. 18 May 2018, no. 51, which implements the Directive 2016/680/EU of the European Parliament and Council of 27 April 2016 on the protection of natural persons with regard to the processing of personal data by the competent authorities for the purpose of the prevention, investigation, detection or prosecution of criminal offences or the execution of criminal penalties, and on the free movement of such data.

According to art. 3.1 of L.D. 51/2018, personal data[216] shall be collected for specified, explicit and legitimate purposes and not processed in a manner that is incompatible with those purposes (art. 3.1(b)), and shall kept in a form which permits identification of data subjects for no longer than is necessary for the purposes for which they are processed, periodically examined in order to check the actual need for conservation, and deleted or anonymised once this need has ceased (art. 3.1(e)).

2. *Access to Other Public Data Banks*

The FIU has direct and unrestricted access to the public data banks mentioned at art. 6.6 of L.D. 90/2017.[217]

The FIU has no access to data banks of public authorities, with the sole exception of the Customs and Monopoly Agency. According to a memorandum of understanding signed between the two authorities, the FIU is allowed to access the Customs and Monopoly Agency's database containing declarations related to cash movements for an amount of, or greater than, €10,000.[218]

Except for these cases, data can only be accessed through collaboration between authorities, in the form of exchange of information, based on protocol agreements, according to art. 12 of L.D. 90/2017.[219]

3. *Access to Private Data Banks*

The ordinary way to acquire data and information is based on the active collaboration of obliged entities, through the submission of SARs (art. 35 of

215 See below, sections VI.B.1 and VI.C.1.
216 According to art. 2.1(a), "personal data" means any information relating to an identified or identifiable natural person.
217 See above, section IV.D.1.
218 The document is available at www.uif.bancaditalia.it.
219 See below, section V.B.

L.D. 90/2017) and SARAs (art. 33 of L.D. 90/2017). Art. 33.2 of L.D. 90/2017 – with reference to aggregate AML reports – provides that the FIU shall verify, through direct access to data and information, that obliged entities are complying with the duty to report.

The Italian FIU does not have direct access to data banks of private entities, except in the case of its monitoring and inspections, which are considered to be extraordinary activities.[220] The AML law does not provide for any further information on the conditions of such access.

4. *Data Analytics*

The law does not provide any particular information on FIU's data matching or data mining. Technical information is contained in the FIU's Annual Reports.[221]

The financial analysis process is described as a series of activities designed to identify those SARs deemed to be well founded and warranting further investigation, to assess the actual degree of risk involved and to decide how they should be handled by drawing upon a variety of information sources.[222] To do this, the analysis process uses the RADAR (*Raccolta e analisi dati antiriciclaggio*) platform to gather and manage reports and to perform the data enrichment. The FIU's data warehouse has made it possible to use most of the accessible information, both internal and external, on an integrated basis. The data warehouse also facilitates the processing of massive quantities of information and therefore supports the identification and analysis of phenomena of interest. It can be used in support of the entire range of the FIU's official duties (management, inspections, strategic analysis, determination of patterns and models of conduct, and information exchange with judicial authorities, foreign FIUs and sectoral supervisory authorities). Data integration creates an environment that allows the use of vaster and overall more comprehensive and cogent information. The data warehouse also offers visual analysis tools inspired by social network models (link analysis or social network analysis).[223]

5. *International Cooperation*

Art. 13-*bis* of L.D. 90/2017, as introduced by L.D. 125/2019 regulates the FIU's international cooperation. According to the first paragraph, the Italian FIU, upon request or on its own initiative, can – under the condition of reciprocity,

---

220 For more details, see Unità di Informazione Finanziaria, *Annual Report for 2017*, May 2018, no. 10, 93 ff., at www.uif.bancaditalia.it. See also above, section IV.C.

221 Unità di Informazione Finanziaria, *Annual Report for 2017*, May 2018, no. 10, 41, at www.uif.bancaditalia.it.

222 Ibid., 41.

223 Unità di Informazione Finanziaria, *Annual Report for 2016*, May 2017, 46, at www.uif.bancaditalia.it.

also with regard to confidentiality – exchange information and collaborate with foreign FIUs for the processing or analysis of information related to the offences of money laundering and terrorist financing and to the persons involved, regardless of the type of predicate offence and its ascertainment.[224] The provision also clarifies that the request shall indicate all pertinent facts, information on the context, reasons and methods of using the information requested. From an operative point of view, the law requires the Italian FIU to cooperate with other FIUs using secure and protected channels of communication: in particular, to access the FIU.net network and to use appropriate technologies to allow the anonymous cross-referencing of data concerning the information being exchanged with the other FIUs.[225]

According to paragraph 2, the Italian FIU shall use the information obtained from other FIUs for the performance of "the processing or analysis of information related to the offences of money laundering and terrorist financing and to the persons involved" and for the purposes for which such information has been provided.[226]

According to paragraph 3, for the above-mentioned purposes the FIU may stipulate memoranda of understanding. The FIU currently has memoranda of understanding with the foreign counterparts of the following countries: Australia, Belgium, Bulgaria, Canada, China, Croatia, Czech Republic, France, Greece, Guernsey, Guatemala, the Holy See, Indonesia, Japan, Latvia, Monaco,

---

224 Paragraph 5 also specifies that the different definitions of criminal offences in force in the legal systems of the Member States shall not hinder cooperation and the exchange of information between FIUs.

225 The Report for 2016 underlines the problem arising from the international collaboration between FIUs, in particular in terms of limitations that reduce its effectiveness. These difficulties arise from the insufficient scope of information powers available to foreign authorities and on the conditions placed on the information exchange, for example the existence of investigations or criminal proceedings in the foreign requested country. Significant limitations also arise in the investigation's use of such information or in the necessary prior consent of the foreign sending FIU, which is subject to numerous conditions. Obstacles to collaboration stem from multiple factors, like the diversity of FIUs in terms of their nature, organisation and institutional and regulatory frameworks. To this is added the frequent confusion between financial analysis and investigation, the lack of adequate information powers and the inadequate ability to exchange information. Significant obstacles to the FIU's activity also stem from the levels of autonomy and independence between the different FIUs. See Unità di Informazione Finanziaria, *Annual Report for 2016*, May 2017, 101 ff., at www.uif.bancaditalia.it.

226 The provision specifies that such information may be used for further purposes or transmitted by the FIU to the competent national authorities with the prior consent of the foreign FIU providing the information and in accordance with any limits or conditions imposed by it. The Italian FIU may give such consent to a foreign FIU to which it has provided information or may refuse it if, on the basis of the evidence available, it is likely to prejudice the investigations or if it conflicts with constitutional rights or fundamental principles of the Italian law. Such exceptions shall be specified in such a way as to avoid any abuse or restriction of the communication of such information.

Panama, Poland, Romania, Russia, Singapore, Slovenia, Spain, the United States and Ukraine.[227]

According to paragraph 4, in addition to the requests and spontaneous exchange of information, the FIU shall participate with the FIUs of other Member States to joint analyses on cross-border cases and shall provide the FIUs with information on SARs involving those States.[228]

The Annual Report explains that such exchanges involve financial, investigative and administrative data and clarifies that the requests usually aim to trace the origin or the use of transferred funds to or from other jurisdictions, to identify the existence and consistency of properties abroad, and to clarify the actual ownership of companies established abroad.[229]

E. PARTICIPATION OF "SUSPECTS"

1. *Defence Rights*

As was observed above,[230] the FIU's analysis might frequently go beyond mere statistical and economic analysis of transactions and instead focus, at least implicitly, on an individual person suspected of money laundering or terrorism financing. This can seem problematic, as investigations against individuals who are suspected of criminal offences are normally subject to a number of defence rights, in particular those in the CCP. The performance of *de facto* investigative tasks by the FIU might therefore raise the question of whether such defence rights can also be applicable as regards the FIU. However, the Italian AML law does not address this issue. The suspect does not enjoy any particular rights vis-à-vis the FIU with regard to its analysis.[231]

2. *Judicial Review or Other Remedies*

With regard to the suspect, the Italian AML system does not provide for judicial review of the FIU's actions nor for (non-judicial) remedies. Remedies are

227 Unità di Informazione Finanziaria, *Annual Report for 2017*, May 2018, no. 10, 111, at www.uif.bancaditalia.it.

228 According to this provision, the Italian FIU, with the authorisation of foreign FIUs, shall, where necessary, transmit the data and results of such analyses to the National Anti-Mafia and Counter-Terrorism Directorate, to the Finance Police and to the Bureau of Anti-Mafia Investigation, for the exercise of their respective powers.

229 Unità di Informazione Finanziaria, *Annual Report for 2017*, May 2018, no. 10, 104 ff., at www.uif.bancaditalia.it.

230 See above, section IV.C on proactive investigations.

231 Another issue concerns the possible application to the banks of the principle of *nemo tenetur se detegere*, in the case of requests for further information by the FIU.

available within the sphere of any subsequent criminal proceedings, but not in relation to the FIU's actions.

Art. 39 of L.D. 51/2018, on the protection of natural persons with regard to the processing of personal data by authorities competent for the purpose (among others) of preventing criminal offences, should also be noted. It recognises the suspect's right to complain to the Italian Guarantor for Privacy (*Garante per la protezione dei dati personali*) and to apply for judicial remedies, if the suspect considers that the FIU's data processing has violated his/her rights under the law.

F. SIMILAR POWERS OF SUPERVISORY BODIES

1. *Financial Supervision*

Despite the fact that the supervisory bodies of financial markets often became aware of suspected money laundering, the law does not assume that the supervisory authorities investigate money laundering. The Italian supervisory bodies of financial markets do not have the right to investigate suspected money laundering on their own.[232]

2. *Non-Financial Sector Supervision*

None of the other non-financial sector supervisory bodies, for example the bar associations, seem to be required to investigate suspected money laundering of which they become aware. Beyond the supervisory duty to uncover violations of CDD and reporting obligations, the other Italian supervisory bodies do not have the right to investigate suspected money laundering on their own.

With regard to non-financial sector supervision, the role of the Special Foreign Exchange Unit of the Finance Police is slightly different. On the one hand, this authority can count as a non-financial sector supervisory authority, and has the duty to verify compliance with CDD and related AML obligations, carrying out monitoring and inspections.[233] On the other hand, this authority is an investigative body. Although the coexistence of these two roles is not defined by the AML law, they overlap, and therefore the Finance Police does have the right to investigate suspected money laundering on its own, as part of its institutional tasks.

232 Art. 7.1(b) of L.D. 90/2017, which describes the preventive powers of such authorities and states that they shall carry out inspections and controls, including through the request of documents, in order to obtain information useful for the performance of their supervisory functions. They also have the power to request the sending of periodic reports relevant to the prevention of money laundering or terrorism financing. These reports technically are not SARs, according to art. 35 of L.D. 90/2017.

233 See above, section II.D.6.

G. REPORTING OBLIGATIONS OF SUPERVISORY AUTHORITIES

Neither supervisory authorities nor self-governing bodies have to submit SARs to the FIU. Art. 37 of L.D. 90/2017 does not contradict this statement. Paragraphs 1 and 2 provide that professionals – as obliged entities – directly report to the FIU or, in line with art. 11.4 L.D. 90/2017, to their self-governing bodies. These, upon receiving an SAR from one of their members, shall immediately transmit the full SAR to the FIU, without the name of the reporter.

H. REPORTING BY OTHER AUTHORITIES

Other Italian authorities do not have to submit SARs to the FIU. The communication of data and information between the FIU and other Italian authorities follows the rules about national and international cooperation set out in art. 12 of L.D. 90/2017.[234]

I. STATISTICS

1. *Number of Reports by Supervisory Authorities and Other Authorities*

Statistics regarding SARs can be found in the Annual Reports of the Italian FIU, but they only concern reports filed by obliged entities.[235]

2. *FIU Analysis*

There are no statistics on the number of FIU investigations and the value of transactions associated with these investigations. The FIU's "Notebook of Anti-Money Laundering" only contains data on the SARs received, analysed and archived, or on FIU's monitoring and checks on irregularities (see next section).[236]

---

234 According to art. 331 CCP, members of the Italian authorities – such as public officials (art. 357 CC) or officials in charge of a public service (art. 358 CC) – who, in the course or because of the exercise of their office or service, have notice of a crime indictable by office, should file a written denunciation, even if the person to whom the offence is attributed is not identified. The denunciation shall be presented or transmitted without delay to the public prosecutor or to a police officer. Non-compliance with this provision is punished with a fine, under arts. 361, 362 and 363 CC.

235 See above, section III.I.

236 Unità di Informazione Finanziaria, *Quaderni dell'antiriciclaggio. Dati statistici*, I semester 2017, September 2017, at www.uif.bancaditalia.it.

3. *Communications to Law Enforcement Authorities*

Statistics on the number of communications by the FIU to other authorities can be found in the Annual Reports of the Italian FIU.[237] They include the number of reports to the judicial authorities, in particular information for investigative purposes and the number of complaints under art. 331 CCP, divided into complaints submitted to the judicial authorities and complaints made in connection with the technical report sent to the investigative bodies. The Annual Report for 2017 shows a downward trend in the number of complaints compared to previous years: from 233 complaints under art. 331 CCP in 2015 to 157 in 2016 and 115 in 2017. With regard to the information for investigative purposes, the Annual Report for 2017 shows an increase in their number, from 17 in 2015 to 26 in 2017.[238]

With regard to the requests for cooperation by the FIU, the Annual Report for 2017 shows a downward trend in the complaints compared to previous years: from 265 in 2014 to 259 in 2015, 241 in 2016 and 226 in 2017.[239]

In addition to the Annual Reports, the Italian FIU used to published, up to the first half of 2012, a "Half-Yearly Bulletin" and a yearly "Notebook of Anti-Money Laundering", both available on the FIU's website, which offer more detailed data than the Annual Reports.

V. DATA FLOW AND DATA PROTECTION

A. DATA EXCHANGE BETWEEN FIU AND PRIVATE SECTOR

1. *From FIU to Private Sector*

The Italian AML system does not in general provide either for the transfer of personal data from the FIU to the private sector or for the existence of any data protection restrictions related to the data transfer.

Different considerations may apply with regard to the FIU's feedback to obliged entities. According to art. 41.2 of L.D. 90/2017, the FIU – ensuring

---

237 Some evaluation regarding the forwarding of SARs by the Italian FIU to other authorities are available on the international level. According to Europol, *From suspicion to action. Converting financial intelligence into greater operational impact*, 2017, at www.europol.europa.eu: "the Italian FIU reports a conversion rate of in excess of 100% due to the fact they forward more reports than they receive (some carried on from previous years) to police authorities (Guardia di Finanza (GdF) and Direzione Investigativa Antimafia (DIA)) after a preliminary analysis process by the FIU".

238 Unità di Informazione Finanziaria, *Annual Report for 2017*, May 2018, no. 10, 98, at www.uif.bancaditalia.it.

239 Ibid., 97.

the protection of confidentiality – shall communicate to the reporting entity, directly or through the self-governing bodies, the outcome of the reports, also taking into account the information received from the Bureau of Anti-Mafia Investigation and the Special Foreign Exchange Unit of the Finance Police.

The question of limits on data flow from the FIU to the private sector might arise where the exchange of information from the FIU to the private sector goes beyond the content of SARs. Notwithstanding the fact that art. 41.2 does not define the content of communicable data from the FIU to the obliged entities or the scope of the duty to ensure confidentiality, the provision seems to distinguish between data relating to the reports and information received from the investigative and judicial authorities forwarded to the obliged entities. With regard to the protection of confidentiality, the provision does not clarify whether this concept totally overlaps with that of the protection of personal data. Therefore, it seems appropriate to keep the two concepts separate.

The Italian National Data Protection Supervisor has criticised this lack of legislative protection, stating that L.D. 90/2017 should have specified the manner in which the FIU communicates the outcome of the reports to the obliged entities and accesses their data banks. In particular, on its view, the introduction of a provision that includes, among the FIU's obligations, the duty to identify appropriate measures to ensure the protection of personal data should be considered.[240]

The absence of further legislative provisions that would address the criticisms of the National Data Protection Supervisor leads us to consider the contents of L.D. 51/2018[241] and the Personal Data Protection Code.[242]

In particular, according to art. 2.1(b) of L.D. 51/2018, the communication of data from the FIU to the obliged entities can be considered a form of processing of personal data.[243]

---

240 Garante per la protezione dei dati personali, *Parere su uno schema di decreto legislative volto ad attuare la direttiva (UE) 2015/849 relativa alla prevenzione dell'uso del sistema finanziario a fini di riciclaggio o finanziamento del terrorismo*, 9 March 2017, 2, at www.garanteprivacy.it. The Italian National Data Protection Supervisor has reiterated the same considerations in its *Parere sullo schema di decreto legislativo recante modifiche ed integrazioni ai d.lgs. 25 maggio 2017 n. 90 e 92 concernenti la prevenzione dell'utilizzo del sistema finanziario a fini di riciclaggio o finanziamento del terrorismo*, 24 July 2019, at www.garanteprivacy.it.

241 The law implements Directive 2016/680/EU on the protection of natural persons with regard to the processing of personal data by competent authorities for the purpose of the prevention, investigation, detection or prosecution of criminal offences or the execution of criminal penalties.

242 The law was recently modified by L.D. 10 August 2018, no. 101, which implements Regulation (EU) 2016/679 of the European Parliament and the Council of 27 April 2016 on the protection of natural persons with regard to the processing of personal data.

243 Indeed, according to this provision, the processing of personal data means any operation or set of operations which is performed on personal data or on a set of personal data, whether or not by automated means, such as – among the others – disclosure by transmission and dissemination or otherwise making available. With regard to the kind of data that can be

With regard to data protection restrictions, art. 5.1 of L.D. 51/2018 provides that the processing of data is lawful if and to the extent that it is necessary for the performance of a task carried out by a competent authority for the purposes set out in art. 1.2,[244] and that it is based on the law. Therefore, while L.D. 51/2018 recognises in the AML Law a legal basis for the processing of data, in particular with regard to the FIU's feedback to obliged entities, it does not define when the processing of data can be said to be "necessary" for the purpose of the prevention of money laundering by identifying the limits of its scope. Furthermore, given that the AML Law is not explicit on the topic, it is not clear whether the FIU is allowed to share personal data with obliged entities outside its feedback obligation.

2. *From Private Sector to FIU*

Personal data transferred from the private sector to the FIU consist of personal data contained in the SARs and data and information sent to the FIU, according to arts. 6.4(f) and 6.5(a) of L.D. 90/2017.[245]

L.D. 90/2017 does not provide for data protection restrictions applicable to the transfer of personal data from the private sector to the FIU.

The data transferred from obliged entities to the FIU represent common data, according to the definition of art. 4.1(a) of the EU Regulation: they consist in "any information relating to an identified or identifiable natural person", and their transfer can be traced back to the "disclosure by transmission or otherwise making available" of personal data, as a form of personal data processing according to art. 4.1(b).[246]

Personal data processed and transferred from obliged entities to the FIU shall comply with the principles relating to the processing of personal data, according to art. 5 of the EU Regulation, in particular the principles of lawfulness; purpose limitation; data minimisation; and accuracy. The data protection restrictions arising from the application of these principles, although not defined by the law, shall be applied.

---

transmitted by the FIU to the private sector, art. 2.1(a) of L.D. 51/2018 defines personal data as *any information* relating to an identified or identifiable natural person. Financial data or judicial data, which are relevant in the present context, are not specifically mentioned as personal data to this effect and do not enjoy particular protection. The same can be said for strategic data.

244 According to art. 1.2 of L.D. 51/2018 applies to the processing of personal data wholly or partly by automated means, and to the processing other than by automated means of personal data that form part of a filing system or are intended to form part of a filing system, by competent authorities for the purposes of the prevention, investigation, detection or prosecution of criminal offences or the execution of criminal penalties, including the safeguarding against and the prevention of threats to public security.

245 See above, section IV.A.2.

246 See above, section V.A.1.

Art. 6 of the Regulation should also be recalled: according to art. 6(1)(c), the processing is lawful when it "is necessary for compliance with a legal obligation to which the controller is subject". In this case, consent to the processing of personal data does not have to be given. In the context of the AML, this can mean that obliged entities are allowed to transfer to the FIU any information relating to customers without their consent.

B. DATA EXCHANGE BETWEEN FIU AND CRIMINAL JUSTICE SYSTEM

1. *From FIU to Criminal Justice System*

Art. 12 of L.D. 90/2017,[247] concerning collaboration and exchange of information between Italian authorities, also provides for the data exchange between FIU and other national authorities. With particular regard to the transfer of personal data from the FIU to the criminal justice system,[248] the relevant provisions are those of paragraphs 3, 5 and 8. In particular, the FIU shall provide to the judicial authority, upon request, the results of its analysis and any other information necessary for starting criminal proceedings. The FIU shall also automatically provide the results of its analysis to the police, the Bureau of Anti-Mafia Investigation and the Special Foreign Exchange Unit of the Finance Police.[249] All the information relevant for the purpose of the AML/CTF legislation is covered by official secrecy, which also applies to the public administration. However, official secrecy cannot be refused to the judicial authority when the information is necessary for an investigation or criminal proceedings. It emerges, therefore, that there are no data protection restrictions on the transfer of personal data from the FIU to the criminal justice system.[250] The provision

247 The provision has been modified by L.D. 125/2019.

248 The Italian criminal justice system is composed of investigative authorities, such as the police, and judicial authorities, such as public prosecutors and judges.

249 The Special Foreign Exchange Unit of the Finance Police has both repressive and preventive powers. The Italian law, namely L.D. 19 March 2001, n. 68, does not separately regulate the two tasks. Art. 220 of the implementing provisions of CCP provides that, when in the course of inspection activities, there are clues of a crime, the activity necessary to ensure the sources of evidence and collect anything else that may serve for the application of criminal law shall be carried out in line with the provisions of the CCP. The provision describes the legal effect of the change from the preventive to the repressive functions. In the context of the prevention of money laundering, it is not easy to clearly keep the distinction and exactly define the data involved and the applicable data protection restrictions.

250 The FIU does not provide for further information. It briefly refers to a new information exchange system, called SAFE, aimed at expanding the use of telecommunications channels between FIU and investigative authorities, by creating an electronic dossier. See Unità di Informazione Finanziaria, *Annual Report for 2016*, May 2017, 95, at www.uif.bancaditalia.it.

of art. 12 only refers to the need, within the collaboration and exchange of information between authorities, to protect the reporter's identity.[251]

The absence of further legislative provisions makes it necessary to consider the contents of the above-mentioned L.D. 51/2018, which recognises the legal basis for the processing of data in the AML/CTF provisions, but does not define when the processing of data is necessary by identifying its limits.[252]

2. *From Criminal Justice System to FIU*

Art. 12 of L.D. 90/2017, concerning the collaboration and exchange of information, deals with the data exchange between the FIU and other national authorities. With particular regard to the transfer of personal data from the criminal justice system to the FIU, the relevant provisions are those in paragraphs 4 and 7.

Unlike the above-mentioned cases, art. 12.4 expressly provides for data protection restrictions. In particular, while investigative bodies shall provide the FIU with the investigative information necessary to enable the FIU to carry out its analysis, under the law, protocol agreements shall regulate the exchange of information in a way that guarantees the prompt availability of such information and the respect of the principles of purpose limitation and proportionality of the processed personal data. If the information is covered by the investigative secrecy, the law also requires the authorisation of the judicial authority before the information can be transmitted from the criminal justice system to the FIU.[253]

With regard to the transfer of personal data from the judicial authority to the FIU, art. 12.7 provides that the information shall be communicated when there is reason to believe that money laundering, self-money laundering, or the use of money, goods or other benefits of illicit provenance or activities intended to carry out one or more acts that have the purpose of financing terrorism is being carried out through financial transactions. This information is covered by official secrecy. The absence of further data protection restrictions, makes it necessary to consider the contents of the above-mentioned L.D. 51/2018, which recognises

---

251 Art. 38 of L.D. 90/2017 contains a general provision on the protection of the SAR's source. The third paragraph of the provision specifies that in any phase of the criminal proceedings, from the inquiry to the trial, the judicial authorities shall adopt appropriate measures to ensure the confidentiality of the reporter's identity. In any case, the name of the reporter cannot appear in either the public prosecutor's folder or the hearing's folder. His/her identity cannot be revealed, unless the judicial authority differently so provides in a reasoned decision ensuring the adoption of appropriate measures to guarantee the protection of the reporter and only if it is necessary for the detection of the offence.

252 See above, section V.A.1.

253 The provision has been modified by L.D. 125/2019, pointing out that in case of a police investigation for which a report has already been sent to the judicial authority, the information cannot be sent to the FIU until the judicial authority has taken its determinations with regard to the prosecution.

the legal basis of the processing of data in the AML/CTF provisions, without defining when the processing of data is necessary by identifying its limits.[254]

C. DATA EXCHANGE BETWEEN FIU AND INTELLIGENCE AGENCIES

1. *From FIU to Intelligence Agencies*

The only provision within the Italian AML/CTF system that refers to the transfer of personal data from the FIU to intelligence agencies is art. 40.1(e) of L.D. 90/2017. It provides that in cases of specific relevance to the security of the State, the FIU shall communicate the results of the analysis carried out, including information pertinent to the predicate offences, to the intelligence agencies, which are regulated by L. 3 August 2007, no. 124, according to memoranda of understanding. However, the provision does not clarify which data protection restrictions exist in relation to the transfer of personal data from the FIU to the Italian intelligence agency. Furthermore, L. 3 August 2007, no. 124, containing provisions on the information system for the security of the State, does not contain any reference either to the collaboration between intelligence authorities and FIU or to data protection restrictions.[255]

The absence of further legislative provisions makes it necessary to consider the Data Protection Code and L.D. 51/2018. According to art. 58 of the Data Protection Code, some of the provisions of L.D. 51/2018 are also applicable to the processing of personal data for national security and defence purposes, where compatible.[256]

---

254 See above, section V.A.1.

255 Art. 4.1(c) only provides, with reference to the functions of the Department of Security Information, that this authority shall collect information, analysis and reports coming from intelligence agencies, armed forces and police, public administrations and research institutions, even private ones. According to art. 13, which regulates the collaboration between the intelligence agencies and the public administrations, the Department and the information agencies for the domestic and foreign security can communicate with all the public administrations and with entities that provide public services and ask them for the collaboration necessary for the fulfilment of their institutional functions. On the basis of an implementing decree, the necessary provisions are adopted in order to ensure the access to the databases of the public administration and of the entities that provide public services and the software and hardware that allow the verification of the access to personal data, even after the fact. The decree was adopted on 29 April 2016, but is currently not available. Art. 26, covering the processing of personal data, only specifies that the collection and processing of news and information is aimed solely at the pursuit of institutional tasks of the security information system. See L. 3 August 2007, no. 124, in *Gazzetta Ufficiale*, 13 August 2007, no. 187.

256 See above, section V.A.1.

2. *From Intelligence Agencies to FIU*

Neither L.D. 90/2017 nor L. 124/2007 provides for the transfer of personal data from intelligence agencies to the FIU.

Art. 13 of L. 124/2007 only provides that intelligence agencies can ask for such collaboration from public authorities, including the FIU, as is necessary for the fulfilment of their institutional functions. Art. 26 of L. 124/2007 specifies that the collection and processing of news and information are solely aimed at pursuing the institutional tasks of the intelligence agencies, but the data protection restrictions are not defined.

The absence of further legislative provisions makes it necessary to consider the Data Protection Code and L.D. 51/2018, as already seen above.[257]

D. DATA EXCHANGE BETWEEN FIU AND TAX AUTHORITIES

1. *From FIU to Tax Authorities*

In the Italian system, the term "tax authorities" can refer both to the Special Foreign Exchange Unit of the Finance Police, which also has preventive powers, and to the Revenue Agency.

With regard to the Special Foreign Exchange Unit of the Finance Police in its preventive capacity, art. 9.9 of L.D. 90/2017 only provides that data and information can be used for "fiscal purposes".

No provision of L.D. 90/2017 concerns either the exchange of data and information between the FIU and the Revenue Agency, or data protection restrictions related to the transfer of data.

However, L.D. 51/2018 seems to be applicable. Indeed, according to art. 2.1(g), both authorities can be defined as public authorities competent in the prevention and investigation of criminal offences, such as tax offences.[258]

2. *From Tax Authorities to FIU*

With regard to the flow of information from the tax authorities to the FIU, art. 6.6(a) of L.D. 90/2017 regulates the power of the FIU to access the data and information contained in the tax register,[259] but it does not make any mention of data protection restrictions.

---

257 See above, section V.A.1.
258 See above, section V.A.1.
259 See above, section IV.D.2.

The Italian Supervisor for Data Protection has highlighted this lack of legislative protection.[260] The Supervisor noted that the archive of financial relationships has been expanded in terms of the type of relationships that are subject to disclosure by financial operators, and the amount of information relating to the business relationships. Therefore, according to the opinion of the Supervisor, art. 6.6 of L.D. 90/2017 should specify that the FIU can also access account data.[261] However, the Italian legislator has not implemented the Supervisor's advice.

The absence of further legislative provisions makes it necessary to consider L.D. 51/2018, as already seen above.[262]

E. DATA EXCHANGE BETWEEN FIU AND CUSTOMS AUTHORITIES

1. *From FIU to Customs Authorities*

In the Italian system, the term "custom authorities" refers to the Custom and Monopolies Agency.

L.D. 90/2017 does not expressly regulate either the transfer of personal data from the FIU to the Custom and Monopolies Agency, or data protection restrictions related to the transfer of data.

However, L.D. 51/2018 seems to be applicable. Indeed, according to art. 2.1(g), the Custom and Monopolies Agency can be defined as a public authority competent in the prevention and investigation of criminal offences, such as tax offences.[263]

2. *From Customs Authorities to FIU*

L.D. 90/2017 does not expressly regulate the transfer of data and information from the Custom and Monopolies Agency to the FIU, or data protection restrictions related to the transfer of data. Art. 8.1(b) only provides for the transfer of all the

---

260 Garante per la protezione dei dati personali, *Parere su uno schema di decreto legislative volto ad attuare la direttiva (UE) 2015/849 relativa alla prevenzione dell'uso del sistema finanziario a fini di riciclaggio o finanziamento del terrorismo*, 9 March 2017, 2, at www.garanteprivacy.it. The Italian National Data Protection Supervisor has reiterated the same considerations in its *Parere sullo schema di decreto legislativo recante modifiche ed integrazioni ai d.lgs. 25 maggio 2017 n. 90 e 92 concernenti la prevenzione dell'utilizzo del sistema finanziario a fini di riciclaggio o finanziamento del terrorismo*, 24 July 2019, at www.garanteprivacy.it.

261 Garante per la protezione dei dati personali, *Parere su uno schema di decreto legislative volto ad attuare la direttiva (UE) 2015/849 relativa alla prevenzione dell'uso del sistema finanziario a fini di riciclaggio o finanziamento del terrorismo*, 9 March 2017, 2, at www.garanteprivacy.it.

262 See above, section V.D.2.

263 See above, section V.A.1.

data necessary to identify possible correlations between commodity flows and suspect financial flows from the Custom and Monopolies Agency to the Bureau of Anti-Mafia Investigation.

However, L.D. 51/2018 seems to be applicable. Indeed, according to art. 2.1(g), the Custom and Monopolies Agency can be defined as a public authority competent in the prevention and investigation of criminal offences, such as tax offences.[264]

F. INFORMATION FLOW BETWEEN FIU AND FOREIGN COUNTERPARTS

1. *Restrictions on Data Transfer from FIU to Foreign FIUs*

Art. 13-*bis* of L.D. 90/2017, introduced by L.D. 125/2019, provides for the transfer of personal data from the FIU to foreign FIUs. According to this provision, the FIU, derogating from official secrecy, can exchange information and collaborate – upon request or spontaneously – with foreign FIUs, with the following conditions: (i) that the information flow is reciprocal; (ii) that the information shared is kept confidential; (iii) that investigative secrecy is maintained with regard to the information received from the investigative authorities; and (iv) that the information exchange respects constitutional provisions and fundamental principles of national law. The provision clarifies that the FIU can exchange information related to money laundering or terrorist financing and to the persons involved, including the data coming from the investigative bodies. Except for these conditions, the provision does not mention further reasons for refusing to exchange information with foreign FIUs.

2. *Restrictions on Use of Data Obtained from Foreign FIUs*

L.D. 125/2019, introducing art. 13-*bis*, specifically deals with the use of personal data the FIU receives from a foreign FIU, but not for the related data protection restrictions.[265] According to this provision, the information received from foreign

264 See above, section V.A.1.

265 Unità di Informazione Finanziaria, *Annual Report for 2016*, May 2017, 101 ff., at www.uif.bancaditalia.it. See n. 219 for discussion of the problems this causes. To this is added the frequent confusion between financial analysis and investigation, the lack of adequate information powers and the inadequate ability to exchange information. Significant obstacles to the FIU's activity also stem from the levels of autonomy and independence between the different FIUs.

FIUs can be transmitted to the competent Italian authorities, with the consent of the foreign FIU that provided the information and in accordance with any limits or conditions imposed by the foreign FIU. In case of information coming from joint analyses of cases of cross-border relevance, the FIU communicates such information to the investigative and judicial authorities where necessary and upon authorisation of the foreign FIU.

G. INFORMATION FLOW BETWEEN FIU AND FOREIGN NON-COUNTERPARTS

1. *Restrictions on Data Transfer from FIU to Other Foreign Authorities*

L.D. 125/2019, rewriting art. 13 on international cooperation, deals with the transfer of personal data from the FIU to other foreign authorities, but not for the related data protection restrictions. According to art. 13.1, all authorities – including the FIU – shall cooperate with the competent authorities of other Member States in order to ensure the exchange of information and assistance necessary for AML/CTF purposes. The following circumstances shall not be considered to be an obstacle to the exchange of information: the relevance of the information to tax matters; the different legal nature or status of the requesting competent authority; the existence of an investigation or criminal proceedings, unless the exchange or assistance could prevent such an investigation or criminal proceeding.

According to art. 13.2, the Italian FIU shall draw up memoranda of understanding with the competent authorities of the other Member States, aimed at regulating the process of timely sharing of the above-mentioned information.

Restrictions on data transfer come from L.D. 51/2018. In particular, art. 31, providing for the principles applicable to data processing, allows the data transfer when: (i) it is necessary for AML/CTF purposes; (ii) the foreign authority is competent for AML/CTF purposes; and (iii) in relation to personal data transmitted or made available from another Member State, that Member State has given its prior authorisation to the transfer.

2. *Restrictions on Use of Data Obtained from Other Foreign Authorities*

Art. 13.2, as rewrote by L.D. 125/2019, also deals with the use of personal data that the FIU receives from a foreign authority, but not for the related data protection restrictions.[266] The absence of further legislative provisions in L.D. 90/2017 makes it necessary to consider the contents of L.D. 51/2018. In

[266] See above, section V.G.1.

particular, art. 31, providing for the principles applicable to data processing, allows the data transfer when: (i) it is necessary for AML/CTF purposes; (ii) the authority is competent for AML/CTF purposes; and (iii) in relation to personal data transmitted or made available from another Member State, that Member State has given its prior authorisation to the transfer.

H. EVIDENTIAL VALUE OF FIU-GENERATED DATA IN COURT PROCEEDINGS

Apart from the above-mentioned provisions, concerning collaboration and exchange of data between FIU and judicial authorities,[267] L.D. 90/2017 does not contain special rules on the admissibility of FIU-generated information as evidence in court proceedings. Following the general rules on evidence in criminal proceedings, FIU-generated information, such as SARs, can be admitted as documentary evidence or its content can be included in the FIU's testimony.

I. USE OF CDD DATA FOR PROFIT MAKING

L.D. 90/2017 does not explicitly prohibit the use of personal data gathered by obliged entities for the purpose of CDD, or received from the FIU, for profit-oriented purposes.

However, art. 32.1 provides that obliged entities shall guarantee that they process data and information exclusively for the purposes of the AML Law, i.e. for purposes directly related to the prevention of financial crimes, and that they respect the Data Protection Code.[268]

J. DATA SHARING BETWEEN OBLIGED ENTITIES REGARDING SARs AND FIU REQUESTS

1. *Data Sharing Inside a Group*

Art. 39 of L.D. 90/2017 provides for a general prohibition on disclosure regarding the submission of SARs or additional information to the FIU, and of the probable

[267] See above, sections V.B.1 and V.B.2.

[268] According to art. 2.1 of L.D. 90/2017, the provisions set up in the Legislative Decree apply for the purpose of preventing and countering the use of the economic and financial system for money laundering and terrorism financing. It imposes measures aimed at protecting the integrity of the economic and financial system and the correctness of the operators' conduct, required to comply with it (art. 2.2). According to art. 2.3, the prevention is carried out in

existence of an investigation on money laundering or terrorism financing.[269] According to art. 39.3, the prohibition laid down in paragraph 1 shall not prevent disclosure between credit and financial institutions in the same group.[270]

The sharing of information regarding the filing of SARs or requests from the FIU with other obliged entities within the same group of companies is therefore allowed and is not subject to particular conditions.

2. *Data Sharing with Similar Professions*

According to art. 39.4, of L.D. 90/2017, the prohibition on disclosure, laid down in paragraph 1,[271] shall not prevent disclosure between professionals who perform their professional activities in an associated form, for example as employees or collaborators.[272]

With regard to data protection, the provision points out that the information exchanged can only be used for the purpose of preventing money laundering and terrorism financing.

3. *Data Sharing with Obliged Entities Outside the EU*

Art. 39.3, 4 and 5 of L.D. 90/2017 authorise obliged entities and professionals to share information regarding the filing of SARs or requests from the FIU with other obliged entities or professionals in third countries in two cases.

The first case is that of communications between obliged entities and their branches and majority-owned subsidiaries located in third countries, if those branches and majority-owned subsidiaries fully comply with the group-wide policies and procedures, including procedures for sharing information within the group. The same applies to communications between professionals located in third countries who perform their professional activities in an associated form, as long as they adopt measures equivalent to those provided for in the AML/CTF legislation.

The second case is that of communications relating to the same customer and the same transaction involving two or more obliged entities, as long as obliged

---

coordination with the repression of crimes such as money laundering, its predicate offences and terrorism financing.

269 From another perspective, art. 41.3. regulating the "return flow" of the report's outcome from the FIU to the reporting entity, maintains the same prohibition on communication provided in art. 39.

270 The provision does not refer to credit institutions and financial institutions belonging to the same group, as required by art. 24 5AMLD.

271 See above, section V.J.1.

272 Art. 39.6 clarifies that the case of a professional who dissuades his/her customer committing an illicit activity is not a violation of the obligation not to disclose.

entities or professionals located in third countries are subject to obligations equivalent to those provided for in the AML/CTF legislation.[273]

K. DATA SHARING BETWEEN OBLIGED ENTITIES REGARDING POSSIBLE CASES OF MONEY LAUNDERING

1. *Data Sharing Inside a Group*

There is no provision in L.D. 90/2017 that explicitly authorises the sharing of information regarding suspicious transactions or similarly unusual events by obliged entities within the same group of companies.

Such sharing of information is then subject to the limits of the Data Protection Code and the GDPR.

2. *Data Sharing with Similar Professions*

Likewise, there is no provision in L.D. 90/2017 that explicitly authorises the sharing of information regarding suspicious transactions or similarly unusual events with other obliged entities outside the group, but within a similar profession.

The absence of such authorisation does not mean the sharing is categorically prohibited. It should be possible, so long as professional secrecy is respected and within the limits of Data Protection Code and the GDPR.

3. *Data Sharing with Obliged Entities Outside the EU*

Finally, there is also no provision in L.D. 90/2017 that explicitly authorises the sharing of information regarding suspicious transactions or similarly unusual events with other obliged entities in third countries.

Again, the absence of such authorisation does not mean that such sharing is prohibited, but that it is subject to the limits of the Data Protection Code and the GDPR.

L. DATA MINING BY OBLIGED ENTITIES

L.D. 90/2017 does not deal with the case of data mining, instead of data matching by obliged entities within their own data banks, in order to identify possible cases of money laundering.

---

273 In this case, according to art. 39.5 of L.D. 90/2017, the above-mentioned provisions of arts. 42, 43 and 44 of the Personal Data Protection Code, concerning the transfer of data flows, are applicable. See above, section V.F.1.

Such processing of personal data should be possible within the limits of the Data Protection Code and art. 22 of the GDPR, concerning automated individual decision making, including profiling.

VI. BENEFICIAL OWNERSHIP TRANSPARENCY

A. BENEFICIAL OWNERSHIP INFORMATION

1. *General Framework*

The Italian AML legislation imposes obligations on legal entities and trusts to disclose their beneficial ownership situation.[274]

Within Italian civil law, legal entities are organisations of people and goods that aim to achieve a certain objective and are recognised by the State as subjects of law. Associations, foundations and other institutions of private nature can acquire legal personality by being recognised, via registration in the Register of Legal Persons, at the prefectures. In terms of enterprises, capital companies (joint stock companies, partnerships partially limited by shares, limited liability companies) and cooperative societies can acquire legal personality by registering themselves in the Register of Companies as a limited liability company. Within Italian civil law, there is no legal definition of trusts.[275]

According to art. 22 of L.D. 90/2017, corporate entities, legal entities and trusts shall obtain and hold for a period of no less than five years information on their beneficial ownership. This information shall be adequate, accurate and current.

In case of corporate entities, according to art. 22., the management shall collect the information on beneficial ownership on the basis of the results of the accounting records, the balance sheet, the shareholder's register, communications on the ownership or control structure of the entity, communications received from the shareholders, and on the basis of any other available data. In the event that doubts remain regarding the beneficial ownership, the management shall expressly ask the shareholders to provide the information. The unjustified inaction or refusal of the shareholders to provide the management with the information they deem necessary for the identification of the beneficial owner

274 The obligation was already present in L.D. 231/2007. See, in particular, arts. 1.2(u), 18.1(b) and 19.1(b).

275 Art. 73 of D.P.R. 22 January 1986, no. 917, containing the "Consolidated Text of the Laws on Income Tax", in *Gazzetta Ufficiale*, 31 December 1986, no. 302, only identifies entities subject to corporate income tax, without defining them. The figure has been already recognised by the Italian jurisprudence. See C. Cass., sentence no. 975, 17 January 2018, in *Ced Cass.*, RV 646913.

or the provision of clearly fraudulent information render their voting rights not exercisable and entail the appeal of any resolutions taken with his/her decisive vote. In the case of legal entities that are not corporate entities, according to art. 22.4, the same information shall be collected by the founder or the management on the basis of its charter, the accounting records or any other available data.

In the case of trusts, according to art. 22.5, the trustee shall collect and hold adequate, accurate and up-to-date information relating to the identity of the founder, the trustee, the guardian, the beneficiary, or any other person who exercises control over the trust, and of any other person exercising, in the final instance, control over the assets transferred to the trust by direct or indirect ownership or by other means.[276]

2. *Definition of "Beneficiary" and "Effective Control"*

According to art. 20.1 of L.D. 90/2017, the beneficiary is defined as the natural person who ultimately owns or controls the legal entity through direct or indirect ownership.

According to art. 20.2 of L.D. 90/2017, a shareholding of 25% plus one share or an ownership interest of more than 25% in the customer held by a natural person shall be an indication of direct ownership (art. 20.2(a)). A shareholding of 25% plus one share or an ownership interest of more than 25% in the customer held by a corporate entity that is under the control of a natural person(s), or held by multiple corporate entities that are under the control of the same natural person(s), shall be an indication of indirect ownership (art. 20.2(b)).

According to art. 20.3 of L.D. 90/2017, if the application of the above-mentioned criteria does not make it possible to definitively identify the direct or indirect owner of the legal entity, the beneficiary is the natural person who holds control. The concept of control is defined as the control of the majority of exercisable votes, or the control of votes sufficient to exercise a dominant influence, or the existence of particular contractual obligations that allow the exercise of a dominant influence.

According to art. 20.4 of L.D. 90/2017, as modified by L.D. 125/2019, if the legal entity is a private legal entity, the founders (if alive), the beneficiaries (if identified or easily identifiable) and the manager are jointly identified as the effective owners.[277]

---

276 The provision has been modified by L.D. 125/2019.

277 L.D. 90/2017 does not refer to trusts, since they may follow different legal rules according to the reason for which they are established, for example whether they are family, testamentary or commercial trusts.

According to art. 20.5 of L.D. 90/2017, as modified by L.D. 125/2019, if the application of the above-mentioned criteria does not make it possible to definitively identify the beneficial owner, the beneficiary is the natural person who holds the position of manager.

L.D. 90/2017 does not refers to trusts, since they may follow different legal rules depending on the reason for which they were established, for example whether they are family, testamentary or commercial trusts.

3. *Definition of "Information"*

In relation to the beneficial owner, L.D. 90/2017 does not define the term "information".

4. *Special Rules for Entities with a Cross-Border Dimension*

L.D. 90/2017 does not provide for foreign legal entities or foreign trusts. The legal entities subject to Italian civil law are those with a registered office in Italy. Consequently, it does not provide for special requirements or mechanism for the disclosure of beneficial ownership.

B. BENEFICIAL OWNERSHIP REGISTRIES

1. *Scope and General Procedure*

The Italian AML legislation provides for a centralised mechanism to disclose beneficial ownership information. According to art. 21 of L.D. 90/2017, companies with legal personality, trusts and private legal entities shall communicate the information about their beneficial owner to the Register of Companies, so that it can be recorded in a special section with restricted access. The registry is nationwide.

In accordance with art. 21.1 of L.D. 90/2017, corporate and legal entities with legal personality that are required to be registered in the Register of Companies referred to in art. 2188 CC and private legal entities required to be registered in the Register of Private Legal Entities pursuant to Presidential Decree (P.D.) 10 February 2000, no. 361, shall communicate their beneficial ownership information to the Register of Companies, so that it can be recorded in a special section with restricted access.

In accordance with art. 21.3 of L.D. 90/2017, trusts that produce legal effects relevant for tax purposes, pursuant to art. 73 of D.P.R. 22 January 1986, no. 917, are also required to be registered in a special section of the Register of Companies.

The information about their beneficial ownership is communicated by the trustee or by another person on behalf of the trustee, so that it can be recorded.

The law does not define which information the registry shall contain.[278]

2. *Standard Verification of Accuracy*

L.D. 90/2017 does not provide for procedures to verify the accuracy of the beneficial ownership information before it is fed into the special section of the above-mentioned registry.

From this perspective, the Italian AML system makes the client responsible for providing all the necessary and up-to-date information to allow obliged entities to fulfil their CDD obligations, including information on beneficial ownership (art. 22.1).

3. Ex Post *Review of Accuracy*

L.D. 90/2017 does not provide for procedures to verify the accuracy of the beneficial ownership information after it has been fed into the special section of the above-mentioned registry.

C. ACCESS TO BENEFICIAL OWNERSHIP INFORMATION

1. *Access by FIU and Other Authorities*

The FIU and the authorities in charge of AML efforts have access to beneficial ownership information about corporate entities, legal entities and trusts.

In particular, arts. 21.2 and 21.4, give access to the special section of the Register of Companies that contains beneficial ownership information to the following authorities:

(i) the Ministry of Economy and Finance, the supervisory authorities, the Italian FIU, the Bureau of Anti-Mafia Investigation and the Special Foreign Exchange Unit of the Finance Police, without any restriction;

278 Art. 21.5 as modified by L.D. 125/2019, clarifies that a decree of the Ministry of Economy and Finance, in agreement with the Ministry of Economic Development, after consulting the Personal Data Protection Supervisor, will establish the data and information on the beneficial owner of companies provided with legal personality, trusts and private legal entities that shall be communicated to the registers, including how it shall be communicated and the time limit for doing so (subpara. (a)). The decree has not been adopted yet. See above, section VI.A.1.c.

(ii) the National Anti-Mafia and Counter-Terrorism Bureau; with regard only to trusts, the provision specifies that the Bureau may have access within the limits of its institutional tasks;
(iii) the judicial authority, within the limits of its institutional tasks;
(iv) the authorities in charge of combating tax evasion, in line with appropriate means of access to guarantee the pursuit of their purposes, established in a specific decree of the Ministry of Economy and Finance in agreement with the Ministry of Economic Development.

2. *Access by Obliged Entities*

Obliged entities have access to beneficial ownership information in two different cases.

According to art. 22.2 of L.D. 90/2017, they will obtain such information from corporate entities and legal entities in carrying out CDD measures. From the perspective of the customer, art. 22.1 requires the customer to provide all the necessary and up-date-date information to allow obliged entities to fulfil their CDD obligations, including information on beneficial ownership.

Art. 21.2(e) of L.D. 90/2017 gives access to the special section of the Register of Companies that contains beneficial ownership information to obliged entities in order to allow them to comply with their CDD obligations, upon accreditation and payment of fees. Art. 21.4(d) of L.D. 90/2017 establishes the same for trusts.

3. *Access by Interested Third Parties*

Art. 21.2(f) of L.D. 90/2017, as modified by L.D. 125/2019, gives access to the special section of the Register of Companies that contains beneficial ownership information about corporate entities and legal entities to the public. In particular, it gives the public access to the following information, upon payment of fees: name, surname, date of birth, country of residence, nationality, and the condition laid down in art. 20 under which the beneficial owner is considered as such. In exceptional cases, access can be refused, in whole or part, where access exposes the beneficial owner to a disproportionate risk of fraud, abduction, kidnapping, extortion, harassment, violence or intimidation or where the beneficial owner is an incapacitated person or a minor of age, on a case-by-case basis and after a detailed assessment of the exceptional nature of the circumstances.

Interested third parties are not allowed to access the special section of the Register of Company that contains information about the beneficial ownership of trusts.

VII. SANCTIONS

A. SANCTIONS FOR MONEY LAUNDERING

1. *Requirement of a Conviction for a Predicate Offence*

The Italian Criminal Code does not specify to what extent the commission of a predicate offence has to be proven in order to apply sanctions for money laundering. However, the Italian jurisprudence is quite clear on this point. For the Italian jurisprudence, neither a definitive sentence on the predicate offence nor the establishment of precisely which predicate offence has been committed is necessary. It is sufficient that the trial court that handles the proceedings on the crime of money laundering ascertains the provenance of criminal assets from a crime (*dolus*).[279] The trial court does not need to identify a particular predicate offence; it is enough that the trial court establishes how the predicate offence was committed, without the need to inquire into the intent behind that predicate offence. In a recent decision, the Italian Court of Cassation confirmed this interpretation, clarifying that for a criminal conviction for money laundering it is not necessary to identify the predicate offence exactly, but it is also not possible to affirm liability for money laundering in a situation in which it is not even possible to establish whether there was a predicate offence.[280]

The perpetrator of money laundering can be convicted for it even in the absence of a criminal conviction or prior judicial proceedings for the predicate offence.[281]

2. *Forms of Sanctions*

Art. 648-*bis* CC punishes the different conducts of money laundering with imprisonment of four to 12 years and with a fine of €5,000–25,000. The penalty

279 See C. Cass., sentence no. 546, 7 January 2011, in *Cass. Pen.*, 2012, 1388 ff.; C. Cass., sentence no. 7795, 19 November 2013, in *Riv. Pen.*, 2014, 394 ff.; C. Cass., sentence no. 10746, 21 November 2014, in *Ced Cass.*, RV 263156; C. Cass., sentence no. 20188, 4 February 2015, in *Ced Cass.*, RV 263521; C. Cass., sentence no. 527, 13 September 2016, in *Ced Cass.*, RV 269017.

280 See C. Cass., sentence no. 13901, 25 February 2016, in *Ced Cass.*, RV 266669.

281 Except for subsequently asking for a review of the sentence for money laundering. See Gambogi, *Riciclaggio e antiriciclaggio*, in *Officina del diritto*, Giuffrè, Milan, 2015, 18–19; Castaldo/Naddeo, *Il denaro sporco. Prevenzione e repressione del riciclaggio*, Cedam, Padua, 2010, 139 ff.

is increased by up to third if the crime is committed during the course of the performance of a professional activity.[282]

The third paragraph of art. 648-*bis* CC introduces an attenuated form of money laundering, depending on the penalty provided for the predicate offence. The sentence for money laundering is reduced by one third if the predicate offence is punishable by a maximum prison sentence of less than five years.

The Italian criminal justice system also provides, at art. 20 CC, that the main penalties imposed after a conviction for money laundering shall be always followed by accessory penalties: they are the "criminal effects" of the conviction. The accessory penalties for crimes are referred to in arts. 28 ff. CC, in particular: being banned from holding public office, being a member of certain professions or arts, and from managing legal entities and companies; the inability to make offers for services to the public administration; termination of employment; forfeiture of or suspension from the exercise of parental responsibility; and having the sentence made public.

Art. 25-*octies* of L.D. 8 June 2001, no. 231, which introduced corporate criminal liability in Italy, punishes the crime of money laundering committed by corporate entities with a fine of €51,600–1,239,200.[283] The system provides for criminal liability for enterprises whose managers or employees commit crimes such as money laundering. In such circumstances, criminal liability has the following requirements. (i) the crime must be listed in the normative catalogue of crimes in arts. 24 ff., which includes money laundering (art. 2); (ii) the crime must have been committed in the interest or for the advantage of the corporate entity (art. 5); and (iii) the crime must have been committed as a result of ineffective adoption of compliance programmes (art. 6.1). According to art. 25-*octies*, disqualification sanctions also apply.[284]

In the event that criminal assets originate from a predicate criminal offence that is punishable by imprisonment of up to five years, art. 25-*octies*.1 imposes a fine of €103,200–1,549,000.

---

282 Another scenario of aggravated money laundering is the one in art. 71.1 of L. 6 September 2011, no. 159, containing the Code of Anti-Mafia Law and Prevention Measures. According to the provision, the penalty provided for by art. 648-*bis* CC increases by from one third to one half when a person under a definitive personal prevention measure commits the offence during its application period and within the three years of its application.

283 According to art. 10.2 of L.D. 231/2001, the fine applies to quotes, with the figure not less than 100 and not more than 1,000. The amount of each quote goes from a minimum of €258 to a maximum of €1,549 (art. 10.3).

284 According to art. 9.2 of L.D. 231/2001, disqualification sanctions are the following: (i) prohibition from the exercise of the corporate activity; (ii) suspension or revocation of authorisations, licences or concessions functional to the commission of the offence; (iii) prohibition from contracting with the public administration; (iv) exclusion from obtaining of public services, loans, grants or subsidies and the possible revocation of those already granted; and (v) ban on advertising goods and services.

3. *Confiscation*

According to art. 648-*quater* CC, introduced by art. 63 of L.D. 231/2007, a conviction for money laundering is always followed by the confiscation of the product and the profits of the crime, except if they belong to a person who acquired the assets *in bona fide*.

According to art. 648-*quater*.2 CC, if the confiscation of the assets is not possible, the court will order a so-called "confiscation by equivalent", i.e. the confiscation of other assets that belong to the convicted person, including if they are in the possession of a third person, up to a value equivalent to the product, profits or reward of the crime.

4. *Statistics*

a. Number of Criminal Proceedings

In Italy, there are no statistics available on the number of criminal proceedings for money laundering and on the value of transactions associated with these proceedings.

On the international level, the mutual evaluation report of the FATF, although quite old, provides some data.[285]

Table 1. Number of criminal proceedings, 2010–2012

	Regulation		**2010**	**2011**	**2012**
Money Laundering	Art. 648-*bis* CC	Cases	1,375	1,292	1,285
		Persons	2,285	2,261	2,189
	Art. 648-*ter* CC	Cases	43	49	77
		Persons	123	134	207
	Art. 12-*quinquies* D.L. 306/92	Cases	68	70	74
		Persons	212	276	229
Tax Crimes	Arts. 2, 4, 5, 8 L. 74/200	Cases	5,270	7,533	7,648
		Persons	7,821	10,692	10,661
Corruption	Arts. 318, 319, 319-*ter*, 320 CC	Cases	349	307	304
		Persons	1,067	719	1,402

Source: FATF, *Anti-money laundering and counter-terrorist financing measures – Mutual Evaluation Report for Italy*.

285 FATF, *Anti-money laundering and counter-terrorist financing measures – Mutual Evaluation Report for Italy*, 53, available at: http://www.fatf-gafi.org. According to the Report, "the average of prosecutions initiated decreases slightly from 2011 to 2012, after an increase in 2010. Money laundering prosecutions are generally linked to the predicate offense and there are

b. Number of Convictions

In Italy, there are no statistics available on the number of convictions for money laundering and on the value of transactions associated with these proceedings.

On the international level the mutual evaluation report of the FATF, although quite old, provides some data.[286]

Table 2. Number of convictions, 2011–2013

	Regulation		2011	2012	2013
Money Laundering	Art. 648-*bis* CC	Cases	1,060	880	941
		Persons	719	642	666
	Art. 648-*ter* Criminal Code	Cases	11	15	20
		Persons	9	8	15
	Art. 12-*quinquies* D.L. 306/92				
		Persons	27	25	36
Tax Crimes	Arts. 2, 4, 5, 8 L. 74/200	Cases	2,593	2,604	2,761
		Persons	1,352	1,588	1,641
Corruption	Arts. 318, 319, 319-*ter*, 320 CC	Cases	313	301	208
		Persons	101	79	91

Source: FATF, Anti-*money laundering and counter-terrorist financing measures – Mutual Evaluation Report for Italy.*

B. SANCTIONS FOR VIOLATIONS OF PREVENTIVE MEASURES

1. *Money Laundering by Violating Preventive Obligations*

Art. 648-*bis* CC does not allow for criminal convictions for money laundering for omissions made in the course of preventive duties. The provision does not refer to any form of criminal liability by omission.[287] Nevertheless, according to the most recent Italian jurisprudence,[288] and a minority doctrine,[289] money

fewer prosecutions for the money laundering as a standalone crime. Foreign predicate offenses are not frequently prosecuted from the money laundering perspective, because Italy does not consider that foreign predicate offenses are major predicates for money laundering in Italy, however there are suspicions about foreign organized crimes laundering their funds in Italy".

286 Ibid., 54.

287 See above, section II.B.2.

288 See C. Cass., no. 9472, 14 January 2016, and C. Cass., no. 29452, 17 May 2013. Both of the decisions are unpublished. For references to less recent decisions, see Manna (a cura di), *Riciclaggio e reati connessi all'intermediazione mobiliare*, Utet, Turin, 2000, 388 ff.

289 Zanchetti, *Il riciclaggio di denaro proveniente da reato*, Giuffrè, Milan, 1997, 374 ff.

laundering by omission could be possible in the form of participation by omission in another's conduct of recycling. The punishment would be that provided for by art. 648-*bis* CC, i.e. four to 12 years' imprisonment and a fine of €5,000–25,000.

2. *CDD, Reporting and Other AML-Related Obligations*

a. Special Criminal Laws against Individuals

Art. 55 of L.D. 90/2017 provides for criminal sanctions for the most serious violations of AML due diligence obligations, namely conduct that concern primarily the agents of obliged entities, such as the falsification of data and information,[290] the use of false data,[291] and the acquisition or maintenance of false data.[292] The different conducts are punishable by imprisonment of six months to three years and with a fine of €10,000–30,000.

According to art. 55.4, unless the fact constitutes a more serious offence, anyone who violates the prohibition on disclosure established by arts. 39.1, and 41.3 is punishable[293] by imprisonment of six months to one year and with a fine of €5,000–30,000.

The AML legislation does not provide for criminal sanctions against individuals for a violation of AML reporting obligations.

The AML legislation provides for criminal sanctions against individuals for the violation of other AML-related obligations in cases where a customer provides false data, with a fine of €10,000–30,000 (art. 55 of L.D. 90/2017).

b. Administrative Sanctions against Individuals

The AML legislation does not provide for administrative sanctions against individuals for a violation of AML due diligence obligations.

---

290 Art. 55.1 punishes anyone obliged to comply with the due diligence obligations who falsifies the data and information relating to the client, the beneficial owner, the executor, and the purpose and nature of the business relationship or the transaction, with imprisonment from six months to three years and with a fine of €10,000–30,000.

291 The same punishment is imposed on anyone required to comply with CDD obligations, on the occasion of the fulfilment of the aforementioned obligations, who uses false data and information relating to the client, the beneficial owner, the executor, and the nature of the ongoing business relationship and the transaction.

292 Art. 55.2 punishes anyone required to comply with the conservation obligations who acquires or keeps false data or untrue information about the customer, the beneficial owner, the executor, and the nature of the ongoing business relationship and the transaction. It also punishes anyone required to comply with the conservation obligations who uses fraudulent means in order to jeopardise the correct conservation of the aforementioned data. Both cases are punished with imprisonment from six months to three years and with a fine of €10,000–30,000.

293 Arts. 39 and 41.3 L.D. 90/2017 concern the refusal to communicate SARs and the "return flow" of the report's outcome from the FIU to the reporting entity. See above, section III.B.1.c.

Art. 11.3 of L.D. 90/2017 specifies that self-regulatory bodies shall apply disciplinary sanctions for the serious, repeated or systematic violations committed by professionals under the AML law and the technical rules.

According to art. 58.3 of L.D. 90/2017, in the event of failure to report suspicious transactions, the same administrative fines provided for obliged entities are applicable to their employees who are in charge of the reporting, independently or in addition to the fine imposed on the obliged entity.

According to art. 5.4 of L.D. 90/2017, the Ministry of Economy and Finance exercises the sanctioning power. The sanctions can be imposed on the initiative of the different authorities mentioned above.

Art. 11.3 specifies that self-regulatory bodies apply disciplinary sanctions for the serious, repeated or systematic violations committed by professionals under the AML law and the technical rules.

Art. 59 of L.D. 90/2017 provides for an administrative sanction against individuals for failure by the members of obliged entities' internal supervisory bodies to comply with the duty to communicate.[294] Each member of the above-mentioned bodies who in the exercise of his/her duty fails to make the mandatory communications pursuant to art. 46 can be punished with an administrative fine of €5,000–30,000.

According to art. 60 of L.D. 90/2017, individuals who, during the FIU's inspections, refuse to produce documents or otherwise refuse to provide news or who provide wrong or incomplete information can be punished with an administrative fine of €5,000–50,000.

According to art. 5.4 of L.D. 90/2017, the Ministry of Economy and Finance exercises the sanctioning power. The sanctions can be imposed on the initiative of the different authorities mentioned above.

Art. 11.3 specifies that self-regulatory bodies shall apply disciplinary sanctions for serious, repeated or systematic violations committed by professionals under the AML law and the technical rules.

c. Sanctions against Legal Entities

Arts. 56 and 57 of L.D. 90/2017 provide for administrative sanctions against obliged entities for violations of AML due diligence obligations. The fines are applicable in line with L. 24 November 1981, no. 689, on administrative offences, whether the violations are committed intentionally or through negligence.

Art. 56 provides for administrative sanctions in the event of failure to comply with the due diligence obligations and the obligation not to carry out the transaction or the business relationship where there is a risk of money laundering.

---

294 See above, section III.F.

According to art. 56.1 of L.D. 90/2017, obliged entities that fail to acquire and verify identification data and information relating to the customer, the beneficial owner, the executor, and the nature of the business relationship and the transaction can be punished with an administrative fine of up to €50,000.[295] The same fine is applicable to obliged entities that – in the event of an objective impossibility of fulfilling their CDD measures – violate the duty to carry out the transaction or the business relationship where there is a risk of money laundering.

According to art. 5.4 of L.D. 90/2017, the Ministry of Economy and Finance exercises the sanctioning power. Art. 65.1 specifies that the Ministry of Economy and Finance imposes these sanctions with reference to obliged entities not subject to the control of supervisory authorities. Sanctions can be applied on the initiative of the FIU (art. 6.4(g)), the Bureau of Anti-Mafia Investigation (art. 9.7), the Special Foreign Exchange Unit of the Finance Police (art. 9.5(a)) or the public administrations and bodies involved if, during the exercise of their functions, they notice that AML provisions are not being observed (art. 12.2).

Within the limits of their competences, supervisory authorities have the power to sanction supervised obliged entities for the non-observance of their CDD obligations (art. 7.2(e) of L.D. 90/2017).

Art. 58 of L.D. 90/2017 provides for administrative sanctions against legal entities for the violations of AML reporting obligations. In particular, obliged entities that fail to send a SAR can be punished with an administrative fine of up to €300,000.[296]

According to art. 5.4 of L.D. 90/2017, the Ministry of Economy and Finance exercises the sanctioning power. The sanctions can be imposed on the initiative of the different authorities mentioned above.

---

295 In the case of serious, repeated or systematic or multiple violations, the administrative fine rises from €2,500 to €50,000. The severity of the violation is also determined considering the intensity and degree of the subjective element, taking into account the possibility of ascribing the violation to the deficiency, incompleteness or inadequate diffusion or spreading of operational practices and internal control procedures. The violation is also determined considering the degree of collaboration with the AML authorities and the relevance of and evidence for the reason for suspicion, taking into account the value of the transaction and its coherency with respect to the characteristics of the customer and the relationship with the customer, as well as considering the repetition and diffusion or spreading of behaviours, also in relation to the dimensions, the organisational complexity and the operability of the obliged entity.

296 In the case of serious, repeated or systematic or multiple violations, the administrative fine rises from €30,000 to €300,000. See n. 284 for further discussion. According to art. 58.4, if the serious, repeated or systematic or multiple violations produce an economic advantage, the maximum amount of the administrative fine rises to twice the amount of the advantage, if it is determined or determinable, and in any case is not less than €450,000; if the amount of the advantage is not determined or determinable, the maximum amount of the fine rises to €1,000,000.

Art. 57 of L.D. 90/2017 provides for administrative sanctions in the event of failure to comply with the obligation to keep records. In particular, art. 57 applies the same sanction as that in art. 56, including in cases of aggravated offences, in the event that obliged entities do not conserve, completely or in part, data, documents and information or do so with a delay.[297]

According to art. 60 of L.D. 90/2017, the failure to provide the FIU with the information and data it requires for the performance of its institutional functions can be punished with an administrative fine of €5,000–50,000.

Obliged entities that fail to execute the suspension of a suspicious transaction ordered by the FIU can be punished with an administrative fine of €5,000–50,000.

According to art. 5.4 of L.D. 90/2017, the Ministry of Economy and Finance exercises the sanctioning power. The sanctions can be imposed on the initiative of the different authorities mentioned above.

Within the limits of their competences, supervisory authorities have the power to sanction supervised obliged entities for the non-observance of other AML-related obligations (art. 7.2(e) of L.D. 90/2017).

3. *Statistics*

a. Number of Investigations and Sanctions

In Italy, there are no statistics available on the number of criminal and administrative investigations launched against individuals and legal entities for the aforementioned offences.

b. Number of Convictions

In Italy, there are no statistics available on the number of criminal and administrative convictions/sanctions imposed on individuals and legal entities for the aforementioned offences.

C. CUMULATION OF MONEY LAUNDERING AND OTHER AML-RELATED SANCTIONS

There is no limit provided by the law governing the cumulation of sanctions for money laundering and sanctions for the violation of preventive obligations.

---

297 In particular, according to art. 31 of L.D. 90/2017, obliged entities shall keep the documents, data and information useful to prevent, identify or verify any money laundering or terrorism financing activity and to allow the FIU or the other competent authorities to carry out their analyses, within the scope of their respective functions.

VIII. THE USE OF CASH AS A MEANS OF PAYMENT

A. LIMITS

In Italy, the use of cash as a means of payment is limited. With the 2016 Stability Law (L. 28 December 2015, no. 208), the Italian legislator raised the threshold for the use of cash and bearer securities, as well as the threshold for currency exchange, from €1,000 to €3,000.

Under art. 49.1 of L.D. 90/2017, the limit for the use of cash as a means of payment carried out for any reason between different subjects, whether they are natural or legal persons, is €3,000. Any transfer above that limit is prohibited even if it is made via several payments below the threshold that appear artificially divided.

B. STATISTICS

The Bank of Italy, through its website, offers information and data on the use of cash alternative payment instruments in relation to the volume of non-cash transactions conducted in the country.[298]

IX. SUMMARY, EVALUATION AND FUTURE PERSPECTIVES

The prevention of money laundering and the role played by the FIU represents a fundamental issue on which the attention of the Italian legislator has been focused in recent decades. The system is conceived as a set of different protagonists, from obliged entities to the various institutions, all engaged in a common effort aimed at the prevention of crimes.

Looking at the different subjects involved in the prevention of money laundering, the Italian AML law delegates a large part of the task of prevention to the obliged entities, in particular, as the statistics show, banks and financial intermediaries. Following the guidelines offered by supervisory authorities and self-governing bodies, obliged entities are first in charge of dealing with the risk of money laundering, by assessing and managing it. The high number of SARs sent to the FIU shows the effects of the lack of definition of the risk of money laundering at the regulatory level, making the system less effective. From this point of view, the recent changes in the obligation to provide feedback should contribute to better guiding obligated entities in their reporting and making the

298 The Bank of Italy's statistical data are published in the "Statistics Series", available at www.bancaditalia.it.

system more efficient. This aspect has a strong impact on the sanctioning system. The recent amendments seem to be more mindful of the important role played by obliged entities in the preventive chain, with the result that criminal penalties have been reduced to the most serious cases, in order to avoid defensive reports.

With regard to the institutions involved in the prevention of money laundering, a leading role is certainly played by the FIU, as an interface between obligated entities and investigative authorities, and by financial analysis. From this point of view, the major area of interest of the new AML law concerns better defining the possibility of information exchange as the core of the prevention system. The exchange of information has not been raised to the point of the FIU having direct access to investigative and judicial information. On the one hand, the role of the Italian FIU remains that of carrying out financial analysis. On the other hand, the need to protect investigative secrecy has been maintained. The distinction between financial analysis and investigative analysis therefore seems to continue to be clear in the Italian system.

Among the other institutions, the new AML law has made an important change to the role assigned to the National Anti-Mafia and Counter-Terrorism Bureau in coordinating the exchange of information between the financial intelligence system and the investigative authorities. The effects of this change are not known yet, and this is linked to the fact that many investigations for money laundering are connected to criminal proceedings for the Mafia association.

Although the new AML law is very strong on the side of prevention and its institutional actors, the rights of the suspect have not been taken into account. The major critical aspect concerns the suspect's awareness of financial analyses regarding his/her transactions, analysis that can lead to criminal investigations against him/her. Another important critical aspect is the limits placed on the processing of the suspect's personal data, since the legislation does not seem to require much more than a legal basis and the existence of an institutional purpose of crime prevention, which are limits that were already in existence before the entry into force of the GDPR.

THE ANTI-MONEY LAUNDERING ARCHITECTURE OF SPAIN

Ana Carolina Carlos de Oliveira

I. INTRODUCTION

The trajectory of the Spanish legislation on AML is one of continued broadening of the scope both of the criminal definition and of the administrative provisions regarding the prevention of money laundering. In addition, the European Directives have had a direct impact on the numerous reforms conducted in the country over the last 20 years.

On a domestic level, Spain is a country that has had to contend with a long history of international organised crime in its territory, as well as with internal terrorism. As a result, the country has developed an intricate net of law enforcement agencies responsible for the fight against terrorism and money laundering (National Police, Civil Guard) and its prevention (Customs Surveillance, FIU, Tax Agency, Intelligence National Centre, Centre for Counter-Terrorism Coordination), as well as a well-organised supervisory system relying on the FIU and other supervisory bodies (supervisory powers of the FIU, and of the Bank of Spain and the National Securities Exchange Commission (CNMV), the latter indirectly cooperating with the supervisory divisions of the FIU).

Nowadays, the Executive Service of the Commission for the Prevention of Money Laundering and Monetary Offences (Servicio Ejecutivo de la Comisión de Prevención del Blanqueo de Capitales e Infracciones Monetarias, SEPBLAC), which is the Spanish Financial Intelligence Unit (FIU), centralises the intelligence tasks regarding the prevention of money laundering, acts as the main supervisory body *in praxis*[1] and coordinates the future supervisory actions taken by the Bank of Spain and CNMV regarding money laundering. The FIU is designed to act with full autonomy and independence in decision-making from

1 According to legal provisions, the Bank of Spain and CNMV are entitled to undertake supervisory tasks for prevention of money laundering. Nevertheless, these bodies focus on the prudential supervision of banks and stock market, and delegate to the FIU the coordination and supervision on preventive measures against money laundering.

the competent government ministry (the State Secretary for Economic Affairs and the Treasury).

On another note, the criminal definition of money laundering is criticised in the literature[2] because of the broad scope of the crime: any criminal activity can be a predicate offence (with some leading to aggravated more severe sanction), all forms of participation in the crime (perpetration and participation) are considered equally severe, and both money laundering by gross recklessness and self-money laundering are also specifically criminalised. This legal landscape leads to difficulties, both theoretically as well as in practice.

Another point to highlight regarding the Spanish AML legislation is the lapse of time between the approval of European Directives, and their transposition in Spain to the AML Law and the Decree that regulates the former (Royal Decree 304/2014). In September 2018, Spain updated the current AML Law (Law no. 10/2010). Initially, Spain planned to comply with the fourth Anti-Money Laundering Directive (4AMLD) via an entirely new AML Law and Decree, with a well-thought-out proposal discussed publicly in late 2017 and early 2018. However, frequent changes in Spain's internal politics in 2018 led to a rapid reform of the existing AML Law, changing the necessary paragraphs and adding others, but there is still no update on the AML Decree. As a result, Spain has an AML Law adapted to the 4AMLD that does not follow the order of topics in the 4AMLD and at a first sight does not look like a law implementing the 4AMLD. In its turn, the AML Decree (from 2014) regulates the AML Law (updated in 2018). However, the Decree follows the rules and logic of the third Anti-Money Laundering Directive (3AMLD), not the 4AMLD. Another example of the mismatch between the Law and Decree can be found in the description of the powers and organisation of the FIU, whistleblower systems and the lack of regulation on the exceptions on customer due diligence (CDD) measures that the reformed AML Law requires. The result is a challenging legal situation that is contradictory on some points. For instance, the regulation on high-risk third countries is different in the AML Law and the Decree. This difference compels this report to interpret both laws in such a way as to harmonise them and to offer a proposal for a practical interpretation, despite the knowledge that the conclusion may not be in accordance with the Decree. Moreover, there is a minimal contribution from supervisory authorities and the jurisprudence to support an interpretation of the Spanish AML system.

---

2 Bajo Fernández/Bacigalupo, *Derecho penal económico*, Madrid, 2012, p. 685; Blanco Cordero, *El delito de blanqueo de capitales*, Madrid, 2015, p. 447; Abel Souto, *El delito de blanqueo de capitales en el Código penal español*, Barcelona, 2005, p. 91; Cobo del Rosal/Zabala López-Gómez, *Blanqueo de capitales: abogados, procuradores y notarios, inversores, bancarios y empresarios*, Madrid, 2005, p. 27; Aránguez Sánchez, *El delito de blanqueo de capitales*, Barcelona, 2000, p. 219; Martínez-Buján Perez, *Derecho penal económico y de la empresa. Parte especial*, Valencia, 2015, p. 486; Del Carpio Delgado, *El delito de blanqueo*, Valencia, 1997, p. 165.

As observed in the interviews conducted for this study, the supervisory authorities are knowledgeable and a substantial number of obliged entities are increasing their interest in compliance programmes. However, as soon as it becomes necessary to delve deep into the details of the legislation, the ultimate meaning of the AML Law and Decree becomes unclear.

Therefore, the Spanish legislation is difficult to understand and adds substantial challenges that must be explained in a comparative study like the present one. Nevertheless, it should be noted that the weaknesses result mainly from the legislative situation, and not necessarily from a misunderstanding of the international AML system or from insufficient efforts on the part of the national authorities to fight this crime.

A. HISTORY OF ANTI-MONEY LAUNDERING IN THE COUNTRY

The Spanish legislator introduced the offence of money laundering in the Penal Code (SPC) in 1988. The first iteration of the offence was art. 546 *bis* (f) SPC. Its creation came at the same time as the preliminary discussions on the Convention of the United Nations against the Illicit Traffic in Narcotic Drugs and Psychotropic Substances in 1988 (Vienna Convention) and it came into force just a few months before the approval of that Convention.[3] As official documents from the Spanish Parliament show, the first draft of art. 546 *bis* (f) was approved even before the final approval of the Vienna Convention, but it was nevertheless directly inspired by the preliminary reports and discussions on that Convention.[4] In fact, art. 546 *bis* (f) initially defined money laundering as an aggravated form of the offence of "handling stolen goods", related to goods obtained through drug trafficking. The criminal definition from 1988 (art. 546 *bis* (f)) established only the acts of acquisition, reception and benefiting from the capital proceeding from drug trafficking as money laundering.

Just four years later, in 1992, a more precise definition was introduced by another reform, under Law no. 8, of 23 December 1992.[5] The explanatory notes to this Law refer to the relevance and binding power of the first Directive of the European Union against Money Laundering (Directive 91/308/EEC).[6]

---

3 Martínez-Buján Perez, *Derecho penal económico y de la empresa. Parte especial*, Valencia, 2015, p. 479.

4 Fiscalía General del Estado, *Memoria Elevada al Gobierno de S.M. presentada al inicio del año judicial por el Fiscal General del Estado Exmo. Sr. D. Leopoldo Torres Boursault*, Madrid, 1990, p. 18.

5 Available at: https://www.boe.es/buscar/doc.php?id=BOE-A-1992-28425.

6 Articles 344 *bis* (h) and 344 *bis* (i) were a translation of arts. 3(1)(b)(i) and (ii) and (c) (i) of the Vienna Convention, and was at the time criticised by the literature, because of the poor technique regarding the translation of the crime into Spanish, which lead to

The 1992 reform created arts. 344 *bis* (h) and 344 *bis* (i),[7] both specifying the criminal definition of money laundering, which from then on included the actions of: (i) conversion or transfer of goods, (art. 344 *bis* (h)(1)); (ii) concealment or disguise of the nature, location, movement or real ownership (art. 344 *bis* (h)(2)); and (iii) possession or purchase of goods originating from predicate offences listed in the article (art. 344 *bis* (i)). All three acts could be punished only if the subject knew, at the time of acting, that those goods originated from any of the predicate offences defined by the article.

Nevertheless, the criminal definition came into force in Spain before the proper administrative regulation. In fact, despite the criminal definition in 1988 and its reform in 1992, it was only in 1993 that the Spanish legislator enacted the preventive regulation, AML Law no. 19/1993. The Law created and regulated the administrative system on prevention of money laundering, also aiming to transpose the first AML Directive into Spanish domestic law. AML Law no. 19/1993 defined which class type of transactions in goods would be considered suspicious and set out for the first time a list of obliged entities,[8] including their duties to maintain data banks and to inform the FIU about suspicious transactions.

The complete system for prevention of money laundering nevertheless took two additional years to be implemented, until the administrative provision (Royal Decree 925/1995) came into force. It may be that the extended period between the enactment of the criminal (1988) and the complete administrative (1995) regulation is one of the reasons why academics in Spain generally dedicate

misunderstandings. Diez Ripolles, "El blanqueo de capitales en el ordenamiento jurídico español", *Revista Actualidad Penal*, no. 32, 1994, p. 601.

7 Art. 344 *bis* (h) states: "1. The one who converts or transfers goods, knowing that those proceed from an offence or offences described in the anterior paragraphs, or to conduct an act of participation in such offence or offences, for the purpose of concealing or disguising the illicit origin of the goods, or to assist any person who participated in the commission of such offences to evade the legal consequences of its acts, will be sanctioned with the penalty of minor imprisonment and fine of one to 100 million pesetas. 2. With the same sanctions will be punished who conceal or disguise the nature, source, location, destination, movement or the real ownership of goods or rights with respect to them, knowing that those proceed from an offence or offences described in the anterior paragraphs or from an act of participation on them. 3. If the acts were committed by inexcusable negligence or ignorance the sanction will the major imprisonment at the maximum level and the fine of one to 50 million pesetas."
Art. 344 *bis* (i) states: "The one who acquires, possesses or uses goods, knowing, in the moment of receiving them, that they proceed from any of the offences described in the previous paragraphs will be sanctioned with the sanction of minor imprisonment and fine from one to 100 million pesetas."

8 They were, at the time: credit institutions; life insurance agencies; stock market societies and agencies; collective investment institutions; pension funds and collective investment management companies; portfolio management companies; credit card issuers; natural and legal persons working on money exchange; casinos; real estate agencies; and any other activity that could be vulnerable to money laundering activities (art. 2 Ley Organica 19/1993, available at: https://www.boe.es/buscar/doc.php?id=BOE-A-1993-30991).

more attention to the criminal implications that to the administrative regulation of money laundering as an offence.[9] Money laundering was a prohibition introduced at first hand in the criminal law, before a comprehensive knowledge of the phenomena outside penal law.

The AML Law no. 19/1993 created the Spanish FIU with the characteristics it still has today,[10] and the Royal Decree 925/1995 specifies its structure and how it operates. At that time, there was no minimum threshold for the duty to implement CDD measures, so all obliged entities should, theoretically, have implemented them. Initially, some authors pointed out that the AML system focused primarily on financial institutions as obliged entities, and considered the system to be tax-oriented,[11] because of the number of investigations into tax fraud as a predicate offence originating from AML policies. Despite the focus of the practice on financial institutions, however, the legal provisions made no distinction between obliged entities.

This situation changed in 2014 with the new administrative regulation (Decree 304/2014), which restricted the duty to implement certain CDD measures to professionals whose annual turnover is under €2 million and who have fewer than 10 employees (art. 31 Decree 304/2014). Such professionals must implement basic CDD measures, but are released from the obligation to implement risk analysis, internal manuals, internal monitoring bodies, external auditing and employee training.

With regard to the *criminal* definition of money laundering, the first significant change came with the reform of the Spanish Penal Code in 1995. After the reform, the Spanish legislator decided to broaden the scope of money laundering to the assets created by any *serious offence* (*felony*). According to the Code at the time, "serious offence" meant any offence with a maximum prison sentence of more than three years. In addition, the reform of 1995 relocated the offence in the structure of the Code, under art. 301 SPC, labelling the chapter "Handling of stolen goods and money laundering". In essence, the text remains the same as art. 3(1)(b)(i) and (ii) and (c)(i) of the Vienna Convention, differing only in the fact that now that money laundering is seen as an autonomous crime the list of predicate offences would be much broader than solely drug trafficking.[12]

9 Fabián Caparrós, *El delito de blanqueo de capitales*, Madrid, 1998, p. 348.

10 SEPBLAC, the FIU in Spain, was created based on the previously existing supervisory body on money exchange, called then the Executive Service of the Supervisory Commission against Fraud in Exchange Control.

11 García Noriega, *Blanqueo y antiblanqueo de capitales: como se lava el dinero, cómo se combate el lavado*, Madrid, 2010, p. 320.

12 In fact, the broad scope of the catalogue of predicate offences included, at first, crimes against private and public property, prostitution, prevarication, corruption, embezzlement of public funds, fraud, insider trading, disclosure of sensitive information from public employees or compromising industrial secrecy, price manipulation in public auctions, drug trafficking, illicit association, arms trafficking and terrorism. Tax fraud would join this list only in cases

The normal prison sentence for money laundering ranges from six months to six years. Nevertheless, laundering the profits of illicit trafficking of drugs (in the beginning the only predicate offence) became an aggravated clause of art. 301.1, second paragraph, SPC. Following the change, this became an aggravating factor that raises the prison sentence for money laundering into the range of two years and nine months to six years.

The next significant change in the Spanish legislation came in 2003, with Law no. 15/2003, which modified the Penal Code of 1995.[13] The reform broadened once more the list of predicate offences for money laundering. Whereas in 1995 only serious offences (which already consisted of an extensive list of crimes) were relevant as predicate offences, after 2003 any *offence*[14] from the Penal Code could lead to a prosecution for money laundering.

The reform of 2003 also altered the regime of sanctions in art. 301 SPC. It included the special option of disqualification from exercising a profession or running a business for a period of one to three years; the possibility of definitively or temporarily (for up to five years) shutting down (the business. Furthermore, art. 301.5 SPC makes specific reference to the confiscation of the goods and profits obtained via the activity of money laundering.

The last decade has been a very important one in the development of the legal framework dealing with money laundering and terrorism financing in Spain,

of non-payment over a certain tax threshold. Furthermore, it also included a list of crimes that are not usually defined as profit generating, such as crimes against life and physical integrity, crimes against the environment, crimes against consumer relations, forfeiture of documents, perjury and so on. To the reader not used to the SPC system, the references to serious offences as predicate offences in the text of art. 301 of the 1995 SPC may seem unclear, since the reader must refer to two different articles to understand the definition of serious offences. In that sense, art. 13 of the 1995 SPC explains that "serious offences are infractions punished with serious sanctions", while art. 33.2 defines serious sanctions as: "(a) crimes with sanctions of imprisonment for a term superior to three years; (b) crimes with sanctions of absolute disqualification; (c) crimes with sanctions of special disqualifications for a term superior to three years; (d) crimes with sanctions of suspension of public employment for a term superior to three years; (e) crimes with sanctions of driving disqualifications for a term superior to six years; (f) crimes with sanctions of suspension of the right to possess a gun for a term superior to six years; (g) crimes with sanctions of banning orders from specific places, or that forbid access to certain places for a term superior to three years". Finally, all these provisions are valid, even if in practice the defendant is sentenced to a term of less than three years, or even if he/she acquitted at the end of the criminal proceedings. It is the definition of the crime in the abstract by the SPC that places the crime in the category of *serious offences*.

13 Aligned with the second AML Directive (Directive 2001/97/EC), which updated the European preventive measures against money laundering and terrorism financing with the aims and recommendations from the FATF.

14 This change meant that the required predicate offence for the purpose of money laundering would be any kind of offence, and no longer only a *serious* offence, ranging from crimes against property and economic crimes to homicides.

motivated to some extent by the publication of the 3AMLD[15] and the country's 2014 mutual evaluation report from the FATF.[16]

It was after 2010 that administrative regulations acquired real prominence, following the publication of Law no. 10/2010 (AML Law). The law establishes the current structure of the FIU, the list of obliged entities and a comprehensive list of CDD measures and sanctions. In addition, the AML Law propelled the growth of the compliance officer services sector, since this sector was becoming an area of increasing interest among legal professionals.[17]

Spain once again altered the criminal definition of money laundering in the Penal Code in 2010. Organic Law no. 5/2010 introduced another expansion of the offence of money laundering. It specifically criminalised self-laundering and added the criminal liability of legal entities for money laundering committed by their employees. Continuously broadening the scope of the criminal definition, since 2010 art. 301 SPC has included any illicit activity as a predicate offence for money laundering, ranging from all minor offences up to serious offences. In short, as will be examined in detail below, there is presently no threshold for predicate offences that can be associated with money laundering in Spain.

In criminalising self-money laundering, the reform of the Penal Code in 2010 also aimed to put an end to a doctrinal and jurisprudential discussion about that possibility. At the time, some authors stressed that self-money laundering involved a situation of double jeopardy for the perpetrator of the predicate offence in the event of use and possession of the illicit gains.[18] It was also argued that money laundering should be crime-oriented to dissuade third persons from helping the perpetrator of the predicate offence to carry out the conversion of the illicit money. On the other hand, the jurisprudence had accepted early on the possibility of self-money laundering, despite the previous, narrower definition of

---

15 Directive 2005/60/EC, which also incorporates the 2003 FATF Recommendations. In 2009, the Court of Justice of the European Union (CJEU) declared Spain a non-compliant country, claiming an incomplete transposition of the 3AMLD in the sentence of the CJEU, Fifth Chamber, 24 September 2009 Case C-504/08, available at: http://curia.europa.eu/juris/liste.jsf?language=es&jur=C,T,F&num=C-504/08&td=ALL.

16 In fact, the Mutual Evaluation Report for Spain from 2006 evaluates the country as having a low level of compliance. See García Noriega, *Blanqueo y antiblanqueo de capitales: como se lava el dinero, cómo se combate el lavado,* Madrid, 2010, p. 313.

17 Bermejo/Palermo, "La intervención delictiva del compliance officer", in Ortiz de Urbina/Kuhlen/Montiel (eds.), *Compliance y teoría del Derecho penal,* Madrid, 2013, p. 179.

18 Corcoy Bidasolo, "Expansión del Derecho penal y garantías constitucionales", *Revista de Derechos fundamentales,* no. 8, 2012, p. 67; Fabián Caparrós, *El delito de blanqueo de capitales,* Madrid, 1998, p. 733; Palma Herrera, *Los delitos de blanqueo de capitales,* Madrid, 2000, p. 386 ff.; Quintero Olivares, "Sobre la ampliación del comiso y el blanqueo, y la incidencia en la receptación civil", *Revista electrónica de ciencia penal y criminología,* no. 12, vol. 2, 2010, p. 20; Abel Souto, "La reforma penal de 22 de junio de 2010, en materia de blanqueo de dinero", in Abel Souto/Sánchez Stewart (coord.), *II Congreso sobre prevención y represión del blanqueo de dinero,* Madrid, 2011; Matalín Evangelio, "El 'autoblanqueo' de capitals", *Revista General de Derecho Penal,* no. 20, 2013, p. 34.

the offence of money laundering.[19] On this basis, the legal reform in 2010 ended the doctrinal claim that self-money laundering should not be criminalised, specifically including this conduct.

Following the latest development of the 4AMLD, Spain had to deal with a particular situation in updating the national legal framework. In February 2018,[20] the legislator approved a reform proposal to implement the recommendations of the 4AMLD. The proposal already anticipated some important topics connected with the fifth Anti-Money Laundering Directive (5AMLD) and incorporated contributions from a public consultation. Nevertheless, in September of the same year (2018), the country adopted a different version of the proposal,[21] with a narrower scope than the original one. This could be seen as a consequence of the change of political groups in the Spanish Parliament during that year, as well as the result of the pressure exerted by the EU following Spain's delay in implementing the 4AMLD.[22] Another reform of the Spanish regulation is therefore expected in the next year, dealing with both the regulation of the AML Law (Decree 304/2014 must be updated) and the implementation of the 5AMLD.

One of the significant points of the current reform of the AML Law (adopted in September 2018) relates to the definition of PEPs and the change in mechanisms to facilitate reporting by obliged entities. In that sense, it is now mandatory for each obliged entity to have an internal whistleblowing system. For the FIU's part, it shall develop a system to receive and process information coming from whistleblowing. Furthermore, Spain allowed obliged entities to share common data banks, in order to reduce the costs of CDD measures.

A particular characteristic of the Spanish AML system after the reform is the inclusion of "external experts"[23] in the list of persons who may be sanctioned, making them responsible for non-compliance with the administrative rules of the AML Law, along with managers or directors (art. 57.2 AML Law), as will be seen in more detail below. The reform also requires the registration of company service providers and raised the maximum amount of the sanctions.

---

19 STS 801/2010, of 23 September 2010. See also, Sentence of the Court of Appeal of Huelva (no. 31/2009, of 5 March 2009) and of the Court of Appeal of the Balearic Islands (no. 25/2010, of 12 March 2010), to mention the most important decisions.

20 Available at: http://www.mineco.gob.es/stfls/mineco/ministerio/participacion_publica/audiencia/ficheros/ECO_Tes_171222_AP_Reglamento_BCFT_fin.pdf.

21 Royal Decree 11/2018, of 4 September, which implemented legislative updates in three different laws, among them the AML Law.

22 The memorandum of the mentioned Royal Decree 11/2018, of 4 September, that altered the AML Law explicitly refers to the formal infringement proceeding against Spain (2017/0527) from the EU, opened as a result of the failure of the country to transpose the 4AMLD in due time.

23 This is the term used by the Spanish AML Law, but may well be understood to refer to external accountants or auditors (in equivalent terms with 4AMLD) who are responsible for the annual evaluation of the preventive measures adopted by obliged entities (art. 28 AML Law). See *infra* section III.G.

Apart from the history of money laundering in Spain, it is worth briefly highlighting the economic context in Spain over the last decade, which has also been reflected in the distribution of supervisory tasks and the exposure of the country to money laundering transactions. The country's financial sector underwent a reorganisation in the years before the acute period of economic crisis in 2011/2012, which persisted afterwards: local and regional savings banks were closed[24] or merged into bigger banks, in order to make them more resilient to economic crises.[25] In that context, it could be said that the focus of the Central Bank in Spain was on regulating the banking sector[26] and dealing with the consequences of the economic crisis in the country, delegating the prevention of money laundering entirely to the FIU. At the same time, the economic crisis made the real estate sector more vulnerable to money laundering transactions, because of the greater availability of properties to foreign investors.

B. CURRENT CONCERNS AND REFORM AGENDA

The concerns raised by the Spanish regulation lay in the excessively broad definition of the crime of money laundering, which softens the focus on the prosecution of major predicate offences[27] and raises issues of constitutional law. These issues notwithstanding, the doctrine argues that such a broad definition of the crime affects *legal clarity.* As a matter of fact, it is still a point of discussion

---

24 Martín-Oliver/Ruano, "Restructuración bancaria y accesibilidad a los servicios financieros en España", *Papeles de economía española*, no. 146, 2015, p. 181. The authors state that 134 banking institutions and thousands (13,721) of bank offices closed between 2007 and 2014.

25 García Montalvo, "Crisis financiera, reacción regulatoria y el futuro de la banca en España", *Estudios de economía aplicada*, no. 32, vol. 2, 2014, p. 521.

26 Bank of Spain, *Memoria de la Supervisión Bancaria en España*, 2017, available at https://www.bde.es/f/webbde/Secciones/Publicaciones/PublicacionesAnuales/MemoriaSupervisionBancaria/17/Capitulo_6_Participacion_del_Banco_de_Espana_en_org_inter_de_regulacion_y_supervision_bancarias.pdf; Alvarez, "La banca española ante la actual crisis financiera", *Revista Estabilidad Financiera*, no. 15, 2008, p. 28 ff.

27 As described above, the offence of money laundering in Spain (art. 301 SPC) foresees that the goods generated by any "illicit activity" are sufficient as precedents. This leads to circumstances where the sanction for money laundering significantly outstrips the sanction applied to the predicate offence. For example, the maximum sanction for regular theft is 18 months, but if its profits are laundered, the sanction for laundering ranges from three to six years. Furthermore, the idea of "illicit activity" places, for instance, both a single act of theft and serious corruption on the same level as predicate offences to money laundering. This distorts a balanced application of the harm principle and the strict proportionality between different sanctions. In the same way, it is said that the money laundering offence includes every bagatelle and reckless crime as a precedent offence. Phrased in such a way, the article includes even those acts perpetrated by non-culpable agents (minors, people that acted in mistake of law) as predicate offences. Finally, the proportionality principle is also affected, since the direct commission and other forms of participation such as aiding should receive the same sanction (art. 301.2 SPC). Martínez/Buján Perez, *Derecho penal económico y de la empresa. Parte especial*, Valencia, 2015, p. 486.

in Spanish doctrine[28] and jurisprudence[29] what actually constitutes the correct interpretation of all the words used to define the offence: acquisition, possession, use, conversion and transfer of illicit capital on the one hand, and "any acts with the intent to conceal or hide the origin of such capital" on the other, as will be discussed below (section II.B.1.b).

Regarding the administrative regulation on money laundering, a current concern in Spain, at the time of writing this report, is the process of adjusting the details of the new data protection regulation and the AML Law following the reform implementing the GDPR. Another aspect that frequently appears in the expert discussion or newspapers is the use of advanced software systems to detect suspicious transactions and protect the data of clients of small obliged entities, including lawyers.[30] The regulation of virtual currencies,[31] crowdfunding platforms and virtual currency service providers also remains on the list of concerns in Spain.

On another note, public prosecutors[32] have officially expressed the difficulties they face in getting conviction sanctions, especially in cases of gross negligence[33] money laundering. At the same time, lawyers complain about the difficulties in preparing defences based on broad suspicions sustained only on vague facts.[34] The interviews conducted for this report also revealed a limited channel of communication between the FIU and obliged entities, which is alleged to have an impact on the quality of SARs. What is more, difficulties with the

---

28 Aránguez Sánchez, *El delito de blanqueo de capitales*, Barcelona, 2000, p. 349; Fabián Caparrós, *El delito de blanqueo de capitales*, Madrid, 1998, p. 378; Blanco Cordero, *El delito de blanqueo de capitales*, Madrid, 2015, p. 465; Quintero Olivares, "Art. 301", in Quintero Olivares (dir.)/Morales Prats (coord.), *Comentarios al Código penal español*, Cizur Menor, 3rd ed., 2004, p. 1496.

29 STS 265/2015, of 22 April 2015; STS 83/2014, of 13 February 2014; STS 350/2014, of 29 April 2014.

30 Fernández Burgueño, "La obligación legal de cifrar información y datos personales", *Diario La Ley* 1/2017.

31 Pérez García, "La regulación de la innovación tecnológica en el mercado financiero: Fintech, Crowdfunding y Bitcoin", *Diario La Ley*, 9132/2018.

32 Fiscalía General del Estado, *Memoria de la Fiscalía General del Estado presentada a S.M. por el Fiscal General del Estado en 2016*, Madrid, 2016, p. 664.

33 The criminal definition of money laundering in Spain foresees the sanction for "gross negligence" conduct that constitutes the crime. According to the Spanish doctrine, "gross negligence" in this context must be interpreted as the negligent ignorance of the origins of the money when the obliged entity has sufficient signs of its criminal origin and still does not ensure reasonable knowledge of the origin of the money. *Pérez Manzano*, "El encubrimiento, la receptación y el blanqueo de dinero", in Consejo General del Poder Judicial (org.), *El encubrimiento, la receptación y el blanqueo de dinero*, Madrid, 1994, p. 248. STS 1034/2005, of 14 September sanctioned a man for gross negligence money laundering for lending his bank account for some days to third parties, allowing them to move small amounts of money into the country, reaching the total of US$135,000 at the time, and then transferring the sum to the US.

34 Fabián Caparrós, "Consideraciones dogmáticas y político-criminales sobre el blanqueo de capitales imprudente", *Revista General de Derecho Penal*, no. 16, 2011.

breadth of the offence are reflected in the jurisprudence. The Spanish Supreme Court has so far not established precise boundaries between the practice of self-money laundering and the mere use of the profits of a crime by its perpetrator. Hence there are different decisions about the baseline conduct that constitutes self-money laundering in cases involving very similar circumstances.[35]

The trade-off between AML measures and lawyers' professional secrecy[36] is also a current concern in Spain. Spanish regulation says that lawyers are obliged to communicate suspicious transactions when acting as an *advisor*. However, it is still not clear which advisory activities are protected by professional secrecy and which are not.[37]

Moreover, the Spanish economy is starting to see an increase in real estate prices,[38] which could indicate another round of the economy warming up and the attraction of foreign capital to this sector, which historically represents a major focus for money laundering in the country. Another current AML concern in Spain relating to the real estate sector lies in the granting of golden visas. After the housing bubble burst in 2012, there were a significant number of forced evictions and an increase in the number of houses available on the market (frequently under the possession of banks). One of the strategies developed by Spain to cope with the effects of the crisis was Law no. 14/2013 "to support entrepreneurial initiatives and its internationalisation".[39] Under the extended provisions to reduce taxes for entrepreneurs, there is a clause that guarantees residence visas (golden visas) for entrepreneurs who purchase housing worth

---

35 STS 350/2014, handed down by magistrate Monteverde; STS 245/2014 of 24 March, handed down by magistrate Sánchez Melgar; STS 809/2014, handed down by magistrate Palomo. In the latter case, the magistrate posited that there is no offence to the *ne bis in idem* principle when the same subject is convicted for the predicate offence and for the self-money laundering, because of the clear legal provision in the Penal Code. In the offence of "handling illicit goods" there is no such provision, which leads to the conclusion that the desire of the legislator was precisely the strong incrimination of self-money laundering. Standing against the majority, magistrate Martínez Arrieta maintains the interpretation that the offence of "handling illicit goods" cannot be a predicate offence for self-money laundering, because to possess or to receive illicit assets would absorb the illicit content of the crime of money laundering.

36 As foreseen in art. 542.3 of the Organic Law for the Judiciary System no. 6/1985 and in art. 32 of the Spanish Bar Association Code.

37 That is the official statement of the General Council of the Spanish Lawyers, recommending that in the event of doubt over the duty to inform, the lawyers should contact the Dean of the Special Commission for the prevention of Money Laundering of the aforementioned Council. See: http://www.abogacia.es/wp-content/uploads/2012/06/RECOMENDACIONES-PBC-ABOGADOS-CGAE.pdf, p. 10.

38 "Precio de la vivienda calienta el temor a una nueva burbuja inmobiliaria", *El País*, 14 April 2018, available at: https://elpais.com/economia/2018/04/13/vivienda/1523635585_471312.html.

39 Law no. 14/2013 brought into being the so-called "golden visa", which allows foreigners to enter and obtain a permanent visa in Spain, if they are bringing foreign investment to the country, intended specifically to cope with the crisis in the real estate market during the financial crisis years.

more than €500,000, or who invest more than €1 million in a Spanish business.[40] This law was an important measure in coping with the economic crisis. Nevertheless, it is also plausible that it may create incentives for illicit money flows, since it automatically guarantees a residence visa for the investor.

Finally, the empirical study for this report revealed a common point of concern between the public and the private sectors: the fact that outside financial institutions, there is still a proportion of obliged entities that are not properly aware of their duties regarding AML and that are still not compliant with the preventive measures.

One last word must be said regarding the reform agenda. There is currently another Proposal under discussion from the Spanish Parliament and already submitted to the public consultation. The proposal aims to transpose the 5AMLD to the country's regulation and states that it was also an opportunity for the Spanish legislator to incorporate the latest recommendations of the FATF. Within the modifications derived from the 5AMLD, one must highlight the incorporation of new obligated entities, in particular the virtual currency and virtual wallets service providers, and providers of exchange or security tokens, crowdfunding platforms and real estate investment companies. The regulation of the virtual currency and virtual assets providers will mean a significant effort on the part of the Bank of Spain, which will hold the responsibility of regulating and registering those services.

Also, in order to meet the provisions of the 5AMLD with respect to the BOR, the Proposal creates a single Beneficial Ownership Registry. The Registry will be held by the Ministry of Justice, which will obtain information directly from companies, foundations and associations obliged to declare their BO. The Beneficial Ownership Registry will also centralise the information contained in the databases of the General Council of Notaries and the Commercial Registry, to add it to its own database and will be interconnected with other Beneficial Ownership registries across the EU. To complete this register, legal persons and entities without legal personality of Spanish nationality or subject to Spanish legislation will have the duty to obtain, keep and update the information regarding beneficial ownership and provide it to authorities and obliged entities. By the

---

40 The requirements to obtain a visa are: (i) the investment can be done by a natural or legal person, as long as that legal person is not registered in a country listed as a tax heaven by Spanish authorities; and (ii) in the case of a legal entity, the natural person who applies for the visa must hold the majority of voting rights. The investment can be: (i) buying a minimum of €2,000,000 of public debt; (ii) buying Spanish company stocks or shares from a minimum value of €1,000,000; (iii) having bank deposits above the threshold of €1,000,000; or (iv) buying real estate valued over €500,000 (art. 63 Law no. 14/2013). To request a "golden visa", the investor needs first to apply for a one-year visa, and after the authorisation of the first visa, he/she can then apply for specific authorisation for residency of investors, which allows them to live in the country initially for two years, renewed every two years. Jimenez Mateo, "El visado de residencia para inversores introducido por la Ley 14/2013 ('Golden Visa')", *Revista Actualidad Juridica Uría Menéndez*, no. 38, Oct/Dec. 2014.

time of the writing of this report (2020), the access to BO registries remains exclusive to public authorities (police, tax administration, FIU, etc.) and obliged entities. Any person outside the provided list would have access only to name and surname, month and year of birth, country of residence and nationality of the current beneficial owner. On this point, the Proposal indicates that the regulation on the BOR will be of "transcendental dimensions" in comparison with the current regulation.

Still regarding centralised files, the proposal adds the obligation to declare the rental of safety boxes, payment accounts, and virtual currency accounts to the already existing Financial Ownership File, giving the authorities access to the information contained in it.

On another note, the Proposal expressly recognises the link with the AML regulation and the GDPR and allows the creation of common systems for storing due diligence information.

Another point to highlight is the accountability of the external experts. The internal control measures and bodies shall be subject to annual review by an external expert, who will become directly responsible for the mandatory reports they sign and subject to administrative sanctions. The Proposal expands the list of PEPs, including those persons who perform or have performed important public functions in the Spanish autonomous region (i.e. mayors, councillors) of the provincial capital municipalities, or of the autonomous region and local entities with more than 50,000 inhabitants. In the case of a merger, the obliged entities shall continue to apply the CDD measures for a period of one year and after this period they shall apply adequate diligence measures in accordance with the risk.

The Proposal is supposed to be voted on and come into force in June 2021 (if there are no major political factors to impose its postponement). For the time being, however, one must note that the Reform Proposal mentioned several times in the footnotes of this report is still a draft (it is not even a definitive proposal) and is therefore still under discussion and could be altered before its publication. However, there is apparently little reason to believe that there will be major changes to the draft since Spain is currently late on the transposition of the 5AMLD.[41]

II. AIMS AND SCOPE OF AML SYSTEM

A. AIMS OF AML REGIME

According to official statements (the explanatory memorandum of the AML Law), the first and primary objective of the AML policies in Spain is to incorporate the international standards of money laundering prevention, such as the

41 Proposal available at: https://www.mineco.gob.es/stfls/mineco/ministerio/participacion_publica/audiencia/ficheros/ECO_TES_20200612_AP_V_Directiv_Blanqueo.pdf.

recommendations from the FATF and the European Directives, and to unify the legal efforts in the country to prevent money laundering and terrorism financing.[42]

By the time money laundering was first described as a crime after the reform of the Penal Code in 1988, the aim of the regime was focused on combating drug trafficking and organised crime in the country.[43] However, the developments of the AML regime in the last 15 years have moved toward the protection of the integrity of the financial system, which is explicitly recognised by art. 1.1 AML Law.[44] It should also be underlined that there has been a focus on using a risk-based approach to drive preventive measures.[45]

In addition, the doctrine points to other aims of the system, such as the confiscation of illicit gains,[46] and a particular focus on a tax-oriented system,[47] through a growing integration of cooperation and data sharing between the FIU and the tax agencies.[48] In fact, since 2003, art. 301.5 SPC has specifically mentioned the confiscation of the gains obtained via money laundering up to the estimated amount gained via the crime. To contribute to this goal, Spain has created a special office under the auspices of the Attorney General, the Asset Recovery and Management Office (Oficina de recuperación y gestión de activos).[49]

On the other hand, interviews conducted for this report showed different perspectives on the aims of the AML regime. The private sector emphasises the expansion of data collection, as well as a tax-oriented approach. From another standpoint, the law enforcement agencies underline that the original aims of the AML are still the primary objectives of the system: dismantling organised crime, identifying the author(s) of the predicate offence and mainly protecting the legality of financial flows.

---

42 The Explanatory Memorandum of the AML Law refers to the 3AMLD, and states that a "total transposition ha[s] being made". In the case of the measures against terrorism financing, the strategies of the country are part of the efforts of the political negotiations to free former convicted members of national terrorist organisations (ETA).

43 Introduction to the reform of the Spanish Penal Code of 1973, followed by the Organic Law no. 1 on 24 March 1988 (Ley Organica no.1/1988), which intensified the fight against illicit drug trafficking. The full text of the law is available at https://www.boe.es/buscar/doc.php?id=BOE-A-1988-8031.

44 See art. 1.1 AML Law: "The purpose of this Law is to safeguard the integrity of the financial system and other economic sectors by establishing obligations in respect of the prevention of money laundering and terrorist financing".

45 In accordance with Introductory Note 18 to the 3AMLD.

46 Bermejo, *Prevención y castigo del blanqueo de capitales. Una aproximación desde el análisis económico del derecho*, PhD Thesis, Universidad Pompeu Fabra, 2010, p. 230; Ragués i Vallès, "Lavado de activos y negocios standard", in Silva Sánchez, *Blanqueo de capitales y negocios standard. Con especial mención a los abogados como potenciales autores de un delito de blanqueo*, Córdoba, 2001, p. 621.

47 García Noriega, *Blanqueo y antiblanqueo de capitales: como se lava el dinero, cómo se combate el lavado,* Madrid, 2010, p. 319.

48 See *infra* section V.D.

49 See http://www.mjusticia.gob.es/cs/Satellite/Portal/es/ministerio/organigrama/secretaria-estado-justicia/oficina-recuperacion-gestion.

However, from a practitioner perspective, the recent report from the Public Prosecutor's Office states that the AML Law and its preventive measures are the main instrument they have available to them to fight organised crime in the country. Since the AML Law allows a more homogeneous regulation of the crime, it also facilitates international cooperation to exchange intelligence data with third countries like Italy, Russia and others.[50]

B. SCOPE OF MONEY LAUNDERING

1. *Definition of Money Laundering in Criminal Law*

a. *Actus Reus*

i. Predicate Offences

Spain follows an all-crimes approach to predicate offences. Since 2010, any illicit activity can be a predicate offence for money laundering in Spain. As indicated above, there is also *no seriousness threshold* for predicate offences in the Spanish system, neither in terms of the gravity of the offence nor in terms of the amount of money laundered. Nevertheless, the term "illicit activity" used in art. 301 SPC shall be interpreted as a criminal offence, not as an administrative offence.[51]

With respect to tax offences, any tax evasion above a value of €120,000 is a criminal activity (art. 305 SPC) and can, therefore, be a predicate offence. The doctrine is not universally in agreement with this provision, but the jurisprudence largely accepts the link between the gains from tax evasion and money laundering.[52]

ii. Definition of Money Laundering Acts

To better understand the criminal definition of money laundering (art. 301 SPC), the objective and subjective elements will be examined separately. Nevertheless, it is necessary to highlight that the objective definition of the crime is substantially intertwined with the expression that refers to the subjective element, namely intent

---

50 Fiscalía General del Estado, *Memoria de la Fiscalía General del Estado presentada a S.M. por el Fiscal General del Estado en 2016*, Madrid, 2016, Chapter VI, p. 386.

51 At the time of the reform of the Law in 2010, the expression "illicit activity" meant to include the entire chapter of "minor offences" from the SPC as predicate offences, including cases of very low-level crimes against property (without the use of violence). This amendment is of no relevance now, because in 2015 another reform extinguished the category of minor offences, placing them among the regular crimes, regardless of the lower severity of the offence they may represent.

52 STS 974/2012, of 5 December 2012.

or gross negligence on the part of the subject, as discussed in the next section (*mens rea*). Moreover, an explanation of the definition of money laundering in Spain would not be complete without a comment on the debate in the doctrine and jurisprudence regarding the interpretation of the part of the definition of the crime that deals with wrongful acts, which is discussed in this section.

The criminal definition in art. 301.1 SPC lists three main types of criminal conduct:

(a) acquisition, possession, use, conversion and transmission of assets;
(b) carrying out any other act aiming to hide or disguise the illicit origins of the assets, or for the purpose of helping someone to evade any legal consequences of previous criminal activity; and
(c) concealing or disguising the true nature, source, location, destination, movements or rights over assets.

The acts of acquisition, possession, use, conversion and transmission of assets are crimes when the assets originate from a predicate offence "committed by the perpetrator of the predicate crime itself or by third persons".[53] Via the expression "any illicit activity, committed by him or by any third person", Spanish law has since 2010 specifically criminalised self-money laundering (art. 301.1 SPC, first paragraph).

Both the doctrine and jurisprudence in Spain have made efforts to provide a coherent and more restrictive interpretation of the definition of the crime, rooted in the subjective element of intent and gross negligence. In summary, the doctrine and jurisprudence strongly bind the criminal definition mentioned in points (*a*)[54] and (*b*)[55] above to the subjective aim of hiding or disguising the criminal origins of the money.[56]

Finally, the last group of activities described as money laundering (art. 301.2 SPC) is the concealment or disguise of the true nature, source, location, destination, movements or rights over the assets, knowing that they derive from any of the offences described in the previous paragraph or from an act of participation in such offences. Concealment or disguise involves the layering of transactions with the aim of giving the appearance of licit gains.

Nevertheless, it is worth mentioning a detail about the language of the criminal definition on this point, since the word "disguise" is a source of interpretative problems. Indeed, instead of using a term that more accurately

53 Art. 301, first paragraph, SPC. Moreover, the crime states that the predicate offence can be "committed by him or by any third person", in a literal translation of the law, which explicitly criminalises self-money laundering.

54 Art. 301, first paragraph, SPC: "acquisition, possession, use, conversion and transmission of assets".

55 Art. 301, second paragraph, SPC: "to carry on with any other act aiming to hide or disguise the illicit origins of the assets".

56 See *infra* section II.B.1.b.

translates the expression "disguise" (such as *disimular*, used in other legislation in the Spanish language, e.g. in Argentina[57] and Chile[58]), the Spanish legislator opted for the verb *encubrir. Encubrir* means, *groso modo*, to hide. And for the purposes of money laundering, it means "to hide" the illicit origins of the money, which excludes any sort of deliberate concealing that the English word "disguise" implies. By doing so, the legislation essentially allows the incrimination of acts of simply "hiding" the origins of the money, without applying any method of disguise.

Regarding tax evasion, art. 301 SPC makes no explicit mention of it as a predicate offence. However, such a provision does exist in the administrative definition of the offence in the AML Law.[59] The latter helped to make the juridical interpretation of tax fraud as a predicate offence more uniform, despite some criticism from the Spanish doctrine.[60] In this sense, when tax evasion passes the threshold of €120,000, it is enough to constitute a crime and therefore to be a predicate offence for money laundering. Nonetheless, Supreme Court jurisprudence has stressed that even though tax fraud is considered a predicate offence for money laundering,[61] the use of the defrauded tax for the business's ordinary expenses (without the intent of laundering the defrauded payment) should not be considered as such.[62]

Similarly, neither the criminal (art. 301 SPC) nor the administrative (art. 1 AML Law) definition of money laundering make any explicit reference to the laundering of surrogate goods. There is also no mention of the conditions of "decontamination" of the illicit assets. According to the administrative definition of the crime (art. 2 AML Law), illicit assets are any "assets deriving from criminal activity", i.e. "anything whose acquisition or possession originates from a crime, whether corporeal or incorporeal, movable or immovable, tangible or intangible, and legal documents or instruments in any form including electronic or digital, evidencing title to or an interest in such assets". The Spanish jurisprudence has not yet established restrictive guidelines on the laundering of surrogate goods and refers to illicit assets as those directly or indirectly proceeding from a crime, and the cases of chains of money laundering.[63]

---

57 Art. 303 Argentinian Penal Code.

58 Art. 27 Chilean Anti Money Laundering Act (Law no. 19913/2003).

59 See *infra* section II.C.

60 Some authors argue that the provision of tax fraud as a predicate offence means converting prosecution for money laundering into a strategy to shore up the country's tax revenue. Martínez-Buján Perez, *Derecho penal económico y de la empresa. Parte especial*, Valencia, 2015, p. 486; Bacigalupo, *Sobre el concurso de delito fiscal y blanqueo de dinero*, Madrid, 2012, p. 9. There is also criticism to the effect that the evaded tax will always remain for a while the taxpayer's property, which would immediately represent the "possession" of illicit goods, enough to constitute money laundering according to the definition in the SPC.

61 STS 947/2012, of 5 December 2012.

62 STS 265/2015, of 29 April 2015.

63 Audiencia Provincial de Les Illes Balears, Sentence no. 161/2015, of 29 October 2015.

Finally, even though the jurisprudence in Spain has adopted self-money laundering and the laundering of money originating from tax evasion, it has made efforts to limit the scope of the criminal definition of money laundering, indicating a focus on the acts of disguising and not merely use of the illicit gains.

b. *Mens Rea*

Art. 301 SPC criminalises money laundering under two circumstances: (a) when committed intentionally and with the knowledge that the assets derive from criminal activity, and (b) when committed by gross negligence. Art. 301 does not explicitly refer to wilful blindness as a way to commit the crime. Nevertheless, wilful blindness is often found in the interpretation by tribunals, since the doctrine and jurisprudence describe it as a form of intent (*dolus*).[64] Indeed, there are decisions from the Supreme Court describing money laundering for wilful blindness as *dolus eventualis* (which is a form of intent).[65] Meanwhile, the SPC does not provide a legal definition of intent.[66]

As mentioned above, the objective definition of money laundering is closely related to the intent of the agent and, as a consequence, the debate around intent and gross negligence are of great relevance.

It is generally understood that art. 301 SPC describes intent in money laundering acts as the *aim of hiding or disguising* the illicit origins of the assets, or the *aim of helping someone* to evade any legal consequences of the previous criminal activity.

In particular, art. 301.1, first paragraph, SPC defines the first group of money laundering acts as acquisition, possession, use, conversion and transmission of assets, "knowing that it originated in any illicit activity". The law does not require subjective certainty of the origins of the money; likelihood suffices to constitute *mens rea*.[67] Nor does it specify the timeframe for such awareness: it does not require that the money launderer knows the illicit origins of the funds *at the time of receipt*. Nevertheless, the jurisprudence requires that the *awareness* of the illicit origins of the gains should be the minimum threshold to find intent: that is to say, mere *suspicion* of illicit origins is not enough for intent.[68]

---

64 Ragués i Vallès, *La ignorancia deliberada en Derecho penal*, Barcelona, 2007, p. 199.

65 STS 961/2010, of 11 November 2010; STS 279/2012, of 9 April 2012; STS 974/2012, of 5 December 2012; STS 238/2016, of 29 March 2016; STS 228/2013, of 22 March 2013.

66 Art. 5 SPC reads that there will be no sanction without intent or recklessness, and art. 10 SPC establishes that crimes are intentional or reckless actions and omissions punished by the law. But besides that, there is no legal definition of such concepts.

67 Art. 301 SPC refers to acquisition, possession, use, conversion or transfer of goods "knowing that those have their origins in an illicit activity". Similarly, art. 301.2 SPC refers to concealment or disguise "knowing that such assets are derived from criminal activity".

68 STS 1822/2001, of 10 October 2001; STS 1637/1999, of 10 January 2000; STS 157/2003, of 5 February 2003; STS 1070/2003, of 22 July 2003; STS 308/2004 of 12 March 2004; STS 1113/2004, of 9 October 2004; STS 33/2005, of 19 January 2005; STS 1034/2005, of 14 September 2005; STS 557/2012, of 9 July 2012; STS 228/2013, of 22 March 2013.

Complementing this, art. 301.1 second paragraph, SPC refers to the second group of criminal activity as carrying on with "any other act aiming to hide or disguise the illicit origins of the assets, or for the purpose of helping someone to evade any legal consequences of the previous criminal activity". Notwithstanding this, some authors conclude that, ultimately, art. 301, second paragraph, SPC invalidates all the objective elements that come before it (acquisition, use, conversion, transfer, possession) and defines money laundering *as any act aiming to hide or disguise the illicit origins of the goods*.[69] In fact, this is the interpretation upheld by the current jurisprudence on this topic, following a court decision from 2015: STS 265/2015 established that art. 301.1 SPC, in summary, contains only a legal category – "to commit any act" – with two different aims: "aiming to hide or disguise the illicit origins", or "aiming to help someone to evade legal consequences of the previous criminal activity".

According to this interpretation, then, the acts of art. 301.2 SPC (concealment or disguise of the true nature, source, location, destination, movements or rights over the assets, knowing that they derive from any of the offences described in the previous paragraph or from an act of participation in such offences) are the only ones that could be carried out by gross negligence.[70] Nevertheless, the text of art. 301 SPC allows any criminal conduct of money laundering to be understood as having been committed by gross negligence. Gross negligence lies in the failure to recognise basic signs of the illicit origins of the goods.

It is worth highlighting that the concept of gross negligence has no precise definition in the SPC, being more commonly interpreted as the breach of a very basic duty of care. There is currently a discussion in the Spanish doctrine as to whether gross negligence money laundering is a special crime, i.e. one only liable to be committed by obliged persons in relation to their duties to implement preventive measures, or if it is a common crime, i.e. a crime committed by everyone inside and outside of the list of obliged persons. Despite the discussions on this topic, the jurisprudence and the majority of the doctrine considers it to be a common crime, i.e. one that any citizen is liable to commit if they are in some way related or exposed to money laundering activities.[71]

---

69 Martínez/Buján Perez, *Derecho penal económico y de la empresa. Parte especial*, Valencia, 2015, pp. 311, 486.

70 Calderón Tello, *El delito de blanqueo de capitales: problemas en torno a la imprudencia y la receptación*, Cizur Menor, 2016, p. 187. In the jurisprudence, see also: STS 506/2015, of 27 July 2015; STS 228/2013, of 22 March 2013; STS 2545/2001, of 4 January 2002; STS 16/2009, of 27 January 2009; STS 1034/2005, of 14 September 2005.

71 Calderón Tello, *El delito de blanqueo de capitales: problemas en torno a la imprudencia y la receptación*, Cizur Menor, 2016, p. 199; Blanco Cordero, *El delito de blanqueo de capitales*, Madrid, 2015, p. 744; Palma Herrera, *Los delitos de blanqueo de capitales*, Madrid, 2000, p. 419; Aránguez Sánchez, *El delito de blanqueo de capitales*, Barcelona, 2000, p. 284. In the jurisprudence, STS 5782/2015, of 13 November 2015, convicted the mother of a drug dealer for reckless money laundering for lending bank accounts and helping her son to buy properties to launder the gains of drug trafficking.

Finally, concerning gross negligence money laundering, it must be stressed again that the gross negligence refers to the recklessness or lack of skill to acknowledge the illicit origins of the goods, and not to the reckless conduct itself.

2. *Money Laundering by Omission*

The SPC does not provide a criminal description of money laundering by failure to inform about suspicious transactions, nor by failure to implement preventive measures. Nevertheless, combining arts. 301 SPC and 11 SPC, the general clauses of the Penal Code on commission by omission, is, in principle, possible. Doing so would be valid in particular for cases where the obliged persons are guarantors,[72] having previously put themselves in place to prevent money laundering.

Compliance officers are, in principle, more exposed to the risks of sanctions for money laundering by omission, due to the criminal liability of legal entities for this offence in Spain (art. 31*bis* SPC). Indeed, the criminal liability of legal entities is possible only in relation a restricted list of crimes, and money laundering is among them. Because of that, in the scenario where some employee or manager takes advantage of an ineffective compliance programme to use the enterprise to commit money laundering, there would be the possibility that the person directly responsible for the AML policies in the enterprise would be investigated for money laundering by omission (with intent or gross negligence). Nevertheless, there is not enough evidence that the jurisprudence in Spain would follow a path for broad sanctioning of compliance officers. As yet, there is no jurisprudence on this topic.[73]

As mentioned above, the Spanish legislation punishes gross negligence money laundering. As a result, one could raise the concern that on some occasions the negligence of an obliged person to forward information about suspicious transactions or to take measures to avoid money laundering activities could lead to criminal responsibility for gross negligence omission. Nonetheless, the Spanish courts still remain sceptical about the criminalisation of gross negligence money laundering by omission.[74] In that sense, the question about intentional or gross negligence money laundering by omission is more a theoretical than a practical problem. However, it is necessary to stress that the concerns from the doctrine are not unfounded, because the legal definition of money laundering in Spain indeed allows for a wide degree of variation in the attribution of liability.

---

72 For example, compliance officers from obliged entities.

73 There are, on the other hand, many administrative sanctions for non-compliance with AML measures.

74 In the only case where the argument of money laundering by omission appears, involving partners of a company (Juzgado de Instrucción no. 3, Palma de Mallorca, Sentence of 7 January 2014, Appeal no. 2677/2008), the Court decided that there was no criminal liability because partners cannot be considered guarantors.

3. *Aggravated Forms of Money Laundering*

In order to establish a distinction between minor and serious cases of money laundering, art. 301 SPC increases the sanction for laundering in cases pertaining to a specific range of predicate offences. The aggravated form of money laundering corresponds to an exhaustive list of crimes related to the laundering of goods originating from the following sources: drug trafficking, corruption, influence peddling, embezzlement and fraud against the public treasury (Chapters V, VI, VII, VIII, IX and X of Title XIX SPC), and crimes against historic heritage and against the environment (Chapters I, II, III and IV of Title XVI SPC).

Another aggravated form of money laundering relates to the authors of the offence: serious sanctions are foreseen when the offence is committed by members of criminal organisations.

4. *Statutes of Limitation*

Art. 131 SPC[75] defines the statute of limitation in the Spanish legal system. In the case of the offence of money laundering, its length depends on the authors of the crime. For the basic crime described in art. 301 SPC, the statute of limitation is 10 years (art. 131.1 SPC). However, when the person suspected of money laundering falls within the aggravated category sanctioned by art. 303 SPC (businessmen, financial brokers, public employees, social workers, teachers or professors carrying out money laundering during the course of their duties), the statute of limitation will be 15 years, as a result of the higher sanctions foreseen by art. 303 SPC.

On the other hand, there are no temporal limits regarding the predicate offence that would preclude criminal liability for money laundering. The only limitation refers to the statute of limitation for the offence of money laundering itself.

5. *Jurisdictional Rules*

Art. 301.4 SPC provides for an expanded jurisdiction rule applicable to money laundering, and in principle[76] does not require the predicate offence to be

---

75 The statutes of limitation in Spain, as defined by art. 131 SPC, consider for its calculation general frames of maximal penalty provided by the articles of the penal code.

76 Some authors try to restrict the criminal proceedings for money laundering to cases where there is double incrimination of the predicate offence, both in Spain as well as in the country where it took place. Nevertheless, according to a literal interpretation of the law, art. 301.4 SPC does not require dual incrimination. A sanction for money laundering would be allowed only if the conduct is a criminal offence in both countries (Spain and the country where the offence took place entirely or partially). Fabián Caparrós, *El delito de blanqueo de capitales*, Madrid, 1998, p. 384; Aránguez Sánchez, *El delito de blanqueo de capitales*, Barcelona, 2000, p. 196; Fabián Caparrós, "La aplicación territorial del delito de blanqueo de capitales en el Derecho español", in Pérez Cepeda (ed.), *El principio de justicia universal: fundamentos y límites*, Valencia, 2012, p. 470.

criminalised in both Spain and the third country (dual incrimination of the predicate offence). To better understand art. 301.4 SPC, though, one needs to distinguish between two situations: (a) the jurisdiction rules of Spanish courts when that predicate offence is committed totally or partially abroad, and (b) the jurisdictional rules applicable to money laundering in general.

In the first case, i.e. when the predicate offence is committed totally or partially abroad, but the acts of money laundering take place on Spanish territory, the ubiquity principle applies. Even if the predicate offence is committed entirely abroad, Spanish courts have jurisdiction over the laundering of money resulting from it. Art. 301.4 SPC is silent on the issue of dual incrimination of the predicate offence. This allows Spanish courts to prosecute the gains resulting from conduct that is, in theory, not criminalised abroad if such conduct would have constituted a predicate offence had it occurred domestically. Despite the doctrinal criticism on this matter,[77] the reason for it lies in the autonomy of the money laundering offence in relation to the predicate offence.[78] So far, there has been scarce jurisprudence on this topic, and the Supreme Court has not yet come to an agreement regarding the need for dual incrimination for the prosecution of money laundering of illicit gains entirely perpetrated abroad.[79]

Regarding the general jurisdictional rules applicable to money laundering, some authors argue that because of the bad legislative technique of art. 301.4 SPC,[80] and on the basis of the Vienna Convention of 1988, one could interpret art. 301.4 SPC as giving Spain universal jurisdiction over money laundering activities committed entirely abroad.

Nevertheless, the general procedural rule in Spain does not foresee money laundering as one of the crimes that could be prosecuted by Spanish courts under the rule of universal jurisdiction (art. 23.3 Law no. 6/1985). Therefore, under a strict interpretation of the law, it can be concluded that Spain does not have universal jurisdiction over the prosecution of money laundering.

---

77 Totally critical of the provision in Spanish law, Blanco Cordero, *El delito de blanqueo de capitales*, Madrid, 2015, p. 395.

78 Fabián Caparrós, "La aplicación territorial del delito de blanqueo de capitales en el Derecho español", in Pérez Cepeda (ed.), *El principio de justicia universal: fundamentos y límites*, Valencia, 2012, p. 475.

79 STS 974/2016, of 23 December 2016 required dual incrimination, with a dissenting vote from one of the judges. On the other hand, STS 1501/2003, of 19 December 2003 seemed to exclude the requirement for dual incrimination.

80 Art. 301.4 SPC says prosecution of money laundering will take place "even though … the acts punishable pursuant to the preceding Sections may have been committed, full or partially, abroad". Martínez-Buján Perez, *Derecho penal económico y de la empresa. Parte especial*, Valencia, 2015, p. 581; Martín Sagrado, "Principio de justicia universal y blanqueo de capitales: dificultades interpretativas derivadas de la deficiente técnica legislativa", *La Ley* 4732/2017.

C. NON-CRIMINAL DEFINITION OF MONEY LAUNDERING

Spanish law has two definitions of money laundering: the criminal definition in art. 301 SPC and the non-criminal one in art. 1.2 AML Law. The text of the latter is largely based on art. 1.2 3AMLD and 4AMLD, and its content has close similarities with the criminal definition.

Comparing the text of the two articles (art. 301 SPC and art. 1.2, first paragraph, AML Law),[81] one notices that the text of the non-criminal definition of money laundering seems more precise than that of the criminal definition, although not more restrictive. In essence, both cover the same activities: acquisition, possession and use of illicit goods, transfer, concealment and disguising of the illicit origin of the goods, with knowledge of those illicit origins, and participation in any of the above activities. Nevertheless, the non-criminal definition clarifies some points of previous doctrinal discussion, extending the definition to tax fraud as a predicate offence[82] and to the acts of facilitating and advising actions aiming at the laundering of illicit assets.

Like the criminal definition, the non-criminal definition covers self-money laundering. It also requires knowledge of the illicit origins of the goods at the time of receipt. Moreover, the non-criminal definition is more specific about what can be an object of money laundering: tangible or intangible assets, real estate or personal property, as well as documents and legal documents, regardless of their form, attesting property or rights to assets.

However, the non-criminal definition offers a more extensive description (in comparison with the criminal definition) of the circumstances under which

---

81 Art. 1.2 AML Law: "For the purposes of this Act, the following conduct shall be regarded as money laundering: (a) The conversion or transfer of assets, knowing that such assets are derived from criminal activity or from an act of participation in such activity, for the purpose of concealing or disguising the illicit origin of the assets or of assisting any person who is involved in such activity to evade the legal consequences of his or her actions. (b) The concealment or disguise of the true nature, source, location, disposition, movement, beneficial ownership of assets or rights, knowing that such assets are derived from criminal activity or involvement in criminal activity. (c) The acquisition, possession or use of assets, knowing, at the time of receipt, that such assets are derived from criminal activity or from an act of participation in criminal activity. (d) Participation in, association to commit, attempts to commit and aiding, abetting, facilitating and counselling the actions mentioned in the foregoing points. (e) Money laundering shall exist even where the conduct described in the foregoing points was carried out by the person or persons who carried out the criminal activity that generated the assets. For the purposes of this Law, assets deriving from criminal activity means assets of every kind whose acquisition or possession originates from a crime, whether corporeal or incorporeal, movable or immovable, tangible or intangible, and legal documents or instruments in any form including electronic or digital, evidencing title to or an interest in such assets, including the amount defrauded in the case of tax crime. Money laundering shall be regarded as such even where the activities which generated the assets were carried out in the territory of another Member State or in that of a third country".

82 Blanco Cordero, "El delito fiscal como actividad delictiva previa del blanqueo de capitales", *Revista electrónica de ciencia penal y criminología*, no. 13, vol. 1, 2011, p. 3.

someone is deemed to be committing the offence, referring to the acts of "participation in, association to commit, attempts to commit and aiding, abetting, facilitating and counselling" the actions described above as money laundering. In doing so, the non-criminal definition covers preparatory activities (i.e. attempts to commit) at the same level as money laundering acts themselves.

Finally, extended jurisdiction is also adopted by the non-criminal definition, understanding activities (which generated illicit assets) carried out abroad as enough to place money laundering activity inside Spain.

Above all, an important feature of the non-criminal definition is that it mentions tax evasion as a predicate offence for money laundering, which is not explicit in the criminal definition in art. 301 SPC. In doing so, the AML Law serves as an official interpretation[83] of the criminal definition, contributing to resolve a doctrinal discussion about the use of the money saved via tax fraud as a predicate offence for money laundering.[84] In that regard, it is to should be mentioned that, for criminal law purposes, the tax evasion needs to be above €120,000 to figure as a crime (art. 305 SPC). Consequently, only amounts above this threshold can be an object of money laundering for law enforcement purposes, under both the criminal and non-criminal definitions.

D. SCOPE OF OBLIGED ENTITIES

1. *Financial and Banking Institutions*

The AML Law provides a list of the financial institutions that form the main category of obliged entities. The reform of the AML Law in 2018 slightly altered the list of obliged entities, including details and changing the category of some financial providers.

---

83 Nevertheless, the idea that art. 1.2 AML Law is an official (authentic) interpretation of the criminal definition is not a consensus opinion in the Spanish doctrine. In favour of this conclusion: Blanco Cordero, "El delito fiscal como actividad delictiva previa del blanqueo de capitales", *Revista electrónica de ciencia penal y criminología*, no. 13, vol. 1, 2011, p. 5; Mallada Fernández, "El delito fiscal como delito previo del blanqueo de capitales", *Revista Quincena Fiscal*, no. 10, 2012, p. 3. Against: Martínez-Bujan Perez, *Derecho penal económico. Parte especial*, Valencia, 2015, p. 549; Bacigalupo, *Sobre el concurso de delito fiscal y blanqueo de dinero*, Madrid, 2012, p. 9.

84 Abel Souto, "La reforma penal española de 2010 sobre el blanqueo, las nuevas técnicas de comisión delictiva y el uso de las telecomunicaciones para el blanqueo", in Abel Souto/Sánchez Stewart (eds.), *III Congreso sobre prevención y represión del blanqueo de dinero*, Valencia, p. 207; Choclán Montalvo, "Delito fiscal y blanqueo de capitales", *La Ley* 7743/2016, p. 3; Mallada Fernández, "El delito fiscal como delito previo del blanqueo de capitales", *Revista Quincena Fiscal*, no. 10, 2012. Lately, an important decision of the Supreme Court also stated that the tax fraud could be a predicate offence for money laundering (STS 974/2012, of 5 December 2012, known as the "Ballena Blanca" Operation).

Art. 2.1 AML Law[85] states that "financial and banking institutions" covers banks (including savings banks and cooperative credit companies), life insurance companies (and natural persons acting as insurance brokers), securities agencies and companies, portfolio management companies, investment funds, securities dealers,[86] and pension funds management companies.

"Financial service providers" also covers asset management companies, venture capital management companies, payment institutions[87] and companies dealing with currency exchange,[88] and mutual guarantee companies.[89] Financial and banking service providers shall implement all preventive duties set out by the AML Law.

Finally, the AML Law includes within its scope *de facto* financial activities that are not included in its list of financial institutions, namely: persons acting professionally as intermediaries in brokering loans or credit provisions, as well as persons who, without being licensed as credit institutions, carry out professionally credit and loan activities, factor and finance commercial transactions, make leasing agreements, issue and manage credit cards, or provide

---

85 Art. 2.1 AML Law: "(a) Credit institutions. (b) Insurance companies authorised to operate in the field of life insurance and insurance brokers acting in connection with life insurance or other investment related-services, with the exceptions laid down in the regulations (currently, the regulation of the AML Law establishes no exceptions). (c) Investment services firms. (d) Management companies of investment funds and investment companies whose management is not assigned to a management company. (e) Pension fund management entities. (f) Management companies of venture capital entities and venture capital companies whose management is not assigned to a management company. (g) Mutual guarantee companies. (h) Payment institutions and electronic payment institutions. (i) Persons whose business activity includes currency exchange."

86 The Society for the Management of Assets Proceeding from Bank Restructuring (SAREB), created in 2012 after the economic crisis in Spain, was included officially in the reform of 2018 as a financial institution in the terms of art. 2.d AML Law (list of obliged entities). SAREB is an entity to aid in the restructuring of the Spanish financial sector. 45% of its funds are public (coming from the Fund for the Orderly Restructuring of the Banking Sector (FROB) and 55% are private, coming from Spanish banks. Art. 24.2 Decree 1559/2012, of 15th November 2012, which determines the Regimen of Asset Management Companies. See https://www.sareb.es/es_ES/conoce-sareb/quienes-somos/que-es-sareb. Access: 24.10.2017.

87 For instance, services such as Western Union or PayPal. Art. 41 AML Law determines that the payment institutions shall transfer the funds through accounts opened in credit institutions, both in the destination country of the funds and in any other in which the overseas correspondents or intermediate clearing systems operate. That means that the payment institution itself must use the banking system to transfer its payment orders, but it remains responsible for the risks of money laundering and for the preventive measures adopted by the correspondent banking institution.

88 For example, *bureaux de change* and tourism agencies. Art. 3 Decree 304/2014 *excludes* such companies as obliged entities under the definition of a financial institution "when the currency services are incidental, parallel to the main activity". With this exception, the Decree complements the AML Law and specifies exceptions of the situations where some person or activity remains out of the list of obliged entities, which will be the case, for example, of travel agencies.

89 Regulated by Law no. 1/1994, mutual guarantee companies were created to facilitate access to credit for small and medium-sized companies, and provide services only for those companies under each Spanish administrative region (Comunidades Autónomas).

guarantees or similar commitments;[90] persons engaged in the deposit, custody or professional transfer of funds or means of payment; and managers of payment systems, clearing systems and financial derivatives, as well as managers of credit or debit cards issued by other entities.[91]

2. *Virtual Currency System Participants*

The AML Law does not mention virtual currency system participants as obliged entities, and it could be considered a blind spot in the Spanish regulation on money laundering.

In February 2018, the Central Bank of Spain and the National Securities Exchange Commission delivered a joint statement[92] pointing out that no cryptocurrency has been registered, authorised or verified by the competent Spanish authorities.

As far as the jurisprudence goes, there is only one sentence from the Supreme Court in the context of civil proceedings that underlines the link between virtual currencies and the risk of money laundering.[93] However, it is not explicitly applicable to the interpretation of the AML system or regular criminal law.

Currently, notaries are able to accept virtual currency as a mean of payment. Although such currency is not a legal tender, it could be used in a barter transaction.

Nevertheless, a Proposal to transpose the 5AMLD to the Spanish AML Law does include the virtual currency system participants. According to the Proposal, providers of virtual currency exchange, virtual currency to fiat exchange, virtual currency transfer and wallet services will be added as obliged entities for the purposes of the prevention of ML (art. 2.1, v). Moreover, it will be mandatory for all virtual currency providers operating for residents in Spain to register as such in the Bank of Spain.[94]

---

90 The AML Law refers to the activities covered by the first additional provision of Law no. 3/1994, which adapts Spanish legislation on credit institutions to the Second Banking Coordination Directive and introducing other changes related to the financial system.

91 Those obliged entities are under the obligations of AML Law only in terms of art. 40 AML Law, which defines the managers of payment systems and other persons listed in this item as "collaborative entities". It reads: "Collaborative entities. Managers of payment systems and of systems for the clearing and settlement of securities and financial derivatives, together with managers of credit cards or debit cards issued by other entities shall cooperate with the Commission for the Prevention of Money Laundering and Monetary Offenses and its support bodies by delivering the information they possess on conducted transactions, as provided in article 21.1".

92 https://www.bde.es/f/webbde/GAP/Secciones/SalaPrensa/NotasInformativas/18/presbe2018_07.pdf.

93 STS 37/2015, of 6 February 2015.

94 In this respect, the Proposal provides the following definitions:

5. "Virtual currency shall mean a digital representation of value not issued or guaranteed by a central bank or public authority, not necessarily associated with a legally established

3. *Legal Profession and Tax Advisors*

Notaries and land, commercial and moveable property registrars[95] (art. 2.1(n) AML Law), as well as lawyers and barristers[96] (art. 2.1(ñ) AML Law), count as obliged persons under the AML Law.

In the case of "lawyers, barristers and other independent professionals", their duties as obliged persons are restricted to specific transactions or triggered by pre-defined situations: "when they participate in the design, implementation or advice on activities on behalf of clients relating to the buying and selling of real estate or business entities, the management of funds, securities or other assets, the opening or management of current, savings or securities accounts, the organisation of contributions necessary for the creation, operation or management of companies or the creation, operation or management of trusts, companies or similar structures, or when acting on behalf of clients in any financial or real estate transaction" (art. 2.1(ñ) AML Law).

In the same context, art. 22 AML Law does not answer the question regarding the professional activities of lawyer subject to the duty to inform, because it determines that lawyers are exempt from communicating suspicious transactions when "ascertaining the legal position for the client". Nevertheless, it is a vague expression to use to specify the situation in which a lawyer performs such acts (of ascertaining the legal position for the client). Later on, art. 22 AML

---

currency and not having the legal status of currency or money, but accepted as a means of exchange and capable of being transferred, stored or traded electronically.

6. Exchange between virtual currencies means exchange between one or more types of virtual currencies.
7. Exchange of virtual currency for fiduciary currency shall mean the purchase and sale of virtual currency by the delivery or receipt of euros or any other foreign currency of legal tender or electronic money accepted as a medium of exchange in the country where it is issued.
8. Providers of electronic purse storage services shall mean natural or legal persons providing safeguarding or custody services for cryptographic private keys on behalf of their customers for the holding, storage and transfer of virtual currency."

Proposal available at: https://www.mineco.gob.es/stfls/mineco/ministerio/participacion_publica/audiencia/ficheros/ECO_TES_20200612_AP_V_Directiv_Blanqueo.pdf.

95 The movable property registrar legally registers ownership and burdens regarding movable property, such as rights, contractual terms, vehicles and any movable property financially evaluated.

96 In Spain, legal professionals are heavily regulated at the federal level. In order to be a lawyer in Spain, one needs to follow the terms of the Spanish Bar Association (*Colegio de Abogados*): to hold a law degree, to hold a specific Master's degree that enables one to exercise of the profession (only for students who applied to the Bar Association after 2011, the year when the new Law related to Access to the Legal Profession, Decree 775/2011, started to require enrolment in a specific Master's course, where more practical aspects of the profession are taught), to pass the national test of the Bar Association, and then to be registered with one of the provincial sections of the Association.

Law states that lawyers are not obliged to carry out due diligence measures when they are involved in the legal defence of their client, "including the *advisory* activities about ways to avoid a legal proceeding, regardless the fact that they have received this information before, after or during the aforementioned proceeding" (art. 22 AML Law).[97]

It is clear in the AML Law that lawyers are obliged entities when creating and managing companies and trusts and representing clients in operations not exclusively performed by legal professionals (i.e. management of funds, buying and selling real estate property).[98]

Nevertheless, there is a discussion in Spanish doctrine about the extent of lawyers' duties to inform when acting as advisors and the potential conflict with professional secrecy. This is a recognised problem within the legal professions under the money laundering regime, and the doctrine in Spain mainly adopts the interpretation of the European Court of Human Rights.[99] It highlights that any pre-judicial consultation with lawyers must be exempt from the duty to inform, because acts aiming to "ascertain the legal position of the client" coincide with the core of constitutional defence rights, and therefore are not subject to the AML Law.[100]

As yet, there is no jurisprudence in Spain on this topic. However, based on the theoretical conclusions mentioned above, the litigation and pre-litigation phases shall remain exempt from the duty to inform, respecting the need for professional secrecy.[101] In that sense, lawyers must carry out their CDD and reporting obligations when representing their client outside of the litigation and pre-litigation phases.

The above-mentioned art. 2.1(ñ) AML Law obliges lawyers to report when exercising *advisory* functions in some operations or in relation to the legal

97 Art. 22 AML Law: "Exemption. Lawyers shall not be subject to the obligations under articles 7.3, 18 and 21 with respect to the information that they receive from any of their clients or obtain on the latter when ascertaining the legal position for their client or performing their duty of representing that client in or concerning judicial proceedings, including advice on instituting or avoiding proceedings, irrespective of whether such information was received or obtained before, during or after such proceedings. Notwithstanding the provisions of this Law, lawyers shall remain subject to their obligation of professional secrecy in accordance with the legislation in force".

98 Coca Vila, "El abogado frente al blanqueo de capitales. ¿Entre Escila y Caribdis?", *InDret*, no. 4, 2013, p. 19.

99 ECtHR, *Michaud v. France*, Application no. 12323/11.

100 Coca Vila, "El abogado frente al blanqueo de capitales. ¿Entre Escila y Caribdis?", *InDret*, no. 4, 2013, p. 20.

101 In fact, in 2014 SEPBLAC published a document notifying about the beginning of inspections of law firms to look for suspicious activities. The document from the Bar Association of Barcelona indicates the notification from the FIU: http://web.icam.es/bucket/REQUERIMIENTO%20SEPBLAC%20FEBRERO%202014.pdf.

position of the client.[102] In this case, there is an example of a transplant straight from a European Directive into Spanish law, where, however, a slightly different translation presents problems.

Moreover, there is no institution in Spain ready to counsel law firms on the specific risks of each legal area or to serve as an intermediary between lawyers and the FIU.[103] Because of this, the FATF has stated that lawyers in Spain are "an outlier, with limited awareness of their ML/FT risks and obligations, and little evidence that effective controls are in place".[104]

Finally, notaries and civil registrars have one of the most developed structures of money laundering prevention by obliged entities, since the Notary Regulation Act and the Notary Act make it mandatory for notaries and civil registrars to cooperate in relation to AML policies.[105]

4. *Informal Value Transfer Systems*

According to art. 41 AML Law, money remittance transactions shall be made through accounts opened with credit institutions "both in the destination country of the funds and in any other in which the overseas correspondents or intermediate clearing systems operate". If the money remittance service is organised like a business, it must be conducted by a credit institution, the creation of which must be previously authorised by the Ministry of Economy or the Bank of Spain.[106]

Following that, one concludes that there is no legal gap in Spanish regulation allowing informal value transfers, but these shall be considered illegal.[107]

---

102 The advisory activity goes further than merely *participating* or *assisting*. Sánchez Stewart. *Abogados y prevención del blanqueo de capitales*, Málaga, 2014, p. 19.

103 There is no organisation similar to the role performed, for instance, in France by the President of the Bar Association, who serves as a special filter for the information provided by lawyers.

104 FATF, *Mutual Evaluation Report – Spain*, 2014, p. 13.

105 Art. 24 Notary Act (Law of 28 May 1982).

106 Moreover, art. 1.2 Law no. 19/2003 on the Legal Regime of Capital Movement and Economic Transactions Abroad states that any acts of business, transactions and operations between residents and non-residents are unrestricted if the transaction "involves or may involve overseas receipts and payments, as well as transfers from or to a foreign country, or any variations in accounts or financial debtor or creditor positions with regard to foreign companies, apart from any special limitation imposed by law". In addition, art. 3.2 Law no. 19/2003 establishes that any natural or legal person that carries out one of those transactions must communicate it to the Ministry of Economy and the Central Bank of Spain. The same is true for credit entities, investment services companies and other financial intermediates, which must equally communicate to the above-mentioned organs their clients' transactions.

107 As is well known, hawala is one type of informal value transfer system, and therefore forbidden in Spain. Nevertheless, according to current investigations, this system is responsible for the circulation of large amounts of illicit money in Spain for terrorist purposes. There are news reports revealing a network of 250 Spanish butchers and phone shops funding jihadists in

5. *Non-Profit Sector*

Foundations and associations are obliged entities under art. 2.1(x) AML Law. However, the empirical study carried out for this report suggests that the non-profit sector is not fully aware of its duties regarding the prevention of money laundering.

6. *Overview of Other Obliged Entities*

Besides the obliged entities listed above, the AML Law also applies to other obliged entities listed under art. 2.1 AML Law, such as auditors, external accountants and tax advisers; postal services in respect of *giro* or transfer activities; property developers and activities related to real estate agencies, commission or brokerage in real estate trading; trust and company service providers; casino; and professional dealers in jewels, precious stones or precious metals and in works of art or antiques. Art. 2.3 AML Law establishes, however, that these activities can be totally or partially excluded from the obligations when they present a low risk of money laundering.

Persons responsible for the management, operation and marketing of lotteries or other gambling activities in respect of prize payment transactions[108] and natural persons engaged in the movement of means of payment above the threshold of €10,000, or its equivalent in foreign currency,[109] also fall within the scope of the AML Law. In addition, persons whose business activity includes selling to consumers in hiring of goods with the offer of restitution of the price[110] and dealers in goods when receiving cash payments above the threshold of €15,000[111] are also obliged entities. Finally, the recent reform added electronic gambling providers as obliged entities[112] (art. 2.1(p) AML Law).

Syria; see https://elpais.com/elpais/2015/02/02/inenglish/1422892172_955064.html. The Supreme Court has also handed down decisions regarding money laundering via hawala systems (STS 2754/2008, of 4 June 2008; STS 4947/2007, of 15 June 2007; Sentence from the National High Court 6284/2006, of 9 May 2006 and Sentence from the National High Court 2591/2010, of 26 February 2010). In detail, Lombardero Expósito, *El Nuevo marco regulatório del blanqueo de capitales*, Barcelona, 2015, p. 408 ff.

108 According to the AML Law, persons responsible for lotteries, sport bets, bingo and type B gaming machines are only obliged entities in relation to prize payment transactions.

109 The list of obliged entities refers to art. 34 AML Law, which sets the threshold at €10,000.

110 Art. 1 of Consumer Protection in the Procurement of Goods with a Price Refund Offer (Law 43/2007, of 13 December) regulates commercial activities in which the consumer has the right to return the product within 15 days and receive a full refund.

111 The threshold is established by art. 38 AML Law.

112 According to art. 3.3(h) Law no. 13/2011, gambling by electronic, informatic, telematic or interactive means are that which one uses any mechanism or installation allowing the production, storage or transmission of documents, data, information or communication, such as television, internet, and fixed-lined or mobile phones.

A current Proposal to adapt the Spanish regulation to the 5 AMLD defines as obliged entities crowdfunding platforms, professional dealers of arts and antiquities and those intermediating such transactions, external experts, real estate developers and those professionally engaged in agency, commission or brokerage activities in the purchase and sale of real estate and in the leasing of real estate involving a total annual rent of EUR 120,000 or more or a monthly rent of EUR 10,000 or more.[113]

E. RELATIONSHIP BETWEEN AML AND ANTI-TERRORISM FINANCING FRAMEWORK(S)

Historically, Spain has experienced domestic terrorist attacks from groups such as ETA (in particular in the 1970s) and in the recent years has also been a victim of jihadist attacks.[114]

For this reason, the SPC has an entire section dedicated to the prevention of and fight against terrorism. This section includes the crime of terrorism financing (art. 576 SPC), which is independent from the definition of money laundering (art. 301 SPC). In fact, the treatment of both conducts is very different under the criminal law,[115] since the SPC dedicates a whole chapter to defining, in detail, a variety of conducts related to terrorism and its financing. On the other hand, the administrative preventive system is largely the same for money laundering and terrorism financing. The main difference between the AML and anti-terrorism systems is the broad possibility of freezing assets[116] when there is a suspicion of terrorism financing. A further difference is the existence of a special administrative body responsible for counter-terrorism financing.

As a result, two additional administrative laws provide for increased safeguards against terrorism financing, complementary to the AML Law: the Terrorism Financing Blocking Act and its associated regulation.[117]

113 The above-mentioned changes will be added to the list of current art. 2 of AML Law, along with other paragraphs to reorganise the current list of obliged entities. The Proposal also provides further details on the activities of company service providers under the duty to prevent money laundering. Proposal available at: https://www.mineco.gob.es/stfls/mineco/ministerio/participacion_publica/audiencia/ficheros/ECO_TES_20200612_AP_V_Directiv_Blanqueo.pdf.

114 De la Rosa, "Financiación del terrorismo", in González Cussac (ed.), *Financiación del terrorismo, blanqueo de capitales y secreto bancario: un análisis crítico*, Valencia, 2009, p. 255.

115 The two actions (money laundering and terrorism financing) come under very different sections of the Penal Code: money laundering is defined in a chapter dedicated only to money laundering and "handling stolen goods", while terrorism financing is defined within a much larger chapter, which sets out the multiple forms of terrorist acts and sanctions against all such forms, their financing included.

116 See *infra* section III.C.1.d, "Power or duty to freeze".

117 Law no. 12/2003 (Terrorism Financing Blocking Act) and Decree 413/2015 (which regulates the former), both dedicated to countering the financing of terrorism.

The first creates the Committee for Surveillance on Terrorism Financing Activities, whose main task is to determine cases that require asset freezing, the prohibition of account deposits or the opening of bank accounts, without consulting the owner of such assets.[118]

The duty to freeze assets in Spain in this context is restricted to cases of terrorism financing and regulated by the Terrorism Financing Blocking Act.[119] The Committee for Surveillance on Terrorism Financing Activities has the exclusive competence to determine the amount and timeframe of the asset freezing.[120,121] Institutionally, the FIU answers to the Treasury, while the Committee for Surveillance on Terrorism Financing Activities answers to the Secretary of Home Affairs.

The Committee for Surveillance on Terrorism Financing Activities shall act in cooperation with the FIU in tasks relating to the notification of obliged entities about the asset freezing, "in order to guarantee the effectiveness of the asset freezing agreement".[122] The director of the FIU has a right to speak but not to vote in the Committee.[123] Once the Committee for Surveillance on Terrorism Financing Activities identifies the assets to be frozen, it is then the Commission for the Prevention of Money Laundering and Monetary Offences (Comisión Nacional de Prevención del Blanqueo de Capitales e Infracciones Monetarias, CPMLMO) that must notify the obliged entity about the freezing. CPMLMO is also responsible for supervising and sanctioning the obliged entities who infringe freezing orders.[124]

Once the Commission of Surveillance on Terrorism Financing Activities has notified the obliged entities, they must then proceed to block "the accounts, balances, financial positions as well as the transactions and movement of funds, even if occasional, and any corresponding operations involving charges, payments or transfers in which the payer, the sender, the owner, the recipient or beneficiary is a person or entity with ties to terrorist groups or organisations, or if the transaction, movement or operation was performed as a consequence

---

118 Art. 10 Decree 413/2015 and Arts. 1.1 and 1.2 Terrorism Financing Blocking Act.

119 Art. 1.2 Terrorism Financing Blocking Act defines very broadly the acts of freezing assets, i.e. "the blocking of any movement, transfer, exchange, use or transaction in capital or financial assets, which result in or may result in a change in the amount, value, location, property, possession, nature or destination of said capital or assets or any other change that may facilitate its utilisation, including the management of a portfolio asset".

120 Memorandum to the Terrorism Financing Blocking Act.

121 According to the Proposal to implement the 5AMLD (art. 42.1), the duty to freeze will be applicable by the obliged entities to any natural or legal person from the time of their publication by the UN Security Council. Proposal available at: https://www.mineco.gob.es/stfls/mineco/ministerio/participacion_publica/audiencia/ficheros/ECO_TES_20200612_AP_V_Directiv_Blanqueo.pdf.

122 Art. 9 Decree 413/2015.

123 Art. 9.2(c) Law no. 12/2003.

124 Art. 6 Law no. 12/2003.

due to or for the reason of perpetrating terrorist activities or to contribute to the goals pursued by terrorist groups or organisations" (art. 1.1 Terrorism Financing Blocking Act).

All obliged entities and public administrations must comply with the Terrorism Financing Blocking Act, and the maximum period for which they can maintain the asset freeze is six months (art. 2.5 Terrorism Financing Blocking Act). The particular mechanism of freezing assets, though, works independently of the filing of an SAR from the obliged entity.

At the same time, the AML Law sets out sanctions and international financial counter-measures that include the freezing of assets in the case of terrorism financing. The sanctions imposed by the United Nations Security Council Resolutions (relating to the prevention and suppression of terrorism financing, the proliferation of weapons of mass destruction and their financing) must be transposed to the domestic financial system (art. 42 AML Law). Here, again, the obliged entity does not have autonomy to decide on the freezing of assets, since the body responsible for the decision is the Council of Ministers, on the motion of the Spanish Minister of Finance. In turn, the obliged entities must freeze the assets immediately after receiving the order from CPMLMO.[125,126]

Spain also relies on another specific body dedicated to preventing the financing of terrorism, which works in close cooperation with the FIU. In 2004, the country's authorities created the National Centre for Counter-terrorism Coordination (Centro Nacional de Coordinación Antiterrorista, CNCA). It has different purposes from the FIU, but it is also an intelligence body, and the link between the CNCA and the FIU is essentially one of the former receiving information collected by the latter. After 2017, the Secretary of Home Affairs merged the activities of the CNCA with the Intelligence Centre against Organised Crime, creating a new body, the Intelligence Centre against Terrorism and Organised Crime (CITCO), maintaining the tasks formerly attributed to the CNCA.[127] The CITCO answers to the Secretary of Home Affairs, and has the characteristics of an intelligence agency, and the duty to collect sensitive

---

125 Nevertheless, the FATF Mutual Evaluation Report on Spain of 2014 points out that freezing orders and implementation of targeted financial sanctions are "the major weakness in Spain CFT regime", because of deficiencies in the framework of applicable EU regulations. The report also states that "Spain has no clear channels or procedures for directly receiving foreign requests to take freezing actions pursuant UNSCR 1373". FATF, *Mutual Evaluation Report – Spain*, 2014, p. 77.

126 According to the Proposal of the AML Law (waiting for parliamentary debate and approval) it will be mandatory for the obliged entities to proceed with the freezing of assets right after the decision of the United Nations Security Council. There will be no need anymore to wait for the decision of the Spanish Council of Ministers and following communication from the CPMLMO.

127 Decree 770/2017, of 28 July 2017.

information and coordinate the strategies of police bodies (National Police and the Civil Guard).[128]

III. THE SYSTEM OF MONEY LAUNDERING PREVENTION

A. CUSTOMER DUE DILIGENCE

1. *Standard CDD Rules*

a. Triggers and Timing

Generally speaking, it is always mandatory for obliged entities to perform CDD measures if they identify any suspicion of money laundering (art. 7.1 AML Law), regardless of any exemption or threshold. As to the additional triggers, CDD measures must be undertaken in regard to all new customers, as well as existing customers when they contract new products or conduct a transaction that is significant in terms of its volume or complexity (art. 7.2 AML Law). Obliged entities shall apply CDD measures to new and existing customers on a risk-sensitive basis (art. 7.2 AML Law).

In addition, obliged entities shall proceed to the *formal identification* of the client when the following thresholds are met:

(i) when the customer (whether a natural or legal person) intends "to establish business relationships or to take part in any occasional transactions whose amount is equal to or greater than EUR 1 000" (art. 4.1 Decree 304/2014) – though obliged entities are exempted from the formal identification if there are no doubts about the identity of the client;
(ii) exceptionally, prior to the payments of prizes for lotteries and other games of chance where the amount is equal to or greater than €2,500, unless there are no doubts surrounding the identity of the party involved.

Spanish law provides different triggers for the *identification of the beneficial ownership*, which shall be done *prior* to:

(i) the establishment of a business relationship;
(ii) wire transactions above a threshold of €1,000 (art. 9 Decree 304/2014);
(iii) occasional transactions above a threshold of €15,000 (art. 9 Decree 304/2014).
(iv) in cases of lottery or betting transactions, in the payment of prizes above €2,500 (art. 4.1 Decree 304/2014).

---

[128] https://www.intelpage.info/centro-nacional-de-coordinacion-antiterrorista.html.

Besides those general rules, some groups of obliged entities face special thresholds and situations in relation to CDD measures. Life insurance dealers shall identify the policyholder before the conclusion of the contract, and "the identity of the beneficiary of the life insurance must be verified *in all cases before payment of the benefit under the contract* or the exercise of the rights of redemption, payment or pledge granted by the policy" (art. 3.3 AML Law, art. 5 Decree).

Moreover, all obliged entities shall undertake CDD measures in their business relationships with trusts or other legal arrangements or patrimonies which, despite lacking legal personality, may act in the course of trade (art. 7.4 AML Law). On the same note, professional dealers in goods are obliged to perform CDD measures when dealing with means of payment[129] above a threshold of €10,000 *done by non-residents* in Spain (art. 38 AML Law), be that a single transaction or a sum of smaller transactions that appear to be linked.[130]

According to art. 14.5 AML Law, obliged entities shall apply adequate risk management procedures in order to determine whether or not the customer or the beneficial owner is a politically exposed person (PEP).[131]

As regards the timing of CDD measures, they must be applied prior to the beginning of the business relationship, with one exception: obliged entities are allowed to establish a business relationship or execute transactions by phone or other electronic means without the client being present (art. 12 AML Law). That is the case only under specific circumstances: (i) when the customer's identity is accredited in accordance with the definition in the applicable regulations on electronic signatures; (ii) if the first deposit originates from a bank account in the same client's name opened in Spain, the EU or in equivalent third countries;[132] or (iii) if the requirements set out in the regulations are judged to be met.[133]

---

129 These are cash, cash checks (or cashier's checks) and any other means made payable to the bearer (art. 34.2 AML Law).

130 These rules apply to general dealers in goods, however, since dealers in jewellery, precious stones and antiques have lower thresholds (€1,000). See *infra* section III.A.2.a.

131 The rules regarding the admission of PEPs as clients shall be detailed in the client's admission policy in the internal monitoring manual.

132 According to Resolution of 10 August 2012 of the General Secretariat of the Treasury and Financial Policy, Spain considers the following to be equivalent jurisdictions: Australia, Brazil, Canada, Hong Kong, India, Japan, Mexico, Singapore, South Africa, South Korea, Switzerland and the United States.

133 With respect to the latter (point (iii)), although the AML Law is silent regarding which regulations should be consulted, one can interpret it to mean that obliged entities are allowed to establish a business relationship without the client's presence if it was possible to remotely request the information necessary to fulfil the CDD measures. Moreover, in addition to the AML legislation (AML Law and Decree), there is other relevant legislation that could be considered by the obliged entity, as recently highlighted by a sentence of the CJEU (Judgment of the CJEU, Fifth Chamber, 10 March 2016, Case C-235/14) regarding the Spanish banking system and prevention of money laundering, including: the data protection law and the regulation of payment services (Law no. 16/2009, of 13 November 2009).

But in any case, the obliged entity must proceed to the formal identification of the client within one month of establishing the remote business relationship. Within this timeframe, they shall obtain a copy of the necessary documents from the customer for the purposes of CDD (art. 21 Decree 304/2014).

Moreover, art. 9 Decree 304/2014 requires obliged entities to also verify the identity of the beneficial ownership using independent, trustworthy sources when there are reasons to suspect that the information provided by the client is not accurate, or when a special review (art. 17 AML Law) is required to determine the risks of the transaction, based on its unusual, economically unreasonable or overly complex character. In the event of the customer's reluctance or refusal to provide the required information or documentation, obliged entities shall refrain from establishing or maintaining the business relationship or from executing the transaction (art. 9.3 Decree 304/2014).

Furthermore, some obliged entities not operating in the financial sector have a list of occasions that shall trigger CDD measures. Casinos must apply CDD measures "to all persons intending to enter the establishment" and before following situations: (i) the issuances of cheques to customers as a result of the exchange of chips; (ii) transfers of funds made by casinos at the request of customers; and (iii) the issue by casinos of certificates providing evidence of the gains obtained by players. Finally, casinos must also apply CDD measures to any person who carries out transactions with a value of €2,000 or more, whether in a single transaction or a sum of smaller transactions that appear to be linked, by the collection of winnings, or by the purchase or exchange of gambling chips (art. 7.5 AML Law).

Having regard to the particular situation of lawyers and other privileged professions as obliged persons, their triggers for applying CDD measures are related to the legal service they provide, and arise in the following situations: (i) when they participate, on behalf of clients, in the design, implementation or advice on activities relating to the buying and selling of real estate or business entities; (ii) the management of funds, securities or other assets; (iii) the opening or management of current, savings or securities accounts; (iv) organisation of contributions necessary for the creation, operation or management of companies; (v) creation, operation or management of trusts, companies or similar structures; and (vi) when acting on behalf of clients in any financial or real estate transaction (art. 2.1(ñ) AML Law).

When dealing with specific situations,[134] notaries shall undertake measures to identify natural and legal persons, based on documentation and following procedures established by law (art. 6 Decree 304/2014).

[134] Transactions of forming companies, associations, foundations or similar legal arrangements, or undertaking any legal acts or legal proceedings related to their functioning or management, or when dealing with clients constituting, transmitting or extinguishing any actual rights upon real estate or commercial entities, or the purchasing or sale of stocks, shares or any other exchangeable securities or financial instruments.

In addition, due to the higher risk of terrorism financing, foundations and associations shall identify and verify the identity of every person who donates funds or resources voluntarily here the amount exceeds €100 in cash or where the person uses an anonymous means of payment. If the donation comes from a Spanish bank account, then the threshold for the duty to identify rises to €1,000 (art. 42.2 Decree 304/2014).

Finally, according to art. 7.3 AML Law, if the obliged entity is unable to comply with the due diligence requirements, it shall not establish any business relationship nor proceed to any transaction. If this situation arises during an ongoing business relationship, the obliged entity shall terminate the relationship and proceed to a special review (art. 17 AML Law), which may eventually lead to the filing of an SAR.[135]

b. CDD Measures

The CDD measures demanded by the AML Law in Spain include the duties to perform: (i) formal identification; (ii) identification of the beneficial owner; (iii) identification of the purpose and nature of the business relationship; and (iv) ongoing monitoring, for the time periods and other specific situations described in the section above.

Obliged entities shall formally identify their clients and obtain information about the *purpose and nature* of the business relationship, sufficient to allow them to know the nature of their clients' professional or entrepreneurial activity (art. 5 AML Law), with no exceptions. If formal identification is not possible, or if a client refuses to provide the means for identification, obliged entities are forbidden to establish or maintain the business relationship (art. 3.2 AML Law, art. 9.3 Decree 304/2014). If the difficulties in applying CDD measures arise within an ongoing business relationship, the obliged entity shall proceed to the special review (art. 17 AML Law). If there is a suspicion of money laundering, the obliged entity shall report it to the FIU (art. 18 AML Law).

The CDD measures shall also make it possible to determine the ownership and control structure of legal persons (art. 4.4 AML Law). Additionally, in the course of CDD proceedings the obliged entity will request information from its

135 This particular situation will be altered after the approval of the current Proposal to adapt the AML Law to the 5AMLD. Art. 7.3 of the Proposal determines that if the obliged entity is unable to comply with the due diligence requirements prior to or during the business relationship, those shall not be initiated or shall be terminated. When appropriate, the obliged entity shall perform a special examination to verify a suspicion of money laundering. Nevertheless, if further CDD measures may tip-off the client regarding the existence of a suspicion of money laundering in the eyes of the obliged entity, the obliged entities are allowed to proceed with the transaction without completing the CDD and shall then file an SAR immediately. Proposal available at: https://www.mineco.gob.es/stfls/mineco/ministerio/participacion_publica/audiencia/ficheros/ECO_TES_20200612_AP_V_Directiv_Blanqueo.pdf.

clients to determine whether they are acting of their own accord or on behalf of a third party.[136] If the obliged entity finds indications or suspicion that a natural person is acting on behalf of a client, the obliged entity shall request additional information to determine the identity of the client (natural or legal person) on whose behalf the person is acting.

Alongside initial CDD measures, obliged entities must continuously monitor business relationships (art. 6 AML Law) to ensure that the information about and profile of the client's transactions are up to date.

In addition, Spanish law provides further details on the CDD measures applying to particular types of obliged entities or clients. Insurance intermediaries are required to register the beneficiary of the insurance as soon as the policyholder designates who they are. If this is not done,[137] the obliged entity shall determine the identity of the beneficiary at the time of the payout (art. 5 Decree 304/2014). If there is some difficulty in the identification, the obliged entity shall apply the special measures foreseen in art. 17 AML Law.[138]

When dealing with trusts, obliged entities must request the founding document of the trust, the identification, and verification of the identity of the person acting on behalf of the beneficiaries or in the terms of the trust or legal instrument (art. 6.3 Decree 304/2014).

Finally, the Spanish AML Law allows financial institutions and other obliged persons to delegate the fulfilment of CDD measures to third parties, in part or entirely, though remaining ultimately accountable for any legal consequences. The only exception is the ongoing monitoring of the business relationship, which shall always be undertaken by the obliged entity itself. This provision does not apply to groups, in whose case the ongoing monitoring can be done through the group (art. 8 AML Law, art. 13.2 Decree 304/2014).

c. Individual Responsibility

All obliged entities are required to appoint a person as a representative before SEPBLAC, who shall be responsible for fulfilling reporting obligations and responding to requests from the FIU. The representative shall be at the level of manager or director in the company.[139] The FIU shall be promptly informed

136 See *infra* section VI.A.1.b (Definition of "Beneficiary" and "Effective Control").

137 The AML Law uses the expression "generically designated beneficiaries", such as wills or by other means.

138 These are special review of the patterns of operations, complex or unusual transactions, or transactions lacking a rational and legal apparent purpose.

139 Spanish law follows the interpretative note to the 15th FATF Recommendation, which reads: "compliance management arrangements should include the appointment of a compliance officer at the management level".

of the representative's nomination, and can raise reasoned objections to or comments about the nomination (art. 35 Decree). In the case of individual professionals, the owner of the business will be the designated representative.

It is not mandatory for the obliged entity to wait for the FIU's approval for the representative to be appointed, but once the FIU sends its observations, they shall be considered and implemented. The failure of the obliged entity to adopt the FIU's recommendations regarding the representative is sanctioned as a serious offence (art. 52.1(n) AML Law).

To fulfil its duties before SEPBLAC, the obliged entity shall give the designated person unlimited access to any internal information available (art. 26.2 AML Law). Furthermore, the representative is allowed to nominate two additional representatives to work under their direction and supervision.

The law does not make a distinction between categories of obliged entities in relation to the nomination of a representative to SEPBLAC.

d. Further CDD Guidance

The Spanish FIU (SEPBLAC) provides some guidance to obliged entities by providing both typologies lists and recommendations[140] to give advice on the implementation of internal monitoring measures. According to SEPBLAC, the list of recommendations is a result of its supervisory experience and intelligence analysis and is also based on the information received from obliged entities. In this light, SEPBLAC recognises the range of obliged entities and highlights the fact that each one must make their best efforts to *recognise and be aware of the specific risks* of their professional activity. In that sense, SEPBLAC also stresses that the information proposed in the list of recommendations may not be totally relevant to every obliged entity listed in the AML Law.

The list of recommendations emphasises the need for measures of internal monitoring appropriate to the professional activity, volume of business, number of employees and the business areas in which the obliged entity operates. Keeping these factors in mind, all obliged entities shall draw up a self-evaluation report on money laundering. The report shall be practical and adapted to the business area, reporting the products and services, the channels used to transfer money, the characteristics of the clients, specifying the ones that are potentially more vulnerable to money laundering, the risks of the geographic areas of activity and the steps that employees shall adopt in each case. In that sense, SEPBLAC's recommendations are not equally binding on all obliged entities,

140 SEPBLAC Recommendations on Measures for Internal Control for Prevention of AML/TF, http://www.sepblac.es/espanol/informes_y_publicaciones/documento%20_recomendaciones_sobre_medidas%20_control_interno_PBCFT.pdf.

since it depends on the level of exposure to risks of money laundering. Thus, the obliged entity itself needs to adapt the duties and CDD measures from the AML Law, after undertaking a self-evaluation regarding its exposure to risks of money laundering.

Besides the recommendations regarding the acknowledgment of the activity's risk, SEPBLAC stresses that the relationship with clients (KYC) is the key for the CDD measures.[141] The obliged entity must ensure proper internal feedback mechanisms within the company to identify risk patterns and prevent future illegal transactions. Moreover, SEPBLAC recommends that the CDD measures be performed according to an "universal principle", i.e. applied to each one of the clients with whom that obliged entity has a business relationship. The cornerstone of the KYC is to determine the client's beneficial ownership and the origin of the funds.

Most of all, following the creation of an internal self-evaluation risk report, SEPBLAC recommends that obliged entities classify the typology of risky transactions, risky clients and regions, the policy on accepting clients, rules for internal procedures to collect data, the KYC database and alert systems, in order to help the employees recognise the risk of the operation and apply the corresponding strength of CDD measures. SEPBLAC also recommends the creation of practical guidelines, as well as a list of all public and internal norms and general procedures available to the employees. The list of recommendations stresses on many occasions the need for an external expert/auditor, who should evaluate the internal preventive measures and provide the obliged entity with a well-founded opinion about the effectiveness of its system.

Another CDD measure required by SEPBLAC is a formalised contract signed between the obliged entity and the client, explaining the mutual obligations regarding the prevention of money laundering.[142]

Besides the general recommendations above mentioned, the Spanish FIU provides a typology list with the most common risks for a variety of obliged entities,[143] focusing on the following sectors: insurance service providers;[144] credit institutions;[145] payment institutions;[146] dealers in jewellery, precious

[141] See: https://www.sepblac.es/wp-content/uploads/2018/03/recomendaciones_sobre_medidas_de_control_interno_pbcft.pdf.

[142] Ibid., p. 13.

[143] The current catalogues are available in the website from the National Treasury (not from SEPBLAC): http://www.tesoro.es/prevencion-del-blanqueo-y-movimiento-de-efectivo/legislación/guias-y-orientaciones.

[144] http://www.tesoro.es/sites/default/files/cor_entidades_aseguradoras.pdf.

[145] http://www.tesoro.es/sites/default/files/cor_entidades_de_credito.pdf.

[146] http://www.tesoro.es/sites/default/files/cor_entidades_de_pago.pdf.

stones, antiques and art;[147] the real estate sector;[148] investment service companies;[149] casinos;[150] and non-profit organisations. Each list focuses on the phenomenology of suspicious transactions, client and employee behaviour, typical fraud in documents and so on. In addition, SEPBLAC also offers an easy-to-understand guide to dealing with third countries, establishing parameters for identifying high-risk third countries,[151] in which case enhanced CDD measures shall apply.

Overall, however, the Spanish supervisory bodies are not prolific in providing the obliged entities with specific guidance or with analysis by sector. There is no information on the most recent update to the typology lists, but it is noticeable that the typologies of credit institutions is the most extensive one.

Finally, the Colleges of Notaries and Mercantile Registrars, in fulfilment of their duties to cooperate with regard to AML policies, created centralised prevention bodies for each profession (notaries and registrars).

In 2005, the Notary Regulation Act and the Notary Act[152] created the Centralised Prevention Body of the College of Notaries (Organo Centralizado de Prevención de Blanqueo de Capitales del Colegio Notarial, OCP). Some years later, in 2015, the College of Property and Mercantile Registrars also created a Registrar Center against Money Laundering to act as the prevention body for registrars[153] (Centro Registral Anti-blanqueo de Capitales, CRAB), on the same basis as the OCP.[154]

The task of both the OCP and CRAB is to centralise the reports from notaries and registrars, cooperate with the FIU and mediate the relationship between notaries and registrars – as obliged entities – and the FIU, and to provide further CDD measures. The OCP is widely assessed as very effective at raising awareness of the risks inherent in the sector, as well as carrying out case studies about high-risk operations.[155]

---

147 http://www.tesoro.es/sites/default/files/cor_joyerias.pdf.

148 http://www.tesoro.es/sites/default/files/cor_sector_inmobiliario.pdf.

149 http://www.tesoro.es/sites/default/files/cor_valores.pdf.

150 http://www.tesoro.es/sites/default/files/cor_valores.pdf.

151 http://www.tesoro.es/sites/default/files/guia_riesgo_geografico_en_materia_de_bc-ft_.pdf.

152 Art. 24 Notary Act (Law of 28 May 1982).

153 Order ECC/2402/2015, of 11 November 2015.

154 Put simply, the functions of notaries and registrars are complementary. Notaries have the power to officially attest the public validity of a document and attest the veracity of legal acts performed in their presence (the legitimacy of the signatories of a document, declarations with public effects (last wills, declaration of societies, etc.)). After the public attestation from the notary, the document can be used for any official and public purposes. On the other hand, registrars publicise legal acts, to make them known to and effective against third parties (marriage, mortgage, registration of companies). The Instruction of 10 December 1999 from the General Directory for Notary and Registrars (BOE 311, of 29 December 1999) establishes their general duties regarding the prevention of money laundering.

155 See also FATF, *Mutual Evaluation Report – Spain*, 2014, p. 15.

2. *Simplified CDD*

a. Scope

Spanish law allows obliged entities to apply simplified CDD measures to a list of clients and operations that are considered by the law to have a lower risk of money laundering (art. 9 AML Law). According to the Decree, in principle, public law companies or other legal persons controlled or majority owned by public entities from the EU or equivalent third countries[156] are subject to simplified CDD measures (art. 15 Decree 304/2014). The same applies to financial institutions,[157] as well as their branches and subsidiaries,[158] domiciled in the EU or in equivalent third countries, and to listed companies that trade securities on a regulated market in the EU or equivalent third countries. The only exception is money service providers,[159] which cannot apply simplified measures.

According to the Proposal to transpose the 5AMLD, the Spanish Council of Ministers may decide to require obliged entities to apply enhanced CDD measures to correspondent banking from high risk third countries and may also determine them to review, modify or terminate their business relationship.[160]

In the same way, simplified CDD measures may also be applied in the case of low-risk products or transactions (art. 16 Decree 304/2014), such as life insurance policies where the premium is low;[161] collective insurance for complementary social welfare;[162] life insurance policies solely insuring the risk of death;[163] and prepaid cards, when not rechargeable and the amount stored does not exceed €250, or where, if rechargeable, the total amount transacted in a calendar year is limited to €2,500.

---

156 According to Resolution of 10 August 2012 from the General Secretariat of the Treasury and Financial Policy, Spain considers the following to be equivalent jurisdictions: Australia, Brazil, Canada, Hong Kong, India, Japan, Mexico, Singapore, South Africa, South Korea, Switzerland and the United States.

157 See section II.D.1.

158 Only when they are subject by the parent company to procedures to prevent money laundering and terrorism financing.

159 See n. 86.

160 Art. 42.2, k under the modifications of the Proposal. Proposal available at: https://www.mineco.gob.es/stfls/mineco/ministerio/participacion_publica/audiencia/ficheros/ECO_TES_20200612_AP_V_Directiv_Blanqueo.pdf.

161 Simplified CDD measures apply to those only when the annual premium does not exceed €1,000, or the single premium does not exceed €2,500; in the case of pension plans and mutual societies, when liquidity is limited they may not be used as collateral for a loan.

162 Under the following conditions: (i) that it implements pension collective agreements or an employment regulation procedure; (ii) that it does not allow the payment of premiums by the insured worker that, together with those paid by the insurance policyholder employer, reach an amount exceeding €8,000 per year; and (iii) that cannot be used as a guarantee for a loan and do not include other forms of surrender other than exceptional liquidity.

163 Including those that also provide additional guarantees of financial compensation for permanent or partial, total or absolute disability or temporary disability, serious illness and dependency.

Other cases where simplified CDD measures may be applied are money orders of public administrations or their agencies and official money orders for postal service payments to and from the Postal Service itself; collections or payments regarding low commissions generated by tourism bookings (when not exceeding €1,000); consumer credit contracts for amounts under €2,500;[164] syndicated loans;[165] and credit card contracts for amounts less than €5,000.[166] The rule for simplified CDD measures applies to the cases mentioned above, unless the electronic money holder requests reimbursement of an amount equal to or greater than €1,000 during the same calendar year. Electronic money issued upon receipt of the means of payment under art. 34.2(a) AML Law is excluded.

Finally, in the case of retail operations by professional dealers in jewels, precious stones or precious metals, and professional dealers in works of art or antiques, there is a special provision. In the case of retail operations with clients who are natural persons in transactions under €1,000 they are exempted from all CDD measure.[167] If the transaction is over €1,000, and is with a natural person, they need only conduct formal identification (art. 18 Decree 304/2014) and shall store relevant information in such a way that it is available to CPMLMO if requested. Regular CDD measures would include, in addition to the formal identification, the identification of the beneficial owner and the purpose and nature of the professional or business activity of the client. In the case of the latter, a National Treasury recommendation states that a signed statement from the client with that information (beneficial ownership and purpose and nature of the professional or business activity) suffices.

b. Requirements

The risk assessment of the clients and financial transactions is a key element for the definition of the level of CDD measures. Simplified CDD measures must always be in accordance with the previous risk assessment conducted by the obliged entity.

164 Only if the reimbursement is made exclusively by debiting a bank account held by the debtor in a credit institution domiciled in the EU or in equivalent third countries.

165 Syndicated loans in which the agent bank is a credit institution domiciled in the EU or in equivalent third countries, in respect of the participating entities that are not the agent bank.

166 Only when the amount withdrawn can only be refunded from an account held by the customer in a credit institution domiciled in the EU or equivalent third country. The above-mentioned list is not a literal translation or a copy of the Law, but an interpreted version, providing the reader with the result of the references made by the AML Law and Decree to Royal Decree 1588/1999 on the regulation on the implementation of pension agreements between companies and employees and beneficiaries, and to Law no. 35/2006 on Income Tax of Individuals and Partial Amendment of the Corporation Tax, Non-resident Income and Wealth.

167 http://www.tesoro.es/sites/default/files/orientaciones_joyeros.pdf.

In addition, if the obliged entity encounters one of the cases listed above,[168] and if there is no evident risk, it may apply one or more of the following measures (art. 17 Decree 304/2014): reducing the frequency of customer identification updates and the degree of ongoing monitoring of the client's transactions, or not collecting specific information or carrying out specific measures to understand the customer's professional or business activities. In the case of low risk and simplified CDD measures, obliged entities are also allowed to postpone the verification of the customer's identity and the beneficial ownership until after the establishment of the business relationship and after the quantitative threshold[169] is exceeded.

c. Further Simplified CDD Guidance

None of the supervisory bodies (SEPBLAC, Bank of Spain, the College of Notaries) offer special guidance on simplified CDD measures.

3. *Enhanced CDD*

a. Scope

The provisions on enhanced CDD measures in the Spanish legislation deal mainly with the prevention of money laundering in high-risk third countries and in relation to politically exposed persons (PEPs),[170] in accordance with obliged entities' own risk exposure or when higher-than-average risks are detected (art. 11 AML Law).[171] The AML Law also refers to cross-border correspondent banking (art. 13 AML Law) and transactions made by electronic means (telephone, internet) without the client being present (art. 12 AML Law) as cases where enhanced CDD measures should be applied.

According to the Proposal to transpose the 5AMLD, the Spanish Council of Ministers may decide to require obliged entities to apply enhanced CDD measures to correspondent banking from high risk third countries and may also determine them to review, modify or terminate their business relationship.[172]

---

168 See *supra* section III.A.2.a.

169 See thresholds mentioned in the previous section III.A.2.a. (scope of simplified CDD).

170 See *infra* section III.4.

171 Art. 11 AML Law refers to "countries with strategic deficits in the prevention of money laundering" as those which pose significant threats to the financial system of the EU, and which will be defined at European supervisory level, as states in art. 9 4AMLD.

172 Art. 42.2, k under the modifications of the Proposal. Proposal available at: https://www.mineco.gob.es/stfls/mineco/ministerio/participacion_publica/audiencia/ficheros/ECO_TES_20200612_AP_V_Directiv_Blanqueo.pdf.

Art. 19 Decree 304/2014 specifies the aforementioned high-risk scenarios requiring enhanced CDD measures:

(i) private banking services;[173]
(ii) remittance transactions whose individual or aggregate value per calendar quarter exceed €3,000 and foreign currency exchange transactions whose individual or aggregate value per calendar quarter exceeds €6,000;
(iii) transactions with bearer shares, where they are permitted (they are not permitted, however, where the obliged entity cannot ascertain by other means the ownership and control structure of the company);
(iv) business relationships and transactions with customers from high-risk countries[174] (as specified *infra* section III.A.5);
(v) transfer of shares or stocks in pre-established companies (shelf companies).[175]

In addition, obliged entities shall proceed to closer risk analysis at their own discretion. Thus, the list in the Decree must be seen only as an initial guideline to what constitute higher-risk cases. Obliged entities shall strive to verify the accuracy of the information provided by the client (art. 5 AML Law), and are obliged to confirm it when the client or the nature of the business: (i) presents higher risks according to external recommendations; (ii) presents higher risks according to the risk evaluation conducted internally by the obliged entity; or (iii) when the active and passive transactions do not correspond to the declared business activity or to the previous transactions (art. 10 Decree 304/2014).

In the first place, obliged entities shall dedicate attention to the characteristics of their clients. Clients not residing in Spain, companies whose ownership and control structure is not transparent or is unusual or overly complicated, and asset-holding companies may all be high-risk clients (art. 19.3(a) Decree 304/2014).

---

173 "Private banking services" is the Spanish term for activities similar to wealth management services or family office (the latter is more commonly used in Spanish financial jargon). Its main activity is the tailored wealth management of families, groups of families, the foundation of trusts and general management of patrimony. Cf. Rivo López/González Vázquez/Rodríguez López, "Family office: instrumento de gestión del patrimonio familiar", *Revista de Empresa Familiar*, no. 2, vol. 1, 2011.

174 High-risk third countries shall include, in all cases, those countries in relation to which the FATF requires the application of enhanced due diligence measures, according to art. 19 Decree 304/2014.

175 For these purposes, shelf companies are pre-established companies incorporated without a real economic activity, in order to be subsequently sold to third parties. For explanatory purposes, it should be noted that pre-established companies are not the same as domiciliary companies. The main idea behind pre-established or shelf companies is to save time for entrepreneurs that decide to start a business. The average time needed to establish a company in Spain ranges from 30 to 60 days. Because of this, there are law firms and other professionals that create and register companies with very general scopes and aims, and leave those companies "on the shelf", waiting to operate. When a client needs one, he or she can acquire a shelf company, change the corporate statute and start to use the company in a very short period of time.

Secondly, the characteristics of the operation, business relationship or distribution channel may also lead to enhanced CDD measures, if they consist in business relationships or transactions in unusual circumstances, with clients that frequently use bearer means of payment, or when executed through intermediaries (art. 19.3(b) Decree 304/2014).[176]

There is still no administrative jurisprudence or further guidance (and there not be without a deepening of the case law) on what is considered an "unusual circumstance". However, the lists of typologies drawn up by the FIU may be a starting point for some obliged entities to determine when business activity is unusual, although the lists are not exhaustive and in the case of some obliged entities are not regularly updated. The only list continually updated is the one regarding risks for financial institutions.

In any case, according to the amended art. 11 AML Law, private banking activity,[177] money remittance services[178] and foreign exchange operations shall be considered high risk when their activity exceeds the limits of the regulation.[179] Nevertheless, despite the mention of the "limits of the regulation", there is still no regulation, given the short amount of time that has elapsed since the approval of the reform of the AML Law (September 2018). In the meantime, one could refer to those limits by analogy to the limits applicable to financial activities, as described above (transactions whose individual or aggregate amounts per calendar quarter exceed €3,000 and foreign currency exchange transactions whose individual or aggregate amounts per calendar quarter exceed €6,000). Nevertheless, it is not possible to infer the limits the legislator will establish for private banking and money remittance services.

In respect of cross-border correspondent banking, obliged entities shall apply the following enhanced CDD measures: (i) gather sufficient information about a respondent institution to understand the nature of the respondent's

176 The list provided by Annex III of the 4AMLD, which Spain is yet to implement domestically, provides a more extensive range of potentially higher-risk situations. Just in terms of customer risk factors, the 4AMLD extends the list of higher risks to (i) companies that have nominee shareholders or shares in bearer form and (ii) businesses that are cash-intensive. On the other hand, in terms of the product, service, transaction or delivery channel customer risk factors, the 4AMLD extends the list of higher risks to: (i) products or transactions that might favour anonymity; (ii) non-face-to-face business relationships or transactions, without certain safeguards, such as electronic signatures; (iii) payment received from unknown or unassociated third parties; and (iv) new products and new business practices, including new delivery mechanisms, and the use of new or developing technologies for both new and pre-existing products.

177 See n. 164.

178 For example, Western Union, MoneyGram, etc.

179 In the case of the need for enhanced CDD measures for all money remittance services, the former version of the AML Law (in force until September 2018) considered such services to always be high risk. In 2016, however, a decision of the CJEU (Case C-235/14, of 10 March 2016) considered that the Spanish regulation was too strict and lacked proportionality, stating that it should be possible for money remittance services to tailor the CDD measures to the risk exposure. After the reform, the AML Law maintained the provision, describing those services as high risk only when above certain thresholds, which are still to be determined by the regulation.

business and to determine from publicly available information its reputation and the quality of its supervision; (ii) assess the respondent institution's AML controls; (iii) obtain approval from senior management before establishing new correspondent relationships; (iv) document the respective responsibilities of each institution; and (v) conduct enhanced, ongoing monitoring of the business relationship, taking into consideration the geographical, customer or service risk factors (art. 13 AML Law).

The Spanish legislation (art. 12 AML Law) allows obliged entities to carry out transactions with customers who are not physically present under the following circumstances: (i) if the customer's identity can be assured by means of electronic signatures; (ii) if the first deposit originates from an account in the same client's name opened in Spain, the EU or equivalent third countries; and (iii) if the requirements to be set out in the regulations are judged to be met. In those cases, enhanced CDD measures shall be undertaken when in the course of the business relationship the obliged entity perceives the risk to be above average.

Finally, art. 16 AML Law does mention technological innovations as a focus of enhanced CDD measures to be adopted by obliged entities.[180]

b. Requirements

If they identify a higher risk of money laundering, obliged entities must examine the activities declared by their clients and their client's beneficial ownership. Additionally, and depending on the risk identified, they shall apply one or more of the measures below (art. 20 Decree 304/2014): (i) updating the data obtained in the customer acceptance process; (ii) obtaining additional documentation or information on the purpose and nature of the business relationship, on the source of funds, on the customer's source of wealth, or on the purpose of the transactions; (iii) obtaining senior management authorisation to establish or maintain the business relationship or to carry out the transaction; (iv) enhancing monitoring of the business relationship; (v) reviewing and documenting the consistency of the business relationship or transactions; (vi) requiring that payments or deposits are made into an account in the customer's name at a credit institution domiciled in the EU or in equivalent countries; and (vii) limiting the amount or nature of the transactions or the means of payment used.

Moreover, the beneficiary of a life insurance policy must be included as a relevant risk factor for the purposes of deciding whether enhanced CDD

[180] Literally, under art. 16 AML Law: "Products or transactions favouring anonymity and new developing technologies. Obliged subjects shall pay special attention to any money laundering or terrorist financing threat that may arise from products or transactions that might favour anonymity, or from new developing technologies, and take appropriate measures to prevent their use for money laundering or terrorist financing purposes. In such cases, obliged subjects shall conduct a specific analysis of possible money laundering or terrorist financing threats, which should be documented and made available to the competent authorities."

measures shall be applied. If the beneficiary poses a higher-than-average risk, he or she shall be identified prior to the payment of the benefit resulting from the contract or prior to the policyholder's exercise of the right of surrender, deposit or pledge granted by the policy.

Besides the requirements described above, the AML Law and Decree do not offer further guidance and details to obliged entities. In that sense, one might have difficulties in interpreting what the legislator meant, for example, by requiring "senior management authorisation to carry out the transaction", since that would represent a challenge for any major corporation.

c. Further Enhanced CDD Guidance

Supervisory authorities provide special local guidance for enhanced CDD measures. CPMLMO has published on its website the Joint Guidelines on the 4AMLD,[181] with further recommendations on enhanced and simplified CDD measures, but those were not drafted specifically for Spain, nor are they drawn up solely by Spanish authorities.

4. Rules on Politically Exposed Persons

a. Definition

The Spanish AML Law[182] uses the expression "persons with public responsibility" to refer to "politically exposed persons" (PEPs). According to the Explanatory Memorandum of the AML Law, the legislator understood that the Spanish translation ("persons with public responsibility") was more in line with the meaning of the Directive, and clearer in the Spanish language. However, this choice is confusing, because it leads to an interpretation that only those with "public responsibility" are PEPs, when in reality the AML Law also refers to relatives and close associates.

That being said, in the definition of PEP, the Spanish AML Law focuses on high-ranking members of the executive, legislative and judicial branches (art. 14 AML Law), close relatives,[183] and closely associated persons.[184]

---

181 Risk factor Guidelines, http://www.cpbc.tesoro.es/sites/default/files/2_ba_directrices_sobre_factores_de_riesgo.pdf.

182 Directive 2006/70/EC, which implements measures for Directive 2005/60/EC of the European Parliament and of the Council regarding the definition of 'politically exposed person' and the technical criteria for simplified customer due diligence procedures and for exemption on grounds of a financial activity conducted on an occasional or very limited basis.

183 Art. 14.4 AML defines as family members for the purpose of the law: the spouse or stable partner, as well as parents and children, and the spouses and stable partners of the children.

184 Art. 14.4 AML defines as close associates for the purpose of the law: any natural person who is known to hold the ownership or control of a legal instrument or person jointly with a PEP, or who maintains some other kind of close business relationship with a PEP, or who holds

After the reform, art. 14.2 AML Law divides PEPs into two groups, national and international. It also standardises the treatment of international PEPs, such that both international and European "persons with public responsibility" (or PEPs) shall now undergo enhanced CDD measures.

International PEPs (foreign PEPs and PEPs from international organisations) are those who perform or have performed prominent public functions, such as: heads of state; heads of government; ministers or other members of government; secretaries of state or undersecretaries; members of parliament; Supreme Court judges, Constitutional Court judges or other senior judicial officials whose decisions are generally not appealable, outside of exceptional circumstances, including the equivalent members of the Public Prosecution Service; members of courts, auditors or members of boards of directors of central banks; ambassadors and *chargés d'affaires*; senior staff of the Armed Forces; members of the administrative, management or supervision bodies of government-owned enterprises; directors, assistant directors or members of the board or those with an equivalent function in international organisations; and those who hold senior management positions in charge of political parties with parliamentary representation.

The list provided above also applies to local Spanish PEPs. In addition to the above list, at a local level PEPs are those who hold senior management positions in the Spanish state administration,[185] in the administration of the Spanish

the ownership or control of a legal instrument or legal person that is known to have been established for the benefit of a PEP. In that sense, the definition in the AML Law does not differ significantly from the provisions of art. 3(11) 4AMLD.

185 Art. 14 AML Law refers to the Law no. 3/2015, of 30 March 2015, who regulates the exercise of senior management positions in the general administration of the State. According to the latter, those positions are: (a) The members of the Government and the Secretaries of the State; (b) The Undersecretaries and assimilated; the Secretaries-General; the Delegates of the Government in the Autonomous regions and in Ceuta and Melilla; the Delegates of the Government in Public law entities; and the chiefs of permanent diplomatic mission, as well as the chiefs of permanent representation before international organisations; (c) Technical Secretaries, or Directors of the General Administration of the State and assimilated; (d) Presidents, the Vice-presidents, the Directors-general, the Executive directors and assimilated in entities of the public sector, foundations or enterprises which are linked or dependent on the General Administration of the State, if they hold the management position and at the same time were nominated after a decision of the Cabinet or by its own governmental bodies and, in any case, the Presidents and the Directors with status of Director-general of the Managing Entities and Common Services of the Social security; the Presidents and the Directors of the State Agencies, the Presidents and the Directors of the Port Authorities and the President and the Secretary-General of the Economic and Social Advice; (e) the President, the Vice-president and the rest of the members of the Council of the National Antitrust Commission, the President of the Council of Transparency and Good Government, the President of the Independent Authority from Fiscal Accountability, the President, Vice-president and the Members of the Council of the National Commission of the Stock market, the President, the Advisers and the Secretary-General of the Nuclear Security Council, as well as the President and the members of the governing organs of any other regulatory organism or of supervision; (f) the Directors, Executive directors, Secretaries-General or equivalents of the regulatory organisms and of supervision; and (g) the holders of any other job in the state, any

Autonomous Regions or Provinces and those who perform or have performed prominent public functions in the Autonomous Regions[186] (art. 14.3 AML Law). Moreover, still at the local level in Spain, mayors, council members and persons who hold senior management positions in the capitals of the Autonomous Regions or Local Entities[187] with more than 50,000 inhabitants, or senior management positions in trade unions or employers' organisations or Spanish political parties, are also PEPs.

The decision to limit the PEP requirements to mayors and councillors of towns with more than 50,000 inhabitants was based on the size of the municipality's budget and potential real estate activities, and "the responsibilities and functions of municipal governments (as higher-level functions and actions are required from towns with more than 50.000 inhabitants)".[188]

Article 14.3 AML Law, moreover, determines that CPMLMO shall publish a list detailing which functions and posts determine whether someone is a PEP in Spain. However, this paragraph came into force in the AML Law reform of September 2018, and so the list is not yet available.

Finally, it should be noted that the definition of PEPs does not include intermediary or lower-level civil servants (art. 14. 4 AML Law).

b. Requirements

The first particularity of enhanced CDD measures for PEPs, close relatives[189] and closely associated persons in Spain is that the obliged entities must keep performing the enhanced measures up to two years after the person loses their status as a PEP (art. 14.9 AML Law). After this period, obliged entities shall adopt adequate CDD measures, in accordance with an analysis of the risk posed by the former PEP.

In addition, obliged entities shall also adopt special procedures when doing business with PEPs. After determining whether the customer or the beneficial owner is a PEP, obliged entities shall obtain approval from at least the immediate senior management[190] in order to establish or maintain business relationships. They shall also perform enhanced ongoing monitoring of the business

public sector that is its denomination, which appointment is carried out by the Cabinet, except for those that have the Assistant general directors consideration and assimilated.

186 Such as presidents, members of governing councils and deputies of Autonomous Communities (art. 14.3(b) AML Law).

187 "Local Entity" is the denomination some territories receive in Spain, when they have autonomy to set their budget and administrative decisional authority within a municipality. It is, in short, an autonomous territory located inside a municipality. That is the case of the Community of Andalucia, regulated by Law 7/1993, of 27 July.

188 FATF, *Mutual Evaluation Report – Spain*, 2014, p. 169.

189 See note 174.

190 According to art. 14.5 AML Law, the obliged entity shall define in the internal procedures the minimum managing level necessary to provide the authorisation to establish or maintain

relationship and adopt "appropriate measures" in order to determine the origin of the assets and of the funds.

Obliged entities shall also apply "reasonable measures" to determine whether the beneficiary owner of a life insurance policy is a PEP before the payment of the premiums (art.14.7 AML Law). In this case, obliged entities shall: (i) immediately inform management before the payment of any premium; (ii) encourage a closer review of the whole business relationship with the policyholder; and (iii) proceed to a special review[191] to determine whether the situation merits filing an SAR.

In addition, in any situation in which the obliged entity identifies a suspicious transaction, it shall adopt "adequate measures" to verify whether a PEP is involved.[192]

Nevertheless, despite the extensive requirements for CDD measures regarding PEPs, one common difficulty faced by the private sector is accessing lists to identify PEPs. There are companies that provide updated lists,[193] but their costs mean they are not easily accessible for small or medium-sized obliged entities.

c. Further Enhanced CDD Guidance on PEPs

Neither the public administration nor the supervisory authorities provide special guidance for enhanced CDD measures on PEPs in Spain.

5. *Rules on High-Risk Third Countries*

a. Scope

The scope of the Spanish regulation on high-risk third countries is to provide rules and guidance on the enhanced CDD measures applicable to such jurisdictions. Art. 11 AML Law defines high-risk third countries as those identified in the European Commission decision adopted in accordance with art. 9 4AMLD. On the other hand, art. 19.2(e) Decree 304/2014 refers to the lists of high-risk third countries provided by the FATF.[194] In short, obliged entities shall apply

business relationship with PEPs. This managing level shall be adapted according to the risk of the transaction or of the specific client and the persons responsible for the authorisation shall have sufficient knowledge of the level of exposure of the PEP to risk of money laundering. Finally, they shall have sufficient authority to take decisions regarding the level of risk exposure.

191 See *infra* section III.C.1.a.

192 The specification of these legal expressions ("reasonable", "adequate", "appropriate" measures), however, is left for the obliged entity, since neither the AML Law nor the Decree specify which measures could be appropriate or reasonable.

193 Lists commonly mentioned by obliged entities are Factiva (from Dow Jones), Compliance and Accuity.

194 The Ministry of Economy highlights the FATF's updated list of high-risk third countries (from 25 February 2019) for AML purposes. See http://www.cpbc.tesoro.es/sites/default/files/lista_gafi_jurisdicciones_de_riesgo_y_monitoreadas._febrero_2019.pdf.

enhanced CDD measures to business relationships with the countries listed by the EU and the FATF. However, it should be noted that this difference between the AML Law and the Decree could lead to a potential conflict in obligations, should the lists of the EU and the FATF differ at any point.[195]

b. Requirements

As mentioned in the previous section, the requirements relating to high-risk third countries are characterised by the need to apply enhanced CDD measures on a permanent basis. These measures shall be applied when establishing a business relationship or transactions with clients from high-risk countries, territories or jurisdictions, or that in relation to the transfer of funds from or to such countries. However, the doctrine calls attention to the fact that the Decree does not say how clients from high-risk countries should be defined, i.e. whether a national of or just a resident in such countries, although the criterion of residency seems to prevail.[196]

c. Further Enhanced CDD Guidance on High-Risk Third Countries

Moreover, art. 22 Decree 304/2014 provides additional guidance for the cases in which obliged entities *may* consider a country to be high risk, after its own risk assessment. Following the guidance of art. 22, obliged entities shall proceed to an internal risk assessment to determine their exposure to the risk of money laundering depending on countries or geographic areas in which their clients operate, and then decide on the enhanced CDD measures to be taken.

Art. 22 Decree 304/2014 indicates that the obliged entities may consider to be high risk those countries that: (i) do not have appropriate AML systems; (ii) are subject to sanctions, embargoes or similar measures adopted by the EU; (iii) are experiencing significant levels of corruption or other criminal activities; (iv) where the funding or support of terrorist activity is promoted; (v) are known to be significant offshore areas; or (vi) that are considered tax havens. The Decree

195 One reason for this difference could be that the current Decree was amended to comply with the 3AMLD, when the approach on high-risk third countries in the AML Law was in early development. Nevertheless, the proposal for the Decree (which was not approved) included the same list as the current art. 22. This leads to two possible interpretations. First, that the obliged entities shall apply enhanced CDD measures only to the list of countries provided by the European Commission and, at its own discretion, proceed to the risk assessment, taking in consideration the listing provided by the Decree. Second, that the obliged entities shall apply enhanced CDD measures to the countries listed by the European Commission, and also to those considered to be of high-risk of money laundering by other sources such as the Mutual Evaluation Reports of the FATF or reports from other international organisations.

196 Mallada Fernández et. al. *Guía práctica de prevención del blanqueo de capitales*, Madrid, 2015, p. 259.

also mentions that obliged entities shall use to credible sources to determine whether, in its assessment, a country is high risk, such as the FATF's mutual evaluation reports or reports from other international organisations. Moreover, CPMLMO shall publish guidelines to assist obliged subjects in determining geographical risk, something CPMLMO does provide,[197] although the guidance is not currently being updated. Obliged entities shall also refer to reliable sources of information to keep the list of high-risk third countries up to date, such as the FATF's mutual evaluation reports or the equivalent local or international reports.

The Geographic Risk Guide, created by CPMLMO for guidance purposes, provides obliged entities with a list of places to consult to determine whether a country is high risk: obliged entities can consult the FATF list of non-cooperative jurisdictions on prevention of money laundering, the EU list of high-risk third countries, the Basel Institute list and the countries listed on the United Nations Convention against corruption, as well as the information provided by the World Economic Forum, Transparency International, Global Financial Integrity and the Tax Justice Network, especially as it relates to offshore companies. The Geographic Risk Guide also refers to the lists provided by the Financial Stability Board, and the evaluations carried out by the International Monetary Fund and the Offshore Group of Banking Supervisors. Obliged entities shall also refer to a list of tax havens[198] and systematically report transactions with a given set of countries.[199]

The most recent guidance regarding high-risk third countries comes from the Spanish Treasury,[200] despite not having binding force, and suggests a special review of transactions with the following countries: Anguilla, Antigua and Barbuda, Bermuda, Brunei, Cayman Islands, Cook Islands, Dominican Republic, Falkland Islands, Fiji, Gibraltar, Grenada, Guernsey, Jersey, Jordan, Lebanon, Liberia, Liechtenstein, Macao, Mariana Islands, Mauritius, Monaco, Montserrat, Nauru, Saint Vincent and the Grenadines, Saint Lucia, Seychelles,

197 http://www.tesoro.es/sites/default/files/guia_riesgo_geografico_en_materia_de_bc-ft_.pdf.

198 According to the Guide, at present the tax heavens are: Antigua and Barbuda, Bahrain, Brunei, Bermuda, the Cayman Islands, the Cook Islands, Dominican Republic, Fiji, Gibraltar, Granada, Guernsey, Jersey, Jordan, Lebanon, Liberia, Liechtenstein, Macao, Malvina Island, Mariana Island, Mauritius, Monaco, Montserrat, Nauru Republic, the Salomon Islands, San Vicente, Santa Lucia, Seychelles, the Turks and Caicos Islands, Vanuatu Islands, the British Virgin Islands, and the US Virgin Islands.

199 Countries considered by the FATF to be non-cooperative are: North Korea and Iran. Countries considered to be in an ongoing process to improve global AML/CTF: Bahamas, Botswana, Cambodia, Ethiopia, Ghana, Pakistan, Panama, Syria, Sri Lanka, Trinidad and Tobago, Tunisia, and Yemen. See the FATF's updated list available from the Spanish Ministry of Finances: http://www.cpbc.tesoro.es/sites/default/files/lista_gafi_jurisdicciones_de_riesgo_y_monitoreadas._junio_2019.pdf.

200 http://www.tesoro.es/sites/default/files/guia_riesgo_geografico_en_materia_de_bc-ft_.pdf.

Solomon Islands, Turks and Caicos Islands, Vanuatu, British Virgin Islands, and United States Virgin Islands.

The existence of the lists mentioned above does not prevent obliged entities from setting up initiatives to make their own evaluation of high-risk third countries. The OCP, for instance, provides notaries with their own lists and ranking of countries.

Finally, Spanish law requires obliged entities to forward systematic communication (not SARs) when dealing with the following countries: Egypt, Guatemala, Indonesia, Iran, Myanmar, Nigeria, the Philippines and Ukraine.[201]

Despite the regulation described above, major changes are expected regarding business relationships with high-risk third countries under the Proposal to transpose the 5AMLD. According to the Proposal, the Spanish Council of Ministers in compliance with the European regulations and on a proposal from the Minister of Economic Affairs and Digital Transformation, may agree on the adoption of international financial sanctions and countermeasures regarding those countries. The Council of Ministers' agreement may be adopted autonomously or pursuant to decisions or recommendations of international organisations, institutions or groups. The agreement may impose on the obliged entities, inter alia, a series of financial countermeasures, such as: a) prohibiting, limiting or conditioning capital movements from or to the third country or nationals or residents thereof; b) subjecting to prior authorisation the opening of payment accounts; c) freezing the assets of residents from the third country; d) prohibiting the making available of funds and economic resources belonging to, owned, held or controlled by natural or legal persons who are nationals or residents of the third country; e) requiring the application of enhanced CDD measures, f) requiring the systematic reporting of transactions by nationals or residents of the third country or involving financial movements to or from the third country; g) prohibiting, limiting or conditioning the establishment or maintenance of subsidiaries, branches or representative offices of financial institutions from the third country; h) prohibiting, limiting or imposing conditions on financial institutions to establish or maintain subsidiaries, branches or representative offices in the third country; i) prohibiting, limiting or conditioning business relations or financial transactions with the third country or with nationals or residents of the third country; j) prohibiting the acceptance by the obliged entities of CDD measures carried out by obliged entities located in the third country; k) requiring financial institutions to review, modify and, where appropriate, terminate correspondent relationships with financial

201 Order ECO/2652/2002, of 24 October 2002, last updated in 2010 by Order EHA/1464/2010, which included Iran on the list.

institutions in the third country; and l) making subsidiaries or branches of financial institutions in the third country subject to enhanced supervision or to external examination or audit; m) imposing enhanced reporting or auditing requirements on financial groups' external auditing regarding subsidiaries or branches located or operating in the third country. Finally, the SEPBLAC shall be responsible for supervising and inspecting compliance with those provisions.[202]

6. *Private Sector CDD Guidance*

Notaries have a well-developed system to provide further guidance on the exercise of CDD within the sector. The OCP of the Notaries[203] has the aim of collaborating with the law enforcement authorities in the prevention of money laundering. The OCP has an Analysis and Communication Unit that is responsible for examining suspicious operations of which it has been informed by individual notaries across the country, and for providing notaries with further guidance. On the same basis, the CRAB performs similar tasks in relation to the activity of registrars, and will acquire more significance in Spain in the near future, since it is currently responsible for beneficial ownership registries.

Moreover, notaries must identify the beneficial ownership and the shareholding and control structure of legal entities before registering the legal entity's activities when it identifies the signs of high-risk transactions outlined by the OCP, or when the legal entity has been established in a jurisdiction listed as tax haven (art. 3 Order EHA/114/2008).

Finally, the General Council of Spanish Lawyers also provides brief and simplified guidance for the sector, giving some examples of what might trigger CDD measures.[204]

B. PRELIMINARY RISK ANALYSIS

As mentioned above, the AML Law and Decree always establish the minimum standards regarding the CDD measures to be applied by obliged entities. After a special review (art. 17 AML Law), the obliged entity shall always determine whether the risk relating to the client or transaction requires a more extensive application of enhanced CDD measures.

---

202 Art. 42 of the Proposal, available at: https://www.mineco.gob.es/stfls/mineco/ministerio/participacion_publica/audiencia/ficheros/ECO_TES_20200612_AP_V_Directiv_Blanqueo.pdf.

203 Regulated by Ministry Order EHA/2963/2005, of 20 September 2005.

204 http://www.abogacia.es/wp-content/uploads/2012/06/RECOMENDACIONES-PBC-ABOGADOS-CGAE.pdf.

C. REPORTING AND ASSET FREEZING

1. *First-Time Reporting*

a. Trigger for/Degree of Suspicion

Art. 18 AML Law indicates transactions that may give rise to suspicions of money laundering to be those that reveal an "obvious inconsistency with the nature, volume of activity or customer operating history" or transactions that do not have any economic, professional or business justifications. These inconsistencies can be identified by the obliged entity when following the steps of the special review established in art. 17 AML Law and they shall be reported to the FIU in the form of an SAR if there is any suspicion of money laundering. More precisely, if after the analysis there are "indications" or the "confirmation" of money laundering,[205] it is mandatory for all types of obliged entities to file an SAR, even if the transaction was only attempted, but not completed.

In the face of a suspicious transaction, the obliged entity must analyse it through the special review process (art. 17 AML Law). This review consists in analysing, "with special attention", any fact or transaction, regardless of its amount, that is unnecessarily complicated, apparently without economic purpose or shows signs of fraud or dissimulation, and that by its nature could be related to money laundering.

The special review (art. 17 AML Law) consists of further investigation of the characteristics of the transaction which gave rise to a suspicion of money laundering.

There is a second trigger, based on fixed thresholds, that shall give rise to systematic reporting (art. 27 Decree 304/2014). However, SARs should not be confused with systematic reporting, since the latter does not involve any level of suspicion of money laundering. Only financial institutions are obliged to carry out systematic reporting, and they shall communicate to the FIU the following transactions on a monthly basis: (i) physical movement of cash or other forms of bearer documents issued by credit institutions exceeding €30,000 (except when is a client's account deposit); (ii) money remittances on payment services, the physical movement of cash or other form of bearer documents for amounts exceeding €1,500 or the equivalent amount in foreign currency; (iii) wire transfers exceeding €30,000 with natural or legal persons who are resident, or representing a resident, in a listed high-risk third country; and (iv) cross-border movements, or movements within Spanish territory, of amounts over €100,000.

---

[205] Art. 18 AML Law uses both expressions to refer to the level of suspicion that shall lead to a SAR: indication or certainty that the transaction is related to money laundering, according to the internal analysis of the obliged entity.

Finally, the lists prepared, on a risk-sensitive basis, by the internal monitoring body[206] of some obliged entities can provide their own typologies to help the employees recognise the degree of suspicion according to parties and amounts involved in the suspicious transactions. These lists shall generate an alert and the transactions shall be reviewed to determine whether they need to undergo special review.

b. Content and Direct Addressee(s) of SARs

The SAR must be addressed "without delay" to the FIU through the person registered as the obliged entity's designated person to contact the FIU. The procedures for filing an SAR will follow the steps established by the obliged entity's manual of internal monitoring and then will be forwarded to the FIU, containing (art. 18 AML Law): (i) the identification of the natural or legal persons taking part in the transaction and the nature of their participation; (ii) the activities that such persons are known to engage in; (iii) a list of transactions and their dates, stating their nature, the currency, the amounts and place or places involved, their purpose, and the means of payment or receipt used; (iv) steps taken by the obliged entity to investigate the transactions; (vi) a statement of all the circumstances of whatever kind giving rise to the suspicion of a link with money laundering or terrorism financing; and (vii) any other data relevant to the prevention of money laundering.

Spanish law also foresees that the obliged entity shall include in the SAR "information on the decision adopted or expected to be adopted by the obliged subject regarding continuation or discontinuation of the business relationship with the customer(s) involved in the transaction, as well as the reasons for this decision" (art. 26.3 Decree 304/2014). If the business relationship is not discontinued to avoid interfering with an ongoing police investigation previously notified to the obliged entity,[207] this shall be explicitly mentioned.

c. Duty not to Disclose

Under art. 24 AML Law, obliged entities and their directors and employees are forbidden to disclose to their customers or third parties[208] that an SAR has been filed. Outside the company, however, the duty not to disclose is defined strictly

---

206 See *infra* section III.F.

207 Under art. 263 *bis* of the Criminal Procedure Law.

208 One might interpret the expression "third parties" to refer to other clients or persons intervening in the transaction, but that are not the legitimate recipient of the information, such as the FIU or legal enforcement agencies. Cf. Aliaga Mémdez, *Normativa comentada de prevención del blanqueo de capitales*, Madrid, 2010, p. 206.

in the Spanish legislation, to the point that obliged entities are allowed *not* to undertake certain aspects of CDD if they can reasonably foresee that, in doing so, they might reveal to the client that the transaction has been scrutinised or communicated to the FIU (art. 12 Decree 304/2014).

d. Power or Duty to Freeze

The primary duty to freeze in Spanish legislation refers only to cases of terrorism financing, following a direct order from the Surveillance Commission for Terrorist Financing Activities (Comisión de Vigilancia de Actividades de Financiación del Terrorismo),[209] and the freezing is not related to or bound by the filing of an SAR. The Surveillance Commission is under the control of the Ministry of Internal Affairs (art. 2.1 Terrorism Financing Blocking Act).

Other than in cases of terrorism financing, however, obliged entities shall freeze and block assets owned, controlled or held by persons, entities or organisations "in respect of which a European Union Regulation or Resolution of the Council of Ministers has established this restrictive measure" (art. 48 Decree 304/2014). In Spain, the body responsible for determining the freezing of assets and their liberation[210] (art. 49 Decree 304/2014) in cases of money laundering is the Secretariat General of the Treasury and Financial Policy, following the regulation of the EU Council of Ministers.

In both cases (money laundering and terrorism financing), obliged entities are not free to decide when to freeze accounts and financial movements of specific individuals suspected of money laundering or terrorism financing.[211] One of the two bodies just mentioned (the Surveillance Commission or the Secretariat General of the Treasury) will decide on the freezing of assets and then communicate the order to the obliged entities. This procedure, however, does not necessarily have to follow a report; it can equally be the result of an international order or a decision from the Ministry of Interior, not related to the filing of an SAR. After receiving the order to freeze assets, the obliged entity shall report any attempt by the client to carry out a transaction.

There is another distinct option, namely to confiscate assets on the basis of a suspicion of money laundering outside of the freezing system. This, however, does not depend on obliged entities; it falls within the competence of the customs authorities.[212]

---

209 Art. 10 Decree 413/2015, which regulates the powers and competence of the Surveillance Commission for Terrorist Financing Activities.

210 The liberation shall also be in accordance with a EU Regulation or Resolution of the Council of Ministers and shall be decided within a maximum of six months after the submission of the plea (art. 49.5 Decree 304/2014).

211 See *infra* section III.E.

212 According to art. 45 Decree 304/2014, the customs authorities shall confiscate the non-declared means of payment carried internally or cross-border, or when there is suspicion that

If approved, the current Proposal to transpose the 5AMLD will allow the Council of Ministers to deliberate and then impose on obliged entities the freezing of assets belonging to, owned, held or controlled by natural or legal persons who are nationals or residents of high risk third countries.[213]

e. Instant Collateral Duties

After filing an SAR, the obliged entity has the obligation to further monitor the client's activities and shall immediately adopt "additional risk management and mitigation measures, which must take into account the risk of disclosure" (art. 26.2 Decree 304/2014).

2. Follow-Up

a. Duty to Provide FIU with Additional Data

According to the AML Law (art. 18.2), if the FIU considers the information contained in the SAR to be insufficient, it can request additional information from the obliged entity. It will return the SAR to the obliged entity and justify the reasons for the return, as well as stating the matter that needs to undergo further examination. The obliged entity, in turn, shall then make a closer examination of the reported transaction. As a complement to the this, art. 64 AML Law[214] specifies that if the FIU has difficulties in reaching a conclusion about the suspicion of money laundering based on the filed SAR, it shall request that the reporting entity explain the content of the report or complement it with additional information.

However, neither AML Law nor its regulation (Decree 304/2014) specify the limits of the information that the FIU is allowed to procure from obliged entities or the methodology or procedures to be followed after the return of the SAR. An obliged entity's refusal to cooperate with the FIU is a serious offence (art. 52.1(k) AML Law).[215]

---

the declaration is not accurate, and may derive from money laundering activities. In this case, customs can apprehend the money, deposit it in a judicial account, and send the information to the FIU. As explained *supra* in section III.C.1.a, it is mandatory to declare (i) incoming or outgoing *cross-border movements* of means of payment for an amount of €10,000 or more, or its equivalent in foreign currency, or (ii) movements *within national territory* of means of payment for an amount of €100,000 or more, or its equivalent in foreign currency.

213 According to the proposed reform of art. 42 AML Law. Proposal available at: https://www.mineco.gob.es/stfls/mineco/ministerio/participacion_publica/audiencia/ficheros/ECO_TES_20200612_AP_V_Directiv_Blanqueo.pdf.

214 Added in the reform of September 2018.

215 See art. 33(1)(a) 4AMLD.

b. Continued Duty not to Disclose SAR to Client

The AML Law makes no distinction in terms of time limits or other limits to the duty not to disclose. Obliged entities are forbidden to reveal information to their clients both before and after they file an SAR (art. 24 AML Law). Breaching prohibition on disclosure is categorised as a very serious offence and subject to the highest category of sanctions (art. 51.1(c) AML Law).[216]

c. Continued Collateral Duties

There are no continued collateral duties under the Spanish AML Law.

3. Special Rules for Privileged Professions

a. Trigger for/Degree of Suspicion

Spanish law in principle sets out for privileged professions the same requirements regarding the degree of suspicion for filing an SAR.

Nevertheless, as mentioned above,[217] legal professionals are excluded from the duty to file SARs[218] (art. 22 AML Law) when they receive information "in the course of ascertaining the legal position of their client, or performing their task of defending or representing that client in, or concerning, judicial proceedings, including providing advice on instituting or avoiding such proceedings, whether such information is received or obtained before, during or after such proceedings".[219]

Moreover, an Instruction from 1999,[220] though not updated, provides some indications of triggers in relation to the tasks of notaries and registrars. The Instruction defines the following as giving rise to a suspicion of money laundering: (i) the constitution of more than three societies at the same day, when at least one of the partners in those societies is the same person; (ii) if the partners or directors are not Spanish nationals; (iii) foundation of companies with under-age partners; (iv) apparent lack of professional expertise of the partners; (v) naming the same manager in three or more companies simultaneously; and (vi) indications that the client is taking measures to hide the beneficial owner. The Instruction also gives some indication of the values that will give rise to

216 In this sense, Spain is considered compliant with the FAT recommendations. See FATF, *Mutual Evaluation Report – Spain*, 2014, p. 178.
217 See *supra* section II.D.3.
218 See art. 34(2) 4AMLD.
219 See *supra* section II.D.3.
220 Instruction of 10 December 1999 of the General Directory for Notary and Registrars (BOE 311, of 29 December 1999), http://noticias.juridicas.com/base_datos/Privado/i101299-mj.html.

suspicion (establishing companies with bearer means of payment exceeding €300,000). However, given the age of the Instruction, it can be inferred that these monetary thresholds may already have been surpassed in practice.

The Instruction also mentions regular triggers for suspicion, such as a business relationship with companies established in high-risk third countries or with non-nationals, payment of more than 25% of real estate transactions in cash, and successive transfers.

b. Content and Addressee(s) of SAR's

The content and addressee of the SARs filed by the privileged professions in Spain are the same as those pertaining to other obliged entities, except for notaries and registrars. Lawyers, auditors, external accountants and tax advisors shall report directly to the FIU, while notaries and mercantile registrars have their own supervisory body. The OCP is the addressee of SARs filed by notaries. The body has an Analysis Unit that receives the SARs from the sector, analyses them and forwards the information to the FIU[221] in the name of the intervening notary.[222] Similarly, the CRAB performs the same tasks as the OCP in relation to registrars, receiving and analysing SARs submitted by property and mercantile registrars. After carrying out their analysis),[223] the CRAB and the OCP shall forward the SARs to the FIU.[224]

There are no significant differences in the content of SARs filed by notaries and registrars as privileged professions. According to specific regulation on the sector,[225] however, the minimum information that SARs from notaries shall contain is the identity of all the natural and legal persons involved in the transaction, the nature of their participation and a list of transactions and all the details pertaining to them.[226] The minimum information also includes a brief description of every circumstance that gives rise to the suspicion or reliable identification of ties to money laundering. The regulation on property registrars has no further details on the content of SARs.

Notaries are exempted from filing SARs in cases with no economic or patrimonial elements (i.e. last wills, power of attorney, simple statutory modifications) or notarial acts that do not have any relevance to money laundering (art. 3.2 Decree 304/2014), with one exception, i.e. setting up companies, associations, foundations or similar legal arrangements, or undertaking any legal acts or legal proceedings related to their functioning or management. In the case of setting up

221 Art. 27.2 AML Law, art. 44 Decree 304/2014. See *infra* section III.C.3.b.

222 Art. 4 Ministry Order EHA/2963/2005.

223 Art. 27.2 AML Law, art. 44 Decree 304/2014, art. 5 Ministerial Order ECC/2402/2015.

224 Art. 6 Ministerial Order ECC/2402/2015.

225 Art. 9 Ministry Order EHA/2963/2005.

226 These are: their dates, indicating nature, currency used, amount, place or places of execution, purposes and means of payment used.

companies, even if there is no economic element, the notary and registrar shall evaluate the risk of money laundering and, if there is a suspicion, file an SAR.

The unique feature of the reporting regime for privileged professions is the possibility of creating centralised prevention bodies for collegiate professions, similar to the OCP, which may assume responsibility for reviewing suspicious transactions and filing SARs in the name of professionals. Other than that, all obliged entities and persons in privileged professions shall respect the general triggers[227] and degree of suspicion described above[228] to evaluate the transactions.

c. Duty not to Disclose to Client

According to art. 24.3 AML Law, obliged entities and their directors and employees are forbidden to disclose to their customers or third parties that an SAR has been. However, there is an exception in the case of auditors, external accountants, tax advisors and legal professionals. These professionals are allowed to inform the client about the possibility that an SAR could be filed when trying to dissuade their client from committing an illegal activity (art. 24.3 AML Law).[229] In that sense, the General Council of Spanish Lawyers' manual on money laundering prevention stresses that such warning and guidance do not infringe the duty not to disclose information to clients.[230]

Art. 64 AML Law, added in the reform of September 2018, provides that the filing of an SAR or sending of any information to fulfil the requirements of the AML regulation is by no means a breach of an eventual contractual secrecy agreement between the parties.

4. *Protection of SAR's Source*

The AML Law (art. 30) establishes the protection of the SAR's source: employees, directors or agents who send an internal communication to the internal monitoring body.[231] The identity of the reporting person shall be kept secret in relation to any external communication or representation, and the obliged entity

---

227 In a public statement in a seminar run by the College of Notaries, the director of the OCP emphasised the need for more precise rules to indicate triggers and suspicious transactions. The reference to screening the functioning of companies to identify the risk of money laundering is considered to be vague, in particular because a significant proportion of money laundering relates to activities in shell companies and tax havens. See "El papel del notariado en la prevención del blanqueo de capitales", p. 4, http://www.notariado.org/liferay/c/document_library/get_file?folderId=12092&name=DLFE-149784.pdf.

228 See *supra* section III.C.1.a.

229 See *infra* section III.C.6.c.

230 See http://www.abogacia.es/wp-content/uploads/2012/06/RECOMENDACIONES-PBC-ABOGADOS-CGAE.pdf.

231 See *infra* section III.G.

shall adopt sufficient measures to protect him or her from any threat or hostile act, although the article does not clarify what kinds of internal or external threat. The consequence of this is that the person who filed the SAR cannot be called to serve as a witness in any judicial or administrative proceedings.[232] Such tasks may only be required of and performed by the company's representative to the FIU.

Obliged entities shall have a person registered to represent them to the FIU, who is responsible for forwarding the SARs (art. 26.2 AML Law) and who will be the only person identified when an SAR is submitted. Any further communications will be directed to the representative, and it is their obligation to manage the anonymity of their sources.

All communications forwarded to the FIU beyond SARs shall also be treated as confidential in nature by the FIU. Art. 65.3 AML Law determines that if the FIU receives a communication from a whistleblower, it shall not reveal identifying data about the source. Even if sanctioning proceedings against a natural or legal person follows as a consequence of the communication, the FIU shall not reveal the data about the person who filed the complaint.

D. RECORD KEEPING

According to art. 25 AML Law, obliged entities shall keep the documentation gathered in compliance with their obligations for a period of ten years, after which they shall eliminate it. Five years after the end of the business relationship or the execution of the occasional transaction, the retained documentation shall be accessible only to the internal control units and, where applicable, the parties responsible for its legal defence.

They shall keep all documents obtained or generated in the due diligence process, including, in particular, copies of verified identification documents, customer statements, documents and information provided by the customers or obtained from reliable third-party sources, contract documents and the results of any analysis carried out (art. 28 Decree).

E. COMPLIANCE OFFICERS

The AML Law determines (art. 26 *ter*) that all obliged entities shall appoint a director or senior manager to act as a representative to SEPBLAC. The representative may or not be the entity's compliance officer, but appointing the that person as a representative will be a natural path for the obliged entity to

232 Blanco Cordero, *El delito de blanqueo de capitales*, Madrid, 2015, p. 259.

follow. The representative to the FIU (that may or not be the compliance officer) must be guaranteed "the necessary material, human and technical resources for the exercise of their functions". The representative shall operate separately from the internal auditing department or unit and shall have unlimited access to any information in possession of the obliged entity (art. 26 *ter.*5 and 6 AML Law).

The representative shall also be the person designated to act in any kind of legal proceedings regarding the data collected and forwarded to the FIU, and the person the FIU will contact if additional information is needed (art. 30.1 AML Law).[233]

Moreover, obliged entities employing more than 50 persons and with an annual turnover or total annual balance above €10 million must set up an internal compliance committee (the internal monitoring body).[234] Representatives from the obliged entity's different business areas of the obliged entity (art. 35 Decree 304/2014, art. 26 AML Law) shall be part of the internal monitoring body, meeting periodically and keeping a record of those meetings.

However, small obliged entities that do not operate in the field of financial services and that are not obliged to set up an internal monitoring body do not have to appoint a representative to the FIU. When such obliged entities report a suspicious transaction, they shall include the identification data of the representative of the obliged entity (art. 26.4 Decree 304/2014).

Finally, in the case of individual entrepreneurs or individual professionals, the business owner shall act as the representative to the FIU. He or she will be competent to represent the obliged entity to the FIU, to approve the internal preventive manual, to apply adequate procedures concerning CDD measures, preservation of documents, internal monitoring, evaluation and risk assessment, and to ensure compliance with the rules regarding communication with the FIU.

F. INTERNAL COMPLAINT MECHANISM

Until September 2018, the Spanish legislation did not include a clear reference to the need for internal complaint mechanisms. After the reform, art. 26 *bis* AML Law sets out that obliged entities shall establish internal procedures so that its personnel are able to communicate, even anonymously, relevant information about possible breaches of or offences regarding prevention of money laundering committed in the course of the obliged entity's professional activity.

The AML Law allows the internal complaint mechanisms regarding money laundering to be integrated into the general whistleblowing system. Nevertheless,

[233] There is currently an informal discussion among compliance officers and external consultants in Spain regarding the regulation of those professions by the FIU. Nevertheless, there has been no official statement on the forthcoming regulation.

[234] See *infra* section III.G.

those mechanisms cannot be a substitute for the internal monitoring body,[235] which is the only body within the obliged entity that is responsible for receiving and processing information regarding suspicious transactions (art. 26 *bis*.4 AML Law).

All the information managed through internal complaint mechanisms shall be protected under the data protection regulation, and the employees, directives or agents that communicate any infringement of the money laundering legislation by the obliged entity shall be protected from any form of discrimination or unfair treatment[236] (art. 26 *bis*.3 AML Law).

A recent reform in Spanish data protection law, following the implementation of the General Data Protection Regulation, offers further guidance on the creation of internal complaint systems. According to art. 24 of the new Data Protection

---

235 The majority of obliged entities in Spain are under the obligation to put in place an internal monitoring body: financial institutions, insurance brokers and groups of obliged entities that employ more than 50 persons, and whose annual turnover or total annual balance exceeds €10 million (or who are part of a business group that exceeds these figures). In the last group are: "(i) Persons whose business activity includes currency exchange. (j) Postal services in respect of giro or transfer activities. (k) Persons professionally involved in brokering loans or credits, as well as persons who, without being licensed as credit institutions, carry out professionally credit and loans activities, factoring and financing of commercial transaction, leasing agreements, issuing and managing credit cards and that provides guarantees or similar commitments. (l) Property developers and persons whose business activities include those of agency, commission or brokerage in real state trading. (m) Auditors, external accountants and tax advisers. (n) Notaries and land, commercial and moveable property registrars. (ñ) Lawyers, barristers and other independent professionals when they participate in the design, implementation or advice on activities on behalf of clients relating to the buying and selling of real estate or business entities, the management of funds, securities or other assets, the opening or management of current, savings or securities accounts, the organisation of contributions necessary for the creation, operation or management of companies or the creation, operation or management of trusts, companies or similar structures, or when acting on behalf of clients in any financial or real estate transaction. (o) Persons who on a professional basis and in accordance with the specific rules applicable in each case provide the following services to third parties: forming companies or other legal persons; acting as or arranging for another person to act as a director or secretary of a company, a partner of a partnership or a similar position in relation to other legal persons; providing a registered office, business address, correspondence or administrative address and other related services for a company, a partnership or any other legal person or arrangement; acting as or arranging for another person to act as a trustee of an express trust or similar legal arrangement, or acting as or arranging for another person to act as a shareholder for another person, other than a company listed on a regulated market that is subject to disclosure requirements in conformity with Community legislation or subject to equivalent international standards. (p) Casinos. (q) Professional dealers in jewels, precious stones or precious metals. (r) Professional dealers in works of art or antiques. (s) Persons whose business activity includes those set down in article 1 of Consumer Protection in the Procurement of Goods with a Price Refund Offer. (t) Persons engaged in the deposit, custody or professional transfer of funds or means of payment. (u) Persons responsible for the management, operation and marketing of lotteries or other gambling activities in respect of prize payment transactions."

236 The law does not provide specify whether this means internal or external discrimination or unfair treatment.

Law (Law no. 3/2018), the complaints may be anonymous, and the company shall inform employees and third parties about the existence of its internal complaint system. In principle, only the employees responsible for the complaint system shall have access to the data stored in it. However, the information may be disclosed whenever necessary to adopt disciplinary measures or to submit the information to judicial proceedings. If an internal disciplinary measure is taken against an employee, the disclosure of information shall be restricted to the employees responsible for human resources. In all cases, however, the company shall adopt measures to preserve the identity and *confidentiality* of the data regarding (primarily) the whistleblower, as well as the person who is the subject of the complaint.

Art. 24.4 Data Protection Law states that the company has three months to process the data collected through its internal complaint channels. After that period, the company's body responsible for investigating the complaints may keep processing the data, but in a separate database, outside the internal complaint system. In addition, if no investigation is held, the company shall delete this information from the system, *unless* it decides to keep the data with the purpose of maintaining some evidence of the correct functioning of its internal complaint system. If this is the case, every complaint shall remain anonymised.

G. ADDITIONAL PREVENTIVE MEASURES

The AML Law and its regulation set out an extensive list of duties to be followed by obliged entities, oriented as auxiliary to ensure effective CDD measures. It is mandatory for all financial institutions and insurance brokers to implement a system of internal risk analysis. They shall also create a prevention manual, request reports from an external expert and create systems of training their employees (art. 31 Decree 304/2014).

Outside of financial services, the internal monitoring measures are only mandatory if the obliged entity[237] employs more than 10 people *and* has an annual turnover or total annual balance of over €2 million (or is part of a business group that exceeds that threshold).

Here is a brief description of the obligations:

- *Internal risk analysis* (art. 32 Decree 304/2014): The analysis must create internal typologies.[238] It shall be reviewed periodically, and a specific risk

[237] See note 224.

[238] The analysis shall identify and assess the obliged entity's risks based on types of customers, countries or geographic areas, products, services, operations and distribution channels, considering variables such as the purpose of the business relationship, the level of customer assets, the volume of transactions and the regularity or duration of the business relationship.

analysis shall be conducted before the launch of a new product, the provision of a new service, the use of a new distribution channel or the use of new technology.

- *Prevention manual* (art. 33 Decree 304/2014): The manual shall contain a description of: (i) the obliged entity's customer acceptance policy, with an accurate description of customers that potentially pose a higher-than-average risk; (ii) a structured due diligence procedure; (iii) a structured, risk-based procedure for identifying the CDD measures applicable to existing customers; (iv) a list of events or transactions which, due to their nature, may be related to money laundering and terrorism financing, i.e. typologies of such events or transactions, as well as establishing periodic reviews and disseminating them to the obliged entity's managers, employees and agents; (v) a detailed description of the internal flow of information, with precise instructions to the obliged entity's managers, employees and agents on how to proceed in relation to events or transactions which, by their nature, may be related to money laundering and terrorism financing; (vi) a procedure for detecting events or transactions subject to special review; (vii) a structured special review procedure; (viii) a detailed description of how the internal monitoring bodies operate, including their composition, powers and meeting schedule; (ix) measures to ensure that the obliged entity's managers, employees and agents are familiar with the internal monitoring procedures; (x) measures to be adopted to verify compliance with internal monitoring procedures by the obliged subject's managers, employees and agents; (xi) agent recruitment requirements and criteria; (xii) measures to be taken to ensure that the obliged entity's correspondents apply appropriate procedures for the prevention of money laundering and terrorism financing; (xiii) a procedure for the periodic verification of the adequacy and effectiveness of internal monitoring measures; (xiv) regular updating of internal monitoring measures in the light of the developments observed in the sector and of the obliged entity's business and operational profile analysis; and (xv) a method of record keeping ensuring proper management and immediate availability.
- *External and independent review* (art. 28 AML Law, art. 38 Decree 304/2014): A report detailing the internal monitoring procedure shall document the measures in place, assessing their operational efficiency and eventually proposing changes or improvements as required, in both majority-owned branches and subsidiaries. The senior management of the obliged entity must be informed of the results of the evaluation of the external expert within three months.[239, 240]

[239] Details on the content of the report of the external experts are regulated in Order EHA/2444/2007.

[240] The proposal to reform the AML Law to transpose the 5AMLD will provide for a review of the AML compliance systems by an external expert, who will be held responsible for its evaluation.

- *Ongoing training of employees* (art. 29 AML Law, art. 39 Decree): The training plan shall be based on the risks internally identified in the activity of the obliged entity and provide specific training activities which must be consistent with the degree of responsibility of the recipients and the level of risk of the activities carried out.
- *Record keeping obligations* (art. 25.1 AML Law): Obliged entities shall keep the documentation gathered for CDD for a period of 10 years, after which they shall delete it. Five years after the end of the business relationship or the execution of the occasional transaction, only the internal monitoring units of the obliged entity may have access to the information.

Moreover, all financial institutions, insurance brokers and obliged entities[241] that employ more than 50 persons *and* whose annual turnover or total annual balance exceeds €10 million (or who are part of a business group that exceeds those thresholds) must set up an internal monitoring body. The internal monitoring body is placed under the responsibility of the FIU representative, i.e. the compliance officer,[242] and shall implement adequate policies and procedures on CDD, reporting, record keeping, internal monitoring of employee activities, risk assessment and management, ensuring reporting and compliance (art. 26 *ter* AML Law). It will consist of representatives from the different business areas of the obliged entity and shall meet with the frequency determined in the internal monitoring procedures. All meetings shall be recorded. Moreover, the internal monitoring body shall operate separately from the obliged entity's internal audit department (art. 26 *ter*.6 AML Law).

In the case of obliged entities whose annual turnover exceeds €50 million or whose general annual balance exceeds €43 million, the internal monitoring body may approve the procedures for the implementation of money laundering and terrorism financing prevention policies (art. 31.2 Decree 304/2014). Obliged entities of this size shall also establish a technical unit for data processing and analysis. Its function will be that of a specialised technical unit, responsible for data mining and analysis of the whole company (art. 35.3 Decree 304/2014).

Aside from the specific measures described above, which guide the preventive measures of medium and large-scale companies, the Spanish legislation also prescribes a list of auxiliary measures to prevent money laundering and terrorism financing that must be implemented by all obliged entities. There are: *record keeping* for at least 10 years after the end of the business relationship or the transaction[243] (art. 28 Decree 304/2014, art. 25 AML Law), the development

241 See note 224.

242 See *supra* section III.F.

243 Under art. 29 Decree 304/2014, the records shall allow for the reconstruction of individual transactions to provide, if necessary, evidence at trial. After five years of the end of the

of structured *internal communication channels*[244] (art. 24 Decree 304/2014), and *screening of employees*[245] (art. 37 Decree 304/2014).

Additionally, all of the above-mentioned obligations shall also apply to branches or subsidiary companies in third -countries, with the proper adjustment to local AML regulation at group level.[246] In any event, these measures must be "at least equivalent to those laid down by community law".[247]

H. RULES ON OBLIGED ENTITIES' CIVIL LIABILITY TOWARDS CLIENT

The Spanish AML Law has no specific provision regarding obliged entities' civil liability towards the client in the event that the fulfilment of CDD measures causes any kind of economic damage to the client or its business (interruption of banking services, delay of the transaction, etc.). Nevertheless, an analogical interpretation with art. 23 AML is perfectly possible: according to this article, the obliged entity will not have any civil liability towards the client, if there was good faith in its communication of a suspicious transaction to the FIU. In that sense, one may conclude that, if the obliged entity undertakes the CDD measures in good faith, no civil liability shall arise in relation to possible negative consequences for the client.

I. SUPERVISORY AUTHORITIES' ROLE

1. Supervisory Measures to Ensure the Application of CDD Obligations and Other AML-Related Obligations

According to art. 47.1 AML Law, the FIU is the supervisory body responsible for ensuring that all obliged entities[248] have consistent systems of money laundering

business relationship, the information regarding the client of business relationship shall be available only to the internal monitoring body of the obliged entity.

244 According to the art. 24 Decree 304/2014 the obliged entities shall establish an internal communication channel to spread information about news patterns of money laundering, with clear and precise guidelines to the employees and directors, and they shall guarantee the confidentiality of the reports on risky operations carried out by their employees.

245 The Decree foresees, above all, high ethical standards in the hiring of personnel, requiring that past professional activities be scrutinised (no criminal conviction for crimes against patrimony, for economic crimes, or for crimes against the public administration).

246 Art. 26.3 AML Law and arts. 36 and 37 Decree 304/2014.

247 FATF, *Mutual Evaluation Report – Spain*, 2014, p. 175.

248 According to Recommendation 28 of the FATF: "Countries should ensure that the other categories of DNFBPs are subject to effective systems for monitoring and ensuring compliance with AML/CFT requirements. This should be performed on a risk-sensitive basis".

prevention. Nonetheless, in the case of banks, the FIU shares its supervisory responsibility with the Central Bank of Spain. Moreover, in the securities and insurance sectors, the FIU carries out AML inspections and also directs the National Securities Exchange Commission (CNMV) and the Directorate-General for Insurance and Pension Funds (DGSFP) to conduct financial institution-specific inspections as needed.[249]

On another note, art. 2.3. AML Law states that obliged entities conducting occasional financial transactions and gambling service providers with a low risk of money laundering may be exempted from the supervision of the FIU. Still, the FIU may decide to perform supervisory visits to those obliged entities to ensure that they have not misused the exemption (47.1 AML Law). The supervisory tasks may occur, thus, in all individual or group of obliged entities and in subsidiary companies, and shall follow an Annual Guiding Plan approved by CPMLMO.[250]

The Annual Guiding Plan schedules the on-site supervisory visits from the FIU or other supervisory bodies and aims to ensure the monitoring of obliged entities selected for annual review by the FIU, based on the risk level of each professional activity. It shall also determine the type, depth and frequency of the supervision (art. 47.3 AML Law). At present, the OCP of the College of Notaries[251] and the CRAB of the College of Registrars are the only bodies exclusively dedicated to AML supervision, together with the FIU.

As a result of the on-site supervisory visits, the FIU completes an "inspection report" with recommendations that the obliged entity shall implement. If these recommendations are not followed, the FIU can propose to CPMLMO that formal requirements urging the obliged entity to adopt the corrective measures indicated in the inspection report be drawn up.[252] The inspection report may have evidential value for the sanctioning proceedings before CPMLMO (but not for evidentiary purposes in a criminal investigation).

Independently of the Annual Guiding Plan, the FIU can propose to CPMLMO the adoption of new requirements for the obliged entities under annual supervision, urging them to adopt the corrective measures deemed necessary.

Moreover, the FIU may inspect or monitor the effective implementation of the internal monitoring measures provided by the internal manual of the obliged entities. It may also analyse the list of employees of the obliged entity and the names of the designated representatives[253] (compliance officers) to ensure their ethical and professional background (art. 37 Decree 304/2014).

---

249 FATF, *Mutual Evaluation Report – Spain*, 2014, p. 104.

250 See infra section IV.A.1.

251 See *supra* section III.C.3.b.

252 Arts. 26.6 and 47.5 AML Law and art. 67.2 Decree 304/2014.

253 The FIU must be provided with a detailed description of the career of the representative nominated by the obliged entity and may make reasoned objections or observations (art. 35 Decree 304/2014).

On the other hand, in the case of financial institutions, some CDD measures, such as customer identification or the creation and maintenance of data banks, are also monitored by sector-specific oversight bodies (i.e. the National Securities Exchange Commission (CNMV) and the Central Bank of Spain). Nevertheless, the control of the risk assessments carried out by obliged entities, and of their obligation to file SARs, are still the exclusive responsibility of the FIU.

2. *Complaint Mechanism*

As mentioned in a previous section,[254] it is possible for employees to communicate directly with the FIU.

Employees may communicate a transaction that gives rise to a suspicion of money laundering directly to the FIU under two conditions: (i) of the internal monitoring body has already been informed of the indications or certainty of a link to money laundering, and (ii) if the obliged entity fails to inform the reporting director or employees of the outcome of the SAR (art. 18.4 AML Law).

Moreover, the reform of the AML Law introduced brief regulations on a whistleblowing system (art. 63 AML Law).[255] Following this provision, employees are able to communicate breaches of an obliged entity's money laundering preventive system directly the FIU.

J. STATISTICS ON SARS BY OBLIGED ENTITIES

The website of the Spanish FIU (SEPBLAC) compiled and made available data on the number of SARs that it received in the 2015 and 2016 from the private sector. In 2015, the FIU received 4,757 SARs (the most significant proportion from financial institutions, which filed 3,948 SARs). In 2016 the number rose slightly to 4,990 (with a greater proportion from non-financial obliged entities, increasing from 654 SARs in 2015 to 922 SARs in 2016) and in 2017 to 4,999.[256] According to the empirical study carried out for this report, the lack of a list or of minimum thresholds for predicate offences (which followed the reform of the Spanish Penal Code in 2010) did not have a significant impact on the number of communications from obliged entities. In fact, the interviews carried out for this report showed that the slight increase in the number of SARs filed is more

---

254 See *supra* section III.D.

255 The Proposal for a new Decree (currently under parliamentary debate and waiting for approval) determines that the manual of internal control for the prevention of money laundering shall describe an internal procedure for anonymous reporting of violations of preventive regulations or procedures adopted by the obliged entity to ensure compliance with them (art. 33.1, o).

256 https://www.sepblac.es/wp-content/uploads/2019/01/memoria_2017.pdf, p. 2.

connected to the FIU's intensified supervision than to the criminal definition of money laundering.

On the other hand, the FATF considered the absolute number of SARs relatively low for a country of Spain's size. However, at the same time, it draws attention to the fact that a single SAR routinely involves a high number of individual transactions,[257] that the reports are considered useful, and that a high proportion of SARs give rise to further investigations.[258]

IV. THE SYSTEM OF FINANCIAL INTELLIGENCE UNITS

A. INSTITUTIONAL AND FUNCTIONAL CHARACTERISTICS

1. *Organisational Position*

The general structure of AML units in Spain is as follows: there is the National Commission for the Prevention of Money Laundering and Monetary Offences (Comisión Nacional de Prevención del Blanqueo de Capitales e Infracciones Monetarias, CPMLMO), and two supportive bodies: the Executive Service of the Commission for the Prevention of Money Laundering and Monetary Offences (Servicio Ejecutivo de la Comisión de Prevención del Blanqueo de Capitales e Infracciones Monetarias, SEPBLAC), which is Spain's FIU, and the Secretariat of CPMLMO.

CPMLMO is a collegiate body subordinated to the Treasury and acts via plenary meetings or through the permanent Financial Intelligence Committee.

Originally SEPBLAC was part of the Spanish Central Bank, but since 2014 it has been defined as an independent authority affiliated only to CPMLMO (art. 67.4 Decree 304/2014). The director of SEPBLAC is nominated by CPMLMO, following the consultation with the Bank of Spain.

The chairman of CPMLMO is the Minister of Finance,[259] and some members of SEPBLAC are seconded employees of the Spanish Central Bank (art. 45.3 AML Law). As a result, the institutional position of SEPBLAC is that of an administrative agency inside the Treasury. Structurally, the SEPLAC includes public employees seconded from five public institutions: the Bank of Spain, the Tax Agency, the Treasury, the National Police and the Civil Guard. It should be noted, however, that the representatives of the Tax Agency, the National Police and the Civil Guard are not covered by the budget of the FIU but by the budget

---

257 The FATF Mutual Evaluation Report for Spain mentions that one SAR (3310/2014) involved 153 separate transactions. FATF, *Mutual Evaluation Report – Spain*, 2014, p. 97.

258 Ibid., pp. 96–97.

259 Art. 44.3 AML Law.

of their home institutions.[260] Moreover, SEPLAC has a budget to hire additional personnel (art. 67.7 Decree 304/2014), but the majority of its funding is assigned by the Bank of Spain.

On another note, art. 65 Decree 304/2014 creates the Financial Intelligence Committee. It shall approve the general criteria for disseminating financial intelligence reports, provide guidance on financial and intelligence analysis (art. 65 I(d) Decree 304/2014) and coordinate risk analysis in relation to money laundering. The aim of such analysis is to provide recommendations regarding risk sectors to be included in the Annual Guiding Plan for supervision by the FIU.

The AML Law also defines the relationship between the FIU and the Secretariat of CPMLMO. The results of all supervisory visits undertaken by the FIU shall be forwarded to the Secretariat, which shall deliver them to CPMLMO for sanctioning proceedings, if relevant (art. 64.3 AML Law). The Secretariat (art. 66 Decree 304/2014) is responsible for executing the resolutions of CPMLMO, defining the initiation or dismissal of disciplinary proceedings, establishing how to collect evidence, and defining additional measures to be taken before the initiation of disciplinary proceedings. The Secretariat shall also submit proposals to CPMLMO in disciplinary proceedings for serious and very serious offences, and to the Secretary General of the Treasury in disciplinary proceedings for minor offences. In that sense, its function is complementary to that of the FIU in relation to CPMLMO: the FIU carries out supervisory and intelligence tasks, while the Secretariat supports CPMLMO in sanctioning proceedings and international representation.

The FIU in Spain has a little more than 100 members, approximately 60 of them dedicated to financial intelligence analysis.

2. *Purpose and Tasks*

SEPBLAC carries out various types of tasks. It serves as an intelligence analysis unit for SARs and as a supervisory body for obliged entities. It cooperates with the international counterparts, manages the Financial Ownership File,[261] supervises and checks the fulfilment of applied sanctions and provides information regarding the creation of new financial entities, as will be explained below.

The AML Law foresees the following tasks under the *financial analysis functions* of the FIU: (i) to receive and analyse SARs, systematic communications[262] and wire transfer reports; (ii) to draw up financial intelligence reports where there is a reasonable suspicion of money laundering or administrative breaches, based on the SARs; (iii) to cooperate with and provide assistance to the judicial bodies,

260 Arts. 68 and 69 Decree 304/2014.

261 See *infra* section IV.D.1.

262 See *supra* section III.A.5.a.

the Public Prosecutor's Office, the police (Policía Nacional and Guardia Civil) and the competent administrative bodies and submit to them those reports with reasonable indications of a crime or breach of administrative law; and (iv) to undertake operational and strategic analysis to identify patterns, trends and typologies to inform CPMLMO (art. 45.4 AML Law, art. 67.5 Decree 304/2014).

The *supervisory functions* of the FIU are as follows: (i) to supervise the fulfilment of the duties of obliged entities[263] or the execution of the sanctions imposed on them by CPMLMO; (ii) to propose recommendations to the obliged entities with the aim of improving their internal monitoring measures (art. 67.2 Decree 304/2014);[264] (iii) to execute the orders of CPMLMO; (iv) to propose to CPMLMO the sanctioning of obliged entities, the creation of guidance on the fulfilment of the AML Law by obliged entities and the adoption of key requirements for obliged entities to fulfil their duties (art. 45.4 AML Law).

Following the reform of the AML Law, art. 63 created the possibility of direct communication between the FIU and whistleblowers. In that situation, if there is reasonable suspicion of money laundering following the communication from the employees, managers or agents of the obliged entity, the FIU may undertake additional supervisory acts *propio motu*, independently from the Annual Guiding Plan.[265]

The FIU also has the power to give general instructions to legislative authorities, through the manuals and recommendations published by CPMLMO.

As part of one of its main tasks – cooperation with other authorities – SEPBLAC must cooperate with the criminal justice system, its international counterparts, other national supervisory bodies (the CNMV and OCP), the tax authorities and the Bank of Spain.

The Annual Guiding Plan approved by CPMLMO may determine that in AML-related situations SEPBLAC's supervisory tasks should be coordinated with other supervisory bodies, such as the Bank of Spain, the CNMV and the Directorate-General for Insurance and Pension Funds (DGSFP) (art. 47.2 AML Law). The FIU supports the activity of the Bank of Spain by informing it about its precautionary assessment of acquisitions and increases in shareholdings in the financial sector (art. 45.4(j) AML). It shall also write reports for the Bank of Spain evaluating the adequacy of the internal monitoring mechanisms against money laundering of new financial institutions in Spain, before the Bank of Spain authorises those financial institutions to operate in the country.

SEPBLAC's cooperation with tax authorities is regulated by both the AML Law and the General Taxation Law. Art. 94.4 of the General Taxation Law[266]

---

[263] With exception of notaries, since the OCP is the body responsible for the supervision of notaries.

[264] See *supra* section III.G.

[265] See *supra* section IV.A.1.

[266] *Ley General Tributaria*, Law no. 58/2003, of 17 December 2003.

states that SEPBLAC shall forward any information *with tax relevance* to the tax administration office. This means that the FIU shall forward to the tax authorities any information that could indicate tax fraud or be in any way relevant to the tax authorities (i.e. if it relates to tax evasion). In addition, SEPBLAC *can* also submit its financial intelligence report to tax authorities, without being requested to do so (art. 67.4 Decree 304/2014).

Likewise, SEPBLAC shall cooperate with the law enforcement authorities (public prosecutors, National Police, Civil Guard) and judicial bodies by forwarding its financial intelligence reports when they support a reasonable indication of a crime (art. 45.4(a) AML Law). SEPBLAC shall also cooperate with the above-mentioned bodies by answering further questions regarding transactions that give rise to a suspicion of money laundering. The FIU also cooperates with its international counterparts, as will be seen in detail in section IV.D.5.

The FIU is part of the Ministry of the Treasury. It is mandatory for it to centralise any relevant information regarding suspicions of a money laundering offences or administrative wrongdoings, and then to analyse that information and distribute the result of this analysis internally to the competent authorities. It is also responsible for cooperating as regards further strategic information related to money laundering, always following the rule of autonomy and independence that characterises the FIU.

3. *Independence*

Regarding its institutional organisation, the FIU is functionally allocated within the CPMLMO. Nevertheless, Decree 304/2014, amended to comply with the 2012 FATF Recommendations, explicitly granted the FIU "autonomy and operative independence", which established its decision-making autonomy from CPMLMO (art. 67.4 Decree 304/2014). All in all, SEPBLAC's operations are not controlled by any authority, and its analysts have a duty of secrecy in relation to any investigation conducted within the FIU.

4. *Powers*

SEPBLAC has broad investigative powers related to the information already sent by obliged entities. It is empowered to request any additional information and documents from obliged entities[267] to carry out its activities (art. 47.4 AML Law), both from internal data banks[268] and international sources.[269] Also within

[267] Art. 9 of Order EHA/2963/2005, establishes the OCP, specifically mentions the duty of notaries to send any information that SEPBLAC requests in order to carry out its functions.
[268] See *infra* section VII.
[269] See *infra* section IV.D.5

its powers is the capacity to access tax data or data related to money laundering from all public authorities and law enforcement agencies (police and security bodies).[270]

In addition, the FIU can propose that CPMLMO adopt key measures for obliged entities in order to comply with AML policies (independently of the opening of administrative sanctioning proceedings, art. 67.3 Decree 304/2014). SEPBLAC may decide on a case-by-case basis what "indispensable measures" are considered to be for a particular obliged entity.

B. TREATMENT OF SARS

1. *Data Processing*

Under art. 45 AML Law, one of the main tasks of the FIU is to receive SARs, analyse the information received, create financial intelligence reports and disseminate the reports to the competent authorities (i.e. public prosecutors, police forces, foreign counterparts[271]). Additionally, the FIU shall submit to the Tax Agency reports with fiscally relevant information and shall respond to information requests from legally authorised authorities (art. 67.4 Decree 304/2014).[272]

The FIU analyses SARs with the goal of reasonably determining if it concerns a money laundering operation. As soon as a suspicion is confirmed, the FIU draws up a financial intelligence report, which shall be sent directly to the law enforcement or administrative authorities (art. 46.1 AML Law), such as the National Police, Civil Guard, tax authorities, criminal law system (judicial system, public prosecutors) and foreign counterparts.

The AML Law does not provide further information on data processing by the FIU. This information is, however, available in academic works.[273] According to these sources, once SEPBLAC receives the information from the reporting entities through an online platform, it is processed by the FIU's software, called TAIS (the Spanish acronym for Automatic Treatment of Service Information[274]). The next steps are as follows:

(a) *Registration:* The analyst registers the communications and adds them via the software, which constitutes the FIU's database.

---

270 FATF, *Mutual Evaluation Report – Spain*, 2014, p. 56.

271 See *supra* section IV.A.2.

272 See *infra* section V.

273 Mallada Fernández et. al., *Guia prática de prevención del blanqueo de capitales*, Madrid, 2015, p. 313.

274 See *infra* section V.A.3.

(b) *Valuation*: The reports are then put together with the records from previous communications about clients or transactions (data matching). At this point, a decision is made as to whether a case shall be opened and assigned to one of the units of the FIU.
(c) *Analysis*: Within the FIU, the file is received by the Investigative Unit, or by one of the police units that is part of it. Within the framework of one of these units, an analyst determines whether further investigative measures are to be adopted, or whether the SAR does not give concrete signs of money laundering. In the latter case, the analyst will close the file.
(d) *Request for additional information*: If the case is not closed in the previous phase, the analyst will request complementary data, including information from other sources (additional information from obliged entities or information from international sources) connected to the FIU.[275]
(e) *Disseminating*: With all the information in hand, the analyst will generate a financial intelligence report setting out the conclusions of the previous investigations. Based on that, the analyst will forward the financial intelligence report to the appropriate authorities. The financial intelligence report can conclude that a money laundering operation does not exist and proceed to close the proceedings, without the report being forwarded to any authority. On the other hand, if there is a suspicion of money laundering, the analyst shall forward this conclusion to the law enforcement agencies (police offices, public prosecutors) and tax authorities, so they can decide upon further measures to be taken.

Art. 63 AML Law creates the possibility of direct communication between employees of obliged entities and the FIU (whistleblowers). Following communication from a whistleblower, art. 64.2(a) AML Law allows the FIU and other supervisory authorities to access the information shared by the whistleblower to define the plan for their next supervisory visits to the obliged entity.

2. *Special Procedures for Privileged Professions*

In Spain, notaries and registrars are the privileged professions that possess a mandatory supervisory body for AML purposes (art. 27.3 AML Law), OCP for notaries and the CRAB for registrars. As a result, both notaries and registrars shall first forward the SARs generated by them to their supervisory body, which will then analyse and forward the SARs to the FIU (art. 27.2 AML Law, art. 44 Decree 304/2014, art. 5 Order ECC/2402/2015).[276]

---

275 For a complete list of the sources of information that the FIU can have access to, see *infra* section IV.D.

276 See *infra* section III.B.3.b.

Other independent legal professionals, auditors, external accountants and tax advisors do not currently have their own supervisory bodies (besides the recommendations of art. 27 AML Law) and therefore shall file SARs directly with the FIU via an online form.[277]

3. *Feedback Obligations*

a. Obligation of the FIU

SEPBLAC is allowed, but not obliged, to inform the reporting entity about the outcome of an SAR (art. 46.2 AML Law). The information that can be provided is restricted to the action that has been taken after the SAR, and must be kept confidential by the obliged entity. Nevertheless, the results of the empirical research carried out for this report highlighted that the FIU gives limited feedback and provides insufficient information.

b. Obligation of Investigative Authorities

According to art. 46 AML Law, after receiving information from SEPBLAC, the recipients of the reports (Public Prosecutor's Office or competent judicial, police or administrative authorities) are obliged to provide regular feedback about the destination of the reports from the FIU.

Complementary to the legislation, the interviews conducted for this report indicated a closer feedback mechanism between the police and the supervisory bodies, in particular the OCP for notaries and the CRAB for registrars. In practice, the law enforcement agencies participate in meetings to provide some feedback about the quality of the information sent by these groups of obliged entities.

4. *Disclosure Obligations Towards "Suspect"*

The AML Law does not oblige the SEPBLAC to disclose any information towards the suspect.

C. PROACTIVE INVESTIGATIONS

Spanish law does not provide information about the possible proactive powers of the FIU; it only states that it must conduct investigations based on the information it receives (art. 45.4(d) AML Law).

---

[277] Form F 19-1, available on SEPBLAC's website.

Because there are other possible sources not listed in the law, one can assume that some situations could trigger an investigation: spontaneous information from a foreign FIU, news from the press, communications from administrative authorities, and information from sector supervisors (such as the customs agency, the Central Bank, etc.).[278] Nevertheless, the empirical study carried out for this report points to the majority of the FIU's investigations being triggered by SARs.

D. ACCESS TO DATA

1. *Design and Content of FIU's Own Data Banks*

SEPBLAC collects SARs, systematic communications,[279] cross-border declarations and seizures.[280] It also gathers information from the supervisory bodies (OCP for notaries, CRAB for registrars, the Bank of Spain, the CNMV, the Social Security Registry, and the Ministry of Justice's Register of Life Insurance) related to suspicion of money laundering and spontaneous information from its foreign counterparts. The judicial system (after a request from the Public Prosecutor's Office) and any public employee who identifies a suspicious transaction (art. 48 AML Law) also report to the FIU, and this information will be added to its data banks.

Under art. 27 Decree 304/2014, systematic communications from obliged entities include cash transactions reports, wire transfer reports, operations with PEPs and operations with listed high-risk third countries. In summary, the monthly systematic reporting/communication contains information regarding: (a) the physical movement of cash or other forms of bearer documents issued by credit institutions with a value over €30,000 (except when is a client's account deposit); (b) money remittances on payment services, the physical movement of cash or other forms of bearer documents for amounts exceeding €1,500 or the equivalent amount in foreign currency; (c) wire transfers over €30,000 with natural or legal persons resident, or representing a resident, in a listed high-risk third country; and (d) cross-border movements, or within the national territory, of amounts over €100,000.[281]

SEPBLAC is also responsible for the management of the Financial Ownership File, established by art. 43.1 AML Law. The File, which became operational in June 2016, contains information from every bank and securities account in Spain, and is provided with data by all Spanish financial institutions. They are to

278 FATF, *Mutual Evaluation Report – Spain*, 2014, item 3.3.

279 See *supra* section III.C.1.a.

280 See *infra* section V.E.2.

281 See *supra* section III.B.1.a.

send information related to the opening and closing of bank accounts, savings accounts and security accounts, as well as fixed-term deposits, in addition to the name of the account holder, the name of the beneficial owner, the name of the financial institution and the branch location. Details about the account balance or financial transactions do not, however, have to be shared with the File. The File contains exclusive information regarding bank accounts and is, therefore, substantially different from the beneficial ownership files carried out by notaries and registrars.

The design of the FIU's data bank follows, to some extent, the general rules set out in the Spanish Data Protection Law and the GDPR on minimum standards for the creation of a data bank.

According to the Data Protection Law (Law no. 3/2018), the minimum rules for creating and running a public database are: the duty of accuracy of the data (art. 4) and confidentiality in its treatment (art. 5); purpose limitation (art. 16); and high levels of security of the data (art. 8 and additional provisions nos. 1 and 18). In the case of communications from whistleblowers, the AML Law foresees a special secrecy duty for SEPBLAC regarding the identity of the whistleblower (art. 65.3 AML Law). Nevertheless, two of the main principles of the Data Protection Law do not apply to SEPBLAC's data bank: there is no need to obtain the data subject's consent and no rights to access, amend, suppress or oppose the data (art. 32 AML Law, additional provision no. 10 Data Protection Law).

Finally, there is no legal limit on how long SEPBLAC can store the data. The limit of 10 years of storage applies only to the data banks of obliged entities (art. 29.1 Decree 304/2014). Since there is no specific regulation, one may conclude that limits directly result from basic principles of data protection, such as purpose limitation and data minimisation (arts. 5 and 25 GDPR).

2. *Access to Other Public Data Banks*

SEPBLAC has full direct access to a wide variety of information relevant for money laundering investigation purposes, *independent of prior judicial authorisation*. The FIU has access to: (a) data on the Balance of Payments from the Bank of Spain and statistical information on capital movements, and foreign economic transactions reported to the Bank of Spain; (b) data from the CNMV; (c) data from the Registry of Social Security of the DGSFP; and (d) data from the Ministry of Justice's Register of Life Insurance. The FIU also has direct access to criminal records and information on cross-border declarations and seizures.[282] Furthermore, when relevant for a money laundering-related investigation, the FIU has access to police databases via the representatives of the police forces working within the FIU. These police officers retain their normal access to the database of their original institution (Civil Guard or National Police)

282 FATF, *Mutual Evaluation Report – Spain*, 2014, p. 48.

and may refer to it to complement their analysis within the FIU of transactions giving rise to a suspicion of money laundering.

Similarly, SEPBLAC has a close, two-way collaboration with the tax authorities: the exchange of tax information is open to SEPBLAC and correspondingly SEPBLAC's information can be requested by the tax authorities (art. 49.2 AML Law, art. 67.4 Decree 304/2014) when it has tax relevance. Like police officers, the representatives of the tax authorities working within the FIU may access tax data if deemed necessary for the analysis of a suspicion of money laundering by the FIU.

Moreover, SEPBLAC process the data of the Financial Ownership File,[283] so it has full access to its content. It also has access to the data from the public land, companies, real estate and moveable property registers held by the College of Notaries (art. 45 Decree 304/2014).

More recently, the reform of the AML Law added a Register of Trust or Company Service Providers. Any legal person that provides trust or company services[284] must register its activities in the Mercantile Registry, and any natural person must register directly with the Ministry of Justice, by filling in a form that is available online. All changes in the management board or in the company's register shall also be notified to the Mercantile Registry. These obliged entities shall provide information on the type of services they offer, their location, whether the services are provided to residents or non-residents, the turnover of the services provided, the number of transactions by class and any change in the beneficial ownership. Therefore, the Register of Trust or Company Service Providers will be another public database available for consultation by the FIU.

3. *Access to Private Data Banks*

SEPBLAC has unlimited access to supervisory information from the supervisory bodies. So far, the main private data bank in Spain is that held by the OCP of the College of Notaries and the notary profession's Single Computerised Index.[285]

---

[283] See *supra* section IV.D.1.

[284] Trust and company service providers, according to art. 2.1 o AML Law, are persons who, on a professional basis, provide the following services to third parties: forming companies or other legal persons; acting as or arranging for another person to act as a director or secretary of a company, a partner of a partnership or a similar position in relation to other legal persons; providing a registered office, business address, correspondence or administrative address and other related services for a company, a partnership or any other legal person or arrangement; or acting as or arranging for another person to act as a trustee of an express trust or similar legal arrangement, or acting as or arranging for another person to act as a shareholder for another person, other than a company listed on a regulated market that is subject to disclosure requirements in conformity with Community legislation or subject to equivalent international standards.

[285] Created according to the art. 10 Order EHA/114/2008. For the functioning of the Notary Index, see http://www.notariado.org/liferay/web/notariado/e-notario/indice-unico.

The latter contains information from the real estate register[286] and beneficial ownership register for limited liability companies. In addition, the FIU has unrestricted access to private commercial databases such as Informa,[287] which provides commercial and financial information about Spanish enterprises and independent professionals.[288]

4. *Data Analytics*

The AML Law does not foresee any definition or constraints on the activity of the FIU concerning data analytics. The information available on this topic is provided by the FATF Mutual Evaluation Report for Spain, which states that SEPBLAC has "state of the art" software, analytical and data mining tools, allowing it to conduct effective investigations.[289] There is no official information available regarding the technique the FIU uses to perform data mining.

5. *International Cooperation*

International cooperation was one of the topics of the legal reform of the AML Law in 2018. The Spanish FIU shall fully cooperate *propio motu* or following a request from a European FIU (art. 48 *bis* AML Law), whenever necessary for the proper fulfilment of its tasks, according to the guidelines set out in arts. 51–57 4AMLD as modified by the 5AMLD: cooperation to the greatest extent possible, using and requiring the use of the FIU's full research powers to access AML-related data, and limiting the use of the information to AML-related purposes or at the request of the FIU providing the data.[290]

The exchange of information between SEPBLAC and non-European FIUs shall be in accordance with the Egmont Group Principles or with the terms of the relevant memorandum of understanding. Finally, the exchange of information

---

286 Art. 17 Organic Law for the Notaries, of 28 May 1862. See FATF, *Mutual Evaluation Report – Spain*, 2014, p. 15.

287 See FATF, *Mutual Evaluation Report – Spain*, 2014, p. 46.

288 According to information available on the Informa website, "the database INFORMA D&B has been fed from multiple public and private information sources, such as the Borme (Official Gazette of the Commercial Registry), Official Filed Accounts, BOE (Official State Gazette), Provincial and autonomous regions' Official Gazettes, National and Regional Press, ad hoc Investigations and Several Publications". The data bank offers national business, financial and marketing information, with 6.6 million national economic agents; 3.4 million companies and active sole proprietors with ratings; more than 14 million companies' balance sheets; more than 14.4 million administration positions; more than 2.6 million corporate links; and more than 150,000 data updated on a daily basis. See https://www.informa.es/en/about-us/our-database.

289 FATF, *Mutual Evaluation report – Spain*, 2014, p. 48.

290 See *infra* sections V.F and V.G.

between SEPBLAC and other competent authorities (besides FIUs) from non-European countries shall rely on international agreements or the reciprocity principle, as long as the foreign jurisdictions have the same data protection standards as Spain.[291]

The exchange of information between the Spanish FIU and its European counterparts goes through the encrypted system of the FIU.net, a secure network available solely to FIU members. In the case of non-European FIUs, SEPBLAC uses the encrypted system of the Egmont Group.

E. PARTICIPATION OF "SUSPECTS"

1. *Defence Rights*

According to art. 32 AML Law, the data subject has no access to data related to them stored in the FIU data bank. Moreover, obliged entities are not allowed to inform the data subject[292] about the information collected (which will be the general rule for other databases), and the data subject does not have any right to access, correct or delete the data.

2. *Judicial Review or Other Remedies*

The Spanish AML Law does not include any particular provision about judicial review of the FIU's actions but refers instead to the general principles of the judicial review of administrative sanctions (art. 61 AML Law).

A specific provision regarding the possibility of a judicial remedy is provided by the Notary Services Regulation:[293] according to art. 145.6 of this Regulation, notaries may refuse to register if there is a suspicion of a crime, especially in cases of money laundering. In that case, the "suspect" could make a judicial appeal against the decision in administrative court, for the registration of the property to be performed.

291 According to the Proposal to transpose the 5AMLD, the SEPBLAC shall cooperate with the the European Banking Authority, providing it with the necessary information to enable it to carry out its obligations regarding the prevention of money laundering (art. 48.1). Proposal available at: https://www.mineco.gob.es/stfls/mineco/ministerio/participacion_publica/audiencia/ficheros/ECO_TES_20200612_AP_V_Directiv_Blanqueo.pdf.

292 According to Art. 2(i) Europol Databank Regulation, "'data subject' means an identified or identifiable natural person, an identifiable person being a person who can be identified, directly or indirectly, in particular by reference to an identifier such as a name, an identification number, location data or an online identifier or to one or more factors specific to the physical, physiological, genetic, mental, economic, cultural or social identity of that person".

293 Decree of 2 June 1944.

F. SIMILAR POWERS OF SUPERVISORY BODIES

1. *Financial Supervision*

According to art. 67.1 Decree 304/2014, SEPBLAC is the FIU and AML supervisor for all sectors. In the financial sector, however, SEPLAC coordinates its supervisory activities with the prudential regulators: the Bank of Spain, the DGSFP and the CNMV.[294]

The supervisory bodies for the financial markets supervise the implementation of CDD measures[295] and record keeping by financial institutions. However, they are not autonomous supervisory bodies in relation to AML prevention, since their supervisory activity in that respect takes place exclusively in partnership with, or coordinated by, the FIU (art. 44(m) AML Law).[296]

The primary purpose of the Bank of Spain is to ensure the stability of the financial system.[297] The cooperation with the FIU is foreseen in its regulation,[298] but not as a supervisory authority regarding money laundering. Neither the AML Law nor the law that regulates the functions of the Bank of Spain[299] establishes the possibility of investigations undertaken by the Bank of Spain for AML purposes. The same can be said about the DGSFP[300] and the CNMV.[301]

---

294 See *supra* section III.E.

295 The supervisory functions of the Bank of Spain regarding AML/CTF follow the guidelines of the Basel Committee on Banking Supervision, which states (Principle 29 of the Basel III Agreement on Banking Supervision): "The supervisor determines that banks have adequate policies and processes, including strict customer due diligence (CDD) rules to promote high ethical and professional standards in the financial sector and prevent the bank from being used, intentionally or unintentionally, for criminal activities". *Basel Committee on Banking Supervision*, Guidance on the application of the Core principles for effective banking supervision to the regulation and supervision of institutions relevant to financial inclusion, Basel, 2001, p. 5, https://www.bis.org/bcbs/publ/d351.pdf.

296 FATF, *Mutual Evaluation Report – Spain*, 2014, p. 104.

297 See https://www.bde.es/bde/es/areas/supervision/funcion/objetivos_basico/Objetivos_basicos.html.

298 The authorisation for establishing a financial institution in Spain is conditional on the approval of SEPBLAC, and the adequacy of their AML/CTF preventive measures (arts. 6 and 7 of Law no. 10/2014, of 26 June 2014, on the Planning, Supervision and Creditworthiness of the Financial System).

299 Law no. 10/2014, of 26 June 2014, on the Planning, Supervision and Creditworthiness of the Financial System.

300 Art. 7 Decree 531/2017, which establishes the functions of the DGSFP.

301 Art. 4. Act on the National Securities Exchange Commission determines its functions as follows: "1. The CNMV shall perform the following tasks: a) The supervision of bond markets, b) The supervision and inspection of the activity of all legal or natural persons involved in trade within these markets, c) The exercise of sanctioning authority over said persons, d) The authorisation and inspection of subjects and entities that are active in bond and financial instrument markets, whenever this is prescribed by current regulations, e) All remaining tasks prescribed to it by the current legal framework".

In principle, the CNMV and DGSFP are also tasked with AML supervision but, in practice, they do not focus on AML. According to the FATF, "both CNMV and DGSFP have AML supervisory methodologies of their own but … they are less proactive than the Bank of Spain in their AML supervision. Rather than developing a specific ML inspection program, they provide SEPBLAC with a list of planned prudential inspections and seek SEPBLAC's advice on which companies shall have an AML inspection".[302] Despite this conclusion on the part of the FATF, the empirical research carried out for this report revealed that practitioners have the perception that the Bank of Spain does not prioritise the inspection of money laundering-related administrative wrongdoings, delegating the task to the FIU.

Therefore, to conclude, the supervisory bodies for the financial markets in Spain have no similar powers to the FIU in terms of the power to investigate suspicions of money laundering, nor do they seem to focus on such tasks, except when cooperating with the FIU.

2. *Non-Financial Sector Supervision*

The OCP for the notaries has the right to investigate activities that give rise to a suspicion of money laundering, in line with its function as a special review body (art. 27 AML Law). The investigation can be carried out on its own initiative, or after a request from one of the affiliate obliged persons (notaries). Nevertheless, the findings of the OCP's investigations must be forwarded to the FIU (by filing an SAR), and the OCP is not allowed to apply coercive measures directly.

G. REPORTING OBLIGATIONS OF SUPERVISORY AUTHORITIES

Art. 48.2 AML Law states that the Bank of Spain, the CNMV, the DGSFP, the National Directory of Registrars and Notaries, the Spanish Accounting and Account Auditing Institute (ICAC), professional chambers, and public authorities at the national and autonomous region levels shall inform SEPBLAC about suspicious activities related to money laundering they encounter when performing their inspection or supervisory tasks.

Besides the FIU, there are two other supervisory bodies exclusively dedicated to AML in Spain: the OCP for notaries and the CRAB for registrars. All other supervision relating to AML is conducted by the FIU. As supervisory authorities, the OCP and the CRAB are obliged to file SARs with the FIU, after verifying[303] the information sent by their members and conducting further investigations to

---

302 FATF, *Mutual Evaluation Report – Spain*, 2014, p. 109.

303 See *infra* section V.L. regarding the methods used by the OCP to verify and filter information.

establish the existence of an effectively suspicious transaction[304] (art. 27 AML Law, art. 44 Decree 304/2014). The OCP can proceed with data matching within its own database, request further information from its members, and filter that information, with the goal of making its SARs more accurate.

H. REPORTING BY OTHER AUTHORITIES

All employees and public authorities in Spain are obliged to communicate to the FIU the results of its investigations related to transactions giving rise to a suspicion of money laundering that they discover in the course of performing their inspections or tasks (art. 48.1 AML Law).[305]

Moreover, courts shall forward evidence to SEPBLAC, on the instruction of the Public Prosecutor's Office or of their own volition, when they detect signs indicative of a breach of obligations that does not constitute a criminal offence (art. 48.3 AML Law). Along these lines, the customs authorities and police officers seconded to customs shall immediately communicate to the FIU any cases of non-conviction-based confiscations of means of payment (art. 35 AML Law).

Furthermore, the judicial authorities are obliged to report to the FIU any breaches or inadequacies of the preventive measures adopted by obliged entities. If they identify criminal activity, then they must proceed to a proper judicial investigation, without filing an SAR.[306]

Besides the OCP, the National Administrator of the Registry of Emissions Allowances[307] is a Spanish body responsible for regulating the trading of

---

304 According to art. 34 4AMLD, the supervisory body (self-regulatory body) may send unfiltered information to the FIU. However, art. 27 AML Law requires that the supervisory bodies review the information prior to submitting it.

305 According to art. 48.1 AML Law, "any authority or official discovering facts that may constitute an indication or evidence of money laundering or terrorist financing, either during the inspections of monitored institutions or in any other way, shall report such circumstance to the SEPBLAC."

306 The FATF Mutual Evaluation Report for Spain reads: "The Tax Auditing Department of the AEAT undertakes administrative investigations of the predicate offence of tax crimes ... If ML/TF is detected during an investigation, it must be reported to a prosecutor or judge, along with any recommendations for invoking provisional measures". FATF, *Mutual Evaluation Report – Spain*, 2014, p. 148. Aliaga Méndez, "Normativa comentada del blanqueo de capitales, adaptada a la Ley 10/2010", *La Ley*, 2010, p. 353.

307 A body established in 2005, by Law no. 1/2005, to regulate the system for trading greenhouse gas emission allowances. The Law transposes Directive 2003/87/EC of the European Parliament and of the Council, establishing a scheme for greenhouse gas emission allowance trading within the European Community. See http://www.renade.es/esp/QueEsIberclear.aspx.

greenhouse gas emissions allowances. The body is a subsidiary of the CNMV, but is not an obliged entity since it does not have to perform CDD measures (and is not listed as such by the AML Law). Nevertheless, art. 41.2(d) Decree 304/2014 determines that the Registry of Emissions Allowances shall adopt internal monitoring measures to identify transactions giving rise to a suspicion of money laundering in the trading of greenhouse gas emissions allowances and shall report them to the FIU.[308]

Furthermore, public administrations or their subordinate bodies granting subsidies to associations and foundations – along with protectorates[309] – shall report to SEPBLAC any situations detected in the exercise of their powers that may be related to money laundering (art. 42. 4. Decree 304/2014).

I. STATISTICS

1. *Number of Reports by Supervisory Authorities and Other Authorities*

According to information available on the FIU's website, in 2017 the OCP filed 383 SARs, the Mercantile Registrars[310] filed 158 SARs, and "public bodies" filed 52 SARs.[311] There is no information on the value of transactions associated with these SARs, nor any clarification on which the "public bodies" mentioned in the statistics are.

2. *FIU Analysis*

There are no statistics available on the FIU's analysis.

---

308 According to the FATF: "A positive feature is that the reporting obligation has also been extended to the SAREB, and also to the national administrator of the emission allowance registry which was established in 2005 to regulate the system for trading greenhouse gas emission allowances, given the risks of ML and VAT fraud through this sector". FATF, *Mutual Evaluation Report – Spain*, 2014, p. 89.

309 A protectorate is a body inside a foundation responsible for ensuring the correct exercise of the foundation's rights and the constitutionality of its activities, ensuring that the foundation's capital is used for the aims of the foundation, and nominating directors and supervising their activities. In public foundations, this role must be performed by the state administration.

310 See *infra* section VI.B.1.

311 Committee for the Prevention of Money Laundering and Monetary Offences, *Statistical Information 2012–2016*, p. 6, https://www.sepblac.es/wp-content/uploads/2019/01/report_2017.pdf.

3. *Communications to Law Enforcement Authorities*

SEPBLAC states that a high number[312] of SARs were communicated to law enforcement agencies and other authorities. Of the total of 4,999 SARs received in 2017:

- 105 were forwarded to international cooperation;
- 94 went to special police forces or to judicial authorities;
- 2,743 to the National Police;
- 1,648 to the Civil Guard;
- 1,078 to the Inspection Unit of the Tax Agency;
- 165 to the Customs Unit of the Tax Agency; and
- 81 to other bodies.[313]

V. DATA FLOW AND DATA PROTECTION

The general regulation of data protection in Spain changed recently to comply with the GDPR. The new Spanish Data Protection Law altered the data protection system significantly, but did not have significant impacts on the prevention of money laundering, since the AML Law makes some exceptions to data protection regarding the exchange of information. Nevertheless, the adoption of the GDPR provides some guidance in the cases where the AML Law is silent.

As a general rule, the GDPR[314] (recital 112) and the Data Protection Law in Spain[315] (art. 8) do not require the data subject to consent to the exchange of his or her personal data between the public administration bodies dealing with

---

312 According to the FATF, there are "numerous case examples and statistics demonstrating how the vast majority of SEPBLAC's analysis is actionable (either initiate investigations or support existing ones); the numerous case examples demonstrating the ability of the law enforcement agencies to develop evidence and trace criminal proceeds, based on their own investigations or by using the financial intelligence reports from SEPBLAC". FATF, *Mutual Evaluation Report – Spain*, 2014 p. 15.

313 Committee for the Prevention of Money Laundering and Monetary Offences, *Statistical Information 2012–2016*, p. 8, https://www.sepblac.es/wp-content/uploads/2019/01/report_2017.pdf.

314 As an European Regulation, the GDPR (General Data Protection Regulation – Regulation (EU) no. 2016/679 of the European Parliament and of the Council of 27 April 2016 on the protection of natural persons with regard to the processing of personal data and on the free movement of such data) applies directly to the internal legal system in Spain, without the need for legal transposition (as is the case with the AML Directives). Nevertheless, the GDPR provides only general guidance, and needs further regulation in each Member State. In Spain, Law no. 3/2018 adapts the Spanish data protection system to the GDPR (dealing mainly with the sanctioning regime and the Spanish Data Protection Agency's internal processes).

315 Law no. 3/2018 of 5 December 2018.

different topics, if there is a public interest. The Spanish Data Protection Agency published very general guidance[316] on the concept of "public interest" mentioned by the Data Protection Law: any interest established *by law* is of public interest. Moreover, more recent guidance from the Data Protection Agency mentions that there is "legitimate interest" in the access and exchange of data according to the balance between the purpose and aims of the exchange of information and the fundamental rights of the data subject.[317]

Therefore, one may conclude that the provisions of the AML Law are adequate for the requirements of the GDPR and the proposal of the new Data Protection Law, since the AML Law highlights the need for cooperation and data sharing between the public administration, the FIU and the private sector. What remains open to interpretation are the limits on the exchange of data.

One of the key topics treated by the Proposal to transpose the 5AMLD into Spanish AML Law is data protection. The Proposal stresses the application of the data protection rules in obliged entities' data processing, but does not provide any particular limitation beyond the information mentioned above.[318]

A. DATA EXCHANGE BETWEEN FIU AND PRIVATE SECTOR

1. *From FIU to Private Sector*

The data collected by the FIU must be subject to a high level of security (art. 32.5 AML Law) and, according to art. 49 AML Law, the FIU has a duty of secrecy related to all the information contained in its database. Given that there is no

---

316 Available at https://www.aepd.es/media/docs/impacto-rgpd-en-aapp.pdf.

317 Available at https://www.aepd.es/media/informes/informe-juridico-rgpd-interes-legitimo.pdf, p. 6.

318 According to the proposal for art. 32, dedicated to data protection rules applied to the results of CDD measures:

"2. The data collected by obliged entities for the fulfillment of due diligence obligations may not be used for purposes other than those related to the prevention of money laundering and the financing of terrorism without the consent of the data subject, unless the processing of such data is necessary for the ordinary management of the business relationship.
3. Prior to the establishment of the business relationship or the performance of an occasional transaction, reporting parties must provide new customers with the information required by Article 11 of Organic Law 3/2018 of 5 December on the Protection of Personal Data and the Guarantee of Digital Rights. Such information shall contain, in particular, a general notice on the legal obligations of the obliged entities with respect to the processing of personal data for the purpose of preventing money laundering and the financing of terrorism."

Proposal available at: https://www.mineco.gob.es/stfls/mineco/ministerio/participacion_publica/audiencia/ficheros/ECO_TES_20200612_AP_V_Directiv_Blanqueo.pdf.

exception in the Law regarding data sharing with the private sector, one may thus conclude that the FIU is not allowed to transfer personal data to obliged entities. Indeed, the FIU may request additional information from the obliged entity if it finds it has a need for complementary data, but even in this case, the AML Law does not explicitly foresee the exchange of information from the FIU to the private sector.

2. *From Private Sector to FIU*

As already seen above, it is mandatory for all obliged entities to provide the FIU with information regarding activities that give rise to a suspicion of money laundering. Firstly, they shall file an SAR with relevant information related to the money laundering suspicion and, if requested by the FIU, provide the additional information required. A manual drawn up by SEPBLAC[319] regarding CDD measures indicates that obliged entities shall create an archive for each client centralising the information about the transactions and the business relationship. Besides those general remarks, though, the AML Law does not provide further detail on the possible limits of the data exchange from the private sector to FIU.

On the other hand, the general principles of both the Spanish Data Protection Law and the GDPR (art. 4 Law no. 3/2018)[320] are proportionality, purpose limitation and security in the treatment of personal data. This means that public or private entities shall collect data only when such data are adequate, relevant and not excessive in relation to the scope and purpose for which they were collected (in this case, prevention of money laundering and terrorism financing).

Still, under the Data Protection Law, art. 8 (in coordination with art. 6(1) GDPR) determines that processing data is lawful only when necessary for compliance with a legal obligation if the law requires it. Since the AML Law governs the transfer of data from the private sector to FIU, obliged entities only have permission to use the data for sharing purposes defined in the Law.

Moreover, the Spanish Data Protection Agency[321] has underlined the application of the principle of data minimisation laid out in art. 5 Data Protection Law. According to that principle, the collection of data must be limited to the minimum amount, and kept for the minimum timeframe, necessary for the data bank.

It should be stressed that the proportionality principle informs the entire Spanish data protection system in terms of the exchange of data, as the national

---

319 Available at https://www.sepblac.es/wp-content/uploads/2018/03/recomendaciones_sobre_medidas_de_control_interno_pbcft.pdf, p. 15.

320 Organic Law no. 15/1999, of 13 December 1999, updated in 2018 to comply with the requirements of the GDPR.

321 Available at https://www.aepd.es/media/informes/informe-juridico-rgpd-interes-legitimo.pdf, p. 10.

jurisprudence highlights.[322] Therefore, the exchange of information between obliged entities and the FIU must also be carried out in line with the principle of proportionality.

On another note, art. 32.2 AML Law specifies that the transfer of personal data from the private sector to the FIU is not subject to the following restrictions on handling personal data set out by the Data Protection Law: there is no need to request the consent of the data subject, to inform them or to allow them to access the information, since this would mean tipping the data subject off. However, the exceptions to the data protection regime mentioned in the AML Law do not intend to exclude the general principles of data protection, but instead aim to clarify obliged entities' legal authorisation to collect relevant information for the purposes of prevention of money laundering.[323]

To sum up, it may be concluded that obliged entities shall exchange information with the FIU in line with the principle of purpose limitation[324] (only data relevant for the prevention of money laundering) and limited to the minimum data necessary for the FIU to carry out its financial intelligence analysis (art. 5 GDPR).

B. DATA EXCHANGE BETWEEN FIU AND CRIMINAL JUSTICE SYSTEM

1. *From FIU to Criminal Justice System*

Cooperation between the FIU and the criminal justice system takes place through the submission of financial intelligence reports (art. 67.4 Decree 304/2014) based on reasonable grounds for suspected money laundering transactions (art. 45.4(b) AML Law), which can eventually trigger an investigation by law enforcement agencies. In this sense, the FIU does not share its entire database, but rather the result of the "reports with reasonable indications of a crime or, where appropriate, breach of the administrative law" (art. 45.4(b) AML Law). The report consists of an initial intelligence analysis from the FIU but is not meant to meet the need for further investigation from the law enforcement

322 A relevant decision of the Spanish Constitutional Court (Sentence no. 292/2000) declared unconstitutional some articles of the current Data Protection Law for lack of proportionality.

323 Martín, "El tratamiento de datos personales amparado en el interés legítimo en el marco del régimen especial de protección de datos de la Ley 10/2010, de 28 de abril, de prevención del blanqueo de capitales y la financiación del terrorismo ('LPBC')", *Diario La Ley*, no. 8153, 2013.

324 Available at https://www.aepd.es/media/informes/informe-juridico-rgpd-interes-legitimo.pdf, p. 6.

agencies. In practice, there is still room for improvement in the filtering and financial analysis by the FIU in terms of the amount of information forwarded to the investigative authorities.

Art. 49.2(e) AML Law states explicitly that the FIU can share information with legally entitled criminal justice and administrative authorities when so requested. The request, nevertheless, needs to refer to the precise legal precept that grants the authorisation for it. That means that it must indicate the law that supports it (Penal Code, Tax Law, etc.) and the use the criminal justice or administrative authorities wish to give to the information: which offence from the Penal Code, the overall content of the criminal investigation (if it is related to money laundering offences), and if the legal proceeding is open to the public or is under legal secrecy. The aim of art. 49.2(e) AML Law is to ensure that the requesting authority is responsible for the content of the information shared, and also to guarantee that intelligence data are not disseminated before the FIU concludes its internal analysis.

The FIU has operational autonomy and independence to decide whether to share data (art. 44.3 Decree 304/2014) and to determine which cases it will supervise and investigate. However, once it has the reasonable suspicion of a crime, the FIU shall send the information to the criminal justice system (since doing so is one of its main tasks). Nevertheless, besides the legal provision that the FIU shall inform the criminal justice system, the extent of information the FIU shall share remains open to interpretation (i.e. whether the FIU can decide to hold back some of the data under analysis in ongoing investigations).

In the light of all this, it may be concluded that the FIU has discretionary powers to limit the information it shares with the criminal justice system, without a judicial order, if it is beyond the minimum necessary to inform the reasonable suspicion of a crime. However, practice shows that the FIU is very cooperative with the law enforcement agencies. As reported by the FATF, SEPBLAC cooperates and exchanges information and financial intelligence on a regular basis, in an arrangement that facilitates cooperation and data exchange between the FIU and the National Police, Civil Guard, Tax Agency and customs authorities.[325]

Here, again, it is necessary to refer to the general principles of the Data Protection Law regarding the limits on the information the FIU shall share, since the AML Law is silent on this issue. It may be concluded that the proportionality principle of art. 5 GDPR applies.

---

325 FATF, *Mutual Evaluation Report – Spain*, 2014, p. 51.

2. *From Criminal Justice System to FIU*

As described above, the criminal justice system and the FIU are both entitled to investigate money laundering and terrorism financing transactions, thus allowing for data sharing under the Data Protection Law (art. 8 and additional provisions 1 and 10). Nevertheless, there is no clear rule regarding the extent or possibility of data exchange from the criminal justice system to the FIU.

Likewise, there is no explicit regulation in Spain regarding the limits of data transfer between the bodies of the criminal justice system,[326] in relation to which parallels could be drawn to the transfer of data from those bodies to the FIU. Obviously, such questions do not apply to judges, since they are members of the judicial branch and have independence and autonomy to decide about the information under their purview.

On the other hand, art. 284 of the criminal Prosecution Law[327] mentions that the police shall communicate all relevant information about wrongdoings to the public prosecutors, except when there is no known perpetrator or when they cannot forward the information "without ceasing the preventive diligences". In that sense, it may be concluded by analogy that the exchange of data from the criminal justice system to the FIU is allowed, but that it may be limited by the interests of the investigation.

In practice, however, it should be noted that the structure of the FIU[328] includes secondments from the police bodies (Civil Guard and National Police), which facilitate the exchange of data between those bodies and the FIU, despite the absence of specific regulation.

C. DATA EXCHANGE BETWEEN FIU AND INTELLIGENCE AGENCIES

1. *From FIU to Intelligence Agencies*

The AML Law does not address the question of data exchange between the FIU and intelligence agencies. However, art. 8 and additional provisions 1 and 10 of the Data Protection Law (and art. 10 Decree no. 1720/2007) allow the bodies of the public administration to share information when it is geared towards these same AML purposes.

---

326 Law no. 2/1986, which regulates the police corps in Spain, does not provide further guidance on this topic.

327 Ley de enjuiciamiento criminal, Royal Decree of 14 September 1882.

328 See *supra* section IV.A.

As mentioned above,[329] art. 45.4(a) AML Law defines as one of the tasks of the FIU "render[ing] the necessary assistance" to the "*competent administrative authorities*" in relation to suspicions of money laundering, i.e. the spontaneous dissemination of relevant information related to money laundering crimes and violations of the AML Law by obliged entities. More precisely, the Spanish National Intelligence Agency (Centro Nacional de Inteligencia, CNI) is an autonomous legal entity under the Ministry of the Presidency that provides support to the public administration.[330] Nevertheless, the Director of the CNI is a permanent member of the plenary of CPMLMO[331] (art. 63.1(q) Decree 304/2014), suggesting that there is a close cooperation between the FIU and the CNI.

In summary, despite the legislative lacuna, it can be assumed that under art. 45.4(a) AML Law the FIU is allowed to exchange relevant information on money laundering activities[332] with the CNI; however, the limits of the right to communicate are not subject to debate. It can be assumed here that the FIU has autonomy to decide on those limits.[333]

2. *From Intelligence Agencies to FIU*

Law no. 11/2002 regulates the functioning of the Spanish National Intelligence Service (CNI). In it, art. 5.1 states that all information or sources of information are classified, but that the CNI will maintain the necessary cooperation and coordinative measures with the rest of the public administration "where applicable".[334] In practice, the CNI cooperates with authorities focused on the prevention of terrorism at a high level of sensitivity, which excludes, for instance, the police units solely dedicated to investigating money laundering.

Therefore, even if there is no clear mention of data sharing between the FIU and the CNI, it can be concluded that the cooperation between the two agencies is not only possible but also fall under the administrative regime on data sharing, since both authorities are competent to investigate money laundering and terrorism financing. In other words, anti-money laundering and terrorism financing investigations shall be an area where said cooperation is "applicable".

---

329 See *supra* section V.B.1.

330 Piqueras/Cisternes, *El régimen jurídico de los servicios de inteligencia en España*, Valencia, 2015, p. 107.

331 See http://www.cpbc.tesoro.es/la-comision.

332 See art. 49 4AMLD.

333 The Proposal to transpose the 5AMLD refers clearly to the access of the CNI to the Financial Ownership Registry (art. 43.3) and Beneficial Ownership Registry (Additional provision number 4). Proposal available at: https://www.mineco.gob.es/stfls/mineco/ministerio/participacion_publica/audiencia/ficheros/ECO_TES_20200612_AP_V_Directiv_Blanqueo.pdf.

334 The FATF states that the CNI is particularly active in the "investigative efforts related to terrorism and TF". FATF, *Mutual Evaluation Report – Spain*, 2014, p. 68.

D. DATA EXCHANGE BETWEEN FIU AND TAX AUTHORITIES

1. *From FIU to Tax Authorities*

Art. 49.2(e) AML and art. 67.4 Decree 304/2014 rule that the FIU *shall* forward to the Tax Agency all reports containing fiscally relevant information. Likewise, art. 49.2(e) AML Law determines that the exchange of data between the FIU and the tax authorities shall "preferably" take place under the terms of an agreement between CPMLMO and the Tax Agency.[335]

The FIU depends on public employees from the Tax Agency (art. 69 Decree 304/2014) working within its structure. They are responsible for the financial analysis within the FIU of activities giving rise to a suspicion of money laundering. Moreover, the Director of Financial and Tax Inspection from the Tax Agency is a member of the plenary of CPMLMO. Such legal provisions make it clear that their purpose is to unite the efforts of the Tax Agency and the FIU regarding the investigation of money laundering and tax offences. That results in tax offences taking on a prominent role among the predicate offences for money laundering transactions.

Nevertheless, it is not possible to infer from the purposes of the AML Law the extent of the "fiscally relevant" data that the FIU may exchange with the tax authorities. Therefore, there is a need for clarification regarding the limits of the information *with tax relevance* that the FIU can share. Again, one must refer to the decision-making autonomy of the FIU (44.3 Decree 304/2014), to the level of confidentiality of the information handled and to the principle of minimisation in the exchange of data to conclude that the FIU may restrict such transfer of information to the minimum necessary to support the suspicion of tax fraud.[336]

2. *From Tax Authorities to FIU*

Art. 45.4(a) and (b) AML Law authorise data exchange between competent administrative authorities. The tax authorities are responsible for investigating tax fraud and providing the FIU with data. Moreover, art. 95.1(i)of the General Tax Law[337] expressly sets out the data sharing regime for tax data from the Tax Agency to the FIU.

Beyond the two articles mentioned above, art. 49.2(e) AML Law indicates that the exchange of data between the tax authorities and the FIU will be carried

---

335 There is at present no signed agreement, or, if there is, then its terms are not available for public consultation.

336 See *supra* section V.B.1.

337 Law no. 58/2003 of 17 December 2003. Art. 95.1(i) of the General Tax Law determines that all information handled by the Tax Agency must be protected and kept for the exclusive use of the Agency, except when the transfer of information had the aim of cooperating with the FIU, among other law enforcement agencies and public authorities listed by the article.

out in accordance with a specific agreement between the two bodies. However, there is at present no signed agreement.

According to Order HAC/232/2002, the Tax Agency holds different classes of data from the tax authorities and sorts the data according to the level of sensitivity of the information and the employees authorised to access them. A Resolution from 15 February 2018[338] establishes a new order for such data banks, creating a new file, File 56, aimed exclusively at the exchange of information, with the maximum level of security. The File collects information from obliged entities and legal representatives of companies, such as personal or legal entities IDs, nationality, register on financial transactions, "social circumstances", details of employment history, and economic and financial data. The definition of the File itself states that its main aim is to share such data with the FIU.

It should also be noted that, according to art. 69.1 Decree 304/2014, employees are seconded from the Tax Agency to the FIU to assist with the financial and intelligence analysis. That indicates the existence of a close cooperation between the two bodies. Therefore, it may be concluded that there shall be no restrictions on the exchange of information about activity flagged as giving rise to a suspicion of money laundering on reasonable grounds. Moreover, tax authorities have direct access (with no need for judicial authorisation) to some sources of personal data that are also available to the FIU.

E. DATA EXCHANGE BETWEEN FIU AND CUSTOMS AUTHORITIES

1. *From FIU to Customs Authorities*

There is no specific rule regarding the exchange of information between customs authorities and the FIU. Structurally, the customs authorities in Spain are part of the tax authorities, and the Director of Customs is a member of the plenary of CPMLMO (art. 63.1(u) Decree 304/2014). However, there is no information on the AML regulation that allows the definite conclusion that customs could have the same level of data exchange with the FIU as the tax authorities.

Nevertheless, given the institutional position of the customs authorities (an investigative unit within the tax authorities),[339] it may be concluded that the tax authorities centralise the information and the eventual exchange of data takes place directly between the tax authorities and the FIU.

---

338 https://www.boe.es/buscar/doc.php?id=BOE-A-2018-2742.

339 A statement of the customs authority on its website mentions that "to be inside the AEAT allows the customs to be connected with investigations on property and assets that could have its origins in a predicate offence and that constitutes an money laundering offence, or

As mentioned above,[340] under art. 45.4(a) and (b) AML Law one of the tasks of the FIU is the duty to bring proceedings that derive from reasonable grounds to suspect money laundering crimes or breaches of AML preventive measures by obliged entities before the "competent administrative authorities".[341] The customs authorities are a normal administrative authority as part of the Tax Agency, so, in principle, it may be concluded that the FIU could share information with them. However, again, there is a need for further clarification on this issue.

2. *From Customs Authorities to FIU*

SEPBLAC receives direct reports on inbound/outbound cross-border transport of currency and bearer negotiable instruments above EUR 10,000 (art. 34 AML Law)[342] from customs agents. In addition, according to the FATF, officers from the customs administration work within SEPBLAC in an arrangement that facilitates cooperation and information exchange between the two bodies.[343]

F. INFORMATION FLOW BETWEEN FIU AND FOREIGN COUNTERPARTS

1. *Restrictions on Data Transfer from FIU to Foreign FIUs*

According to art. 48 *bis*.3 AML Law, the exchange of information between SEPBLAC and FIUs from EU Member States shall follow arts. 51–57 4AMLD, as modified by the 5AMLD. In summary, the 4AMLD foresees maximum cooperation between EU Member States. A refusal to exchange information is an exceptional circumstance, in cases where the exchange could be contrary to fundamental principles of national law.

Nevertheless, some restrictions on data transfer may apply. The information shall be used only for the purpose for which the information was sought or provided. Moreover, the transmitting FIU may impose restrictions and

---

that could justify the confiscation of illicit gains". See http://www.investigacionaduanerafiscal.es/bienvenida/. The FATF explains that customs authorities are located within the Tax Agency in Spain, and that the customs surveillance authorities have "exclusive jurisdiction over issues involving foreign trade (cargo movements in and out of Spain, including those made by planes and lorries, with countries that are not part of the Customs Territory of the European Union)", and that the customs surveillance authorities are authorised to investigate and pursue certain crimes, and are also part of the judicial police. FATF, *Mutual Evaluation Report – Spain*, 2014, p. 34.

340 See *supra* section V.B.1.

341 See http://www.cpbc.tesoro.es/la-comision.

342 FATF, *Mutual Evaluation Report – Spain*, 2014, p. 47.

343 Ibid., p. 50.

conditions for the use of the information provided, through a method of "previous authorisation". The sending FIU restricts the exchange of information to the pre-established purposes or limits and the receiving FIU shall comply with those restrictions and ask for the consent of the sending FIU to disseminate the data. Nevertheless, the sending FIU may only refuse permission if the use of the information would go beyond AML purposes and if the dissemination could lead to the impairment of a criminal investigation.

On the other hand, the exchange of data between the Spanish FIU and third countries shall follow the principles set out by the Egmont Group[344] and the memorandum of understanding between FIUs. As regards data protection rules, Principle 32 of the Egmont Group[345] states that the exchanged data shall be used only for the purpose for which the information was sought or provided.

On another note, art. 37 AML Law mentions that beyond the information regarding suspicion of money laundering, the FIU may share with the competent authorities of other countries data obtained in Spain by the FIU from the declaration of means of payment and the seizure of means of payment by customs authorities. Nonetheless, more clarification is needed in Spanish law regarding the limits of the transfer of this type of information.

2. *Restrictions on Use of Data Obtained from Foreign FIUs*

Art. 48 *bis*.5 AML establishes that the FIU may only use the information received for the purposes to which the providing authorities have consented. Furthermore, art. 48 *bis* AML Law makes clear reference to the principles of the Egmont Group and to the 4AMLD for the restrictions on the use of data shared between FIUs.

Both art. 55(1) 4AMLD (as modified by the 5AMLD) and the aforementioned Principle 32 of the Egmont Group establish that the information may be exchanged under strict limitations, *only* for the purpose for which the information was sought or provided, i.e. prevention or investigation of money laundering. Art. 55(1) 4AMLD (referred by art. 48 *bis* AML Law) states that the requesting FIU shall ask for the prior consent of the providing FIU to use the information for purposes beyond those originally approved.

Still, under the general guidance of the Principles of the Egmont Group, the requesting FIU shall disclose to the providing FIU "the reason for the request, and to the extent possible the purpose for which the information will be used and provide enough information to enable the FIU receiving the request to provide information lawfully".

344 Available at https://egmontgroup.org/en/document-library/8.

345 The Egmont Group is a united body of 159 FIUs, which "provides a platform for the secure exchange of expertise and financial intelligence to combat ML".

The Egmont Group Principles underline that both FIUs must have similar data protection standards. If the foreign FIU cannot protect the information adequately, the providing FIU may refuse to share it.[346] Finally, the Egmont Principles state that the cooperation may also be refused if there is a lack of reciprocity or recurring inadequate cooperation.

G. INFORMATION FLOW BETWEEN FIU AND FOREIGN NON-COUNTERPARTS

1. *Restrictions on Data Transfer from FIU to Other Foreign Authorities*

According to art. 37 AML Law, information obtained from the declaration of means of payment and the seizure of means of payment by customs authorities obtained in Spain by the FIU may be transferred to the competent authorities of other countries. However, the AML Law does not specify who the foreign competent authority is. Since this article of the AML Law is placed in the chapter regarding "Means of Payment", and not mentioned in the chapters dedicated to cooperation, it may be concluded that the FIU could share information regarding means of payment with other foreign authorities, in diagonal cooperation.

Moreover, if there is any suspicion of fraud or of any other illegal activity that affects the interests of the EU, the FIU shall forward the information to the European Commission.[347]

Outside the AML Law, guidance on data exchange can be found in the Egmont Group Principles. Paragraph 18 of the Principles states that "FIUs may decide to exchange information indirectly with non-counterparts in response to requests from competent authorities". In that sense, since art. 48 *bis* AML Law expressly adopts the Egmont Group Principles (even though only referring to them regarding the exchange of information between FIUs outside the EU), it could be concluded that SEPBLAC *may* share data with non-counterparts at least within the same limits as those imposed on data sharing between the Spanish FIU and non-European counterparts.

According to the FATF, Spain has signed several Memoranda of Understanding with non-EU countries establishing international cooperation between law enforcement agencies and FIUs.[348]

---

346 Principle no. 27 of the Egmont Group of Financial Intelligence Units Principles for Information Exchange between Financial Intelligence Units, p. 6. Available at https://egmontgroup.org/en/document-library/8.

347 To this effect, the European Commission is represented by OLAF: the European Commission Anti-fraud Office. See https://ec.europa.eu/anti-fraud/home_en.

348 As mentioned in the FATF's Report, Spain has signed specific Memoranda of Understanding with countries in North Africa and the Maghreb, Latin America and Asia to counter specific money laundering and terrorism financing threats originating in certain countries. FATF, *Mutual Evaluation Report – Spain*, 2014, p. 131.

2. *Restrictions on Use of Data Obtained from Other Foreign Authorities*

There is no specific rule in the AML Law about the use of data obtained from foreign authorities. Nevertheless, art. 48 *bis*.5 AML Law mentions that the FIU may only use the information received for the purposes that the "providing authorities" have permitted. In that sense, it may be concluded that the same restrictions on the information sent by foreign FIUs shall apply to the data shared by foreign authorities.[349]

Moreover, according to the general principles of the 4AMLD (art. 55) and the Egmont Group Principles (paragraph 32) mentioned in art. 48 *bis*.3 and 4 AML Law, there is, in principle, purpose limitation regarding the use of the data exchanged. Moreover, according to the Egmont Group, the providing foreign authority may impose limits on the use of the shared data.

H. EVIDENTIAL VALUE OF FIU-GENERATED DATA IN COURT PROCEEDINGS

According to art. 46 AML Law, the financial intelligence reports sent from the FIU to the competent authorities will have *no* evidential value and cannot be directly used in trial and pre-trial judicial proceedings.

On the other hand, the inspection reports carried out by the FIU on the obliged entities – in the fulfilment of its supervisory function – will have evidential value for sanctioning purposes; furthermore, evidence contained in these reports may be cited by the interested parties in defence of their rights or interests (art. 47 AML Law).

In practice, most of the financial intelligence reports produced by the FIU are forwarded to the police and trigger an investigation from the police authorities. On that basis, the criminal justice authorities proceed to complement the financial intelligence report with their own investigations. Later on, if they have a strong suspicion of money laundering, the result is forwarded to the Public Prosecutor's Office. As a consequence, the law enforcement agencies have to follow criminal procedural law to use the information from the financial intelligence reports, and the latter shall not be used directly as evidence in judicial proceedings.

I. USE OF CDD DATA FOR PROFIT MAKING

Under art. 60 Decree 304/2014, obliged entities can only use data gathered through CDD measures for specific purposes related to prevention of money

---

349 See *supra* section V.F.2.

laundering. Thus, they are not allowed to use the information for any other purposes, unless the processing of such data is necessary for the normal management of the business relationship. It is, however, doubtful what "normal management" means, since it could coincide with the commercial purpose of the obliged entity, and the law would forbid this.

Spanish banks use the data generated by their clients' use of financial products (money transfers, payments, etc.) to create patterns of consumption to sell to companies.[350] The data is anonymised and aggregated in software made available for use via a subscription. Given that the service concentrates on consumption patterns, it may be inferred that the information gathered through CDD measures is not used, since that data is not necessary to identify such patterns.

J. DATA SHARING BETWEEN OBLIGED ENTITIES REGARDING SARS AND FIU REQUESTS

In principle, art. 24.2 AML Law does not differentiate between data sharing in relation to SARs, transactions under evaluation or transactions that "may be evaluated in the future". It is clear, however, that the data refers to suspicious transactions. On this basis, data sharing between obliged entities mentioned in this section relates to SARs and suspicious transactions that could lead to an SAR.[351]

1. *Data Sharing Inside a Group*

In a general way, art. 24.2(a) AML Law allows the disclosure that an SAR was filed with the FIU between *financial entities* belonging to the same group.[352] Given that groups shall adopt, at a minimum, Spanish AML preventive standards

350 Bank Santander offers a service called "Mi Comercio", which helps business managers to identify the patterns of its clients (time of the day and day of the week, amount spent, means of payment used, etc.). See https://www.bancosantander.es/es/empresas/banca-online/apps/mi-comercio-santander.

351 According to the Proposal to transpose the 5AMLD, obliged entities may delegate the administration of the database that is used to share data with other obliged entities. In this case, the parties responsible for developing or running the system used for sharing information shall carry out a data protection impact assessment of the processing operations in question with a view to adopting enhanced technical and organisational measures to guarantee the integrity, confidentiality and availability of personal data. These measures must in any case ensure the traceability of access to and communication of the data (art. 33.2). Proposal available at: https://www.mineco.gob.es/stfls/mineco/ministerio/participacion_publica/audiencia/ficheros/ECO_TES_20200612_AP_V_Directiv_Blanqueo.pdf.

352 The concept of a "group" is defined in art. 42 Spanish Commercial Code as follows: "A group exists when a society exercises or may exercise, directly or indirectly, control over others".

across the entire group (art. 26.3 AML Law), the disclosure of information is only allowed between obliged entities domiciled inside the EU or located in third countries with similar data protection regulations.[353]

In particular, the group's internal monitoring bodies shall have unrestricted access to any information held by the subsidiaries and branches needed for the performance of their duties for the prevention of money laundering. The parameters and rules for this internal information exchange shall be described in the company's internal manual on money laundering prevention (art. 36.2 Decree 304/2014).

2. *Data Sharing with Similar Professions*

Spain allows auditors, external accountants, tax advisers and notaries – acting within the same legal person or in a network[354] – to share information regarding the filing of SARs or suspicious transactions, provided that they belong to the same professional category and are subject to equivalent obligations as regards professional secrecy and personal data protection (art. 24.1 *c* AML Law).

Outside of the privileged professions, when extraordinary risks are identified according to the typologies and recommendations of the Financial Intelligence Committee,[355] obliged entities *outside* the group, but *within a similar profession*, may disclose information under the strict circumstances detailed by art. 61.2 Decree 304/2014:

(a) when they refrain from undertaking the client's transaction and file an SAR; and
(b) when they have a reasonable suspicion that the client may try the same operation in a similar or identical manner with another obliged entity;
(c) they shall share the information only through shared files.

The creation of the aforementioned shared files requires the authorisation of CPMLMO, which shall first consult the Spanish Data Protection Agency. The obliged entities may request the creation of the file directly through their representative professional bodies (art. 61.2 Decree 304/2014).

---

353 The countries that Spain considers as having equivalent data protection standards are: Andorra, Argentina, Canada, Faroe Islands, Guernsey, Isle of Man, Israel, Jersey, New Zealand, Switzerland, Uruguay and the USA. The list is available at the website of the Spanish Data Protection Agency: https://www.aepd.es/reglamento/cumplimiento/transferencias-internacionales.html.

354 For these purposes, a network shall mean the larger structure to which a person belongs and which shares common ownership, management or compliance control.

355 According to art. 65.1(i) Decree 304/2014, the Financial Intelligence Committee of CPMLMO is responsible for creating and approving guidelines and typologies regarding money laundering transactions, after receiving proposals from the FIU. See *supra* section IV.A.1.

If all the previous conditions are fulfilled, the information shall be added to a centralised fraud prevention file created by the obliged entities, only accessible by the persons responsible for the internal monitoring body (art. 33.4 AML Law). Access to the centralised common files is also restricted to those obliged entities that could be exposed to the same specific threat of money laundering (art. 61.2, d Decree 304/2014), and shall be limited to the extent necessary for the fulfilment of their duties regarding preventing money laundering.

3. *Data Sharing with Obliged Entities Outside the EU*

Under art. 24.2 AML Law,[356] financial institutions inside the same group are allowed to disclose information when carrying out their activities within EU member states or in third countries "with equivalent standards". The AML Law does not specify, however, when the equivalent standards from third countries refer to AML[357] or data protection standards. Nevertheless, a broader understanding of the AML Law and Decree[358] allow the conclusion that the Law points to equivalent standards regarding *data protection*.[359]

Moreover, if a third country does not offer an adequate level of data protection, the obliged entities need to request a special authorisation from the Data Protection Agency to proceed with the data sharing (art. 36 Decree 304/2014).

Outside of the financial sector, other Spanish obliged entities may exchange data with entities outside the EU if the destination country is listed as having the same data protection standards. Otherwise, the obliged entity shall request an authorisation from the Data Protection Agency.

K. DATA SHARING BETWEEN OBLIGED ENTITIES REGARDING POSSIBLE CASES OF MONEY LAUNDERING

1. *Data Sharing Inside a Group*

As mentioned above,[360] art. 24.2(a) AML Law does not make a distinction between data sharing regarding SARs, transactions under evaluation and

356 See *supra* section V.J.1.

357 According to art. 1.4 AML Law, equivalent third countries are those states, territories or jurisdictions so determined by the Commission for the Prevention of Money Laundering and Monetary Offences due to their having established equivalent requirements to those of Spanish law.

358 In this context, arts. 26 and 31.1 AML Law determines that obliged entities must ensure that all of the group has AML preventive measures according to the standards set by Spanish AML Law. On this basis, one can conclude that the information sharing inside the group already takes place in an environment with the same AML standards.

359 See note 351.

360 See *supra* section V.J.

transactions that "may be evaluated in the future", so one must assume that the sharing of information beyond the filing of an SAR is permissible, even if the information does not ultimately give rise to an SAR.

2. *Data Sharing with Similar Professions*

Firstly, as mentioned above,[361] art. 24.2(b) of the AML Law allows similar categories of obliged persons listed in the Law – e.g. lawyers and notaries[362] – to exchange information amongst themselves regarding possible cases of money laundering. The main precondition to exchange information in the case of an extraordinary risk of money laundering is to file an SAR (art. 61.1 Decree 304/2014). In addition, they shall have a reasonable suspicion that the client may try the same operation in a similar or identical manner with another obliged entity. If these two conditions are fulfilled, the obliged entity may exchange data within similar professions after authorisation from CPMLMO, which should first consult the Data Protection Agency.

More specifically, after the above-mentioned authorisation from the CPMLMO, art. 33.1 AML Law allows financial institutions and legal professionals to share information that is "different" from the fact that an SAR was filed or a suspicious transaction found, but it does not specify what this information might be. Therefore, it can be concluded that it includes the exchange of personal data and less sensitive information regarding clients and transactions[363] (such as the class of operation and the category or type of clients in terms of their risk levels), but the law is not clear in this respect.

Finally, the exchange of information within similar professions shall take place through shared files with prior authorisation from the Data Protection Agency.[364]

3. *Data Sharing with Obliged Entities Outside the EU*

On this see *supra*, section V.J.3.

L. DATA MINING BY OBLIGED ENTITIES

As a general matter, the AML Law does not specify data mining powers of obliged entities, thus the general rules of art. 21 of the GDPR should apply.

---

361 See *supra* section V.J.1.
362 See *supra* section V.J.2.
363 Aliaga Méndez, "Normativa comentada de prevención del blanqueo de capitales", *La Ley*, 2010, p. 269.
364 See *supra* section V.J.2.

The main database of obliged entities in Spain is the Single Computerised Index of the College of Notaries.[365] According to the College of Notaries, it is the second-biggest database in Spain, after the database of the Tax Agency. The College of Notaries combines within a single database all the information collected as part of the exercise of its functions, with an exception made for last wills. As a result, the Index contains information on 390 different kinds of notarial acts, such as selling and buying of real estate (location, use and size of the estate, method and means of payment used, taxes collected, register of former owners, the e-mails addresses of the buyers and sellers, etc.), founding of companies, identification of legal persons, historical registry of company owners, incorporation of companies owned by foreign-based legal entities, borrowings, mortgages, endorsements of debts, etc. The Index also contains the largest list of PEPs in Spain.

Besides the general Index, containing all the above-mentioned information, there are satellite databases, with the task of checking double entries in the system and bringing them together under a single reference (because the same person can have transactions registered with their passport, national resident's ID and national ID; in principle, different IDs appear in the Index as different people, so the satellite databases process and bring this information together under a separate entry for further consultation). If one notary communicates a suspicious transaction to the OCP (supervisory body for notaries), the members of the OCP may consult the Index to look for further information about the person or company that is the subject of the communication. Moreover, the Index has the capacity to carry out data mining itself, using the 28 typologies developed and updated for the functioning of the software. According to the requests received (from the police, tax authorities, FIU, obliged entities, etc.), the software generates a spreadsheet with the information, whose scope will be limited by the purpose of the information request.

VI. BENEFICIAL OWNERSHIP TRANSPARENCY

A. BENEFICIAL OWNERSHIP INFORMATION

1. *General Framework*

In Spain, there are two forms of anonymous company ownership: joint stock companies[366] and private limited companies,[367] which shall keep a record

365 More general information can be found in the website of the Single Computerised Index: http://www.notariado.org/liferay/web/notariado/e-notario/indice-unico.

366 Regulated by art. 41 ff. of the Venture Capital Company Law (Royal Decree 1/2010).

367 These are companies created with one up to the maximum of 50 bearers, which must invest a minimum of €3,000 in cash, rights or property, to create a legal entity. Art. 4 Venture Capital Company Law (Royal Decree 1/2010).

of the legal ownership of shares and registered shares. Art. 94 of the Market Shares Law[368] foresees that the buyer of bearer shares acquires "ownership" after the registration of the securities accounts in its name.

Nevertheless, it is the AML legislation[369] that introduces the concept of beneficial ownership[370] in Spanish law. Thus, the AML Law (art. 4) deals with beneficial ownership as a CDD matter under the responsibility of obliged entities and defines it according to the effective control or, in the absence of this information, it points to the legal entity's board of directors or manager,[371] as detailed in the following section.

The AML Law is silent regarding how these obligations differ depending on the subject's nationality, so it may be concluded that the duty to disclose the beneficial ownership applies equally to citizens and domestic entities, as well as legal entities incorporated in the country and legal arrangements administered in the territory. As an exception, companies on the stock market are exempted from declaring their beneficial owner (art. 9.4 Decree 304/2014).

2. *Definition of "Beneficiary" and "Effective Control"*

Art. 4.2 AML Law and art. 8 Decree 304/2014 define the beneficiary in a corporate entity the one who has "effective control" of it.[372] This could be: (i) the natural person(s) on whose behalf a business relationship is to be established or a transaction conducted; or (ii) the natural person(s) who ultimately own or control, directly or indirectly, more than 25% of the share capital or voting rights of a legal person, or who through agreements or statutory provisions or other means exercise direct or indirect control in the management of a legal person (art. 8 Decree 304/2014).

The criteria in the European Directive on Annual Financial Statements[373] provides indicators about the control, such as a majority of shareholders, the

---

368 Royal Decree 4/2016, of 26 October 2016.

369 In fact, the College of Notaries created a guide to inform small and medium-sized companies about the meaning of beneficial ownership and the duties set out by the AML Law. See https://www.notariabierta.es/guia-teorico-practica-titularidad-real-i/.

370 One detail regarding the translation of the term "beneficial ownership" into the AML Law that may lead to confusion should be noted. Art. 4 AML Law adopted the term *titular real*, which means "real bearer" and does not exactly translate the sense of the owner who receives the benefits of the company. As a consequence, national jurisprudence on *titular real* frequently refers to simulated contracts and frauds, and not to beneficial ownership.

371 See *infra* section VI.A.1.b.

372 For details of the FATF's recommendations on beneficial ownership, see *FATF Guidance: Transparency and beneficial ownership*, 2014, http://www.fatf-gafi.org/media/fatf/documents/reports/Guidance-transparency-beneficial-ownership.pdf.

373 Directive 2013/34/EU of the European Parliament and of the Council of 26 June 2013 on the annual financial statements, consolidated financial statements and related reports of certain types of undertakings. Art. 22 (requirement to prepare consolidated financial statements) reads:

right to appoint or remove a majority of the members of the administrative body, or having authority over a subsidiary company, if mother and subsidiary company are under the direction of another mother company.

If no natural person has direct or indirect control over more than 25% of the shares of the legal entity, or in any other way exercises control over the company, the managers or directors shall be considered the beneficial owners. Where the

---

"1. A Member State shall require any undertaking governed by its national law to draw up consolidated financial statements and a consolidated management report if that undertaking (a parent undertaking): (a) has a majority of the shareholders' or members' voting rights in another undertaking (a subsidiary undertaking); (b) has the right to appoint or remove a majority of the members of the administrative, management or supervisory body of another undertaking (a subsidiary undertaking) and is at the same time a shareholder in or member of that undertaking; (c) has the right to exercise a dominant influence over an undertaking (a subsidiary undertaking) of which it is a shareholder or member, pursuant to a contract entered into with that undertaking or to a provision in its memorandum or articles of association, where the law governing that subsidiary undertaking permits its being subject to such contracts or provisions. A Member State need not prescribe that a parent undertaking must be a shareholder in or member of its subsidiary undertaking. Those Member States the laws of which do not provide for such contracts or clauses shall not be required to apply this provision; or (d) is a shareholder in or member of an undertaking, and: (i) a majority of the members of the administrative, management or supervisory bodies of that undertaking (a subsidiary undertaking) who have held office during the financial year, during the preceding financial year and up to the time when the consolidated financial statements are drawn up, have been appointed solely as a result of the exercise of its voting rights; or (ii) controls alone, pursuant to an agreement with other shareholders in or members of that undertaking (a subsidiary undertaking), a majority of shareholders' or members' voting rights in that undertaking. The Member States may introduce more detailed provisions concerning the form and contents of such agreements. Member States shall prescribe at least the arrangements referred to in point (ii). They may subject the application of point (i) to the requirement that the voting rights represent at least 20% of the total. However, point (i) shall not apply where a third party has the rights referred to in points (a), (b) or (c) with regard to that undertaking. 2. In addition to the cases mentioned in paragraph 1, Member States may require any undertaking governed by their national law to draw up consolidated financial statements and a consolidated management report if: (a) that undertaking (a parent undertaking) has the power to exercise, or actually exercises, dominant influence or control over another undertaking (the subsidiary undertaking); or (b) that undertaking (a parent undertaking) and another undertaking (the subsidiary undertaking) are managed on a unified basis by the parent undertaking. 3. For the purposes of points (a), (b) and (d) of paragraph 1, the voting rights and the rights of appointment and removal of any other subsidiary undertaking as well as those of any person acting in his own name but on behalf of the parent undertaking or of another subsidiary undertaking shall be added to those of the parent undertaking. 4. For the purposes of points (a), (b) and (d) of paragraph 1, the rights mentioned in paragraph 3 shall be reduced by the rights: (a) attaching to shares held on behalf of a person who is neither the parent undertaking nor a subsidiary of that parent undertaking; or (b) attaching to shares: (i) held by way of security, provided that the rights in question are exercised in accordance with the instructions received, or (ii) held in connection with the granting of loans as part of normal business activities, provided that the voting rights are exercised in the interests of the person providing the security. 5. For the purposes of points (a) and (d) of paragraph 1, the total of the shareholders' or members' voting rights in the subsidiary undertaking shall be reduced by the voting rights attaching to the shares held by that undertaking itself, by a subsidiary undertaking of that undertaking or by a person acting in his own name but on behalf of those undertakings."

manager is another legal entity, the beneficial owner shall be the manager (natural person) appointed in the managing legal entity (art. 8 Decree 304/2014).

On the other hand, art. 4.2 AML Law defines beneficial owners in trusts or other similar legal entities as: (i) the settlor; (ii) the trustee(s); (iii) the protector, if any; (iv) the beneficiaries, or where the individuals benefiting from the legal arrangement or entity have yet to be determined, the class of persons in whose main interest the legal arrangement or entity is set up or operates; or (v) any other natural person exercising ultimate control over the trust by means of direct or indirect ownership or by different means.

For foundations and associations, the beneficial owners shall be those natural persons who own or control 25% or more of the voting rights of the board (in the case of a foundation) or of the representative body (in an association). Where there is no natural person(s) who meet these criteria, the board members and, in the case of associations, the members of the representative body or board shall be deemed the beneficial owners (art. 8(c) Decree 304/2014).

3. *Definition of "Information"*

Spanish law does not have a precise definition of the term "information" in the context of beneficial ownership. Nevertheless, art. 9.5 Decree 304/2014 mentions that information is the data necessary to establish the identity of the beneficial owner.[374]

4. *Special Rules for Entities with a Cross-Border Dimension*

The Spanish legislation on companies with a cross-border dimension does not have special rules for companies operating within the European Union: the same registration rules apply to national and European companies.

On the other hand, in the case of companies operating outside the European Union, Spain requires that they be registered in the country before they are allowed to operate at a national level[375] (art. 300 Mercantile Registry Law[376]).

---

374 Nevertheless, the reform proposal of Decree 304/2014, with no prospect of being approved sooner, would foresee a reform of art. 9.5 of the Decree. Art. 9.5 would add that the information regarding the identification of beneficial owner should include the ID number, nationality, country of residency and date of birth, as well as the nature of the interest or participation which determine the recognition of a person as a beneficial owner. (The proposal can still be found on some websites and is available at http://www.tesoro.es/sites/default/files/audiencia_e_informacion_publica_del_proyecto_de_real_decreto_de_modificacion_del_reglamento.pdf.).

375 The World Bank ranked Spain's regulation on the establishment of a company by a foreigner or a cross-border company among the most demanding in Europe. Spain is 86th out of 186 countries in the World Bank's ranking regarding the difficulty of creating a company. Available at https://datos.bancomundial.org/indicator/IC.REG.PROC?name_desc=false&view=chart.

376 Law no. 1784/1996.

Foreign companies shall declare their registered office, their activities, the identity of their permanent representatives, with a clear indication of their faculties and powers, the identity of the legal entity outside the country, and the identity of their managers, indicating the position they hold in the company (art. 297 Mercantile Registry Law).

There is no particular requirement for foreign nationals or entities in terms of the procedure for identifying the beneficial owner, but Spain does have special regulations for trusts that operate in the country. Trusts and any similar legal arrangements must disclose the constituent document of the trust to the obliged entities. The obliged entities then shall identify and take appropriate measures to verify the "identity of the settler, the trustees, the protector, the beneficiaries or types of beneficiaries and of any other individual who exercises ultimate effective control over the trust, even if through a chain of control or ownership. For beneficiaries designated based on features or types, the required information must be obtained to establish the beneficiary's identity at the time of payment or when the beneficiary intends to exercise rights conferred" (art. 9.5 Decree 304/2014).

Art. 9.1 Decree 304/2014 also introduces a direct obligation on trustees (of express trusts) to disclose to obliged entities their status as such when opening a business relationship or executing wire transfers for an amount exceeding €1,000 or performing other occasional transactions exceeding €15,000.

B. BENEFICIAL OWNERSHIP REGISTRIES

1. *Scope and General Procedure*

There are two categories of anonymous companies in Spanish mercantile law: joint-stock companies (*sociedad anonima*, SA)[377] and limited liability companies (*sociedad limitada*, SL), both of which must declare their beneficial ownership.

Currently, Spain has two different beneficial ownership registries: one with the Central Mercantile Registry, created in 2018, and the beneficial ownership database of the College of Notaries (the OCP[378]).

---

377 Regulated by art. 41 ff. of the Venture Capital Company Law (Royal Decree 1/2010).

378 The duplication of registers gave rise to a lawsuit proposed by the College of Notaries against the competence of the Mercantile Registrar to collect beneficial ownership information. The College of Notaries argued that it would give rise to a duplication and possible contradiction of information and the violation of privacy rights (given the public character of the mercantile registries), and that the College of Notaries should be the ones responsible for the centralised database, given its expertise and more extensive database. The National High Court decided preliminarily against the petition from the College of Notaries, maintaining the validity of Order JUS/319/2018, but a final decision is still pending (Sentence from the High Court – Audiencia Nacional, Section 3ª, Auto 89/2018 of 28 May 2018, Rec. 427/2018).

The local or Central Mercantile Registries[379] shall register the shares, shareholders and address and statute of private limited and joint-stock companies,[380] as well as, since 2018, data regarding the beneficial ownership of such companies. In 2018, Order JUS/319/2018, of 21 March established that every company registered in Spain or that reports annual accounts in the country shall declare to the Mercantile Registry its beneficial ownership along with its yearly accounts. The Order provides online forms to help companies report the natural person(s) who own more than 25% of the company and the details of companies in the chain of command.[381]

Moreover, the CNMV registers information on shareholders or persons controlling public companies.[382] The Spanish Securities Market Law[383] requires the recording of holdings of negotiable securities in a depository institution (i.e. Iberclear[384] or an investment firm, subject to AML supervision).

As mentioned above,[385] however, it is the AML Law which introduces the mandatory declaration of beneficial ownership in Spain. In accordance with the AML Law (art. 4), the College of Notaries created a beneficial ownership database in 2012. The database collects beneficial ownership data from limited liability companies for the purposes of preventing money laundering, although it still does not include the registers of joint-stock companies, which are held by the CNMV or the Mercantile Registry. Nevertheless, limited liability companies represent almost 90% of Spanish companies.

The Single Computerised Index[386] manages this database, and the OCP of the College of Notaries, in its role as a supervisory body (art. 44.2(c) Decree 304/2014), has full access to the information stored in it. The database contains the identification of beneficial owners of new Spanish companies and other companies that have an act before a notary, such as changes to the board of directors or the company's capital, transfers of shares in limited liability companies, etc. The information is generally reliable, accurate and up-to-date.[387]

The database, which is integrated into the Index, offers two levels of information: (i) the beneficial ownership information obtained by the individual notary in carrying out standard CDD requirements; and (ii) for limited liability

---

379 See http://www.rmc.es/.

380 Regulated by art. 9 ff. of the Venture Capital Company Law (Royal Decree 1/2010).

381 See https://www.boe.es/diario_boe/txt.php?id=BOE-A-2018-4243.

382 See https://www.cnmv.es/Portal/quees/Funciones/ValSocEmisor.aspx.

383 Decree 4/2015, of 23 October 2015, which unifies dispositions regarding Securities Market Law.

384 Iberclear is the Spanish Central Securities Depository and a subsidiary of Bolsas y Mercados Españoles (BME), the operator of all stock markets and financial systems in Spain. See: http://www.iberclear.es/ing/Home.

385 See *supra* section IV.A.1.a.

386 See http://www.notariado.org/liferay/web/notariado/e-notario/indice-unico.

387 FATF, *Mutual Evaluation Report – Spain*, 2014, p. 14.

companies (SL), the beneficial ownership information obtained through aggregating the information on successive transfers of shares.[388]

Nevertheless, according to a Proposal for the transposition of the 5AMLD, the rules on Beneficial Ownership will be substantially altered in the coming reform of the AML Law. The Proposal provides for a Beneficial Ownership Registry under the Ministry of Justice, which will obtain information directly from companies, foundations and associations obliged to declare their beneficial owner. These entities will provide the obliged entities and the Registry with detailed information regarding the beneficial ownership. All natural persons who have the status of beneficial owners will be required to supply this information immediately to the Beneficial Ownership Registry, as soon as they become aware of this fact.[389]

2. Ex Ante *Verification of Accuracy*

The collection of beneficial ownership information by notaries and registrars relies on the client's declaration and the history of the company. In addition, software from the Single Computerised Index is used to work out the data match to calculate the beneficial ownership.

There are no specific legal mechanisms to ensure the accuracy of declarations by customers, or of the records held by companies on beneficial ownership, nor penalties for providing false or incomplete information or, lastly, in cases where the company fails to maintain accurate information on its beneficial ownership. Finaly, according to a Proposal for the transposition of the 5AMLD, the Beneficial Ownership Registry will be responsible for the verification of accuracy of the information provided by the legal entities, those required to provide information may be held accountable if they fail to do so.[390]

3. *Ex Post Review of Accuracy*

The Spanish legislation does not provide for any procedure to verify the accuracy of beneficial ownership information after it has been fed into the Mercantile Registries or the Single Computerised Index.

---

388 Ibid., p. 121.

389 Art. 4 bis of the Proposal, available at: https://www.mineco.gob.es/stfls/mineco/ministerio/participacion_publica/audiencia/ficheros/ECO_TES_20200612_AP_V_Directiv_Blanqueo.pdf.

390 According to the Proposal, the beneficial ownership information shall be kept up-to-date, as applicable, by the sole administrator or joint administrators, by the board of directors, its chairman, and, in particular, the secretary of the board of directors, whether or not they are a director, and by the owners of the association's governing body. Proposal available at: https://www.mineco.gob.es/stfls/mineco/ministerio/participacion_publica/audiencia/ficheros/ECO_TES_20200612_AP_V_Directiv_Blanqueo.pdf.

C. ACCESS TO BENEFICIAL OWNERSHIP INFORMATION

1. *Access by FIU and Other Authorities*

The information contained in the beneficial ownership database of the College of Notaries and the Mercantile Registries is available to all public authorities, such as law enforcement agencies, public prosecutors, the customs authorities and SEBPLAC. All of them have direct, online access via a token system, with results delivered in real time. Other authorities (e.g. the judiciary, the Secretariat of the Commission and the OLAF) may request access to specific information.

For older information, the OCP coordinates the digitalisation of documents from notaries regarding beneficial ownership dating from before 2010, year in which the AML Law required the creation of the beneficial ownership database. Therefore, if the public authorities request beneficial ownership information that is not yet available in the database, the OCP will require the individual notary – the owner of the data – to digitalise it and send to the database, and the OCP shall then forward it to the requesting authority.

The official website of the Single Computerised Index of the College of Notaries states that notaries' offices shall transfer notarised documents to the Index once a fortnight. The information then is forwarded to the following key recipients:

(a) autonomous regions, for notification of operations with tax relevance;
(b) the Directorate-General for the Land Survey, for notification of operations altering the land survey;
(c) local councils and provincial authorities, for notification of operations affecting the municipal property gains tax;
(d) the public registries of commerce, property, foundations, cooperatives, etc., for awareness of a large number of acts related to these organisations (constitutions, extensions, sales, powers, appointments, dismissals, etc.);
(e) the General Council of the Judiciary, for notification of procedural powers granted by notaries and what they involve;
(f) the Tax Agency, for notification on fiscal matters;
(g) notarial colleges, for the administration of the notary colleges themselves.[391]

2. *Access by Obliged Entities*

Under art. 9.6 Decree 304/2014, the beneficial ownership database can be made available to obliged entities to help them carry out their CDD obligations required by art. 8 AML Law, on the basis of an agreement between the obliged

[391] See http://www.notariado.org/liferay/web/notariado/e-notario/indice-unico.

entity and the Colleges of Notaries or Registrars. The aforementioned agreement is signed between the OCP, CRAB and professional representative bodies. In the future, according to a Proposal to transpose the 5AMLD, the obliged entities will also have access to the Beneficial Ownership Registry to be created by the Ministry of Justice.[392]

3. *Access by Interested Third Parties*

Spanish law is silent on the possibility of third parties or the public at large accessing the beneficial ownership information, which leads to the conclusion that such information is not open to the public. As mentioned above, a Proposal to transpose the 5AMLD foresees the creation of the Beneficial Ownership Registry. Besides the public authorities and obliged entities, the general public may only access data consisting of the name and surname, month and year of birth, country of residence and nationality of the current real owners of a legal person or entity or structure without legal personality, as well as information on the nature of such real ownership.[393]

D. NON-FINANCIAL BENEFICIAL OWNERSHIP REGISTRIES

The Spanish AML Law does not mention the need to disclose beneficial ownership information beyond that of legal entities and trusts, such as the beneficial ownership of real estate or bank vaults. Nevertheless, as mentioned above,[394] Order JUS/319/2018, of 21 March, determines that the Mercantile Registry shall collect beneficial ownership information along with the annual accounts declarations. According to art. 16 of the Commerce Code, the Mercantile Registry shall include: (i) individual owners; (ii) mercantile societies; (iii) credit and insurance companies, as well as mutual societies; (iv) collective investment institutions and pension funds; (v) economic interest groups;[395] and (vi) professional civil societies constituted in line with the requirements established in the specific legislation on professional societies. Thus, beyond the aforementioned database of the OCP, the Mercantile Registry collects the non-beneficial ownership information above.

---

392 Art. 4 bis of the Proposal, available at: https://www.mineco.gob.es/stfls/mineco/ministerio/participacion_publica/audiencia/ficheros/ECO_TES_20200612_AP_V_Directiv_Blanqueo.pdf.

393 Additional art. 3 of the Proposal, available at: https://www.mineco.gob.es/stfls/mineco/ministerio/participacion_publica/audiencia/ficheros/ECO_TES_20200612_AP_V_Directiv_Blanqueo.pdf.

394 See *supra* section VI.B.1.

395 These are groups of companies or individuals organised for better coordination to achieve a mutual interest (e.g. consortiums to build aeroplanes or to manage nuclear plants) or to standardise the performance of all associated persons (i.e. providing Visa credit card services). Those companies are regulated by Law no. 12/1991.

VII. SANCTIONS

A. SANCTIONS FOR MONEY LAUNDERING

1. *Requirement of a Conviction for a Predicate Offence*

The criminal definition of money laundering in art. 301 SPC does not require any previous conviction or investigation for the predicate offence.

In addition, it is not necessary that all the factual elements and circumstances relating to the predicate offence be established.[396] A decision from the Spanish Supreme Court summarises the requirements for the proof of the predicate offence: "the illicit origins can be proven through indirect or circumstantial evidence and … the assessment of criminal origins … does not require the identification of concrete criminal operations, provided that criminal activity is sufficiently proven in a general sense".[397]

2. *Forms of Sanctions*

In Spain, both natural and legal entities can be sanctioned for money laundering. For regular money laundering, the sanction ranges from six months to six years, and the aggravated forms of the offence change the minimum sanction. In brief, the criminal conviction of natural persons for money laundering shall lead to the following sanctions (art. 301 SPC):

(a) imprisonment from six months to six years, the minimum sanction rising to two years and nine months in the case of aggravated offences[398] or if the money laundering was committed by members of organised crime;
(b) temporary closure of the business for up to five years, or permanent closure;

In accordance with the seriousness of the crime and the personal circumstances of the perpetrator, the judges or the court *may* impose, additionally, the following sanctions:

(c) a monetary fine of up to three times the amount of the money laundered; or
(d) special disqualification from the exercise of the profession or business from one to three years, the minimum sanction rising to one year and six

[396] Just to refer to some relevant decisions on this topic: STS362/2017, of 19 May 2017; STS 238/2016, of 29 March 2016; STS 699/2015, of 17 November 2015; STS 508/2015, of 27 July 2015; STS 910/2014, of 2 January 2014; STS 801/2010, of 23 September 2010.

[397] STS 974/2012, of 5 December 2012.

[398] See *supra* section II.B.3.

months in the case of aggravated offences[399] or if the money laundering was committed by members of organised crime.

Moreover, aggravated sanctions are provided for particular groups of people. If the money laundering offence is committed by businessmen, financial brokers, state employees, social workers, doctors, psychologists, veterinarians, pharmacists, teachers or professors during the discharge of their duties, sanctions (a)–(c) above will apply, plus special disqualification from the exercise of their profession or from public service or office for three to 10 years (art. 303, first part SPC).

If the money laundering offence is committed by employees of public authorities during the discharge of their duties, sanctions (a)–(c) above will apply, plus special disqualification from the exercise of their profession or from public service or office for 10–20 years (art. 303, second part SPC).

Art. 301.3 SPC establishes a minimum prison sentence of six months to two years for gross negligence money laundering.

Spain also foresees the criminal liability of legal entities (art. 31 *bis* SPC), which can be sanctioned for acts of money laundering. Although this is not a universally accepted interpretation, a possible summary is that Spain has adopted a hybrid system,[400] based firstly on "vicarious liability" as well as on the autonomous liability of the obliged entity. Under vicarious liability, the criminal liability of the legal entity depends on the crime committed by the natural person, making the legal entity accountable for the actions of its directors, managers and people acting on its behalf, as a mean of supplementing the principle of individual liability. For vicarious liability, it is enough that the natural person is prosecuted for the crime; there is no need for a conviction.[401] Vicarious liability also applies in cases where: (i) the perpetrator of the crime cannot be identified; (ii) it was not possible to initiate legal proceedings against him/her; (iii) the person cannot be held accountable because he/she lacks culpability; or (iv) if the person has evaded law enforcement (art. 31 *bis* SPC).

However, there is also the possibility of the autonomous liability of the legal entity (without the incrimination of a natural person) for crimes committed for

---

399 See *supra* section II.B.3.

400 The text of art. 31 *bis* ff. SPC are confusing for a reader not acquainted with the topic and are difficult to interpret. The doctrine, jurisprudence (in favour of autonomous liability, see, for instance, Sentence of the Supreme Court 2ª, no. 668/2017, Rec. 1625/2016) and official guidance of the public prosecutors (Circular no. 1/2016 in favour of vicarious liability) hold different interpretations of the character of the criminal liability of legal entities. The explanation above is a summary of this debate, but it should be noted that this is a topic subject to ongoing interpretation. Gómez Martin, "La responsabilidad penal para personas jurídicas en el Código Penal español: una visión panorámica tras la reforma de 2015", *Revista Aranzadi Doctrinal*, no. 1, 2016.

401 Memento Penal Lefebvre, *Commentary on art. 31 bis, criminal liability of legal entities*, 2015, updated online as at September 2018, no. 3111.

its benefit due to a serious breach in the duties of supervision, surveillance and monitoring. The legal entity is responsible, then, when an organisational failure inside the company is decisive for the commitment of the crime, for instance if the company fails to implement compliance systems and preventive measures against crimes, and creates an environment within the organisation that facilitates people acting on its behalf to commit a crime. However, the crime committed must be in the name of the company or directly or indirectly benefit the company.

It is a commonplace in the Spanish doctrine that the compliance officer's material resources and independence to carry out their role must be guaranteed for the legal entity to be released from responsibility. Theoretically, if the company does not provide the compliance officer with the resources to carry out his/her preventive tasks, the legal entity may be criminally accountable for acts of money laundering committed by its clients. Therefore, the application of the correct preventive measures and the independence of the compliance officer may clear the company from criminal sanctions, passing the responsibility on to the natural person who committed the crime (art. 31 *bis*.1 SPC). In that context, the Public Prosecutor's Office published an interpretative recommendation on art. 31 *bis*.1 SPC (which describes the possible non-criminal liability of legal entities),[402] establishing that the prosecutor will interpret an effective internal compliance system as a sign that the enterprise is free from blame with regard to the crimes committed by its employees or clients.[403]

The criminal sanctions provided for legal entities (art. 33.7 SPC) in the event of the commitment of money laundering offence (art. 302 SPC) are:

(a) fine of six months to two years of daily fines, calculated according to daily fees;[404]
(b) fine of two to five years of daily fines,[405] calculated according to quotes, if the crime committed by the natural person is punishable by more than five years' imprisonment.

Beyond of these sanctions, judges may opt for one or more of the following sanctions (art. 33.7 SPC):

---

402 Circular no. 1/2016 of the Public Prosecutors Head Office.

403 Circular no. 1/2016 from the Public Prosecutors Head Office on the criminal liability of legal entities according the reform of the Penal Code realised by the Organic Law no. 1/2015, which altered the parameters for the sanctioning of legal entities.

404 According to art. 50 SPC, daily fees for legal entities shall vary from €30 to €5,000. After defining the value of the daily fee, the judge determines the number of the days or years of sanction. Judges shall take into consideration the patrimony and economic circumstances of the defendant in establishing the daily quotes (art. 66 SPC).

405 For instance, a maximum criminal fine that a conviction of legal entity can reach is five years of criminal sanctions calculated over the maximum amount of the daily quote (€5,000): 1,825 days (five years) multiplied by €5000 (daily quote), i.e. €9,125,000.

(a) termination of the legal entity;
(b) suspension of its activities for a maximum of five years;
(c) closure of its offices and facilities for a maximum of five years;
(d) prohibition on exercising in the future the activity through which the crime was committed, enabled or hidden; the activity will remain forbidden definitively or for a limited period no longer than 15 years;
(e) disqualification from receiving public subventions and subsidies for a maximum of 15 years;
(f) being subject to judiciary intervention to secure the rights of employees and creditors for a maximum term of five years.

3. *Confiscation*

Confiscation is the auxiliary measure foreseen by art. 127 SPC following a conviction for money laundering under art. 301 SPC. The options include confiscation of the gains originating from the crime, as well as any physical assets that may result from it, following conviction for offences committed with intent or for gross negligence offences with sanctions lasting more than one year. In the case of convictions for reckless money laundering (art. 301.3 SPC), the sanctions range is imprisonment from six months to two years, and so is also subject to the confiscation rule.

The general rule in art. 127 *bis*.1(i) SPC establishes the expanded confiscation[406] of the assets of a person convicted for money laundering when there are signs that they are of illicit origin and the defendant is not able to prove otherwise. The limits of expanded confiscation are the acquisition of the assets by a third party in good faith. However, art. 127 *quarter* SPC foresees that if the person received the property as a donation, bought it for a price lower than the market value, or had reasonable grounds to suspect the illicit origins of the goods, the purchase cannot be considered to be in good faith. Moreover, if the confiscation of the illicit gains is for any reason no longer possible, art. 127.3 SPC foresees the confiscation of other goods of an equivalent value (compensation claim).

4. *Statistics*

a. Number of Criminal Proceedings

According to statistics gathered by CPMLMO, 540 investigations on money laundering were started in 2016, with a total of 334 persons investigated, and 49 conviction decisions.[407] CPMLMO does not provide statistics on the origin

406 Memento Penal Lefebvre, *Commentary on art. 31 bis, criminal liability of legal entities*, 2015, updated online as at September 2018, no. 12242.

407 Commission for the Prevention of Money Laundering and Monetary Offences, *Memoria de Información Estadística 2012–2016*, p. 40, http://www.cpbc.tesoro.es/sites/default/files/memoria_estadistica_2012-2016_def.pdf.

of the proceedings (SAR or another origin) or on the individual value of transactions associated with these proceedings.

In the same year, 2016, financial intelligence reports from SEPBLAC triggered 37 investigations into money laundering and 182 investigations into predicate offences.

SEPBLAC contributed to 341 ongoing judicial proceedings on money laundering and predicate offences by drawing up financial intelligence reports following requests from the police authorities. Moreover, 992 ongoing investigations on money laundering and predicate offences made use of reports from SEPBLAC.

Of the 4,039 financial intelligence reports received by all police authorities in 2016, 243 cases had results directly connected to the FIU report, leading to 1,684 provisional detentions in police operations related to reports from the FIU.[408]

However, there is no official information available on the value of transactions associated with each SAR, nor about the precise outcome of such reports. But all in all, the result is considered adequate by the FATF Mutual Evaluation Report, which states that "the vast majority of SEPBLAC's analysis is actionable (either initiate investigations or support existing ones)".[409]

b. Number of Convictions

CPMLMO's statistics from 2016 report that 192 persons were convicted of money laundering that year.[410] However, there is no information available on whether the convictions were the result of an SAR or another source. Also in 2016, €5,286,430 in cash or other means of payment, 71 real estate properties (houses, warehouses, parking lots, etc.), 13 vehicles and 36 horses were confiscated.[411]

B. SANCTIONS FOR VIOLATIONS OF PREVENTIVE MEASURES

1. *Money Laundering by Violating Preventive Obligations*

Spanish law does not provide a specific criminal provision on the violation of preventive obligations.

---

408 Ibid., p. 83.

409 FATF, *Mutual Evaluation Report – Spain*, 2014.

410 Commission for the Prevention of Money Laundering and Monetary Offences, *Memoria de Información Estadística 2012–2016*, p. 41, http://www.cpbc.tesoro.es/sites/default/files/memoria_estadistica_2012-2016_def.pdf.

411 Ibid., p. 53.

2. *CDD, Reporting and Other AML-Related Obligations*

a. Special Criminal Laws against Individuals

Spanish law does not provide for criminal sanctions against individuals for a violation of AML due diligence obligations, whether for a violation of AML reporting obligations or any violation of other AML-related obligations.

b. Administrative Sanctions against Individuals

The AML Law foresees sanctions for obliged entities as natural or legal persons. If the obliged entity is a legal person, art. 54 AML states that it is the legal person that will primarily be sanctions. Nevertheless, art. 54 AML also foresees the imposition of administrative sanctions on the obliged entity's directors or managers (whether individually or as part of a collegiate body), as well as on external experts[412] if the company's violation of the obligations in the AML Law can be attributed to their wilful or negligent misconduct (derived liability).

According to art. 51.1(a) AML Law, failure to fulfil the reporting duty (file an SAR) when a director or employee of the obliged entity has internally revealed the existence of indications or certainty that a fact or transaction was related to money laundering is considered a very serious offence.[413]

The AML Law also foresees other AML violations not related to CDD or reporting obligations. The following violations are *very serious* administrative offences (art. 51 AML):

(a) failure to fulfil the obligation to cooperate with the FIU or CPMLMO, following a request from CPMLMO;
(b) tipping off;
(c) resistance to or obstruction of inspections, following an explicit request in writing from the acting inspectors;
(d) failure to comply with the following obligations, in the event of unwillingness to comply:
    (i) to adopt an internal control manual;
    (ii) to adopt enhanced money laundering preventive measures (beyond CDD measures) in subsidiaries acting in high-risk third countries;
    (iii) to comply with the decisions of the Cabinet[414] (Council of Ministers) related to counter-measures against high-risk third countries; and

---

412 See *supra* section III.G.

413 See *supra* section III.F.

414 The Cabinet may decide to adopt additional counter measures against high-risk third countries, beyond the Resolutions of the United Nations Security Council. The measures

(iv) to take corrective action at the formal request of the Standing Committee;

(e) in the event of recidivism of a serious offence (listed below) within five years.

The sanctions for these very serious offences are as follows (art. 56.3 AML Law):

- a fine of €60,000–10,000,000 per natural person; and
- removal from office and disqualification from holding the position of manager or director in the same legal entity or any other obliged entity for a maximum of 10 years; or
- public reprimand.[415]

The fine is mandatory and may be combined with one of the other available sanctions. All sanctions for very serious offences shall be accompanied by an order requiring the person concerned to cease the conduct and to desist from repeating that conduct (art. 57.4 AML Law).

---

are as follows (art. 42.2 AML Law): "a) Prohibit, restrict or condition the movements to the third country or made by its nationals or residents; b) subject the transactions to prior authorisation as well as the transfers from or to the third country or made by its nationals or residents; c) Freeze or block funds and economic resources when the ownership, possession or control thereof pertains to natural or legal persons who are nationals or residents of the third country; d) Prohibit the disposition of funds or economic resources when the owners are nationals or residents of the third country; e) Require the application of enhanced due diligence measures to the business relations or transactions of nationals or residents of the third country; f) Establish the systematic reporting of transactions of nationals or residents or involving financial movements from or to the third country; g) Prohibit, restrict or condition the establishment or maintaining of subsidiaries, branches or representative offices of the financial institutions of the third country; h) Prohibit, restrict or condition the establishment or maintaining by financial institutions of subsidiaries, branches or representative offices in the third country; i) Prohibit, restrict or condition business relations or financial transactions with the third country or with its nationals or residents; j) Prohibit obliged subjects from accepting the due diligence performed by institutions located in the third country; k) Require financial institutions to review, modify and, if appropriate, terminate their correspondent banking relations with the financial institutions of the third country; l) Subject the subsidiaries or branches of the financial institutions of the third country to enhanced supervision or to external screening or auditing; m) Impose enhanced reporting requirements or external auditing upon financial groups with respect to any subsidiary or branch located or operating in the third country."

415 A public reprimand consists in a public statement which identifies the natural or legal person and the nature of the breach, warning of the possible consequences if the sanctioned person or entity repeats the wrongdoing in the future and exhorting them to amend their conduct. The public reprimand is published by the administrative sanctioning authority on the BOE (Official Bulletin of the State) and on the website of the Commission (art. 61.5 AML Law) and shall be available for consultation for five years.

The list of violations of due diligence obligations that lead to an administrative sanction is provided by art. 52 AML Law, and are described, in principle, as *serious* administrative offences:

(a) failure to comply with the obligation to formally identify the client in CDD measures;
(b) failure to comply with obligations to identify the beneficial owner;
(c) failure to comply with the obligation to obtain information on the purposes and nature of the business relationship;
(d) failure to comply with the obligation to implement ongoing monitoring of the business relationship;
(e) failure to comply with the obligation to apply CDD measures for existing customers when contracting new products or conduct a transaction that is significant in terms of its volume or complexity;
(f) failure to comply with the obligation to apply enhanced CDD measures, where applicable;
(g) failure to comply with the obligation to carry out a special review[416] of suspicious transactions.

Furthermore, of the failure to comply with the following reporting obligations is also a *serious* offence:

(a) failure to comply with the obligation to report suspicious transactions (art. 52.1(h) AML Law);
(b) failure to comply with systematic reporting obligation (art. 52.1(j) AML Law);

Art. 52(k)–(y) AML Law provides a list of *serious* AML administrative offences not related to CDD or reporting obligations:

(a) failure to comply with the obligation to abstain from executing suspicious transactions;
(b) failure to comply with the obligation to cooperate with the FIU after a written request from CPMLMO or one of its organs (FIU, Secretariat of the Commission);
(c) failure to comply with the record keeping obligation;
(d) failure to comply with the obligation to approve and implement adequate internal monitoring measures, including the written approval and implementation of an explicit customer acceptance policy;
(e) failure to comply with the obligation to report to the FIU on the proposed appointment of a representative of the obliged entity vis-à-vis the FIU or the refusal to address the observations from the FIU regarding the appointee;

416 See *supra* section II.A.1.a.

(f) failure to comply with the obligation to set up an adequate internal monitoring body including, where appropriate, technical units;
(g) failure to comply with the obligation to provide a representative to the FIU with the necessary material, human and technical resources to exercise his/her functions;
(h) failure to comply with the obligation to adopt and make available to the FIU an appropriate and updated internal manual for the prevention of money laundering;
(i) failure to comply with the obligation to carry out an independent audit;
(j) failure to comply with the employee training obligation;
(k) failure to comply with the obligation for obliged entities to adopt appropriate measures for maintaining the confidentiality of the identity of employees, directors or agents who have reported suspicious transactions to internal monitoring bodies;
(l) failure to comply with the obligation to apply the same preventive measures as the EU standards in branches and majority-owned subsidiaries located in third countries;
(m) failure to comply with the obligation to report on the opening or cancellation of a current account, savings accounts, security accounts or fixed-term deposits;
(n) failure to comply with the obligation to take corrective action at the formal request of the Financial Intelligence Committee, where there is *no* unwillingness to comply;
(o) entering into or continuing prohibited business relationships or executing prohibited transactions;
(p) resistance or obstruction of inspections, when there is no express written request from acting inspectors;
(q) failure to comply with the obligation to declare to the customs authorities the movement of means of payment (art. 51.3(a) AML Law).
(r) infraction of the duty to inform about transfers of funds requested by the EU Regulation on information accompanying transfers of funds[417] (art. 52.5 AML Law).

The sanctions for serious offences for individuals are (art. 57.2 AML Law):

- public reprimand;[418]
- private reprimand;[419]

417 Regulation (EC) no. 2015/847 of the European Parliament and of the Council of 20 May 2015 on information accompanying transfers of funds and repealing Regulation (EC) No 1781/2006.

418 See note 409.

419 A private reprimand consists in a communication from the administrative sanctioning authority to the person or entity who committed the administrative offence. It contains

- a fine of €3,000–5,000,000;
- disqualification for the exercise of the profession for a maximum of five years.

If there is a conviction, then the imposition of the fine is mandatory, unless it is a case of a minor offence according to art. 52.2 AML Law. Beyond the fine, one of the three other available sanctions above shall be simultaneously applied.

In the case of a public reprimand, CPMLMO may decide to postpone the disclosure of the sanction. Alternatively, CPMLMO may decide not to disclose the sanction, if doing so could affect the stability of the financial markets (art. 57.5 AML Law).

The authority responsible for the imposition of sanctions is the Secretariat of CPMLMO (art. 45 AML Law, art. 58 Decree 304/2014). The Secretariat can use the following criteria to decide on the amount and the proportion of sanctions, according (art. 59.2 AML Law) to:

(a) the level of responsibility or fault in the facts of the particular case;
(b) the past conduct of the person concerned, in the respective entity or any other entity, in connection with the requirements on AML prevention;
(c) the person's position in the hierarchy of the legal entity;
(d) the financial situation of the person concerned, when the penalty is a fine;
(e) the benefits obtained following the breach of administrative rules;
(f) the losses caused to third parties following the breach of administrative rules; and
(g) the level of cooperation of the person concerned with the competent authorities (e.g. FIU, police).

Finally, art. 52.2 AML Law establishes that the non-fulfilment of the duties related to points (a)–(f) can be sanctioned as minor offences when the institution or obliged entity's breach is considered merely occasional or isolated on the basis of the percentage of instances in the sample of compliance controls. It is not mandatory to impose a penalty for minor offences, but the penalty may be:

- a private reprimand;
- fines of up to €60,000.

---

a warning of the possible consequences of future wrongdoing and exhorts the person or entity to amend their conduct. Some data regarding the public reprimand may be published, but the identity of the obliged entities or persons sanctioned may not (art. 61.6 AML Law). Nevertheless, as one author notes, the private reprimand is already included in the decision (sentence) of the administrative authority that imposes the sanction, in such way that it is unnecessary to mention a "private reprimand". Aliaga Mendez, *Normativa comentada de la Ley de blanqueo de capitales*, Madrid, 2010, p. 411.

c. Sanctions against Legal Entities

According to arts. 51 and 52 AML Law, the violation of AML reporting obligations can be a serious offence or a very serious offence. The violation of reporting obligations is a *very serious* offence in in the case of failure to fulfil the reporting duty (file an SAR) when a director or employee of the obliged entity has internally revealed the existence of indications or certainty that a fact or transaction was related to money laundering or terrorism financing (art. 51.1(a) AML Law).

The AML Law also foresees other AML violations by legal entities not related to CDD or reporting obligations. These are the same mentioned above, in section VII.B.2.b.

The sanctions for these very serious offences are the most severe available under the law, and include:

- a public reprimand;
- fines from €150,000 up to whichever of the following is higher: 10% of the annual turnover of the obliged entity; double the financial value of its operations plus 50%; five times the value of the benefits gained via the wrongdoing, insofar as they can be determined; or €10,000,000;
- if the obliged entity's activity is subject to public authorisation, the temporary suspension of that authorisation.

The fine is mandatory, and one of the above-mentioned sanctions shall be imposed simultaneously with the fine (art. 57.1 AML Law).

On the same basis, the violation of AML reporting obligations is considered a *serious* offence in the case of:

(a) failure to comply with the obligation to report suspicious transactions (art. 52.1(h) AML Law); or
(b) failure to comply with the systematic reporting obligation (art. 52.1(j) AML Law).

The violation of due diligence obligations also constitutes a *serious* administrative offence. The list of violations is provided by art. 52 AML Law:

(a) failure to comply with the obligation to formally identify the client in CDD measures;
(b) failure to comply with obligations to identify the beneficial owner;
(c) failure to comply with the obligation to obtain information on the purposes and nature of the business relationship;
(d) failure to comply with the obligation to implement ongoing monitoring of the business relationship;

(e) failure to comply with the obligation to apply CDD measures for existing customers when contracting new products or conduct a transaction that is significant for its volume or complexity;
(f) failure to comply with the obligation to apply enhanced CDD measures, where applicable;
(g) failure to comply with the obligation to carry out a special review[420] of suspicious transactions.

On the other hand, art. 52(k)–(y) AML Law provides a list of *serious* AML administrative offences not related to CDD or reporting obligations:

(a) failure to comply with the obligation to cooperate with the FIU after a written request from the Commission or one of its organs (FIU, Secretariat of the Commission);
(b) failure to comply with the record keeping obligation;
(c) failure to comply with the obligation to approve and implement adequate internal monitoring measures, including the written approval and implementation of an explicit customer acceptance policy;
(d) failure to comply with the obligation to report to the FIU on the proposed appointment of a representative of the obliged entity vis-à-vis the FIU or the refusal to address the observations from the FIU regarding the appointee;
(e) failure to comply with the obligation to set up an adequate internal monitoring body including, where appropriate, technical units;
(f) failure to comply with the obligation to provide a representative to the FIU with the necessary material, human and technical resources to exercise his/her functions;
(g) failure to comply with the obligation to adopt and make available to the FIU an appropriate and updated internal manual for the prevention of money laundering;
(h) failure to comply with the obligation to carry out an independent audit;
(i) failure to comply with the employee training obligation;
(j) failure to comply with the obligation for obliged entities to adopt the appropriate measures for maintaining the confidentiality of the identity of employees, directors or agents who have reported suspicious transactions to internal monitoring bodies;
(k) failure to comply with the obligation to apply the same preventive measures as the EU standards in branches and majority-owned subsidiaries located in third countries;

420 See *supra* section II.A.1.a.

(l) failure to comply with the obligation to report on the opening or cancellation of a current account, savings accounts, security accounts or fixed-term deposits;
(m) failure to comply with the obligation to take corrective action at the formal request of the Financial Intelligence Committee, where there is *no* unwillingness to comply;
(n) entering into or continuing business relationships or executing prohibited transactions;
(o) resistance or obstruction of inspections, when there is no express written request from acting inspectors.

The difference between sanctions against legal entities and individuals lies in the size of the sanction. The sanctions applicable to legal entities for the *serious* administrative offences described above are as follows (art. 57.1 AML Law):

- a public reprimand;
- a private reprimand;
- fines from €60,001 up to whichever of the following is higher: 10% of the annual turnover of the obliged entity; the value of the transaction plus 50%; triple the value of the benefits gained via the wrongdoing, insofar as they can be determined; or €5,000,000;
- if the obliged entity's activity is subject to public authorisation, the temporary suspension of that authorisation.

The fine is mandatory, and it has to be combined with one of the other available sanctions. The authority responsible for the imposition of the sanctions is the Secretariat of CPMLMO (art. 45 AML Law, art. 58 Decree 304/2014). The Secretariat has the scope to decide on the amount of and the proportion of sanctions, according (art. 59 AML Law) to:

(a) the sum of the transaction or the proceeds obtained, if any, as a result of the omissions or acts constituting the offence;
(b) the benefits obtained following the breach of administrative rules;
(c) the circumstance of having acted or failing to act to remedy the breach on one's own initiative;
(d) final administrative penalties imposed on the obliged entity for various types of offence in the preceding five years;
(e) the level of responsibility or fault in the facts of the particular case;
(f) the gravity and duration of the administrative offences;
(g) the losses caused to third parties following the administrative offences;
(h) the financial situation of the legal entity concerned;
(i) the level of cooperation of the person concerned with the competent authorities (e.g. FIU, police).

In all cases, the measure of the aforementioned sanctions shall not be higher than the benefits obtained via the breach of the administrative offence.

Nevertheless, under certain circumstances the non-fulfilment of duties related to CDD measures can be sanctioned as a minor offence: if there was no suspicion of money laundering attached to the transaction, and if the infringement of the CDD measures mentioned above by the obliged entity was only occasional, and if it is an isolated occurrence considering the percentage of instances within the overall sample of duties fulfilled (52.2 AML Law). The sanctions applicable to obliged entities in the case of minor offences are (art. 58 AML Law):

- a private reprimand;
- fines of up to €60,000.

Finally, art. 57.3 AML Law establishes another category of sanctions for the failure to comply with the following reporting duties:

(a) failure to comply with the obligation to declare the movement of means of payment (art. 52.3(a) AML Law);
(b) failure to comply with the obligation to declare money remittances via an informal value transfer system[421] (art. 52.3(a) AML Law);

The sanctions for these breaches of reporting duties are:

- fines from €600 up to the maximum of 50 times the amount the means of payment transferred;
- a public reprimand;
- a private reprimand.

3. *Statistics*

a. Number of Investigations and Sanctions

According to statistics provided by CPMLMO, in 2015 the supervisory authorities (FIU, Bank of Spain and CNMV) conducted 79 on-site inspections (65 conducted by the FIU) and 284 off-site inspections.[422] Those inspections resulted in 14 administrative sanction proceedings in relation to the non-fulfilment of preventive measures exclusively by obliged entities.[423] Sanctions

421 See *supra* section II.D.4.

422 Commission for the Prevention of Money Laundering and Monetary Offences, *Memoria de Información Estadística 2012–2016*, p. 71, http://www.cpbc.tesoro.es/sites/default/files/memoria_estadistica_2012-2016_def.pdf.

423 The statistics do not specify which preventive measure was sanctioned.

imposed in 2016 came to €10,034,159, double the amount from the previous year (€5,605,690).[424]

Nevertheless, besides that information, there are no details available on the number of criminal and administrative investigations launched against individuals and legal entities for the offences above.

b. Number of Convictions

The statistics on criminal sanctions do not specify whether the criminal proceedings had their origins in the violation of preventive measures. Nevertheless, the Spanish jurisprudence includes cases of criminal sanctions against legal entities for money laundering offences in which the lack of an effective system of AML preventive measures was relevant for the criminal conviction.

C. CUMULATION OF MONEY LAUNDERING AND OTHER AML-RELATED SANCTIONS

As described in the sections above, there is no criminal liability against individuals or legal entities for any other conduct besides money laundering activity itself. Notwithstanding, if an obliged entity conducts acts of money laundering, it can violate administrative and criminal rules at the same time, and therefore will be subject to both jurisdictions. If that is the case, it is possible to be held criminally responsible for money laundering and subjected to criminal or administrative sanctions for the same criminal conduct. Nevertheless, as a general rule in Spain, and in line with the prohibition on double jeopardy, someone cannot be sentenced twice for the same facts.[425] As a consequence of this rule, the criminal jurisdiction decision prevails over the administrative one. Thus, if there is already ongoing administrative proceedings and the public prosecutors initiate criminal proceedings, the administrative proceedings will be suspended until the conclusion of the criminal investigation or conviction.[426]

After the decision of the criminal court, if the person is criminally acquitted, the administrative proceedings can resume. On the other hand, if there is a criminal conviction, the criminal sanction will prevail, and if the person has already paid any economic sanction within the administrative proceedings, the amount would be deducted from the criminal fine.

---

424 See Commission for the Prevention of Money Laundering and Monetary Offences, *Memoria de Información Estadística 2012–2016*, p. 73, http://www.cpbc.tesoro.es/sites/default/files/memoria_estadistica_2012-2016_def.pdf.

425 Art. 25 of the Constitution of Spain.

426 Art. 7.2 of Decree 1398/1993, which regulates the proceedings for the exercise of the power to impose administrative sanctions.

VIII. THE USE OF CASH AS A MEANS OF PAYMENT

A. LIMITS

In Spain, the upper limit on the use of cash as a means of payment is €2,500, or its equivalent in a foreign currency, for any transaction.[427] In cases where the payer is a natural person without tax residence in Spain (e.g. tourists), the limit is €15,000 in the equivalent currency. Since 2015 there have been reports that the government intends to reduce the limit the use of cash to €1,000, but as yet no law makes specific concrete reference to this lower amount.

B. STATISTICS

Statistics are not available on the use of cash in relation to the overall volume of transactions conducted in Spain. The Bank of Spain provides statistics on electronic means of payment (non-cash),[428] but does not provide information on the proportion of cash/non-cash transactions.

IX. SUMMARY, EVALUATION, AND FUTURE PERSPECTIVES

A notable feature of the regulation of the money laundering system in Spain is the complexity of the terms of the law and its interpretation, both in the criminal definition and in the administrative regulation, and the differences between the literature in the two areas. On the one hand, there is prolific literature on the criminal definition. This may point to the fact that the doctrine has needed to delimit and interpret the money laundering acts defined in the Penal Code, as well as to the phenomenon of money laundering itself. On the other hand, there is not the same level of bibliographical support on the administrative regulation and sanctions, despite the complexity of the AML Law.

Regarding the criminal definition of the offence, the cautious approach of the jurisprudence and the law enforcement agencies in the interpretation of criminal wrongdoings must be highlighted. They understand the broad terms of the definition of the crime and require the disguising of illicit gains, with the tendency to reject the use of money laundering as a circumvention of criminal

427 Art. 7.1 of Law no. 7/2012, which modifies the tax regulation to intensify the measures to prevent tax fraud.

428 See https://www.bde.es/f/webbde/SPA/sispago/ficheros/es/estadisticas.pdf.

procedure to identify the predicate offence. All in all, one can note an intent from the doctrine and jurisprudence to provide limits to the broader definition and to respect the principles of legal certainty and legality. Nevertheless, until the moment, there are no unified guidelines in the jurisprudence on the limits of surrogate goods[429] or on the limits of the interpretation of self-money laundering.

Spain's AML preventive system has some unique features. The historical reliance on notaries makes them an intermediary between the private and public sector. Even more peculiar is the figure of the "external expert", who specialises in developing preventive systems and in the risk analysis of the systems put in place by obliged entities. The objective of these professionals is similar to an auditor, but they aim to provide specialised support for obliged entities in developing and implementing their internal preventive measures, such as risk evaluation of the sector, a client acceptance policy and an internal manual. Their service is not designed exclusively for small and medium-sized obliged entities, but they are the natural addressees, since large obliged entities – such as banks and investment funds – usually implement their own independent system. The reform of the AML Law in 2018 included the external expert in the list of sanctions for individuals, therefore acknowledging the legitimacy of these professionals as providing support to and supervision of obliged entities.

Spain has a robust system for collecting SARs and other information from different sources, with a well-integrated system between the law enforcement agencies and close cooperation from notaries. The prevention bodies of the Colleges of Notaries and Registrars provide the law enforcement agencies with up-to-date and accurate information about the transactions registered by them (real estate, company registration, etc.). However, despite these well-organised systems, the registration of beneficial ownership information is still ongoing and will need further regulation, since there is no consensus regarding the profession that should be responsible for the establishment of a single register (notaries or mercantile registrars).

Still, supervisors and some practitioners interviewed for this report often mentioned the need to improve the awareness of some sectors of obliged entities, such as lawyers, real estate agents and small-scale jewellery dealers, of their obligations. In fact, it can be seen that the AML system focuses on the financial sector as its main addressee, which raises difficulties in adapting the requirements to non-financial obliged entities. This fact makes some demands disproportionate for small-scale or non-financial obliged entities, which are expected to understand and comply with complex preventive duties. Among other measures Spain may decide to adopt, a good idea could be a census for each sector, encouraging the self-regulation of each group of obliged entities.

---

429 Surrogate goods are the replacement values of the proceeds of a predicate offence.

Alternatively, given the resources that would be required for such a task, the FIU could instead implement communication channels to promote a better understanding of the needs and risks of the most common activities of obliged entities outside the financial sector. Naturally, the significance of the money laundering risks in the financial sector justifies the focus on this group of obliged entities, and the resources of these institutions fosters the exchange of information between them and the FIU. Nevertheless, an improvement on the guidance and organisation from the public authorities to the non-financial sector could strengthen the overall preventive system in Spain.

Therefore, a concern of the system now is the further regulation of the AML Law after its reform in September 2018. A forthcoming update of Decree 304/2014 may provide better alignment regarding preventive measures, in accordance with the scale of the obliged entity.

In a general sense, the FIU in Spain acts in practice as the sole supervisory authority, and it is also responsible for the intelligence reports. A very positive feature of the Spanish system is that the intelligence reports from the FIU cannot be used as evidence in criminal proceedings. Therefore, every financial intelligence report received by the law enforcement agencies must be complemented with further investigation and collection of evidence, which preserves the individual's defence rights.

On the other hand, the lack of guidance and communication from the FIU to obliged entities in noticeable. The website of the FIU, although easily understandable, provides very little information to obliged entities. For instance, there is no public list of Spanish PEPs, no further guidance on enhanced CDD measures, and some of the information on typologies or high-risk third countries are not up-to-date. Overall, there is room for improvement in the role of the FIU in terms of its communication with obliged entities and civil society and in the tasks of updating the typology lists. Moreover, the FIU could adopt a more proactive role on the reorganisation of the complex legislative situation regarding the AML system in Spain. The performance of the FIU in Spain is strongly shaped by the FATF's Mutual Evaluation Reports and recommendations, in such a way that the guidelines of the FATF seem to preponderate over European ones. As a consequence, concerns regarding individual rights might take longer to gather momentum in Spain, as the standards of the FATF may differ from those of the EU.

A common complaint among many professionals dedicated to the prevention of money laundering is the lack of guidance from public authorities regarding their duties, in particular the limited communication from the FIU. Obliged entities also have to deal with limited feedback from the law enforcement agencies and almost non-existent feedback from the FIU. One of the reasons for the restricted communication from the FIU's side, however, is the shortage of personnel, as well as a culture of limited communication between public authorities and the citizens. As a result, the present study suggests that better feedback between the public and the private sector could improve the quality of the SARs sent by obliged entities. At the moment, the gap in official guidance is filled by service providers such as compliance officers, external experts and companies providing lists of PEPs and beneficial owners.

Concerning data analytics systems, the empirical study carried out for this report showed that both the law enforcement agencies and larger obliged entities use state-of-the-art software, well adapted to the specific features of the AML system, facilitating a rapid response to requested information.

The exchange of information between the FIU, police and tax authorities within Spain is fluid, and it can be noted that the public authorities beyond the FIU benefit from the AML system in terms of the investigation of crimes and tax fraud. Nevertheless, much legal clarification on the limits of the exchange of information between these authorities is needed. The new Data Protection Law improved the regulation on access to data banks and led to a redesign in the public authorities' data, in particular within the tax authorities. However, it is still not enough to provide clear regulation of the mechanisms and limits of the exchange of data that is relevant for AML purposes. Moreover, although the data protection system in Spain is well developed, some modifications can be expected in the near future, including the creation of the role of the "data protection officer", who in the future may be intertwined with AML compliance.

On another note, there is close cooperation between the tax authorities, the FIU and the law enforcement agencies in Spain, and there is no question that tax fraud is a predicate offence. As a result, the AML system provides added resources for the investigation of tax evasion and tax fraud. In that sense, the practice of the AML system seems to support the indications from the doctrine, with some authors pointing out that the AML system in Spain is strongly oriented towards the investigation of tax fraud as a predicate offence.

International cooperation is also well developed in Spain, and representatives of the FIU participate in the main fora of discussions regarding legal updates in the prevention of money laundering. However, there is the perception that some foreign FIUs do not have the same well-organised system for international cooperation, therefore delaying the exchange of information requested by Spain. One possibility to counter such delay could be a list of the highly cooperative FIUs.

To address the situation that there is not enough clarity about lawyers' duties to inform and professional secrecy, it would be a recommended improvement in the Spanish AML system to create a supervisory body that could guide and collect information from law firms and serve as an intermediary between lawyers and the FIU, similar to the OCP of the College of Notaries. However, it should be recognised that it could be difficult in Spain to make it mandatory for lawyers to subscribe to an AML supervisory body, because it would go against the tendency in Spain to preserve lawyers as independent liberal professionals.

Virtual currencies and crowdfunding platforms are another point of concern among practitioners and law enforcement agencies. In fact, they were included as triggers for enhanced CDD measures in a previous proposal, which was not adopted at the last moment. Nevertheless, one can assume that virtual currencies will be soon addressed by the Spanish authorities since it remains a weakness in the AML prevention system.

In the near future, an update to the regulation of the AML Law (the Decree that implements the AML Law) can be expected, since the reform of September 2018 altered only the AML Law. In addition, another to AML Law can be expected soon, following the guidelines of the 5AMLD.

THE ANTI-MONEY LAUNDERING ARCHITECTURE OF SWITZERLAND

Jean-Baptiste MAILLART*

I. INTRODUCTION

A. HISTORY OF ANTI-MONEY LAUNDERING IN THE COUNTRY

The offence of money laundering was introduced in Switzerland in 1990 under art. 305bis of the Criminal Code (CC)[1] following a series of high-profile scandals that tarnished the Swiss financial centre's reputation in the 1980s, such as the so-called "Banco Ambrosiano", "Pizza Connection" and "Lebanon Connection" scandals.[2] At the same time, the legislator added art. 305ter to the CC, which rendered financial intermediaries criminally liable for failing to ascertain the identity of the beneficial owner of the assets with the care that is required in the circumstances. Art. 305ter CC was then amended four years later when a second paragraph was inserted, providing for financial intermediaries' right to report to the criminal justice authorities any observations that indicate that assets originate from a felony.[3]

Until 1997, art. 305ter CC was the only provision providing for preventive measures against money laundering applicable to all financial intermediaries.[4] The private law Agreement on the Swiss banks' code of conduct with regard to the exercise of due diligence (CDB), which was enacted in 1977 by the Swiss

* The author would like to thank Dr Katia Villard from the University of Geneva for her valuable comments.

1 Art. 305bis was inserted into the CC (RS 311.0) by the Federal Act of 23 March 1990, in force since 1 August 1990 (RO 1990 1077; FF 1989 II 961).

2 For more on these scandals and the origins of the offence of money laundering, see e.g. FF 1989 II 961, 966; FF 1993 III 269, 277–278; P. Bernasconi, *Finanzunterwelt*, Zurich, 1988, p. 20 ss.

3 Art. 305ter(2) was inserted into the CC by the Federal Act of 19 March 1994, in force since 1 August 1994 (RO 1994 1614; FF 1993 III 269).

4 For more on this, see FF 1996 III 1057, 1060.

Bankers Association (SBA) following the Chiasso Credit Suisse/Texon banking scandal,[5] was indeed only applicable to banks, obliging them to identify the contracting parties and beneficial owners of funds.[6] This led to the adoption of the Federal Act on Combating Money Laundering and Terrorist Financing (Anti-Money Laundering Act, AMLA) on 10 October 1997, which significantly strengthened Switzerland's preventive-regulatory approach to money laundering in two main ways.[7] Firstly, the AMLA imposed detailed customer due diligence (CDD) obligations upon the entire financial sector, including both the banking and the para-banking sectors. Secondly, the AMLA introduced an obligation to report suspicious transactions for all financial intermediaries and established the Money Laundering Reporting Office Switzerland (MROS) as a relay and filtration point between financial intermediaries and law enforcement authorities.[8]

The AMLA has been amended multiple times in the past two decades.[9] A major development took place in 2008 when the scope of the AMLA was expanded to cover the financing of terrorism.[10] The 2013 revision of the AMLA, which finally allowed MROS to exchange financial information with foreign counterparts, should also be mentioned.[11] Up until then, MROS could not indeed exchange any financial data with foreign financial intelligence units (FIUs), such as information about a reporting entity (e.g. its name) or specific data related to a suspicious activity report (SAR) like bank account numbers, account balances, names of contracting parties or names of beneficial owners, because these date were protected by Swiss banking secrecy and professional secrecy legislation.[12] Foreign FIUs that wanted to obtain financial information held by MROS had to make a request for mutual legal assistance, a slow and

5 The Chiasso Credit Suisse/Texon scandal started out as a simple fraud in the 1960s and turned into a major public embarrassment for Credit Suisse and much of the Swiss banking system.

6 The CDB is normally revised on a five-year cycle. The current version was adopted on 13 June 2018 and entered into force on 1 January 2020 (available at: https://www.swissbanking.org/library/richtlinien/vereinbarung-ueber-die-standesregeln-zur-sorgfaltspflicht-der-banken-vsb-20/vsb_2020_einzelseiten_print_en.pdf/@@download/file/VSB_2020_Einzelseiten_Print_EN.pdf). It applies "to the banks and securities dealers and all their branch offices domiciled in Switzerland, but not to their foreign branches, representative offices and subsidiary companies" (art. 1).

7 RS 955.0. The AMLA entered into force on 1 April 1998 (RO 1998 892; FF 1997 IV 723).

8 On the benefits from the establishment of MROS foreseen by the Federal Council at the time, see FF 1996 III 1057, 1086–1087.

9 All successive amendments to the AMLA can be found at: https://www.admin.ch/opc/fr/classified-compilation/19970427/history.html.

10 The AMLA was amended by the Federal Act of 3 October 2008 for Implementing the Revised FATF Recommendations of 2003, in force since 1 February 2009 (RO 2009 361; FF 2007 5919).

11 The AMLA was amended by the Federal Act of 21 June 2013 on AML/CTF in the Financial Sector, in force since 1 November 2013 (RO 2013 3493; FF 2012 6449).

12 FF 2012 6449, 6460.

cumbersome process.[13] As emphasised in the deliberations of the Council of States[14] about the revised FATF Recommendations, which took place in the autumn of 2008, this clearly reflected the intention of the law makers for whom bank secrecy in Switzerland prevailed over international cooperation and the global fight against illicit financial flows for many years.[15] However, this situation was no longer tenable after the 2012 FATF Recommendations were adopted, the Interpretative Note to Recommendation 40 providing that FIUs should have the power to exchange "all information required to be accessible or obtainable directly or indirectly by the FIU under the FATF Recommendations, in particular under Recommendation 29",[16] i.e. all information contained in SARs as well as any additional financial information that the FIU should be able to obtain from reporting entities and other sources in order to perform its analysis properly.[17] Moreover, it should be noted that MROS's lack of cooperation with regard to the exchange of financial information had long been criticised by the Egmont Group of FIUs, of which MROS has been a member since it (MROS) was set up in 1998, because it violated one of the Group's *Principles for Information Exchange between FIUs for Money Laundering and Terrorism Financing Cases* adopted in 2001, namely Principle 9, according to which information exchange between FIUs "should produce any available information that may be relevant to an analysis or investigation of financial transactions and other relevant information and the persons or companies involved".[18] The Heads of FIUs, the Egmont Group's governing body, even issued a suspension warning about MROS in July 2011, giving Switzerland one year to implement concrete measures to address the non-compliance issue.[19]

The AMLA was last amended significantly by the Federal Act for Implementing the Revised FATF Recommendations of 2012 (FATF Implementation Act).[20] The bill, which was adopted by the Swiss Parliament on 12 December 2014 after a long and difficult political process, aimed to: (i) tighten the duties of financial intermediaries with regard to the identification of the beneficial owner of legal entities; (ii) broaden the definition of politically exposed persons (PEPs) to

13 FF 2012 6449, 6461.

14 The Council of States is the smaller chamber of the Federal Assembly of Switzerland, and is considered the Assembly's upper house, with the National Council being the lower house. It has 46 members who represent the cantons.

15 See BO 2008 E 674.

16 Interpretative Note to FATF Recommendation 40 (2012), para. 9.

17 See Interpretative Note to FATF Recommendation 29 (2012), paras. 2, 5 and 6.

18 For more on this, see FF 2012 6449, 6465–6466. It should be noted that the Egmont Principles for Information Exchange between FIUs for Money Laundering and Terrorism Financing Cases were revised in 2013 and that Principle 9 now reads as follows: "FIUs should exchange information with foreign FIUs, regardless of their status; be it administrative, law enforcement, judicial or other".

19 For more on this, see FF 2012 6449, 6467–6468.

20 RO 2015 1389; FF 2014 585.

include domestic and international organisations PEPs and clarifying the CDD measures to be taken when conducting business with them; (iii) bring natural persons and legal entities that deal in goods commercially and in doing so accept more than CHF 100,000 in cash (dealers) within the scope of the AMLA;[21] and (iv) give MROS new powers to analyse SARs (more time given for the analysis and right to request other public authorities in Switzerland to pass on all the data required for analysing SARs). The FATF Implementation Act also amended other legal instruments, such as the Criminal Code, the Civil Code, the Code of Obligations (CO),[22] by: (i) introducing provisions to improve the transparency of legal persons; (ii) extending the spectrum of tax-related predicate offences for money laundering to include qualified tax offences with respect to direct taxation; and (iii) tightening financial sanctions related to terrorism financing. The FATF Implementation Act entered into force on 1 January 2016, except for the various provisions on the transparency of legal entities and bearer shares, which were already brought into force on 1 July 2015. The evaluation of Switzerland by the Global Forum on Transparency and Exchange of Information for Tax Purposes was indeed due in the autumn of 2015 and required the swiftest possible entry into force of the provisions.[23]

The AMLA is a framework law in that it sets out principles that are specified in several ordinances and regulations. The Anti-Money Laundering Ordinance (AMLO)[24] sets out notably the requirements for the professional practice of financial intermediation, as well as the CDD obligations and reporting duties that dealers must fulfil. The Swiss Financial Market Supervisory Authority Anti-Money Laundering Ordinance (AMLO-FINMA)[25] specifies in detail the preventive obligations for the financial intermediaries under FINMA supervision, whilst self-regulatory organisations' regulations do the same for their affiliates.[26]

---

21 It should be noted that the designation of dealers in high-value goods as obliged entities under the AMLA was foreseen by the Federal Council since 1996 (see FF 1996 III 1057, 1071).

22 In total, the bill entailed extensive changes to eight different acts, namely the AMLA, the CC, the Civil Code (RS 210), the Code of Obligations (RS 220), the Federal Act of 11 April 1889 on Debt Enforcement and Bankruptcy Law (RS 281.1), the Federal Act of 22 March 1974 on Administrative Criminal Law (RS 313.0), the Federal Act of 23 June 2006 on Collective Investment Schemes (RS 951.31) and the Federal Act of 3 October 2008 on Intermediate Securities (RS 957.1).

23 More specifically, the amendments to the CO, the Federal Act on Collective Investment Schemes and the Federal Act on Intermediate Securities came into force on 1 July 2015.

24 RS 955.01. The AMLO was adopted on 11 November 2015 and entered into force on 1 January 2016 (RO 2015 4819). Its latest modification dates back to 27 November 2019 and entered into force on 1 January 2020 (RO 2019 4701).

25 RS 955.033.0. The AMLO-FINMA was adopted on 3 June 2015 and entered into force on 1 January 2016 (RO 2015 2083). Its latest modification dates back to 20 June 2018 and entered into force on 1 January 2020 (RO 2018 2691).

26 For more details on institutional arrangements for supervision and oversight with respect to financial intermediaries, see *infra* section II.D.1.

With respect to casinos and promoters of large-scale games, preventive measures are stipulated in the Federal Gaming Board Anti-Money Laundering Ordinance (AMLO-CFMJ)[27] for the former, and in the Federal Department of Justice and Police Anti-Money Laundering Ordinance (AMLO-DFJP)[28] for the latter. Lastly, the Ordinance on MROS (O-MROS)[29] regulates in detail the work of MROS, that is to say its tasks and its handling of sensitive financial disclosures.

B. CURRENT CONCERNS AND REFORM AGENDA

In past years, the Swiss authorities have demonstrated a clear commitment to strengthening the fight against money laundering and enhancing the transparency of financial flows. In addition to the aforementioned legislative improvements, one should point out the Federal Act on Implementation of Recommendations of Global Forum[30] that recently came into force and which notably specifies the beneficial ownership reporting obligations of shareholders and provides a fine to be imposed on them and/or companies that fail to report beneficial owners or fail to keep the list of the beneficial owners of shares up-to-date.[31]

Switzerland also set up on 29 November 2013 the Interdepartmental Coordinating Group on Combating Money Laundering and the Financing of Terrorism (GCMF), a permanent body mandated to coordinate AML/CFT policy matters within the Federal Administration.[32] In particular, the GCMF carries out an ongoing assessment of ML/TF risks, thereby identifying new threats and vulnerabilities, and proposes any measures needed to reduce these risks.[33] The GCMF includes three standing technical working groups that carry

---

27 RS 955.021. The AMLO-CFMJ was adopted on 12 November 2018 and entered into force on 1 January 2019 (RO 2018 5307).

28 RS 955.022. The AMLO-DFJP was adopted on 7 November 2018 and entered into force on 1 January 2019 (RO 2018 5319).

29 RS 955.23. The O-MROS was adopted on 25 August 2004 and entered into force on 1 October 2004 (RO 2004 4181). Its latest modification dates back to 27 November 2019 and entered into force on 1 January 2020 (RO 2019 4701).

30 RS 220. The Federal Act of 21 June 2019 on Implementation of Recommendations of Global Forum entered into on 1 November 2019 (RO 2019 3161; FF 2019 277).

31 For more on this, see *infra* section VI.

32 Acting under the aegis of the Federal Department of Finance, and more specifically the State Secretariat for International Financial Matters, the GCMF is made up of representatives of the Federal Customs Administration, the Federal Office of Police (which includes the FIU), the Federal Office of Justice, the Federal Gaming Board (part of the Federal Department of Justice and Police), the Swiss Federal Intelligence Service (part of the Federal Department of Defense, Civil Protection and Sport), the Directorate of International Law and the Sectoral Foreign Policies Division (parts of the Federal Department of Foreign Affairs), the FINMA and the Office of the Attorney General of Switzerland.

33 The first risk assessment of this kind was published in 2015. The report draws on data obtained from public agencies both at the federal and regional levels, as well as by private-sector entities, non-governmental organisations and academia (public sources). However, no direct

out operational tasks in risk assessment, information exchange and coordination, and the processing of terrorist lists. Moreover, money laundering was defined as a priority issue by the Office of the Attorney General (OAG) for the period 2016–2019.[34] This prompted the establishment of two specialised units within the OAG: the *Zentrale Aufbereitung Geldwäschereiverdachtsmeldung* (ZAG), a unit made up of the Attorney General and the Deputy Attorney Generals, federal prosecutors specialised in money laundering, and representatives of the OAG's Mutual Legal Assistance Division, which centralises the processing of MROS reports; and the Forensic Financial Analysis (FFA), a department that provides prosecutors with economic and financial expertise. When a new SAR is received, the ZAG Secretariat first checks whether the SAR is directly related to a case in progress, in which case the SAR is forwarded to the prosecutor concerned. If there is no direct connection, a prosecutor is appointed to carry out a preliminary analysis of the SAR, if necessary with support from economic and financial analysts from the FFA. The ZAG meets twice a week (or more often if necessary) to examine the preliminary analyses and decide whether to open criminal proceedings.[35] According to the FATF, this new organisational arrangement "has already optimized resources, improved the way proceedings are conducted (because a strategy is drawn up right from the beginning of the proceeding) and led to an increase in the spontaneous sharing of information with foreign authorities".[36]

Yet, despite all the efforts provided by the federal authorities, weaknesses in certain areas were identified by the FATF in its fourth review of Switzerland, which was conducted in 2016 using the 2013 Methodology. Although the mutual evaluation report acknowledges the generally good quality of the Swiss system for combating money laundering and terrorist financing, and confirms that the level of effectiveness and technical compliance in Switzerland has improved since the last evaluation in 2005[37] and that the Swiss authorities are deeply committed

---

consultation with stakeholders took place. The overall assessment of the risks of money laundering resulted in a medium risk for banks and enhanced risks for universal and private banks. The report did not focus on the money-laundering risks posed by legal entities and arrangements operating in Switzerland. The evaluation recommended eight measures to improve the current system, including promoting dialogue between the public and private sectors, developing and systemising statistics and specific recommendations for future analyses as well as with regard to the examinations of the areas not covered by the AMLA, namely the real estate sector, the commodities industry, foundations and free ports. The report is available at: https://www.newsd.admin.ch/newsd/message/attachments/42276.pdf.

34 See https://www.bundesanwaltschaft.ch/mpc/en/home/die-bundesanwaltschaft/strategie-2016-2019-breit.html.

35 FATF (2016), *Anti-money laundering and counter-terrorist financing measures – Switzerland*, Fourth Round Mutual Evaluation Report, para. 135.

36 *Ibid.*, para. 162.

37 The 2005 mutual evaluation, conducted on the basis of the 2004 Methodology, concluded that Switzerland was compliant or largely compliant with 11 Core or Key Recommendations. However, it was rated partially compliant with the former Recommendations 5 and 13, as well

to preventing and prosecuting money laundering,[38] it also points out multiple deficiencies in the AML/CFT regime, including the following:

- dealers in precious metals and precious stones only have to perform CDD measures when they receive cash payments of more than CHF 100,000;[39]
- acts related to the creation of companies, legal persons and legal arrangements, in which lawyers, notaries, legal professionals, accountants, or trust and company service providers are involved without being parties to transactions, fall outside the scope of the AMLA;[40]
- the criteria used by obliged entities for classifying customers into risk categories are sometimes incomplete and do not always provide a satisfactory risk profile;[41]
- banking institutions do not sufficiently review and update information on longstanding customers, classified as low risk at the beginning of the relationship, and check the identity of beneficial owners;[42]
- the number of SARs is too low, and most of them are produced in response to external information sources;[43]
- the dual legal regime (right and obligation) for SARs affects the understanding and interpretation by financial intermediaries of the circumstances in which there is a requirement to report suspicions to MROS;[44]
- MROS may request information from a financial intermediary on behalf of a foreign FIU, but only if the financial intermediary had previously submitted an SAR or has a link with an SAR received by MROS, which limits the effectiveness of MROS's cooperation with foreign counterparts;[45]
- sanctions for serious violations of AML/CTF obligations imposed by supervisory authorities appear to be insufficient and thus not dissuasive.[46]

---

as with the former Special Recommendations I, III and IV. For this reason, Switzerland was put on the FATF regular follow-up process. In 2009, the Plenary decided that Switzerland's compliance level with the Core Recommendations was largely compliant, but that the measures taken to comply with the Key Recommendations were insufficient. Given the progress achieved by Switzerland on other Recommendations rated partially compliant, the Plenary used the flexibility the procedures give it and placed Switzerland on the biennial monitoring process.

38 Switzerland was deemed compliant with six and largely compliant with 25 of the 40 FATF Recommendations.

39 For more on this, see FATF (2016), *Anti-money laundering and counter-terrorist financing measures – Switzerland*, Fourth Round Mutual Evaluation Report, para. 303.

40 For more on this, see *ibid.*, paras. 81 and 293.

41 For more on this, see *ibid.*, paras. 286–289.

42 For more on this, see *ibid.*, paras. 295–301.

43 For more on this, see *ibid.*, paras. 315–317.

44 For more on this, see *ibid.*, para. 315.

45 For more on this, see *ibid.*, paras. 459–460.

46 For more on this, see *ibid.*, paras. 375–380 and 384.

In response, the Federal Council instructed the Federal Department of Finance (FDF) in June 2017 to prepare a preliminary draft bill implementing the most important recommendations of the FATF.[47] The preliminary draft bill was subject to public consultation from 1 June 2018[48] to 21 September 2018.[49] On 26 June 2019, the Federal Council published the draft bill (DB-AMLA) and the related message,[50] taking into account the responses received during the consultation phase. In comparison to the preliminary draft bill, only a few significant changes were made.[51] Among the key measures proposed in the DB-AMLA, which will be further detailed throughout this report, are the following: (i) introducing due diligence and reporting obligations for certain persons providing services in connection with companies or trusts (advisors); (ii) obliging financial intermediaries to verify information on beneficial owners and to regularly check that client data is up to date; (iii) abolishing the 20-day period imposed on MROS to inform the financial intermediary that fulfilled its obligation to file an SAR whether or not it is forwarding the case to the law enforcement authorities, and replacing it with a 40-day period at the end of which the financial intermediary may terminate the business relationship (though always retaining the paper trail) unless MROS has informed it that it will forward the case to the prosecuting authorities; and (iv) reducing the threshold for applying CDD measures for dealers in precious metals and gems from CHF 100,000 to CHF 15,000. Switzerland will be subject to a follow-up review with respect to improving effectiveness in 2021.

Another important component of the reform agenda in Switzerland that must be mentioned is the set of measures proposed by the Federal Council on 14 September 2018 to enhance the fight against terrorism (DB-Terr),[52] which is currently being discussed by Parliament. Although not all the measures proposed

---

47 See the Federal Council's media release of 28 June 2017, https://www.admin.ch/gov/en/start/documentation/media-releases.msg-id-67338.html.

48 The opening of the consultation procedure coincided with the publication of the GCMF's report on the risks of money laundering for legal entities. This report analyses the risks associated with various legal forms in Switzerland and abroad, and reinforces the draft's proposed measures concerning services for companies and trusts. The report is available at: https://www.sif.admin.ch/dam/sif/fr/dokumente/Integrit%C3%A4t%20des%20Finanzplatzes/national-risk-assessment.pdf.download.pdf/National%20Risk%20Assessment%20(NRA)%20-%20F.pdf.

49 In total, 79 opinions were received. The bill subjected to public consultation and the Federal Council's corresponding message are available at: https://www.ejpd.admin.ch/dam/data/ejpd/aktuell/news/2018/2018-06-01/bericht-f.pdf.

50 The DB-AMLA and the Federal Council corresponding message are available at: https://www.efd.admin.ch/efd/fr/home/dokumentation/nsb-news_list.msg-id-75603.html.

51 In comparison to the preliminary draft bill, the most important change was certainly to maintain the right to report (art. 305ter(2) CC. For more on this, see *infra* section III.C.1.a.

52 FF 2018 6469.

by the Swiss Government are relevant in the context of the present study, one does directly impact the AML legal framework. It is proposed to grant MROS the power to request additional information from financial intermediaries in the absence of SAR.[53] One should also note that the Federal Council proposes to expressly extend the scope of art. 260ter CC (participation in or support for a criminal organisation) to terrorist organisations.[54] However, this will not change the state of the law as 260ter CC is already deemed to be covering terrorist financing.[55]

II. AIMS AND SCOPE OF AML SYSTEM

A. AIMS OF AML REGIME

When money laundering was introduced into the CC in 1990 under art. 305bis,[56] the latter was inserted in Title Seventeen of Book Two, entitled "Felonies and Misdemeanours against the Administration of Justice". The Federal Council explained this choice by the fact that criminals who launder money primarily aim at frustrating the forfeiture of dirty money.[57] However, although no link with organised crime is required for the offence of money laundering to be deemed to have been committed,[58] the Swiss Government's ultimate objective in the fight against this offence in the 1990s was primarily to track down criminal groups and disrupt their activities by taking away their criminal proceeds. This is very clear from the first sentence of the Government's message of 1989, which reads as follows: "[m]oney laundering is a phenomenon which is closely related to organised crime".[59] Further, the Federal Council indicates that art. 305bis CC is "fit for combatting in an effective way the laundering of dirty money and, consequently, drug trafficking which constitutes the main form of predicate offences to money laundering".[60] In the same vein, it is mentioned in the message of 1996 related to the AMLA that "the main objective of the AML regime is to fight against organised crime".[61]

---

53 See *infra* section IV.A.4.
54 See FF 2018 6469, 6506 ff.
55 FF 2002 5014, 5061; ATF 128 II 355; ATF 125 II 569.
56 See *supra* section I.A.
57 FF 1989 II 961, 981.
58 On this point, see ATF 119 IV 59.
59 FF 1989 II 961, 962.
60 FF 1989 II 961, 962.
61 FF 1996 III 1057, 1072.

Currently, the federal authorities' discourse on AML is significantly different, as it mainly focuses on the protection of the integrity of the financial sector with the aim of promoting the country's competitiveness. This paradigm shift in the objective of the AML legal framework, which is to be connected with other measures recently undertaken by Switzerland to sanitise the financial industry, such as initiatives to limit banking secrecy and proactively combat tax evasion,[62] is clearly reflected in the Federal Council report "Financial market policy for a competitive Swiss financial centre", adopted in October 2016.[63] Complying with international standards in the area of money laundering and taxation is indeed considered in this report to be one of the five key priorities of the Government to ensure that Switzerland remains one of the world's leading locations for financial business.[64] A similar argument had already been put forward a few years before, after Switzerland received a suspension warning from the Egmont Group for not allowing MROS to exchange financial information with its foreign counterparts.[65] For the Federal Council, writing in 2012, a suspension of MROS's participation to the Egmont Group after 14 years of membership would "seriously damage the reputation of the Swiss financial place … [as] being a member [of the Egmont Group] provides a sort of quality label".[66] One should also mention the 2014 dispatch on the FATF Implementation Act, in which the Federal Council explained that "it is in the interest of the Swiss financial centre, in particular the preservation of its integrity and its competitiveness, to take the necessary measures to implement the key aspects of the revised [FATF] Recommendations"[67] and amend the AMLA. Another example is that of the National Risk Assessment (NRA) conducted by the GCMF in 2015, in which it is written that "Switzerland attaches great importance to maintaining a honourable, attractive and efficient financial centre on its territory [and] makes every effort to protect it against any criminal use, in particular money laundering and terrorist financing".[68]

---

62 Since 2009, Switzerland has been implementing the OECD international standard relative to the exchange of information upon request, which it has used as the basis for adapting and extending its network of agreements regarding double taxation. In 2014, it established the aggravated tax offence related to direct tax as a predicate offence for money laundering. Since 2018, it exchanges tax information with designated partner States and the EU on the basis of the OECD international standard on the automatic exchange of financial account information (AEOI Standard). In the area of corporate taxation, Switzerland is actively involved in the Base Erosion and Profit Shifting project of the OECD and G20.

63 https://www.sif.admin.ch/sif/en/home/dokumentation/publikationen/bericht-finanzmarktpolitik.html. See also e.g. FF 2019 5237, 5243.

64 The four other key thrusts of the financial market policy are monitoring and improving market access, allowing for innovation, optimising regulatory content and processes and limiting systemic risks.

65 For more on this, see *supra* section I.A.

66 FF 2012 6449, 6467–6468.

67 FF 2014 585, 587. See also 591.

68 GCMF, *National Risk Assessment*, 2015, p. 8.

B. SCOPE OF MONEY LAUNDERING

1. *Definition of Money Laundering in Criminal Law*

a. *Actus Reus*

i. Predicate Offences

Pursuant to art. $305^{bis}(1)$ CC, two categories of offences are regarded as predicate offences to money laundering: felonies and aggravated tax misdemeanours.

Felonies are defined in art. 10(2) CC as "offences that carry a custodial sentence of more than three years".[69] Examples include fraud (art. 146 CC),[70] computer fraud (art. 147 CC), handling stolen goods (art. 160 CC), theft (art. 139 CC), robbery (art. 140 CC), active and passive public bribery (arts. 322ter, 322^{quater} and $322^{septies}$ CC),[71] participation or support for a criminal organisation (art. 260ter CC), trafficking in human beings (art. 182 CC), certain drug-related offences (art. 19(2) Federal Act of 3 October 1951 on Narcotic and Psychotropic Substances),[72] and qualified duty fraud (art. 14(4) Federal Act of 22 March 1974 on Administrative Criminal Law).[73,74]

---

69 Under Swiss criminal law, felonies are distinguished from misdemeanours and contraventions according to the severity of the penalties that the offence carries. Misdemeanours "carry a custodial sentence not exceeding three years or a monetary penalty" (art. 10(3) CC) and contraventions are "acts that are punishable by a fine" (art. 103 CC).

70 According to the 2015 NRA, fraud was the most frequently suspected predicate offence in Switzerland for the period 2004–2014 (see GCMF, *National Risk Assessment*, 2015, p. 36). Since 2015, fraud and bribery have alternated in first place.

71 In 2018, bribery once again overtook fraud as the most frequently suspected predicate offence, with 1,639 SARs (see MROS Annual Report 2018, p. 18). As a result, the GCMF published on 15 July 2019 a report on corruption as a predicate offence to money laundering (available at: https://www.sif.admin.ch/dam/sif/fr/dokumente/Integrit%C3%A4t%20des%20Finanzplatzes/nra_bericht_korruption.pdf.download.pdf/20190710_ber-korruption-geldwaescherei-f_final.pdf). The report concludes that there is a high risk of money laundering from foreign corruption in Switzerland but also underlines Switzerland has adopted the necessary legislative and administrative measures to address it and has already started to improve them.

72 RS 812.121. In practice, the offence of money laundering is very often applied to drug-related offences; see e.g. ATF 122 IV 211 and ATF 119 IV 242.

73 RS 313.0. Since 1 January 2016, art. 14(4) Federal Act on Administrative Criminal Law is applicable to all qualified duty offences and not only to those in the realm of the international movement of goods (customs contraband). This provision is indeed also applicable to the withholding tax and stamp duties and also includes VAT on inland deliveries, provision of services and alcohol, beer and tobacco taxes on inland production. On this provision, see U. Cassani, "Evolutions récentes en matière de droit pénal économique: blanchiment d'argent et corruption privée", *Revue pénale suisse* 2018, p. 185.

74 Art. 14(4) Federal Act on Administrative Criminal Law is the only tax offence that qualifies as a felony under Swiss criminal law. It should be mentioned, however, that the Federal Supreme Court considers that fraud committed by misuse of a fiscal instrument (VAT carrousel fraud) falls under the definition of a criminal fraud in the sense of art. 146 CC, which is a felony,

Aggravated tax misdemeanours in the sense of art. 305bis(1) CC refers to tax frauds in respect of direct taxes as defined in art. 186 of the Federal Act of 14 December 1990 on Direct Federal Taxation[75] and art. 59(1) of the Federal Act of 14 December 1990 on the Harmonization of Direct Federal Taxation at Cantonal and Communal Levels,[76] when the embezzled taxes are in excess of CHF 300,000 per tax period.[77] Tax fraud as per these two provisions is committed if forged or falsified documents or documents with untrue content, such as accounting records, balance sheets, income statements, wage statements or other statements of third parties, are used to deceive the authorities for the purpose of tax evasion. It is applicable both in respect of the income and property taxes of natural persons and the profits and capital taxes of legal persons, as well in respect of property gains taxes, but not taxes on inheritance and donations.[78]

ii. Definition of Money Laundering Acts

Pursuant to art. 305bis(1) CC, money laundering is defined as any "act that is aimed at frustrating […] the forfeiture of assets which [the perpetrator] knows or must assume originate from a felony or aggravated tax misdemeanour". The notion of act has been interpreted quite broadly by the jurisprudence, in that it covers acts of conversion, transfer, concealment and disguise, which aim at removing the paper trail and thus preventing forfeiture in the sense of art. 70 CC.[79] Since money laundering under Swiss criminal law is a conduct offence, what matters is that the act is aimed at frustrating the forfeiture of assets. Whether such a frustration actually occurs has no importance.[80]

According to the Federal Supreme Court, the person committing the predicate offence can concurrently incur liability based on art. 305bis CC, meaning that under Swiss criminal law an offender can be convicted for laundering the

---

and could therefore be considered a predicate offence to money laundering (among others, see ATF 110 IV 24, c. 2e; FT 6B_461/2018 of 24 January 2019, c. 6.4.1).

75 RS 642.11.

76 RS 642.14.

77 Art. 305bis(1bis) CC.

78 On the issues raised by the notion of aggravated tax misdemeanour as predicate offence to money laundering, see U. Cassani, "Nuances de gris: la politique criminelle suisse en matière de blanchiment de fraude fiscale", *Archives de politique criminelle* 2017, p. 145; B. Chappuis, *La profession d'avocat. Tome I: Le cadre légal et les principes essentiels*, 2nd ed., Schulthess, Geneva/Zurich, 2016, pp. 261–264.

79 Among several others, examples of money laundering acts in the jurisprudence include: exchanging cash (ATF 122 IV 211); concealment of cash in a hiding place (ATF 119 IV 59, c. 2e; ATF 122 IV 211, c. 2b; ATF 127 IV 20, c. 3b); check cashing based on the conversion of a contaminated asset (FT 6B_209/2010, c. 6.4). The mere possession of proceeds does not in principle constitute an act of money laundering (ATF 128 IV 117, c. 7a; ATF 127 IV 20, c. 3a).

80 FF 1989 II 961, 983; ATF 127 IV 20, c. 3a; ATF 126 IV 255 c. 3a; ATF 124 IV 274, c. 2; ATF 119 IV 59, c. 2e.

proceeds of his or her own criminal behaviour.[81] However, it is important to stress that this position is criticised by the majority of the doctrine.[82]

The notion of assets in the sense of art. $305^{bis}(1)$ CC is extensive and includes any type of financial instruments (like Swiss and foreign banknotes and coins, precious metals and securities)[83] and, more generally, assets of every kind, whether corporeal or incorporeal, movable or immovable, and legal documents or instruments evidencing title to, or interest in, such assets.[84]

With respect to the requirement that assets must "originate from a felony or aggravated tax misdemeanour", the Federal Council[85] as well as the Federal Supreme Court[86] and most scholars[87] consider that it shall be interpreted in light of art. 70 CC related to forfeiture of assets in that only assets which are liable to forfeiture can be the subject of money laundering. Assets directly originating from a felony (*productum sceleris*) as well as assets intended to persuade or reward the perpetrator of such an offence (*praetium sceleris*) therefore undoubtedly qualify as assets as per art. $305^{bis}(1)$ CC. However, the question of whether surrogate assets, i.e. the replacement values of the proceeds of a predicate offence, are equally covered by art. $305^{bis}(1)$ CC remains controversial. Some authors indeed consider that surrogate assets cannot be confiscated and thus cannot be the subject of money laundering.[88] On the other hand, the majority

81 See e.g. ATF 126 IV 255, c. 3a; ATF 124 IV 274, c. 3; ATF 122 IV 211, c. 3; ATF 120 IV 323, c. 3e.

82 See e.g. G. Arzt, "Das schweizerische Geldwäschereiverbot im Lichte amerikanischer Erfahrungen", *RPS* 1989, p. 190; C.K. Graber, *Geldwäscherei: ein Kommentar zu Art. 305bis und 305ter StGB*, Berne, 1990, p. 111; J.-B. Ackermann, "Geldwäscherei (StGB Art. $305^{bis)}$", in N. Schmid (ed.), *Kommentar Einziehung, Organisiertes Verbrechen, Geldwäscherei*, vol. 1, Zurich, 1998, N 115; J.-B. Ackermann, "Geldwäschereistrafrecht", in J.-B. Ackermann and G. Heine (eds.), *Wirtschaftsstrafrecht der Schweiz*, Berne, 2013, N 14 f.; J.-B. Ackermann and S. Zehnder, "Art. 305bis StGB Geldwäscherei", in J.-B. Ackermann, *Kommentar Kriminelles Vermögen Kriminelle Organisationen*, vol. II, Zurich, 2018, N 226 ff. *Contra:* G. Stratenwerth and F. Bommer, *Schweizerisches Strafrecht, Besonderer Teil II, Straftaten gegen Gemeininteressen*, 6th ed., Berne, 2008, para. 55, n. 43.

83 FF1989 II 961, 982; GCMF, *National Risk Assessment*, 2015, p. 11. Financial instruments are required, however, to have an intrinsic value. Counterfeit banknotes could not therefore be the subject of money laundering (FT 6S.426/2006 of 28 December 2006, c. 2.2; J.-B. Ackermann and S. Zehnder, "Art. 305bis StGB Geldwäscherei", in J.-B. Ackermann, *Kommentar Kriminelles Vermögen Kriminelle Organisationen*, vol. II, Zurich, 2018, N 338).

84 FF 1989 II 961, 982.

85 FF 1989 II 961, 983.

86 See e.g. ATF 137 IV 79, c. 3.2; ATF 129 IV 238, c. 3.3.

87 See e.g. G. Arzt, "Wechselseitige Abhängigkeit der gesetzlichen Regelung der Geldwäscherei und der Einziehung", in S. Trechsel (ed.), *Geldwäscherei*, Zurich, 1997, pp. 25–26 ff.; J.-B. Ackermann and S. Zehnder, "Art. 305bis StGB Geldwäscherei", in J.-B. Ackermann, *Kommentar Kriminelles Vermögen Kriminelle Organisationen*, vol. II, Zurich, 2018, N 400 ff.; U. Cassani, in A. Macaluso, L. Moreillon and N. Queloz (eds.), *Commentaire Romand Code pénal II*, Basel, 2017, N 27; G. Stratenwerth and F. Bommer, *Schweizerisches Strafrecht, Besonderer Teil II, Straftaten gegen Gemeininteressen*, 6th ed., Berne, 2008, para. 55, n. 28; V. Delnon and M. Hubacher, "Geldwäscherei und Teilkontamination", *RPS* 2016, 340 f.

88 G. Stratenwerth and F. Bommer, *Schweizerisches Strafrecht, Besonderer Teil II, Straftaten gegen Gemeininteressen*, 6th ed., Berne, 2008, para. 55, n. 28.

of the doctrine[89] and the Federal Supreme Court[90] regard the money laundering offence as applicable to such assets, provided that the link with the property obtained directly from the predicate offence can be evidenced.[91]

b. *Mens Rea*

In order to be liable to prosecution for money laundering, the perpetrator must have acted intentionally, since art. 305bis CC does not provide otherwise.[92] Mere negligence is therefore not sufficient. Pursuant to art. 12(2) CC, a person acts intentionally if he/she "carries out the act in the knowledge of what he[/she] is doing and in accordance with his[/her] will". Intention includes *dolus eventualis*, an element which is already met when the perpetrator considers the harmful outcome as possible, but acts nevertheless because he/she accepts the possibility of the outcome and resigns him/herself to it.[93]

Art. 305bis(1) CC requires that the perpetrator of money laundering "knows or must assume" that the assets originate from a felony or aggravated tax misdemeanour. The wording "must assume" refers to the *dolus eventualis* and does not mean that negligence is already punishable.[94] In this context, it is also important to stress that the perpetrator is not required to know precisely the legal nature and definition of the predicate offence. The fact that he/she regards the facts as being more serious than a mere wrongdoing is deemed to be sufficient.[95]

According to the federal jurisprudence, intent and knowledge may be inferred from factual circumstances.[96]

---

89 See e.g. J.-B. Ackermann, "Geldwäscherei (StGB Art. 305bis)", in N. Schmid (ed.), *Kommentar Einziehung, Organisiertes Verbrechen, Geldwäscherei*, vol. 1, Zurich, 1998, N 211 f.; J.-B. Ackermann Jand S. Zehnder, "Art. 305bis StGB Geldwäscherei", in J.-B. Ackermann, *Kommentar Kriminelles Vermögen Kriminelle Organisationen*, vol. II, Zurich, 2018, N 346 ff.; U. Cassani, in A. Macaluso, L. Moreillon and N. Queloz (eds.), *Commentaire Romand Code pénal II*, Basel, 2017, N 28; B. Corboz, "Le blanchiment d'argent", *SJ* 1998, p. 79; H. Vest, "Probleme des Herkunftsprinzips bei der Geldwäscherei", in J.-B. Ackermann, A. Donatsch and J. Rehlberg (eds.), *Wirtschaft und Strafrecht, Festschrift für Niklaus Schmid*, Zurich, 2001, pp. 417 f. and 428 f.; S. Trechsel and M. Pieth, in S. Trechsel and M. Pieth (eds.), *Schweizerisches Strafgesetzbuch: Praxiskommentar*, 3rd ed., Zurich, 2018, art. 305bis CC, N 14.

90 See e.g. ATF 137 IV 79, c. 3.2; FT 6S.426/2006 of 28 December 2006, c. 2.2.

91 On this requirement specifically, see e.g. ATF 129 II 453, c. 4.1; ATF 137 IV 79, c. 3.2; ATF 126 I 97, c. 3c.

92 Art. 12(1) CC: "Unless the law expressly provides otherwise, a person is only liable to prosecution for a felony or misdemeanour if he commits it intentionally".

93 Art. 12(2) CC. Examples of cases which discuss the question of the *dolus eventualis* in the context of money laundering include ATF 119 IV 242 and FT 6B_900/2009 of 21 October 2010.

94 FF 1989 II 961, 984; ATF 119 IV 242, c. 2b.

95 FF 1989 II 961, 984; ATF 119 IV 242, c. 2b; ATF 122 IV 211, c. 2e; FT 6S.426/2006 of 28 December 2006, c. 2.3.

96 See e.g. FT 6B_879/2013 of 18 November 2013.

2. *Money Laundering by Omission*

As it stands, art. 305bis CC only covers money laundering by commission. However, pursuant to art. 11(1) CC, money laundering may also be committed by omission when the perpetrator fails "to comply with a duty to act", which is the case when he/she "does not prevent a legal interest protected under criminal law from being exposed to danger or from being harmed even though, due to his[/her] legal position, he[/she] has a duty to do so".[97] For instance, prosecutors, police officers or customs agents, who have the duty to protect the administration of criminal justice, could be held accountable for money laundering by omission in the event that they intentionally fail to comply with such a duty and this failure leads to money laundering.

According to a 2010 landmark decision of the Federal Supreme Court, money laundering can also be committed through omission by financial intermediaries, since the AML-related obligations imposed upon them by the AMLA, in particular the duty to clarify the economic background and the purpose of a transaction or a business relationship (art. 6) and the duty to report to the FIU (art. 9), provide them with the status of guarantor.[98] In December 2016, the FATF reported that five bankers – former top managers and senior executives of a major Swiss bank – had already been convicted for money laundering by omission in Switzerland and that other prosecutions initiated on this basis were pending.[99]

3. *Aggravated Forms of Money Laundering*

Art. 305bis(2) CC provides for the following non-exhaustive list of serious cases of money laundering:[100] where the offender acts as a member of a criminal organisation,[101] where the offender acts as a member of a group that has

---

97 Art. 11(2) CC.

98 ATF 136 IV 188, c. 6. See also FT 6B_729/2010 of 8 December 2011, c. 4.3.1, in which the Federal Supreme Court considers that the status of guarantor of financial intermediaries may also be inferred from internal regulations.

99 FATF (2016), *Anti-money laundering and counter-terrorist financing measures – Switzerland*, Fourth Round Mutual Evaluation Report, para. 179.

100 The non-exhaustive character of this list, which is evidenced by the use of the expression "in particular" (see in this sense FF 1989 II 961, 985), is considered by some authors as a violation of the principle of legality (see e.g. C.K. Graber, *Geldwäscherei: ein Kommentar zu Art. 305bis und 305ter StGB*, Berne, 1990, p. 153; J.-B. Ackermann, "Geldwäscherei (StGB Art. 305bis)", in N. Schmid (ed.), *Kommentar Einziehung, Organisiertes Verbrechen, Geldwäscherei*, vol. 1, Zurich, 1998, N 440; U. Cassani, in A. Macaluso, L. Moreillon and N. Queloz (eds.), *Commentaire Romand Code pénal II*, Basel, 2017, N 48).

101 Art. 305bis(2)(a) CC. Pursuant to art. 260ter(1) CC, a criminal organisation is "an organisation, the structure and personal composition of which is kept secret and which pursues the objective of committing crimes of violence or securing a financial gain by criminal means". According to the Federal Supreme Court, this definition also applies to art. 305bis(2)(a) CC (ATF 129 IV 271, c. 2.3.1).

been formed for the purpose of the continued conduct of money laundering activities[102] or where the offender achieves a large turnover or substantial profit through commercial money laundering.[103]

4. *Statutes of Limitation*

Like any offence which carries a custodial sentence of three years,[104] the limitation period for money laundering is 10 years.[105] However, in serious cases, a non-exhaustive list of which is provided in art. 305bis(2) CC, the limitation period is 15 years because such cases carry a custodial sentence of more than three years.[106] The limitation period begins either on the day on which the offender committed the offence, or on the day on which the final act was carried out if the offence consists of a series of acts carried out at different times, or on the day on which the criminal conduct ceases if the criminal conduct continued over a period of time.[107] Pursuant to art. 97(3) CC, the time limit ceases to apply "if a judgment is issued by a court of first instance before expiry of the limitation period". This provision only applies in the case of conviction, however. In the case of acquittal, the limitation period continues to run so that the right to prosecute can still be limited during the appeals proceedings.[108]

It should be noted that the limitation period for the prosecution of the relevant predicate offence may bar prosecutors from bringing money laundering charges. If the predicate offence is barred by a statute of limitation, then no forfeiture or money laundering in terms of forfeiture will be possible.[109]

---

102 Art. 305bis(2)(b) CC.

103 Art. 305bis(2)(c) CC. The Federal Supreme Court has considered CHF 100,000 to be a large turnover (ATF 129 IV 188 c. 3.1; ATF 117 IV 63, c. 2b), and CHF 10,000 as a substantial profit (ATF 129 IV 253, c. 2.2). With respect to the notion of commercial money laundering, the Federal Supreme Court requires that the perpetrator acts at least two times (ATF 116 IV 319, c. 2) but does not require the laundered proceeds to originate from different predicate offences (FT 6P.125/2005 and 6S.399/2005 of 23 January 2006, c. 12.2). Moreover, the perpetrator must be ready to act on an undetermined number of occasions, as soon as a favourable opportunity arises (ATF 116 IV 319, c. 2), with the intention of obtaining income from his/her offences (ATF 116 IV 319, c. 2), and to conduct his criminal activity in a professional manner, either by virtue of the time and resources devoted to it, the frequency of the acts committed, or the importance of the income which he/she seeks to obtain or has actually obtained (ATF 116 IV 319, c. 4).

104 On criminal sanctions for money laundering, see *infra* section VII.A.2.

105 Art. 97(1)(c) CC.

106 Art. 97(1)(b) CC. On criminal sanctions for aggravated forms of money laundering, see *infra* section VII.A.2.

107 Art. 98 CC.

108 ATF 134 IV 328 c. 2.1; ATF 137 IV 59, c. 4.

109 J.-B. Ackermann and S. Zehnder, "Art. 305bis StGB Geldwäscherei", in J.-B. Ackermann, *Kommentar Kriminelles Vermögen Kriminelle Organisationen*, vol. II, Zurich, 2018, N 894.

The limitation period for predicate offences (felonies and aggravated tax misdemeanours) is 15 years.[110]

5. *Jurisdictional Rules*

According to the territoriality principle, which is set forth in art. 3 CC and further specified in art. 8 CC, Swiss criminal law is applicable to every person who commits an offence in Switzerland, whether in whole or in part.[111] Therefore, any person who commits an act of money laundering in the territory of Switzerland, whether in whole or in part, falls within the jurisdiction of Swiss criminal courts. Additionally, art. 305bis CC is applicable when the perpetrator or the victim is a Swiss national, provided that the dual incrimination requirement is met and that the person concerned is in Switzerland or is extradited to Switzerland due to the offence.[112] Neither the protective principle (art. 4 CC) nor the universality principle (art. 6 CC) apply, however, since money laundering does not qualify as an offence against the State or its national security[113] and Switzerland is not obliged by any international convention to prosecute money laundering on the basis of universal jurisdiction.[114]

Finally, considering that Switzerland is an attractive location for laundering assets acquired as a result of offences committed abroad,[115] it is important to stress that money laundering is also punishable when the predicate offence was committed in the territory of another country, provided that it is a criminal offence in that country and would have constituted a criminal offence had it been carried out domestically.[116]

C. NON-CRIMINAL DEFINITION OF MONEY LAUNDERING

The only definition of money laundering under Swiss law is the one contained in art. 305bis CC. Art. 1 AMLA directly refers to it.

---

110 Art. 97(1)(c) CC; art. 60 Federal Act of 14 December 1990 on the Harmonization of Direct Federal Taxation at Cantonal and Communal Levels; art. 189 Federal Act of 14 December 1990 on Direct Federal Taxation.

111 An offence is considered to be committed in part in Switzerland when only the criminal conduct or the result of this offence occurs in Switzerland (art. 8(1) CC).

112 Art. 7(1) CC.

113 Offences against the State or its national security are listed in arts. 265–278 CC.

114 The situation is different with regard to terrorist financing (see art. 7(4) of the International Convention for the Suppression of the Financing of Terrorism of 9 December 1999, ratified by Switzerland on 23 September 2003).

115 See in this respect the 2015 NRA, according to which, for the period 2004–2014, 56% of predicate offences to money laundering taking place Switzerland were committed abroad (GCMF, *National Risk Assessment*, 2015, p. 33).

116 Art. 305bis(3) CC. On this provision, see e.g. ATF 136 IV 179, c. 2; ATF 126 IV 255, c. 3b; ATF 120 IV 323 c. 3d.

D. SCOPE OF OBLIGED ENTITIES

1. *Financial and Banking Institutions*

The AMLA is applicable to so-called "financial intermediaries".[117] Pursuant to art. 2(2), the following qualify as financial intermediaries:

a. banks as defined in article 1*a* of the Banking Act of 8 November 1934 and persons as per Article 1*b* of the same Act;

a^{bis}. asset managers and trustees mentioned in article 2(1)(a) and (b) of the Financial Institutions Act of 15 June 2018 and precious metal testers as defined in article 42bis of the Precious Metals Control Act of 20 June 1933;

b. fund managers in the sense of article 2(1)(d) of the Financial Institutions Act;

b^{bis}. investment companies with variable capital, limited partnerships for collective investments, investment companies with fixed capital and asset managers of collective investments within the meaning of the Collective Investment Schemes Act of 23 June 2006, and portfolio managers as defined in article 2(1)(c) Financial Institutions Act;

c. insurance institutions as defined in the Insurance Supervision Act of 17 December 2004 that deal in direct life insurance or offer or distribute shares in collective investment schemes;

d. securities firms mentioned in article 2(1)(e) of the Financial Institutions Act;

d^{bis}. central counterparties and central securities depositories in accordance with the Financial Market Infrastructure Act of 19 June 2015;

d^{ter}. payment systems that require authorisation from the FINMA in accordance with Article 4 paragraph 2 of the Financial Market Infrastructure Act of 19 June 2015;

e. casinos, as defined in the Federal Gambling Act of 29 September 2017;

f. promoters of large-scale games, as defined in the Federal Gambling Act.

Except for casinos and promoters of large-scale games, which are respectively supervised by the Federal Gaming Board and the Intercantonal Supervisory and Executive Authority referred to in art. 105 Federal Act on Gambling of 29 September 2017,[118] FINMA, which came into being on 1 January 2009 as a result of the Swiss Federal Banking Commission, the Federal Office of Private Insurance and the AML Control Authority being merged together,[119] is in charge

---

117 Art. 2(1)(a) AMLA.

118 Arts. 12(b) and 12(b^{bis}) AMLA. For more on specific CDD requirements for casinos and promoters of large-scale games, see *infra* section III.A.1.d; for more on supervision, see *infra* section III.H.1.

119 FINMA was created by the Federal Act of 22 June 2007 on the Swiss Financial Market Supervisory Authority (RS 956.1), which came into force on 1 January 2009 (RO 2008 5207; FF 2006 2741).

of specifying and supervising implementation of AMLA requirements by all the aforementioned financial intermediaries.[120]

Pursuant to art. 2(3) AMLA, financial intermediaries are also all "persons who on a professional basis accept or hold on deposit assets belonging to others or who assist in the investment or transfer of such assets". This second category of financial intermediaries includes in particular lending businesses,[121] providers of money or value transfer services,[122] issuers or managers of means of payment (such as credit card and travellers cheques),[123] dealers in banknotes and coins,[124] dealers in precious metals,[125] *bureaux de change*,[126] and traders in commodities and securities.[127] This category also includes persons who "make investments as investment advisers"[128] and persons who "hold securities on deposit or manage securities"[129] but no longer includes asset managers as of 1 January 2020.[130] The AMLO as well as the FINMA circular "Activité d'intermédiaire financier au sens de la LBA" set out the rules regarding when these financial activities are deemed to be carried out "on a professional basis"[131] and further specify which activities amount to financial intermediation in the sense of art. 2(3) AMLA and which do not.[132]

Since 1 January 2020, financial intermediaries as per art. 2(3) AMLA must now all become members of a self-regulatory organisation (SRO)[133] and can no longer opt to be directly supervised by FINMA.[134] According to art. 14(2) AMLA,

120 Arts. 12(a) and 17(a) AMLA. For more on specific CDD requirements for financial intermediaries as per art. 2(2)(a)–(d^{ter}) AMLA, see *infra* section III.A.1.d; for more on supervision, see *infra* section III.H.1.

121 Art. 2(3)(a) AMLA.

122 Art. 2(3)(b) AMLA.

123 *Ibid.*

124 Art. 2(3)(c) AMLA.

125 *Ibid.*

126 *Ibid.*

127 *Ibid.*

128 Art. 2(3)(f) AMLA.

129 Art. 2(3)(g) AMLA.

130 All asset managers are now (since 1 January 2020) subject to the supervision of FINMA regarding their AML/CTF-related obligations according to art. 2(2)(a^{bis}) *cum* art. 12(a) AMLA. FINMA supervision is, however, merely indirect as direct supervision of asset managers falls under the responsibility of one or several oversight bodies authorised by FINMA (art. 43*a* Federal Act on the Swiss Financial Market Supervisory Authority *cum* arts. 7(2) and 61 Federal Act on Financial Institutions).

131 Arts. 7–10 AMLO; Circ.-FINMA 11/1, "Activité d'intermédiaire financier au sens de la LBA", 20 October 2010, updated on 26 October 2016, Cm 142–153.

132 Arts. 2–6 AMLO; Circ.-FINMA 11/1, "Activité d'intermédiaire financier au sens de la LBA", 20 October 2010, updated on 26 October 2016, Cm 3–141.

133 Art. 12(c) and 14(1) AMLA.

134 According to art. 42 AMLA, financial intermediaries as per art. 2(3) AMLA which, on 1 January 2020, were still directly supervised by FINMA are compelled to become member of a recognised SRO by 31 December 2020. Such financial intermediaries are, however, allowed to pursue their activities until a decision on their affiliation is taken.

affiliation to an SRO shall be granted only if the financial intermediary guarantees compliance with its duties in accordance with the AMLA by means of its internal regulations and organisation, and if itself and the persons responsible for its administration and management, as well as the persons who hold a qualifying participation in it, enjoy a good reputation.[135] Governed by private law, SROs are structures which must be recognised by FINMA.[136] This notably requires that they issue regulations (approved by FINMA) specifying the due diligence obligations with which their affiliates must comply, that they oversee compliance with these rules and that they ensure the persons and bodies they instruct to carry out controls are independent and professionally qualified.[137] In total, 11 SROs are recognised by FINMA at the moment.

Table 1. SROs recognised by FINMA

SRO	Type of affiliates
Verein zur Qualitätssicherung von Finanzdienstleistungen (VQF)	All types of non-banking sector financial intermediary
Swiss Association of Asset Managers (SAAM)	Asset managers
Organismo di Autodisciplina dei Fiduciari del Cantone Ticino (FCT)	Fiduciaries
Selbstregulierungsorganisation des Schweizerischen Anwaltsverbandes und des Schweizerischen Notarenverbandes (SAV/SNV)	Lawyers and notaries
Association Romande des Intermédiaires Financiers (ARIF)	All types of non-banking sector financial intermediary
Schweizerischer Leasingverband (SLV)	Leasing companies
PolyReg General SRO (PolyReg)	All types of non-banking sector financial intermediary
Organisme d'Autorégulation des Gérants de Patrimoine (OAR-G)	Asset managers
SRO-TREUHAND | SUISSE	Fiduciaries
Selbstregulierungsorganisation des Schweizer Verbandes der Investmentgesellschaften (SVIG)	Investment companies
Geschäftsstelle (SVV)	Insurance companies

135 Moreover, persons who enjoy a qualifying reputation in the financial intermediary must guarantee that their influence is not detrimental to a sound and prudent management of the institution.

136 Art. 18(1)(a) AMLA.

137 Art. 24(1) AMLA. If a SRO fails to meet these conditions, FINMA can issue a warning and then withdraw its recognition (arts. 18(1)(a) and 28 AMLA). For more on specific CDD requirements for financial intermediaries affiliated to SROs, see *infra* section III.A.1.d. For more on supervision, see *infra* section III.H.1.

2. Virtual Currency System Participants

Virtual currency system participants are not explicitly designated as obliged entities under the AMLA. Nevertheless, in a report published on 14 December 2018, the Federal Council explains that a wide range of activities in the crypto area qualify as financial intermediary activities within the meaning of the AMLA and are thus subject to the latter.[138]

- Custodian Wallet Providers

Unlike non-custodian wallet providers, providers of custodian wallets hold clients' private keys in safekeeping and enable them to send and receive virtual currencies. Custodian wallet providers have power of disposal and can thus trigger transactions.[139]

According to the Federal Council, "[i]f custodian wallet providers order the transfer of cryptocurrencies in the name and on behalf of contractual parties, they are providing a payments transaction service" and are therefore subject to the AMLA.[140] As already described, persons that provide services related to payments on a professional basis indeed qualify as financial intermediaries according to art. 2(3)(b) AMLA and thus fall within the scope *ratione personae* of the latter.[141] Art. 4(1)(a) AMLO specifies that a service constitutes a service relating to payments in the sense of art. 2(3)(b) AMLA notably when the financial intermediary "issues instructions for the transfer of the assets in the name and on behalf of the contractual party".

- Centralised Trading Platforms

Centralised trading platforms are also covered by the AMLA, the Federal Council's report suggests.[142] As these platforms accept money or cryptocurrencies

138 Federal Council, *Legal framework for distributed ledger technology and blockchain in Switzerland: An overview with a focus on the financial sector*, 14 December 2018, https://www.newsd.admin.ch/newsd/message/attachments/55153.pdf. This report also highlights that certain specific crypto-related activities are currently not subject to the AMLA, namely providers of non-custodian wallets, certain decentralised trading platforms, and the issue of pure assets and utility tokens (see pp. 141–142).

139 Federal Council, *Legal framework for distributed ledger technology and blockchain in Switzerland: An overview with a focus on the financial sector*, 14 December 2018, p. 137, https://www.newsd.admin.ch/newsd/message/attachments/55153.pdf. In contrast, providers of non-custodian wallets "merely make software available and are not involved in the transfer of assets. Clients can transfer cryptocurrencies without the involvement of their non-custodian wallet providers. Such transfers are peer-to-peer transactions" (p. 137).

140 *Ibid.*

141 See *supra* section II.D.1.

142 Federal Council, *Legal framework for distributed ledger technology and blockchain in Switzerland: An overview with a focus on the financial sector*, 14 December 2018, p. 138, https://www.newsd.admin.ch/newsd/message/attachments/55153.pdf.

from clients and transfer them to other clients, thereby acting as an intermediary between clients in a trilateral relationship, they can be considered to be providing a service relating to payments within the meaning of art. 2(3)(b) AMLA *cum* art. 4(1)(a) AMLO.[143]

- Currency Exchange Offices

According to the Federal Council, "[t]he professional purchase and sale of cryptocurrencies in return for conventional currencies (e.g. CHF) or for other cryptocurrencies constitute exchange activities subject to AMLA".[144] Persons involved in such activities indeed qualify as *bureaux de change* in the sense of art. 2(3)(c) AMLA in conjunction with art. 5(1)(a) AMLO.

- Issuing of Payment Tokens as Part of an Initial Coin Offering

According to the Swiss Government, the issuing of tokens within the framework of an initial coin offering (ICO) qualifies as a financial intermediation activity if they are to be used or intended by the issuer to be used as a means of payment for the purchase of goods or services.[145] In such a case, the Federal Council indeed considers that the issuing of tokens amounts to the issuance of means of payment subject to the AMLA pursuant to art. 2(3)(b) AMLA in conjunction with art. 4(1)(b) AMLO.[146]

3. *Legal Profession and Tax Advisors*

Legal professionals, such as lawyers, notaries and tax advisors, only fall within the scope of the AMLA to the extent that they perform financial intermediation in the sense of art. 2(3), that is when they qualify as "persons who on a professional basis accept or hold on deposit assets belonging to others or who assist in the

---

143 *Ibid.*

144 *Ibid.*, p. 139. See also Federal Council, *Report on virtual currencies in response to the Schwaab (13.3687) and Weibel (13.4070) postulates*, 25 June 2014, p. 14; FINMA, *Guidelines for enquiries regarding the regulatory framework for initial coin offerings (ICOs)*, 16 February 2018, p. 7; Circ.-FINMA 11/1, "Activité d'intermédiaire financier au sens de la LBA", 20 October 2010, updated on 26 October 2016, Cm 84.

145 Federal Council, *Legal framework for distributed ledger technology and blockchain in Switzerland: An overview with a focus on the financial sector*, 14 December 2018, p. 138, https://www.newsd.admin.ch/newsd/message/attachments/55153.pdf. See also GCMF, *National Risk Assessment: Risk of money laundering and terrorist financing posed by crypto assets and crowdfunding*, October 2018, p. 14.

146 Art. 4(1)(b) AMLO specifies that the professional issuance of a cashless means of payment qualifies as a financial intermediary activity and is thus subject to the AMLA. In accordance with art. 4(2)AMLO, means of payment are instruments that allow third parties to transfer assets. The article mentions some examples, including virtual currencies.

investment or transfer of such assets". Such professionals are therefore not subject to the AMLA when their work is limited to preparing or executing non-financial aspects of the transactions concerned. As underlined by the FATF, "[t]his means in particular that acts related to setting up companies, legal persons and legal arrangements, in which lawyers, notaries or fiduciaries may be involved without being parties to transactions such as transfers, are outside the scope of the [AMLA]".[147] However, as explained *infra*,[148] this situation will change (as regards due diligence obligations) if the Federal Council's recent proposal to extend the scope of the AMLA to so-called "advisors" is adopted by the legislator.

4. *Informal Value Transfer Systems*

All providers of payment services in Switzerland should be appropriately registered and regulated. *Hawala* and other such informal value transfer services, however, usually qualify as illegal since they are usually not registered. It should be noted that, according to the federal authorities, there is no evidence that such alternative money-transfer networks are present in Switzerland.[149]

5. *Non-Profit Sector*

The AMLA does not explicitly mention non-profit entities in the list of obliged entities. However, non-profit entities can be payment institutions, and thus obliged entities, where they transfer money from the donor to the ultimate beneficiary if the selection of the ultimate beneficiary is done by the donor him/herself and not left to the transferring non-profit entity. Non-profit entities may furthermore fall under other categories of obliged entities if they fulfil the respective statutory criteria, for example a credit institution that provides loans and thus banking services to beneficiaries.

6. *Overview of Other Obliged Entities*

In addition to financial intermediaries, the AMLA also applies to so-called "dealers",[150] defined in art. 2(1)(b) as "natural persons and legal entities that deal in goods commercially and in doing so accept cash",[151] including "persons that commercially trade with goods on behalf and on account of third parties".[152]

---

147 FATF (2016), *Anti-money laundering and counter-terrorist financing measures – Switzerland*, Fourth Round Mutual Evaluation Report, para. 81.

148 See *infra* section II.D.6.

149 GCMF, *National Risk Assessment*, 2015, p. 93.

150 Art. 2(1)(b) AMLA.

151 *Ibid.*

152 Art. 13 AMLO.

Pursuant to art. 15 AMLO, goods are deemed to be any tangible movable object that is not real estate as per art. 187 CO, as well as any immovable object for which the purchase is defined in art. 216 CO.[153] Whether the trading is performed as a principal or secondary activity is irrelevant.[154] What matters is that the trading "constitutes an independent economic activity aimed at generating an ongoing income".[155]

At the time of writing, the Swiss prevention system only designates financial intermediaries and dealers as obliged entities. However, in line with the consultation draft, the DB-AMLA published by the Federal Council on 26 June 2019 proposes to extend the scope of the AMLA to a third category of obliged entities, so-called "advisors", defined as follows:

> Natural or legal person who, on a professional basis, prepare for or carry out one or several of the following activities on behalf of third parties:
>
> - Incorporation, management or administration of domiciliary companies or trusts in the sense of article 2 of the Convention of 1 July 1985 on the law applicable to trusts and on their recognition;
> - Organisation of contributions for the incorporation, management or administration of domiciliary companies or trusts;
> - Purchasing and selling of domiciliary companies;
> - Providing a business address or premises to a domiciliary company or a trust;
> - Acting (or arranging for another person to act as) as a nominee shareholder for another person.[156]

According to the Federal Council, such an enlargement of the ambit of the AMLA will ensure compliance with FATF Recommendation 22,[157] thereby taking into account one of the most important criticisms from the intergovernmental organisation's latest mutual evaluation report.[158] It will also implement the

---

153 Real estate agents are therefore deemed to be considered dealers when accepting cash payments. As rightly underlined by the FATF, real estate agents are also deemed to be considered financial intermediaries "when they transfer or pay the amount of the sale price to the seller at the buyer's instruction" (FATF (2016), *Anti-money laundering and counter-terrorist financing measures – Switzerland*, Fourth Round Mutual Evaluation Report, para. 109).

154 Art. 14(2) AMLO.

155 Art. 14(1) AMLO.

156 Art. 2(1)(c) DB-AMLA. It should be noted that operating companies in Switzerland are excluded from the scope of the DB-AMLA due to their low risk (for more on this, see FF 2019 5237, 5255).

157 FF 2019 5237, 5244 and 5253.

158 FATF (2016), *Anti-money laundering and counter-terrorist financing measures – Switzerland*, Fourth Round Mutual Evaluation Report, paras. 81 and 293. One should note that the lack of compliance of the Swiss AML legislation with FATF Recommendation 22 was already mentioned in the 2005 mutual evaluation report (paras. 882–892) as well as in the 2009 follow-up report (para. 10).

recommendations of many parliamentarians who, following the Panama Papers scandal, required the strengthening of the Swiss AML legal framework with respect to legal professionals who carry out acts related to setting up companies, legal persons and legal arrangements without being parties to transactions.[159] The information leaked in April 2016 indeed revealed the misuse of offshore companies and other corporate vehicles by many Swiss lawyers and company/trust service providers for tax evasion and money laundering purposes.[160]

A few comments should be made about the definition of advisors as provided by the Federal Council. First, advisors are subject to the AMLA only in so far as they operate on a professional basis, that is when they carry out their activities in the aim of obtaining a regular income.[161] Second, advisors are deemed obliged entities when they carry out certain activities but also when they *prepare* them. That said, according to the Federal Council, the notion of "preparation", does not include "a first exchange with a client with the aim, for example, of clarifying his/her intentions, the possible services and, if necessary, the consequences in terms of costs."[162] Third, with respect to the notion of domiciliary company, the Swiss Government refers to art. 2(1)(a) AMLO-FINMA which defines domiciliary companies as "legal entities, companies, institutions, foundations, trusts, fiduciary companies and similar associations that do not operate a trading, manufacturing or other commercial business." According to the same provision, the following are not deemed to be domiciliary companies: (i) "legal entities and companies that aim to safeguard their members' or beneficiaries' interests by means of mutual self-help or that pursue political, religious, scientific, artistic, charitable, sociable or similar aims"; (ii) "legal entities and companies that hold a majority of equity interest of one or several operating companies in order to reunite these under a single management by means of voting majority or otherwise and whose main business is not the management of assets of others (holding companies or sub-holding companies). In the process, the holding or sub-holding company shall factually exercise its management and controlling influence."

E. RELATIONSHIP BETWEEN AML AND ANTI-TERRORISM FINANCING FRAMEWORK(S)

Money laundering and terrorism financing are two different phenomena and thus two separate offences in the CC. While the former is defined in art. 305bis

159 FF 2019 5237, 5253.
160 *Ibid.*
161 FF 2019 5237, 5292.
162 *Ibid.*

CC, introduced in 1990,[163] the latter has been criminalised under art. 260^{quinquies} CC since 2003.[164]

However, with respect to the prevention of money laundering and terrorism financing, the applicable legal regime is the same since the scope of the AMLA was expanded to the financing of terrorism in 2008.[165] There is one difference that is worth noting, however. Financial intermediaries shall, in addition to performing standard CDD measures, clarify the economic background and the purpose of a transaction or of a business relationship if the data on a customer, a beneficial owner or an authorised signatory in a business relationship or transaction are identical or very similar to the data contained in the national terrorist lists established pursuant to Resolution 1373 (2001) of the UN Security Council that they shall receive from the supervisory authorities by virtue of art. 22*a* AMLA.[166] Financial intermediaries shall then file an SAR with MROS when, based on these clarifications, they know or have reason to assume that the data correspond.[167] In such a case, assets shall be immediately frozen (and kept frozen until the reporting financial intermediary receives a ruling from the competent prosecution authority but at most five working days from the date on which it filed the SAR with MROS).[168] This is an exception to the rule provided by art. 10(1) AMLA, according to which the financial intermediary that filed an SAR shall only freeze the assets that are related to the report upon receiving a notification from MROS stating that it has forwarded the case to the law enforcement authorities.[169]

---

163 See *supra* section I.A. On the criminal definition on money laundering see, *supra* section II.B.1.

164 Art. 260^{quinquies} was inserted into the CC by the Federal Act of 21 March 2003, in force since 1 October 2003 (RO 2003 3043; FF 2002 5014). One should also note that terrorist financing also falls under art. 260ter CC (see *supra* section I.B).

165 See *supra* section I.A.

166 Art. 6(2)(d) AMLA. FINMA and the Federal Gaming Board receive these lists from the FDF (art. 22*a*(1) AMLA). FINMA then sends these lists to (i) the financial intermediaries that are subject to FINMA supervision (i.e. those listed under art. 2(2)(a) and (b)-(d^{ter}) AMLA), (ii) the oversight bodies in the sense of art. 43*a* Federal Act on the Swiss Financial Market Supervisory Authority, which then must transmit the lists to the asset managers, trustees and precious metal testers that they are in charge of supervising, and (iii) SROs, which then must transmit the lists to their affiliated members (art. 22*a*(2) AMLA). The Federal Gaming Board must also send the received lists to casinos (art. 22*a*(3) AMLA). One should note that the FDF shall not pass any data on to FINMA or the Federal Gaming Board if, after consulting the Federal Department of Foreign Affairs, the Federal Department of Justice and Police, the Federal Department of Defence, Civil Protection and Sport and the Federal Department of Economic Affairs, Education and Research, it must assume that human rights or principles of the rule of law would be violated (art. 22*a*(4) AMLA).

167 Art. 9(1)(c) AMLA.

168 Art. 10(2) AMLA.

169 For more on this, see *infra* section III.B.1.d.

III. THE SYSTEM OF MONEY LAUNDERING PREVENTION

A. CUSTOMER DUE DILIGENCE

1. *Standard CDD Rules*

a. Triggers and Timing

– Financial Intermediaries

In the context of AML, the AMLA requires financial intermediaries to undertake CDD measures in the following four situations: (i) when establishing a business relationship,[170] unless it only involves assets of low value (petty cases);[171] (ii) when, in the course of a business relationship, doubts arise as to the identity of the customer or of the beneficial owner;[172] (iii) when carrying out an occasional transaction (as defined in art. 2(b) AMLO-FINMA) of significant financial value, whether that transaction is carried out in a single operation or in several operations that appear to be linked;[173] or (iv) when there is a suspicion of money laundering, regardless of any derogation, exemption or threshold.[174]

– Dealers

In the case of dealers, CDD measures shall be performed when accepting cash payments of more than CHF 100,000, including where this amount is exceeded upon aggregating several partial payments.[175] However, an exception applies if the payment(s) exceeding CHF 100,000 is carried out through a financial intermediary that is subject to the AMLA, in which case the dealer will not have to comply with the due diligence requirements for such payment(s).[176] Moreover, it should be noted that the DB-AMLA provides for a reduction of the threshold for cash payments in trading in precious metals and precious stones from CHF 100,000 to 15,000,[177] thereby addressing one of the main criticisms in the FATF's 2016 mutual evaluation report.[178] According to the Swiss Government's

170 Arts. 3, 4 and 6 AMLA.
171 Art. 7*a* AMLA.
172 Art. 5(1) AMLA.
173 Art. 3(2) AMLA.
174 Arts. 3(4) and 7*a* AMLA.
175 Art. 8*a*(1) and (3) AMLA.
176 Art. 8*a*(4) AMLA.
177 Art. 8*a*(4bis) DB-AMLA.
178 For more on this, see FATF (2016), *Anti-money laundering and counter-terrorist financing measures – Switzerland*, Fourth Round Mutual Evaluation Report, para. 303.

proposal, this only concerns the trading of gold, silver, platinum and palladium in the form of semi-finished products, melt products and melt material – and not also precious metal articles and multi-metal articles – as well as the trading of rubies, sapphires, emeralds and diamonds that are not yet threaded, assembled or mounted.[179] In other words, the trading in precious metals and precious stones that are typically intended to be sold to end-customers is excluded from the scope of the proposed rule.[180]

– Advisors

Surprisingly enough, with respect to advisors, the Federal Council does not specify in the DB-AMLA or the associated message in which circumstances exactly CDD measures would have to be fulfilled.

b. CDD Measures

– Financial Intermediaries

The AMLA requires financial intermediaries to take the three following CDD measures.

First, the financial intermediary must verify the identity of the customer on the basis of a document of evidentiary value.[181] Where the customer is a legal entity, the financial intermediary must acknowledge the provisions regulating the power to bind the legal entity, and verify the identity of the persons who enter into the business relationship on behalf of the legal entity.[182]

Second, the financial intermediary must identify the beneficial owner with the due diligence required in the circumstances except with respect to contracting parties that are listed on a stock exchange or that are subsidiaries of listed companies.[183] If the customer is not the beneficial owner or if there is any

179 See FF 2019 5237, 5259–5260 and 5297–5298.

180 *Ibid.*

181 Art. 3(1) AMLA.

182 *Ibid.*

183 Art. 4(1) AMLA. In addition, one should also note that, if a bank has no doubts that the contracting partner is identical to the beneficial owner, it is exempt from the duty to require from the contracting partner a statement concerning the beneficial ownership of the assets (art. 29 CDB). Moreover, it is important to highlight that the bank "can abstain from establishing the beneficial owners for accounts and securities accounts that are held by attorneys or notaries licensed in Switzerland or firms of attorneys or notaries organised in the form of a company on behalf of their clients provided they declare in writing that a) they are not themselves the beneficial owners as far as the assets are concerned; and b) they are subject to the corresponding cantonal and federal legislation in their capacity as attorneys or notaries; and c) they are bound by professional confidentiality (Article 321 Swiss Criminal Code) in respect of the assets deposited; and d) the account/securities account is exclusively used for the purposes of their activity as attorneys or notaries." (art. 36(1) CDB).

doubt about the matter, if the customer is a domiciliary company (as defined in art. 2(a) AMLO-FINMA) or a legal entity with an operational activity, or if it involves an occasional transaction of considerable value in the sense of art. 3(2) AMLA,[184] the financial intermediary shall require a written declaration from the customer regarding the identity of the beneficial owner.[185] Moreover, in the case of collective accounts or collective deposits,[186] the financial intermediary must require the customer to provide a complete list of the beneficial owners and to give notice of any change to the list immediately.[187] Pursuant to art. 4(1) DB-AMLA, the financial intermediary shall not only identify the beneficial owner but also critically verify his/her identity and take, with the diligence required by the circumstances, the measures necessary to ensure its plausibility (just asking to provide a copy of an identity document of the beneficial owner for the file is not deemed enough for the Federal Council).[188] However, this merely creates a legal basis for existing practice and enshrines case law. As regards art. 305ter(1) CC, which punishes any person who fails to ascertain the identity of the beneficial owner of the assets with the care that is required in the circumstances, the federal jurisprudence indeed already requires not only ascertaining but also verifying the beneficial owner's identity so that the obliged entity is satisfied that it knows who the beneficial owner is.[189] More precisely, the Federal Supreme Court considers that any person who is satisfied with the declarations of the client concerning the beneficial owner and who, despite implausibilities, does not proceed to subsequent clarifications has not properly identified the beneficial owner and has therefore breached his/her duty of diligence.[190]

Third, the financial intermediary is required to ascertain the nature and purpose of the business relationship wanted by the customer.[191] The extent of the information that must be obtained, the hierarchical level at which the decision to enter into or continue a business relationship must be taken and the regularity of checks are determined by the customer.[192]

De lege lata, there is no general and explicit obligation for the financial intermediary to ensure that data obtained as part of due diligence remains current and relevant during the business relationship. The situation may change though, as the DB-AMLA explicitly includes an obligation to regularly check

184 See *supra* section III.A.1.a.
185 Art. 4(2) AMLA.
186 On collective accounts and collective deposits, see FF 1996 III 1060, 1082.
187 Art. 4(3) AMLA.
188 FF 2019 5237, 5295.
189 ATF 125 IV 139, c. 4.
190 *Ibid.*
191 Art. 6(1) AMLA.
192 *Ibid.*

that client data is up to date.[193] According to the Federal Council's proposal, the frequency and scope of reviews should be based on the degree of risk posed by the contracting party.[194]

– Dealers and advisors

Pursuant to arts. 8*a*(1)(a)–(b) AMLA and 8*b*(1)(a)–(b) DB-AMLA, dealers and advisors shall verify the identity of the customer and establish the identity of the beneficial owner in the same way as financial intermediaries.

Additionally, the Federal Council deems it necessary to oblige advisors to always clarify the economic background and purpose of any operation wanted by the customer.[195] Dealers are only bound by this obligation in specific circumstances.[196]

c. Individual Responsibility

The AMLA does not require that a particular person within the obliged entity is responsible for the implementation and application of CDD measures. Art. 26(1) AMLO-FINMA provides, however, that the Board of Directors or the supreme management board of financial intermediaries must approve internal directives on the combating of money laundering and terrorist financing.

d. Further CDD Guidance

As mentioned *supra*,[197] the AMLA is a framework law, meaning that it sets out basic requirements, in particular CDD requirements, which are further specified and completed in several ordinances and regulations. In this regard, the AMLO specifies in detail the CDD measures that dealers must take.[198] Whilst the AMLO is the only instrument which defines the due diligence requirements under the AMLA for dealers, CDD obligations for financial intermediaries are stipulated in various instruments, depending on the type of financial intermediary.[199] The AMLO-FINMA sets out the rules regarding the implementation of the due diligence requirements by the financial intermediaries as per art. 2(2) AMLA

---

193 Art. $7(1^{bis})$ DB-AMLA.

194 *Ibid.*

195 Art. 8*b*(2) DB-AMLA.

196 Art. 8*a*(2) AMLA. See *infra* section III.A.3.a.

197 See *supra* section I.A *in fine*.

198 More specifically, see arts. 17–21 AMLO.

199 On the different categories of financial intermediaries, see *supra* section II.D.1.

which are supervised by FINMA.[200] As regards financial intermediaries as per art. 2(3) AMLA, due diligence requirements are provided by the SROs' regulations[201] (which must be approved by FINMA).[202] Regarding casinos and promoters of large-scale games, preventive measures are stipulated in the AMLO-CFMJ for the former, and in the AMLO-FDJP for the latter.[203] Lastly, one should not forget the CDB, which aims at substantiating due diligence rules for banks (as defined in art. 2(2)(a) AMLA) and securities dealers (as defined in art. 2(2)(d) AMLA) concerning the identification of contracting partners along with the establishment of the controlling persons and beneficial owners.[204] Although this is formally a private law agreement between the SBA, on the one hand, and the signatory banks, on the other hand, most financial intermediaries in the sense of art. 2(2) AMLA have to abide by it according to arts. 35, 40(4) and 41(3) AMLO-FINMA. The provisions of the CDB are thus an integral part of the regulatory framework that applies to all banks and securities traders in Switzerland.

It would fall outside the ambit of this study to go into detail about the content of each of these regulatory instruments. However, it is deemed appropriate to highlight and illustrate some of their main characteristics in terms of CDD requirements for obliged entities.

– Applicable Threshold for Transactions

The AMLA requires financial intermediaries to take CDD measures when carrying out an occasional transaction of significant financial value, but does not determine what constitutes a significant financial value.[205] Quite the opposite, the AMLA explicitly requires FINMA, the Federal Gaming Board and SROs to define the applicable threshold in their respective fields and adjust such values as required.[206] According to the relevant legal instruments, this threshold is set at CHF 15,000 for all financial intermediaries since 1 January 2020.[207] Pursuant to arts. 2(1) and 3 AMLO-CFMJ, casinos must apply CDD measures to all transactions of more than CHF 4,000, whether these transactions are carried

200 Art. 3(1) AMLO-FINMA.
201 Art. 25(2) AMLA.
202 Art. 18(1)(c) AMLA.
203 Art. 17(b) and (c) AMLA; art. 1(1) AMLO-CFMJ; art. 1(1) AMLO-FDJP.
204 More specifically, see arts. 4–41 CDB 20.
205 Art. 3(2) AMLA. See *supra* section III.A.1.a.
206 Art. 3(5) AMLA.
207 See e.g. arts. 40(1) and 41(1)(c) AMLO-FINMA; Art. 3(1) R SVV; §14(2)(a) R PolyReg General SRO (PolyReg); art. 22 R VQF. One should note, however, that, in the case of a money-changing transaction, the threshold is set at CHF 5,000 (see e.g. art. 51(1)(a) AMLO-FINMA; art. 10(2) R OAR-G).

out in a single operation or in several operations during a 24-hour period. Alternatively, offline casinos may also choose to apply CDD measures to all customers at the entry to a casino.[208]

– Timing of Verification of the Identity of the Customer and Beneficial Owner

The AMLA does not specify when exactly obliged entities are supposed to verify the identity of the customer and beneficial owner.

As regards dealers, art. 17(1) AMLO provides that such a verification shall be performed in all cases "at the conclusion of the agreement". No exception applies.

The rules are slightly more complex with respect to financial intermediaries. In principle, the financial intermediaries must obtain the documents and information required to verify the identity of the customer and the beneficial owner before executing the transaction or establishing the business relationship.[209] However, if particular information and/or documents are not available or particular documents have not been provided in the appropriate form and on the basis of a risk-based assessment, banks and securities dealers are authorised to open the account by way of exception, so that the ordinary course of business is not disrupted, but such information and/or documents must be obtained as soon as possible and no later than 30 days after the opening of the account.[210] Failing that, the bank must freeze the account for all incoming and outgoing assets, and decide the next steps to take based on a risk analysis. In the case where the missing information and/or documents cannot be provided, the bank is required to end the relationship.

– Required CDD Measures

The AMLA imposes several CDD measures on obliged entities but does not specify exactly how to implement them.[211] The AMLO and the various regulatory texts applicable to financial intermediaries fill this gap.

For instance, the AMLA imposes on all obliged entities the principle of customer identification and verification of identity on the basis of a document of evidentiary value, but does not indicate the type of document that shall be used.[212] Against this background, the AMLO-FINMA specifies that any identification document bearing a photo is acceptable for natural persons[213] and

208 Art. 2(3) AMLO-CFMJ.

209 See e.g. art. 55(1) AMLO-FINMA; art. 12 R OAR-G; §7(2) R PolyReg; art. 45(4) CDB 20.

210 Art. 6(3) R SAAM; art. 45(4) CDB 20.

211 See *supra* section III.A.1.b.

212 Arts. 3(1) and 8*a*(1) AMLA. See *supra* section III.A.1.a.

213 Art. 45(3) AMLO-FINMA.

that legal persons must show an extract from the commercial register or another official document.[214] It also provides that when the customer does not have identification, the financial intermediary may verify identity on an exceptional basis using other "documentary evidence".[215] Similar rules are applicable to financial intermediaries affiliated to SROs, casinos, promoters of large-scale games and dealers.[216]

– Failure to Satisfactorily Complete CDD

Another important characteristic of the regulatory texts that specifies the CDD requirements set out in the AMLA is that they indicate what financial intermediaries shall do in the event of a failure to comply with relevant CDD measures. The AMLA itself is indeed silent on this point.

When the obligations to verify the identity of the customer or the beneficial owner cannot be carried out, certain affiliates of SROs, must refuse to establish the business relationship or must terminate it.[217] On the other hand, when banks have not obtained the missing documents within a period of 90 days, they are not obliged to terminate the business relationship but only to block all outgoing funds (which does not rule out the possibility of incoming funds during this period being of illicit origin).[218] Banks must, however, terminate the business relationship as soon as possible if doubts persist concerning the beneficial owners following a second procedure to confirm their identity or if it has been confirmed that they were knowingly supplied with erroneous information.[219]

2. *Simplified CDD*

a. Scope

The AMLA allows for simplified CDD measures in only one case, which is when the customer is a listed company or a subsidiary over which a listed company has majority control.[220]

---

214 Art. 47 AMLO-FINMA.

215 Art. 50(2) AMLO-FINMA. One could think, for instance, of a confirmation from a public authority or a business report signed by an auditor.

216 See e.g. arts. 8 and 9 CDB 20; arts. 4(1), 5 and 6 R SVV; §§9 and 11 R PolyReg; arts. 15, 16 and 21 R VQF; art. 5(1) AMLO-CFMJ; arts. 6–8 AMLO-FDJP; art. 17 AMLO.

217 See e.g. §§17 and 25 R PolyReg; art. 6(3) R SAAM.

218 Art. 45 CDB 20. See *supra* section III.A.1.d.

219 Art. 46(2) CDB 20.

220 Art. 4(1) AMLA.

b. Requirements

Pursuant to art. 4(1) AMLA, when the customer is a listed company or a subsidiary over which a listed company has majority control, the identity of the beneficial owner need not be established by the financial intermediary. This also applies to dealers.[221]

c. Further Simplified CDD Guidance

Except in the aforementioned case where a customer is a listed company or a subsidiary over which a listed company has majority control, financial intermediaries cannot decide to apply simplified CDD measures on their own. They can only do it within the framework set out by FINMA. Pursuant to art. 3(2) AMLO-FINMA, FINMA may take into account specific information related to the activities of financial intermediaries by reducing requirements, depending on the level of risk involved. Financial intermediaries are not authorised to reduce their level of due diligence in the event of low risk that they may have identified outside the provisions expressly made by the AMLO-FINMA.

The AMLO-FINMA only provides for simplified CDD measures for issuers of means of payment.[222] According to art. 12(1) AMLO-FINMA, issuers of means of payment are exempted from having to collect copies of documents for the identification of contractual parties and the establishment of the controlling person and beneficial owner of the assets for their files if they have a delegation agreement with a bank authorised in Switzerland that contains certain specific clauses, such as the obligation for the bank to inform the issuer of means of payment whether the contractual party, the controlling person or the beneficial owner of the assets is a PEP.[223] Moreover, art. 12(2) AMLO-FINMA provides that, under certain conditions, issuers of means of payment do not need to obtain a certification of authenticity for copies of identification documents when the business relationship was contracted directly and by mail. For instance, this exemption applies when the means of payment that allows private persons to receive or send money by cashless payment between private persons domiciled in Switzerland does not exceed CHF 1,000 per month and CHF 5,000 per year and per contractual party.[224]

---

221 Art. 8*a*(1)(b) AMLA.

222 Simplified CDD measures are not to be confounded with exemptions from CDD. On exemptions from CDD, see art. 11 AMLO-FINMA.

223 Art. 12(1)(b) AMLO-FINMA.

224 Art. 12(2)(c) AMLO-FINMA.

3. *Enhanced CDD*

a. Scope

- Financial Intermediaries

In the context of AML, the AMLA requires financial intermediaries to apply enhanced CDD measures in the following circumstances: (i) if the transaction or the business relationship appears unusual, unless its legality is clear;[225] (ii) if there are indications that assets are the proceeds of a felony or an aggravated tax misdemeanour or are subject to the power of disposal of a criminal organisation;[226] or (iii) if the transaction or the business relationship carries a higher risk.[227]

- Dealers

In the case of dealers, the AMLA requires them to apply enhanced CDD measures in two situations: (i) if a transaction appears to be unusual (unless its legitimacy is clearly recognisable);[228] or (ii) if there are indications that assets are the proceeds of a felony or of an aggravated tax misdemeanour or are subject to the power of disposal of a criminal organisation.[229]

b. Requirements

Under the AMLA, enhanced CDD measures consist of clarifying the economic background and the purpose of a transaction or of a business relationship.[230]

c. Further Enhanced CDD Guidance

The AMLA does not further specify the scope and requirements of enhanced CDD measures. Similarly to standard CDD measures, further guidance is to be found in the various regulatory texts which complete the Swiss AML legal framework,[231] with the notable exception of the CDB.[232] Here again, it would fall outside the ambit of this study to go into detail about the content of each of

225 Art. 6(2)(a) AMLA.
226 Art. 6(2)(b) AMLA.
227 Art. 6(2)(c) AMLA.
228 Art. 8*a*(2)(a) AMLA.
229 Art. 8*a*(2)(b) AMLA.
230 Arts. 6(2) and 8*a*(2) AMLA.
231 See *supra* section III.A.1.d.
232 Art. 2(2) CDB 20: "The special duties of investigation for business relationships and transactions involving higher risks are set out in the AMLO-FINMA".

these ordinances and regulations. However, it is deemed appropriate to provide a brief overview of the most relevant binding guidance they provide with respect to enhanced CDD measures.

– Indications that Assets are the Proceeds of a Felony or of an Aggravated Tax Misdemeanour or are Subject to the Power of Disposal of a Criminal Organisation

Art. 8*a*(2)(b) AMLA requires dealers to clarify the economic background and the purpose of a transaction when there are indicators of money laundering, but does not specify either the nature or the content of these indicators. Art. 19 AMLO partially fills the gap by providing the following non-exhaustive list of indicators of money laundering:

> a. the person pays predominantly with small denomination bank notes;
> b. primarily easily marketable goods with a high degree of standardization are purchased;
> c. the person does not provide any or only insufficient identification information … or insufficient data to determine the beneficial owner;
> d. the person provides obviously false or misleading information;
> e. there are doubts as to the authenticity of the identification documents.

– Business Relationships and Transactions Carrying a Higher Risk

Pursuant to art. 6(2)(c) AMLA, financial intermediaries shall clarify the economic background and the purpose of any business relationship and transaction which they have identified as carrying a higher risk. In this context, all ordinances and regulations applicable to financial intermediaries include a non-exhaustive list of criteria that the latter shall take into account to identify higher-risk situations.

As regards criteria for spotting business relationships carrying a higher risk, some are very often brought up, such as: the registered office or domicile of the customer, controlling person or beneficial owner of the assets;[233] the nationality of the customer or beneficial owner;[234] the nature and location of the business activity of the customer or beneficial owner of the assets;[235] a lack of personal contact with the customer and beneficial owner;[236] the amount of

233 See e.g. art. 13(2)(a) AMLO-FINMA; art. 13(2)(b) AMLO-CFMJ; art. 31(2)(a) R SAAM; art. 57(5)(a) R VQF; art. 27(2)(a) R OAR-G; §32(3)(a) R PolyReg.

234 *Ibid.*

235 See e.g. art. 13(2)(b) AMLO-FINMA; art. 13(2)(c) AMLO-CFMJ; art. 31(2)(b) R SAAM; art. 57(5)(b) R VQF; art. 27(2)(b) R OAR-G; §32(3)(b) R PolyReg.

236 See e.g. art. 13(2)(c) AMLO-FINMA; art. 31(2)(c) R SAAM; art. 57(5)(b) R VQF; §32(3)(b) R PolyReg.

assets deposited;[237] the amount of inflowing and outflowing assets;[238] or the use of complex legal structures, in particular domiciliary companies.[239] On the other hand, some criteria are more specific and only applicable to certain types of obliged entities. Such is the case, for instance, of the request for a mortgage credit in a currency other than the Swiss franc or for a building that is not located in Switzerland, a criterion which only applies to insurance companies.[240]

Regarding criteria that financial intermediaries shall use to identify higher-risk transactions, three are always mentioned: the amount of inflowing and outflowing assets; significant variations from the normal transaction type, volume and frequency for the business relationship in question; and significant variations from the usual transaction type, volume and frequency of for comparable business relationships.[241] However, some criteria are only relevant to specific sectors and thus are only mentioned in certain instruments. For instance, the fact that a payment of more than CHF 25,000 made to a beneficiary who is not the policyholder either because of family reasons, personal reasons or business relations is only considered a relevant criterion in the SRO-SVV regulation applicable to insurance companies that are not under FINMA supervision.[242] Moreover, federal ordinances and SROs' regulations differ with respect to the types of transactions that shall always be considered by financial intermediaries as carrying a higher risk. For instance, the AMLO-CFMJ exclusively refers to transactions that amount to CHF 30,000 or more,[243] whilst the Verein zur Qualitätssicherung von Finanzdienstleistungen (VQF) regulation refers to transactions where assets with an equivalent value of CHF 100,000 are physically introduced at the beginning of the business relationship, either at once or in a staggered manner, and to money and asset transfers whereby a single transaction, or multiple transactions that appear to be related, reach or exceed CHF 5,000.[244]

- Additional Clarifications for Business Relationships and Transactions Carrying a Higher Risk

Ordinances and regulations that further specify the AMLA not only clarify the scope of enhanced CDD measures but also define what is meant by clarifying

237 See e.g. art. 13(2)(e) AMLO-FINMA; art. 13(2)(d) AMLO-CFMJ; art. 31(2)(e) R SAAM; art. 57(5)(e) R VQF; art. 27(2)(c) R OAR-G; §32(3)(e) R PolyReg.

238 See e.g. art. 13(2)(f) AMLO-FINMA; art. 13(2)(e) AMLO-CFMJ; art. 31(2)(f) R SAAM; art. 57(5)(f) R VQF; §32(3)(f) R PolyReg.

239 See e.g. art. 13(2)(h) AMLO-FINMA; art. 31(2)(h) R SAAM; art. 57(5)(h) R VQF; art. 27(2)(e) R OAR-G, §32(3)(h) R Polyreg.

240 Art. 13bis(2)(m) R SVV.

241 See e.g. art. 14(2) AMLO-FINMA; art. 15(2) AMLO-CFMJ; art. 32(2) R SAAM; art. 58(2) R VQF; art. 28(2) R OAR-G.

242 Art. 13ter(2)(g) R SVV.

243 Art. 15(3) AMLO-CFMJ.

244 Art. 58(3) R VQF.

the economic background and the purpose of a business relationship or transaction which carries a higher risk. Depending on the circumstances, financial intermediaries shall then for instance clarify whether the customer is the beneficial owner of the assets,[245] the origin of the assets,[246] the intended use of withdrawn assets,[247] the background and plausibility of large incoming payments,[248] the source of wealth of the contracting party and beneficial owner,[249] or the professional or business activity of the customer, controlling person or beneficial owner of the assets.[250]

4. *Rules on Politically Exposed Persons*

a. Definition

The AMLA refers to three different types of PEPs – foreign PEPs, domestic PEPs and PEPs in international organisations – which it defines as follows:

- *foreign PEPs* are "individuals who are or have been entrusted with prominent public functions by a foreign country, such as heads of state or of government, senior politicians at national level, senior government, judicial, military or political party officials at national level, and senior executives of state-owned corporations of national significance".[251]
- *domestic PEPs* are "individuals who are or have been entrusted with prominent public functions at national level in Switzerland in politics, government, the armed forces or the judiciary, or who are or have been senior executives of state-owned corporations of national significance".[252]
- *PEPs in international organisations* are "individuals who are or have been entrusted with a prominent function by an intergovernmental organisation or international sports federations, such as secretaries general, directors, deputy directors and members of the board or individuals who have been entrusted with equivalent functions".[253]

245 See e.g. art. 15(2)(a) AMLO-FINMA; art. 16(a) and (b) AMLO-CFMJ; art. 55(3)(a) R VQF.
246 See e.g. art. 15(2)(b) AMLO-FINMA; art. 16(c) AMLO-CFMJ; art. 14(1)(b) R SVV; art. 34(2)(a) R SAAM; art. 29(1)(b) R OAR-G; art. 55(3)(b) R VQF; §35(2)(a) R PolyReg.
247 See e.g. art. 15(2)(c) AMLO-FINMA; art. 14(1)(f) R SVV; art. 29(1)(c) R OAR-G; art. 55(3)(c) R VQF; §35(2)(b) R PolyReg.
248 See e.g. art. 15(2)(d) AMLO-FINMA; art. 55(3)(d) R VQF.
249 See e.g. art. 15(2)(e) AMLO-FINMA; art. 16(d) AMLO-CFMJ; art. 55(3)(e) R VQF; art. 14(1)(c) R SVV; art. 34(2)(e) R SAAM; §35(2)(d) R PolyReg.
250 See e.g. art. 15(2)(f) AMLO-FINMA; art. 16(e) AMLO-CFMJ; art. 55(3)(f) R VQF; §35(2)(e) R PolyReg.
251 Art. 2*a*(1)(a) AMLA.
252 Art. 2*a*(1)(b) AMLA. The precise list of domestic PEPs is provided in FF 2013 607, 657.
253 Art. 2*a*(1)(c) AMLA. An international sports federations in the terms of this provision is the International Olympic Committee and the non-governmental organisations that it recognised that regulate one or more official sports at global level (art. 2*a*(5) AMLA).

In the case of domestic PEPs, the PEP status ends 18 months after the person's retirement from the relevant function.[254] For foreign PEPs and PEPs in international organisations, no such pre-defined period is applicable. For these persons, one could argue that a risk-based approach shall be used to define whether the status must be maintained.

Obliged entities in Switzerland reportedly determine the PEP status by researching public information sources and lists prepared by external service providers, as well as by using external companies for specific research in the case of foreign customers.[255] This approach corresponds to the minimum procedures required by the Federal Supreme Court case law.[256]

b. Requirements

According to the AMLA, business relationships with foreign PEPs and their family members or close associates (as defined in art. 2*a*(2) AMLA) shall always be deemed by financial intermediaries to be higher-risk business relationships.[257] On the other hand, relationships with domestic PEPs and PEPs in international organisations and their family members or close associates shall only be considered as carrying a higher risk when combined with one or more further risk criteria.[258]

The AMLA itself does not set out specific enhanced CDD measures with respect to PEPs. In other words, it does not require anything other than the clarification of the economic background and the purpose of the business relationship.

c. Further Enhanced CDD Guidance on PEPs

As just mentioned, the AMLA itself does not set out specific enhanced CDD measures with respect to PEPs. However, regulatory texts sometimes require additional measures. For instance, the establishment of a business relationship with a PEP may be subject to the approval of management at its highest level or at least one of its members.[259] Financial intermediaries may also have to implement regular monitoring for transactions with foreign PEPs.[260] Another example is that of continued heightened monitoring, which may have to be put in place with the involvement of the management body, which each year

---

254 Art. 2*a*(4) AMLA.

255 FATF (2016), *Anti-money laundering and counter-terrorist financing measures – Switzerland*, Fourth Round Mutual Evaluation Report, para. 306.

256 FT 6B_729/2010 of 8 December 2011, c. 3.5.5.

257 Art. 6(3) AMLA.

258 Art. 6(4) AMLA.

259 See e.g. art. 19(1) AMLO-FINMA; art. 15(1) R SRO-SVV; §34(4) R PolyReg; art. 60 R VQF, §2.6.9.1 R SVIG; art. 27(5) R OAR-G.

260 See e.g. art. 19 AMLO-FINMA; art. 15(1)(b) R SVV; art. 60(2) R VQF; §2.6.9.1 R SVIG.

must receive the information required to decide whether to pursue the business relationships.[261]

5. *Rules on High-Risk Third Countries*

a. Scope

As mentioned *supra*,[262] when assessing money laundering risks, financial intermediaries must take into account the customer's country/place of business or establishment to identify higher-risk business relationships and transactions. For some financial intermediaries, the criteria for identifying increased risk also refer to the customer's links with countries whose AML/CFT measures do not comply with the core principles of the AMLA,[263] or with "countries or territories that are non-cooperative or subject to international sanctions recognised by Switzerland".[264] Until recently, however, there was no set list of high-risk third countries in relation to which financial intermediaries had to take enhanced CDD measures. That said, it should be pointed out that since 1 January 2020 financial intermediaries under FINMA supervision have to apply enhanced CDD measures with respect to any kind of business relationship or transaction involving a high-risk third country identified as such by the FATF.[265] The SROs also modified their requirements on this point and have introduced similar measures, particularly on the classification of business relationships and transactions presenting a higher risk.

b. Requirements

Neither the AMLA nor the ordinances and regulations which specify it set out particular enhanced CDD measures with respect to higher-risk countries.

c. Further Enhanced CDD Guidance on High-Risk Third Countries

There is no further enhanced CDD guidance on high-risk third countries in Switzerland.

6. *Private Sector CDD Guidance*

The CDB aims at substantiating due diligence rules for banks (as defined in art. 2(2)(a) AMLA) and securities dealers (as defined in art. 2(2)(d) AMLA) concerning the identification of contracting partners, along with the establishment of the

---

261 See e.g. art. 25(1)(e) AMLO-FINMA; §34(4)(a) R Polyreg.
262 See *supra* section III.A.3.c.
263 See e.g. art. 13bis(2)(k) R SVV.
264 See e.g. art. 31(7)(c) R SAAM.
265 See in particular arts. 13(3)(d) and 14(3)(b) AMLO-FINMA.

controlling persons and beneficial owners.[266] Although this is formally a private law agreement between the SBA, on the one hand, and the signatory banks, on the other hand, most financial intermediaries in the sense of art. 2(2) AMLA have to abide by it according to arts. 35, 40(4) and 41(3) AMLO-FINMA. The provisions of the CDB are thus an integral part of the regulatory framework that applies to all banks and securities traders in Switzerland.

B. PRELIMINARY RISK ANALYSIS

The AMLA does not impose an obligation on obliged entities to carry out a risk analysis of their business operations prior to carrying out any client-specific or transaction-specific CDD measures in order to assess their risk exposure and adapt their CDD practice accordingly. However, according to art. 25(2) AMLO-FINMA, financial intermediaries are required to prepare a risk analysis for money laundering and terrorist financing, specifically taking into account the client's domicile or residence, the client segment, and the products and services offered. The risk analysis shall be approved by the board of directors or executive management and updated periodically.[267]

C. REPORTING AND ASSET FREEZING

1. *First-Time Reporting*

a. Trigger for/Degree of Suspicion

– Financial Intermediaries

The reporting system currently used in Switzerland with respect to financial intermediaries draws a distinction between the right to report, in the case of "mere" suspicion of money laundering (voluntary SARs), and the obligation to report, in the case of "well-founded" suspicion (mandatory SARs). These two categories are dealt with in two separate pieces of legislation, respectively art. $305^{ter}(2)$ CC and art. 9(1) AMLA. However, the distinction between voluntary and mandatory SARs has become blurred in recent years and the same level of suspicion seems now to be covered by both provisions.

The right to report was introduced into the CC in 1994, four years before the entry into force of the AMLA, which provided for mandatory SARs.[268]

---

266 More specifically, see arts. 4–41 CDB 20.
267 Art. 25(2) AMLO-FINMA.
268 See *supra* section I.A.

Art. 305ter(2) CC was therefore the first provision under Swiss law that addressed the question of reporting cases of suspected money laundering to competent authorities. At the time, the legislator's concern was to provide a basis of justification in the sense of art. 14 CC so that financial intermediaries could report to the prosecution authorities cases where they suspected assets originated from a felony without themselves becoming the subject of legal proceedings for breach of professional secrecy, like bank secrecy or manufacturing/trade secrecy.[269] The text of art. 305ter(2) CC refers to "any observations that indicate that assets originate from a felony or an aggravated tax misdemeanour in terms of Article 305bis(1bis) CC". The Federal Council defines "observations" as "elements based on suspicion, likely to be supported by the prosecution authorities".[270] According to the Swiss Government, art. 305ter(2) CC allows financial intermediaries to "communicate to the competent authorities the relevant facts of an individual case – their observations, questions, misgivings and all documentary evidence – which lead them to believe that the assets may be of criminal origin".[271] In other words, as explained by MROS, financial intermediaries can use their right to report "on account of a suspicion based on probability, doubt or a sense of unease about entering into a business relationship".[272]

Under the obligation to report set forth in art. 9(1)(a) AMLA, financial intermediaries must immediately file an SAR in the context of AML if they know or assume, based on a "well-founded suspicion", that assets involved in a business relationship are connected to an offence in terms of art. 260ter(1) (support or participation to a criminal organisation) or 305bis CC (money laundering),[273] or that they derive from a felony or an aggravated tax misdemeanour in the sense art. 305bis(1bis) CC,[274] or that they are subject to the power of disposal of a criminal organisation.[275] The reporting requirement also applies where a financial intermediary breaks off negotiations aimed at establishing a business relationship because of a well-founded suspicion that the assets involved are connected to an offence defined under art. 9(1)(a) AMLA (cases of attempted money laundering).[276] According to the Federal Council's interpretation at

269 FF 1993 III 269, 314–315. Bank secrecy is provided for in art. 47 of the Federal Act of 8 November 1934 on Banks and Savings Banks (RS 952.0). Breach of manufacturing or trade secrecy is provided for in art. 162 CC.

270 FF 1993 III 269, 317.

271 *Ibid.*

272 MROS Annual Report 2012, p. 10.

273 Art. 9(1)(a)(1) AMLA.

274 Art. 9(1)(a)(2) AMLA.

275 Art. 9(1)(a)(3) AMLA.

276 Art. 9(1)(b) AMLA. According to the Swiss FIU, "[s]ubmitting a SAR under article 9(1)(b) AMLA allows MROS to gather information on assets of doubtful origin and on suspect persons, and pass this information on to prosecution authorities or to its counterparts abroad" (MROS Annual Report 2017, p. 13). For further information on art. 9(1)(b) AMLA, see FF 2007 5919, 5936.

the time the reporting obligation was introduced, a suspicion is deemed well founded "where there are concrete signs or several clues that spark fear that the assets involved are of criminal origin".[277] However, the interpretation of this notion was broadened over time. In its 2007 Annual Report, MROS explained that the Government did not intend to establish a duty to report only when there are concrete facts to submit the report.[278] Rather, according to MROS's interpretation, "mandatory SARs should be submitted when a financial intermediary is required to clarify an unusual transaction or business connection under art. 6 AMLA and has evidence that assets either originate from criminal activity or at least that this possibility cannot be excluded".[279] Pursuant to this interpretation, which was upheld several times by the Federal Supreme Court[280] and the Federal Criminal Court,[281] a mere doubt therefore becomes a well-founded suspicion when clarifications of the economic background and the purpose of a transaction or business relationship do not enable the suspicion that the assets are of legal origin to be dismissed.

In this context, there is now very little scope for the application of art. 305ter(2) CC. According to the federal jurisprudence, the circumstances covered by the right to report indeed largely fall under the obligation to report. The Federal Council therefore initially proposed repealing the right to report.[282] As pointed out by both the Swiss Government in the explanatory report on the proposal[283] and the FATF,[284] the suppression of the dual legal regime for reporting would have prevented legal uncertainty for financial intermediaries as to the circumstances in which there is a requirement to report suspicious activities. However, based on the results of the public consultation, the Federal Council finally decided to maintain the right to report in the DB-AMLA and to clarify at a later stage the meaning of "well-founded suspicion", and thereby the difference between the right and the obligation to report, in the AMLO.[285] The definition provided will be aligned on the aforementioned jurisprudential interpretation.[286] Without providing any explanation as to such a radical change

277 FF 1996 III 1057, 1086.
278 MROS Annual Report 2007, p. 3.
279 *Ibid.*
280 See in particular FT 4A_313/2008 of 27 November 2008 and FT 1B_433/2017 of 21 March 2018, c. 4.5.1.1.
281 See in particular FT SK.2014.14 of 18 March 2015, c. 4.5.1.1 and FT SK.2017.54 of 19 December 2017, c. 2.2.3.1.
282 See the explanatory report of the preliminary draft bill (available at: https://www.newsd.admin.ch/newsd/message/attachments/52555.pdf), pp. 16–20.
283 *Ibid.*, p. 18.
284 FATF (2016), *Anti-money laundering and counter-terrorist financing measures – Switzerland*, Fourth Round Mutual Evaluation Report, para. 315.
285 See FF 2019 5237, 5264–5265.
286 *Ibid.*, p. 28.

of vision, the Federal Council now considers that "the right to report should in no case be seen as competing with the obligation to report. The same case can never fall under both the right and the obligation to report."[287]

– Dealers

Contrary to financial intermediaries, dealers in Switzerland are only subject to an obligation to report and not also to a right to report.[288] Under art. 9(1bis) AMLA, dealers have a duty to report if they know or assume, on the basis of a well-founded suspicion, that the cash used for payment has to do with offences mentioned in art. 260ter(1) (support or participation to a criminal organisation) or art. 305bis CC (money laundering), that the cash comes from a felony or an aggravated tax misdemeanour under art. 305bis(1bis) CC, or that the cash in question is at the disposal of a criminal organisation. According to art. 20 AMLO, a suspicion is deemed well founded in the sense of art. 9(1bis) AMLA "if there is concrete evidence or several clues that the cash payment stems from a punishable act, which cannot be dismissed despite additional clarifications as per Article 19 AMLO".

Art. 9(1bis) AMLA does not specify whether the threshold of CHF 100,000 applicable for CDD measures also applies to the reporting obligation or if this obligation applies to all cash payments. MROS clarifies this point as follows:

> [Well-founded] grounds for suspicion requires a certain level of knowledge about the client. This knowledge may be acquired after having carried out due diligence required under Article 8*a* AMLA. However, this latter provision only applies if the payment exceeds CHF 100'000. It logically ensues that the only SARs to be received from merchants are those relating to amounts exceeding CHF 100'000 and for which there are [well-founded] grounds for suspicion after due diligence has been carried out.[289]

– Advisors

With respect to advisors, the Federal Council had initially not provided for an obligation to report. However, the Swiss Government finally decided to include an obligation for advisors to file an SAR with MROS in the event that they know or have well-founded grounds to suspect that a transaction they prepare for

287 *Ibid.*, p. 29.

288 According to one author though, art. 305ter(2) CC should be applied to dealers by analogy (U. Cassani, "Commentaire de l'article 305ter CP", in A. Macaluso, L. Moreillon and N. Queloz (eds.), *Commentaire romand, Code penal II (art. 311–392) CP, Partie spéciale, Helbing Lichtenhahn*, Basel, 2017, p. 2019).

289 MROS Annual Report 2014, p. 55.

or carry out is connected to an offence in terms of art. 260ter(1) (support or participation to a criminal organisation) or 305bis CC (money laundering), or that they derive from a felony or an aggravated tax misdemeanour in the sense art. 305bis(1bis) CC, or that they are subject to the power of disposal of a criminal organisation.[290] No obligation to report arises if no transaction is involved. According to the Federal Council, this is in line with FATF Recommendation 23, which indeed only requires trust and company service providers to report suspicious *transactions*.[291]

b. Content and Direct Addressee(s) of SARs

Financial intermediaries and dealers shall send all their SARs to MROS,[292] which is the only contact point for the submission of SARs in Switzerland.[293] Since 1 January 2020, SARs must now be submitted exclusively via the goAML Web application, an online platform,[294] and no longer by fax or mail. The goAML Web application, which was developed by the United Nations Office on Drugs and Crime as one of its strategic responses to financial crime, but to which MROS made specific customisation changes,[295] provides a secure web interface between MROS and the reporting entities (for which a prior registration in the system is required).[296] It allows the submission of SARs using the XML upload functionality[297] or manually filling the reports online.[298]

---

290 Art. 9(1ter) DB-AMLA.

291 See the explanatory report of the preliminary draft bill, available at: https://www.newsd.admin.ch/newsd/message/attachments/52555.pdf, pp. 10–11.

292 Art. 9(1) and (1bis) AMLA.

293 One should note, however, that voluntary SARs could be sent directly either to MROS or to the law enforcement authorities up until 2008. The Federal Act of 3 October 2008 for Implementing the Revised FATF Recommendations of 2003 abolished this dual channel system.

294 Art. 3*a* O-MROS. For more on this new information system, see https://www.fedpol.admin.ch/fedpol/en/home/kriminalitaet/geldwaescherei/meldung.html and https://www.fedpol.admin.ch/dam/data/fedpol/kriminalitaet/geldwaescherei/aml/faq-e.pdf.

295 For more on the specific customisation changes introduced by MROS into the goAML Web system, see https://www.fedpol.admin.ch/dam/data/fedpol/kriminalitaet/geldwaescherei/aml/goaml-web-manual-e.pdf.

296 Art. 3*a*(2) O-MROS. Registration can be completed via the registration page available at: https://www.fedpol.admin.ch/fedpol/en/home/kriminalitaet/geldwaescherei/meldung/registrierung.html.

297 XML is an IT format used to structure large volumes of data such as might exist in an SAR. For more on XML reporting for goAML, see https://www.fedpol.admin.ch/dam/data/fedpol/kriminalitaet/geldwaescherei/aml/goaml-xml-schema.pdf.

298 Until 30 June 2020 (end of the transition period), however, obliged entities will also be able to submit their SARs following a third procedure. For further information on this procedure, see https://www.fedpol.admin.ch/fedpol/en/home/kriminalitaet/geldwaescherei/meldung.html.

Regarding the content of SARs, all SARs must include the following information, regardless of whether they are filed by financial intermediaries or dealers:[299]

- name and address of the reporting entity;
- name and details of a contact person within the reporting entity (though this information can also be provided on a separate document);
- date of reporting;
- data on the contracting party (in the case of individuals, at least the name, address, date of birth and nationality; in the case of legal entities, at least the name and domicile);
- name and address of residence of the ultimate beneficial owner(s) if the customer is not the (only) beneficial owner (dealers must also mention the date of birth and the nationality of the beneficial owner(s) in accordance with art. 18(4)(c) and(d) AMLO); and
- description of why the activity is suspicious.

Additionally, all SARs filed by financial intermediaries must contain the following:[300]

- name of the supervisory authority;
- thorough description of the business relationship, including in particular the place of the business relationship (or place where the activity prompting the report took place), the date of establishment/termination of the relevant account(s), the account(s) number(s); the type of accounts (e.g. individual/joint account, numbered/personal account, global account);
- details on the assets involved, including the account(s) balance;
- type and number of the identification document obtained from the contracting party, as well as the issuing agency and the date of issuance;
- way in which mail is delivered to the contracting party;
- data on third parties involved (e.g. payee, payor, deliverer of checks, stocks, guarantee beneficiary, guarantee surety, third-party security creditors);
- other existing business relationships with the contracting party (if applicable);
- data on persons with power of attorney/authorised signatory (at least the name and address of residence);

---

299 See the reporting forms available on MROS's website (for financial intermediaries: https://www.fedpol.admin.ch/fedpol/en/home/kriminalitaet/geldwaescherei/meldung/meldeformular.html; for dealers: https://www.fedpol.admin.ch/fedpol/en/home/kriminalitaet/geldwaescherei/meldung/meldeformular-haendler.html).

300 See art. 3(1) O-MROS and the reporting forms available for financial intermediaries on MROS's website (https://www.fedpol.admin.ch/fedpol/en/home/kriminalitaet/geldwaescherei/meldung/meldeformular.html).

- type of source that triggered suspicion (e.g. media, information received from law enforcement authorities, information received from third parties like potential victims or business partners);
- description of the suspicious activity, including account statements and detailed documentary evidence of suspicious transactions as well as potential links with other business relationships in the sense of art. 9 AMLA and art. $305^{ter}(2)$ CC and the results of the clarifications carried out pursuant to art. 6 AMLA;
- documentation on suspicious elements (e.g. printouts of World Check entries, press/media reports, decisions from prosecution authorities).

c. Duty not to Disclose

Under the AMLA, financial intermediaries and dealers are prohibited from informing the persons concerned that they have filed an SAR with MROS.[301] However, the prohibition on tipping off "does not apply to protecting personal interests in the context of a civil action or criminal or administrative proceedings".[302] The purpose of this provision is to give the financial intermediary or the dealer that filed an SAR the possibility to defend itself in the event that a lawsuit is filed against it under civil, criminal or administrative law. The existence of such a lawsuit is therefore an important factor in the application of this provision. As underlined by MROS, "[t]he requirement not to inform the client, however, cannot be lifted within the framework of preliminary discussions between the financial intermediary and its client (e.g. aimed at avoiding a court case under civil, criminal or administrative law)".[303]

d. Power or Duty to Freeze

While in the past any SAR filed with MROS led to an immediate freezing of assets, the act of submitting an SAR in the context of AML is now dissociated from the act of freezing assets.[304] Pursuant to art. 10(1) AMLA, freezing of assets related to an SAR shall only be initiated following a notification from MROS stating that the relevant information contained in the SAR have been forwarded to the competent prosecution authority. Pending such notification, which, at the time of writing shall be received within 20 working days in the case

---

301 Art. 10*a*(1) and (5) AMLA. Art. 10*a*(5) DB-AMLA provides the same prohibition for advisors that have filed an SAR.

302 Art. 10*a*(6) AMLA.

303 MROS Annual Report 2014, p. 53.

304 The new system was introduced by the Federal Act of 12 December 2014 for Implementing the Revised FATF Recommendations of 2012.

of a mandatory SAR,[305] the financial intermediary shall continue executing the orders of the customer.[306]

Once the financial intermediary is notified by MROS that the relevant information contained in its SAR was forwarded to the competent prosecution authority, it shall immediately freeze the underlying assets until a ruling is received from the latter, but at most for five working days.[307] If the financial intermediary itself is unable to freeze the assets, it may inform the financial intermediary subject to the AMLA that is able to do so.[308] This is particularly relevant for asset managers who usually do not have power of disposal over the assets of their clients, unlike banks, which hold the assets on deposit.[309]

e. Instant Collateral Duties

Financial intermediaries that are supervised by FINMA shall always inform the latter whenever they file an SAR that relates to a business relationship that involves significant assets.[310] In particular, they must inform FINMA when, in view of the circumstances, it must be assumed that the case that was reported will have an impact on the reputation of the financial intermediary or Switzerland as a financial place.[311] Regarding financial intermediaries that are supervised by SROs, some of them are obliged to inform the SRO to which they are affiliated of every single SAR they send to MROS.[312]

2. Follow-Up

a. Duty to Provide FIU with Additional Data

According to art. 11*a*(1) AMLA, financial intermediaries that have filed a voluntary or mandatory SAR with MROS shall, if requested to do so, provide to the latter any additional information it may need to carry out the analysis of the SAR.[313] Financial intermediaries shall, however, only provide additional

---

305 Art. 23(5) AMLA. In contrast, there is no timeframe imposed on MROS to analyse SARs filed by financial intermediaries on the basis of art. 305ter(2) CC. The Federal Council now suggests that the same applies to all SARs, whether they are filed on the basis of art. 9(1) AMLA or 305ter(2) CC. For more on this, see *infra* section IV.B.1.

306 Art. 9*a* AMLA. Art. 9*a*(2) DB-AMLA provides that, during MROS's analysis of an SAR, financial intermediaries shall ensure that they execute client orders involving significant amounts in such a manner as to leave a paper trail.

307 Art. 10(2) AMLA.

308 Art. 10(3) AMLA.

309 FF 2007 5919, 5937.

310 Art. 34 AMLO-FINMA.

311 *Ibid.*

312 See e.g. art. 75(1) R VQF.

313 Art. 11*a*(1) DB-AMLA provides the same obligation for advisors that have filed an SAR.

information of a financial nature which directly relates to the SAR they have filed and which is either in their possession or in the hands of entities in Switzerland which form part of them.[314] It should also be noted that MROS shall specify a deadline for the provision of the information.[315]

Dealers are not bound by the obligation to provide additional information to MROS after having a filed an SAR.[316]

b. Continued Duty not to Disclose SAR to Client

According to arts. 10*a*(1) and 11*a*(4) AMLA, the ban on tipping off the client about the filing of an SAR or the provision of additional information to MROS is not limited in time. Therefore, obliged entities shall never[317] disclose to a client the fact that they filed an SAR with MROS or that they provided additional information to the latter, unless it is necessary for protecting their personal interests in the context of a civil action or criminal or administrative proceedings.[318] Moreover, as explained above, art. 9*a* AMLA requires financial intermediaries to execute client orders while MROS is carrying out its analysis.[319] This obligation is aimed at preventing the client from being indirectly informed that an SAR has been sent to MROS.

c. Continued Collateral Duties

During MROS's analysis of an SAR, financial intermediaries placed under FINMA supervision shall ensure that they execute client orders involving significant amounts in such a manner as to leave a paper trail.[320] The same also applies to financial intermediaries subject to certain SROs.[321] Article 9*a*(2) DB-AMLA renders this obligation applicable to all financial intermediaries.

---

314 FF 2012 6449, 6481.

315 Art. 11*a*(3) AMLA.

316 Art. 11*a*(1) AMLA *a contrario.*

317 One should note, however, that, according to art. 34(3) AMLA, the right to information of persons concerned in accordance with art. 8 of the Federal Act on Data Protection shall only be suspended from the filing of an SAR until the time when MROS informs the financial intermediary whether it passes on the SAR to a prosecution or not and for as long as assets are frozen in accordance with art. 10 AMLA. Given that this provision contradicts arts. 10*a*(1) and 11*a*(4) AMLA, the Federal Council suggests in the DB-AMLA to rewrite it in order to make clear that obliged entities shall never disclose to a client the fact that they filed an SAR with MROS or that they provided additional information to the latter. For more on this, see FF 2019 5237, 5270.

318 Art. 10*a*(6) AMLA. See *supra* section III.B.1.c.

319 See *supra* section III.B.1.d.

320 Art. 33 AMLO-FINMA.

321 See e.g. Art. 50 R SAAM; art. 70 R VQF; art. 62(3) R SAV/SNV.

3. *Special Rules for Privileged Professions*

a. Trigger for/Degree of Suspicion

As already mentioned, lawyers and notaries are so far only subject to the AMLA to the extent that they perform financial intermediation in the sense of art. 2(3), i.e. when they qualify as "persons who on a professional basis accept or hold on deposit assets belonging to others or who assist in the investment or transfer of such assets".[322] Art. 9(2) AMLA[323] provides, however, an exception with respect to the reporting requirement. According to this provision, lawyers and notaries are not subject to the obligation to report insofar as they are bound in their (financial intermediation) activities by professional secrecy in terms of art. 321 CC.[324]

According to the Federal Supreme Court, financial intermediation activities where lawyers and notaries are bound by professional secrecy in the sense of art. 321 CC are those which are specific to the profession (*activités typiques; anwaltsspezifische Dienstleistungen*).[325] FINMA provides some examples.[326] With respect to lawyers, professional secrecy applies, for instance, to "deposit transactions and, if appropriate, related short-term investments in relation to upfront payments or procedural fees, securities, public-law contributions, etc., as well as payments to or from a party, a third party or an authority relating to an inheritance partition in progress or to the execution of dispositions because of death, the pending liquidation of a matrimonial regime in the context of a divorce or separation, a civil or public law before ordinary or arbitral tribunals as well as enforcement proceedings".[327] As regards notaries, professional secrecy could apply to "the transfer of the purchase price of a real state through the notary's client assets account which authenticates the deed of sale".[328] Professional secrecy could also for instance apply to "the reimbursement by the notary of mortgage debts on the purchase price or the payment of taxes related to a real estate transaction using funds transferred by a co-contractor".[329]

322 See *supra* section II.D.3. See also art. 9(2)(b) DB-AMLA.

323 Art. 9(2)(a) DB-AMLA.

324 In this regard, see FF 2019 5237, 5300.

325 ATF 132 II 103, c. 2. *Contra:* B. Chappuis, *La profession d'avocat. Tome I: Le cadre légal et les principes essentiels*, 2nd ed., Schulthess, Geneva/Zurich, 2016, pp. 295–296. According to this author, financial intermediation activities carried out by lawyers and notaries are never specific to the profession. As a result, the author considers that lawyers and notaries who carry out financial intermediation activities are always subject to the obligation to report.

326 See also GCMF, *National Risk Assessment: Risque de blanchiment d'argent associé aux personnes morales*, November 2017, pp. 84–85, https://www.sif.admin.ch/dam/sif/fr/dokumente/Integrit%C3%A4t%20des%20Finanzplatzes/national-risk-assessment.pdf.download.pdf/National%20Risk%20Assessment%20(NRA)%20-%20F.pdf.

327 Circ.-FINMA 11/1, "Activité d'intermédiaire financier au sens de la LBA", 20 October 2010, updated on 26 October 2016, Cm 116.

328 Circ.-FINMA 11/1, "Activité d'intermédiaire financier au sens de la LBA", 20 October 2010, updated on 26 October 2016, Cm 123.

329 *Ibid.*

Conversely, financial intermediation activities in the context of which lawyers and notaries are *not* bound by professional secrecy in the sense of art. 321 CC and are therefore subject to the reporting requirement as per art. 9 AMLA are those which are not specific to the profession (*activités accessoires*; *akzessorische (anwaltliche) Geschäftstätigkeit*).[330] FINMA defines such activities as those where "the commercial component prevails over the activity of lawyer".[331] This includes notably activities which are usually carried out by asset managers, fiduciaries or banks, like asset management or investment.[332]

b. Content and Addressee(s) of SAR

Swiss law does not allow lawyers and notaries to send their SARs to their SRO (Selbstregulierungsorganisation des Schweizerischen Anwaltsverbandes und des Schweizerischen Notarenverbandes, SAV/SNV). Lawyers and notaries must send their mandatory and voluntary SARs directly to MROS,[333] which will then forward the relevant information as well as the results of its analysis to the competent prosecution authority if deemed necessary.[334] The Federal Council indeed considers that "it is up to the lawyers and notaries themselves to distinguish, in the context of their practice and in each individual case, whether it is a case related to their main or accessory activity",[335] and therefore whether they are bound by professional secrecy or not.

Likewise, there is no special rule regarding the content of SARs filed by privileged professions. These SARs must include the same information as those filed by any other financial intermediaries.[336]

c. Duty not to Disclose to Client

Under Swiss law, there are no special rules on the prohibition on tipping off for privileged professions. In particular, there is no derogatory provision allowing them to dissuade a client from engaging in illegal activity.

---

330 ATF 132 II 103, c. 2.

331 Circ.-FINMA 11/1, "Activité d'intermédiaire financier au sens de la LBA", 20 October 2010, updated on 26 October 2016, Cm 117.

332 *Ibid.* See also ATF 112 IB 608; FF 1996 III 1057, 1088.

333 Art. 61 R SAV/SNV.

334 Art. 23(4) AMLA. See *infra* section IV.B.1.

335 FF 1996 III 1057, 1089. During the consultation process preceding the Federal Council's decision on the AMLA, the Swiss Bar Association and the Swiss Association of Notaries proposed, however, a special regulation on reporting by lawyers and notaries. Under this proposal, lawyers and notaries would not submit their reports to MROS, but to their self-regulatory body. This body would be responsible for deciding whether the report concerned facts covered by professional secrecy or whether it could be transmitted to MROS.

336 See *supra* section III.B.1.b.

4. *Protection of SAR's Source*

According to art. 9(1ter) AMLA, the name of the financial intermediary or dealer must appear in any SAR filed with MROS. The identity of the financial intermediary's or dealer's employees who are in charge of the case may, however, be made anonymous in the SAR, provided it is guaranteed that MROS and the competent prosecution authority are able to contact them without delay.[337]

D. RECORD KEEPING

Obliged entities in Switzerland are subject to a duty to keep records on transactions and clarifications required under the AMLA for 10 years after the transaction has been performed or the business relationship terminated.[338] The records must give "experts an objective idea about the transactions and business relationships as well as compliance with the provisions of the AMLA"[339] and must be kept in such a manner as to be able to respond within a reasonable time to any requests from law enforcement authorities[340] and other authorised authorities.[341] Financial intermediaries must also keep all SAR-related data.[342] These data must be kept separately for five years.[343]

E. COMPLIANCE OFFICERS

The Swiss AML legal framework requires financial intermediaries to establish a special department responsible for the prevention of money laundering. The duties of this department are further explained *infra*.[344]

F. INTERNAL COMPLAINT MECHANISM

In Switzerland, obliged entities are not required to have in place an internal complaint mechanism that would allow employees or third persons to inform senior management about violations of AML-related obligations committed within the obliged entity.

---

337 Art. 9(1ter) AMLA.
338 Arts. 7(1), 7(3) and 8*a*(1)(c) AMLA. See also art. 8*b*(1)(c) DB-AMLA (advisors).
339 Art. 7(1) AMLA.
340 Art. 7(2) AMLA.
341 See e.g. art. 22(1) AMLO-FINMA; art. 21(1) AMLO-CFMJ; art. 41(1) R SAAM; §37(4) R PolyReg.
342 Art. 34 AMLA.
343 Art. 34(1) and (4) AMLA.
344 See *infra* section III.G.

G. ADDITIONAL PREVENTIVE MEASURES

The Swiss AML legal framework requires financial intermediaries to take the necessary organisational measures to prevent money laundering in their field of business.[345] In particular, this includes providing employees with adequate training on all relevant aspects of AML[346] and, in the majority of cases, ensuring that employees meet the integrity criteria and are selected in compliance with the duty of care.[347] This also includes having a special department responsible for the prevention of money laundering. Depending on the financial intermediary, this special department shall, for instance, support and advise line managers and management in the implementation of AML measures,[348] organise and monitor training of staff,[349] define the parameters for the transaction monitoring system,[350] carry out or order additional clarifications,[351] ensure that the responsible management body is provided with sufficient information to approve business relationships with PEPS,[352] and/or prepare a risk analysis in relation to its field of activity and type of business relationships, especially taking into account the domicile or residence of the customers, the customer segment and the products and services offered.[353] Where applicable (indeed, not all financial intermediaries are obliged to have internal directives),[354] the special department shall also be in charge of preparing and/or supervising the adherence to internal directives for the prevention of money laundering.[355]

345 The Swiss AML legal framework does not include any corresponding duties for dealers. Regarding advisors, however, art. 8c DB-AMLA requires them to take organisational measures. In particular, they shall ensure that their staff receive adequate training and that internal controls are carried out.

346 Art. 8 AMLA. See also e.g. art. 27 AMLO-FINMA; art. 24 AMLO-CFMJ; art. 26 AMLO-FDJP; art. 39 R OAR-G; §60(1) R PolyReg; art. 21(1) R ASA; art. 79 R VQF.

347 See e.g. art. 27 AMLO-FINMA; art. 2(1)R OAR-G; art. 42(1) R SAAM. *Contra* R PolyReg, which does include an equivalent provision.

348 See e.g. art. 24(1) AMLO-FINMA; art. 23(2)(e) AMLO-CFMJ; art. 25(2)(e) AMLO-FDJP; §41(1) R PolyReg.

349 See e.g. art. 24(2) AMLO-FINMA; art. 23(2)(b) AMLO-CFMJ; art. 25(2)(b) AMLO-FDJP; art. 44(4)(b) R SAAM; §41(2) R PolyReg; art. 21(1) R ASA.

350 See e.g. art. 25(1)(b) AMLO-FINMA; art. 25(2)(d) AMLO-DFJP; art. 38(2) R OAR-G; §41*bis*(b) R PolyReg.

351 See e.g. art. 25(1)(d) AMLO-FINMA; art. 25(2)(c) AMLO-DFJP; art. 23(2)(c) AMLO-CFMJ; art. 21(1) R ASA; art. 38(2) R OAR-G; §41*bis*(c) R PolyReg.

352 See e.g. art. 25(1)(e) AMLO-FINMA; art. 38(2) R OAR-G; §41*bis*(e) R PolyReg.

353 See e.g. art. 25(2) AMLO-FINMA; art. 38(3) R OAR-G; §41(2) R PolyReg; art. 77(3) R VQF; art. 21(5) R ASA.

354 For instance, affiliates to certain SROs are only obliged to have internal directives if they have more than 10 employees concerned with activities subject to AMLA. See e.g. art. 43 R SAAM; art. 78 R VQF; art. 36 R OAR-G.

355 See e.g. arts. 24(2) and 25(1)(a) AMLO-FINMA; art. 38(2) R OAR-G; art. 21(2) R ASA; art. 44(4)(a) R SAAM; art. 77(1)(c) R VQF.

Such directives shall address, *inter alia*, the criteria applied to define business relationships with increased risk and to detect transactions with increased risk; the transaction monitoring requirements; the cases in which the internal AML specialists or body must be involved and the senior executive body notified; the basic principles on the training of employees; the company policy on PEPs; the responsibility to file reports with MROS; the method in which the financial intermediary records, limits and monitors increased risks; the criteria pursuant to which third parties can be involved in order to identify the contracting party or the beneficial owner, or to fulfil the duties concerning further clarification with regard to a business relationship or transactions; and the internal division of responsibilities between the specialist AML unit and the other units concerned with AML compliance.[356]

H. RULES ON OBLIGED ENTITIES' CIVIL LIABILITY TOWARDS CLIENT

According to art. 11 AMLA, any obliged entity that in good faith files an SAR with MROS,[357] or that freezes assets in accordance with art. 10 AMLA,[358] may not be prosecuted for a breach of official, professional or trade secrecy or be held liable for breach of contract. This rule also applies when financial intermediaries provide upon request additional information to MROS for the fulfilment of its analysis function.[359]

I. SUPERVISORY AUTHORITIES' ROLE

1. *Supervisory Measures to Ensure Application of CDD and Other AML-Related Obligations*

In order to provide a clear and comprehensive picture of the various measures that supervisory authorities shall or can take to prevent money laundering and ensure application of CDD and other AML-related obligations by obliged entities, it is deemed appropriate to address separately the measures that FINMA shall/can take towards the financial intermediaries under its supervision, the

356 See e.g. art. 26(2) AMLO-FINMA; art. 36(4) R OAR-G; art. 43(2) R SAAM; art. 78(2) R VQF; art. 21(3) R ASA.

357 See *supra* section III.B.1.a.

358 See *supra* section III.B.1.d.

359 Art. 11*a*(5) AMLA. For more on the provision of additional information to MROS by financial intermediaries, see *supra* section III.B.2.a and *infra* section IV.A.4.

measures that FINMA shall/can take towards the SROs, the measures that the Federal Gaming Board and the Intercantonal Supervisory and Executive Authority referred to in art. 105 Federal Act on Gaming shall/can take towards casinos and promoters of large-scale games, and the measures that SROs shall/can take towards their affiliates.[360] Dealers are not *stricto sensu* supervised but still must appoint an audit firm to verify that they comply with their AML-related duties. This obligation (which may also apply to advisors, should they become a third category of obliged entities) will therefore also be addressed herein.

- FINMA's Supervisory Measures towards the Financial Intermediaries under its Supervision

As part of its prudential supervision responsibilities, FINMA has the duty to supervise compliance with the AML/CTF requirements by financial intermediaries in the sense of art. 2 (a)–(d^{ter}) AMLA.[361] The range of supervisory activities carried out by FINMA in this context includes in particular the application of the fit and proper test with respect to managers and directors, audits and on-site supervisory reviews at the premises of supervised institutions.

FINMA uses the "*garantie d'activité irréprochable*" mechanism to ensure that managers and directors of financial intermediaries under its supervision are fit and proper, the aim being to ensure that only individuals who meet the proper business conduct requirements under financial market law are involved in the strategic or executive management of financial institutions. FINMA applies this mechanism at the time of application for licensing[362] and also, in certain cases, at the time of changes of managers and/or directors.[363] FINMA maintains a watch list of persons whose business conduct does not meet the fit and proper requirements or whose fitness and propriety need to be confirmed should the person assume a position subject to these requirements.[364] The file only contains

360 On the different categories of financial intermediaries and institutional arrangements for supervision and oversight, see *supra* section II.D.1.

361 Art. 12(a) AMLA.

362 See e.g. art. 3(2)(c) Federal Act on Banks and Savings Banks; art. 10(2)(d) Federal Act of 24 March 1995 on Stock Exchanges and Trading in Securities (RS 954.1); art. 14(1)(a) Federal Act on Collective Investment Schemes; art. 14(1)(a) Federal Act of 17 December 2004 on the Supervision of Insurance Companies (RS 961.01). It should be noted that sector-specific provisions also require that, at the time of authorisation, holders of at least 10% of the equity or voting rights or a qualified shareholding guarantee that their influence will not be wielded to the detriment of sound and prudent management (see e.g. art. 3(2)(c^{bis}) Federal Act on Banks and Savings Banks).

363 See e.g. art. 10(6) Federal Act on Stock Exchanges and Trading in Securities; art. 16 Federal Act on Collective Investment Schemes.

364 Art. 1*a*(1) FINMA Ordinance of 8 September 2011 on Data Processing (RS 956.124).

information that is necessary to perform the "*garantie d'activité irréprochable*" assessment.[365] This includes: identifying information (surname, first name, date of birth, gender, place of origin, nationality, address and first language); education and professional activities (qualifications, further training, expertise, employer and workplace); financial situation and insurances; extracts from commercial, debt enforcement, bankruptcy and criminal registers; criminal charges and criminal complaints launched by authorities; court decisions, decrees and other official documents; reports and decisions by self-regulatory and professional organisations; measures imposed under employment law, administrative law and criminal law; reports by auditors and third parties appointed by FINMA; and reports on internal audits and investigations of supervised institutions.[366] FINMA informs the person concerned in writing about any data collection entry.[367] It can defer informing the person concerned if there are predominant interests for doing so.[368]

Auditing is also an important part of FINMA's supervisory work in the area of AML vis-à-vis the financial intermediaries under its direct supervision. Audits can be carried out either by FINMA itself or by audit firms licensed by the Federal Audit Oversight Authority.[369] FINMA's approach to AML auditing is risk-oriented in the sense that the intensity of auditing depends on the risk posed by the respective financial market participant. For each category of financial intermediary under its supervision (e.g. banks, security dealers, insurance companies, etc.), FINMA sets out a minimum standard strategy whereby it defines the frequency and scope of the so-called "basic audit".[370] For instance, the minimum standard strategy currently applicable for banks and securities dealers includes an annual critical review (whereby the auditor attests that there is no element allowing him/her to conclude that there are irregularities) and a more in-depth audit (whereby the auditor gives a positive assurance of the lack of irregularities) every three years.[371] Certain AML-related aspects are however subject to an annual in-depth audit, which involves carrying out sampling of a group of files selected randomly, for example the application of CDD measures, in particular with regard to higher-risk customers.[372] Moreover, additional audits

---

365 Art. 3(1) FINMA Ordinance on Data Processing.

366 Art. 3(2) FINMA Ordinance on Data Processing.

367 Art. 5*a* FINMA Ordinance on Data Processing.

368 Art. 18*b* Federal Act of 19 June 1992 on Data Protection (RS 235.1), to which art. 5*a* FINMA Ordinance on Data Processing refers.

369 Art. 24(1) Federal Act on the Swiss Financial Market Supervisory Authority.

370 Art. 3(1) Federal Council Financial Market Audit Ordinance of 5 November 2014 (RS 956.161); Circ.-FINMA 2013/3, "Activités d'audit", 6 December 2012, updated on 20 June 2018, Cm 28–29.

371 See Appendix I (Presentation of the audit strategy – banks/securities dealers) to Circ.-FINMA 2013/3, "Activités d'audit", 6 December 2012, updated on 20 June 2018.

372 See e.g. footnote 1 of Appendix I (Presentation of the audit strategy – banks/securities dealers) to Circ.-FINMA 2013/3, "Activités d'audit", 6 December 2012, updated on 20 June 2018.

will be carried out if the risk analysis of the supervised institution highlights a medium to high net risk exposure. For medium- and high-risk institutions, FINMA indeed defines additional actions – either a supplementary audit to widen the scope of the elements reviewed (for example, verifying whether the irregularities found during the previous year's review concern other areas of activity)[373] or a targeted audit conducted by a third party ("*chargé d'audit*") – in order to examine an aspect of the audit in depth.[374]

In addition to audits, FINMA may also carry out on-site checks using its own resources, which allows it to conduct in-depth and exhaustive checks of the entire AML/CFT mechanism. As a rule, on-site supervisory reviews are performed as part of annual planning. However, additional unscheduled supervisory reviews may also be performed due to specific events. The duration of an on-site supervisory review may be from a few days to a few weeks, if a more in-depth assessment of the situation is required.

– FINMA's Supervisory Measures towards SROs

FIMMA monitors compliance with AML/CTF requirements by financial intermediaries under its direct supervision but also by SROs from the date on which they are recognised.[375]

FINMA undertakes a risk analysis and classification of SROs once a year. The annual classification is based on the number and the structure of the affiliates, the inherent risk of the affiliates as well as the assessment of FINMA of the supervision policy and the organisation of the SRO itself. The risk category (high, medium or low) to which a SRO is assigned determines the intensity and frequency of the supervisory tools used by FINMA in each case.

Supervisory tools include periodic on-site supervisory reviews, regular bilateral supervisory consultations and analysis of a SRO's annual reports. Once a year, all SROs are sent assessment letters detailing any weak points and indicating where action is required. In addition, FINMA organises meetings with all SROs as a forum for discussing general challenges in the operational implementation of AML requirements.

– Federal Gaming Board and Intercantonal Supervisory and Executive Authority's Supervisory Measures towards Casinos and Promoters of Large-scale Games

---

373 Art. 4 Financial Market Audit Ordinance.

374 Arts. 24(1)(b) and 24*a* Federal Act on the Swiss Financial Market Supervisory Authority. For example, in 2011, at the time of the movements connected with political developments in North Africa (the "Arab Spring"), FINMA asked for a more in-depth analysis of the PEP customers of 20 banks.

375 Art. 18(1)(b) AMLA. On the recognition of SROs by FINMA, in particular the conditions which must be fulfilled for recognition, see *supra* section II.D.1.

As part of their duties, the Federal Gaming Board and the Intercantonal Supervisory and Executive Authority referred to in art. 105 Federal Act on Gambling are in charge of monitoring compliance with AML requirements by casinos and promoters of large-scale games.[376] To achieve this task, the two supervisory authorities can notably request and obtain all the information and documents they deem necessary, carry out on-site checks, order provisional measures while the investigation is in progress, and appoint experts.[377]

– SROs' Supervisory Measures towards their Affiliates

The AMLA gives the SROs general powers to supervise their affiliated financial intermediaries with regard to compliance with the AML requirements enshrined in the regulations they issue.[378] FINMA cannot act directly with the SROs' affiliates, nor can it act in the place of the SROs with regard to the affiliates. Similarly to FINMA regarding the financial intermediaries under its supervision, SROs' supervisory responsibilities primarily consist of verifying that the supervised financial intermediaries are fit and proper, and conducting audits.

The SROs set out their membership conditions either in their statutes or in their AML regulations. These conditions generally require that affiliates, their directors, managers and employees and anyone who holds a significant share of their capital enjoy a good reputation and provide guarantee of proper business conduct and compliance with AML duties.[379] The SROs must be informed of changes in the data or information given to them at the time of joining, and in some cases must approve these changes.[380]

With respect to AML auditing, which can be carried out by the SROs themselves or be delegated,[381] audit cycles vary depending on the SRO. In general, however, audits take place every year,[382] but can be spaced out upon request of the affiliate

376 Art. 12(b) and (b^{bis}) AMLA; arts. 97(1)(a)(2) and 107(1)(a)(2) Federal Act on Gambling.

377 See arts. 98 and 108(1) Federal Act on Gambling.

378 Arts. 24(1)(b) and 25(3)(b) AMLA. On the issuance of AML regulations by SROs, see *supra* section II.D.1. For an overview of the content of these regulations, see *supra* section III.A.

379 See e.g. Cm 11(b) R ASSL; art. 2(1) R OAR-G; art. 4 By-Laws VQF; §4(1)(b) R Polyreg; art. 4(a) Statutes SAAM.

380 See e.g. §52(3) R Polyreg; art. 7(2) R VQF.

381 Art. 24(1)(d) AMLA. FATF (2016), *Anti-money laundering and counter-terrorist financing measures – Switzerland*, Fourth Round Mutual Evaluation Report, para. 365. With respect to AML auditing of lawyers and notaries who qualify as financial intermediaries, the lawyers and notaries instructed to carry out AML controls pursuant to art. 18(3) AMLA, shall meet the following requirements: lawyer's or notary's practicing certificate; guarantee that inspections will be carried out properly; proof of the relevant knowledge of AMLA, practical experience and continuing professional development; and independence from the member being checked (art. 18(4) AMLA).

382 See e.g. §51(1) R Polyreg; art. 4(3)(b) Audit concept VQF; Cm 38 ASSL Regulation related to the control procedure.

and following a risk-based approach.[383] For example, affiliates of the Organisme d'Autorégulation des Gérants de Patrimoine (OAR-G) can be audited every two years unless one or several of the following conditions are met: blame inflicted less than three years ago; unjustified delay of the member's obligations vis-à-vis the SRO over the last two years (reminder fees); major breach or recidivism of minor breach in one of the last two AML reports; compliance action plan in progress; new area of activity subject to the AMLA in the last revised period; exchange activity or transfer of funds or transport and storage of payments or payment transactions; and/or new director with responsibilities for activities subject to the AMLA.[384] Conversely, irrespective of the determined audit frequency, special (extraordinary) audits can be ordered at any time, in particular where there is a suspicion of money laundering, irregularities or violations of AML duties.[385] In terms of the scope of the checks, the most widespread practice is that of a standard review of compliance with AML preventive obligations (notably CDD, reporting and record keeping obligations).[386] However, the audit activity may also call for deeper examination and investigates the transactions of the business.[387] In such a case (transaction-based auditing), the auditor inspects a random sample of files (which must guarantee a representative overview of the customer base) with regard to compliance with AMLA duties and duties pursuant to the SRO's regulations.[388]

– Dealers and Advisors' Obligation to Appoint an Audit Firm

Dealers are not *stricto sensu* supervised in the sense that, contrary to financial intermediaries, they are not subject to the supervision of a particular institution. Dealers shall, however, appoint an audit firm to verify that they comply with their due diligence obligations and to produce a report to the relevant corporate body.[389] In this context, dealers shall provide the audit firm with all the information and documents required to conduct the audit.[390] Art. 22(1) AMLO specifies that the obligation to appoint an auditor is deemed to be independent of the obligation to have its (consolidated) annual financial statements audited.

383 See e.g. §51(3) R Polyreg; Cm 39 ASSL Regulation related to the control procedure; Cm 11–12 OAR-G Regulation related to the AMLA revision procedure, sanctions, ad hoc controls and special investigations.

384 Cm 11–12 OAR-G Regulation related to the AMLA revision procedure, sanctions, ad hoc controls and special investigations.

385 See e.g. §§50 and 53 R Polyreg; art. 4(4) Audit concept VQF; Cm 26–29 OAR-G Regulation related to the AMLA revision procedure, sanctions, ad hoc controls and special investigations.

386 See e.g. §52 R Polyreg.

387 See e.g. art. 8 Audit concept VQF.

388 *Ibid.*

389 Art. 15(1) and (4) AMLA.

390 Art. 15(3) AMLA.

Art. 15 DB-AMLA provides the exact same obligation of monitoring for advisors.

2. *Complaint Mechanism*

Swiss law does not provide for a mechanism (at the level of supervisory authorities or other competent authorities) that allows individuals (in particular employees of obliged entities) to report violations of CDD and related obligations by an obliged entity.

J. STATISTICS ON SARS BY OBLIGED ENTITIES

Pursuant to arts. 1(d) and 23(1)(a) O-MROS, one of MROS's duties is to provide annual statistics on SARs in order to inform the public about the evolution of the fight against money laundering, predicate offences to money laundering, organised crime and terrorism financing. Once a year (usually in April), MROS then publishes a report including very detailed statistics about the SARs it received during the previous year, in particular, but not limited to, the number, the total asset value, the type (mandatory/voluntary) and the origin (type and home canton of reporting entities) of the SARs received. At the time of writing, the most recent available statistics are from 2018.[391]

In 2018, MROS received a total of 6,126 SARs, representing an increase of 31% compared to the previous year, of 110% compared to 2016 and of 720% compared to 2008 (see Figure 1).[392] This made 2018 yet another record-breaking year. As a result, MROS reports that it was unable, for the third year in a row, to process all the SARs received.[393] The total asset value of all the SARs received also increased in 2018. It reached CHF 17.5 billion, compared to CHF 16.47 billion in 2017 and CHF 5.32 billion in 2016 (see Figure 2).[394] According to MROS, the significant increase in 2017 compared to previous years can be explained by a higher reporting volume, but first and foremost by the fact that it received in that year 31 SARs involving assets amounting to more than CHF 10.6 billion, or almost two-thirds of the total asset value of the SARs received.[395]

---

[391] MROS Annual Report 2018 (April 2019), https://www.fedpol.admin.ch/dam/data/fedpol/kriminalitaet/geldwaescherei/jabe/jb-mros-2018-e.pdf.

[392] MROS Annual Report 2018, pp. 8–9.

[393] MROS Annual Report 2018, p. 6. According to MROS, 3,590 SARs were still awaiting processing at the end of 2018, including 984 SARs received in 2017 and 60 from the 2016 reporting year (MROS Annual Report 2018, pp. 8–9).

[394] MROS Annual Report 2018, p. 9 and MROS Annual Report 2017, p. 15.

[395] MROS Annual Report 2017, p. 15.

In particular, MROS reports having received in 2017, for the first time ever, two SARs involving assets of over CHF 1 billion each and one SAR involving assets of over CHF 500 million.[396]

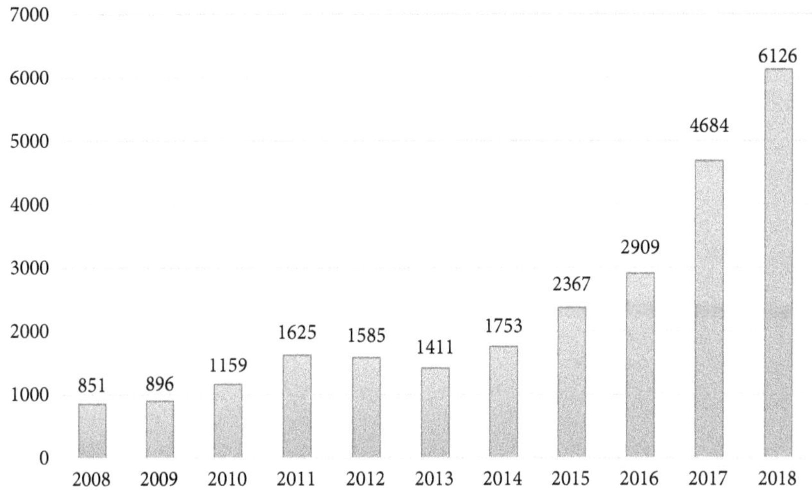

Figure 1. SAR reporting volume 2008–2018

Source: MROS Annual Report 2018, p. 9.

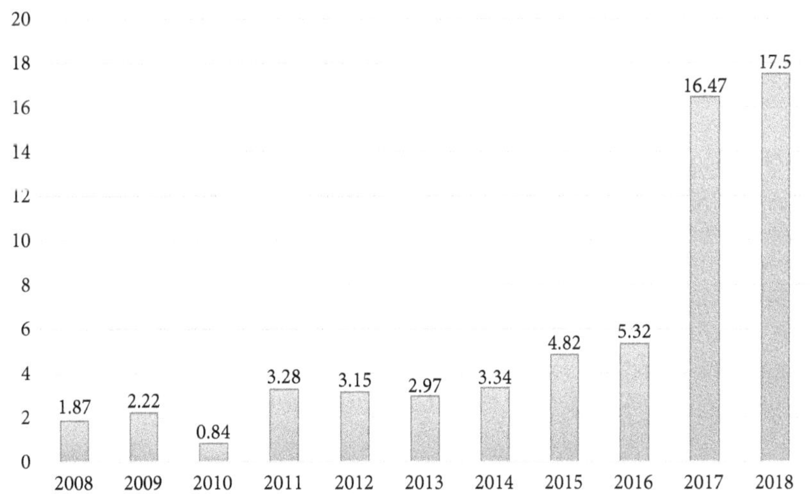

Figure 2. Total asset value of all SARs received 2008–2018 (in billions)

Source: MROS Annual Reports 2008–2018.

[396] *Ibid.* Additionally, the Swiss FIU reports having received 10 SARs relating to amounts of CHF 200 million and 18 SARs that involved sums greater than CHF 75 million.

Of the 6,126 SARs submitted to MROS in 2018, 51% were voluntary SARs and 49% were mandatory SARs.[397] For the fourth consecutive year, MROS received more voluntary SARs than mandatory SARs (see Figure 3).[398] The gap between the two types of SARs was, however, narrower than in 2017. While the number of SARs submitted under art. 305ter(2) CC (voluntary SARs) increased from 2,562 to 3,147, the number of SARs submitted under art. 9 AMLA (mandatory SARs) rose from 2,122 to 2,979.[399]

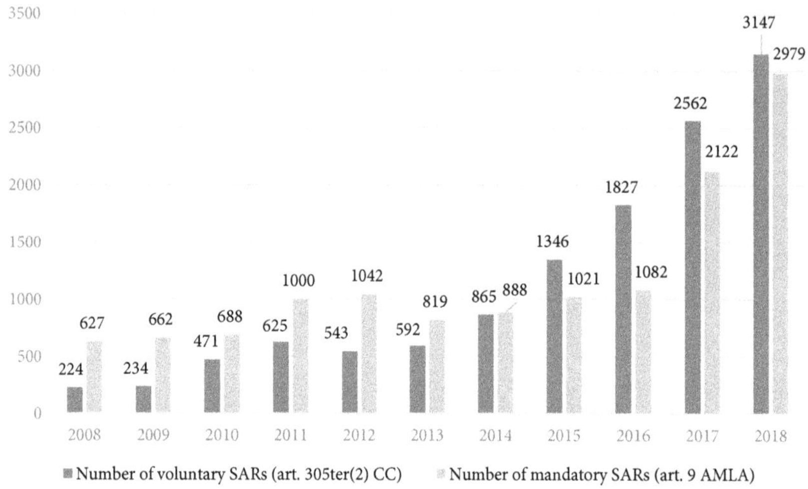

Figure 3. Number of voluntary and mandatory SARs 2008–2018
Source: MROS Annual Report 2018, p. 10.

Another interesting figure revealed in MROS's statistics is the comparison of the reporting volume between the different types of obliged entities. As shown in Figure 4, banks have always been by far the largest submitter of SARs, making up 89% of the total of SARs received in 2018 (see Figure 5),[400] and it is therefore unsurprising that the great majority of SARs received by MROS always come from the three cantons with a highly developed financial sector, i.e. Zurich, Geneva and Ticino (see Figure 6).[401] On the other end of the spectrum, dealers did not file any SARs in 2018.[402] Considering that the number of SARs from

397 MROS Annual Report 2018, p. 10.
398 *Ibid.*
399 *Ibid.*
400 *Ibid.*, p. 16.
401 *Ibid.*, p. 14.
402 *Ibid.*, p. 16.

other sectors (other types of financial intermediaries and dealers) has not changed significantly over the years, it can be observed that banks are the ones responsible for the rise in SARs over the past 10 years.

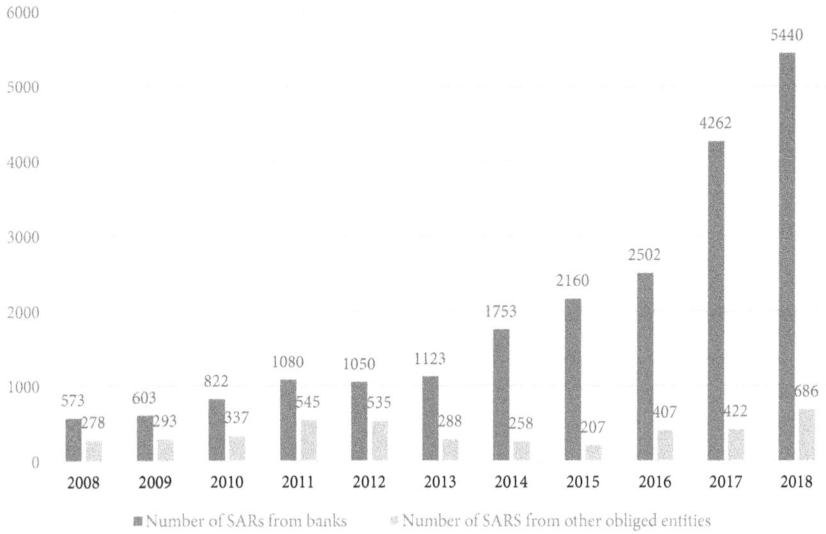

Figure 4. Number of SARs from banks and other obliged entities 2008–2018
Source: MROS Annual Report 2018, p. 16.

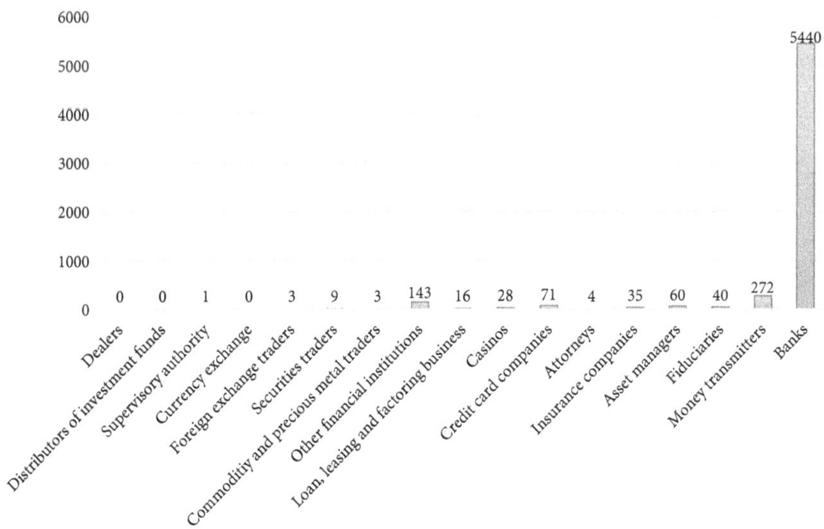

Figure 5. Number of SARs from banks and other obliged entities 2018
Source: MROS Annual Report 2018, p. 16.

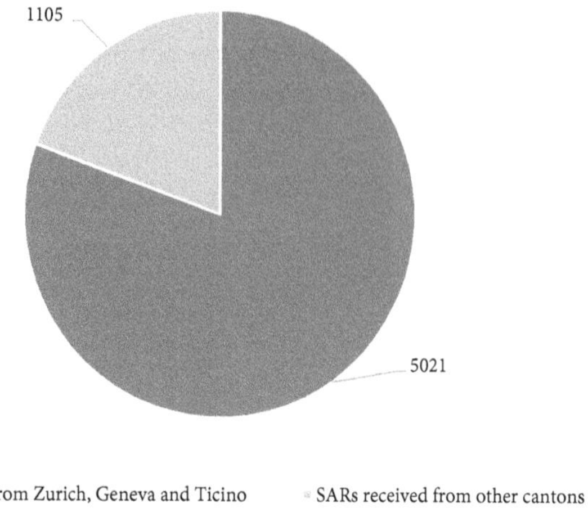

Figure 6. Home cantons of reporting entities 2018
Source: MROS Annual Report 2018, p. 14.

IV. THE SYSTEM OF FINANCIAL INTELLIGENCE UNITS

A. INSTITUTIONAL AND FUNCTIONAL CHARACTERISTICS

1. *Organisational Position*

MROS is managed by the Federal Office of Police (FedPol).[403] However, it is important to note that MROS is not a law enforcement authority, but rather an administrative unit with special tasks.

2. *Purpose and Tasks*

MROS carries out three core functions. First, it serves as the national centre for the receipt of SARs in connection with money laundering, predicate offences to money laundering, organised crime and terrorism financing, which are filed by financial intermediaries and dealers but also by supervisory authorities and audit firms.[404] Second, MROS examines and analyses the reports received.[405] Third, where there appears to be reasonable grounds for opening criminal proceedings,

---

403 Art. 23(1) AMLA.

404 On financial intermediaries and dealers' reporting obligation, see *supra* section III.B; on supervisory authorities and audit firms' reporting obligation, see *infra* section IV.G.

405 Art. 23(2) AMLA. For more on MROS's analysis function, see *infra* sections IV.A.4, IV.B.1 and IV.D.

MROS disseminates the results of its analysis and other relevant information to the competent prosecution authority.[406]

In addition to these three core functions, MROS also has the duty to raise the awareness of financial intermediaries by providing trainings.[407] For instance, in 2018, MROS held more than 40 conferences and presentations for the Swiss financial community.[408] Moreover, another responsibility of MROS is to provide annual statistics on developments in combating money laundering, predicate offences to money laundering, organised crime and terrorism financing.[409]

3. *Independence*

Although MROS is administratively part of FedPol, it is operationally independent and autonomous. Decisions to analyse, request and disseminate information are taken freely by the head of MROS or his/her deputy. Moreover, MROS decides in complete independence whether or not to engage with other domestic authorities or foreign counterparts on the exchange of information.[410]

4. *Powers*

Being administrative in nature, MROS is not empowered to order the freezing of assets or to suspend or withhold consent to a suspicious transaction that is proceeding in order to analyse the transaction, confirm the suspicion and disseminate the results of the analysis to the competent prosecution authority. However, MROS has extensive powers to fulfil its operational analysis function properly. More specifically, it is able to request and obtain from domestic authorities as well as financial intermediaries all the information it deems necessary for its analysis of suspicious activities.

– Power to Obtain Additional Information from Financial Intermediaries

As already mentioned, MROS has the power to request from a financial intermediary that has submitted a SAR any additional information it may need to carry out its analysis as long as the information is directly related to the SAR in question and is either in the possession of the financial intermediary or in the hands of one its subsidiaries in Switzerland.[411]

---

406 Art. 23(4) AMLA. For more on MROS's dissemination function, see *infra* section IV.B.1.

407 Art. 1(c) O-MROS.

408 MROS Annual Report 2017, p. 7.

409 Arts. 1(d) and 23 O-MROS.

410 Arts. 29(2bis) and 30 AMLA. For further details on these two provisions, see *infra* sections V.C.1, V.D.1, V.E.1 and V.F.1.

411 See *supra* section III.B.2.a.

By virtue of art. 11*a*(2) AMLA, MROS can also formally request additional information from financial intermediaries that have not submitted an SAR when, on the basis of its analysis of an SAR, it becomes apparent that these financial intermediaries are or were involved in a suspicious transaction or business relationship.[412] For MROS, "the additional information provided by third-party financial intermediaries allows it to analyse an SAR in greater detail and is often decisive for its decision on whether or not to discontinue its analysis or forward the case to the prosecution authorities".[413] With respect to art. 11*a*(2) AMLA, MROS also specifies that a request form submitted on the basis of this article does not necessarily constitute adequate grounds for suspicion and must not therefore automatically trigger the submission of a mandatory SAR.[414] Nevertheless, the financial intermediary which receives such a request for additional information cannot ignore the fact that this request arose in relation to an SAR submitted by another obliged entity.[415] According to MROS, the third-party financial intermediary is therefore required to carry out clarifications under art. 6(1) AMLA (ascertain the nature and purpose of the business relationship wanted by the customer) to determine whether it also has specific grounds for suspicion.[416] If that is the case, then it shall file an SAR with MROS, including the documents that MROS has requested pursuant to art. 11*a*(2) AMLA.[417] If there are no specific grounds for suspicion, then the financial intermediary will merely provide MROS with the additional information requested.[418]

At the time of writing, MROS does not have the authority to request additional information from a third-party financial intermediary if this request is only based on information provided in a source other than an SAR and its subsequent analysis. In other words, MROS is authorised to request additional information only if it has previously received an SAR requiring an in-depth analysis and additional information from other financial intermediaries. As a result, "[i]f MROS receives a spontaneous tip-off, or a request from a foreign counterpart, but does not find any corresponding SAR in its database, it is not permitted to use the information that has come into its possession, even though this might be reliable information on serious violations of the law".[419] In its draft bill published on 14 September 2018 (DB-Terr), the Federal Council proposed, however, to insert a new paragraph (paragraph 2bis) into art. 11*a* AMLA, which would give MROS the power to approach financial intermediaries on the sole

412 It should be noted that the DB-AMLA extends the scope of this provision to advisors.
413 MROS Annual Report 2017 p. 19.
414 MROS Annual Report 2013, p. 56; MROS Annual Report 2017, p. 19.
415 MROS Annual Report 2017, p. 19.
416 *Ibid.*
417 *Ibid.*
418 *Ibid.*
419 MROS Annual Report 2017, p. 57. See also FF 2018 6469, 6537.

basis of information received from a foreign counterpart.[420] According to the Swiss Government, MROS needs to be granted such a power so that it can fight against money laundering and terrorism financing in the most effective manner.[421]

– Power to Obtain Additional Information from Domestic Authorities

MROS's operational analysis of SARs is also based on a large body of financial intelligence and other useful information that MROS can obtain from domestic authorities in the following two ways: (i) through direct access to public databases (see *infra* section IV.D.2) and (ii) through mutual administrative assistance.

Regarding mutual administrative assistance, art. 29(1) AMLA allows FINMA, the Federal Gaming Board and the Intercantonal Supervisory and Executive Authority referred to in art. 105 Federal Act on Gambling to provide MROS with any information or documents required for the fulfilment of its duties. In the DB-AMLA, the Federal Council suggests extending the scope of providing authorities to SROs.[422] Even more importantly, art. 29(2) AMLA authorises MROS to request and obtain from the federal, cantonal and municipal authorities any information it needs to perform analyses related to money laundering, predicate offences, organised crime or terrorism financing, in particular financial information and other sensitive personal data and personality profiles obtained in criminal, administrative criminal and administrative proceedings, including those from pending proceedings. According to the Federal Council, any public authority can be requested by MROS to pass on relevant data, notably the tax authorities, the customs authorities, the land registries and the residents' registration offices.[423] Information can be provided orally, by e-mail or by writing.[424]

B. TREATMENT OF SARS

1. *Data Processing*

MROS receives SARs from financial intermediaries and dealers, as well as from supervisory authorities and audit firms.[425] Pursuant to art. 4(1) O-MROS, SARs

---

420 For more details about this paragraph, see FF 2018 6469, 6536–6543.

421 FF 2018 6469, 6541.

422 Art. 29*b*(1) DB-AMLA.

423 FF 2014 585, 672. See also art. 4(1) Federal Act of 7 October 1994 concerning the Central Criminal Police Offices of the Federal Government (RS 360), which art. 7(1) O-MROS refers to.

424 Art. 7(2) O-MROS.

425 On financial intermediaries and dealers' reporting obligation, see *supra* section III.B; on supervisory authorities and audit firms' reporting obligation, see *infra* section IV.G.

data received from financial intermediaries are entered into MROS's database.[426] Until recently, data was entered manually by MROS's staff. However, as mentioned *supra*,[427] MROS set up a new computer system that automatically enters SARs into its database. This system has been operational since 1 January 2020.

On the basis of the information received, MROS carries out both strategic and operational analysis.[428] With respect to its operational analysis function, MROS shall immediately notify the competent prosecution authority if it has reasonable grounds to suspect that an offence as defined in arts. $260^{ter}(1)$ (participation in or support for a criminal organisation), 305bis (money laundering) or 305ter CC (insufficient diligence in financial transactions and right to report) has been committed, that assets are the proceeds of a felony or an aggravated tax misdemeanour under art. $305^{bis}(1^{bis})$ CC, that assets are subject to the power of disposal of a criminal organisation, or that assets serve the financing of terrorism (art. $260^{quinquies}(1)$ CC).[429] The choice of the prosecuting authority depends on the nature of the offence, art. 22 ff. of the Criminal Procedure Code serving as the frame of reference in this regard. If MROS determines, at the end of its analysis of an SAR, that there are no reasonable grounds for opening criminal proceedings, the data contained in the SAR are archived but remain accessible for a period of 10 years,[430] during which they can be passed on to the prosecution authorities if, on the basis of new information, there are reasonable grounds to suspect money laundering, predicate offences to money laundering, organised crime or terrorism financing.[431]

Where an SAR is made by a dealer, by a financial intermediary on a voluntary basis, by a supervisory authority or by an audit firm, MROS is not bound by any deadline for analysing the SAR. On the contrary, where an SAR is filed by a financial intermediary on the basis of the reporting obligation, MROS's decision on whether or not to disseminate the results of its analysis and relevant information to the competent prosecution authority must be taken by the statutory deadline of 20 working days after receipt of the SAR.[432] In the DB-AMLA, however, the Federal Council suggests suppressing the 20-day period for the analysis of mandatory SARs.[433] As explained by the Swiss Government, MROS cannot respect this timeframe since, in many cases, it needs to request

426 For further information about MROS's database, in particular its content, see *infra* section IV.D.1.
427 On this new computer system, see *supra* section III.C.1.b.
428 Art. 1(2)(f) O-MROS.
429 Art. 23(4) AMLA.
430 Art. 28(1) O-MROS.
431 Art. 8(2) O-MROS.
432 Art. 23(5) AMLA.
433 Art. 23(5) DB-AMLA.

additional information from obliged entities or foreign counterparts to perform its analysis, which takes time.[434] The Federal Council also explains that the suppression of the temporal limit on processing mandatory SARs should give MROS the necessary leeway to deal as a priority with SARs relating to serious cases.[435] In lieu of the 20-day period for the analysis of mandatory SARs, the Federal Council suggests a 40-day period at the end of which the financial intermediary may terminate the business relationship (though always retaining the paper trail) unless MROS has informed it that it will forward the case to the prosecuting authorities.[436] This rule will apply to both mandatory SARs and voluntary SARs.[437] Should the financial intermediary decide to terminate the business relationship, the obligation not to tip off the client will remain.[438]

2. *Special Procedures for Privileged Professions*

As already mentioned, there are no special procedures in Switzerland for privileged professions with respect to the processing of SARs.[439] Swiss law does not allow lawyers and notaries to send their SARs to their SRO (SAV/SNV). Lawyers and notaries must send their mandatory and voluntary SARs directly to MROS, which will then forward them to the competent prosecution authority if deemed necessary.

3. *Feedback Obligations*

a. Obligation of the FIU

At the end of its analysis of an SAR received from a financial intermediary, MROS shall always inform the latter whether or not it will pass on the results of its analysis and other relevant information to the competent prosecution authority.[440] However, with respect to dealers, supervisory authorities and audit firms, MROS does not have the obligation to inform them about the outcome of their SARs. Art. 10(1) O-MROS merely provides for the possibility for MROS to inform supervisory authorities about the measures taken on the basis of the SARs it received from them.

434 FF 2019 5237, 5266.
435 *Ibid.*
436 Art. 9*b*(1) and (2) DB-AMLA.
437 *Ibid.*
438 Art. 9*b*(5) DB-AMLA.
439 See *supra* section III.B.3.b.
440 Art. 23(5) and (6) AMLA.

b. Obligation of Investigative Authorities

In order for MROS to assess the quality of its work and establish statistics,[441] art. 29*a*(2) AMLA requires the prosecution authorities to automatically and immediately inform MROS of the decisions reached in relation to the SARs forwarded to them. These decisions are established in the Criminal Procedure Code and are listed below:

- opening of a criminal investigation (art. 309);
- issuance of no-proceedings order (art. 310);
- decision to extend a criminal investigation (art. 311(2));
- suspension of a criminal investigation (art. 314);
- resumption of a suspended criminal investigation (art. 315);
- ruling to suspend proceedings (art. 320); and
- reopening of a criminal investigation (art. 323).

In addition, art. 29*a*(1) AMLA requires the prosecution authorities to immediately notify MROS of any pending proceedings, judgments and decisions on the closure of proceedings connected with arts. 260ter(1) (participation in or support for a criminal organisation), $260^{quinquies}$(1) (terrorism financing), 305bis (money laundering) and 305ter(1) CC (insufficient diligence in financial transactions).

4. Disclosure Obligations Towards "Suspect"

On the basis of art. 8(1) Federal Act on Data Protection, any person may request information from MROS as to whether data concerning him/her is being processed. MROS must then usually provide the person with all available data in its database concerning him/her, including the available information on the source of the data, and inform him/her of the purpose of and, if applicable, also the legal basis for the processing, as well as the categories of the personal data processed, the other parties involved with the file and the data recipients.[442]

However, pursuant to art. 8 Federal Act of 13 June 2008 on the Federal Police Information Systems,[443] to which art. 35(1) AMLA refers, MROS shall defer providing information to the requesting person in the following cases: if the data processed concerning the requesting person relate to overriding interests for criminal prosecution that require the maintenance of secrecy, or if no data concerning him/her are being processed. In these two cases, MROS must inform the person concerned of the postponement of its reply and let him/her know that

441 FF 2007 5919, 5954.
442 Art. 8(2) Federal Act on Data Protection.
443 RS 361.

he/she can ask the Federal Data Protection and Information Commissioner to verify whether any data concerning him/her are being processed in accordance with the law and whether overriding interests related to the maintenance of secrecy justify the postponement.[444] MROS provides the information to the requesting persons as soon as the interests relating to the maintenance of secrecy can no longer be invoked, but at the latest after the expiry of the retention period, provided that this does not cause excessive work.[445] Individuals for whom no data has been processed are informed by MROS three years after receipt of their request.[446] If a person shows plausibly that he/she will be seriously and irreparably damaged by the postponement of the reply, the Federal Data Protection and Transparency Officer may recommend that MROS immediately and exceptionally provide the requested information, as long as this does not pose a threat to internal or external security.[447]

C. PROACTIVE INVESTIGATIONS

As noted above, MROS does not at the moment have the power to request additional information from financial intermediaries in the absence of an SAR.[448] MROS can only request additional information from financial intermediaries that have submitted an SAR, as well from those that have not submitted an SAR when, on the basis of its analysis of an SAR, it becomes apparent that these financial intermediaries are or were involved in a suspicious transaction or business relationship.

D. ACCESS TO DATA

1. *Design and Content of FIU's Own Data Bank*

MROS manages its own data processing system in relation to money laundering.[449] According to art. 15 O-MROS, the data contained in this system come in particular from the following sources:

- SARs received from financial intermediaries, dealers, supervisory authorities and audit firms;
- mutual administrative assistance requests received from domestic authorities;

---

444 Art. 8(2) Federal Act on the Federal Police Information Systems.
445 Art. 8(6) Federal Act on the Federal Police Information Systems.
446 *Ibid.*
447 Art. 8(7) Federal Act on the Federal Police Information Systems.
448 See *supra* section IV.A.4.
449 Art. 23(3) AMLA. See also art. 1(2)(e) O-MROS.

- mutual administrative assistance requests received from foreign FIUs;
- mutual legal assistance requests received from foreign prosecution authorities;
- notices received from police authorities regarding inquiries carried out before the opening of an investigation;
- notices received from federal and prosecution authorities about the decisions reached in relation to the SARs forwarded to them;
- notices received from federal and prosecution authorities about any pending proceedings, judgments and decisions on the closure of proceedings connected with arts. 260ter(1), 260^{quinquies}(1), 305bis and 305ter(1) CC;
- lists of individuals and companies annexed to UN Security Council resolutions related to suspicions of money laundering, predicate offences or terrorist financing;
- lists of individuals and companies suspected by the Swiss authorities of laundering money, committing money laundering offences, belonging to a criminal organisation or financing terrorism; and
- the results of MROS's own analysis.

Pursuant to art. 16(1) O-MROS, the data processed in MROS's database must relate to one of the three following scenarios: (i) suspicious financial transactions; (ii) persons/companies suspected of laundering money, attempting to launder money, participating in a criminal organisation in the sense of art. 260ter CC (participation in or support for a criminal organisation) or facilitating the financing of terrorism as defined in art. 260^{quinquies} CC; or (iii) persons/companies suspected of preparing, committing or facilitating acts which can be assumed to be constitutive of predicate offences to money laundering or to be accomplished by a criminal organisation in the sense of art. 260ter CC. Data on persons/companies that do not relate to one of these three scenarios can still be entered into the database as long as they are necessary for MROS in the performance of its tasks, in particular its duties to carry out operational and strategic analyses and to collaborate with national and foreign authorities.[450]

2. *Access to Other Public Data Banks*

In order to fulfil its operational analysis function properly, MROS uses publicly available (open source) information such as that found on the Internet or in the company registry.[451] Additionally, MROS has direct access to RUMACA, the customs database, which contains information about declarations of cross-border currency transportation and ancillary offences.[452] In terms of

450 Art. 16(2) O-MROS.
451 FF 2013 607, 614.
452 Art. 110*e*(3)(a)(2) Federal Act of 18 March 2005 on Customs (RS 631.0).

access to databases of domestic authorities, MROS also has access, pursuant to art. 35*a*(1) AMLA, to the following data banks: the National Police Index, the Central Migration Information System (SYMIC), the Computerised Criminal Records Database (VOSTRA), the State Security Information System, and the Federal Office of Justice's Person, File and Case Management Electronic System in the field of mutual legal assistance in criminal matters. Direct access does not mean, however, unrestricted access, but rather that MROS can autonomously verify, by means of a computerised access procedure, whether a person reported or notified to it is listed in any of these databases.[453] Following this verification, if MROS wants to obtain further information, it has to file a request for administrative assistance with the competent authority on the basis of art. 29(2) AMLA.[454]

- National Police Index

Pursuant to art. 17(1) Federal Act on the Federal Police Information Systems, the National Police Index is used to determine whether data related to a specific person are processed in one or several of the following police databases:

- Police Information Systems of the Cantons;
- Support System for Judicial Police Investigations of the Confederation;[455]
- Federal Offences Data Processing System;[456]
- Data Processing System for International and Intercantonal Police Cooperation;[457]
- Support System for Cantonal Investigations in Criminal Matters;[458]
- System for the Identification of Persons in Criminal Proceedings and the Search for Missing Persons;[459]
- Police Computerised Research System (RIPOL);[460] or
- Schengen Information System's National Part (N-SIS).[461]

---

453 Art. 35*a*(1) AMLA.
454 On art. 29(2) AMLA, see *supra* section IV.A.4.
455 For more information about this database, in particular its content, see art. 10 Federal Act on the Federal Police Information Systems.
456 For more information about this database, in particular its content, see art. 11 Federal Act on the Federal Police Information Systems.
457 For more information about this database, in particular its content, see art. 12 Federal Act on the Federal Police Information Systems.
458 For more information about this database, in particular its content, see art. 13 Federal Act on the Federal Police Information Systems.
459 For more information about this database, in particular its content, see art. 14 Federal Act on the Federal Police Information Systems.
460 For more information about this database, in particular its content, see art. 15 Federal Act on the Federal Police Information Systems.
461 For more information about this database, in particular its content, see art. 16 Federal Act on the Federal Police Information Systems.

The information contained in the National Police Index is limited to the identity of the person (in particular his/her name, date and place of birth and the names of his/her parents), the name of the database(s) in which the person is registered, the date(s) of registration in the database(s), the reason(s) for the registration(s) and the authority(ies) responsible for the management of the database(s).[462]

- Central Migration Information System

The Central Migration Information System (SYMIC) was established in 2006 to replace the Central Register of Foreigners (RCE) and the Automated Registration System of Persons (AUPER), two databases that had become obsolete and no longer met the technical and data protection requirements. SYMIC is managed by the State Secretariat for Migration[463] and contains personal data about foreigners and asylum seekers in Switzerland.[464]

- Computerised Criminal Records Database

The Computerised Criminal Records Database (VOSTRA) is managed by the Federal Office of Justice.[465] VOSTRA lists persons who have been convicted in the territory of the Confederation, Swiss nationals who have been convicted abroad, and persons in respect of whom proceedings for felonies or misdemeanours are pending in Switzerland.[466] VOSTRA also includes in particular:

- convictions for felonies and misdemeanours in cases where a sentence or measure has been imposed;[467]
- convictions for contraventions in three cases: (i) where a fine of more than CHF 5,000 or community service of more than 180 hours has been imposed; (ii) where the applicable federal law gives the authority that decides on the merits an express right or obligation to issue, in the event of a second or subsequent offence, a fine of a specified minimum amount or, in addition to a fine, a pecuniary penalty or custodial sentence; or (iii) when a prohibition to carry on an activity, a prohibition of contact or a geographical prohibition are imposed;[468]

---

462 Art. 17(3) Federal Act on the Federal Police Information Systems.

463 Art. 2 Federal Act of 20 June 2003 on the Common Information in the Areas of Foreigners and Asylum (RS 142.51).

464 For further information on SYMIC, see Federal Council Ordinance on Central Migration Information System (RS 142.513).

465 Art. 365(1) CC; art. 2(1) Federal Council Ordinance of 29 September 2006 on the Criminal Records Database (RS 331).

466 Art. 366(1) and (4) CC.

467 Art. 366(2)(a) CC; art. 3(1)(a) and (b) Federal Council Ordinance on the Criminal Records Database.

468 Art. 366(2)(b) CC; art. 3(1)(c) Federal Council Ordinance on the Criminal Records Database.

- notifications received from abroad of convictions there that must be recorded in accordance with the Criminal Code;[469] and
- information on the circumstances leading to the amendment of existing entries.[470]

- State Security Information System

The State Security Information System is managed by the Federal Intelligence Service.[471] It is primarily made up of the two following databases: the IASA-EXTR SRC database, which contains data relating to violent extremism, and the IASA SRC database, which contains information pertaining to a wide array of areas, such as terrorism, espionage and dissemination of nuclear, chemical and biological weapons.[472] As mentioned *supra*,[473] MROS does not have unrestricted access to these two databases. It can only verify on the Federal Intelligence Service's indexing system (INDEX SRC) whether data related to a specific person reported or notified to it are processed in one of these two databases.

- Federal Office of Justice's Person, File and Case Management Electronic System in the Field of Mutual Legal Assistance in Criminal Matters

The Federal Office of Justice's Person, File and Case Management Electronic System in the field of mutual legal assistance in criminal matters contains information pertaining in particular to extradition, other forms of mutual legal assistance, delegation of prosecution and repression of offences, and transfer of sentenced persons.[474]

3. *Access to Private Data Banks*

Neither the AMLA nor the O-MROS address the question of MROS's access to private databases. This does not mean, however, that MROS does not use data banks of private entities to perform its operational analysis function. The Federal Council recently reported[475] that MROS uses the three following private

469 Art. 366(2)(c) CC; art. 3(1)(e) Federal Council Ordinance on the Criminal Records Database.
470 Art. 366(2)(d) CC; art. 5 Federal Council Ordinance on the Criminal Records Database.
471 Art. 47(1) Federal Act of 25 September 2015 on Intelligence (RS 121).
472 For further information on these two databases, in particular their content, see arts. 49 and 50 Federal Act on Intelligence. See also arts. 16–28 Federal Council Ordinance of 16 August 2017 on Information Systems and Data Storage Systems of the Federal Intelligence Service (RS 121.1).
473 Art. 51(4)(c) Federal Act on Intelligence.
474 Art. 3(a) Federal Council Ordinance of 23 September 2016 on the Federal Office of Justice's Person, File and Case Management Electronic System (RS 351.12).
475 FF 2013 607, 614.

databases: (i) Dow Jones Factiva's global news database, which, according to the company's website, is fed by nearly 33,000 premium sources, including licensed publications, influential websites, blogs, images and videos;[476] (ii) Dun & Bradstreet's data cloud, which, allegedly, delivers comprehensive business data and analytical insights on the basis of over 300 million business records, from more than tens of thousands sources, updated 5 million times per day;[477] and (iii) CRIF's Teledata database, which links information about companies and individuals in both the national and international environment.[478]

4. *Data Analytics*

MROS only conducts data matching. MROS does not conduct data mining in or between the aforementioned data banks, in particular to automatically process the content of such data banks in order to identify possible suspects.

5. *International Cooperation*

As already mentioned, MROS has been a member of the Egmont Group since 1998 and can therefore use Egmont's Secure Web system to submit requests for operational information to one or several of the 158 other FIUs that are members of Egmont. In addition, MROS is now authorised to negotiate and sign memorandums of understanding (MoUs) directly with foreign FIUs in order to establish the terms for the exchange of information (before 2013, only the Federal Council had the right to enter into such agreements).[479] As of December 2016, MROS had allegedly signed 10 MoUs with foreign FIUs, according to the FATF.[480] At the time of writing, there does not seem to be more recent figures available.

E. PARTICIPATION OF "SUSPECTS"

1. *Defence Rights*

MROS's operational analysis can focus on, at least implicitly, individual persons suspected of money laundering. This can seem problematic as investigations against individuals that are suspected of criminal offences are normally subject

[476] https://www.dowjones.com/products/factiva/.

[477] https://www.dnb.com/about-us.html.

[478] https://www.teledata.ch/td-web/anonymousAbout.

[479] Art. 30(6) AMLA.

[480] FATF (2016), *Anti-money laundering and counter-terrorist financing measures – Switzerland*, Fourth Round Mutual Evaluation Report, p. 213.

to a number of defence rights, in particular those contained in the Code of Criminal Procedure. The use of *de facto* investigative powers by MROS might therefore raise the question of whether such defence rights also apply as regards the FIU. However, the AMLA does not address the issue. The "suspect" does not enjoy any particular rights vis-à-vis MROS with regard to its analysis.

2. *Judicial Review or Other Remedies*

The "suspect" cannot apply for review of MROS's action, whether judicial or otherwise.

F. SIMILAR POWERS OF SUPERVISORY BODIES

1. *Financial Supervision*

Neither FINMA, the SROs, the Federal Gaming Board or the Intercantonal Supervisory and Executive Authority referred to in art. 105 Federal Act on Gambling have the right to investigate a suspicion of money laundering on their own.

2. *Non-Financial Sector Supervision*

Similarly, audit firms do not have the right to investigate a suspicion of money laundering on their own.

G. REPORTING OBLIGATIONS OF SUPERVISORY AUTHORITIES

In addition to financial intermediaries and dealers,[481] the AMLA also provides for a reporting obligation to MROS for supervisory authorities, as well as audit firms appointed by dealers to verify that they comply with their AML-related duties.[482]

Pursuant to arts. 16(1) and 27(4) AMLA, FINMA, the Federal Gaming Board, the oversight bodies in the sense of art. 43*a* Federal Act on the Swiss Financial Market Supervisory Authority and the SROs shall immediately file an SAR with MROS if they have reasonable grounds to suspect that a criminal offence under art. $260^{ter}(1)$ (support for or participation in a criminal organisation) or 305bis CC (money laundering) has been committed, that assets are the proceeds of a felony

481 On financial intermediaries and dealers' reporting obligation, see *supra* section III.B.

482 On dealers' obligation to appoint an audit firm, see *supra* section III.H.1.

or an aggravated tax misdemeanour in the sense art. 305bis(1bis) CC, that assets are subject to the power of disposal of a criminal organisation, or that assets serve the financing of terrorism (art. 260^{quinquies}(1) CC). This duty shall only apply, however, if the financial intermediary has not already submitted an SAR.[483]

Regarding audit firms, the reporting obligation applies if they notice that a dealer has failed to comply with its duty to report and that they have reasonable grounds to suspect that money laundering or a criminal offence under art. 260ter(1) (participation in or support for a criminal organisation) has been committed, that assets are the proceeds of a felony or an aggravated tax misdemeanour in the sense of art. 305bis(1bis) CC, or that assets are subject to the power of disposal of a criminal organisation.[484] Art. 15(6) DB-AMLA provides the same for audit firms in charge of advisors.[485]

H. REPORTING BY OTHER AUTHORITIES

Under the Swiss AML legal framework, only financial intermediaries, dealers, supervisory authorities and audit firms are bound by a reporting obligation. No other authorities have to file SARs with MROS.

I. STATISTICS

1. *Number of Reports by Supervisory Authorities and Other Authorities*

The statistics that MROS annually publishes include figures not only about SARs filed by obliged entities[486] but also about SARs filed by supervisory authorities.[487] These figures reveal that the number of SARs filed by supervisors is always extremely small. Between 2008 and 2017, FINMA, the Federal Gaming Board and SROs only made 11 reports out of a total of over 19,000 SARs.[488] Of the 6,126 SARs submitted to MROS in 2018, only two were submitted by supervisors.[489] According to the FATF, "[t]here are insufficient checks on whether financial intermediaries observe their obligation to report, and failures to meet this obligation are not systematically and immediately reported to MROS".[490]

---

483 Arts. 16(2) and 27(5) AMLA.

484 Art. 15(5) AMLA.

485 One should note, however, that the preliminary draft bill initially provided for a reporting obligation not to MROS but rather to the FDF.

486 See *supra* section III.I.

487 On supervisory authorities' reporting obligation, see *supra* section IV.A.4.

488 MROS Annual Report 2018, p. 16.

489 *Ibid.*

490 FATF (2016), *Anti-money laundering and counter-terrorist financing measures – Switzerland*, Fourth Round Mutual Evaluation Report, p. 51.

2. *FIU Analysis*

MROS does not provide detailed statistics on how many analyses it carries out and the value of the transactions associated with these investigations. Between 2014 and 2018, however, MROS included in its annual reports the number of information requests sent to third-party financial intermediaries on the basis of art. 11*a*(2) AMLA.[491] Although this figure should not be seen as corresponding to the number of investigations by MROS, it still provides a good indication of MROS's investigative activity. In 2017, MROS sent 289 requests for information by virtue of art. 11*a*(2) AMLA, representing an increase of over 50% compared to 2015 (see Figure 7).

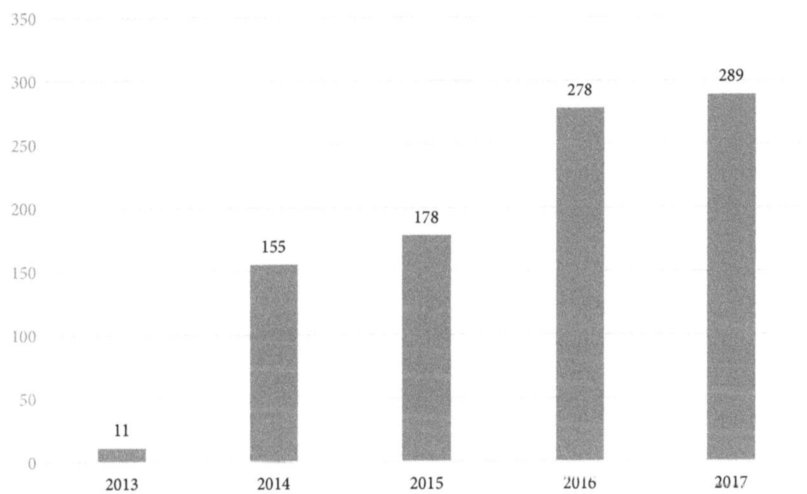

Figure 7. Number of information requests to third-party financial intermediaries on the basis of art. 11*a*(2) AMLA 2013–2017
Source: MROS Annual Report 2017, p. 19.

3. *Communications to Law Enforcement Authorities*

The proportion of SARs forwarded to the law enforcement authorities (conversion rate) steadily declined from 2011 to 2017, before rising again slightly in 2018 (see Figure 8). Of all the SARs forwarded by MROS in 2018, 48% (1,146 SARs) were forwarded to the OAG, a 4% decrease compared to 52% in 2017 (see Figure 9).

According to MROS, "the falling proportion of forwarded SARs in no way reflects a decline in the quality of the reports from financial intermediaries".[492] For the Swiss FIU, this trend must rather be explained by the fact that it has

[491] On art. 11*a*(2) AMLA (MROS's power to request additional information from financial intermediaries that have not submitted an SAR), see *supra* section IV.A.4.

[492] MROS Annual Report 2017, p. 14.

recently received additional human resources as well as more powers for gathering information, and that it is not bound by any deadline for analysing voluntary SARs submitted under art. 305ter(2) CC.[493] Altogether, these three factors "mean that MROS has the capacity to analyse SARs in greater detail and set aside cases that are insubstantial or cannot be proven with a reasonable amount of effort".[494]

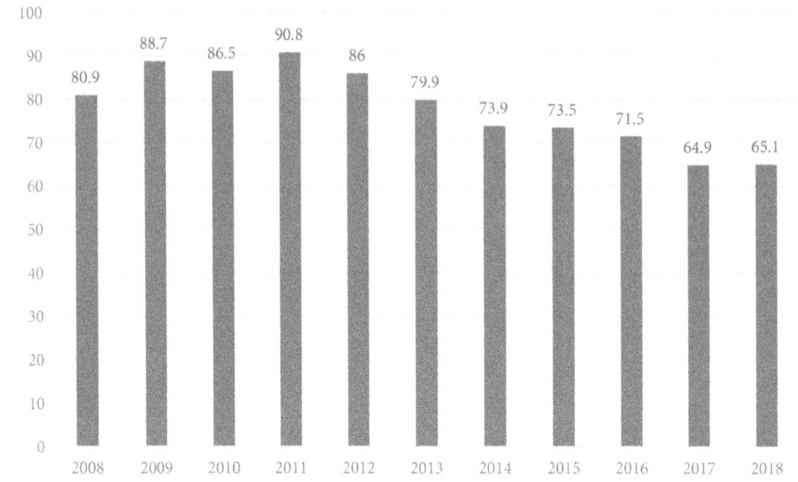

Figure 8. Rate of SARs forwarded to the prosecution authorities 2008–2018
Source: MROS Annual Report 2018, p. 111.

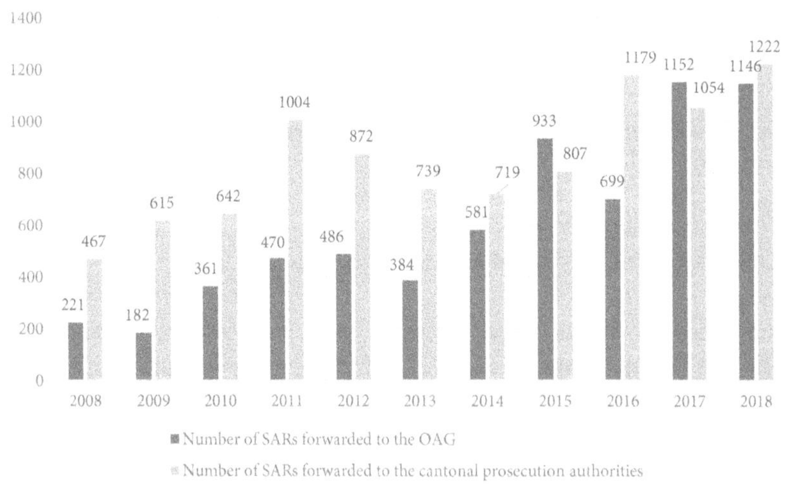

Figure 9. Number of SARs forwarded to the OAG and the cantonal prosecution authorities 2008–2018
Source: MROS Annual Report 2018, p. 20.

493 *Ibid.*
494 *Ibid.*

V. DATA FLOW AND DATA PROTECTION

A. DATA EXCHANGE BETWEEN FIU AND PRIVATE SECTOR

1. *From FIU to Private Sector*

Swiss law does not give MROS the power to share its data with the private sector. Art. 11*a* AMLA gives MROS the power to directly request from financial intermediaries any additional information that is deemed necessary to analyse an SAR.[495] Nothing in the AMLA, however, indicates that this request allows MROS to communicate more information than is strictly necessary for specifying the scope of its request.

2. *From Private Sector to FIU*

Swiss law, in particular the AMLA, does not set out specific data protection requirements for the transfer of personal data from the private sector to MROS, whether such transfer takes place in the context of reporting pursuant to art. 9 AMLA or art. 305ter(2) CC, or in the context of the provision of additional information on the basis of art. 11*a* AMLA. This does not mean, however, that no data protection restrictions apply. According to art. 33 AMLA, the processing of personal data by obliged entities is governed by the Federal Act on Data Protection. As the processing of personal data covers notably its transfer,[496] the relevant data protection principles set out in this Act apply to the transfer of information from obliged entities to MROS. Additionally, one should note that, with respect to the provision of additional information to MROS by financial intermediaries that have filed an SAR (art. 11*a*(1) AMLA), the Federal Council made clear that financial intermediaries shall only provide additional information of a financial nature which directly relates to the SAR they have filed and which is either in their possession or in the hands of entities in Switzerland that form part of them.[497]

B. DATA EXCHANGE BETWEEN FIU AND CRIMINAL JUSTICE SYSTEM

1. *From FIU to Criminal Justice System*

As seen earlier, MROS shall immediately notify the competent prosecution authority if it has reasonable grounds to suspect that an offence as defined in

495 See *supra* sections III.B.2.a and IV.A.4.
496 Art. 3(e) Federal Act on Data Protection.
497 FF 2012 6449, 6481.

arts. $260^{ter}(1)$ CC (participation in or support of a criminal organisation), 305bis CC (money laundering) or 305ter CC (insufficient diligence in financial transactions and right to report) has been committed, that assets are the proceeds of a felony or an aggravated tax misdemeanour under art. $305^{bis}(1^{bis})$ CC, that assets are subject to the power of disposal of a criminal organisation, or that assets serve the financing of terrorism (art. $260^{quinquies}(1)$ CC).[498] Swiss law does not set out specific data protection restrictions regarding the transfer of personal data from MROS to the criminal justice authorities in this context.

According to art. $29(2^{bis})$ AMLA, MROS may also provide information to criminal justice authorities upon request or spontaneously outside the context of mandatory notification. However, such data sharing shall only be carried out on a case-by-case basis and provided that the authorities use the information exclusively for combating money laundering, its predicate offences, organised crime or the financing of terrorism.[499] Dissemination upon request shall never be mandatory for MROS.[500] Additionally, art. $29(2^{bis})$ AMLA provides that art. 30(2) and (5) AMLA applies by analogy,[501] which means that, regarding the sharing of information from MROS to criminal justice authorities, the latter must be treated in the same way as foreign FIUs that receive information from MROS.[502] In particular, the same restrictions on the dissemination of the information received to third authorities shall apply.[503] It could also be mentioned that information shall only be passed in the form a report.[504]

Regarding information received from foreign FIUs, MROS can pass it on to national criminal justice authorities only if it receives the express consent of the FIU that provides the information.[505]

2. *From Criminal Justice System to FIU*

According to art. 29(2) AMLA, criminal justice authorities shall, if requested to do so, pass on to MROS all the data required to perform its analysis function properly. Such data include, in particular, financial information and other sensitive personal data and personality profiles obtained in criminal or administrative criminal proceedings, including those from pending proceedings.[506]

498 See *supra* section IV.B.1.
499 Art. $29(2^{bis})$ AMLA.
500 *Ibid.*
501 On art. 30(2)–(5) AMLA, see *infra* section V.F.1.
502 FF 2014 585, 671.
503 Art. 30(4) and (5) AMLA. See *infra* section V.F.1.
504 Art. 30(3) AMLA.
505 Art. $29(2^{ter})$ AMLA. See *infra* section V.F.2.
506 Art. 29(2) AMLA.

C. DATA EXCHANGE BETWEEN FIU AND INTELLIGENCE AGENCIES

1. From FIU to Intelligence Agencies

According to art. 20(1)(j) Federal Act on Intelligence, MROS is required to pass on to the Swiss Federal Intelligence Service any information pertaining to the financing of terrorism or the proliferation of nuclear, biological or chemical weapons. Additionally, MROS is required to share spontaneously with the Federal Intelligence Service all relevant information relating to any serious and concrete threat to internal or external security it spots.[507]

The Federal Act on Intelligence does not address the question of the transfer of information from MROS to the Federal Intelligence Service in matters relating exclusively to money laundering, or its predicate offences, in the absence of a serious and concrete threat to internal or external security. One can therefore assume that such transfer of data is regulated by the same rules as those referred to above that apply to the transfer of data from MROS to the criminal justice authorities.[508]

2. From Intelligence Agencies to FIU

Pursuant to art. 29(2) AMLA, the Federal Intelligence Service shall, if requested to do so, pass on to MROS all the data required to perform its analysis function properly. Moreover, it should be noted that, according to art. 60(1) Federal Act on Intelligence, the Federal Intelligence Service is required to share personal data with the competent Swiss authorities when it is deemed necessary for the protection of internal or external security.

D. DATA EXCHANGE BETWEEN FIU AND TAX AUTHORITIES

1. From FIU to Tax Authorities

The transfer of data from MROS to the tax authorities is regulated by the same rules as those referred to above that apply to the transfer of data from MROS to the criminal justice authorities outside of the context of mandatory notification.[509]

---

507 Art. 20(3) Federal Act on Intelligence.

508 See *supra* section V.B.1.

509 See *supra* section V.B.1.

2. *From Tax Authorities to FIU*

According to the Federal Council, the tax authorities fall within the scope *ratione personae* of art. 29(2) AMLA.[510] Therefore, the tax authorities shall, if requested to do so, pass on to MROS all the data required to perform its analysis function properly.

E. DATA EXCHANGE BETWEEN FIU AND CUSTOMS AUTHORITIES

1. *From FIU to Customs Authorities*

The transfer of data from MROS to the custom authorities is regulated by the same rules as those referred to above that apply to the transfer of data from MROS to the criminal justice authorities outside of the context of mandatory notification.[511]

2. *From Customs Authorities to FIU*

According to the Federal Council, the custom authorities fall within the scope *ratione personae* of art. 29(2) AMLA.[512] Therefore, the tax authorities shall, if requested to do so, pass on to MROS all the data required to perform its analysis function properly.

F. INFORMATION FLOW BETWEEN FIU AND FOREIGN COUNTERPARTS

1. *Restrictions on Data Transfer from FIU to Foreign FIUs*

Pursuant to art. 30(1) AMLA, MROS may, upon request or spontaneously, share information and personal data with a foreign FIU provided that the latter: (i) guarantees that it will use the information solely for the purpose of analysis in the context of combating money laundering, its predicate offences, organised crime or terrorist financing; (ii) guarantees that it will reciprocate on receipt of a similar request from MROS; (iii) guarantees that official and professional secrecy will be preserved; (iv) guarantees that it will not pass on the

---

510 FF 2014 585, 672.

511 See *supra* section V.B.1.

512 FF 2014 585, 672.

information received to third parties without MROS's express consent; and (v) will comply with the conditions and restrictions imposed by MROS. If one of these conditions is not met, MROS shall not transmit the information and/or personal data. Moreover, a request for information from a foreign FIU shall not be granted by MROS in the three following cases: (i) where the request has no connection with Switzerland (fishing expedition); (ii) where the request requires the application of procedural compulsion or other measures or acts for which Swiss law stipulates mutual assistance procedures or another procedure regulated in special legislation or an international treaty; and (iii) where national interests or public security and order will be prejudiced.[513] With respect to the last mandatory clause, MROS specifies that it "will not, for example, send information about political opponents to countries or regimes, which persecute dissidents".[514]

As regards the content of the information and personal data that MROS is allowed to share with foreign counterparts, the principle of availability applies, meaning that MROS can only share personal data and information that are in its possession or that it may obtain on the basis of the AMLA.[515] This includes, in particular, data from SARs,[516] as well as all the data it can request and obtain from financial intermediaries and domestic authorities in accordance with art. 11*a*(1) and (2), and art. 29(1) and (2) AMLA.[517] The fact that, according to art. 11*a*(2) AMLA, MROS does not (yet) have the power to request information from a financial intermediary on behalf of a foreign counterpart in the absence of a link to an SAR previously filed with MROS by a Swiss financial intermediary[518] is a major obstacle to the cooperation between MROS and its foreign counterparts.[519] It also prevents equal treatment between national-level SARs and information received from foreign FIUs,[520] which is incompatible with the Egmont Group principles.

As mentioned above, MROS can authorise a foreign FIU to further disseminate the information and/or personal data it received from MROS to

513 Art. 31 AMLA.

514 MROS Annual Report 2017, p. 59.

515 Art. 30(1) AMLA.

516 With respect to SARs data, art. 30(2) AMLA provides that MROS may, in particular, pass on the following information: (i) the name of the financial intermediary or the dealer who filed the SAR, provided that the anonymity of the person who has made the report or who has provided additional information to the FIU is preserved; (ii) the name of the account holder, the account number and the account balance; (iii) the identity of the beneficial owners; and (iv) details of transactions.

517 See *supra* section IV.A.4.

518 *Ibid.*

519 According to MROS, 60% of information requests it receives from foreign counterparts are rejected because of the current art. 11*a*(2) AMLA (FF 2018 6469, 6539).

520 MROS Annual Report 2017, p. 57.

third-party authorities. This authorisation power is, however, not absolute. Pursuant to art. 30(4) AMLA, MROS must ensure that the third-party authorities that will receive the information and/or personal data: (i) will use the information solely to institute criminal proceedings or for the purpose of analysis in the context of combating money laundering, its predicate offences, organised crime or terrorist financing, or to obtain evidence in response to a request for mutual legal assistance relating to such criminal proceedings; (ii) will not use the information to prosecute offences that are not offences predicate to money laundering under Swiss law; (iii) will not use the information as evidence in court proceedings; and (iv) will preserve official or professional secrecy. Moreover, one should note that, according to art. 30(5) AMLA, if the request to pass on the information to a foreign third-party authority concerns a matter that is the subject of criminal proceedings in Switzerland (in the sense of art. 308 ff. Code of Criminal Procedure), MROS shall first obtain the consent of the public prosecutor's office responsible for the proceedings.

2. *Restrictions on Use of Data Obtained from Foreign FIUs*

Once MROS receives information from a foreign FIU, it can only use it for the purpose for which it was sought or provided, that is to perform its analysis function.[521] Furthermore, according to art. 29(2ter) AMLA, any dissemination of the information to other federal, cantonal and communal authorities in Switzerland is dependent on the express consent of the providing FIU and shall only be done for the purposes of combating money laundering, its predicate offences, organised crime or the financing of terrorism.[522]

When MROS is authorised by a foreign FIU to share information with a prosecution authority in Switzerland, it is very often, if not always, subject to the condition that the information will not be used as evidence in court proceedings, so that the mutual legal assistance procedure is not circumvented.[523] It follows from this restriction that the information shall not be made part of the records of the proceedings.[524] However, the problem is that, in practice, some prosecutors in Switzerland interpret defence rights in such a broad way that they feel compelled to include in the case file all the information they receive from MROS even if this information cannot be used as evidence.[525] In order to prevent such inclusion and avoid compliance issues, the Federal Council suggested introducing a new

521 On MROS's analysis function, see *supra* section IV.B.1.

522 Art. $29(2^{ter})$ and 29*b*(3) DB-AMLA provide that, under the same two conditions, MROS should also be able to share information with supervisory authoritie23s.

523 FF 2019 5237, 5269–5270 and 5310–5311.

524 *Ibid.*

525 *Ibid.*

provision in the AMLA explicitly to provide that the restrictions imposed by foreign FIUs when sharing information with MROS shall also be respected by the criminal justice authorities that receive the information from the latter.[526]

G. INFORMATION FLOW BETWEEN FIU AND FOREIGN NON-COUNTERPARTS

1. *Restrictions on Data Transfer from FIU to Other Foreign Authorities*

MROS is not only authorised, under certain conditions, to share information and personal data with foreign counterparts,[527] but it can also directly cooperate with foreign prosecution authorities. Pursuant to art. 13 O-MROS, however, MROS can only share information and personal data with such authorities provided that the following four conditions are met: (i) the information and/or personal data relates to suspicions of money laundering, predicate offences to money laundering, organised crime or terrorism financing; (ii) the provision of information and/or personal data is necessary to obtain information that MROS needs; (iii) the provision of information and/or personal data does not aim at circumventing international mutual legal assistance; and (iv) that reasons are given for the administrative assistance request. Moreover, art. 13(2) Federal Act on the Central Criminal Police Offices of the Federal Government, which art. 32(1) AMLA and art. 13(1)(a) O-MROS explicitly refer to, requires at least one of the following conditions to be met in order for MROS to be allowed to pass on personal data to foreign prosecution authorities: (i) the information is required in order to prevent or elucidate an offence in an area within MROS's competence; (ii) a Swiss request for information must be substantiated; and/or (iii) the transfer of personal data is in the interest of the person concerned, and the person concerned has consented to it or the circumstances permit to assume his/her consent. In any case, MROS shall never disclose the name of the person who filed the SAR on behalf of the financial intermediary or the dealer or who complied with the duty to provide information under art. 11*a* AMLA.[528]

2. *Restrictions on Use of Data Obtained from Other Foreign Authorities*

There are no special data protection restrictions regarding MROS's use of personal data it receives from other foreign authorities.

---

526 Art. 29*a*(2bis) DB-AMLA.

527 See *supra* section V.F.

528 Art. 32(3) AMLA.

H. EVIDENTIAL VALUE OF FIU-GENERATED DATA IN COURT PROCEEDINGS

There are no special rules on the admissibility of FIU-generated information as evidence in court proceedings.

I. USE OF CDD DATA FOR PROFIT MAKING

Neither the AMLA nor the various AML regulations and ordinances specify to what extent personal data gathered by obliged entities for the purpose of CDD, or received by them from the FIU, can be used for profit-oriented purposes. This does not mean, however, that obliged entities are allowed to process personal data collected in the AML context for other purposes, in particular commercial purposes. Quite the contrary, according to art. 4(3) Federal Act on Data Protection, which obliged entities have to comply with when gathering data for the purposes of the prevention of money laundering and terrorist financing:[529] "[p]ersonal data may only be processed for the purpose indicated at the time of collection, that is evident from the circumstances, or that is provided for by law".

J. DATA SHARING BETWEEN OBLIGED ENTITIES REGARDING SARS AND FIU REQUESTS

1. *Data Sharing Inside a Group*

According to art. 10*a*(3)(b) AMLA, a financial intermediary is authorised to inform another financial intermediary within the same corporate group that a mandatory SAR has been filed with MROS. Two conditions, however, have to be met. First, the information may only be provided insofar as this information is necessary for the fulfilment of the obligations imposed by the AMLA.[530] Second, the information may only be passed on to a financial intermediary domiciled in Switzerland.[531] In other words, it is not possible for a financial intermediary to inform a group member domiciled abroad about the submission of an SAR.

---

529 Art. 33 AMLA.
530 Art. 10*a*(3) AMLA.
531 *Ibid.*

This fact is derived from the formulation of art. 10*a*(3) AMLA, whereby a financial intermediary may only inform another financial intermediary that is "subject to the AMLA". One should note, however, that the Federal Council now proposes to grant financial intermediaries the possibility to inform their parent company abroad that an SAR has been filed with MROS.[532]

According to the Federal Council, the authorisation contained in art. 10*a*(3)(b) AMLA is limited to the information that an SAR has been filed.[533] The financial intermediary shall therefore limit the information transmitted to what is strictly necessary, in particular to identify the customer or, where applicable, the account in question.[534] The financial intermediary shall not transmit the content of the SAR, in particular the elements that led it to conclude that its suspicion was well founded.[535]

2. *Data Sharing with Similar Professions*

According to art. 10*a*(3) AMLA, a financial intermediary is not only authorised to inform another financial intermediary within the same corporate group that a mandatory SAR has been filed with MROS, but it can also inform, under the same conditions,[536] another financial intermediary outside the group provided, however, that both financial intermediaries provide joint services for one customer in connection with the management of that customer's assets on the basis of a contractual agreement to cooperate.[537] In the case of asset management for which there would be a contract between a bank and an asset manager, the bank would therefore be allowed, for instance, to inform the asset manager that it has filed an SAR with MROS, and vice versa. Another example would be that of a contractual relationship between a bank and a credit card company with respect to a bank account for which there is a credit card.

3. *Data Sharing with Obliged Entities Outside the EU*

Swiss law does not provide for special rules regarding data sharing regarding SARs and FIUs requests between obliged entities in Switzerland and obliged entities outside the EU.

---

532 Art. 10*a*(3bis) DB-AMLA.
533 FF 2007 5919, 5952.
534 *Ibid.*
535 *Ibid.*
536 See *supra* section V.J.1.
537 Art. 10*a*(3)(a).

K. DATA SHARING BETWEEN OBLIGED ENTITIES REGARDING POSSIBLE CASES OF MONEY LAUNDERING

1. *Data Sharing Inside a Group*

With respect to art. 10*a*(3) AMLA described above,[538] the Federal Council explains that it only applies after an SAR was filed with MROS.[539] Financial intermediaries are therefore not allowed to share information with other financial intermediaries within the same corporate group about suspicious transactions or similarly unusual events in the absence of an SAR, or at least not until they submit a SAR to MROS.

2. *Data Sharing with Similar Professions*

Similarly, according to the Federal Council's interpretation of art. 10*a*(3) AMLA,[540] financial intermediaries are also prohibited, in the absence of an SAR, from sharing information regarding possible cases of money laundering with those other financial intermediaries outside the group with whom they provide joint services for one customer in connection with the management of that customer's assets on the basis of a contractual agreement to cooperate.

3. *Data Sharing with Obliged Entities Outside the EU*

Swiss law does not provide for special rules on data sharing regarding suspicious transactions or similarly unusual events between obliged entities in Switzerland and obliged entities outside the EU.

L. DATA MINING BY OBLIGED ENTITIES

Under the Swiss AML legal framework, obliged entities are not explicitly obliged, prohibited or authorised to conduct data mining within their data banks in order to identify possible cases of money laundering. Art. 20 AMLO-FINMA merely requires banks and securities dealers to implement an IT-based transaction monitoring system (except in cases where they have few contractual parties and beneficial owners or if they carry out few transactions). This provision, however, does not specify how precisely this IT system to monitor transactions shall be operated, in particular whether it could/should/shall involve data mining.

---

538 See *supra* section V.J.

539 FF 2007 5919, 5952.

540 See *supra* section V.K.1.

Despite the lack of a proper legal framework regarding the use of data mining technologies by obliged entities, it should be pointed out that certain financial institutions have recently started using such tools and techniques to help patch up holes in their defence against money laundering. Such is the case, for instance, of Credit Suisse. Since 2015[541] to early 2020,[542] the bank indeed used Foundry, software developed by the US company Palantir Technologies that seeks to aggregate the complete data of any particular client as well as his/her connections within the bank at the push of a button. In September 2018, FINMA ordered Credit Suisse to finish the implementation of this "single client view" programme for all relationships and for all relevant functions by the end of 2019.[543] This order was taken in the context of an enforcement procedure against Credit Suisse for its involvement in a series of scandals, including corruption at Brazilian state-controlled oil firm Petrobras and Venezuela's state oil company PDVSA.[544]

VI. BENEFICIAL OWNERSHIP TRANSPARENCY

A. BENEFICIAL OWNERSHIP INFORMATION

1. *General Framework*

– Corporate Entities

According to art. 697*j*(1) CO, any person who, alone or in concert with third parties, acquires shares representing 25% or more of the share capital or voting rights in a non-listed[545] Swiss company limited by shares, must within one month notify the latter of the first name, last name and address of the natural person for whom it is ultimately acting (the beneficial owner). Later changes regarding the name or address of the beneficial owner must be disclosed within three months.[546] According to the Federal Government, the acquiring person

541 https://www.finews.com/news/english-news/34113-credit-suisse-palantir-single-client-view-compliance-finma-foundry-boersengang-tidjane-thiam-lara-warner-alex-karp-cia.

542 https://www.finews.com/news/english-news/39599-credit-suisse-palantir-signac-colleen-graham-lara-warner-surveillance-software-tidjane-thiam.

543 https://www.finma.ch/en/news/2018/09/20180917-mm-gwg-cs/.

544 *Ibid.*

545 According to art. 697*j*(3) CO, if the shareholder is a company whose participation rights are listed on a stock exchange, if the shareholder is controlled by such a company in accordance with art. 963(2) CO, or if the shareholder controls such a company in this sense, it must only give notice of this fact and provide details of the company's name and registered office. Further disclosure obligations are provided by art. 663*c* CO and art. 120 Federal Act on Financial Market Infrastructures and Market Conduct in Securities and Derivatives Trading.

546 Art. 697*j*(4) CO.

must undertake inquiry efforts and make that notification to the best of its knowledge.[547] If the shareholder is a legal entity or partnership, each natural person that controls the shareholder must be recorded as a beneficial owner in analogous application of art. 963(2) CO.[548] According to this provision, control is given when the person directly or indirectly holds a majority of votes in the highest management body, directly or indirectly has the right to appoint or remove a majority of the members of the supreme management or administrative body, or is able to exercise a controlling influence based on the articles of association, the foundation deed, a contract or comparable instruments.

Identical reporting obligations also exist for any person acquiring capital contribution and thus reaching or exceeding the threshold of 25% of the nominal capital or voting rights in a Swiss limited liability company.[549]

In the event of failure to comply with the aforementioned disclosure obligations, the holder of the shares/parts can be punished with a fine up to CHF 10,000.[550] Moreover, art. 697*m*(1) CO provides that such failure leads to the suspension of all voting rights until notification is made. Further, the acquiring shareholder's right to dividends (and repayment of capital) is irrevocably forfeited for the period until disclosure is made.[551] Any dividends paid out prior to a notification could be reclaimed by the company, which could primarily become relevant in the event of the company's bankruptcy and may impact dividend recapitalisation. The board of a Swiss company must ensure that no shareholder exercises voting rights or receives dividends while it is in violation of its disclosure obligation.[552] Board members not living up to this duty may become liable for damage caused,[553] which is again primarily relevant in a bankruptcy scenario. They are also liable to criminal sanctions if they unduly pay dividends to shareholders or partners who have failed to fulfil their duties of disclosure.[554]

– Trusts

Domestic trusts and other similar legal arrangements are not available in Switzerland. Nonetheless, Switzerland's ratification of the Hague Convention on the Law applicable to Trusts and on their Recognition, in 2007, allowed foreign

547 FF 2014 585, 639.
548 Art. 697*j*(2) CO.
549 Art. 790*a* CO.
550 Art. 327 *cum* 106(1) CC. Art. 327 CC was introduced by the Federal Act of 21 June 2019 on Implementing the Recommendations of the Global Forum on Transparency and Transfer of Information for Tax Purposes, in force since 1 November 2019. It should be noted that the Federal Council had initially suggested introducing criminal sanctions for violations of the disclosure obligation under art. 697*j* CO in 2014. See FF 2014 585, 620 ff.
551 Art. 697*m*(2) and (3) CO.
552 Art. 679*m*(4) CO.
553 Arts. 754 and 827 CO.
554 Art. 158 CC.

trusts to be recognised under civil law. Trustees administrating foreign trusts in Switzerland are deemed financial intermediaries in certain circumstances and, as such, are required to obtain and verify information about the beneficial ownership of their customers, the trusts, when the business relationship is formed.[555] Trustees managing trusts in Switzerland are notably considered to be financial intermediaries in their capacity as "governing bodies of domiciliary companies"[556] where they provide wealth management services, make investments as advisers, or hold or manage securities on behalf of the trust, on a professional basis.[557]

2. *Definition of "Beneficiary" and "Effective Control"*

As already explained,[558] arts. 697*j*(1) and 790*a*(1) CO define the beneficial owner of a company limited by shares or a limited liability company as the natural person who ultimately controls the company in that he/she, alone or in concert with third parties, holds at least 25% of the capital or voting rights in the company.

The AMLA's definition of beneficial ownership, which is particularly relevant in the context of CDD, is more extensive in that, according to art. 2*a*(3), the beneficial owners of an operating legal entity do not necessarily need to hold at least 25% of the capital or voting rights to qualify as such provided, however, that they "otherwise control it". Moreover, art. 2*a*(3) AMLA provides that "[i]f the beneficial owners cannot be identified, the most senior member of the legal entity's executive must be identified".

3. *Definition of "Information"*

Pursuant to arts. 697*j*(1) and 790*a*(1) CO, the information about the beneficial owner that must be disclosed includes his/her first name, last name and address. In contrast, art. 4 AMLA, which provides for the obligation of obliged entities to establish the beneficial owner in circumstances which require the performance of CDD measures,[559] does not specify what information shall be collected.

4. *Special Rules for Entities with a Cross-Border Dimension*

Swiss law does not provide for special requirements and mechanisms for the disclosure of foreign nationals, foreign entities or foreign trusts.

---

555 Art. 4 AMLA. See also art. 64 AMLO-FINMA.
556 Art. 6(1)(d) AMLO.
557 Art. 2(3) AMLA.
558 See *supra* section VI.A.1.a.
559 See *supra* section III.A.1.b.

B. BENEFICIAL OWNERSHIP REGISTRIES

1. *Scope and General Procedure*

There is no centralised beneficial ownership registry in Switzerland.[560] Since 2015, however, non-listed companies limited by shares and limited liability companies are required to keep a list of the beneficial owners disclosed to them.[561] The aim of this rule is to ensure that companies know their substantial beneficial owners and can quickly relay such information to governmental authorities on request. The register, which shall contain the first name, surname and address of the beneficial owners,[562] must be kept in such a manner that it can be accessed in Switzerland at any time.[563] Furthermore, the documents on which notice of beneficial owners of shares are based must be retained for 10 years following the person's deletion from the register.[564]

Since 1 November 2019, in case a company limited by shares or a limited liability company fails to comply with the aforementioned obligations, it is liable to a fine up to CHF 10,000.[565] Furthermore, any shareholder, creditor or the commercial registrar may now request the court to take some measures in such circumstances.[566] The court may, in particular, allow the company a period of time, under threat of its dissolution, within which to re-establish the lawful situation, appoint the required corporate body or an administrator, or dissolve the company and order its liquidation according to the regulations on insolvency proceedings.[567]

2. *Verification of Accuracy*

Swiss law does not require companies to verify the accuracy of the beneficial ownership information disclosed to them. Arts. 697*l*(1) and 790*a*(5) CO only require companies to keep a list of the beneficial owners disclosed to them.

---

560 It should be noted that the Swiss socialist party proposed introducing such a register in Switzerland in 2016 (Postulat 16.3315, https://www.parlament.ch/fr/ratsbetrieb/suche-curia-vista/geschaeft?AffairId=20163315#/!). However, upon recommendation of the Federal Council, the Federal Assembly rejected this proposal the following year.

561 Arts. 697*l*(1) and 790*a*(5) CO.

562 Arts. 697*l*(2) and 790*a*(5) CO.

563 Arts. 697*l*(4) and 790*a*(5) CO.

564 Arts. 697*l*(3) and 790*a*(5) CO.

565 Art. 327*a*(a) and (b) CC. Art. 327 CC was introduced by the Federal Act of 21 June 2019 on Implementing the Recommendations of the Global Forum on Transparency and Transfer of Information for Tax Purposes, in force since 1 November 2019.

566 Art. 731*b*(1)(3) CO.

567 Art. 731*b*(1)(3) CO.

C. ACCESS TO BENEFICIAL OWNERSHIP INFORMATION

1. *Access by FIU and Other Authorities*

In the absence of a central beneficial ownership registry in Switzerland, MROS and other competent authorities, such as investigation and prosecution authorities, rely only on beneficial ownership information maintained by companies themselves or collected by financial intermediaries in the framework of CDD. According to Transparency International, this situation is problematic as "[c]ompetent authorities are ... unable to access this information without having to request it to the company or financial institution, which could potentially tip companies or individuals off that there might be an ongoing investigation".[568]

In the case of beneficial ownership registers maintained by companies limited by shares and limited liability companies, the law states that competent authorities shall be able to access it in Switzerland at any time.[569] In the case of financial intermediaries, the AMLA requires them in particular to respond to requests for additional information, including beneficial ownership information, made by MROS.[570] Swiss law also notably provides that FINMA and prosecution authorities are allowed to request from financial institutions further information and documents.[571]

Regarding trusts, competent authorities can obtain information concerning the beneficial owners of trusts from the trustees in Switzerland as they are financial intermediaries subject to all of the obligations which come with this status, in particular the obligation to collect beneficial ownership information, and they are not subject to professional secrecy.[572]

2. *Access by Obliged Entities*

As already seen, obliged entities are required to take CDD measures in certain situations.[573] One of these CDD measures is to identify the beneficial owner with the due diligence required in the circumstances,[574] which entails requesting and obtaining beneficial ownership information from the client.

568 Transparency International, *Switzerland Beneficial Ownership Transparency*, 2018, p. 2, https://transparency.ch/wp-content/uploads/2018/04/TI_G20_Country-Report-Switzerland.pdf.

569 Arts. 697*l*(5) and 790*a*(3) CO.

570 Art. 11*a* AMLA. See *supra* section IV.A.4.

571 See in particular art. 29 Federal Act on the Swiss Financial Market Supervisory Authority; arts. 244, 246 and 263 ff. Code of Criminal Procedure.

572 See *supra* section VI.A.1.

573 See *supra* section III.A.1.a.

574 See *supra* section III.A.1.b.

3. *Access by Interested Third Parties*

Neither the public at large nor interested third parties have access to beneficial ownership information in Switzerland at the moment.

VII. SANCTIONS

A. SANCTIONS FOR MONEY LAUNDERING

1. *Requirement of a Conviction for a Predicate Offence*

Under Swiss criminal law, the money laundering offence is punishable regardless of whether there is or is not a prior or simultaneous conviction for the predicate offence.[575] It is also irrelevant whether or not criminal proceedings have been opened against the perpetrator(s) of the predicate offence.[576] It is not even necessary to establish in detail the circumstances relating to that offence or the identity of the perpetrator(s).[577] For a person to be sentenced for money laundering, it is merely required to prove that the assets that are deemed to be the subject of money laundering originate from a predicate offence, whether a felony or an aggravated tax misdemeanour.[578] The Federal Supreme Court is particularly lenient with respect to this requirement when the assets originate from the activities of a criminal organisation.[579]

2. *Forms of Sanctions*

Under Swiss criminal law, both natural and legal persons can be prosecuted for money laundering.

Pursuant to art. 305bis(1) CC, money laundering is punishable by a custodial sentence not exceeding three years or by a monetary penalty. In serious cases, a non-exhaustive list of which is provided for in art. 305bis(2) CC, the sanction is a maximum penalty of five years' imprisonment and a monetary penalty of up to 500 daily penalty units, or just a monetary penalty.[580] According to art. 34 CC, a monetary penalty amounts to a maximum of 180 daily penalty units (unless the law provides otherwise, as is the case for serious cases of money

575 See e.g. ATF 138 IV 1, c. 4.2.2.
576 See e.g. ATF 120 IV 323, c. 3d.
577 ATF 138 IV 1, c. 4.2.2; FT 6B_91/2011 of 26 April 2011, c. 2.1.
578 See e.g. ATF 138 IV 1, c. 4.2.2; ATF 120 IV 323, c. 3d; FT 6B_141/2007 of 24 September 2007, c. 3.3.3.
579 See e.g. ATF 138 IV 1, c. 4.2.3.2.
580 Art. 305bis(2) CC.

laundering), and a daily penalty unit is a maximum of CHF 3,000. Consequently, money laundering is punishable by a monetary penalty of up to CHF 540,000, and up to CHF 1,500,000 in serious cases when a penalty of imprisonment is also imposed. Additionally, pursuant to art. 67(1) CC, if a person has committed money laundering while carrying on a professional activity or an organised non-professional activity, if, as a result, he/she receives a custodial sentence in excess of six months and if there is a risk that he/she will abuse his/her activity in order to commit a further felony, the court may prohibit him/her totally or partially from carrying on this activity or comparable activities for a period of six months to five years. The sentences handed down take into account the seriousness of the money laundering act, the amounts laundered, the time elapsed between the offence and the judgment, and whether it was a repeat offence.

The rules governing the criminal liability of undertakings are set out in art. 102 CC. In this context, undertakings are any legal entity under private law or any legal entity under public law (with the exception of local authorities), companies and sole proprietorships.[581] Art. 102 distinguishes between two types of corporate criminal liability but only one applies with respect to money laundering. Pursuant to art. 102(2) CC, if money laundering is committed in an undertaking in the exercise of commercial activities in accordance with the objects of the undertaking, the undertaking is penalised irrespective of the criminal liability of any natural persons, provided the undertaking has failed to take all the reasonable organisational measures that are required in order to prevent such an offence.[582] In such a case, the undertaking is liable to a fine up to CHF 5 million.[583]

With respect to corporate criminal liability, it is important to stress that, in September 2015, the OAG set up an internal working group, called "Group 102", made up of several prosecutors with experience in the economic and money laundering field and in legal mutual assistance, which maintains consistent

581 Art. 102(4) CC.

582 On the conditions set out in art. 102(2) CC, see ATF 142 IV 333 and, more recently, FT 6B_31/2019 of 12 December 2019. The facts of the former case were as follows: one day after €5 million was received by the Swiss Post on an account held for one its clients, most of it was withdrawn in cash. The assets were later found to be the proceeds of a crime. The prosecution did not supply evidence that any of the involved employees fulfilled both the objective and subjective constitutive elements of money laundering. The Swiss Federal Supreme Court denied criminal corporate liability of Swiss Post, based on the lack of proof that the crime of money laundering had been committed by at least one individual within the corporation. It confirmed that corporate liability under art. 102(2) CC does not require an individual to be convicted of money laundering, but requires proof that at least one individual in the corporation fulfils all objective and subjective elements of money laundering.

583 Art. 102(1) CC.

doctrine in the prosecution of legal persons (for both the opening of a preliminary investigation and its subsequent conduct). The group ensures that prosecutors are assisted by a superior when they deal with this sort of case, especially if simplified proceedings are initiated. It is also a supervisory body, tasked with ensuring that legal persons do not obtain an overly favourable end result that would not be consistent with the requirements of the criminal prosecution. According to the FATF, this group is equipped to heighten the effectiveness of the prosecution of legal persons in Switzerland".[584]

3. *Confiscation*

As noted by the FATF, "[c]onfiscation is a priority for the Swiss authorities".[585] Pursuant to art. 70(1) CC, confiscation of assets shall be ordered by the court following any conviction for money laundering.[586] Confiscation is, however, excluded if a third person has acquired the assets in good faith, provided that the person has paid a consideration of equal value in return or confiscation would cause him/her disproportionate hardship.[587] If confiscation is impossible because the assets are no longer available, the court may uphold a claim for an equivalent sum (compensation claim).[588] The court may dismiss an equivalent claim in its entirety or in part if the claim is likely to be unrecoverable or if the claim would seriously hinder the rehabilitation of the person concerned.[589] The investigating authority may seize assets of the person concerned with a view to the enforcement of an equivalent claim.[590] Such seizure does not, however, accord the State preferential rights in the enforcement of the equivalent claim.[591]

4. *Statistics*

a. Number of Criminal Proceedings

Swiss authorities do not provide statistics on the number of criminal proceedings for money laundering in Switzerland. The only relevant figures available relate to 2014 and are included as follows in the 2016 FATF Mutual Evaluation Report.

---

584 FATF (2016), *Anti-money laundering and counter-terrorist financing measures – Switzerland*, Fourth Round Mutual Evaluation Report, para. 186.

585 *Ibid.*, para. 14.

586 It should be noted that, in addition to ancillary confiscation, Swiss law (arts. 376–378 Code of Criminal Procedure) also provides for independent confiscation (imposed when no criminal procedure can be launched, including when the offence has been committed abroad).

587 Art. 70(2) CC.

588 Art. 71(1) CC.

589 Art. 71(2) CC.

590 Art. 71(3) CC.

591 *Ibid.*

Table 2. Number of criminal proceedings for money laundering in 2014

Number of money laundering proceedings opened at the MPC and in the canton	Based on MROS reports	Based on other sources	Total
MPC	72	16	88
Cantons	184	173	357
Total	256	189	445

Source: FATF (2016), *Anti-money laundering and counter-terrorist financing measures – Switzerland*, Fourth Round Mutual Evaluation Report, para. 166.

The FATF also indicates that, in February 2016, nine proceedings against legal persons for money laundering were in progress within the MPC.[592] Five had been opened just for money laundering and four had been opened for both money laundering and corruption of foreign public officials.[593]

b. Number of Convictions

According to the Federal Office of Statistics, there were 416 convictions for money laundering in 2017 at both federal and cantonal levels. This represents an increase of more than 200% compared to 2008 (see Figure 10).

Figure 10. Number of convictions for money laundering 2008–2017
Source: Federal Office of Statistics.

592 FATF (2016), *Anti-money laundering and counter-terrorist financing measures – Switzerland*, Fourth Round Mutual Evaluation Report, para. 185.

593 *Ibid.*

B. SANCTIONS FOR VIOLATIONS OF PREVENTIVE MEASURES

1. *Money Laundering by Violating Preventive Obligations*

As seen earlier,[594] the Federal Supreme Court ruled in 2010 that money laundering can be committed through omission by financial intermediaries since the AML-related obligations imposed upon them under the AMLA, in particular the duty to clarify the economic background and the purpose of a transaction or a business relationship (art. 6) and the duty to report to the FIU (art. 9), give them the status of guarantor.[595]

2. *CDD, Reporting and Other AML-Related Obligations*

a. Special Criminal Laws against Individuals

According to art. 305ter(1) CC, "[a]ny person who as part of his profession accepts, holds on deposit, or assists in investing or transferring outside assets and fails to ascertain the identity of the beneficial owner of the assets with the care that is required in the circumstances is liable to a custodial sentence not exceeding one year or to a monetary penalty". Failure to ascertain the identity of the beneficial owner of the assets with the care that is required in the circumstances is a special offence (*délit propre pur*; *echtes Sonderdelikt*), in that it may only be committed by financial intermediaries as defined in art. 2(2) and (3) AMLA,[596] and not also by dealers in the sense of art. 2(1)(b) AMLA. It should also be noted that art. 305ter(1) CC only refers to one specific CDD measure, namely the obligation to identify and verify the identity of the beneficial owner of the assets. Yet the Federal Supreme Court has considered in one case that failure to correctly identify the customer who is not the beneficial owner also falls within the scope of art. 305ter(1) CC.[597]

Criminal sanctions for violations of AML preventive measures are also provided for under the AMLA. According to art. 37 AMLA, a financial intermediary or dealer that fails to comply with the duty to report suspicious activities to MROS (art. 9 AMLA)[598] is punishable with a fine not exceeding CHF 500,000 if committed intentionally, or CHF 150,000 if committed through negligence. Moreover, art. 38 AMLA provides that dealers can be fined up to

---

594 See *supra* section II.B.2.

595 ATF 136 IV 188, c. 6. See also FT 6B_729/2010 of 8 December 2011, c. 4.3.1 in which the Federal Supreme Court considers that the status of guarantor of financial intermediaries may also be inferred from internal regulations.

596 ATF 129, c. 2.3; ATF 129 IV 329, c. 2.2.

597 ATF 138 IV 1.

598 See *supra* section III.B.1.a.

CHF 100,000 (CHF 10,000 if the offender acts through negligence) for failure to appoint an audit firm to verify that they are complying with their preventive duties (art. 15 AMLA).[599]

The Federal Act on Gambling stipulates a maximum fine of CHF 500,000 for casinos and promoters of large-scale games in the event of intentional failure to exercise due diligence in the area of AML/CTF.[600]

b. Administrative Sanctions against Individuals and Legal Entities

In order to provide a clear and comprehensive picture of the various administrative sanctions that can be imposed on financial intermediaries, it is deemed appropriate to address financial intermediaries under FINMA supervision, financial intermediaries under SRO supervision, and casinos/ promoters of large-scale games separately.

– Financial Intermediaries under FINMA Supervision

In the context of its supervisory functions, FINMA is required to ensure the restoration of compliance with the law when irregularities in the application of AML/CTF obligations by supervised institutions arise. Art. 31 Federal Act on the Swiss Financial Market Supervisory Authority empowers FINMA to issue a ruling ordering proportionate measures to address the problem. FINMA can restore compliance with the law through mere investigations and injunctions to comply with the law, or with enforcement proceedings as described below. In contrast to the enforcement instruments set out in arts. 32–37 Federal Act on the Swiss Financial Market Supervisory Authority, art. 31 also applies if no serious violation of supervisory law has occurred.

FINMA's enforcement proceedings always result in binding decisions that are subject to appeal.[601] In order to decide on the appropriateness of opening an enforcement action, FINMA relies on a matrix that combines the interest in undertaking a procedure (such as the protection of creditors and investors, fair competition and the stability of the financial system) on the one hand, and the seriousness of the violation (such as systematic and repeated infringements or the performance of unauthorised activities) on the other hand. Depending on the nature of the violation or irregularity, FINMA can impose, possibly cumulatively, various enforcement measures. In particular, art. 9(1) AMLO-FINMA provides that any infringement of the provisions of

599 See *supra* section III.H.1. It should be noted that the DB-AMLA extends the scope of article 38 to advisors.

600 Art. 131(1)(f) Federal Act on Gambling.

601 Art. 44 ff. Federal Act of 20 December 1968 on Administrative Procedure (172.021).

the AMLO-FINMA may call into question the required guarantee for proper business conduct of financial intermediaries. Since the *garantie d'activité irréprochable* is a precondition for a bank licence,[602] an infringement of the AMLO-FINMA may result in the revocation of the licence by FINMA.[603] Serious infringements of the AMLO-FINMA may also lead to a practicing ban for a period of up to five years,[604] and the confiscation of the profits procured in the process.[605] The enforcement tools at FINMA's disposal also include declaratory rulings (reprimands),[606] and the publication of the final ruling naming those involved.[607] It should be noted that monetary sanctions can never be applied by FINMA.

In parallel with the actions of FINMA, the supervisory board of the SBA is responsible for sanctioning violations of the CDB by signatory banks.[608] According to art. 64(1) CDB 16,[609] banks can be fined up to CHF 10 million by the supervisory board in the event of a violation of the CDB.[610] In assessing the level of the fine, due account must be taken of the seriousness of the violation, the degree of culpability and the bank's financial situation.[611] Measures imposed by other authorities with respect to the same issue must also be taken into account.[612]

---

602 See *supra* section III.H.1.

603 Art. 37 Federal Act on the Swiss Financial Market Supervisory Authority.

604 Art. 33 Federal Act on the Swiss Financial Market Supervisory Authority.

605 Art. 35 Federal Act on the Swiss Financial Market Supervisory Authority.

606 Art. 32 Federal Act on the Swiss Financial Market Supervisory Authority. Declaratory rulings have no direct legal effect and do not give rise to any liability under civil or criminal law. They represent the mildest form of official sanctions and are intended to encourage compliance with supervisory law and prevent repeated violations.

607 Art. 34 Federal Act on the Swiss Financial Market Supervisory Authority.

608 Art. 61(1) CDB 16 (same provision in CBD 20).

609 Same provision in CDB 20.

610 It should be noted, however, that, according to art. 63 CDB 16, the proceedings against the bank at fault must be closed without any sanction in minor cases. According to this provision, a violation of the code of conduct will in particular be considered minor if the objective of the agreement, i.e. the identification of the contracting partner, the establishment of the controlling person and of the beneficial owner, has been achieved despite formal shortcomings. The following are examples of minor violations mentioned by art. 63 CDB 16: (i) use of documents that are more than 12 months old to identify a legal entity or partnership; (ii) use of an incomplete or incorrectly completed Form A, provided that the last name and first name (or company name) of the beneficial owner are stated and the contracting partner has signed the form; the same applies to incomplete Forms I, K, S and T; (iii) where the volume of assets involved does not exceed CHF 25,000; (iv) where the matter has not been recorded in accordance with regulations in an appropriate way; or (v) if particular information and/or documents are missing or documents are not available in the appropriate form, this was only determined after the account opening and the correction was undertaken with 30 days.

611 Art. 64(1) CDB 16 (same provision in CDB 20).

612 *Ibid.*

– Financial Intermediaries under SRO Supervision

According to art. 25(3)(c) AMLA, SROs are required to define appropriate penalties in their regulations. SROs shall also submit a list of sanctions rulings regarding their affiliates to FINMA.[613] The sanctions applicable in the event of any breach of the SROs regulations include fines in all cases,[614] and also warnings or exclusion.[615] The maximum fine varies between CHF 100,000 and CHF 1,000,000. As rightly underlined by FINMA, "[t]his heterogeneous range of sanctions may play a role in the choice of affiliation with an SRO".[616] The amount is usually set in light of the seriousness of the violation, as well as the extent of guilt and the financial capacity of the financial intermediary,[617] or of the existence of a fine imposed by the courts.[618] In the cases of minor offences or negligence, it is possible that a fine will not be imposed, but a warning or reprimand given instead.[619]

– Casinos and Promoters of Large-scale Games

The CFMJ can suspend, restrict or withdraw the concession of a casino, or place it under additional conditions and requirements, if it fails to fulfil certain essential conditions, notably the implementation of AML/CTF obligations.[620] The Intercantonal Supervisory and Executive Authority referred to in art. 105 Federal Act on Gambling has the same powers at its disposal vis-à-vis promoters of large-scale games.[621]

3. *Statistics*

a. Number of Investigations and Sanctions

Swiss law does not provide statistics on the number of criminal and administrative investigations launched in Switzerland against individuals and legal entities for the aforementioned offences.

613 Art. 27(3) AMLA.
614 E.g. art. 88 R VQF; art. 6 SAAM Disciplinary Regulations.
615 E.g. art. 37 SRO-SVV Regulations related to Control, Audit and Sanctions; §54 PolyReg; art. 47 R OAR-G.
616 FATF (2016), *Anti-money laundering and counter-terrorist financing measures – Switzerland*, Fourth Round Mutual Evaluation Report, para. 384.
617 See e.g. art. 6 R SAAM.
618 See e.g. §53 R Polyreg.
619 See e.g. art. 6 R SAAM; §55 R Polyreg.
620 Art. 15 Federal Act on Gambling.
621 Art. 31 Federal Act on Gambling.

b. Number of Convictions

Swiss law does not provide statistics on the number of convictions imposed in Switzerland on individuals and legal entities for the aforementioned offences.

C. CUMULATION OF MONEY LAUNDERING AND OTHER AML-RELATED SANCTIONS

In principle, nothing in Swiss law prevents sanctions for money laundering being combined with sanctions for the violation of preventive obligations. However, a cumulation of art. 305bis CC (money laundering) and art. 37 AMLA (violation of the duty to report) would only be possible if the relevant criminal conduct did not take place at the same time. If a financial intermediary commits money laundering by omission because it violated its reporting obligation, he/she cannot also be convicted for a violation of the duty to report under art. 37 AMLA, as this would amount to convicting someone for not having reported an offence that he/she committed himself/herself.

VIII. THE USE OF CASH AS A MEANS OF PAYMENT

A. LIMITS

There is no general limit on cash payments in Switzerland, a country where the use of cash is in fact widespread, mainly for cultural reasons. It should be mentioned, however, that since 1 January 2016, cash payments are only allowed up to CHF 100,000 in forced sales of movable goods and real property.[622] Moreover, it is important to note that, in the context of the 2014 AML reform, the Federal Council proposed introducing two new provisions into the AMLA (arts. 2*b* and 2*c*) requiring that all payments in excess of CHF 100,000 for sales and purchases of movable or immovable properties be arranged through a financial intermediary subject to AMLA.[623] However, after an extremely controversial debate, to be seen against the backdrop of today's tendency to view large cash payments in sales transactions as unusual and, from a money laundering point of view, potentially suspicious, Parliament rejected the Federal Council's proposal.

---

622 Arts. 129(2) and 136(2) Federal Act on Debt Enforcement and Bankruptcy. See FF 2014 585, 647–648.

623 See FF 2014 585, 658–661.

B. STATISTICS

In 2017, the Swiss National Bank conducted a survey on payment methods with the aim of obtaining representative information on payment behaviour and the use of cash by households in Switzerland, and to ascertain the underlying motives for this behaviour.[624] This study revealed that cash is the most common method of payment for households in Switzerland. Of all the payments recorded, 70% were processed with cash.[625] However, when measured in terms of value, cash accounted for just 45% of the recorded expenditure.[626] According to the Swiss National Bank, this difference is attributable to the fact that cash is a particularly popular payment method for small amounts.[627] Nevertheless, cash is also often used when larger sums are involved. According to the study, 35% of non-recurring payments that involve amounts of more than CHF 1,000 are settled with cash.[628]

IX. SUMMARY, EVALUATION AND FUTURE PERSPECTIVES

International cooperation has never been Switzerland's strength. Quite legitimately, the lack of cooperation by the Swiss authorities with foreign authorities in the field of AML/CTF has very often been the source of criticism from the international community. In particular, the fact that MROS refused to cooperate with foreign counterparts regarding the exchange of financial information until 2013 has long been criticised by the Egmont Group of FIUs and even led to the issuance by the Heads of FIUs, the Egmont Group's governing body, of a suspension warning in 2011.[629] It should also be pointed out that several stakeholders interviewed in the framework of this analysis underlined the lack of international cooperation by certain Swiss authorities, in particular judicial authorities, and identified this as a major weakness in the global fight against money laundering and terrorist financing.

It would be wrong to assume, however, on the basis of the aforementioned lack of international cooperation, the poor reputation that the Swiss financial place held for many decades and the numerous scandals that shook it, that

624 Swiss National Banks, *Survey on Payment Methods*, 2017, https://www.snb.ch/en/mmr/reference/paytrans_survey_report_2017/source/paytrans_survey_report_2017.en.pdf.

625 *Ibid.*, pp. 16–17.

626 *Ibid.*, p. 5.

627 *Ibid.*, p. 6.

628 *Ibid.*, p. 19.

629 See *supra* section I.A.

Switzerland has always had a weak and permissive AML/CTF legal framework. In fact, with the enactment in 1977 by the Swiss Bankers Association of the private law Agreement on the Swiss banks' code of conduct with regard to the exercise of due diligence,[630] Switzerland was one of the very first countries to oblige the private sector to take measures to prevent money laundering. Furthermore, the offence of money laundering was introduced in Switzerland in 1990,[631] just two years after the United Nations Convention against Illicit Traffic in Narcotic Drugs and Psychotropic Substances (Vienna Convention),[632] which is the first international convention addressing money laundering, and before many other countries, including European countries.[633] Additionally, one could mention the adoption in 1997[634] of the comprehensive AMLA which, since then, was revised multiple times, thereby demonstrating the authorities' commitment to progressively strengthening the fight against money laundering and enhancing the transparency of financial flows. In this regard, it is interesting to note that the FATF Recommendations and mutual evaluations have always led to positive awareness and driven forward numerous legislative reforms in Switzerland over the years, thereby forming a blueprint for the AML/CTF legal framework.[635] The ongoing reform of the AMLA (DB-AMLA), following the 2016 mutual evaluation, which notably aims at introducing due diligence and reporting obligations for certain persons providing services in connection with companies or trusts (advisors), reflects this very well.

From a comparative point of view, the Swiss AML law distinguishes itself in many ways. Five significant peculiarities are worth mentioning here.[636] First, the money laundering offence (art. 305bis CC) does not cover the acquisition, possession and use of criminal proceeds,[637] whilst most jurisdictions include this set of criminal conducts under the definition of money laundering.[638] Second, contrary to many other countries, Swiss courts have recognised that money laundering can also be committed through omission by financial intermediaries.[639] Money laundering by omission can result from a failure to comply with a reporting duty but also from the duty to clarify the economic

630 *Ibid.*

631 *Ibid.*

632 United Nations, Convention against Illicit Traffic in Narcotic Drugs and Psychotropic Substances, Vienna, 19 December 1988.

633 See notably Germany report in this volume, section I.A.

634 See *supra* section I.A.

635 *Ibid.*

636 For a comprehensive review of all the peculiarities of the Swiss AML/CTF framework in comparison with the FATF Recommendations, the EU legal framework, and the German, Spanish, Italian and UK AML laws, see the comparative analysis in this volume.

637 See *supra* section II.B.1.a.ii.

638 See the comparative analysis in this volume, section II.B.1.a.ii.

639 See *supra* section II.B.2.

background, the purpose of a transaction or a business relationship, as well as from internal regulations.[640] Third, one should point out certain distinctive features of the reporting regime in Switzerland. The reporting system currently used in Switzerland with respect to financial intermediaries indeed draws a unique distinction between the right to report, in the case of "mere" suspicion of money laundering (voluntary SARs), and the obligation to report, in the case of "well-founded" suspicion (mandatory SARs), though the distinction between voluntary and mandatory SARs has become blurred in recent years and the same level of suspicion seems now to be covered by both types of SARs.[641] Furthermore, obliged entities are not only compelled to file an SAR if they know or assume, based on a "well-founded suspicion", that assets involved in a business relationship are connected to money laundering, terrorist financing or that they derive from a predicate offence, but also if they are related to an offence in terms of art. 260ter(1) CC (support or participation to a criminal organisation) or that they are subject to the power of disposal of a criminal organisation.[642] This explicit organised crime dimension of the reporting regime is unique among all the jurisdictions that fall within the scope of this study. The fourth distinctive feature worth mentioning is the impossibility for MROS, at the moment, to request additional information from a financial intermediary that has not submitted an SAR if this request is only based on information provided in a source other than an SAR and its subsequent analysis.[643] Last but not least, the fifth peculiarity of the Swiss AML/CTF legal framework which should be underlined is the fact that the AMLA itself is relatively short (only 37 provisions in total) in that it is deemed a framework law merely setting out principles. Those principles are further specified in several ordinances and regulations, most of which being issued by supervisory authorities. In fact, supervisors in Switzerland, in particular FINMA, play a key role in the implementation and compliance with AML-related norms, not only by specifying the latter in accordance with the needs, capabilities and resources of the entities which fall under their supervision, but also by taking a wide range of measures to prevent money laundering, ensure application of CDD and other AML-related obligations by obliged entities and effectively sanction violations of such obligations.[644]

---

640 *Ibid.*

641 See *supra* section III.C.1.a.

642 *Ibid.*

643 See *supra* section IV.A.4.

644 See *supra* sections III.I and VII.B.

THE ANTI-MONEY LAUNDERING ARCHITECTURE OF THE UNITED KINGDOM

Michael Levi and Liliya Gelemerova

I. INTRODUCTION

A. HISTORY OF ANTI-MONEY LAUNDERING IN THE COUNTRY

The history of anti-money laundering (AML) efforts will be divided into two sections: criminalisation of money laundering, and preventative control efforts.

– *Criminalisation of Money Laundering*

Following closely on the heels of US legislation of 1986, the 1980s saw an incoherent development of the criminalisation regime, based on what the political market could bear and on the social problems that were at the forefront of political and media consciousness. The UK's legislative AML efforts began formally with the Drug Trafficking Offences Act 1986, which introduced drugs-only money laundering offences, in keeping with the view that drug trafficking was the most serious and fastest-growing problem connected with "organised crime".[1] This was extended by the Criminal Justice Act 1988, section 98 of which gave protection from civil lawsuits to those who reported their suspicions of non-drugs serious offences, but did not criminalise laundering of their proceeds. From the beginning, however, the government and the private sector cooperated on the regime, with some early hiccups, such as when the police claimed that

[1] There was not seen to be any need in the UK to criminalise organised crime membership *per se* because the conspiracy legislation was considered adequate to the task and because there was substantial opposition to the use of wiretaps in evidence, which is often required to prove membership. See Michael Levi and Alaster Smith, *A comparative analysis of organised crime conspiracy legislation and practice and their relevance to England and Wales*, London: Home Office, 2002.

they could transfer their own suspicions to the banks, by-passing the requirements under the Police and Criminal Evidence Act 1984 to get a Production Order *ex parte* (i.e. without the defendant being present) from a court when they sought access to bank accounts.[2] Their threat to arrest a major bank compliance officer for money laundering was sorted out by negotiation in a characteristically British way, and they backed off while the banks developed a more cooperative regime. Since that study in the late 1980s, the UK (and the world) has witnessed an extraordinary growth in efforts to control crime for economic and political gain (and, especially since 9/11, terrorism) via measures to identify, freeze and confiscate the proceeds of crime nationally and transnationally.

– *Development of the AML Preventive-Regulatory Regime*

There was an informal reporting process before 1986 based around personal relationships and trust. Some bankers would open the paper records of an account on the table and walk out of the room, while police looked at them in their absence; but this was intelligence only, as civil rulings were quite strict about when banks could violate customer confidentiality other than in their own interests as victims of fraud. After the Drug Trafficking Offences Act 1986, informal reporting by some bankers increased to the National Drugs Intelligence Unit (NDIU) (created in 1985). The SAR regime was introduced in 1986/87[3] and, as the name of the NDIU suggests, the regime focused at the time on proceeds from drug trafficking. Essentially, the regime was introduced in the Drug Trafficking Offences Act 1986, which focused on the proceeds from drug trafficking. This law originally did not refer to the phenomenon as "money laundering" but described it under the heading "Assisting another to retain the benefit of drug trafficking".[4] It focused on third-party laundering as opposed to self-laundering. It did not specifically create an obligation for certain types of businesses, e.g. financial institutions, to report suspicious activity (Suspicious Activity Report or SAR); however, it created a defence for an individual involved in an arrangement that facilitates another person in retaining or controlling the proceeds of drug trafficking if that individual were to disclose their suspicion or belief to a constable. Under the SAR regime, the NDIU became the body

---

2 Michael Levi, "Pecunia non olet: cleansing the money launderers from the Temple", *Crime, Law, and Social Change*, 16 (1991) 217–302, at p. 217.

3 According to the Information Commissioner's Report to the House of Lords European Union Committee entitled "The Serious Organised Crime Agency's operation and use of the ELMER database". It is unclear when it was published but the website of the UK Parliament shows copyright of 2011, https://publications.parliament.uk/pa/ld201011/ldselect/ldeucom/82/8205.htm.

4 http://www.legislation.gov.uk/ukpga/1986/32/contents.

designated to receive SARs. Both informal and formal reporting gradually increased as the police and governments increasingly took the view that greater centralisation of national and international police problems was required, and banks needed to play their part in fighting drugs and Irish terrorism.[5] To try to coordinate financial sector behaviour, a public-private body – the Joint Money Laundering Steering Group – was set up in 1990, in collaboration with their (then) regulator, the Bank of England, to produce formal Money Laundering Guidance for the financial sector. This, over the next years, produced regularly updated guidance on the various Money Laundering Regulations which were promulgated and enhanced, often in response to EU Directives.[6] In the event of civil and criminal cases, this guidance would be taken into account by the courts as a guide to best practice.

The NDIU became the National Criminal Intelligence Service (NCIS) in 1992. This appears to have signified the beginning of a move towards making the reporting of non-drugs related suspicious activity mandatory (which move was completed in 1993 – see the end of this paragraph). The First European Money Laundering Directive (1991/308/EEC) obliged credit and financial institutions to put in place and act upon AML procedures, the most significant of which was the duty to report suspicion of money laundering. The Directive was implemented through the Criminal Justice Act 1993, which amended the existing legislation, and the Money Laundering Regulations 1993. The preventive obligations imposed by the law applied to all persons in their business capacity, including solicitors; the Money Laundering Regulations 1993 applied to solicitors carrying on regulated activities under the Financial Services and Markets Act. The Criminal Justice Act and the Money Laundering Regulations introduced in 1993 made voluntary reporting of non-drugs related "suspicious activity"[7] mandatory.

– *2000 to date*

The UK's AML and counter-terrorist financing framework consists of primary and secondary legislation and industry guidance. Industry guidance has no direct legal applicability but it is admissible in court and in regulatory adjudications as evidence of 'best practice'.

The Proceeds of Crime Act 2002 (POCA) introduced a range of new provisions – substantive criminal law – aimed at strengthening crime proceeds

5 Michael Levi interviews, 1988–1994.

6 See http://www.jmlsg.org.uk/. Prior to 2006, only paper records are available.

7 A more analytically accurate term would be "suspected activity", since "suspicious" implies that there is something inherent in the activity that provokes the report.

recovery. This also included provisions that aimed at strengthening the AML regime. The Act (Part 7) – as amended by subsequent legislation – now contains the principal (also known as "primary") AML legislation.[8]

For the purpose of crime proceeds recovery post-conviction, POCA removed the requirement for prosecutors to prove that the assets were the proceeds of crime (beyond reasonable doubt) and from what type(s) of crime (e.g. drugs versus no-drug crime). More specifically, it allowed the application of civil rules and procedure, i.e. it is sufficient to prove that the assets are the proceeds of any sort of crime, based on the balance of probabilities. This means that post-conviction, for the confiscation element, prosecutors can apply a lower threshold of evidence and do not have to prove the predicate offence and what type it is, so long as an inference can be properly made that the proceeds come from crime. POCA consolidated, updated and reformed previous UK legislation relating to money laundering and criminal property.[9]

The second EU Directive was implemented in the UK through the Money Laundering Regulations 2003, which were linked to POCA. The Money Laundering Regulations 2003 came into force on 1 March 2004. They brought within the regulated sector the category of "legal or natural persons acting in the exercise of their professional activities" (designated non-financial businesses and professions, DNFBPs).

In short, there was a rationalisation (i.e. strengthening and harmonising the preventive measures) in the process of customer identification and reporting for different crimes, via the Money Laundering Regulations 1993,[10] further formalised in POCA and the Money Laundering Regulations 2003, reflected also in successive drafts of the Joint Money Laundering Steering Group guidance. However, different banks then and now took different approaches to the amount of internal filtering of suspicions they undertook before reporting (or not reporting) to the Financial Intelligence Unit (FIU), the body designated to receive SARs. (In the UK, it sits within the National Crime Agency or NCA).[11] This may be viewed by some as inconsistency of approach, but by others as

---

8 The Act has been amended several times since its introduction, most particularly by the Serious Organised Crime and Police Act 2005, the Serious Crime Act 2007 and the Serious Crime Act 2015. Of these latter acts, the key change in regards to the AML regime was introduced by the Serious Organised Crime and Police Act 2005 which established the Serious Organised Crime Agency (SOCA), replacing NCIS. SOCA operated from 1 April 2006 until 7 October 2013 when it was, in turn, replaced by the National Crime Agency (NCA).

9 https://www.supremecourt.uk/cases/docs/uksc-2010-0190-judgment.pdf, https://www.cps.gov.uk/legal-guidance/proceeds-crime-act-2002-part-7-money-laundering-offences.

10 The Money Laundering Regulations, SI 1993/1933, http://www.legislation.gov.uk/uksi/1993/1933/contents/made. See Gary Hagland, "The Money Laundering Regulations 1993: Their Implementation And Implications For Securities Houses", *Journal of Financial Regulation and Compliance*, 2(3), 1994, pp. 227–233.

11 Michael Gold and Michael Levi, *Money-Laundering in the UK: an Appraisal of Suspicion-Based Reporting*, London: Police Foundation, 1994. Michael Levi interviews, 1988–1994, and intermittently to the present.

reflecting the thinking behind the shift from rules-based to risk-based or principles-based reporting.

POCA and the Terrorism Act 2000[12] are supported by the Money Laundering, Terrorist Financing and Transfer of Funds (Information on the Payer) Regulations 2017 (referred to as Money Laundering Regulations 2017, which replaced the earlier money laundering regulations),[13] which is secondary legislation. The Money Laundering Regulations 2017 transposed the Fourth Anti-Money Laundering Directive (4AMLD) into UK law.

Most importantly, the Money Laundering Regulations 2017 support POCA in that they set out a number of obligations for the regulated sector that are aimed at preventing or detecting money laundering and terrorist financing risk. These include the requirement for each firm (including law firms) to conduct a money laundering and terrorist financing risk assessment, to set up internal controls, train staff and implement due diligence measures.

The UK has thus far adopted all EU AML directives. Notwithstanding Brexit, the UK has implemented the Fifth Anti-Money Laundering Directive[14] (5AMLD) (in regard to the Sixth Anti-Money Laundering Directive see section Vii. A, 2. Forms of sanctions),[15] in order to retain an EU-equivalent anti-financial crime standard. It was transposed into UK legislation through the Money Laundering and Terrorist Financing (Amendment) Regulations 2019. These regulations came into force 10 January 2020, creating, among other things, further risk factors to assess, including whether:

a) the customer is the beneficiary of a life insurance policy;
b) the customer is a third country national who is applying for residence rights in or citizenship of an EEA state in exchange for transfers of capital,

---

12 Since 2000 there have been a series of amendments and further acts aimed at terrorism, including the Anti-Terrorism, Crime and Security Act (ATCSA) of 2001. POCA and ATCSA have been amended by the Criminal Finances Act 2017. The National Crime Agency's guidance of May 2019 "Requesting a defence from the NCA under POCA and TACT" refers to the Terrorism Act 2000 (TACT).

13 Money Laundering, Terrorist Financing and Transfer of Funds (Information on the Payer) Regulations 2017, SI 2017/692. These Regulations replace the Money Laundering Regulations 2007 (SI 2007/2157) and the Transfer of Funds (Information on the Payer) Regulations 2007 (SI 2007/3298) with updated provisions that implement in part the Fourth Money Laundering Directive 2015/849/EU of the European Parliament and of the Council of 20 May 2015 on the prevention of the use of the financial system for the purpose of money laundering or terrorist financing (OJ L 141, 05.06.2015, p. 73) and the Funds Transfer Regulation 2015/847/EU of the European Parliament and of the Council of 20 May 2015 on information accompanying transfers of funds (OJ L 141, 05.06.2015, p. 1). See https://www.legislation.gov.uk/uksi/2017/692/note/made.

14 Directive (EU) 2018/843 of the European Parliament and of the Council of 30 May 2018 amending Directive (EU) 2015/849 on the prevention of the use of the financial system for the purposes of money laundering or terrorist financing, and amending Directives 2009/138/EC and 2013/36/EU.

15 Directive (EU) 2018/1673 of the European Parliament and of the Council of 23 October 2018 on combating money laundering by criminal law PE/30/2018/REV/1.

purchase of a property, government bonds or investment in corporate entities in that EEA state;

c) transactions related to oil, arms, precious metals, tobacco products, cultural artefacts, ivory and other items related to protected species, or other items of archaeological, historical, cultural and religious significance, or of rare scientific value.[16]

These factors are to be considered when assessing whether there is a high risk of money laundering or terrorist financing in a particular situation, and the extent of the measures which should be taken to manage and mitigate that risk. Further enhancements include lowering thresholds for due diligence in e-money products and requiring firms to report to Companies House discrepancies between the information the firm holds on their customers compared with the information held in the Companies House Register (on this point see also next section).[17] Obliged entities also need to understand the ownership and control structure of their corporate customers, and record any difficulties encountered in identifying beneficial ownership. In relation to the requirement to apply enhanced due diligence, this now explicitly includes any customer or transaction where either of the parties to the transaction is established in a high-risk third country (as defined by the European Commission in the Fourth Anti-Money Laundering Directive). Additionally, where the customer (a) is the beneficiary of a life insurance policy, (b) is a legal person or a legal arrangement, and (c) presents a high risk of money laundering or terrorist financing for any other reason, an obliged entity that is a credit or financial institution must take reasonable measures to identify and verify the identity of the beneficial owners of that beneficiary before any payment is made under the policy.

The 2019 updates also added to the list of obliged entities (defined as 'relevant persons' in UK legislation) the following: letting agents, art market participants and cryptoasset exchange providers. The requirement for an obliged entity to establish and maintain, throughout its group, policies, controls and procedures for data protection and sharing information for the purposes of preventing money laundering and terrorist financing with other members of the group, now explicitly also includes policies on the sharing of information about customers, customer accounts and transactions. In addition to training employees on AML, obliged entities are now also explicitly required to train any agents they use for the purposes of their business.

---

16 Some AML professionals and business already considered these as high risk factors, from a smuggling, corruption, terrorist financing and money laundering perspective. The new enhancement helps achieve a more consistent approach.

17 (SI 2019/1511). See also https://www.fca.org.uk/firms/financial-crime/money-laundering-regulations.

One entirely new section concerns requests for information about accounts with credit institutions and safe-deposit boxes. The Secretary of State or the Treasury must ensure that a central automated mechanism is established for making and responding to requests for information. Credit institutions and safe custody services providers, accordingly, must establish and maintain systems which enable them to respond, using the central automated mechanism, to requests for information from law enforcement authorities or from the Gambling Commission.

A notable update concerns the NCA's relationship with other authorities. Where the NCA has, in its performance of FIU functions, disseminated any information to a United Kingdom competent authority, that authority must, upon request, provide a report to the NCA about the authority's use of that information, including the outcome of any investigations or inspections conducted on the basis of that information.[18] This may enhance the ability of the UK to report on the investigative impact of SARs and of any further intelligence development made by the FIU.[19] This is important for domestic as well as for international accountability and legitimacy. However it should be noted that this does not require *routine* reporting back.

B. CURRENT CONCERNS AND REFORM AGENDA

– *Beneficial Ownership Register*

The UK has registers of beneficial ownership for three different types of assets: companies, properties and land, and trusts. Information on the beneficial ownership of companies is publicly available. For properties owned by overseas companies and legal entities, the government plans to launch a public beneficial ownership register in 2021. The register for trusts is not public, nor is it planned to make it so.[20]

The register of beneficial owners of companies as well as properties and the recently introduced unexplained wealth orders[21] are among the key measures

---

18 This chapter was submitted around the time when the new regulations were issued – 20 December 2019. They came into force on 10 January 2020. While every effort was made to update this chapter, some citations of the earlier regulations may remain.

19 While the proofs of this chapter were being finalised, a revised version of the JMLSG guidance on the ML Regulations 2019 was issued in June 2020, but we were unable to include this guidance at this late stage.

20 Federiko Mor, "Registers of beneficial ownership", House of Commons Library, Briefing Paper No 8259, 24 August 2018, https://researchbriefings.parliament.uk/ResearchBriefing/Summary/CBP-8259.

21 Incorporated into UK law as part of the Criminal Finances Act 2017, an unexplained wealth order is a court order issued to compel someone to reveal the sources of their unexplained wealth.

the UK has introduced in response to criticism that the country is a key crime proceeds destination. Scholars, NGOs (e.g. Transparency International UK, Global Witness, Spotlight on Corruption and Shadow World Investigations) and practitioners have raised questions about the effectiveness of UK's AML regime and the credibility of FATF's overall evaluation in relation to these reforms.[22] At least one significant problem is that Companies House has never had either the resources or the role of checking the veracity of data sent to it – for the beneficial ownership or other registers – but external bodies may be unaware of this fact.[23] Furthermore, the issue has raised tensions between the UK and its overseas territories over the attempts to impose public registers on them.

According to a Europol report published on 5 September 2017, the UK is one of the top countries from which both individuals and companies feature most in STRs/SARs across the EU:

> This may be related to a perceived increasing use of UK LLPs in money laundering schemes, given that there is some scope to conceal beneficial ownership through designating ownership to entities located in jurisdictions with significant banking secrecy (i.e. on the face of it the company may appear to be a UK company, however ultimate ownership details will in fact rest elsewhere). This issue has already been addressed through the recent UK Small Business Enterprise and Employment Act 2015, which requires most UK companies, including LLPs, to maintain registers of persons with significant control over a company (essentially a register of beneficial owners).[24]

Although this is administrative data, it has some relevance because it reflects active financial investigation in other EU countries.

---

22 Ron Pol, "Ron Pol reflects on effectiveness issues revealed by the UK's leaked AML/CFT evaluation & shares new visualisations of the ratings methodology that will be used to assess NZ's regime", interest.co.nz, 20 October 2018, https://www.interest.co.nz/opinion/96510/ron-pol-reflects-effectiveness-issues-revealed-uk%E2%80%99s-leaked-amlcft-evaluation-shares.

23 In September 2019, Company Watch, which provides credit reports on thousands of private companies every year, added a disclaimer to its assessments amid fears that the Companies Register is being used by fraudsters. Among faults are that directors who misspell their names may appear multiple times. Also, companies with turnover less than £10.2m – the vast majority of those registered – can claim exemption from audits of their annual accounts. Companies House cannot remove bankrupt directors from their register: they have to ask them to resign.

24 Europol, "From suspicion to action. Converting financial intelligence into greater operational impact", 2017, https://www.europol.europa.eu/publications-documents/suspicion-to-action-converting-financial-intelligence-greater-operational-impact.

Additionally, a 2019 enhancement to the Money Laundering Regulations (discussed in section I.A) is worth noting. Specifically, before establishing a business relationship with a company or partnership, obliged entities must:

a) collect proof of registration or an excerpt of the register from the prospect customer; and
b) report to the registrar any discrepancy between information relating to the beneficial ownership of the customer which the relevant person collects (under a) above) and which otherwise becomes available to the obliged entity in the course of carrying out its duties under the Money Laundering Regulations.

It is unclear, however, how the registrar will make use of this information while guaranteeing the obliged entity's disclosure confidentiality and without the prospective customer realising that a disclosure had been made. The implications of this reporting must also be considered in the context of obliged entities having to report suspicion-triggering discrepancies to the FIU in the form of SARs. It is also unclear why the provision focuses on proof collected before the start of a business relationship instead of specifically also including proof collected at later stages (for instance, when, during a periodic customer file review, the customer provides documents on changes). (One possible reason is to collect data on intermediary-shopping by offenders.)

Also, in the context of new technologies and digital onboarding, obliged entities seek to obtain certain documentation about their prospective or existing customers from official repositories, such as company registries or exchanges, through automated software tools. This automation means that a customer outreach is not always necessary and is aimed at speeding up the process of onboarding a customer or updating a customer's file. However, the abovementioned 2019 enhancement to the regulations appears to require reaching out to the client for proof of registration in any event. This may defeat the purpose of automation, particularly for the entities that are on the lower end of the risk spectrum and have simpler ownership structures. It is yet to be seen how the JMLSG and other industry bodies will interpret this and other new enhancements.

– *Statistics*

Although not exclusive to the UK, the lack of comprehensive and consistent statistics has been noted by scholars and authoritative bodies. The Europol report, discussed above (and the subsequent FATF Mutual Evaluation Report), highlights that the UK has not provided statistics on the financial amounts in SARs and on the conversion rate (whether an SAR has resulted in any follow-up activity, not necessarily a conviction). Such data are not collected, and feedback from police and non-police bodies with SAR access has been a problem ever since the beginning of what we might term the "loose-coupled system" in the 1980s.[25] This has a cultural explanation that is unlikely to be unique to the UK. Investigators may not see it as a priority to tell the FIU when an SAR has been useful for either investigation or asset recovery purposes (see, however, section I.A. above for 2019 updates to the regulations), and the FIU may not prioritise telling the SAR reporters even when it is notified by investigators that an SAR has been useful. The FATF Evaluation criticises the UK's FIU for the absence of its own SAR follow-up investigation and for what may be described as the distributed model of sending out SARs and leaving it up to the individual recipients to investigate (or, more often, not). It should be noted that this reflects UK (or certainly England and Wales) police culture (and constrained resources): this lack of internal investigation and follow-up also happens with the centralised fraud victim complaints distributed to other police forces by Action Fraud and the National Fraud Intelligence Bureau in the City of London Police.[26]

– *Defensive/Precautionary Reporting and Alleged Over-reporting (Over-compliance)*

Defensive, also known in the industry as "precautionary", reporting appears to be an issue in the UK. (This is not to be confused with the "defence regime" or also known as "consent" requests under the UK AML regime "defence against money laundering" (DAML) or, similarly, under the counter-terrorist financing (CTF) regime – see section III.C.1.d – although it may well be that it is the "consent regime" that contributes to high levels of defensive reporting). This means that obliged entities feel safer if they file an SAR as a precaution even where they do not know or suspect money laundering or terrorist financing but they fear that their thought process may be later subject to critical interpretation by regulators or courts. In other words, filing the SAR requires less effort than trying to prove the negative to auditors and regulators at a later stage, even though the latter proof may never be required.

---

25 Michael Levi, "Pecunia non olet: cleansing the money launderers from the Temple", *Crime, Law, and Social Change*, 16 (1991) 217–302; Michael Gold and Michael Levi, *Money-Laundering in the UK: an Appraisal of Suspicion-Based Reporting*, London: Police Foundation, 1994; M Levi, "Incriminating disclosures: an evaluation of money-laundering regulation in England and Wales", *European Journal of Crime, Criminal Law, and Criminal Justice*, 3(2) (1995) 202–217.

26 Alan Doig, "Fraud: from national strategies to practice on the ground – a regional case study" *Public Money & Management*, 38(2) (2018) 147–156; Home Affairs Select Committee, *Policing for the Future*, House of Commons, 2018, 515; Police Foundation, *More Than Just A Number: Improving the Police Response to Victims Of Fraud*, London: Police Foundation, 2018; HMICFRS, *Fraud: Time to choose – An inspection of the police response to fraud*, 2019.

The above-mentioned Europol report identified that of all the regulated sectors in the EU, it is the UK that produces the most SARs. Between 2006 and 2014, UK SARs accounted for 36% of all SARs submitted across all EU Member States. Dutch SARs accounted for 31%. SARs submitted from each of the remaining states accounted for between 1% and 5%. According to the report:

> It is of course understandable that the UK would generate one of the highest reporting volumes in the EU: not only is it home to one of the largest financial markets in Europe, but in addition, it operates a Suspicious Activity Regime (SAR), which broadens the types of reports it can receive. Nonetheless, the figures are extremely high in comparison to other countries, which may also be a result of defensive or over reporting.

A footnote in the same Europol report further explained:

> Although reporting guidance from the FCA, JSMLG and NCA is quite comprehensive on obligations, and the UK FIU analysis of reports suggests that the majority of the financial institutions that submit SARs conduct at least a basic level of research and analysis prior to submission, and in some cases undertake quite substantial pre-submission examination.[27]

There is some ambiguity or indeed contradiction in this perspective. The FATF pressurises countries to make more reports, and particular sectors, such as the legal and accountancy professions and estate agents, are often criticised in the media and by NGOs for making an insufficient number of reports. There is a general lack of clarity in the evaluation and enforcement community (and, for that matter, among NGOs) about what constitutes the right number of reports, and there is a systemic failure to address this in terms of ratios to clear denominators. There is no consistency in the use of either numbers or percentages of reports, and little evidenced thinking about the value (indeed, the point) of firms making reports that have no serious chance of leading to action.

– *De-risking*

A report commissioned by the Financial Conduct Authority (FCA) and published in 2016 observes:

> The Financial Conduct Authority ... is aware that over recent years some banks have removed bank accounts/services from customers or other relationships which they associate with higher money laundering risk. This process has been termed

27 Europol, "From suspicion to action. Converting financial intelligence into greater operational impact", 2017, https://www.europol.europa.eu/publications-documents/suspicion-to-action-converting-financial-intelligence-greater-operational-impact.

'de-risking' and it has been attributed to the increasing overall cost of complying with regulatory requirements. These include prudential and conduct obligations and, standards as well as the threat of enforcement action for failing to meet such obligations, particularly in relation to anti-money laundering/combating financing of terrorism (AML/CFT). However, there appear to be other factors at play too, including ethical, reputational and commercial considerations.[28]

– *JMLIT*

In the UK, we believe, there is an efficient and useful form of sharing intelligence between law enforcement and regulatory authorities on the one hand and the regulated sector on the other. Specifically, through the Joint Money Laundering Intelligence Taskforce (JMLIT) – a private-public partnership – regulated entities, the NCA and HM Revenue & Customs (HMRC) can sit around the table and discuss law enforcement and regulatory investigations and share intelligence – both ways – thanks to enabling legislation which allows for regulated entities to share sensitive information if the NCA is sitting at the table and requesting information. Such intelligence sharing is considered particularly valuable when it comes to targeting human trafficking, and it is becoming increasingly popular outside Europe.

– *UK Government Plan of January 2019 to Reform the SAR Regime*

The UK Law Commission issued a report in 2018 proposing changes to the SAR regime. Notable proposals include modifications to the test of suspicion required for filing an SAR, allowing banks to process mixed criminal and legitimate funds in limited circumstances. The Commission also proposed the introduction of a corporate criminal offence of failure to ensure the reporting of suspected money laundering.[29] Its consultation paper highlighted that the low suspicion threshold for SAR filing combined with the individual criminal liability resulted in large-scale defensive (also known as precautionary) SAR filing (see subsection "Defensive/Precautionary Reporting and Alleged Over-reporting (Over-compliance)" above). It was proposed that increasing the threshold to "reasonable grounds" would help reduce defensive SAR filing.[30]

---

[28] David Artingstall, Nick Dove, John Howell, Michael Levi, "Drivers & Impacts of Derisking. A study of representative views and data in the UK", by John Howell & Co. Ltd. for the Financial Conduct Authority, February 2016, https://www.fca.org.uk/publication/research/drivers-impacts-of-derisking.pdf.

[29] "UK Law Commission Proposes Reforms to Suspicious Activity Reports for Money Laundering", Debevoise & Plimpton, 28 August 2018, https://www.debevoise.com/insights/publications/2018/08/uk-law-commission-considers-reforms-to-suspicious.

[30] https://www.nortonrosefulbright.com/en-gb/knowledge/publications/5ed49740/the-law-commission-consultation-on-reforming-the-sars-regime-key-takeaways-for-the-financial-sector.

In January 2019 the Home Secretary and Chancellor of the Exchequer announced that they would chair the new Economic Crime Strategic Board, a taskforce that brings together representatives from the private sector (such as financial institutions), law enforcement agencies and regulatory bodies to tackle the economic crime threat. The Board will meet biannually to set its priorities and direct its resources.[31] This model has been criticised by some NGOs, such as Global Witness and Corruption Watch, for including the major banks at its centre when, in their view, they are part of the problem.[32]

It is yet to be seen to what degree the UK policymakers will adopt the recommendations made by the UK Law Commission.

– *The Primary Criticisms of the FATF 2018 Mutual Evaluation Report*

The FATF has highlighted that the UK needs to strengthen the capacity and capabilities of the UK's FIU and the ability of the authorities to conduct systematic and strategic assessments of the UK money laundering threat. The limited role, resourcing and IT capacity of the FIU resulted in the FATF rating the overall effectiveness of UK financial intelligence regime as "moderate".

Supervision of the legal and accounting industries for AML and CTF purposes and the general understanding of financial-crime risks among professionals in these sectors was also rated "moderate".

The report has also highlighted the need to keep accurate and up-to-date the data in the beneficial shareholder public register (UK Companies House).

Those issues and the FIU's judged lack of autonomy from the NCA "in defining its role or its priorities," resulted in one of two "partially compliant" grades.

The UK has pledged to increase the staff of the FIU, and has increased it by half by mid-2020. The UK government is considering how to improve the accuracy of data in Companies House and what further measures to take, and has issued a (now completed) consultation paper discussing long-pressed-for enhancements to the validity of the public register, and other changes.[33]

Think tanks, academia and members of the industry have noted that to justify its high ratings, they would have expected the UK to have achieved more.

---

31 "The law commission consultation on reforming the SARs regime: Key takeaways for the financial sector", Norton Rose Fulbright, August 2018, https://www.whitecase.com/publications/alert/sar-reform-case-causey-and-its-effect.

32 "To all intents and purposes the [strategic board] is formalised policy capture of the economic crime agenda by precisely the corporations it ought to be policing": "Overhaul of financial crime rules too weak, warn critics", Financial Times, 12 July 2019, https://www.ft.com/content/0a4ed736-a400-11e9-974c-ad1c6ab5efd1.

33 https://www.gov.uk/government/consultations/corporate-transparency-and-register-reform.

In particular, it has been stressed that the UK remains a key destination for tainted funds. Some of the key shortcomings highlighted in UK's report, including issues with Companies House data and the inconsistent scrutiny into the real estate sector and certain professions (compared to scrutiny into banks) are viewed as significant. The Royal United Services Institute's (RUSI) head of financial crime Tom Keatinge expressed the view of many organisations when he observed:

> The UK has achieved top-of-the-class marks from the FATF – government officials will be both surprised and relieved. However, the fact that the UK remains central to global money laundering schemes brings into question the relevance of this evaluation. Furthermore, we have cause to question some of the findings in the report, in particular, the assessment in relation to the effective use of financial intelligence by UK law enforcement.[34]

II. AIMS AND SCOPE OF AML SYSTEM

A. AIMS OF AML/CTF REGIME

Generally, the language used in legislation implies that the AML/CTF regime aims to prevent the corruption and misuse of the financial system for the purposes of money laundering and the furthering of crime (including terrorism). More specifically, the Money Laundering Regulations state in the introductory part that they transpose the EU Directive on the prevention of the use of the financial system for the purposes of money laundering and terrorist financing. Subsequently, the phrase "prevention of the use of the financial system for the purposes of money laundering or terrorist financing" is reiterated multiple times throughout the regulations.

However, a key and direct objective is to help confiscate the assets of criminals and, as a result, channel those assets to better use and prevent criminals from enjoying them.[35] The key AML piece of legislation is POCA, amended subsequently and supported by the Money Laundering Regulations of 2017 (previously of 2007) and 2019. This law aims at supporting the

---

34 "RUSI Experts React to UK's Financial Action Task Force Mutual Evaluation Report", RUSI, 7 December 2018, https://rusi.org/rusi-news/rusi-experts-react-uk-financial-action-task-force-mutual-evaluation-report.

35 In the Serious and Organised Crime Strategy 2018, the Home Secretary notes (p. 2): "Our revised approach puts greater focus on the most dangerous offenders and the highest harm networks. Denying perpetrators the opportunity to do harm and going after criminal finances and assets will be key to this." The first objective of the strategy states (p. 6): "We will use new and improved powers and capabilities to identify, freeze, seize or otherwise deny criminals access to their finances, assets and infrastructure, at home and overseas including Unexplained Wealth Orders and Serious Crime Prevention Orders."

confiscation of crime proceeds, including through civil recovery channels. The law states in its introductory part:

> An Act to establish the Assets Recovery Agency and make provision about the appointment of its Director and his functions (including Revenue functions), to provide for confiscation orders in relation to persons who benefit from criminal conduct and for restraint orders to prohibit dealing with property, to allow the recovery of property which is or represents property obtained through unlawful conduct or which is intended to be used in unlawful conduct, to make provision about money laundering, to make provision about investigations relating to benefit from criminal conduct or to property which is or represents property obtained through unlawful conduct or to money laundering, to make provision to give effect to overseas requests and orders made where property is found or believed to be obtained through criminal conduct, and for connected purposes.

We note that the Assets Recovery Agency was subsequently abolished because of its failure to confiscate funds in excess of its costs. Its civil recovery functions were subsumed into SOCA (now the NCA), and have not been utilised extensively since then.

As the POCA section of the website of the CPS[36] notes:

> Therefore, where there is sufficient evidence to meet the evidential test under the Code for Crown Prosecutors, the following Public Interest factors in favour of prosecution for offences of money laundering should be very carefully considered:
>
> - The importance of making it more difficult for criminals to legitimise their ill-gotten gains;
> - The importance of deterring professional launderers;
> - The importance of protecting the integrity of financial institutions domestically and internationally.

B. SCOPE OF MONEY LAUNDERING

1. *Definition of Money Laundering in Criminal Law*

a. *Actus Reus*

i. Predicate Offences

Under POCA, the Crown has to prove that the laundered proceeds are "criminal property", as defined in section 340 POCA: that is to say that the property

36 https://www.cps.gov.uk/legal-guidance/proceeds-crime-act-2002-part-7-money-laundering-offences.

constitutes a person's *benefit* from *criminal conduct* (whether via a criminal prosecution or a civil recovery path under which evidence has only to meet the balance of probabilities test).

"Criminal conduct" is all conduct which constitutes an offence in any part of the UK (which means that an "all crimes" approach is adopted in respect of predicate crimes committed in the UK).[37]

Under POCA, any criminal conduct which generates proceeds or other economic benefit (e.g. criminal tax savings) can be considered a predicate offence regardless of whether it has occurred in the UK or abroad, subject to the condition that if it had had occurred abroad, even if lawful in that country at the time it occurred, it had to be a criminal offence in the UK and punishable (in principle) by more than a year of imprisonment.

The Government and Parliament took the above approach when POCA was being debated. According to a Government 2008 report, the main reasons for the "all crimes" approach are:

- that there may be very little correlation between sums laundered and the seriousness of an offence. Reports on the laundering of small amounts can help solve serious crime;
- that the introduction of a *de minimis* monetary threshold would be easy for launderers to circumvent through "smurfing" – splitting money into sums coming below the threshold to avoid detection;
- that having a threshold linked only to serious crimes relies on a person (e.g. a bank clerk) being able to distinguish between serious crime and other crime in identifying the source of criminal property.[38]

POCA does set a £250 threshold for deposit-taking bodies, stipulating that they do not commit a money laundering offence if the amount in the account operated by them is under this threshold. As the NCA's guidance of May 2019, "Guidance on submitting better quality Suspicious Activity Reports (SARs)", explains:

> S339A of POCA makes provision for deposit taking institutions only to process individual transactions or activity on an account that do not exceed £250, and where there is a suspicion of money laundering – without the need to request a defence under s335 to a principal money laundering offence.

---

37 *Ibid.* In some cases there is extra-territorial jurisdiction, most notably the Bribery Act 2010.

38 The government reply to the 19th report from the House of Lords, European Union Committee Session 2008–09 HL Paper 132, Money laundering and the financing of terrorism Presented to Parliament by the Secretary of State for the Home Department by Command of Her Majesty October 2009.

While from POCA it appears that deposit-taking entities do not need to file an SAR for amounts under the threshold (or is not clear enough whether they have to), the above guidance issued by the NCA states:

> The reporter should still consider making a disclosure in respect of the initial opening of an account. Or, if different, the time when the deposit-taking body first suspects that the property is criminal property.

Having to file an SAR for an amount under £250 would appear to defeat the purpose of setting this threshold in the first place. It is possible that, considering the above reasons for the "all crimes" approach, the UK authorities wanted to ensure that smurfing through the use of different deposit-taking bodies is captured.

However, prosecutors will not pursue *de minimis* amounts, which means that if a crime generates a small amount/economic benefit (e.g. shoplifting), prosecutors are very unlikely to pursue a money laundering charge. The website of the Crown Prosecution Service (CPS) notes:

> A money laundering charge ought to be considered where the proceeds are more than *de minimis* in any circumstances where the defendant who is charged with the underlying offence has done more than simply consume his proceeds of crime. A charge under section 329 of possession of laundered proceeds, however, may not be necessary, for instance where proceeds were simply 'kept under the bed'. An application for confiscation of the actual benefit of the offence may be sufficient in those circumstances.[39]

See Appendix E Crown Prosecution Service for more details on proving the predicate offence.

ii. Definition of Money Laundering Acts

In short, POCA describes the money laundering offences as follows:

- A person commits an offence if he conceals, disguises, converts, or transfers criminal property, or removes criminal property from England and Wales, Scotland or Northern Ireland. Concealing or disguising criminal property includes concealing or disguising its nature, source, location, disposition, movement, ownership or any rights connected with it.
- A person commits an offence if he enters into, or becomes concerned in an arrangement which he knows or suspects facilitates the acquisition, retention, use or control of criminal property by or on behalf of another person.

---

39 See https://www.cps.gov.uk/legal-guidance/proceeds-crime-act-2002-part-7-money-laundering-offences.

- A person commits an offence if he acquires, uses or has possession of criminal property: this includes the proceeds of his own crimes.

See Appendix A Criminal Offences under POCA for more details.

Under POCA, prosecutors have to prove that the laundered proceeds are "criminal property", as defined in section 340 POCA: that is to say that the property constitutes a person's benefit from criminal conduct.

There is no certainty in regards to how commingled property (i.e. legitimate and illegitimate) should be treated. The general understanding of the law is that dealing with mixed funds can give rise to criminal liability. There have been multiple instances of financial institutions in the UK being fined for weakness in their AML systems and controls. From a disclosure perspective, it is irrelevant whether the funds are solely of criminal origin or mixed. Regulators do not even have to prove that there are crime proceeds at all if they see what they define as a "weakness" (which can be broadly interpreted to include a range of issues), though this can lead to remedial action rather than to a formal penalty under the discretionary model or both. The Law Commission (as discussed above in subsection "UK Government Plan of January 2019 to Reform the SAR Regime" of section I.B) proposed in 2018 changes to the SAR regime to raise the reporting threshold and allow, within limited circumstances, dealing with mixed funds. We are not suggesting that prosecutions are the only index of seriousness or effectiveness, but an article in the FCPA blog in March 2018 highlighted that, "[d]espite the UK's rhetoric about wanting a 'world leading reputation for integrity' as a financial center, it has never prosecuted a single company or bank for money laundering."[40] As the Law Commission noted in their 2018 consultation paper, in the absence of significant case law, the broadly drafted legislation combined with inconsistent sector-specific guidance makes it difficult for obliged entities to understand their obligations.[41]

Where the illegitimate property/funds/benefit cannot be ring-fenced, value-based (as opposed to object-based) confiscation may be pursued, which in any event has always been the UK model other than for cash and instrumentalities of crime forfeiture. In such instances, the equivalent of what is believed to be the illegitimate portion of the commingled property will be subject to confiscation.

40 Susan Hawley, "The UK doesn't prosecute money laundering (and that should change)", FCPA blog, 20 March 2018, http://www.fcpablog.com/blog/2018/3/20/susan-hawley-the-uk-doesnt-prosecute-money-laundering-and-th.html.

41 "The law commission consultation on reforming the SARs regime: Key takeaways for the financial sector", Norton Rose Fulbright, August 2018, https://www.nortonrosefulbright.com/en-gb/knowledge/publications/5ed49740/the-law-commission-consultation-on-reforming-the-sars-regime-key-takeaways-for-the-financial-sector.

As explained in a 2017 UNODC report, in the UK

> default of payment of a value based confiscation order can result in an additional period of imprisonment being levied. The convicted person may however apply for a reduction in the value of the order if he or she can show that they have no other assets from which to pay. If the convicted person refuses to pay or claims he or she has no assets from which to pay, apart from an additional period of imprisonment being levied, the following enforcement mechanism are typically available for the collection of unfulfilled value based confiscation orders.
>
> - The confiscation order has the status of a civil judgment and the government becomes a judgment creditor. The debt can be collected through ordinary civil law enforcement mechanisms, such as insolvency/bankruptcy proceedings; or
> - Special realisation procedures are provided for as part of the asset recovery law.[42]

Tax evasion is a predicate offence to money laundering. In *R v Allen*, the Court decided that a person who "benefits" from tax evasion benefits to the extent of the tax evaded, although scholars have noted that this is not straightforward.[43] Given that tax evasion is a predicate offence, but one that generates illegal savings as opposed to profit in the ordinary sense of that word, and given that mixed funds give rise to liability, it is unclear where a line should be drawn and whether funds should be treated differently for the tax evasion charges as opposed to the money laundering charges.[44]

b. *Mens Rea*

Knowledge or suspicion that the property is of criminal origin is an essential requirement for liability and, therefore, the *mens rea*, under each of the principal money laundering offences under POCA sections 327, 328 and 329 (see Appendix A Criminal offences under POCA and Appendix E Crown Prosecution Service).

The Court of Appeal has held that the meaning of "suspicion" under the Criminal Justice Act 1988 (the predecessor of POCA) is that "the defendant

---

42 Study prepared by the Secretariat on effective management and disposal of seized and confiscated assets, Open-ended Intergovernmental Working Group on Asset Recovery, UNODC, 23 August 2017, https://www.unodc.org/documents/treaties/UNCAC/WorkingGroups/workinggroup2/2017-August-24-25/V1705952e.pdf.

43 *R v Allen* [2001] UKHL 45; Peter Alldridge, "Smuggling, Confiscation and Forfeiture", *The Modern Law Review*, 65(5) (2002) 781–791.

44 "The wide definition of criminal property may result in a relatively small amount of criminal property tainting a significantly larger asset [...] in cases of tax evasion, failure to declare turnover upon which tax should be paid generally renders the entire turnover criminal property", SARs Regime Good Practice Frequently Asked Questions Defence Against Money Laundering (DAML), NCA, May 2019, https://www.nationalcrimeagency.gov.uk/who-we-are/publications/167-defence-against-money-laundering-daml-faq-may-2018/file#:~:text=A%20DAML%20does%20not%20provide,of%20the%20funds%20in%20question.

must have thought that there was a possibility, which was more than fanciful, that the other person was or had been engaged in or had benefited from criminal conduct. A vague feeling of unease would not suffice. This is subject, in an appropriate case, to the further requirement that the suspicion so formed should be of a settled nature".[45] The same meaning is to be adopted in civil proceedings that arise out of the money laundering provisions under Part 7 of the POCA.[46] It is noteworthy that there is no requirement for suspicion to be reasonable.[47] It is not necessary to know the precise details of the predicate offence and prosecutors do not have to prove the predicate offence at the criminal law standard. In fact, they do not need to know what type of predicate offence generated the proceeds (see also section VIIA.1).

2. *Money Laundering by Omission*

It is commonly understood that there is criminal liability if the omission is the result of gross negligence, akin to recklessness,[48] or deliberate non-disclosure rather than the result of money laundering being impossible to detect within the due process that the regulated sector can reasonably put in place. The Money Laundering Regulations require that regulated entities and regulated professionals undertake due diligence on customers to confirm their bona fides. Section 331 POCA creates an offence of failure to disclose in respect of nominated officers (i.e. compliance officers) in the regulated sector who receive disclosures based under section 330 and who do not pass the information to the FIU as the disclosure-receiving unit when they:

- know or suspect; or
- have reasonable grounds for knowing or suspecting that another person is engaged in money laundering.[49]

---

45 *R v Da Silva* [2006] EWCA Crim 1654, although in *Shah and another v HSBC Private Bank (UK) Ltd [2012] EWHC 1283* the judge ruled that this formulation ("of a settled nature") is only applicable in limited circumstances (see https://www.bclplaw.com/en-GB/thought-leadership/landmark-decision-in-shah-v-hsbc-private-bank-brings-welcome-relief-for-firms.html).

46 *K Ltd v National Westminster Bank Plc* [2007] 1 WLR 311.

47 Paul Marshal, Chancery Bar Association, Money Laundering Explanatory Note, Part 1, Substantive Law, May 2013.

48 In the law of England and Wales, recklessness may be defined as the conscious taking of an unjustified risk. Negligence is unreasonable conduct that creates risk, while gross negligence is a high degree of negligence that may deserve criminal punishment. In *R v G & R* [2003] UKHL 50, it was determined that recklessness was punishable criminally where: (i) a circumstance when he is aware of a risk that it exists or will exist; (ii) a result when he is aware of a risk that it will occur; and it is, in the circumstances known to him, unreasonable to take the risk.

49 See https://www.cps.gov.uk/legal-guidance/proceeds-crime-act-2002-part-7-money-laundering-offences.

However, when it comes to mere negligence (as opposed to gross negligence), there are different schools of thought.

One school of thought argues that POCA effectively criminalises negligence in the regulated sector.[50] In particular, section 330(3) POCA states: "The second condition is that the information or other matter – (a) on which his knowledge or suspicion is based, or (b) which gives reasonable grounds for such knowledge or suspicion, came to him in the course of a business in the regulated sector."

Lawyers have highlighted:

> The consensus of the learned authors of Archbold (2018) and of the leading specialist textbook 'Mitchell, Taylor and Talbot on Proceeds of Crime' (which is reproduced in the CPS's legal guidance) is that subsection 330(2)(b) is an offence committed by negligence. Archbold instructs its readers that section 330 (and section 331) 'introduce a negligence test.' Accordingly, a person may commit an offence under it 'even if he did not actually know or suspect' (para 26–22). The latter textbook endorses this interpretation: 'The offence is committed by a person who has the necessary knowledge or suspicion but also where, in the circumstances, he should at least have suspected that the other person was engaged in money laundering.'[51]

It can be argued that policymakers have deliberately included the "reasonable grounds" provision to enforce the expectation that firms and professionals in the regulated sector follow a process, which includes Know-Your-Customer (KYC) and due diligence checks and transactions monitoring, in finding out whether there are reasonable grounds to suspect the property is of criminal origin. If firms and professionals are able to demonstrate they have followed an appropriate process and have taken all reasonable steps, then they can claim that defence. Section 331 POCA, as well the availability of the aforementioned defence, do not depend on whether money laundering is actually taking place or has ever taken place.

It is notable that the 'reasonable grounds" provision does not apply outside of the regulated sector, according to POCA. Additionally, the CPS explicitly states that the offence of failure to disclose by nominated officers outside the regulated sector (section 332 POCA) cannot be committed by negligence. The mental element of this offence is knowledge or suspicion.[52] This supports the argument that nominated officers in the regulated sector, in theory, may be prosecuted for negligence.

---

50 Outside of the regulated sector this offence cannot be committed by negligence. See https://www.cps.gov.uk/legal-guidance/proceeds-crime-act-2002-part-7-money-laundering-offences.

51 David Corker, "Failure to disclose does not equate to negligence", Corker Binning blog, 7 February 2018, https://www.corkerbinning.com/failure-to-disclose-does-not-equate-to-negligence/.

52 https://www.cps.gov.uk/legal-guidance/proceeds-crime-act-2002-part-7-money-laundering-offences.

As there is significant scope for interpretation as to what appropriate process should entail, the regulated sector faces difficulty in ensuring that regulators concur with their assessment, though regulators may not themselves be able to specify a process for detecting money laundering in those circumstances. As the risk of nominated officers in the regulated sector facing liability is perceived to be high, there is significant defensive SAR reporting (as highlighted by the Law Commission) and de-risking (see above section I.B).

A second school of thought argues:

> these odd and ambiguous words [came to] mean that negligence alone is insufficient to create criminal liability. They do so by requiring proof that the information about which a prosecutor contends constitutes the reasonable grounds was at the material time actually known to the accused. These words mean more than that this information was merely available or accessible to him.

And:

> Bearing in mind that an individual convicted of this offence is subject to a maximum sentence of five years' imprisonment and that ancillary professional ruin would accompany any conviction, it would be remarkable if Parliament had ordained that one could commit it based on mistake, ignorance and/or stupidity. One could be guilty of it despite not foreseeing or understanding that the transaction created a money laundering risk. Absent the common law offence of manslaughter by gross negligence, subsection 330(2)(b) would be unique amongst the calendar of serious criminal offences. Even this common law offence is a weak analogue however, as the courts have emphasised that mere negligence is insufficient to commit it; the conduct must be so reprehensible, so grossly out of order, to warrant criminalising.

However, even this second school of thought admits that the wording is ambiguous and it will be up to the courts to decide. While there are reported sentencing cases under subsection 330(2)(a), there is no jurisprudence yet concerning subsection 330(2)(b).

If it is expected that information will "come to" the nominated officer if he has ensured adequate anti-financial crime processes, controls and supervision, then the question is whether, once the information is with the nominated officer, if he fails to correctly assess this information, he can be prosecuted for negligence. This is perhaps where a line can be drawn between, on the one hand, negligently ignoring information and the need for adequate processes, and, on the other, making a genuine error in judgment when assessing the information. It would seem to make sense that at least in the latter case, prosecutors will have to prove beyond reasonable doubt that the nominated officer knew, suspected or had – in the sense of understanding – reasonable grounds to know or suspect. But more criminal trials and perhaps sentencing are required for there to be certainty about this.

We note that a conviction for the primary money laundering offences carries a maximum punishment of imprisonment for 14 years or a fine or both. The secondary offence of failure to disclose carries a maximum punishment of five years.[53]

3. *Aggravated Forms of Money Laundering*

An individual found guilty of one of the primary offences (sections 327–329) is liable to a maximum term of imprisonment of 14 years and an unlimited fine, if sentenced in a Crown Court. Beyond this, the law does not define in detail what an aggravated form of money laundering is, but the courts would decide through case law – influenced by Sentencing Council guidelines[54] – in what instances higher sentences in the range of 14 years' imprisonment should be imposed. There are no extra powers for the more serious end of the spectrum cases, but these may sometimes be sought after for their publicity and associated both special and general deterrent value.

4. *Statutes of Limitation*

As is common in UK legislation, no limitation period applies to money laundering and terrorist financing offences committed under POCA. (Offences committed before POCA came into force are subject to previous legislation, but these are unlikely now to be prosecuted 17 years later.)

However, the principal/primary money laundering offences under POCA are subject to a defence of assumed consent where an SAR is made to the authorities and, if consent is refused during the seven working days' notice period, a moratorium period has elapsed. The moratorium is 31 days, but under the Criminal Finances Act 2017 a senior officer will be able to apply to the Crown Court to increase the moratorium in up to 31-day increments, up to a total of 217 days.[55] Consent is requested where there is a pending transaction (i.e. in only some types of relationships/products will a consent be needed). This pending transaction cannot lawfully be executed in the 31 days.

---

[53] *Ibid.*

[54] *Fraud, Bribery and Money Laundering Offences: Definitive Guideline*, Sentencing Council, 2014.

[55] BCL Solicitors LLP, "Anti-money laundering and fraud in the United Kingdom", Lexology, 28 December 2018, https://www.lexology.com/library/detail.aspx?g=f0870ad8-910f-4bef-a6f3-5445c93bd94d; "Criminal Finances Act 2017 provisions to come into force tomorrow", Herbert Smith Freehills, 30 October 2017, https://hsfnotes.com/fsrandcorpcrime/2017/10/30/criminal-finances-act-2017-provisions-to-come-into-force-tomorrow/.

5. *Jurisdictional Rules*

In short, both for some predicate offences and for money laundering, there is extraterritorial effect that the courts can pursue if there are harmful consequences in the UK.

Under POCA, any criminal conduct which generates proceeds or other economic benefit can be considered a predicate offence regardless of whether it has occurred in the UK or abroad, subject to the condition that if it had had occurred abroad and, even if not unlawful in that country at the time it occurred, it was criminal in the UK and punishable (in principle) by more than a year of imprisonment. The CPS notes, however, that the laundering act must have occurred within the UK jurisdiction.[56]

In other words, for conduct punishable by less than a year of imprisonment, there is an exception to the extraterritorial reach described as the "overseas conduct defence". A person will not be liable under sections 327–329 if:

- he or she knew or reasonably believed that the relevant criminal conduct occurred abroad; and
- that relevant criminal conduct was not, when it took place, unlawful under the criminal law of that other country.

The "overseas conduct defence" does not apply to conduct that (despite being legal under local law) would constitute an offence punishable by a maximum sentence of imprisonment over 12 months in the UK if it had occurred in the UK. Hence there are very few offences to which the defence applies.

There is scope for interpretation as to what extent the primary money laundering offences under POCA (see section II.B.1.a.ii) have extraterritorial jurisdiction. However, through case law the courts have stipulated that the UK jurisdiction can extend to money laundering conduct abroad and that the language in POCA indicated that Parliament had intended for the Part 7 offences to be extraterritorial in effect. In *R v Rogers & ors*,[57] the Court of Appeal of England and Wales held that the three money laundering offences in Part 7 POCA have extraterritorial effect, such that an offence of converting criminal property under section 327(1)(c) POCA could be tried in the UK even where the defendant, who lived and worked in Spain, committed no part of the offence

56 "For the purpose of Part 7 the Proceeds of Crime Act 2002, offences which were committed abroad are relevant predicate crimes if laundering acts are committed within our jurisdiction where the predicate offence committed abroad (from which proceeds were generated) would also constitute an offence in any part of the United Kingdom if it occurred here (section 340 (2)(b)) (see Archbold)." See: https://www.cps.gov.uk/legal-guidance/jurisdiction.

57 [2014] EWCA Crim 1680.

within the UK.[58] This is because the conduct's harmful consequences – i.e. a significant measure of the criminal conduct – took place in the UK (see also section II.B.1.a.i).

C. NON-CRIMINAL DEFINITION OF MONEY LAUNDERING

The legal system in the UK uses one definition of money laundering which is based on the definition of money laundering in the EU directives.

D. SCOPE OF OBLIGED ENTITIES

The obliged entities which form the regulated sector are:

- credit institutions (banks, building societies, others);[59]
- financial institutions,[60] Money Service Businesses, electronic money institutions, auction platforms, recognised investment exchanges, payment service providers;

---

58 See for more details: "Money laundering offences apply to conduct occurring entirely outside the UK", Allen & Overy, 20 April 2015, http://www.allenovery.com/publications/en-gb/Pages/Money-laundering-offences-apply-to-conduct-occurring-entirely-outside-the-UK.aspx.

59 According to the Anti-Money Laundering Regulations, "credit institution" means:

"(a) a credit institution as defined in Article 4.1(1) of the capital requirements regulation; or
(b) a branch (as defined by Article 4.1(17) of that regulation) located in an EEA state of an institution falling within sub-paragraph (a) (or an equivalent institution whose head office is located in a third country) wherever the institution's head office is located, when it accepts deposits or other repayable funds from the public or grants credits for its own account (within the meaning of the capital requirements regulation), or when it bids directly in auctions in accordance with the emission allowance auctioning regulation on behalf of its clients." According to the FCA Handbook, a credit institution is: "(1) (except in REC): (a) has the meaning in article 4(1)(1) of the EU CRR; or (b) [deleted] (c) [deleted] (d) [deleted] (2) (in REC and in SUP 11 (Controllers and close links) and SUP 16 (Reporting requirements)): (a) a credit institution authorised under the CRD; or (b) an institution which would satisfy the requirements for authorisation as a credit institution under the CRD if it had its registered office (or if it does not have a registered office, its head office) in an EEA State. (3) (in relation to the definition of electronic money issuer and payment service provider) a credit institution as defined by (1)(a) and includes a branch of the credit institution within the meaning of article 4(1)(17) of the EU CRR which is situated within the EEA and which has its head office in a territory outside the EEA in accordance with article 47 of the CRD." https://www.handbook.fca.org.uk/handbook/glossary/G239.html.

60 According to the Money Laundering Regulations, "'financial institution' means—

(a) an undertaking, including a money service business, other than an institution referred to in paragraph (3), when the undertaking carries out one or more listed activity;
(b) an insurance undertaking duly authorised in accordance with the Solvency 2 Directive, when it carries out any activities or operations referred to in Article 2.3 of that Directive;

- auditors, insolvency practitioners, external accountants and tax advisers;
- independent legal professionals;[61]

(c) a person (other than a person falling within Article 2 of the markets in financial instruments directive), whose regular occupation or business is the provision to other persons of an investment service or the performance of an investment activity on a professional basis, when—
  (i) providing investment services or performing investment activities (within the meaning of that directive); or
  (ii) bidding directly in auctions in accordance with the emission allowance auctioning regulation on behalf of its clients;

(d) a person falling within Article 2.1(j) of the markets in financial instruments directive, when bidding directly in auctions in accordance with the emission allowance auctioning regulation on behalf of clients of the person's main business;

(e) a collective investment undertaking, when marketing or otherwise offering its units or shares;

(f) an insurance intermediary as defined in Article 2.5 of Directive 2002/92/EC of the European Parliament and of the Council of 9th December 2002 on insurance mediation(1), with the exception of a tied insurance intermediary as mentioned in Article 2.7 of that Directive, when it acts in respect of contracts of long-term insurance;

(g) a branch located in an EEA state of a person referred to in sub-paragraphs (a) to (f) (or an equivalent person whose head office is located in a third country), wherever the person's head office is located, when carrying out any activity mentioned in sub-paragraphs (a) to (f);

(h) the National Savings Bank;

(i) the Director of Savings, when money is raised under the auspices of the Director under the National Loans Act 1968." According to the FCA Handbook, a financial institution is: "(1) (in accordance with paragraph 5(c) of Schedule 3 to the Act (EEA Passport Rights: EEA firm) and article 3 (22) of the CRD (Definitions)), but not for the purposes of GENPRU, BIPRU and IFPRU), an undertaking, other than a credit institution, the principal activity of which is to acquire holdings or to carry on one or more of the listed activities listed in points 2 to 12 and 15 of Annex I to the CRD, which is a subsidiary of the kind mentioned in article 34 of the CRD and which fulfils the conditions in that article (2) for the purposes of GENPRU (except GENPRU 3), BIPRU (except in BIPRU 12) and in accordance with Articles 1(3) (Scope) and 4(5) (Definitions) of the Banking Consolidation Directive): (a) an undertaking, other than a credit institution or an investment firm, the principal activity of which is to acquire holdings or to carry on one or more of the listed activities listed in points 2 to 12 and 15 of Annex I to the Banking Consolidation Directive including the services and activities provided for in Sections A and B of Annex I of the MIFID when referring to the financial instruments provided for in Section C of Annex I of that Directive (b) (for the purposes of consolidated requirements) those institutions permanently excluded by Article 2 of the Banking Consolidation Directive (Scope), with the exception of the central banks of EEA States (3) (except in (1) and (2) and subject to (4)) has the meaning in article 4(1)(26) of the EU CRR. (4) (for the purposes of consolidated requirements in IFPRU and in accordance with article 2(6) of CRD) the following: (a) financial institutions within the meaning in article 4(1)(26) of the EU CRR; and (b) those institutions permanently excluded by article 2(5) of CRD (Scope) with the exception of the ESCB central banks as defined in article 4(1)(45) of the EU CRR." https://www.handbook.fca.org.uk/handbook/glossary/G418.html.

61 Independent legal professionals include firms or sole practitioners that provide, by way of business, legal or notarial services to other people, for instance when participating in financial or real property transactions.

- trust or company service providers;
- estate agents and letting agents;
- high-value dealers;[62]
- casinos;
- art market participants;
- cryptoasset exchange providers; and
- custodian wallet providers.

Every business covered by the Money Laundering Regulations must be monitored by a supervisory authority. A large part of the financial institutions and financial services providers, such as banks, are supervised by the FCA.

According to the Money Laundering Regulations:

> 7.—(1) Subject to paragraph (2), the following bodies are supervisory authorities—
>
> (a) the FCA is the supervisory authority for—
> (i) credit and financial institutions which are authorised persons but not excluded money service businesses;
> (ii) trust or company service providers which are authorised persons;
> (iii) Annex 1 financial institutions;
> (iv) electronic money institutions;
> (v) auction platforms;
> (vi) credit unions in Northern Ireland;
> (vii) recognised investment exchanges within the meaning of section 285 of FSMA(b);
> (viii) cryptoasset exchange providers;
> (ix) custodian wallet providers.
>
> (b) each of the professional bodies listed in Schedule 1 is the supervisory authority for relevant persons who are regulated by it;
>
> (c) the Commissioners for Her Majesty's Revenue and Customs are the supervisory authority for—
> (i) high value dealers;
> (ii) money service businesses which are not supervised by the FCA;
> (iii) trust or company service providers which are not supervised by the FCA or one of the professional bodies listed in Schedule 1;
> (iv) auditors, external accountants, insolvency practitioners, tax advisers and independent legal professionals who are not supervised by one of the professional bodies listed in Schedule 1;
> (v) bill payment service providers which are not supervised by the FCA;

62 A high-value dealer under Money Laundering Regulations is any business or sole trader that accepts or makes high-value cash payments of €10,000 or more (or equivalent in any currency) in exchange for goods.

(vi) telecommunication, digital and IT payment service providers which are not supervised by the FCA;
(vii) estate agents who are not supervised by one of the professional bodies listed in Schedule 1;
(viii) art market participants;
(d) the Gambling Commission is the supervisory authority for casinos.

(2) Where under paragraph (1) there is more than one supervisory authority for a relevant person, the supervisory authorities may agree that one of them will act as the supervisory authority for that person.Telecommunications, digital and IT payment service providers are considered obliged entities as providers of payment services.

A range of professional services regulated by their own professions (see (b) above, referring to Schedule 1, self-regulatory organisations[63]) – 22 Professional Body Supervisors (PBSs) responsible for AML supervision for the accounting and legal sectors – are under the meta-supervision of OPBAS (the Office for Professional Body Anti-Money Laundering Supervision), a new (2018) regulator set up by the government to try to ensure that these 22 AML supervisors provide consistently high standards of AML supervision set out in the Money Laundering Regulations.[64] OPBAS is housed at the FCA.

1. Financial and Banking Institutions

Credit institutions (banks, building societies, others) and financial institutions (Money Service Businesses and others) are among the obliged entities.

2. Virtual Currency System Participants

Virtual currency system participants are not yet regulated. There is a plan for self-regulation, but it is unclear at this stage how this will progress.

If a virtual currency system is also deemed to be a financial institution, then it will be regulated by either the FCA or HMRC (or both) and will be covered by

63 The Association of Accounting Technicians; the Association of Chartered Certified Accountants; the Association of International Accountants; the Association of Taxation Technicians; the Chartered Institute of Legal Executives/CILEx Regulation; the Chartered Institute of Management Accountants; the Chartered Institute of Taxation; the Council for Licensed Conveyancers; the Faculty of Advocates; the Faculty Office of the Archbishop of Canterbury; the General Council of the Bar/Bar Standards Board; the General Council of the Bar of Northern Ireland; the Insolvency Practitioners Association; the Institute of Certified Bookkeepers; the Institute of Chartered Accountants in England and Wales; the Institute of Chartered Accountants in Ireland; the Institute of Chartered Accountants of Scotland; the Institute of Financial Accountants; the International Association of Bookkeepers; the Law Society/Solicitors Regulation Authority; the Law Society of Northern Ireland; and the Law Society of Scotland. See http://www.legislation.gov.uk/uksi/2017/692/schedule/1/made.

64 https://www.fca.org.uk/opbas. See Schedule 1 Money Laundering Regulations.

the Money Laundering Regulations. See also section I.A. for 2019 amendments to the regulations in regard to cryptoasset exchange providers.

3. *Legal Profession and Tax Advisors*

These are covered by the Money Laundering Regulations regardless of the nature of activity they perform (e.g. financial intermediation, setting up companies and so on). However, their obligations and criminal law risks are affected by whether they are performing these acts as part of the regulated sector or not.

4. *Informal Value Transfer Systems*

Informal value transfer systems are not part of the AML regulated sector. If such providers are informal, i.e. not registered as such, they may be unknown to the authorities, though it is an offence to supply financial services without being registered. However, if they agree to comply with the Money Laundering Regulations and register (at a cost)[65] with HMRC, they will be regulated for AML purposes.

5. *Non-Profit Sector*

NGOs and charities are not covered by the Money Laundering Regulations, although the NCA's annual SAR reports indicate that there is a certain percentage of SARs filed by charities. Charities are required by their own sector oversight body – the Charity Commission – to report suspicious activity.[66]

---

65 https://www.gov.uk/guidance/money-laundering-regulations-registration-fees.

66 https://www.charitycommissionni.org.uk/charity-essentials/controlling-against-terrorist-financing-and-money-laundering/. Of course, where those running the charity are also engaged in crime, this is unlikely. The most recent public case is the Orthodox Jewish charity network which had an "enormous jump" in income in 2012 to £8 million, having recorded an annual income of £1.7 million between 2008 and 2011, due to sales of counterfeit Viagra and allied products. The principal was sentenced to seven and a half years' imprisonment in 2019 (though he fled while on bail), and only then was the Charity Commission able to announce its investigation. The case appears to have been launched after customers complained the online-purchased drugs did not work, and the investigators discovered large numbers of online card payments to the charities' accounts. See Isabella Nikolic, "Money launderer, 67, who tried to buy a knighthood is convicted in his absence of £10 million Jewish charities scam after going on the run", Daily Mail, 24 June 2019, https://www.dailymail.co.uk/news/article-7174919/Money-launderer-67-convicted-10million-Jewish-charities-scam-going-run.html; Emma Bartholomew, "Stamford Hill Orthodox Jewish charity finance boss laundered £10m through selling 'dangerous' fake Viagra and diet pills", Hackney Gazette, 10 July 2019, https://www.hackneygazette.co.uk/news/crime-court/charities-laundered-10m-through-fake-viagra-sales-1-6153522. It allegedly warned Medical Aid for Palestinians to be careful that it did not distribute funds inappropriately, following a complaint by Jewish organisations, but took no formal action: Zachary Keyser, "Charity Commission Warns

The Charity Commission has the power to strike them (and individual trustees) off if they violate the criteria, including failing to have adequate standards of identification of where money goes to. There is particular concern about terrorism finance risks in the charity sector.

According to the UK government,[67] services that are provided by certain charities and public sector bodies are not covered by the Money Laundering Regulations. This is because the services are not carried out by way of business. The types of charity and public body that do not have to register with HMRC under the Money Laundering Regulations are:

- UK-registered charities that provide these services free or for a nominal charge;
- public authorities serving members of the public free of charge, or for a fee to cover the cost of providing the service only;
- public authorities that provide these services as part of their statutory duties and charge a fee;
- public authorities that are funded by the Exchequer or council tax payers, and not by the person who receives the service;
- public authorities or joint ventures (where 50% or more of the shares are owned by the public body) that provide services only to other public authorities;
- public authorities or joint ventures (where 50% or more of the shares are owned by the public body) that provide services to a firm authorised by a public body to act on their behalf – for example a housing association.

6. *Overview of Other Obliged Entities*

See the list at the beginning of this section D. Scope of Obliged Entities.

E. RELATIONSHIP BETWEEN AML AND ANTI-TERRORISM FINANCING FRAMEWORK(S)

SARs relating to terrorist financing are submitted to the UK's FIU under the Terrorism Act 2000.[68] The preventive regime is currently combined (in the

---

Medical Aid for Palestinians about Funding Misuse", Jerusalem Post, 25 March 2019, https://www.jpost.com/Middle-East/Charity-Commission-warns-Medical-Aid-for-Palestinians-about-funding-misuse-581860.

67 https://www.gov.uk/guidance/money-laundering-regulations-who-needs-to-register#charities-and-public-sector-bodies. See also https://www.charitycommissionni.org.uk/charity-essentials/controlling-against-terrorist-financing-and-money-laundering/.

68 There have been amendments/enhancements to the Act since 2000.

aftermath of 9/11) and the regulated sector has to have an anti-financial crime programme that covers terrorist financing risk alongside money laundering risk. But the UK's FIU separates the terrorist financing-related SARs from the rest of the SARs and has a dedicated specialist team reviewing them. According to the HM Treasury's UK National Risk Assessment of Money Laundering and Terrorist Financing (October 2015), the Terrorism Finance Team (TFT) within the FIU identifies and acts upon submitted reports relating to terrorist financing.[69] Terrorism-related SARs are disseminated to the National Terrorist Financial Investigation Unit (the NTFIU is part of the Metropolitan Police Service Counter Terrorism Command) and other counterterrorism-related agencies. Additionally, under the "consent"/"defence" regime (see sections II.B.4 and III.C.1.d), where the consent request has been refused under the Terrorism Act, there is no moratorium period, and there is no defence unless and until the request is granted by the NCA. Other than that, there are no formal and material differences between the AML and counter-terrorist financing regimes.

While there is the acknowledgement that in terrorist financing amounts are often small and not necessarily from illegal sources, there is hardly any notable debate about how these phenomena should be treated differently by practitioners, regulators or regulated entities. It could be argued that in practice, the (politically and socially) acceptable risk level in terrorist financing is zero. But there is an ongoing discussion about how the perception that charities are high risk from a terrorist financing perspective harms the charitable sector in the UK.

As the UK Charity Commission's chairman William Shawcross has stressed, "terrorist abuse is one of the greatest risks facing the charitable sector today"[70] as it seriously undermines public confidence in providing humanitarian aid. (Though this preceded the scandals involving major charities' suppression of scandals involving staff engaged in sexual oppression in overseas operations, it may remain the Commission's view today.) However, as noted recently by UK authorities, de-risking by withdrawing bank services to charities may mean "charitable funds may go underground, increasingly transacted in cash, or moved off-shore via cash couriers or alternative remittance systems."[71]

---

69 The UKFIU's Terrorist Finance Team identifies, assesses and exploits SARs submitted under both TACT and POCA.
Due to the additional sensitivity around SARs submitted under TACT, and those SARs submitted under POCA identified as having a terrorist financing link, these SARs are made available only to a restricted group of end users. See https://assets.publishing.service.gov.uk/government/uploads/system/uploads/attachment_data/file/655198/National_risk_assessment_of_money_laundering_and_terrorist_financing_2017_pdf_web.pdf.

70 Andrew Gilligan, "'Terror link' charities get British millions in Gift Aid", Daily Telegraph, 29 November 2014.

71 HM Treasury and Home Office, *UK national risk assessment of money laundering and terrorist financing*, October 2015.

III. THE SYSTEM OF MONEY LAUNDERING PREVENTION

A. CUSTOMER DUE DILIGENCE

1. *Standard CDD Rules*

a. Triggers and Timing

According to the Money Laundering Regulations and the JMLSG,[72] an obliged entity/obliged professional must apply CDD measures when it does any of the following:

- establishes a business relationship;
- carries out an occasional transaction;
- suspects money laundering or terrorist financing; or
- doubts the veracity of documents or information previously obtained for the purpose of identification or verification.[73]

The above applies to all types of obliged entities.

According to the Money Laundering Regulations, an "occasional transaction" for CDD purposes means:

- a transfer of funds within the meaning of article 3.925 of the Funds Transfer Regulation exceeding €1,000; or
- a transaction carried out other than in the course of a business relationship (e.g. a single foreign currency transaction, or an isolated instruction to purchase shares), amounting to €15,000 or more, whether the transaction is executed in a single operation or in several operations which appear to be linked.

A casino must also apply customer due diligence measures in relation to any transaction amounting to €2,000 or more, whether the transaction is executed in a single operation or in several operations which appear to be linked.

---

72 The JMLSG is made up of the leading UK Trade Associations in the Financial Services Industry (http://www.jmlsg.org.uk/), which themselves have undergone some rationalisation under the banner of UK Finance. It produces guidance for firms in the financial services sector, most notably banks. This guidance must be approved by the Treasury.

73 For more details see JMLSG, Regulation 27(1), 5.2.1, http://www.jmlsg.org.uk/industry-guidance/article/jmlsg-guidance-current.

A letting agent must also apply customer due diligence measures in relation to any transaction which consists of the conclusion of an agreement for the letting of land —

(i) for a term of a month or more, and
(ii) at a rent which during at least part of the term is, or is equivalent to, a monthly rent of €10,000 or more.

The letting agent must apply customer due diligence measures in relation to both the person by whom the land is being let and the person who is renting the land.

An art market participant must also apply customer due diligence measures—

(a) in relation to the trade of a work of art when the firm or sole practitioner carries out, or acts in respect of, any such transaction, or series of linked transactions, whose value amounts to €10,000 or more;
(b) in relation to the storage of a work of art, when it is the operator of a freeport and the value of the works of art so stored for a person, or series of linked persons, amounts to €10,000 or more.

A cryptoasset exchange provider of the kind who operates a machine which utilises automated processes to exchange cryptoassets for money, or money for cryptoassets, must also apply customer due diligence measures in relation to any such transaction carried out using that machine.

b. CDD Measures

UK regulators do not take a prescriptive approach and expect the regulated sector to take a risk-based approach and decide what measures to take depending on the level of risk. Separate guidance has been issued to the regulated sector by the relevant industry associations or supervisory bodies.

It does not necessarily matter in which part of the regulated sector the obliged entity operates; rather, what matters is the size and complexity of the entity's business and the risks it faces along a range of dimensions.

According to the Money Laundering Regulations:

> Customer due diligence measures
>
> 28.—(1) This regulation applies when a relevant person is required by regulation 27 to apply customer due diligence measures.
>
> (2) The relevant person must—
>
> (a) identify the customer unless the identity of that customer is known to, and has been verified by, the relevant person;

(b) verify the customer's identity unless the customer's identity has already been verified by the relevant person; and
(c) assess, and where appropriate obtain information on, the purpose and intended nature of the business relationship or occasional transaction.

(3) Where the customer is a body corporate—

(a) the relevant person must obtain and verify—
  (i) the name of the body corporate;
  (ii) its company number or other registration number;
  (iii) the address of its registered office, and if different, its principal place of business;
(b) subject to paragraph (5), the relevant person must take reasonable measures to determine and verify—
  (i) the law to which the body corporate is subject, and its constitution (whether set out in its articles of association or other governing documents);
  (ii) the full names of the board of directors (or if there is no board, the members of the equivalent management body) and the senior persons responsible for the operations of the body corporate.

(3A) Where the customer is a legal person, trust, company, foundation or similar legal arrangement the relevant person must take reasonable measures to understand the ownership and control structure of that legal person, trust, company, foundation or similar legal arrangement.

(4) Subject to paragraph (5), where the customer is beneficially owned by another person, the relevant person must—

(a) identify the beneficial owner;
(b) take reasonable measures to verify the identity of the beneficial owner so that the relevant person is satisfied that it knows who the beneficial owner is; and
(c) if the beneficial owner is a legal person, trust, company, foundation or similar legal arrangement take reasonable measures to understand the ownership and control structure of that legal person, trust, company, foundation or similar legal arrangement.

(5) Paragraphs (3)(b) and (4) do not apply where the customer is a company which is listed on a regulated market.

(6) If the customer is a body corporate, and paragraph (7) applies, the relevant person may treat the senior person in that body corporate responsible for managing it as its beneficial owner.

(7) This paragraph applies if (and only if) the relevant person has exhausted all possible means of identifying the beneficial owner of the body corporate and—

(a) has not succeeded in doing so, or
(b) is not satisfied that the individual identified is in fact the beneficial owner.

(8) If paragraph (7) applies, the relevant person must—

(a) keep records in writing of all the actions it has taken to identify the beneficial owner of the body corporate; (b) take reasonable measures to verify the identity of the senior person in the body corporate responsible for managing it, and keep records in writing of—
   (i) all the actions the relevant person has taken in doing so, and
   (ii) any difficulties the relevant person has encountered in doing so.

See Appendix B Customer Due Diligence for more details.

c. Individual Responsibility

According to 2017 changes in the Money Laundering Regulations, obliged entities must now appoint a money laundering compliance principal (MLCP) and that individual must be on the board of directors (or equivalent management body), or a member of senior management, where appropriate to the size and nature of the business. Essentially this aims to ensure that responsibility rests with the board as well as with the money laundering reporting officer (MLRO) and it is in the interest of the board to fully understand the financial crime risks their organisation faces and how these are mitigated. MLCPs do not get involved in the day-to-day decision making as to whether to file an SAR and how to conduct investigations. They take part in the more strategic decisions such as defining the organisation's risk appetite. It is theoretically possible (and indeed is intended) that this upwards responsibilisation of the Board of Directors may increase the risks of corporate criminal liability, which in the UK is dependent on being able to prove that the acts were at the behest of the 'directing mind' of the corporation.

d. Further CDD Guidance

Various bodies provide guidance to the various parts of the regulated sector (e.g. accountancy, legal sector, financial services).

For instance, for audit, accountancy, tax advisory, accountancy-related services firms and trust and company services firms guidance on how to help prevent money laundering and terrorist financing has been produced by the Consultative Committee of Accountancy Bodies and is based on law and regulations as of 26 June 2017. This guidance has to be approved by HM Treasury in order to be published as final. Among other things, the guidance explains what the concept of a "risk-based approach" means, how to assess risk, and what CDD is, in what situations it is required and what it entails; it also discusses suspicious activity reporting, record keeping, and training and awareness.

Similarly, the various iterations of the guidance produced by the JMLSG undergo a process of approval by the HM Treasury.

The FCA Handbook also contains guidance relevant to FCA-regulated firms.

The AML/counter-terrorist financing guidance produced by the legal sector AML supervisors, including the Law Society, in March 2018, has also received the approval of HM Treasury.[74]

The various pieces of guidance are not dissimilar from each other in approach and concepts.

2. *Simplified CDD*

a. Scope

Before the 4AMLD was transposed into national legislation through the 2017 regulations (Money Laundering, Terrorist Financing and Transfer of Funds (Information on the Payer) Regulations 2017), simplified due diligence was commonly applied automatically in cases of regulated and/or listed companies, particularly in "lower-risk" jurisdictions (as judged by the FATF and the international consensus, whether analytically justified or not). With the 2017 change in regulations, simplified CDD can now be applied by any obliged entity only upon appropriate risk assessment to evidence that the client subject to due diligence is low risk. The risk assessment should include looking at geography risk, industry risk and risk associated with the product and delivery channels (see Appendix C Simplified Due Diligence for more details).

b. Requirements

UK legislation and relevant guidance do not prescribe the exact steps that customer due diligence and simplified due diligence have to entail.

According to the JMLSG guidance, simplified due diligence means not having to apply CDD measures, but this is only upon adequate risk assessment that can demonstrate that risk is low. In practice, this means not having to verify the customer's identity, or, where relevant, that of a beneficial owner, nor having to obtain information on the purpose or intended nature of the business relationship, although there is some scope for interpretation. It is, however, still necessary to conduct ongoing monitoring of the business relationship to avoid the risk that a change in account behaviour raises the risks. Firms must have reasonable grounds for believing that the customer, transaction or product relating to such transaction falls within one of the categories set out in the

---

[74] Law Society, "Anti-money laundering guidance", 6 March 2018, https://www.lawsociety.org.uk/policy-campaigns/articles/anti-money-laundering-guidance/.

Regulations, and may have to demonstrate this to their supervisory authority. Clearly, for operating purposes, the firm will nevertheless need to maintain a base of information about the customer.

There is no material difference between how simplified due diligence is applied by the different types of obliged entities. However, it can be inferred from legislation that certain businesses, when offering certain products (e.g. a life insurance policy for which the premium is low; see criteria in the Money Laundering Regulations 2017 and 2019), typically face lower risk of money laundering and therefore can take simplified measures.

c. Further Simplified CDD Guidance

As discussed above, guidance is provided by various industry bodies (e.g. JMLSG) but needs to be approved by HM Treasury. The FCA also issues guidance to those firms that are FCA-regulated. As discussed in the section above, legislation and guidance indicate that simplified CDD means that certain CDD measures do not need to be taken. But basic identification and monitoring of the relationship are still required. The approach in the UK is not to provide prescriptive guidance: so obliged entities decide at their own discretion what exactly the various levels of due diligence would entail.

3. *Enhanced CDD*

a. Scope

The 2017 Money Laundering Regulations (as amended in 2019) state:

> 33.—(1) A relevant person must apply enhanced customer due diligence measures and enhanced ongoing monitoring, in addition to the customer due diligence measures required under regulation 28 and, if applicable, regulation 29, to manage and mitigate the risks arising—
>
> (a) in any case identified as one where there is a high risk of money laundering or terrorist financing—
>   (i) by the relevant person under regulation 18(1), or
>   (ii) in information made available to the relevant person under regulations 17(9) and 47;
>
> (b) in any business relationship with a person established in a high-risk third country;
>
> (c) in relation to correspondent relationships with a credit institution or a financial institution (in accordance with regulation 34);
>
> (d) if a relevant person has determined that a customer or potential customer is a PEP, or a family member or known close associate of a PEP (in accordance with regulation 35);

(e) in any case where the relevant person discovers that a customer has provided false or stolen identification documentation or information and the relevant person proposes to continue to deal with that customer;
(f) in any case where—
  (i) a transaction is complex or unusually large,
  (ii) there is an unusual pattern of transactions, or
  (iii) the transaction or transactions have no apparent economic or legal purpose, and
(g) in any other case which by its nature can present a higher risk of money laundering or terrorist financing or in relation to any relevant transaction where either of the parties to the transaction is established in a high-risk third country.

b. Requirements

Legislation does not prescribe exactly what steps enhanced due diligence should entail. But it is clear within the scope of enhanced due diligence it is expected that more in-depth checks are undertaken, particularly source of funds and source of wealth to be understood and verified (especially where politically exposed persons (PEPs) are concerned). The Money Laundering Regulations 2019 (reg. 33) also state that in any case where:

(i) a transaction is complex and unusually large, or there is an unusual pattern of transactions, or
(ii) the transaction or transactions have no apparent economic or legal purpose

the enhanced CDD measures must include:

(a) as far as reasonably possible, examining the background and purpose of the transaction, and
(b) increasing the degree and nature of monitoring of the business relationship in which the transaction is made to determine whether that transaction or that relationship appear to be suspicious.

Additionally, the Money Laundering Regulations (reg. 33) state that depending on the requirements of the case, the enhanced customer due diligence measures may also include, among other things:

(a) seeking additional independent, reliable sources to verify information provided or made available to the relevant person;
(b) taking additional measures to understand better the background, ownership and financial situation of the customer, and other parties to the transaction;
(c) taking further steps to be satisfied that the transaction is consistent with the purpose and intended nature of the business relationship;
(d) increasing the monitoring of the business relationship, including greater scrutiny of transactions.

In regard to customers and transactions in high-risk third countries, the regulations state:

> The enhanced due diligence measures taken by a relevant person for the purpose of paragraph (1)(b) must include—
>
> (a) obtaining additional information on the customer and on the customer's beneficial owner;
> (b) obtaining additional information on the intended nature of the business relationship;
> (c) obtaining information on the source of funds and source of wealth of the customer and of the customer's beneficial owner;
> (d) obtaining information on the reasons for the transactions;
> (e) obtaining the approval of senior management for establishing or continuing the business relationship;
> (f) conducting enhanced monitoring of the business relationship by increasing the number and timing of controls applied, and selecting patterns of transactions that need further examination.

Where the customer: (a) is the beneficiary of a life insurance policy, (b) is a legal person or a legal arrangement, and (c) presents a high risk of money laundering or terrorist financing for any other reason, an obliged entity that is a credit or financial institution must take reasonable measures to identify and verify the identity of the beneficial owners of that beneficiary before any payment is made under the policy.

See Appendix D Enhanced Due Diligence for more details.

In this regard, the legislation does not envisage material differences between the requirements applicable to the various types of obliged entities. It depends mostly on whether there are identified high-risk factors such as geography and the presence of PEPs. As with other uses of the term "high risk", there may be a tension between professional judgment by insiders and more generic available third-party assessments such as by the EC, the Basel Institute or commercial bodies such as Refinitiv. The analytical defensibility of such risk judgments is out of scope for this study.

c. Further Enhanced CDD Guidance

It is the same guidance as above listed. Guidance issued by the various supervisory bodies carries equal weight for the respective parts of the industry. One of the more comprehensive pieces of guidance is the one issued by the JMLSG.[75] We note, however, that the purpose of this guidance is to provide

[75] http://www.jmlsg.org.uk.

direction and examples of best practices. It is not binding, as it leaves scope for flexibility and interpretation of the exact implementation of the key principles. Furthermore, though the guidance can be referenced in a court, compliance with it does not give absolute immunity from prosecution. In terms of enhanced CDD, available guidance articulates the requirements in the Money Laundering Regulations 2017 (as amended in 2019) and also places a focus on understanding the source of wealth and funds of the client, the background to and purpose of the transaction. How a randomly selected jury in a criminal court or how a regulatory tribunal is expected to make sense of these issues is a separate set of problems that are out of scope for this study but would repay social scientifically informed policy analysis.

4. *Rules on Politically Exposed Persons*

a. Definition

The UK's Money Laundering Regulations define a PEP as:

> (a) 'politically exposed person' or 'PEP' means an individual who is entrusted with prominent public functions, other than as a middle-ranking or more junior official;
> (b) 'family member' of a politically exposed person includes—
> (i) a spouse or civil partner of the PEP;
> (ii) children of the PEP and the spouses or civil partners of the PEP's children;
> (iii) parents of the PEP;
> (c) 'known close associate' of a PEP means—
> (i) an individual known to have joint beneficial ownership of a legal entity or a legal arrangement or any other close business relations with a PEP;
> (ii) an individual who has sole beneficial ownership of a legal entity or a legal arrangement which is known to have been set up for the benefit of a PEP.

A reference to a business relationship with an individual includes a reference to a business relationship with a person of which the individual is a beneficial owner.

Individuals entrusted with prominent public functions include:

(a) heads of state, heads of government, ministers and deputy or assistant ministers;
(b) members of parliament or of similar legislative bodies;
(c) members of the governing bodies of political parties;
(d) members of supreme courts, of constitutional courts or of any judicial body the decisions of which are not subject to further appeal except in exceptional circumstances;
(e) members of courts of auditors or of the boards of central banks;

(f) ambassadors, charges d'affaires and high-ranking officers in the armed forces;
(g) members of the administrative, management or supervisory bodies of State-owned enterprises;
(h) directors, deputy directors and members of the board or equivalent function of an international organisation.

According to the Money Laundering Regulations, for the purpose of deciding whether a person is a known close associate of a PEP, a relevant person need only have regard to information which is in its possession, or to credible information which is publicly available. No epistemological guidance is given as to how organisations should judge whether or not information is "credible".

There are no differences in the *legal* definition. However, the FCA's guidance[76] does distinguish between domestic and foreign PEPs. The FCA advises that domestic PEPs can be treated as carrying a lower risk than foreign PEPs, perhaps reflecting its judgment or assumption that there is greater integrity among UK than foreign public officials: "A PEP who is entrusted with a prominent public function in the UK should be treated as low risk, unless a firm has assessed that other risk factors not linked to their position as a PEP mean they pose a higher risk." It appears that the FCA has allowed for such approach based on reg. 33 (6) of the Money Laundering Regulations 2017 (as amended in 2019). This paragraph states that when assessing whether there is a high risk of money laundering or terrorist financing in a particular situation, and the extent of the measures which should be taken to manage and mitigate that risk, obliged entities must take account of risk factors including, among other things, the country risk factors. According to the regulations, in making the assessment, obliged entities must bear in mind that the presence of one or more risk factors may not always indicate that there is a high risk of money laundering or terrorist financing in a particular situation.

The regulations state in what situations risk is typically considered high but also allow for a risk-based approach based on an assessment of the risk, i.e. neither simplified nor enhanced due diligence have to apply automatically – a typical risk factor may be assessed not to pose a high risk in certain situations. Simplified CDD can only take place following risk assessment and if that assessment demonstrates the risk is low, then simplified measures can apply. That said, the actual risk assessment already entails some research, which arguably defeats the purpose of simplified CDD being applied.

---

[76] Financial Conduct Authority, "FG 17/6 The treatment of politically exposed persons for anti-money laundering purposes", July 2017, https://www.fca.org.uk/publication/finalised-guidance/fg17-06.pdf.

When interpreting the legal definition of a PEP, the FCA's guidance advises:

(a) it does not include local government in the UK but it may, where higher risks are assessed, be appropriate to do so in other countries;
(b) in the UK, it will not normally be necessary to treat public servants below Permanent or Deputy Permanent Secretary[77] as having a prominent public function;
(c) firms should note that the Regulations (reg. 35(10)) explicitly state that they cannot apply these measures to those who were not a PEP under the Money Laundering Regulations 2007 (i.e. those who held a prominent public position in the UK (such as a former MP, retired member of the House of Lords or a former UK ambassador) where they ceased that office prior to 26 June 2017).

The FCA guidance allows for lower due diligence standards to be almost automatically applied in regards to local PEPs and excludes local government from the PEP definition even though senior figures at local level (e.g. the Mayor of London) may have access to leverage and public funds equal to that at national level. This appears to contradict the spirit of the 4AMLD, which places scrutiny on both domestic and foreign PEPs and excludes middle and junior ranking officials but not necessarily those at a local level. "Organised crime" penetration and corrupt contracting can also occur at a local level.

b. Requirements

PEPs must be the subject of enhanced due diligence (see the previous section for details in regards to PEPs in the UK context). According to the UK's Money Laundering Regulations, the obliged entity must assess the risk that may arise from a relationship with a PEP/close associate or family member and on this basis determine what risk-management systems and procedures are appropriate.

The obliged entity is required to:

(a) have approval from senior management[78] for establishing or continuing the business relationship with that person;

---

77 A Permanent Secretary is the most senior civil servant of a British government ministry, charged with running the department on a day-to-day basis.

78 According to the regulations, "senior management" means an officer or employee of the relevant person with sufficient knowledge of the relevant person's money laundering and terrorist financing risk exposure, and of sufficient authority, to take decisions affecting its risk exposure.

(b) take adequate measures to establish the source of wealth and source of funds which are involved in the proposed business relationship or transactions with that person; and
(c) where the business relationship is entered into, conduct enhanced ongoing monitoring of the business relationship with that person, including greater scrutiny of transactions.

The obliged entity will have to understand the background and purpose of the transaction and determine what level of monitoring would be appropriate.

Depending on the circumstances of the case, the enhanced due diligence measures may also include:

- seeking additional independent, reliable sources to verify information provided or made available to the obliged entity;
- taking additional measures to understand better the background, ownership and financial situation of the customer, and other parties to the transaction;
- taking further steps to be satisfied that the transaction is consistent with the purpose and intended nature of the business relationship.

The above measures do not always differ from those applied to other high risk factors, although legislation appears to place a focus on understanding the source of wealth and funds and obtaining approval from senior management when the client relationship involves a PEP risk factor.

c. Further Enhanced CDD Guidance on PEPs

See the previous section.

5. Rules on High-Risk Third Countries

a. Scope

A "high-risk third country" means a country which has been identified by the European Commission in delegated acts adopted under Article 9.2 4AMLD as a high-risk third country.

The Money Laundering Regulations (reg. 33.6.c.) explain that enhanced CDD must be applied where risk posed by geographical risk factors is high, including:

(i) countries identified by credible sources, such as mutual evaluations, detailed assessment reports or published follow-up reports, as not having effective systems to counter money laundering or terrorist financing;
(ii) countries identified by credible sources as having significant levels of corruption or other criminal activity, such as terrorism (within the meaning of section 1 of

the Terrorism Act 2000(1)), money laundering, and the production and supply of illicit drugs;

(iii) countries subject to sanctions, embargos or similar measures issued by, for example, the European Union or the United Nations;

(iv) countries providing funding or support for terrorism;

(v) countries that have organisations operating within their territory which have been designated—

   (aa) by the government of the United Kingdom as proscribed organisations under Schedule 2 to the Terrorism Act 2000(2), or

   (bb) by other countries, international organisations or the European Union as terrorist organisations;

(vi) countries identified by credible sources, such as evaluations, detailed assessment reports or published follow-up reports published by the Financial Action Task Force, the International Monetary Fund, the World Bank, the Organisation for Economic Co-operation and Development or other international bodies or non-governmental organisations as not implementing requirements to counter money laundering and terrorist financing that are consistent with the recommendations published by the Financial Action Task Force in February 2012 and updated in October 2016.

b. Requirements

The CDD rules for high-risk countries may be similar to the aforementioned enhanced CDD. For instance, the source of wealth and funds may need to be understood and verified in the case both of a PEP from a low-risk jurisdiction but who has attracted controversy in the media (e.g. for business activities or conspicuous expenditure) and of a client in wealth management who is not a PEP but comes from a high-risk jurisdiction. According to the Money Laundering Regulations, enhanced due diligence and enhanced monitoring must be undertaken to mitigate the risks arising in any business relationship with a person established in a high-risk third country or in relation to any relevant transaction where either of the parties to the transaction is established in a high-risk third country.[79]

The obliged entity will have to understand the background and purpose of the transaction and determine what level of monitoring would be appropriate.

Depending on the circumstances of the case, the enhanced due diligence measures may also include:

- seeking additional independent, reliable sources to verify information provided or made available to the obliged entity;

[79] It remains to be seen how the various industry associations, including the JMLSG, will interpret the 2019 amendments and guide the regulated sector.

- taking additional measures to understand better the background, ownership and financial situation of the customer, and other parties to the transaction;
- taking further steps to be satisfied that the transaction is consistent with the purpose and intended nature of the business relationship;
- increasing the monitoring of the business relationship, including greater scrutiny of transactions.

The enhanced due diligence measures taken by an obliged entity for the purpose of a relationship or transaction with exposure to a high-risk third country must include—

(a) obtaining additional information on the customer and on the customer's beneficial owner;
(b) obtaining additional information on the intended nature of the business relationship;
(c) obtaining information on the source of funds and source of wealth of the customer and of the customer's beneficial owner;
(d) obtaining information on the reasons for the transactions;
(e) obtaining the approval of senior management for establishing or continuing the business relationship;
(f) conducting enhanced monitoring of the business relationship by increasing the number and timing of controls applied, and selecting patterns of transactions that need further examination.

c. Further Enhanced CDD Guidance on High-Risk Third Countries

See the previous section.

6. *Private Sector CDD Guidance*

Various vendors such as Refinitiv and LexisNexis provide guidance. The Wolfsberg principles are also commonly referred to in the industry for legitimation of risk judgments. There are no material differences between the various pieces of guidance.

B. PRELIMINARY RISK ANALYSIS

Obliged entities are required to undertake money laundering and terrorist financing risk assessments both in terms of their enterprise generally (e.g. type of clients, product risk, geography) as well as of their clients and transactions specifically. Even when obliged entities plan to apply simplified CDD, they must first demonstrate that the risk is low by undertaking and documenting risk analysis.

More specifically, according to the Money Laundering Regulations, in carrying out the risk assessment, obliged entities must take into account information made available to them by the supervisory authority and risk factors including factors relating to:

(a) its customers;
(b) the countries or geographic areas in which it operates;
(c) its products or services;
(d) its transactions; and
(e) its delivery channels.

In deciding what steps are appropriate, obliged entities must take into account the size and nature of its business.

C. REPORTING AND ASSET FREEZING

1. *First-Time Reporting*

a. Trigger for/Degree of Suspicion

Under POCA, persons in the regulated sector (i.e. obliged entities) are required to make a report in respect of information that comes to them within the course of a business in the regulated sector:

- where they know; or
- where they suspect; or
- where they have reasonable grounds for knowing or suspecting.[80]

The suspicion threshold is very low. As the JMLSG notes, suspicion is more subjective and falls short of proof based on firm evidence. Suspicion has been defined by the courts as being beyond mere speculation and based on some foundation: "[a] degree of satisfaction and not necessarily amounting to belief but at least extending beyond speculation as to whether an event has occurred or not"; and "[a[lthough the creation of suspicion requires a lesser factual basis than the creation of a belief, it must nonetheless be built upon some foundation."[81]

---

80 https://www.gov.uk/guidance/money-laundering-regulations-report-suspicious-activities.
81 JMLSG Guidance, Part 1, chapter 6 "Suspicious activities, reporting and data protection", 6.11, p. 167, December 2017.

Suspicion might be regarded more analytically as a matter of degree, not a binary construction. It is important to understand that this can be an organisational issue – as many as 150 people or as few as one might work under an MLRO, depending on the size of the regulated body. In *R v da Silva*,[82] the Court of Appeal considered the correct interpretation of suspicion within the meaning of section 93A(1)(a) of the Criminal Justice Act 1988 (the predecessor to POCA). It was defined as:

> a possibility, which is more than fanciful, that the relevant facts exist. A vague feeling of unease would not suffice. But the statute does not require the suspicion to be 'clear 'or 'firmly grounded and targeted on specific facts', or based upon 'reasonable grounds'.

The Law Commission concluded that:

> the large volume of disclosures was caused, in part, by a broad definition of "criminal property" in section 340 of POCA which requires that suspected laundering of the proceeds of any criminal conduct must be reported … Around 15% of authorised disclosure SARs did not meet the threshold of suspicion. If we assume that this proportion is representative across all 27,471 authorised disclosures submitted between October 2015 and March 2017, approximately 4,121 would have been submitted unnecessarily … [R]eporters only articulated reasonable grounds to suspect, by demonstrating one or more objective grounds, in 52.4% of the sample we analysed. This represents a substantial proportion of authorised disclosures which are lodged without objective grounds in support.[83]

In our view, without a statutory definition or well developed guidance as to the meaning of suspicion:

(a) suspicion is a low threshold if it requires only a possibility which is more than fanciful. The application of this criterion will normally lead to a large number of reports, and many false positives and/or SARs that there are insufficient resources to investigate in a more than minimal way;
(b) without a clear definition, guidance or a requirement for reasonable grounds, suspicion can be inconsistently applied by those who have to decide whether or not to report their concerns.

The exception is where there is professional legal privilege, where there is an exception to the duty to report.

---

82 [2006] 2 Cr App R 35.

83 Law Commission, "Money Laundering: Summary", 2019, p. 8, https://s3-eu-west-2.amazonaws.com/lawcom-prod-storage-11jsxou24uy7q/uploads/2019/06/6.5612_LC_Anti-money-laundering-summary_v6.pdf.

b. Content and Direct Addressee(s) of SARs

The SAR is filed with the UK's FIU, which sits within the NCA. It is filed through the SAR online system, though there is a capacity to file manually, which is discouraged by the FIU. How the SAR is filed has no formal bearing on the way SARs are prioritised; it is an issue of administrative cost and convenience, as all bodies seek to promote the shift from manual to electronic communication to reduce the burden on their scarce resources.

According to guidance provided by the NCA,[84] the "Reason For Suspicion" field must set out the facts, focusing on who is involved, what and where the criminal/terrorist property is and its value (estimated as necessary), when and how circumstances arose and are planned to happen, and ultimately why the reporter is suspicious or has knowledge.

Details on the entities involved (these entities may be the subject of the SAR themselves or may be linked to an individual who is the subject of an SAR; they may be the client or a client's counterparty if the SAR is actually not on the client but the client's counterparty) should include:

- subject's full name, date of birth and addresses (including postcode);
- subject details (e.g. National Insurance numbers, vehicle registration, driving licence, passport number, phone numbers, email addresses, etc.;
- subject's occupation/employer;
- details of any associated subjects (including, where appropriate, full details of professionals involved in the activities);
- company details, including full legal name, designation (Ltd, LLP, GmbH, SARL), registration number and tax reference/VAT numbers, country of incorporation and details on beneficial ownership where held);
- if relevant to the business, the subject's financial details (account numbers) and details of associates.

c. Duty not to Disclose

Under POCA, it is a criminal offence to release information to the customer that an SAR has been submitted. This is called a "tipping-off offence". The customer is very likely to suspect that an SAR has been made if the transactions they want to make are significantly delayed or frozen altogether. The banks have developed forms of words to give to customers without committing

[84] National Crime Agency, "Requesting a defence from the NCA under POCA and TACT", April 2018; updated version as of May 2019; https://www.nationalcrimeagency.gov.uk/who-we-are/publications/43-requesting-a-defence-under-poca-tact/file.

tipping-off offences. For instance, where banks need to obtain information from a client about a transaction that has been flagged up by automated systems as potentially suspicious, banks may simply refer to the need to update their KYC. Banks will avoid mentioning suspicion or anything that suggests the transaction is being investigated for money laundering or terrorist financing concerns. Some organisations use general wording such as "compliance with statutory obligations" when they have to explain a delay in a transaction; but in the industry there is a view that this wording will be commonly associated with obligations arising from AML/counter-terrorist financing legislation. What offenders or non-offenders think if and when they are given such explanations is germane to the effectiveness of these anti-tip-off provisions, but not to this report. It is less consequential in the UK, where reporting does not automatically lead to a freeze on the transaction or the account, than in some other jurisdictions.

d. Power or Duty to Freeze

In the UK there is a "defence", also known as "consent", regime. Persons and businesses generally, and not just those in the regulated sectors, may avail themselves of a defence against money laundering charges, referred to colloquially (and somewhat pejoratively, since the implication is that this is not a real request for consent), as DAML or DATF (defence against terrorist financing). This can be done by seeking, via an SAR, the consent of the UK's FIU at the NCA. This consent is to conduct a transaction or undertake other activity about which they have concerns. For DAML the legislation gives the NCA seven working days to respond. Where no reply is provided by the NCA, it is considered that a defence is afforded to a reporter at the end of the seven-day notice period. Where the NCA refuses consent, the transaction or activity must not proceed for a further 31 calendar days, or, if earlier, until further notified by the NCA.[85] The moratorium period of 31 calendar days can be extended (see also section II.B.4). When it comes to terrorist financing, however, where the consent request has been refused, there is no moratorium period, and there is no defence unless and until the request is granted by the NCA.

e. Instant Collateral Duties

The regulated entity is expected to continue monitoring the activity in any event, regardless of whether a consent (see previous section) has been granted. The consent does not absolve the reporter from any of their other AML/counter-terrorist financing obligations.

---

85 This regime has been reviewed by the Law Commission (2018, 2019) and in late 2019 is awaiting a government decision as to what action should be taken.

2. *Follow-Up*

a. Duty to Provide FIU with Additional Data

If the FIU requires further information, the reporting entity will be expected to provide it. In principle, the FIU can ask for any additional information and obliged entities will have to provide it, unless legal privilege applies.

b. Continued Duty not to Disclose SAR to Client

The regulated entity is expected not to disclose the filing of the SAR to the client under any circumstances. The fact that an SAR has been made is not disclosed in evidence to the defence in the event of a criminal trial, though it may be the subject of a civil suit against the disclosing body if a plaintiff/ "victim" claims that it has been improperly harmed by freezing of funds, etc.

c. Continued Collateral Duties

The obliged entity is expected to carry on fulfilling its general AML/counter-terrorist financing duties such as continuing to apply ongoing KYC, due diligence and monitoring measures unless the obliged entity has decided to offboard the client.

3. *Special Rules for Privileged Professions*

a. Trigger for/Degree of Suspicion

There may be a defence where the information has been provided in privileged circumstances and/or is protected by LPP.

Specifically, the above-mentioned Legal Sector Affinity Group's guidance notes:

> When advice is given or received in circumstances where litigation is neither contemplated nor reasonably in prospect, except in very limited circumstances communications between you and third parties will not be protected under the advice arm of LPP.
>
> Privileged circumstances, however, exempt communications regarding information communicated by representatives of a client, where it is in connection with your giving legal advice to the client, or the client seeking legal advice from you.[86]

---

[86] Legal Sector Affinity Group, "Anti-Money Laundering Guidance for the Legal Sector", March 2018.

This guidance applies to the entire legal sector, i.e. tax advisors would be included if they provide tax advice in their capacity as independent legal professionals.

The guidance also explains:

> No offence is committed if the information or other matter giving rise to suspicion comes to a professional legal adviser or relevant professional advisor in privileged circumstances.
>
> You should note that receipt of information in privileged circumstances is not the same as legal professional privilege. It is a creation of POCA designed to comply with the exemptions from reporting set out in the European directives.
>
> Privileged circumstances means information communicated:
>
> - by a client, or a representative of a client, in connection with the giving of legal advice to the client; or
> - by a client, or by a representative of a client, seeking legal advice from you; or
> - by a person in connection with legal proceedings or contemplated legal proceedings.
>
> The exemption will not apply if information is communicated or given to the legal professional with the intention of furthering a criminal purpose.
>
> The Crown Prosecution Service guidance for prosecutors indicates that if a legal professional forms a genuine, but mistaken, belief that the privileged circumstances exemption applies (for example, the client misleads the legal professional and uses the advice received for a criminal purpose) the legal professional will be able to rely on the reasonable excuse defence. …
>
> LPP does not extend to everything that legal professionals have a duty to keep confidential. LPP protects only those confidential communications falling under either of the two heads of privilege – advice privilege or litigation privilege.
>
> The extent to which LPP attaches to a notary's records has not been the subject of a legal decision in England and Wales and is an evolving area of law. Notaries should therefore consider seeking specific legal advice based on the particular circumstances of a given situation if it appears LPP may apply. …
>
> LPP does not extend to documents which themselves form part of a criminal or fraudulent act, or communications which take place in order to obtain advice with the intention of carrying out an offence. …
>
> It is not just your client's intention which is relevant for the purpose of ascertaining whether information was communicated for the furtherance of a criminal purpose. It is also sufficient that a third party intends the legal professional/client communication to be made with that purpose. …

> If you know the transaction you're working on is a principal offence, you risk committing an offence yourself. In these circumstances, communications relating to such a transaction are not privileged and should be disclosed.[87]

As mentioned in previous sections, regulated persons are prevented from disclosing if their knowledge or suspicion is based on privileged information and LPP is not excluded by the crime/fraud exception. It is the Legal Sector Affinity Group's view that under those circumstances, solicitors will have a reasonable excuse for not making an authorised disclosure and will not commit a money laundering offence.

b. Content and Addressee(s) of SARs

SARs are filed with the UK's FIU at the NCA, as for every category of regulated entity. LPP does not extend to everything that legal professionals have a duty to keep confidential. LPP protects only those confidential communications falling under either of the two heads of privilege – advice privilege or litigation privilege. The exemption will not apply if information is communicated or given to the legal professional with the intention of furthering a criminal purpose.

c. Duty not to Disclose to Client

As per the Legal Sector Affinity Group's guidance, a legal professional will not commit a tipping-off offence if the disclosure to a client is made for the purpose of dissuading the client from engaging in conduct amounting to an offence.

It is a defence that a disclosure is made by a legal adviser to a client, or a client's representative, in connection with the giving of legal advice or to any person in connection with legal proceedings or contemplated legal proceedings.

Such a disclosure will not be exempt if it is made with the intention of furthering a criminal purpose.

The guidance from the Legal Sector Affinity Group further advises that enquiries of a client or a third party to help the firm decide whether the professional has a suspicion is not tipping-off unless they disclose that an SAR has been made or that a money laundering investigation is being carried out or contemplated. The offence of tipping-off only applies to the regulated sector.

---

87 *Ibid.*

4. *Protection of SAR's Source*

The source is protected from the discovery process in which parties to litigation must reveal their documents to the other side.[88]

D. RECORD KEEPING

Obliged entities must retain:

- copies of, or references to, the evidence they obtained of a customer's identity, for five years after the end of the customer relationship; and
- details of customer transactions for five years from the date of the transaction.

In regard to suspicious activity reporting, obliged entities should also retain:

- details of actions taken in respect of internal and external reports of suspicions;[89] and
- details of information considered by the nominated officer in respect of an internal report where no external report is made.

Records of all internal and external reports should be retained for at least five years from the date the report was made.

E. COMPLIANCE OFFICERS

Regulated entities must nominate an officer to receive disclosures[90] from the regulated entity's staff under Part 3 (terrorist property) of the Terrorism Act 2000 or Part 7 (money laundering) of POCA.

According to the Money Laundering Regulations, where a disclosure is made to the nominated officer, that officer must consider it in the light of any relevant information which is available to the obliged entity and determine whether it

---

88 Eoin O'Shea, "Civil Liability Protection For Those Making Suspicious Activity Reports (SARs)", Reed Smith Client Alerts, 28 May 2015, https://www.reedsmith.com/en/perspectives/2015/05/civil-liability-protection-for-those-making-suspic?utm_source=Mondaq&utm_medium=syndication&utm_campaign=View-Original.

89 "Internal" is in reference to any internal to the obliged entity escalations of potentially suspicious activity to the nominated officer who then decides whether a SAR needs to be filed "externally", i.e. with the FIU at the NCA.

90 In this context "disclosures" means escalations from internal staff of any suspicious financial activity that may entail money laundering or terrorist financing.

gives rise to knowledge or suspicion or reasonable grounds for knowledge or suspicion that a person is engaged in money laundering or terrorist financing.

It is the nominated officer's responsibility to decide whether they need to send a report or "disclosure" about the incident to the NCA (where the UK's FIU sits) by filing an SAR.[91]

Separately, for those obliged entities that are regulated by UK's financial services regulator (the FCA), the Handbook of the FCA, SYSC[92] 3.2.6I, stipulates that a firm must:

(a) appoint an individual as MLRO, with responsibility for oversight of its compliance with the FCA's rules on systems and controls against money laundering; and
(b) ensure that its MLRO has a level of authority and independence within the firm and access to resources and information sufficient to enable him to carry out that responsibility.

The FCA Handbook, SYSC 3.2.6J, further stipulates that the job of the MLRO within a firm is to act as the focal point for all activity within the firm relating to AML. The FCA expects that a firm's MLRO will be based in the UK.[93]

In FCA-regulated firms, the nominated officer and the MLRO can be the same person (see the JMLSG Guidance, 2017), and usually is; moreover, in non-FCA regulated firms the nominated officer can also be referred to as the MLRO.

Where the MLRO is sufficiently senior, that person can act also as the MLCP (see section III.A.1.c for details on MLCP above).

Depending on the size and nature of the business, the smallest organisations and sole practitioners do not have to have these three controls: (i) to appoint a MLCP, (ii) to screen employees, and (iii) to have an internal audit function. But all regulated persons are still required to comply with AML/counter-terrorist financing legislation and file SARs. Sole practitioners will have to perform the MLRO role.

The MLRO has to have independence and powers within the regulated entity, in order to be able to take decisions as appropriate, and also has to have the technical competence (e.g. for those entities regulated by the FCA, MLROs have to be approved by the FCA and the FCA has to determine if the individual is sufficiently competent; they are expected to have no convictions and to declare any civil judgments against them). Typically, bigger organisations apply a three lines of defence model where the teams

---

91 https://www.gov.uk/guidance/money-laundering-regulations-report-suspicious-activities.

92 The Senior Management Arrangements, Systems and Controls sourcebook (SYSC) is located within the high-level standards block of the FCA Handbook.

93 https://www.handbook.fca.org.uk/handbook/SYSC/3/2.html#DES92.

generating revenue and facing customers and their support functions (e.g. middle office and back office within banks) are within the first line of defence (KYC is often within first line of defence); the second line of defence is compliance and financial crime risk management oversight (including overseeing the KYC process occurring in the first line of defence); and the third line of defence is audit and controls assurance. The nominated officers and MLROs sit within the second line of defence and thus are independent, to the extent possible, from business while exercising oversight over the first line of defence.[94]

F. INTERNAL COMPLAINT MECHANISM

The law does not require that there is a set and specifically designed "whistleblower" mechanism as such. But, generally, reflecting contemporary views about the importance of openness, regulators require that all regulated entities put in place a process that informs senior management of both issues (e.g. violations, weaknesses in the internal systems and controls) and of relationships (e.g. with clients, business partners) that may represent a particularly high risk or even potential risk outside the organisation's acceptable risk parameters/risk appetite. Such mechanisms can be used both by internal and third-party employees. Separately, if employees of third persons know or suspect money laundering or terrorist financing (or, if they are within the regulated sector, have reasonable grounds to know or suspect) within an obliged entity, they should make a disclosure to the NCA (as already discussed in other sections).

FCA-regulated entities are required to appoint an MLRO, as discussed above, who is expected to prepare an annual MLRO report for senior management to inform them of any material issues and AML/counter-terrorist financing developments within the organisation.[95]

Separately, it is also expected from each regulated entity (not just those regulated by the FCA) to have a whistleblowing line. The FCA's Financial Crime Handbook lists as an example of good practice: "Whistleblowing procedures are clear and accessible, and respect staff confidentiality."[96] For firms' obligations in

---

94 See https://www.iia.org.uk/resources/audit-committees/governance-of-risk-three-lines-of-defence/; Institute of Internal Auditors, "The Three Lines of Defense in Effective Risk Management and Control", IIA Position Paper, January 2013, https://global.theiia.org/standards-guidance/recommended-guidance/Pages/The-Three-Lines-of-Defense-in-Effective-Risk-Management-and-Control.aspx; Inês Sofia de Oliveira, David Artingstall and Florence Keen, with Matt Russell and Ben Luddington, "The Cartography of Compliance On Banks, Anti-Money Laundering and Achieving Effectiveness in the UK", Royal United Services Institute for Defence and Security Studies in cooperation with PWC, January 2017.

95 http://www.jmlsg.org.uk/other-helpful-material/article/mlro-annual-report.

96 Financial Conduct Authority, *Financial crime: a guide for firms*, Part 1: A firm's guide to preventing financial crime, July 2016. The FCA has announced a pending upgrading of

relation to whistle-blowers, the FCA Handbook makes reference to the Public Interest Disclosure Act 1998.[97] Barclays Bank's CEO was fined £642,430 and reprimanded in 2018 for actively seeking (though failing) to discover the identity of an internal whistle-blower, though note that this was not in the context of money laundering revelations.[98]

G. ADDITIONAL PREVENTIVE MEASURES

Documenting the CDD and risk assessment process and record keeping is mandatory. UK legislation is not prescriptive, i.e. it does not set out in detail how requirements must be met. However, regulatory guidance indicates what is expected to be seen as best practice; for instance, what due diligence on trade finance transactions should entail, or how guarantors (as opposed to client borrowers or issuers) should be treated. MLROs are expected to record their reasons for not referring internally reported cases onwards to the FIU as SARs. Proper recording of what has been done to assess risk and actual due diligence are reviewed as part of the supervisory process and can lead to fines if considered inadequate.

In addition to the various levels of due diligence and risk assessment of clients, business partners and counterparties, regulated entities are required to undertake enterprise-wide risk assessment, monitoring of transactions and provide training to staff, and are provided guidance as to the respective processes/steps these processes should entail. This applies to all obliged entities.

It is a standard practice for potential employees to be vetted by employers (to verify their CV and check for criminal backgrounds), though MLROs have additionally to be vetted formally by the FCA. In addition, as discussed above, regulated entities are expected to have effective whistleblowing lines.

The FIU publishes annual reports in which it provides statistics and feedback on the SAR regime. It also supports the regulated sector by providing typologies material and general feedback on SARs through seminars aimed at improving

its approach to whistleblowing: see "UK financial regulator to overhaul its treatment of whistleblowers", Financial Times, 30 December 2018. https://www.ft.com/content/3ebb9920-f4ae-11e8-ae55-df4bf40f9d0d. See, more generally, the website of Protect (https://www.pcaw.co.uk/), with whom the FCA is collaborating in these revisions. These are not linked specifically to AML, nor is there any reason why they should be so linked: see, e.g. Financial Conduct Authority, "Retail and Wholesale Banking: review of firms' whistleblowing arrangements", 14 November 2018, https://www.fca.org.uk/publications/multi-firm-reviews/retail-and-wholesale-banking-review-firms-whistleblowing-arrangements.

97 www.legislation.gov.uk/ukpga/1998/23/contents.

98 Financial Conduct Authority, "Final Notice: Mr James Edward Staley", Ref. JXS02208, 11 May 2018, https://www.fca.org.uk/publication/final-notices/mr-james-edward-staley-2018.pdf. As with many fines, the issue of proportionality in relation to income or profits may be queried.

the quality of SARs. An organisation can also arrange a visit from the UK's FIU for feedback on the SARs submitted by the organisation. Indeed, the Money Laundering Regulations state that "the NCA must make arrangements to provide appropriate feedback on the suspicious activity disclosures it has received at least once a year." However, it is not clear whether this provision is about the NCA providing feedback to individual obliged entities or, cumulatively, to the entire regulated sector through its annual reports. Furthermore, the same provision of the Regulations states that the feedback may be provided in any form the NCA thinks fit. In practical terms, this will be general feedback, for example how to get better in terms of level of detail, structure, clarity – as serves the purposes of the FIU within its own staffing and systems constraints – rather than on outcome of the SAR or concrete information on the direction of any formal investigation (although the direction may become clear if there is a freezing order, trial, etc.). The UK's FIU also organises general feedback sessions with regulated bodies, such as the Law Society Money Laundering Task Force, though these too might not discuss specific SARs. There can be tensions with professional bodies, insofar as the FIU may resist improvements that require it to do more with the capacity it does not have. The term 'appropriate' remains undefined.

H. RULES ON OBLIGED ENTITIES' CIVIL LIABILITY TOWARDS CLIENT

If a client suffers economic damage from CDD measures (e.g. by the sudden disruption of banking services) or the freezing of assets after the filing of an unjustified SAR, an obliged entity cannot be held responsible and forced to compensate the client if the SAR is filed in good faith. A 2012 court case – *Shah v HSBC* – supports this,[99] though see *Lonsdale v National Westminster Bank*[100] for a rare exception.

I. SUPERVISORY AUTHORITIES' ROLE

1. *Supervisory Measures to Ensure Application of CDD and Other AML-Related Obligations*

UK Supervisors exercise oversight by undertaking routine checks as well as probes triggered by specific events (e.g. information provided by a whistleblower).

99 [2012] EWHC 1283 (QB); see also Law Society, "Shah v HSBC – an update". 17 May 2012, http://www.lawsociety.org.uk/support-services/advice/articles/case-summaries/shah-v-hsbc-update/.

100 [2018] EWHC 1843 (QB).

They also undertake periodic thematic reviews, which include the treatment of foreign PEPs and e-money risks, which aim to guide practice and may lead to fines or other sanctions for control weaknesses if not adhered to.[101]

For law enforcement authorities, collecting SARs and following up on SARs is a key preventive power allowing them to gather intelligence ahead of potential money laundering transactions. However, in practice, for this preventative role to be applied requires speedier action than is practicable in all but a small number of cases, usually where a DAML request is put in and/or there is an instruction/request to prioritise an SAR.

2. *Complaint Mechanism*

Under the Public Interest Disclosure Act 1998, a worker who reports wrongdoing in the public interest is protected by law – this person cannot lose their job or be treated unfairly for blowing the whistle.[102]

As the UK government's website explains, the practical effect of this legislation (though this is advice, not in the legislation) is that:

> You can tell your employer or a prescribed person anonymously but they may not be able to take the claim further if you haven't provided all the information they need.
>
> You can give your name but request confidentiality – the person or body you tell should make every effort to protect your identity.
>
> If you report your concern to the media, in most cases you'll lose your whistleblowing law rights.[103]

There is not a one single authority to receive complaints. There are various prescribed persons or bodies, each dealing with a different issue. For instance, Chapter 10 of the Law Society Code of Conduct states that solicitors must report serious misconduct by any person or firm authorised by the Solicitors Regulation Authority (SRA), or any employee, manager or owner of such a firm to the SRA. This includes conduct relating to a criminal offence such as money laundering,

---

101 Examples include: Financial Conduct Authority, "TR13/9 Anti-Money Laundering and Anti-Bribery and Corruption Systems and Controls: Asset Management and Platform Firms", October 2013, https://www.fca.org.uk/publication/thematic-reviews/tr13-09.pdf; "TR 13/3 Banks' control of financial crime risks in trade finance", July 2013, https://www.fca.org.uk/publication/thematic-reviews/tr-13-03.pdf; "TR18/3 Money Laundering and Terrorist Financing Risks in the E-Money Sector", 3 October 2018, https://www.fca.org.uk/publications/thematic-reviews/tr18-3-money-laundering-and-terrorist-financing-risks-e-money-sector; and "TR14/16 How small banks manage money laundering and sanctions risk: update", 14 November 2014, https://www.fca.org.uk/publications/thematic-reviews/tr14-16-%E2%80%93-how-small-banks-manage-money-laundering-and-sanctions-risk.

102 https://www.gov.uk/whistleblowing; see also https://www.pcaw.org.uk/a-guide-to-pida/.

103 https://www.gov.uk/whistleblowing/who-to-tell-what-to-expect.

and conduct in relation to breaches of the Money Laundering Regulations.[104] Whistleblowers can report direct to the FCA allegations about regulated firms in the financial sector such as banks and e-money firms.[105]

Where the complaint is not a matter of whistleblowing but is known to the organisation that is the subject of the complaint, it can then be referred to an ombudsman.[106]

J. STATISTICS ON SARs BY OBLIGED ENTITIES

From a few informal tip-offs from bankers to police in 1986, the number of "suspicious transaction reports" by bankers and professionals to the UK NCIS (later replaced by SOCA and then the NCA, which houses the FIU) rose from a few hundred in 1991 to 15,114 in 1999 to 94,708 in 2003 – almost doubling after 9/11 – to 195,000 in 2005 (9, 600 of them from lawyers) to 463,938 in 2017–18 and 478,437 in 2018–19.

The UK's FIU's annual reports provide statistics on the SAR regime, including the number of SARs filed per sector. While a breakdown of amounts per sector is not provided, and neither is the outcome of such reports (which is only partially known by the FIU or by anyone else), the FIU provides the amount of assets seized (but not per sector) which are considered to be the result of actions following up SARs. In addition, the FIU provides case studies with case-specific (but redacted) details, including amounts and the nature of the predicate offence. Given the number of SARs in the UK (and some other EU Member States, such as the Netherlands), follow-ups that might be realistic in a low-reporting jurisdiction would be very ambitious there. However, the lack of feedback reduces the lesson-learning potential of the dataset.

The number of SARs and the sectors from which they emanate are set out below. The sums involved in individual SARs or SARs collectively are unavailable for any sector: indeed given the volume of reports in the UK, it is not clear what the point of collecting amounts would be, and there would be massive resistance to doing so, given the strains on the FIU and the opportunity cost of generating the data.

---

104 https://www.gov.uk/whistleblowing/who-to-tell-what-to-expect; http://www.sra.org.uk/solicitors/enforcement/solicitor-report/whistleblowing-to-the-sra.page.

105 For instance, according to the media, a whistle-blower reported to the FCA allegations that e-money firm Revolut failed to adequately respond to internal compliance concerns. See BBC report, 2 April 2019 https://www.bbc.co.uk/news/technology-47751945. (Accessed 30 December 2019.)

106 https://www.citizensadvice.org.uk/consumer/get-more-help/how-to-use-an-ombudsman-in-england/.

Table 1. SARs submitted by all sectors, April 2018–March 2019

April 2018 to March 2019	Volumes	% of total	% comparison to 2017–18
Credit institution – banks	383,733	80.21%	3.29%
Credit institution – building societies	21,714	4.54%	10.56%
Credit institution – others	10,203	2.13%	–25.41%
Financial institution – MSBs	18,940	3.96%	–10.65%
Financial institution – others	24,911	5.21%	16.16%
Accountants and tax advisers	5,055	1.06%	–1.65%
Independent legal professionals	2,774	0.58%	4.29%
Trust or company service providers	23	0.00%	–56.60%
Estate agents	635	0.13%	–10.56%
High value dealers	481	0.10%	93.17%
Gaming (including casinos)/leisure (including some not under Money Laundering Regulations [MLRs])	4,163	0.87%	93.27%
Not under MLRs	5,805	1.21%	5.78%
Total	**478,437**	**100%**	**3.13%**

Source: National Crime Agency, "Suspicious Activity Reports (SARS) Annual Report 2019"[107]

Further details of reporting are available in the SAR annual reports.[108]

IV. THE SYSTEM OF FINANCIAL INTELLIGENCE UNITS

A. INSTITUTIONAL AND FUNCTIONAL CHARACTERISTICS

1. *Organisational Position*

The UK's FIU sits within the NCA, a UK law enforcement agency established to fight serious and organised crime.[109]

2. *Purpose and Tasks*

The UK's FIU receives, analyses and distributes financial intelligence gathered from SARs, both actively and via its management of its database ELMER, which

---

107 https://www.nationalcrimeagency.gov.uk/who-we-are/publications/390-sars-annual-report-2019.

108 The NCA publishes reports annually.

109 See http://www.nationalcrimeagency.gov.uk/ and https://www.nationalcrimeagency.gov.uk/what-we-do/crime-threats/money-laundering-and-terrorist-financing.

authorised financial investigators can consult. Though its role has remained substantially unchanged since its creation and its absorption into the NCIS in 1992, it has no separate constitutional status from the NCA, and its legal authority for this work derives from subsection (c) of section 1(5) of the Crime and the Courts Act 2013, which states:

> The NCA is to have the function (the 'criminal intelligence function') of gathering, storing, processing, analysing, and disseminating information that is relevant to any of the following – (a) activities to combat organised crime or serious crime; (b) activities to combat any other kind of crime; (c) exploitation proceeds investigations (within the meaning of section 341(5) of the Proceeds of Crime Act 2002), exploitation proceeds orders … and applications for such orders.

The proportion of SARs received that are actually analysed in detail and further intelligence developed before distribution is unknown, but the lack of development by the FIU was one of the issues criticised by FATF both in its recent (2018) and in its previous (2007) evaluation. Common sense would suggest that with a volume of SARs as great as that of the UK's FIU, there would have to be huge centralised staffing in order to develop a "large" proportion of them. In a comparative context, one way of expressing this might be as a ratio of reports received to staff available. Thus, disregarding the post-FATF MER increase in personnel, we note that in 2017–18, 84 staff had to deal with 463,938 SARs, which equals 5,523 SARs per staff member per year or – excluding abstractions, sickness and supervisory responsibilities – around 220 per staff member per working day. Each "SAR development" therefore has a significant opportunity cost in not processing other SARs. However, FATF mutual evaluation reports have not approached this level of sophistication in analysing resource allocation issues and trade-offs hitherto.

3. *Independence*

The UK's FIU is an operationally independent part of the NCA. In accordance with the strategic framework which set up the NCA, the Home Secretary determines the strategic priorities of the NCA and will hold the Director General of the NCA to account for the discharge of the "NCA functions" while also respecting the Director General's operational independence. More specifically, in regard to operational independence, the framework explains that NCA's Director General is:

> responsible (including through a senior NCA officer acting on his or her behalf) for all decisions about which operations to conduct and how they should be conducted.

This would include, for example, decisions about whether to continue or stop a criminal investigation.[110]

Nor can prosecutors or other police forces/non-police agencies such as HMRC instruct it to carry out further investigations without the agreement of the NCA Director General, though they can request further enquiries. By convention, the Director General does not give instructions to the FIU on what to follow up or not follow up, and there is no evidence of political interference in the FIU work, though such interference would be public only in the event of whistleblowing. However, as with many aspects of the unwritten UK constitutional arrangements, this independence operates by convention.

4. Powers

The UK's FIU has analytical but no coercive powers, except limited ones over DAML freezing orders that are carried out by a separate NCA team. In the vast majority of cases, no legal consequences flow from the making of an SAR, and no action is taken automatically against an individual or business that is reported on. It is not known how many subjects of SARs are subsequently de-risked by their bank without being told that they have been reported to the FIU (which would be a criminal tipping-off offence). However, de-risking following SARs is by no means automatic, and we should not underestimate the impact of the cost of enhanced scrutiny impacted by more general risk profiling by regulators and international risk matrices on discouraging risk-averse banks from "risky" clients.

The JMLSG explains that POCA empowers the NCA to conduct an investigation to discover whether a person holds criminal assets and to recover the assets in question.

POCA also creates five investigative powers for the law enforcement agencies, which are therefore available to the NCA and to other agencies (but not to the UK's FIU specifically):

- a production order;
- a search and seizure warrant;
- a disclosure order;
- a customer information order; and
- an account monitoring order.

110 Crime and the Courts Act 2013, sections 3 and 4. See also Home Office and NCA, "Revised Framework document for the National Crime Agency", May 2014, https://www.nationalcrimeagency.gov.uk/who-we-are/publications/29-nca-framework-document/file.

B. TREATMENT OF SARs

1. Data Processing

No SAR leads to the automatic blocking of funds. SARs are increasingly but not exclusively electronic, and since the beginning of the SAR regime, there have never been sufficient resources to do more than analyse a minority of them. The FIU operates an electronic database called ELMER on which SAR data are kept for six years, following intervention by the Information Commissioner to reduce the period for which they were kept.[111] The FIU makes a judgement about which police force to forward the SAR to, but with the exception of the Serious Fraud Office (SFO), the UK does not operate a prosecutor-led system of investigation, and prosecutors do not get access to SARs. The UK's FIU operates a "consent regime",[112] under which SAR reporters can request permission to transact funds transfers (when a suspicion has emerged prior to a transaction), giving them a defence against money laundering or terrorism financing charges.[113] (See also sections II.B.4 and III.C.1.d). Relevant statistics on consent requests is provided in the table below.

Table 2. Statistics on consent requests, 2018–2019

Key statistics	April 2018 to March 2019
Total SARs	478,437
DAML SARs	34,151
DAML SARs refused	1,332
Breaches of confidentiality	3

Source: National Crime Agency.

111 For a thorough Parliamentary report on the data retention and processing issues at the NCA's predecessor agency, SOCA, see https://publications.parliament.uk/pa/ld201011/ldselect/ldeucom/82/8205.htm.

112 Some in the industry view it as controversial because consent should not be seen as "clearance" from the NCA and does not absolve obliged entities from responsibility (other than from the ML offences under POCA) if they believe the funds are criminal; for instance, consent is not a defence under the UK Bribery Act. This appears to defeat the purpose of obtaining consent. Additionally, with the transaction delayed, the client will likely draw the conclusion that an SAR has been made and will in practice be unintentionally tipped off (communications must be carefully worded to avoid the "tipping off" offence). With no *de minimis* thresholds and with loosely defined concepts, the SAR regime has been criticised by the Law Commission for the high volume of low-quality defensive (or precautionary) SARs.

113 For the NCA's interpretation of the issues, see National Crime Agency, "Requesting a defence from the NCA under POCA and TACT", May 2019.

"The NCA is not a crime reporting agency. If the funds involved are not yet the proceeds of crime then it is not money laundering, but attempted fraud."[114] This statement is clearly aimed at reducing defensive (or precautionary; not to be confused with 'defence/consent' requests, see section I.B.) filing but fails to recognise various subtleties. For instance, fraud is typically also laundering at the same time (e.g. tax fraud, investment fraud) and on this basis, attempted fraud is also attempted money laundering. There may be scenarios where the offence is in the process of being committed and so the funds are already tainted, and because of the broad legal definition of money laundering it is difficult for obliged entities to draw a line. For instance, if a bank sees payments from a client to a counterparty suspected to be a public official, with the payments suspected to be bribes for the official to organise a fraudulent bidding process, then the client has not generated proceeds yet, but the funds the client is sending to the official are crime proceeds for the official. Making that corrupt payment, even if the client has not won the bid yet and has not generated corrupt proceeds, is already an offence. Although the NCA probably did not mean to discourage the reporting of such conduct, the NCA's above statement may be interpreted in that manner. It is also worth noting that POCA (section VII, 330) requires not only the reporting of persons involved in laundering and the whereabouts of laundered property, but also any information which an individual believes or it is reasonable to expect him to believe may assist in identifying these persons or the whereabouts of any of the laundered property. What information may assist would be a subjective decision and a difficult one to articulate; and so obliged entities find themselves having to report even a very remote nexus that in reality may be of no help to the NCA.

The UK's FIU receives financial intelligence gathered from SARs, and makes all SARs available to 4,800 authorised financial investigators in law enforcement agencies and to HMRC for their own analysis and investigations (with the exception of SARs in certain sensitive categories such as professional standards investigations).[115]

2. *Special Procedures for Privileged Professions*

There are no specific differences between how an SAR from a non-privileged obliged entity and how an SAR from a privileged profession would be processed. However, LPP can be a reason for not reporting and for having a

---

[114] See National Crime Agency, "Guidance on submitting better quality Suspicious Activity Reports (SARs)", 2019, p. 5, https://www.nationalcrimeagency.gov.uk/who-we-are/publications/42-guidance-on-submitting-better-quality-sars/file.

[115] See HM Treasury and Home Office, *National risk assessment of money laundering and terrorist financing 2017*, October 2017.

defence against a charge of money laundering, except when used to further a crime. But if the FIU is seeking to develop an SAR, it and criminal investigators cannot lawfully read or use material that is under LPP if they come across it, and will be denied access to it if they ask for it. Such claims of LPP are normally given to a separate set of senior lawyers who have no contact with an investigation, to assess whether or not the material is legally privileged.

3. *Feedback Obligations*

a. Obligation of the FIU

According to a provision (Part 11, reg. 104) in the Money Laundering Regulations, "the NCA must make arrangements to provide appropriate feedback on the suspicious activity disclosures it has received at least once a year." See section III.G above for further details.

Indeed the obliged entity will seldom be aware of what has happened to an SAR, neither the court outcome (except where the case is reported in the media and the reporting body is aware of that) nor even the investigative input. This has been the case since the beginning of the system.[116] Except in special circumstances, such as the JMLIT, there is no legal authority for intelligence to be passed from the FIU or police organisation to the reporting entity. Consequently, feedback would be bound to be limited.

However, as discussed above (see sections II.B.4 and III.C.1.d), there is a consent/defence regime, in accordance with which, if the FIU wants a transaction that is subject to an SAR to be blocked, it must notify the obliged entity that had filed the SAR.[117]

---

116 Michael Gold and Michael Levi, *Money-Laundering in the UK: an Appraisal of Suspicion-Based Reporting,* London: Police Foundation, 1994.

117 In *Lonsdale v National Westminster Bank* [2018] EWHC 1843 (QB), the High Court ruled that in some rare circumstances, a customer could challenge the basis for the making of an SAR. In March 2017 the bank froze a joint account belonging to one of its customers, a barrister, for eight days and in December it froze seven other accounts of the same customer. The customer requested access to documents relating to the freezing of his accounts. The bank provided limited documentary evidence and did not disclose the SARs. The judge emphasised that the general rule is that if a document is mentioned in a statement of case or a witness statement the other party has a right to inspect it. However, the right to inspect is not unqualified and a balance must be struck when considering whether, for example, inspection would be disproportionate or should be refused on grounds of confidentiality.
The judge held that there was no evidence that inspection by the plaintiff would amount to tipping-off, nor that the SARs, submitted some 16 months previously, were required still to be kept confidential, since there was no evidence of active investigation. The SARs were plainly relevant to the assessment of whether NatWest genuinely held a relevant suspicion, the key issue in Mr Lonsdale's claim for breach of contract. On that basis the judge ordered that the SARs be disclosed to Mr Lonsdale unless the NCA sought to argue otherwise within 14 days, which it did not.

b. Obligation of Investigative Authorities

The various agencies collaborate to the extent that they have the resources and good institutional and personal relationships to do so. However, the authority receiving the information is not under a formal obligation to provide feedback to the FIU and only sometimes does so. Generally, where an SAR has resulted in the seizure of assets, information is fed back to the FIU and then is reflected in the FIU's annual report as part of its statistics. However, since asset freezing and confiscation are decisions that are not all centralised in CPS, HM Courts and Tribunals Service and individual courts, these data are not guaranteed to be complete. HMRC is bound by its own data protection and secrecy rules, and does not feed back information to the FIU.

4. Disclosure Obligations Towards "Suspect"

The FIU does not inform the "suspect" about an SAR. The suspect's defence cannot know about SARs officially, even if the suspects can work out by the non-availability of financial services that they have been the subject of an SAR and perhaps a DAML report.

C. PROACTIVE INVESTIGATIONS

The UK's FIU has no separate constitutional and legal powers. The FIU are on the staff of the NCA and in principle could conduct investigations without receiving SARs. However, in practice they do not do so, and in any event they would not be doing so as members of the FIU but as NCA staff.

Although the "tipping-off" offence applies to the context of an SAR being filed, it can be inferred from legislation that the same logic applies to instances where an investigation has been initiated without an SAR. That is to say, obliged entities are required not to disclose to the client or the suspect, if different from the client, that there is a formal investigation.

D. ACCESS TO DATA

1. Design and Content of FIU's Own Data Banks

The principal data bank of the UK FIU is its stock of past SARs.

2. Access to Other Public Data Banks

The FIU does not have access to the intelligence data banks of other bodies. It can check the Police National Computer (PNC) for convictions and other data that are on the PNC, but not the tax, welfare payments, trading standards or databases of other public bodies. Those bodies can use the SARs for their own purposes and can collaborate with the NCA/FIU. It can also make requests to access foreign FIU and other data, via the Egmont Group or (via the UK Central Authority) using mutual legal assistance processes. As per the above, the FIU provides data to other parts of the NCA and other agencies. HMRC has direct access to the FIU's data. The FIU does not have access to other agencies' confidential data banks. It (and other law enforcement bodies) can request access to HMRC's register of trusts with UK tax consequences.

3. *Access to Private Data Banks*

The FIU does not have automatic access to confidential private data banks but can request further information following up on an SAR. It purchases access to some commercial databases, as the sometimes quite large private sector FIUs created within large banks can also do.

4. *Data Analytics*

It is not clear that the FIU or any enforcement body would be prohibited from using data mining. However, there is no evidence that they actually are doing or will do so, beyond counter-terrorism. Data protection is explained in section V. The FIU does data matching on its own database consisting of SARs, and it explores possible connectivity via JMLIT cases.[118]

The UK's FIU reports[119] the following activities that it undertakes (though the denotation of this work and of the category of 'vulnerable persons' remains vague):

> The UKFIU screens/analyses SARs daily to identify fast-tracking to LEAs; this is to ensure that the intelligence's maximum value is exploited. Over the year the UKFIU:
>
> – 'read and triaged' 27,586 potential vulnerable person SARs (up 5.84%).

---

118 According to the NCA's website: "JMLIT is a partnership between law enforcement and the financial sector to exchange and analyse information relating to money laundering and wider economic threats. The taskforce consists of: over 40 financial institutions; the Financial Conduct Authority; Cifas; five law-enforcement agencies: the NCA, HMRC, the SFO, the City of London Police, and the Metropolitan Police Service. JMLIT is an innovative model for public/private information sharing that has generated very positive results since its inception in 2015, and is considered internationally to be an example of best practice." See https://www.nationalcrimeagency.gov.uk/what-we-do/national-economic-crime-centre.

119 SARs Annual Report 2019, p. 7. (Below, "Read and triaged" refers to the total number of SARs returned by the UK's FIU keyword searching that require reading and triaging by a UK FIU officer; integrity SARs relate to knowledge or suspicion of money laundering and/or terrorist financing involving an employee of an LEA or the civil service.) See https://www.nationalcrimeagency.gov.uk/who-we-are/publications/390-sars-annual-report-2019.

- disseminated 3,735 vulnerable person SARs (up 3.32%).
- read and triaged 25,800 potential politically exposed person (PEP) SARs (down 3.25%).
- disseminated 2,388 PEP SARs (up 68.29%).
- read and triaged 29,848 integrity SARs (down 4.51%).
- disseminated 788 integrity SARs (down 35.78%).

The above are not substantially different forms of reporting but different statistical categories applied by the FIU. Note that the data are sent to law enforcement bodies and not to prosecutors, who would not know if an SAR had been made.

5. *International Cooperation*

The FIU cooperates with counterparts abroad based on Memoranda of Association. The content of any such agreements is, however, confidential. There is a special agreement with the Crown Dependencies and Overseas Territories for access to beneficial ownership information and other financial intelligence.[120] The NCA maintains a substantial number of international liaison officers internationally who can both make and respond to lawful requests.

E. PARTICIPATION OF "SUSPECTS"

1. *Defence Rights*

In theory, suspects should not be aware of an SAR being filed on them and an obliged entity should not be committing a "tipping-off" offence. Therefore, defence rights do not apply, especially in the context where assets are not frozen.[121] However, as discussed above, if an obliged entity (e.g. a bank) delays or terminates a transaction with a client, the client may begin to suspect that an SAR had been filed despite its confidential nature.

If an SAR is used as part of an investigation that results in a trial, the suspect will have the same defence rights as any other defendant. However, typically

---

120 *Statutory review of the implementation of the exchange of notes on beneficial ownership between the United Kingdom, Crown Dependencies and Overseas Territories*, 2019.

121 The pre-charge restraint order under POCA is a tool that can only be used in rare circumstances and is *not* a power of the FIU but only of the prosecutor. *In re Stanford International Bank Ltd v Serious Fraud Office* [2010] EWCA Civ 137, Hughes LJ said (para 191): "In effect a prosecutor seeking an ex parte order must put on his defence hat and ask himself what, if he were representing the defendant or a third party with a relevant interest, he would be saying to the judge, and, having answered that question, that is what he must tell the judge. … This application came close to being treated as routine and to taking the court for granted. It may well not be the only example."

during trial the fact that an SAR had led to the trial is not disclosed, nor is the name of the obliged entity. In very rare cases, there can be civil litigation in which the plaintiff has discovered the existence of an SAR or has plausibly surmised that one had been made and seeks damages against the reporting entity. As the *Shah v HSBC* case[122] indicates, where an obliged entity has filed an SAR in good faith, the court is expected to decide in favour of the obliged entity. In *Lonsdale v National Westminster Bank*,[123] the High Court ruled that in some rare circumstances a customer could challenge the basis for the making of an SAR, but only after a period of time has elapsed that makes it clear there is no longer any plausible criminal investigation. However, the confidentiality of SARs was created specifically to reduce to a minimum the circumstances under which a suspect would be able to take legal or other (e.g. violent) action against the reporting entity or individuals believed responsible for the reports.

Under the Data Protection Act 2018 (DPA18) and its predecessors, individuals normally can request from an organisation any data held on them within this organisation However under its establishing legislation – the Crime and Criminal Courts Act 2013 – the NCA is exempt from Freedom of Information requests, and the FIU can (and will) refuse access to files if the suspect was to file a "data subject access" request, i.e. a request to see if the organisation has their personal data and, if so, what the data are. Section 45(4) DPA18 makes it clear that data controllers have the right to restrict access.[124]

Under section 40(2) POCA, the Crown Court can make a pre-charge restraint order, but only if it is satisfied that: (a) a criminal investigation has been commenced, and (b) there are reasonable grounds to suspect that the alleged offender has benefited from his criminal conduct. But any restraint order must, under section 41(2A) POCA, contain a legal aid exception. Second, under section 41(7A–C) POCA, a pre-charge restraint order must now "include in the order a requirement for the applicant for the order to report to the court on the progress of the investigation at such times and in such manner as the order may specify (a 'reporting requirement')", unless the Court decides that, in the circumstances of the case, a reporting requirement should not be imposed. However, if the Court so decides, it must give reasons for its decision. Third, the Court must discharge the order if proceedings for the offence are not started within a reasonable time (section 41(7B)(b) POCA), whether or not an application to discharge the order is made. There is active discussion in 2019 of methods by which restraint orders can be incentivised. These are partly an issue of departmental budgets and the caution of prosecutors in risking the costs of applications for restraint.

122 [2012] EWHC 1283.

123 [2018] EWHC 1843 (QB).

124 Section 45 DPA18 reads: "The controller may restrict, wholly or partly, the rights conferred by subsection (1) to the extent that and for so long as the restriction is, having regard to the fundamental rights and legitimate interests of the data subject, a necessary and proportionate measure to – (a) avoid obstructing an official or legal inquiry, investigation or procedure; (b) avoid prejudicing the prevention, detection, investigation or prosecution of criminal offences or the execution of criminal penalties; (c) protect public security; (d) protect national security; (e) protect the rights and freedoms of others. (5) Where the rights of

LPP applies to professionals in the legal sector (as discussed above, section III.C.3.a), but they will still have to file an SAR if the privileged information is communicated to them to further a criminal purpose. If they do not do so, they may be committing a money laundering offence, in addition to any other offences.

2. Judicial Review or Other Remedies

Suspects cannot be involved in the FIU process and, as discussed above, should not be aware of the FIU action. If suspects were to suspect that an SAR had been filed, they can launch litigation. But as the *Shah v HSBC* case (mentioned above) demonstrates, the court is expected to decide in favour of the reporting entity if the SAR has been filed in good faith. *Lonsdale v National Westminster Bank* is a rare exception.

If the suspect were to launch litigation, it would be for the courts to decide whether the FIU has overstepped its authority and treated someone unfairly by passing the SAR to another authority to potentially launch an investigation. Even when an FIU investigation leads to prosecution, FIU material remains confidential as they cannot disclose the name of the source of the SAR.

F. SIMILAR POWERS OF SUPERVISORY BODIES

1. Financial Supervision

In many fraud cases, the fraud automatically involves money laundering as part of the extraction of the funds, so the distinction made in the question is somewhat artificial, a problem also with the FATF evaluators' pressure for money laundering prosecutions that are standalone or at least additional to those for predicate offences. The FCA is an authorised recipient of SAR data, and can investigate the systems and controls of FCA-regulated entities for

---

a data subject under subsection (1) are restricted, wholly or partly, the controller must inform the data subject in writing without undue delay – (a) that the rights of the data subject have been restricted, (b) of the reasons for the restriction, (c) of the data subject's right to make a request to the Commissioner under section 51, so the Commissioner would then review the SAR and his/her decision can be reviewed in a court, (d) of the data subject's right to lodge a complaint with the Commissioner, and (e) of the data subject's right to apply to a court under section 167. (6) Subsection (5)(a) and (b) do not apply to the extent that the provision of the information would undermine the purpose of the restriction. (7) The controller must – (a) record the reasons for a decision to restrict (whether wholly or partly) the rights of a data subject under subsection (1), and (b) if requested to do so by the Commissioner, make the record available to the Commissioner."

AML/counter-terrorist financing weaknesses. It can also launch its own criminal investigations, for example into insider dealing and other market conduct offences within its legal competence (regulated entities file reports with the FCA on transactions suspected to be insider dealing). Many such offences involve money laundering, but quite properly, they are unlikely to be, and certainly will not automatically be, labelled as "money laundering cases". However, specific leads into money laundering cases are investigated (if at all) by the law enforcement authorities (and in some instances, a report on insider dealing will also result in or will be done in parallel with an SAR).

It is sometimes a matter of tension as to which body will have the obligation of regulating particular sectors, an issue which has resource implications, especially at a time of austerity. HMRC can regulate sectors such as money service businesses within its legal competence, as well as investigate money laundering suspicions on its own initiative.[125] Indeed, at the end of 2016–17, the staff resource for HMRC's Anti-Money Laundering Supervision team equated to around 200. In the period 2015–17, HMRC staff carried out activities including:[126]

- Keeping a register of all supervised businesses and publishing a lookup facility on GOV.UK;
- Specifying what information those applying for registration must provide to HMRC.
- Carrying out Fit and Proper tests;
- Requiring information and attendance at meetings of relevant representatives in or connected with the business;
- Entering business premises – inspecting, observing and making copies of information found there;
- Refusing to register a business;
- Imposing civil penalties for failure to meet any requirement of the regulations.
- Where judged by them to be appropriate, instituting proceedings for criminal offences; and
- Making disclosures to other supervisory authorities.

2. *Non-Financial Sector Supervision*

Supervisory bodies can only probe within the scope of their supervisory mandate. Any case-specific leads are followed by law enforcement/investigative bodies (e.g. the NCA, SFO). Those regulators within the OPBAS mandate may

---

125 https://www.gov.uk/guidance/money-laundering-regulations-appeals-and-penalties.

126 HMRC, *Report on Tackling Financial Crime in the Supervised Sectors 2015–2017*, 2018, p. 6.

receive SARs,[127] but there may be a tension between investigating disciplinary offences (e.g. non-compliance with solicitors' client or office account rules) and investigating money laundering or other substantive crime cases. Normally, the disciplinary offences would be made subservient to the criminal ones (if the regulatory body is aware of them), but could be pursued as standalone ones or in the aftermath of a conviction. Prosecutions for money laundering are comparatively rare and there is no requirement that disciplinary offences should reveal their connection with money laundering suspicions. It would usually be easier to pursue them for technical breaches and therefore the true effect of AML provisions in disciplinary cases is obscure. There is no equivalent in the UK of the continental European and Canadian provisions whereby the Bar Association has the mandate to investigate money laundering within their members, as a way of protecting legal confidentiality.

G. REPORTING OBLIGATIONS OF SUPERVISORY AUTHORITIES

Supervisory bodies[128] for the various parts of the AML-regulated sector are not obliged entities but they typically have MOUs or established gateways in

127 OPBAS aims to improve consistency of professional body AML supervision in the accountancy and legal sectors, but *does not* directly supervise legal and accountancy firms. The professional body AML supervisors overseen by OPBAS that may receive SARs are listed in Schedule 1 to the Money Laundering Regulations, and are as follows: the Association of Accounting Technicians; the Association of Chartered Certified Accountants; the Association of International Accountants; the Association of Taxation Technicians; the Chartered Institute of Legal Executives/CILEx Regulation; the Chartered Institute of Management Accountants; the Chartered Institute of Taxation; the Council for Licensed Conveyancers; the Faculty of Advocates; the Faculty Office of the Archbishop of Canterbury; the General Council of the Bar/Bar Standards Board; the General Council of the Bar of Northern Ireland; the Insolvency Practitioners Association; the Institute of Certified Bookkeepers; the Institute of Chartered Accountants in England and Wales; the Institute of Chartered Accountants in Ireland; the Institute of Chartered Accountants of Scotland; the Institute of Financial Accountants; the International Association of Bookkeepers; the Law Society/Solicitors Regulation Authority; the Law Society of Northern Ireland; and the Law Society of Scotland.
OPBAS *does not* supervise: members of professional bodies, such as firms, accountants and solicitors, or any other type of business subject to the requirements of the Money Laundering Regulations; statutory anti-money laundering supervisors such as the Gambling Commission and HMRC; activity carried out by professional body supervisors outside the UK; and the adequacy of any functions performed by professional body supervisors unrelated to AML supervision – this includes any oversight of their members' controls over other types of financial crime, such as those related to the prevention of fraud, improving data security and the implementation of financial sanctions and asset freezes.

128 According to the Money Laundering Regulations (Part 11), the following public authorities must inform the NCA if they know or suspect or have reasonable grounds to suspect money laundering or terrorist financing: "103.—(1) The following bodies and persons

place to notify the NCA if, in the course of their work, they become aware or suspicious that money laundering or terrorist financing is taking place (or has taken or will take place) at an organisation supervised by them. The extent to which this is actually done is unknown.

H. REPORTING BY OTHER AUTHORITIES

Other authorities are not part of the regulated sector, but the expectation is that they will notify the FIU if they consider it to be appropriate. This very rarely happens, but they are free to do so. Unlike some other European countries (e.g. the Netherlands), there are legal provisions about confidentiality within HMRC by the Commissioners for Revenue and Customs Act 2005 that make it criminal for them to communicate suspicions to other bodies except in particular circumstances via specified gateways.[129]

---

must, if they know or suspect or have reasonable grounds for knowing or suspecting that a person is or has engaged in money laundering or terrorist financing, as soon as practicable, inform the NCA – (a) the Auditor General for Scotland; (b) the Auditor General for Wales; (c) the Bank of England; (d) the Comptroller and Auditor General; (e) the Comptroller and Auditor General for Northern Ireland; (f) the FCA; (g) the Gambling Commission; (h) the Official Solicitor to the Supreme Court; (i) the Pensions Regulator; (j) the PRA; (k) the Public Trustee; (l) the Secretary of State, in the exercise of his or her functions under enactments relating to companies and insolvency; (m) the Treasury, in the exercise of their functions under FSMA; (n) the Treasury Solicitor; (o) a designated professional body for the purposes of Part 20 of FSMA (provision of financial services by members of the professions); (p) a person or inspector appointed under section 65 (investigations on behalf of FCA) or 66 (inspections and special meetings) of the Friendly Societies Act 1992(a); (q) an inspector appointed under section 106 of the Co-operative and Community Benefit Societies 2014(b) (appointment of inspectors) or section 18 of the Credit Unions Act 1979(c) (power to appoint inspector); (r) an inspector appointed under section 431 (investigation of a company on its own application), 432 (other company investigations), 442 (power to investigate company ownership) or 446D (appointment of replacement inspectors) of the Companies Act 1985(d); (s) a person or inspector appointed under section 55 (investigations on behalf of FCA) or 56 (inspections and special meetings) of the Building Societies Act 1986(e); (t) a person appointed under section 167 (appointment of persons to carry out investigations), 168(3) or (5) (appointment of persons to carry out investigations in particular cases), 169(1)(b) (investigations to support overseas regulator) or 284 (power to investigate affairs of a scheme) of FSMA(f), or under regulations made under section 262(2)(k) (open-ended investment companies) of that Act(g), to conduct an investigation; and (u) a person authorised to require the production of documents under section 447 (Secretary of State's power to require production of documents) of the Companies Act 1985(h), or section 84 of the Companies Act 1989(i) (exercise of powers by officer)."

129 See https://www.gov.uk/hmrc-internal-manuals/information-disclosure-guide/idg50000. We note that reports on transactions suspected to be insider trading are filed with the FCA.

I. STATISTICS

1. Number of Reports by Supervisory Authorities and Other Authorities

It is unclear whether and how many SARs may have been filed by supervisory or other authorities. There is no such separate category in the FIU's annual reports, which provide the number of SARs filed per sector. There is also a category of SARs filed by non-AML regulated entities.

2. FIU Analysis

There are no statistics on the number of FIU investigations and the value of transactions associated with these investigations. Nor are there any data on what investigations are conducted on their own initiative by the FIU (though these would normally happen only in collaboration with the NCA or another criminal investigation body). However, there are statistical data in the FIU's annual reports on the amounts seized that are attributed by the NCA to DAML and non-DAML SARs. Thus, the 2019 report[130] proclaims "£131,667,477 denied to criminals as a result of DAML requests (refused and granted) – up 153.66% on the previous year's £51,907,067". This rise is attributable mostly to the recently introduced Asset Freezing Orders in the Criminal Finances Act 2017. Note that these are asset *seizures*, not confiscation, so it is not clear at this point for how long the (variable) period of 'denial' to suspected offenders may be. Proper interpretation of such data requires analysis of the attrition between the alleged predicate crimes, SARs, seizures confiscation orders and actual confiscation. We can expect this to vary over time and between jurisdictions.

3. Communications to Law Enforcement Authorities

Statistics on the number of communications by the FIU to other authorities are not normally provided, but the FATF Mutual Evaluation Report has generated the data, at least for recent years.

V. DATA FLOW AND DATA PROTECTION

A. DATA EXCHANGE BETWEEN FIU AND PRIVATE SECTOR

1. From FIU to Private Sector

The FIU does not provide data to the private sector in a regular streamlined manner other than, to a deeply anonymised degree, through the annual reports. Feedback is

130 P.4.

provided generally, for example, through seminars and industry communications (e.g. typologies, how to structure SARs better, what level of detail to provide); it is not case-specific, at least in a formal sense. The FIU will not tell the obliged entity what the outcome of an SAR is and whether it provided helpful investigative leads, although if further cooperation from the obliged entity is required on the SAR, the obliged entity may eventually learn about any potential investigation.

Established in 2015 to complement the SAR framework, the JMLIT is a partnership between law enforcement and the financial sector to exchange and analyse information relating to money laundering and wider economic threats. The JMLIT consists of:

- over 40 financial institutions;
- the FCA;
- CIFAS;[131] and
- five law-enforcement agencies: the NCA, HMRC, the SFO, the City of London Police, and the Metropolitan Police Service.[132]

The JMLIT is not used to get feedback on specific SARs as it is a separate process and the FIU is not central to it. The JMLIT is a forum used to share information on new typologies, existing vulnerabilities and live tactical intelligence. The way it works, when it comes to sharing intelligence, is as follows. The authorities, e.g. the NCA, HRMC or SFO, provide leads, from investigations they are working on, to the representatives of the financial institutions that are members of the JMLIT. They, in turn, then search their internal systems to check for any exposure to the subjects of these investigations (e.g. as clients or counterparties in transactions) and provide the results back to the authorities through the JMLIT. Those security-vetted bank staff that are part of the JMLIT can get limited feedback, in certain circumstances (e.g. if it comes to issuing a freezing order) where they are working on a joint investigation, but that information is classified and is not more widely distributed.

2. *From Private Sector to FIU*

In terms of personal data, there is no limit as to what and how much information is provided by the obliged entity to the FIU, as long as this is for financial crime prevention purposes and the data are relevant to the suspicious

131 CIFAS is a fraud prevention service in the UK. It is a not-for-profit membership association representing organisations from across the public, private and voluntary sectors. See https://www.cifas.org.uk.

132 See https://nationalcrimeagency.gov.uk/what-we-do/national-economic-crime-centre.

(or suspected) activity.[133] One of the FATF-praised initiatives of the JMLIT process is to generate "super-SARs" (this is just borrowing the term, but these are separate to the SAR process as explained above), which combine data from several institutions, and this approach is expected to expand using the gateway provisions.

B. DATA EXCHANGE BETWEEN FIU AND CRIMINAL JUSTICE SYSTEM

1. *From FIU to Criminal Justice System*

The ELMER database of SARs is available to authorised financial investigators only. Their access to it is tracked and they cannot pass on information without the permission of the FIU.

2. *From Criminal Justice System to FIU*

If an SAR has resulted in prosecution, a prosecutor may of their own initiative provide information to the FIU to the extent that it helps the FIU search its database for further SARs relevant to the case, for proceeds of crime confiscation and possibly for evidential purposes. In this regard there is no limit from a data protection perspective. Prosecutors apply a seriousness threshold when deciding whether to pursue a case. As the CPS's website explains: "A money laundering charge ought to be considered where the proceeds are more than *de minimis* in any circumstances where the defendant who is charged with the underlying offence has done more than simply consume his proceeds of crime." However, this consideration plainly does not result in the vast number of prosecutions that it theoretically might do.

According to the 2019 amendments to the Money Laundering Regulations, where the NCA has, in its performance of FIU functions, disseminated any information to a United Kingdom competent authority, that authority must, upon request, provide a report to the NCA about its use of that information, including the outcome of any investigations or inspections conducted on the basis of that information.

The FIU has direct access to NCA databases and national databases such as the PNC and the Police National Database (PND).[134] They would access local data on request using S7 of the Crime and Courts Act 2013.

---

133 There may be client privilege limitations, but that is different from personal data limits. With regard to the FIU requesting data, this can only happen as a follow-up to an SAR, not prior to an SAR. The FIU does not have investigative authority in that sense. But another body can request information, for instance the FCA, the NCA (where the FIU sits), the SFO, etc.

134 The PNC and PND are currently in the process of being merged into the Law Enforcement Data Service. See Home Office, "National Law Enforcement Data Programme.

C. DATA EXCHANGE BETWEEN FIU AND INTELLIGENCE AGENCIES

1. *From FIU to Intelligence Agencies*

There is no limit to information passing to intelligence agencies from the FIU, except where authorisation requirements from third parties exist (see also section IV.D.2). Terrorist financing SARs are dealt with separately from the main body, and though there can be an overlap when terrorists are involved in organised crime to finance their activities, this could be searched by a nominal search from authorised financial investigators, who could then share the data with intelligence agencies via their Memorandum of Understanding (MOU) or established gateways. In the event the FIU has received information from a foreign FIU, this information can be passed on only with the foreign FIU's consent.

2. *From Intelligence Agencies to FIU*

An intelligence agency may provide very limited information to the FIU to the extent that it helps the FIU search its database for further SARs relevant to the intelligence development. It may also provide information to the FIU against targets, though it is not obvious how informing the FIU would assist: disruption would involve other enforcement agencies rather than the FIU. In that sense there is no limit. However, the principal exchanges are with the National Terrorist Financial Investigation Unit (NTFIU), part of the Metropolitan Police Counter Terrorist Command. (The UK's FIU proactively disseminates terrorism-related SARs to the NTFIU and the Counter Terrorism Unit network).

The agencies are specifically excluded from the gateway provisions of S7 of the Crime and Courts Act 2013 (ss2). Therefore, if the FIU needs information from an intelligence agency, this would have to be on a specific request and done through the gateways available to the intelligence agencies under their own legislation and procedures regarding security clearances.

According to the 2019 amendments to the Money Laundering Regulations, where the NCA has, in its performance of FIU functions, disseminated any information to a United Kingdom competent authority, that authority must, upon request, provide a report to the NCA about its use of that information, including the outcome of any investigations or inspections conducted on the basis of that information. However, it is unclear yet whether and how this will apply to intelligence agencies.

Law Enforcement Data Service (LEDS) – Privacy Impact Assessment Report", July 2018, https://assets.publishing.service.gov.uk/government/uploads/system/uploads/attachment_data/file/721542/NLEDP_Privacy_Impact_Assessment_Report.pdf.

D. DATA EXCHANGE BETWEEN FIU AND TAX AUTHORITIES

1. *From FIU to Tax Authorities*

As discussed above, HMRC has direct access to the FIU's data (except for certain sensitive categories such as terrorist financing data).

2. *From Tax Authorities to FIU*

HMRC will provide information to the FIU to the extent that it helps the FIU search its database for further SARs relevant to HMRC's case. However, there has been criticism of past unwillingness of HMRC to pass on information to the FIU or to the intelligence agencies about tax suspects later demonstrated to have terrorist connections.[135] Such issues need to be understood in the context of organisational culture rather than purely in terms of legal gateways.

Further, as per the FATF's UK Mutual Evaluation Report, "HMRC databases, including the register of trusts with UK tax consequences (Trust Registration Service), tax information, and information on UK citizens with overseas bank accounts may be accessed directly by the HMRC's law enforcement arm and are available to other LEAs [law enforcement agencies] upon request."[136] There are dedicated HMRC officers seconded to the FIU to manage this process, but they only have indirect access to the FIU.

The Mutual Evaluation Report also states on cash declarations:

> Criterion 32.6 – Cross-border cash declarations which are reported to HMRC are provided to the NCA on a monthly basis under an MOU between the agencies which has been in place since 22 January 2018, with the first exchange of information under the MOU in February 2018. This information can then be provided to the UKFIU, but there are limitations as to what data can be stored in line with the Operating Procedure for dealing with Bulk Personal Data. This data can also be accessed by HMRC secondees to the UKFIU.[137]

According to the 2019 amendments to the Money Laundering Regulations, where the NCA has, in its performance of FIU functions, disseminated any information to a United Kingdom competent authority, that authority must, upon request, provide a report to the NCA about its use of that information, including the outcome of any investigations or inspections conducted on the basis of that information.

---

135 "Sunbed boss 'linked to £8bn fraud that helped bin Laden'", Sunday Times, 14 April 2019. https://www.thetimes.co.uk/article/sunbed-boss-linked-to-8bn-fraud-that-helped-bin-laden-kkldskl8r.

136 FATF, *Mutual Evaluation Report – UK*, 2018, p. 44.

137 *Ibid.*, p. XX.

E. DATA EXCHANGE BETWEEN FIU AND CUSTOMS AUTHORITIES

1. *From FIU to Customs Authorities*

This is explained in section V.D.1 above (note that customs is part of HMRC, which is also the UK's tax authority).

2. *From Customs Authorities to FIU*

The customs authorities will provide information to the FIU to the extent that it helps the FIU search its database for further SARs relevant to HMRC's case.

According to the 2019 amendments to the Money Laundering Regulations, where the NCA has, in its performance of FIU functions, disseminated any information to a United Kingdom competent authority, that authority must, upon request, provide a report to the NCA about its use of that information, including the outcome of any investigations or inspections conducted on the basis of that information.

F. INFORMATION FLOW BETWEEN FIU AND FOREIGN COUNTERPARTS

If there is a Memorandum of Association (which typically is put in place in accordance with the Egmont Group's standards), the UK's FIU can share information with foreign FIUs, including personal data, to the extent this is relevant to preventing and disrupting crime.

The UK Mutual Evaluation Report noted that:

> 494. The UK generally has good access to basic and BO information ... and can provide this information to foreign jurisdictions in a timely manner upon request. However, foreign LEAs may be directed to the public PSC register for BO information, whereas UK LEAs would typically corroborate this information with BO information from financial institutions and DNFBPs where available ... Where the information is not available from the PSC register, the UK can provide assistance using other sources ...
>
> 495. The UK authorities advised that foreign requests for basic and BO information on legal persons/arrangements are common. Where relevant, the UKFIU and certain LEAs will direct requests for information on legal persons to the public PSC register. In doing so, the requesting agency is not advised that to obtain *verified* BO information it is necessary to seek such information from the relevant FI or DNFBP via a request for formal or informal co-operation. This may result in authorities relying on unverified information (see Chapter 7 on IO.5).

> 496. Where the requested information is not publicly available on the PSC register, it can be obtained through a request to Companies House (for information on legal persons), to HMRC (for information on trusts), or to the relevant LEA (for information held by FIs or DNFBPs where available). These requests can generally be answered in a timely fashion, with non-urgent requests to Companies House and financial institutions typically receiving a response within two weeks.

In 2016 the UK entered into an agreement with three Crown Dependencies and six Overseas Territories with financial centres to enhance the sharing of company beneficial ownership information on a bilateral basis. The Crown Dependencies and Overseas Territories agreed to provide LEAs, including tax authorities, with beneficial ownership information of companies registered in their jurisdiction within 24 hours (or, where urgent, within an hour).[138]

To set the information rules to and from the UK in context, excluding general and informal requests, the inwards and outwards data flow is captured in the following UK FIU data,[139] over half of which may be reduced post-Brexit unless it is re-routed via the Egmont Group and CARIN.[140]

Table 3. Number of financial intelligence requests received and made by the UK FIU, 2018–19 (2017–18 data in brackets)

	Number of financial intelligence requests received	Number of financial intelligence requests made by UK's FIU
Egmont network	1,132 (742)	1,147 (665)
FIU.Net network (EU)	234 (472)	114 (544)
ARO network	244 (224)	227 (311)
CARIN network	29 (17)	30 (39)
Total	**1,639 (1,455)**	**1,518 (1,559)**
Intelligence reports spontaneously received from overseas		1,295 (1,621)
Intelligence spontaneously disseminated (excluding Europol)		399 (470)
Intelligence spontaneously disseminated to Europol		365 (204)

Source: National Crime Agency.

---

138 Home Office, *Statutory review of the implementation of the exchange of notes on beneficial ownership between the united kingdom, crown dependencies and overseas territories*, United Kingdom, June 2019, https://assets.publishing.service.gov.uk/government/uploads/system/uploads/attachment_data/file/812355/Statutory_review_of_the_exchange_of_notes_arrangements.pdf. For a later ministerial statement, see HLWS361 (15 July 2020), https://www.parliament.uk/business/publications/written-questions-answers-statements/written-statement/Lords/2020-07-15/HLWS361/.

139 *Suspicious Activity Reports (SARs) Annual Report 2019*, p. 6. *Suspicious Activity Reports (SARs) Annual Report 2018*, p. 4.

140 The ARO network, which is within the EU, and the CARIN network, which is worldwide but has Europol as its secretariat, are networks (both mentioned in the table) of asset recovery

According to the 2019 amendments to the Money Laundering Regulations:

3. The NCA must take such steps as it considers appropriate to co-operate with foreign FIUs in their performance of FIU functions.

Provision of information in response to external requests

4. In response to an external request, the NCA must (subject to paragraph 10) provide promptly any relevant information in the NCA's possession.

5. Where an external request is received and the NCA does not possess information which the NCA considers relevant to the external request, and it suspects a relevant person possesses such information, the NCA-

a) may exercise its powers under Parts 7(3) and 8(4) (investigations) of the 2002 Act, any orders made under section 445(5) (external investigations) of that Act, or Part 3 of the 2000 Act(6), as applicable, to seek an order for information from such person, and
b) must (subject to paragraph 10 [see restrictions below]) provide any relevant information received in consequence of any such order promptly to the foreign FIU concerned.

6. The NCA must designate at least one point of contact with responsibility for receiving external requests.

7. Where the NCA has provided relevant information to a foreign FIU, and that foreign FIU makes a request for consent to disseminate some or all of the relevant information to a foreign competent authority, the NCA must (subject to paragraph 11 [see restrictions below]) consent to the dissemination of as much of the requested information as possible and communicate its consent promptly to the foreign FIU.

8. Where the NCA provides relevant information in response to an external request in accordance with this Schedule, the NCA shall take such steps as it considers appropriate to ensure that such information is transmitted securely.

The 2019 amended regulations include these conditions and restrictions on provision or further dissemination of relevant information:

9. The NCA may impose such restrictions and conditions on the use of relevant information provided in response to an external request as the NCA considers appropriate.

10. Where an obligation arises under this Schedule for the NCA to provide relevant information in response to an external request, the NCA may decide not to provide some or all of the information where and to the extent that the NCA considers that doing so could be contrary to national law.

---

offices (see https://eucrim.eu/articles/asset-recovery-uncac-convention-possibilities-and-limitations/). As such, it would appear safe to assume that the numbers relating to the Egmont network and the FIU.Net network are FIU-to-FIU requests, while the rest are not necessarily.

11. The NCA is not required to comply with the duty to give consent to the dissemination of information to a foreign competent authority under paragraph 7 if and to the extent that the NCA considers that the giving of such consent could—

(a) prejudice an investigation, whether into a criminal cause or matter or in relation to any investigation referred to in section 341 (investigations) of the 2002 Act(7) or to which Schedule 5A (terrorist financing investigations) to the 2000 Act(8) applies; or
(b) be contrary to national law.

12. The NCA must have particular regard—

(a) where making a decision under paragraph 10, to the need for as unfettered an exchange of relevant information in response to external requests as possible, or
(b) where making a decision under paragraph 11, to the need for as unfettered dissemination of information as possible by a foreign FIU to foreign competent authorities, in order for the foreign FIU concerned to carry out FIU functions efficiently and effectively.

1. Restrictions on Data Transfer from FIU to Foreign FIUs

See previous section. The DPA18 covers the processing of personal data:

- within and outside the scope of the GDPR;
- by competent authorities for law enforcement purposes; and
- by the intelligence services.

Personal data can only be transferred outside the EEA if adequate protections are in place (e.g. contractual clauses) or if the country to which the data is being transferred is deemed "adequate".

On the above basis, in terms of data protection, different requirements will apply depending on whether the foreign FIU is in the EU or outside the EU. Because within the EU the authorities will have to apply EU data protection legislation (the GDPR), EU FIUs and other relevant bodies (including Europol) are considered to adhere to an equivalent standard.[141] Exchanging information with a non-EU FIU is more challenging. But ultimately, the flow of

[141] FIU.Net became operational in 2002 (under Council Decision 2000/642/JHA). In January 2016, FIU.Net was incorporated into Europol. Article 5.4 of the aforementioned Decision stipulates that FIUs "shall undertake all necessary measures, including security measures, to ensure that information submitted under this Decision is not accessible by any other authorities, agencies or departments" than those it is intended for. The extent to which FIU. Net will become a truly fluid pan-EU financial intelligence facility is not currently known. It is doubtful that this UK access will survive Brexit.

information will depend on whether there is a signed MOU and what its terms are. The Egmont Group is attempting to develop inter-FIU SARs sharing on an international basis.

According to section 10(5) DPA18, processing personal data relating to criminal convictions and offences must meet certain conditions, such as the processing being necessary to make a disclosure in good faith under section 339ZB POCA, to detect or prevent illegal acts (paragraph 10, Schedule 1 DPA18), or to comply with or assist others to comply with a regulatory requirement that involves taking steps to establish whether a person has committed an illegal act (paragraph 12, Schedule 1 DPA18).

2. *Restrictions on Use of Data Obtained from Foreign FIUs*

As explained above, the general data protection and privacy laws apply. It will also depend on the relationship between the two countries (e.g. within or outside the EU, as explained above) and whether there is a MOU and its terms.

According to the amended Money Laundering Regulations of 2019, where the NCA receives information from a foreign FIU, the NCA must:

(a) use the information only for the purpose for which it was sought or provided, unless it has obtained the prior consent of the foreign FIU to any other use of the information;
(b) comply with any restrictions or conditions of use which have been imposed by the foreign FIU in respect of the information; and
(c) obtain the prior consent of the foreign FIU to any further dissemination of the information.

G. INFORMATION FLOW BETWEEN FIU AND FOREIGN NON-COUNTERPARTS

1. *Restrictions on Data Transfer from FIU to Other Foreign Authorities*

Typically transfer of data to other foreign authorities, i.e. non FIUs, is done via the respective national FIU. The FIU will exchange information with a counterpart, i.e. a FIU, abroad, based on a MOU. The counterpart abroad can only pass on data to another authority within the same jurisdiction upon the UK FIU's consent. As Table 5 indicates, there may be also transfer of data to non-FIU bodies, for instance the ARO or CARIN network. There are no restrictions if this transfer is done to detect or prevent crime (see section 1 above).

2. *Restrictions on Use of Data Obtained from Other Foreign Authorities*

The situation is similar to that explained in section V.F.1. above. There are no restrictions if the foreign authorities have given the FIU consent to pass the data onto other bodies and this is necessary to detect or prevent crime (see section 1 above).

H. EVIDENTIAL VALUE OF FIU-GENERATED DATA IN COURT PROCEEDINGS

SAR data, generally, cannot be used directly in court proceedings as that would mean disclosing the source of information. In a 2018 case, for the first time, courts allowed the subject of an SAR to see the SAR. This was in *Lonsdale v National Westminster Bank.*[142] David Lonsdale, a barrister, told the media that he had seen the SARs following the court decision, but that the terms of the settlement meant he could not say what they contained. He further stated:

> Money coming into my bank accounts came from transparent and lawful sources, that is to say my rental property and my practice at the Bar. The bank was perfectly well aware of the source of this money. The bank never sought to provide any justification for freezing my accounts and writing to the NCA. It just relied upon a claim that it suspected that money was the proceeds of crime but could not tell me why as this was all 'confidential'.[143]

However, SARs are used for investigative leads and to that extent, indirectly, they can contribute to court proceedings. The UK court disclosure rules require that undisclosed material which contributes to the case must be disclosed to the defence to allow them to develop a defence based not only on the prosecution (or civil plaintiff) case. However, as the SARs, as financial intelligence, are essentially leads, it is the material discovered based on these leads that is disclosed: otherwise the SARs themselves would be disclosed, which is contrary to policy.

The FIU seldom develops its own investigations, and approved financial investigators do so but are attached not to the FIU but to police or other non-police enforcement agencies.

If any non-public information in an SAR is to be used, due process must be followed in order for the information to be admissible in court; for example,

---

142 [2018] EWHC 1843 (QB).

143 Neil Rose, "Barrister wins right to see reports his bank made to police", Legal Futures, 10 October 2018, https://www.legalfutures.co.uk/latest-news/barrister-wins-right-to-see-reports-his-bank-made-to-police.

the obliged entity that had made the disclosure must first provide consent and, as described above, client privileged information cannot be used; further information requests must be based on a magistrates' court order. This, however, is not yet fully tested.

I. USE OF CDD DATA FOR PROFIT MAKING

CDD data, particularly personal data, cannot be used for purposes other than stated. UK data protection laws follow EU regulations.

J. DATA SHARING BETWEEN OBLIGED ENTITIES REGARDING SARs AND FIU REQUESTS

1. Data Sharing Inside a Group

Such sharing inside a group is possible, within a GDPR framework agreement, if necessary to detect and prevent crime. It is now explicitly stated in the amended 2019 Money Laundering Regulations that a group's policies, controls and procedures for data protection and sharing information for the purposes of preventing money laundering and terrorist financing with other members of the group must include policies on the sharing of information about customers, customer accounts and transactions. This may yet give rise to problems with branches or legally separate institutions of the group in financial secrecy jurisdictions.

2. Data Sharing with Similar Professions

The Criminal Finances Act 2017 introduced important changes to the AML regime for the reporting of suspicious activity under Part 7 POCA. A change that had a significant practical impact on lawyers, estate agents and financial sector professionals is the ability for regulated persons to share information relating to a money laundering suspicion. Section 11 of the Criminal Finances Act 2017 inserted sections 339ZB–339ZG into POCA, which enable regulated persons to request and share information with their regulated peers. Any sharing of information will be voluntary. This sharing is relevant to the SAR process to the extent that it can help improve the quality of SARs, as financial institutions can build more clarity around certain events by communicating with each other.[144]

---

144 Obliged entities from the same group can also share intelligence for financial crime prevention purposes within a GDPR framework agreement.

Insulation from resulting claims of breach of confidence or contravention of data protection laws is ensured by section 339ZF POCA, which provides that a relevant disclosure "made in good faith" does not breach any duties of confidence or any other restriction on information disclosure. If information is shared, the new framework then contemplates a joint SAR being made. But see above regarding client privileged information. Information can only be disclosed if four key conditions are met: (a) the person making the request and the would-be discloser must be regulated;[145] (b) the information must have been obtained in the course of regulated business; (c) the FIU (which is within the NCA) must have been properly notified of the information to be disclosed; and (d) for the information to be disclosed, the would-be discloser must be satisfied that it "will or may assist in determining any matter in connection with a suspicion that a person is engaged in money laundering".[146] There are grounds for scepticism about how frequently these provisions will be used and therefore will have practical as well as symbolic importance.

As discussed previously, according to section 10(5) DPA18, the processing of personal data relating to criminal convictions and offences must meet certain conditions: these include the processing being necessary to make a disclosure in good faith under section 339ZB POCA (i.e. an obliged entity can request information about a suspect from another obliged entity), to detect or prevent crime (paragraph 10, Schedule 1 DPA18) or to comply with or assist other persons to comply with a regulatory requirement that involves taking steps to establish whether a person has committed an illegal act (paragraph 12, Schedule 1 DPA18).

Separate to the SAR process, financial institutions are allowed to share information under strict terms through the JMLIT, a private-public partnership whose members include currently over 40 financial institutions, and UK law

---

145 Intelligence can be shared in this form not only upon request but also where one obliged entity shares with another to prevent financial crime. Both must be obliged entities.

146 The threshold for the sharing of information is very low. Any number of personal details in a business's possession, such as a client's former name, family details, historical transactions or names of their business interests could well assist in determining a matter relating to a money laundering suspicion even if, in isolation, those details do not appear very useful. See the Home Office circular, "Money laundering: sharing of information within the regulated sector", https://assets.publishing.service.gov.uk/government/uploads/system/uploads/attachment_data/file/679032/HO_Circular-_Sharing_of_information_within_the_regulated_sector_1.0.pdf. In this context, in relation to point (c) we add that by sharing information, regulated entities may determine that actually there were no valid grounds for an SAR, which means that in retrospect, the FIU had been notified for no good reason (which just adds to the clutter they need to deal with). If, on the other hand, the shared information results in better analysis and a joint SAR, then that (rather than a notification based on uncertain facts) is what the FIU needs to see.

enforcement and regulatory authorities[147] (explained in earlier sections). The members of the operational group of JMLIT discuss specific investigations with the authorities that are members of the JMLIT and share intelligence with the authorities, as well as with each other, in relation to these formal investigations. The idea of the JMLIT is for member private sector organisations to follow up on law enforcement intelligence and then to report back. A private sector organisation can also provide intelligence in the first place, which is fed to the NCA and then the NCA, if appropriate, loops in the other members of the JMLIT, including private sector organisations. The information does not go outside the JMLIT except via NCA gateways. There are questions about the scalability of this process, which depends also on trust between members, but it has been heralded by the FATF and by some jurisdictions (e.g. Singapore and Hong Kong).

3. *Data Sharing with Obliged Entities Outside the EU*

The above-discussed data sharing provisions (see section 2 above) apply to entities that are AML-regulated in the UK. Data relating to SARs cannot be shared with entities in other countries unless they are part of the same organisation – a group – and data are shared for the purposes of crime prevention and detection (UK-headquartered obliged entities are expected to have a group-wide compliance programme, although this does not necessarily mean that identical processes are applied everywhere). However, even in this instance, the organisation must adhere to data protection laws. This means that while within the EU there are shared GDPR standards, outside of the EU data can be shared only with parts of the organisation that are in GDPR-equivalent jurisdictions within a GDPR framework agreement.

K. DATA SHARING BETWEEN OBLIGED ENTITIES REGARDING POSSIBLE CASES OF MONEY LAUNDERING

See section V.J.2 above. As explained in the previous sections, even if an SAR has not been filed yet, group entities can share information about suspected financial crime, as relevant, but under a GDPR framework agreement.

L. DATA MINING BY OBLIGED ENTITIES

Data mining in the sense of "profiling" can be done for the purposes of financial crime prevention, as appropriate, with consideration for data protection and privacy laws.

[147] https://www.nationalcrimeagency.gov.uk/what-we-do/national-economic-crime-centre.

GDPR has been transposed into UK legislation. According to the Data Protection Act 2018, Schedule 2 "Exemptions etc from the GDPR", Part 1":

> Crime and taxation: general
>
> 2(1) The listed GDPR provisions and Article 34(1) and (4) of the GDPR (communication of personal data breach to the data subject) do not apply to personal data processed for any of the following purposes—
>
> (a) the prevention or detection of crime,
> (b) the apprehension or prosecution of offenders, or
> (c) the assessment or collection of a tax or duty or an imposition of a similar nature,
> to the extent that the application of those provisions would be likely to prejudice any of the matters mentioned in paragraphs (a) to (c).

VI. BENEFICIAL OWNERSHIP TRANSPARENCY

A. BENEFICIAL OWNERSHIP INFORMATION

1. *General Framework*

The Companies Act 2006, the People with Significant Control Regulations 2016 and Parts 5 and 6 of the Money Laundering Regulations 2019 contain provisions relating to beneficial ownership. Any entity registered in the UK must disclose its beneficial owners through documentation filed with Companies House (the UK's company registry). A beneficial owner or a Person of Significant Control (PSC)[148] is anyone in the company who meets one or more of the conditions listed in the People with Significant Control Regulations 2016, which applies to registered and unregistered companies, societates Europaeae, limited liability partnerships and eligible Scottish partnerships (Scottish limited partnerships and Scottish qualifying partnerships).[149] A company can have more than one beneficial owner.

Once a company has identified its PSCs, it needs to record their details in its own PSC register and inform Companies House.[150]

---

148 The definitions of beneficial owner in the ML Regulations and of PSC do not overlap word for word and different tests might apply, despite the government using "the existing definition of 'beneficial ownership' … as the basis for our statutory definition of a PSC" (see https://assets.publishing.service.gov.uk/government/uploads/system/uploads/attachment_data/file/395478/bis-14-1145-the-register-of-people-with-significant-control-psc-register-register-final-1.pdf).

149 Department for Business, Energy and Industrial Strategy, "Register of People with Significant Control", June 2017, https://assets.publishing.service.gov.uk/government/uploads/system/uploads/attachment_data/file/753027/170623_NONSTAT_GU__1_.pdf.

150 Companies to which Chapter 5 of the FCA's Disclosure and Transparency Rules (DTR5) applies are subject to these requirements, as DTR5 (which deals with disclosure of voting rights) already requires disclosure of major shareholdings to the market, including interests that are held indirectly. UK-incorporated companies with shares listed in London or another

The information it must obtain, confirm and enter in the company's own PSC register will depend on whether the PSC is a person or a registrable relevant legal entity (RLE). Where it is a RLE within the PSC regime, other than the RLE's ownership, there is no need for the entire ownership chain to be reflected in files as the RLE's ownership should be reflected in the RLE's own PSC statement. Where the legal entity is outside the PSC regime (e.g. registered offshore), then its ultimate ownership must be reflected in the subject company's PSC register.

If, for some reason, the PSC information cannot be provided, other statements will need to be made instead to explain why the PSC information is not available. The register can never be blank.

Information on the company's register and on the PSC register at Companies House must be kept up to date. New information must be entered onto the register within 14 days.

2. *Definition of "Beneficiary" and "Effective Control"*

The definition of ultimate beneficial owner/PSC is based on the EU directives. A beneficial owner in the context of PSC[151] is a person who:

- holds, directly or indirectly, more than 25% of the shares;
- holds, directly or indirectly, more than 25% of the voting rights;
- holds the right, directly or indirectly, to appoint or remove a majority of directors;
- otherwise has the right to exercise, or actually exercises, significant influence or control over the company; or
- has the right to exercise, or actually exercises, significant influence or control over the activities of a trust or firm which is not a legal person, the trustees or members of which would satisfy any of the four conditions above.

Most small companies' PSCs are likely to fall into the first and second, and possibly the third, categories above. The fourth and fifth categories are typically associated with more complex corporate structures.

EEA regulated market or on specified markets in Switzerland, the USA, Japan and Israel are exempt since they already have to disclose detailed ownership information under the EU Transparency Directive or similar transparency rules. However, all other UK-incorporated companies (including UK-incorporated subsidiaries of UK Main Market and AIM companies) will be required to maintain a PSC register.

151 ML Regulations – "beneficial owner" of a non-listed corporate means: (a) any individual who exercises ultimate control over the management of the body corporate; (b) any individual who ultimately owns or controls (in each case whether directly or indirectly), including through bearer share holdings or by other means, more than 25% of the shares or voting rights in the body corporate; or (c) an individual who controls the body corporate.

3. *Definition of "Information"*

"Information" in the sense of "personal data" – considering Regulation (EC) No 45/2001 – is defined in data protection legislation as any information relating to an identified or identifiable natural person.

4. *Special Rules for Entities with a Cross-Border Dimension*

Entities may be able to share information between branches in different countries, subject to data protection laws that may inhibit this. There are no special rules, since the UK cannot force companies to break the secrecy laws in their other places of business. This can be a source of tension.

B. BENEFICIAL OWNERSHIP REGISTRIES

1. *Scope and General Procedure*

Companies registered in the UK are required to disclose their beneficial ownership through a centralised government company registry, Companies House.

2. Ex Ante *Verification of Accuracy*

The information is entered into the company registry based on documents provided by the company. The information entered is checked against the original documents and companies are required to provide accurate information. The Companies Act 2006 sets out the criminal offence of providing false information on the company register. In 2018, the first company director was successfully prosecuted for falsifying company information under this law. He was ordered to pay over £12,000 after he pleaded guilty to filing false information on the UK's company register.[152] However, this prosecution attracted severe criticism because the person convicted was aiming to expose the absurdity of the lack of controls over the quality of filing information.

Late filing penalties were introduced in 1992 to encourage directors of companies to file their accounts and reports on time, because this information is

---

[152] Companies House Press Release, "UK's 'first ever' successful prosecution for false company information", 23 March 2018, https://www.gov.uk/government/news/uks-first-ever-successful-prosecution-for-false-company-information.

required for the public record. All companies – private or public, large or small, trading or non-trading – must send their accounts and reports to Companies House every year. If company accounts and reports are submitted late, the law imposes an automatic penalty. The period allowed for filing a company's accounts depends on whether the company is filing its first accounts since incorporation or subsequent accounts.[153]

Failure to file confirmation statements, annual returns or accounts is a criminal offence that can result in directors being fined personally in the criminal courts. Failure to pay the late filing penalty can result in enforcement proceedings. Any criminal proceedings taken as a result of non-filing of confirmation statements, annual returns or accounts is separate from, and in addition to, any late filing penalty imposed against the company for filing accounts late. There is no late filing penalty imposed on confirmation statements or annual returns that have been filed late. The registrar may also take steps to strike the company off the public record if these documents are delivered late.[154]

However, the company registry does not vet or verify that the individuals identified as owners in the company's documentation are indeed its true owners. Though the study is now a decade old, in 2008, an independent study found that a large number of individuals featuring as company directors in the UK were disqualified directors or linked to risk in some other way.[155] Government decisions are awaited but in May 2019, the *Financial Times* reported that:

> the UK is planning the biggest overhaul of its official corporate register in 170 years following criticism that it is being used by criminals around the world to launder ill gotten gains through shell companies. Companies House is to be given more power to check information and the identities of people setting up businesses, as well as the individuals who control them.[156]

---

153 https://www.gov.uk/government/publications/late-filing-penalties/late-filing-penalties. In 2014/15, the number of penalties issued in England and Wales stood at 165,000, with a total value of around £78 million. However, in 2017/18 the number had reached 204,000. with a cost to businesses of around £87m. See James Bunney, "Late filing of annual accounts up 23% since 2014", Accountancy Daily, 26 September 2018, https://www.accountancydaily.co/late-filing-annual-accounts-23-2014.

154 https://www.gov.uk/government/publications/late-filing-penalties/late-filing-penalties.

155 Antony Savvas, "UK Companies House register contains 3,994 high-risk individuals, Datanomic finds", Computer Weekly, 21 February 2008, https://www.computerweekly.com/news/2240085116/UK-Companies-House-register-contains-3994-high-risk-individuals-Datanomic-finds.

156 "Companies House faces biggest overhaul in 170 years", Financial Times, https://www.ft.com/content/f4ade274-6dc6-11e9-a9a5-351eeaef6d84. See for proposals, https://www.gov.uk/government/consultations/corporate-transparency-and-register-reform. We note that even if extra powers to check data are granted, this will have a modest effect (other than possible deterrence) unless staffing resources exist to conduct the checks and amend the Register.

3. Ex Post *Review of Accuracy*

See comments in the previous section. Global Witness has reviewed the data and concluded:[157]

- Almost 3,000 companies listed their beneficial owner as a company with a tax haven address – something that is not allowed under the rules. There are problems with how the data has been inputted. For example, you can write anything in the nationality field and we found over 500 ways of putting 'British', including ten people who wrote 'Cornish'.
- 76 beneficial owners share the same name and birthday as someone on the U.S. sanctions list. We have to do more digging to find out whether these are actually the same people, but it's an insight into what is possible with this new information.
- Most beneficial owners are from the UK, followed by a number from other European countries and India and China.

According to 2019 amendments to the Money Laundering Regulations, obliged entities must report to the company registry discrepancies they see between beneficial ownership information available to them and company registry records. How active they are required to be in seeking out potential discrepancies is not yet resolved. See also section I.B.

C. ACCESS TO BENEFICIAL OWNERSHIP INFORMATION

1. *Access by FIU and Other Authorities*

The information filed with Companies House is a matter of public record. All information that appears on the register can be accessed by the public. In 2016 the UK, three Crown Dependencies and six British Overseas Territories committed to enhance the effectiveness of sharing company beneficial ownership information on a bilateral basis between the UK and the Crown Dependencies and major Overseas Territories. They agreed to provide law enforcement agencies with this information on request for companies (also referred to in the agreements as "corporate and legal entities") incorporated in their respective jurisdictions. These arrangements were called the Exchange of Notes (EoN) for Information Sharing and came into force on 1 July 2017.

---

157 Robert Palmer and Sam Leon, "What does the UK beneficial ownership data show us?", Global Witness blog, 22 November 2016, https://www.globalwitness.org/en/blog/what-does-uk-beneficial-ownership-data-show-us/.

A Statutory Review was required by section 445A POCA, as amended by section 9 of the Criminal Finances Act 2017, to assess the effectiveness of the arrangements. It covers the period from 1 July 2017 to 31 December 2018.[158]

The key findings of this Review are:

- UK Law Enforcement Agencies (LEAs) report that the EoN has been extremely useful in accessing the information needed to support ongoing investigations.
- This process gives UK LEAs rapid access to beneficial ownership information on over half a million entities based in the 3 CDs and 6 participating OTs. This represents 87% of businesses in scope of the scheme. Plans are in place for this to reach 100% by December 2020. In addition, these jurisdictions have reciprocal access to information on 3.8 million UK entities through the UK's People with Significant Control public register.
- During the first 18 months of operation, 296 requests were made. Nearly all of these were originated by UK law enforcement agencies and 118 asked for multiple pieces of information in a single request. This equates on average to nearly 4 requests per week. Responses were provided for all requests made and all but 4 were provided within the agreed time frame.

2. *Access by Obliged Entities*

Companies must identify the PSCs and record their details with Companies House. As per Companies House's website, a PSC is someone who owns or controls the company, also called "beneficial owners". More specifically, as explained on the website of Companies House:

> A PSC must meet one or more of the following conditions of control.
>
> Most PSCs are likely to be people who hold:
>
> - more than 25% of shares in the company
> - more than 25% of voting rights in the company
> - the right to appoint or remove the majority of the board of directors
>
> If a PSC holds more than 25% of shares, they are likely to hold the same amount of voting rights. …
>
> Your PSC might influence or control your company through other means. This could be directly, or on behalf of someone else. For example, someone who tells the directors or shareholders what to do.[159]

---

158 *Statutory review of the implementation of the exchange of notes on beneficial ownership between the United Kingdom, Crown Dependencies and Overseas Territories*, 2019.

159 Companies House, "People with significant control (PSC): who controls your company?", 20 February 2018, https://www.gov.uk/government/news/people-with-significant-control-psc-who-controls-your-company.

This information is filed with Companies House and is accessible to the public, including obliged entities. The register for trusts is not public (see also section I.B. Beneficial Ownership Register).

3. Access by Interested Third Parties

As stated above, the Beneficial Owners Register is a public one and is thus accessible to all. The register for trusts is not public (see also section I.B. Beneficial Ownership Register).

D. NON-FINANCIAL BENEFICIAL OWNERSHIP REGISTRIES

Regulated entities must collect KYC data including beneficial ownership of property. But the KYC records held will not themselves be public (although the data may well have been retrieved from public sources like Land Registry). The Land Registry contains information on real estate ownership but if a property is owned by a company, as opposed to being owned directly by individuals, the beneficial ownership is not disclosed in records held by the Land Registry. Currently the UK authorities are taking steps to introduce more transparency in this regard in the property sector. Bank vault storage is also subject to KYC, and this will be strengthened by the 5AMLD implementation.

VII. SANCTIONS

A. SANCTIONS FOR MONEY LAUNDERING

1. Requirement of a Conviction for a Predicate Offence

There can be a standalone prosecution and conviction for money laundering as long as there is at least circumstantial evidence, i.e. it can be inferred (e.g. from the suspect's lifestyle) that the subject of laundering is a benefit derived through criminal conduct. This is set out also in the UK Mutual Evaluation Report 2018, though the report notes that it could not separate out the statistics of standalone cases from those where money laundering is the principal charge (i.e. cases where the launderer is different from the predicate offender).[160] Moreover, based

160 The MER states: "UK authorities demonstrated their ability to prosecute and obtain convictions for a full range of ML cases, including stand-alone and self-laundering, third-party laundering and the laundering of foreign predicates." But, according to the report, statistics provided by the UK authorities cannot be disaggregated based on the type of ML pursued.

on the case cited in the MER as an example of a standalone prosecution, it is difficult to assess to what extent law enforcement bodies and prosecutors actually benefit from the standalone prosecution provision.[161] The MER also notes that there are as of yet no statistics on high-end money laundering prosecution and convictions, although the number of ongoing investigations is "positive".

2. *Forms of Sanctions*

Under POCA (sections 327–329), the three principal money laundering offences (the concealing offence, the arranging offence, and the acquisition, use and possession offence) are very serious, carrying a maximum of 14 years' imprisonment and/or an unlimited fine (POCA, section 334):

(a) on summary conviction, to imprisonment for a term not exceeding six months or to a fine not exceeding the statutory maximum or to both, or
(b) on conviction on indictment, to imprisonment for a term not exceeding 14 years or to a fine or to both.

For the ancillary offences of tipping off and failure to disclose (sections 330–332 of POCA) a person is liable (section 334 of POCA):

(a) on summary conviction, to imprisonment for a term not exceeding six months or to a fine not exceeding the statutory maximum or to both, or
(b) on conviction on indictment, to imprisonment for a term not exceeding five years or to a fine or to both.

The principal money laundering offences potentially carry heavier penalties than most predicate offences. Theft, for instance, carries seven years.

The Money Laundering Guideline issued by the Sentencing Council for England and Wales[162] covers three offences with the same statutory maximum of 14 years' custody. The lowest volume of the three offences (the "arrangements" offence) showed no clear trend in volumes over the period 2006–2015 (see Figure 1), with 190 offenders sentenced in 2015. The offence of "concealment"

161 "The defendant in this case, Katchi, was a collector for an organised criminal group operating throughout the UK. During a traffic stop, Katchi was found to be in possession of large amounts of cash, with further quantities found at his residence upon a search. Katchi was charged with two counts of ML, and received a sentence of six years' imprisonment." FATF, *Mutual Evaluation Report – UK*, 2018, p. 67.

162 Sentencing Council, *Assessing the impact of the Sentencing Council's Fraud, Bribery and Money Laundering Definitive Guideline*, 2018, pp. 15–16. According to the Coroners and Justice Act 2009, a court must follow any relevant sentencing guidelines, unless it is contrary to the interests of justice to do so. The newly created Scottish Sentencing Council has not yet developed such guidance.

saw a gradual increase, reaching 530 offenders sentenced in 2015. Volumes for the offence of "acquisition" increased to 780 offenders sentenced in 2010, but then dropped sharply in 2013, with 550 offenders sentenced in 2015.

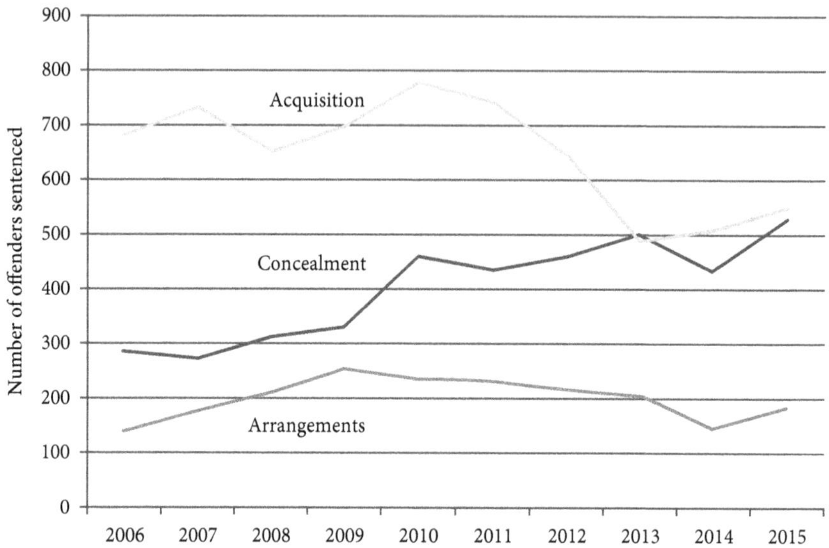

Figure 1. Adult offenders sentenced for money laundering offences, 2006–2015
Source: Sentencing Council, 2018, *Assessing the impact of the Sentencing Council's Fraud, Bribery and Money Laundering Definitive Guideline*, p. 6.

In terms of prosecution approaches, the CPS's website gives advice on the use of discretion, which feeds into the sentencing decisions above, because what is not prosecuted cannot be sentenced:

- A money laundering charge ought to be considered where the proceeds are more than *de minimis* in any circumstances where the defendant who is charged with the underlying offence has done more than simply consume his proceeds of crime.
- A charge under section 329 of possession of laundered proceeds, however, may not be necessary, for instance where proceeds were simply 'kept under the bed'. An application for confiscation of the actual benefit of the offence may be sufficient in those circumstances.
- Where, however, there is any significant attempt to transfer or conceal ill-gotten gains money laundering should normally be considered as an additional charge, in part because the purpose of the concealment will be to defeat or avoid prosecution and confiscation.
- A careful judgement will need to be made as to whether it is in the public interest to proceed with the money laundering offence in the event of a plea to the underlying criminality by a defendant who is also indicted for laundering his own proceeds. The prosecutor should take into account whether the laundering

> activity involves such a significant attempt to conceal ill-gotten gains that a court may consider a consecutive sentence. Prosecutors should not simply proceed with a money laundering charge in this situation to trigger the lifestyle assumptions in respect of convictions for money laundering under S.327 or S.328. To do so, for no other reason, could attract abuse of process arguments.

In 2015–16, HMRC achieved 30 convictions for POCA money laundering or money laundering-related regulatory offences, resulting in total custodial sentences of 1,033 months.[163] In the same period, using the confiscation and cash forfeiture powers in POCA, HMRC recovered £26.9 million of criminal proceeds, of which £6.5 million was associated with money laundering. In 2016–17 HMRC, achieved 42 convictions for POCA money laundering or money laundering-related offences, resulting in a sum of custodial sentences of 1,115 months. It recovered £24.9 million, of which £6.2 million was associated with money laundering.[164]

HMRC will charge up to £1,500, as well as the penalty for breaches of the Money Laundering Regulations, for failures in relation to, for example:

- CDD;
- risk assessment;
- policies, controls and procedures; or
- record keeping.

HMRC will charge up to £350, as well as the penalty, for failures to, for example:

- register;
- tell HMRC of changes to the business; or
- provide information.[165]

These penalty sums are not very substantial.

A person convicted of one of the "failure to disclose" offences (under sections 330, 331 or 332 POCA) can be subject to criminal prosecution or regulatory censure. On indictment to the Crown Court, that person would be liable to imprisonment for a term not exceeding five years or to an unlimited fine or to both.

A person guilty of an offence of tipping-off is liable following conviction on indictment to imprisonment for a term not exceeding two years and/or a fine.

---

163 This is a problematic and unilluminating way of representing penalties, as it does not tell us about their distribution, but there is no way of disentangling the official data. It is presumably aimed at producing an apparently large total amount to deter. Its impact on the potential offender population is unknown.

164 HMRC, *Report on Tackling Financial Crime in the Supervised Sectors 2015–2017*, 2018, p. 10.

165 https://www.gov.uk/guidance/money-laundering-regulations-appeals-and-penalties.

For offences committed in England and Wales on or after 12 March 2015, there is no upper limit to the fine that the magistrates can impose.

A person guilty of an offence of prejudicing an investigation is liable on conviction on indictment to a maximum prison term of five years and/or to an unlimited fine.[166]

Where the record keeping obligations under the Money Laundering Regulations are not observed, a firm or person is open to prosecution, including imprisonment for up to two years and/or a fine, or regulatory censure.

In regard to legal entities, there is a range of remedial actions and sanctions. FATF's 2018 MER states that "criminal liability and proportionate, dissuasive sanctions apply to legal persons convicted of ML, without prejudice to the criminal liability of natural persons. Legal persons are punishable by an unlimited criminal fine (POCA, ss.327–329, 334; Interpretation Act 1978, sch.1)."

FATF's 2018 MER notes: "Supervisors use a range of remedial actions to encourage compliance. The three statutory supervisors, FCA, HMRC and the Gambling Commission, have demonstrated their ability to sanction individuals in addition to corporations." For instance, the FCA has a range of remedial actions including:

a) the use of action plans;
b) attestations by firms that required improvements have been completed; and
c) early interventions using power under s.166 of the FSMA to require a firm to engage the services of Skilled Person to carry out a review and provide a report to the FCA.

FCA's sanctions include:

a) restricting or suspending a firm's business or licence on either a voluntary basis by the firm or through the use of the FCA's powers to require the business or licence restriction;
b) prohibitions, banning individuals from an industry;
c) fines and disgorgement; and
d) public censures.

However, in regard to criminal liability for legal entities there are caveats, as some industry commentators have noted.[167] The UK Government declined

166 "Money laundering under the Proceeds of Crime Act 2002 – overview", https://www.lexisnexis.com/uk/lexispsl/corporatecrime/document/391421/55KB-9471-F188-N12W-00000-00/Money_laundering_under_the_Proceeds_of_Crime_Act_2002_overview#.

167 Bright Line Law (Russel Hopkins and Olivia English), "The EU's latest money laundering directive: Does the UK comply?", Lexology, 3 December 2018, https://www.lexology.com/library/detail.aspx?g=7d1db7a3-04b5-4d25-8e6a-f29eaec24cb2.

to "opt in" to Directive (EU) 2108/1673 (the sixth AMLD) on the following basis:

> The UK's domestic legislation is already largely compliant with the Directive's measures, and in relation to the offences and sentences set out in the Directive, the UK already goes much further. Therefore, the Government decided not to opt in as we did not consider that opting in would enhance the UK approach to tackling money laundering.[168]

Although UK legislation does go further than the EU directives in many respects, that is not the case in regard to liability for legal entities; hence, we can assume, these inadequacies prompted the caveat "largely compliant" (as opposed to "fully compliant"). As explained in FATF's UK 2018 MER, in regard to small companies, shell and front companies, the authorities tend to use the Insolvency Service to wind them up but the difficulty is imposing criminal sanctions on larger corporates. As noted in the 2018 UK MER:

> Where legal persons are involved in offending, the UK will wind up shell or front companies and pursue prosecution of the natural persons or civil or regulatory actions. Complicit legal persons are investigated as part of the broader investigation, but rarely convicted. This is because the UK's ability to prosecute large legal persons for criminal ML offences under POCA and notable predicates such as fraud remains limited due to difficulties in proving criminal intent. Under the 'Identification Doctrine' established in UK case law, a criminal act can only be attributed to a legal person where the natural person committing the offence can be said to represent the "directing mind and will" of the legal person. In large companies with diffused decision-making responsibilities, proving this is extremely difficult, as was acknowledged by the NCA and the SFO. In response to this issue, the UK has made legislative changes to ease the intent requirements with respect to certain offences, including bribery and corruption and, with the enactment of the Criminal Finances Act 2017, tax evasion.

The MER also notes that: "The ability to impose effective sanctions for legal persons could not be assessed due to a lack of ML convictions in this area."[169] We add that the presence of sanctions for some legal persons does not enable us to make ready judgments about their being 'effective' or otherwise. Neither special nor general deterrence of legal persons has been adequately researched

168 "Eighth Annual Report to Parliament on the Application of Protocols 19 and 21 to the Treaty on European Union (TEU) and the Treaty on the Functioning of the Union (TFEU) in Relation to EU Justice and Home Affairs (JHA) Matters (1 December 2016–30 November 2017)", Home Office and Ministry of Justice, February 2018.

169 We note that while the MER says in one place that legal persons are "rarely convicted", elsewhere the report states that there is a lack of money laundering convictions.

scientifically, especially not in the context of large financial services firms. The Identification Doctrine gives rise to problems in fraud and corporate homicide as well as in money laundering cases.

3. *Confiscation*

The recoverable criminally derived benefit can be confiscated. Under POCA, if the court rules that the defendant has benefited from criminal conduct, the court can decide to make a confiscation order requiring the defendant to pay that amount. The UK has an *in personam* confiscation regime, and many confiscation orders are not paid or are paid only in part, despite the risk of extra prison sentences being imposed.[170] The regime is under review by the Law Commission in 2019–20.

4. *Statistics*

a. Number of Criminal Proceedings

The official statistics relating to crime and policing are maintained by the Home Office. Official statistics relating to sentencing, criminal court proceedings, et cetera are maintained by the Ministry of Justice. No data are available on the value of transactions involved in money laundering prosecutions, but there are 2,000 prosecutions annually for standalone money laundering or where money laundering is the principal offence.[171] As a point of comparison, there were only

---

170 "The gross value of confiscation order debt as at 31 March 2019 is £2,065 million (2017–18: £1,961 million) and has been impaired for accounting purposes to a net present value of £161 million (2017–18: £152 million), which is the estimate of the amount that is ultimately collectable." *HM Courts & Tribunals Service Trust Statement 2018–19*, p. 8. In other words, only 7.8% of the amount currently owing is collectible.

171 FATF's 2018 MER states: "The UK routinely and aggressively identifies, pursues and prioritises ML investigations and prosecutions. It achieves around 7 900 investigations, 2 000 prosecutions and 1 400 convictions annually for standalone ML or where ML is the principal offence. The UK investigates and prosecutes a wide range of ML activity. Investigations of high-end ML (a long-standing risk area for the UK) have increased since being prioritised in 2014. These cases generally take years to progress to prosecution and conviction and limited statistics are available on high-end ML investigations, prosecutions and convictions prior to its prioritisation in 2014. As a result, it is not yet clear whether the level of prosecutions and convictions of high-end ML is fully consistent with the UK's threats, risk profile and national AML/CFT policies." The same report also notes: "Prosecution and conviction figures are notably lower in Scotland. This may be due to Scotland's higher evidentiary threshold which can pose challenges in prosecuting criminal cases, particularly ML leading authorities to place a greater emphasis on general or catch-all offences."

65 prosecutions and 27 convictions of anyone for section 24 Drug Trafficking Offences Act 1986 money laundering offences between 1986 and the end of 1992, including probably only one non-conspiring banker.[172] In its annual reports, the UK's FIU provides some statistics on SARs that have resulted in seized cash and case studies.

A government reply to a detailed question about prosecutions and convictions led to the following answer:

Table 4. Number of prosecutions and convictions for offences under sections 327–330 POCA, 2013–2017

	2013	2014	2015	2016	2017
Prosecutions					
Section 327	981	880	1,063	841	878
Section 328	310	266	317	355	288
Section 329	1,050	944	921	797	737
Section 330	3	3	5	1	1
Convictions					
Section 327	520	447	550	601	537
Section 328	213	150	188	257	225
Section 329	527	541	594	567	581
Section 330	6	4	2	3	1

Note: The figures given in the pivot table relate to defendants for whom these offences were the principal offences for which they were dealt with. When a defendant has been found guilty of two or more offences it is the offence for which the heaviest penalty is imposed. Where the same disposal is imposed for two or more offences, the offence selected is the offence for which the statutory maximum penalty is the most severe.

Source: HC Deb, 24 October 2018, cW.

b. Number of Convictions

Evidence presented to the FATF stated that there are about 1,400 convictions annually.[173]

[172] Michael Levi, "Incriminating disclosures: an evaluation of money-laundering regulation in England and Wales", *European Journal of Crime, Criminal Law, and Criminal Justice*, 3(2) (1995) 202–217.

[173] FATF, *Mutual Evaluation Report – UK*, 2018, p. 59.

Table 5. Number of persons prosecuted and convicted for money laundering in the UK, 2013–2016

	2013	2014	2015	2016
	England and Wales			
Proceeded against	2,349	2,095	2,307	1,998
Convictions	1,269	1,143	1,336	1,435
	Scotland			
Proceeded against	13	42	18	21
Convictions	5	16	11	12
	Northern Ireland			
Proceeded against	156	135	133	125
Convictions	129	118	95	58
	TOTAL			
Proceeded against	2,518	2,272	2,458	2,144
Convictions	1,403	1,277	1,442	1,505

Source: FATF, *Mutual Evaluation Report – UK*, 2018.

There are substantial sums restrained and confiscated,[174] but these are not tracked back to SARs, nor did the UK Mutual Evaluation Report attempt to do so except via a few case studies.

Table 6. Assets restrained and confiscated 2014–2017

	2014/15		2015/16		2016/17	
	Number of orders	Amount (million GBP)	Number of orders	Amount (million GBP)	Number of orders	Amount (million GBP)
Total assets restrained	1,297	396.9	1 499	473	1,422	382.8
Total assets recovered		200.85		321.72		483.64
POCA confiscation	6,126	160.8	6,117	211.4	5,649	165.6
POCA civil and tax recovery	24	6.55	15	11.33	13	8.52
POCA cash forfeiture	3,111	33.5	3,336	40.49	3,560	42.22
SFO disgorgement	0	0	1	6.2	1	258.2
FCA disgorgement	0	0	1	52.3	1	9.1

Source: FATF, *Mutual Evaluation Report – UK*, 2018.

174 *Ibid.*, p. 74.

Nor are confiscation data tracked routinely to types of offending, though some broad categories of data are revealed in the Mutual Evaluation Report.[175]

Table 7. Confiscation orders as a percentage of total value of offence types, 2014–2017

	2014/15	**2015/16**	**2016/17**
Total value of confiscation orders	**244.5**	**454.6**	**185.1**
Offence type			
Money laundering	38.4	59.5	26.5
– as a percentage of total value	16%	13%	14%
Fraud	75.2	61.8	60.5
– as a percentage of total value	31%	14%	33%
Tax-related offending	61.1	259.7	18.6
– as a percentage of total value	25%	57%	10%
Drug offending	37.2	49.0	57.2
– as a percentage of total value	15%	11%	31%
Immigration crime	1.1	0.5	1.4
– as a percentage of total value	~0%	~0%	1%
Acquisitive crime	6.7	5.8	6.6
– as a percentage of total value	3%	1%	4%
Total (above offences)	**219.7**	**436.3**	**170.8**
– as a percentage of total value	**~90%**	**~96%**	**~92%**

Source: FATF, *Mutual Evaluation Report – UK*, 2018.

A separate issue relates to so-called "high-end" money laundering, where initiatives were praised by the FATF but described by them as too early to show impact. One of the senior law officers, the Solicitor General, was asked in Parliament about the number of prosecutions and convictions, and replied:[176]

> There is no legal definition or specific criminal offence of "high end" money laundering. The CPS does not maintain a central record of the number of defendants prosecuted for, and convicted of these offences. This information could only be obtained by examining CPS case files, which would incur disproportionate cost.
>
> CPS holds limited information on the number of offences which were charged and which reached a first hearing in the Magistrates Court. This does not equate to the number of defendants charged as single defendant may be charged with more than one offence.

175 *Ibid.*, p. 83.

176 HC Deb, 27 November 2018, cW.

The figures for the period since 2014 are provided in the table below.

	2015–2016	2016–2017	2017–2018
Sections 327–330 POCA	4,542	4,866	4,813

The SFO has prosecuted four individuals for money laundering offences since 2014. Two of these prosecutions resulted in a successful conviction in 2018. One of the two individuals unsuccessfully prosecuted was legally qualified.

(We add that it is important to separate out those charged with laundering the proceeds of crimes including fraud and corruption in which they were directly involved, and those charged with laundering the proceeds of others' crimes: only some of the latter may be accurately described as professional money launderers.[177])

B. SANCTIONS FOR VIOLATIONS OF PREVENTIVE MEASURES

1. *Money Laundering by Violating Preventive Obligations*

As previously discussed, certain preventive measures are mandatory (e.g. KYC, due diligence). Typically, the responsibility rests with the MLRO and senior management. If they fail to implement an effective AML programme, including systems and controls in the regulated entity they work for, they can be held personally liable by criminal and regulatory authorities.

But in regard to the offence of failure to disclose, there are two schools of thought, with one arguing that an offence can be committed by negligence and the other arguing that negligence alone is not grounds for prosecution. According to this second school of thought, the state of mind required is that the offender must know or suspect or be reckless about whether the funds were proceeds of crime, and without some forensic evidence, such as a recorded phone call or email/file note, it may be difficult to prove beyond reasonable doubt.[178] For more details, see also section II.B.2. above and the next section.

---

177 See Michael Levi and Melvin Soudijn. Forthcoming 2020. 'Understanding the Laundering of Organized Crime Money', *Crime and Justice*. It is also important to distinguish between professional money launderers and launderers who have professionally qualifications, though the categories may sometimes overlap.

178 In the law of England and Wales, recklessness may be defined as the conscious taking of an unjustified risk. Negligence is unreasonable conduct that creates risk, while gross negligence is a high degree of negligence that may deserve criminal punishment. In *R v G & R* [2003] UKHL 50, it was determined that recklessness was punishable criminally where: (i) a circumstance when he is aware of a risk that it exists or will exist; (ii) a result

2. *CDD, Reporting and Other AML-Related Obligations*

a. Special Criminal Laws against Individuals

See the previous section. Chapter 3 of Part 9 of the Money Laundering Regulations discusses the criminal penalties. A person is not guilty of an offence if that person has taken all reasonable steps and conducted all due diligence to avoid committing an offence.

Additionally, failure to make a disclosure on the PSC register and failure to comply with notices requiring someone to provide information are criminal offences.

The information is entered into the central companies registry based on documents provided by the company. The information entered is checked against the original documents. However, the central companies registry is not currently responsible for investigating and confirming that the individuals identified as owners in the company's documentation are indeed its true owners.

According to regulation 88 of the Money Laundering Regulations, a person commits an offence if, in purported compliance with the Regulations, this person provides information to any person which is false or misleading and:

(a) that person knows that the information is false or misleading; or
(b) that person is reckless as to whether the information is false or misleading.

A person guilty of an offence under the above paragraph is liable:

(a) on summary conviction—
  (i) in England and Wales, to imprisonment for a term not exceeding three months, to a fine or to both,
  (ii) in Scotland or Northern Ireland, to imprisonment for a term not exceeding three months, to a fine not exceeding the statutory maximum or to both;
(b) on conviction on indictment, to imprisonment for a term not exceeding two years or to a fine or to both.

The above applies to the obliged entities in the context of the requirement to comply with the Money Laundering Regulations. It includes false statements made by the first line of defence of an obliged entity to the second line of defence of the same obliged entity or by an obliged entity to the authorities or to other obliged entities.

Regulation 86 states that in deciding whether a person has committed an offence the court must decide whether that person followed guidelines issued

---

when he is aware of a risk that it will occur; and it is, in the circumstances known to him, unreasonable to take the risk."

by the European Supervisory Authorities in accordance with the EU Money Laundering Directive, the UK Money Laundering Regulations or guidance issued by the FCA or another body and approved by the UK Treasury. A person is not guilty if that person took all reasonable steps and exercised all due diligence to avoid committing the offence.

Regulation 87 relates to persons in the regulated sector knowingly prejudicing an investigation into a violation of the regulations.

According to regulation 90, even if the offence was committed outside of the UK by a person in the UK, it will be treated, for the purposes of legal proceedings, as if it has been committed within the UK.

Additionally, according to the Companies Act, criminal sanctions may be imposed on companies and their officers for not complying with their beneficial ownership information obligations.

b. Administrative Sanctions against Individuals

Administrative sanctions include suspension or cancellation of authorised status or prohibition imposed on managers. If solicitors allow their client accounts to be used for banking activities by clients that are not related to the provision of particular legal services, or fail to take due diligence measures required, they can be sanctioned by the Solicitors Disciplinary Tribunal following action that is normally taken by the SRA or by the Law Society's regular inspection of records.

c. Sanctions against Legal Entities

The range of sanctions are as above. The various supervisory bodies can initiate the sanctions (e.g. the FCA, HMRC). More specifically, in regard to civil penalties, according to Part 9 of Chapter 2 of the Money Laundering Regulations, sanctions may include financial penalties, a censuring statement, cancellation or suspension of regulatory permissions, payment services provider registration or authorisation, or other restrictions, as well as prohibitions on management.

3. *Statistics*

a. Number of Investigations and Sanctions

The UK's FIU annual report provides statistics on how many SARs have been filed, how many have been passed onto other bodies, intelligence disseminated to foreign agencies, and:

- restraint sums;
- cash seizure sums;
- funds indemnified by HMRC;

- funds recovered by HMRC;
- some cases with arrests recorded.

There is no consistent and regular publication of statistics, and no collated list of sanctions against regulated or other persons for violations of prevention measures, though the FATF Mutual Evaluation Report stimulated regulators to produce data, which may continue hereafter.

In the period 2012–2018, the FCA concluded 14 AML/counter-terrorist financing enforcement cases relating to 10 firms and four individuals. HMRC undertook a modest number of cases against breaches of the Money Laundering Regulations: in the period June 2017–2018, four firms were issued with penalties (all under £6,000) for breaches; two firms were fined a total of £466.50 (but names were not published because the acts were minor); while in the period 2007–2017 (when the Regulations were revised), 535 firms were fined a total of £2.4 million.[179] A total of 101 individuals were convicted of money laundering in the period April 2010–April 2018 as a result of HMRC investigations. The average size of fine for HMRC breaches went up from £1,310 in 2016/17 to £3,450 in 2017/18.

The UK Mutual Evaluation Report provides limited information on sanctions by the FCA, set out below:[180]

Table 8. Penalties for money laundering imposed by the Financial Conduct Authority, 2012–2017

	2012/13	2013/14	2014/15	2015/16	2016/17	Total
Fines	5	4	1	1	3	14
Section 166 FSMA	11	14	6	6	5	42
Attestations	15 between June 2013 and June 2016					15
Business restrictions	12 between 2012–14			2	6	20
Early Interventions		4	8	8	7	27

Source: FATF, *Mutual Evaluation Report - UK*, 2018.

Section 166 FSMA refers to the appointment of skilled persons (e.g. senior money laundering experts from the private sector) to monitor the firm's AML activities and to suggest enhancements, for which monitoring the firm has to pay.

179 https://www.gov.uk/government/publications/businesses-not-complying-with-money-laundering-regulations-in-2018-to-2019/current-list-of-businesses-that-have-not-complied-with-the-2017-money-laundering-regulations. See https://www.gov.uk/guidance/money-laundering-regulations-appeals-and-penalties for the procedures.

180 FATF, *Mutual Evaluation Report - UK*, 2018, p. 134.

Another way of looking at the data in the context of the other responsibilities of the FCA is provided by Duff and Phelps:

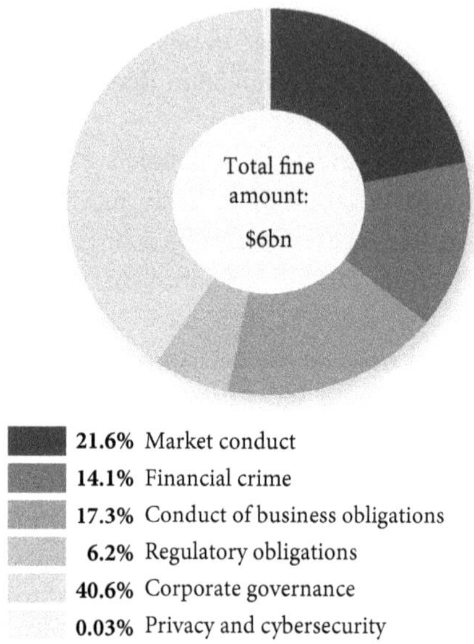

Figure 2. UK fine amounts by regulatory category, 2013–2017
Source: Duff and Phelps, Global Enforcement Review 2018.

Subsequently, consulting firm Encompass has reviewed regulatory penalties imposed for AML violations in calendar year 2019 around the world, and (including regulators such as the Gambling Commission as well as the FCA), the UK was second to the US, with 12 fines totalling $388.4m.[181] Note that in our view, the imposition of regulatory penalties is an activity measure, not necessarily an effectiveness measure, though the absence of penalties may be a sign of merely formal or symbolic compliance.

The Law Society's Solicitors' Disciplinary Tribunal publishes its decisions, but in the case of money laundering or predicate crimes, such sanctions would normally occur post-conviction, and "money laundering" is not available as a search term on its case database.[182] The SRA also publishes a selection of cases, but these give little insight into their relationship to money laundering and are intended to enable the public to check whether a particular solicitor has been subject to sanctions or not.[183] The SRA usually prosecute via the Solicitors' Disciplinary Tribunal because the latter has the power to strike off lawyers.

181 https://www.encompasscorporation.com/blog/encompass-aml-penalty-analysis-2019/.

182 See http://www.solicitorstribunal.org.uk/judgment-search-results#judgment-list.

183 See https://www.sra.org.uk/consumers/solicitor-check/recent-decisions/ for recent decisions; and https://www.sra.org.uk/consumers/solicitor-check.page for individual lawyers' checks.

The SRA also conducted a thematic review of law firms.[184] In that review of 50 firms, designed to test the sector's compliance with new, tougher AML regulations, the SRA found only a third had carried out a mandatory risk assessment of their AML procedures or were in the process of implementing one. In six of the 50, which ranged from high street to City firms, the SRA found serious concerns that merited "ongoing disciplinary processes".

In 2015–18, the SRA closed down eight law firms over money laundering concerns, although in some cases the action was preventive and took place without definitive proof of their wrongdoing. A further 14 companies shut down of their own accord after it raised concerns. The SRA has also referred 49 lawyers to the solicitors' disciplinary tribunal.

In 2017–18, HMRC imposed 655 penalties against accountants, estate agents and dealers in luxury goods such as art and jewellery, down from 901 in 2016–17. This may have reflected a greater focus on more complex cases.

The UK Gambling Commission's principal role is to protect customers from misconduct by gambling firms and to protect "vulnerable" gamblers from being encouraged to gamble. It has also imposed some penalties, though only one for money laundering breaches alone: the AML actions relate to failure to pursue checks on the source of funds that were later discovered to be stolen. One recent case – a £7.1 million fine on Daub Alderney – was part of an announced crackdown by the Commission in 2018 and was for failure to conduct a money laundering risk assessment on their customers as required under the conditions of licence, as well as under money laundering legislation.[185] Another recent case – a £6.2 million penalty on William Hill bookmakers – is set out in the following footnote.[186] Another £2.2 million penalty was imposed on

---

184 https://www.sra.org.uk/sra/how-we-work/reports/preventing-money-laundering-financing-terrorism.page.

185 Gambling Commission, "Daub Alderney to pay £7.1m fine for anti-money laundering and social responsibility failures", 13 November 2018, https://www.gamblingcommission.gov.uk/news-action-and-statistics/news/2018/Daub-Alderney-to-pay-7.1m-fine-for-anti-money-laundering-and-social-responsibility-failures.aspx.

186 Gambling Commission, "William Hill to pay £6.2m penalty package for systemic social responsibility and money laundering failures", 20 February 2018, https://www.gamblingcommission.gov.uk/news-action-and-statistics/news/2018/William-Hill-to-pay-6.2m-penalty-package.aspx.

"A Gambling Commission investigation revealed that between November 2014 and August 2016 the gambling business breached anti-money laundering and social responsibility regulations. Senior management failed to mitigate risks and have sufficient numbers of staff to ensure their anti-money laundering and social responsibility processes were effective. This resulted in ten customers being allowed to deposit large sums of money linked to criminal offences which resulted in gains for WHG of around £1.2m. WHG did not adequately seek information about the source of their funds or establish whether they were problem gamblers.

WHG will pay more than £5m for breaching regulations and divest themselves of the £1.2m they earned from transactions with the ten customers. Where victims of the ten customers are identified, they will be reimbursed. If further incidents of failures relating to this case emerge, WHG will divest any money made from these transactions.

Paddy Power,[187] a £2.3 million penalty on Gala Interactive,[188] and a £80,000 penalty on Stan James Online.[189] In May 2019, The Gambling Commission imposed £4.5 million in "penalty packages" on online casinos,[190] and this was

---

WHG will also appoint external auditors to review the effectiveness and implementation of its anti-money laundering and social responsibility policies and procedures and share learning with the wider industry ...

Examples of WHG's failures include (all figures are approximate):

- A customer was allowed to deposit £654,000 over nine months without source of funds checks being carried out. The customer lived in rented accommodation and was employed within the accounts department of a business earning around £30,000 per annum.
- A customer was allowed to deposit £541,000 over 14 months after the operator made the assumption that the customer's potential income could be £365,000 per annum based on a verbal conversation and without further probing. The reality was that the customer was earning around £30,000 a year and was funding his gambling habit by stealing from his employer.
- A customer who was allowed to deposit £653,000 in an 18 month period activated a financial alert at WHG. The alert resulted in a grading of 'amber risk' which required, in accordance with the licensee's anti-money laundering policy, a customer profile to be reviewed. The file was marked as passed to managers for review but this did not occur due to a systems failure. The customer was able to continue gambling for a further six months despite continuing to activate financial alerts.
- A customer was identified by WHG as having an escalating gambling spend with deposit levels exceeding £100,000. WHG interacted with the customer seeking assurance that the customer was 'comfortable with their level of spend'. After receiving verbal assurance and without investigating the wider circumstances the operator continued to allow the customer to gamble. In our view that interaction was inadequate and did not review the customer's behaviour sufficiently to identify if their behaviour was indicative of problem gambling.
- A customer exceeded deposits of £147,000 in an 18 month period with an escalating spend and losses of £112,000. WHG systems identified the issue but its only response over a 12 month period was to send two automated social responsibility emails. Our view is that this action alone was not sufficient given the customer's gambling behaviour coupled with the severity of the losses."

187 Gambling Commission, "Paddy Power Betfair to pay penalty package for social responsibility and money laundering failures on its gambling exchange", 16 October 2018, https://www.gamblingcommission.gov.uk/news-action-and-statistics/news/2018/Paddy-Power-Betfair-to-pay-penalty-package-for-social-responsibility-and-money-laundering-failures-on-its-gambling-exchange.aspx.

188 Gambling Commission, "Gala Interactive to pay £2.3m penalty package following social responsibility failures", 6 November 2017, https://www.gamblingcommission.gov.uk/news-action-and-statistics/news/2017/Gala-Interactive-to-pay-2.3m-penalty-package.aspx.

189 Gambling Commission, "Stan James Online to pay £80,000 penalty package for social responsibility and money laundering failures", 30 October 2017, https://www.gamblingcommission.gov.uk/news-action-and-statistics/news/2017/Stan-James-Online-to-pay-80000-penalty-package.aspx.

190 "InTouch Games Limited will pay £2.2m, Betit Operations Limited will pay £1.4m, and MT Secure Trade will pay £700,000 in lieu of financial penalties, and BestBet will pay a financial penalty of £230,972. The penalty packages relate to the businesses failings to put in place effective safeguards to prevent money laundering and keep consumers safe from gambling harm. The penalty packages form part of an ongoing investigation into the online casino sector. Over the last 18 months the regulator has conducted assessments of, or engaged with, 123 online operators – and of the 45 told to submit an action plan to raise standards 38 have already showed signs of improvement. A further 34 were compliant with standards expected

followed by further penalties, the largest of which was a £5.9 million fine on Ladbrokes for "past failures".[191] Other sanctions are published, but none visibly relates to money laundering failures.[192] In none of them is it clear that the firms were actively assisting people to launder money in the sense of concealing the source of funds in order to hide the audit trail: the gambling firms were increasing their turnover by failing to carry out their licence responsibilities or failing to think through the control process. Nor is it clear that any of the gamblers were doing this as a placement or layering exercise: it appears that they were simply obsessed with gambling. So it is plain that as with the SRA, the Gambling Commission conducted a "blitz" on its regulatees as part of an attempt to get them to take their AML responsibilities more seriously.

HM Treasury produces a consolidated annual report on the sanctions imposed by the AML/counter-terrorist financing supervisory bodies under its jurisdiction. The most recent report reveals the following (with data from the previous year in brackets, where available):

Table 9. Enforcement action by members of the Accountancy Affinity Group

2017–2018	Expulsion/ Withdrawal of membership	Suspension	Fine
Institute of Chartered Accountants of England & Wales	8 (11)	0 (1)	11 – £77,625 (9)
Association of Chartered Certified Accountants	9 (0)	1 (0)	0 (0)
Association of Accounting Technicians	4 (1)	0 (0)	53 – £47,112.92 (23 – £30,047.09)
Association of Taxation Technicians	0 (1)	0 (0)	12 – £2,394 (13 – £1,534)
Chartered Institute of Taxation	0 (–)	0 (–)	28 – £3,378 (12 – £6,708.13)
International Association of Bookkeepers	1 (5)	0 (0)	0 (0)

(continued)

by the Commission or had minor issues which have been, or are in the process of being, remedied. Since the investigation began five operators have surrendered their licence and can no longer transact with consumers in Britain. In November 2018 three companies paid nearly £14m in penalty packages as result of their failings to put in place effective safeguards to prevent money laundering and keep consumers safe from gambling-related harm." https://www.gamblingcommission.gov.uk/news-action-and-statistics/News/widespread-regulator-action-results-in-further-45m-in-penalty-packages-for-online-gambling-sector.

191 https://www.gamblingcommission.gov.uk/news-action-and-statistics/news/news.aspx?searchKeywords=&categories=0/1/24/41&page=0.

192 Gambling Commission, "Operator licences – regulatory decisions", https://www.gamblingcommission.gov.uk/PDF/Regulatory-sanctions-register-operators.pdf

Table 9 *continued*

2017–2018	Expulsion/ Withdrawal of membership	Suspension	Fine
Institute of Certified Bookkeepers	0 (–)	0 (–)	16 – £4115 (–)
Institute of Chartered Accountants of Ireland	0 (0)	0 (0)	2 – £750 (0)
Institute of Chartered Accountants of Scotland	0 (1)	0 (0)	0 (0)
Association of International Accountants	1 (–)	0 (–)	2 – £400 (–)
Chartered Institute of Management Accountants	1 (0)	0 (0)	1 – £675 (0)
Insolvency Practitioners Association	2 (–)	1 (–)	0 (–)
Institute of Financial Accountants	2 (2)	0 (–)	1 – £500 (–)

Source: HM Treasury, *Anti-money laundering and counter- terrorist financing: supervision report 2017–18*, 2019.

The Legal Sector Affinity Group sanctions 2017–18 were as follows:

Table 10. Sanctions on UK lawyers, 2017–2018

Body	Expulsion/Withdrawal of Membership	Suspension	Fine
Solicitors Regulation Authority	1 (3)	1 (2)	7 – 70,500 (2–£60,000)
Law Society of Scotland	1 (1)	0 (0)	2–£4,000 (0)
Law Society of N. Ireland	0 (0)	0 (0)	0 (0)
Council of Licenced Conveyancers	1 (0)	0 (0)	0 (0)
Chartered Institute of Legal Executives	0 (0)	0 (0)	0 (0)
General Council of Bar	0 (0)	0 (0)	0 (0)
General Council of the Bar of N. Ireland	(–) (–)	– (–)	– (–)

(*continued*)

Table 10 *continued*

Body	**Expulsion/Withdrawal of Membership**	**Suspension**	**Fine**
Faculty of Advocates	0 (–)	0 (–)	0 (–)
Faculty Office of the Archbishop of Canterbury	1 (–)	0 (–)	0 (–)

Source: HM Treasury, *Anti-money laundering and counter- terrorist financing: supervision report 2017–18*, 2019.

b. Number of Convictions

There is no one single source that would consistently publish this data. The most likely agency to prosecute for regulatory failures is the FCA, and penalties imposed by the FCA 2012–2018 totalled £343,346,924 on firms and £92,700 on individual MLROs. However, these include regulatory penalties, and criminal prosecutions are not separated out. Moreover, totals can be distorted by the effect of individual cases or connected cases that are unlikely to recur. We would add that the collateral financial consequences for individual MLROs are not included but may be considerable.

The 49 lawyers referred to the Solicitors' Disciplinary Tribunal resulted in 12 being struck off, the suspension of 13 and more than £800,000 in fines. In April 2017, the international firm Clyde & Co was ordered to pay a fine of £50,000 and three of its lawyers were fined £10,000 each over various allegations, including failure to comply with accounting rules and to act in accordance with money laundering regulations. The three partners allowed a client account to be used as a banking facility in breach of accounting rules and the code of conduct, a failure to act in accordance with their obligations under the Money Laundering Regulations 2007.[193]

HMRC fined companies £2.3 million in 2017–18, up from £1.2 million a year earlier. This constituted £3,500 per penalty, and unless the businesses were very unprofitable, this looks like a modest sanction.[194] In 2018–2019, HMRC

---

193 Max Walters "Clyde & Co faces £50,000 fine after SDT ruling", Law Society Gazette, 4 April 2017, https://www.lawgazette.co.uk/law/clyde-and-co-faces-50000-fine-after-sdt-ruling-/5060549.article.

194 In *N Bevan Limited v HMRC* [2016] TC 05404 the First Tier Tribunal (FTT) upheld a HMRC penalty imposed on a small one-person accountancy firm not supervised by any professional body for not keeping up with their AML obligations. Following two site visits and a warning letter, HMRC imposed a penalty on the taxpayer for failure to comply with its requirements in respect of customer due diligence, ongoing monitoring of clients, record keeping, and

recovered more than £41 million using the confiscation, civil recovery and cash forfeiture regimes in POCA and successfully prosecuted 32 individuals for money laundering offences and failing to follow regulations. West London money transmitter Touma Foreign Exchange Ltd received a £7.8 million penalty for a wide range of serious failures under the Money Laundering Regulations. Between June 2017 and September 2018, the business breached rules on risk assessments and associated record keeping; policies, controls and procedures; CDD measures; and adequate staff training.[195] This included a failure to submit its MLRO for vetting by HMRC.

C. CUMULATION OF MONEY LAUNDERING AND OTHER AML-RELATED SANCTIONS

There is no prohibition on combining sanctions for money laundering with sanctions for the violation of preventive obligations, but in a UK context this would be regarded as a highly theoretical question. Someone could be subject to professional disciplinary sanctions on the same set of facts as a criminal prosecution – whether successful or not – and, if the evidence was different, to support parallel charges, this would not offend any *ne bis in idem* principle, in the same way that alternative charges of differential seriousness for violence, sex and motoring offences could be indicted. This might be the basis for plea bargaining, or the court or disciplinary body might produce a different verdict on the parallel charges.

---

risk assessment. The taxpayer argued he had not breached any requirements. Although he could not produce client or other records to show procedures undertaken, he only acted for clients known for many years, only taking on new clients where they were connected to existing clients, and he used HMRC's authorised agent facilities to confirm the information provided to him by clients and as an electronic record of the information he gathered.

The Tribunal in reaching its decision considered the guidance issued by the Consultative Committee of Accountancy Bodies (CCAB) in August 2008, noting that if a taxpayer had complied with this guidance, it would not have breached the regulations. It upheld the penalty, finding that: the taxpayer had failed to establish proper verification, monitoring and record keeping processes despite a clear warning to do so; the only evidence provided that these were in place was the taxpayer's assertion; and using HMRC's online tax agent system to record information on clients does not comply with money laundering requirements.

The FTT did however change the level of the penalty: it was limited to 10% of the firm's gross revenue, and the mitigation factor was reduced from 50% to 20%: HMRC had been "over generous" as the taxpayer had been given the opportunity to address their concerns but did nothing.

195 HMRC Press Release, "Money sender fined record £7.8 million in money laundering crackdown", 4 September 2019, https://www.gov.uk/government/news/money-sender-fined-record-78-million-in-money-laundering-crackdown.

VIII. THE USE OF CASH AS A MEANS OF PAYMENT

A. LIMITS

There are no legislative limits on the use of cash as a means of payment in the UK, though there are requirements on the reporting of large cash payments in line with EU requirements.

B. STATISTICS

In the UK, cash has dropped from 60% of all payments in 2008 to 28% in 2018. In 2017, debit card payments overtook cash as the most popular form of payment in the UK.[196] Consumers used their debit cards 15.1 billion times in 2018, up 14% each year compared to 2016. The number of cash transactions fell by 31% to 11 billion transactions in the same period, though it remained the second most frequent means of payment, with 1.9 million people who almost always used cash. Use of contactless payment cards has been rising very rapidly to 7.4 billion transactions. Over two thirds (69%) of people in the UK now use contactless payments.

By the end of 2018 there were nearly 124 million contactless cards in circulation, with 84% of debit cards and 64% of credit cards in Britain having contactless functionality. UK Payments has provided the chart below, containing historical and predicted data.

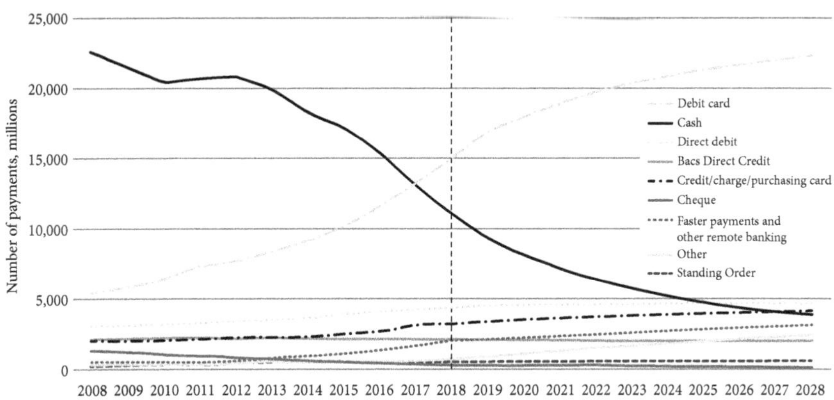

Figure 3. Payment volumes (millions), 2008–2028
Source: UK Finance, *UK Payment Markets Summary 2019*, June 2019.

---

196 https://www.ukfinance.org.uk/wp-content/uploads/2018/06/Summary-UK-Payment-Markets-2018.pdf; UK Finance, *UK Payment Markets Summary 2019*, June 2019, https://www.ukfinance.org.uk/sites/default/files/uploads/pdf/UK-Finance-UK-Payment-Markets-Report-2019-SUMMARY.pdf.

IX. SUMMARY, EVALUATION AND FUTURE PERSPECTIVES

The 2018 FATF evaluation of the UK generated more data from different components of the complex AML regime in the UK than had been available previously, though the validity of these data is difficult to assess, with only modest published research. The UK does not lack rules and processes for dealing with suspicion and SARs, and in that sense the difference between common law and continental models may be exaggerated. Thus, there are significant legal constraints of intra-public sector communications (HMRC personal data on individual and business taxpayers to anyone) and public to private communications (police/NCA to private sector and individuals lack sufficient legal gateways for communication; we note that the JMLIT is accessed by only a limited number of financial institutions). However, once a SAR has been made, there are few constraints from private to public, ever since the Drug Trafficking Offences Act 1986 made a first small breach in the dam of customer confidentiality by protecting banks from liability for making disclosures in suspected drug trafficking cases.[197] However, discretion continues to be a central feature of British policing and prosecutions, as does the decentralised/distributed nature of the loose-coupled AML process, in which the role of the FIU is less important than appears to be envisaged in the questionnaire.[198]

One important feature of UK policing has been its flexible approach to the policing of the public sphere, with no firm line as to where the state ends and private collective or individual governance begins. Thus, an early study of data matching three decades ago showed the importance of large scale *private* sector data sharing in payment card fraud prevention,[199] later developing more broadly in public–private anti-fraud and counterfeiting efforts, including even the private sector financing of police units in the City of London police to deal with "organised" payment card fraud and insurance fraud cases (which otherwise would have received police and prosecution support only intermittently), under police command but with public–private joint steering committees on policy.[200]

---

197 Michael Levi, "*Pecunia non olet*: cleansing the money launderers from the Temple", *Crime, Law, and Social Change*, 16 (1991) 217–302; Michael Levi, "Pecunia non olet? The control of money-laundering revisited", in Frank Bovenkerk and Michael Levi (eds.), *The Organised Crime Community*, New York: Springer, 2007, pp. 161–182.

198 See Eleanor Gale and Jessica Kelly, *Exploring the Role of the Financial Investigator*, Home Office Research Report 104, November 2018.

199 Michael Levi, Paul Bissell and Tony Richardson, *The Prevention of Cheque and Credit Card Fraud,* CPU Paper 26, London: Home Office, 1991.

200 Michael Levi, "Public and Private Policing of Financial Crimes: the Struggle for Co-ordination", *Journal of Criminal Justice and Security*, 4 (2010) 343–357. See also https://www.cityoflondon.police.uk/advice-and-support/fraud-and-economic-crime/Pages/default.aspx.

In the control of cybercrimes in many parts of the world, it is a conscious strategy to extend the use of the private sector as part of "the policing family",[201] and also (in the UK) to recruit private sector experts as unpaid "special constables" to assist, at times, under-trained and (outside specialist units such as the National Cyber Security Centre) inexpert police. Alongside what has become known in the Netherlands, Sweden and, to a lesser extent, other parts of Europe generally as the administrative approach to organised crime, the successive Serious and Organised Crime Strategies of the UK government stress the importance of Protect and Prepare alongside the Pursue (law enforcement) function in the general ambition of harm reduction. There is no suggestion that these (and Prevent) are the exclusive roles of the public police.

Returning to AML, the UK (like the Netherlands) has always operated in a relatively high-volume reporting environment compared with other police FIU systems, and whatever the formal regulatory environment may be, even though they have been expanded somewhat following the criticisms in the 2018 Mutual Evaluation Report, the 127 (up from 80) or so UK FIU staff (in 2020) cannot deal very comprehensively with 478,437 SARs as well as carrying out the outreach and other activities required of them, especially given the complexity of many financial crime cases and of DAML requests. The AML regime of the UK and of other EU countries places significant demands on an ever-larger range of private sector actors, but the appropriate balance between public and private AML resources has not been the subject of clear public debate in the UK or in the national or international arenas elsewhere. In this sense, the extension of the public into the private has crept upon us, just as the pervasive impact of private technology into the private sphere has. The FIU resource scarcity long preceded the UK public sector austerity programme, in which policing is not a protected area of public finance: but the reduction in UK police numbers has had an inevitable impact on financial investigation in practice, even though some investigation costs are recoverable from the government's Asset Recovery Incentivisation Scheme, making it profitable or at least cost-neutral

201 Michael Levi, Alan Doig, Rajeev Gundur, David Wall and Matthew Williams, "Cyberfraud and the Implications for Effective Risk-Based Responses: Themes from UK Research", *Crime, Law and Social Change*, 67(1) (2017) 77–96. See also HMICFRS, *Fraud: Time to Choose. An inspection of the police response to fraud*, 2019. This is not only occurring in the UK but also internationally: see Benoit Dupont, "Bots, cops, and corporations: on the limits of enforcement and the promise of polycentric regulation as a way to control large-scale cybercrime", *Crime, Law and Social Change*, 67(1) (2017) 97–116; Benoit Dupont, "The global anti-cybercrime network", in Lennon Y.C. Chang and Russel Brewer (eds.), *Criminal Justice and Regulation Revisited: Essays in Honour of Peter Grabosky*, Abingdon: Routledge, 2018, p. 163; David Mussington, Brent J. Arnold, Benoit Dupont, Scott Hilts, Timothy Grayson, Christian Leuprecht, Liam Nevill, Brian O'Higgins and Josh Tupler, *Governing Cyber Security in Canada, Australia and the United States*, Centre for International Governance Innovation, 2018; S. Boes. and E.R. Leukfeldt, "Fighting cybercrime: A joint effort", in Robert M. Clark and Simon Hakim (eds.), *Cyber-Physical Security*, Cham: Springer, 2017, pp. 185–203.

for forces to devote some resources to them *provided this leads to actual proceeds of crime recoveries*.[202] This may be one reason why the number of accredited financial investigators has risen from 837 in 2004,[203] then mainly in the police and customs, to 4,800 today, spread across 77 agencies[204] – though we would point out that they may not all be currently engaged in financial investigation work. Nevertheless, a review of financial investigation by Gale and Kelly concluded:[205]

> It also became apparent that there were challenges to the effective use of financial investigation, which were often systemic in nature. For instance, financial investigation was often considered and used as a tool for investigating economic crime and undertaking asset recovery only, despite the numerous benefits reported by both the FIs [financial investigators] and the non-FIs when it had been used during investigations of non-economic crime.
>
> This may be due to a limited understanding of financial investigation among key partners. The FIs reported that non-FI colleagues from their organisations as well as partners from the criminal justice system and other organisations sometimes lacked understanding of financial investigation. This could frustrate the progress of financial investigations – particularly the use of additional charges for money laundering and recovering criminal assets through confiscation.

Although a much broader problem than in the UK, which globally is a leader in sophisticated crime statistics, the lack of comprehensive and consistent statistics on the AML process has been noted by scholars and official bodies. The UK does not collect and never has collected systematically statistics on amounts in SARs and their conversion rate into subsequent action; this is a hydraulic system in which it is arguable that one might as well have only the number of reports one is prepared to deal properly with, unless the system is *de facto* a mass dataset, which is a half-way house between an unusual transaction reporting model (Dutch-style) and a refined SAR system with far fewer reports but whose reports

---

202 This can have unintended impacts in skewing investigations towards cases where assets have not been dissipated or are more readily recoverable (i.e. are not overseas, and are in cash or other recoverable form). ARIS divides recovered assets between operational agencies and the Home Office on a 50/50 basis. While the Home Office portion of ARIS is earmarked as part of its core budget – making it a sort of hypothecated taxation – operational partners may use these funds as they see fit. Law enforcement agencies received £56 million in 2017 from ARIS. See Home Office, Asset recovery statistical bulletin 2012/13–2017/18", Research Report 18/18, September 2018, https://assets.publishing.service.gov.uk/government/uploads/system/uploads/attachment_data/file/739567/asset-recovery-financial-years-2013-to-2018-hosb1818.pdf. There is, however, considerable attrition between the sums ordered to be confiscated and actual confiscation levels.

203 Richard J Harding, *Evaluation of the Assets Recovery Agency training provision* (unpublished).

204 Law Commission SARs Regime Consultation Review, 2018.

205 Eleanor Gale and Jessica Kelly, *Exploring the Role of the Financial Investigator*, Home Office Research Report 104, November 2018, p. 43.

are more thoroughly followed up.[206] This has a "police culture" dimension, in that few investigators see it as a priority to tell the FIU when a SAR has been useful for either crime investigation or asset recovery purposes, and the FIU is too busy processing its vast volume of SARs to tell the private sector reporters, even when they are notified by LEAs, of how useful or otherwise the SAR has been. In more formal terms, the national College of Policing gives some guidance as to how to conduct financial investigation,[207] and Gale and Kelly make some recommendations,[208] as others have done before them about the plugging of intelligence gaps and better partnership work oriented towards disruption.[209]

In a review that generally praises the UK's initiatives (whose outputs and outcomes often lie in the future, after the MER and the Plenary which awards its final grades), the FATF Mutual Evaluation Report criticises the UK's FIU for the absence of its own SAR follow-up investigation and for what may be described as the distributed model of sending out SARs and leaving it up to the individual recipients to investigate (or, more often, not to do so). The resource implications of giving the UK's FIU a much larger role in intelligence development have not been examined fully. (Although substantially more FIU staff have been promised – and some already employed – following the FATF report, as they were when the previous one was finalised in 2007). However, it is not clear that law enforcement would do much more with the intelligence if it was developed more fully by the FIU. (If nothing is actually done with it, what is the point of developing the SARs further?) This relative lack of follow-up is a problem with all forms of intelligence packages to and by the NCA and its predecessor agencies,[210] and it is also true of the centralised fraud reports made to Action

206 Michael Gold and Michael Levi, *Money-Laundering in the UK: an Appraisal of Suspicion-Based Reporting*, London: Police Foundation, 1994; Michael Levi, "Incriminating disclosures: an evaluation of money-laundering regulation in England and Wales", *European Journal of Crime, Criminal Law, and Criminal Justice*, 3(2) (1995) 202–217; Michael Levi, Peter Reuter and Terence Halliday, "Can the AML/CTF System Be Evaluated Without Better Data?", *Crime, Law and Social Change*, 69(2) (2018) 307–328.

207 https://www.app.college.police.uk/app-content/investigations/investigative-strategies/financial-investigation-2/.

208 Eleanor Gale and Jessica Kelly, *Exploring the Role of the Financial Investigator*, Home Office Research Report 104, November 2018.

209 See Nick Maxwell and David Artingstall, *The Role of Financial Information-Sharing Partnerships in the Disruption of Crime*, London: RUSI, 2017; and Helena Wood, David Artingstall, Haylea Campbell and Anton Moiseienko, *Known Unknowns: Plugging the UK's Intelligence Gaps on Money Laundering Involving Professional Services Providers*, London: RUSI, 2018.

210 Michael Levi and Mike Maguire, "Something old, something new; something not entirely blue: Uneven and shifting modes of crime control", in Tim Newburn and Jill Peay (eds.), *Policing: Politics, Culture and Control*, Oxford: Hart Publishing, 2012, pp. 195–218.

Fraud and (after filtering for expected investigatability) distributed on to forces around the country by the National Fraud Intelligence Bureau in the City of London Police.[211] There is simply far too much "intelligence" around from which to develop Pursue actions, whether because of limited personnel or of cross-border obstacles, which include overburdened FIUs elsewhere and domestic political resistance to serving the interests of foreign states when their own domestic cases cannot be investigated and there are other needs expressed by their citizens and politicians. (We contend that this is a problem in all jurisdictions, even in "legality principle" ones where there is an obligation to prosecute once there is 'sufficient' evidence; the broader question of how much expenditure on financial investigation – or indeed expenditure on the criminal prosecution of money laundering or any other offence – is socially optimal is out of scope for this study.) There are also serious limits from austerity to prosecutors' resources in cases high and low, both in the UK and, we suspect, elsewhere. The implications of these practical limitations of criminal justice outputs for the earlier stages of AML system as a whole remain inchoate and have not been considered seriously.[212]

The Executive Summary of the FATF report on the UK states, positively:[213]

Overall Level of Compliance and Effectiveness ...

4. The UK has implemented an AML/CTF system that is effective in many respects. Particularly good results are being achieved in the areas of investigation and prosecution of ML/CTF, confiscation, the implementation of targeted financial sanctions related to terrorism and proliferation, protecting the non-profit sector from terrorist abuse, understanding the ML/CTF risks facing the country, preventing misuse of legal structures and co-operating domestically and internationally to address them. However, major improvements are needed to strengthen supervision and implementation of preventive measures, and ensure that financial intelligence is fully exploited.
5. In terms of technical compliance, the legal framework is particularly strong with only two areas in need of significant improvements – measures related to correspondent banking and the UKFIU.

---

211 Alan Doig, "Fraud: from national strategies to practice on the ground – a regional case study", *Public Money & Management*, 38(2) (2018) 147–156; Michael Levi and Alan Doig, "Exploring the 'Shadows' in the Implementation Processes for National Anti-fraud Strategies at the Local Level: Aims, Ownership, and Impact", *European Journal on Criminal Policy and Research* (2019), https://doi.org/10.1007/s10610-019-09422-6; Home Affairs Select Committee, *Policing for the* Future, HC 515, 2018; Michael Skidmore, Josephine Ramm, Janice Goldstraw-White, Clare Barrett, Sabina Barleaza, Rick Muir and Martin Gill, *More Than Just A Number: Improving the Police Response to Victims Of Fraud*, London: Police Foundation, 2018; HMICFRS, *Fraud: Time to Choose. An inspection of the police response to fraud*, 2019.

212 We are not arguing that such a pursuit of every case would be a fiscally sensible policy.

213 FATF, *Mutual Evaluation Report – UK*, 2018, p. 6.

6. The UK has significantly strengthened its AML/CTF framework since its last evaluation particularly in relation to operational co-ordination among law enforcement agencies, stronger investigative tools, mechanisms to facilitate public/private information sharing, and the creation of an authority to address inconsistencies in the supervision of lawyers and accountants. One important issue which is outstanding from the previous assessment is the need to enhance the resources and capabilities available to the UKFIU.

The issue of *effectiveness at what* is not addressed, and the report stays at the level of activity indicators.[214] The metrics of success remain under-explored, nor is the proportionality of reporting issue tackled other than by assertion, for example: "there remains an underreporting of suspicious transactions by higher risk sectors such as trust and company service providers (TCSPs), lawyers, and accountants."[215] What actually would or should happen in the aftermath of these extra exhorted reports remains an intellectual work in progress. The scalability of the JMLIT for dealing with larger numbers of cases than the (undeclared) number currently done remains an open question that has not been publicly examined.

The UK is a jurisdiction that is serious about major crime control that aims to make progress against identified social harms, using AML as one of several mechanisms to reduce crimes and the harms from them. Its offshore roles and relationships are a legacy of Empire, and they have not been considered in this review, but they continue to shape the perception of the UK externally and are a source of tension within the UK government and between it and the Overseas Territories and Crown Dependencies. The compliance function of the private sector has been transformed into an ally of policing by a combination of criminal and regulatory threats and recommendations, and the long tradition of public- private cooperation in the UK[216] has been deployed to make this a collaborative as well as top-down endeavour. The effects of these actual and prospective changes on crime rates and harms remains under-explored, but this seems not to have inhibited this inexorable trend towards "responsibilisation" of the private sector to play public roles, even if implementation test mechanisms like mystery shopping have not yet been systematically deployed in the thematic reviews that have become part of the regulatory toolbox. Brexit will have an impact on the international networking process, and access to Europol:

214 In its one-page statement in December 2019, the Wolfsberg Group expressed its frustration at the lack of developed thinking on effectiveness: see https://www.wolfsberg-principles.com/sites/default/files/wb/pdfs/Effectiveness%201%20pager%20Wolfsberg%20Group%202019%20FINAL_Publication.pdf.

215 *Ibid.*, p. 6.

216 Sir Robert Peel's 1829 principle that "the police are the public and the public are the police" was a very different model from the Continental models.

the clunky Council of Europe Mutual Legal Assistance mechanisms have been allowed to get rusty and despite improvements, Egmont has accounted for the majority of inter-FIU exchanges (see Table 3 earlier this chapter), and in the past year surged in popularity, while exchanges via the EU (including the FIU. Net at Europol) fell significantly. The explanation for these changes is out of scope. But many of the issues raised in this review will still be able to operate relatively unimpeded.

The technological features of the electronic database ELMER have been in need of refashioning for well over a decade, but this is a difficult time for costly changes, quite apart from the cost and delay issues that habitually befall government technology projects in the UK. Some investment by the private sector will be used to co-fund with the public sector. Whether post-Brexit Britain will have economic strains that tempt more organisations to launder money and more private sector enterprises to protest about their own *over*-investment and public *under*-investment in action on SARs remains to be seen. Hitherto, apart from specialist concern about de-risking of customers, correspondent banking facilities, and Global South nations as an unintended counter-productive consequence of AML regulation, there has been little sustained popular or political protest about the social, economic or privacy costs of AML in the UK. So unless there is a determined shift in the direction of travel of AML in the UK – rare in the aftermath of a positive AML Mutual Evaluation Report – or a shift in thinking by the FATF itself as part of its self-review in 2020, the most likely future direction is more of the same, with some additional attention being paid to the areas such as FIU investigation levels and its outdated technological systems on which the MER recommends the need for improvement.

APPENDIX

A. CRIMINAL OFFENCES UNDER POCA

POCA lists the following money laundering offences:

"327. Concealing etc

(1) A person commits an offence if he—

(a) conceals criminal property;
(b) disguises criminal property;
(c) converts criminal property;
(d) transfers criminal property;
(e) removes criminal property from England and Wales or from Scotland or from Northern Ireland.

(2) But a person does not commit such an offence if—

(a) he makes an authorised disclosure under section 338 and (if the disclosure is made before he does the act mentioned in subsection (1)) he has the appropriate consent;
(b) he intended to make such a disclosure but had a reasonable excuse for not doing so;
(c) the act he does is done in carrying out a function he has relating to the enforcement of any provision of this Act or of any other enactment relating to criminal conduct or benefit from criminal conduct.

[F1(2A) Nor does a person commit an offence under subsection (1) if—

(a) he knows, or believes on reasonable grounds, that the relevant criminal conduct occurred in a particular country or territory outside the United Kingdom, and
(b) the relevant criminal conduct—
    (i) was not, at the time it occurred, unlawful under the criminal law then applying in that country or territory, and
    (ii) is not of a description prescribed by an order made by the Secretary of State.

(2B) In subsection (2A) "the relevant criminal conduct" is the criminal conduct by reference to which the property concerned is criminal property.]

[F2(2C) A deposit-taking body that does an act mentioned in paragraph (c) or (d) of subsection (1) does not commit an offence under that subsection if—

(a) it does the act in operating an account maintained with it, and
(b) the value of the criminal property concerned is less than the threshold amount determined under section 339A for the act.]

(3) Concealing or disguising criminal property includes concealing or disguising its nature, source, location, disposition, movement or ownership or any rights with respect to it."

328. Arrangements

(1) A person commits an offence if he enters into or becomes concerned in an arrangement which he knows or suspects facilitates (by whatever means) the acquisition, retention, use or control of criminal property by or on behalf of another person.

(2) But a person does not commit such an offence if—

(a) he makes an authorised disclosure under section 338 and (if the disclosure is made before he does the act mentioned in subsection (1)) he has the appropriate consent;
(b) he intended to make such a disclosure but had a reasonable excuse for not doing so;
(c) the act he does is done in carrying out a function he has relating to the enforcement of any provision of this Act or of any other enactment relating to criminal conduct or benefit from criminal conduct.

[F3(3) Nor does a person commit an offence under subsection (1) if—

(a) he knows, or believes on reasonable grounds, that the relevant criminal conduct occurred in a particular country or territory outside the United Kingdom, and
(b) the relevant criminal conduct—
    (i) was not, at the time it occurred, unlawful under the criminal law then applying in that country or territory, and
    (ii) is not of a description prescribed by an order made by the Secretary of State.

(4) In subsection (3) 'the relevant criminal conduct' is the criminal conduct by reference to which the property concerned is criminal property.]

[F4(5) A deposit-taking body that does an act mentioned in subsection (1) does not commit an offence under that subsection if—

(a) it does the act in operating an account maintained with it, and
(b) the arrangement facilitates the acquisition, retention, use or control of criminal property of a value that is less than the threshold amount determined under section 339A for the act.]

329. Acquisition, use and possession

(1) A person commits an offence if he—

(a) acquires criminal property;

(b) uses criminal property;
(c) has possession of criminal property.

(2) But a person does not commit such an offence if—

(a) he makes an authorised disclosure under section 338 and (if the disclosure is made before he does the act mentioned in subsection (1)) he has the appropriate consent;
(b) he intended to make such a disclosure but had a reasonable excuse for not doing so;
(c) he acquired or used or had possession of the property for adequate consideration;
(d) the act he does is done in carrying out a function he has relating to the enforcement of any provision of this Act or of any other enactment relating to criminal conduct or benefit from criminal conduct.

[F5(2A) Nor does a person commit an offence under subsection (1) if—

(a) he knows, or believes on reasonable grounds, that the relevant criminal conduct occurred in a particular country or territory outside the United Kingdom, and
(b) the relevant criminal conduct—
    (i) was not, at the time it occurred, unlawful under the criminal law then applying in that country or territory, and
    (ii) is not of a description prescribed by an order made by the Secretary of State.

(2B) In subsection (2A) 'the relevant criminal conduct' is the criminal conduct by reference to which the property concerned is criminal property.]

[F6(2C) A deposit-taking body that does an act mentioned in subsection (1) does not commit an offence under that subsection if—

(a) it does the act in operating an account maintained with it, and
(b) the value of the criminal property concerned is less than the threshold amount determined under section 339A for the act.]

(3) For the purposes of this section—

(a) a person acquires property for inadequate consideration if the value of the consideration is significantly less than the value of the property;
(b) a person uses or has possession of property for inadequate consideration if the value of the consideration is significantly less than the value of the use or possession;
(c) the provision by a person of goods or services which he knows or suspects may help another to carry out criminal conduct is not consideration.

330. Failure to disclose: regulated sector

(1) A person commits an offence if [F7the conditions in subsections (2) to (4) are satisfied].

(2) The first condition is that he—

(a) knows or suspects, or
(b) has reasonable grounds for knowing or suspecting, that another person is engaged in money laundering.

(3) The second condition is that the information or other matter—

(a) on which his knowledge or suspicion is based, or
(b) which gives reasonable grounds for such knowledge or suspicion, came to him in the course of a business in the regulated sector.

[F8(3A)The third condition is—

(a) that he can identify the other person mentioned in subsection (2) or the whereabouts of any of the laundered property, or
(b) that he believes, or it is reasonable to expect him to believe, that the information or other matter mentioned in subsection (3) will or may assist in identifying that other person or the whereabouts of any of the laundered property.

(4) The fourth condition is that he does not make the required disclosure to—

(a) a nominated officer, or
(b) a person authorised for the purposes of this Part by [F9the Director General of the National Crime Agency], as soon as is practicable after the information or other matter mentioned in subsection (3) comes to him.

(5) The required disclosure is a disclosure of—

(a) the identity of the other person mentioned in subsection (2), if he knows it,
(b) the whereabouts of the laundered property, so far as he knows it, and
(c) the information or other matter mentioned in subsection (3).

(5A) The laundered property is the property forming the subject-matter of the money laundering that he knows or suspects, or has reasonable grounds for knowing or suspecting, that other person to be engaged in.

(6) But he does not commit an offence under this section if—

(a) he has a reasonable excuse for not making the required disclosure,
(b) he is a professional legal adviser [F10 or F11 … relevant professional adviser] and—
    (i) if he knows either of the things mentioned in subsection (5)(a) and (b), he knows the thing because of information or other matter that came to him in privileged circumstances, or

(ii) the information or other matter mentioned in subsection (3) came to him in privileged circumstances, or

(c) subsection (7) [F12or (7B)] applies to him.]

(7) This subsection applies to a person if—

(a) he does not know or suspect that another person is engaged in money laundering, and
(b) he has not been provided by his employer with such training as is specified by the Secretary of State by order for the purposes of this section.

[F13(7A) Nor does a person commit an offence under this section if—

(a) he knows, or believes on reasonable grounds, that the money laundering is occurring in a particular country or territory outside the United Kingdom, and
(b) the money laundering—
    (i) is not unlawful under the criminal law applying in that country or territory, and
    (ii) is not of a description prescribed in an order made by the Secretary of State.]

[F14(7B) This subsection applies to a person if—

(a) he is employed by, or is in partnership with, a professional legal adviser or a relevant professional adviser to provide the adviser with assistance or support,
(b) the information or other matter mentioned in subsection (3) comes to the person in connection with the provision of such assistance or support, and
(c) the information or other matter came to the adviser in privileged circumstances.]

(8) In deciding whether a person committed an offence under this section the court must consider whether he followed any relevant guidance which was at the time concerned—

(a) issued by a supervisory authority or any other appropriate body,
(b) approved by the Treasury, and
(c) published in a manner it approved as appropriate in its opinion to bring the guidance to the attention of persons likely to be affected by it.

(9) A disclosure to a nominated officer is a disclosure which—

(a) is made to a person nominated by the alleged offender's employer to receive disclosures under this section, and
(b) is made in the course of the alleged offender's employment F15 …

[F16(9A) But a disclosure which satisfies paragraphs (a) and (b) of subsection (9) is not to be taken as a disclosure to a nominated officer if the person making the disclosure—

(a) is a professional legal adviser [F17 or F18 … relevant professional adviser],
(b) makes it for the purpose of obtaining advice about making a disclosure under this section, and
(c) does not intend it to be a disclosure under this section.]

(10) Information or other matter comes to a professional legal adviser [F19 or F20 … relevant professional adviser] in privileged circumstances if it is communicated or given to him—

(a) by (or by a representative of) a client of his in connection with the giving by the adviser of legal advice to the client,
(b) by (or by a representative of) a person seeking legal advice from the adviser, or
(c) by a person in connection with legal proceedings or contemplated legal proceedings.

(11) But subsection (10) does not apply to information or other matter which is communicated or given with the intention of furthering a criminal purpose.

(12) Schedule 9 has effect for the purpose of determining what is—

(a) a business in the regulated sector;
(b) a supervisory authority.

(13) An appropriate body is any body which regulates or is representative of any trade, profession, business or employment carried on by the alleged offender.

[F21(14) A relevant professional adviser is an accountant, auditor or tax adviser who is a member of a professional body which is established for accountants, auditors or tax advisers (as the case may be) and which makes provision for—

(a) testing the competence of those seeking admission to membership of such a body as a condition for such admission; and
(b) imposing and maintaining professional and ethical standards for its members, as well as imposing sanctions for non-compliance with those standards.]

331. Failure to disclose: nominated officers in the regulated sector

(1) A person nominated to receive disclosures under section 330 commits an offence if the conditions in subsections (2) to (4) are satisfied.

(2) The first condition is that he—

(a) knows or suspects, or

(b) has reasonable grounds for knowing or suspecting, that another person is engaged in money laundering.

(3) The second condition is that the information or other matter—

(a) on which his knowledge or suspicion is based, or
(b) which gives reasonable grounds for such knowledge or suspicion, came to him in consequence of a disclosure made under section 330.

[F22(3A) The third condition is—

(a) that he knows the identity of the other person mentioned in subsection (2), or the whereabouts of any of the laundered property, in consequence of a disclosure made under section 330,
(b) that that other person, or the whereabouts of any of the laundered property, can be identified from the information or other matter mentioned in subsection (3), or
(c) that he believes, or it is reasonable to expect him to believe, that the information or other matter will or may assist in identifying that other person or the whereabouts of any of the laundered property.

(4) The fourth condition is that he does not make the required disclosure to a person authorised for the purposes of this Part by [F23 the Director General of the National Crime Agency] as soon as is practicable after the information or other matter mentioned in subsection (3) comes to him.

(5) The required disclosure is a disclosure of—

(a) the identity of the other person mentioned in subsection (2), if disclosed to him under section 330,
(b) the whereabouts of the laundered property, so far as disclosed to him under section 330, and
(c) the information or other matter mentioned in subsection (3).

(5A) The laundered property is the property forming the subject-matter of the money laundering that he knows or suspects, or has reasonable grounds for knowing or suspecting, that other person to be engaged in.

(6) But he does not commit an offence under this section if he has a reasonable excuse for not making the required disclosure.]

[F24(6A) Nor does a person commit an offence under this section if—

(a) he knows, or believes on reasonable grounds, that the money laundering is occurring in a particular country or territory outside the United Kingdom, and

(b) the money laundering—
   (i) is not unlawful under the criminal law applying in that country or territory, and
   (ii) is not of a description prescribed in an order made by the Secretary of State.]

(7) In deciding whether a person committed an offence under this section the court must consider whether he followed any relevant guidance which was at the time concerned—

(a) issued by a supervisory authority or any other appropriate body,
(b) approved by the Treasury, and
(c) published in a manner it approved as appropriate in its opinion to bring the guidance to the attention of persons likely to be affected by it.

(8) Schedule 9 has effect for the purpose of determining what is a supervisory authority.

(9) An appropriate body is a body which regulates or is representative of a trade, profession, business or employment.

332. Failure to disclose: other nominated officers

(1) A person nominated to receive disclosures under section 337 or 338 commits an offence if the conditions in subsections (2) to (4) are satisfied.

(2) The first condition is that he knows or suspects that another person is engaged in money laundering.

(3) The second condition is that the information or other matter on which his knowledge or suspicion is based came to him in consequence of a disclosure made under [F25the applicable section].

[F26(3A) The third condition is—

(a) that he knows the identity of the other person mentioned in subsection (2), or the whereabouts of any of the laundered property, in consequence of a disclosure made under the applicable section,
(b) that that other person, or the whereabouts of any of the laundered property, can be identified from the information or other matter mentioned in subsection (3), or
(c) that he believes, or it is reasonable to expect him to believe, that the information or other matter will or may assist in identifying that other person or the whereabouts of any of the laundered property.

(4) The fourth condition is that he does not make the required disclosure to a person authorised for the purposes of this Part by [F27 the Director General of

the National Crime Agency] as soon as is practicable after the information or other matter mentioned in subsection (3) comes to him.

(5) The required disclosure is a disclosure of—

(a) the identity of the other person mentioned in subsection (2), if disclosed to him under the applicable section,
(b) the whereabouts of the laundered property, so far as disclosed to him under the applicable section, and
(c) the information or other matter mentioned in subsection (3).

(5A) The laundered property is the property forming the subject-matter of the money laundering that he knows or suspects that other person to be engaged in.

(5B) The applicable section is section 337 or, as the case may be, section 338.

(6) But he does not commit an offence under this section if he has a reasonable excuse for not making the required disclosure.]

[F28(7) Nor does a person commit an offence under this section if—

(a) he knows, or believes on reasonable grounds, that the money laundering is occurring in a particular country or territory outside the United Kingdom, and
(b) the money laundering—
    (i) is not unlawful under the criminal law applying in that country or territory, and
    (ii) is not of a description prescribed in an order made by the Secretary of State.]

333. Tipping off

333A. Tipping off: regulated sector

(1) A person commits an offence if—

(a) the person discloses any matter within subsection (2);
(b) the disclosure is likely to prejudice any investigation that might be conducted following the disclosure referred to in that subsection; and
(c) the information on which the disclosure is based came to the person in the course of a business in the regulated sector.

(2) The matters are that the person or another person has made a disclosure under this Part—

(a) to a constable,
(b) to an officer of Revenue and Customs,
(c) to a nominated officer, or

(d) to a [F31 National Crime Agency officer] authorised for the purposes of this Part by the Director General of that Agency, of information that came to that person in the course of a business in the regulated sector.

(3) A person commits an offence if—

(a) the person discloses that an investigation into allegations that an offence under this Part has been committed is being contemplated or is being carried out;
(b) the disclosure is likely to prejudice that investigation; and
(c) the information on which the disclosure is based came to the person in the course of a business in the regulated sector.

(4) A person guilty of an offence under this section is liable—

(a) on summary conviction to imprisonment for a term not exceeding three months, or to a fine not exceeding level 5 on the standard scale, or to both;
(b) on conviction on indictment to imprisonment for a term not exceeding two years, or to a fine, or to both.

(5) This section is subject to—

(a) section 333B (disclosures within an undertaking or group etc),
(b) section 333C (other permitted disclosures between institutions etc), and
(c) section 333D (other permitted disclosures etc).

333B. Disclosures within an undertaking or group etc

(1) An employee, officer or partner of an undertaking does not commit an offence under section 333A if the disclosure is to an employee, officer or partner of the same undertaking.

(2) A person does not commit an offence under section 333A in respect of a disclosure by a credit institution or a financial institution if—

(a) the disclosure is to a credit institution or a financial institution,
(b) the institution to whom the disclosure is made is situated in an EEA State or in a country or territory imposing equivalent money laundering requirements, and
(c) both the institution making the disclosure and the institution to whom it is made belong to the same group.

(3) In subsection (2) "group" has the same meaning as in Directive 2002/87/EC of the European Parliament and of the Council of 16th December 2002 on the supplementary supervision of credit institutions, insurance undertakings and investment firms in a financial conglomerate.

(4) A professional legal adviser or a relevant professional adviser does not commit an offence under section 333A if—

(a) the disclosure is to professional legal adviser or a relevant professional adviser,
(b) both the person making the disclosure and the person to whom it is made carry on business in an EEA State or in a country or territory imposing equivalent money laundering requirements, and
(c) those persons perform their professional activities within different undertakings that share common ownership, management or control.

333C. Other permitted disclosures between institutions etc

(1) This section applies to a disclosure—

(a) by a credit institution to another credit institution,
(b) by a financial institution to another financial institution,
(c) by a professional legal adviser to another professional legal adviser, or
(d) by a relevant professional adviser of a particular kind to another relevant professional adviser of the same kind.

(2) A person does not commit an offence under section 333A in respect of a disclosure to which this section applies if—

(a) the disclosure relates to—
    (i) a client or former client of the institution or adviser making the disclosure and the institution or adviser to whom it is made,
    (ii) a transaction involving them both, or
    (iii) the provision of a service involving them both;
(b) the disclosure is for the purpose only of preventing an offence under this Part of this Act;
(c) the institution or adviser to whom the disclosure is made is situated in an EEA State or in a country or territory imposing equivalent money laundering requirements; and
(d) the institution or adviser making the disclosure and the institution or adviser to whom it is made are subject to equivalent duties of professional confidentiality and the protection of personal data (within the meaning of section 1 of the Data Protection Act 1998).

333D. Other permitted disclosures etc

(1) A person does not commit an offence under section 333A if the disclosure is—

(a) to the authority that is the supervisory authority for that person by virtue of the Money Laundering Regulations 2007 (S.I. 2007/2157); or

(b) for the purpose of—
   (i) the detection, investigation or prosecution of a criminal offence (whether in the United Kingdom or elsewhere),
   (ii) an investigation under this Act, or
   (iii) the enforcement of any order of a court under this Act.

(2) A professional legal adviser or a relevant professional adviser does not commit an offence under section 333A if the disclosure—

(a) is to the adviser's client, and
(b) is made for the purpose of dissuading the client from engaging in conduct amounting to an offence.

(3) A person does not commit an offence under section 333A(1) if the person does not know or suspect that the disclosure is likely to have the effect mentioned in section 333A(1)(b).

(4) A person does not commit an offence under section 333A(3) if the person does not know or suspect that the disclosure is likely to have the effect mentioned in section 333A(3)(b)."

B. CUSTOMER DUE DILIGENCE

According to the Money Laundering Regulations, CDD measures means in summary:

(a) identifying the customer and verifying the customer's identity on the basis of documents, data or information obtained from a reliable and independent source;
(b) obtaining information on the purpose and intended nature of the business relationship;
(c) identifying, where there is a beneficial owner who is not the customer, the beneficial owner and taking adequate measures, on a risk-sensitive basis, to verify his identity so that the relevant person is satisfied that he knows who the beneficial owner is, including, in the case of a legal person, trust or similar legal arrangement, measures to understand the ownership and control structure of the person, trust or arrangement; and
(d) if the customer is an entity, in addition to determining the ownership (as per the above), the relevant person must obtain and verify:
   (i) the name of the body corporate;
   (ii) its company number or other registration number;
   (iii) the address of its registered office, and if different, its principal place of business;

(iv) and (unless the entity is listed on a regulated market), the law to which the entity is subject, and its constitution (whether set out in its articles of association or other governing documents) and the full names of the board of directors (or equivalent management body) and the senior persons responsible for the operations of the entity.[217]

---

217 See https://www.legislation.gov.uk/uksi/2017/692/part/3/made; https://www.fca.org.uk/firms/money-laundering-terrorist-financing/high-risk-customers-politically-exposed-persons. Further details on the CDD measures provision:

28.—(1) This regulation applies when a relevant person is required by regulation 27 to apply customer due diligence measures.

(2) The relevant person must—

(a) identify the customer unless the identity of that customer is known to, and has been verified by, the relevant person;
(b) verify the customer's identity unless the customer's identity has already been verified by the relevant person; and
(c) assess, and where appropriate obtain information on, the purpose and intended nature of the business relationship or occasional transaction.

(3) Where the customer is a body corporate—

(a) the relevant person must obtain and verify—
    (i) the name of the body corporate;
    (ii) its company number or other registration number;
    (iii) the address of its registered office, and if different, its principal place of business;
(b) subject to paragraph (5), the relevant person must take reasonable measures to determine and verify—
    (i) the law to which the body corporate is subject, and its constitution (whether set out in its articles of association or other governing documents);
    (ii) the full names of the board of directors (or if there is no board, the members of the equivalent management body) and the senior persons responsible for the operations of the body corporate.

(3A) Where the customer is a legal person, trust, company, foundation or similar legal arrangement the relevant person must take reasonable measures to understand the ownership and control structure of that legal person, trust, company, foundation or similar legal arrangement.

(4) Subject to paragraph (5), where the customer is beneficially owned by another person, the relevant person must—

(a) identify the beneficial owner;
(b) take reasonable measures to verify the identity of the beneficial owner so that the relevant person is satisfied that it knows who the beneficial owner is; and
(c) if the beneficial owner is a legal person, trust, company, foundation or similar legal arrangement take reasonable measures to understand the ownership and control structure of that legal person, trust, company, foundation or similar legal arrangement.

(5) Paragraphs (3)(b) and (4) do not apply where the customer is a company which is listed on a regulated market.

The guidance issued by the JMLSG is directed at financial services companies regulated by UK's financial watchdog, the FCA. But the approach taken by other parts of the regulated sector is not dissimilar. More specifically, interpreting the JMLSG guidance states that the regulated firm's CDD procedures should include procedures to:

- Identify and verify the identity of each customer on a timely basis
- Identify and take reasonable measures to verify the identity of any ultimate beneficial owner
- Obtain appropriate additional information to understand the customer's circumstances and business, including the expected nature and level of transactions.

---

(6) If the customer is a body corporate, and paragraph (7) applies, the relevant person may treat the senior person in that body corporate responsible for managing it as its beneficial owner.

(7) This paragraph applies if (and only if) the relevant person has exhausted all possible means of identifying the beneficial owner of the body corporate and—

(a) has not succeeded in doing so, or
(b) is not satisfied that the individual identified is in fact the beneficial owner.

(8) If paragraph (7) applies, the relevant person must—

(a) keep records in writing of all the actions it has taken to identify the beneficial owner of the body corporate;
(b) take reasonable measures to verify the identity of the senior person in the body corporate responsible for managing it, and keep records in writing of—
    (i) all the actions the relevant person has taken in doing so, and (ii) any difficulties the relevant person has encountered in doing so.

(9) Relevant persons do not satisfy their requirements under paragraph (4) by relying solely on the information—

(a) contained in—
    (i) the register of people with significant control kept by a company under section 790M of the Companies Act 2006 (duty to keep register)(1);
    (ii) the register of people with significant control kept by a limited liability partnership under section 790M of the Companies Act 2006 as modified by regulation 31E of the Limited Liability Partnerships (Application of Companies Act 2006) Regulations 2009(2); or
    (iii) the register of people with significant control kept by a European Public Limited-Liability Company (within the meaning of the Council Regulation 2157/2001/EC of 8 October 2001 on the Statute for a European Company which is to be, or is, registered in the United Kingdom) under section 790M of the Companies Act 2006 as modified by regulation 5 of the European Public Limited Liability Company (Register of People with Significant Control) Regulations 2016(3);
(b) referred to in sub-paragraph (a) and delivered to the registrar of companies (within the meaning of section 1060(3) of the Companies Act 2006 (the registrar)) under any enactment; or
(c) contained in required particulars in relation to eligible Scottish partnerships delivered to the registrar of companies under regulation 19 of the Scottish Partnerships (Register of People with Significant Control) Regulations 2017(4).

The guidance further states:

A customer identification programme that is graduated to reflect risk will involve:

- a standard information dataset to be held in respect of all customers;
- a standard verification requirement for all customers;
- more extensive due diligence (more identification checks and/or requiring additional information) on customer acceptance for higher risk customers;
- where appropriate, more limited identity verification measures for specific lower risk customer/product combinations; and
- an approach to monitoring customer activities and transactions that reflects the risk assessed to be presented by the customer, which will identify those transactions or activities that may be unusual or suspicious.

---

(10) Where a person ("A") purports to act on behalf of the customer, the relevant person must—

(a) verify that A is authorised to act on the customer's behalf;
(b) identify A; and
(c) verify A's identity on the basis of documents or information in either case obtained from a reliable source which is independent of both A and the customer.

(11) The relevant person must conduct ongoing monitoring of a business relationship, including—

(a) scrutiny of transactions undertaken throughout the course of the relationship (including, where necessary, the source of funds) to ensure that the transactions are consistent with the relevant person's knowledge of the customer, the customer's business and risk profile;
(b) undertaking reviews of existing records and keeping the documents or information obtained for the purpose of applying customer due diligence measures up to date.

(12) The ways in which a relevant person complies with the requirement to take customer due diligence measures, and the extent of the measures taken—

(a) must reflect—
    (i) the risk assessment carried out by the relevant person under regulation 18(1);
    (ii) its assessment of the level of risk arising in any particular case;
(b) may differ from case to case.

(13) In assessing the level of risk in a particular case, the relevant person must take account of factors including, among other things—

(a) the purpose of an account, transaction or business relationship;
(b) the level of assets to be deposited by a customer or the size of the transactions undertaken by the customer;
(c) the regularity and duration of the business relationship.

(14) If paragraph (15) applies, a relevant person is not required to continue to apply customer due diligence measures under paragraph (2) or (10) in respect of a customer.

(15) This paragraph applies if all the following conditions are met—

(a) a relevant person has taken customer due diligence measures in relation to a customer;
(b) the relevant person makes a disclosure required by—
    (i) Part 3 of the Terrorism Act 2000(5), or
    (ii) Part 7 of the Proceeds of Crime Act 2002(6); and

The JMLSG guidance further states:

> The firm identifies the customer by obtaining a range of information about him. The verification of the identity consists of the firm verifying some of this information against documents or information obtained from a reliable source which is independent of the customer.

C. SIMPLIFIED DUE DILIGENCE

According to the Money Laundering Regulations:

"37.—(1) A relevant person may apply simplified customer due diligence measures in relation to a particular business relationship or transaction if it determines that the business relationship or transaction presents a low degree of risk of money laundering and terrorist financing, having taken into account—

(a) the risk assessment it carried out under regulation 18(1);
(b) relevant information made available to it under regulations 17(9) and 47; and
(c) the risk factors referred to in paragraph (3).

(c) continuing to apply customer due diligence measures in relation to that customer would result in the commission of an offence by the relevant person under—
(i) section 21D of the Terrorism Act 2000 (tipping off: regulated sector)(7); or
(ii) section 333A of the Proceeds of Crime Act 2002 (tipping off: regulated sector)(8).

(16) The relevant person must be able to demonstrate to its supervisory authority that the extent of the measures it has taken to satisfy its requirements under this regulation are appropriate in view of the risks of money laundering and terrorist financing, including risks—

(a) identified by the risk assessment carried out by the relevant person under regulation 18(1);
(b) identified by its supervisory authority and in information made available to the relevant person under regulations 17(9) and 47.

(17) Paragraph (16) does not apply to the National Savings Bank or the Director of Savings.

(18) For the purposes of this regulation—

(a) except in paragraph (10), "verify" means verify on the basis of documents or information in either case obtained from a reliable source which is independent of the person whose identity is being verified;
(b) documents issued or made available by an official body are to be regarded as being independent of a person even if they are provided or made available to the relevant person by or on behalf of that person.

There are also additional CDD measures for credit and financial institutions in regard to long-term insurance.

(2) Where a relevant person applies simplified customer due diligence measures, it must—

(a) continue to comply with the requirements in regulation 28, but it may adjust the extent, timing or type of the measures it undertakes under that regulation to reflect its determination under paragraph (1); and
(b) carry out sufficient monitoring of any business relationships or transactions which are subject to those measures to enable it to detect any unusual or suspicious transactions.

(3) When assessing whether there is a low degree of risk of money laundering and terrorist financing in a particular situation, and the extent to which it is appropriate to apply simplified customer due diligence measures in that situation, the relevant person must take account of risk factors including, among other things—

(a) customer risk factors, including whether the customer—
  (i) is a public administration, or a publicly owned enterprise;
  (ii) is an individual resident in a geographical area of lower risk (see sub-paragraph (c));
  (iii) is a credit institution or a financial institution which is—
    (aa) subject to the requirements in national legislation implementing the fourth money laundering directive as an obliged entity (within the meaning of that directive), and
    (bb) supervised for compliance with those requirements in accordance with section 2 of Chapter VI of the fourth money laundering directive;
  (iv) is a company whose securities are listed on a regulated market, and the location of the regulated market;
(b) product, service, transaction or delivery channel risk factors, including whether the product or service is—
  (i) a life insurance policy for which the premium is low;
  (ii) an insurance policy for a pension scheme which does not provide for an early surrender option, and cannot be used as collateral;
  (iii) a pension, superannuation or similar scheme which satisfies the following conditions—
    (aa) the scheme provides retirement benefits to employees;
    (bb) contributions to the scheme are made by way of deductions from wages; and
    (cc) the scheme rules do not permit the assignment of a member's interest under the scheme;
  (iv) a financial product or service that provides appropriately defined and limited services to certain types of customers to increase access for financial inclusion purposes in an EEA state;

(v) a product where the risks of money laundering and terrorist financing are managed by other factors such as purse limits or transparency of ownership;
(vi) a child trust fund within the meaning given by section 1(2) of the Child Trust Funds Act 2004(1);
(vii) a junior ISA within the meaning given by regulation 2B of the Individual Savings Account Regulations 1998(2);

(c) geographical risk factors, including whether the country where the customer is resident, established or registered or in which it operates is—
(i) an EEA state;
(ii) a third country which has effective systems to counter money laundering and terrorist financing;
(iii) a third country identified by credible sources as having a low level of corruption or other criminal activity, such as terrorism (within the meaning of section 1 of the Terrorism Act 2000(3)), money laundering, and the production and supply of illicit drugs;
(iv) a third country which, on the basis of credible sources, such as evaluations, detailed assessment reports or published follow-up reports published by the Financial Action Task Force, the International Monetary Fund, the World Bank, the Organisation for Economic Co-operation and Development or other international bodies or non-governmental organisations—
(aa) has requirements to counter money laundering and terrorist financing that are consistent with the revised Recommendations published by the Financial Action Task Force in February 2012 and updated in October 2016; and
(bb) effectively implements those Recommendations.

(4) In making the assessment referred to in paragraph (3), relevant persons must bear in mind that the presence of one or more risk factors may not always indicate that there is a low risk of money laundering and terrorist financing in a particular situation.

(5) A relevant person may apply simplified customer due diligence measures where the customer is a person to whom paragraph (6) applies and the product is an account into which monies are pooled (the 'pooled account'), provided that—

(a) the business relationship with the holder of the pooled account presents a low degree of risk of money laundering and terrorist financing; and
(b) information on the identity of the persons on whose behalf monies are held in the pooled account is available, on request to the relevant person where the pooled account is held.

(6) This paragraph applies to—

(a) a relevant person who is subject to these Regulations under regulation 8;
(b) a person who carries on business in an EEA state other than the United Kingdom who is—
    (i) subject to the requirements in national legislation implementing the fourth money laundering directive as an obliged entity (within the meaning of that directive), and
    (ii) supervised for compliance with those requirements in accordance with section 2 of Chapter VI of the fourth money laundering directive.

(7) In determining what simplified customer due diligence measures to take, and the extent of those measures, when paragraph (1) applies, credit institutions and financial institutions must also take account of any guidelines issued by the European Supervisory Authorities under Article 17 of the fourth money laundering directive.

(8) A relevant person must not continue to apply simplified customer due diligence measures under paragraph (1)—

(a) if it doubts the veracity or accuracy of any documents or information previously obtained for the purposes of identification or verification;
(b) if its risk assessment changes and it no longer considers that there is a low degree of risk of money laundering and terrorist financing;
(c) if it suspects money laundering or terrorist financing; or
(d) if any of the conditions set out in regulation 33(1) apply."[218]

D. ENHANCED DUE DILIGENCE

The Money Laundering Regulations stipulate:

"Obligation to apply enhanced customer due diligence

33.—(1) A relevant person must apply enhanced customer due diligence measures and enhanced ongoing monitoring, in addition to the customer due diligence measures required under regulation 28 and, if applicable, regulation 29, to manage and mitigate the risks arising—

(a) in any case identified as one where there is a high risk of money laundering or terrorist financing—
    (i) by the relevant person under regulation 18(1), or

[218] There are also provisions in regard to electronic money and anonymous prepaid cards issued in a third country.

(ii) in information made available to the relevant person under regulations 17(9) and 47;

(b) in any business relationship with a person established in a high-risk third country or in relation to any relevant transaction where either of the parties to the transaction is established in a high-risk third country;

(c) in relation to correspondent relationships with a credit institution or a financial institution (in accordance with regulation 34);

(d) if a relevant person has determined that a customer or potential customer is a PEP, or a family member or known close associate of a PEP (in accordance with regulation 35);

(e) in any case where the relevant person discovers that a customer has provided false or stolen identification documentation or information and the relevant person proposes to continue to deal with that customer;

(f) in any case where—

(i) a transaction is complex or unusually large, or there is an unusual pattern of transactions, and

(ii) the transaction or transactions have no apparent economic or legal purpose, or

(g) in any other case which by its nature can present a higher risk of money laundering or terrorist financing.

(2) Paragraph (1)(b) does not apply when the customer is a branch or majority owned subsidiary undertaking of an entity which is established in an EEA state if all the following conditions are satisfied—

(a) the entity is—

(i) subject to the requirements in national legislation implementing the fourth money laundering directive as an obliged entity (within the meaning of that directive), and

(ii) supervised for compliance with those requirements in accordance with section 2 of Chapter VI of the fourth money laundering directive;

(b) the branch or subsidiary complies fully with procedures and policies established for the group under Article 45 of the fourth money laundering directive; and

(c) the relevant person, applying a risk-based approach, does not consider that it is necessary to apply enhanced customer due diligence measures.

(3) For the purposes of paragraph (1)(b)—

(a) a 'high-risk third country' means a country which has been identified by the European Commission in delegated acts adopted under Article 9.2 of the fourth money laundering directive as a high-risk third country;

(b) a "relevant transaction" means a transaction in relation to which the relevant person is required to apply customer due diligence measures under regulation 27;
(c) being "established in" a country means—
   (i) in the case of a legal person, being incorporated in or having its principal place of business in that country, or, in the case of a financial institution or a credit institution, having its principal regulatory authority in that country; and
   (ii) in the case of an individual, being resident in that country, but not merely having been born in that country.

(3A) The enhanced due diligence measures taken by a relevant person for the purpose of paragraph (1)(b) must include—

(a) obtaining additional information on the customer and on the customer's beneficial owner; (b) obtaining additional information on the intended nature of the business relationship;
(c) obtaining information on the source of funds and source of wealth of the customer and of the customer's beneficial owner;
(d) obtaining information on the reasons for the transactions;
(e) obtaining the approval of senior management for establishing or continuing the business relationship;
(f) conducting enhanced monitoring of the business relationship by increasing the number and timing of controls applied, and selecting patterns of transactions that need further examination.

(4) The enhanced customer due diligence measures taken by a relevant person for the purpose of paragraph (1)(f) must include—

(a) as far as reasonably possible, examining the background and purpose of the transaction, and
(b) increasing the degree and nature of monitoring of the business relationship in which the transaction is made to determine whether that transaction or that relationship appear to be suspicious.

(4A) Where the customer—

(a) is the beneficiary of a life insurance policy, (b) is a legal person or a legal arrangement, and
(c) presents a high risk of money laundering or terrorist financing for any other reason,

a relevant person who is a credit or financial institution must take reasonable measures to identify and verify the identity of the beneficial owners of that beneficiary before any payment is made under the policy.

(5) Depending on the requirements of the case, the enhanced customer due diligence measures required under paragraph (1) may also include, among other things—

(a) seeking additional independent, reliable sources to verify information provided or made available to the relevant person;
(b) taking additional measures to understand better the background, ownership and financial situation of the customer, and other parties to the transaction;
(c) taking further steps to be satisfied that the transaction is consistent with the purpose and intended nature of the business relationship;
(d) increasing the monitoring of the business relationship, including greater scrutiny of transactions.

(6) When assessing whether there is a high risk of money laundering or terrorist financing in a particular situation, and the extent of the measures which should be taken to manage and mitigate that risk, relevant persons must take account of risk factors including, among other things—

(a) customer risk factors, including whether—
    (i) the business relationship is conducted in unusual circumstances;
    (ii) the customer is resident in a geographical area of high risk (see sub-paragraph (c));
    (iii) the customer is a legal person or legal arrangement that is a vehicle for holding personal assets;
    (iv) the customer is a company that has nominee shareholders or shares in bearer form;
    (v) the customer is a business that is cash intensive;
    (vi) the corporate structure of the customer is unusual or excessively complex given the nature of the company's business;
    (vii) the customer is the beneficiary of a life insurance policy;
    (viii) the customer is a third country national who is applying for residence rights in or citizenship of an EEA state in exchange for transfers of capital, purchase of a property, government bonds or investment in corporate entities in that EEA state;
(b) product, service, transaction or delivery channel risk factors, including whether—
    (i) the product involves private banking;
    (ii) the product or transaction is one which might favour anonymity;
    (iii) the situation involves non-face-to-face business relationships or transactions, without certain safeguards, such as an electronic identification process which meets the conditions set out in regulation 28(19);
    (iv) payments will be received from unknown or unassociated third parties;

(v) new products and new business practices are involved, including new delivery mechanisms, and the use of new or developing technologies for both new and pre-existing products;
(vi) the service involves the provision of nominee directors, nominee shareholders or shadow directors, or the formation of companies in a third country;
(vii) there is a transaction related to oil, arms, precious metals, tobacco products, cultural artefacts, ivory and other items related to protected species, or other items of archaeological, historical, cultural and religious significance, or of rare scientific value;

(c) geographical risk factors, including—
(i) countries identified by credible sources, such as mutual evaluations, detailed assessment reports or published follow-up reports, as not having effective systems to counter money laundering or terrorist financing;
(ii) countries identified by credible sources as having significant levels of corruption or other criminal activity, such as terrorism (within the meaning of section 1 of the Terrorism Act 2000(86)), money laundering, and the production and supply of illicit drugs;
(iii) countries subject to sanctions, embargos or similar measures issued by, for example, the European Union or the United Nations;
(iv) countries providing funding or support for terrorism;
(v) countries that have organisations operating within their territory which have been designated—
(aa) by the government of the United Kingdom as proscribed organisations under Schedule 2 to the Terrorism Act 2000(87), or
(bb) by other countries, international organisations or the European Union as terrorist organisations;
(vi) countries identified by credible sources, such as evaluations, detailed assessment reports or published follow-up reports published by the Financial Action Task Force, the International Monetary Fund, the World Bank, the Organisation for Economic Co-operation and Development or other international bodies or non-governmental organisations as not implementing requirements to counter money laundering and terrorist financing that are consistent with the recommendations published by the Financial Action Task Force in February 2012 and updated in June 2019.

(7) In making the assessment referred to in paragraph (6), relevant persons must bear in mind that the presence of one or more risk factors may not always indicate that there is a high risk of money laundering or terrorist financing in a particular situation.

(8) In determining what measures to take when paragraph (1) applies, and what the extent of those measures should be, credit institutions and financial institutions must also take account of any guidelines issued by the European Supervisory Authorities under Article 18.4 of the fourth money laundering directive.

Enhanced customer due diligence: credit institutions, financial institutions and correspondent relationships

34.—(1) A credit institution or financial institution (the 'correspondent') which has or proposes to have a correspondent relationship with another such institution (the 'respondent') from a third country must, in addition to the measures required by regulation 33—

(a) gather sufficient information about the respondent to understand fully the nature of its business;
(b) determine from publicly-available information from credible sources the reputation of the respondent and the quality of the supervision to which the respondent is subject;
(c) assess the respondent's controls to counter money laundering and terrorist financing;
(d) obtain approval from senior management before establishing a new correspondent relationship;
(e) document the responsibilities of the respondent and correspondent in the correspondent relationship; and
(f) be satisfied that, in respect of those of the respondent's customers who have direct access to accounts with the correspondent, the respondent—
    (i) has verified the identity of, and conducts ongoing customer due diligence measures in relation to, such customers; and
    (ii) is able to provide to the correspondent, upon request, the documents or information obtained when applying such customer due diligence measures.

(2) Credit institutions and financial institutions must not enter into, or continue, a correspondent relationship with a shell bank.

(3) Credit institutions and financial institutions must take appropriate enhanced measures to ensure that they do not enter into, or continue, a correspondent relationship with a credit institution or financial institution which is known to allow its accounts to be used by a shell bank.

(4) For the purposes of this regulation—

(a) 'correspondent relationship' means—
    (i) the provision of banking services by a correspondent to a respondent including providing a current or other liability account and related

services, such as cash management, international funds transfers, cheque clearing, providing customers of the respondent with direct access to accounts with the correspondent (and vice versa) and providing foreign exchange services; or

(ii) the relationship between and among credit institutions and financial institutions including where similar services are provided by a correspondent to a respondent, and including relationships established for securities transactions or funds transfers;

(b) a 'shell bank' means a credit institution or financial institution, or an institution engaged in equivalent activities to those carried out by credit institutions or financial institutions, incorporated in a jurisdiction in which it has no physical presence involving meaningful decision-making and management, and which is not part of a financial conglomerate or third-country financial conglomerate;

(c) in sub-paragraph (b), 'financial conglomerate' and 'third-country financial conglomerate' have the meanings given by regulations 1(2) and 7(1) respectively of the Financial Conglomerates and Other Financial Groups Regulations 2004(88).

Enhanced customer due diligence: politically exposed persons

35.—(1) A relevant person must have in place appropriate risk-management systems and procedures to determine whether a customer or the beneficial owner of a customer is—

(a) a politically exposed person (a 'PEP'); or
(b) a family member or a known close associate of a PEP,

and to manage the enhanced risks arising from the relevant person's business relationship or transactions with such a customer.

(2) In determining what risk-management systems and procedures are appropriate under paragraph (1), the relevant person must take account of—

(a) the risk assessment it carried out under regulation 18(1);
(b) the level of risk of money laundering and terrorist financing inherent in its business;
(c) the extent to which that risk would be increased by its business relationship or transactions with a PEP, or a family member or known close associate of a PEP, and
(d) any relevant information made available to the relevant person under regulations 17(9) and 47.

(3) If a relevant person has determined that a customer or a potential customer is a PEP, or a family member or known close associate of a PEP, the relevant person must assess—

(a) the level of risk associated with that customer, and
(b) the extent of the enhanced customer due diligence measures to be applied in relation to that customer.

(4) In assessing the extent of the enhanced customer due diligence measures to be taken in relation to any particular person (which may differ from case to case), a relevant person—

(a) must take account of any relevant information made available to the relevant person under regulations 17(9) and 47; and
(b) may take into account any guidance which has been—
    (i) issued by the FCA; or
    (ii) issued by any other supervisory authority or appropriate body and approved by the Treasury.

(5) A relevant person who proposes to have, or to continue, a business relationship with a PEP, or a family member or a known close associate of a PEP, must, in addition to the measures required by regulation 33—

(a) have approval from senior management for establishing or continuing the business relationship with that person;
(b) take adequate measures to establish the source of wealth and source of funds which are involved in the proposed business relationship or transactions with that person; and
(c) where the business relationship is entered into, conduct enhanced ongoing monitoring of the business relationship with that person.

(6) A relevant person which is providing a customer with a contract of long-term insurance (an 'insurance policy') must take reasonable measures to determine whether one or more of the beneficiaries of the insurance policy or the beneficial owner of a beneficiary of such an insurance policy are—

(a) PEPs, or
(b) family members or known close associates of PEPs.

(7) The measures required under paragraph (6) must be taken before—

(a) any payment is made under the insurance policy, or
(b) the benefit of the insurance policy is assigned in whole or in part to another person.

(8) A relevant person must, in addition to the measures required by regulation 33, ensure that—

(a) its senior management is informed before it pays out any sums under an insurance policy the beneficiary of which is a PEP or a person who comes within paragraph (6)(b) in relation to a PEP, and
(b) its entire business relationship with the holder of the insurance policy ('the policy holder') is scrutinised on an ongoing basis in accordance with enhanced procedures, whether or not the policy holder is a PEP or a family member or known close associate of a PEP.

(9) Where a person who was a PEP is no longer entrusted with a prominent public function, a relevant person must continue to apply the requirements in paragraphs (5) and (8) in relation to that person—

(a) for a period of at least 12 months after the date on which that person ceased to be entrusted with that public function; or
(b) for such longer period as the relevant person considers appropriate to address risks of money laundering or terrorist financing in relation to that person.

(10) Paragraph (9) does not apply in relation to a person who—

(a) was not a politically exposed person within the meaning of regulation 14(5) of the Money Laundering Regulations 2007(89), when those Regulations were in force; and
(b) ceased to be entrusted with a prominent public function before the date on which these Regulations come into force.

(11) When a person who was a PEP is no longer entrusted with a prominent public function, the relevant person is no longer required to apply the requirements in paragraphs (5) and (8) in relation to a family member or known close associate of that PEP (whether or not the period referred to in paragraph (9) has expired).

(12) In this regulation—

(a) 'politically exposed person' or 'PEP' means an individual who is entrusted with prominent public functions, other than as a middle-ranking or more junior official;
(b) 'family member' of a politically exposed person includes—
    (i) a spouse or civil partner of the PEP;
    (ii) children of the PEP and the spouses or civil partners of the PEP's children;
    (iii) parents of the PEP;

(c) 'known close associate' of a PEP means—
  (i) an individual known to have joint beneficial ownership of a legal entity or a legal arrangement or any other close business relations with a PEP;
  (ii) an individual who has sole beneficial ownership of a legal entity or a legal arrangement which is known to have been set up for the benefit of a PEP.

(13) For the purposes of paragraph (5), a reference to a business relationship with an individual includes a reference to a business relationship with a person of which the individual is a beneficial owner.

(14) For the purposes of paragraphs (9), (11) and (12)(a), individuals entrusted with prominent public functions include—

(a) heads of state, heads of government, ministers and deputy or assistant ministers;
(b) members of parliament or of similar legislative bodies;
(c) members of the governing bodies of political parties;
(d) members of supreme courts, of constitutional courts or of any judicial body the decisions of which are not subject to further appeal except in exceptional circumstances;
(e) members of courts of auditors or of the boards of central banks;
(f) ambassadors, charges d'affaires and high-ranking officers in the armed forces;
(g) members of the administrative, management or supervisory bodies of State-owned enterprises;
(h) directors, deputy directors and members of the board or equivalent function of an international organisation.

(15) For the purpose of deciding whether a person is a known close associate of a politically exposed person, a relevant person need only have regard to information which is in its possession, or to credible information which is publicly available.

Politically exposed persons: other duties

36.—(1) The duty under section 30(1) of the Bank of England and Financial Services Act 2016 (duty to ensure that regulations or orders implementing the fourth money laundering directive comply with paragraphs (a) to (d) of that subsection)(90) does not apply if, and to the extent that, the duty is otherwise satisfied as a result of any provision contained in these Regulations, or any guidance issued by the FCA under these Regulations.

(2) The duty under section 333U(1) and (2) of FSMA (duty to issue guidance in connection with politically exposed persons)(91) does not apply if, and to the

extent that, the duty is otherwise satisfied as a result of guidance issued by the FCA under these Regulations."

E. CROWN PROSECUTION SERVICE

The CPS's guidance on POCA states:[219]

"Proving that proceeds are the benefit from criminal conduct in money laundering prosecutions (proving the predicate offence).

Proving that proceeds are the benefit of 'criminal conduct' will usually be done by circumstantial evidence.

Where money laundering offences are proceeded with on the same indictment as the underlying crimes, the underlying criminal conduct will be proved as part of the proceedings to the requisite standard. Where the money laundering proceedings are 'standalone', there are two ways of proving criminal property, firstly by proving the type of offending that gave rise to the criminal property and secondly by relying upon circumstantial evidence (R v Anwoir [2008] EWCA Crim 1354).

It is not necessary in 'stand alone' money laundering prosecutions to wait for a conviction in relation to the 'criminal conduct' (i.e. the underlying or predicate offences giving rise to the criminal property).

Prosecutors are not required to prove that the property in question is the benefit of a particular or a specific act of criminal conduct, as such an interpretation would restrict the operation of the legislation. The prosecution need to be in a position, as a minimum, to be able to produce sufficient circumstantial evidence or other evidence from which inferences can be drawn to the required criminal standard that the property in question has a criminal origin.

Typically evidence of the criminal origin of proceeds may be provided in money laundering proceedings by:

- Accomplice evidence;
- Circumstantial evidence and/or other evidence;
- Forensic evidence (e.g. contamination of cash with drugs) from which inferences can be drawn that money came from drug trafficking;
- Evidence of complex audit trails, from which an accountancy expert may be able to conclude that the complexity of the transactions indicate that the property was the proceeds of crime. (Archbold 2006 10–66). While this was not a money laundering prosecution, by analogy, it would seem permissible

219 https://www.cps.gov.uk/legal-guidance/proceeds-crime-act-2002-part-7-money-laundering-offences.

for a witness to give expert evidence that the facts lead him to the conclusion that the property was the proceeds of crime);

- Evidence of the unlikelihood of the property being of legitimate origin – Where the prosecution proves D has no legitimate explanation for possessing the property in question a jury may be willing to draw an inference that it is proceeds of crime;
- Criminals often attempt to launder proceeds through a cash intensive business. Where the cash flows appear too large or the profit margins too high this may be capable of giving rise to expert evidence that the business will usually give rise to a particular level of profit and the profits are clearly excessive which together with other available evidence can be sufficient to prove the underlying criminality. See R. v. Boam 1998 Cr. Law Bulletin."

ANTI-MONEY LAUNDERING ARCHITECTURES

Between Structural Homogeneity and Functional Diversity

Jean-Baptiste MAILLART*

I. INTRODUCTION

A. HISTORY OF ANTI-MONEY LAUNDERING IN THE COUNTRY

In the five national jurisdictions which fall within the scope of this study, namely Germany, Italy, Spain, Switzerland and the UK, anti-money laundering (AML) efforts started with the introduction of the criminal offence of money laundering into national law. Among the five jurisdictions examined, Italy was the first country to criminalise money laundering (1978), whilst Germany was the last one (1992). What is interesting to note from a comparative point of view is not so much *when* money laundering was criminalised but rather *why* national legislators decided to make it a criminal offence. In Spain and the UK,[1] the objective pursued initially was to track down organised criminal groups involved in drug trafficking and disrupt their activities by seizing their criminal proceeds. In contrast, AML was conceived at first in Germany and Switzerland[2] as a tool to fight organised crime in general and not just organised crime in relation to the trafficking of drugs. In Italy, finally, money laundering was introduced as a

* In this chapter, references in footnotes to specific sections of national and supranational reports are only provided when those sections are different from the ones in which such references are made.

1 In the UK, it should be noted that the law originally did not refer to money laundering but rather described it under the heading "Assisting another to retain the benefit of drug trafficking".

2 Switzerland report, section II.A.

criminal offence in the late 1970s with the aim of dismantling terrorist groups, such as the Red Brigades, by taking away these groups' criminal assets originating from certain offences such as extortion, robbery or kidnapping. Over the years, the AML frameworks have however expanded beyond their initial focus and have been increasingly including types of predicate offences, and thus criminal policy goals, that are not necessarily related to organised crime and potentially not even to serious criminality.[3]

When the original 40 Financial Action Task Force (FATF) Recommendations were issued in 1990, only Germany had not yet criminalised money laundering. The early influence of the FATF framework on the development of the criminal law approach to money laundering in the jurisdictions analysed was originally therefore quite limited. It should, however, be noted that the FATF, by stressing the criminalisation of self-laundering[4] and promoting an ever-growing scope of predicate offences,[5] has increasingly impacted the development of the money laundering offence. Its impact has even been greater on the preventive-regulatory approach to money laundering. Over the past three decades, the FATF has indeed undoubtedly functioned as the universally recognised standard-setter not only regarding the preventive measures that the financial sector and other designated sectors should have in place, but also with respect to the powers and responsibilities that the competent authorities (e.g. investigative, judicial and supervisory authorities) should have. The FATF Recommendations and mutual evaluations have driven forward numerous legislative reforms over the years, to the extent that the inter-governmental body could be labelled as a quasi-legislator in the field of AML/CTF.

As just explained, national AML frameworks have been significantly influenced by the FATF Recommendations and mutual evaluations over the past 30 years. One should note, however, that European Union Directives have also played an important role by making FATF standards binding for Member States. The EU legal framework is even more relevant today as the EU is somewhat emancipating itself from the FATF in the fight against financial crime by imposing its own rules and not merely rules arising from the FATF Recommendations.[6]

At this point, it is not necessary to compare the chronological development of the AML regulatory framework in each jurisdiction examined. However, three observations are worth making. First, it is important to highlight the fact that the range and complexity of measures that obliged entities must take to prevent

3 See *infra* section II.A.
4 See *infra* section II.B.1.a.ii.
5 See *infra* section II.B.1.a.i.
6 On the emancipation of the EU from the FATF in the fight against money laundering and terrorist financing, see EU report, section VIII.

money laundering has been constantly extending in all the jurisdictions analysed since the inception of the AML regime. Second, it is worth observing that the scope of obliged entities, which initially covered only credit institutions and financial institutions, was expanded in EU Member States to other professions, such as lawyers, tax advisors and trust and company service providers, following notably the second AML Directive adopted in 2001 (Directive 2001/97/EC)[7] implementing the revised FATF Recommendations. The only exception in this regard is Spain, where customer due diligence (CDD) and reporting obligations were imposed on such professions from 1993. Third and last, it should be pointed out that financial intelligence units (FIUs) have undergone profound changes over the years. While they were first created as bodies to collect suspicious activity reports (SARs),[8] they have, especially under the fourth Anti-Money Laundering Directive (4AMLD), increasingly been transformed into operational intelligence units with the aim of proactively gathering relevant information.

B. CURRENT CONCERNS AND REFORM AGENDA

From a comparative point of view, it is important to point out the fact that such concerns widely differ from one jurisdiction to another, thereby clearly reflecting the strong heterogeneity of AML regimes and the lack of common AML policy and objective, notably within Europe.

The FATF, for instance, is currently mostly concerned by questions related to the transparency of beneficial ownership and information sharing between relevant stakeholders. In contrast, the EU's current work in the area of AML is primarily focused on reshaping the supervision system and trying to establish its own autonomous list of high-risk third countries.

At national level, ongoing debate about AML in Germany primarily relates to the quality of the FIU's operational analysis and the insufficiency of supervision over non-financial obliged entities. In Switzerland, the main AML-related concern that the legislator is discussing at the moment is the idea of expanding the scope of the AML law in order to make lawyers obliged entities, not only when they qualify as financial intermediaries,[9] that is when they perform financial

[7] Directive 2001/97/EC of the European Parliament and of the Council of 4 December 2001 amending Council Directive 91/308/EEC on prevention of the use of the financial system for the purpose of money laundering (OJ L 344, 28.12.2001, p. 76).

[8] Germany, Italy, Switzerland, Spain and the UK established a national financial intelligence unit (FIU) at very different times. The UK FIU, for instance, was created in 1985, whereas, at the other end of the spectrum, the German FIU was only established in 2002.

[9] On the definition of financial intermediaries, see *infra* section II.D.3 and Switzerland report, section II.D.3.

transactions, but also when their work consists in setting up companies, legal persons and legal arrangements and where no transactions are involved.[10] Debates in Italy also pertain to the scope of obliged entities but rather concern virtual currency system participants. In the UK, questions arise notably about defensive reporting and how to increase the quality of SARs (through public-private partnerships for instance).[11] Finally, in Spain, discussions mainly relate the new data protection requirements and their applicability in the AML context.

II. AIMS AND SCOPE OF AML SYSTEM

A. AIMS OF AML REGIME

The FATF and EU's current discourse on AML primarily focuses on the protection of the soundness, integrity and stability of the financial system. That said, it is worth noting that, in addition to this objective, both the FATF Recommendations and the relevant EU Directives suggest that AML also aims at tracking down criminals and protecting society from crime. The original 40 Recommendations of the FATF were specifically designed to track down organised criminal groups involved in drug trafficking and to disrupt their activities by seizing their criminal proceeds. This is echoed in Article 35(1) 4AMLD, according to which obliged entities shall not carry out transactions which they know or suspect to be related to money laundering or terrorist financing unless refraining from carrying out such transactions is impossible or is likely to hinder investigations or judicial proceedings.[12] Even more clearly, recital (2) 4AMLD provides that "the objectives of protecting society from crime and protecting the stability and integrity of the Union's financial system should be balanced against the need to create a regulatory environment that allows companies to grow their businesses without incurring disproportionate compliance costs".

The protection of the financial sector is also explicitly considered as the main objective in implementing AML measures in all the national jurisdictions analysed, thereby reflecting the FATF Recommendations and the 4AMLD. This holds true particularly in Switzerland where, nowadays, the financial industry's competitiveness largely depends on how its commitment to AML is perceived. Besides preserving the financial sector from the threat of money laundering, certain national AML laws also emphasise other objectives, either explicitly or implicitly. In Italy, for instance, the fight against organised crime is at the core of the AML preventive regime, as reflected notably in the prominent coordinating

---

10 See *infra* II.D.3 and Switzerland report, sections II.D.3 and II.D.6.

11 On public-private partnerships in the UK, see *infra* section IV.B.3.a.

12 See *infra* section III.C.1.d.

role given to the National Anti-Mafia and Counter-Terrorism Bureau.[13] One could also mention Spain, which very clearly treats AML as a tool to fight against tax offences. The obligation of the Spanish FIU to forward any relevant tax-related information to the tax authorities is probably the best illustration of this.[14]

B. SCOPE OF MONEY LAUNDERING

1. *Definition of Money Laundering in Criminal Law*

a. *Actus Reus*

i. Predicate Offences

Both the FATF Recommendations and Directive 2018/1673/EU require countries to consider applying the offence of money laundering to the widest range of predicate offences possible and at least to all serious offences. In this regard, both supranational frameworks still allow for considerable flexibility of countries when it comes to the definition of predicate offences, insofar as they require countries that have a minimum threshold for offences in their legal system to apply money laundering to all offences that are punishable by a minimum penalty of more than six months' imprisonment. Moreover, to the extent that the application of those penalty thresholds does not already do so, the FATF Recommendations and Directive 2018/1673/EU require countries to include a range of offences within specific categories of offences (e.g. terrorism, drug trafficking, tax crimes, extortion, illicit arms trafficking, fraud, corruption). With the only exception of cybercrimes, the scope of these categories of offences is broadly similar under both the EU and FATF legal frameworks.

At national level, Spain[15] and the UK[16] follow an all-crimes approach with respect to the scope of predicate offences for money laundering. In Germany, Italy and Switzerland, the definition of criminal activities which constitute predicate offences is narrower. In fact, German law provides for an exhaustive catalogue of predicate offences which contains only serious offences, whereas the catalogue in Swiss law goes beyond this and also includes some less serious

---

13 See Italy report, section VIII.

14 See Spain report, sections IV.A.2 and V.D.1.

15 The all-crimes approach was adopted in Spain in 2010.

16 It is reported, however, that prosecutors will not pursue *de minimis* amounts, which means that if a crime generates a small amount/economic benefit (e.g. shoplifting), prosecutors are very unlikely to pursue a money laundering charge.

offences.[17] In Italy, courts can only apply money laundering in relation to serious offences.

ii. Definition of Money Laundering Acts

Pursuant to Article 3(1)(b) and (c) of the of the 1988 United Nations Convention against Illicit Traffic in Narcotic Drugs and Psychotropic Substances (Vienna Convention)[18] and Article 6(1) of the 2000 United Nations Convention against Transnational Organized Crime (Palermo Convention),[19] which set out minimum rules relating to the definition of money laundering acts at international level, money laundering refers to three distinct sets of conduct: (i) conversion or transfer of property; (ii) concealment or disguise of the true nature, source, location, disposition, movement, rights with respect to, or ownership of property; and (iii) acquisition, possession or use of property. Directive 2018/1673/EU adopts the same definition and so do all the national jurisdictions within the scope of this study, with the exception of Switzerland where the money laundering offence does not cover the possession of criminal proceeds. It should be pointed out that only UK and Spanish laws explicitly cover all three sets of money laundering acts. In Germany and Italy, the definition of money laundering appears narrower but has been interpreted broadly by national courts as essentially comprising all the aforementioned forms of money laundering.

As regards self-laundering, the criminalisation of this specific form of money laundering is required by Directive 2018/1673/EU with respect to the first and second sets of money laundering conducts (see variants (i) and (ii) above), but not by the FATF. At national level, Germany remains the only country that still provides certain limits to the definition of self-laundering. In Switzerland, Spain, Italy and the UK, criminal law indeed covers the laundering of the proceeds of one's own criminal activity, whether explicitly (Spain, Italy[20] and the UK) or by virtue of jurisprudential interpretation (Switzerland).

---

17 In Switzerland, predicate offences include offences that carry a custodial sentence of more than three years, as well as aggravated tax misdemeanours. In Germany, predicate offences include criminal acts that are punishable by a minimum sentence of one year's imprisonment as well as wide range of other offences, such as taking or giving bribes for the exercise of the function of an elected representative, commercial or armed smuggling, or the incitement to submit fraudulent asylum applications when committed the form of organised criminality.

18 United Nations, Convention against Illicit Traffic in Narcotic Drugs and Psychotropic Substances, Vienna, 19 December 1988.

19 United Nations, Convention against Transnational Organised Crime, New York, 15 November 2000.

20 It should be noted that in Italy self-laundering is contained in a separate provision and not in the general money laundering provision. On the introduction of self-laundering as an autonomous criminal offence in Italy, see Italy report, section I.A.

b. *Mens Rea*

Each jurisdiction that falls within the scope of this study requires that, in order to be liable for money laundering, the perpetrator must have acted intentionally, in particular with respect to the criminal origin of the property. This is in line with the minimum rules set out under the Vienna Convention, the Palermo Convention and Directive 2018/1673/EU. It is worth pointing out that each jurisdiction's definition of the *mens rea* element requires less than full knowledge of the criminal origin, either because intention includes *dolus eventualis*[21] or, as is the case in the UK, because the law already provides for liability when the offender only suspects the criminal origin of the property. Moreover, the jurisprudence in each jurisdiction specifies that the perpetrator is not required to know precisely the type or the precise circumstances of the predicate offence.

Partially departing from money laundering as being an intent-based crime, Germany and Spain also provide for criminal liability when money laundering is committed by lesser fault standards. The jurisprudence in Germany defines gross negligence in the context of money laundering as cases where, in light of the circumstances, the criminal origin of the object was blatant and the perpetrator demonstrated particular indifference or gross carelessness towards its origin.

2. *Money Laundering by Omission*

All the jurisdictions do in principle accept some form of liability for money laundering by omission regarding persons who are under the duty to prevent money laundering when they fail to comply with such a duty and this failure leads to money laundering. However, the scope of persons who are under a legal duty to avert money laundering is not the same everywhere. All the jurisdictions recognise that state agents, such as prosecutors, customs agents, police officers or FIU officers, can in principle be convicted of money laundering by omission, as they are tasked under law with averting crime, but the approach of the jurisdictions beyond state agents varies. UK law provides for an offence of failure to disclose for certain employees in obliged entities who do not pass on relevant information. Furthermore, courts in Switzerland and Italy have already recognised criminal responsibility of obliged entities' employees for money laundering by omission.[22] According to the Italian jurisprudence, money laundering by omission can, in this context, only result from a failure

---

[21] It is worth noting that, in Spain, *dolus eventualis* includes wilful blindness.

[22] See also Italy report, section VII.B.1 and Switzerland report, section VII.B.1.

to comply with a reporting obligation, whereas in Switzerland the status of guarantors of obliged entities' employees may also be inferred from the duty to clarify the economic background and the purpose of a transaction or a business relationship, as well as from internal regulations.

3. *Aggravated Forms of Money Laundering*

Unlike the Vienna Convention, which merely imposes an obligation on States parties to ensure that their courts are able to take into account aggravated circumstances, Article 6(1) Directive 2018/1673/EU requires EU Member States to ensure that aggravated circumstances apply when money laundering is committed within the framework of a criminal organisation or where the perpetrator is an obliged entity within the meaning of Article 2 4AMLD and has committed the offence in the exercise of his/her professional activities. According to Article 6(2) Directive 2018/1673/EU, further aggravating circumstances may include the fact that the laundered property is of considerable value or that it derives from certain predicate offences (namely participation in an organised criminal group and racketeering, terrorism, trafficking in human beings and migrant smuggling, sexual exploitation, illicit trafficking in narcotic drugs and psychotropic substances, corruption).

With the exception of the UK, all the jurisdictions analysed provide for a non-exhaustive list of aggravated forms of money laundering in serious cases. The German and Swiss Criminal Codes thus specify that this covers cases where money laundering is done on a commercial basis or as a member of a criminal group the purpose of which is the continued commission of money laundering. While section 261(4) of the German Criminal Code does not explicitly provide for additional aggravated forms of money laundering, Article $305^{bis}(2)$ of the Swiss Criminal code further specifies that money laundering committed by a person who acts as a member of a criminal organisation also constitutes a serious case. As regards Italy and Spain, the scope of aggravated forms of money laundering in these two countries is, in comparison, quite different. In Italy, money laundering is deemed serious when the perpetrator is acting in a professional capacity or when he/she is subject to a personal preventive order in application of the anti-mafia code. In Spain, money laundering is deemed serious when the property derives from a number of specifically listed predicate offences, such as drug trafficking, corruption, embezzlement or crime against the environment.

4. *Statutes of Limitation*

Neither the FATF Recommendations nor Directive 2018/1673/EU specify what statute of limitation should or could apply to money laundering. This question is left entirely to the discretion of States. In the UK, no limitation period applies to money laundering. In contrast, in Spain and Switzerland, the limitation period for money laundering is 10 years after the offence has ended, and 15 years in the case of aggravated forms of money laundering. In Germany, intentional and grossly negligent money laundering carry in principle a limitation period of five years after the offence has ended. In the event of interruption (when certain procedural measures are carried out, such as the interrogation of the suspect or the issuance of a search warrant), the limitation period restarts but may not exceed 10 years. In Italy, the ordinary statute of limitation for money laundering is 12 years from the moment of the commission of the offence. In the event that a qualified activity of investigation is carried out within that period, the limitation period is extended to 15 years from the commission of the offence. If no final conviction is reached within 15 years after the offence has ended, the crime is considered time-barred.

It is worth noting that in Germany, Italy and Spain, the fact that the predicate offence is declared time-barred is of no relevance for liability for money laundering. In contrast, the limitation period for the prosecution of the relevant predicate offence may bar prosecutors from bringing money laundering charges in Switzerland. If the predicate offence is barred by a statute of limitation, then no forfeiture or money laundering in terms of forfeiture will be possible. The limitation period for predicate offences in Switzerland is 15 years.

5. *Jurisdictional Rules*

In the five national jurisdictions that fall within the scope of this study, criminal law is applicable to anyone who commits an offence, in whole or in part, on their territory (territoriality principle).[23] Therefore, any person who commits, in whole or in part, an offence of money laundering in the territory of these five countries falls within the jurisdiction of their respective criminal courts. Criminal law in Germany, Spain, Italy, Switzerland and the UK also applies to money laundering offences committed abroad when the perpetrator is one of their nationals (active personality principle).[24] In respect of money

---

23 The approach to the territoriality principle is even broader in the UK, as UK courts have already asserted their jurisdiction over money laundering cases on the basis of the effects doctrine where the conduct had harmful consequences in the UK but no constituent element of money laundering occurred on the territory of the UK.

24 In a similar way, at least German law extends its jurisdiction for money laundering committed abroad to cases where the victim is a German national (passive personality principle).

laundering offences committed abroad, German and Swiss criminal law require dual incrimination, meaning that the act constitutes an offence at the place of its commission and would have constituted an offence had it occurred domestically. In contrast, dual incrimination is not a requirement in Spain, Italy and the UK.

As regards predicate offences committed abroad, paragraph 5 of the Interpretative Note to FATF Recommendation 3 and Article 3(3)(c) Directive 2018/1673/EU require countries to ensure that the money laundering offence can be applied in relation to such offences when the conduct would have constituted a predicate offence had it occurred domestically. Under both legal frameworks, countries may further require that the relevant conduct constitutes a criminal offence under the national law of the country where that conduct was committed. In this regard, Directive 2018/1673/EU is, however, more restrictive as it lists six predicate offences with respect to which the dual incrimination requirement cannot be applied (namely participation in an organised criminal group and racketeering, terrorism, human trafficking, sexual exploitation, illicit trafficking in narcotic drugs and psychotropic substances, and corruption). At the time of writing, Italy, Spain and the UK do not require dual incrimination with respect to predicate offences committed abroad. What matters in these three jurisdictions is that the relevant conduct would have constituted a predicate offence had it occurred there.[25] In contrast, in Germany and Switzerland, money laundering is punishable only provided that the predicate offence constitutes a criminal offence in the country where it was committed and would have constituted a criminal offence had it been carried out domestically.

C. NON-CRIMINAL DEFINITION OF MONEY LAUNDERING

In line with the FATF Recommendations,[26] the Swiss, German and UK legal frameworks include only one definition of money laundering, which serves as the criminal law definition and also as the relevant definition for the application of the preventive AML regime.[27]

---

25 One should note, however, that in case of predicate offences for money laundering committed abroad and punishable by less than 12 months of imprisonment in the UK, a person will not be liable for money laundering if he/she knew or reasonably believed that the relevant criminal conduct occurred abroad, and that relevant criminal conduct was not, when it took place, unlawful under the criminal law of that other country.

26 One should recall that the FATF Recommendations do not define themselves the offence of money laundering, but rather explicitly refer to the money laundering definition contained in the Vienna Convention and the Palermo Convention. See *supra* section II.B.1.a.ii and FATF report, section II.B.1.a.ii.

27 See *supra* section II.B.1.a.ii.

In contrast, since the adoption of Directive 2018/1673/EU, the EU legal framework now contains two money laundering definitions which are identical in terms of *actus reus* and *mens rea*,[28] but which provide for slightly different rules with respect to property derived from conduct that occurred on the territory of another Member State or of a third country, as well as regarding the scope of predicate offences for money laundering.[29] In the same vein, the Italian and Spanish legal systems also provide for a separate definition of money laundering outside criminal law, in the AML law. The differences between the two definitions should not, however, be overestimated. Though in both jurisdictions the money laundering definition provided by the AML law seems more extensive and precise than its criminal law counterpart, jurisprudential interpretation and special provisions of the Criminal Code lead one to conclude that money laundering is defined in the same way in criminal law and in the AML preventive-regulatory law. In particular, both Spanish and Italian AML law explicitly cover self-laundering, whereas this form of money laundering is absent from the criminal definition of money laundering in these two countries. Self-laundering is, however, criminalised in a separate provision in Italy[30] and was considered to fall within the criminal definition of money laundering by the Spanish jurisprudence.

D. SCOPE OF OBLIGED ENTITIES

1. *Financial and Banking Institutions*

Under both the FATF and EU legal frameworks, the scope of financial and banking institutions considered to be obliged entities is very extensive and similar, the 4AMLD defining "credit institutions" and "financial institutions" on the basis of EU law. As regards the five national jurisdictions analysed, the range of financial and banking institutions is also very broad, with no major differences from one country to another. In all the jurisdictions, examples of obliged entities in the financial sector include in particular banks, asset management

---

28 See *supra* sections II.B.1.a.ii and II.B.1.b.

29 The money laundering definition provided in Art. 1(4) 4AMLD is broader than its criminal law counterpart (Art. 3(3)(c) and (4) Directive 2018/1673/EU) in that it extends to such property regardless of whether the dual incrimination requirement is met. In contrast, the 4AMLD is much less extensive than Directive 2018/1673/EU regarding the scope of predicate offences for money laundering. Art. 2(1) Directive 2018/1673/EU indeed refers to 22 categories of offences, within which Member States are required to include a range of predicate offences, whereas Art. 3(4) 4AMLD only refers to six categories, namely terrorism, illicit trafficking in narcotic drugs and psychotropic substances, organised crime, fraud, corruption, and tax offences.

30 Art. 648*ter* Italian Criminal Code.

companies, insurance undertakings, securities dealers, investment companies, providers of money or value transfer services, and issuers or managers of means of payment.

2. *Virtual Currency System Participants*

A few years ago, virtual currency (increasingly also known as virtual assets) system participants (VCSPs) were not considered to be obliged entities in any jurisdiction, as virtual currencies and related financial services were still at an early stage of development. The anonymity of the rapidly emerging virtual currency payment products and services rapidly allowed, however, for their potential misuse for criminal purposes. As a result, VCSPs now fall within the ambit of the FATF Recommendations and the 4AMLD (as modified by the 5AMLD) and are subject to AML/CTF regulations in all the jurisdictions analysed, except for Spain so far. It is worth noting that VCSPs are explicitly designated as obliged entities only under the FATF legal framework, the 5AMLD and Italian law. In Germany, Switzerland and the UK, VCSPs are deemed obliged entities because they qualify, more broadly, as financial or banking institutions. Moreover, it should be mentioned that the scope of VCSPs covered differs quite significantly from one legal framework to another. The FATF Recommendations and Italian law provide for a very extensive definition of VCSPs as it includes wallet providers, providers engaged in exchange services between virtual currencies and fiat currencies as well as exchangers between virtual currencies and providers of financial services for initial coin offerings (ICOs). In contrast, the 5AMLD and Swiss law only consider custodial wallet providers and providers engaged in exchange services between virtual currencies and fiat currencies to be obliged entities. In Germany, the range of VCSPs covered includes all types of virtual currency exchange platforms, including custodial wallet providers and persons participating in or providing financial services related to an issuer's offer and/or sale of a virtual asset.

3. *Legal Profession and Tax Advisors*

Legal professionals, in particular lawyers and notaries, and tax advisors fall within the scope of the FATF Recommendations and the 4AMLD and are subject to AML/CTF regulations in all the jurisdictions analysed. It should be noted, however, that at the moment tax advisors and legal professionals in Switzerland fall within the scope of the AML law only insofar as they act as financial intermediaries, i.e. when they qualify as "persons who on a professional basis accept or hold on deposit assets belonging to others or who assist in the investment or transfer of such assets". Such professionals are therefore not subject to the AML law when their work is limited to preparing or executing non-financial aspects of the transactions concerned. In particular, this means that acts related to setting up companies, legal persons and legal arrangements, in which lawyers, notaries or fiduciaries may be involved without being involved in transactions such as transfers, are outside the scope of the AML law.[31] In contrast, under the 4AMLD as well as under German, Italian, Spanish and UK laws, legal professionals are deemed obliged entities when they participate, whether by acting on behalf of and for their client in any financial or real estate transaction, or when they assist their clients in the carrying out or the planning of transactions concerning: (i) the buying and selling of real property or business entities; (ii) the management of client money, securities or other assets; (iii) the opening or management of bank, savings or securities accounts; (iv) the organisation of contributions necessary for the creation, operation or management of companies; or (v) the creation, operation or management of trusts, companies, foundations or similar structures. As regards tax advisors, EU, German, Spanish, Italian and UK laws designate such professionals as obliged entities irrespective of any particular type of professional activity.

4. *Informal Value Transfer System*

Informal value transfer systems may fall within the scope of certain categories of obliged entities if the relevant definitional requirements are met. In Germany, for instance, value transfer systems will usually constitute a provision of payment services and, if conducted commercially or otherwise at a scale that requires business-like organisational arrangements, constitute payment institutions thereby requiring permission by the Financial Supervisory Authority and the obligation to comply with AML/CTF requirements.

5. *Non-Profit Sector*

Similar to informal value transfer systems, non-profit entities are not explicitly designated as obliged entities in any of the jurisdictions analysed, with the exception of Spain, where foundations and associations are specifically covered by AML law. Nonetheless, to the extent that they meet the respective statutory criteria, non-profit entities can always qualify as certain types of obliged entities (e.g. payment service providers).

---

31 It should be noted, however, that the Federal Council published on 26 June 2019 a draft bill introducing due diligence and reporting obligations for persons, such as lawyers, notaries or fiduciaries, providing services in connection with the creation of companies or trusts without being involved in transactions. See notably Switzerland report, section II.D.6.

6. *Overview of Other Obliged Entities*

In addition to the aforementioned, the scope of obliged entities in the four jurisdictions based on EU law extends to auditors, external accountants, providers of gambling services, real estate agents, dealers in high-value goods, and trust and company service providers.[32] While this is in line with the 4AMLD requirements, it goes beyond the FATF Recommendations, which do not cover auditors and do not cover all dealers but only dealers in precious stones and/or precious metals.

As regards Switzerland, providers of gambling services,[33] real estate agents and traders in high-value goods are also covered by the AML legislation. However, auditors are not covered and, like legal professionals and tax advisors, trust and company service providers are only covered (for the moment)[34] to the extent that they perform financial intermediation, i.e. when they qualify as "persons who on a professional basis accept or hold on deposit assets belonging to others or who assist in the investment or transfer of such assets".[35]

E. RELATIONSHIP BETWEEN AML AND ANTI-TERRORISM FINANCING FRAMEWORK(S)

Money laundering and terrorist financing are often very different phenomena insofar as they can pursue very different objectives, and in that funds used to support terrorist groups may have their origin in legitimate sources, whereas the source of funds for money laundering is always of an illegitimate origin.

As regards the preventive-regulatory regime for AML and counter-terrorism financing (CTF), however, national jurisdictions have mainly opted for one single regime (AML/CTF). This is in line with the 4AMLD, where all the preventive and reporting measures set out address both money laundering and terrorist financing, as well as with the FATF Recommendations which, except for three of them that are unique to terrorist financing (namely Recommendations 5, 6 and 8), cover both phenomena.

---

32 UK report, section II.D.1.

33 Switzerland report, section II.D.1.

34 Switzerland report, section II.D.6.

35 However, as noted *supra* in footnote 31, the Federal Council recently published a draft bill introducing due diligence and reporting obligations for trust and company service provides who are not involved in transactions.

In Spain, Germany, Switzerland and the UK, the set of preventive measures applicable to both AML and CTF is rather similar. That said, it is important to point out that each legal framework provides for some special rules applying only to the fight against terrorist financing. In this regard, the UK deserves a particular mention as it provides special rules for TF within the regulatory and reporting framework. The FIU must treat terrorist financing-related SARs separately and subject them to the review of a dedicated team of specialists. Additionally, if consent to conduct a dubious transaction or another activity is sought by an obliged entity but refused by the National Crime Agency (NCA) on the basis of the Terrorism Act, the obliged entity cannot proceed with the transaction unless it has received a subsequent authorisation from the NCA; otherwise, the obliged entity remains criminally liable.[36] In contrast, when consent is refused by the NCA in cases where the obliged entity reports a money laundering suspicion, a moratorium period of 31 calendar days applies, meaning that the obliged entity can proceed with the reported transaction at the end of this period provided it has not received a definitive veto from the NCA during this period.[37] It should be noted that Spain, Germany and Switzerland also have a separate asset-freezing regime for terrorist financing.

III. THE SYSTEM OF MONEY LAUNDERING PREVENTION

A. CUSTOMER DUE DILIGENCE

1. *Standard CDD Rules*

a. Triggers and Timing

Performing customer due diligence (CDD) measures constitutes one of the three main AML obligations of the private sector, the two others being the reporting obligation[38] and the record keeping obligation.[39] Obliged entities are not required, however, to apply CDD measures in all circumstances. In all the jurisdictions, obliged entities shall perform CDD measures in certain circumstances specified by the law. As emphasised below, CDD triggers are similar under the FATF

36 On the so-called "consent regime" in the UK, see UK report, section III.C.1.d.
37 See *infra* section IV.A.4.
38 See *infra* section III.C.
39 See *infra* section III.D.

Recommendations and the 4AMLD, as well as in Germany, Spain, Italy, the UK and Switzerland. Some differences are, however, worth noting.

Under all legal frameworks, obliged entities are required to apply CDD measures: (i) when establishing a business relationship; (ii) when carrying out a wire transfer;[40] (iii) when carrying out an occasional transaction above a certain threshold, whether that occasional transaction is carried out in a single operation or in several operations which appear to be linked; (iv) when there is a suspicion of money laundering, regardless of any derogation, exemption or threshold; and (v) when, in the course of a business relationship, doubts arise as to certain information previously obtained. In accordance with FATF Recommendation 10 and Article 11 4AMLD, the threshold mentioned under circumstance (iii) is set at €15,000 in all the jurisdictions.[41] With respect to circumstance (v), it is interesting to note that, whereas the FATF, the 4AMLD, Italy and Spain refer to "doubts about the veracity and adequacy of previously obtained customer identification data", Germany refers to both customer and beneficial owner identification data but mentions the accuracy of the information, which seems to be less demanding than veracity and adequacy in that it would most likely not cover the case in which the information is accurate but not sufficient. Swiss law provides an intermediate position as it talks about customer and beneficial owner identification information, and refers to any kind of doubt which may arise in the course of a business relationship with respect to this information.

In addition to the aforementioned general circumstances, all the legal frameworks provide further specific CDD triggers for certain types of obliged entities. It would fall outside the ambit of this analysis to list them all, but it should be highlighted in particular that significant differences exist with respect to persons trading in goods. Whereas the 4AMLD and the four countries based on EU law analysed require all dealers in goods to undertake CDD measures when accepting cash payments amounting to €10,000 or more, the FATF is less demanding in that it sets the threshold at €15,000 and only requires certain types of dealers to perform CDD, namely dealers in precious metals and dealers in precious stones. As regards Switzerland, the AML law is even less stringent, as dealers must apply CDD measures only when they engage in a cash transaction with a customer of more than CHF 100,000 (about €91,380).[42] Swiss law even provides for an exception if the cash payment exceeding CHF 100,000 is carried

[40] Under EU law, which is reflected in the national law of all EU-based jurisdictions analysed, CDD measures shall be applied with respect to any wire transfer as defined in Art. 3(9) of Regulation (EU) 2015/847 (funds transfer regulation), exceeding €1,000.

[41] CHF 15,000 in Switzerland.

[42] The draft bill published by the Federal Council on 26 June 2019 proposes, however, reducing the threshold for applying CDD measures for dealers in precious metals and gems from CHF 100,000 to CHF 15,000.

out through a financial intermediary who is subject to the AML law, in which case the dealer will not have to comply with any due diligence requirements for such payments.

b. CDD Measures

Consistent with FATF Recommendation 10 and Article 13 4AMLD, German, Spanish, Italian and UK AML law require obliged entities to perform the following CDD measures vis-à-vis all customers: (i) identify the customer and verify the customer's identity on the basis of documents of evidentiary value obtained from a reliable and independent source; (ii) verify that any person purporting to act on behalf of the customer is so authorised and identify and verify the identity of that person; (iii) identify the beneficial owner and take reasonable measures to verify the identity of the beneficial owner (German and UK laws further specify that such verification should not rely exclusively on the beneficial ownership registry); (iv) understand the ownership and control structure of the customer when the customer is a legal entity or a legal arrangement;[43] (v) understand the purpose and intended nature of the business relationship; and (vi) conduct ongoing monitoring of the business relationship to ensure that the transactions conducted are consistent with the obliged entity's knowledge of the customer, the business and risk profile, and that the documents, data or information held are kept up to date.

In contrast, CDD measures required by Swiss law are more limited. Obliged entities in Switzerland are indeed only obliged to apply CDD measures (i), (ii) and (iv). Obliged entities must also identify the beneficial owner, but they are not required by law to verify his/her identity. With respect to CDD measures (v) and (vi), such measures are simply not imposed on obliged entities at the moment by the law. In other words, there is not yet a general obligation to conduct ongoing due diligence on the business relationship and no obligation to understand the ownership and control structure of customers which are either legal entities or legal arrangements.

c. Individual Responsibility

Contrary to the FATF Recommendations, the 4AMLD requires obliged entities to "identify the member of the management board responsible for the

[43] There is no explicit requirement to understand the ownership and control structure of customers that are legal persons under UK law. However, financial institutions are likely to collect some of this information as a step in identifying the customer's beneficial owners and Joint Money Laundering Steering Group (JMLSG) Guidance suggests that it is good practice to take reasonable measures to do so.

implementation of the laws, regulations and administrative provisions necessary to comply with [AML/CTF requirements]".[44]

Among the five national jurisdictions examined in the framework of this study, Switzerland is the only one where the AML law does not require obliged entities to appoint an individual to the board of directors (or equivalent management body), or a member of senior management, where appropriate to the size and nature of the business, tasked with certain duties related to AML.[45] In contrast, German, Italian, Spanish and UK laws all require the appointment of someone at the executive level who is responsible for the implementation AML/CTF obligations. This person is not involved in the day-to-day implementation of AML obligations but rather takes part in more strategic decisions, such as defining the organisation's risk appetite, and ensures that AML and CTF is duly taken into account at board or directorate level. Accordingly, this member of the executive management bears total responsibility for compliance with AML obligations.

d. Further CDD Guidance

In the UK, Switzerland and Italy, the AML laws are merely framework laws in the sense that they only set out basic requirements. As a result, supervisory authorities are required to regularly provide obliged entities with updated guidance on the interpretation and application of CDD requirements and internal controls. Depending on the country, supervisors may for instance specify risk factors, how exactly to perform CDD duties, what to do in case of failure to satisfactorily complete CDD or when exactly obliged entities are supposed to verify the identity of the customer and beneficial owner. In contrast, in Germany and Spain, the AML laws are more extensive, and therefore detailed, and the supervisory authorities' role in providing further CDD guidance is therefore much more limited.

2. *Simplified CDD*

a. Scope

In accordance with the Interpretative Note to FATF Recommendation 10 and Article 15 4AMLD, the four EU-based legal frameworks analysed allow obliged entities to perform simplified CDD measures in circumstances where the risks

---

44 Art. 46(4) 4AMLD.

45 It should be noted, however, that the board that the Board of Directors or the supreme management board of financial intermediaries is not completely exempted from AML-related duties as it must approve internal directives on the combating of money laundering and terrorist financing.

of money laundering are lower on the basis of a predefined risk assessment and provided that, before applying such measures, obliged entities always ascertain that the business relationship or the transaction in the particular case does in fact present a lower degree of risk. When assessing the risks of money laundering and terrorist financing relating to types of customers, geographic areas, and particular products, services, transactions or delivery channels, obliged entities in the four EU-based jurisdictions shall take into account at least the factors that usually contribute to a low-risk situation and which are set out in Annex II of the 4AMLD and restated in national law. Examples of such factors include business relationships and transactions with public companies listed on a stock exchange and subject to disclosure requirements, life insurance policies for which the premium is low and business carried out with Member States or third countries identified by credible sources as having a low level of corruption or other criminal activity.

Compared to the EU, Swiss law allows for fewer exceptions as regards the scope of simplified CDD measures. The Swiss AML legal framework indeed allows for simplified CDD measures in only one case, that is when the customer is a listed company or a subsidiary over which a listed company has majority control.

b. Requirements

Neither the FATF Recommendations nor the 4AMLD specify the minimum content of CDD measures that obliged entities are required to take in situations deemed to present a low risk of money laundering. Such is the case also of the UK and Italian AML laws. In contrast, Spanish, German and Swiss laws explicitly provide for certain simplified CDD measures, though in different ways. In Germany and Spain, recourse to simplified CDD does not in principle exempt obliged entities from their standard CDD obligations, but only affects the intensity and/or frequency of measures to this effect. In other words, when they are entitled to apply simplified CDD measures, obliged entities in Germany and Spain shall still apply all the usual CDD measures,[46] but can do so in a more flexible way, such as verifying the identity of the customer and the beneficial owner after the establishment of the business relationship (Spain), or on the basis of other documents than the usual official ones like ID cards or passports (Germany). In contrast, Swiss law exempts obliged entities from the application of specific CDD obligations in low-risk situations. More specifically, when the customer is a listed company or a subsidiary over which a listed company has majority control (the only situation in which obliged entities in Switzerland are

[46] See *supra* section III.A.1.b.

allowed to apply simplified CDD),[47] obliged entities are not required to establish the identity of the beneficial owner.

c. Further Simplified CDD Guidance

As prescribed in Articles 17 and 18(4) 4AMLD, the European Supervisory Authorities (ESAs), namely the European Banking Authority (EBA), the European Securities and Markets Authority (ESMA) and the European Insurance and Occupational Pensions Authority (EIOPA), issued guidelines on 26 June 2017 with the aim of promoting the development of a common understanding, by credit and financial institutions across the EU, of what the risk-based approach to AML/CTF entails and how it should be applied.[48] These guidelines set out risk factors credit and financial institutions should consider when assessing the risk of money laundering and terrorist financing associated with individual business relationships and occasional transactions. Moreover, these guidelines set out how firms can adjust the extent of their CDD measures in a way that is commensurate to the risk of money laundering and terrorist financing they have identified.

At national level, with the exception of Spain, financial supervisors in all the countries analysed provide at least basic guidance on simplified CDD measures to obliged entities.[49] More specifically, supervisors specify low risk factors that obliged entities should take into consideration when assessing the money laundering or terrorist financing risks associated with business relationships and transactions, as well as the simplified CDD measures that obliged entities are allowed to take in low-risk situations. It should be noted, however, that the level of guidance provided by supervisors in this respect differs quite significantly from one jurisdiction to another. For instance, the Bank of Italy's guidance is relatively extensive in terms of the scope of low-risk situations, whereas the Swiss Financial Market Supervisory Authority (FINMA) only authorises issuers of means of payment to apply simplified CDD measures.

3. Enhanced CDD

a. Scope

In accordance with the Interpretative Note to FATF Recommendation 10 and Article 18(1) 4AMLD, the AML laws in the four EU-based countries analysed,

---

47 See *supra* section II.A.2.a.

48 ESAs, Joint Guidelines under Articles 17 and 18(4) of Directive (EU) 2015/849 on simplified and enhanced due diligence and the factors credit and financial institutions should consider when assessing the money laundering and terrorist financing risk associated with individual business relationships and occasional transactions, JC 2017 37, 26 June 2017.

49 UK report, section III.A.2.b.

namely Germany, Spain, Italy and the UK, require obliged entities to apply enhanced CDD measures in all circumstances where the risks of money laundering are higher. When assessing the risks of money laundering relating to types of customers, geographic areas, and particular products, services, transactions or delivery channels, obliged entities in the four jurisdictions based on EU law shall take into account at least the factors of potentially high-risk situations set out in Annex III of the 4AMLD and restated in national law. Examples of such factors include business relationships and transactions conducted with businesses that are cash-intensive, non-face-to-face business relationships or transactions without certain safeguards, such as electronic signature, and business carried out with countries identified by credible sources as having significant levels of corruption or other criminal activity.

In line with the requirements set out in the FATF Recommendations and the 4AMLD as modified by the 5AMLD, the following circumstances shall always be treated as high risk in the four EU legal frameworks analysed: (i) business relationships and occasional transactions involving natural persons or legal entities established in high-risk third countries identified as such; (ii) cross-border correspondent relationships with a third-country respondent institution; (iii) business carried out with politically exposed persons (PEPs);[50] and (iv) transactions which are either complex, unusually large, conducted in an unusual pattern or which do not have an apparent or economic lawful purpose. In Switzerland, the AML law only considers circumstances (iii) and (iv) as carrying a high risk at all times.

Two additional comments must be made regarding the national lists of high-risk situations requiring the application of enhanced CDD measures. First of all, the Spanish list is broader than the four aforementioned circumstances as it also requires enhanced CDD in a number of other predefined circumstances, namely private banking, companies that have shares in bearer form, products or transactions that might favour anonymity, and foreign currency exchange transactions that amount to €6,000 or more. Second, it is worth pointing out that the Swiss AML law explicitly qualifies as high risk situations in which there are indications that assets are the proceeds of a predicate offence to money laundering, thereby clarifying the relationship between the reporting obligation and enhanced CDD measures.

b. Requirements

The FATF Recommendations and the 4AMLD set out specific CDD measures with respect to situations that are always deemed to carry a high risk, namely

50 Under the FATF framework, business carried out with foreign PEPs only.

business relationships/transactions with PEPs,[51] business relationships/ transactions involving high risk third countries,[52] cross-border correspondent relationships, and transactions which are either complex, unusually large, conducted in an unusual pattern or which do not have an apparent economic or lawful purpose. Neither the FATF Recommendations nor the 4AMLD include, however, a list of minimum enhanced CDD measures that would be applicable in all high-risk situations.

In contrast, the AML law in each of the five national jurisdictions analysed provides, in addition to specific enhanced CDD measures applicable to predefined categories of high-risk situations, a list of minimum enhanced CDD measures applicable in all other cases where obliged entities determine that there might be a higher risk. However, the list of measures to be taken in such cases widely differs from one jurisdiction to another, both in terms of their content and their nature (cumulative or alternative measures). Spanish law, for instance, provides an extensive list of alternative measures that obliged entities shall consider taking in cases of high risk, including *inter alia* obtaining additional information on the purpose and nature of the business relationship, and obtaining senior management authorisation to establish or maintain the business relationship or to carry out the transaction. In comparison, enhanced CDD measures under Swiss law only consist of clarifying the economic background and the purpose of a transaction or of a business relationship. The Italian and German AML laws provide a more demanding solution as both legislations include a cumulative list of three minimum enhanced CDD measures, notably the submission of the business relationship to enhanced ongoing monitoring.

c. Further Enhanced CDD Guidance

As seen earlier,[53] the ESAs issued in 2017, in accordance with Articles 17 and 18(4) 4AMLD, joint guidelines on simplified and enhanced CDD measures and the factors credit and financial institutions should consider when assessing the money laundering and terrorist financing risk associated with individual business relationships and occasional transactions. In particular, these guidelines provide guidance on how enhanced CDD measures set out in Article 18(2) 4AMLD (enhanced CDD measures applicable to all complex and unusually large transactions, and all unusual patterns of transactions which have no apparent economic or lawful purpose) and Article 19 4AMLD (enhanced CDD measures applicable to cross-border correspondent relationships with third-country respondent institutions) could be applied.

---

51 See *infra* section II.A.4.b.

52 See *infra* section II.A.5.b.

53 See *supra* section III.A.2.c.

With the exception of Spain, financial supervisory authorities in all the countries analysed provide guidance on enhanced CDD measures to obliged entities. More specifically, supervisors specify high risk factors that obliged entities should take into consideration when assessing the money laundering or terrorist financing risks associated with business relationships and transactions, as well as the enhanced CDD measures that obliged entities should take in high-risk situations.

4. *Rules on Politically Exposed Persons*

a. Definition

Politically exposed persons (PEPs) are individuals who are or have been entrusted with a prominent public function, either domestically, in a foreign country or in an international organisation. Under the FATF and EU legal frameworks, the following persons qualify as PEPs: heads of states, heads of governments, senior members of government, members of parliament or of similar legislative bodies, important political party officials, high-ranking officers in the armed forces, high-ranking judicial officials, members of the administrative, management or supervisory bodies of state-owned enterprises, and directors, deputy directors and members of the board or equivalent function of an international organisation. The EU scope of PEPs also includes members of courts of auditors or of the boards of central banks, as well as ambassadors and *chargés d'affaires*. With respect to the EU scope of PEPs, it should also be noted that, with respect to judicial officials, the 4AMLD only refers to members of supreme courts, of constitutional courts or of other high-level judicial bodies, the decisions of which are not subject to further appeal except in exceptional circumstances. Furthermore, one should point out the new mechanism established by the 5AMLD requiring that EU Member States create and publicly release a functional list of PEPs. The list features the name of the positions that are considered to be politically exposed but does not actually name the person who is occupying the position as that changes periodically. This requirement extends to accredited international organisations, and the EU shall also release an EU-level version of the list. The purpose of this is to make it easier for compliance teams to identify the PEPs that they should be screening and monitoring for changes to risk.

The German, Italian, Spanish and UK AML laws follow the aforementioned EU definition of PEPs, while Switzerland defines PEPs in the exact same way as the FATF does. One should note, however, that the Italian legislation goes beyond international standards as the national definition of PEPs includes other individuals such as mayors and heads of regions. Similarly, under Spanish law, persons like mayors of towns of more than 50,000 people or persons holding senior management positions in trade unions or employers' organisations also fall within the scope of PEPs.

b. Requirements

In line with Article 20 4AMLD, obliged entities in Germany, Italy, Spain and the UK are required to take the following enhanced CDD measures whenever they conduct business relationships or carry out occasional transactions with PEPs: (i) obtain senior management approval for establishing or continuing business relationships with such persons; (ii) take adequate measures to establish the source of wealth and source of funds that are involved in business relationships or transactions with such persons; and (iii) conduct enhanced, ongoing monitoring of those business relationships. These measures must also be applied to family members and close associates of PEPs. Moreover, obliged entities must monitor the risk posed when a person ceases to hold the title yielding PEP status for a period of 12 months in Germany, Italy and the UK, and 24 months in Spain.

The FATF Recommendations are less demanding with respect to enhanced CDD measures applicable to PEPs as they do not provide that the risk specific to PEPs must be taken into account by obliged entities after the person left the respective public function, and also because they only require the aforementioned measures (i)–(iii) to be taken with respect to foreign PEPs. Regarding domestic and international organisation PEPs, obliged entities must only take reasonable measures, based on the assessment of the level of risk, to determine whether the customer or beneficial owner is a domestic/international organisation PEP. If a customer or beneficial owner is determined to be a domestic PEP or an international organisation PEP, enhanced CDD measures do not automatically have to be applied. It is only in cases of a higher-risk business relationship that obliged entities should take enhanced CDD measures consistent with those applicable to foreign PEPs. If the risk assessment establishes that the business relationship with the domestic/international organisation PEP presents a normal or low risk, the obliged entity is not required to apply enhanced due diligence measures.

Switzerland follows the same approach as the FATF in that only business relationships with foreign PEPs and their family members or close associates shall be deemed by financial intermediaries to carry a higher risk at all times. However, contrary to the FATF Recommendations, the AML law does not itself set out specific enhanced CDD measures with respect to PEPs.

c. Further Enhanced CDD Guidance on PEPs

With the exception of Spain, supervisory authorities in all the countries analysed provide guidance specifying the law's definition of PEPs, how to appropriately identify PEPs and/or the enhanced CDD measures applicable to business relationships and occasional transactions involving PEPs. The Bank of Italy, for instance, specifies what sources obliged entities shall use to identify PEPs, emphasising in particular the necessity for obliged entities to consult open access resources. Another example is that of the Financial Conduct Authority (FCA) in the UK, which further refines the scope of PEPs by excluding public servants below Permanent or Deputy Permanent Secretary from it.[54] The FCA also advises that domestic PEPs can be treated as carrying a low risk unless a firm has assessed that other risk factors not linked to the person's position as a PEP mean they pose a higher risk.[55] In that regard, the FCA's guidance departs from the 4AMLD, which treats domestic and foreign PEPs equally.[56]

5. *Rules on High-Risk Third Countries*

a. Scope

Germany, Italy, Spain and the UK require obliged entities to always apply enhanced CDD measures with respect to business relationships and transactions involving high-risk third countries identified as such by the European Commission pursuant to Article 9(2) 4AMLD as modified by the 5AMLD. At the time of writing, the EU list of high-risk third countries is aligned with the FATF list as updated after the Plenary meeting which took place on 24–29 June 2018, and is composed of the following countries: Ethiopia, Iran, the Democratic Republic of Korea, Pakistan, Serbia, Sri Lanka, Syria, Trinidad and Tobago, Tunisia and Yemen. This list is slightly different from the FATF list as it stands in April 2020.[57]

Regarding Switzerland, before 31 December 2019 there was no set list of high-risk third countries towards which financial intermediaries shall take enhanced CDD measures. Since 1 January 2020, however, financial intermediaries under FINMA supervision have to apply enhanced CDD measures with respect to any business relationship or transaction involving a high-risk third country identified as such by the FATF.

b. Requirements

With the exception of Italy and Germany, none of the national legal frameworks examined provide for specific enhanced CDD measures that obliged entities shall take with respect to business relationships and occasional transactions involving high-risk third countries. Such is the case also of the FATF Recommendations, which do not specify the type of enhanced CDD measures to be taken with regard to high-risk third countries.

---

54 UK report, section IV.A.4.a.

55 *Ibid.*

56 See *supra* section III.A.4.a.

57 As of April 2020, the FATF list includes Albania, the Bahamas, Barbados, Botswana, Cambodia, Ghana, Iceland, Iran, Jamaica, Democratic Republic of Korea Mauritius, Mongolia, Myanmar, Nicaragua, Pakistan, Panama, Syria, Uganda, Yemen and Zimbabwe.

In contrast, the 4AMLD as modified by the 5AMLD requires obliged entities to apply a minimum set of predefined enhanced CDD requirements when dealing with high-risk third countries as identified by the Commission, including notably obtaining additional information on the customer and on the beneficial owner(s), obtaining additional information on the intended nature of the business relationship, and obtaining information on the source of funds and source of wealth of the customer and of the beneficial owner(s). This formalised approach which, at the time of writing, is only followed in Italy, Germany and the UK, aims to lessen differences in the application of regulatory requirements between obliged entities, harmonising these measures on an EU level.

c. Further Enhanced CDD Guidance on High-Risk Third Countries

Supervisory authorities in the five national jurisdictions examined provide no extensive guidance specifying the law's enhanced CDD requirements applicable in relation to high-risk third countries. As far as the EU context is concerned, this guidance gap at national level is not so problematic as the three ESAs published in 2017 quite detailed guidance on what the enhanced CDD measures that obliged entities subject to the 4AMLD shall take with respect to all business relationships and transactions involving high-risk third countries identified as such by the European Commission could entail.

As already highlighted,[58] Spanish supervisors do not provide any guidance on CDD to obliged entities. An exception applies, however, regarding the scope of high-risk third countries in relation to which obliged entities should perform enhanced CDD measures. The National Commission for the Prevention of Money Laundering and Monetary Offences (COPBLAC), the Spanish Treasury and the General Council of Notaries Centralised Prevention Unit indeed consider more countries to carry a high risk than those listed by the European Union.[59]

6. *Private Sector CDD Guidance*

In all the jurisdictions, various private entities provide guidance to obliged entities for the management of financial risks and the implementation of CDD measures. These entities may for instance be firms specialising in financial risk management, such as Refinitiv, law firms, or even associations or consortiums of certain types of obliged entities, such as bar associations or associations of financial intermediaries. In this respect, the Swiss Bankers Association's Agreement on the Swiss Banks' Code of Conduct with Regard to the Exercise of Due Diligence (CDB), which was enacted for the first time in 1977 and which

---

58 See *supra* sections II.A.2.c, II.A.3.c and II.A.4.c.

59 See *supra* section II.A.5.a.

aims at substantiating due diligence rules for banks and securities dealers in Switzerland concerning the identification of contracting partners along with the establishment of the controlling persons and beneficial owners, deserves to be acknowledged. Although this is formally a private law agreement between the Swiss Bankers Association on the one hand and the signatory banks on the other, most financial intermediaries in Switzerland are indeed legally obliged to abide by it. The provisions of the CDB are thus an integral part of the regulatory framework that applies to all banks and securities traders in Switzerland.

B. PRELIMINARY RISK ANALYSIS

The risk-based approach is at the core of the 2012 FATF Recommendations, the 4AMLD and all national legal frameworks. In this context, obliged entities are notably required to conduct a preliminary risk analysis, proportionate to their nature and size, which consists of identifying and assessing, prior to the conduct of any client-specific or transaction-specific CDD measures, the risks related to money laundering and terrorist financing that come along with the business activities they engage in, having regard to certain risk factors, including those relating to their customers, countries or geographical areas, products, services, transactions or delivery channels. This aims at tailoring the particular entity's subsequent CDD to its individual risk exposure and risk appetite. The preliminary risk assessment procedure shall be documented, periodically updated and made available to the competent supervisory authorities.

C. REPORTING AND ASSET FREEZING

1. *First-Time Reporting*

a. Trigger for/Degree of Suspicion

In line with FATF Recommendations 20 and 23 and Article 33 4AMLD, obliged entities in Germany, Italy, Spain, Switzerland and the UK are all required to submit an SAR to the FIU in the event of suspicion that funds, regardless of the amount involved, are the proceeds of criminal activity, which could constitute a predicate offence to money laundering, or are related to terrorist financing.

In addition, it is interesting to note that particular reporting duties exist in most national legal frameworks examined, with the exception of Italy and the UK. In Spain, for instance, financial institutions shall report to the FIU on a monthly basis on certain types of transactions, regardless of any suspicion.[60]

---

60 See notably Spain report, section IV.A.2.

Such transactions notably include wire transfers amounting to €30,000 or more involving a high-risk third country, and transactions that amount to €100,000 or more, whether these transactions are carried out nationally or transnationally. The German AML legal framework does not (yet) include comparable automatic reporting, but does also include a particular reporting obligation, which arises when the contracting party has not fulfilled its obligation to disclose to the obliged entity whether it intends to establish, continue or perform the business relationship or transaction on behalf of a beneficial owner. As for Switzerland, it provides a reporting requirement in the event an obliged entity terminates or does not establish a business relationship after having failed to satisfactorily complete CDD. This requirement goes beyond FATF Recommendation 10 and Article 14(4) 4AMLD, which only require obliged entities, in this case, to "consider making a STR [suspicious transaction report] in relation to the customer" in such a case, but without imposing an explicit obligation to this effect.

Besides the aforementioned particular reporting obligations, it is worth noting, from a comparative point of view, that all five national legal frameworks analysed lack clarity as regards the degree of suspicion to trigger a duty to report. Whereas the AML laws in Germany, Spain and the UK refer to mere suspicion that a transaction involves money laundering or terrorist financing or is related to a predicate offence, Italian law requires "reasonable grounds" of suspicion and Swiss law calls for a "well-founded suspicion". National practice, and in particular case law, reveals that the level of required suspicion is relatively low in all the jurisdictions considered in the study, though important differences remain. In Italy and the UK, and increasingly also Germany, the very high number of SARs filed each year by obliged entities[61] necessarily entails a low level of suspicion being applied.[62] In contrast, in Spain, the low level of suspicion as well as the amount of SARs filed annually,[63] indicate a comparatively higher threshold; Spain does however compensate this situation by requiring obliged entities to automatically file reports regarding predefined types of transactions. In Germany, the legislative drafting history of section 43 of the AML law, which includes the duty to report, makes clear that the standard of suspicion for reporting money laundering or terrorist financing cases remains below the standard of suspicion of a criminal complaint and that obliged entities should submit an SAR whenever a money laundering or terrorist financing background cannot be excluded, in view notably of the circumstances of the case and professional

61 See Italy report, section III.J and UK report, section III.J.

62 In this regard, see in particular UK Law Commission, "Money Laundering: Summary", 2019, p. 8.

63 See Spain report, section III.J.

experience. Interestingly enough, the Swiss FIU has also been following this negative approach to suspicion since 2007. According to the Swiss FIU, obliged entities shall indeed submit SARs when, after having performed enhanced CDD measures, they have "evidence that assets either originate from criminal activity or at least that this possibility cannot be excluded".[64] Accordingly, a mere doubt therefore becomes a well-founded suspicion when clarifications of the economic background and the purpose of a transaction of business relationship did not enable the suspicion that the assets are of illegal origin to be dismissed.

b. Content and Direct Addressee(S) of SARs

In all the jurisdictions, obliged entities shall file their SARs directly with the FIU.[65] As regards the content of SARs, neither the FATF Recommendations nor the 4AMLD further specify it. The same applies to the national AML laws examined. It is therefore left entirely to FIUs to define SARs' content requirements.

c. Duty not to Disclose

The prohibition of disclosure is a key component of the reporting regime, mainly because it ensures the confidentiality of investigations and thereby prevents suspected persons from absconding with or disposing of assets. In line with FATF Recommendation 21, the Spanish and Swiss AML laws prohibit obliged entities from disclosing to the customer concerned or other third persons the fact that they have submitted an SAR to the FIU. In contrast, the scope of the tipping-off prohibition is broader under EU, German, Italian and UK laws as it also covers the analysis carried out before the filing of an SAR, as well as the period prior to it when the obliged entity is merely contemplating the possibility of carrying out such an analysis.

d. Power or Duty to Freeze

The freezing of assets in the AML context is one of the very few issues that is addressed by the 4AMLD and not also by the FATF. According to Article 35(1) 4AMLD, the content of which is reflected in Italian, UK and German laws (but not Spanish law), obliged entities shall not carry out transactions which they know or suspect to be related to money laundering or terrorist financing until they have filed an SAR and have complied with any further specific instructions

64 MROS Annual Report 2007, p. 3.

65 For corresponding exceptions pertaining to independent legal professions, see *infra* section III.B.3.b.

from the FIU.[66] An exception applies, however, where refraining from carrying out transactions is impossible or is likely to hinder investigations or judicial proceedings.[67] In contrast, obliged entities in Switzerland shall only freeze assets upon receiving a notification from the FIU stating that the SAR has been forwarded to the competent authorities. Pending such a notification, which should be received within 20 working days, the financial intermediary shall continue executing the orders of the customer. Another distinctive feature of the Swiss legal framework as regards the freezing of assets is that, compared to the other legal frameworks analysed, it specifies the maximum amount of time during which assets shall be frozen (five working days).

e. Instant Collateral Duties

Neither the FATF Recommendations nor the 4AMLD specify whether obliged entities should be under any collateral obligations after having filed an SAR, and the same can be said about Italian and German laws. In contrast, Spanish and UK laws expressly provide that, after having filed an SAR, the reporting entity is compelled to further monitor the client's activities and shall take additional risk management and mitigation measures. Swiss law does not impose such an obligation upon obliged entities[68] but rather requires two other measures to be taken by financial intermediaries under FINMA supervision following the filing of an SAR. First, such financial intermediaries are compelled to inform FINMA whenever they file an SAR that relates to a business relationship that involves significant assets. In particular, they must inform FINMA when, in view of the circumstances, it must be assumed that the case that was reported will have an impact on the reputation of the financial intermediary or Switzerland as a financial place. Second, in the case of orders involving significant amounts, financial intermediaries under FINMA supervision which have filed an SAR are required, during the FIU's analysis of the SAR, to execute the suspected client's orders but in such a manner as to leave a paper trail.[69]

---

66 It should be noted that German law is more permissive than Art. 35(1) 4AMLD as it allows the obliged entity which has filed an SAR to carry out the suspicious transaction once the third working day (which does not include Saturdays) after the day on which the SAR was filed has elapsed without the execution of the transaction having been prohibited by the FIU or the competent public prosecution office. Similarly, but in a more lenient way from the perspective of the FIU, if no reply is provided by the UK FIU within seven working days, it is considered that a defence is afforded to the reporting obliged entity and that it is allowed to carry out the suspicious transaction. Where the UK FIU refuses consent, however, the transaction or activity must not proceed for a further 31 calendar days, or, if earlier, until further notified by the FIU. The moratorium period of 31 calendar days can be extended.

67 In such cases, the FIU shall be immediately informed afterwards.

68 One should point out, however, that the filing of an SAR will very often constitute a crucial factor to guide the obliged entity's CDD towards the same client or business relationship and should insofar usually give rise to enhanced CDD measures.

69 Switzerland report, section III.C.2.c.

2. *Follow-Up*

a. Duty to Provide FIU with Additional Data

In line with FATF Recommendation 29 and Article 33(1)(a) 4AMLD, the five national legal frameworks analysed require obliged entities which have submitted an SAR to provide additional data to the FIU if requested to do so. The Swiss legal framework differs, however, in two respects. First, it only applies this obligation to financial intermediaries, and not also to dealers in goods. Second, it is the only country analysed in this study which specifies the content and thereby the limits of the additional information that obliged entities may be requested to provide to the FIU. Accordingly, financial intermediaries shall only provide additional information of a financial nature which directly relates to the SAR they have filed and which is either in their possession or in the hands of entities in Switzerland forming part of them.

b. Continued Duty not to Disclose SAR to Client

Pursuant to FATF Recommendations 21 and 23, obliged entities should be prohibited by law from disclosing the fact that an SAR "is being filed" with the FIU. The FATF does not, however, indicate whether there should also be a continued duty on the part of the reporting obliged entity not to disclose to the client the filing of an SAR, even if this has not led to a discovery of illegal conduct. In contrast, EU, German, Italian, Spanish, Swiss and UK laws explicitly provide that the ban on tipping-off the client about the filing an SAR also applies after such a filing (but does not specify until when). In Switzerland, an explicit exception applies when the disclosure is necessary for protecting the obliged entity's personal interests in the context of a civil action or criminal or administrative proceedings.

3. *Special Rules for Privileged Professions*

a. Trigger for/Degree of Suspicion

Under the 4AMLD, as well as under German, Italian and Spanish laws, notaries and other independent legal professionals are bound by the reporting obligation where they participate, whether by acting on behalf of and for their client in any financial or real estate transaction, or by assisting in the planning or carrying out of transactions for their client concerning: (i) the buying and selling of real property or business entities; (ii) the management of client money, securities or other assets; (iii) the opening or management of bank, savings or securities accounts; (iv) the organisation of contributions necessary for the creation, operation or management of companies; or (v) the creation, operation or management of trusts, companies, foundations, or similar structures.[70] Interestingly, the scope of the reporting duty of privileged professions is narrower under the FATF Recommendations as it only covers cases where, on behalf of a client, they *engage* in a financial transaction in relation to one of the aforementioned activities, and not also when they assist in the planning or carrying out of the transaction. Switzerland is even more restrictive as legal professions are deemed obliged entities only to the extent that they perform financial intermediation in the sense of Article 2(3) of the AML law, that is when they qualify as "persons who on a professional basis accept or hold on deposit assets belonging to others or who assist in the investment or transfer of such assets" (the thresholds associated with this definition are very high and thus often not met by legal professions).[71]

Whatever the ambit of the reporting obligation is, the law in all the jurisdictions provides that notaries and other independent legal professionals are not subject to the obligation to report insofar as they are bound by professional secrecy, that is when the matter relates to information that they receive from, or obtain on, one of their clients, in the course of ascertaining the legal position of their client, or performing their task of defending or representing that client in, or concerning, judicial proceedings, including providing advice on instituting or avoiding such proceedings.[72] In Germany, however, the reporting obligation remains in force if the obliged entities knows (and not merely suspects) that the contracting party has used or is using the client relationship for the purpose of money laundering or terrorism financing or another criminal offence. A mere suspicion is not enough; the respective professional must, from his or her subjective perspective, be sure that the client relationship has been used or is used for a criminal purpose.[73]

b. Content and Addressee(S) of SARs

In Germany, the UK and Switzerland, all obliged entities are required to submit their SARs directly to the FIU. In contrast, Spanish law requires notaries and registrars to submit their SARs to their designated self-regulatory bodies, which then have to forward the information to the FIU promptly and unfiltered.

---

70 German law specifies further cases, in particular advising clients on capital structure or industrial strategies, that in substance, however, seem to not significantly go beyond the five listed categories.

71 See Switzerland report, section II.D.1.

72 This exemption also extends to tax advisors, external accountants and auditors in the three EU countries analysed.

73 One should note, however, that according to section 43 para. 6 of the AML Law, the Federal Ministry of Finance can, in agreement with the Ministry of Justice, through legislative degree, determine certain types of real estate transactions in which the aforementioned privilege does not apply.

As regards Italian law, lawyers, notaries, other independent legal professionals, as well as tax advisors, auditors and external accountants, can choose whether to file their SARs with the FIU or with their self-governing organisations. Such special rules as regards the addressee of SARs from privileged professions provided by Spanish and Italian laws are in line with Article 34(1) 4AMLD and the Interpretative Note to FATF Recommendation 23.

c. Duty not to Disclose to Client

In principle, the law does not exempt privileged professions from the obligation not to disclose the fact that an SAR was filed with the FIU. However, according to the FATF Recommendations, as well as EU, German, Italian, UK and Spanish laws, where lawyers, notaries, other independent legal professionals and external accountants seek to dissuade a client from engaging in illegal activity, this does not constitute disclosure.[74] This exception thereby goes beyond dissuasion from money laundering, its predicate offences and terrorism financing, and extends to cases where privileged professionals try to dissuade their clients from other illegal acts, including acts that are merely unlawful and not criminal. In contrast, there are no special rules on the prohibition of tipping-off for privileged professions in Switzerland. In particular, there is no derogatory provision allowing them to dissuade a client from engaging in illegal activity.

4. Protection of SAR's Source

Neither the FATF Recommendations nor the 4AMLD address the question of whether the identity of the obliged entity's employee who filed an SAR should or could be made anonymous in the SAR. Article 33(2) 4AMLD only provides that the person in charge of forwarding the SAR to the FIU shall be the compliance officer appointed at management level in accordance with Article 8(4)(a) of that Directive. In contrast, Italian, Spanish and UK laws provide that the reporter's identity shall always remain anonymous. Swiss law is less stringent in this respect as it leaves it up to the obliged entity to decide whether the reporter's identity shall remain anonymous or not, provided then that it is guaranteed that the FIU and the competent prosecution authority are able to contact him/her without delay. By comparison, in Germany, the FIU may be under an obligation to provide the SAR's source. Where the FIU provides information to a person affected by an SAR, it must redact the personal data of the individual who filed the SAR, except if legitimate interests of the requesting person are preponderant.

---

74 This exception also extends to tax advisors and auditors under the 4AMLD as well as under German, Italian and Spanish laws.

In a similar vein, another question relating to the protection of an SAR's source is that of his/her protection from punitive action by the obliged entity concerned. The FATF Recommendations do not address this question and neither does Swiss and UK laws, though both legal orders would extend labour law protection to abusive or punitive employment actions. In contrast, EU, Italian, German and Spanish laws provide that individuals, including employees and representatives of the obliged entity who report suspicions of money laundering or terrorist financing internally or to the FIU, shall not be exposed to threats or retaliatory or hostile action, and in particular shall be protected from adverse or discriminatory employment actions.

D. RECORD KEEPING

In line with FATF Recommendation 11 and Article 40(1) 4AMLD, obliged entities in the five jurisdictions analysed are subject to a duty to keep records of transactions and all information obtained through the performance of CDD measures. In Spain, Italy and Switzerland, obliged entities are required to maintain the records for 10 years after the business relationship ends, or after the date of the occasional transaction, whereas the FATF, the 4AMLD, German and UK laws impose a five-year retention period.[75] Swiss AML law also imposes on financial intermediaries an explicit obligation to keep SARs.

E. COMPLIANCE OFFICERS

Under the FATF legal framework, all obliged entities are required to appoint a compliance officer at the management level. The 4AMLD specifies that the appointment of a compliance officer is required only when deemed appropriate "with regard to the size and nature of the business". Moreover, unlike the FATF Recommendations, the 4AMLD specifies the main duties which compliance officers shall carry out, namely the implementation of the AML law and other regulations and administrative provisions, and the transmission of SARs to the FIU.

At national level, quite similar solutions have been adopted. The Italian AML law is the most stringent one with respect to the obligation to appoint a

---

[75] One should note, however, that Art. 40(1)(a) 4AMLD allows Member States to extend the retention period for up to an additional five years if deemed necessary for the purposes of prevention, detection or investigation of money laundering and terrorist financing, and after carrying out an assessment of the necessity and proportionality.

compliance officer, as this obligation is imposed on all obliged entities which have a corporate structure, regardless of the size of the entity. Germany is similarly extensive but provides exceptions by supervisory authorities. The appointment of a compliance officer in Spain is only required by law of obliged entities of a certain scale (outside of financial services, obliged entities with more than 10 employees and an annual turnover above EUR 2 million)[76] and never from obliged entities structured as individual entities. In Switzerland, the law does not expressly require obliged entities to appoint a compliance officer, but specifies an obligation to set up a special department responsible for the prevention of money laundering.

F. INTERNAL COMPLAINT MECHANISM

The FATF does not require obliged entities to have in place an internal complaint mechanism that would allow employees to inform senior management about violations of AML-related obligations committed within the obliged entity.

In contrast, Article 61(3) 4AMLD as modified by the 5AMLD requires obliged entities "to have in place appropriate procedures for their employees, or persons in a comparable position, to report breaches internally through a specific, independent and anonymous channel, proportionate to the nature and size of the obliged entity concerned". Such procedures now exist in the four EU-based jurisdictions.

G. ADDITIONAL PREVENTIVE MEASURES

All the AML legal frameworks analysed require obliged entities to take the necessary organisational measures to prevent money laundering in their field of business. In line with the requirements set out in the FATF Recommendations and the 4AMLD, such organisational measures must include notably, in each jurisdiction, the following: (i) the development of internal policies, controls and procedures, including model risk management practices; (ii) employee screening; (iii) an independent audit function; and (iv) training programmes to help employees recognise operations that may be related to money laundering or terrorism financing and to instruct them as to how to proceed in such cases.

---

[76] See Spain report, section III.G.

H. RULES ON OBLIGED ENTITIES' CIVIL LIABILITY TOWARDS CLIENT

In line with the FATF Recommendations and the 4AMLD, Spanish, Italian, German, Swiss and UK laws provide that, when an obliged entity files an SAR in good faith or provides additional information to the FIU upon request, it cannot be held liable under civil law for breach of any restriction on disclosure of information imposed by contract or by the law. In addition, it should be noted that Spanish and Italian laws specify that the protection from civil liability extends to circumstances where the person who disclosed the information was not precisely aware of the underlying criminal activity, regardless of whether illegal activity actually occurred.

I. SUPERVISORY AUTHORITIES' ROLE

1. *Supervisory Measures to Ensure Application of CDD and Other AML-Related Obligations*

In all the jurisdictions analysed, supervisory authorities have the duty to verify that the supervised obliged entities comply with their AML-related preventive obligations. This is in line with the FATF Recommendations and the 4AMLD as modified by the 5AMLD. The range of supervisory measures that Swiss, Spanish, German, Italian and UK supervisors can carry out include the following: (i) ensuring that managers and directors are fit and proper, the aim being to ensure that only individuals who meet the proper business conduct requirements under financial market law are involved in the strategic or executive management of obliged entities; (ii) conducting audits, the intensity and frequency of which depending on the risk profile, the size and the nature of the obliged entity; (iii) conducting scheduled or unscheduled on-site inspections at the premises of supervised institutions; and (iv) compelling obliged entities to produce any information that is relevant to monitoring compliance with AML-related obligations.

With respect to obliged entities outside the financial sector, Spanish, Italian and Swiss laws provide for very different solutions in terms of the scope of the supervisory measures that can be taken to ensure application of CDD and other AML-related obligations. In Italy, the Special Foreign Exchange Unit of the Finance Police has the power to conduct inspections and controls of non-financial obliged entities. Similarly, the Spanish FIU, which has AML supervisory competences for all obliged entities, can conduct supervisory visits of obliged entities outside the financial sector, namely those which only carry out occasional transactions and certain gambling service providers. In contrast, dealers in Switzerland, which are not placed under the supervision of a specific authority, cannot be subject to inspection or control from a supervisory authority, such as FINMA. The only obligation imposed upon dealers is to appoint an audit firm whose duty is to verify that they comply with their due diligence obligations and to produce a report for the relevant corporate body. In this context, dealers shall provide the audit firm with all the information and documents required to conduct the audit.

2. *Complaint Mechanism*

Unlike the FATF Recommendations, the 4AMLD as modified by the 5AMLD requires the competent authorities, as well as, where applicable, self-regulatory bodies, to have in place effective and reliable mechanisms to encourage the reporting of AML-related violations within obliged entities. While these mechanisms shall, in principle, include clear rules that ensure that the identity of the reporting person is kept confidential and not revealed to the obliged entity, it is important to stress that Article 61(1)(e) 4AMLD gives Member States the possibility not to apply these rules if this is "required by national law in the context of further investigations or subsequent judicial proceedings".

Among the five jurisdictions analysed, only Spain and Germany so far require supervisory authorities to provide a specific mechanism for receiving notices from individuals about potential and actual contraventions of AML/CTF obligations committed within the obliged entity of which they are employees. Notifiable violations notably include the case where an obliged entity's employee internally reported a case of money laundering to the compliance officer who then did not file an SAR. Notifications should in principle be done anonymously.[77] Employees of obliged entities in Spain may submit SARs directly to the FIU, which is the supervisory body responsible for all obliged entities,[78] provided, however, that the following two conditions are met: (i) the internal control body (which shall be established in obliged entities of a certain nature and size and put in place under the responsibility of the compliance officer)[79] was informed of the suspicion; and (ii) the internal control body failed to inform the compliance officer of this suspicion. In contrast, German law does not require such conditions to be met in order for an employee who spotted a violation of an AML/CTF-related obligation to notify the competent supervisory authority directly.

---

77 According to German law, the supervisory authority must not disclose the identity of a notifying person without this person's explicit consent, and must furthermore not disclose the identity of the person that forms the object of the notification. These disclosure prohibitions do not however apply if the transfer of the information, due to a legal requirement, is necessary in the context of further investigations or in subsequent administrative or court proceedings, or if the disclosure is ordered by a court.

78 See *supra* section III.I.2.

79 See Spain report, sections III.E and III.G.

J. STATISTICS ON SARs BY OBLIGED ENTITIES

The number of SARs filed every year by obliged entities significantly differs from one jurisdiction to another. In the UK, for instance, over 450,000 SARs were filed with the FIU from April 2017 to March 2018, whereas approximately 6,000 SARs were submitted to the Swiss FIU in 2018. Although the difference between jurisdictions in terms of reporting volume is very large, it is however impossible to properly and appropriately compare the statistics available as the details of these statistics are not provided in most jurisdictions,[80] in particular the total value of the assets involved, the content and usefulness of SARs and the type of predicate offence(s) to which they relate. Moreover, the fact that the jurisdictions analysed differ in size and in terms of the importance of their financial market substantially reduces the comparative value of the annual reporting volume.

IV. THE SYSTEM OF FINANCIAL INTELLIGENCE UNITS

A. INSTITUTIONAL AND FUNCTIONAL CHARACTERISTICS

1. *Organisational Position*

Neither the FATF Recommendations nor the EU AML legal framework require FIUs to be of any particular type. That means that countries are free to establish their FIU in the institutional context of their choice, notably within administrative authorities or police authorities. Among the jurisdictions studied, only the UK has opted for a law enforcement model.[81] In contrast, the German,[82] Italian,[83] Spanish[84] and Swiss FIUs are all administrative FIUs. As regard the latter, it is important to note that the fact that it is managed by the Federal Office of Police does not imply that it has law enforcement status. The Swiss FIU is not considered to be a law enforcement authority, but rather an administrative unit with special tasks.

---

80 One should note, however, that the Swiss FIU in particular publishes every year very detailed statistics about the SARs it received during the previous year.

81 The UK FIU sits within the National Crime Agency (NCA).

82 The German FIU is now integrated into the General Directorate of Customs and therein attached to the Customs Criminal Office. The FIU is thereby subordinated to the Federal Ministry of Finance. Previously, the FIU was of a law enforcement nature.

83 The Italian FIU sits within the Bank of Italy.

84 The Spanish FIU is part of the Treasury.

2. *Purpose and Tasks*

In line with FATF Standards and EU requirements, all FIUs carry out the three following core functions: (i) collecting information related to money laundering, associated predicate offences and terrorism financing, in particular SARs; (ii) analysing the information received[85] and obtaining additional information from obliged entities and other sources in order to perform their analysis properly; and (iii) disseminating the results of their analysis and other relevant information to the relevant competent authorities[86] and, where appropriate,[87] to obliged entities. FIUs also have the duty to raise the awareness of obliged entities about money laundering and terrorism financing risks by developing and circulating typologies. Certain FIUs, such as the Swiss FIU, even go beyond typologies and provide training to obliged entities, in particular those belonging to the financial sector.

In addition to the aforementioned tasks, the Spanish and Italian FIUs perform supervisory functions. The scope of duties carried out by the Spanish FIU in this respect is however broader as it consists of ensuring that all AML-related preventive obligations are complied with, whereas the Italian FIU only has the duty to ensure that obliged entities correctly fulfil their duty to report.[88] As a supervisor, the Spanish FIU also aims to protect the integrity of the Spanish financial market by assessing the robustness of the programmes against money laundering and terrorism financing in financial institutions wanting to start operating in Spain, and reporting the results of this assessment to the Bank of Spain before the latter's authorisation.

3. *Independence*

Both the FATF Recommendations and the 4AMLD require FIUs to be "operationally independent and autonomous".[89] This means in particular that decisions to analyse SARs and disseminate information to the competent authorities shall be taken freely. The FATF further specifies that operational independence and autonomy of the FIU also means that if it is established within the existing structure of another authority, its core functions should remain distinct from those of the other authority, and that it should always be able

---

85 On the difference between strategic and operational analysis, see *infra* section IV.B.1.

86 With respect to the range of competent authorities to whom the FIU shall disseminate information, triggers for dissemination, and content of disseminated information, countries follow very different approaches. See *infra* section IV.B.1.

87 See *infra* section IV.B.1.

88 See Italy report, section IV.A.4.

89 Interpretative Note to FATF Recommendation 29 (2012), para. 8; Art. 32(3) 4AMLD.

"to make arrangements or engage independently with other domestic competent authorities or foreign counterparts on the exchange of information".[90]

Regardless of their legal nature, the German, Italian, Spanish, Swiss and UK FIUs provide safeguards against the influence of other government bodies, through their level of independence. Two national peculiarities can serve as examples in this respect as they imply a certain restriction of the independence of the FIU in the conduct of its operational actions. First, the German FIU is subject to the legal supervision of the Ministry of Finance insofar as it collects SARs, analyses the information received and disseminates relevant information to the competent authorities, meaning that the Ministry can interfere where it deems an FIU's action to be illegal. In other areas of the FIU's activity, notably the information exchange with other FIUs and other domestic supervisory authorities, supervision may even extend to questions of policy. Second, potentially contributing to external influence, the Spanish FIU's staff includes representatives from five public authorities, namely the Bank of Spain, the tax authorities, the Treasury, the National Police and the *Guardia Civil*.[91] These representatives are seconded employees within the FIU who remain part of their home authority and who take full part in the work of the FIU, notably the operational analysis of SARs.

4. *Powers*

In order to perform their analysis function properly, all FIUs have, in line with the FATF Recommendations and the 4AMLD, the power to request and obtain additional information from obliged entities and domestic authorities, insofar as no transmission restrictions preclude this. With respect to the power to obtain additional information from obliged entities, it is important to note that the German and Italian FIUs are able to request and obtain additional information from *any* obliged entity, even if no prior SAR was filed. In contrast, the UK and Spanish FIUs may usually request additional information only from obliged entities which have previously filed an SAR. As for the Swiss FIU, it does have the authority to request additional information from financial intermediaries that have not submitted an SAR but only when, on the basis of its analysis of an SAR, it becomes apparent that these financial intermediaries are or were involved in a suspicious transaction or business relationship (third-party financial intermediaries). At the time of writing, the Swiss FIU does not (yet) have the authority to request data from a third-party financial intermediary if

90 *Ibid.*

91 Spain report, section IV.A.1.

this request is only based on information provided in a source other than an SAR and its subsequent analysis.[92]

Certain FIUs, namely the German and the Italian FIUs, also have the power to suspend the execution of suspicious transactions in order to analyse the transaction and confirm the suspicion.[93] In this respect, the main difference between the two FIUs relates to the duration of the suspension. The Italian FIU can suspend the execution of a suspicious transaction for a maximum of five working days provided that it does not impede the investigation or prosecution of crimes. Measures taken by the German FIU shall end at the latest one month after the ordering of the transaction, or when the fifth day has elapsed since the matter was passed on to the competent law enforcement agency. Moreover, unlike the Italian FIU, the German FIU is also able to instruct a credit institution to deny access to a safe deposit box, and it can issue orders to an obliged entity in relation to a transaction.

The power to suspend suspicious transactions described above is similar to the authority of the UK FIU to reject so-called Defense Against Money Laundering (DAML) requests. If the UK FIU rejects a DAML request, the requesting obliged entity is prohibited from carrying out the transaction and the moratorium period then begins. The moratorium period extends to 31 calendar days following the notice of refusal. During this time, the UK FIU will be examining the transaction and, where appropriate, working to take positive enforcement action against any criminal assets the obliged entity has identified.

Lastly, the supervisory powers of the Italian and Spanish FIUs must be mentioned here. While the Italian FIU has the power to carry out inspections and audits within obliged entities to ensure compliance with certain AML-related obligations,[94] Spanish law explicitly obliges the FIU to provide advice to obliged entities on how to improve their programmes against money laundering and terrorist financing, and to coordinate the imposition and execution of AML-related sanctions with the National Commission for the Prevention of Money Laundering and Monetary Offences (COPBLAC).[95]

---

92 In its draft bill published on 14 September 2018, the Federal Council proposed, however, to give the Swiss FIU the power to approach financial intermediaries on the sole basis of information received from foreign counterparts.

93 Such power complies with Art. 32(7) 4AMLD according to which FIUs shall be empowered "to suspend or withhold consent to a transaction that is proceeding, in order to analyse the transaction, confirm the suspicion and disseminate the results of the analysis to the competent authorities".

94 Those obligations are the reporting obligation and the obligation to submit aggregated customer data to the FIU. On the duty of obliged entities to provide aggregated data to the Italian FIU, see *infra* section IV.B.1.

95 Spanish report, section IV.A.2.

B. TREATMENT OF SARs

1. Data Processing

FIUs' processing of data follows a two-step approach: (i) the analysis of information received, in particular SARs from obliged entities; and (ii) the dissemination of relevant information to the competent authorities, in particular investigative and prosecuting authorities.

– Analysis

SARs and other information related to money laundering, associated predicate offences and terrorist financing received by FIUs are used by the latter to perform both strategic and operational analyses.[96] Strategic analysis aims to identify the underlying patterns and trends related to money laundering and terrorist financing, thereby enabling the FIU to define an adequate prevention strategy and set operational priorities. From a comparative point of view, it is interesting to note that, in Italy, financial intermediaries are required to submit, on a monthly basis, aggregated data concerning their activities, which are then used by the FIU in the framework of its strategic analysis to reveal possible money laundering or terrorist financing contingencies in specific geographical areas.[97] Such a duty to report, which aims at helping the FIU to further refine its strategic analysis, does not exist, in a comparable way, outside of Italy.

In contrast, operational analysis focuses on specific targets (e.g. persons, assets, criminal networks and associations) and aims at deciphering the links between those targets and possible money laundering, associated predicate offences or terrorist financing. In all the jurisdictions analysed, the FIU benefits from a margin of appreciation as to when, how, and for what purpose it processes the information received, notably SARs from obliged entities. The reason why the FIU enjoys such discretionary power differs, however, from one jurisdiction to another. In Germany, for instance, the FIU is not subject to a duty to comprehensively investigate each SAR, mainly because the AML legislation does not specify to what extent the FIU shall analyse SARs.[98] In comparison, according to the UK report, the fact that the UK FIU is not able to look at all the SARs it receives primarily results from the very high reporting volume in the UK.[99]

---

96 Italy report, section IV.A.2; Germany report, section IV.A.2.
97 Italy report, section IV.A.2.
98 Germany report, section IV.C.
99 UK report, sections IV.A.2 and IV.B.1.

- Dissemination

Under the EU and FATF frameworks, FIUs shall be responsible for disseminating the results of their analyses and any additional relevant information to the competent authorities where there are grounds to suspect money laundering, associated predicate offences or terrorist financing.[100] In these specific circumstances, FIUs shall therefore be authorised to disseminate information to the competent authorities. However, neither the FATF Recommendations nor the 4AMLD indicate whether FIUs shall also be obliged to this effect. Yet it is worth noting that all FIUs in the jurisdictions analysed are compelled – and not merely authorised – to disseminate information to the competent authorities in specific circumstances. However, the range of information that must be disseminated, and thereby also the scope of recipient authorities of this information, significantly differ from one jurisdiction to another.

In Germany, Italy and Spain, the FIU shall transfer to the competent authorities any relevant information for the investigation, prevention and prosecution of all criminal offences, and not only information relating to suspicions of money laundering, associated predicate offences and terrorist financing.[101] Furthermore, the German FIU shall, where necessary, inform the competent tax authorities or authorities charged with the protection of the social security systems of matters which come to its knowledge in the performance of its tasks and which it has not transmitted to another competent government agency.[102] In Spain, the FIU shall report any information relating to a breach of administrative law.[103] In particular, the FIU shall transmit to the tax authorities any information with tax relevance.[104]

At the other end of the spectrum, Switzerland follows a much more restrictive approach to the FIU's obligation to pass on information to the competent authorities. First, the FIU shall only provide information to the competent prosecution authorities, and not to any domestic authority which could potentially make use of certain information held by the FIU. Second, the transfer shall only concern information relating to money laundering, terrorist financing and associated predicate offences, namely felonies and aggravated tax misdemeanours.[105] Information relating to suspicions of misdemeanours, contraventions or breaches of any other area of law shall therefore not be transmitted by the FIU. Third, the grounds of suspicion necessary to trigger

100 FATF report, e.g. section V.B.1.
101 Germany report, section IV.A.2; Italy report, section IV.A.2; Spain report section IV.A.2.
102 Germany report, section IV.A.2.
103 Spain report, section IV.A.2.
104 *Ibid.*
105 See *supra* section II.B.1.a.i; Switzerland report, section II.B.1.a.i.

the dissemination of information must qualify as "reasonable",[106] thus implying compliance with the proportionality principle.

2. *Special Procedures for Privileged Professions*

As was already observed,[107] Article 34(1) 4AMLD and the Interpretative Note to FATF Recommendation 23 permit countries to allow privileged professions to report their suspicions to their appropriate self-regulatory bodies, provided however that the latter then forward the information to the FIU promptly and unfiltered. However, neither the FATF nor the 4AMLD nor the jurisdictions analysed provide for a specific procedure for analysing SARs from privileged professions.

3. *Feedback Obligations*

a. Obligation of the FIU

Unlike the FATF Recommendations, the 4AMLD does not provide for an explicit obligation of the FIU to inform obliged entities about the outcome of SARs. According to Article 46(3) 4AMLD, "Member States shall ensure that, where practicable, timely feedback on the effectiveness of and follow-up to reports of suspected money laundering or terrorist financing is provided to obliged entities". The 4AMLD does not specify, however, the authority or authorities which shall provide this feedback and whether case-by-case feedback is required for each individual SAR.

At national level, the German and Italian FIUs are compelled by law to provide feedback to all reporting entities,[108] although the law does not further specify the content of such feedback and in particular whether or to what extent

---

106 That is also the case in Spain. See Spain report, sections IV.A.2 and V.B.1.

107 See *supra* section III.C.3.b.

108 Germany report, section IV.A.2. One should note that the Joint Money Laundering Intelligence Taskforce (JMLIT) established in the UK in 2015 is characterised by a mutual dialogue and in this respect is not part of the traditional SAR framework. The JMLIT is a forum used to share information on new typologies, existing vulnerabilities and live tactical intelligence. The way it works, when it comes to sharing intelligence, is as follows. The authorities, e.g. the NCA, HM Revenue and Customs or the Serious Fraud Office, provide leads notably from ongoing investigations to the representatives of the financial institutions that are members of the JMLIT. They, in turn, then search their internal systems to check for any exposure to the subjects of these investigations (e.g. as clients or counterparties in transactions) and provide the results back to the authorities through the JMLIT. Those security-vetted bank staff that are part of the JMLIT can get limited feedback, in certain circumstances (e.g. if it comes to issuing a freezing order) where they are working on a joint investigation, but that information is classified and is not more widely distributed.

the feedback must contain specific information on the particular reported activity or whether it might perhaps suffice that the reporting entity is only informed about the nature of the FIU's follow-up measures without providing the specific results of an operational analysis. The Swiss FIU is also bound by such an obligation, but only with respect to financial intermediaries, and not regarding SARs from dealers. Insofar as FIUs do not provide feedback on SARs, obliged entities might however learn about any potential investigation if required to provide further information on a specific SAR to the competent authorities

b. Obligation of Investigative Authorities

Unlike the 4AMLD, the FATF Recommendations do not explicitly require investigative authorities to provide feedback to the FIU about the use made of the information provided and about the outcome of the investigations or inspections performed on the basis of that information.

With the sole exception of the UK (where in any case the FIU already sits within the NCA), the investigative authorities in all the national jurisdictions analysed are required to inform the FIU of the decisions reached in relation to the SARs forwarded to them. In addition, it should be noted that the Swiss prosecution authorities shall immediately, independently of any SAR, notify the FIU of any pending proceedings, judgments and decisions on the closure of proceedings connected with a specific set of criminal offences, namely participation in a criminal organisation, terrorism financing, money laundering and insufficient diligence in financial transactions.[109] This obligation, which goes beyond merely informing the FIU about the outcome of SARs, only exists in Switzerland.

4. FIU's Disclosure Obligations Towards "Suspect"

Neither the FATF Recommendations nor the EU legal framework specify to what extent FIUs shall be entitled or obliged to inform the individuals or entities that appear as possible "suspects" in SARs about the analyses they conduct. The same observation can be made about the Italian legal regime. In contrast, the Spanish, German, UK and Swiss legislation address the issue, though providing very different answers to it.

In Spain and the UK, the FIU is allowed to refuse access to its files by persons whose personal data are being processed or held by it.[110]

---

109 On insufficient diligence in financial transactions as a criminal offence, see Switzerland report, section VII.B.2.a. See also *infra* section VII.B.2.a.

110 Spain report, section IV.E.1; UK report, section IV.E.1.

In comparison, German law allows the FIU to provide the person concerned, upon request, with details of the available information concerning him/her if the analysis of an SAR has not yet been concluded and provided that this will not interfere with the purpose of the analysis. At the request of the person concerned, the FIU may also provide such information if the analysis of an SAR has been concluded but its results were not forwarded to the criminal justice authorities. The German FIU is however no longer allowed to provide information to the person concerned once it has transmitted the matter to the criminal justice authorities and as long as the procedure by these authorities is ongoing. The FIU must also refuse to provide information if such disclosure would negatively impact international relations, matters concerning the internal or external security of Germany, the conduct of another criminal investigation, or the conduct of ongoing judicial proceedings.

The Swiss FIU is also authorised to disclose details about an operational analysis to the person concerned under specific circumstances. According to Swiss data protection law, to which the AML law frequently refers, any person may request information from the Swiss FIU as to whether data concerning him/her is being processed. The FIU shall then provide the person with all available data concerning him/her, including the available information on the source of the data, and inform him/her of the purpose of, and if applicable also the legal basis for, the processing, as well as the categories of personal data processed, the other parties involved with the file and the data recipients. The FIU shall however defer the disclosure of information to the requesting person if the data processed concerning him/her relate to overriding interests for criminal prosecution which require the maintenance of secrecy.

C. PROACTIVE INVESTIGATIONS OF THE FIU

Considering that, in line with the requirements set out in the FATF Recommendations and the 4AMLD, all FIUs shall serve as the central agency for receipt and analysis of SARs filed by obliged entities but also of any other information related to money laundering, associated predicate offences and terrorism financing,[111] one can argue that FIUs' operational analysis does not require an SAR as a starting point, as such analysis may also be triggered by information spontaneously shared by foreign counterparts, the press or another third party.

Despite the above, it is worth noting that, in Spain and the UK, the FIU reportedly always launches an operational analysis on the basis of an SAR. To some extent, this could be explained by the fact that neither the Spanish nor

[111] See *supra* section IV.A.2.

the UK FIU have the authority to request additional information from financial intermediaries that have not previously submitted an SAR.[112]

D. ACCESS TO DATA

1. Design and Content of FIU's Own Data Banks

As already explained,[113] one of the main tasks of FIUs is to receive SARs as well as any other information relevant to money laundering, associated predicate offences and terrorist financing. The breadth of each FIU's own data bank thus depends on how much information national legislation requires the FIU to collect within the framework of AML/CTF. In this regard, Spanish law is particularly extensive as it tasks the FIU with serving as the national centre for the receipt of a wide array of systematic reports, namely (i) domestic cash movements of €100,000 or more; (ii) transfers exceeding €30,000 to/from designated territories or countries (high-risk jurisdictions, including tax havens);[114] (iii) transactions involving the physical movement of cash exceeding €30,000 or more (as reported by banks); (iv) aggregate information on the international transfers of credit institutions (broken down by country of origin or destination); and (v) all money transfers involving cash or bearer negotiable instruments of €1,500 or more.[115]

Furthermore, in accordance with the 5AMLD[116] but unlike the FATF Recommendations, it is worth noting that the Spanish FIU has control over the so-called "Financial Ownership File", a database established at the Bank of Spain containing prescribed information on all customers' bank and securities accounts in Spain. The information in this database is filed by financial institutions, and includes the date of account opening, the name of the account holder, the name of the beneficial owner, the name of the financial institution and the branch location.[117] It does not contain, however, information on the account balance or financial transactions.[118]

2. Access to Other Public Data Banks

In order to perform their analysis function properly, all FIUs have access to various public authorities' data banks. However, the number and relevance

---

112 See *supra* section IV.A.4.

113 See *supra* section IV.A.2.

114 As listed in Royal Decree 1080/1991.

115 Spain report, section III.C.1

116 Yet the transposition deadline for setting up these mechanisms, such as central registries or central electronic data retrieval systems, is 10 September 2020.

117 Spain report, section IV.D.2.

118 *Ibid.*

of the databases that FIUs can access greatly differ from one jurisdiction to another despite the fact that both the FATF Recommendations and the 4AMLD provide that FIUs shall have access to all the administrative and law enforcement information they need to carry out their tasks (though it does not further clarify what data this would require and for what purposes). It would fall outside the ambit of this comparative analysis to list all the databases that each FIU may access, but it is worth highlighting some key differences between the different legal regimes analysed.

First, it should be pointed out that the five national jurisdictions considered follow very different approaches as regards the way(s) the FIU can access law enforcement data. Whilst in Italy[119] and Switzerland, law enforcement data can only be retrieved by the FIU following an administrative assistance procedure request, the German, Spanish and UK FIUs have access to such data more directly. In Germany, though the FIU only has indirect access to the Länder police databases, it has direct access to the Federal police database. Moreover, it is interesting to note that the German FIU seems to be more and more in favour of having a police representative within its own staff, something that the Spanish FIU has been implementing now for a few years now and which considerably eases access to law enforcement data. As regards the UK FIU, the fact that it is part of the NCA entails that it has direct access to the Police National Computer (police information system).

Second, with the exception of the UK and Swiss FIUs, all FIUs can retrieve data from the tax authorities' database. However, while the Italian and Spanish FIUs have very extensive access to it,[120] the German FIU is usually only entitled to retrieve, by transmitting the name and address or date of birth and by automated means, a person's tax number and the address of the competent tax office as preparation to request information from tax offices.

It is also important to mention the fact that, with the notable exception of the UK FIU, all FIUs considered already have direct access, through an automated mechanism, to information on the identity of holders of bank and payment accounts.[121] The information on the identity of holders of bank and payment accounts may be stored in a file directly under the control of the FIU (Spain),[122] in a separate public database (Italy),[123] or in a decentralised way within each financial institution (Germany).[124] It may however also be stored in financial institutions' own data banks, as is the case in Germany as explained below.[125]

---

119 Italy report, section V.B.2.
120 Italy report, section IV.B.1.
121 *Ibid.*
122 See *supra* section IV.D.1.
123 Italy report, section IV.B.1.
124 Germany report, section IV.D.3.
125 See *infra* section IV.D.3.

3. *Access to Private Data Banks*

Neither the FATF Recommendations nor the 4AMLD require that FIUs have direct access to private data banks in order to perform their analysis function properly.

National AML frameworks do not explicitly address the access to private databases by the FIU. Nevertheless, FIUs often purchase access to private commercial databases to widen their data stock and thereby enhance their operational analyses. It has for instance been reported that the Swiss FIU uses three private databases – namely Dow Jones's global news database, Dun & Bradstreet's database and CRIF's Teledata database – and that the Spanish FIU has full access to Informa, a private data bank that provides commercial and financial information about Spanish companies and independent professionals.[126]

4. *Data Analytics*

In an age where the flow of data, in particular financial data, is constantly increasing, and thus where a clear understanding of rules applicable to the processing of data by public authorities for the prevention of crime seems crucial, one would expect national laws to tackle the issue of the FIU's use of data analytics.[127] Amongst the national jurisdictions analysed, only German law, however, though not in the framework of AML/CTF, seems to address the issue of to what extent authorities are authorised to conduct data analytics in or between their own data banks and the other public and private databases they can retrieve information from.[128] In light of German constitutional jurisprudence, the FIU can only to a limited extent use data analytics technologies for the operational analysis of personal data, and in particular cannot use access to various public databases for the purpose of an operational analysis that is not yet directed at a particular business relationship or transaction.

As regards data mining, it is subject to comparatively strict standards in Germany. To what extent the use of data mining tools is authorised in other jurisdictions remains unclear. However, even if authorised, the right to obtain human intervention on the part of the FIU shall at least be provided according

---

126 FATF, *Anti-money laundering and counter-terrorist financing measures – Spain, Fourth Round Mutual Evaluation Report*, 2014, p. 46.

127 After all, the FATF reports that SEPBLAC, the Spanish FIU, "has state-of-the-art software, analytical and data-mining tools" (FATF, *Anti-money laundering and counter-terrorist financing measures – Spain, Fourth Round Mutual Evaluation Report*, 2014, p. 48) and that the Italian FIU's analytical system "has some data mining features" (FATF, *Anti-money laundering and counter-terrorist financing measures – Italy, Fourth Round Mutual Evaluation Report*, 2016, para. 134).

128 See *supra* sections IV.D.1, 2 and 3.

to Directive 2016/680/EU.[129] In any case, EU FIUs' decisions "shall not be based on special categories of personal data [namely personal data revealing racial or ethnic origin, political opinions, religious or philosophical beliefs, or trade union membership, … genetic data, biometric data for the purpose of uniquely identifying a natural person, data concerning health or data concerning a natural person's sex life or sexual orientation], unless suitable measures to safeguard the data subject's rights and freedoms and legitimate interests are in place".[130] Furthermore, profiling resulting in discrimination against natural persons on the basis of these special categories of personal data is prohibited.[131] This limitation is particularly important because of the inherent potential of CDD measures (following a risk-based approach) to apply unfounded discrimination criteria between groups.

5. *International Cooperation*

The German, Spanish, Italian, Swiss and UK FIUs are all members of the Egmont Group and can therefore use Egmont Secure Web, a secure communication channel, to submit requests for operational information to one or several of the FIUs which are part of Egmont. EU FIUs may also request information from their EU counterparts using FIU.net. Compared to Egmont Secure Web, FIU.net, which was established in 2007 and embedded in Europol in 2016, is a much more sophisticated and technologically advanced computer network. FIU.net is not just a channel of communication; it is rather a platform on which FIUs can retrieve financial information and integrate it directly into their own database. FIU.net also enables multilateral exchanges, which may vary from a minimal approach (such as "known/unknown requests" to check whether individuals' names are found in another EU Member State's database), to a "case file" approach (giving further details and justification for obtaining information from the other FIUs.)

With regard to the specific terms for the exchange of information between FIUs, these are usually specified in memorandums of association the content of which usually remains confidential.

---

129 Art. 11(1) Directive 2016/680/EU. On the applicability of Directive 2016/680/EU, or possibly Regulation (EU) 2016/679, to the processing of data by FIUs, see EU report, section IV.D.4.

130 Art. 11(2) Directive 2016/680/EU.

131 Art. 11(3) Directive 2016/680/EU.

E. PARTICIPATION OF "SUSPECTS"

1. *Defence Rights*

FIUs' operational analysis may focus on, at least implicitly, individual persons suspected of money laundering. This can seem problematic as investigations against individuals that are suspected of criminal offences are normally subject to a number of defence rights, in particular those contained in the Code of Criminal Procedure. The performance of *de facto* investigative powers might therefore raise the question of whether such defence rights apply as regards the FIU. However, neither international instruments nor national AML legislations address the issue, and the "suspect" thus does not enjoy any particular rights vis-à-vis the FIU with regard to its analysis. National AML laws usually provide that lawyers, legal advisors who are members of a chamber of lawyers, patent attorneys, notaries, auditors, tax advisors and tax agents may refuse to provide information to the FIU insofar as the request relates to information they obtained in the context of providing legal advice or of the legal representation of the contracting party, and provided that the obliged entity does not know that the contracting party has used or is using its legal advice for the purpose of money laundering or terrorist financing.

2. *Judicial Review or Other Remedies*

Neither supranational instruments nor Italian, Spanish and Swiss laws specify to what extent the FIU's action can be reviewed, either judicially or otherwise. In contrast, German law explicitly provides that the obliged entity or another adversely affected party, such as the obliged entity's contracting party, may lodge an objection against provisional measures imposed by the FIU,[132] leading to an administrative review of measures. Following an unsuccessful objection, the interested parties can apply to the administrative court for judicial review. Similarly, as regards the UK FIU's position within the NCA, UK courts should be able to review any decision made by the FIU, in particular whether the FIU has overstepped its authority and treated someone unfairly by passing an SAR on to another authority to potentially launch an investigation.

[132] See *supra* section IV.A.4.

F. SIMILAR POWERS OF SUPERVISORY BODIES

1. *Financial Supervision*

To the extent that violations of AML by obliged entities' employees can, and if committed intentionally will, constitute money laundering, the question arises whether supervisory authorities are also allowed to investigate the criminal offence of money laundering. However, neither the FATF Recommendations nor the 4AMLD indicate whether supervisory bodies of financial markets should or could have the right to investigate a suspicion of money laundering on their own. The Italian, Spanish, Swiss and German legal frameworks are clear on this issue, in that supervisory authorities are not authorised to investigate suspicions of money laundering. In contrast, supervisors in the UK can investigate money laundering suspicions on their own initiative. The Financial Conduct Authority has the authority to investigate a suspicion of money laundering insofar as such suspicion appears in a broader investigation relating to insider dealing or another market offence.

2. *Non-Financial Sector Supervision*

As regards non-financial sector supervisors, these do not have the task of investigating a suspicion of money laundering on their own in Italy, Germany, Switzerland and the UK. In contrast, the General Council of Notaries Centralised Prevention Unit (OCP) in Spain has the function of examining potentially suspicious activities, or patterns of activity, conducted through notaries. If suspicions are confirmed, the OCP must file an SAR with the FIU.

G. REPORTING OBLIGATIONS OF SUPERVISORY AUTHORITIES

Contrary to the FATF Recommendations, the 4AMLD requires Member States to ensure that AML supervisory authorities promptly inform the FIU of any fact related to possible money laundering (or terrorist financing) that they discover when performing checks on the obliged entities. In this context, if Spanish, German or UK supervisors, in the course of their work, become aware or suspicious that money laundering is taking (or has taken or will take) place within an obliged entity supervised by them, they shall file a report with the FIU. In Switzerland, supervisory authorities also have a reporting obligation, not only if money laundering/terrorist financing suspicions arise (like in Spain, Germany and the UK), but also if supervisors have grounds to suspect that a predicate offence has been committed. This duty to report shall only apply, however, if an SAR has not already been submitted by the obliged entity.

H. REPORTING BY OTHER AUTHORITIES

Pursuant to Article 36(2) 4AMLD, Member States shall ensure that supervisory bodies empowered by law or regulation to oversee the stock, foreign exchange and financial derivatives markets inform the FIU if they discover facts that could be related to money laundering or terrorist financing.

Beyond the aforementioned authorities, any authority or official in Spain discovering facts that may constitute an indication or evidence of money laundering or terrorist financing, either during the inspections of monitored institutions or in any other way, shall report such circumstance to the FIU. Moreover, Spanish courts shall forward evidence to COPBLAC, on the instruction of the Prosecutor's Office or upon their own motion, when they detect signs indicative of a breach preventive obligations that do not constitute criminal offences. In Germany, if facts indicate that assets are related to money laundering or terrorist financing, the revenue authorities must report these facts to the FIU without delay. In the UK, other public authorities are not obliged but merely authorised to report their suspicions to the FIU.

I. STATISTICS

1. *Number of Reports by Supervisory Authorities and Other Authorities*

The UK and Italy do not provide statistics on the number of reports about suspicious activities filed by supervisory authorities and other authorities. However, Germany, Switzerland and Spain provide such statistics. Although it would not be very relevant here to compare numbers *per se*, as the authorities' reporting duties differ from one jurisdiction to another, it is worth noting that, in each of these three countries, the number of reports about suspicious activities filed by supervisory authorities and other authorities is always very small compared to the overall reporting volume. In Switzerland, for instance, supervisors only made 11 reports out of a total of over 19,000 SARs between 2008 and 2017. In Germany, supervisory authorities filed 54 reports with the FIU in 2008 out of a total of over 77,000 SARs.

2. *FIU Analyses*

None of the jurisdictions analysed expressly provide statistics on how many analyses the FIU carries out and the value of transactions associated with these analyses. In certain jurisdictions, however, such statistics may be deduced from other figures, such as the number of feedback reports provided to the FIU by the criminal justice authorities or the number of SARs forwarded by the FIU to the law enforcement authorities.[133] In Switzerland, the FIU's analysis activity may also be inferred from the number of requests for additional information sent to third-party financial intermediaries.[134]

3. *Communications to Law Enforcement Authorities*

The proportion of SARs forwarded to the law enforcement authorities by the FIU (the conversion rate) significantly differs from one jurisdiction to another. However, here again, it would be of reduced value to compare the numbers available, as not only the overall reporting volume but also the total value of the assets involved, the ultimate usefulness and relevance of the SARs, and the type of predicate offence(s) to which they relate differ widely from one jurisdiction to another. It can be noted, however, that the conversion rate has been declining in recent years in most jurisdictions. In this regard, Switzerland is a striking example as the percentage of SARs forwarded to the prosecution authorities went from 90.8% in 2008 to 65.1% in 2018.

V. DATA FLOW AND DATA PROTECTION

A. DATA EXCHANGE BETWEEN FIU AND PRIVATE SECTOR

1. *From FIU to Private Sector*

Like the FATF Recommendations and the 4AMLD, national laws do not explicitly allow FIUs to share personal data with obliged entities. That said, all FIUs are empowered, under certain conditions previously described,[135] to request and obtain additional information from obliged entities. In this context, one must therefore assume that FIUs are authorised to share with the requested obliged entities as much information as needed so that they are able to provide a meaningful response to the request. In the absence of a specific legislative authorisation, FIUs from the four continental jurisdictions covered (namely Germany, Spain, Italy and Switzerland) are not, however, allowed to share more information than is strictly necessary for specifying the scope of their requests. The situation is less clear in the UK. In fact, the UK has developed quite an extensive approach to the sharing of personal data between the competent authorities and the private sector, notably through the development and implementation of the Joint Money Laundering Intelligence Taskforce (JMLIT),

---

133 In this regard, see Germany report.

134 On the notion of third-party financial intermediaries and the power of the FIU to request information from them, see Switzerland report, section IV.A.4.

135 See *supra* section IV.A.4.

which allows the NCA (which includes the FIU) to share tactical intelligence related to ongoing investigations directly with vetted representatives from over 40 financial institutions.[136]

2. *From Private Sector to FIU*

Obliged entities must very often share personal data with the FIU, either *ex officio*, through the filing of SARs[137] or following requests for additional information.[138] However, it is interesting to note that, while the FATF Recommendations and the 4AMLD (as modified by the 5AMLD) require FIUs' requests for additional information to be based on sufficiently defined conditions so that they do not amount to fishing expeditions, national AML legal frameworks do not further specify these conditions.[139] This does not mean, however, that no data protection restrictions apply and that any personal data can be transferred to the FIU. Obliged entities in the EU shall respect the requirements set out in Regulation (EU) 2016/679 when deciding whether or not to share information with the FIU, notably the purpose limitation, proportionality and data minimisation principles. As for Switzerland, the same general principles enshrined in the Federal Act on Data Protection apply to the transfer of personal data from obliged entities to the FIU.

B. DATA EXCHANGE BETWEEN FIU AND CRIMINAL JUSTICE SYSTEM

1. *From FIU to Criminal Justice System*

Although not required by the FATF Recommendations and the 4AMLD, all FIUs are compelled under national law to disseminate without delay the results of their analysis and relevant information to the competent criminal justice authorities when there are grounds to suspect that money laundering, terrorist financing or an associated predicate offence has been committed.[140] As already seen,[141] the relevant suspicion threshold may differ from one jurisdiction to another. Additionally, one should recall that certain jurisdictions, namely Germany, Spain and Italy, require the FIU to transfer any relevant information

---

136 On JMLIT, see *supra* section IV.B.3.a.
137 See *supra* section III.C.1.a.
138 See *supra* section III.C.2.a.
139 "Relevant information" and "results of analysis", which are expressions used in every single AML legal framework, are rather vague and equivocal, possibly covering a wide range of personal information, including CDD-related data going beyond the reported transaction.
140 See *supra* section IV.B.1.
141 *Ibid.*

for the investigation, prevention and prosecution of all criminal offences, whereas Switzerland and the UK limit the range of information that must be disseminated to information relating to suspicions of money laundering, associated predicate offences and terrorist financing.[142] Besides this, however, all the jurisdictions analysed share one common feature in that the law does not specify the exact scope of information that the FIU must transfer to the criminal justice authorities. "Relevant information" and "results of analysis", which are expressions used in every single AML legal framework, are rather vague and equivocal, possibly covering a wide range of personal information, including CDD-related data going beyond the reported transaction.

In addition to the aforementioned mandatory transfer of information to the criminal justice authorities, FIUs may also be requested by the latter to share information. Pursuant to FATF Recommendation 31 and Article 32(4) 4AMLD *cum* recital (44) 5AMLD, such requests must be motivated by concerns relating solely to money laundering, associated predicate offences or terrorist financing.[143] However, among the five national legal frameworks analysed, only Switzerland and the UK adopted this limitation. In Germany, Spain and Italy, requests for information from criminal justice authorities may relate to the investigation or the conduct of criminal proceedings related to any criminal offence. Another difference among the various jurisdictions examined which is worth noting is that not all FIUs are allowed to refuse to provide information to the criminal justice authorities when requested to do so. Contrary to the FATF Recommendations and the 4AMLD, which explicitly state that dissemination upon request shall never be mandatory for the FIU, the Italian FIU is indeed obliged to transmit information to investigative or prosecuting authorities if this information is deemed necessary in the context of an investigation or criminal proceeding. As for the UK FIU, its autonomy is even further weakened as its SAR database is directly accessible by authorised financial investigators. In contrast, the decision to disclose the information always remains with the FIU in Germany, Switzerland and Spain. In Germany, notably, where there are objective grounds for assuming that the provision of such information would have a negative

---

142 *Ibid.*

143 One should note, however, that, according to Art. 7(1) Directive 2019/1153/EU of the European Parliament and of the Council of 20 June 2019 laying down rules facilitating the use of financial and other information for the prevention, detection, investigation or prosecution of certain criminal offences, and repealing Council Decision 2000/642/JHA (OJ L 186, 11.07.2019, p. 122), EU law enforcement authorities shall now be given the possibility to request information from the FIU for the wider purpose of fighting serious crime, rather than being limited to money laundering and terrorist financing. More precisely, FIUs shall "be able to reply, in a timely manner, to reasoned requests for financial information or financial analysis by those designated competent authorities in their respective Member State, where that financial information or financial analysis is necessary on a case-by-case basis and where the request is motivated by concerns relating to the prevention, detection, investigation or prosecution of serious criminal offences."

impact on ongoing investigations or analyses, or in exceptional circumstances where disclosure of the information would be clearly disproportionate to the legitimate interest of a natural or legal person or irrelevant with regard to the purposes for which it has been requested, the FIU shall be under no obligation to comply with the request for information.

2. *From Criminal Justice System to FIU*

In line with FATF Recommendation 29 and Article 32(4) 4AMLD, all national AML laws permit the FIU to request information, in particular personal data, from the relevant criminal justice authorities insofar as this is necessary for the performance of its functions. None of the AML laws examined explicitly specify further transmission limitations as regards information flows from criminal justice authorities to the FIU. However, this does not mean that no data protection restrictions apply in this context. Quite the contrary in fact, all data protection principles which apply to data processing by the competent authorities must be respected. An assessment of the proportionality of a transfer of personal data from the criminal justice authorities to the FIU is important not least because the FIU also extensively interacts with obliged entities and data that the FIU has received from criminal justice authorities can then have an indirect but nevertheless detrimental effect on obliged entities' clients, without the FIU being in a position to assess the substance of the suspicion underlying the criminal justice's investigation.

C. DATA EXCHANGE BETWEEN FIU AND INTELLIGENCE AGENCIES

1. *From FIU to Intelligence Agencies*

Neither the FATF Recommendations nor the EU legal framework address the relationship between the FIU and intelligence agencies, notably the question of the sharing of information.[144] However, with the exception of Spain, this question is specifically addressed in each of the national frameworks analysed. In Germany, for instance, the FIU is compelled by law to transmit the results of its operational analysis and all relevant information to the Federal Office for the Protection of the Constitution and to the Federal Intelligence Service insofar as there are factual indications that this transmission is necessary for the performance of their functions. The German FIU must also transmit without

144 With respect to the EU legal framework, this is simply because the EU does not have jurisdiction in matters of national security, which usually include legislation on information sharing involving intelligence agencies.

delay SARs from obliged entities and supervisory authorities to the Federal Office for the Protection of the Constitution when the transmission of this information is deemed necessary for the Federal Office to carry out its duties. This latter obligation is particularly interesting when compared to Italian law, which only allows the FIU to pass on to the intelligence agencies the results of its analysis, including information relevant to predicate offences, but not also SARs themselves.

Where the transfer of information from the FIU to intelligence agencies is authorised, it shall always take place within the limits set out by data protection law. In particular, personal data shall not be transmitted insofar as the dissemination of the data would be disproportionate to the legitimate interests of a natural or legal person. However, these considerations are only vaguely addressed in the jurisdictions studied.

2. *From Intelligence Agencies to FIU*

In Germany, Switzerland and the UK, the law permits the FIU, for the performance of its functions, to request and obtain data from domestic public authorities, which in principle also covers the intelligence services. Limits on this power are set by the data transfer provisions of the laws regulating the respective intelligence services. In contrast, neither Italian nor Spanish laws provide for special rules regulating the transfer of information from intelligence agencies to the FIU.

D. DATA EXCHANGE BETWEEN FIU AND TAX AUTHORITIES

1. *From FIU to Tax Authorities*

Neither the FATF Recommendations nor the 4AMLD require FIUs to transfer information to the tax authorities, whether *ex officio* or upon request. However, it is worth noting that, with the exception of Switzerland[145] and Italy, FIUs in all the

---

[145] In Switzerland, the transfer of data from the FIU to the tax authorities is regulated by the same rules as those that apply to the transfer of data from the FIU to the criminal justice authorities outside the context of mandatory notification. See *supra* section V.B.1 and Switzerland report, section V.B.1. As a result, data sharing shall only be carried out on a case-by-case basis and provided that the authorities use the information exclusively for combating money laundering, its predicate offences, organised crime or the financing of terrorism. Dissemination upon request shall never be made mandatory for the FIU. Additionally, Art. 29(2bis) AMLA provides that Art. 30(2) and (5) AMLA applies by analogy, which means that, regarding the sharing of information from MROS to criminal justice authorities, the latter must be treated in the same way as foreign FIUs that receive information from MROS. In particular, the same restrictions on the dissemination of the information received to third authorities shall apply. It could also be mentioned that information shall only be passed on in the form a report.

jurisdictions analysed are compelled by law to transfer to the tax authorities on their own initiative any relevant information that points toward the commission of a tax offence as a predicate offence to money laundering.

Where tax authorities do not qualify as "competent authorities" investigating tax offences but carry out purely administrative functions (e.g. processing of tax declarations), information sharing is not addressed under EU law.[146] The purpose limitation principle enshrined in Article 4(2) Directive 2016/680/EU can be taken to exclude the sharing of information with authorities which do not process data for the purposes of the prevention, investigation, detection or prosecution of criminal offences or the execution of criminal penalties, including the safeguarding against and the prevention of threats to public security.[147] That said, the Spanish and the UK FIUs are both required to share with the tax authorities not only information relating to tax offences but, more generally, any information with tax relevance.[148] At first glance, the same could be said about the German FIU. German law indeed broadly provides that the FIU shall transmit personal data, *ex officio* or upon request, to the competent domestic authorities insofar as this is necessary for taxation procedures. However, in light of the proportionality standard developed by the Federal Constitutional Court's jurisprudence, it would seem that a transfer of personal data by the FIU to the tax authorities is admissible only where the information is meant to prevent or investigate serious tax crimes.

2. *From Tax Authorities to FIU*

Among the five national legal frameworks which fall within the scope of this study, the Spanish one is by far the most permissive regarding the transfer of information, notably personal data, from the tax authorities to the FIU. First of all, the Spanish FIU has direct and unrestricted access to the tax authorities' database.[149] Second, the Spanish FIU's staff includes a representative from the tax authorities who contributes to the FIU's operational analyses and who can, in this context, share knowledge and information from his/her home institution. Third, since 2018, the tax authorities automatically share with the FIU information contained in a new data bank (so-called "File 56"), which includes

146 The FATF Recommendations do not address the question of the transfer of data from the FIU to tax authorities where tax authorities carry out purely administrative functions.

147 Indeed, cross-border information sharing between criminal justice authorities could otherwise be hampered if data they provided to counterparts with other Member States could further be shared with purely administrative authorities.

148 In the UK, the HM Revenue and Customs even has direct access to the FIU's SARs database, except for certain sensitive data such as terrorist financing-related data. See UK report, section IV.D.2.

149 See *supra* section IV.D.2.

information from obliged entities and legal representatives of companies, such as identification details, nationality, employment-related information, and economic and financial data.

As regards the other jurisdictions examined, they should be divided into three groups that provide very different data protection restrictions for the transfer of personal data from the FIU to the tax authorities. The first group consists of Italy, where, like in Spain, the FIU has direct and unrestricted access to the tax authorities' database. The second group comprises Germany, where, as an exception to the tax secrecy governing the treatment of personal data in tax proceedings, the revenue authorities are obliged, *ex officio* or upon request, to transfer personal data, insofar as such disclosure serves the performance of the FIU's tasks. The German revenue authorities are even under an obligation to report to the FIU any facts indicating that assets is the object of money laundering or related to terrorism financing. Finally, the third group consists of Switzerland and the UK, where the FIU can obtain data from the tax authorities but only upon request. In Switzerland, such data include in particular financial information and other sensitive data and personality profiles obtained in criminal or administrative proceedings, including those from pending proceedings.

E. DATA EXCHANGE BETWEEN FIU AND CUSTOMS AUTHORITIES

1. *From FIU to Customs Authorities*

Under the EU and FATF frameworks, the FIU is responsible for disseminating *ex officio* the results of its analyses and any additional information to the customs authorities provided that: (i) there are grounds to suspect a customs-related offence has been committed; (ii) this offence is a predicate offence to money laundering; and (iii) the customs authorities have the duty to investigate customs-related offences. In these circumstances, both the FATF Recommendations and the 4AMLD invite the FIU to disseminate information to the customs authorities, but neither of them indicates whether the FIU has a corresponding obligation.

At national level, Spanish, Italian and Swiss laws do not specifically address the issue of information sharing from the FIU to the customs authorities, and thus do not compel the former to transfer personal data to the latter in the above-mentioned circumstances. In contrast, as already explained,[150] HM Revenue and Customs in the UK, where the customs authorities sit, has direct

[150] See *supra* section V.D.1.

access to the FIU's database. In Germany, the FIU is obliged to inform the customs authorities about customs-related money laundering and customs-related predicate offences and, in this context, transmit relevant personal data to them. Such transmission in view of suspected criminal offences is reportedly however subject to the proportionality principle, which excludes the sharing of information relating to less serious forms of criminality.

2. *From Customs Authorities to FIU*

As already stated,[151] the FATF Recommendations and the 4AMLD require countries to ensure that the FIU, in order to conduct proper analysis, has access to the widest possible range of administrative and law enforcement information, which includes information held by the customs authorities. However, none of these two frameworks address the question of data sharing with the customs authorities. The regulation of this question is therefore left to the discretion of national jurisdictions.[152] Yet not all countries specifically address the question of information sharing from the customs authorities to the FIU. Such is the case in Italy, for instance, where the transfer of information is simply subject to the general data protection rules that apply to the processing of data by the competent authorities, notably the proportionality principle. In comparison, other jurisdictions provide special rules explicitly allowing for the transfer of information from the customs authorities to the FIU. For example, in Spain, the customs authorities must share with the FIU all reports on inbound and outbound cross-border transportations of currency and bearer negotiable instruments. Another example is that of Switzerland and Germany, where the law gives the FIU direct access to certain customs databases, which notably contains information on customs-related crimes, but also on non-crime related personal information regarding the domestic and cross-border movement of goods, capital and services.

F. INFORMATION FLOW BETWEEN FIU AND FOREIGN COUNTERPARTS

1. *Restrictions on Data Transfer from FIU to Foreign FIUs*

Enhancing information sharing between FIUs has long been high on the agenda of both the FATF and the EU. Throughout the years, both have

---

151 See *supra* sections IV.A.4 and IV.D.2.

152 It should be noted, however, that the requirements set out in Art. 4(2) Directive 2016/680/EU shall be respected by any EU FIU processing the information received from the custom authorities.

developed standards and rules aiming at stimulating information exchange and overcoming obstacles preventing cross-border information sharing between FIUs. In addition to various legislative changes to the EU AML legal framework introduced by the 5AMLD in this regard,[153] one could for instance mention the report entitled "Mapping Exercise and Gap Analysis on FIUs' powers and obstacles for obtaining and exchanging information" commissioned by the European Commission and published in 2016.[154] This report aims to assist FIUs in improving their cooperation, facilitate the implementation of the EU legislation, and identify areas where further initiatives are needed to remove obstacles or remedy existing deficiencies in order to foster the widest possible cooperation between FIUs.

Information sharing between FIUs is, however, still subject to many limitations and restrictions, whether sharing takes place upon request or on the FIU's own initiative. Although not all national laws necessarily provide for the exact same list of limitations and restrictions,[155] the same key requirements can be found in each legal framework and are described below. In fact, those arise from the Egmont Group Principles for Information Exchange between Financial Intelligence Units, adopted in 2001 and updated in 2013, to which paragraph 13 of the Interpretative Note to FATF Recommendation 29 and recital (18) 4AMLD explicitly refer. All FIUs examined are members of the Egmont Group of FIUs and are thus bound by the Egmont Principles. Cases of significant and relevant non-compliance are subject to the Egmont Group Support and Compliance Process.[156]

The first requirement which applies to the transfer of information from an FIU to a foreign counterpart is that information can only be shared for the processing or analysis of information by the FIU if it is related to money laundering or terrorist financing.[157] Furthermore, the exchange of information shall be refused if the foreign FIU does not guarantee that it will reciprocate on receipt of a similar request from the FIU, that it will not pass on the information received to third parties without the requested FIU's express consent, or that it will protect the information effectively. Beyond these limitations, FIUs may,

153 See Arts. 53 and 55 4AMLD as modified by the 5AMLD.

154 EU FIU's Platform, *Mapping exercise and gap analysis on FIUs powers and obstacles for obtaining and exchanging information*, 15 December 2016, http://ec.europa.eu/transparency/regexpert/index.cfm?do=groupDetail.groupDetailDoc&id=33583&no=2.

155 See e.g. Arts. 30(4) and 31 AMLA (Switzerland).

156 For an example of non-compliance with the Egmont Principles and the resulting sanction taken by the Egmont Group, see Switzerland report, section I.A.

157 It is worth noting, however, that the German FIU is also entitled, upon request, to transmit personal data to a foreign FIU for the purpose of a planned urgent measure (in particular the temporary prohibition of transactions), insofar as facts indicate that the property in question is located in Germany and is connected with a matter which is before the foreign FIU, as well as for the performance of the functions of another foreign public authority acting against money laundering, its predicate offences or terrorist financing.

in principle, impose additional conditions and restrictions on the sharing of information, in particular personal data, with foreign counterparts.[158] However, both the FATF Recommendations and the 4AMLD require that FIUs do not prohibit or place unreasonable or unduly restrictive conditions on exchanging information or providing assistance. In particular, FIUs shall not refuse a request for assistance on the grounds that:

> (a) the request is also considered to involve fiscal matters; and/or (b) laws require financial institutions or designated non-financial businesses and professions (except where the relevant information that is sought is held under circumstances where legal privilege or legal professional secrecy applies) to maintain secrecy and confidentiality; and/or (c) there is an inquiry, investigation or proceeding underway in the country receiving the request, unless the assistance would impede that inquiry, investigation or proceeding; and/or (d) the nature or status (civil, administrative, law enforcement etc.) of the requesting counterpart authority is different to its foreign FIU.[159]

Within the EU, the exchange of data with the FIUs of other EU Member States is to be ensured irrespective of the type of predicate offence for money laundering and also if the type of predicate offence has not been established. This principle is enshrined in Article 53(3) 4AMLD.

2. *Restrictions on Use of Data Obtained from Foreign FIUs*

In all the jurisdictions analysed, the overarching principle with respect to the use of information obtained by the FIU from foreign counterparts is that information can only be used for the purpose for which the information was sought or provided. In this context, any further use of that information, as well as its dissemination to other authorities, is subject to prior authorisation by the providing FIU. It is important to stress, however, that Egmont Group Principle 26 provides that "[t]he FIU receiving the request should not refuse consent to such dissemination unless this would fall beyond the scope of application of its AML/CFT provisions, could impair a criminal investigation, would be clearly disproportionate to the legitimate interests of a natural or legal person or the State of the providing FIU, or would otherwise not be in accordance with fundamental principles of its national law".

---

158 For instance, this can be relevant if the use of the data is limited by national proportionality considerations or limitations stipulated by another authority from whom the data was originally obtained.

159 Interpretative Note to FATF Recommendation 40 (2012), para. 2. See also Egmont Group, *Principles for Information Exchange Between Financial Intelligence Units for Money Laundering and Terrorism Financing Cases*, 2013, Principle 24.

G. INFORMATION FLOW BETWEEN FIU FOREIGN NON-COUNTERPARTS

1. *Restrictions on Data Transfer from FIU to Other Foreign Authorities*

With respect to the transfer of information, in particular personal data, from one FIU to a foreign non-counterpart, it is crucial to distinguish between direct exchange of information and indirect exchange of information through one or more domestic or foreign authorities.

Because it carries the risk of circumventing international cooperation rules, such as mutual legal assistance rules, direct exchange of information is rarely authorised. In fact, among the seven legal frameworks analysed, only the Spanish, Swiss and Italian ones specifically authorise this kind of information sharing.[160] Under Spanish law, the FIU is authorised to transfer information contained in declarations of means of payment and related to the seizure of means of payment to foreign competent authorities. Although the law does not specify which authorities qualify as foreign competent authorities, one must assume that this is primarily customs authorities of other countries. As regards Swiss law, the FIU is authorised to share information, including personal data, with foreign prosecution authorities, provided, however, that several conditions are met, notably that: (i) the information and/or personal data relates to suspicions of money laundering, predicate offences to money laundering, organised crime or terrorism financing; (ii) the provision of information and/or personal data is necessary to obtain information that the FIU needs; (iii) the provision of information and/or personal data does not aim at circumventing international mutual legal assistance; and (iv) reasons are given for the administrative assistance request.

By contrast, in line with the Interpretative Note to FATF Recommendation 40, indirect exchange of information is broadly allowed. In particular, the forwarding of data by the requesting foreign FIU to other national authorities of the same country with the prior consent of the providing FIU is permitted everywhere, either on the basis of a special provision in this regard (Germany, Switzerland)[161] or by analogy with the aforementioned rules regulating the FIU's use of data obtained from foreign FIUs (Spain, Italy, the UK).[162]

2. *Restrictions on Use of Data Obtained from Other Foreign Authorities*

Among the seven frameworks analysed, only the FATF Recommendations set out specific rules regarding the FIU's use of personal data it directly receives

160 One should note, however, that under the 2012 FATF Recommendations, direct exchange of information between the FIU and foreign non-counterparts is "encouraged".

161 Switzerland report, section V.F.1.

162 See *supra* section V.F.2.

from foreign non-counterparts, such as foreign prosecution authorities. As for the exchange of information between FIUs,[163] the Interpretative Note to FATF Recommendation 40 provides that information received by FIUs from foreign non-counterparts should be used only for the purpose for which the information was sought or provided. In this context, any further use beyond that originally approved or dissemination to further authorities should be authorised by the authority that provided the information.

H. EVIDENTIAL VALUE OF FIU-GENERATED DATA IN COURT PROCEEDINGS

Neither the FATF Recommendations nor the 4AMLD specify whether FIU-generated data could or should be used as evidence in court proceedings. Similarly, the law in Germany, Switzerland, Italy and the UK does not explicitly address the admissibility of FIU-generated information as evidence in court proceedings, and notably does not provide for a prohibition of disclosure. In this context, admissibility before a court will thus depend primarily on whether the transfer of information to the criminal justice authorities was allowed in the first place.[164] It will also depend on to what extent SARs can be used as evidence in court proceedings, given that FIUs rely mainly on SARs to perform their operational analysis, which is usually treated as confidential.

In contrast, Spanish law explicitly prohibits the use of FIU information in court proceedings. However, this prohibition only concerns the results of the FIU's operational analysis, and not also information included in inspection reports produced by the FIU in the fulfilment of its supervisory functions.[165]

I. USE OF CDD DATA FOR PROFIT MAKING

The FATF Recommendations do not address possible limits on the use of data collected through CDD, in particular regarding the possible use of such data for purely commercial purposes. In contrast, the 4AMLD makes clear that processing of personal data by obliged entities for commercial purposes shall be strictly prohibited. Obliged entities shall process personal data on the basis of this Directive only for the purpose of the prevention of money laundering and terrorist financing, or for other purposes as long as they are not incompatible with AML/CTF.

---

[163] See *supra* section V.F.2 and FATF report, section V.F.2.

[164] See *supra* section V.B.1.

[165] On the dual functions of the Spanish FIU, see *supra* section IV.A.4. See also Spain report, section IV.A.2.

At national level, all the jurisdictions examined prohibit the use of personal data gathered by obliged entities in the framework of CDD for profit-oriented purposes. In this regard, Spanish law deserves particular attention for two reasons. First, the prohibition of the use of CDD data for profit making arises directly from AML law in Spain, whereas, in all the other jurisdictions analysed, such prohibition results from the application of the purpose limitation principle enshrined in data protection law. Second, Spanish law does not provide for a complete prohibition of the use of data collected through CDD for commercial purposes. Indeed, Article 60 Decree 304/2014 prohibits such use "unless the processing of such data is necessary for the normal management of the business relationship". Although "normal management of the business relationship" does not equal commercial purposes, it cannot be excluded that there exists a potentially broad overlap between the two notions.

J. DATA SHARING BETWEEN OBLIGED ENTITIES REGARDING SARs AND FIU REQUESTS

1. *Data Sharing Inside a Group*

As stated by the FATF Guidance on Private Sector Information Sharing, group-wide sharing of SARs "allows financial institutions to identify higher risk customers across the group's business and deploy specific monitoring mechanisms or enhanced measures [and] enables emergence of a global picture of the risk exposure of the financial institution to such customers, thereby promoting implementation of an effective risk-based approach".[166] On this basis, one might think that the FATF would require a broad and unrestricted sharing of SARs between financial institutions that belong to the same group. Yet FATF Recommendation 18 and its Interpretative Note do not require but merely invite financial institutions' group-level AML/CTF functions and branches/subsidiaries to share SARs between themselves. The sharing of SARs between branches and subsidiaries belonging to the same financial corporate group is not explicitly permitted under FATF Recommendation 18.

In comparison, the 4AMLD does not require that obliged entities belonging to the same group have to be able to share SARs *per se*. The 4AMLD only permits credit institutions and financial institutions to inform other credit institutions and financial institutions from the same group and established in the EU that they have filed an SAR or responded to a request from the FIU. Similarly, in the five national jurisdictions which fall within the scope of this study, group-wide

166 FATF Guidance, *Private Sector Information Sharing*, 2017, para. 43.

sharing of SARs is allowed. The prohibition not to disclose the filing of an SAR or a request for information by the FIU[167] does not apply to disclosure between obliged entities which are part of the same group, provided, however, that the information disclosed is solely used for the purpose of preventing money laundering or terrorism financing.

2. *Data Sharing with Similar Professions*

The FATF Recommendations do not specify to what extent obliged entities should be authorised to share information regarding the filing of SARs or regarding requests by the FIU with other obliged entities outside the group, but within a similar profession. In contrast, the 4AMLD as well the four EU states examined permit certain categories of obliged entities, namely credit institutions, financial institutions, auditors, external accountants, tax advisors, notaries and other independent legal professionals, in cases relating to the same customer and the same transaction involving two or more obliged entities, to share information about the filing of an SAR (but not the content of the SAR) and the FIU's request for additional information with obliged entities from the same professional category, provided that they are subject to obligations as regards professional secrecy and personal data protection. Furthermore, it is worth noting that Germany also allows, independently of the identity of the particular transaction and contracting party, disclosure between certain obliged entities which are self-employed, notably attorneys at law, patent attorneys, notaries, independent legal advisors that are not members of a bar association, tax advisors, and auditors. In this respect, Germany goes well beyond what is authorised under the 4AMLD.

In Switzerland, a financial intermediary is not only authorised to inform another financial intermediary within the same corporate group that a mandatory SAR[168] has been filed with the FIU,[169] but it can also, under the same conditions,[170] inform another financial intermediary outside the group, provided, however, that both financial intermediaries provide joint services for one customer in connection with the management of that customer's assets on the basis of a contractual agreement to cooperate.

---

167 See *supra* sections III.C.1.c and III.C.2.b.

168 The reporting system currently used in Switzerland with respect to financial intermediaries draws a distinction between the right to report, in the case of "mere" suspicion of money laundering (voluntary SARs), and the obligation to report, in the case of "well-founded" suspicion (mandatory SARs).

169 See *supra* section V.J.1.

170 See Switzerland report, section V.J.1.

3. *Data Sharing with Obliged Entities Outside the EU*

The 4AMLD has established a special regime regulating the sharing of information regarding the filing of SARs and regarding requests by the FIU with other obliged entities in third countries. This regime, which was slightly amended by the 5AMLD, was comprehensively implemented in the four EU-based jurisdictions. According to Article 39(3) 4AMLD as modified by the 5AMLD, credit and financial institutions from the EU are allowed to share information regarding the filing of SARs and FIUs' requests for additional information with their branches and majority-owned subsidiaries established in third countries, provided, however, "that those branches and majority-owned subsidiaries fully comply with the group-wide policies and procedures, including procedures for sharing information within the group, in accordance with Article 45, and that the group-wide policies and procedures comply with the requirements set out in the Directive." Data sharing regarding SARs and FIUs' requests with credit and financial institutions established in a third country, but which are not part of the same group, is also allowed if the third country "imposes requirements equivalent to those laid down in this Directive and that they are from the same professional category and are subject to obligations as regards professional secrecy and personal data protection".[171]

As regards auditors, external accountants, tax advisors, notaries and other independent legal professionals, such entities are allowed, in cases relating to the same customer and the same transaction involving two or more obliged entities, to share information about the filing of SARs and FIUs' requests for additional information with obliged entities from the same category who are established outside the EU, provided, here again, that the relevant third country imposes requirements equivalent to those laid down in the 4AMLD.[172]

K. DATA SHARING BETWEEN OBLIGED ENTITIES REGARDING POSSIBLE CASES OF MONEY LAUNDERING

1. *Data Sharing Inside a Group*

Contrary to the above-explained regime on SARs (FATF) and information regarding the filing of SARs (EU),[173] the FATF Recommendations and the 4AMLD do not merely authorise but require group-wide sharing of information on activities and transactions which appear unusual, in that they could be related to money laundering or terrorist financing, but which have not (at least yet) been

171 Art. 39(5) 4AMLD.
172 *Ibid.*
173 See *supra* section V.J.1.

reported to the FIU. Both legal frameworks, however, provide for exceptions to this requirement. Under the 4AMLD, information sharing shall not take place if instructed to this effect by the FIU. Under the FATF Recommendations, information sharing shall not occur if there is no cross-jurisdictional element to it, "such as a customer that has exposure to operations of the group in more than one location or aspects of the flow of transactions or funds that affect operations in the relevant jurisdictions".[174]

Interestingly, none of the five national AML laws examined explicitly[175] clarify to what extent obliged entities which are part of the same group must share information on possible cases of money laundering which are not yet constitutive of suspicion giving rise to an SAR. German law, for instance, only allows certain obliged entities from the same group[176] to share information about specific matters which involve abnormalities or unusual circumstances indicating money laundering, one of its predicate offences or terrorism financing, if they can assume that other obliged entities from the same group require this information for their risk assessment of a corresponding or similar transaction or business relationship or the assessment whether an SAR or a criminal complaint should be filed. In comparison, Swiss law does not allow but prohibits financial intermediaries to share information with other financial intermediaries within the same corporate group about suspicious transactions or similarly unusual events in the absence of an SAR, or at least not until they submit an SAR.

2. *Data Sharing with Similar Professions*

Neither the FATF Recommendations nor the 4AMLD specify to what extent obliged entities are required or authorised to share information regarding suspicions beyond SARs and FIU requests with other obliged entities outside the group, but within a similar profession. The same applies to Italian and UK laws.

In contrast, German law allows such sharing of information under the same conditions as those listed for obliged entities within the same group. Spanish law also allows such sharing of information, though not under those conditions but under the conditions applying to the sharing of information

---

174 FATF Guidance, *Private Sector Information Sharing*, 2017, para. 51.

175 It should however be remembered that internal information sharing is usually part of group-wide compliance regulations which may explain why it is not explicitly explained by national laws.

176 Namely credit institutions, financial services institutions, payment institutions and electronic money institutions, agents of payment institutions and agents of electronic money institutions, independent traders that sell or re-exchange electronic money of a credit institution, other financial undertakings, insurance undertakings, insurance agents and investment management companies.

regarding the filing of SARs.[177] As regards Switzerland, financial intermediaries are prohibited, in the absence of an SAR, from sharing information regarding possible cases of money laundering with those other financial intermediaries outside the group.

3. *Data Sharing with Obliged Entities Outside the EU*

The 4AMLD requires countries to ensure that, unless otherwise instructed by the FIU, obliged entities are allowed to share information regarding suspicious transactions or similarly unusual events with their branches and majority-owned subsidiaries established in third countries, provided, however, that those branches and majority-owned subsidiaries fully comply with the group-wide policies and procedures, including procedures for sharing information within the group, in accordance with Article 45, and that the group-wide policies and procedures comply with the requirements set out in the Directive. None of the four jurisdictions based on EU law analysed, however, explicitly specify to what extent such data sharing with obliged entities outside the EU should be allowed.

L. DATA MINING BY OBLIGED ENTITIES

None of the seven AML legal frameworks analysed, whether international or national, explicitly specify to what extent obliged entities are authorised to conduct data mining (instead of mere data matching) within their data banks in order to identify possible cases of money laundering. However, it is important to note that Article 22 Regulation (EU) 2016/679, which directly applies in all Member States, includes a right not to be subjected to decisions that are based purely on automated decision-making. According to this provision, each data subject "shall have the right not to be subject to a decision based solely on automated processing, including profiling, which produces legal effects concerning him or her or similarly significantly affects him or her." In practical CDD terms, this means that data mining can be used to help guide the obliged entities' work within the EU but that an employee must always verify that the correlation established by the software is in fact reasonable, so that the risks of illegitimate profiling and hidden discrimination are diminished.

177 See *supra* section V.J.2 and Spain report, section V.J.2.

VI. BENEFICIAL OWNERSHIP TRANSPARENCY

A. BENEFICIAL OWNERSHIP INFORMATION

1. *General Framework*

Regarding the question of transparency and beneficial ownership, the fundamental requirement underlying the FATF Recommendations is that the competent authorities, and obliged entities when performing CDD measures, are able to access adequate, accurate and current information on the beneficial ownership of legal entities, and trusts and similar legal arrangements, in a timely fashion. Apart from express trusts for which trustees are required to obtain and hold beneficial ownership information regarding the trust, the FATF however allows countries to choose the mechanisms they rely on to achieve this objective.[178]

In contrast, the 4AMLD requires Member States to ensure that beneficial ownership information is quickly accessible by the competent authorities and obliged entities, but it also specifies the means through which information on the beneficial ownership of trusts and similar legal arrangements, and legal persons, other than companies listed on a regulated market that are subject to disclosure requirements consistent with Union law or subject to equivalent international standards, shall be made available.[179] Under the EU legal framework, beneficial ownership information shall indeed be (i) obtained and held by legal entities as well as trustees of express trusts and similar legal arrangements, and (ii) held, at national level, in a central register.[180] Another difference between the FATF legal framework and the 4AMLD is that the latter, in particular since it was amended by the 5AMLD, requires Member States to ensure that beneficial ownership information is not only accessible by the competent authorities, and obliged entities within the framework of CDD, but also by other persons, i.e. any member of the general public (as regards corporate and other legal entities) or any person that can demonstrate a legitimate interest (as regards trusts and similar legal arrangements).[181]

At national level, the four EU-based jurisdictions which fall within the scope of this study have all implemented the aforementioned EU dual approach to obtaining[182] and disclosing beneficial ownership information, with the exception

---

178 FATF report, section VI.B.1.

179 EU report, section VI.B.1.

180 *Ibid.*

181 EU report, section VI.C.3. See *infra* section VI.C.3.

182 It is worth noting that, to enable legal persons to comply with this duty, German, Swiss and Italian laws provide for corresponding duties of shareholders. In comparison, the UK emphasises the responsibility of beneficial owners (which are not necessarily shareholders known to the company) to provide the relevant information.

of the UK where companies can opt not to hold the beneficial ownership information at their registered address or another location of which the relevant authorities are notified, but to have it only available at the central registry. In Switzerland, there is no centralised beneficial ownership registry.[183] Since 2015, however, companies limited by shares not listed on the stock exchange and limited liability companies are required to keep a list of the beneficial owners disclosed to them.[184]

2. *Definition of "Beneficiary" and "Effective Control"*

With respect to the definition of "beneficial owner",[185] it is deemed necessary to follow a differentiated approach, distinguishing between legal entities on the one hand, and trusts and similar legal arrangements on the other hand.

– Legal Entities

The FATF definition of beneficial owner in the context of legal persons refers to "[t]he natural persons who ultimately have a controlling ownership of the structure in a legal person".[186] In comparison, the EU definition is more precise. Article 3(6)(a)(i) 4AMLD as modified by the 5AMLD indeed provides that the term "beneficial owner" covers at least the following: "natural person(s) who ultimately owns or controls a legal entity through direct or indirect ownership of a sufficient percentage of the shares or voting rights or ownership interest in that entity, including through bearer shareholdings, or through control via other means". In addition, the very same article defines what it means by "direct or indirect ownership", and thereby further specifies the meaning of beneficial ownership.[187] Furthermore, both the FATF Recommendations and the 4AMLD provide that the natural person(s) who holds the position of senior managing official(s) shall always be designated as a last resort as the beneficial owner in the event that, after having exhausted all possible means, no natural person(s) is identified or if there is any doubt that the person(s) identified is the beneficial owner.

---

183 Switzerland report, section VI.B.1.

184 *Ibid.*

185 In the UK, beneficial owner is known as the "person with significant control" (PSC). See UK report, section VI.A.1.a.

186 Interpretative Note to FATF Recommendation 10 (2012), para. 5(b)(i.i).

187 First, Art. 3(6)(a)(i) 4AMLD states that "[a] shareholding of 25% plus one share or an ownership interest of more than 25% in the customer held by a natural by a natural person shall be an indication of direct ownership." Second it provides that "[a] shareholding of 25% plus one share or an ownership interest of more than 25% in the customer held by a corporate entity, which is under the control of a natural person(s), or by multiple corporate entities, which are under the control of the same natural person(s), shall be an indication of indirect ownership".

The definition of beneficial owner in Germany, Italy, Spain and the UK follows Article 3(6)(a)(i) 4AMLD. In Switzerland, a beneficial owner is someone who, alone or in concert with third parties, acquires shares representing 25% or more of the share capital or voting rights, though one must point out that Swiss law uses a different definition of beneficial ownership in the context of CDD.[188]

– Trusts and Similar Legal Arrangements

With respect to trusts, the EU definition of beneficial owner reads as follows: "(i) the settlor(s); (ii) the trustee(s); (iii) the protector(s), if any; (iv) the beneficiaries or where the individuals benefiting from the legal arrangement or entity have yet to be determined, the class of persons in whose main interest the legal arrangement or entity is set up operates; (v) any other natural person exercising ultimate control over the trust by means of direct or indirect ownership or by other means".[189] This definition, which is slightly more specific than the one provided by the FATF, was applied by Germany, Italy, Spain and the UK. As regards other legal arrangement similar to trusts, beneficial owner refers everywhere to any person(s) holding equivalent or similar positions to those referred to with respect to trusts. Domestic trusts and other similar legal arrangements cannot be created in Switzerland.

3. *Definition of "Information"*

Neither the FATF nor the 4AMLD provide details on what information about the beneficial owner shall be collected. Italian, Spanish and UK laws are rather silent on this issue. In contrast, Swiss law provides that the information about the beneficial owner that shall be disclosed includes the first name, the last name and the address of the latter. German law specifies further that the information must contain the nature and extent of the economic interest.[190]

---

188 It is important to note, however, that the definition of beneficial ownership in the context of CDD under Swiss law is more extensive in that, according to Art. 2a(3) AML Act, the beneficial owners of an operating legal entity do not necessarily need to hold at least 25% of the capital or voting rights to qualify as such, provided, however, that they "otherwise control it". Moreover, this article provides that "[i]f the beneficial owners cannot be identified, the most senior member of the legal entity's executive must be identified".

189 Art. (3)(6)(b) 4AMLD as modified by the 5AMLD.

190 According to section 19 para. 3 GWG, information on the nature and extent of the economic interest must show why the person is a beneficial owner, in the case of legal persons (with the exception of foundations) and registered partnerships requiring information about: (i) the person's share in the entity, in particular the extent of capital or voting shares; (ii) the exercise of control in any other way, in particular due to an agreement between the person and a shareholder or between multiple shareholders or due to the person's entitlement to appoint legal representatives or members of executive bodies of the company; or (iii) the person's function as the company's legal representative or managing partner.

B. BENEFICIAL OWNERSHIP REGISTRIES

1. *Scope and General Procedure*

As previously underlined,[191] the FATF Recommendations maintain a certain level of flexibility as to the means through which information on the beneficial ownership of legal persons[192] should be made available to the competent authorities and obliged entities. Countries may choose to rely on a national beneficial ownership registry which would hold the beneficial ownership information of all legal persons incorporated or created by any other mechanism in their territory, but they do not have to. They may also, for instance, merely require companies themselves to obtain and hold information on the companies' beneficial ownership without also imposing on them an obligation to disclose the information to a beneficial ownership registry. In fact, as mentioned above, this is what Switzerland chose to do.[193]

In contrast, the 4AMLD requires Member States to ensure that legal persons, trusts and other similar legal arrangements obtain and hold information on their beneficial ownership, and communicate it to a central beneficial ownership register at national level. The nature and relevant institutional framework of such a register is, however, not specified by EU law. Member States are therefore free to choose, for instance, whether to make the beneficial ownership register a special section of the company registry or create a special agency in charge of it. While Germany opted for the latter option, Spain, Italy and the UK integrated the beneficial ownership registry within the company registry. Interestingly, Spanish notaries also created in 2012 their own beneficial ownership registry outside the company registry. This second database does not, however, hold information on the beneficial ownership of all legal persons, rather only private limited liability companies.

2. Ex Ante *Verification of Accuracy*

EU law as well as German, Italian, Spanish and UK laws require the information held in the beneficial ownership register to be adequate, accurate and current. However, none of them provide for a verification procedure of the accuracy of the beneficial ownership information before it is entered into the register. In the UK, the information entered is checked against the original documents, but

---

191 See *supra* section VI.A.1.

192 The FATF is less flexible as regards express trusts since it requires countries to ensure that trustees and persons in equivalent or similar positions obtain and hold beneficial ownership information. See *supra* section VI.A.1.

193 See *supra* section VI.A.1.

the company registry does not vet or verify that the individuals identified as beneficial owners in the original documentation are indeed its true beneficial owners.[194]

3. Ex Post *Review of Accuracy*

Before being modified by the 5AMLD, the 4AMLD did not specify any procedure that Member States shall put in place in order to ensure that information held in the beneficial ownership register is kept up to date. Since the adoption of the 5AMLD, however, Member States are required to establish specific mechanisms to this effect. According to Articles 30(4) and 31(5) 4AMLD as modified by the 5AMLD, "[s]uch mechanisms shall include requiring obliged entities and, if appropriate and to the extent that this requirement does not interfere unnecessarily with their functions, competent authorities to report any discrepancies they find between the beneficial ownership information available in the central registers and the beneficial ownership information available to them". In the case of reported discrepancies, "Member States shall ensure that appropriate actions be taken to resolve the discrepancies in a timely manner and, if appropriate, a specific mention be included in the central register in the meantime."[195]

Among the four EU-based jurisdictions which fall within the scope of this study, only Germany has so far implemented the aforementioned mechanisms into its national law.

C. ACCESS TO BENEFICIAL OWNERSHIP INFORMATION

1. *Access by FIU and Other Authorities*

In line with the FATF Recommendations and the 4AMLD, German, Italian, Spanish, Swiss and UK laws provide that the FIU and other competent authorities, such as the criminal justice authorities, have unrestricted access (though within the limits of data protection law) to beneficial ownership information, whether this information is held by the legal entities and legal arrangements themselves and/or in the central register. Swiss law also explicitly requires financial intermediaries to respond to requests for additional beneficial ownership information made by the FIU, the Financial Market Supervisory Authority or any prosecution authorities.

194 See also UK report, section VII.B.2.a.

195 Arts. 30(4) and 31(5) 4AMLD as modified by the 5AMLD.

2. *Access by Obliged Entities*

In line with the FATF Recommendations and the 4AMLD, German, Italian, Spanish, Swiss and UK laws provide that obliged entities have access to the beneficial ownership information of legal persons and legal arrangements when performing CDD measures.

With respect to beneficial ownership information held in central registers, the 4AMLD specifies, however, that where such access "would expose the beneficial owner to disproportionate risk, risk of fraud, kidnapping, blackmail, extortion, harassment, violence or intimidation, or where the beneficial owner is a minor or otherwise legally incapable, Member States may provide for an exemption from such access to all or part of the information on the beneficial ownership on a case-by-case basis."[196] Contrary to Spain, Germany, Italy and the UK explicitly provide for such an exemption.

3. *Access by Interested Third Parties*

In Switzerland, neither the public at large nor interested third parties have access to beneficial ownership information. As previously stated, only the competent authorities and obliged entities can request and obtain information on companies' beneficial ownership.[197] This corresponds to the FATF Recommendations, which do not specify to what extent access to beneficial ownership information could or should be expanded beyond the competent authorities and obliged entities.

In contrast, since it was amended by the 5AMLD, the 4AMLD grants access to a limited set of information on the beneficial ownership of corporate and other legal entities held in the central beneficial ownership register to any member of the general public. Moreover, as regards information on the beneficial ownership of trusts and similar legal arrangements held in the central register, this information shall, since the adoption of the 5AMLD, be accessible to any person that can demonstrate a "legitimate interest". Independently of such legitimate interest, access shall also now be granted in relation to a trust or similar legal arrangement which holds or owns a controlling interest in any corporate or other legal entity incorporated outside the EU, through direct or indirect ownership, including through bearer shareholdings, or through control via other means.

Among the five national jurisdictions which fall within the ambit of our study, Germany, Italy and the UK are the only ones so far where the information on the beneficial ownership of corporate and other legal entities held in the central beneficial ownership register can be accessed by the public.

---

196 Arts. 30(9) and 31(7a) 4AMLD as modified by the 5AMLD.

197 See *supra* sections VI.A.1.a, VI.C.1 and VI.C.2.

As regards Spanish law, it is silent on the possibility of interested third parties or the public at large accessing the information held in the two beneficial ownership registers.[198]

VII. SANCTIONS

A. SANCTIONS FOR MONEY LAUNDERING

1. *Requirement of a Conviction for a Predicate Offence*

In line with the Interpretative Note to FATF Recommendation 3 and Article 3(2)(a) Directive 2018/673/EU, it is not necessary under German, Swiss, Spanish, Italian and UK laws that a person be convicted of a predicate offence or that the predicate offence was subject to prior criminal proceedings in order to secure a conviction for money laundering. In other words, there can be a standalone prosecution and conviction for money laundering, provided, however, that there is at least some circumstantial evidence that the assets which are deemed to be the subject of money laundering originate from a predicate offence, so that it is indubitably excluded that the assets were acquired legally or that they originate from an offence which is not a predicate offence. In this context, it is not necessary that all the factual elements and circumstances relating to the predicate offence (e.g. the identity of the perpetrator and the victim, the place of commission of the predicate offence, the exact modality of its commission) be established in detail.

2. *Forms of Sanctions*

With respect to the different types of sanctions which can be applied following a criminal conviction for money laundering, it is deemed necessary to follow a differentiated approach, distinguishing between natural persons, on one hand, and legal persons, on the other hand.

- Natural Persons

Both the FATF Recommendations and Directive 2018/673/EU require countries to apply criminal sanctions to natural persons convicted of money laundering. The EU Directive specifies that national law must provide a maximum

198 On the two beneficial ownership registers in Spain, see *supra* section VI.B.1. See also Spain report, section VI.B.1.

punishment of at least four years' imprisonment. Member States shall also ensure that natural persons who have committed money laundering are, where necessary, subject to additional sanctions or measures, such as fines, exclusion from access to public funding or temporary disqualifications from the practice of commercial activities.

At national level, the main sanctions applicable in the event of conviction for money laundering are imprisonment and pecuniary penalties, applied either cumulatively (Italy, Spain, the UK) or alternatively (Germany, Switzerland, the UK).[199] The level of sanctions varies quite significantly, however, from one jurisdiction to another. In the UK, money laundering offences are punishable on indictment by up to 14 years' imprisonment, an unlimited fine, or both.[200] In Italy, natural persons convicted of money laundering are subject to four to 12 years' imprisonment and a fine of €5,000–25,000 (two to eight years' imprisonment and a fine of €5,000–25,000 for the crime of self-money laundering).[201] Comparatively, money laundering is punishable in Switzerland and Spain by lower custodial sentences but much higher fines. In Switzerland, money laundering is punishable by a custodial sentence not exceeding three years or a monetary penalty up to CHF 540,000. In Spain, imprisonment ranges from six months to six years for intentional money laundering and the fine imposed may be up to three times the value of the assets laundered. In all countries, more stringent sanctions are imposed on individuals in serious cases of money laundering.[202]

– Legal Persons

Neither the FATF Recommendations nor Directive 2018/673/EU require countries to hold legal entities involved in money laundering criminally liable. However, with the exception of Germany, all the jurisdictions analysed recognise corporate criminal liability for money laundering. In particular, according to Spanish, Italian and Swiss laws, a corporation can be held liable for money laundering if it has failed to take all the reasonable preventive measures that

---

199 Further, additional sanctions and measures are provided for in certain national laws. In Spain, for instance, judges may also, in view of the severity of the act and the personal circumstances of the offender, sentence him/her to the punishment of special barring from exercise of his profession or industry for a term from one to three years, and order the measure of temporary or definitive closure of the establishment or premises. If the closure is temporary, the duration may not exceed five years.

200 Lower penalties apply on summary conviction.

201 If the predicate offence is punishable by a custodial sentence not exceeding five years, the sentence of money laundering is, however, reduced by one third.

202 For instance, in Switzerland, the sanction is a maximum penalty of five years' imprisonment and a monetary penalty of up to CHF 1,500,000, or just a monetary penalty.

were required to prevent such an offence, regardless of the criminal liability of any natural persons.[203] Moreover, Swiss and Spanish laws provide for vicarious liability. According to this additional form of responsibility, an undertaking will be held liable if money laundering is committed in the exercise of its commercial activities in accordance with the objects of the undertaking and if it is not possible to attribute this act to any specific natural person due to the inadequate organisation of the undertaking. In all the jurisdictions, the penalties applicable to legal entities include fines, which can be quite high (up to CHF 5 million in Switzerland, unlimited in the UK) and disqualifications. Disqualifications can include the suspension or revocation of government concessions, debarment, exclusion from government financing and even prohibition from carrying on business activity.

3. *Confiscation*

With the exception of the UK, all the legal frameworks analysed provide for compulsory confiscation of the relevant assets following a conviction for money laundering. This complies with FATF Recommendation 4 and Article 4 of Council Framework Decision 2001/500/JHA. Confiscation is, however, excluded if a third person has acquired the assets in good faith, provided that the person has paid a consideration of equal value in return or confiscation would cause him/her disproportionate hardship. If confiscation is impossible because the assets are no longer available, courts may, under certain conditions,[204] uphold a claim for an equivalent sum (compensation claim).

It is also worth noting that, although neither the FATF Recommendations nor Directive 2018/1673/EU require it, all national laws provide for civil forfeiture, i.e. non-conviction based confiscation.

4. *Statistics*

a. Number of Criminal Proceedings

Although FATF Recommendation 33 and Article 44(2)(b) 4AMLD require countries to maintain, on an annual basis, statistics on the number of cases

[203] In addition, Spanish and Italian laws require that the offence was committed in the interest or for the benefit of the corporation.

[204] In Switzerland, for instance, the court may dismiss an equivalent claim in its entirety or in part if the claim is likely to be unrecoverable or if the claim would seriously hinder the rehabilitation of the person concerned. In the UK, if the prosecution can prove that the defendant had a "criminal lifestyle", there is a presumption that any property transferred to the defendant in the six years prior to criminal proceedings or held by the defendant at any time after conviction is subject to confiscation (sections 10, 142 and 223 Proceed of Crime Act 2002).

investigated and the number of persons prosecuted for money laundering, such statistics are not available everywhere. Among the five national jurisdictions analysed, only the Spanish and UK authorities provide annual statistics on the number of criminal proceedings for money laundering. Whilst more than 2,000 prosecutions for money laundering are carried out every year in the UK, only a few hundred take place every year in Spain. However, such numbers are of limited comparative value insofar as they do not specify the value of transactions associated with the proceedings, the relationship between self-laundering and investigations for predicate offences, and the types and levels of sanctions applied.

b. Number of Convictions

FATF Recommendation 33 and Article 44(2)(b) 4AMLD require countries to maintain, on an annual basis, statistics on the number of convictions for money laundering. With the exception of Italy, all the jurisdictions examined provide such statistics. Whereas 1,400 persons are convicted for money laundering every year in the UK, only a few hundred are convicted in Spain and Switzerland. However, for the same reasons as those mentioned in the previous section,[205] comparing national statistics is of limited value.

B. SANCTIONS FOR VIOLATIONS OF PREVENTIVE MEASURES

1. Money Laundering by Violating Preventive Obligations

Neither the FATF Recommendations nor the EU AML legal framework address the question of whether a violation of an AML-related preventive obligation by an obliged entity's employee could, should or shall give rise to a criminal responsibility for money laundering by omission. Yet, as previously explained,[206] Swiss and Italian courts have already explicitly recognised a criminal liability of obliged entities' employees for money laundering by omission. According to the Italian jurisprudence, money laundering can, in this context, only result from a failure to comply with a reporting obligation, whereas in Switzerland the status of guarantor of obliged entities' employees may also be inferred from the duty to clarify the economic background and the purpose of a transaction or a business relationship, as well as from internal regulations. One should also note that Germany punishes money laundering by gross negligence.

---

205 See *supra* section VII.A.4.a.

206 See *supra* section II.B.2.

2. *CDD, Reporting and Other AML-Related Obligations*

a. Special Criminal Laws against Individuals

Neither the FATF Recommendations nor the EU AML legal framework require countries to provide for and apply criminal sanctions to natural persons who fail to comply with AML-related preventive obligations, such as CDD, reporting and record keeping obligations. While, in this context, the FATF allows countries to choose among civil, criminal and administrative sanctions, the 4AMLD requires Member States to impose administrative sanctions and measures,[207] except for breaches which are subject to criminal sanctions in their national law and for which Member States may decide not to lay down rules for administrative sanctions or measures. Yet it is interesting to note that Switzerland, Italy and the UK provide for criminal sanctions in the case of failure to comply with certain AML/CTF requirements. However, the scope of conducts which amount to criminal offences and the range of sanctions applied differs quite significantly from one jurisdiction to another.

The UK is certainly where the most violations of AML/CTF requirements have been criminalised. In fact, it is deemed a criminal offence, punishable by a custodial sentence not exceeding two years and/or an unlimited fine, to breach any "relevant requirement" under the 2017 Money Laundering Regulations, unless the person took all reasonable steps and exercised all due diligence to avoid committing the offence.[208] Relevant requirements include notably performing appropriate risk assessments and refraining from undertaking activities unless the proper policies and procedures are in place and followed. The same penalties also apply to anyone who violates the non-disclosure obligation or who, in purported compliance with a requirement imposed on him/her by or under these Regulations, provides information to any person which is false or misleading in a material particular.[209] Additionally, failing to report a suspicious transaction[210] and prejudicing a criminal investigation are two offences punishable on indictment by up to five years' imprisonment, an unlimited fine, or both.

In comparison with the UK, the scope of violations of AML-related preventive obligations which amount to criminal offences is much narrower in Italy and

[207] See *infra* section VII.B.2.b.

[208] In deciding whether a natural person has contravened a relevant requirement, the court must decide whether that person followed guidelines issued by the European Supervisory Authorities, the UK Money Laundering Regulations or guidance issued by the Financial Crime Agency or another supervisor body and approved by the UK Treasury.

[209] This includes notably false statements made by the first line of defence of an obliged entity to the second line of defence of the same obliged entity or by an obliged entity to the authorities or to other obliged entities.

[210] See also UK report, section IV.A.4.

Switzerland. As outlined below, one should also note the particular uniqueness of some of these offences, in that they are unique to the legal framework to which they belong. Swiss law thus criminalises the failure to file an SAR (punishable by a fine not exceeding CHF 500,000 if committed intentionally, or CHF 150,000 if committed through negligence), but it also provides the following offences: (i) the fact of a financial intermediary not identifying the beneficial owner of the assets with the care that is required in the circumstances (punishable by up to one year's imprisonment or a monetary penalty), and (ii) the fact of a dealers not appointing an audit firm to verify that they are complying with their preventive duties (punishable by a fine of up to CHF 100,000 if committed intentionally, or CHF 10,000 if committed through negligence). One should however note that Swiss law does not differentiate between criminal and administrative offences. Therefore, the aforementioned sanctions may be called administrative sanctions in other jurisdictions as they do not imply that action is taken by the criminal justice authorities. As regards Italian law, it requires the application of criminal sanctions in the case of tipping-off (imprisonment for between six months and one year and a fine of €5,000–50,000), as well as in case of forgery in CDD and forgery in record keeping (imprisonment for between six months and three years, and a fine of €10,000–30,000). Forgery in CDD consists, for a natural personal who is himself/herself an obliged entity or the employee of an obliged entity, in falsifying the data and information concerning the client, the beneficial owner, the executor, the scope and nature of the continuative relation or of the professional service, or of the transaction. Forgery in record keeping obligations consists in acquiring false data or untrue information concerning the client, the beneficial owner, the executor, the scope and nature of the continuative relation or of the professional service, or of the transaction, or in using fraudulent means for the purpose to jeopardise the correct keeping of such data and information.

b. Administrative Sanctions against Individuals

All national AML laws set up a comprehensive system of administrative penalties applicable to natural persons who are liable for failing to comply with the AML/CTF requirements. Such administrative penalties must be split into two categories: (i) sanctions and measures applicable to individuals who are themselves obliged entities, and (ii) where AML/CTF obligations apply to obliged entities that are legal persons, sanctions and measures applicable to the obliged entities' employees who are, under national law, responsible for the breach.

As noted above,[211] the FATF Recommendations do not require sanctions imposed on natural persons, who are themselves obliged entities and who violated

[211] See *supra* section VII.B.2.a.

one of their preventive obligations, to be of an administrative nature, whereas the 4AMLD requires administrative sanctions, except, however, where the wrongdoing already constitutes a criminal offence.[212] Pursuant to Article 59(2) 4AMLD, Member States shall ensure that the range of administrative sanctions and measures that can be applied in case of serious, repeated, systematic, or a combination thereof, violations of the CDD, reporting, record keeping and internal controls requirements set out in the Directive, include at least the following:

(a) a public statement which identifies the natural … person and the nature of the breach;
(b) an order requiring the natural … person to cease the conduct and to desist from repetition of that conduct;
(c) where an obliged entity is subject to an authorisation, withdrawal or suspension of the authorisation;
(d) a temporary ban against any person discharging managerial responsibilities in an obliged entity, or any other natural person, held responsible for the breach, from exercising managerial functions in obliged entities;
(e) maximum administrative pecuniary sanctions of at least twice the amount of the benefit derived from the breach where that benefit can be determined, or at least EUR 1 000 000.

Derogating from Article 58(2)(e) 4AMLD, for breaches involving financial institutions, to the extent that they can be natural persons, Article 59(3)(b) 4AMLD provides specific sanctions in that it specifies the maximum administrative fine to be no less than €5,000,000.

At national level, the array of administrative sanctions and measures available to punish natural persons, who are themselves obliged entities and who violated one or several preventive obligations, ranges from fines (imposed by the designated supervisory authorities, or in some cases another authority)[213] to suspension or withdrawal of the licence and critical public statements. In accordance with EU law, punishments in EU Member States are usually

212 *Ibid.*

213 In Germany, for instance, competence for administrative sanctions proceedings against tax advisors and tax agents lies with the local tax office; for attorneys at law, patent attorneys, notaries and auditors, the law of some federal states designates as the competent authority for administrative sanctions proceedings not the respective supervisory authority (that is, the respective professional chamber or, for notaries, the president of the respective Regional Court) but particular central authorities whose intervention can be triggered by a notice from the competent supervisory authority. In Switzerland, the Swiss Banking Association (which is not considered a supervisory authority) is competent for sanctioning violations of the Agreement on the Swiss Banks' Code of Conduct with Regard to the Exercise of Due Diligence (CDB) by signatory banks. Banks can be fined up to CHF 10,000,000 by the supervisory board of the Swiss Banking Association in the event of a violation of the CDB.

increased in case of serious, repeated or systematic violations, or a combination thereof. In Italy, for instance, punishments are tripled in such circumstances. In Germany, a fine can be up to €1,000,000 or up to twice the economic benefit derived from the offence if the offence was serious, repeated or systematic, whereas, in the absence of those aggravating circumstances, the offence may only be punished by a monetary penalty of up to €100,000.

FATF Recommendation 35 provides that, where financial institutions and designated non-financial businesses and professions that are legal persons are liable for failing to comply with AML/CTF requirements, "[s]anctions should be applicable not only to [them], but also to their directors and senior management". In comparison, Article 58(3) 4AMLD merely provides that "where obligations apply to [obliged entities that are] legal persons … sanctions and measures *can* be applied to the members of the management body". However, the scope of natural persons concerned is broader under the 4AMLD than under FATF Recommendation 35. Pursuant to Article 58(3) 4AMLD, sanctions and measures can indeed also be applied "to other natural persons who under national law are responsible for the breach".

At national level, all the jurisdictions provide for administrative sanctions and measures applicable to the obliged entities' employees who are responsible for the breach of the AML/CTF obligations. Italian law requires applying administrative fines to employees of obliged entities who are not directors or part of the senior management in certain circumstances. More specifically, a=Article 58(3) Italian AML law provides that any employee who fails to comply with the reporting requirement shall be subject to an administrative fine, independently or in addition to the fine imposed on the obliged entity. One should however note that administrative sanctions are not limited to fines. Germany, for instance, has quite an extensive regime in this regard. Instead of revoking the licence of an obliged entity, the designated supervisory authorities may indeed demand the dismissal of executive management officials responsible for a sustained violation by AML-related preventive obligations. Competent supervisors can furthermore prohibit such officials from exercising their activity for another legal person and, in the case of some violations, for any obliged entity. Responsibility in this sense does not require that the executive management official personally committed the offence, but rather that an offence which was committed by another employee could have been prevented, for example through adequate internal controls or other organisational measures. Additionally, in the case of some particular offences by an obliged entity (notably as regards the prohibition on certain dealings with shell banks), the designated supervisory authorities can prohibit a company official who was responsible for the violation from assuming an executive management position with any obliged entity for up to two years, even if this official had not been acting in an executive management position.

c. Sanctions against Legal Entities

FATF Recommendation 35 requires countries to apply either civil, criminal or administrative penalties to obliged entities that are legal persons and which violate preventive obligations, while the 4AMLD requires in principle the application of administrative sanctions and measures. As regards financial institutions, however, FATF Recommendation 27 specifies that the designated supervisory authorities "should have powers to impose a range of disciplinary and financial sanctions, including the power to withdraw, restrict or suspend the financial institution's license, where applicable". One should also note that the 4AMLD requires Member States to ensure "that legal persons can be held liable for the breaches ... committed for their benefit by any person, acting individually or as part of an organ of that legal person, and having a leading position within the legal person based on any of the following: (a) power to represent the legal person; (b) authority to take decisions on behalf of the legal person; or (c) authority to exercise control within the legal person".

Penalties provided by national laws for failure by legal persons to comply with AML/CTF requirements are very similar, if not identical, to the ones applicable to natural persons described above. One difference though is that administrative fines that can be imposed on legal persons are usually much higher than those applicable to natural persons. Following the 4AMLD, Germany, for instance, provides, with respect to serious, repeated or systematic breaches involving credit or financial institutions that are legal persons, that the maximum fine that can be imposed is €5,000,000, or 10% of the entity's total annual turnover according to the latest available accounts approved by the management body.

3. *Statistics*

a. Number of Investigations and Sanctions

Unlike Switzerland and Italy, Spain and the UK provide statistics on the number of investigations and sanctions in relation to identified violations of AML preventive measures. However, from a comparative perspective, the statistics provided are of limited value as the value of transactions associated with the proceedings is not provided, nor are the types and levels of sanctions applied and the types of violations involved.

b. Number of Convictions

None of the jurisdictions which fall within the scope of this study provide statistics on the number of convictions for violations of AML preventive measures.

C. CUMULATION OF MONEY LAUNDERING AND OTHER AML-RELATED SANCTIONS

None of the jurisdictions analysed does in principle exclude the combination of sanctions for money laundering with sanctions for the violation of preventive regulations, provided that the respective wrongs are substantially different.[214] The latter caveat will usually prohibit the imposition of sanctions for violations of CDD or reporting obligations that are committed by one and the same offender for the purpose of a money laundering offence.[215]

VIII. THE USE OF CASH AS A MEANS OF PAYMENT

A. LIMITS

Like in Switzerland, there is no limit on cash payments imposed at EU level. However, a number of Member States have in place restrictions for cash payments above a specific threshold. In Italy, for instance, cash payments are only allowed up to an amount of €3,000. In Spain, the limit is €2,500 for residents and €15,000 for non-residents. In contrast, some Member States do not cap cash payments at a certain amount; this is the case in Germany and the UK.

B. STATISTICS

Not all the jurisdictions provide statistics on the use of cash in relation to the overall value of transactions conducted in the country. In Spain, for instance, the Bank of Spain does not provide such statistics. In contrast, such statistics are provided in the UK, Switzerland and Italy by the competent authorities. While cash is still the most common method of payment for households in Switzerland, it only amounted to 28% of all payments in the UK in 2018.

IX. CONCLUSION

On the basis of the comparative analysis above, one can first observe that the AML frameworks analysed by this study are marked by a high level of formal homogeneity, especially when compared to other examples of transnational

---

214 See Germany, VII.C; Spain report, section VII.C; UK report, VII.C.

215 See Switzerland report, section VII.C.

criminal policy. In every single national jurisdiction analysed, the AML regime is in principle based on very similar pillars, namely roughly the same definition of the money laundering offence in the criminal law, an extensive list of preventive obligations binding a wide-ranging list of obliged entities and an FIU operating as a filter between these entities and the law enforcement authorities. This state of affairs is largely due to the FATF, which has over the least thirty years undoubtedly played a crucial role as both global standard setter and watchdog, thereby raising problem awareness and driving numerous legislative reforms at national level. That said, one must not overlook that, on closer examination, the five national AML regimes analysed by this study are by no means identical to each other, but in many ways substantially heterogeneous. By inspecting the details of each framework, the comparative analysis has revealed numerous important discrepancies in how national legislators have implemented FATF standards and EU law. These discrepancies evidence that the FATF and even the EU framework still grant national legislators with considerable flexibility. Differences may be relatively minor, such as, for instance, the minimum content of CDD measures that obliged entities are required to take in situations deemed to present a low risk of money laundering. They may, however, also be rather fundamental in that they imply very different visions of how key elements of AML (in particular FIUs) are supposed to function and what purpose they are meant to serve (for example, to what extent AML is primarily conceived as an instrument to tackle organised crime or used against profit-generating crime more generally). As a result, formal compliance with FATF and EU demands alone does not necessarily reveal much about the functioning of a particular national AML framework, as this functioning can depend on many aspects that have not yet been addressed at the supranational level. In order to move towards greater functional coherence in the design of AML, any assessment and further development of supranational standards therefore needs to be more precise about the ultimate purpose as opposed to merely the formal characteristics of a particular instrument. Only then is it possible to scratch beyond the surface of national frameworks and understand how AML instruments need to be designed in order to accommodate supranational demands within the context of a particular legal order.

REINVENTING EU ANTI-MONEY LAUNDERING

Towards a Holistic Legal Framework

Benjamin VOGEL

I. INTRODUCTION

In the European Union, recent years have seen a remarkable revitalisation of anti-money laundering (AML).[1] Today's debates have the potential to provoke a significant shift from the state of play that had been developed over the last three decades.[2] Not least, widespread concerns about the actual performance of the private sector's customer due diligence (CDD) and reporting practices, difficulties in the cooperation between criminal justice authorities[3] and Financial Intelligence Units (FIUs), greater awareness of the impact of high-risk third countries on preventive efforts in the EU, and inconsistencies in the supervision of obliged entities reflect persistent and possibly growing doubts about the shape of today's AML. The present analysis aims to identify where the existing EU framework and, as a result, national laws demonstrate contradictions and other deficiencies that will most probably affect the system's overall ability to serve its purposes. To this end, it is necessary to clarify how various parts of the AML architecture relate to and impact on each other, and thereby provide a common starting point for reflection about possible reform at the level of the EU and of Member States.

Some introductory observations will first provide an overview of key structural questions that are of overarching concern for any holistic policy approach, followed by an analysis of the role of fundamental rights and in particular data protection, before moving to a detailed examination of the core pillars of the AML architecture. While some elements of the following analysis may be more relevant in some Member States than in others, many concerns point towards a need to further harmonise AML within the EU. Encompassing homogeneity throughout Member States would seem unrealistic and insufficiently accommodate legitimate disagreements over national policy priorities. However, greater consistency of the European framework seems necessary in order to remedy deficiencies at the national level and improve Union-wide cooperation between the competent authorities.

A. OVERARCHING CONCERNS

1. *Ambiguity of the Objectives of AML*

To begin with, AML is today often marked by ambiguity of its objectives. While the prevention of money laundering might at first glance seem to be a rather

---

1 See European Union, section I.A.

2 See FATF, section I.A.

3 Note that "criminal justice authorities" is, for the present analysis, meant to refer not only to criminal courts and prosecutors, but also to police authorities tasked with investigating criminal conduct.

straightforward aim, a closer view will often uncover much more uncertainty. Following Directive (EU) 2015/849 and Directive (EU) 2018/1673,[4] AML is said to serve the protection of the integrity, stability and reputation of the financial sector. This formula is obviously rather vague and invites interpretations that would deprive AML of genuine meaning. In particular, it is not obvious that the inflow of criminal assets necessarily has an impact on the stability of financial institutions;[5] such effect can of course result from AML measures adopted against deviant institutions,[6] but this rationale then seems to rely on AML, rather than to offer a justification for it. It is equally not plausible that purely reputational concerns could, to any significant degree, explain the existence of a legal framework of such magnitude. As regards the protection of the integrity of financial institutions, AML is obviously concerned with the aim of avoiding the possibility that these institutions could, through their services, facilitate criminal endeavours. Still more importantly, however, the overall design of today's frameworks, despite a somewhat inconclusive historic origin,[7] suggest that financial institutions are essentially meant to provide a firewall between illegal and legal economies. Underlying this concept is seemingly the assumption that, if not prevented by financial institutions, illegal assets and the criminal players they embody can infiltrate and gain control over parts of the economy. Indirectly, such control can penetrate wider society, for example through sponsoring of social events or politicians, through the creation of employment for followers, or through the provision of scarce resources.[8] The principal rationale for protecting the integrity of financial institutions thus seems to reflect concerns that financial services can, wittingly or unwittingly, serve as a gateway for criminal actors to engage in legitimate commercial activity and thereby ultimately embolden such actors. This risk does not seem far-fetched, especially when one considers the substantial economic power of some forms of organised crime, but the actual risk

---

4 Recital 1 of Directive (EU) 2015/849 of the European Parliament and of the Council of 20 May 2015 on the prevention of the use of the financial system for the purposes of money laundering or terrorist financing, amending Regulation (EU) No 648/2012 of the European Parliament and of the Council, and repealing Directive 2005/60/EC of the European Parliament and of the Council and Commission Directive 2006/70/EC; recital 1 of Directive (EU) 2018/1673 of the European Parliament and of the Council of 23 October 2018 on combating money laundering by criminal law.

5 PC van Duyne/MS Groenhuijsen/AAP Schudelaro, Balancing financial threats and legal interests in money-laundering policy, 43 *Crime, Law and Social Change* (2005), pp. 123–125.

6 See A Amicelle, When finance met security: back to the war on drugs and the problem of dirty money, 3 *Finance and Society* (2017), p. 118.

7 See PC van Duyne/JH Harvey/LY Gelemerova, The Critical Handbook of Money Laundering: Policy, Analysis and Myths, 2018, pp. 41–90.

8 To this effect, see already the preamble of the United Nations Convention against Illicit Traffic in Narcotic Drugs and Psychotropic Substances of 20 December 1988, United Nations Treaty Series, vol. 1582, p. 95; see also P van Duyne, Money laundering policy: fears and facts, in P van Duyne/K von Lampe/JL Newell (eds.), Criminal Finances and Organised Crime in Europe, 2003, p. 76.

to this effect will of course vary from place to place and depend on the aims and *modi operandi* of particular criminal actors.[9] On this account, the prohibition and prevention of money laundering is thus meant not so much to de-incentivise predicate offences though hampering the use of ill-gotten gains,[10] but to prevent criminal actors from using the financial system and the wider commercial sphere for the purpose of expanding their power and operational freedom. Even where such actors are using commerce for purely economic (as opposed to power-oriented) reasons, efforts to prevent them from operating legitimate businesses can furthermore also serve to prevent a corrosive effect of criminal assets on norms in the respective market, not least because initially lawful businesses may themselves feel the need to have recourse to unlawful practices in order to compensate for the more advantageous financing costs of their criminal competitors, but also because crime-related businesses may have a comparatively greater inclination to flout applicable regulations. The concurrence of criminal actors' aim to use businesses for advancing their criminal activities and the profit interests of business owners that are utilised for these aims can ultimately lead to predatory competition and thereby stifle law-abiding businesses.[11]

Additionally to the purpose of separating illegal from legal economies, and again reflecting the above-mentioned EU legislation, the ultimate objective of AML is however also meant to serve the aim of detecting predicate offences of money laundering, not least organised crime[12] and tax offences,[13] and to facilitate

---

9 See for example P van Duyne, Organised crime, corruption and power, 26 *Crime, Law and Social Change* (1997), pp. 201–238; M Dugato/S Favarin/L Giommoni, The risks and rewards of Organized Crime investments in real estate, 55(5) The British Journal of Criminology (2015), p. 944; M Riccardi/C Soriani/V Giampietri, Mafia infiltration in legitimate companies in Italy, in EU Savona/M Riccardi/G Berlusconi (eds.), Organised Crime in European Businesses, 2016; PA Bianchi/A Marra/D Masciandaro/N Pecchiari, Is it worth having the Sopranos on board? Corporate governance pollution and organized crime: The case of Italy, Baffi Carefin Working Paper Series, 2017. See also P van Duyne, Organised crime, corruption and power, 26 *Crime, Law and Social Change* (1997), pp. 214–215.

10 On the weakness of this concept, see P Reuter/EM Truman, Chasing Dirty Money: The Fight against Money Laundering, 2004, p. 128.

11 D Gambetta/P Reuter, Conspiracy among the Many: the Mafia in Legitimate Industries, in NG Fielding/A Clarke/R Witt (eds.), The Economic Dimension of Crime, 2000, pp. 100–120.

12 On the role of AML as part of a comprehensive preventative strategy against organised crime, see M Levi/M Maguire, Reducing and preventing organised crime: An evidence-based critique, 41 *Crime, Law and Social Change* (2004), pp. 397–469. For the scope and nature of the phenomenon, see notably the working definition of the Joint Working Party of the German Police and Judicial Authorities of May 1990: "Organised Crime is the planned commission of criminal offences determined by the pursuit of profit or power which, individually or as a whole, are of considerable importance if more than two persons, each with his/her own assigned tasks, collaborate for a prolonged or indefinite period of time (a) by using commercial or business-like structures, (b) by using force or other means of intimidation, or (c) by exerting influence on politics, the media, public administration, judicial authorities or the business sector"; see Bundeskriminalamt, Organised Crime – National Situation Report 2018, p. 10.

13 See Directive (EU) 2018/1673 of 23 October 2018. For doubts on the role of the organised crime policy narrative in practice, see e.g. PA Sproat, To what extent is the UK's anti-money

the prosecution of predicate offenders. In this sense, AML, through CDD, documentation and reporting obligations, is a tool to ensure greater transparency of financial dealings in order to facilitate investigations.[14] On this account, both the preventive obligations of obliged entities and the criminal prohibition of money laundering are meant to serve as a tool to tackle profit-generating crime. Unlike in the above integrity-oriented rationale, which focuses on the criminogenic potential of criminal assets as a means for criminals to exercise power or distort markets, a predicate offence-oriented understanding of AML is quintessentially retrospective in that is treats the processing of criminal assets as an opportunity to uncover predicate offences, sanction predicate offenders and, through confiscation, possibly also rectify the harm brought about by these offences.

Both above-mentioned objectives can of course be realised in more or less mixed forms, and they often are, but despite their similarities, one should not underestimate the potentially significant differences between them. Where policymakers or the competent authorities give preference to one of those two visions of AML, this can be to the detriment of the other. For example, an AML system might apply a very high suspicion threshold to suspicious activity reports (SARs), requiring obliged entities to report transactions to the FIU only where the reporting entity is almost certain that the transaction is linked to money laundering. Such an approach can make sense in particular if obliged entities' CDD obligations are primarily taken to be a preventive tool to protect the inflow of criminal assets. In this case, the FIU will normally receive only a comparatively small number of reports, meaning that the reporting system is unlikely to be a major source of financial data in proceedings against predicate offenders. This would contrast rather sharply with a reporting system in which obliged entities are expected to report even low degrees of suspicion and where SARs are extensively used in criminal proceedings against predicate offenders, even if in view of the low reporting threshold investigations will only in a relatively small number of cases uncover more than the activities of the predicate offender.

AML, in particular the criminalisation of money-laundering committed by predicate offenders themselves, has in some jurisdictions facilitated the prosecution of (suspected) predicate offenders, especially in cases where

laundering and asset recovery regime used against organised crime?, 12 *Journal of Money Laundering Control* (2009), p. 134. For the initially limited role of tax offences, see M Levi, Pecunia Non Olet? The Control of Money-laundering Revisited, in F Bovenkerk/M Levi (eds.), The Organised Crime Community, Essays in Honor of Alan A. Block, 2006, p. 173.

14 Controversially, the criminalisation of money laundering is in the eyes of many also meant to effectively lower the standard of proof required for sanctioning predicate offenders. While this view does certainly reflect a widely shared practice, it largely rests on an uncoherent understanding of the rationale of the prohibition of money laundering, see *infra* section III.B.1.b.

mens rea requirements for money laundering are less demanding than for the predicate offence. However, a focus on predicate offences is unlikely to address large-scale and complex money laundering.[15] If money laundering charges are only a quasi-automatic auxiliary charge to the predicate offence, or where money laundering offences primarily serve to trigger criminal investigations into the predicate offence by following the "money trail", an AML system risks paying insufficient attention to more sophisticated[16] and more important threats to the integrity of financial institutions.[17] In other words, the claim that AML is meant to serve the protection of the integrity of those institutions becomes rather weak if AML in practice primarily serves to prosecute medium- or even low-level predicate offences and at the same time fails to uncover criminal actors within the regulated sector.

A focus on predicate offences is not necessarily the result of policy choices by police and prosecutors but can directly result from the shape of relevant laws. If a country's definition of money laundering is comparatively broad and includes low- and medium-level crime as well as self-laundering, it cannot come as a surprise that AML will become a major tool to facilitate the prosecution of predicate offenders. If, at the same time, SARs in practice serve primarily as an information source for the investigation of predicate offences and less as an instrument to better understand complex money laundering schemes, one may conclude that the respective national AML system has effectively side-lined the objective of protecting the integrity of the financial sector. In contrast, when legislation and the competent authorities stress the role of the effectiveness of CDD and, as a consequence, the effectiveness of the supervision of obliged entities, emphasis is placed on the aim of protecting the financial sector and the wider economy from criminal assets.[18] The level of commitment to this aim, however, also depends on the extent to which FIUs and criminal justice authorities seek to identify actors that undermine obliged entities' gatekeeping function.

---

15 For criticism to this effect, see for example FATF, Mutual Evaluation Report Germany, 2010, p. 64; also inconclusive also in this respect, FATF, Mutual Evaluation Report United Kingdom, 2018, pp. 58–64.

16 For such more complex phenomena, see E van der Does de Willebois/EM Halter/RA Harrison/JW Park/JC Sharman, The Puppet Masters: How the Corrupt Use Legal Structures to Hide Stolen Assets and What to Do About It, The World Bank 2011, pp. 11–68.

17 See MF Cuéllar, The tenuous relationship between the fight against money laundering and the disruption of criminal finance, 93(2/3) *The Journal of Criminal Law and Criminology* (2003), pp. 405–406.

18 Political commitment to enhance obliged entities' gatekeeping function is brought to the fore not least in recent calls at EU level, in response to past money laundering scandals, to improve the quality of supervision throughout the Union; see European Commission, Report from the Commission to the European Parliament and the Council on the assessment of recent alleged money laundering cases involving EU credit institutions of 24 July 2019, COM(2019) 373 final.

The weighting of the two above-described primary objectives of AML is thus relevant not least for understanding the relationship between the competent authorities and the private sector. Insofar as obliged entities are taken to be auxiliaries to help the competent authorities in the investigation of crime, the primary focus of authorities is on obliged entities' criminal customers. Insofar as the law emphasises the role of obliged entities as gatekeepers of the financial system, the primary focus of authorities is on obliged entities and their employees. The design of AML measures therefore always requires careful scrutiny as to what purpose they are likely to serve in practice, and whether such a practice might eventually be detrimental to other and possibly more important objectives.

2. *Fragmentation of the AML Framework*

AML consists of a framework of distinct but interrelated areas of law, in particular criminal law, regulatory law and data protection law. The relationship between those different areas of law not only give rise to often great complexity and complicate both the political as well as the academic engagement with the subject matter. The heterogeneity of applicable legal frameworks is also reflected at the level of relevant players; here it is not only criminal justice authorities, FIUs, supervisory authorities and obliged entities that play a crucial role, but increasingly also less obvious actors, such as intelligence agencies, whistleblowers, investigative journalists and broader civil society.

As the analysis of supranational and national legal frameworks shows, the interdependence between the various constitutive elements of AML are not yet approached in a sufficiently holistic manner. Criminal justice and the obligations of obliged entities are frequently perceived as related, but insufficient thought is given to how one impacts on the other. FIUs are often seen as being primarily merely a collection point for SARs, whereas FIUs' growing operational role and their relationship with other authorities, especially criminal justice and supervisory authorities, remains rather nebulous. Supervisory authorities and their importance for AML have often been underappreciated, and so has their relationship with the criminal justice authorities. Of at least no lesser importance, the exact impact of data protection law on both the duties of obliged entities and the powers of relevant authorities (in particular FIUs) remains somewhat ambiguous. Finally, even within the regulatory framework applicable to obliged entities, major questions can exist as regards the relationship between various obligations, notably between due diligence and reporting duties. Recent reforms in EU law, not least the Fourth AML Directive, while having expanded the complexity of the system, have further amplified the need to balance the various elements of the AML architecture, yet in many cases without clarifying how exactly this should be done.

This fragmentation of AML underlines the need for a cross-disciplinary policy approach that sees each institution, power or duty in the context of the wider AML framework. While it has rightly been recognised that the prevention of money laundering requires the combination of various instruments, there is now a growing need to develop legislative solutions which ensure coherence and synergies between those instruments. Thus, AML must not be understood as an assemblage of different tools, but as an architecture. Otherwise, there is a real risk that the multitude of different actors involved (such as supervisors, obliged entities, criminal justice authorities or FIUs), instead of mutually supporting each other, will develop a life of their own, with little regard to how their practice impacts on the wider system.

3. *AML between Crime Prevention and Economic Freedom*

The conventional understanding of AML, as it developed at least since the 1990s,[19] was based on the idea that the private sector could identify cases of money laundering and then report these to the authorities, and that responsibility for the prevention of money laundering largely rests with obliged entities. The information flow was thus primarily conceptualised as a one-way street from the private to the public sector. Obliged entities, being much closer to economic operators, were expected to identify illicit flows in a more effective way than would be possible for the competent authorities. This concept was arguably based on the view that the identification of illicit flows by private entities is essentially a rather clear-cut task. Whenever obliged entities had doubts that a business was perfectly legal, they would keep the client only if they could positively confirm the legality of the assets. If things were as simple as this, obliged entities' obligation to prevent money laundering would indeed seem straightforward and not subject to inverse considerations, especially profit interests.

Over recent years, confidence in the workability of private sector detection has been muted. As revelations of large-scale money laundering through major banks have demonstrated, the effectiveness of CDD is in many cases at least dubious. This might partially be due to insufficient internal procedures of obliged entities or sometimes even a willingness of staff to close their eyes to manifest risks.[20] It has however also become clear that obliged entities are in very many cases not able to spot whether a client relationship or transaction is related to money laundering. While transactions from jurisdictions known for endemic criminality or anonymity-friendly business patterns might initially raise some red flags, the ability of obliged entities to inquire into the actual

---

19 See FATF, section I.A; European Union, section I.A.

20 European Commission, Report on the assessment of recent alleged money laundering cases involving EU credit institutions of 24 July 2019, COM(2019) 373 final.

origin of assets will often remain limited. Inquiries with the customer are frequently the primary source for finding out more, but this is obviously not a very promising path when dealing with a *mala fide* customer. In cases where unusual transactions relate to persons or geographical areas that are of limited economic interest for the obliged entity and its home market, the decision to cease business with the client will be less problematic. Things may however be much more complex where obliged entities find themselves confronted with more significant economic interests, for example wider expectations not to impede external trade relations. In these cases, precautionary de-risking might be rejected for having a disproportionate impact on legitimate businesses and the wider economy. Parallel to obliged entities, it is not least the supervisory authorities who, through their standards of what constitute acceptable risks, seek to find a balance between an open economy and crime prevention, in other words between freedom and security. It then becomes clear that private sector due diligence obligations are oftentimes not that straightforward after all.

4. *The Relationship between the Public and the Private Sector*

Given that AML essentially constitutes a partial outsourcing of criminal policy tasks to obliged entities, it is also necessary to keep in mind that the relationship between the private sector and the authorities is of major importance for understanding the potential of, and limits to, the delegation of preventive and investigative functions. In this respect, the EU legislator should one the one hand take into consideration not least that continental European jurisdictions are often attached to a vision of the relationship between public service and private enterprise that can be in rather stark contrast to the vision followed in major common law jurisdictions.[21] Such differences concern not least the question to what extent national legislators are willing and, according to their constitutional law, able to delegate law enforcement functions to for-profit actors.[22] Diverging traditions can also be observed in how a country's public service is more or less open to career switches from private practice to public function, and *vice versa*, a factor that can be significant not least with regard to the professional

---

21 See M Bevir/RAW Rhodes, Searching for civil society: changing patterns of governance in Britain, 81 *Public Administration* (2003), pp. 41–62; W Jann, State administration and governance in Germany: Competing traditions and dominant narratives, 81 *Public Administration* (2003), pp. 95–118; E Ongaro, Public Management Reform and Modernization: Trajectories of Administrative Change in Italy, France, Greece, Portugal and Spain, 2009, Chapter 7.

22 See G Katrougalos, Constitutional Limitations of Privatization in the USA and Europe: A Theoretical and Comparative Perspective, 17(3) *Constellations* (2010), pp. 407–425; M Bergstrom/K Svedberg Helgesson/U Mörth, A New Role for for-Profit Actors: The Case of Anti-Money Laundering and Risk Management, 49 *Journal of Common Market Studies* (2011), pp. 1043–1064.

background of obliged entities' compliance officers and of FIU staff. Though the relevance of differences in institutional culture must always be assessed with regard to particular tasks, it should not be neglected. For in arguably no other area of criminal law enforcement are the public and the private sector as intimately intertwined as in AML/CTF. Where such collaboration is meant to play a key role, the culture that defines the relationship between state bodies, businesses and wider civil society in a country becomes crucial.

On the other hand, the potential for private sector involvement in criminal policy of course also depends on the extent to which businesses in a particular jurisdiction are potentially vulnerable to infiltration by criminal actors. Insofar as the situation in a particular jurisdiction makes employees of obliged entities vulnerable to threats and intimidation, it would seem problematic to greatly rely on the private sector to address the very criminals that AML seeks to constrain, let alone to entrust obliged entities extensively with sensitive information.[23] The level of support that can realistically be expected from the private sector will not least depend on the ability of the competent authorities to protect obliged entities' employees from repercussions. Consequently, insofar as authorities in a particular context find it difficult to protect employees from harm or to protect their anonymity when they report criminal transactions to the authorities,[24] the effectiveness of any AML obligations imposed on such employees will necessarily be limited.

5. *Aligning AML to Constitutional Orders*

Finally, and crucially, a set of norms with global vocation such as the FATF Recommendations is necessarily limited in its ability to shape a global consensus.[25] National constitutional laws and principles usually vary significantly from one country to another. Consequently, national legislators' ability to agree on common rules globally remain limited. A particular AML instrument that may function well in one national legal system can at the same time conflict with core principles of another national legal system and therefore lead to sometimes radically different views on whether the respective instrument would constitute best practice. Where core constitutional principles of one jurisdiction are of

---

23 See S Caneppele/F Calderoni/ S Martocchia, Not only banks. Criminological models on the infiltration of public contracts by Italian organized crime, 12 *Journal of Money Laundering Control* (2009), p. 168, highlighting the need to inquire whether new legislation may inadvertently produce new opportunities for crime.

24 See M Levi, How Well Do Anti-Money Laundering Controls Work in Developing Countries?, in P Reuter (ed.), Draining Development? Controlling Flows of Illicit Funds from Developing Countries, 2012, p. 403.

25 See B Zagaris/SM Castilla, Constructing an International Financial Enforcement Subregime: The Implementation of Anti-Money-Laundering Policy, 19 *Brooklyn Journal of International Law* (1993), pp. 873–878.

direct relevance for AML but of much less relevance for other jurisdictions,[26] it is unsurprising that the former jurisdictions will tend to develop policy solutions that will vary significantly. In the worst case, national legislators copy international standards without sufficient domestic contextualisation and thereby leave practitioners with no guidance on how to overcome the resulting conflicts between those standards and relevant domestic principles. Greater autonomous rule-making by the EU or national legislators, if done in good faith, can therefore constitute not a weakening of the global AML framework, but potentially reflect a much more serious commitment to this framework than a domestic policy that is blindly following the international standards without looking at their actual merits in the context of a particular domestic legal system.[27]

In this respect, a more autonomous AML policy of the EU seems pertinent not least because of the great importance of data protection law in the EU legal order, a preoccupation that is not shared to a similar extent by many FATF members. Given that AML is quintessentially about (financial) personal data, it seems almost unavoidable that disagreement on the status of data protection within domestic legal orders will have significant repercussions on the shape of individual AML frameworks.

As another example of the importance of constitutional context, one can point to the differences even between EU Member States as to what extent they allow for the gathering of intelligence within criminal proceedings. The more national law requires that trial courts and defendants have, at the latest during the trial, in principle full access to the information gathered by the police and prosecutors during the investigation, the less these authorities can safeguard the confidentiality of sources of information. While this might not exclude the possibility that intelligence gathering (notably by intelligence agencies) plays a significant role as a trigger for criminal investigations, procedural systems with strong limitations on the use of secretly obtained information in criminal proceedings can contrast rather sharply with procedural systems that allow investigative authorities greater leeway to pre-select the information they want to provide to the trial court.

As a final example of fundamental constitutional differences, one can point to the impact of police or prosecutorial discretion and how the extent of such discretion potentially impacts on the shape of an individual AML framework and in particular on the shape of the criminal law. In a system where criminal

---

26 To this effect see also Opinion of the European Data Protection Supervisor (EDPS) on a proposal for a Directive of the European Parliament and of the Council on the prevention of the use of the financial system for the purpose of money laundering and terrorist financing, and a proposal for a Regulation of the European Parliament and of the Council on information on the payer accompanying transfers of funds of 4 July 2013, para. 10.

27 For an account of tendencies in public management to envisage context-specific solutions in response to unsatisfactory experience with uniform global standards, see C Pollitt, Towards a new world: some inconvenient truths for Anglosphere public administration, 81 *International Review of Administrative Sciences* (2015), pp. 3–17.

justice authorities enjoy little discretion, they have, in principle, no power to select charges; rather it is the substantive criminal law that tells them what to investigate and to charge. This can contrast sharply with criminal justice systems that recognise broad police or prosecutorial discretion and thereby may treat the substantive criminal law more as a tool in the hands of the competent authorities than as an inflexible command addressed to them. As a consequence, legislators in a discretionary system find it easier to define criminal offences more broadly, as criminal justice authorities will be allowed to select cases in light of criminal policy considerations. The less a criminal justice system allows for such discretion, the more legislators will have to specify and limit the scope of the definition of a criminal offence. Otherwise, broad criminal laws will force the competent authorities to increasingly deal with low-scale criminality, thereby taking up prosecutorial resources that could have been better spent on investigating more complex serious criminality.

B. MEASURING EFFECTIVENESS AND EFFICIENCY

Like any other legal framework, the legitimacy of AML depends not least on its ability to serve its objectives. Without reliable findings about their effectiveness, one cannot determine whether, in view of their direct costs and any detrimental side-effects, AML measures are adequate. In this regard, today's frameworks are confronted with two primary challenges. On the one hand, and as already mentioned, the pursued objectives are frequently not clear. On the other hand, AML suffers from a lack of reliable data to assess its performance and unintended side-effects.[28] Both points put a given framework's very lawfulness into question, as without a clearly defined objective and findings on effectiveness, any determination of the proportionality of individual instruments and of a framework as a whole are impossible. There is therefore an urgent need for policymakers to more clearly express their goals and gather data about the extent to which various instruments contribute to these goals.[29]

---

28 RT Naylor, Wash-out: A critique of follow-the-money methods in crime control policy, *Crime, Law and Social Change* (2000), pp. 1–57; PC van Duyne, (Transnational) Organised Crime, Laundering and the Congregation of the Gullible, Valedictory by Professor Petrus C van Duyne, 2011; T Halliday/M Levi/P Reuter, Anti-Money Laundering: An Inquiry into a Disciplinary Transnational Legal Order, 4 *UC Irvine Journal of International, Transnational, and Comparative Law* (2019), pp. 10–11; RF Pol, Response to money laundering scandal: evidence-informed or perception-driven?, 23 *Journal of Money Laundering Control* (2020), p. 103.

29 See now also Article 44 of Directive (EU) 2015/849 of 20 May 2015, as amended by Directive (EU) 2018/843 of the European Parliament and of the Council of 30 May 2018 amending Directive (EU) 2015/849 on the prevention of the use of the financial system for the purposes of money laundering or terrorist financing, and amending Directives 2009/138/EC and 2013/36/EU, which requires Member States to maintain comprehensive data to review the effectiveness of their AML/CTF system.

An assessment of the effectiveness of AML can depart from the assumption that the system is supposed to facilitate the investigation of predicate offences and the sanctioning of predicate offenders, ultimately in order to more effectively deter future offenders, render the acquisition of ill-gotten assets less attractive and facilitate their restitution. One must however question whether it is really helpful to assess the role of AML primarily in the light of this particular objective. Of course, national and supranational instruments frequently refer to the "fight against crime" as one of their objectives.[30] Yet it would appear that AML's role as an instrument to facilitate the detection and investigation of predicate offences can hardly serve as the primary yardstick for the prohibition of money laundering and for the resulting legal framework. After all, the effectiveness of criminal policy first and foremost depends on the overall performance of a country's criminal justice system, not on the performance of AML. To the extent that AML serves the role of producing financial information and thereby contributing to a "follow-the-money" approach in the investigation of profit-generating crime, it might expand the capacities of criminal justice authorities. However, the actual value of AML instruments in this regard will primarily depend on whether these instruments do – against the background of a particular national criminal justice system and with regard to the ultimate objective – really add anything substantial to what is already possible under the general powers of criminal procedure. The practical relevance of SARs or of other private–public data sharing mechanisms may for example also depend on the investigative powers and resources of criminal justice authorities to access financial data, in particular their actual ability to seize or otherwise compel the production of financial institutions' customer data. Similarly, depending on the shape of a jurisdiction's substantive criminal law, as well as on the flexibility of its law of evidence, criminal proceedings against money laundering can be more or less relevant as a tool to curtail the commission of predicate offences. The number of money laundering convictions will by itself tell little about the performance of a national criminal justice system, for the accomplishment of this objective depends first and foremost on the effectiveness of investigations into predicate offences.[31] AML offers, at best, supplementary tools for the investigation of predicate offences and the sanctioning of predicate offenders. The effectiveness of a national framework to this end primarily depends on the overall investigative powers and resources available to criminal justice authorities. The question whether AML enhances the effectiveness of a legal order in addressing predicate offences can therefore only be determined in view of the features of

---

30 On the lack of conclusive evidence for AML's effectiveness in this regard, see PC van Duyne/JH Harvey/LY Gelemerova, The Critical Handbook of Money Laundering: Policy, Analysis and Myths, 2018, pp. 260–266.

31 See RF Pol, Anti-money laundering effectiveness: assessing outcomes or ticking boxes?, 21 *Journal of Money Laundering Control* (2018), pp. 223–224.

the particular criminal justice framework. In other words, insofar as AML is said to serve the investigation and sanctioning of predicate offenders, there is little point in assessing the effectiveness of a criminal justice system on the basis of the performance of an ancillary subsystem, namely AML. Consequently, it is not possible to infer from the application of AML instruments whether or not a legal order is successful in tackling predicate offences. Fundamentally different considerations may apply to those predicate offences (such as corruption by foreign officials) which, because they are committed abroad and due to the absence of predicate offenders or for evidentiary reasons, cannot be prosecuted by domestic authorities. Insofar as AML then also serves objectives of foreign and security policy, any effectiveness assessment would also need to have regard in particular to whether the domestic confiscation of assets has the desired effects in the respective foreign jurisdiction.

As already mentioned above, AML does however also serve to protect the integrity of financial institutions in the sense of preventing them from becoming a tool in the hands of criminal actors to integrate proceeds of crime into legal businesses. To the extent that the prohibition of money laundering and of the wider AML framework constitute instruments to separate legal and illegal economies, an effectiveness assessment is not concerned with the effectiveness of criminal justice, but, much more specifically, with the ability of a legal order to prevent the exploitation of legitimate businesses and legitimate business activities by criminal actors.[32] Here again, the lack of adequate data pertaining to the amount of laundered assets[33] is obviously of concern for evaluating a framework's legitimacy. Yet, unlike regarding AML's function as a tool to facilitate the investigation of predicate offences, any assessment of AML's effectiveness regarding the protection of the integrity of financial institutions requires one to look for a more distinct outcome, namely the ability of a legal order to render the investment and other use of ill-gotten gains more difficult. In this respect, criminal justice is thus not an objective, but rather an element of AML. The latter's performance will rely on various elements which will supplement and, to some extent, possibly even substitute criminal justice. Furthermore, while AML measures can, notably through deception or infiltration of obliged entities, be weakened, it would nevertheless appear rather obvious that the mere existence of obliged entities' AML obligations will, in comparison to a pre-AML state of affairs, in any case complicate criminal efforts to expand into legal markets.[34] Assessing the effectiveness of AML in this respect, and consequently the

32 See e.g. S Caneppele/F Calderoni/ S Martocchia, Not only banks. Criminological models on the infiltration of public contracts by Italian organized crime, 12 *Journal of Money Laundering Control* (2009) 151, pp. 156–170.

33 See M Levi/P Reuter/T Halliday, Can the AML system be evaluated without better data?, 69 *Crime, Law and Social Change* (2018), pp. 307–328.

34 In a similar vein also P Reuter/EM Truman, Chasing Dirty Money: The Fight against Money Laundering, 2004, pp. 137–138.

legitimacy of unintended side-effects, does of course require empirical findings on the overall volume of criminal finance, on the actual ability of obliged entities to avert the inflow of the assets and on the effects of interaction between crime-funded businesses and legitimate businesses.[35] Yet, even without extensive data, one may still conclude that it would in all likelihood expand the operational freedom and thus power of criminal actors if they were (again) allowed to freely (that is, with no questions being asked) invest in lawful businesses. Insofar as the interaction between lawful businesses and criminal actors appears, at least in some countries, to be rather rare, any assessment of AML should also ask to what extent such a state of affairs, instead of constituting proof of the redundancy of AML, may rather be its effect, and to what extent AML may meanwhile have contributed to a change in business ethics.[36]

Resulting from the preceding observations, the design of the various elements of an AML framework must always be founded on a clear determination of the objectives pursued with a particular measure. Only then is it possible to understand the role that this measure plays within the framework and how it interacts with other elements. And only such understanding can then allow one to formulate questions to test the underlying factual assumptions. For any normative theory is conditioned and thus confined by facts, but such theory (such as a particular concept of the objectives of AML) is at the same time a precondition to identify the relevant factual questions. In this sense, the following normative reflections about a desirable shape of AML are at the same time meant to identify areas that are in need of clarification through additional empirical research. Reflecting this mutual interdependence between normativity and facts, the proposed solutions are thus an attempt to overcome the many contradictions and resulting deficits of today's AML framework by approaching them in a comprehensive and thus systematic way, an attempt that must then in many respects be further advanced by empirical inquiries.

II. CONSTITUTIONAL FRAMEWORK

A. APPLICABLE RIGHTS

AML measures of the EU must conform to the European constitutional order, including to the Charter of Fundamental Rights and the European Convention

---

35 See PC van Duyne, Money laundering policies: fears and fact, in P van Duyne/K von Lampe/JL Newell (eds.), Criminal Finances and Organised Crime in Europe, 2003, pp. 67–104.

36 See already D Garland, The Limits of the Sovereign State, 36 *British Journal of Criminology* (1996), p. 454, who highlights that what he labels "responsibilisation" of non-state actors "does not entail the simple off-loading of state functions", but also "aims to bring about marginal but effective changes in the norms, the routines, and the consciousness of everyone."

of Human Rights. Two characteristics of the AML architecture are of particular relevance for identifying the applicable fundamental rights limits, namely the obligations imposed on private businesses in the context of CDD (in particular the monitoring of business relationships and transactions, as well as the retention of customer data) and the operational function of FIUs and resulting from it the nature of AML as a tool of state surveillance. Relevant in this respect are in particular the right to respect for private and family life according to Article 8 of the Convention and Article 7 of the Charter, and the right to the protection of personal data according to Article 8 of the Charter.[37]

B. THE PROCESSING OF PERSONAL DATA BY OBLIGED ENTITIES

1. *The Law*

The processing of data of individuals and legal entities[38] by obliged entities for the purpose of CDD is obviously a cornerstone of the AML system. This processing forms the basis for obliged entities' reporting obligations and thus the basis for the data processing of FIUs and the sharing of such data between the FIU and the competent authorities. According to Article 52(1) of the Charter, limitations on the right to the protection of personal data must be provided for by law, and, subject to the principle of proportionality, may be made only if they are necessary and genuinely meet objectives of general interest recognised by the Union or the need to protect the rights and freedoms of others. These limiting principles are taken up in particular by Articles 5 para. 1(c) and Article 6 para. 1 s. 1(f) of Regulation (EU) 2016/679 (the General Data Protection Regulation, applicable notably to data processing by private persons), which require the processing to follow a legitimate interest, and the processed personal data to be adequate, relevant and limited to what is necessary in relation to the purposes for which they are processed.

---

37 Other elements of AML can obviously also infringe fundamental rights, though they will, in principle, have a comparatively more limited impact on the overall design of the framework. This concerns not least limitations on the right to a fair trial under Article 6 ECHR as regards the evidentiary standards required for a conviction for money laundering (see ECtHR, Zschüschen v. Belgium, decision of 2 May 2017, app. no. 23572/07) and limitations on the confidentiality of lawyer–client relations under Article 8 ECHR (see ECtHR, Michaud v. France, judgment of 6 December 2012, app. no. 12323/11). For potential challenges resulting from the broad definition of money laundering in view of the principle of legality under Article 7 ECHR, see *infra* section III.B.1.c.

38 For the applicability of the right to the protection of personal data to legal entities, see ECJ (Grand Chamber), judgment of 9 November 2010 (Schecke GbR/Eifert v. Land Hessen), C-92/09 and C 93/09, para. 53. H Johlen, in K Stern/M Sachs, Europäische Grundrechte-Charta, Kommentar, 2016, Art. 8, paras. 26–27.

Beyond the identification of the required general interest pursued, the main question from a fundamental rights perspective then is whether the processing of personal data conforms to the principle of proportionality. According to the jurisprudence of the EU Court of Justice, respect for the principle of proportionality of the processing of personal data must, as a starting point, have regard to the nature of the processed data and the effect of the data processing on rights holders. In its 2014 decision on Directive (EC) 2006/24 on the retention of communications traffic data, the Court found a "particularly serious [interference]" with the rights laid down in Articles 7 and 8 of the Charter because the obligation of telecommunications providers to retain traffic data applied "to all means of electronic communication, the use of which is very widespread and of growing importance in people's everyday lives", and thus entailed "an interference with the fundamental rights of practically the entire European population."[39] Even though the Directive did not extend to the retention of the content of communications, the Court observed that the traffic data "may allow very precise conclusions to be drawn concerning the private lives of the persons whose data has been retained, such as the habits of everyday life, permanent or temporary places of residence, daily or other movements, the activities carried out, the social relationships of those persons and the social environments frequented by them."[40] It furthermore noted that the fact that data are retained and used without the person being informed was "likely to generate in the minds of the persons concerned the feeling that their private lives are the subject of constant surveillance."[41]

In assessing the proportionality of the data retention, the Court underlined the importance of the protection of personal data for the right to respect for private life. As a result, the EU legislator "must lay down clear and precise rules governing the scope and application of the measures in question and imposing minimum safeguards so that persons whose data have been retained have sufficient guarantees to effectively protect their personal data against the risk of abuse and against unlawful access and use of that data". Such safeguards were particularly important where personal data "are subject to automatic processing and where there is a significant risk of unlawful access to those data".[42]

---

39 ECJ (Grand Chamber), judgment of 8 April 2014 (Digital Rights Ireland), C-293/12 and C-594/12, paras. 37, 56; see also ECJ (Grand Chamber), judgment of 21 December 2016 (Tele2 Sverige), C-203/15 and C-698/15, para. 97.

40 ECJ (Grand Chamber), judgment of 8 April 2014 (Digital Rights Ireland), C-293/12 and C-594/12, para. 27; see also ECJ (Grand Chamber), judgment of 21 December 2016 (Tele2 Sverige), C-203/15 and C-698/15, para. 99.

41 ECJ (Grand Chamber), judgment of 8 April 2014 (Digital Rights Ireland), C-293/12 and C-594/12, para. 37; see also ECJ (Grand Chamber), judgment of 21 December 2016 (Tele2 Sverige), C-203/15 and C-698/15, para. 100.

42 ECJ (Grand Chamber), judgment of 8 April 2014 (Digital Rights Ireland), C-293/12 and C-594/12, para. 54; see also ECJ (Grand Chamber), judgment of 21 December 2016 (Tele2 Sverige), C-203/15 and C-698/15, para. 110.

The Court found that Directive (EC) 2006/24 failed to circumscribe the interference with Articles 7 and 8 with sufficient precision, taking into account several considerations. The data retention covered "in a generalised manner, all persons and all means of electronic communication as well as all traffic data without any differentiation, limitation or exception being made in the light of the objective of fighting serious crime." The Directive covered all persons using electronic communication "without the persons whose data are retained being, even indirectly, in a situation which is liable to give rise to criminal prosecutions"; thus it applied "even to persons for whom there is no evidence capable of suggesting that their conduct might have a link, even an indirect or remote one, with serious crime", and even to communications that, according to national law, are subject to professional secrecy. The Directive did not

> require any relationship between the data whose retention [was] provided for and a threat to public security and, in particular, it [was] not restricted to a retention in relation (i) to data pertaining to a particular time period and/or a particular geographical zone and/or to a circle of particular persons likely to be involved, in one way or another, in a serious crime, or (ii) to persons who could, for other reasons, contribute, by the retention of their data, to the prevention, detection or prosecution of serious offences.[43]

As regards the need to provide sufficiently precise limits to the interference with Articles 7 and 8 of the Charter, the Court also highlighted that Directive (EC) 2006/24

> fail[ed] to lay down any objective criterion by which to determine the limits of the access of the competent national authorities to the data and their subsequent use for the purposes of prevention, detection or criminal prosecutions concerning offences that, in view of the extent and seriousness of the interference with the fundamental rights enshrined in Articles 7 and 8 of the Charter, may be considered to be sufficiently serious to justify such an interference.[44]

In this respect, the Court noted in particular that the Directive referred "in a general manner to serious crime, as defined by each Member State in its national law", thereby lacking any precision on what level of criminality would justify the use of the retained data by national authorities. The Directive did also "not contain substantive and procedural conditions relating to the access of the

43 ECJ (Grand Chamber), judgment of 8 April 2014 (Digital Rights Ireland), C-293/12 and C-594/12, paras. 57–59; see also ECJ (Grand Chamber), judgment of 21 December 2016 (Tele2 Sverige), C-203/15 and C-698/15, paras. 105–106.

44 ECJ (Grand Chamber), judgment of 8 April 2014 (Digital Rights Ireland), C-293/12 and C-594/12, paras. 60.

competent national authorities to the data and to their subsequent use." It did notably not "expressly provide that that access and the subsequent use of the data in question must be strictly restricted to the purpose of preventing and detecting precisely defined serious offences or of conducting criminal prosecutions relating thereto". In this regard, the Court considered it as particularly significant "that the access by the competent national authorities to the data retained [was] not made dependent on a prior review carried out by a court or by an independent administrative body whose decision seeks to limit access to the data and their use to what is strictly necessary for the purpose of attaining the objective pursued".[45]

Furthermore, in finding that Directive (EC) 2006/24 did not "provide for sufficient safeguards, as required by Article 8 of the Charter, to ensure effective protection of the data retained against the risk of abuse and against any unlawful access and use of that data" and thereby sustaining its conclusion that the Directive did not comply with the principle of proportionality, the Court had regard notably "to (i) the vast quantity of data whose retention is required by that directive, (ii) the sensitive nature of that data and (iii) the risk of unlawful access to that data". In that regard, it pointed out in particular that the Directive did "not require the data in question to be retained within the European Union, with the result that it cannot be held that the control, explicitly required by Article 8(3) of the Charter, by an independent authority of compliance with the requirements of protection and security, as referred to in the two previous paragraphs, is fully ensured." The Court stressed that "[s]uch a control, carried out on the basis of EU law, is an essential component of the protection of individuals with regard to the processing of personal data".[46]

2. *Relevance for AML*

The judgment of the EU Court of Justice regarding Directive (EC) 2006/24 applies to the retention of communications traffic data, not financial data. It is thus not directly applicable to AML. Nevertheless, the judgment does offer some important insights into the data protection limits applicable to the processing of financial data by obliged entities and the competent authorities. To assess its relevance for AML, one must begin by comparing the processing of communications traffic data and the processing of financial and other customer data with respect to their impact on citizens. At first glance, it may seem as if the retention and use of communications data is of far greater intrusiveness than the

---

[45] ECJ (Grand Chamber), judgment of 8 April 2014 (Digital Rights Ireland), C-293/12 and C-594/12, paras. 60–62; see also ECJ (Grand Chamber), judgment of 21 December 2016 (Tele2 Sverige), C-203/15 and C-698/15, paras. 115 and 120.

[46] ECJ (Grand Chamber), judgment of 8 April 2014 (Digital Rights Ireland), C-293/12 and C-594/12, paras. 66–68; see also ECJ (Grand Chamber), judgment of 21 December 2016 (Tele2 Sverige), C-203/15 and C-698/15, para. 122.

processing of obliged entities' customer data, not least because of the difference in the quantity of relevant data. Today, a huge part of the private interactions between individuals takes place through electronic communication. Most individuals will usually engage in a multitude of electronic communications every day, thereby enabling third parties, through access to the traffic data, to acquire a more or less detailed picture of individuals' private and social lives. As the Court of Justice rightly observed, if communications traffic data are comprehensively retained, access to these data allows very precise conclusions to be drawn about a person's life.

Compared to communications traffic data, the volume of a person's financial transactions is normally smaller and, in most cases, will allow less direct insights into individuals' daily interactions. Furthermore, while communications are usually private and shielded from the eyes of third parties, the same is not the case for a large part of business relationships and transactions, as they will in many cases be visible to third parties, for example to sales assistants and bank employees. Despite these differences, the processing of financial data can today allow for insights into a person's private life to an extent that, if not equal to the level of detail of communications traffic data, may effectively be similarly intrusive. In that regard, one must in particular note that in today's economies, cash payments are increasingly replaced by electronic transactions. Not least due to new payment technologies, even the smallest transactions are conducted electronically, meaning that it becomes possible to track a person's conduct and thereby discover habits, daily movements and social environments simply by accumulating transaction data.

Furthermore, in order to appreciate the relevance of data for the right to respect for private life, importance must also be accorded to the further processing they allow. Financial transaction data will often allow indirect access to vast amounts of customer data, including customer data of businesses that are not obliged entities. For unlike in the case of cash transactions, electronic transaction data will normally enable investigators to link a business's customer data (in particular the identity of the goods and services sold, the place of the purchase and additional purchase-specific circumstances) to clearly identifiable customers. Especially as regards online providers of goods and services, this customer data can be very detailed, not least because the customer's purchasing behaviour will often be recorded for commercial purposes (including for example details about a customer's habits and political, cultural, sexual and other preferences resulting not only from the type of goods and services purchased, but also from the manner of their consumption). While customer data would to some extent have been available to the authorities even where the goods and services were paid for in cash (for example by asking the shop assistant whether he or she remembered a particular client), today's dominance of electronic payment technologies allows authorities to access and bring together businesses' customer data in a way that can lead to a very comprehensive picture of a person's private life. Consequently, while financial transaction data does at first glance usually offer less information about a person's private life than a comprehensive record of his or her communications traffic data, the potential of financial data for exploring a person's private life by identifying and exploring corresponding stocks of private customer data may ultimately not lag behind the potential of traffic data. In fact, unlike financial transaction data, retained communications traffic data will in many cases not offer additional insights into a communication, not least because the recorded content of a communication will very frequently be encrypted and thus inaccessible to investigators.

As importantly, any assessment of the intrusiveness of obliged entities' data processing must consider that the processing of data through CDD data extends well beyond transaction and other financial data and includes personal data that obliged entities gathered from the customer him- or herself and from third parties in order to establish or verify a customer's personal background and business relationships, the purpose of business relationships and transactions, or the origin of funds.[47] Depending on the applicable limits of the respective national legal framework[48] and the practice of obliged entities, CDD data can thereby potentially also include large amounts of additional information originating from the processing of personal data by a third party, for example data resulting from the analysis of social networks and search engines or data stemming from criminal justice and other authorities. Especially insofar as obliged entities make extensive use of such third-party sources of personal data, the combination of financial data and CDD data can then lead to a very detailed picture of a person's private life and thereby to extensive personal profiles.

The very purpose of data processing by obliged entities pursuant to their CDD and reporting duties suggests that a comparison between the retention of communications traffic data on the one hand and the processing of customer data in AML one the other hand must not be confined to the nature of the processed data, but must furthermore adequately appreciate the respective methods of data processing. In this respect, it is noteworthy that the EU Court of Justice already qualified as a particularly serious interference with Articles 7 and 8 of the Charter the fact that traffic data was simply retained, independently of any actual further processing of such data. The mere availability of the data for their potential subsequent use by the competent authorities was enough to constitute, in the eyes of the Court, a serious interference with the right to privacy. The situation is markedly different in AML. Here obliged entities are of course also required to document their CDD measures,[49] thereby potentially allowing criminal justice

47 For the scope of CDD data gathering, see European Union, section III.A.

48 On the lack of specificity of national frameworks in this respect, see Comparative Analysis, sections III.C.1.b, III.C.2.a and V.A.2.

49 Article 8 para. 4(a) of Directive (EU) 2015/849 of 20 May 2015.

authorities and FIUs to request financial and other relevant data. Going beyond mere data retention, obliged entities are however also required to analyse the customer data by themselves in order to identify and report cases of money laundering and terrorism financing. For example, the obligation according to Article 18 para. 2 of Directive 2015/849 to adopt enhanced CDD measures in cases of unusual transactions or patterns of transactions will regularly require obliged entities to apply data analysis technologies to detect such unusual events.[50] This effectively means that obliged entities are required to monitor even inconspicuous or unsuspicious customers and transactions. In view of the vast amounts of transaction data processed especially by credit institutions, it is obviously necessary that obliged entities rely on automated processing systems to identify anomalies. However, the automated and thus largely statistical analysis of customer relationships also exposes customers to risks, not least the risk of being erroneously subjected to account closures and assets freezes[51] as a consequence of overly broad or otherwise defective screening parameters. More importantly, one must also note that, while the monitoring is conducted by obliged entities and thus normally private, not public, bodies, it also serves the purpose of identifying reportable activities in view of obliged entities' obligation to file SARs. Consequently, obliged entities' monitoring of their customers is a key element of FIUs' data gathering.[52] Given that this monitoring, despite being geared towards reporting and thus criminal investigations, in principle covers every business relationship or transaction independently of any prior suspicion of criminal wrongdoing,[53] CDD exposes every user of financial services to a risk of being subjected to preventive and investigative measures of domestic or foreign authorities as a result of on erroneous data processing.[54] In light of these potentially serious detrimental consequences of private-sector CDD, and depending on the scope and sensitivity of the financial and CDD data processed by obliged entities, the performance of CDD by obliged entities can then constitute a very serious interference with a customer's private life even before steps have been taken by the FIU and other competent authorities. This view is strengthened by the fact that CDD is usually conducted by employees of obliged entities who are not qualified in the same way as state authorities to conduct inquiries in an impartial and diligent manner, and who will frequently be motivated more by their employer's economic interest than by considerations pertaining to truth and fairness towards the client.

---

50 See for the obligation to apply electronic screening technologies for example Germany, section III.G and Spain, section III.G.

51 See on these consequences in more detail *infra* section III.D.1.b.

52 See Comparative Analysis, section IV.B.1.

53 See European Union, section III.A.1.b, and Comparative Analysis, section III.A.1.b.

54 See ECtHR, Weber and Saravia v. Germany, judgment of 29 June 2006, app. no. 54934/00, para. 125.

In light of both the scope and intrusiveness of financial data, the potential inclusion of sensitive personal data from third parties, and the processing purpose and methods, one must assume that obliged entities' CDD and reporting can, in principle, trigger a duty for EU and national legislators to respect standards and safeguards similar to those determined by the Court of Justice with regard to the retention of communications traffic data. To what extent the safeguards applicable to the retention of communications traffic data also apply to obliged entities' CDD will ultimately depend in particular on the nature and scope of personal data gathered for the purpose of CDD and thus on whether the accumulation and analysis of financial and CDD data can allow for insights into a person's private life similar to the level of detail provided by communications data. In addition, this question will also depend on further aspects of the particular AML framework, notably on whether obliged entities' CDD and reporting is subject to effective remedies, on the impact of an obliged entity's CDD on the behaviour of other obliged entities (possibly both within and outside its group of companies), and on the manner in which SARs are subsequently processed by the FIU and other competent authorities (in particular whether SARs are thoroughly scrutinised by the FIU before forwarding them to criminal justice authorities, and whether the forwarding of SARs is conditioned by a particular seriousness threshold regarding the suspected crime). Insofar as the financial and CDD data retained and thereby made accessible to the competent authorities under the AML framework could effectively reach a level of intrusiveness of CDD similar to the retention of telecommunications traffic data, legislators must, in line with the above safeguards developed by the EU Court of Justice, notably limit the scope of retention by defining adequate guidance for obliged entities' CDD data gathering, confine the ultimate purpose of CDD and reporting to the detection and prevention of serious crime, adequately specify the grounds that can give rise to a reportable suspicion, and provide for independent scrutiny of the sharing of sensitive personal data by obliged entities.[55]

C. THE PROCESSING OF PERSONAL DATA BY FINANCIAL INTELLIGENCE UNITS

1. *The Law*

Before identifying the fundamental rights standards applicable to the processing of data by FIUs, one must first determine what this processing essentially entails. Obviously, FIUs are in particular tasked with analysing financial data submitted

[55] See ECJ (Grand Chamber), judgment of 21 December 2016 (Tele2 Sverige), C-203/15 and C-698/15, paras. 108 and 117.

by obliged entities and, insofar as they find the suspicion confirmed, forwarding the reports or the results of their analysis to criminal justice authorities. Yet FIUs' powers go well beyond the mere analysing and forwarding of financial data and also comprise extensive data gathering, in particular data about the customers of obliged entities. Of course, FIUs are (beyond the data contained in the centralised account registries)[56] usually not enabled to directly access customer data. However, while it is primarily obliged entities (and not FIUs) who are required to gather information about their customers and to perform continuous monitoring,[57] if an obliged entity discovers grounds for a suspicion of money laundering (or terrorism financing), it is then under an obligation to inform the competent FIU and enjoys no discretion in this regard.[58] While the gathering of data about business relationships and transactions is thus performed by obliged entities, their obligation to this effect together with their obligation to report suspicious activities to the FIU lead to the conclusion that legislators have effectively delegated the central part of FIUs' data-gathering functions to obliged entities,[59] in this respect making the latter an instrument of FIUs. Furthermore, even where an FIU requests information about a business relationship or transaction from an obliged entity, this information can in some cases go beyond data already held by this obliged entity and instead extend to information that the obliged entity will then gather only following the FIU's request.[60] Due to an information request by the FIU, the requested obliged entity might then for example approach the customer to clarify certain aspects of his or her personal background or business activities and then inform the FIU about its findings.

To identify the applicable fundamental rights standard in particular within the jurisprudence of the European Court of Human Rights, it should be recalled that customer information processed by obliged entities and FIUs regularly falls under the category of data relating to a person's private life within the meaning of

---

56 Article 32 of Directive (EU) 2015/849 of 20 May 2015, as amended by Directive (EU) 2018/843 of 30 May 2018. Those registries contain in particular information on the identity of the holder and of the beneficial owner of any payment accounts and bank accounts identified by IBAN.

57 European Union, sections III.A.1 and III.A.3, and Comparative Analysis, sections III.A.1. and III.A.3.

58 European Union, section III.C.1.a, and Comparative Analysis, section III.C.1.a.

59 On a similar delegation, see ECtHR, Vukota-Bojic v. Switzerland, judgment of 18 October 2017, app. no. 61838/10, para. 47.

60 An obligation to gather information due to an FIU request is not explicitly provided by EU law; see Article 32 para. 9 of Directive (EU) 2015/849 of 20 May 2015, as amended by Directive (EU) 2018/843 of 30 May 2018. However, it is clear that such an information request will often trigger enhanced CDD obligations and thus the obligation to collect additional information about the customer (see European Union, section III.A.3), especially where the information request implies that a specific customer is of interest to the FIU or criminal justice authorities.

Article 8 of the European Convention of Human Rights. As set forth by the Court, the scope of such data not only covers information about a person's relationships with others, but extends to information about that person's professional or business activities.[61] While customers may not necessarily have an expectation of privacy when performing an individual transaction (notably when the transaction is usually witnessed by third parties, for example shop assistants), the creation of a systematic record and the analysing of transactions, and even more of CDD information related to the customer's personal background and to the sources of his or her assets, will constitute an interference with private life.[62] When done by a pubic authority, or by a private entity obliged by law to this effect, such interference must be justified under Article 8 of the Convention, having regard to the requirements developed by the jurisprudence of the Court. These requirements depend on the nature of the interference, notably on the question whether the FIU's gathering of customer data is essentially based on mere data requests, or instead on surveillance of customers.[63]

In order to establish whether the interaction between FIUs and obliged entities is primarily characterised by requests for customer data or instead also constitutes surveillance of customers, one must note that data processing under the AML framework does not merely consist of the gathering and analysing of customer data that would have been obtained by obliged entities irrespective of their AML/CTF obligations. In fact, through the performance of CDD, obliged entities obtain data that is specifically gathered for the very purpose of detecting and, where appropriate, reporting cases of money laundering (and terrorism financing) to the FIU. Consequently, through obliged entities' reporting and further communication, the FIU is thus not merely accessing information that had already been obtained by obliged entities for purposes other than the prevention and detection of criminal activity. Instead, at least insofar as the grounds for an SAR were uncovered through the performance of CDD, the FIU receives information that the reporting obliged entity acquired for the very purpose of determining whether the matter should be reported to the FIU. Consequently, the FIU does not merely request information, but through delegation of this task to obliged entities, effectively subjects customers to continuous monitoring. One must therefore conclude that FIUs' gathering of

---

61 ECtHR (Grand Chamber), Amann v. Switzerland, judgment of 16 February 2000, app. no. 27798/95, para. 65; ECtHR, Vukota-Bojic v. Switzerland, judgment of 18 October 2017, app. no. 61838/10, para. 53.

62 See. ECtHR, Uzun v. Germany, judgment of 2 September 2010, app. no. 35623/05, para. 44; ECtHR, P.G. and J.H. v. United Kingdom, judgment of 25 September 2001, app. no. 44787/98, para. 57.

63 ECtHR, P.G. and J.H. v. United Kingdom, judgment of 25 September 2001, app. no. 44787/98, para. 42; ECtHR, Ben Faiza v. France, judgment of 8 February 2018, app. no. 31446/12, para. 74.

customer data, insofar as it is meant to serve CDD and reporting obligations, constitutes a form of surveillance.

Furthermore, it is important to recall that this surveillance is normally done without the suspicious customer being informed about the FIU's processing of his or her data. Of course, customers may (at least in the context of credit institutions) today increasingly be aware that business relationships and transactions are subject to some level of monitoring by obliged entities, even if they might know little or nothing about the scope of such monitoring. In any case, resulting from the tip-off prohibition imposed on obliged entities,[64] a customer will be informed neither about the obliged entity's suspicion regarding his or her business relationship, nor about the filing of a report by the obliged entity to the FIU, nor about any operational analysis undertaken by the FIU as a result of the report.[65] Therefore, at the latest by the time an obliged entity singles out a particular business relationship or particular transaction as being potentially reportable and therefore performs CDD measures by acquiring additional information from the customer him- or herself or from third parties, this performance of CDD must already be categorised as essentially constituting secret surveillance.

According to Article 8 para. 2 of the Convention, any interference with the right to private life must be "in accordance with the law" and "necessary in a democratic society" for one of a number of purposes, notably "in the interests of national security" or for the "prevention of disorder or crime". While the legal basis for such interference must be accessible and its consequences foreseeable to the person concerned, the European Court of Human Rights has, with regard to secret surveillance measures, developed more detailed requirements. The required precision of the legal basis will depend in particular on the level of interference of the surveillance measure with the individual's right to respect for his or her private life. In any case, "the law must be sufficiently clear in its terms to give citizens an adequate indication of the conditions and circumstances in which the authorities are empowered to resort to any such measures". The Court adds that, "[i]n view of the risk of abuse intrinsic to any system of secret surveillance, such measures must be based on a law that is particularly precise, especially as the technology available for use is continually becoming more sophisticated".[66] Furthermore, it provides that, "because of the lack of public scrutiny and the risk of misuse of power" that are characteristic of secret surveillance measures, "compatibility with the rule of law requires that

64 Comparative Analysis, section III.C.1.c.

65 On the continuing obligation of obliged entities not to disclose, see Comparative Analysis, section III.C.2.c.

66 ECtHR, Uzun v. Germany, judgment of 2 September 2010, app. no. 35623/05, para. 61; see also ECtHR, Vukota-Bojic v. Switzerland, judgment of 18 October 2017, app. no. 61838/10, para. 67.

domestic law provides adequate protection against arbitrary interference with Article 8 rights". The presence of "adequate and effective guarantees against abuse … depends on all the circumstances of the case, such as the nature, scope and duration of the possible measures, the grounds required for ordering them, the authorities competent to permit, carry out and supervise them, and the kind of remedy provided by national law".[67] For the interception of telecommunications and other secret surveillance measures whose level of interference with the right to private life is analogous to such interception,[68] the European Court of Human Rights has developed more specific safeguards that must be set out in statute law. These include in particular:

> the nature of the offences which may give rise to an interception order; a definition of the categories of people liable to have their communications intercepted; a limit on the duration of interception; the procedure to be followed for examining, using and storing the data obtained; the precautions to be taken when communicating the data to other parties; and the circumstances in which intercepted data may or must be erased or destroyed.[69]

2. *Relevance for AML*

The jurisprudence of the European Court of Human Rights highlights the close correlation between a public authority's data processing powers, the extent of the secrecy of its operations and the applicable safeguards. In order for them to ensure effective intelligence gathering, FIUs' data stocks must usually to a significant degree be shielded from external scrutiny in order to honour confidentiality assurances towards foreign FIUs and potentially also towards other public and private sources.[70] The level of safeguards will then depend in particular on the scope of sensitive personal data being secretly processed by FIUs. In this regard, it is of particular importance that FIUs' gathering of financial and CDD data is done in collaboration with obliged entities. In principle, an FIU will in most cases not have extensive direct access to customer data. The more extensive FIUs' access to financial data, the stronger the safeguards that will however be

---

67 ECtHR, Uzun v. Germany, judgment of 2 September 2010, app. no. 35623/05, para. 63; see also ECtHR, Vukota-Bojic v. Switzerland, judgment of 18 October 2017, app. no. 61838/10, para. 68.

68 ECtHR, R.E. v. United Kingdom, judgment of 27 October 2015, app. no. 62498/11, paras. 130–131.

69 ECtHR, Big Brother Watch and others v. United Kingdom, judgment of 13 September 2018, app. no. 58170/13, 62322/14 and 24960/15, para. 307; ECtHR, Weber and Saravia v. Germany, judgment of 29 June 2006, app. no. 54934/00, para. 95.

70 See for example Germany, sections III.I.2. and IV.B.4; Comparative Analysis, sections IV.B.4 and V.F.1.

required. Legislators thus have to make a choice not least between the volume of data available to the FIU and the level of secrecy to which its data gathering and data analyses should be subjected.

In any case, the law must lay down limits on the gathering and recording of information in secret files, for example on "the kind of information that may be recorded, the categories of people against whom surveillance measures such as gathering and keeping information may be taken, the circumstances in which such measures may be taken or the procedure to be followed."[71] To ensure adequate foreseeability of FIUs' powers, legislators will therefore need to specify in particular the types of sensitive information that may be included in the FIU's operational analysis, especially insofar as such information can originate from other confidential sources than SARs (such as domestic and foreign intelligence services). Furthermore, and crucially, to the extent that an FIU should be empowered to request financial or CDD data from an obliged entity without this request being disclosed to the affected customer, the law must conclusively specify the circumstances that shall allow such a request, as well as the nature and scope of the information sought.

Insofar as the FIU would be authorised to secretly access data of such a scope and nature that the level of sensitivity as regards private life is deemed to be comparable to the interception of telecommunications (for example because the scope and content of the financial and CDD data allows detailed insights into a person's behaviour, feelings and opinions), the law would furthermore need to provide additional safeguards to ensure adequate processing. Such safeguards may in particular include an enhanced authorisation regime regarding the FIU's internal decision-making (including for example the requirement that the respective measure be authorised by a senior-rank officer and only on the basis of a written application setting out in detail the grounds for the application).[72] In addition, insofar as an operational analysis is allowed to focus on an activity that neither forms the object of an SAR nor is otherwise suspected of criminality (for example if there are merely indications that a bank account is used by a person who is personally linked to criminal actors, but against whom there are no indications that he or she committed a crime him- or herself), legislators should define the circumstances under which such activities and unsuspected persons may be targeted and the internal procedure for selecting them.[73]

---

71 ECtHR (Grand Chamber), Rotaru v. Romania, judgment of 4 May 2000, app. no. 28341/95, para. 57.

72 ECtHR, R.E. v. United Kingdom, judgment of 27 October 2015, app. no. 62498/11, para. 161.

73 See ECtHR, Weber and Saravia v. Germany, judgment of 29 June 2006, app. no. 54934/00, para. 97; cf. ECtHR, R.E. v. United Kingdom, judgment of 27 October 2015, app. no. 62498/11, paras. 134–136. See similarly ECJ (Grand Chamber), judgment of 21 December 2016 (Tele2 Sverige), C-203/15 and C-698/15, para. 119.

As the European Court of Human Rights furthermore requires the existence of "adequate and effective safeguards against abuse", the law must also provide for procedures to supervise the secret processing of information.[74] As long as the FIU's secret collection of financial and other customer data does not reach a level of intrusiveness comparable to a telecommunications interception, it will normally not be necessary for the individual measure to be authorised by an independent body, although, even if the interception threshold is reached, that body does not necessarily need to be of judicial nature.[75] Otherwise, if this threshold is reached, the affected person must be notified about the data gathering as soon as the notification is no longer liable to jeopardise the investigation.[76] In any case, the overall operational activity of FIUs has to be subject to adequate judicial or independent administrative supervision.[77] This is in particular necessary insofar as details of the FIU's decision-making and the content of the processed data are neither thoroughly scrutinised in subsequent criminal proceedings nor otherwise disclosed to the affected person.[78]

Finally, in order for secret surveillance to be necessary in a democratic society, the purpose of FIUs' operational analyses, when based on covert measures, will usually have to be limited to the protection of national security or to the detection and prevention of serious crime.[79] In order to thus ensure proportionality, FIUs' operational analysis must in this respect not be allowed to aim at criminal conduct that, in the particular instance, cannot be described as significantly more serious than the average level of criminal wrongdoing.[80] This will usually include money laundering only in cases where the offence is linked to organised crime or where the offender, in terms of scope and complexity,

---

74 ECtHR (Grand Chamber), Rotaru v. Romania, judgment of 4 May 2000, app. no. 28341/95, para. 59.

75 See ECtHR, Klass and others v. Germany, judgment of 6 September 1978, app. no. 5029/71, para. 56; ECtHR, Kennedy v. United Kingdom, judgment of 18 May 2010, app. no. 26839/05, paras. 166–169; ECtHR, Uzun v. Germany, judgment of 2 September 2010, app. no. 35623/05, para. 72; ECtHR, R.E. v. United Kingdom, judgment of 27 October 2015, app. no. 62498/11, paras. 133 and 161. See also ECJ (Grand Chamber), judgment of 21 December 2016 (Tele2 Sverige), C-203/15 and C-698/15, para. 120.

76 See ECJ (Grand Chamber), judgment of 21 December 2016 (Tele2 Sverige), C-203/15 and C-698/15, para. 121.

77 See *supra* section II.C.2.

78 See ECtHR, Dumitru Popescu v. Romania, judgment of 26 April 2007, app. no. 71525/01, paras. 75–76 and 78; ECtHR, Uzun v. Germany, judgment of 2 September 2010, app. no. 35623/05, para. 72.

79 See ECtHR, Malone v. United Kingdom, judgment of 2 August 1984, app. no. 8691/79, p. 76; ECtHR, Uzun v. Germany, judgment of 2 September 2010, app. no. 35623/05, para. 80; Weber and Saravia v. Germany, judgment of 29 June 2006, app. no. 54934/00, paras. 114–115; Ben Faiza v. France, judgment of 8 February 2018, app. no. 31446/12, para. 79.

80 See ECtHR, Iordachi and others v. Moldova, judgment of 10 February 2009, app. no. 25198/02, para. 44; ECtHR, R.E. v. United Kingdom, judgment of 27 October 2015, app. no. 62498/11, paras. 57 and 160.

made extensive efforts to conceal the origins of ill-gotten assets or to otherwise frustrate their recovery. FIUs will however frequently not be able to assess the seriousness of the potentially underlying criminality at an early stage of an operational analysis, not least because a small-value transaction may at a later point turn out to be linked to much more serious criminality. The proportionality of FIUs' data processing will therefore need to be ensured not only, and not even primarily, by defining limits on the kind of offences that can motivate an operational analysis, but in particular by limiting the FIU's power to share the results of its analysis with criminal justice authorities to cases of serious crime.[81]

III. THE PILLARS OF ANTI-MONEY LAUNDERING

A. PRELIMINARY REMARKS

AML can be understood as a system whose architecture comprises several distinct but interrelated key elements, or pillars. The role of each of these pillars must be assessed in the context of other areas of law and of the institutions involved in its application. While supranational norm-setters provide general objectives and concepts that national legislators are expected to follow, the design of national legislation will thus largely depend on the particularities of national law. Supranational AML frameworks are therefore only a crucial starting point of the analysis of any national framework, and their demands need to be specified in light of applicable fundamental rights standards and other hallmarks of national law. As a consequence, AML legislation of different countries, even when transposing EU law, can be marked by profound differences and be founded on different premises and indeed objectives.[82] Despite such diversity, it remains the case that, not least due to the FATF Recommendations as a common reference point, national AML systems usually share many common characteristics. Naturally, commonalities are even more developed in the EU Member States, which are bound by more specific rules that those of the FATF.

For drawing conclusions about the current state of the EU framework and, on this basis, developing recommendations for the future, the following observations are based on the analysis of the national AML frameworks covered by this study. The main aim of this approach is to understand how current EU legislation impacts on the national level and what lacunas or inconsistencies surface in the design or the application of national laws. Insofar as the identified

81 See ECtHR, Kennedy v. United Kingdom, judgment of 18 May 2010, app. no. 26839/05, paras. 42 and 46; ECtHR, R.E. v. United Kingdom, judgment of 27 October 2015, app. no. 62498/11, para. 139.

82 See for example Comparative Analysis, sections IV.B.1, IV.D and V.B.

deficiencies could in principle also be remedied by national laws independently of EU legislation, they do not of course necessarily require supranational solutions. Nevertheless, such findings remain relevant not only in view of potential EU harmonisation, but more importantly for understanding where EU (and indeed FATF) standards will need to accommodate sufficient flexibility in order to avoid counterproductive distortions at the national level. Obviously, not least as this study could only analyse a limited number of national frameworks, it certainly does not claim to offer an exhaustive inventory of the deficits suffered by national AML frameworks. Yet, due to the selection of underlying jurisdictions, the following analysis was able to identify major points of contention that, due to concurring observations at national level, provide insights into some major structural weaknesses of supranational frameworks. To this end, the analysis of the relevant laws of Germany, Italy, Spain and the United Kingdom (the latter, while now no longer a Member State, having still implemented recent EU instruments) showed how EU law impacts on national legal orders. The inclusion of Switzerland served to check to what extent the challenges identified for Member States are primarily the cause of EU legislation or are to be expected even of the implementation of FATF standards. This allowed the following analysis to approach EU law both in view of national laws and in view of the global standards on which EU AML law for its part is largely built. Lastly, while it was in many respects tempting to include singular experiences and best practices from countries other than those analysed by this study, this option was discarded for methodological reasons. Much as particular legislative innovations and possible success stories may provide guidance for other jurisdictions, the problem remains that it is, in light of the complexity of AML architectures, usually impossible to deduce meaningful insights without a thorough understanding of the respective national framework. De-contextualised legal transplants offer rather unreliable support, especially with regard to a framework that, as in the case of AML, is heavily dependent on particularities of national constitutional law. They should therefore be treated with caution; in any case, they must not (but unfortunately often seem to) replace a thorough analysis of the structural reasons for one national framework's deficits.

The following analytical structure depicts AML through five central pillars that are considered to be its main functional elements, comprising the following: criminal justice as the elements that addresses money laundering through investigation, prosecution, punishment and confiscation (section III.B); FIUs as the dedicated agencies for analysing financial data and that are meant to provide strategic information on money laundering threats and detect individual cases (section III.C); private sector prevention, that is the function of obliged entities to serve as gatekeepers of the financial system to prevent the inflow of criminal assets (section III.D); private sector reporting, that is the function of obliged entities to provide financial intelligence for the detection and prosecution of crime (section III.E); and AML supervision that serves to ensure obliged entities' compliance with their obligations and provide guidance to this effect (section III.F). Other elements than those mentioned can of course also be of great relevance, not least the scope of investigative powers of criminal justice authorities and confiscation powers. However, they are usually not particular to AML, despite their undeniable relevance for its effectiveness, and are therefore only taken into account for the purpose of contextualisation, not however as research objects in their own right.

B. CRIMINAL JUSTICE

1. *Substantiating the Definition of Money Laundering*

a. Current State

Current definitions of money laundering focus on the concealment and disguise of the proceeds of crime and their integration into the legal economy, extending to those who provide the criminal assets, those who receive them and those who provide assistance in the process. The 2018 EU Directive on combating money laundering by criminal law continues to use this internationally widely accepted understanding.[83] The offence is primarily characterised by the criminal origin of assets and not by objective features that would specify the conduct of the offender. In the absence of findings as to the origin of assets, this definition of money laundering conduct (in particular the acquisition, possession or use of property) thus does not usually allow one to differentiate the wrongdoing of money laundering from legitimate conduct. Only two variations of the offence (that is the concealment or the disguise of the assets' background) can be understood as describing a discernible objective wrongdoing that is independent of the assets' criminal background; however, in the absence of further statutory details on the manner of the concealment or disguise, the application of these two variations is also likely to be guided not by the presence of specific objective features of the conduct, but by the question whether somebody's action aimed to conceal or disguise the criminal origin of assets, and thus again primarily by the origin of the assets and the perpetrators' mindset to this effect.

Given the retrospective focus of the offence, money laundering is usually rather easy to prosecute if the criminal origin of assets is beyond doubt. This makes the offence particularly straightforward to apply if criminal assets are processed by persons that are closely related to the commission of the predicate offence. An orientation of money laundering offences to this effect

[83] Article 3 para. 1 of Directive (EU) 2018/1673 of 23 October 2018.

has been further amplified by calls from the FATF and now in particular by Directive (EU) 2018/1673 to extend criminal liability for money laundering to the predicate offender, thus to so-called self-laundering.[84] The offence of money laundering is however much more difficult to apply to those forms of processing of criminal assets where the launderer is far removed in time and space from the predicate offence, even though EU law now provides that a conviction for money laundering is possible "without it being necessary to establish all the factual elements or all circumstances relating to that criminal activity, including the identity of the perpetrator".[85] While the predicate offence thus has to be proven only in a rather approximate manner, it must usually still be established beyond reasonable doubt that the assets' origin is in fact criminal.[86] This poses great problems for example in cases of long chains of complex and cross-border transactions where the launderer was not involved in the commission of the predicate offence and might not even know from where exactly the assets originated. Criminal justice authorities must then undertake an investigation that it is clear from the very start will be time – and resource – intensive. Furthermore, not least due to the complexity of the subject matter and the heavy reliance on evidence from foreign jurisdictions, criminal justice authorities will have many reasons to doubt that such an investigation will, after many months or even years, ultimately lead to a successful confirmation of the assets' criminal origin. In other words, the outcome of an investigation into more complex forms of money laundering offences can from an investigator's perspective often appear too speculative to undertake it in the first place, even if the criminal origin of the assets looks likely. As a result, investigations into money laundering will in practice oftentimes be quickly discontinued even in cases where, due to a client's behaviour vis-à-vis an obliged entity, it seems rather obvious that somebody wants to conceal the background of a business dealing. Incidentally, this can also explain why in many cases suspicious conduct is reported by obliged entities but then not followed up by investigative authorities – for dissimulating conduct by

84 Article 3 para. 5 of Directive (EU) 2018/1673 of 23 October 2018.

85 Article 3 para. 3(b) of Directive (EU) 2018/1673 of 23 October 2018.

86 For less demanding standards, see notably the evidentiary thresholds applicable in the United Kingdom, section VII.A.1, which go further by merely requiring circumstantial evidence, allowing courts to base the finding of assets' criminal origin notably on the suspect's lifestyle and thereby ultimately on the question whether the origin of assets can be explained by legal income. A similar approach is also followed in Spain, section VII.A.1. Such evidentiary approach does effectively further facilitate the application of the money laundering offence against persons who are clearly related to criminal activity. Ultimately, such a lowering of the evidentiary standard is therefore further strengthening the tendency to use the offence as a prosecutorial tool against predicate offences; not however facilitating the prosecution of laundering committed by perpetrators whose criminal involvement, notably in light of their seemingly legitimate professional activity, is less obvious.

a client in itself is usually in this respect irrelevant from the criminal law's point of view as long as one is not able to establish the asset's criminal origin.

b. Challenges

Due to their breadth and lack and specificity, (i) today's money laundering offences suffer from ambiguity as regards their actual purpose, an ambiguity that surfaces in particular with regard to the criminalisation of self-laundering; (ii) the resulting uncertainty frequently invites incoherent policy that fails to address primary threats to the integrity of financial institutions and that might even constitute a major obstacle to the wider acceptance of AML efforts.

(i) Ambiguity of money laundering offences and related incoherence of prosecutorial policy first and foremost result from uncertainty about those offences' objectives. At first sight, their rationale could seem rather straightforward. A great deal of criminality is profit-driven. To enjoy their ill-gotten gains, as well as to avert asset recovery by the competent authorities, criminals will usually need to insert these gains into the legal economy. In order to impede predicate offences, it does therefore seem sensible to reduce opportunities for criminal assets to access legitimate businesses and at the same time increase the likelihood for predicate offenders to be detected when undertaking business activities.[87] Insofar as individuals assist criminals to overcome or circumvent regulatory barriers that have been erected between illegal and legal economies, they might then, according to this view, justly be subjected to sanctions. This understanding of the prohibition of money laundering, which would in essence treat it as a form of assistance to the predicate offender, can be derived from the wording of the money laundering definition especially insofar as it criminalises "the conversion or transfer of property ... for the purpose ... of assisting any person who is involved in the commission of [criminal] activity to evade the legal consequences of that person's action".[88]

However, the rationale for money laundering as a form of assistance to the predicate offence does not fit together with the criminalisation of self-laundering, that is money laundering by persons who were already involved in the commission of the predicate offence. Self-laundering does in fact provide a focal point for understanding the criminal policy objective underlying the "concealment" and "disguise" variations of money laundering. For insofar as the criminalisation of self-laundering allows for charges against one and the same person for both the predicate offence and for subsequent money laundering, and if self-laundering is nevertheless meant to constitute a serious offence in its

87 On this essentially predicate offence-focused rational, see *supra* section I.A.1.

88 Article 3 para. 1(a) of Directive (EU) 2018/1673 of 23 October 2018.

own right, it becomes clear that the wrong of money laundering is necessarily fundamentally different from the wrong of the predicate offence and not merely a form of assistance to the latter. Obviously, the core objective of punishing the concealment and disguise of criminal assets cannot consist merely of the aim of deterring or detecting predicate offences, for this would mean that in this respect the criminalisation of money laundering would add little to nothing to the criminalisation of the predicate offence itself. Due to the lack of clarity, under EU and national laws, of the distinct wrong of money laundering,[89] prosecutors and judges will often find it difficult to make sense of the offence. After all, in any criminal justice system based on the moral credibility of its judgments,[90] courts need to persuasively explain why the conduct constitutes serious criminality and is deserving of punishment additional to the punishment imposed for the predicate offence.

Anti-money laundering, including the prohibition of money laundering, does of course also serve the purpose of shielding financial institutions from the inflow of proceeds of crime, an objective that is, in principle, distinct from addressing predicate offences.[91] Yet in current definitions of money laundering, this objective does not become very clear either.[92] Some indication of a distinct wrong to this effect is provided insofar as the offence of money laundering mentions the concealment or disguise of illegal assets, because those two variations imply wrongs that are not necessarily closely linked to the predicate offence, in particular violations of laws aimed at ensuring the transparency of financial dealings. Other variations of money laundering, in particular the acquisition, possession or use of assets, do not however allow one to discern a wrong that would, in the absence of findings as to the predicate offence, explain the reprehensibility of the conduct, thereby reiterating uncertainty regarding the offence's objective as a whole. EU law does now of course clarify that Member States are not required to criminalise the last-mentioned variations also in the form of self-laundering,[93] thereby indicating that in this respect the offence of money laundering pursues a different purpose than the concealment and disguise variations.[94] While this exception confirms that the concealment or

89 See P Alldridge, What went wrong with money laundering law?, 2016, pp. 34–39.

90 See A von Hirsch, Deserved Criminal Sentences: An Overview, 2017, pp. 29–44; R Williams, Criminal Law in England and Wales: Just Another Form of Regulatory Tool?, in M Dyson/ B Vogel (eds.), The Limits of Criminal Law: Anglo-German Concepts and Principles, 2018, pp. 217–234.

91 See *supra* section I.A.1.

92 See Comparative Analysis, section II.B.1.

93 Article 3 para. 5 of Directive (EU) 2018/1673 of 23 October 2018.

94 In line with the two primary objectives of AML (see *supra* section I.A.1.), it would appear that the wrongfulness of the acquisition, possession or use of criminal assets consists in the fact that the perpetrator provides assistance to the predicate offender and/or (if he or she is acting for an obliged entity) allows the inflow of criminal assets into the financial system.

disguise variations entail wrongs that are distinct from the predicate offence, it however adds little to clarify the substance of these wrongs.

(ii) As a consequence of the uncertainty surrounding the rationale of money laundering offences, criminal justice authorities will often remain ignorant as to why they should charge a person with money laundering, and which criteria they should use, at sentencing or in the context of procedural diversion strategies, in order to determine the seriousness of a conduct that falls under the wording of the money laundering definition. In the absence of a coherent explanation for the criminalisation of money laundering, some will even assume that punishment of self-laundering constitutes double punishment for essentially one and the same wrongdoing.[95] Application of the money laundering offence (which might in some cases even be equipped with a more severe sentencing range than that applicable to the predicate offence) can then sharply conflict with societal perceptions of wrongfulness. Such a discrepancy between on the one hand legal norms that – as in the case of money laundering – designate an offence as "serious" and on the other hand the lack of a sufficiently clear justification that explains this seriousness in a way that is coherent with social conceptions of wrongfulness, undermines political as well as judicial comprehension of the offence of money laundering and can thereby be detrimental to the wider effectiveness of AML.

Questions about the rationale of the criminalisation of money laundering are closely connected to another area of concern, namely that money laundering charges are in many cases used as little more than as an instrument to facilitate the prosecution of (suspected) predicate offenders.[96] The relatively low standard of proof of money laundering offences pertaining to the establishment of the predicate offence does indeed offer a strong incentive for criminal justice authorities to charge and convict the predicate offender only or primarily for money laundering. For it is in this case not even necessary to show that the suspect did participate in the commission of the predicate offence, provided that it is established that he or she was aware of the asset's criminal origin or, depending on the scope of the respective national money laundering offence, that he or she suspected or must have be aware of such origin.[97] However, if the offence of money laundering is in fact used as a tool to punish predicate offences, it is overlooked that the predicate offence and money laundering are two distinct wrongs whose respective seriousness must be assessed on the basis of distinct

---

95 MF Cuéllar, The tenuous relationship between the fight against money laundering and the disruption of criminal finance, 93 *The Journal of Criminal Law and Criminology* (2003), pp. 412–414.

96 MF Cuéllar, The tenuous relationship between the fight against money laundering and the disruption of criminal finance, 93 *The Journal of Criminal Law and Criminology* (2003), pp. 405–410; V Zoppei, Anti-Money Laundering Law: Socio-Legal Perspectives on the Effectiveness of German Practices, 2017, p. 189 f.

97 See comparative analysis *supra* section II.B.1.b.

considerations. At least insofar as predicate offenders are concerned, the degree of wrongfulness of money laundering conduct must not primarily and, in the absence of detailed evidence to this effect, not even to a significant extent depend on the predicate offence. Misconceptions about the nature of the wrong of money laundering, and thus of its criminal policy function, are particularly evident when predicate offenders are charged only with money laundering and the predicate offence is not further investigated. Such cases suggest that the respective authorities do not fully appreciate the difference between predicate offences and money laundering and in particular that the application of both offences must follow categorically different objectives.

Resulting from uncertainty about the rationale of the money laundering prohibition as well as from the attractiveness of the offence from an evidentiary point of view, the competent authorities will frequently fail to invest energy and resources on cases in which the origin of assets has been successfully concealed through elaborate dissimulation methods. Instead, they will focus on less complex dissimulation efforts and on cases where the criminal origin of assets is not dissimulated at all.[98] Current money laundering offences thus effectively discourage criminal justice authorities from investigating suspects who are not directly related to predicate offenders and where, as a result, the tainted origin of assets is not easy to establish. This notably concerns offenders who act as professional service providers and, to this end, design complex laundering schemes for predicate offenders. For professional launderers will in many (if not most) cases have no close connection to,[99] and therefore also no detailed knowledge of, the origin of assets, not least because neither they nor their criminal clients have an interest in sharing such information. In this respect, the structural dependence of current money laundering offences on the assets' criminal origin frequently requires the criminal justice authorities to know more about the origin of the assets than does the launderer him- or herself. Today's definition of the offence of money laundering thereby essentially fails to deal with those activities that, for the purpose of preventing the inflow of criminal assets into the legal economy, seem most relevant.

---

98 See for example on the one hand the impressive number of investigations for "money laundering", and on the other hand the number of investigations for "high-end money laundering" in FATF, Mutual Evaluation Report United Kingdom, 2018, pp. 58 and 64 respectively. Note in this respect Crown Prosecution Service, Legal Guidance Proceeds Of Crime Act 2002 Part 7 – Money Laundering Offences, as updated on 1 March 2018: Charging practice, plea acceptance and other issues "Mixed cases" (where the perpetrator of the predicate offence can also be charged with laundering): "A money laundering charge ought to be considered where the proceeds are more than *de minimis* in any circumstances where the defendant who is charged with the underlying offence has done more than simply consume his proceeds of crime. A charge … of possession of laundered proceeds, however, may not be necessary, for instance where proceeds were simply 'kept under the bed'."

99 See M Levi/M Soudijn, Understanding the Laundering of Organized Crime Money, *Crime and Justice* (2020), section III.B.

c. Reform

Following from the above observations, it is desirable to reform the criminal law in a way that reinforces money laundering offences' practical relevance as an instrument to counter the inflow of criminal assets into the legal economy. Unlike current definitions of money laundering, (i) the focus of a reformed money laundering offence should lie not on assets' origin, (ii) but on the perpetrator's conduct, and thereby at the same time (iii) provide judicial authorities with guidance as to how to assess the seriousness of individual money laundering offences.

- Avoid a further blurring of the boundaries of money laundering offences resulting from the "all-crimes approach"

(i) Instead of being merely a supplement to charges for profit-generating predicate offences or a tool to lower the evidentiary burden in this respect, money laundering offences should be the primary criminal policy tool to address conduct that, while not necessarily being closely connected to the commission of predicate offences, ultimately helps predicate offenders by providing the circumvention of AML as a service.[100] More recent developments in the definition of money laundering offences might appear to have already moved in the proposed direction. In particular, some national legal frameworks have extended the scope of predicate offences to all crimes,[101] thereby effectively lessening the emphasis on predicate offences. The so-called "all-crimes approach" avoids the need to specify even the type of the predicate offence if, in light of the perpetrator's conduct (in particular because of extensive concealment efforts), it is clear that the origin of the assets cannot be anything other than criminal. Despite this lesser emphasis on the assets' origin, the all-crimes approach is however unlikely to provide a satisfactory remedy to the above-mentioned deficiencies. For as long as the conduct of money laundering is not defined more clearly than has so far been the case, less specificity regarding the origin of assets will even reinforce the tendency to use money laundering offences as a convenient tool to punish predicate offenders. More importantly, if the offence of money laundering does not convey a clear vision of the pursued criminal policy objectives, criminal justice authorities will, also under an all-crimes approach, often see little incentive to focus investigative efforts on conduct where, despite or indeed because of complex dissimulation efforts, the criminal origin of the assets is merely highly likely but not certain. Furthermore, given that today's

---

100 For findings on the market characteristics of money laundering, see M Levi/P Reuter, Money Laundering, 34 *Crime and Justice* (2006), pp. 320–322.

101 See Spain, section II.B.1.a.i, and United Kingdom, section II.B.1.a.i.

definitions of money laundering often already suffer from a lack of clarity as regards their conduct elements, an additional blurring of the boundaries by the all-crimes approach further weakens the rule of law credentials of money laundering offences. For the definition of money laundering, because of its criminalisation of *prima facie* inconspicuous conduct, already operates at the borders, or even in a grey area, of what is required of criminal statutes under the legality principle, according to which criminal conduct must be clearly defined by law.[102]

- Align money laundering offences with CDD obligations while insofar attenuating the relevance of the detection of predicate offences

(ii) To overcome an overly strong conceptual dependence of money laundering offences on the assets' origin and at the same time ensure that criminal conduct is primarily defined by clear objective wrongdoing, legislators should aim at adapting the criminal law to the CDD obligations provided under preventive AML law. This would offer an opportunity to strengthen the effectiveness of preventive rules while at the same time leading to an enforcement practice in which criminal investigations into money laundering are only incidentally concerned with predicate offences and predominantly with the aim of protecting obliged entities from being abused or infiltrated by criminal actors. Convergence between the criminal law definition of money laundering and preventive AML laws would thus ensure that the criminal law is better integrated into the wider AML landscape and focuses on those actors who, through their deliberate violation of preventive safeguards, constitute the primary door openers for the inflow of criminal assets into the legal economy. The offence of money laundering should thus operate largely independently of the detection of predicate offences and primarily target professional money laundering providers and crime-facilitating employees of obliged entities. More precisely, instead of focusing on the identification of criminal assets, the criminal law should emphasis liability for efforts to conceal the background of a business relationship or transaction.

- Concretise the concealment and disguise variations of money laundering as a fraud pertaining to key CDD risk parameters in cases where a legal origin of assets is doubtful

Resulting from this objective, the money laundering definition should be closely tied to CDD obligations that aim to ensure transparency of financial dealings. In most cases of money laundering, the (prospective) client or an employee

---

102 See ECtHR, Navalnyye v. Russia, judgment of 17 October 2017, app. no. 101/15, paras. 59–68.

of an obliged entity will need to violate at least some of these transparency obligations in order to convince an obliged entity to enter into or continue a business relationship. Of particular relevance are the customer's duties to disclose his or her identity, the identity of the beneficial owner, the purpose and nature of the envisaged business relationship and the origin of the assets. As regards employees of obliged entities, of particular relevance are obligations to communicate CDD-related information internally to competent colleagues, in particular to compliance officers. Accordingly, insofar as money laundering is characterised by the "concealment or disguise" of assets,[103] legislators should specify the objective wrongdoing and in turn abandon the offence's emphasis on the criminal origin of assets. A reformed definition of money laundering through "concealment or disguise" should thus consist of the following elements:

- deliberately making a false representation to the employee of an obliged entity or to the employee of a third party entrusted with the performance of CDD,
- about one's own or about a client's identity, the beneficial owner's identity, the purpose and nature of the envisaged business relationship or the origin of assets,
- in order to enter into or continue a business relationship with an obliged entity or perform a transaction through an obliged entity, or in order to help a third person to enter into or continue a business relationship with or perform a transaction through this or another obliged entity,
- in the knowledge of specific circumstances pertaining to the origin of assets and to the products, services or transaction methods used in the business relationship or transaction that suggest an obvious possibility that the assets' origin is illegal.

Based on this definition, criminal liability would no longer require that assets were in fact of criminal origin, but instead the two following elements. First, the suspect must have intentionally misled an obliged entity about his or her or a third person's identity, beneficial owner, business purpose or the origin of assets, with the aim of convincing the obliged entity to enter into or continue a business relationship or perform a transaction. Second, in view of the particular circumstances of the case any belief in a legal origin of the assets must have been merely speculative and the suspect must have been aware of this. Such an offence would in many cases significantly reduce the evidential burden, but at the same time would ensure that criminal liability extends only to sufficiently blameworthy conduct. For the new offence would only cover individuals who

103 Article 3 para. 1(b) of Directive (EU) 2018/1673 of 23 October 2018.

deliberately circumvent obliged entities' preventive measures knowing that their conduct will probably allow the integration of illegal assets into the legal economy.

- Emphasise that enforcement practice should focus on those forms of money laundering that are characterised by extensive and complex concealment efforts

(iii) Moreover, under the proposed offence, it would also become clear that the seriousness of varying acts of "concealment" and "disguise" of money laundering depends on the complexity of the deception and on the volume of assets, and not on the nature of the predicate offence. The offence would therefore at the same time provide guidance to investigators and judges to focus efforts and resources on complex and professional laundering activities. If scarce investigative resources so require, laundering schemes of low complexity could then be diverted from the criminal justice system or otherwise dealt with in a way that complies with the rationales of AML. For irrespective of whether the criminal prohibition of the concealment and disguise of criminal assets is primarily taken to serve the prevention of the inflow of such assets into the financial system, or instead to serve the production of greater financial transparency with the ultimate aim of facilitating the investigation of predicate offences, the nature of these wrongs is primarily characterised by the level of deception they entail, not by the wrong of the predicate offence.[104]

2. *Clarifying the Role of Obliged Entities in the Investigation of Crime*

a. Current State

In addition to the protection of the integrity of the financial sector, AML serves the objective of strengthening the ability of the competent authorities to detect and investigate money laundering and predicate offences and confiscate proceeds of crime.[105] These aspects underlie particular obliged entities' duty to file SARs,[106] and the prohibition imposed on them to inform suspicious customers as well as other third parties about the filing of an SAR or about requests from the FIU.[107] The current AML framework is thereby shaped by

104 To this effect also MF Cuéllar, The tenuous relationship between the fight against money laundering and the disruption of criminal finance, 93 *The Journal of Criminal Law and Criminology* (2003), p. 418.

105 See *supra* section I.A.1.

106 Article 33 para. 1(a) of Directive (EU) 2015/849 of 20 May 2015, as amended by Directive (EU) 2018/843 of 30 May 2018.

107 Article 39 para. 1 of Directive (EU) 2015/849 of 20 May 2015.

the idea that criminal investigations will regularly be triggered by SARs, and thus attributes a central place to the ability of obliged entities to detect criminal wrongdoing through the performance of CDD. While continuing to attribute a key role to the initial detection of crime by obliged entities, not least today's design of the function of FIUs does however indicate that, in the eyes of the EU legislator, increasing reliance may also be placed on an obliged entity's ability to supplement information that the FIUs or criminal justice authorities already obtained from other sources (for example through SARs from another obliged entity or through criminal investigations).[108] In fact, insofar as FIUs are not limited to exclusively relying on SARs as starting point for their operational analysis,[109] the law implicitly acknowledges that an SAR will, by itself, often not provide sufficient substance to trigger a criminal investigation. That FIUs shall now have the power to request information from obliged entities independently of the prior filing of an SARs[110] further confirms that EU law sees individual SARs increasingly as only one source of information for the purpose of detecting money laundering, a source that will in many cases need to be complemented by other SARs, information requested by the FIU, and information from criminal justice and other security authorities. In any case, the identification of criminal assets is no longer only a one-way street of information flowing from reporting obliged entities via FIUs to criminal justice authorities. Instead, the identification of criminal assets increasingly relies on a collaborative effort between FIUs and obliged entities that will entail the filing of SARs, but potentially also information requests from FIUs addressed to other authorities and other obliged entities, enhanced monitoring of suspected customers by obliged entities as part of their CDD obligations,[111] and follow-up reporting by obliged entities to the FIU.

Despite the moving away from a one-way reporting regime to a more collaborative regime, EU law does not currently provide much detail about the cooperation between obliged entities and FIUs or between obliged entities and criminal justice authorities. Questions in this respect arise not least as regards the rules applicable to the monitoring of business relationships that have already been reported to the FIU, in particular in view of the fact that such monitoring may in essence constitute covert surveillance of the suspected customer.[112] This would be the case especially if obliged entities' obligation to provide information

---

108 See Comparative Analysis, section IV.D.

109 See Article 32 para. 3 of Directive (EU) 2015/849 of 20 May 2015.

110 Article 32 para. 9 of Directive (EU) 2015/849 of 20 May 2015, as amended by Directive (EU) 2018/843 of 30 May 2018: "each FIU shall be able to request, obtain and use information from any obliged entity for the purpose [of preventing, detecting and combating money laundering and terrorist financing] even if no prior report is filed".

111 Article 13 para. 1 s. 1 (d) and Article 18 para. 2 s. 2 of Directive (EU) 2015/849 of 20 May 2015, as amended by Directive (EU) 2018/843 of 30 May 2018.

112 See *supra* section II.C.1.

to the FIU, or directly to criminal justice authorities, would go beyond a mere screening of available customer data and instead extend to information about a customer's current and future conduct. More importantly still, while EU law has seemingly moved beyond the idea that FIUs' operational analyses should be exclusively guided by SARs, it so far does not clarify whether the FIU or criminal justice authorities may be authorised to provide obliged entities with specific information about particular crimes or particular suspects in order to trigger enhanced CDD.[113] Some national frameworks have now already allowed the competent authorities to share with obliged entities strategic and sometimes even personal data from recently concluded or ongoing criminal investigations,[114] a practice often called "public–private partnerships".[115] Such rather specific information can enable obliged entities to screen their data stocks in a much more specific and timely way than would be possible when done on the basis of rather broad and abstract typologies produced by supranational or national bodies, not least by supervisory authorities. Currently, the EU AML framework does not however clarify whether or to what extent FIUs and criminal justice authorities should be authorised to utilise obliged entities' enhanced CDD measures for monitoring suspects, be it for purely preventive purposes or for conducting criminal investigations.

b. Challenges

Data sharing by criminal justice authorities and FIUs (i) can contribute in particular to investigations against predicate offenders, though not necessarily to an improvement of obliged entities' gatekeeping function. Data sharing can take different shapes, (ii) depending primarily on the type of the respective data, and can then pose significant challenges to both (iii) the rights of suspects and (iv) unrelated third parties, as well as to (v) the integrity of criminal proceedings.

(i) Before addressing challenges to data sharing by competent authorities, a preliminary caveat seems necessary. The more specific or even personalised the data shared by authorities with obliged entities, the less appropriate it would seem to label the sharing as an instrument that serves CDD in a conventional sense. For the provision of data by the competent authorities will often not so much be about helping an obliged entity to identify criminal customers for the

---

113 See European Union, section V.A.1, and Comparative Analysis, section V.A.1.

114 See United Kingdom, section V.A.1; for comprehensive accounts of these developments, see NJ Maxwell/D Artingstall, The Role of Financial Information-Sharing Partnerships in the Disruption of Crime, RUSI Occasional Paper, 2017.

115 In this vein already P Reuter/EM Truman, Chasing Dirty Money: The Fight against Money Laundering, 2004, pp. 176–177. To designate new forms of public–private information sharing as "public–private partnerships" is admittedly somewhat misleading, as this label is also appropriate for describing AML as a whole.

purpose of reporting them to the authorities, but rather about enlisting the obliged entity in the monitoring of customers that are already of interest to these authorities or about using the framework of AML to collect information outside the formal requirements of criminal procedure law. If the competent authorities share specific names of individual convicts or suspects, the use of such information by obliged entities can resemble more a targeted surveillance or a partial outsourcing of a criminal investigations than the performance of preventive due diligence.[116] An increasingly collaborative approach between investigative authorities and obliged entities will in this respect not constitute an improvement of conventional CDD, but instead something different.[117] While such public–private partnerships can supplement the existing AML framework, they are unlikely to significantly improve the quality of obliged entities' risk detection and thus gatekeeping capacity outside the confines of the particular information disclosed by the competent authorities. It is important to keep this point in mind, especially insofar as the success of information sharing is sometimes measured by the number of SARs attributed to shared data. Obviously, if the competent authorities provide obliged entities with information related to ongoing criminal investigations, it is rather likely that especially big financial institutions, in light of their extensive customer data stocks, will be able to provide the authorities with some actionable information. One must however not confuse this with the capacity of obliged entities to effectively prevent the inflow of criminal assets into the financial sector. It is one thing for authorities to solicit the assistance of obliged entities in an already ongoing investigation by providing these entities with personal or similarly specific data, and another to enhance obliged entities' ability to detect criminality on their own by providing them with typologies and other strategic data.[118]

(ii) Moving beyond these preliminary observations, one must note that any assessment of data sharing by competent authorities does primarily depend on the nature of the data. Unlike traditional typologies that largely focus on rather abstract information, public–private data sharing mechanisms often aim to provide obliged entities with a more specific or detailed knowledge about strategic threats and vulnerabilities, money laundering methods or about the underlying predicate offences.[119] As regards strategic information, criminal justice authorities may for example disclose details about types of crime in

---

116 For the form of obliged entities' enhanced CDD obligations, including enhanced continuous monitoring of customer relationships, see European Union, section III.A.3.b., and for example Germany, section III.A.3.b.

117 See also United Kingdom, section V.A.1.

118 On the sharing of information by supervisory authorities and FIUs for the purpose of improving the performance of CDD, see *infra* section III.F.2.

119 See NJ Maxwell, Expanding the Capability of Financial Information-Sharing Partnerships, RUSI Occasional Paper, 2019, pp. 6–7.

a particular country or region that are likely to lead to money laundering or details about particular money laundering methods frequently used by specific criminal groups. In this case, public–private partnerships will not necessarily entail the provision of personal data, but nevertheless provide information that is sufficiently specific to raise relatively detailed red flags within obliged entities' CDD. The more narrowly defined such information is (for example by pointing to a particular kind of criminality or to particular criminal groups within a specific city), the more targeted the information sharing, possibly even up to a point where obliged entities are enabled to identity a small number of targeted individuals even if their identity had not explicitly been disclosed by the authorities. Beyond that, the provided data may in principle also include information about specific individuals with the aim of uncovering their past or monitoring their future conduct or of incentivising the obliged entity to screen other individuals so far unknown to the authorities who were or are in contact with the primary target.

(iii) The question about the type of information that might be shared by criminal justice authorities or FIUs already points to one central challenge to such a mechanism: the risk that individuals may be stigmatised and economically and socially excluded if they are explicitly identified or otherwise, in the case of rather narrow risk parameters, if they fall within the confines of a category of people considered of interest by the competent authorities. The problem of potential discrimination and de-risking due to overly generalising risk patterns is of course not something new to AML,[120] but it is likely to become even more prominent in the case of more frequent and more extensive data sharing by the competent authorities. It is evident that such mechanisms can be particularly fruitful if based on information originating from ongoing or recently concluded investigations by criminal justice authorities. The authorities might then for example inform the receiving obliged entities about a particular suspicion that they have against a more or less clearly defined group of people or even against specific individuals. It is then important to remember that awareness of criminal investigations against a client does normally constitute a central parameter for obliged entities' CDD[121] and very often leads to the termination of the business relationship, not least in banking practice. The more data is shared by criminal

---

120 See *infra* section III.D.1.b.

121 To this effect also European Banking Authority et al., Joint Guidelines under Articles 17 and 18(4) of Directive (EU) 2015/849 on simplified and enhanced customer due diligence and the factors credit and financial institutions should consider when assessing the money laundering and terrorist financing risk associated with individual business relationships and occasional transactions of 4 January 2018, para. 20, which explicitly mentions allegations of criminality against the customer as a potentially relevant risk factor, and further specifies that "[f]irms should note that the absence of criminal convictions alone may not be sufficient to dismiss allegations of wrongdoing."

justice authorities or FIUs, the more frequently such de-risking is likely to lead to the termination of provision of banking and related other services to suspects and closely related individuals. Such data sharing-induced de-risking practice is problematic not only because, as a collateral consequence, unrelated and law-abiding clients may also be subject to preventive CDD measures, but in particular because the respective suspicion might not be founded on sufficient evidence and at a later stage of the investigation be discarded as erroneous in a court of law. By then it will often be too late to undo severe economic and social damage that has already unjustly been caused to the affected individuals or companies. This effect is particularly severe if obliged entities are allowed or even expected to share information that they received from the authorities with other obliged entities inside or even outside a group of companies, as this will multiply the effects of premature or otherwise erroneous investigative leads. After all, criminal justice authorities' initial suspicion, and even more so a suspicion of FIUs, is frequently based on as-yet uncorroborated information and not on conclusive evidence. It is precisely because of the oftentimes rather hypothetical quality of such intelligence that limitations on suspects' rights before a criminal conviction – such as asset freezing – are usually conditioned by rather demanding procedural safeguards.[122] If, as a result of a criminal suspicion that through public–private information sharing finds its way into CDD practice, clients are comprehensively blacklisted by the financial sector, they might find it hard or even impossible to dispose of their assets, leading to what can then resemble a comprehensive freezing of the client's assets.[123] Especially data emanating from ongoing criminal investigations thus entails a significant risk of individuals as well as companies being subjected to detrimental measures in the form of extensive de-risking without the underlying suspicion having been thoroughly tested or even disclosed.

(iv) Data sharing by competent authorities can, however, also impact on persons that are neither suspects nor related to suspects. For insofar as the sharing is usually meant to trigger a subsequent processing of customer data by obliged entities, such a mechanism can question the fundamental separation between the authorities and the data stocks of obliged entities. Criminal justice authorities or the FIU may for example provide obliged entities with a typology about certain criminal conduct (such as the national origin, profession and other personal traits of the offender for example) in the expectation that the obliged entities filter their data stocks in order to identify a narrow group of individuals that can then be subject to further, more targeted investigative measures. If the receiving obliged entities are legally obliged or otherwise willing to comply with the authorities' demand, the data sharing mechanism opens up the possibility

122 For an example of non-conviction based confiscation, see Germany, section VII.A.2.

123 See United Kingdom, section V.H.

for competent authorities to make extensive use of obliged entities' customer data stocks. Of course, FIUs are, under the current EU AML framework, already allowed to request information from obliged entities, thereby enabling the FIU to indirectly access extensive private data stocks, especially those of financial institutions. The same will usually be true for criminal justice authorities. Yet, information requests are normally only meant to retrieve a more or less specific set of information (in particular information related to a suspicious transaction), not, however, also to require the requested obliged entity to perform an extensive analysis of their customer data or to monitor particular customers. In contrast, insofar as a public-private data sharing mechanism results in criminal justice authorities or FIUs defining detailed criteria used by obliged entities in analysing and monitoring their customer data, it can become increasingly difficult to say that this processing is still in the hands of the respective obliged entity. In other words, the more competent authorities get, through the provision of personal or strategic data, intimately involved in the definition of obliged entities' search algorithms, and thus the greater their influence over obliged entities data processing, the more this formally private processing becomes a measure of competent authorities. Given the vast customer data stocks of obliged entities, such an ability to indirectly process this data can potentially multiply the amount of personal data screened by competent authorities and FIUs and then raise serious proportionality concerns. As obliged entities' customer data stocks will primarily include data of persons that are not involved in the commission of crime, an indirect processing of obliged entities' data stocks by competent authorities exposes a high number of innocent persons to the risk of being treated as suspects.[124] As highlighted by the Court of Justice of the European Union, access by competent authorities to vast private sector data stocks thus entails considerable risks of an unlawful use of such data.[125] Such risks are to some extent already concomitant of the performance of CDD when performed by obliged entities without any assistance from competent authorities, in that customers may be unjustly subject to an SAR. However, the potential for discriminatory or otherwise unlawful processing of customer data significantly increases if obliged entities' filter function is diminished and private data pools thereby effectively become the object of data processing by competent authorities.

(v) Besides their potential impact on both suspects and unrelated third persons, data sharing by criminal justice authorities and FIUs also entail risks for the integrity of criminal proceedings. For data collected through criminal investigations can lead to a partial disclosure of sensitive information, not

---

124 See Germany, section IV.D.4.

125 See *supra* section II.B.1.

only about suspects and witnesses but also about investigative strategies of the authorities. The more detailed the disclosure, the higher the risk that sharing will prejudice ongoing or future investigations by tipping off suspects or otherwise providing criminal actors with information about ways to avoid detection. Even if regulation imposes a duty of confidentiality on receiving obliged entities, for example in that shared sensitive information must not be widely shared within the receiving obliged entity, and even if the use of the data is tightly restricted to particular purposes, the risk of abuse can be considerable. For oversight and accountability standards applicable to competent authorities are normally far greater than respective standards in the private sector.[126] Laws can of course threaten employees of obliged entities with sanctions in the event of the illegal processing of shared data, but the ability of the competent authorities to detect data breaches and resulting abuse within large private institutions will remain much more constrained[127] than their ability to detect similar wrongdoing committed within their own institutional sphere. Insofar as individual employees of obliged entities might undergo background checks and thereby receive official security clearance, the risk of an abuse is potentially somewhat limited. However, as the shared data must always be somehow used within the obliged entity's CDD decision-making, the chance of an unwarranted disclosure of sensitive information to colleagues remains even if the security-cleared employee acts in good faith. In the absence of robust safeguards to control the use of shared data by the receiving obliged entity, trust between participants of a data sharing mechanism is obviously as insufficient a safeguard as it is for any other handling of sensitive information by state authorities. The risk of abuse is heightened if participating private actors wield considerable influence over the selection of topics and objectives addressed within the mechanism, as this can provide malign actors in the private sector with opportunities to solicit sensitive information from the authorities. Finally, risks for the integrity of criminal proceedings as well as for suspects and other affected persons will be increased where the data sharing between public and private authorities is done in the absence of adequate oversight mechanisms. For the secrecy of such public–private interaction can easily stimulate an excessive disclosure of information that, while being detrimental from the viewpoint of broader policy considerations, is perceived as mutually beneficial by the acting public and private agents, not least because both sides can have a significant reputational stake in the successful outcome of a particular partnership. If not equipped with adequate safeguards, the exchange of information can then effectively entail a

[126] On this weakness see in more detail *infra* section III.D.2.b.

[127] On the challenges posed to the detection of internal deliberate wrongdoing, see also *supra* section III.F.1.b.

considerable risk of corruption, in extreme cases even allowing private actors to support the authorities against competitors while at the same time shielding themselves from scrutiny by those same authorities.[128]

c. Reform

To address the above concerns, public-private data sharing mechanisms must be equipped with adequate safeguards. Insofar as these mechanisms are meant to support ongoing criminal investigations or FIUs' operational analyses,[129] the shape of such safeguards will depend on whether the data sharing (i) targets already known suspects and persons related to them or rather (ii) aims at identifying yet unknown suspects. In any case, the law (iii) needs to address risks for the integrity of criminal proceedings and (iv) provide effective oversight.

- Ensure that any detrimental effects on suspects caused by the public-private data sharing are limited to what is strictly necessary and, where appropriate, require an enhanced suspicion threshold

(i) In light of the above-described risk of erroneous suspicions, particularly demanding safeguards are required if personal data about specific suspects or about narrowly defined groups of persons is to be shared. Insofar as an individual is already targeted by an investigation but has not been convicted of the offences that underpin the suspicion, criminal justice authorities and the FIU must ensure that, in view of its potential detrimental effects on the suspect, the provision of data to obliged entities is proportionate.[130] As the intrusiveness of the data sharing does in particular depend on the likelihood that targeted customers might, as a consequence of the data sharing, experience economic and other disadvantages,[131] the law may therefore prohibit obliged entities from adopting, on the basis of the received data, adverse measures against a customer. Such prohibitions may in particular apply to the termination of a business relationship[132] and to the internal disclosure of the received data to more employees than are strictly necessary for retrieving the information sought

128 See P van Duyne, Organised crime, corruption and power, 26 *Crime, Law and Social Change* (1997), pp. 209–210.

129 On public-private data sharing for the purpose of improving the quality of obliged entities' CDD, see in more detail *infra* section III.F.2.c.

130 See by analogy ECtHR, Sidabras and Džiautas v. Lithuania, judgment of 27 July 2004, app. nos. 55480/00 and 59330/00, para. 56.

131 See in more detail *infra* section III.D.1.b.

132 On the limits of any obligation to continue a business relationship in cases where the suspicion is substantiated, see *infra* section III.D.1.c.

by the authorities. Insofar as such limitations are not feasible,[133] or if the sharing is even meant to prevent transactions by the suspect, additional substantive safeguards will be required to address the risk of unwarranted stigmatisation and of causing serious difficulties to the individual concerned to engage in economic activity.[134] In these cases, the provision of data by the authorities may need to be preconditioned by a suspicion threshold similar to those applicable to comparable provisional measures existing within pre-trial proceedings, for example the suspicion threshold required for the provisional freezing of suspects' assets under criminal procedure law.[135]

- Ensure that the sharing by competent authorities of the personal characteristics of potential suspects does not have a disproportionate effect on affected individuals

(ii) The provision of data by competent authorities that is not directly targeting particular individuals does in many cases not require similarly demanding safeguards. However, insofar as the data nevertheless entails the risk of stigmatisation and financial exclusion of individuals, for example those from a particular professional, national or religious background, legislators must ensure that the sharing of information with obliged entities remains proportionate to the objectives pursued. As a starting point, the authorities therefore need to differentiate between on the one hand information about money laundering threats and methods that is not likely to have a discriminatory effect and, on the other hand, information about personal characteristics of potential suspects that entail such an effect.[136] In the latter case, legislation must ensure that public-private data sharing mechanisms do not result in a *de facto* dissolution

---

133 On ways to enforce a prohibition of unlawful de-risking criteria, see *infra* section III.D.1.c.

134 For the relevance of such effects with regard to right to private life under Article 8 ECHR, see ECtHR, Taliadorou and Stylianou v. Cyprus, judgment of 16 October 2008, app. nos. 39627/05 and 39631/05, para. 54.

135 For a comparative account of non-conviction based confiscation standards in numerous national jurisdictions, see JP Rui/U Sieber (eds.), Non-Conviction-Based Confiscation in Europe: Possibilities and Limitations on Rules Enabling Confiscation without a Criminal Conviction, 2016.

136 See Article 10 of Directive (EU) 2016/680 of the European Parliament and of the Council of 27 April 2016 on the protection of natural persons with regard to the processing of personal data by competent authorities for the purposes of the prevention, investigation, detection or prosecution of criminal offences or the execution of criminal penalties, and on the free movement of such data, and repealing Council Framework Decision 2008/977/JHA, which highlights as particularly sensitive "[t]he processing of personal data revealing racial or ethnic origin, political opinions, religious or philosophical beliefs, or trade union membership, and the processing of genetic data, biometric data for the purpose of uniquely identifying a natural person, data concerning health or data concerning a natural person's sex life or sexual orientation".

of the borders between competent authorities and the data stocks of obliged entities, as such dissolution would effectively subject an almost infinite number of unsuspected customers to data processing by criminal justice authorities or FIUs. The jurisprudence of the Court of Justice of the European Union indicates two key substantive safeguards to this effect, namely limits on the scope of accessible data and conditions under which the authorities may access this data.

- In case of the sharing of the personal characteristics of potential suspects, limit the scope of personal data that obliged entities may process on the basis of such information

First, the law must limit the scope of customer data that is in principle available to competent authorities via a public-private data sharing mechanism. Insofar as the authorities provide personal characteristics of potential suspects in order to trigger a processing of customer data by obliged entities based on this information, the proportionality standards of the Court of Justice suggest that such data processing must not extend indiscriminately to all customer data held by the obliged entity, but only to customer data that gives rise to an enhanced probability that it may be related to the particular crimes that underpin the authorities' data sharing.[137] To this end, legislation could for example limit the processing of customer data done as part of a data sharing mechanism to the data of customers that are in some specific way related to known suspects or that are active in a particular professional and geographical area closely related to known suspects. In the same vein, and in the absence of a case-specific authorisation to this effect, obliged entities should not be allowed to share with other obliged entities potentially discriminatory data that they received through the data sharing. These limitations would confine the danger that public-private data sharing might lead to an indiscriminate and ultimately arbitrary processing of customer data that could allow the targeting of individuals and businesses for discriminatory or otherwise illegitimate reasons.

- Limit the public-private sharing of information on the personal characteristics of potential suspects to the detection, investigation and prevention of particularly serious crimes

Second, the law must ensure that the transfer by competent authorities of information about personal traits of potential suspects is limited to cases where

137 See ECJ (Grand Chamber), judgment of 8 April 2014 (Digital Rights Ireland), C-293/12 and C-594/12, paras. 58–59; see also ECJ (Grand Chamber), judgment of 21 December 2016 (Tele2 Sverige), C-203/15 and C-698/15, paras. 110–111.

the pursued objective is proportionate to the nature and scope of the customer data that obliged entities process on the basis of the received information.[138] The more extensive and sensitive the personal data of *prima facie* unsuspected customers processed as a result of public-private data sharing, the more the use of such data sharing as an instrument to identify unknown suspects must be limited. Limitation criteria to this effect will notably require a clear and sufficiently specific definition of purposes for which the data sharing mechanism may be used. These purposes may include in particular the detection, investigation or prevention of particular serious crimes whose type and case-specific degree of seriousness should be defined in more detail by legislation. In addition, legislators may also consider limits as to the threshold of suspicion underlying the transfer of data to obliged entities.

- Prevent the abuse of public-private data sharing by criminal actors, in particular by providing for an appropriate vetting of information prior to its disclosure

(iii) To protect the integrity of criminal proceedings, the law must furthermore ensure that public–private data sharing does not compromise the competent authorities' control over their data stocks, both as regards their decision on the scope of the data disclosure and as regards guarantees to ensure that disclosed data is only used for predefined and legitimate purposes, and also does not impair the impartiality and soundness of the authorities' case selection. In this respect, one should in particular point out that, while public–private data sharing may be able to satisfy proportionality requirements in particular insofar as the data provided is aimed at the activities of organised criminal groups, the focus of data sharing mechanisms on organised crime will at the same time be especially at risk of being exploited by those criminal actors. For especially powerful criminal organisations may want to abuse public-private data-sharing as an opportunity to collect information about the authorities' investigative strategies. Already at the level of determining what data is potentially to be shared with whom and for which purposes, legislators should therefore anticipate the possibility that criminal actors within obliged entities might try to infiltrate such mechanisms. To this effect, the law should in particular require that any information is, prior to its sharing with obliged entities, vetted through a collective decision-making process within the respective authorities. Such vetting would ensure that shared information does not contain elements that may be prejudicial to ongoing

[138] See ECJ (Grand Chamber), judgment of 8 April 2014 (Digital Rights Ireland), C-293/12 and C-594/12, paras. 60–61; see also ECJ (Grand Chamber), judgment of 21 December 2016 (Tele2 Sverige), C-203/15 and C-698/15, para. 115.

investigations and furthermore that the sharing is not left to the individual decision of a single official. In a similar vein, where shared data relates to particular individuals or particular groups, the law should require that such data is solely shared on the initiative of the respective authority and never on the basis of a solicitation from an obliged entity.

- Provide for a review by a court or independent administrative body when sharing information about particular suspects or personal characteristics of potential suspects

(iv) The proportionality of data sharing also depends on the availability of procedural safeguards to ensure respect for the applicable substantive limitations.[139] Insofar as mechanisms provide obliged entities with personal data or personal characteristics of potential suspects, independent review by a court or an independent administrative body is crucial. Given that risks for the rights of affected customers as well as for the integrity of criminal proceedings arise already at the moment of the transfer of data to obliged entities and not only when obliged entities communicate results of their data processing to competent authorities or the FIU, such review should (except in cases of urgency) intervene before such transfer. Insofar as shared information does not disclose personal data or personal traits of potential suspects, less demanding forms of oversight may suffice. Even then, legislation should however require that the public-private information sharing is subject to some form of effective control that protects both the authority from an unreasonable disclosure of strategic data and private entities (notably non-participating obliged entities) from competitive disadvantages. Regarding this second concern, adequate oversight could in particular be achieved by involving the competent supervisory authorities within the respective mechanism.[140] In any case, if a criminal investigation is already assigned to a judicial authority, it would seem imperative that the same authority also decides about the sharing of data gathered through this investigation in order not to compromise its control over the case file.

139 See ECJ (Grand Chamber), judgment of 8 April 2014 (Digital Rights Ireland), C-293/12 and C-594/12, para. 62; see also ECJ (Grand Chamber), judgment of 21 December 2016 (Tele2 Sverige), C-203/15 and C-698/15, para. 120.

140 Insofar as the sharing of information is not part of an ongoing criminal investigation or an FIU's operational analysis and instead aims at improving the quality of obliged entities' CDD, it should in any case be performed either directly by the competent supervisory authority or by the FIU under the control of this authority; see in more detail *infra* section III.F.2.c.

C. FINANCIAL INTELLIGENCE UNITS

1. *Clarifying FIUs' Role in the State Security Architecture*

a. Current State

Having developed only since the 1990s,[141] FIUs are a rather new element within states' security architecture. As a result not least of differences in the institutional shape of national criminal justice and supervisory frameworks, the design of national FIUs varies in important ways between Member States.[142] While (i) some of their core functions are defined by EU law, (ii) FIUs' purpose and institutional nature remain in many ways still vague. Despite such divergences, (iii) one can, in view of recent developments in EU law, nevertheless discern an increasing convergence in what FIUs are meant to accomplish and how they should operate.

(i) As regards the core of FIUs' operational hallmarks, one must start with their function of collecting SARs and other information, their tasks of analysing the information obtained and, if they have grounds to suspect money laundering, related predicate offences or terrorism financing, of communicating the results of their analysis and other relevant information to the competent authorities.[143] From this it results that FIUs are effectively conceptualised as a filter between reporting obliged entities and criminal justice authorities and, as regards their operational analyses, as a precursor to criminal investigations. In this respect, it is particularly noteworthy that, following Directive 2018/843, the FIU must now be empowered to request information from obliged entities irrespective of whether an SAR was already filed.[144] While FIUs are tasked with both operational and strategic analyses (the former targeting particular situations, individuals or entities, the latter aimed at the detection of trends and patterns), it is furthermore

---

141 A Amicelle/K Chaudieu, In Search of Transnational Financial Intelligence: Questioning Cooperation between Financial Intelligence Units, in C King/C Walker/J Gurulé (eds.), The Palgrave Handbook of Criminal and Terrorism Financing Law, Vol. 1, 2018, pp. 649–650.

142 See Comparative Analysis, sections IV.A.1, IV.A.4, IV.B.1 and IV.D.2, and also V Mitsilegas, New Forms of Transnational Policing: The Emergence of Financial Intelligence Units in the European Union and the Challenges for Human Rights: Part 1, 3 *Journal of Money Laundering Control* (1999), pp. 147–154; I Deleanu, FIUs in the European Union – facts and figures, functions and facilities, in B Unger et al. (eds.), The Economic and Legal Effectiveness of the European Union's Anti-Money Laundering Policy, 2014, pp. 97–124.

143 Article 32 para. 3(1) of Directive (EU) 2015/849 of 20 May 2015.

144 Article 32 para. 9 of Directive (EU) 2015/849 of 20 May 2015, as amended by Directive (EU) 2018/843 of 30 May 2018.

crucial to note that FIUs shall enjoy operational autonomy in the sense that the decision to conduct an analysis remains with them.[145] Consequently, they are not only simple assistants of the criminal justice authorities, but are expected to perform their tasks on the basis of autonomous policy choices and priorities. Importantly, EU legislation also provides that communication between FIUs and obliged entities cannot be disclosed to the clients affected by an SAR or by an operational analysis.[146] In carrying out an operational analysis, FIUs are in principle not expected to enter into direct contact with targeted individuals or entities, let alone under an obligation to provide the suspect with a hearing.[147] Finally, as results from the rules applicable to cross-border cooperation, the applicable EU rules require that FIUs must be able to share information spontaneously or upon request with other EU FIUs, and that the exchange of information may only be refused in exceptional circumstances.[148] It is thus clear that cross-border cooperation between FIUs follows not the rules of mutual legal assistance in criminal matters, but is characterised by a much greater level of informality.[149]

(ii) Many aspects of the FIU framework do however remain rather unspecified in several important ways. To begin with, while EU law defines FIUs' operational task as being aimed at the detection of money laundering, related predicate offences or terrorism financing, it does not exclude that Member States may opt for a broader scope of operational analyses and dissemination. Member States may therefore potentially extend the FIU's mission to other criminal offences and even non-criminal conduct, for example conduct that may be relevant for taxation purposes only.[150] EU law also does not give details about the institutional nature of FIUs. Depending on the policy choice of individual Member States, the FIU can therefore be located in particular within, or attached to, criminal justice authorities, customs or supervisory authorities. Closely related to this, while Member States are required to ensure that FIUs have access, in a timely manner, to law enforcement and administrative information that they require for the performance of their tasks,[151] EU law does not specify the exact content and scope of the information that must be accessible to the FIU. Against the background of the fact that FIUs are required to enjoy wide autonomy, their institutional affiliation should in principle not be an overly decisive factor. Yet, due to the lack of legislative detail as regards FIUs' power to access data of other

145 Article 32 para. 3(1) s. 1, para. 4 s. 3 and para. 8 of Directive (EU) 2015/849 of 20 May 2015.
146 Article 39 para. 1 of Directive (EU) 2015/849 of 20 May 2015.
147 See Comparative Analysis, section IV.E.
148 Article 53 para. 1(1) and para. 3 of Directive (EU) 2015/849 of 20 May 2015, as amended by Directive (EU) 2018/843 of 30 May 2018.
149 See European Union, section V.F.
150 See Comparative Analysis, section IV.B.1.
151 Article 32 para. 4 s. 1 of Directive (EU) 2015/849 of 20 May 2015.

authorities, the simultaneous indeterminacy under EU law of their institutional affiliation is bound to raise further doubts about FIUs' precise function.[152] It therefore does not come as a surprise that EU law remains rather vague with regard to the design and depth of FIUs' operational analysis, only stating that the analysis will depend "on the type and volume" of the information that FIUs received and on the "expected use of the information" that they disseminate to the competent authorities.[153] Furthermore, EU law is not very specific about the question to what extent FIUs' actions can be constraint by requirements for judicial authorisation. While communication between the FIU and obliged entities in the context of the filing of an SAR shall clearly be "direct",[154] which excludes the interposition of a judicial or any other authority, FIU access to "financial, administrative and law enforcement information" can be provided "directly or indirectly", which would seem to allow national legislators to require prior authorisation by a judicial or other authority. Similarly, FIU information requests to obliged entities which had not filed an SAR in the matter may also seem to allow for only indirect access,[155] thus possibly allowing national legislators to require prior authorisation. Finally, EU law stresses FIUs' autonomy over their decision to disseminate information and also provides for a right of the FIU to refuse the disclosure of information especially if this would have "a negative impact on ongoing investigations or analyses, or, in exceptional circumstances, where disclosure of the information would be clearly disproportionate to the legitimate interests of a natural or legal person";[156] however it is less clear to what extent FIUs' decisions to this effect can be subject to judicial scrutiny and whether FIU information may even be used as evidence in court proceedings.

(iii) Despite those open questions, the overall legislative framework allows one to deduce certain characteristics of FIUs that, while not explicitly clarified in EU legislation, do nevertheless specify their intended purposes and design. First, an FIU in the sense of EU law is not, within its operational mission, tasked with a mere superficial plausibility check of incoming SARs. Rather, through access to the data of other authorities and notably through the power to request information from obliged entities independently of the filing of a prior SAR, FIUs are empowered to extensively scrutinise SARs, but also other relevant information coming from public and private sources. As the commencement

152 See Comparative Analysis, section IV.D.2.

153 Article 32 para. 8 of Directive (EU) 2015/849 of 20 May 2015.

154 Article 33 para. 1 of Directive (EU) 2015/849 of 20 May 2015.

155 Article 32 para. 9 of Directive (EU) 2015/849 of 20 May 2015.

156 Article 32 para. 4 s. 3 and para. 5 of Directive (EU) 2015/849 of 20 May 2015; Article 7 of Directive (EU) 2019/1153 of the European Parliament and of the Council of 20 June 2019 laying down rules facilitating the use of financial and other information for the prevention, detection, investigation or prosecution of certain criminal offences, and repealing Council Decision 2000/642/JHA.

of an operational analysis is subject to the autonomous decision of the FIU,[157] it is furthermore clear that FIUs are not required by law to conduct an analysis with regard to every single SAR they receive. While incoming SARs may be subject to a preliminary inspection (notably through automated means) to provisionally assess their value and determine further action, EU law gives FIUs extensive discretion to determine their own autonomously set policy priorities. Consequently, they can define criteria to guide the selection of situations and targets of an operational analysis, for example by focusing on threats and methods that, from a criminal policy perspective and in light of resource constraints, seem most relevant. Given that FIUs are meant to serve as a precursor to subsequent proceedings by the competent authorities, especially criminal justice authorities and supervisory authorities,[158] but at the same time enjoy discretion as to whether or not to analyse information and disseminate information, it is furthermore evident that FIUs, despite EU law's silence regarding their institutional nature, can usually not operate under the control of criminal justice authorities. As resulting not least from the little-formalised framework for cross-border cooperation between FIUs inside and outside the EU, and from the absence of mandatory judicial safeguards, it is also clear that the dissemination of information to the competent authorities is primarily meant to provide these authorities with mere intelligence to commence investigations and is, in principle, not meant to serve as evidence. The intelligence focus of FIUs is confirmed by the fact that their enforcement powers are very limited to none. In particular, EU law does not require them to have the power to directly enforce information requests against obliged entities. While FIUs must have the power "directly or indirectly" to temporarily suspend a suspicious transaction, they shall only do so insofar as this is necessary to establish whether there are grounds to suspect relevant criminal activity and to disseminate this result to the competent authorities, implying that more permanent provisional measures shall only be taken by those authorities.[159] Finally, it is important to again refer to the power of FIUs, already mentioned above, to reject information requests from other authorities, including from criminal justice authorities,[160] if the disclosure would be clearly disproportionate to the legitimate interests of a natural or legal person. This is seemingly meant to provide the FIU with the means in particular to protect the identity of its sources even in subsequent criminal proceedings.

---

157 Article 32 para. 3 s. 1 of Directive (EU) 2015/849 of 20 May 2015.

158 See Article 32 para. 6 of Directive (EU) 2015/849 of 20 May 2015, which specifies that the competent authorities shall provide feedback to the FIU "about the outcome of the *investigations* or *inspections* performed on the basis of [FIU] information" (emphases added).

159 Article 32 para. 3 s. 3 and para. 7 s. 1 of Directive (EU) 2015/849 of 20 May 2015.

160 Article 7 paras. 2 and 4 of Directive (EU) 2019/1153 of 20 June 2019.

b. Challenges

Uncertainty about the role of FIUs in Member States' security architecture (i) concerns in particular their relationship with criminal justice authorities; (ii) confusion in this regard risks undermining FIUs' operational advantages.

(i) The above-mentioned points of ambiguity regarding FIUs' institutional nature and exact functioning can, and not infrequently do, give rise to uncertainty at national level and even at EU level,[161] in particular given that the depth of FIUs' operational analysis is not conclusively defined. Uncertainty regarding the FIUs' role does not only have the potential to raise contradictory or unrealistic expectations with policymakers and the wider public; an erroneous understanding of their role can also undermine political support for FIUs, because they will sometimes be criticised for failing to accomplish functions that, on closer inspection, are not necessarily theirs. This concerns not least the relationship between FIUs and criminal justice authorities. At first sight, it may seem desirable for the law to foster close cooperation between FIUs and criminal justice authorities or even to integrate the former into the latter. An FIU's data stocks and in particular the information it receives from obliged entities may offer valuable clues for a criminal investigation even if the FIU's own analysis of the data proves inconclusive. At the same time, the FIU will obviously in many cases greatly benefit from knowing that individuals or companies appearing in an SAR are already the object of a criminal investigation. In light of those observations, one could indeed think that the gathering of financial intelligence and criminal investigations should as much as possible be interlinked.[162]

Calls for proximity between FIUs and criminal justice authorities are however only convincing as long as legislators want to grant them merely a very limited operational role. Some FIUs indeed remain attached to a role that is usually limited to a mere plausibility assessment of SARs before forwarding the reports to the competent authorities.[163] As long as the FIU subjects SARs

---

161 Compare, on the one hand, the initial Proposal for a Directive laying down rules facilitating the use of financial and other information for the prevention, detection, investigation or prosecution of certain criminal offences, 2018/0105(COD) at draft recital 15 and draft article 7, and, on the other hand, Directive (EU) 2019/1153 of 20 June 2019, at recital 15 and at Article 7 paras. 1 and 4. See also Opinion of the European Data Protection Supervisor (EDPS) on a proposal for a Directive on the prevention of the use of the financial system for the purpose of money laundering and terrorist financing of 4 July 2013, para. 32.

162 See on continuing ambiguity of national legal orders in this respect Comparative Analysis, section V.B.1.

163 The level of an FIU's operational role depends not least on the scope of its access to data stocks of other authorities; see for an example United Kingdom, section IV.D.2.

only to a preliminary (maybe even extensively automated) assessment on the basis of typologies and other more statistical information or on the basis of data that is already available in its own and in other public databases, it essentially performs little more than an input control that aims to protect criminal justice authorities from being overwhelmed by low-quality SARs. In this respect, the relationship between these authorities and the FIU raises no questions of principle. The same is all the more true if an FIU is, most of the time, not looking into individual SARs at all, and instead focuses on strategic analyses and the maintenance of an SAR database that is to a large extent accessible to criminal justice authorities.[164]

Close interlinkage of FIUs and criminal justice authorities is however less plausible if FIUs are meant to assume a much stronger filter function. Such FIUs develop a pronounced intelligence-gathering profile and assume the right to autonomously set their own operational priorities and to disseminate information only in a selective way. This is the case in particular if the FIU does not only run automated data matching with its own or other data banks or conduct a mere plausibility check of individual SARs in order to assess their *prima facie* relevance, but instead conducts an in-depth operational analysis on the basis of certain predefined policy priorities. Where the FIU is not primarily guided by the aim of assessing each and every individual SAR, but autonomously selects its cases on the basis of a multitude of different information sources (including information from criminal justice authorities, foreign FIUs, intelligence services and possibly even media reports),[165] the FIU effectively becomes an agency for preliminary investigations. As seen above, today's EU legislative framework has moved in the direction of the latter vision by stressing FIUs' operational autonomy both as regards the selection of grounds to commence analyses and as regards the decision to disseminate information to the competent authorities.

(ii) This enhanced operational vision of FIUs opens up new opportunities from a criminal policy point of view, but it also explains that there are rather important limits to any cooperation between the FIU and criminal justice authorities. While FIUs will usually not have the power to apply the coercive investigative measures available to a criminal justice authority,[166] their potential advantage lies in the ability to collect a multitude of information from various public and private sources, and despite their crime-detection purpose to do so largely unconstrained by the requirements and limits of criminal procedure law.[167] Three characteristics of FIUs are particularly important in

---

164 See also A Scherrer, Fighting tax crimes: Cooperation between Financial Intelligence Units, Ex-Post Impact Assessment, European Parliamentary Research Service 2017, p. 41.

165 See in particular Germany, section IV.D.2, and Switzerland, section IV.D.2.

166 See Comparative Analysis, section IV.A.4.

167 See Comparative Analysis, section IV.E.

this regard, namely their power to analyse a case independently of an initial criminal suspicion, the confidentiality of their information gathering, and their cross-border cooperation outside the formal requirements of mutual legal assistance. FIUs will preserve these advantages only if they are kept clearly apart from criminal justice authorities.

First, criminal investigations are usually preconditioned by the presence of a specific suspicion, substantiated by specific facts, that a crime has been committed. Such a suspicion can however be particularly difficult to establish in the area of illicit financial flows. The more organised the underlying predicate offending and the greater their scale, the more likely it is that the criminal origin of assets will remain hidden behind complex chains of shell companies, stooges and anonymity-friendly foreign jurisdictions.[168] As a consequence, and as was already observed above,[169] criminal justice authorities will often find it difficult to commence a criminal investigation into complex money laundering because the criminal origin of assets will in many cases remain far from clear and therefore too speculative to trigger resource-intensive investigative efforts. Criminal justice authorities will furthermore be aware that an investigation into complex money laundering carries a significant risk that they will, even after many months or years of investigation, ultimately not be able to establish the assets' origin. FIUs' operational analyses, through their much more informal and thereby also less time-intensive collection of data, have the potential to considerably ease the burden of criminal justice authorities and, through their preliminary findings, provide these authorities with clearer guidance on whether a particular case merits being investigated in depth.

Second, compared to criminal justice authorities, FIUs provide a more suitable cooperation environment for the exchange of sensitive information. Due to the right of suspects to access the investigative file, the ability of criminal justice authorities to collect information from confidential sources is often subject to significant limitations.[170] In contrast, FIUs, because of their place outside criminal proceedings, enjoy extensive autonomy to disclose, or not to disclose, information to other public authorities and suspects.[171] The resulting

168 See E van der Does de Willebois/EM Halter/RA Harrison/JW Park/JC Sharman, The Puppet Masters: How the Corrupt Use Legal Structures to Hide Stolen Assets and What to Do About It, The World Bank 2011, pp. 11–68.

169 See *supra* section III.B.1.a.

170 See the comparative account in B Vogel (ed.), Secret Evidence in Criminal Proceedings (forthcoming).

171 While FIUs will frequently be under an obligation to disclose substantiated suspicions of money laundering or other criminal activity, this obligation will usually not extend to the information underlying the suspicion; see Comparative Analysis, section V.B. For the disclosure to suspects and other persons affected by FIUs' data processing, see Comparative Analysis, section IV.B.4.

greater level of confidentiality of the communication between the FIU and obliged entities outside criminal proceedings is not only much less formalised and thus easier than what would be possible under the rules of criminal procedure law pertaining to witnesses, but can stimulate the willingness of private persons and other public authorities to report wrongdoing or respond to information requests. This concerns first and foremost FIUs' power to protect the identity of reporting obliged entities and their employees, but also the cooperation with foreign FIUs and with intelligence agencies. Resulting from the confidentiality-fostering legal status, FIUs are enabled to assemble information from various sources which would be unwilling to disclose their information to criminal justice authorities.

Third, given that FIUs, due to their operational autonomy, operate outside criminal proceedings, they are also not bound by the rules applicable to mutual legal assistance in cross-border cases.[172] This aspect is particularly important in money laundering investigations,[173] as these have frequently a cross-border component, reflecting the fact that organised crime has often a transnational element and that the effective dissimulation of large-scale proceeds of crime will almost necessarily include some form of cross-border transfer.[174] As a reaction to these cross-border characteristics of money laundering, cooperation between FIUs is marked by a high level of informality and, compared to traditional mutual legal assistance, also speed.[175] In fact, as real-time cross-border transactions have become a ubiquitous feature of both global trade and of complex money laundering, the separation between mutual legal assistance and FIU–FIU cooperation seems inevitable. Here again, the operational autonomy of FIUs and thus their location outside criminal proceedings is a vital precondition, as informal cross-border cooperation largely relies on the mutual trust that shared information will not, without the consent of the foreign authority providing the information, be disclosed to third parties, not even in criminal proceedings.

---

172 See Comparative Analysis, section V.F.

173 In a similar vein in this respect, see European Commission, Impact assessment accompanying the document proposal for a directive of the European Parliament and of the Council on laying down rules facilitating the use of financial and other information for the prevention, detection, investigation or prosecution of certain criminal offences and repealing council decision 2000/642/JHA, Commission Staff Working Document of 17 April 2018, SWD(2018) 114, at 2.1.1.

174 See P Reuter/EM Truman, Chasing Dirty Money: The Fight against Money Laundering, 2004, p. 185.

175 On the speed of FIU–FIU cooperation, see: EU FIUs' Platform, Mapping Exercise and Gap Analysis on FIUs' Powers and Obstacles for Obtaining and Exchanging Information of 15 December 2016, p. 154; Amicelle/K Chaudieu, In Search of Transnational Financial Intelligence: Questioning Cooperation between Financial Intelligence Units, in C King/ C Walker/J Gurulé (eds.), The Palgrave Handbook of Criminal and Terrorism Financing Law, Vol. 1, 2018, pp. 651–559.

c. Reform

In order to safeguard FIUs' autonomy and also clarify their role within the state security architecture vis-à-vis other authorities, the EU legal framework should further specify existing rules. Legislation should ensure that FIUs (i) are kept institutionally separate from criminal justice authorities and (ii) enjoy considerable latitude on whether or not to disclose their data, and furthermore that (iii) the use of FIU data as evidence in criminal proceedings remains limited and that (iv) FIUs do not command extensive powers to freeze assets.

- Keep a clear institutional and operational separation between FIUs and criminal justice authorities

(i) Resulting from the above considerations, FIUs' ability to add value to AML usually depends on a clear distinction between them and criminal justice authorities. This is particularly so in national legal orders where the gathering of information in criminal investigations is overseen by judicial authorities and subject to rather comprehensive disclosure obligations.[176] FIUs' ability in this regard may be less relevant in legal orders that establish a clear separation between the police's pre-trial investigations and the trial file of the criminal court, and thereby facilitate the withholding of information by investigative authorities. However, even insofar as the police are allowed to withhold particular pieces of information from the suspect and the court, third parties (in particular foreign FIUs) will frequently have doubts about to what extent a requesting police authority will really be able to honour a pledge not to share the requested data with other authorities. It is therefore both unsurprising and sensible that the EU legal framework stresses the need for FIUs' autonomy as regards the dissemination of information.[177] It is this autonomy that forms the basis of FIUs' ability to gather information about the deeper structures of complex and transnational illicit financial flows, thereby not only providing criminal justice authorities with operational guidance but also, through their strategic analyses, enhancing the understanding of threats and vulnerabilities within the wider economy.

- Exclude direct access to FIU data stocks by other authorities insofar as information could reveal details about suspicious activities or FIUs' sources

(ii) As already provided for by EU law, FIUs must enjoy a considerable margin of appreciation to decide about the dissemination of information, which shall

176 See S Ruggeri, Audi Alteram Partem in Criminal Proceedings, Towards a Participatory Understanding of Criminal Justice in Europe and Latin America, 2017, pp. 310–311; see also Germany, section III.C.2.b, Spain, section V.H, and United Kingdom, section V.H.

177 Article 32 para. 4 of Directive (EU) 2015/849 of 20 May 2015; Article 7 para. 4 of Directive (EU) 2019/1153 of 20 June 2019.

in principle first and foremost exclude the possibility that other authorities have direct access to the FIU's data. Operational autonomy presupposes that any dissemination of information is subject to a case-by-case decision by the FIU. This does not however exclude the possibility of the FIU opening up some of its own databases to electronic queries by other authorities, provided that such queries do not already provide access to the sought data, but merely serve the purpose of informing the FIU about the interest of the enquiring authority or informing the enquiring authority that the FIU is in possession of potentially relevant data.[178] In the event that the electronic query produces a hit in its database, the FIU can then, in view of the circumstances of the individual case, decide whether it is willing to share the data. Only in narrowly confined cases and only with regard to less sensitive data should other authorities be allowed to automatically retrieve data from the FIU. This might notably include direct access by criminal justice authorities to some limited elements of SARs (such as account numbers and names of related individuals and companies), provided that this information does not already disclose details about the suspicious activity or the source of the report.

- Provide for an obligation of FIUs to disclose information to other authorities only insofar as this is strictly necessary for the prevention or prosecution of serious crime

As with any public authority under the rule of law, the FIU's autonomy must not mean that it is exempted from obligations resulting from the legitimate interests of third parties, not least of judicial authorities.[179] This in particular means that legislators should define conditions that trigger a duty of the FIU to share information with other authorities, notably criminal justice authorities, either on request or spontaneously. The FIU should in principle not be allowed to withhold information required for the prevention or prosecution of serious crime, except in cases where the negative effects of such disclosure outbalance the public interest in the prevention or prosecution of crime (for example where the disclosure would damage the relationship between the FIU and one of its foreign counterparts and this consequence would not be adequate in view of

---

178 See already the Ma3tch technology of FIU.net for the purpose of information exchange between EU FIUs: A Amicelle/K Chaudieu, In Search of Transnational Financial Intelligence: Questioning Cooperation between Financial Intelligence Units, in C King/C Walker/J Gurulé (eds.), The Palgrave Handbook of Criminal and Terrorism Financing Law, Vol. 1, 2018, pp. 657–658.

179 See notably ECJ (Grand Chamber), judgment of 3 September 2008 (Kadi v. Al Barakaat), C-402/05 and C-415/05, paras. 342–344; ECJ (Grand Chamber), judgment of 18 July 2013 (Kadi II), C-584/10, para. 125.

the limited seriousness of the suspected offence).[180] Legislators must define such cases in balancing the seriousness of the suspected crime and the need to safeguard the FIU's autonomy (not least with regard to the need to protect its sources and analytical methods and to honour confidentiality assurances it has given to foreign authorities). Usually this will require that, in the case of serious crime, the FIU may be required to share the substance of the information held by it without however disclosing details from which one could infer the identity of the sources or about the FIU's operational methods.

- Regulate and limit the use as evidence in court proceedings of findings produced by FIUs' operational analyses

(iii) In a similar vein, while the results of the FIU analyses can, subject to the applicable limits of the respective procedural law, be used as evidence in court proceedings,[181] the content of such disclosure will normally have to be limited to information that does not negatively affect the confidentiality interests of the FIU. In practice, this means that the FIU's documents or testimony will oftentimes only be of reduced value as the courts will usually not be able to comprehensively scrutinise the factual basis of the FIU's findings. This limited evidentiary role of FIUs' findings is ultimately a necessary price to pay for their intelligence focus and the resulting importance of confidentiality in its information gathering. Intelligence gathering on the one hand and the publicity governing criminal trials on the other hand are largely antagonistic in nature. As a consequence, the criminal courts will be prevented from accessing FIUs' data insofar as such access would adversely affect FIUs' functioning and, by producing less financial intelligence, ultimately impede the effective administration of justice.

- Limit any asset-freezing powers of FIUs to cases of special urgency and then require prompt transfer of the case to criminal justice authorities

(iv) Finally, it results from the forgoing observation that FIUs should in principle not be equipped with extensive enforcement powers, in particular long-lasting asset-freezing powers.[182] Otherwise, they would frequently be subject to judicial review proceedings[183] and thereby be forced to disclose the information underlying a measure, thus potentially compromising sources and methods.

---

180 See above Germany, sections III.C.2.b. and IV.B.3.

181 On the different national approaches in this regard, see Comparative Analysis, section V.H and in particular Spain, section V.H, where the use of FIU reports as evidence is explicitly disallowed.

182 For diverging approaches to this effect, see in particular Germany, section IV.A.4, and Italy, section IV.A.4.

183 See the explicit provision in this respect in Germany, section IV.E.2.

The results of the FIU's analyses are of course ultimately meant to guide coercive action of other authorities, in particular criminal justice authorities and also supervisory authorities. Yet such action must then be subject to ordinary procedural remedies that include a comprehensive judicial review and in which these authorities will be required to substantiate the lawfulness of their measures on the basis of publicly disclosed evidence. In this way, legislators can ensure that the FIU's autonomy over the disclosure of its data is respected while at the same upholding the right of affected persons to have the coercive measures comprehensively review by a court of law. This does not exclude the possibility that the FIU can adopt provisional measures regarding a particular transfer or asset,[184] but such cases should, following their adoption, without undue delay be transferred to the competent authorities than can then confirm the provisional measure, and thereby assume responsibility for it in case of judicial review, or end the measure. Conversely, the more provisional powers are given to the FIU, the more it will become entangled in court proceedings and the more likely it is that its data and thereby its autonomy will be compromised.

2. *Specifying the Data Processing Powers of FIUs*

a. Current State

As already observed, FIUs under the EU legal framework have today developed into strongly autonomous information-gathering bodies whose operational analysis is aimed at laying the groundwork for criminal investigations. FIUs' powers are so far however only broadly defined and allow considerable flexibility for national legislators. This concerns most notably FIUs' power to request information from any obliged entity irrespective of whether this entity had previously filed an SAR. EU law so far merely specifies that the request must relate to the purpose of detecting, preventing and combating money laundering and terrorism financing.[185] Except for a limitation regarding the professional secrecy applicable to notaries, other independent legal professionals, auditors, external accountants and tax advisors,[186] EU law does not however add details about the purpose of such requests (for example whether the requested information must relate to a particular suspicion or can also be performed for the purpose of the gathering of merely strategic information),[187] about the target of the request (especially whether it can also be aimed at personal data of customers that

184 See for example Italy, section IV.A.4.

185 See Article 32 para. 9 in conjunction with para. 1 of Directive (EU) 2015/849 of 20 May 2015, as amended by Directive (EU) 2018/843 of 30 May 2018.

186 Article 32 para. 9 in conjunction with Article 34 para. 2 of Directive (EU) 2015/849 of 20 May 2015, as amended by Directive (EU) 2018/843 of 30 May 2018.

187 See Comparative Analysis, section IV.A.2.

are not directly related to a suspicious transaction) and about the scope of the information sought (in particular to what extent it can go beyond transaction data and also include other information gathered by the obliged entity through CDD measures). EU legislation also is not very clear, and thereby seems to leave it open to national legislators, on whether to require the FIU to obtain judicial authorisation prior to any FIU information request that had not been preceded by the filing of an SAR from the same obliged entity.[188] Similarly, while requests for additional information from an obliged entity following its filing of an SAR must be direct and thus exclude the possibility of a prior judicial authorisation requirement,[189] the EU does not specify the exact content of the request, merely stating that the requested obliged entity must provide "all necessary information".[190] Again, this leaves open the question about the scope of FIUs' power and in particular how national legislators are supposed to balance the purpose of the request and the fundamental rights of the obliged entities' clients.

Other than FIUs' power to request information from obliged entities, EU legislation does not provide much further detail on FIUs' powers to access information of other authorities, in particular criminal justice authorities. It does specify that such access can be direct or indirect, thus allowing national legislators to require additional procedural safeguards, for example case-by-case consent by the requested authority or even a prior judicial authorisation.[191] While a literal interpretation of Directive 2015/849 could lead to the understanding that FIUs must be enabled to access all administrative and law enforcement data that they require for the fulfilment of their tasks, this can obviously not exempt the FIU from complying with the principle of proportionality.[192] The latter requires the purpose of the processing of personal data by the FIU to be appropriate to the level of intrusiveness of the initial gathering of this data and to its significance.[193] This caveat is relevant not least for the question whether the FIU can have access to personal data gathered by criminal justice authorities through particularly intrusive measures, such a telecommunications surveillance

---

188 Article 32 para. 9 of Directive (EU) 2015/849 of 20 May 2015, as amended by Directive (EU) 2018/843 of 30 May 2018. It remains open whether Article 33 para. 1 s. 1(a), which requires that information be "directly" provided to the FIU, also applies to requests that are not preceded by an SAR. Given that Article 32 para. 9 does, in principle, greatly enhance the scope of FIUs' access to customer data, one must doubt that information requests with and without prior filing of an SAR are supposed to entail the same (limited) procedural safeguards.

189 See European Union, section IV.A.4.

190 Article 33 para. 1(b) of Directive (EU) 2015/849 of 20 May 2015, as amended by Directive (EU) 2018/843 of 30 May 2018.

191 Article 32 para. 4 s. 1 of Directive (EU) 2015/849 of 20 May 2015.

192 See also Article 8 of Directive (EU) 2019/1153 of 20 June 2019.

193 See Articles 7, 8 and 52 para. 1 s. 2 of the Charter of Fundamental Rights of the European Union; Article 4 para. 1(c) and para. 2(b) of Directive (EU) 2016/680 of 27 April 2016.

or the bugging of private premises.[194] In this regard, the FIU's access to such personal data gathered will usually be limited to cases where the purpose of the FIU's analysis (notably in view of the suspected value of the laundered assets or the complexity of a money laundering scheme) is not less important than the purposes for which the data was initially gathered.[195]

Lastly, EU law states that FIUs shall analyse SARs and other information relevant to money laundering, associated predicate offences or terrorist financing.[196] The law does not however further elaborate on the nature and scope of those other sources or on FIUs' data processing methods. In a similar vein, while it is clear that FIUs do increasingly rely on powerful data analysis technologies, the scope and limits of automated data processing powers are not specified.[197] Consequently, insofar as the applicable national law does not entail an authorisation, an FIU's decisions that significantly affect an individual must not be based solely on automated processing of data.[198] Finally, Member States' FIUs are required to exchange "any information" that may be relevant for the analysis of money laundering and terrorism financing. Yet, while it exceptionally allows an FIU to refuse the exchange of information where the exchange could be contrary to fundamental principles of its national law,[199] EU law itself does not further elaborate on such limits.[200]

b. Challenges

In order to determine the limits of FIUs' data gathering and analysis powers, it is necessary to assess to what extent their data processing is relevant to the rights of affected persons, in particular with regard to the right to private life according to Article 7 and the right to the protection of personal data according to Article 8

194 See Germany, section V.B.2.

195 For the purpose limitation requirement in the jurisprudence of the ECJ, see *supra* section II.B.1.

196 Article 32 para. 3 subpara. 1 s. 2 of Directive (EU) 2015/849 of 20 May 2015, as amended by Directive (EU) 2018/843.

197 On fundamental rights challenges of such technologies, see Germany, section IV.D.4, and *infra* section E.2.b.

198 See Article 11 para. 1 of Directive (EU) 2016/680 of 27 April 2016; see also Article 22 of Regulation (EU) 2016/679 of the European Parliament and of the Council of 27 April 2016 on the protection of natural persons with regard to the processing of personal data and on the free movement of such data, and repealing Directive (EC) 95/46; on the question of the applicability of Directive (EU) 2016/680 on FIUs see European Union, section V.B.1.

199 Article 53 para. 1 subpara. 1 and para. 3 of Directive (EU) 2015/849 of 20 May 2015, as amended by Directive (EU) 2018/843.

200 On the lack of specificity of the rules governing FIU–FIU data sharing, see V Mitsilegas/ N Vavoula, The Evolving EU Anti-Money Laundering Regime: Challenges for Fundamental Rights and the Rule of Law, 23 *Maastricht Journal of European and Comparative Law* (2016), pp. 289–292.

of the Charter of Fundamental Rights.[201] In line with the jurisprudence of the EU Court of Justice, such assessment must have regard in particular to the objective pursued by the interference and by the nature and seriousness of the interference.[202] Consequently, FIUs' data processing must be considered as highly intrusive because of the (i) objective of their processing, (ii) the very extensive scope of their data gathering through SARs, (iii) their power to request information from an obliged entity independently of whether or not the latter had filed an SAR, (iv) their influence over criminal proceedings, and (v) a lack of comprehensive judicial or other independent scrutiny.

(i) To begin with the objective of FIUs' data processing, it is important to recall that their operational analyses are meant to serve as a precursor to criminal investigations by the competent authorities in that FIUs are meant to establish whether SARs or other relevant information that had come to their attention merits being investigated for a suspicion of money laundering, related predicate offences or terrorism financing.[203] As operational analyses are thus designed to prepare criminal investigations, their relevance for affected persons is potentially very serious. For if the FIU reaches the conclusion that there are grounds to suspect criminal activity and disseminates this finding to the competent authorities, then there is a significant probability that the affected person will be subjected to investigative measures (such as covert surveillance measures) and also provisional measures (such as the freezing of assets).

(ii) Moving to the nature and seriousness of the interference, one must recall that dominant sources of information for FIUs are SARs and follow-up communications from obliged entities, thus information that is initially gathered by obliged entities' CDD measures. As was already observed above,[204] this data is of potentially great relevance for the individuals affected, as, not least due to the decline of cash as a means of payment, it allows the authorities, through the transaction history and the contracting partners identifiable therein, to build a fairly detailed picture of large parts of the private life of an obliged entity's customer. Given that obliged entities' CDD covers almost the entirety of a country's non-cash transactions, and furthermore given that these obliged entities are under an obligation to continuously monitor their business relationships and report suspicious activities,[205] FIUs' data gathering is thus

201 See *supra* sections II.B.1 und II.C.1.

202 See ECJ (Grand Chamber), judgment of 8 April 2014 (Digital Rights Ireland), C-293/12 and C-594/12, para. 47.

203 Though some national frameworks may go beyond this in that they empower FIUs to also disseminate information regarding other crimes or even non-criminal conduct; see Comparative Analysis, section IV.B.1.

204 See *supra* section II.B.2.

205 Article 13 para. 1(d) of Directive (EU) 2015/849 of 20 May 2015.

based on the monitoring of vast amounts of financial data. While this monitoring is primarily done by the obliged entities and not by FIUs themselves, the obliged entities' reporting obligation effectively makes them agents of the FIU. Their customer monitoring and reporting is in the end an essential part of the FIUs' function. The scope and thus intrusiveness of FIUs' data gathering therefore depends largely on the reporting threshold applicable to SARs and the amount of data communicated through an SAR, in particular on whether obliged entities are required to report only very substantiated suspicions or rather also mere indications of illegal activity or even merely unusual transactions.[206] The scope of FIUs' data gathering furthermore also depends on whether the content of the obliged entities' reports is limited to the suspicious or unusual transaction itself or also extends to the wider transaction history of the respective customer or even to personal data gathered by the obliged entity as part of its CDD.[207] The lower the reporting threshold and the more comprehensive the transmitted customer data, and thus the greater the amount of data that the FIU receives, and the more restricted the level of discretion that obliged entities enjoy in filing a report, the less obliged entities effectively play a filter role between their customers and FIUs and instead become a mere data procurement tool for FIUs. Similarly, insofar as obliged entities increasingly report activities merely because these activities are unusual or are typically relate to criminal activity, the more data FIUs will gather data about clients that are in fact not connected to criminal activity. As a result, individuals and legal entities are then exposed to the risk of being erroneously targeted by a criminal investigation merely on the basis of quintessentially statistical assumptions instead of on the basis of the specific circumstances of the particular case.

(iii) Crucially, FIUs' gathering of personal data trough obliged entities is not limited to receiving SARs. As already pointed out, FIUs have the power to request additional information following receipt of an SAR. Still more importantly, EU FIUs shall now also have the power to request information from obliged entities independently of the prior filing of an SAR.[208] In particular, the power to request information irrespective of the prior filing of an SAR by the requested obliged entity has potentially very significant consequences for assessing the serious of the interference into rights by FIUs. For insofar as all obliged entities (with the exception of certain privileged professions)[209] are required to respond

[206] For differences between national frameworks as regards the definition of reporting triggers, see Comparative Analysis, section III.C.1.a.

[207] The question of scope remains largely unaddressed by national laws; see Comparative Analysis, section III.C.1.b.

[208] Though now required by EU law, this power may not be available to all FIUs yet; see Comparative Analysis, section IV.C.

[209] See Article 32 para. 9 and Article 34 para. 2 of Directive (EU) 2015/849 of 20 May 2015, as amended by Directive (EU) 2018/843 of 30 May 2018.

to the FIU's request, FIUs can now utilise the vast network of obliged entities to access financial data irrespective of whether this obliged entity had already detected suspicious conduct. Depending on the scope of information provided by obliged entities in response to a request, the FIU is then no longer tasked with assessing the relevance of information that, in the eyes of the reporting obliged entity, seemed relevant. Instead, the FIU can itself determine which information it considers relevant, subject of course to the (so far barely specified)[210] threshold defined by law, namely that the request serves the purposes of preventing, detecting or combating money laundering or terrorism financing. This power of FIUs to indirectly access financial data on their own initiative in principle profoundly changes the relationship between obliged entities and FIUs and thereby affects any assessment of the intrusiveness of FIUs' data gathering. For as it is now no longer required to wait for the filing of an SAR in order to request information from an obliged entity, the FIU's ability to access private financial data is sweepingly extended. As, unlike in the case of the filing of an SAR, FIUs' data requests essentially allow for a transfer of personal data independently of whether the obliged entity considered the requested information to be relevant, obliged entities' role as a filter between their customers and the FIU is considerably reduced or, depending on the scope of the requested information, even largely dissolved. One then must again recall that obliged entities, through their financial data, have access to almost all non-cash financial transactions. Their power to request information from obliged entities, subject to legislative restrictions, then means that FIUs can potentially access large amounts of financial data pertaining to suspects as well as to individuals and companies that are not suspected of any wrongdoing.

(iv) The level of intrusiveness of FIUs' data gathering and further data processing obviously also depends on FIUs' influence on subsequent criminal proceedings against persons related to suspicious financial activity. Due to their operational autonomy, including their extensive discretion to disclose data, FIUs internal decision-making is usually only scrutinised by judicial or other authorities to a limited degree.[211] This concerns not least their decision as to whether or not, or how thoroughly, to analyse transactions and to forward particular information to criminal justice authorities. While the handling of case-relevant information by criminal justice authorities is usually subject to some form of judicial control (either by the trial court or through separate judicial review)[212] and is thereby scrutinised for possible discriminatory or other

[210] See Article 32 paras. 9 and 1 of Directive (EU) 2015/849 of 20 May 2015, as amended by Directive (EU) 2018/843 of 30 May 2018.

[211] See Comparative Analysis, section IV.E.2.

[212] See ECtHR (Grand Chamber), Jasper v. United Kingdom, judgment of 16 February 2000, app. no. 27052/95, paras. 51–52; ECtHR, Edwards v. United Kingdom, judgment of 6 December 1992, app. no. 13071/87, paras. 33–39.

arbitrary considerations, the grounds for the FIUs' decision in the particular case will be subject to much less, or even no, independent scrutiny. In view of their extensive access to public and private data, FIUs' function as a precursor to criminal investigations in combination with a lack of external scrutiny as regards their internal decision-making raises a significant risk regarding FIUs' integrity. In fact, insofar as FIUs function as a specialised intelligence service for financial sector activities and thus have unparalleled access to extensive private data stocks, their potential to serve as an instrument of political[213] or other abuse is obvious.[214] On the one hand, a lack of independent scrutiny of its decision not to analyse or disseminate particular information can allow an FIU to shield particular individuals from criminal investigations. On the other hand, extensive access to public and private data, and in particular a close working relationship with obliged entities, can in some cases enable an FIU to build a *prima facie* plausible case against an individual or company even if, to the acting official's knowledge, the suspicion is in fact unsubstantiated. While the facts might come out through the subsequent criminal investigations, the triggering of such investigations alone can pose a significant threat not only to the reputation of targeted individuals, but also to the reputation and creditworthiness of companies.[215]

Closely related to the issue of FIUs' influence on the conduct of criminal investigations is the question of FIUs' access to the data of criminal justice authorities. Given the potentially already strong influence of FIUs on follow-up action by criminal justice authorities, extensive direct access by FIUs to the data of criminal justice authorities would only increase the aforementioned concerns. For it would bring about a knowledge divide, or asymmetry, between FIUs and criminal justice authorities. While being empowered to deny access to its own data, the FIU would then be able to inform itself about the level of knowledge of the criminal justice authorities in a particular case.[216] Beyond what it can already achieve through the dissemination of the results of its operational analyses, the FIU's power to steer the investigative focus of criminal justice authorities would thereby be further expanded. Consequently, while direct

---

213 Note that enhanced due diligence must be performed in particular with regard to politically exposed persons (who notably include members of national parliaments); see Comparative Analysis, section III.A.4.a. AML frameworks thus presuppose that such persons shall be subject to particular scrutiny. While this may in principle make sense in order to address corruption, it also raises the spectre of abuse, in particular in situations where the independence of a national FIU is politically compromised.

214 See K Strauss, The Situation of Financial Intelligence Units in Central and Eastern Europe and the Former Soviet Union, Basel Institute on Governance Working Paper Series No. 09, 2010, pp. 25–26.

215 See L Campbell, Criminal Labels, the European Convention on Human Rights and the Presumption of Innocence, 76 *Modern Law Review* (2013), pp. 695–697.

216 See Germany, section V.B.2.

access to the data of criminal justice authorities could of course often be helpful for FIUs when analysing SARs and other information, such access does at the same time significantly increase the intrusiveness of FIUs' data processing in that it enhances the risk of criminal investigations being steered by a selective dissemination of FIU data without it being possible to independently scrutinise the motives behind the selection.

(v) Finally, the intrusiveness of FIUs' data processing is particularly aggravated by a lack of judicial scrutiny. As already observed, the lack of judicial supervision and thus the power to keep information and its sources hidden from the suspect and the wider public does of course constitute one of the greatest operational advantages of FIUs. Yet the secrecy of their analyses at the same time constitutes a key weakness from a rule of law point of view, as a non-disclosure of the processing of personal data exposes suspects and other affected persons to a heightened risk of being targeted for factually unfounded allegations or illegitimate considerations. Even after the conclusion of an operational analysis, FIUs will frequently not be able to fully disclose their findings as such disclosure might compromise confidential methods and sources. In the absence of full disclosure, affected persons will usually not be able to comprehensively challenge an FIU's conclusions and, as a consequence, challenge the FIU's follow-up action. This not only concerns the FIU's decision to disseminate personal data to the criminal justice authorities, in which case a suspect might still be able to implicitly challenge the result of the operational analysis in a criminal court. As importantly, the lack of comprehensive judicial review reduces the opportunity for affected persons to effectively challenge the dissemination of personal data to other actors, in particular to intelligence services and foreign FIUs, and possibly also to domestic and foreign obliged entities.[217] Once data has been communicated to such third parties, it will usually be very difficult or virtually impossible for the affected person to challenge its further use. Dissemination therefore entails a substantial risk of individuals and companies being subjected, on the basis of erroneous conclusions, to additional monitoring and even further secret precautionary measures (such as formal or informal blacklisting) by state authorities and the private sector[218] without having a realistic opportunity to correct the FIU's version of events.

As, under the rule of law, effective judicial review constitutes a bedrock of the protection of rights against measures by the executive, the lack of such review

217 In a similar vein M Mitsilegas, New Forms of Transnational Policing: The Emergence of Financial Intelligence Units in the European Union and the Challenges for Human Rights: Part 2, 3 *Journal of Money Laundering Control* (2000), pp. 252–256.

218 On the frequently unpredictable content of public as well as commercial databases used for the identification of risk, see M de Goede/G Sullivan, The politics of security lists, 34 *Environment and Planning D: Society and Space* (2016), pp. 67–88.

profoundly deepens the intrusiveness of a measure.[219] This is especially so if there are apparent reasons to assume that the measure might in many cases be influenced by considerations other than those justified by the law. In this respect, it must be considered as particularly relevant that FIUs' analyses are frequently or even regularly carried out in what can be described as a collaboration between the FIU and the reporting obliged entity. Given that the customer is usually informed neither about an ongoing operational analysis nor about the content of the FIU's communication with the obliged entity,[220] it should be highlighted that the result of the operational analysis is usually as much the result of the FIU's data processing as it is the result of the obliged entity's willingness to disclose customer data to the FIU in the first place. To the extent that the result of an operational analysis is then based on two different and partially overlapping interests, namely the FIU's interest in detecting financial wrongdoing and the obliged entity's in being perceived as a good corporate citizen, one should not ignore the risks that this can entail for the customer. In particular, the risk that an obliged entity might not fully disclose relevant information or in some cases even make misleading statements in order to deflect possible criticism of its own CDD practice, thereby potentially making the customer appear in a less favourable light, should be highlighted. Not least also in view of this risk, the fact that FIUs will often be allowed to deny disclosure of information and thereby avert a comprehensive judicial review leads its data processing to be particularly intrusive.

c. Reform

Given that FIUs' operational analyses are usually aimed at the detection and monitoring of criminal activity, but are conducted outside the confines of criminal procedure law and thus notably in the absence of comprehensive judicial scrutiny, legislators need to balance the need for information gathering with respect for fundamental rights safeguards. As part of this balancing, the EU legislator must, (i) within the limits of its legislative competence, ensure an adequate balance between secrecy and the protection of procedural rights. To this end, particular consideration must be given to (ii) the scope of FIUs' power to secretly collect personal data from obliged entities, (iii) the availability of judicial review and (iv) the authority of the FIU to share information with criminal justice authorities. Within each of those three parameters, legislators essentially will have to make a policy choice between the level of transparency of FIUs' action and their powers.

---

219 See *supra* section II.C.1.

220 Article 39 para. 1 of Directive (EU) 2015/849 of 20 May 2015.

- Provide sufficient flexibility that allows national legislators to adapt the design of the FIU to the particularities of a country's constitutional order

(i) In light of FIUs' function as an information-gathering body, the above-mentioned challenges are far from unusual and largely reflect the problems typically connected to the role of intelligence agencies in the administration of criminal justice, in particular the inherent tension between secrecy and the rule of law.[221] Confronted with the need to address particularly serious threats such as terrorism and organised crime, authorities will oftentimes need to collect information outside the highly formalised framework of criminal proceedings. As questions of national security are largely outside of the area of competence of the EU,[222] and in light of the usually close correlation between national security, a country's constitutional identity and its institutional framework applicable to intelligence services,[223] the nature of FIUs' function might prevent the EU legislator from exhaustively regulating their exact competences and powers. It is therefore all the more important that supranational norm-setters anticipate tensions that might arise from national constitutional laws, in particular as regards the relationship between criminal justice and intelligence gathering, and thereby ensure that national legislators keep sufficient flexibility to coherently integrate FIUs into the national security architecture.

- Limit the scope of customer data that obliged entities must disclose to FIUs while being under a prohibition to tip off the customer

(ii) As regards the scope of FIUs' power to obtain personal data from obliged entities, proportionality considerations suggest that secret access to customer data must, in light of the extensive scope and sensitivity of transaction data and CDD documentation kept by obliged entities, be restricted.[224] After all, this data can, directly or as a lead for further inquiries, provide much detail about an individual's private and even intimate life.[225] Similarly, companies, in order to

---

221 See for example J Vervaele, Terrorism and information sharing between the intelligence and law enforcement communities in the US and the Netherlands: emergency criminal law?, 76 *Revue internationale de droit penal* (2005), pp. 409–443; European Union Agency for Fundamental Rights, Surveillance by intelligence services: fundamental rights safeguards and remedies in the EU, Vol. I, 2017.

222 Article 4 para. 2 of the Treaty on European Union; see M Den Boer, Counter-Terrorism, Security and Intelligence in the EU: Governance Challenges for Collection, Exchange and Analysis, 30 *Intelligence and National Security* (2015), pp. 402–419.

223 On the relationship between EU law and national constitutional law, see A von Bogdandy/ S Schill, Overcoming Absolute Primacy: Respect for National Identity under the Lisbon Treaty, 48 *Common Market Law Review* (2011), pp. 1–37, esp. pp. 25–27.

224 See *supra* section II.B.2 and also ECtHR, M.N. and others v. San Marino, judgment of 7 July 2015, app. no. 28005/12, paras. 73 and 83.

225 See *supra* section II.B.2.

enter into or continue a business relationship, are regularly expected to disclose to an obliged entity a vast amount of information about their business model, clients and shareholder structure. Allowing the FIU to comprehensively access this information in secret and thus without any independent scrutiny would give rise to considerable risks that, through FIUs' subsequent data processing and dissemination, highly sensitive information could end up in the hands of domestic and foreign officials and private entities that might exploit it for purposes that are not compatible with the purposes for with the data was initially obtained. As a consequence, insofar as it expects individuals and companies to provide obliged entities with sensitive information in the context of CDD, the legislator must ensure that adequate and effective remedies are in place to prevent abuse.

- In defining FIUs' power to covertly request customer data, limit the scope of such requests to transaction data and to the main findings of the obliged entity's CDD

In designing those remedies, the legislator should as a starting point differentiate between different types of data and adapt the level of scrutiny to the sensitivity of the particular type and to the relevance of the data for FIUs' analyses. As a matter of principle, one should differentiate between on the one hand *basic data* that the FIU should normally be allowed to request without the need to inform the affected individual or company in a timely manner, and on the other hand *extended data* that will require the obliged entity, after having provided the requested data to the FIU, to inform affected persons about the request. *Basic data* would refer to personal data of comparatively limited sensitivity. This category should comprise in particular the identity of a customer or beneficial owner, information about the purpose of a business relationship or transaction, findings regarding the status of a customer or beneficial owner as being a politically exposed person, and information about the origin of assets used in suspect transactions. FIU requests for *basic data* would thus aim to establish what conclusions the requested obliged entity reached with regard to a particular business relationship or transaction – in other words, the outcomes of the performance of its CDD. In contrast, *extended data* would potentially cover all other information lawfully collected by the requested obliged entity for the purpose of CDD, in particular information considered by the requested obliged entity to establish the identity of the beneficial owner or the purpose of the business relationship or to trace the origin of assets. This covers notably documents and other material produced by the customer him- or herself and information collected by the requested obliged entity from third parties. Legislators should also consider differentiating between extended data pertaining to individuals and extended data pertaining to companies, in that an individual's right to private life will usually require particular protection.

(iii) As regards the availability of judicial review against FIUs, it must be recalled that their nature as an intelligence body and the resulting need to protect sources of information usually hinders a comprehensive review of FIUs' actions in a court of law and in the presence of the complainant. Judicial review can normally not be directed against FIUs' data processing as such, but only against follow-up action by other actors, in particular by criminal justice authorities. Nevertheless, as with any other state authority operating under the rule of law, the FIU must be subject to some form of independent oversight. Given that the FIU not only analyses strategic data, but also serves as a precursor to criminal investigations, it would furthermore seem that oversight must extend to individual cases of operational data processing and must offer some form of review mechanism for individuals and companies affected by the FIU's operational analysis. Two aspects of the FIU's action deserve particular attention.

- Require obliged entities, after a standstill period, to inform the affected customer that they provided the FIU with CDD documentation

First, as just explained above, a request for extended CDD data by the FIU from an obliged entity does, in view of the potential scope and sensitivity of such data, require the requested obliged entity to inform the affected customer about the FIU's request and about which data it provided in response to the FIU.[226] Obviously, this obligation could potentially impede the success of the FIU's operational analysis, in particular because the targeted person may transfer suspicious assets to another jurisdiction or destroy evidence. In view of the FIUs' legitimate interest to conclude their operational analyses in secret and thereby protect ensuing criminal investigations, legislators should therefore provide for a temporary suspension of the obliged entities' duty to inform the customer. To determine an appropriate period to this effect, legislators should have regard to the time usually required for the conclusion of operational analysis, also taking into account that FIUs will frequently have to wait for additional information from obliged entities and domestic and foreign authorities.[227] In light of such considerations, it would, in principle, seem adequate to suspend the FIU's duty to inform the customer for four weeks, though in cases where the FIU needs more time to conclude the analysis, the head of the FIU should be empowered to order the obliged entity to prolong the period of non-disclosure to the client for up to another four weeks. The customer's interest in being protected against the use

226 In this vein already United Kingdom, section V.H.

227 See also A Amicelle/K Chaudieu, In Search of Transnational Financial Intelligence: Questioning Cooperation between Financial Intelligence Units, in C King/C Walker/J Gurulé (eds.), The Palgrave Handbook of Criminal and Terrorism Financing Law, Vol. 1, 2018, p. 654.

of inaccurate extended CDD data could in turn be safeguarded by an obligation on the part of the FIU not to forward the results of its operational analysis to other authorities until and unless the affected customer has been informed about the transfer of the extended CDD data to the FIU and thereby put in a position to trigger a judicial examination of the content of the transferred data. Importantly, in order to protect the secrecy interests of the FIU, judicial review of the disclosure of extended CDD data should however not include a review of the FIU's power to request extended CDD data, but only a review to the effect of whether the extended CDD data provided by the obliged entity to the FIU was factually accurate.

- Provide for an independent mechanism that allows affected individuals and companies to request a review of FIUs' refusal to disclose information

Second, in order to mitigate the risk of unlawful data processing by the FIU, individuals affected by its data collection and data processing should in principle be entitled to request from the FIU personal data that it holds about him or her.[228] In order to protect their sources and methods of data processing, FIUs must obviously be entitled to withhold relevant data. Yet, at least in cases where data from the FIU, including reports specifying the results of an operational analysis, are used as evidence in criminal proceedings or otherwise used by another law enforcement authority or obliged entity in a way that is detrimental to a particular person, this person must be entitled to apply for disclosure of the relevant data from the FIU. A refusal by the FIU to disclose such data should, in line with the respective national legal framework, be subject to judicial review or to another similarly effective independent remedy to review the FIU's decision to refuse disclosure, and, if the complainant's interests outweigh the FIU's confidentiality interests, order disclosure.[229] Within this review mechanism, the competent body should be able to see itself the data withheld by the FIU in order to determine whether this data should, in the particular case, be treated as confidential, having regard to both the FIU's interests and the case-specific interests of the complainant. This review mechanism should in particular apply in cases where there are reasons to believe that a person has, outside the context of criminal proceedings, been subject to detrimental measures due to information stemming from the FIU.

---

228 See also G Pavlidis, Financial information in the context of anti-money laundering: Broadening the access of law enforcement and facilitating information exchanges, *Journal of Money Laundering Control* (2020) (ahead-of-print).

229 For conceivable procedural mechanisms to this effect, see ECtHR (Grand Chamber), Chahal v. United Kingdom, judgment of 15 November 1996, app. no. 22414/93, paras. 131–144; ECJ (Grand Chamber), judgment of 4 April 2013 (ZZ), C-300/11, paras. 57–59.

- Limit FIUs' power to disseminate the results of their operational analyses to cases of terrorism and other forms of serious criminality

(iv) Finally, as FIUs' power stems primarily from their function of serving as a precursor to criminal investigations and thereby ultimately from their influence on criminal justice authorities, the level of intrusiveness of the FIUs' data gathering and data processing largely depends on the extent to which the FIUs' action does provide leads for criminal investigations. Legislators must avoid FIUs being put in a position where, despite their data processing being largely exempted from oversight by the judiciary, they are allowed to effectively control the work of criminal justice authorities. As explained above, this risk primarily emanates from the FIUs' autonomy as regards whether or not to disseminate information and from their power to at the same time have more or less extensive access to operational data of criminal justice authorities. Legislators could somewhat remedy this asymmetry by largely reducing FIUs' access to criminal justice data. However, such restrictions would almost necessarily negatively affect the effectiveness of FIUs' analyses. In order to avoid such restrictions while at the same time considerably restricting the risk of abusive data processing and data dissemination by the FIU, legislators should therefore instead clearly limit the FIU's area of operational competence in assigning to it, beyond terrorism financing, the task of addressing only those forms of money laundering that, in view of their scope and purpose, constitute organised crime or that are processing the profits of organised crime or of similarly serious criminality. Similar to existing restrictions with regard to the competences of other intelligence agencies, FIUs' operational analyses should not target criminality the seriousness of which, in light of the security threat it poses, is merely low or does not require more than a short custodial sentence. Given that FIUs' analyses are largely excluded from external impartial scrutiny, such a limitation of the FIUs' data processing is however usually not enough to effectively prevent their analyses from being used in a disproportionate way. Rather, legislators will need to set limits on the dissemination of information by FIUs to criminal justice authorities. Again in line with the generally high intrusiveness of their operational analyses, FIUs should be allowed to disseminate information to criminal justice authorities only if the information is relevant for the investigation and prosecution of serious crime, that is crime of a particular seriousness that usually calls for more than short custodial sentences.[230] In order

[230] To the extent that it would have regard to the seriousness of the particular case and not (only) the abstract categorisation of an offence, this standard would, in principle, be more restrictive than the meaning of "serious criminal offences" used in Article 2 para. 12 of Directive (EU) 2019/1153 of 20 June 2019 and Annex I of Regulation (EU) 2016/794 of the European Parliament and of the Council of 11 May 2016 on the European Union Agency for Law Enforcement Cooperation (Europol) and replacing and repealing Council Decisions 2009/371/JHA, 2009/934/JHA, 2009/935/JHA, 2009/936/JHA and 2009/968/JHA.

to ensure effectiveness of this safeguard and prevent FIUs' powers from being used against individuals and companies irrespective of the seriousness of the suspected crime, this limitation on the FIUs' dissemination power must also apply to information that the FIU claims is only a chance discovery and not the product of a deliberate effort, because due to the confidentiality of the FIU's operations this claim can usually not be independently verified.

D. PRIVATE SECTOR PREVENTION

1. *Improving Coherence of "De-Risking"*

a. Current State

The AML framework attributes a key role to the private sector to prevent money laundering. Obliged entities are required to know their customers and understand the purpose of business relationships and transactions in order to be able to detect cases of money laundering. However, while the law defines when and which CDD measures have to be performed, it is much less clear about when obliged entities should or must abstain from entering a business relationship or performing a transaction. On closer inspection, there are three distinct triggers that can lead to an AML-related termination of a business relationship or transaction: (i) the offence of money laundering, (ii) the inability to perform required CDD measures and (iii) de-risking, that is the precautionary avoidance of clients. In addition, obliged entities are, under EU law, also under an obligation to suspend a business relationship or transaction if they suspect money laundering and therefore file an SAR,[231] but such a suspicion as well as the filing of a report do not on their own usually yet give rise to a duty to permanently terminate the reported activity.[232]

(i) To begin with, obliged entities and their employees have of course to comply with the prohibition of money laundering under criminal law. In line with Directive 2018/1673,[233] this means that obliged entities and their employees are not allowed to entertain a business relationship or perform a transaction if they *know* that relevant property is the proceeds of crime; otherwise they will usually be criminally liable themselves for money laundering, either as a principal or as an accessory. Depending on the form of money laundering offences under the respective national criminal law, criminal liability for money

231 For a different approach in this regard, see Switzerland, section III.C.1.d, which even provides an obligation *not* to suspend a suspicious transaction upon the filing of an SAR.

232 See Article 35 para. 1 of Directive (EU) 2015/849 of 20 May 2015.

233 Article 3 para. 1 of Directive (EU) 2018/1673 of 23 October 2018.

laundering might already be triggered by a less demanding *mens rea* standard than the one set forth by Directive 2018/1673,[234] for example *dolus eventualis* (meaning that it is enough that the employee merely *suspected* a criminal origin of assets and consciously accepted money laundering as a possible consequence of his or her behaviour),[235] suspicion[236] or gross negligence (meaning that the employee might be liable even where he or she was not aware of an unreasonably high risk).[237] Insofar as the threshold of the applicable national criminal law is reached, obliged entities and their employees have to abstain from the respective activity irrespective of CDD and reporting obligations.

(ii) Furthermore, under the EU legal framework, obliged entities are under an obligation to abstain from a business relationship or transaction if they are unable to perform the CDD measures required in the particular case.[238] Accordingly, obliged entities are prevented from entering or continuing a business relationship or performing a transaction if they are *unable* to verify the identity of the client and of any beneficial owner and assess the nature and purpose of a business relationship. Such inability can notably result from an unwillingness of the client to provide relevant information and documentation, but also from legal or factual limits to the obliged entity's ability to gather sufficiently reliable information. The obligation to abstain from a business relationship or transaction in the case of incomplete compliance with the applicable CDD requirements is in fact the core rational underpinning the CDD framework. Both the obliged entity and the client are thereby forced to either make sufficient efforts to provide the required financial transparency or, otherwise, to abstain from the relationship or transaction.

(iii) Finally, the aforementioned obligation to abstain from business relationships or transactions does lead to another form of their termination on AML grounds, namely termination due to the obliged entity's *unwillingness* to perform the applicable CDD measures. As the performance of those measures leads to expenses, not least to staff costs and potentially also costs incurred through the outsourcing of some measures, obliged entities will usually balance those costs against the potential gains expected from the respective client. The higher the risk that a client is presumed to constitute, and therefore the more comprehensive the required CDD and in particular enhanced CDD measures, the less attractive it will in principle be for the obliged entity to keep the client.[239]

---

234 Article 3 para. 2 of Directive (EU) 2018/1673 of 23 October 2018.

235 See for example Germany, section II.B.1.b, Italy, section II.B.1.b, and Spain, section II.B.1.b.

236 See United Kingdom, section II.B.1.b.

237 See Germany, section II.B.1.b, and Spain, section II.B.1.b.

238 Article 14 para. 4(1) of Directive (EU) 2015/849 of 20 May 2015.

239 See T Durner/L Shetret, Understanding bank de-risking and its effect on financial inclusion, Oxfam, 2015, pp. 9–12.

The termination of a business relationship and the non-performance of a transaction are thus not least also the result of an economic balancing between expected costs and the economic potential that a particular client poses. In other words, the less economically attractive a client is, and the higher the risk attributed to him or her, the higher the chance of a termination of the client relationship. Besides direct economic costs, the decision of obliged entities will furthermore also often be guided by reputational concerns regarding possible bad media coverage in the event of an involvement in money laundering and terrorism financing.[240] Given that private businesses usually enjoy a wide margin of freedom of contract following from the freedom to conduct business according to Article 16 of the Charter of Fundamental Rights, the law provides very few limits to an obliged entity's decision to abandon a client even if, from a purely objective point, the risk posed by him or her seems hardly significant. Directive 2014/92, which provides for a right to a payment account with basic features,[241] constitutes a notable exception to this rule. In fact, in light of the costs of CDD, as well as the threat of sanctions and possible reputational damages, obliged entities are usually not expected to assume risks to which they did not consent. As a consequence, while CDD is today expected to follow a risk-based approach, the determination of an unacceptable risk remains contingent upon considerations other than the risk that a particular client entails, first and foremost upon economic considerations. In other words, the level of risk underlying de-risking remains largely unspecific.

b. Challenges

De-risking poses three interrelated questions, namely (i) to what extent it is acceptable for customers to be subjected to potentially discriminatory preventive measures by obliged entities and thus by private bodies, (ii) whether such discriminatory effects of CDD can be attributed to states and what legal consequences would result from such attribution, and finally (iii) whether incoherence in de-risking practice, besides its potentially discriminatory effect, also reflects uncertainty about the primary purpose of obliged entities' involvement in AML.

(i) The ambiguity of de-risking standards and the resulting extensive flexibility that obliged entities enjoy in determining their risk appetite is not without major

240 See K Kirschenmann/L Borchert, The Fight Against Financial Crime: How Global Banks' De-Risking Affects Trade and the Local Economy, 2017, available at SSRN https://ssrn.com/abstract=3088506; M Brei/L Cato/R DeLisle Worrell, Credibility, Reputation and De-Risking in Global Banking: Evidence from a Theoretical Model, 11 *Journal of Globalization and Development* (2020) (ahead-of-publication).

241 Article 16 of Directive (EU) 2014/92 of 23 July 2014 on the comparability of fees related to payment accounts, payment account switching and access to payment accounts with basic features.

drawbacks. Obviously, the termination of business relationships and the rejection of transactions due to a heightened money laundering risk are a crucial part of the obliged entities' preventive function. However, the lack of clear de-risking criteria[242] increases the probability that business relationships and transactions will be abandoned due to essentially unfounded suspicions or discriminatory criteria.[243] As is now widely recognised and has been acknowledged by the FATF,[244] the partial delegation of crime prevention inherent in AML will thereby lead to frequent collateral damage. This concerns in particular the concern that legitimate businesses and private activities of individuals are impeded less because they entail a substantiated unreasonable risk, and more because obliged entities are unwilling to assume even little-substantiated risks if commercial considerations do not clearly favour retention of the client.[245] Furthermore, especially insofar as obliged entities are under their respective national law allowed to share with other obliged entities information related to the de-risking of particular clients even in the absence of the filing of an SAR,[246] de-risking decisions can take effect beyond the relationship between the individual client and the de-risking obliged entity. For other obliged entities' policy towards the same client may then be adversely influenced by prior de-risking decisions and thereby potentially lead to a wider stigmatisation.

The described drawbacks of little-defined de-risking standards also raise a more general question, namely how far it is acceptable to subject individuals to potentially serious consequences solely on the basis of a private risk assessment. After all, with the decline of cash as the primary means of payment, economic and thereby social inclusion relies more and more on the access to financial services.[247] Even if the provision of basic banking services can to some extent

242 L Levi, Punishing Banks, Their Clients and Their Clients' Clients, in C King/C Walker/J Gurulé (eds.), The Palgrave Handbook of Criminal and Terrorism Financing Law, Vol. 1, 2018, pp. 277–279.

243 Concerns to this effect also in Opinion of the European Data Protection Supervisor (EDPS) on a proposal for a Directive on the prevention of the use of the financial system for the purpose of money laundering and terrorist financing of 4 July 2013, especially at para. 78.

244 FATF, Guidance on AML/CFT measures and financial inclusion, with a supplement on customer due diligence, 2017.

245 See in more detail Center for Global Development, Unintended Consequences of Anti-Money Laundering Policies for Poor Countries, 2015; T Durner/L Shetret, Understanding Bank De-Risking and its Effects on Financial Inclusion: An exploratory study, 2015, pp. 19–23; D Artingstall/N Dove/J Howell/M Levi, Drivers & Impacts of Derisking, 2016, pp. 17–27; A Amicelle/V Iafolla, Suspicion-in-the-making: Surveillance and Denunciation in Financial Policing, 58(4) *The British Journal of Criminology* (2018), pp. 857–858.

246 For the diverging solutions of national laws in this respect, see Comparative Analysis, section V.K.

247 See AY Shehu, Promoting financial inclusion for effective anti-money laundering and counter financing of terrorism, 57 *Crime, Law and Social Change* (2012), pp. 307–310.

be guaranteed by an individual right to a basic payment account, the scope of such a guarantee does not extend to legal entities and partnerships, even if they pursue legitimate aims protected as such under constitutional law. It is then not unlikely that de-risking will in many cases interfere with perfectly legal and even desirable activities, including political and wider civil society activities. The effect of a de-risking can be particularly problematic in cases where numerous obliged entities, possibly triggered by extensive data sharing between them[248] or due to the need to conform to the risk standards of more powerful parties within a correspondent banking relationship,[249] adopt similar de-risking strategies and can thereby effectively bring about a market-wide blacklisting of particular individuals and entities.

(ii) At first glance, detrimental effects of de-risking on legitimate activities could be taken to be solely the result of obliged entities' freedom of contract and not impact on the legality of the AML framework. After all, obliged entities can rarely be forced to enter into or continue a client relationship. Such a perspective would however be too narrow and overlook the fact that de-risking essentially results from the legislators' decision to partially delegate certain crime prevention functions to the private sector. Any governmental decision addressed to a private business prohibiting the provision of services to a particular client would usually constitute a state interference with the client's applicable rights and, depending of the nature of the rights concerned, require adequate justifications. Insofar as a legislator delegates this decision to the private business, one must then ask to what extent the cessation of services is imputable to the state. This question becomes all the more acute if the private business's decision to de-risk is based on relevant money laundering typologies or even more detailed information about particular money laundering threats and vulnerabilities which are provided by national or supranational public authorities.[250] According to the European Court of Human Rights, a state cannot absolve itself of its responsibility to respect fundamental rights by delegating its obligations to private bodies.[251] In some

248 On the lack of legislative frameworks as regards a non-SAR-related data sharing, see Comparative Analysis, section V.K.

249 On the impact of de-risking on correspondent banking, see Center for Global Development, Unintended Consequences of Anti-Money Laundering Policies for Poor Countries, 2015, pp. 29–34; V Ramachandran/M Collin/M Juden, De-risking: An Unintended Negative Consequence of AML/CFT Regulation, in C King/C Walker/J Gurulé (eds.), The Palgrave Handbook of Criminal and Terrorism Financing Law, Vol. 1, 2018, pp. 252–257.

250 See also A Amicelle/G Favarel-Garrigues, La lutte contre l'argent sale au prisme des libertés fondamentales : quelles mobilisations?, 76 *Cultures & Conflits* (2009), pp. 62–63, with an account of the changing face of the relationship between financial institutions and their clients as a result of the former being frequently perceived as performing quasi-administrative functions.

251 ECtHR (Grand Chamber), Kotov v. Russia, judgment of 3 April 2012, app. no. 54522/00, para. 92; ECtHR, Vukota-Bojic v. Switzerland, judgment of 18 October 2017, app. no. 61838/10, para. 47.

cases, it would indeed seem that the interaction between a competent authority and an obliged entity may lead to a direct imputation of the obliged entity's action to the state, in particular where the obliged entity is adopting measures against a customer on the instruction of a competent authority and thus enjoys little or no discretion.[252] Yet, even insofar as the decision to de-risk is taken by the obliged entity on the basis of an autonomous assessment of the risk of the particular case, one cannot overlook the fact that the performance of CDD directly results from the AML/CTF obligations imposed by the state on obliged entities.[253] To the extent that these obligations result in discriminatory or otherwise arbitrary effects to the detriment of individuals, legislators must, especially in view of Article 21 of the Charter of Fundamental Rights, take partial responsibility and ensure that, to the extent that this is adequate, such effects are averted.[254] The more CDD and de-risking practice is predetermined by information provided to obliged entities by the competent authorities,[255] the more legislation must address the resulting risk of unsubstantiated discrimination.[256]

Legislation must therefore ensure that it establishes the right balance between the conflicting interests at stake, namely on the one hand the obliged entity's need not to be exposed to overly burdensome constraints and risks, including reputational risks and the risk of sanctions, and on the other hand the need for respect of clients' legitimate interests, in particular their interest in not being

252 See ECtHR (Grand Chamber), Kotov v. Russia, judgment of 3 April 2012, app. no. 54522/00, paras. 102–103.

253 The state's responsibility does thus not so much result from a (positive) obligation of the state to protect customers against rights infringements by private parties, but rather from the state's (negative) obligation to itself refrain from such infringements; cf. for the former case (with regard to the right to private life under Article 8 ECHR), ECtHR, de la Flor Cabrera v. Spain, decision of 27 May 2014, app. no. 10764/09, paras. 32–33.

254 On the horizontal effect of fundamental rights between private parties in particular as regards the right to non-discrimination, see ECJ (Grand Chamber), judgment of 9 January 2010 (Seda Kücükdevec v. Swedex GmbH & Co. KG), C-555/07, para. 50, and ECJ (Grand Chamber), judgment of 15 January 2014 (Association de Médiation Sociale v. Hichem Laboubi), C-176/12, para. 47; ECJ (Grand Chamber), judgment of 17 April 2018 (Vera Egenberger v. Evangelisches Werk für Diakonie und Entwicklung eV), C-414/16, paras. 76–78; M de Mol, The novel approach of the CJEU on the horizontal direct effect of the EU principle of non-discrimination: (unbridled) expansionism of EU law?, 18 *Maastricht Journal of European and Comparative Law* (2011), esp. pp. 123–128; E Frantziou, The Horizontal Effect of the Charter of Fundamental Rights of the EU: Rediscovering the Reasons for Horizontality, 21 *European Law Journal* (2015), pp. 661–665. Note also the recognition of a horizontal effect of Articles 7 and 8 of the Charter of Fundamental Rights in ECJ (Grand Chamber), judgment of 13 May 2014 (Google Spain, SL, Google Inc v. Agencia Espanola de Proteccion de Datos), C-131/12, paras. 74, 81.

255 On the increasingly collaborative design of the EU framework with regard to the preliminary identification of ML/TF threats and vulnerabilities by EU and national authorities, see *infra* section III.F.2.a.

256 Note that, according to recital 66 of Directive (EU) 2015/849 of 20 May 2015, Member States are to ensure respect, within the context of CDD, for the prohibition of discrimination enshrined in Article 21 of the Charter.

subjected to discriminatory or otherwise arbitrary de-risking standards. The need for respect of the clients' interests within what is essentially a criminal policy framework does not mean that obliged entities are comprehensively held accountable to the same standards as state authorities, but it indicates a need to have in place substantive and procedural safeguards that prevent the abuse of de-risking. The more obliged entities are included in the prevention of crime (in particular by increasingly closer cooperation between them and the FIU through higher numbers of SARs and FIU information requests), the greater the risk this cooperation poses for fundamental rights, and thus the more important the need to adequately prescribe limits for de-risking.

(iii) Unclear de-risking standards can also have the potential to negatively affect criminal investigations in that an information request by criminal justice authorities or the FIU will frequently cause the requested obliged entity to reassess their business relationship with individuals who have been named by the requesting authority as being the target of a criminal investigation or an operational analysis. The obliged entity will then often decide to terminate its relationship with such clients, which – even without an explicit disclosure to the client – can easily result in a tip-off that allows the targeted client to inhibit the success of subsequent investigative measures. In this respect, de-risking also raises a basic question about the intended objectives of CDD. For the more extensively obliged entities have recourse to de-risking, the more clients, in particular clients that pose a higher risk, will disappear from the radar of obliged entities' CDD and thus become invisible to the FIU. On the one hand, in view of the aim of AML to protect the integrity of the financial sector and the wider economy, it would of course be counterproductive to allow high-risk clients and their assets into obliged entities. On the other hand, the more rigorous obliged entities' de-risking standards, the less capable CDD and reporting obligations will be of detecting criminal activity. In other words, and similarly to questions highlighted above[257] with regard to the purposes of AML, the question arises whether obliged entities are meant primarily to be gatekeepers of the financial system or rather to serve as a tool to facilitate the detection and investigation of predicate offences. The more the law aims at the latter function, the more limited obliged entities' discretion to de-risk. In contrast, if obliged entities are allowed or even obliged to extensively de-risk clients, the more limited the value of CDD and suspicious activities reporting is for the FIU and criminal investigations.

c. Reform

A legislative framework for de-risking must address two primary problems, namely (i) unintended collateral damage that results from obliged entities'

---

[257] See *supra* section I.A.1.

preventive efforts to the detriment of customers, and (ii) the concern that de-risking may sometimes undermine the gathering of valuable information.

(i) As regards unintended consequences caused by de-risking, it must be recalled that, while obliged entities usually enjoy freedom of contract, they exercise this freedom within, and with a view to, the confines of the AML/CTF framework. To the extent that the legislator has set limits to the exercise of freedom of contract, the legality of actions undertaken by obliged entities due to these limits can of course not be assessed in isolation from the legislative demands. If these demands lead to an interference with individual rights, this is then not only a consequence of obliged entities' freedom of contract, but also a consequence of the legislation. By imposing an obligation on obliged entities to screen their clients and subject them to a preventive risk assessment, legislators expose individuals and companies to the risk of being subjected to limitations on the exercise of various rights conditioned by the availability of adequate financial services. Insofar as such limitations are attributable more to the legislative framework than to obliged entities' autonomous business choices, the legislator cannot remain indifferent to unintended results, at least in cases where the interests of affected clients clearly outweigh the public interest in an effective prevention of money laundering and the respective obliged entities' interest in not seeing its freedom of contract unduly restricted.

- Require obliged entities not to terminate business relationships for reasons of AML/CTF in cases where a risk is not substantiated by more than general statistical assumptions

Resulting from the legislator's responsibility for the consequences of its framework, a decision to de-risk, insofar as based on AML considerations, is subject to limitations. As a minimum constraint, de-risking cannot be justified by the obliged entity's AML/CTF obligations if it is obvious that the termination of a business relationship or the rejection of a transaction is not rationally comprehensible or if this decision is merely speculative. For while obliged entities enjoy freedom of contract, they cannot be allowed to base legally relevant decisions to the detriment of a client on preventive considerations that, in the instance of the particular case, are not relevant or merely fanciful and that seemingly do not also indicate a significant reputational risk for them. This limitation obviously puts some limits on obliged entities' freedom of contract, but such limits are necessary in order not to leave individuals and legal entities unprotected from unintended consequences of obliged entities' CDD obligations. The necessary balance between the interests of the obliged entity and the client is upheld by the requirement that only obviously incorrect de-risking decisions are invalidated. Any remaining marginal risk that the client might be related to financial crime is an operational hazard that is an unavoidable part of the provision of financial services and that, in light of the legitimate interests of other rights holders, the obliged entity cannot be allowed to avoid through an arbitrary or speculative termination of contractual obligations. To assess the proportionality of this moderate limitation of obliged entities' freedom of contract, one should also recall that the AML framework does ultimately also serve obliged entities themselves in that it aims at protecting them from being exposed to, or even infiltrated by, criminal players, in particular powerful transnational organised criminal groups. As AML is thus put in place not least also for the benefit of the private sector, obliged entities can be expected to ensure that their CDD practice as far as reasonably feasible avoids excessive side-effects that may put the proportionality of the framework into question. At least insofar as any continuation of services does not put an extensive economic burden on the concerned obliged entity and is limited to clients where from an objective point of view the exposure to financial crime risks is clearly not substantiated by more than general statistical considerations, obliged entities can be required by law to contribute to the avoidance of collateral damage by refraining from de-risking.

- Provide for a review of obliged entities' decision to terminate services if affected customers present reasonable grounds that the termination was AML/CTF-related

This restriction on AML/CTF-based de-risking of course does not exclude the possibility that the obliged entity may terminate a business relationship for other reasons unrelated to the risk of financial crime. To protect clients' legitimate interests and thereby ensure that the legislator takes its responsibility for unintended consequences of the AML/CTF framework seriously, the law should therefore ensure that alternative grounds of termination are not used to circumvent the aforementioned limitations. If the client can establish reasonable grounds that he or she was subjected to a suspension or termination of services due to an obliged entity's AML/CTF obligations, the obliged entity, in order to uphold the validity of its measures, should then be required to conclusively demonstrate that these measures were in fact based on grounds other than the risk of financial crime. Otherwise, insofar as de-risking would be allowed to extensively operate as a means of cost reduction rather than a tool to adequately address risks of financial crime, the legitimacy of the preventive framework and thereby ultimately its proportionality would be increasingly eroded.

(ii) As regards the loss of potentially valuable information due to de-risking, one must recall that the continuation of a business relationship between an obliged entity and a suspected client might even after the detection and reporting of money laundering provide the authorities with valuable information through follow-up reports. If, as will regularly be the case, the obliged entity decides to terminate the business relationship after having reported a suspicion, the authorities will lose this opportunity. It is equally clear that the decision to de-risk will in many situations constitute a tip-off that implicitly tells the suspect client that he or she is targeted by the authorities, and thereby sometimes endanger the success of criminal investigations. However, obliged entities should, in principle, not be required to monitor particular suspects and for this reason alone maintain the relationship; at most, they can be expected to temporarily keep silent about an ongoing criminal proceeding or an operational analysis that, to their knowledge, is targeting one of their clients. For employees of obliged entities are usually not trained investigators capable of communicating with the suspect client over a long period of time in a way that maintains the secrecy of the investigation or of the operational analysis. Furthermore, obliged entities do not operate under a level of judicial scrutiny comparable to investigators that would allow the legislator to entrust them with surveillance tasks. Finally, as can be learned from the experience with police informers, any deeper involvement of private actors as a source of information in criminal investigations can carry significant personal risks for the employees involved, especially in the area of organised crime.

- Empower FIUs to order obliged entities to temporarily continue a suspicious business relationship without however requiring them to actively engage with the suspect customer

As a consequence, and in light of the fact that the more time passes, the more difficult the obliged entity will find it to hide the criminal investigation or operational analysis from the client and to adapt its communication with him or her accordingly, any obligation not to de-risk despite the detection of criminal activity must be temporally limited to reasonably short periods that limits the danger that the obliged entity's employees are getting deeply involved in the criminal investigation. As importantly, any temporary prohibition on de-risking for the protection of the secrecy of state proceedings should not at the same time require the obliged entity to actively engage with the suspect client for the purpose of collecting more information. For such interaction would be very likely both to disclose relevant information to the client and at the same time endanger the respective employee. Thus, while the obliged entity would still be able to report new observations to the FIU and criminal justice authorities, it would usually only notify information that the client on his or her own initiative (including through the performance of transactions) chose to disclose. The authorities must finally also ensure that the ongoing communication between the obliged entity and the client is not abused for the purpose of circumventing the suspect's procedural rights, in particular the privilege against self-incrimination, through deceptive schemes and the exercise of inadequate pressure.

- Require obliged entities to notify the FIU and the competent supervisory authority of any instance of AML/CTF-based de-risking

In order to protect the interests of clients in line with the above substantive criteria and at the same time ensure that valuable information is not lost due to early de-risking, legislators should provide adequate mechanisms. To this end, obliged entities could be required to communicate to the FIU and also to the competent supervisory authority basic information about any instance of AML/CTF-based de-risking, at least the identity of the (prospective or former) client, the nature of the terminated or rejected business and a brief explanation of the reasons for de-risking. Such notification would have two distinct functions. On the one hand, it would prevent a loss of potentially relevant information to the detriment of the FIU even if the obliged entity did not, or not yet, suspect criminal conduct and therefore did not file an SAR. On the other hand, the notification would provide supervisory authorities with a comprehensive picture of obliged entities' de-risking standards, which could help to detect cases or patterns of excessive de-risking as well as of an obliged entity's above-average risk appetite. Individual clients that can demonstrate reasonable grounds to believe that they were suspect to AML/CTF-based de-risking could then apply to the competent supervisory authority to trigger an administrative review of the obliged entity's conduct and, where applicable, also ensure that insufficiently substantiated claims shared with other obliged entities are marked as such by the supervisory authority.

2. *Preventing Deliberate Wrongdoing Inside Obliged Entities*

a. Current State

The quality of CDD of course depends not only on the ability of obliged entities to detect criminal assets, but equally on the prevention of deliberate violations of the law by obliged entities' employees. This includes the case where employees collaborate with criminal clients, as well the case where employees otherwise consciously accept inappropriate money laundering risks in order to make use of profitable business opportunities. EU law anticipates the possibility of such deliberate wrongdoings in various ways, in particular through requiring obliged entities to document and thereby render traceable their CDD practice and through the Member States' obligation to equip supervisory authorities with adequate powers.[258] Beyond this, EU law also addresses decision-making within obliged entities by measures to ensure illegal assets and wrongdoing are

[258] Article 8 para. 4(a) and Article 48 paras. 2 and 3 of Directive (EU) 2015/849 of 20 May 2015.

not shielded from the competent authorities. Four elements are of particular relevance in this respect.

First, "where appropriate with regard to the size and nature of the business", obliged entities are required to appoint a compliance officer and to perform "employee screening".[259] As regards compliance officers, their very purpose implies that they are meant to serve as control bodies that operate outside the sphere of an obliged entity's primarily economic considerations and, as such, require independence vis-à-vis the obliged entity's executive management and its commercial decision-makers. EU law does not however further specify when exactly the appointment of a compliance officer is deemed appropriate or what particular powers such officer shall have in the exercise of his or her function. In a similar vein, EU law does not specify when exactly and to what extent employee screening is required.

Second, employees and representatives of obliged entities who report suspicious activities internally or to the FIU must be protected from "threats and hostile action", in particular from adverse measures under employment law. Employees who, as a consequence of their reporting, are subject to retaliatory or other adverse actions are entitled to present a complaint to the respective competent authorities.[260]

Third, EU law today emphasises the role of whistleblowers in reporting relevant wrongdoing within obliged entities. Supervisory authorities, or, where applicable, self-regulatory bodies, are required to establish mechanisms to encourage the reporting of potential or actual violations of relevant obligations. Such mechanisms shall ensure confidentiality of the identity of the reporting person, unless disclosure is required by national law in the context of further investigations or judicial proceedings. A comparable mechanism must, in a way that is proportionate to their nature and size, also be put in place by obliged entities to enable employees to report violations internally.[261]

Fourth, obliged entities are required to put in place internal control procedures and, where appropriate to their size and nature, an independent audit function to test internal policies, controls and procedures.[262] Again EU AML law does however not specify the design of such internal controls and audits.

b. Challenges

The current EU AML framework (i) provides little detail about the prevention of wrongdoing committed inside obliged entities, and thereby fails to adequately

---

259 Article 8 para. 4(a) and Article 48 paras. 2 and 3 of Directive (EU) 2015/849 of 20 May 2015. Note that the Directive's use of the term "compliance officer" refers to the head of AML compliance; see European Union, section III.E.

260 Article 38 of Directive (EU) 2015/849 of 20 May 2015.

261 Article 61 of Directive (EU) 2015/849 of 20 May 2015, as amended by Directive (EU) 2018/843 of 30 May 2018.

262 Article 8 para. 4(a)(b) of Directive (EU) 2015/849 of 20 May 2015.

address in particular the risk (ii) that employees may collude with criminal clients and that (iii) relevant information may be internally withheld from compliance departments; the current law thereby ultimately (iv) increases the probability of structural weaknesses of an obliged entity's corporate culture being concealed by the ostensible failures of compliance officers.

(i) As results from the above-mentioned measures, EU law already anticipates that violations of CDD and reporting obligations constitute key obstacles to an effective prevention of money laundering. In particular, compliance officers are meant to ensure that an obliged entity's profit interests do not dominate the design and results of its AML compliance. Furthermore, the prohibition of adverse treatment of those who report suspicious activity or violations of AML obligations evidences the concern that relevant information might deliberately be withheld from the FIU and supervisory authorities. By requiring internal controls and, where appropriate, independent audits, the law acknowledges that employees' respect for AML obligations will also depend on measures that ensure that relevant violations are effectively detected.

Despite these acknowledgements of the challenges posed to AML by deliberate wrongdoing inside obliged entities, the current legal framework largely fails to provide sufficiently effective remedies. Not only do the relevant obligations under EU law remain unspecific, which concerns especially the role and powers of AML compliance officers and the design of internal controls, for which EU law provides no further guidance. More importantly, the law currently does not show sufficient concern for the threat emanating from deliberate wrongdoing inside obliged entities, and, as a consequence, provides hardly any meaningful guidance on how to design adequate mechanisms to address this threat. While the law acknowledges the risk emanating from internal wrongdoing, two omissions of the current law appear to be particularly relevant: lack of regard for the impact of criminal actors within obliged entities, and insufficient regard for the importance of internal information flows.

(ii) Corrupt employees of obliged entities who conspire with clients to circumvent compliance and reporting requirements are arguably the greatest challenge to the effectiveness of AML. However, while the law focuses on the detection of risks amongst the clients of obliged entities, little attention is paid to the detection of criminal employees of obliged entities. The asymmetry between on the one hand the extensively regulated CDD requirement and on the other hand the only brief references in EU law to internal controls, employee screening and audits are clearly unsatisfactory. After all, for criminals it will in many cases be much more useful (and, depending on the circumstances, even easier) to bribe or coerce a key employee of an obliged entity than to conceal the origin of their assets. Especially powerful organised criminal groups will, through a mixture of corruption and threats, often find it easier to manipulate the decision-making of an obliged entity than to merely rely on dissimulation strategies.[263] After all, in order to launder vast amounts of assets over a lengthy period of time, it can suffice for a criminal actor to control a handful of senior management officials of an obliged entity in order to thereby effectively switch off the obliged entity's AML compliance.[264] The ostensive weakness of obliged entities' prevention is today usually attributed to an insufficient quality of CDD. In contrast, policy debates regarding the effectiveness of AML have so far paid little attention to the possibility that the majority of criminal assets are not laundered primarily through complex dissimulation methods, but through the help of *mala fide* employees within obliged entities.[265] While reliable statistics for the volume of laundered assets are still lacking,[266] simply the sparse number of criminal cases involving large-scale laundering for transnational groups could indicate that successful laundering cannot be attributed only or even predominantly to dissimulation efforts by actors outside obliged entities, but rather that criminal actors inside such entities play a crucial role. The EU AML framework however currently contains few elements that would address this particular vulnerability. This concerns not least the possibility that such actors might take steps that, through the dissimulation of traces of criminal wrongdoing (not least by not documenting risk-signalling client information), undermine the ability of the obliged entity's internal control mechanism to detect the wrongdoing.

(iii) As regards the internal flow of information within obliged entities, one must note that EU law is at the moment only concerned with the possibility that employees might withhold relevant information from compliance officers or from the competent authorities due to fear of adverse personal consequences, not least employment-related consequences. It should however not be overlooked that a threat to the effectiveness of CDD and reporting stems not only (and arguably

---

263 For an indication to this effect, see M Levi/M Soudijn, Understanding the Laundering of Organized Crime Money, *Crime and Justice* (2020), section III.C, who quote estimates for the Netherlands that on average one professional money launderer is killed every year, and more are wounded.

264 For an example of the potential effectiveness of such approach, see Danish Financial Supervisory Authority (Finanstilsynet), Report on the Danish FSA's supervision of Danske Bank as regards the Estonia case of 28 January 2019, pp. 11–15.

265 This may also translate into the practice of competent authorities in that investigations into organised crime will oftentimes not pay sufficient attention to the involvement of professional money launderers, that is individuals that are usually not closely related to the predicate offenders; see in this vein the findings in MRJ Soudijn, Using strangers for money: a discussion on money-launderers in organized crime, 17 *Trends in Organized Crime* (2014), pp. 199–217, who argues that the ostensible absence of professional money launderers in the files of large scale organised crime cases is largely due to lacking focus on financial matters in investigative strategy.

266 M Levi/P Reuter/T Halliday, Can the AML system be evaluated without better data?, 69 *Crime, Law and Social Change* (2018), pp. 307–328.

not even primarily) from the non-reporting of CDD-relevant information due to fear of detrimental personal consequences, but also from the non-reporting of relevant information as a consequence of an employee's personal economic interest. Not least the creation of large compliance departments within obliged entities underlines the importance of internal reporting. Compliance officers may make it more likely that compliance-related decisions remain unaffected by profit considerations. However, growing operational autonomy of compliance departments within obliged entities and the professionalisation of such departments by the hiring of staff with a career background in law enforcement[267] at the same time leads to a growing divide between compliance officers and other employees.[268] What at first glance might look like a success story of compliance-oriented management – in particular the hiring of highly skilled and self-confident compliance officers – can on closer inspection in many cases effectively be little more than a form of window-dressing. For the more other employees, especially sales agents and account managers, assume that the compliance officers of their company adopt a thorough and uncompromising approach to money laundering risk prevention, the more hesitant these employees will be to share information with their compliance department. This means that they might withhold information if they assume that this information could call into question the performance of a profitable business relationship or transaction. As a result, while compliance officers are usually a key prerequisite for effective AML, a strengthening of compliance departments will at the same time increase the likelihood that relevant information from within the obliged entity is withheld from compliance officers.

Currently, EU law does not adequately address the challenge posed by deliberate violations of CDD and reporting obligations within obliged entities. Documentation and audits can of course potentially lead to an uncovering of wrongdoing even where relevant information was initially withheld from compliance officers. Yet if such information (for example information that would have triggered enhanced CDD) was not even documented in the first place, compliance officers' power to access internal information and even independent

---

267 See e.g. G Favarel-Garrigues/T Godefroy/P Lascoumes, Sentinels in the banking industry. Private actors and the fight against money laundering in France, 48 *British Journal of Criminology* (2008), pp. 3–6.

268 See however Article 46 para. 4 of Directive (EU) 2015/849 of 20 May 2015, according to which obliged entities are required to identify a "member of the management board who is responsible for the implementation of [AML] laws". As this individual shall (at least in larger obliged entities) not be part of the compliance department, EU law already seemingly indicates a need to bridge the divide between business operations and AML compliance, however without further specifying how the member of the management board is supposed to accomplish this function. For a more specific definition of this function at the national level, see Comparative Analysis, section III.A.1.c.

audits will regularly not lead to the exposure of problematic cases. In a similar vein, measures that stimulate and protect whistleblowers can potentially trigger the uncovering of internal wrongdoing, but these measures will usually provide little substantive insights where deviant actors within an obliged entity have shielded relevant information not only from compliance officers, but also from other colleagues. Altogether, EU law therefore currently lacks sufficient mechanisms to detect internal wrongdoing and to avert the risk that compliance departments may through the withholding of relevant information effectively be isolated from an obliged entity's commercial operations.

(iv) In the end, the centralisation of compliance-related responsibilities in the hands of compliance officers even risks focusing internal and supervisory attention away from employees working within an obliged entity's commercial operations and towards compliance officers. For if respect for AML obligations is perceived primarily as the responsibility of compliance officers, this can invite corporate policies that deliberately shift the blame for an obliged entity's AML deficiencies away from employees operating outside compliance departments. Instead of uncovering the structural reasons for wrongdoing within the wider company (for example, as the case may be, sales agents' unreasonably high risk appetite hidden through the withholding of CDD-relevant information) and thereby addressing systemic failures, compliance officers and their ostensible breaches of duty can then serve as a convenient explanation for CDD and reporting violations. It is obviously important for obliged entities to have adequate internal controls, including where appropriate compliance officers. AML-related failings of the company must however not solely or primarily be attributed to those internal controllers, especially where there are reasons to believe that the failings in essence originate from deliberate wrongdoing by employees other than the controllers.

c. Reform

In order to address the above-mentioned challenges, EU and national legislators should provide additional rules on the internal decision-making of obliged entities. This should include (i) internal rules, especially on the relationship between clients and employees as well as on the relationship between account managers and compliance departments, (ii) obligations to internally investigate possible wrongdoing even in the absence of a particular suspicion, and (iii) powers of supervisory authorities to conduct or order an independent audit of obliged entities' past handling of criminal clients.

- Ensure that obliged entities prevent the withholding of relevant information from compliance officers and that sensitive customers are not handled exclusively by one and the same employee

(i) While it is important to protect the operational independence of compliance officers vis-à-vis the company's profit interests, it is equally necessary to ensure that compliance officers have adequate access to all CDD-relevant information. This of course includes their power to have unhindered and unannounced access to all relevant internal information and to be protected from adverse employment or other consequences of their function. As importantly, legislators must however also provide for mechanisms that avert or hamper the withholding of relevant information by employees and similar individuals within the obliged entity. As a minimum precaution, relationships between an individual high-volume or otherwise sensitive customer and an individual account manager should not be allowed to develop into quasi-personal relationships. Obliged entities should therefore be required to ensure that such customers are not handled exclusively by one and the same employee over a long period of time.[269] Internal procedures should ensure that account managers are in this case regularly rotated or other measures adopted to ensure that the customer relationship is managed and supervised by employees whose selection the customer cannot influence. Similar considerations should apply to the relationship between an individual account manager or sales agent and an individual compliance officer. Here too, the law should provide procedures that ensure regular rotation within compliance departments or that at least ensure that particular high-volume or otherwise sensitive customers are not always checked by the same individual compliance officers over a long period of time.

- Require obliged entities to analyse past CDD processes if they learn that a customer was involved in serious crime and, due to the nature or scope of this criminality, internal failings seem likely

(ii) To improve the detection of deliberate wrongdoing within obliged entities, legislators should furthermore specify procedures to this effect. In particular, large obliged entities offer an opportunity to criminal actors to hide illicit activities behind a greater volume of legitimate transactions and behind a multitude of other employees. Internal control mechanisms, independent audits and even supervisory inspections will often fail because the incriminating information was not documented, and they will instead usually have regard above all to internal documents that were produced by the very employees that might have deliberately circumvented CDD obligations. CDD documentation can therefore be more useful for detecting negligent violations than for detecting

[269] See also European Banking Authority et al., Joint Guidelines under Articles 17 and 18(4) of Directive (EU) 2015/849 on simplified and enhanced customer due diligence and the factors credit and financial institutions should consider when assessing the money laundering and terrorist financing risk associated with individual business relationships and occasional transactions of 26 June 2017, para. 149.

deliberate ones. In the case of heavy reliance on internal CDD documentation, it can hardly come as a surprise that independent audits and supervisory controls might in many cases fail to detect deliberate wrongdoing even where, due to the obliged entity's extensive contact with proven facilitators of money laundering, the absence of at least some level of awareness on the part of an employee of the obliged entity appears rather improbable. To discover the circumstances of a business relationship or transaction beyond of what is readily discernible from the CDD documentation, auditors and supervisors would usually need to gain further information, in particular communication records between employees and clients, observations from third parties (such as business partners of the client) as well as from employees other than those that documented relevant events, and possibly also analyses of bulk data pertaining to the employees that were involved in the respective business dealings. In light of the efforts and resources that this requires, wide-scale or periodic audits and supervisory controls will usually not be able to inquire deeply into the facts behind particular CDD documentation. Criminal justice authorities, in turn, would of course usually be much better positioned to verify these facts. Yet, as long as the obliged entity itself or one of its employees is not suspected of criminal wrongdoing, criminal investigations are normally not feasible. Equally, an obliged entity will most of the time have rather little interest in thoroughly investigating past internal events through an internal investigation as long as this obliged entity is not confronted with, or anticipating, a criminal or supervisory investigation against itself. On the contrary, their understandable interest in not being subjected to sanctions for violations of CDD and reporting obligations might potentially de-incentivise obliged entities from investigating possible internal wrongdoing on their own initiative. Consequently, as long as it is not uncovered by a whistleblower or in the course of an investigation by state authorities, internal wrongdoing, and with it criminal actors inside an obliged entity, are therefore rather likely to go undetected.

In order to increase the probability that internal wrongdoing is detected, the law should therefore require measures that stress the responsibility of obliged entities and the competent authorities to investigate internal business conduct even in cases where neither the respective obliged entity nor one of its employees is so far suspected of having committed a criminal or administrative wrongdoing. For such investigative measures, it should suffice that the circumstances of the particular case suggest that instances of money laundering may have been overlooked by the obliged entity, even if there are no indications that this failure was due to conscious wrongdoing. Such measures should already start at the level of compliance officers. Legislators should clarify that effective AML by an obliged entity requires not only the performance of adequate CDD measures, but also measures that seek to detect past failures in the obliged entity's CDD in order to identify and remedy systemic deficiencies and deliberate violations. The law should therefore at least require that in any case where an obliged entity learns that one of its customers has been involved in criminal activity, this obliged entity must assess to what extent awareness of this criminal activity would have been relevant for assessing the customer's risk profile, and, if it would be relevant in that regard, take the appropriate measures to examine whether its previous business relationship with the said customer had been enabled or facilitated by improper considerations. Compliance officers cannot realistically be expected to perform an internal investigation in every single case where a customer was subsequently found to be or have been engaged in criminal conduct. However, obliged entities should be required to perform a comprehensive analysis of their past CDD practice regarding this particular customer at least where, in light of the nature or scope of the revealed criminal activity, failings in the obliged entity's previous CDD seem likely. In this way, obliged entities would not only review the effectiveness of their internal control mechanisms, but above all increase the probability that deliberate wrongdoing by employees is brought to light.

- Empower supervisory authorities to order an independent audit into an obliged entity's past handling of a particular criminal customer even when this entity is not suspected of wrongdoing

(iii) Beyond such measures as part of obliged entities' compliance, supervisory authorities should be empowered to conduct or order an independent audit into an obliged entity's past handling of a particular client even in the absence of a suspicion of wrongdoing by this entity if there is an obvious possibility (due to the client's involvement in criminal activity or his or her personal links to criminal actors) that this obliged entity may have been used by the client for the purpose of money laundering. To avoid the perception that an audited obliged entity is thereby potentially asked to assist in the building of a case against itself, the law should offer incentives to encourage active cooperation with auditors and supervisory authorities. For otherwise there would be an obvious risk of criminal actors inside obliged entities ultimately remaining undetected because the obliged entities' fear of sanctions might prevail over their interest in protecting themselves from criminal employees. To dissolve this tension, and considering the importance of preventing the infiltration of obliged entities by criminal networks,[270] the law should in particular provide that information about possible AML-related violations disclosed by the obliged entity in the course of a customer-specific audit must not serve as the basis for the imposition of sanctions on the audited entity. Such independent audits would then not only enhance the likelihood of criminal actors inside obliged entities being detected, but would also improve the ability of supervisory authorities to ensure that the

[270] See M Levi/P Reuter, Money Laundering, 34 *Crime and Justice* (2006), p. 322.

responsibility for internal wrongdoing is not primarily attributed to compliance officers where this wrongdoing is first and foremost the result of deliberate deviance by employees outside compliance departments.

E. PRIVATE SECTOR REPORTING

1. *Reshaping the Standards of Obliged Entities' Reporting Duties*

a. Current State

SARs by obliged entities to the FIU constitute a cornerstone of today's AML framework. While the EU provides that SARs must be filed "where the obliged entity knows, suspects or has reasonable grounds to suspect that funds, regardless of the amount involved, are the proceeds of criminal activity or are related to terrorist financing",[271] it does not however further specify the suspicion threshold to be adopted.[272] This ambiguity is particularly surprising in light of the fact that the applicable reporting standard is closely linked to the legality of reported transactions. For obliged entities are not, under EU law, in principle allowed to carry out suspicious transactions unless they have reported the matter and all relevant related information to the FIU and have complied with further instructions from the FIU or the competent authorities.[273] If it reports the respective transaction and receives no further instructions, the obliged entity may however proceed with the transaction even if a suspicion remains.[274] EU law does also not specify conditions (for example a particular threshold or suspicion) under which a competent authority may be required to veto the reported transaction. National legislators are therefore free to determine whether the filing of an SAR will, in principle, mean that a transaction must not be performed for good, or whether the obliged entity should permanently refrain from carrying out the transaction only if this entity does receive an explicit instruction to this effect from a competent authority. Even more far-reaching, EU law does not even exclude the possibility of national law authorising reported transactions even where the reporting person positively knows that a transaction is related to the proceeds of crime or terrorism financing,[275] thereby allowing Member States to one-sidedly prioritise the gathering of financial data over the gatekeeping function of obliged entities.[276] Depending on the

---

271 Article 33 para. 1 subpara. 1(a) of Directive (EU) 2015/849.

272 Comparative Analysis, section III.C.1.a.

273 Article 35 para. 1 in conjunction with Article 33 para. 1 of Directive (EU) 2015/849.

274 See Comparative Analysis, section III.C.1.d.

275 Article 35 para. 1 of Directive (EU) 2015/849.

276 See *supra* section I.A.1.

national framework, the filing of an SAR can therefore have very different effects in law. For it can either in principle negate the legality of a transaction even if the transaction would not fulfil the definition of money laundering, or, on the contrary, effectively constitute an authorisation of transactions that would otherwise lead to criminal liability of the reporting person.[277]

As a result of the vagueness of reporting standards and the indeterminacy of the legal effect of SARs,[278] various approaches to reporting can be adopted. Notwithstanding particular differences in the shape of national frameworks,[279] those approaches can be broadly classified into two groups:

- One ("quantitative") approach favours large numbers of reports and thus a rather low standard of suspicion, even if this means that many reports will eventually turn out to be unsubstantiated. This approach essentially aims to avoid valuable information being withheld from the FIU due to an overly demanding standard of suspicion.[280]
- Another ("qualitative") approach prefers quite a high standard of suspicion, thereby emphasising the ability as well as the responsibility of obliged entities to substantiate initial concerns about a transaction through the performance of CDD and as a result provide the FIU with greater detail as to the presence of a particular suspicion.[281]

Reporting standards will impact on the shape of the wider framework. Quantitative approaches are essentially motivated by the idea that the more unusual activities are reported, the easier it will be for the competent authorities to spot patterns and identify cases of money laundering. Underlying this concept is often the expectation that, with increasing digitalisation of businesses and ever more powerful analytical software, greater data stocks in the hands of the authorities will uncover hidden relations between *per se* inconclusive transactions and thereby eventually enhance detection capabilities.[282] In contrast, qualitative

277 See for example Germany, section II.B.1.a.

278 Note that the term "suspicious activities report" can itself be somewhat ambiguous. The FATF Recommendations and the preamble of Directive (EU) 2015/849 use the term "suspicious transaction report". However, notably with regard to notaries and other independent legal professionals, even the "assisting in the planning [...] of transactions" may give rise to a reporting duty; see Article 2 para. 1(3)(b) in conjunction with Article 33 para. 1 subpara. 2 of Directive (EU) 2015/849.

279 See Comparative Analysis, section III.C.

280 See FATF, section VIII, highlighting that, despite its continuing use of the term "suspicious" activity, the FATF today favours a rather quantitative approach.

281 See D Chaikin, How effective are suspicious transaction reporting systems?, 12 *Journal of Money Laundering Control* (2009), p. 245; for a qualitative approach see also Europol, From Suspicion to Action, Converting financial intelligence into greater operational impact, 2017.

282 See R Coelho/M De Simoni/J Prenio, Suptech applications for anti-money laundering, Financial Stability Institute Insights on policy implementation, no. 18, 2019, p. 10.

approaches assume that the usefulness of reporting does not so much depend on the number of reports, but on the substance of individual communications and their ability to trigger criminal investigations. According to this, obliged entities, through their CDD measures, are best placed to understand their clients and to assess whether a business activity is motivated by unlawful purposes or not. Following a qualitative approach, the law should as much as possible stimulate fact-finding by the private sector in order to identify cases of money laundering.

Quantitative and qualitative approaches can appear to be mutually exclusive. If obliged entities are under an obligation to report even in the presence of only a very low level of suspicion, it means that they are expected to report without having extensively analysed the suspicious facts on their own.[283] Such analysis would be unnecessary because a quantitative reporting standard does not require an initial suspicion to be substantiated beyond the information that was readily available to the obliged entity. In contrast, if obliged entities are required to report only if they have themselves carefully checked their initial suspicion (especially by requiring further documentation and asking questions of the client and by collecting information from third sources), they will not be under an obligation to report as long as they have no more than an initial suspicion. Given the flexibility accorded to national legislators by EU law, it seems however in principle possible for a national framework to combine both approaches by stipulating two distinct reporting obligations.[284]

b. Challenges

Uncertainty about the applicable standard on the part of obliged entities is not only bound to contribute to an incoherent reporting practice but may sometimes also reflect that the EU and national authorities[285] themselves are in doubt as to the purpose of the reporting regime. This uncertainty is unsatisfactory because, as a result, policymakers may fail to consider the impact of a chosen approach on (i) the overall quality of reporting, (ii) on affected persons, and (iii) on the gatekeeping function of obliged entities.

(i) Both qualitative and quantitative approaches entail disadvantages for the quality of reporting. A qualitative reporting standard – thus a rather high standard of suspicion – will necessarily lead to many cases where obliged entities do not report relevant anomalies to the FIU because they do not consider that these already give rise to a suspicion. As a consequence, the FIU and, through it, other competent authorities will potentially miss relevant information that, seen through the bigger picture of the FIU's operational analysis, would have

283 See for example United Kingdom, section III.C.1.a.
284 See (for a non-EU framework) for example Switzerland, section II.C.1.a.
285 See Comparative Analysis, section III.C.1.a.

provided valuable investigative leads. Furthermore, in the absence of extensive data sharing between obliged entities, an individual obliged entity in principle only has access to information pertaining to its own customers, whereas the FIU is able to match information from numerous obliged entities (and from data banks of other public authorities) and thereby spot connections that would be unrecognisable from the individual obliged entity's perspective.[286] It therefore seems more promising to rely primarily on the FIUs' operational analysis rather than on the investigative capabilities of obliged entities, especially insofar as an extensive sharing of personal data between obliged entities would clash with proportionality constrains. Consequently, FIUs should be provided with information about potentially criminal activities even where the reporting obliged entity itself was not able to extensively substantiate its reservations.

A quantitative approach will however necessarily more often produce low-quality reports. After all, it will require obliged entities to report suspicious indications even before these indications are thoroughly substantiated (or indeed subsequently refuted) by the reporting entity's own CDD inquiries. This weakness of the quantitative, low-suspicion approach can in principle be remedied through follow-up requests from the FIU to reporting obliged entities as well as through follow-up communications from the obliged entity to the FIU. Yet, as regards follow-up requests by the FIU, one must remember that a quantitative approach normally leads to higher numbers of SARs. While FIU requests can in principle be a suitable way to expand on the substance of reports, this would require the FIU to proactively monitor the further development of reported circumstances. In view of the sheer number of reports they receive, FIUs do not necessarily have the resources to analyse in depth and follow up on each individual report. Higher numbers of reports may thus effectively lead to valuable reports being overlooked in the shuffle of low-quality information. Depending of course also on the ability of FIUs, not least through data analytics technologies, to remedy this concern, increasing numbers of reports may then, in the case of a resulting diminishing share of valuable reports, also become problematic as regards the proportionality of reporting obligations.

As regards the possible strengthening of quantitative SARs through follow-up reports, the obliged entity would in this case itself complement and thereby potentially substantiate any suspicious indications communicated in its first report as soon as it becomes aware of additional indications, in particular relevant information it discovers through enhanced CDD measures. However, even if the information that formed the object of a report is subsequently further investigated by the reporting entity through CDD measures, or if the reported

[286] RK Gordon, Losing the War against Dirty Money: Rethinking Global Standards on Preventing Money Laundering and Terrorism Financing, 21 *Duke Journal of Comparative & International Law* (2011), p. 546.

event was related to a continuous business relationship through which the reporting entity subsequently learns more about the suspicious circumstances, EU law is in this respect not really clear about the extent to which reporting entities are under a follow-up reporting obligation. Absent any indication to the contrary under national law, obliged entities may therefore refrain from reporting one and the same transaction or one and the same asset more than once, even if, subsequent to the filing of the report, they come across new information that is relevant to the initial suspicion.

(ii) A further concern about a quantitative approach to reporting results from the potential impact of reporting on affected clients. SARs will regularly be accessible not only to the FIU, but also directly or indirectly[287] to investigative and other security authorities.[288] Furthermore, reporting obliged entities are widely allowed to share information about the filing of an SAR with other obliged entities.[289] A report can therefore have effects on the reported client well beyond the mere relationship between him or her and the reporting entity. Depending on the extent of private–private information sharing, reporting can then entail the risk of stigmatising a reported person in the eyes of multiple obliged entities, despite a low and therefore untested suspicion.[290] The existence of a report may for example be considered as a factor by the competent authorities in their decision to commence or continue an investigation.[291] Obviously, under a quantitative approach, both the competent authorities and obliged entities should be expected to credit the term "suspicious" with only limited reliability. In any case, uncertainty as to this meaning between national jurisdictions and sometimes even between different agencies within one and the same jurisdiction risks triggering unwarranted prejudgements in the eyes of those who are used to giving significant credit to such reports.

(iii) Finally, current reporting practice seems to reflect a dilemma that results from the impact of reports on the lawfulness of suspicious transactions. The close correlation under today's EU law between the obligation to report and the obligation not to perform a suspicious transaction before filing a report raises the question what impact reports should have on the legality of reported transactions. It is clear that a quantitative approach to reporting does not fit well

---

287 See Germany, section V.B.1, Italy, section V.B.1, and United Kingdom, section V.B.1.

288 See Article 39 para. 2 of Directive (EU) 2015/849.

289 Article 39 paras. 3–5 of Directive (EU) 2015/849; see Comparative Analysis, section V.J.

290 See European Banking Authority et al., Joint Guidelines under Articles 17 and 18(4) of Directive (EU) 2015/849 on simplified and enhanced customer due diligence and the factors credit and financial institutions should consider when assessing the money laundering and terrorist financing risk associated with individual business relationships and occasional transactions of 4 January 2018, para. 20, which explicitly mentions prior SARs as a potentially relevant risk factor.

291 This seems indeed to be a major rationale insofar as national law requires the FIU to share information with investigative authorities; see Comparative Analysis, section V.B.1.

into a framework in which SARs are meant to temporarily suspend a transaction and enable its prior vetting by the FIU. On the one hand, a *permanent* duty not to perform a reported transaction would likely discourage obliged entities from filing reports and, insofar as it is contrary to the very idea of a quantitative approach, effectively raise the standard of suspicion. For if an obliged entity knows that it needs to suspend a transaction in the event of filing a report, it will presumably think twice before doing so. On the other hand, a close correlation between the reporting obligation and a merely *temporary* suspension of reported transactions is seemingly based on the idea that the FIU would, in each case, analyse the transaction in order to decide about its legality. Even under a qualitative approach, this seems to be a rather unrealistic expectation, as the FIU will usually not be able to provide the reporting entity with a meaningful assessment within a short period of time. Such an expectation will all the more be delusive under a quantitative reporting framework, that is one that aims to produce greater numbers of reports and thus reports that, by themselves, will very frequently contain insufficient information to allow the FIU to quickly check their substance.

Yet a correlation between reporting and the suspension of suspicious transactions might also not easily square with a more qualitative approach to reporting. This is especially so if a particular suspicion has been extensively tested by the obliged entity before reporting it to the FIU and in the eyes of this reporting entity it has thus been established that the suspicion is highly likely to be well founded or that it is at least more likely than the reverse. Insofar as a country's criminal law does not criminalise (grossly) negligent money laundering, the performance of suspicious transactions in such cases will usually still be considered legal.[292] Yet one may question whether it is sensible that the reporting obliged entity should, after a suspension of a couple of days during which it waits in vain for a reaction from the FIU,[293] still be allowed to perform a transaction that this obliged entity itself regarded as highly dubious. In other words, if the reporting entity is of the view that strong indications point towards money laundering, it can seem odd that it should in principle still be allowed to carry out the transaction. In such cases, the correlation between reporting obligations and the suspension of transactions effectively serves as a permit for carrying out suspicious transactions, even if the FIU's non-interference will in many cases mean little more than that the FIU was not able to clear the suspicion up within the available time, and will therefore by no means constitute a rebuttal of the reporting entity's assessment.

---

292 For grossly negligent money laundering, see Germany, section II.B.1.b, and Spain, section II.B.1.b. Note however that criminal liability in Germany is in this respect negated by reporting the transaction to the competent authorities, section II.B.1.a.ii.

293 See for example Germany, section III.C.1.d, and Italy, section III.C.1.d.

c. Reform

In light of the aforementioned weaknesses of the current EU framework, two interconnected questions arise: (i) first, whether it is possible to combine the advantages of the qualitative and of the quantitative approach, while at the same time avoiding their disadvantages; and (ii) second, how to define the relationship between the reporting obligation and the prohibition of transactions.

- Provide for two types of reporting by obliged entities to improve the quality of SARs and at the same time to ensure that FIUs receive relevant information independently of any suspicion

(i) As regards the advantage of the two approaches to reporting, two characteristics seem to be particularly relevant. On the one hand, a quantitative approach is desirable in that it is likely to provide the FIU with a more comprehensive picture of higher-risk situations in the market. Depending on the scope of the definition of enhanced risk adopted by the legislator and by supervisory authorities, this can allow the authorities to know to what extent the national economy is exposed to activities that, by their nature, must be taken to raise the likelihood of money laundering. Such knowledge is particularly useful for the FIU's strategic analysis and can ultimately not only improve the quality of typologies and consequently of CDD, but also guide the FIU and supervisory authorities in their efforts to detect reporting violations. For on the basis of a more extensive picture of enhanced risks, such detection could be facilitated by addressing FIU requests and supervisory controls especially to obliged entities which, in comparison with competitors operating in very much the same market segment, are reporting surprisingly few higher-risk situations. On the other hand, a qualitative approach to reporting leads to a greater involvement of obliged entities in the clearing up of suspicious situations in that, unlike a quantitative approach, it does not limit the reporting to the communication of selective episodes of higher risk, but instead imposes an obligation on obliged entities to clear up such episodes by themselves through the conclusive performance of enhanced CDD measures. A qualitative approach to reporting thereby effectively uses the close relationship between obliged entities and their clients in order to acquire more relevant information and thereby provide an FIU's subsequent operational analysis with an already more substantiated factual starting point. In order to accommodate the advantages of the quantitative and qualitative approaches to suspicion, legislators could combine two cumulative types of reporting.

- Empower FIUs to define situations that usually indicate a high risk of money laundering and require obliged entities to report such situations independently of any suspicion

One type, appropriately labelled "unusual activities reports",[294] should fulfil primarily an oversight function that would provide the FIU with a comprehensive picture of higher-risk situations in particular problem areas, that is situations that usually indicate a heightened risk of money laundering and have been defined as such by the FIU or the supervisory authority.[295] This should in particular cover situations where some facts indicate a possible link to money laundering where these indications do not yet allow the conclusion that the presence of money laundering is more likely than not. Due to their mere oversight function and in order to prevent clients being treated as suspicious merely because they engaged in a higher-risk business relationship or transaction, these unusual activities reports should however not be accessible to criminal justice authorities.

Unusual activities reports would obviously follow a clearly quantitative approach to reporting. As pointed out above, a quantitative threshold can however have the effect of drowning FIUs in worthless information.[296] Even if the growing amount of data in the hands of FIUs may, in particular due to enhanced data analytics abilities, lead to an improved detection capacity, it would seem highly problematic to require obliged entities to invest considerable resources in the production of reports that, for the most part, are of no value to the competent authorities. Triggers for unusual activity reports should therefore be defined by the FIU and follow a clear, evolving and potentially sector-specific strategic vision as regards the particular threats and vulnerabilities defined at the EU or national level. The definition and continued review of such measures should align with thematic focal points expressed in red flags provided to obliged entities by supervisory authorities or FIUs.[297] Unusual activities reports should not require a suspicion, but merely the presence of objective occurrences that are typically indicative of money laundering or at least indicative of a particularly high risk of money laundering. Such reports would thus normally require more substance than simple threshold transaction disclosures or other automatic reporting obligations.[298] Reporting triggers could for example include typical indications of money laundering in connection with certain financial products,

---

[294] While the term "unusual transaction report" is sometimes already used in order to denote reporting obligations that do not require a suspicion, the present proposal is not mean to express support for or criticism of any particular national framework; see for an example Financial Intelligence Unit – the Netherlands, Annual Report 2017, p. 15; cautious in this regard Europol, From Suspicion to Action, Converting financial intelligence into greater operational impact, 2017, p. 10.

[295] In a similar vein also Interpretative Note 14 to FATF Recommendation 29.

[296] Europol, From Suspicion to Action, Converting financial intelligence into greater operational impact, 2017, pp. 29–30.

[297] On the need for more specific guidance for improving the quality of CDD through a more collaborative approach between those authorities and obliged entities, see *infra* section III.F.2.c.

[298] See on the latter for example Germany, section IV.D.1, and Spain, section IV.D.1.

with specific transaction methods or with particular non-EU jurisdictions. The designation of triggers should be guided by the ultimate aim of providing the FIU with a comprehensive picture of money laundering indications within particular problem areas and thereby, through link analyses, increase the probability of detection to an extent that, in view of the resources spent for this purpose by reporting entities, would seem appropriate.

- Limit SARs to cases where money laundering is more likely than not, the customer tried to misrepresent key risk parameters or the obliged, due to other indications, refuses to serve a customer

Another type of reporting, aptly labelled "suspicious activities reports", should be triggered if a particular suspicion is, in light of the facts known to the reporting obliged entity, so much substantiated that this entity decides to abstain from the business relationship or transaction. This should cover:

- situations in which, in view of the facts known to the obliged entity, a link to money laundering is more likely than not;
- situations in which the obliged entity has reasons to believe that a customer or a customer's representative intended to mislead the obliged entity about the customer's or the beneficial owner's identity, the origin of funds or the purpose of a business relationship or transaction;[299] and
- other situations where, in view of specific indications of money laundering, the obliged entity is unwilling to go ahead with a particular business relationship or transaction.

SARs will then be triggered possibly even before the performance of enhanced CDD, provided that at this stage strong indications already point to the presence money laundering. However, an SAR in the proposed sense will usually be the product of enhanced CDD measures that lead to the discovery of strong indications of money laundering.[300] SARs would then reflect the reporting obliged entity's view that the presence of money laundering is more likely than not or that there are at least substantial indications to this effect. Accordingly, these reports (unlike the above-proposed unusual activities reports) would not be a mere oversight tool and should therefore be accessible not only to the FIU, but also (through a hit/no hit data retrieval system which ensures the FIU's control over the data)[301] indirectly to criminal justice authorities.

---

299 See *supra* section III.B.1.c.

300 See Switzerland, section III.C.1.a.

301 On the need to safeguard FIUs' control over information contained in SARs, see *supra* section III.C.1.c.

- Consider a short-time mandatory suspension of any type of transaction that was defined by the FIU as usually indicative of a high risk of money laundering

(ii) As regards the relationship between the reporting obligation and the prohibition of transactions, and in particular in order to ensure proportionality of any interference with the fundamental right to conduct business, unusual activities reports should in principle not inhibit a transaction. A different conclusion might be reached in the case of a particularly high-volume transaction if the transaction, in light of its characteristics, has been predefined by the FIU or the supervisory authority as posing a particularly high abstract risk, in which case it might be admissible to require a preliminary authorisation by the FIU. Transactions that were subject to an unusual activities report might however be suspended for a short time – for example, as already the case under some existing reporting regimes, for a couple of working days[302] – in order to allow the FIU to check the reported situation by means of automated data processing. While the current practice of FIUs indicates that they will in most cases be unable to reach a conclusive judgment within only a few days, a short suspension of reported unusual transactions might nevertheless be appropriate, not least as advances in data processing technologies will in the future arguably strengthen FIUs' ability, if not to conclusively assess the present money laundering indications, but at least to significantly substantiate these indications or also to rebut them.

- Prohibit obliged entities from performing a transaction if a link to money laundering is more likely than not or if the customer tried to misrepresent key risk parameters

In any case, obliged entities should in principle not be allowed to carry out a transaction if they consider it to be more likely than not that the respective assets are related to money laundering or if they have reasons to believe that the customer or customer's representative tried to mislead them about the aforementioned key elements of CDD. A transaction should in these cases only be allowed and even required if the transaction would not impair the competent authorities' access to the respective assets, in particular where the transaction will bring the presumably tainted assets under the reporting entity's control. The reporting entity should however be able to apply to the competent supervisory authority or to the FIU to authorise a suspicious transaction. In order to be meaningful, such authorisation would however need to be explicit (thus not be the result of fictitious consent triggered by the expiration of a standstill period) and require the prior performance by the FIU of an individual operational

302 See for example Germany, section III.C.1.d, and Italy, section III.C.1.d.

analysis through which the FIU was unable to confirm a more-likely-than-not standard of suspicion.

2. *Clarifying Obliged Entities' Powers to Process Personal Data*

a. Current State

To prevent and detect money laundering, the EU AML framework in large parts relies on the processing of personal data by obliged entities, in particular as regards the collection and processing of transaction and other customer data through CDD, the sharing of some of this data between obliged entities, the retaining of customer data, and the reporting of suspicious activities to the FIU. While EU law specifies the respective purposes of the processing of personal data, it usually provides no details about the scope of the data processing. In fact, obliged entities may determine the extent of CDD measures on a risk-sensitive basis, thus depending on the money laundering risk associated with a particular business relationship or transaction.[303] Obliged entities are, as part of their standard CDD obligations, notably required to conduct "ongoing monitoring" of a business relationship.[304] EU law does not however specify the degree and nature of such monitoring, for example to what extent it must entail the collection of additional customer data, if applicable the nature and scope of such additional customer data, and the data processing techniques that can or should be used for the monitoring.[305] Similarly, in case of certain transactions that pose an enhanced risk, obliged entities must examine "as far as reasonably possible" the background and purpose of transactions,[306] yet again the law does not provide further details or limits on the sources of personal data and on the data processing methods that such examination might allow or require.[307]

303 Article 13 para. 2 of Directive (EU) 2015/849 of 20 May 2015.

304 Article 13 para. 1 s. 1(d) of Directive (EU) 2015/849 of 20 May 2015.

305 See also European Banking Authority et al., Joint Guidelines under Articles 17 and 18(4) of Directive (EU) 2015/849 on simplified and enhanced customer due diligence and the factors credit and financial institutions should consider when assessing the money laundering and terrorist financing risk associated with individual business relationships and occasional transactions of 4 January 2018, paras. 49–69, whose examples suggest that obliged entities shall enjoy extensive flexibility.

306 Article 18 para. 2 of Directive (EU) 2015/849 of 20 May 2015, as amended by Directive (EU) 2018/843.

307 See however the broad examples in European Banking Authority et al., Joint Guidelines under Articles 17 and 18(4) of Directive (EU) 2015/849 on simplified and enhanced customer due diligence and the factors credit and financial institutions should consider when assessing the money laundering and terrorist financing risk associated with individual business relationships and occasional transactions of 4 January 2018, in particular para. 14: "Where possible, information about these ML/TF risk factors should come from a variety of sources, whether these are accessed individually or through commercially available tools or databases that pool information from several sources. Firms should determine the type and numbers of sources on a risk-sensitive basis."

As regards obliged entities' obligation to file SARs, EU law requires them to provide the FIU with "information", and, following an FIU's request, with "all necessary information".[308] No details are however provided on the scope of such information, in particular to what extent the obliged entity can or must submit customer data that, while not directly relevant for the suspicious character of a transaction, could provide the FIU with further clues for its operational analysis. As regards information pertaining to a particular suspicious activity, EU law does under certain conditions allow for its sharing between different obliged entities, notably if these entities belong to the same group or if they are connected to the suspicious activity by the same customer and the same transaction.[309] Yet EU AML law does not specify to what extent the shared information can also include customer data that goes beyond the mere identification of the suspicious activity and would allow the receiving entity to enrich its information base for the purpose of its own CDD regarding the same customer.

In a similar vein, while obliged entities must, over a period of at least five years, retain documents and information which are "necessary" to comply with CDD requirements,[310] the meaning of "necessary" is not more clearly defined. It may therefore be understood to cover only documents and information that were extracted from a larger data pool because they contained relevant information (for example information about particular transactions gathered through the continuous monitoring of a business relationship) or instead all information that had to be analysed in order to uncover relevant bits of information (for example all data considered for the purpose of continuous monitoring). Finally, EU law prohibits the processing of personal data on the basis of AML/CTF legislation for any other purpose, in particular for commercial purposes. However, the law excludes any further processing of such data only if it is done in a way that is "incompatible" with those purposes.[311] This seemingly allows, in principle, information obtained through CDD to be subsequently used for other purposes, including commercial purposes, insofar as such subsequent use does not have repercussions that run counter the prevention of money laundering or terrorism financing.

Processing of personal data for the purpose of AML is also subject to EU data protection legislation as regards obliged entities' CDD, notably Regulation 2016/679.[312] However, while the prevention of money laundering is

308 Article 33 para. 1 of Directive (EU) 2015/849 of 20 May 2015, as amended by Directive (EU) 2018/843.

309 Article 39 paras. 3 and 5 and Article 45 para. 8 of Directive (EU) 2015/849 of 20 May 2015, as amended by Directive (EU) 2018/843.

310 Article 40 para. 1 s. 1(a) of Directive (EU) 2015/849 of 20 May 2015, as amended by Directive (EU) 2018/843.

311 Article 41 para. 2 of Directive (EU) 2015/849 of 20 May 2015.

312 Article 41 para. 1 of Directive (EU) 2015/849 of 20 May 2015; Regulation (EU) 2016/679 of 27 April 2016.

a matter of public interest and thereby serves a legitimate aim, Regulation 2016/679 does in itself not provide much further guidance for clarifying the scope of interpretation of the above-mentioned powers.[313] This concerns *inter alia* the questions to what extent the collection of personal data through the performance of CDD and the processing of CDD data for other purposes are proportionate.[314] As a notable exception, Regulation 2016/679 contains limits on the automated processing of personal data. Customers have the right not to be subjected to a decision based solely on automated processing, including profiling, if this decision produces legal effects concerning the customer or similarly affects him or her. While EU law allows such automated processing notably if it is authorised by EU or Member State law which also lays down suitable measures to safeguard the rights and freedoms and legitimate interests of the affected person, the EU AML framework does currently not contain such authorisation. If it is not authorised by the national law of a Member State, automated processing of customer data can therefore only assist the performance of CDD, but must not replace human decision-making, that is decision-making that is in essence based on the judgement of a human actor, or must at least offer the customer the opportunity to obtain human intervention.[315]

b. Challenges

The above-mentioned features of the data processing provisions of the EU AML framework are unsatisfactory for two interconnected reasons. On the one hand, lack of precision raises questions about criteria for ensuring the proportionality of the application of data processing powers, potentially calling into question the lawfulness of core elements of money laundering prevention.[316] On the other hand, uncertainty regarding the limits of their powers will in some cases discourage public and private actors from making use of these powers, as they might rightly be concerned that their action could overstep the legal limits and provoke challenges in the courts. To comprehend the intrusiveness of obliged entities' data processing, four particular considerations deserve particular attention, namely (i) the scope of the processed financial data, (ii) the nature of further personal data gathered in the performance of CDD, (iii) the difficulty of

313 See Article 43 of Directive (EU) 2015/849 of 20 May 2015, as amended by Directive (EU) 2018/843; Article 6 para. 3 subpara. 2 s. 3 of Regulation (EU) 2016/679 of 27 April 2016.

314 See Article 6 para. 3 and para. 4 of Regulation (EU) 2016/679 of 27 April 2016.

315 Article 22 paras. 1, 2(b) and 3 of Regulation (EU) 2016/679 of 27 April 2016.

316 Similar concerns were also expressed in the Opinion of the European Data Protection Supervisor (EDPS) on a proposal for a Directive on the prevention of the use of the financial system for the purpose of money laundering and terrorist financing of 4 July 2013, especially in paras. 44–47 on data sharing between obliged entities.

differentiating between, on the one hand, AML/CTF data processing purposes and, on the other hand, commercial purposes, and (iv) the increasing use of powerful data analytics processing tools.

(i) It has already been observed above[317] that financial data will regularly entail information that allows one to gain extensive knowledge about a person's social, private and sometimes even intimate life, either directly from the account statement (in particular from the stated purpose of a transaction, the identity of the payment recipient or the location of a transaction) or indirectly in that transaction data will enable the identification of persons that will provide additional information (for example a merchant who can provide details about the goods or services underlying a transaction). With the demise of transactions performed through cash and the ever-increasing digitalisation of financial services, bank account data will provide increasing amounts of information about the account holder, up to a point where it becomes possible to create detailed personality profiles of virtually every user of financial services. Similarly, the financial information of companies can expose sensitive details that harm the legitimate confidentiality interests of the company and of its employees.

Obviously, neither individuals nor companies usually enjoy an absolute claim to have their financial information kept secret, as is evidenced not least by extensive powers of tax authorities and criminal justice authorities under national laws to access account and other financial data. The processing of financial data under the AML framework is however significantly different from the disclosure of such data in tax or criminal proceedings in that data processing and in particular data sharing by obliged entities for the purpose of AML is done largely without it being geared towards the subsequent participation of the affected person in the process. This is evident in particular in the prohibition imposed on obliged entities not to disclose the filing of an SAR to the affected client, the power of obliged entities to share information about suspicious activities with other obliged entities without informing the affected client, and the largely secret nature of FIUs' operational analysis and of data sharing between FIUs.[318] Given that financial data is thus processed and exchanged by obliged entities regularly without being subject to judicial scrutiny and without the affected person being heard as regards the underlying suspicion,[319] there is a significant risk of this data being erroneously processed or deliberately abused. The wealth of information contained in accumulated financial data together with the secrecy of the data processing makes the processing of personal data under the AML framework potentially highly intrusive and thus demanding as regards the proportionality of the measures.

---

317 See section II.B.2.

318 See Comparative Analysis, sections III.C.2.b, III.C.4, IV.E.1, V.F.1 and V.J.

319 See *supra* section II.C.2.

(ii) Besides account data and other financial data directly evidencing the services provided by obliged entities for their customers, the processing of personal data under the AML framework also extends to CDD data, that is information which obliged entities collect and assess in order to satisfy their CDD obligations. Such data can in particular include information gathered for the purpose of establishing the beneficial owner or the purpose of a business relationship or transaction or the origin of assets.[320] Customers will in many cases have to provide obliged entities with a multitude of information to satisfy CDD requirements, thereby allowing the respective obliged entity to gain extensive knowledge about a client's economic situation and personal circumstances, not least as regards his or her relationship with business associates and creditors, ties with family members, sources of wealth, business plans, and other information that can help to establish whether the envisaged business relationship or transaction serves a lawful purpose. Furthermore, as the obliged entity must not in most cases rely exclusively on information it obtained from the client, but must verify such information through independent sources,[321] CDD data may also extend to a multitude of additional sources. This includes not least personal data obtained from public registries, social networks and other sources that provide information that are in the public domain; in some jurisdictions, this may extend to information about individuals' criminal records or arrest history.[322] Depending on the national law applicable to an obliged entity, the latter may also have recourse to information that is not in the public domain, for example by using relevant information provided by social network providers. As a result, the processing of personal data under the AML framework goes well beyond the purely financial data and will often extend to information about customers' activities outside the economic sphere. For the same reasons as explained above for financial data, the intrusiveness of the processing of CDD data and thus the assessment of the proportionality of such processing is amplified by the secrecy of data sharing between obliged entities as well as by the secrecy of FIUs' operational analyses.

(iii) Proportionality standards regarding data processing under the AML framework are further accentuated by purpose limitation concerns. As clarified by EU data protection law, the purpose of the processing of personal data is an integral element of any proportionality assessment.[323] Accordingly, the more the purpose of AML CDD is unclear or might in practice depart form the

[320] See for example Germany, sections III.A.1.b and III.A.3.b, and Spain, sections III.A.1.b and III.A.3.b.

[321] Germany, section III.A.1.b, Italy, section III.A.1.b, and United Kingdom, section III.A.1.b.

[322] For an analysis of the comparatively far-reaching public access to such information in the United States, see JB Jacobs, The eternal criminal record, 2015, pp. 159–223.

[323] See Article 5 para. 1(c) and Article 6 para. 4 of Regulation (EU) 2016/679 of 27 April 2016; see also European Union, section V.

purpose of the prevention of money laundering, the more difficult it becomes to justify an interference into personal data. In this respect, it must be recalled that AML is naturally linked to commercial considerations, due to the fact that CDD usually leads to costs that may affect obliged entities' risk appetite and thus their willingness to onboard or keep customers. The relationship between CDD measures and commercial considerations can however go well beyond such indirect impact, in that commercial considerations can become a major motive for the performance of what may formally be labelled CDD measures.[324] After all, the business model especially of financial service providers is to a large extent built on the management of commercial risk (not least the risk that customers may default on their payment obligations). The better such a service provider knows a customer, the easier it becomes to assess whether this customer is commercially attractive. As pointed out above, obliged entities are not under EU law allowed to use AML/CTF legislation in order to gather information from and about the customer for purposes other than the prevention of money laundering and terrorism financing. Yet insofar as customer information is relevant for both money laundering prevention and the prediction of the commercial risk that a customer poses, such double usefulness of information can in practice invite the use of CDD data also for commercial purposes (for example the creating of customer profiles that help to develop new target groups).[325] This would, in principle, seem to be in conformity with EU law, as the latter prohibits the further processing of CDD data only if it is done in a way that is incompatible with the purposes of AML and CTF. Given that commercial considerations necessarily influence an obliged entity's risk appetite and thereby also the scope of CDD, the commercial use of CDD data will be compatible with the purpose of money laundering prevention at least insofar as such data helps the obliged entity to better understand the commercial risks involved, and on this basis define its risk appetite. In other words, insofar as CDD data helps the obliged entity also to assess the commercial risks of a business relationship, such commercial use of the data is compatible with money laundering prevention because the obliged entity must be able to assess whether, against the background of the costs of ensuing CDD obligations, it is willing to enter into or continue the business relationship. Given that EU law provides obliged entities with a wide margin

[324] For drivers of AML compliance by European financial institutions, see the account by LexisNexis Risk Solutions, The True Cost of Anti-Money Laundering Compliance, European Edition, 2017, pp. 5–6.

[325] In a similar vein, Opinion of the European Data Protection Supervisor (EDPS) on a proposal for a Directive on the prevention of the use of the financial system for the purpose of money laundering and terrorist financing of 4 July 2013, para. 13, expressing concern that it may not be clear for a customer for which purpose data is required and processed.

of discretion to determine their own risk appetite[326] and thereby justify the collection of extensive customer information, the close correlation between the purpose of money laundering prevention and commercial purposes then means that the actual purpose of CDD-related data processing may in practice not always be clearly discernible. This ambiguity can facilitate the gathering and further processing of personal data for commercial purposes in cases where this data was in fact not necessary for the assessment of a money laundering or terrorism financing risk. The resulting uncertainty regarding the purpose of data processing nominally conducted for the purpose of AML/CTF impacts on the proportionality assessment, as it raises the likelihood of data processing powers under the AML/CTF framework in practice serving primarily commercial objectives.

(iv) Finally, similar uncertainty and, resulting from it, concerns about the proportionality of data processing under the AML framework can be observed with regard to automated decision-making by obliged entities. Automated decision-making is of growing relevance for AML, as obliged entities are increasingly making use of data analytics tools for the processing of vast amounts of financial data in order to identify suspicious activities.[327] As already stated, under EU law, AML-related decisions that significantly affect an individual can be based solely on the automated processing of data only if the applicable national law provides for a legal basis to this effect. Otherwise automated processing can usually only be used to assist human decision-makers. This in particular covers decisions about de-risking of clients by obliged entities. In principle, and to the extent that they merely help a human agent to become aware of potentially suspicious activities in order for this agent then to verify whether this judgement is in fact justified, the agent's ensuing decision cannot be said to be based solely on automated processing. Yet, even in cases where ultimate decision-making is apparently left to a human agent, it can be questionable whether the input by this agent adds substantially to the results of the automated process. In particular if the decision-making of a data analytics tool is based on correlations that, due the amount of processed data, are too complex to be readily comprehensible by a human agent, it is not unlikely that the agent will effectively delegate his or her decision by not thoroughly verifying the tool's output.[328] While the human agent might then still verify some basic features that from a statistical point of view indicate a higher risk of money laundering (for example whether the customer has relevant prior criminal convictions or whether the transaction method reflects a money laundering

[326] See *supra* section III.D.1.a.

[327] See for example Spain, section IV.L, and Switzerland, section IV.L.

[328] See Germany, section IV.D.4; T Wischmeyer, Artificial Intelligence and Transparency: Opening the Black Box, in T Wischmeyer/T Rademacher (eds.), Regulating Artificial Intelligence, 2020, pp. 80–81.

typology), the main assumptions underpinning the automated decision might be left unchecked. As a result, the decision to single out a particular customer will then in essence still be based on an automated processing of data, thereby rendering the human intervention effectively of very limited or no value and giving rise to the risk that central assumptions underpinning the decision are founded on erroneous reasons or illegal profiling.[329] Thus, even if automated data processing is only meant to assist human decision-makers, the increasingly heavy reliance in AML on data analytics poses risks that that can in some cases question the proportionality of the use of such technology and thereby possibly even exclude it being authorised by legislation.[330]

c. Reform

In view of the above-mentioned data protection challenges, legislators should provide obliged entities with clearer guidance regarding their powers to process personal data. This essentially means that legislation should specify how the existing EU data protection framework shall be applied in the context of AML. Legislation must on the one hand ensure the proportionality of data processing. On the other hand, it should provide relevant private and public actors with greater confidence about the state of the law, thereby avoiding those actors refraining from using the available tools as a result of doubts about the exact limits for the respective legal basis. It is therefore necessary in particular to resolve the above-mentioned ambiguities in the data processing powers of obliged entities. In order to do so, legislators will need to ensure that, for any of the data processing powers provided to obliged entities, they ensure proportionality by adequately balancing the different factors that influence the intrusiveness, in particular (i) the types and scope of data processed, (ii) the purpose of the processing, (iii) the methods of processing, and (iv) the availability of effective remedies against unlawful processing. (v) While a full harmonisation of the applicable standards through Member States seems unfeasible, the EU legislator should strive to reach greater homogeneity.

- Specify limits of private-private data sharing, thereby differentiating between mere alerts and the sharing of more detailed customer data, and in the latter cases provide independent oversight

(i) To begin with, the types and scope of data is of course of obvious importance for the proportionality of data processing. The more sensitive the data and the

---

329 See Article 22 para. 4 of Regulation (EU) 2016/679 of 27 April 2016. For more detail on such risks, see also Germany, section IV.D.4.

330 To this effect also A Amicelle/G Favarel-Garrigues, La lutte contre l'argent sale au prisme des libertés fondamentales : quelles mobilisations?, 76 *Cultures & Conflits* (2009), pp. 60–61.

broader their scope, the more intrusive their gathering, analysing and sharing. Especially with regard to the sharing of data by obliged entities, legislators should therefore clarify limits that consider both the sensitivity of the data for the person concerned and the risks of abuse to which this data can be exposed through their sharing. If an obliged entity informs another obliged entity that, in its view, a particular business relationship or transaction is suspicious, this assessment can of course still be erroneous. The receiving obliged entity should therefore be required to verify the information on its own before performing any measures detrimental to the respective customer (such as the suspension of transactions or the closure of accounts). However, insofar as this sharing does not include a sharing of additional information underlying the suspicion (such as information about the customer's transaction history or information obtained from the customer through CDD), the sharing between obliged entities of a mere suspicion may in principle constitute an adequate interference into the customer's rights[331] even if he or she is not immediately informed about the sharing and provided with an effective judicial remedy. In contrast, if legislators allow a more extensive sharing of customer data between obliged entities, this entails a much greater risk of data being abused. Such sharing can still be adequate for averting particularly serious threats, especially to allow the receiving obliged entity to detect criminal networks amongst its customers, provided that the scope of the data sharing is limited to what, in the individual case, is strictly necessary for the purpose pursued. However, to address the risk of potentially highly sensitive data being either shared on arbitrary grounds or being used for unlawful purposes (for example to exclusively commercial ends), the legislators must then provide for additional safeguards that effectively protect the rights of the affected client.[332] These safeguards should include substantive conditions for the sharing, especially a definition of the conditions under which what types of customer data can be shared and to what extent this can also include CDD data obtained from the customer. In addition, legislators would need to develop procedural remedies that ensure that these substantive safeguards are properly applied, for example by creating a mechanism within the competent supervisory authority (for example within the office of a public data protection ombudsperson) to authorise the sharing of customer data between obliged entities[333] on a case-by-case basis or by requiring disclosure to the affected

---

331 See Article 5 para. 1(c) of Regulation (EU) 2016/679 of 27 April 2016.

332 To this effect also Opinion of the European Data Protection Supervisor (EDPS) on a proposal for a Directive on the prevention of the use of the financial system for the purpose of money laundering and terrorist financing of 4 July 2013, paras. 65–66.

333 See for example Spain, section V.J.2.

customer in order to enable him or her to seek redress before the supervisory authority or a court.[334]

- Insofar as obliged entities may gather personal data about online behaviour or data provided by an authority, ensure that these are not inappropriately used for commercial purposes

(ii) As proportionality crucially depends on the purposes pursued, legislation must furthermore ensure that the processing of personal data by obliged entities on the basis of AML/CTF obligations is in practice not essentially driven by other motives of lesser importance. Limitations to this effect must take into account the fact that the prevention of money laundering and terrorism financing is, under a risk-based approach to CDD, closely intertwined with obliged entities' commercial interests, and that the processing of CDD data for commercial purposes is therefore not in principle inadmissible. At the same time, legislators will need to consider whether the use of certain data processing powers also for commercial purposes may affect the proportionality and thus potentially the lawfulness of data processing under the AML/CTF framework, in particular insofar as the gathering and analysing of personal data from third parties and the use of automated data processing is concerned. For while, for the purposes of AML/CTF, the use of very intrusive data processing methods may be adequate, the pursuit of primarily private commercial purposes can lead to a different conclusion. Thus, legislators may for example authorise obliged entities to rely for AML/CTF purposes on the analysis of social networks, web analytics data and even personal data provided by the competent authorities, thereby potentially allowing these obliged entities to perform a high level of customer monitoring. While such data processing methods may, on the condition of adequate safeguards, be proportionate for the prevention of serious crime, purely private commercial interests will in many cases not suffice to override the interests and fundamental rights of the customer.[335] Legislators must therefore provide adequate limits for the further use of CDD data, in particular CDD data generated through the use of big data analytics, to prevent the uncontrolled migration of personal data from AML/CTF processing towards a commercial use. In order to avert the misuse of AML/CTF, CDD data must in any case not be used further for commercial purposes if the gathering of the data was obviously not suitable or necessary for AML/CTF purposes in the first place. This may for example concern the processing for commercial purposes of personal data

[334] For the right to lodge a complaint with the competent supervisory authority regarding unlawful data processing and the right to an effective judicial remedy against its decision, see Article 77 para. 1 and Article 78 para. 1 of Regulation (EU) 2016/679 of 27 April 2016.

[335] See Article 6 para. 1 s. 1(f) of Regulation (EU) 2016/679 of 27 April 2016.

received by the obliged entity from the competent authorities or through the use of special AML/CTF data analytics technologies if this processing is done in a way that suggests that the data is essentially used not for assessing the obliged entity's risk appetite, but predominantly to create new business opportunities.

- Specify the methods of automated data processing and the nature and scope of the processed data, and require a regular review of the performance of data analytics technologies

(iii) In order to ensure proportionality of automated data processing, legislators must also strive to prevent CDD from being affected by prejudice and unlawful profiling. They should therefore in particular specify the scope of, and limitations to, the performance of big data analytics, and apply these rules not only to obliged entities, but as far as appropriate also to third parties who perform data analytics of obliged entities' customer data (for example cloud service providers that manage obliged entities' customer data) or who offer products resulting from the analysis of personal data (for example customer profiles gained from the analysis of social network user data).[336] Insofar as reasonably feasible, legislation and supervisory authorities should specify the methods of automated processing and the nature and scope of the processed data, for example by defining the personal data sources that may be included in the automated processing, or by defining particular categories of personal data that must not be included in the automated processing. As regards certain forms of data processing, it will however be more difficult or even impossible to define processing limits through predefined criteria, not least in the case of self-learning analytical tools whose decision-making will often not be completely comprehensible to human agents or whose functioning will not be fully disclosed by their makers. Obliged entities and supervisory authorities should in such cases furthermore be required to regularly review the performance of such tools in order to assess whether the tools' output suggests a reproduction of stereotypes or any other bias likely to attribute excessive weight to particular groups of individuals or to money laundering typologies that are too narrowly defined.

- Specify the scope of obliged entities' obligation to disclose personal data to the respective customer, including by providing temporal limits to the tip-off prohibition

[336] See C Aliprandi et al., CAPER: Crawling and Analysing Facebook for Intelligence Purposes, IEEE/ACM International Conference on Advances in Social Networks Analysis and Mining, 2014, available at https://www.researchgate.net/publication/275207535_CAPER_Crawling_and_Analysing_Facebook_for_Intelligence_Purposes.

(iv) In defining the precise scope of data processing powers, legislators must consider that the proportionality of the interference into customers' fundamental rights depends to a significant degree also on the availability of effective remedies against unlawful data processing. Insofar as customers are not informed about the types of personal data gathered by an obliged entity from third parties,[337] they will usually not be able to make use of available administrative and judicial remedies provided for by EU law.[338] In balancing on the one hand the effectiveness of AML/CTF and on the other hand the need to protect customers against an abusive or otherwise unlawful use of their personal data, legislation should therefore in particular specify to what extent an obliged entity is required to inform its customers about the nature and scope of data collected about them from third parties and to what extent customers enjoy a right to access this data, as in principle provided for by the EU data protection framework.[339] In deciding about the scope of customers' rights to be informed and to access relevant data, one must notably take into account that a higher level of non-disclosure and thus secrecy of obliged entities' data processing will mean that, due to the need to safeguard proportionality, the nature and scope of this processing will need to be more limited. In contrast, allowing customers more extensive access to data held about them by an obliged entity will mean that the obliged entity's data processing powers may be comparatively more intrusive. To protect the confidentiality of the filing of SARs, an obliged entity must in any case be required not to disclose suspicion-raising personal data obtained from third parties if this data would indicate that it will file or has already filed an SAR.[340] In contrast, if personal data that the obliged entity obtained from third parties did not lead to an SAR, the customer's interest in having the data disclosed will usually outweigh the obliged entity's interest in keeping the data confidential. To allow the customer to have the relevant data processing reviewed by an independent body[341] and thereby ensure the proportionality of the data processing, legislators

337 See also V Mitsilegas/N Vavoula, The Evolving EU Anti-Money Laundering Regime: Challenges for Fundamental Rights and the Rule of Law, 23 *Maastricht Journal of European and Comparative Law* (2016), p. 281.

338 Article 77 para. 1 and Article 78 para. 1 of Regulation (EU) 2016/679 of 27 April 2016.

339 See Articles 14 and 15 in conjunction with Article 23 para. 1(d) of Regulation (EU) 2016/679 of 27 April 2016.

340 See Article 41 para. 4 of Directive (EU) 2015/849 of 20 May 2015; in a similar vein V Mitsilegas/N Vavoula, The Evolving EU Anti-Money Laundering Regime: Challenges for Fundamental Rights and the Rule of Law, 23 *Maastricht Journal of European and Comparative Law* (2016), p. 282.

341 In a similar vein, European Parliament, Report on the proposal for a directive of the European Parliament and of the Council on the prevention of the use of the financial system for the purpose of money laundering and terrorist financing of 28 February 2014, A7-0150-2014, p. 69, calling for independent verification by the competent data protection authority and for judicial review mechanisms in cases where access to personal data to the affected person is refused.

should furthermore provide that the information that an obliged entity filed an SAR must not be indefinitely withheld from the affected customer.[342] Stipulating temporal limits to the obliged entities' tip-off prohibition, the law should therefore require obliged entities to inform a customer about the filing of an SAR at least if, even several months after the filing, the obliged entity has not been informed by the FIU or another competent authority of the commencement of a criminal investigation against the customer or been requested to temporarily continue to withhold the information from him or her.

- Provide Member States with more detailed guidance on how to accommodate data protection within AML law while allowing them to introduce additional safeguards

(v) Finally, the question arises as to what extent Member States' legislators should enjoy a margin of appreciation in determining the limits of data processing by obliged entities for AML/CTF purposes under national law. The EU AML/CTF framework suggests that there can be some degree of flexibility in how data processing powers are defined by national law.[343] Yet two primary reasons militate in favour of a higher level of precision of the relevant data processing provisions in EU legislation. First, while EU law may implicitly allow and even require national legislators to transpose EU AML/CTF legislation in line with EU and national data protection law, the national legislator will regularly tend to transpose the AML/CTF legislation in close conformity with the wording in order to avoid the risk of infringement proceedings[344] for not having faithfully transposed EU secondary legislation. As a result, data protection requirements will frequently not be sufficiently addressed in national AML/CTF law, thereby effectively leaving it to obliged entities and the competent supervisory authorities to accommodate data protection law, and as a result often leading to great uncertainty about the limits of data processing in practice. EU legislation should therefore either more clearly insist on the need for Member States to specify the scope of data processing powers when transposing AML/CTF legislation or specify these powers in EU AML legislation. Second, given that commercial operations and thus data sharing of obliged entities are regularly cross-border in nature, divergent rules applicable to the data processing by obliged entities can fragment the EU AML/CTF framework and thereby complicate the implementation of coherent AML/CTF CDD especially in groups of companies

[342] For the current lack of temporal limits to obliged entities obligation not to disclose the filing of an SAR, see Comparative Analysis, section III.C.2.b.

[343] See Article 41 para. 1 s. 1 of Directive (EU) 2015/849 of 20 May 2015; Article 6 para. 1 s. 1(c) and para. 2 of Regulation (EU) 2016/679 of 27 April 2016.

[344] Article 258 para. 2 of the Treaty on the Functioning of the European Union.

whose subsidiaries are domiciled in different Member States. Obviously, the data protection standards significantly vary between Member States,[345] and a full harmonisation of obliged entities' data processing powers would therefore be likely to provoke significant distortions within the law of some Member States. EU law could however at least partially address the risk of fragmentation by specifying the scope of obliged entities' AML/CTF data gathering and data sharing powers in greater detail, and at the same time allow individual Member States to introduce additional safeguards especially as regards limits to automated processing and customers' right to access data held about them by an obliged entity.

F. AML SUPERVISION

1. *Enhancing the Detection Capacity of Supervisory Authorities*

a. Current State

The EU legal framework recognises the role of effective supervision. Three aspects stand out as particularly relevant, namely (i) supervisors' powers, (ii) arrangements for the supervision of groups of obliged entities, and (iii) cooperation between supervisors and other competent authorities.

(i) As regards supervisory powers, EU law provides that adequate supervision includes the power to conduct on-site and off-site checks as well as "appropriate and proportionate administrative measures to remedy the situation in the case of breaches".[346] Supervisory authorities must also have the power "to compel the production of any information that is relevant to monitoring compliance and perform checks".[347] As for credit institutions, financial institutions and gambling service providers, supervisory authorities must enjoy "enhanced powers".[348] EU AML law does not however further specify the form of those standard or enhanced powers.[349] In any case, supervisors must have "on-site and off-site

345 Compare for example Germany, section V.B.1, and Italy, section V.B.1.

346 Article 48 para. 1a subpara. 3 of Directive (EU) 2015/849 of 20 May 2015, as amended by Directive (EU) 2018/843 of 30 May 2018.

347 Article 48 para. 2 of Directive (EU) 2015/849 of 20 May 2015, as amended by Directive (EU) 2018/843 of 30 May 2018.

348 Article 48 para. 3 of Directive (EU) 2015/849 of 20 May 2015, as amended by Directive (EU) 2018/843 of 30 May 2018.

349 See however for the powers of prudential supervisors according to Article 91 para. 1 and Article 97 para. 6 of Directive (EU) 2013/36 of 26 June 2013 on access to the activity of credit institutions and the prudential supervision of credit institutions and investment firms, as amended by Directive (EU) 2019/878 of 20 May 2019. See also European Union, sections I.B and III.I.1.

access to all relevant information on the specific domestic and international risks associated with customers, products and services of the obliged entities" and "base the frequency and intensity of on-site and off-site supervision on the risk profile of obliged entities, and on the risks of money laundering and terrorist financing in that Member State".[350]

(ii) Regarding the supervision of groups of companies, EU law sets out special rules for credit and financial institutions that are part of a group. In these cases, supervisory authorities of the Member State where a parent undertaking is established have to supervise the implementation of the group-wide AML/CTF policies and procedure. Furthermore the supervisory authorities of the Member State where a subsidiary is established and the supervisory authorities of the Member State where the parent undertaking is established are now required to cooperate with each other.[351] Going beyond credit and financial institutions, where obliged entities have branches or majority-owned subsidiaries located in a non-EU country whose law does not permit the implementation of effective group-wide AML/CTF policies and procedures, such obliged entities have to apply additional measures to nevertheless effectively handle the respective risks.[352] If those additional measures are not sufficient, the supervisory authority of the home Member State must then adopt additional supervisory measures, which may include "requiring that the group does not establish or that it terminates business relationships, and does not undertake transactions and, where necessary, requesting the group to close down its operations in the third country."[353]

(iii) EU law also mentions the need for cooperation between supervisors and other relevant authorities, requiring "effective mechanisms to cooperate and coordinate" their AML/CTF activities.[354] No general framework for such mechanisms is provided. However, a specific form of cooperation is required as regards the feeding of central beneficial ownership registers. To improve the accuracy of such registries, the competent authorities must report discrepancies

---

350 Article 48 para. 6(b)(c) of Directive (EU) 2015/849 of 20 May 2015.

351 Article 48 paras. 4(2) and 5(2) of Directive (EU) 2015/849 of 20 May 2015, as amended by Directive (EU) 2018/843 of 30 May 2018.

352 For additional measures to be applied by obliged entities, see Commission Delegated Regulation (EU) 2019/758 of 31 January 2019 supplementing Directive (EU) 2015/849 of the European Parliament and of the Council with regard to regulatory technical standards for the minimum action and the type of additional measures credit and financial institutions must take to mitigate money laundering and terrorist financing risk in certain third countries, and European Union, sections III.A.4.b and V.J.3.

353 Article 45 para. 5 of Directive (EU) 2015/849 of 20 May 2015.

354 Article 49 of Directive (EU) 2015/849 of 20 May 2015. For cooperation between prudential supervisors, AML supervisors and FIUs, see also Article 117 para. 5 of Directive (EU) 2013/36 of 26 June 2013 on access to the activity of credit institutions and the prudential supervision of credit institutions and investment firms, as amended by Directive (EU) 2019/878 of 20 May 2019.

they find between the information available in the central registers and the beneficial ownership information available to them, though an obligation to this effect only applies "if appropriate and to the extent that this requirement does not interfere unnecessarily with their functions".[355] This means that the competent authorities, including presumably supervisory and investigative authorities, are in principle expected to jointly contribute to a high level of beneficial ownership transparency. Furthermore, AML/CTF supervisors as well as prudential supervisors are required to report to the FIU when they discover facts that could be related to money laundering or terrorism financing.[356] Finally, guidelines by the European supervisory authorities, issued in December 2019 for the cooperation between AML supervisory authorities in the supervision of cross-border financial institutions, specify that supervisory colleges,[357] established for this purpose by national supervisory authorities, may also invite the FIU of the lead supervisor's Member State as an observer to foster cooperation and information exchange.[358] Beyond these mechanisms, the EU legal framework does not currently provide for other specific cooperation or coordination mechanisms for effective cooperation between supervisors and other competent authorities.

b. Challenges

Supervision is a key element of a functioning AML framework. Without adequate scrutiny of obliged entities CDD and reporting practice, it is unlikely that the respective obligations will be properly applied. Three elements seem to be particularly important in that they are not yet sufficiently addressed by EU law, namely (i) the limited ability of supervisors to uncover wrongdoing within obliged entities, (ii) the fragmentation of oversight due to the parallel involvement of multiple supervisory authorities, and lastly (iii) the weakening of supervision through obliged entities' operations in third countries.

(i) As regards the ability of supervisors to uncover wrongdoing by obliged entities, it must be recalled that CDD and reporting obligations essentially constitute a partial delegation of criminal policy functions to the private sector. Obliged entities therefore have to learn how to detect crime and thus familiarise

---

355 Article 30 para. 4 and Article 31 para. 5 of Directive (EU) 2015/849 of 20 May 2015, as amended by Directive (EU) 2018/843 of 30 May 2018.

356 Article 36 of Directive (EU) 2015/849 of 20 May 2015, as amended by Directive (EU) 2018/843 of 30 May 2018.

357 See European Union, section I.B.

358 European Banking Authority et al., Joint guidelines on cooperation and information exchange for the purpose of Directive (EU) 2015/849 between competent authorities supervising credit and financial institutions – The AML/CFT Colleges Guidelines of 16 December 2019, Chapter 1 para. 19 and Guideline 5.4.

themselves with characteristics of criminal conduct that they may encounter in their business operations. In order to be able to assess the AML performance of supervised entities, supervisory authorities must as a consequence equally familiarise themselves with relevant criminal conduct and how to detect indications of it. Such a criminal policy perspective is however normally not typical for supervisory authorities in the area of business regulation, meaning that they will often lack adequately qualified staff as well as an institutional attitude used to focusing on criminal activity.[359] Due to the nature of money laundering, effective supervision will usually require supervisors to look beyond the shape of an obliged entity's CDD measures and rather look for a possible criminogenic context of the obliged entity's operations. However, while EU law recognises the need for cooperation between supervisors and other competent authorities, including FIUs, it currently provides few specific mechanisms that would improve the ability of supervisors to integrate criminal policy considerations into supervisory measures, not least in order to guide supervisors' checks with regard to both the selection of targeted obliged entities and the design and intensity of the measures.

Moreover, while central beneficial ownership registries can, as observed above, also constitute an instrument for inter-agency cooperation in order to provide a high level of beneficial ownership transparency and thereby be an important instrument of AML supervision, the existing obligation of some authorities to jointly feed into the central beneficial ownership register is, in its current state, unlikely to yield significant operational outcomes. Not only is the obligation of FIUs and criminal justice authorities to this effect still subject to considerable discretion, but the very content of the central beneficial ownership registers is so far rather fragmentary. For when a company's shareholder structure consists of a chain of other companies, the successful identification of the beneficial owners will frequently not be feasible, in particular because a client's ultimate shareholding structure may simply be too diverse or remain hidden in anonymity-friendly jurisdictions.

Closely related to supervisory authorities' traditional unfamiliarity with a focus on crime is the practical difficulty of detecting CDD violations behind an obliged entity's seemingly flawless CDD documentation. While supervisors might find it somewhat easier to spot violations of relevant AML obligations in cases where an obliged entity lacks adequate internal procedures and documentation, even the existence of such documentation can serve as an effective smokescreen to cover the fact that a business relationship or transaction was in fact

---

[359] See in particular on cultural differences in regulatory enforcement A Carretta et al., Don't Stand So Close to Me: The role of supervisory style in banking stability, 52 *Journal of Banking & Finance* (2015), pp. 180–188; GM Gilchrist, Regulation by Prosecutor, 56 *American Criminal Law Review* (2019), pp. 349–350.

performed in full knowledge of an unreasonably high risk. As already explained above,[360] under the risk-based approach, CDD decisions essentially reflect a risk assessment the lawfulness of which is usually not clear-cut, but which includes a margin of appreciation and crucially depends on the level of knowledge of the decision-maker. As a consequence, as long as key risk-enhancing indicators of the particular case (such as information about a client's criminal background) are not documented, CDD documentation can easily simulate lawful business conduct, unless indications outside the documentation raise doubts about its completeness and thereby trigger a more thorough inspection of the particular case. Such indications can originate not least from other authorities (in particular from the FIU and criminal justice authorities).

(ii) The detection of CDD violations can also be facilitated by the supervisory authority comparing the findings of several obliged entities as regards the same customer. For even before a customer has attracted the attention of the FIU and criminal justice authorities, supervisors may, in principle, benefit from the fact that business relationships and transactions usually do not happen in isolation between a particular customer and an obliged entity; rather, the same commercial activity will most of the time also be visible to other obliged entities that are in some way involved in it (for example, in the case of real estate transaction, by one or more credit institutions, an estate agent, a notary and likely other legal professionals). This increases the chance that suspicious facts that were not recorded by one obliged entity may well have been recorded by another obliged entity and thereby become potentially visible to the supervisor, either because this obliged entity had noticed anomalies or simply because the customer provided conflicting explanations to the different entities involved. However, given that competence for the supervision of obliged entities often varies and depends on the nature of an obliged entity's business type, supervisors will usually not enjoy a cross-sector view of one and the same activity. A similar problem arises with regard to cross-border business relationships and transactions that are supervised by national authorities in different countries, possibly even in cases where two obliged entities belong to the same group. While the fragmentation of the supervisory architecture is, at least to some extent, unavoidable, EU law does so far provide few specific instruments aimed at fostering synergies between different AML supervisors.[361]

(iii) As already acknowledged by the EU legal framework, effective supervision crucially depends on supervisors' access to relevant information,

---

[360] See section III.D.1.b.

[361] For cooperation between supervisors of credit and financial institutions, see however European Banking Authority et al., Joint guidelines on cooperation and information exchange for the purpose of Directive (EU) 2015/849 between competent authorities supervising credit and financial institutions – The AML/CFT Colleges Guidelines of 16 December 2019.

notably to customer data. Operations of obliged entities' branches or subsidiaries in third countries pose a significant obstacle in this respect, as they will limit and, in many cases, prevent supervisory authorities of Member States from understanding the CDD practice of such branches and subsidiaries. From the viewpoint of effective AML, this limitation on supervision is important in particular for two reasons. First, by onboarding customers in non-conformity with EU law's CDD standards, branches or subsidiaries in third countries can serve as a tool to pave a way for dubious assets into the Union.[362] This may be the case even if the third-country customer does not him- or herself perform a transaction into the EU, but merely acquires financial products offered by the branch or subsidiary in the third country. Second, insofar as an obliged entity in the EU is allowed to rely, in the performance of its own CDD, on a third-country branch or subsidiary (especially when the latter are part of a group to which the obliged entity also belongs), CDD in the EU will effectively rely on information whose reliability the competent supervisory authority in the EU cannot fully verify. To the extent that they contribute to opacity or anonymity of a customer's ownership structure or of the origin of funds, branches or subsidiaries in third countries will effectively counteract EU obliged entities' ability to establish the beneficial owner of a customer. This in particular includes the case of branches or subsidiaries operating in a jurisdiction that prevents them from sharing beneficial ownership information with third parties, including other members of their own group or foreign supervisory authorities, or by offering trust services within a jurisdiction with little or no beneficial ownership transparency. While EU legislation requires enhanced CDD for business relationships or transactions involving high-risk third countries,[363] this approach seems unsatisfactory. On the one hand, EU law stipulates that enhanced CDD needs not be invoked automatically with respect to branches or majority-owned subsidiaries of an EU obliged entity that are located in such a third country if they fully comply with the group-wide AML/CTF policies and procedures.[364] This begs the question how, in the absence of unhindered access to the documentation in the third state, such compliance

362 For an indication of the potential scale of the problem, see the calculation of the global volume of undeclared assets in G Zucman, La richesse cachée des nations : Enquête sur les paradis fiscaux, 2017, Chapter 2. Undeclared assets may of course often originate from legal activity. In any case, insofar as tax offences constitute predicate offences, undeclared assets and money laundering will often be closely correlated. More importantly, the volume of undeclared assets may provide estimates for the volume of investments the beneficial owner of which will effectively remain unknown.

363 Article 18a of Directive (EU) 2015/849 of 20 May 2015, as amended by Directive (EU) 2018/843 of 30 May 2018.

364 Article 18 para. 1(2) of Directive (EU) 2015/849 of 20 May 2015.

can be adequately verified by supervisory authorities in the EU. On the other hand, and more fundamentally, the very concept of high-risk third countries is too general and inflexible. Not only is such categorisation of a jurisdiction highly political and therefore difficult to implement,[365] it also appears unfeasible insofar as even major jurisdictions, whose classification as high-risk would be politically and commercially absurd,[366] can effectively offer a high level of financial anonymity, thereby allowing interested clients to move their assets from smaller high-risk jurisdictions into such major jurisdictions. Finally, an undifferentiated classification of all entities from a particular jurisdiction as high-risk would potentially deny that some of those entities adopt thorough and effective AML policies, thereby leading to unjust treatment and missing an opportunity to change business conduct through positive incentives.

Already following a more differentiated approach, current EU regulation on group-wide compliance of credit and financial institutions requires branches or subsidiaries to implement additional risk-mitigation measures if the law of a third state where the branch or subsidiary is located limits their ability to carry out an adequate risk assessment, the sharing and processing of customer data, the disclosure of suspicious transactions within the group, record keeping or the transfer of customer data to the competent authorities of Member States.[367] Yet, while such additional measures by obliged entities may include "enhanced review" of the branch or subsidiary, including "onsite checks and independent audits",[368] insofar as European supervisors have no direct access to the relevant client data and are thus not able verify the situation by themselves, it remains highly questionable whether such extra review can reliably detect failings in the third state.[369] This is even more the case if the independent audit may be conducted by an entity with a commercial self-interest in the high-risk jurisdiction. Current regulation also provides little detail on the criteria to be used by obliged entities when deciding whether an EU obliged entity can, for the purpose of CDD, rely on information from a branch or subsidiary in a third

---

365 See Council of the European Union, Statement of 5 March 2019 on Commission Delegated Regulation (EU) of 13 February 2019 supplementing Directive (EU) 2015/849 of the European Parliament and of the Council by identifying high-risk third countries with strategic deficiencies, C(2019)1326 6964/1/19REV 1; see also above European Union, section I.B.

366 See European Commission, Commission Staff Working Document on Foreign Direct Investment in the EU of 13 March 2019, SWD(2019) 108 final, pp. 10–13.

367 Commission Delegated Regulation (EU) 2019/758 of 31 January 2019.

368 Article 8(c) of Commission Delegated Regulation (EU) 2019/758 of 31 January 2019.

369 See to this effect also European Banking Authority et al., Joint Guidelines on the characteristics of a risk-based approach to anti-money laundering and terrorist financing supervision, and the steps to be taken when conducting supervision on a risk-sensitive basis of 16 November 2016, para. 43.

country.[370] Furthermore, while EU credit institutions and financial institutions are required to close down or limit operations of their branches or subsidiaries in third countries where AML/CTF risks can otherwise not be effectively managed, such measures would likely only lead to a shifting of commercial operations to branches or subsidiaries of groups whose parent company is domiciled outside the EU and thus not regulated by EU law. Even as regards credit institutions and financial institutions, the current framework therefore still provides few obstacles for assets to flow from anonymity-friendly jurisdictions into the EU. Lastly, EU law does not currently provide for common rules for the enforcement of group-wide AML compliance as regards obliged entities other than credit institutions and financial institutions, leaving open in particular operations by obliged entities involved in the provision of trust services.

c. Reform

In light of the above-mentioned deficits of its current framework, the EU should improve the ability of supervisory authorities to understand and verify obliged entities' compliance practice. To this end, legislation should (i) take steps to ensure that independent audits do not suffer from conflicts of interest, (ii) improve supervisory authorities' understanding of criminal threats and vulnerabilities, in particular through better sharing of relevant data with other relevant authorities, (iii) highlight FIUs' potential to trigger supervisory inspections and to prevent a fragmented risk perception amongst different supervisory authorities, and (iv) create a mechanism to isolate third-country obliged entities who undermine AML efforts in the EU.

- Ensure that independent audits are not assigned to auditors whose business model gives rise to conflicts of interest, especially if the auditor itself is involved in the facilitation of financial anonymity

(i) As has already been explained, supervisors should in particular enhance their ability to conduct or order independent audits with the aim, even in the absence of a suspicion of wrongdoing by the obliged entity, to uncover criminality by individual employees in cases where it has already been established that a particular obliged entity had been exposed to a criminal customer.[371] Insofar

370 See Article 26 para. 2 of Directive (EU) 2015/849 of 20 May 2015; for credit and financial institutions see also Article 3 para. 2 of Commission Delegated Regulation (EU) 2019/758 of 31 January 2019.

371 See *supra* section III.D.2.c and also European Commission, Report on the assessment of recent alleged money laundering cases involving EU credit institutions of 24 July 2019, COM(2019) 373 final, p. 5.

as a supervisor makes use of a private third party to carry out an audit, the law should furthermore insist on the need to avoid any perception of a potential conflict of interest as regards this third party.[372] Audits into possible AML failings should therefore not be conducted by a private entity whose business model does to a significant degree conflict with core elements of the EU's AML policy, in particular with the law's insistence on beneficial ownership transparency. This could notably exclude the possibility of AML audits being conducted by companies which, through their group's involvement in the provision of trust services in anonymity-enhancing jurisdictions, at the same time facilitate the weakening of beneficial ownership transparency.

- Provide structures for enhancing data sharing between supervisors, FIUs and criminal justice authorities, including a non-public section of the central beneficial ownership registry

(ii) To improve supervisory authorities' criminal policy perspective in AML supervision, legislation should provide for collaborative mechanisms with other competent authorities as well as relevant data sharing. A better understanding of money laundering risks and thereby also an improved ability to detect compliance violations can be achieved first and foremost by regular briefings of supervisory authorities by the FIU on current strategic and specific threats.[373] Detection skills will also be enhanced by secondments of specialists from the FIU and from criminal justice authorities to particularly relevant AML supervisors.

As for data sharing, supervisory authorities should in particular have an extensive understanding of the beneficial ownership and control structure of obliged entities' customers. This information will not only allow supervisors to detect lacunas in the performance of obliged entities' CDD, but also compare the CDD results of one obliged entity with the results of another obliged entity in order to spot inconsistencies. To improve inter-agency cooperation to this effect, public beneficial ownership registers could be supplemented by a purely non-public version accessible only to the competent authorities. In addition to the publicly available information provided by registered companies and obliged entities,[374] trusts and similar arrangements, such a non-public register should

---

372 See above Switzerland, section III.I.

373 See already European Banking Authority et al., Joint Guidelines on the characteristics of a risk-based approach to anti-money laundering and terrorist financing supervision, and the steps to be taken when conducting supervision on a risk-sensitive basis of 16 November 2016, para. 18.

374 For the obligation of obliged entities to report discrepancies to the register, see Article 30 para. 4 and Article 31 para. 5 of Directive (EU) 2015/849 of 20 May 2015, as amended by Directive (EU) 2018/843 of 30 May 2018.

be fed by criminal justice authorities, the FIU and supervisory authorities every time they discover discrepancies. In order to improve supervisory authorities' as well as other competent authorities' understanding of ownership and control structures, especially with regard to entities domiciled in third countries, and in recognition of the factual limits to the identification of real beneficial owners, the non-publicly accessible register should contain not only the identity of an entity's senior managing officials, but also the identity of senior managing officials as well as the address of the client's major corporate shareholders. In the case of a chain of companies and insofar as they are able to trace back the chain, registered companies, trusts and other arrangements should also retain the identity of senior management officials and the address of the shareholders' corporate shareholders, and make this information available to the registry authority to be accessible, via the non-public section of the register, to the supervisory authority as well as to other competent authorities. While not directly helping to identify an entity's real beneficial owner, such extended register would make it easier for supervisors and the FIU to detect anomalies, especially cases where one and the same individual serves as the representative for multiple companies or where in light of entities' identical or similar address it appears that they are front companies.

- Counter knowledge fragmentation among supervisors by requiring FIUs to detect inconsistencies in how a particular suspicious activity was, or was not, reported by different obliged entities

(iii) To avoid a fragmentation of knowledge gained by supervisory authorities across different sectors, one could in principle contemplate the creation of central supervisory authorities that are competent for AML supervision of obliged entities irrespective of the latter's business type.[375] However, such centralisation is problematic insofar as it will often cause parallel supervision of one and the same obliged entity by the AML supervisors and, for non-AML related regulation, by another supervisory authority. The resulting divided supervision invites duplication of efforts, inconsistency in regulatory expectations and ultimately a less holistic approach to an obliged entity's operations. Furthermore, effective AML supervision will usually suggest that supervisors and supervised entities are geographically close in order to facilitate close cooperation with local competent authorities (a necessity that seems much less relevant outside

---

375 See to this effect already Article 8 para. 1(l) of Regulation (EU) No. 1093/2010 of 24 November 2010 establishing a European Supervisory Authority (European Banking Authority) as amended by Regulation (EU) 2019/2175 of 18 December 2019, which confers to the European Banking Authority some AML/CTF competences to act within the area of competence of the European Insurance and Occupational Pensions Authority and the European Securities and Markets Authority.

AML, for example in prudential supervision).[376] Geographical distance and overly centralised structures will render communication between relevant public parties more difficult, complicate the establishment of a trust-based relationship between them, and likely even lead to information loss due to overly hierarchical structures of information exchange. Central supervisor authorities can nevertheless be desirable so as to ensure a harmonised application of AML obligations throughout particular business sectors, especially where commercial operations of the concerned obliged entities are usually of a transregional or transnational nature. Specialised AML supervisors can also serve as safeguard to ensure that local supervisory authorities do adequately prioritise AML considerations vis-à-vis other regulatory considerations.[377] However, while central authorities can provide oversight over regional or local AML supervisors, they should, in light of the aforementioned concerns, as much as possible be confined to the task of assisting, reviewing and, only in case of failings by the lower-level supervisors, taking over the latter's role. In any case, AML supervision should not be attributed to central authorities with few or no regional offices, or to authorities whose institutional structure entails significant obstacles to close cooperation with FIUs and local law enforcement.

The adverse effect of the proposed decentralised approach is that it can fragment the authorities' understanding of money laundering activities that permeate different business sectors. However, such fragmentation can be mitigated by cooperation mechanisms and data sharing between supervisory authorities. Importantly, fragmentation can also be addressed through collaboration between supervisory authorities and FIUs. For this purpose, one should recall that the current EU AML framework already provides FIUs with the power to request information from obliged entities even without them having already filed an SAR. The FIU is thereby enabled to understand a particular transaction or client from the perspective of several distinct obliged entities that were in some way in contact with this transaction or client. The response given to the FIU by the requested obliged entity can allow the FIU, in view of information it has already acquired from other obliged entities, to detect or at least suspect shortcomings in the requested obliged entity's CDD and reporting practice. If the FIU becomes aware of such shortcomings, it should be required to inform the competent supervisory authority. The latter can then perform controls to check the reliability of the obliged entity's AML measures and thus also the credibility of the information provided to the FIU. At least in the case

376 Calls for a highly centralised form of European supervision may overlook the importance, in AML, of close cooperation between AML supervisors, national FIUs and local criminal justice authorities, a necessity that is less obvious in prudential supervision; but see J Kirschenbaum/N Véron, A Better European Architecture to Fight Money Laundering, 2018, pp. 5–6.

377 See European Commission, Report on the assessment of recent alleged money laundering cases involving EU credit institutions of 24 July 2019, COM(2019) 373 final, p. 8.

of obvious, particularly serious deficits of an obliged entity's AML and in sectors known for weak or deficient AML supervision, legislators should consider imposing an obligation on the supervisory authority to expeditiously act upon a notice from the FIU and report back. Beyond strengthening reliability of FIUs' information requests, such a mechanism would provide a better understanding of regional and sector-specific money laundering risks and prevent a fragmented risk perception among different supervisory authorities. In this way the FIU would particularly improve the quality of supervision outside the financial sector, which in some jurisdictions suffers from ineffective AML prevention. Through such cooperation with FIUs, and thus effectively an intelligence-led approach to supervision, supervisory authorities could in many cases avoid or adequately narrow down the scope of routine audits of obliged entities' AML compliance, allowing them to prioritise cases where compliance violations are likely or already discernible.

- Put in place a framework to prevent designated third-country entities from being directly or indirectly involved in domestic business relationships where such entities obstruct the effectiveness of CDD

(iv) Finally, with regard to operations of branches or subsidiaries of obliged entities in third countries, effective supervision should be guided by the principle that private entities with a commercial stake in the Union should not be allowed to actively counteract core values of the EU's AML framework. This notably includes the requirement of beneficial ownership transparency, and should in principle prevent obliged entities from directly or, through branches or subsidiaries, indirectly transferring assets into the Union in contempt of the EU's AML standards. Given that legal limitations on direct business relationships or transactions between entities from a particular third country and obliged entities in the Union seem rather easy to circumvent (notably by interposing an obliged entity domiciled in another non-EU country), the EU legislator should consider preventive mechanisms that effectively also discourage an indirect weakening of CDD within the EU by businesses in third countries. The shaping of such mechanisms should start with the assumption that the effectiveness of enhanced CDD by obliged entities is often reduced or even rendered ineffective by the fact that customers or customers' shareholders are established in third countries that prevent a verification of customer and beneficial ownership information and of the origin of assets.[378] Once an EU obliged entity, in performance of CDD, concludes that relevant information is shielded by the laws of a third country, this obliged entity will usually not be able to independently verify this information. In this way, operations by financial services providers, company or trust

[378] To this effect, Commission Delegated Regulation (EU) 2019/758, recital 3.

service providers and other relevant businesses in third countries considerably weaken the effectiveness of AML in the EU. While it can obviously not regulate businesses domiciled in third countries, the EU can introduce mechanisms that provide incentives for third-country businesses in order to discourage them from weakening the effectiveness of CDD.

Insofar as the competent supervisory authority, possibly on notice from an FIU, establishes that a particular third-country business repeatedly constituted a key obstacle to the performance of effective CDD, this supervisory authority should adopt preventive measures. These should in particular apply if the services provided by a third-country business were effectively inhibiting an obliged entity in the EU from establishing or verifying a customer's beneficial ownership or the origin of assets, or where the information provided by a third-country business for CDD purposes was not accurate. The supervisory authority should then put the respective third-country business on notice that, if this business does not refrain from such conduct, it will prohibit obliged entities in the respective Member State (or, in the case of a central supervisory authority at EU level, throughout all Member States) from performing transactions or having business relationships with the customers of this particular third-country business. The respective business can then implement changes in its operations in order to ensure that it henceforth enables adequate verification of relevant customer information by obliged entities in the EU.[379] Otherwise, if this third-country business is unwilling or legally unable to do so, the supervisory authority should order obliged entities to no longer accept customers and transactions if, in the performance of CDD, it emerges that this customer or transaction is linked to the tainted third-country business.[380] A relevant link can result from a direct contractual relationship between the customer and the third-country business, but possibly also from an indirect relationship, for example in that the third-country business prevents the customer from establishing the beneficial ownership situation of customer's shareholders.

Instead of adopting an undifferentiated approach towards particular high-risk third countries,[381] supervisory authorities in the EU would thereby incentivise

---

379 For the conceivable design of judicial remedies of the third-country business before EU or national courts, see by analogy B Vogel, Targeted Sanctions against Economic Wrongdoing at the UN and EU Level, in U Sieber (ed.), Prevention, Investigation, and Sanctioning of Economic Crime: Alternative Control Regimes and Human Rights Limitations, 2019, pp. 129–157.

380 For the procedural and especially evidentiary standards appropriate in judicial review if the preventive measure was in essence based on conduct in a third state where EU or Member State authorities had no direct access to the relevant evidence, see by analogy ECJ (Grand Chamber), judgment of 21 April 2015 (Anbouba v. Council), C-630/13 P, paras. 47–55.

381 For similar lessons learned with regard to the shift from country embargos towards targeted sanctions, see I Cameron (ed.), EU sanctions: law and policy issues concerning restrictive measures, 2013.

businesses in third states to engage in more proactive AML, and also ensure that branches or subsidiaries of groups whose parent company is domiciled in a third state are no longer shielded by their group. For other members of the group will usually have little appetite to take the blame for a subsidiary's failures and thereby potentially expose themselves to preventive supervisory measures. In a similar vein, supervisory authorities should specify the conditions in which EU obliged entities, for the purpose of CDD, are allowed to rely on information from third countries, thereby considering in particular the willingness of a third-country business to cooperate with supervisory authorities in the EU and FIUs' assessment of the quality of supervision in the third country.[382]

2. *Enhancing the Effectiveness of Customer Due Diligence*

a. Current State

Following a risk-based approach to CDD, the EU legal framework emphasises the ability of obliged entities to categorise business relationships and transactions according to their risk in order to then perform CDD measures that are appropriate to the risk of the particular case.[383] Given that this approach requires a sound understanding of the nature and shape of risks in order to detect them, European and national authorities are required to assess relevant risks.

At the EU level, the Commission must, within intervals of at least every two years, identify, analyse and evaluate the money laundering and terrorism financing risks affecting the internal market and relating to cross-border activities, and make the resulting report available to Member States and obliged entities. This assessment must cover at least those areas of the internal market that are at the greatest risk, the risks associated with each relevant sector, and the most widespread means used by criminals for the purpose of money laundering, including those means used in relation to third countries.[384] In addition, the European Supervisory Authorities must, every two years, issue a joint opinion on the risks of money laundering and terrorism financing affecting the EU's financial sector; these opinions are to be made available to Member States and obliged entities.[385] At the national level, each Member State must identify and assess relevant risks affecting it, and use these findings in particular to identify areas in which obliged entities are to apply enhanced CDD, and make appropriate information available to obliged entities to facilitate their own risk assessment.[386]

382 Cf. Article 28(c) of Directive (EU) 2015/849 of 20 May 2015.
383 See Preamble of Directive (EU) 2015/849 of 20 May 2015, recitals 22–23, and also FATF Recommendation 1.
384 Article 6 paras. 1–3 of Directive (EU) 2015/849 of 20 May 2015, as amended by Directive (EU) 2018/843 of 30 May 2018.
385 Article 6 para. 5 of Directive (EU) 2015/849 of 20 May 2015.
386 Article 7 paras. 1 and 4(a)(e) of Directive (EU) 2015/849 of 20 May 2015.

Finally, obliged entities are required to identify and assess their individual money laundering and terrorism financing risks, including risk factors relating to customers, countries or geographic areas, products, services, transactions and delivery channels.[387] Obliged entities must then perform enhanced CDD on the basis of the triggers defined by EU law (notably unusually complex transactions, transactions conducted in an unusual pattern, business relationships or transactions involving high-risk third countries or with politically exposed persons, and cross-border correspondent relationships), in other cases of higher risk identified by Member States or cases identified as being high-risk by obliged entities themselves.[388]

For credit institutions and financial institutions, the European Supervisory Authorities must furthermore issue guidelines specifying risk factors to be taken into account and measures to be taken in cases where enhanced CDD is appropriate.[389] Despite EU and national guidance, obliged entities nevertheless retain an extensive margin of appreciation in determining whether to apply enhanced CDD measures, not least insofar as regards whether a transaction is unusual or follows an unusual pattern. While Member States are under an obligation to "ensure that obliged entities have access to up-to-date information on the practices of money launderers and financers of terrorism and on indications leading to the recognition of suspicious transactions",[390] EU law does not specify, beyond the aforementioned risk assessments and guidance, any other mechanisms in this respect. This is so even with regard to communication between obliged entities, the FIU and other competent authorities following the filing of an SAR. In this respect, current law merely requires Member States to "ensure that, where practicable, timely feedback on the effectiveness of and follow-up to reports of suspected money laundering or terrorist financing is provided to obliged entities",[391] though without providing details on the scope and frequency of such feedback.

Besides the involvement of EU and national authorities in the identification of risk criteria, the EU legal framework also stresses the role of sanctions following the violation of obliged entities' CDD violations.[392] By requiring that any final decision imposing sanctions for AML/CTF violations always in principle be published, and by requiring Member States to provide for high levels of administrative fines,[393] especially in case of violations committed by credit and

387 Article 8 para. 1 of Directive (EU) 2015/849 of 20 May 2015.

388 Article 18 paras. 1(1) and 2, and Articles 18a–20 of Directive (EU) 2015/849 of 20 May 2015, as amended by Directive (EU) 2018/843 of 30 May 2018.

389 Article 18 para. 4 of Directive (EU) 2015/849 of 20 May 2015.

390 Article 46 para. 2 of Directive (EU) 2015/849 of 20 May 2015.

391 Article 46 para. 3 of Directive (EU) 2015/849 of 20 May 2015.

392 Article 59 para. 1(a) and Article 60 of Directive (EU) 2015/849 of 20 May 2015.

393 Note that Member States can also opt for criminal sanctions instead of administrative fines, as now provided by Article 58 para. 2 of Directive (EU) 2015/849 of 20 May 2015.

financial institutions,[394] the law attaches considerable weight to deterrence as a prerequisite for the effectiveness of obliged entities' CDD obligations. However, at the same time, the law recognises that, under the risk-based approach, the design of adequate CDD measures is not a clear-cut matter, but usually entails a margin of discretion. In particular, obliged entities "may determine the extent of such measures on a risk-sensitive basis", provided that they can demonstrate to the competent authorities "that the measures are appropriate in view of the risks of money laundering and terrorist financing that have been identified".[395] The law also implies that, for the threat of sanctions to be effective, individual wrongdoing should not be allowed to effectively hide behind the liability of a legal entity. Member States must therefore ensure that "where obligations apply to legal persons in the event of a breach" of obliged entities' AML obligations, "sanctions and measures can be applied to the members of the management body and to other natural persons who under national law are responsible for the breach". While sanctions and measures applicable following violations of CDD and a number of other serious, repeated or systematic AML violations must include also "a temporary ban against any person discharging managerial responsibilities in an obliged entity, or any other natural person, held responsible for the breach, from exercising managerial functions in obliged entities",[396] EU law does not further elaborate on the role of individual responsibility for sanctioned wrongdoing, in particular on whether the competent authorities may be required to hold individual employees to account in addition to any sanctions or measures imposed on the legal person.

b. Challenges

The current AML framework invites a practice that ultimately emphasises formal compliance with CDD obligations over actual effectiveness of money laundering detection and prevention. While (i) this state is partially the result of obliged entities' limited ability to fulfil a criminal policy function, (ii) the law's focus on supervisory sanctions is also partially to blame.

(i) The effectiveness of CDD has increasingly been questioned, primarily due to the fact the great majority of SARs produced through it do not, in the EU, contribute to criminal investigations.[397] Though this correlation may not always

394 Article 59 paras. 2(e) and 3, and Article 60 of Directive (EU) 2015/849 of 20 May 2015.

395 Article 13 paras. 2 and 3 of Directive (EU) 2015/849 of 20 May 2015; see also Article 48 para. 8.

396 Article 58 para. 3 and Article 59 para. 2(d) of Directive (EU) 2015/849 of 20 May 2015.

397 Europol, From Suspicion to Action, Converting financial intelligence into greater operational impact, 2017, pp. 29–30. On the limited reliability of SARs also beyond AML/CTF, see PM Regan/T Monahan/K Craven, Constructing the Suspicious: Data Production, Circulation, and Interpretation by DHS Fusion Centers, 47 *Administration & Society* (2015), pp. 740–762.

be conclusive for assessing the quality of CDD, the ineffectiveness cannot not come as a surprise, even if authorities' failure to establish money laundering following an SAR can say as much about the capacity of the competent authorities to inquire into the origin of assets as about the quality of SARs. Given the complexity that tracking illegal assets back through chains of shell companies and multiple jurisdictions often entails, criminal justice authorities often find it very difficult or even impossible to establish the background of illegal assets. It would be unrealistic to expect obliged entities to be more successful in this regard. The origin of assets is usually out of reach of their investigative abilities, as it requires inquiring into the client's (and all too often also the client's client's) past conduct. Obliged entities' efforts would indeed form a poor substitute for adequate investigative powers and resources in the hands of the competent authorities. Legislators should therefore neither hope nor claim that private actors will be more effective than the competent authorities at uncovering criminal conduct. The main potential of CDD lies in the detection not of illegal assets, but of dissimulation efforts (for example an implausible opacity of a customer's shareholding structure or false representations by the customer towards the obliged entity), and thereby in allowing authorities to connect various instances of unusual but inconclusive transactions to create a meaningful picture. It is in this regard that obliged entities have an important role to play.

However, even when adopting more realistic expectations towards CDD, obliged entities will in many cases still find it hard to detect dissimulation, as in this regard too they will usually have to inquire deep into a customer's background in order to establish inconsistencies between information provided by him or her and independently verifiable information. Furthermore, being confronted with the inherent limits of their detection abilities, many obliged entities will, in view of their reporting obligation, prefer to err on the side of caution and thereby produce a large number of SARs that ultimately remain inconclusive (so-called "defensive reporting").[398] Even if obliged entities perform extensive enhanced CDD measures, they will often not be able to detect such inconsistencies, especially in cases of complex high-yield money laundering. In addition, when considering the difficulties faced by criminal justice authorities in investigating money laundering, the current design of CDD can hardly be satisfactory. For not only do SARs frequently or primarily not lead to any finding of criminal activity,[399] but – arguably still more importantly – it is clear that the vast majority of proceeds of crime are not detected by obliged entities. As was already observed above, the inflow of those proceeds into the legal economy is of

398 See N Ryder, Is It Time to Reform the Counter-terrorist Financing Reporting Obligations? On the EU and the UK System, 19 *German Law Journal* (2018), pp. 1185–1186.

399 See KPMG, Money Laundering: Review of the Reporting System, UK Home Office, 2003; Europol, From suspicion to action: Converting financial intelligence into greater operational impact, 2017, p. 29.

course not only a matter of concern as regards the quality of CDD, but presumably as importantly also as regards the ability of the competent authorities to detect criminal actors within obliged entities.[400] Nevertheless, one cannot deny that a better understanding of money laundering risks by obliged entities would in any case improve their ability to detect relevant cases.[401] Otherwise, in view of its current performance, CDD may to a large extent fail in substance, and in this respect constitute more an end in itself[402] than a useful and proportionate tool of criminal policy.

By requiring Member States to provide obliged entities with strategic information, the EU legislator has already recognised the need for CDD to rely on a good understanding of the nature and appearance of risks. Yet, so far neither the extent of such information nor the precise functioning of information gateways is clear. Even rather detailed supervisory guidance on risk factors necessarily relies on relative or ambiguous criteria that still allow for considerable flexibility in the determination of the risk level.[403] More importantly, even in cases that indicate a need for enhanced CDD, obliged entities will have limited access to independent information to verify the customer's statements, thereby reducing the ability to detect contradictions. It is then likely that CDD will become concerned more with the goal of ensuring formal respect for obligations than effectiveness. Even worse, by sweepingly shifting responsibility for the prevention of money laundering to the private sector while overlooking an effectiveness gap, AML risks being a smokescreen for a government's insufficient commitment to adequately resourcing the competent authorities. Without a clear focus on its effectiveness, CDD can then develop into something – very much opposed to the original idea behind the risk-based approach – that resembles a system more concerned with rules than with outcomes. A focus on effectiveness would require legislators to more clearly acknowledge the limits of obliged entities' detection capacity and emphasise the role of the competent authorities in providing the private sector with the necessary assistance for the identification of money laundering risks. Far from reducing obliged entities' responsibility, a more collaborative approach would ultimately emphasise this responsibility by specifying CDD obligations.

---

400 See *supra* sections I.A.1 and III.D.2.b.

401 L Gelemerova, On the frontline against money-laundering: the regulatory minefield, 52 *Crime, Law and Social Change* (2009), pp. 51–52; A Verhage, Compliance and AML in Belgium: a booming sector with growing pains, 12 *Journal of Money Laundering Control* (2009), pp. 123–124.

402 See W Laufer, The Missing Account of Progressive Corporate Criminal Law, 14 *New York University Journal of Law & Business* (2017), pp. 110–116, who criticises such practice as a "compliance game" that is to a large extent performed as an end it itself.

403 See European Banking Authority et al., Joint Guidelines under Articles 17 and 18(4) of Directive (EU) 2015/849 on simplified and enhanced customer due diligence and the factors credit and financial institutions should consider when assessing the money laundering and terrorist financing risk associated with individual business relationships and occasional transactions of 26 June 2017.

(ii) Besides the level of cooperation between the public and the private sector, the quality of CDD also depends on the incentives underlying the private sector's commitment. In this respect, EU law's emphasis on the role of sanctions can be somewhat questionable, especially insofar as the extent of liability of responsible employees is not clarified. If the threat of sanctions is meant to constitute the main incentive for respecting compliance obligations, money laundering prevention is primarily treated as an insurance against sanctions[404] and, at best, only incidentally as a genuine objective. Furthermore, to the extent that sanctions are primarily imposed on the obliged entity itself and not on the individual employees responsible for the wrongdoing, or similarly, if the obliged entity assumes payment of administrative fines imposed on employees, individual decision-makers may lack any incentive for prioritising compliance over personal profit expectations.

To understand the questionable role of supervisory sanctions in stimulating an effectiveness-driven CDD practice, one should also note that the risk-based approach has introduced a considerable degree of vagueness into the determination of CDD violations that can make it difficult to prove that a risk assessment was in fact objectively inappropriate.[405] The underlying flexibility of the risk-based approach is of course desirable in order to allow obliged entities to adapt the design of their CDD to the particular case. However, experience in other areas of financial regulation has shown that excessive risk-taking is inherently difficult to sanction as, apart from manifestly inadequate standards, the boundaries between acceptable and inacceptable risk are often difficult to draw.[406] To establish inappropriate risk-taking in cases where business conduct was not manifestly inadequate but nevertheless lacking behind what would reasonably have been required from the obliged entity in a particular case, supervisors may then effectively need to prove that the responsible employee did not act in good faith, in the sense that he or she deliberately ignored relevant risk indications. It is usually considerably easier for supervisory sanctioning practice to focus on violations of rather formal obligations that are more readily established, in particular the adequacy and implementation of internal policies, controls and procedures.[407] This however invites business practices that are predominantly concerned with the obliged entity's ability to demonstrate the adequacy of its compliance culture rather than with effectiveness.[408] If the prevention of money laundering is approached primarily as an unavoidable

---

404 To this effect W Laufer, Corporate Liability, Risk Shifting, and the Paradox of Compliance, 52 *Vanderbilt Law Review* (1999), pp. 1402–1404.

405 See *supra* section III.D.1.b.

406 For similar difficulties as regards the sanctioning of excessively speculative trading practices, see B Vogel, Grenzen eines beweisfunktionalen Strafrechts, 2014.

407 See also Article 48 para. 8 of Directive (EU) 2015/849 of 20 May 2015.

408 See A Amicelle/V Iafolla, Suspicion-in-the-making: Surveillance and Denunciation in Financial Policing, 58(4) *The British Journal of Criminology* (2018), pp. 855–857.

hurdle to profit making, not least the interpretation of CDD obligations will tend to adopt a narrow reading rather than one guided by the aim of effective prevention. In essence, this means that CDD is guided first and foremost by the objective of protecting the obliged entity from sanctions, not protecting it from money laundering, thereby signalling an antagonistic relationship between AML and obliged entities.[409]

c. Reform

To overcome the aforementioned challenges to the effectiveness of CDD, two approaches should be followed. On the one hand, (i) legislators need to ensure that obliged entities receive more frequent and more specific guidance from the competent authorities in order to get a better understanding of when and to what extent the performance of enhanced CDD is required; this should be done through the provision of more specific red flags as well as through the introduction of more dialogue between obliged entities and supervisors during the performance of CDD. On the other hand, (ii) the legal framework should, through remuneration-related incentives, strive to ensure that obliged entities and their employees identify with the objective of money laundering prevention.

- Require that any public-private sharing of strategic data by criminal justice authorities and FIUs involves the competent supervisory authority and clearly defines how such sharing affects CDD obligations

(i) As regards an improvement of obliged entities' risk-detection capacity, obliged entities should be provided with more specific information about when they should perform in-depth enhanced CDD measures and when extensive efforts to this effect will not be necessary. Cooperation for the purpose of strengthening CDD would in general exclude the possibility of singling out particular suspects or other individuals and be limited to the transfer of strategic information only. This would respect the separation of tasks between investigative and supervisory authorities and notably the fact that neither their institutional nature nor the usually much weaker procedural safeguards applicable to them would suggest an intimate involvement of supervisory authorities in the targeting of specific individuals for serious crime. Similarly, while strategic information provided

409 To this effect also the findings of A Verhage, Between the hammer and the anvil? The anti-money laundering-complex and its interactions with the compliance industry, 52 *Crime, Law and Social Change* (2009), pp. 29–30. Obviously, this antagonism does not extend to a (booming) business of the providers of compliance solutions and compliance professionals; see E Tsingou, Fighting Financial Crime: Who Designs Global Governance and Who Does The Work?, *Fudan Journal of the Humanities and Social Sciences* (2020).

to obliged entities will usually originate from the FIU, the above-described nature of FIUs and in particular their limited judicial oversight[410] makes them rather unsuitable for defining obligations directly vis-à-vis obliged entities. The involvement of supervisory authorities would serve as a safeguard to ensure that such sharing only extends to strategic information and does not – given the largely confidential nature of the relationship between FIUs and obliged entities –mutate into an unregulated targeting of particular individuals.[411]

It has already been explained above[412] that cooperation between competent authorities and obliged entities aimed at supporting ongoing criminal investigations does not in essence constitute a strengthening of CDD, but is rather an additional procedural tool to investigate criminal activity. Such cooperation should therefore not be confused with assistance provided by supervisory authorities and FIUs to obliged entities with the aim of improving the latter's ability to detect risks. Criminal justice authorities may however also provide obliged entities with purely strategic information (for example about recent trends regarding a particular type of crime). The law should then ensure that, insofar as data sharing by criminal justice authorities is not meant to support particular ongoing investigations, the competent supervisory authority is participating in the respective data sharing mechanisms. Such participation seems desirable not least because legal frameworks should avoid the parallel existence of multiple uncoordinated public–private data sharing mechanisms, as this would invite overlap, duplication and even contradictory communication. Involvement of supervisory authorities in the sharing of strategic information by criminal justice authorities is also important in order to ensure legal certainty for participating obliged entities, as only supervisory authorities are able to reliably clarify how the shared information should impact on the performance of CDD. Lastly, insofar as the data sharing is limited to the participation of a limited number of obliged entities, the involvement of supervisory authorities would also help to ensure that non-participating obliged entities do not suffer a competitive disadvantage, as the supervisory authority could adapt its CDD expectations vis-à-vis participating entities to the content of the shared data.

- Require supervisory authorities, in collaboration with FIUs, to define more specific and up-to-date triggers for enhanced CDD and, on request from an obliged entity, assess particular risk parameters

In designing mechanisms for cooperation between the competent supervisory authority and obliged entities, legislators should (supported by the FIU and,

410 See Comparative Analysis, section IV.B.4, and *supra* section III.C.2.b.

411 On substantive and procedural preconditions for the sharing of personal data, see *supra* section III.B.1.c.

412 See *supra* section III.B.2.b.

where appropriate, criminal justice authorities) strive to specify cases of enhanced risk in order to allow for a more rational, results-oriented use of compliance resources, and to ensure that such cases are frequently updated. Specific "red flags" could consist for example of information about a particular type of criminality in a certain area or particular methods used by particular criminal groups within a particular business sector. This should not however mean that obliged entities would be completely exempted from enhanced CDD obligations once a particular risk indicator has not been provided by the supervisor, but merely that the provision (or non-provision) of a risk indicator by the competent authorities will influence the depth of CDD measures. Obliged entities should still be expected to perform enhanced CDD under the existing general indicators (notably the presence of an unusually complex or unusually large transactions or of transactions that follow an unusual pattern), but they should then be enabled to liaise with the supervisor in order to determine whether or to what extent the performance of enhanced measures is really necessary in a particular case. This would keep obliged entities in principle fully bound by their current obligations, but at the same time allow them to engage with the supervisor in order to shape enhanced CDD measures in a way that is more focused on actual risks and less motivated by fear of subsequent supervisory sanctions. Unlike a model that is exclusively based on the prior determination of more or less specific red flags, a dialogue-based collaboration would also avoid CDD becoming inflexible and thus failing to address the dynamic character of money laundering methods.[413] Supervisors should be required to assess requests for clarification on the basis of the information available to them, without however disclosing confidential strategic or personal data.

The possibility of asking the supervisor for clarification on the required scope of enhanced CDD should in particular apply to the assessment of an obliged entity's general money laundering risks, and more precisely to the question whether or not to qualify certain types of customers or types of products as high risk.[414] In addition, obliged entities should however also be entitled to request prior clarification about particular business relationships or transactions, at least to the extent that the requesting obliged entity has already been confronted repeatedly with similar cases in the past. Instead of waiting for the findings of an *ex post* supervisory review, obliged entities would thereby have the opportunity to proactively align the design of CDD to what is considered useful from the supervisor's point of view.

---

413 See S Ross/M Hannan, Money laundering regulation and risk-based decision-making, 10 *Journal of Money Laundering Control* (2007), pp. 111–112.

414 See Article 8 para. 1 of Directive (EU) 2015/849 of 20 May 2015.

The proposed mechanism would obviously require additional resources at the level of supervisory authorities. To keep it practically feasible, it is therefore important to ensure that the processing of requests for supervisory clarification does not trigger a process akin to FIUs' operational analysis, but remains limited to an assessment of the relevance of risk factors of the particular case (in particular whether a certain set of facts should be treated as indicating a higher risk). Above all, it would not be the supervisor's task to determine whether a particular case should be treated as suspicious. The competent supervisory authority would thus not be required to look into the personal background of any individual customers, but merely to assess whether particular arguments advanced by the requesting obliged entity warrant a reduction or complete waiver of enhanced CDD measures. Such arguments can also include the fact that the obliged entity had in the past in equivalent cases regularly performed CDD without producing any findings that would have confirmed a higher risk. Insofar as the proposed model leads to a much deeper and therefore potentially more resource-intensive engagement of supervisory authorities in the performance of CDD, it merely draws the necessary consequences from the unsatisfactory performance of the existing AML compliance regime. Provided that improvements are envisaged, it is unavoidable that the competent authorities assume greater operational responsibility for the functioning of CDD.

- Provide mechanisms to ensure that, in predefined high-risk situations, the occurrence of money laundering can affect the remuneration of obliged entities' senior employees

(ii) To ensure the effective application of CDD obligations under a risk-oriented compliance framework, obliged entities must also be motivated by more than a fear of sanctions and must concern themselves with the effectiveness of money laundering prevention. Some obliged entities already do follow this logic, to a certain degree, driven particularly by a desire to avoid the reputational damage that any implication in illicit finance might cause.[415] Experience, however, suggests that such reputational concerns are often not a sufficient deterrent to forgo highly profitable business opportunities.[416] One way likely to enhance the quality of compliance lies in the creation of a particular incentive that, while not being a sanction and thus not presupposing proof of wrongdoing, would change the way in which obliged entities and in particular their employees perceive money laundering. This goal could be achieved if the risk of money

415 See J Harvey/SF Lau, Crime-money, reputation and reporting, 52(1) *Crime, Law and Social Change* (2008), p. 59.

416 See also W Laufer, A Very Special Regulatory Milestone, 20 *U. of Pennsylvania Journal of Business Law* (2018), pp. 424–425.

laundering became personally economically significant for employees dealing with high-risk situations.[417] Legislation should therefore provide that in case of high-risk situations that subsequently turn out to be part of money laundering, senior employees of obliged entities who personally profited from a tainted deal through bonuses or similar benefits (for example the director of a local branch or the head of a trading unit) can be ordered by the supervisory authority to pay all or part of these personal benefits back to their employer even if they were not aware of the criminal context of the deal. The power to order such repayment should apply to particular types of business dealings previously designated as being high risk by the supervisory authority or the FIU. To keep his or her personal benefit, however, the respective senior employee should be allowed to positively demonstrate to the supervisory authority that the criminal nature of the deal could not reasonably have been detected. To this end, the employee might then for example be required to establish that all relevant information was duly passed on to the company's compliance department, that apparent violations of internal organisational rules did in fact not occur or that such violations in no way impacted the relevant decision-making.

IV. OUTLOOK

The preceding findings have demonstrated the need to understand AML as an architecture of various interconnected elements the purpose and design of which must be aligned in a coherent manner. Obviously, the functioning of the system crucially depends on the definition of money laundering, and in particular the question of to what extent it should be necessary to make this definition dependent on establishing the actual origin of assets or instead primarily define money laundering on the basis of violations of transparency obligations. Equally important are the objectives of AML instruments, in particular policy choices between the use of AML as an instrument to facilitate the sanctioning of predicate offences and its use as a gatekeeping tool to protect the legal economy from being infiltrated by criminal actors. These two aims are in principle not mutually exclusive, but the design of various AML instruments (such as reporting obligations, or the design of data sharing between the competent authorities and obliged entities) will depend on the objective that is primarily pursued. Furthermore, the substantive and procedural safeguards of AML frameworks

---

417 On the role of remuneration as a compliance incentive see also A Enria, Just a few bad apples? The importance of culture and governance for good banking, speech of 20 June 2019, available at https://www.bankingsupervision.europa.eu/press/speeches/date/2019/html/ssm.sp190620~f9149fe258.en.html.

are in many cases still largely inadequate to deal with the highly sensitive nature of financial data. Legislators need to be alert to the considerable potential for abuse inherent in the secret processing of such data by public and private entities, and therefore carefully balance the potential advantages of various elements of AML with the respective risk of them being abused for illegitimate aims. Finally, legislators have to find the right balance between, on the one hand, the need to actively involve and rely on the private sector in the prevention of crime and, on the other hand, the particular vulnerability of private actors to exploitation by criminals. The competent authorities need to provide obliged entities with greater assistance in the detection of crime; at the same time, legal frameworks must pay increasing attention to the threat emanating from professional money launderers inside the regulated sector and find ways to facilitate their detection. The effectiveness of AML can obviously never be understood in the sense of a complete suppression of the financial links between legal and illegal economies. Yet a holistic approach to AML by policymakers has the potential to significantly impede the ability of criminal actors to instrumentalise the financial system for their purposes and prevent them from using their ill-gotten funds as a tool to expand their power throughout society.

The need for coherence between the different elements of the AML framework is all the more important in view of the rise of virtual assets as an alternative to fiat currencies.[418] While the future shape and role of virtual assets are, to a great extent, still speculative,[419] it seems at this point likely that they will increasingly be used as a means to transfer and store value. The current AML framework of course pivotally relies on financial intermediaries to monitor financial flows and to protect the integrity of the market from criminal actors. Virtual assets, in contrast, are characterised by a much more decentralised approach that allows peer-to-peer transactions without the interposition of an intermediary. Due to their entirely electronic nature, crypto assets are furthermore an easy method of cross-border value transfers. Both features potentially constitute significant challenges to AML, not least as regards providers of virtual asset services domiciled in third countries, but they do not signal an unsurmountable conflict with virtual assets. Despite not being fiat currencies, virtual assets need legal certainty and thus a legal framework that protects their titles, otherwise it is difficult to imagine such assets becoming more widely accepted. As the primary legal framework to protect legal economies from illegal actors, AML will therefore have to play an important role to ensure the sustainability of technical innovation. In moving in this direction, legislators should ensure that regulatory

418 For the integration of virtual assets service providers into the EU AML framework, see now Article 2 para. 1(g)(h) of Directive (EU) 2015/849 of 20 May 2015, as amended by Directive (EU) 2018/843 of 30 May 2018.

419 See M Campbell-Verduyn, Bitcoin, crypto-coins, and global anti-money laundering governance, 69 *Crime, Law and Social Change* (2018), pp. 286–292.

and investigative instruments remain tailored to the particular difficulties and need of virtual assets while at the same time being consistently integrated into the overarching architecture. Depending on how virtual assets develop in form and economic relevance, it may become unavoidable to create tools that in many ways go well beyond the confines of traditional AML, especially as regards the role of internet-based service providers. Such particularities should however not lead to another fragmentation of AML, but from the very start be designed with the aim of ensuring maximum consistency of regulatory approaches to finance and cybersecurity.

INDEX

www.ingramcontent.com/pod-product-compliance
Ingram Content Group UK Ltd.
Pitfield, Milton Keynes, MK11 3LW, UK
UKHW051917100926
8556IPUK00021B/1225

9 781780 689548